Reading Swift

Reading Swift

Papers from
The Seventh Münster Symposium
on
Jonathan Swift

Edited by
Janika Bischof, Kirsten Juhas,
and Hermann J. Real

Wilhelm Fink

Printed with kind support of Sparkasse Münsterland Ost

Cover portrait: Courtesy of The Bodleian Library, Oxford

Bibliographic information published by the Deutsche Nationalbibliothek

The Deutsche Nationalbibliothek lists this publication in the Deutsche Nationalbibliografie; detailed bibliographic data available online: http://dnb.d-nb.de.

Internet: www.fink.de

Cover design: Evelyn Ziegler, München
Production: Brill Deutschland GmbH, Paderborn

ISBN 978-3-7705-6397-5 (hardback)
ISBN 978-3-8467-6397-1 (e-book)

Contents

POETRY AND MUSIC

GULLIVER'S TRAVELS

PHILOSOPHICAL AND RELIGIOUS ISSUES

POLITICAL PROBLEMS

IRELAND

RECEPTION AND ADAPTATION I

RECEPTION AND ADAPTATION II

Preface

The Seventh Münster Symposium on Jonathan Swift was an extraordinary event in many respects. While all of the previous Symposia have enjoyed the reputation of having been wonderful combinations of erudition, stimulation, and friendliness, the Seventh perhaps outdid them, in however small, almost imperceptible ways. In the first place, a festive and exuberant mood pervaded the Alexander-von-Humboldt Haus in June 2017 from the start. To one extent, this atmosphere was created by the fact that the delegates who had gathered from several remote corners of the world – Australia, England, France, Ireland, Scotland, the United States, Wales, and Germany – for three days of learned lectures and animated discussions (including a Round Table on "Reading Swift in the Twenty-First Century") knew that they had come together to celebrate the 350th birthday of the Dean, T H E Dean, the only Dean in the history of Ireland; to another, it was due to the awareness that the event was honoured by the patronage as well as the presence of H. E. Michael Collins, the Irish Ambassador to Germany, who was not only kind enough to open the Symposium with a most complimentary speech, which paid warm tribute to the achievements of the Münster Swift 'industry' (see Derek Scally's report in *The Irish Times* of 20 June 2018), but who also gladly engaged in conversation with the international crowd of Prestophiles. His Excellency was greeted by warm addresses of welcome by Pro-Vice-Chancellor Professor Michael Quante on behalf of the Westfälische Wilhelms-Universität, and Mayor Wendela-Beate Vilhjalmsson on behalf of the City of Münster, and the editors would like to express their deepest gratitude to all three of them.

At times when the struggling for funds has very much become part of the academic routine – and more often than not, with disappointing results – we expressly wish to acknowledge the financial support of the *Deutsche Forschungsgemeinschaft* (German Research Council). Likewise, we extend warmest thanks to our *alma mater*, in particular to Dr Anke Kohl, Head of the University's International Office, and to the Dean of the Faculty of Philology, Professor Eric Achermann. At Headquarters, we are greatly obliged to the professional advice of Vanessa Dartmann and Christiane Thieleke of the University's marketing staff, as well as to our favourite 'ministering angel,' Petra Miech, for her able administrative assistance.

In addition to being a festival of scholarship, a Münster Symposium on Jonathan Swift has always been what the Greek root suggests it is: a convivial meeting. Prestophiles tend to think here of Sir William Temple's apophthegm concluding the *Essay upon Ancient and Modern Learning*, "that among so many things as are by Men possessed or pursued in the Course of their Lives, all the rest are but Bawbles, Besides Old Wood to Burn, Old Wine to Drink, Old Friends to Converse with, and Old Books to Read." In other words, we have reason to be grateful, for genial hospitality and culinary conviviality, to the Hotel Mövenpick and Landhaus Eggert as well as to Franz and Hannah Lauter at Schloss Nordkirchen, truly the Westphalian Versailles. Last but not least, we would like to record our indebtedness to Professor Klaus Stierstorfer, Vice Dean of the Faculty of Philology, who hosted a charming and delightful reception for the conference delegates at the Ehrenpreis Centre.

In Sir William Temple's enumeration, one field is conspicuously absent: that of music. To make up for this failure, the convenors decided to organize a workshop with Gerald Resch, the Austrian composer of a new family opera entitled *Gullivers Reise*, and members of the ensemble of the Oper Dortmund, where the opera had premiered in May 2017. The evening turned out a great success, with Gerald Resch vivaciously explaining origins and intentions as well as the modalities of the creative process, and Hans-Peter Frings, deputy director of the Oper Dortmund, the conductor Ingo Martin Stadtmüller, and the singers Joshua Whitener (Gulliver) and Almerija Delic (Vaniliput) on the panel taking questions from the audience and illustrating their points with samples from the opera. The author John von Düffel, who could not be present due to a commitment in Berlin, was kind enough to send a video message. All this while, Dr Michael Bähr was a brilliant Master of Ceremonies.

However, it takes more than convenors, financiers, and institutions to run the show, and we are therefore eager to show our appreciation to all who watched on the sidelines ready to step in whenever their services – bibliographical and electronic, material and moral – were called for: our dear Julia Barisch, the dutiful Ulrich Elkmann of the Ehrenpreis Centre, our dedicated friends Dr Sabine Baltes-Ellermann and Dr Marga Munkelt, Dr Dirk Passmann, the trusted Vice Chairman of the Friends, and, in fitting conclusion, our loved ones Dr Michael Bähr, George and Holde Juhas, and Erika, the one and only, who has now successfully shouldered the burden of seven Symposia.

Finally, as in 2013, the task always following the party, namely to make the scholarly efforts of the Münster Prestophiles available to the worldwide community of Swiftians, was greatly facilitated by a generous grant of the Sparkasse Münsterland Ost, and our most grateful thanks go again to Julia Bergmann and Anna Boeldicke. Given that *post festum* almost all delegates wrote in praising "the outstanding scholarship," the "intellectual stimulation," and "congenial company," with which the Symposium, "a truly great celebration of Presto," had provided them, we would like to assure our sponsors that their money has been well spent, and in a noble cause, too. *Vivant sequentes!*

Münster, April 2018

Hermann J. Real, Kirsten Juhas, and Janika Bischof

Abbreviations

Prose Works [The Prose Works of Jonathan Swift], eds Herbert Davis *et al.*, 16 vols (Oxford: Basil Blackwell, 1939-68; various reimpressions, sometimes corrected).

Correspondence, ed. Williams The Correspondence of Jonathan Swift, ed. Harold Williams, rev. David Woolley, 5 vols (Oxford: Clarendon Press, 1963-72).

Correspondence, ed. Woolley The Correspondence of Jonathan Swift, D.D., ed. David Woolley, I: Letters 1690-1714 (nos 1-300) (Frankfurt on Main: Peter Lang, 1999); II: Letters 1714-1726 (nos 301-700) (Frankfurt on Main: Peter Lang, 2001); III: Letters 1726-1734 (nos 701-1100) (Frankfurt on Main: Peter Lang, 2003); IV: Letters 1734-1745 (nos 1101-1508) (Frankfurt on Main: Peter Lang, 2007), V: Index (Frankfurt on Main: Peter Lang, 2014).

Poems, ed. Rogers Jonathan Swift, The Complete Poems, ed. Pat Rogers (Harmondsworth, Middlesex: Penguin Books, 1983).

Poems, ed. Williams The Poems of Jonathan Swift, ed. Harold Williams, 2nd ed., 3 vols (Oxford: Clarendon Press, 1958; various reimpressions).

ARBER Edward Arber (ed.), *The Term Catalogues, 1668-1709*, 3 vols (New York and London: Johnson Reprint Corporation, 1965).

DIB *Dictionary of Irish Biography: From the Earliest Times to the Year 2002*, eds James McGuire and James Quinn, 9 vols (Cambridge: Cambridge University Press for the Royal Irish Academy, 2009).

Ehrenpreis,	*Mr Swift*	Irvin Ehrenpreis, Swift: The Man, his Works, and the Age,
	Dr Swift	3 vols (London: Methuen, and Cambridge, Massachusetts:
	Dean Swift	Harvard University Press, 1983 [1962-83]).

FOXON D. F. Foxon, *English Verse, 1701-1750: A Catalogue of Separately Printed Poems with Notes on Contemporary Collected Editions*, 2 vols (Cambridge: Cambridge University Press, 1975).

PASSMANN AND VIENKEN Dirk F. Passmann and Heinz J. Vienken, *The Library and Reading of Jonathan Swift: A Bio-Bibliographical Handbook*, 4 vols (Frankfurt on Main: Peter Lang, 2003).

THE ROTHSCHILD LIBRARY *The Rothschild Library: A Catalogue of the Collection of Eighteenth-Century Printed Books and Manuscripts Formed by Lord Rothschild*, 2 vols (London: Dawsons, 1969 [Cambridge, 1954]).

TEERINK AND SCOUTEN H. Teerink, *A Bibliography of the Writings of Jonathan Swift*, 2nd ed., rev. Arthur H. Scouten (Philadelphia: University of Pennsylvania Press, 1963).

Abbreviations of periodicals are those of the "Master List of Periodicals" of the *MLA International Bibliography*.

BIOGRAPHICAL ASPECTS

Eugene Hammond
Stony Brook University, New York

What Do Young Men Know? All-Too-Powerful Inferences Masquerading as Facts

Abstract. Jonathan Swift's first three full-length biographers – the Earl of Orrery, Deane Swift, and the younger Thomas Sheridan – were all young men when they met Swift, and in preparing for their publications were able to learn very little about Swift's first thirty years. Consequently, they frequently drew ill-founded inferences about Swift's early years, which later biographers have too often taken for facts, and which in turn too often have been used to explain and interpret Swift's later works. As we move forward in Swift biography and criticism, we should be more conscious than we have been of how fragile these inferences are when we are tempted to lean on them.

Nature abhors a vacuum, but biographers get excited about vacuums. For the 265 years since John Boyle, fifth Earl of Cork and Orrery, wrote his *Remarks on the Life and Writings of Dr. Jonathan Swift* (1752), there has been little controversy over Swift's intentions in his *Examiner* papers, about Swift's daily life in London between 1711 and 1713, or about his thinking as he was working on his *Drapier's Letters*, all situations that are well documented. But there has been a great deal of controversy among Swift's biographers about whether or not he married Esther Johnson, about whether or not he ever liked his sister Jane, or about whether his mother neglected him during his childhood. The reason we have these and many other controversies about Swift's life is that his first three full-length biographers – Orrery, Deane Swift, and the younger Thomas Sheridan – were only 25, 31, and 16, respectively, when they first met Swift, or at least when they first dealt with him in anything like an adult friendship. The Dean himself was 64, 70, and 68, respectively, when he began to engage with these young men, and his temperament and his memory were increasingly failing him.[1] The young men not only did not know Swift's youth but did not understand his age. Thomas Sheridan was well aware of these young-man drawbacks. In his Introduction, he wrote of Orrery, "To draw [Swift's] character

1 Swift lost much of his enthusiasm for life in January 1728, shortly after his 60th birthday, with the death of Esther Johnson. His memory began to fail him seriously in 1733, in his 66th year. In that year, he wrote to Charles Ford, who was gathering materials for Swift's collected works: "In Your Catalogue of Pamphlets there are some I do not remember. I mean, *Journy to Paris, Remarks about Greg, Peace and Dunkirk, Windsor Prophesy, Pretenders Lettr to a Whig Lord.* I fancy I did not write any of these" (*Correspondence*, ed. Woolley, III, 708-9).

 | DOI:10.30965/9783846763971_002

at length, from observations made at such a [late] period [in his life], was the height of injustice; and yet his Lordship had no opportunity of knowing any thing of the brighter part of his days, but from common report."[2] But then, we should perhaps be glad not to have several more than the mother, sister, and marriage controversies that we have, because in the enthusiasm of Orrery, Deane Swift, and Sheridan to put together comprehensive biographies of Swift, they frequently followed the temptation of youth and recorded inferences they had drawn about Swift as if they were facts. In many cases, these inferences have been accepted, or nearly accepted, as facts ever since.[3]

Swift wrote gracious compliments of both Orrery and Deane Swift shortly after meeting them. He succumbed to one of his frequent and inaccurate enthusiasms for young men with potential in writing to Pope about Orrery in 1733, "I have not known for his age a more valuable Person."[4] Orrery was well versed in the classics. Otherwise, it is difficult to ascertain what it was about Orrery that led Swift to be even temporarily impressed. In April 1739, he complimented Deane Swift, also in a letter recommending him to Pope:[5] "He hath a very good Taste for Wit, writes agreeable and entertaining Verses, and is a perfect Master equally skilled in the best Greek and Roman Authors. He hath a true Spirit for Liberty, and with all these Advantages, is extremely decent and modest."[6] Swift was apparently forgetting that in 1725 when Deane was 18, he had in a letter to Stafford Lightburne called Deane a "Puppy."[7] But Swift was prone to writing blandly positive letters of recommendation before knowing his subjects very thoroughly. The surviving evidence suggests that Swift held both Orrery and Deane Swift in contempt, at least once he had come to know each better.[8] Of young Thomas Sheridan, Swift seems to have been fond.

2 Thomas Sheridan, *The Life of the Rev. Dr. Jonathan Swift* (London: C. Bathurst, *et al.*, 1784), sig. A5r.

3 Sheridan, John Hawkesworth, and Sir Walter Scott rarely go beyond the earlier biographies of Orrery and Deane Swift, which has strengthened the influence of these earlier biographies, all now conveniently assembled in *The Lives of Jonathan Swift*, ed. Daniel Cook, 3 vols (London and New York: Routledge, 2011).

4 *Correspondence*, ed. Woolley, III, 661. He wrote to Charles Ford in 1732, "Ld Orrery stays here [in Dublin] this winter. I meet him sometimes at dinners ... He seems an honest man, and of good dispositions" (*Correspondence*, ed. Woolley, III, 547).

5 *Correspondence*, ed. Woolley, IV, 576.

6 *Correspondence*, ed. Woolley, IV, 575-76.

7 "I am grieved at the Difficultyes your Adversaryes Family must be under by their own wrong Proceedings, and should be more so if that Puppy who is heir had not so behaved himself as to forfeit all Regard or Pity" (*Correspondence*, ed. Woolley, II, 553).

8 Swift wrote to Lord Orrery on 19 October 1735, beginning with some raillery that is a bit harsh and goes on too long. "I own I have received many very friendly and entertaining Letters from you during your absence, and never answered one of them; And what of all that? Am I

But Sheridan's strength, his skill at storytelling, proved equally to have been a weakness, as he frequently enhanced stories about Swift, already at bottom shaky in their foundations, with additional persuasive-sounding but unlikely details. What we know about Orrery, Deane Swift, and Sheridan does not lead us to trust them, and yet in many cases we continue to believe what they believed, most misleadingly, Swift's brief account of his own first 33 years, probably written in 1738 when he was 71.[9]

I do not mean to suggest that Orrery, Deane Swift, or Thomas Sheridan were fools. They raised many of the issues that are still constructively debated among Swift's readers. All three biographies are impressive in their scope and in the cogency of many of their critical assessments. Both Sheridan and Deane Swift complained that Orrery, the first to publish, was malicious in his biography, but I think that Orrery was *trying* to write an even-handed work. The problem was that he wrote with very little evidence other than the few and widely separated days that he spent with Swift, and Swift's works that had been published by 1752. Orrery honestly felt that Swift was a little odd, and I am sure he was right.

---

bound to acknowledge your Favors? Is it not enough and too much that I do not burn without reading them? Are you not entirely obliged to me for Your titles, your Estate, your Health, your Wit, your Generosity, your Learning, your good Nature; Your every thing? It is a strange Thing the Ingratitude of the World; But I make no Reflections. Thus much for Business" (*Correspondence*, ed. Woolley, IV, 200). Such raillery would not make Orrery feel too fond of Swift, as Swift does not sound too fond of Orrery. Deane Swift unburdened himself to Swift one evening that if he could sell all he knew about Greek and Latin literature, he would do so for £300, for all the good it had done him. Not surprisingly, he reports, Swift "seemed to dislike what I said prodigiously" (*An Eighteenth-Century Correspondence*, eds Lilian Dickins and Mary Stanton [London: John Murray, 1910], p. 39).

9 Deane Swift surmised in 1755 that these notes were "written about six or eight and twenty years ago" (*Prose Works*, V, xxii), that is, during the years 1727-29. He assumed that Esther Johnson's death gave Swift the impetus for writing, and that Swift's trip to Goodrich in 1727 would have put genealogical details fresh in his mind. But the tone, prejudices, and crankiness that come through in Swift's notes are far more characteristic of his 1738 thinking than his 1728 thinking. In addition, Swift wrote "Memoirs of my Grandfather, Thomas Swift, by Mr. Lyons, April 1738" on papers that Revd Lyon had gathered in 1738 to help him with his research for these autobiographical notes (*The Works of Jonathan Swift*, ed. Sir Walter Scott, 2nd ed., 19 vols [Edinburgh: Archibald Constable, *et al.*, 1824], I, 504n). And in 1738, Charles Cobbe, Bishop of Kildare, heard of these notes and asked to copy them. In a letter to Pope dated 28 April 1739, Swift mentions sources and repeats details and phrases that also appear in the fragment of autobiography, which would imply that the materials were more freshly on his mind than they could have been if he had written these notes in 1728 (Ehrenpreis, *Dean Swift*, p. 879). From this evidence, Ehrenpreis concluded, and I agree, that Swift wrote his autobiographical account between April 1738 and April 1739. See, however, the reservations by Hermann J. Real, "The Dean's Grandfather, Thomas Swift (1595-1658): Forgotten Evidence," *Swift Studies*, 8 (1993), 84-93.

Swift's account, in his autobiographical notes, of his being kidnapped by his nurse serves as an excellent illustration of the way that inferences about Swift have metamorphosed into apparent facts:

> When he was a year old,[10] an event happened to him that seems very unusual; for his nurse, who was a woman of Whitehaven, being under an absolute necessity of seeing one of her relations, who was then extremely sick, and from whom she expected a legacy; and being extremely fond of the infant, she stole him on ship-board unknown to his mother and uncle, and carried him with her to Whitehaven, where he continued for almost three years. For, when the matter was discovered, his mother sent orders by all means not to hazard a second voyage, till he could be better able to bear it. The nurse was so careful of him, that before he returned he had learnt to spell; and by the time that he was five years old, he could read any chapter in the bible.[11]

Lest we accept the dates of this account too literally, Swift offers an alternative though more casual explanation of his birth and early years in a letter he wrote to Francis Grant on 23 March 1734: "I happened indeed by a perfect Accident to be born [in Ireland], my Mother being left here from returning to her House at *Leicester*, and I was a Year old before I was sent to *England*."[12] By 1734, when Swift wrote this letter, he was 67 and profoundly discouraged by Irish politics. During his 60s and 70s, he sometimes hated to acknowledge his Irishness, and his inventiveness never failed him when he needed a story.

Swift's casual comment here, implying that his mother was born in Leicester and wanted to return there with him, certainly not true, and primarily a convenience for his 1734 self-image, has coloured the lenses of many biographers, so that they believe that Swift's mother did not stay long in Ireland while Jonathan was growing up. Lord Orrery misled us from the start, writing that "Mrs. SWIFT, about two years after her husband's death, quitted *Ireland*, and retired to *Leicester*, the place of her nativity."[13] Orrery is wrong about Abigail Swift's place of nativity – it was Dublin and not Leicester – and he offers no evidence that she "retired" in 1669, when Swift was two, to Leicester. Presumably, Orrery was inferring from Swift's letter to Grant, which Grant published in

10 Swift wrote of himself in these notes in the third person.

11 Sheridan, *The Life of the Rev. Dr. Jonathan Swift*, p. 552.

12 *Prose Works*, XIII, 111; *Correspondence*, ed. Woolley, III, 730. No evidence survives of who Swift's nurse was, of any further contact with her, or of any visits to Whitehaven. This inattentiveness is uncharacteristic of Swift, and his story of being kidnapped is reminiscent of a fairy tale.

13 Boyle, John, fifth Earl of Cork and Orrery, *Remarks on the Life and Writings of Dr. Jonathan Swift, Dean of St. Patrick's, Dublin, in a Series of Letters ... to his Son, the Honourable Hamilton Boyle* (London: A. Millar, 1752), p. 10.

1749. Neither Deane Swift nor Sheridan thought enough of Orrery's speculation to make any mention of Swift's mother leaving Ireland during Swift's youth. Deane Swift simply follows Swift's own autobiographical account without adding any melodrama except in asserting a strong friendship between *his* grandfather (Swift's uncle), Godwin Swift, and Sir John Temple, Sir William Temple's father. John Hawkesworth, though, in his 1755 biography of Swift, was even more misleading than Orrery. After reporting, in imitation of Orrery, that Abigail left for England while Swift was in the hands of his nurse, Hawkesworth resorts to invention influenced by Deane Swift's partiality towards his grandfather Godwin: "But her son was again carried to *Ireland* by his nurse, and replaced under the protection of his Uncle *Godwin*."[14] None of these men – neither Orrery nor Deane Swift nor Hawkesworth – knew anything at first hand of any of the circumstances that they were talking about.[15] They extrapolate either from Swift's autobiographical account, which never places his mother in England until 1688 when Swift was 21, or from other comments, oral or written, that Swift made in his late 60s and 70s, when he was prone to entertain himself by making up stories. By the time Swift was 60, none of his friends, of course, knew anything about his pre-Trinity-College years, so none of his biographers had any versions of his early years, other than Swift's, to rely on.

The casual, unsubstantiated remarks by Swift's eighteenth-century biographers have been largely accepted even by Swift's recent biographers. Alan Downie, so right about so many aspects of Swift's life and character, conflates the accounts of Orrery and Hawkesworth on this issue: "About two Years after her Husband's Death, [Abigail] quitted the Family of Mr. *Godwin Swift*, in *Ireland*, and retired to *Leicester*."[16] Irvin Ehrenpreis thoughtfully, but with no evidence, includes Swift's sister Jane in their mother's 'move' to Leicester: "While her son was at school, Mrs Swift did not remain in Ireland but moved with his sister to Leicester."[17] More recently, Leo Damrosch also accepts this

---

14 *The Works of Dr. Jonathan Swift, Dean of St. Patrick's, Dublin*, ed. John Hawkesworth, 12 vols (London: Bathurst, 1755-75), I, 5.

15 Laetitia Pilkington, alone of Swift's early biographers, reports that when Swift's nurse "returned to *Ireland*," she "restored the Child to his Mother" (*Memoirs of Laetitia Pilkington*, ed. A. C. Elias, Jr, 2 vols [Athens and London: The University of Georgia Press, 1997 {1748-54}], I, 31-32). But she knew no more than Swift's other early biographers where Swift's mother was living.

16 J. A. Downie, *Jonathan Swift: Political Writer* (London, Boston, Henley: Routledge and Kegan Paul, 1984), p. 4.

17 Ehrenpreis, *Mr Swift*, pp. 31-32. Ehrenpreis pulls back a little from this statement in his footnote: "Although this fact is always assumed, it has not been proved" (p. 32n1). From Orrery to Damrosch (John Stubbs, *Jonathan Swift: The Reluctant Rebel* [New York: W.W. Norton, 2016], pp. 76-77, is skeptical), Swift's biographers have for the most part assumed

story as truth: "When Swift was finally brought back to Dublin ... his mother, Abigail, left for England, taking Jane with her and settling permanently in Leicester ... Jonathan Swift was now effectively an orphan."[18] David Nokes, assuming these 'facts,' speculates: "The evidence suggests that [Swift's mother] neglected him in an age when neglect of children was not the invariable rule that has sometimes been claimed ... It may have been Abigail Swift who instilled in him an instinctive association of love and distance."[19] The apparent callousness of Swift's mother during these early years, attributed to her by so many of Swift's biographers, explains for many readers all too well Swift's peculiarities of character, and stressing those peculiarities of character in turn distracts our attention from Swift's purposes in writing his pamphlets, poems, and satires.

But the commonly accepted story of Abigail Swift's leaving Jonathan in Ireland by the age of six and making a home for herself in Leicester makes little sense, and in most cases fails to consider that she had a daughter as well as a son. If Abigail was eager to live with her relatives in Leicester, why would she have stayed in Dublin with her daughter Jane between 1668 and 1671 when she could have easily reclaimed Jonathan from his nurse on the English side of the Irish sea and brought him to Leicester to grow up? Why, if Abigail and Jane did go to Leicester before Swift started school, did he not come with them and attend the free grammar school in Leicester? With respect to Jane, is it plausible that Abigail left Jane at age eight with relatives in Dublin and settled for her own convenience in Leicester? It is equally unlikely that Abigail took Jane to Leicester and raised her there, because if she did, why would Jane return to Dublin to marry a farrier (a blacksmith/veterinarian)[20] in 1699? We know that Jane was living with her Uncle William in Dublin in 1692. She was also listed as a resident "of Bride Street," as was William, at the time of her marriage in 1699.[21] Her marriage to a Dublin tradesman at the age of 33 suggests that she was raised primarily not in Leicester but in Dublin. We ought to expect stronger

---

that Swift's mother left with Jane for Leicester about the time that Swift began Kilkenny school at age 6 or 8. As Ehrenpreis puts it, "Whenever the child [Jonathan] was returned to his mother [after being three years with his nurse], he did not remain long with her" (p. 31).

18 Leo Damrosch, *Jonathan Swift: His Life and his World* (New Haven and London: Yale University Press, 2013), p. 15.

19 David Nokes, *Jonathan Swift, a Hypocrite Reversed: A Critical Biography* (Oxford: Oxford University Press, 1985), p. 9.

20 Julia G. Longe, *Martha Lady Giffard: Her Life and Correspondence, 1664-1722* (London: George Allen, 1911), p. 36.

21 Ada Peter, *Sketches of Old Dublin* (Dublin: Sealy, Bryers, and Walker, 1907), p. 225.

evidence than Orrery's assertion before we believe that Abigail Swift left either one or two children in Ireland while she lived comfortably in England.

Orrery first set us thinking that Swift had an unhappy and unloved childhood with several assumptions he made: first, he wrote about Swift's first 33 years plagiarizing from Swift's account without attribution, and as if it were fact; second, he assumed that with the 1658 death of Swift's grandfather, his grandmother was consequently out of the picture;[22] third, he inferred, offering no evidence,[23] that "the care, tuition, and expence of [Abigail Swift's] two children devolved upon her husband's elder brother, Mr. GODWIN SWIFT, who voluntarily became their guardian;"[24] fourth, he inferred from Swift's autobiographical notes that while at Trinity Jonathan suffered from the "ill treatment of his nearest Relations,"[25] and that he was ungrateful to his relatives;[26] fifth, Orrery stressed the disappointment of Swift's early years (which is not evident in any surviving source *except* in Swift's autobiographical notes), and then he used that supposed disappointment to explain Swift's later disappointments. Swift noted in his autobiographical account, for example, that King William ignored his "promise" of a Canterbury or Westminster prebend.[27] Orrery from this comment draws a far-too-dramatic inference: "From this first disappointment, may probably be dated that bitterness towards kings, and courtiers, which is to be found so universally dispersed throughout his works."[28] Finally, Orrery assumed that Swift had a youthful moroseness of temper: "The moroseness of his temper, often rendered him very unacceptable to his companions; so that he was little regarded, and less beloved."[29] But there is NO evidence that Swift was morose as a young man.

---

22 Orrery, *Remarks on the Life and Writings of Dr. Jonathan Swift*, p. 9.

23 And swayed, I believe, only by Swift's comment to him that he was born at 7 Hoey's Court (Eugene Hammond, *Jonathan Swift: Irish Blow-In* [Newark, Delaware: University of Delaware Press, 2016], p. 11n).

24 Orrery, *Remarks on the Life and Writings of Dr. Jonathan Swift*, p. 10.

25 *Prose Works*, V, 192. Which could have been Godwin Swift and his wife withholding money from his "portion" that he thought he was due.

26 Orrery includes as evidence Swift's letter to his uncle William, but is disappointed in the style of it. Orrery also draws an inference that taints Swift: "Or perhaps the letter was rather the effect of duty than inclination, and in that case, the style of it must be illaborate, and void of all freedom and vivacity" (Orrery, *Remarks on the Life and Writings of Dr. Jonathan Swift*, p. 18).

27 *Prose Works*, V, 195.

28 Orrery, *Remarks on the Life and Writings of Dr. Jonathan Swift*, p. 29. Orrery comments further, "Disappointments, the earlier they happen in life, the deeper impression they make upon the heart" (p. 12).

29 Orrery, *Remarks on the Life and Writings of Dr. Jonathan Swift*, p. 10. This comment gave birth to the notion that Swift was a difficult young man, a notion that Samuel Richardson

In his biography, Orrery made several other questionable assumptions. He was the first to call Esther Johnson "Stella" outside the poetic context. He assumed that Swift and Esther Johnson married in 1716. He implied that Swift hastened the deaths of the key women in his life, Esthers Johnson and Vanhomrigh.[30] He paints a very ill character of Esther Vanhomrigh. He was the first to tell the improbable story of a Swift ride to Celbridge just before Esther Vanhomrigh died. In *supposed* explanation of Swift's *supposed* objection to his sister Jane's choice of a husband in 1700, and to his unwillingness to avow his *supposed* marriage to Esther Johnson, Orrery projects a class prejudice onto Swift that Swift did not share.[31] Orrery admired Horace greatly, and because Swift as a poet did not behave and carry himself the way that Horace did, Orrery underestimates Swift's poetry. Steeped in his class prejudice, Orrery accused Swift of "depraved taste" in companions after he returned to Dublin in 1714.[32] Taking literary licence, Orrery dramatized the misery of Swift's final years, writing that Swift's lifelong dizziness and deafness eventually "render[ed] him the exact image of one of his own *Struldbruggs*, a miserable spectacle, devoid of every appearance of human nature, except the outward form."[33] Most fundamentally of all, Orrery's view of life was too shallow for him to understand

---

reinforced: Richardson in 1752 claimed to have heard from Jack Temple, who inherited Moor Park, that "Sir William hired Swift, at his first entrance into the world, to read to him and sometimes to be his amanuensis, at the rate of £20 a year and his board, which was then high preferment to him; but Sir William never favoured him with his conversation, because of his ill qualities, nor allowed him to sit down at table with him" (Samuel Richardson to Lady Bradshaigh, 22 April 1752, in *The Correspondence of Samuel Richardson*, ed. Anna Laetitia Barbauld [London: Richard Phillips, 1804], VI, 173-74.)

30 This idea that Swift had life-and-death power over the women in his life has had considerable stamina. Harold Williams wrote in a footnote to Swift's 1700 letter to Jane Waring, "Varina died unmarried, from which, perhaps, evidential conclusions may be drawn" (*Correspondence*, ed. Williams, I, 36n1).

31 Orrery wrote of Swift, "He grew outragious at the thoughts of being brother-in-law to a tradesman. He utterly refused all reconciliation with his sister, *nor* ever would listen to the entreaties of his mother, who came over to *Ireland*, under almost a certainty of pacifying his anger, having, in all other respects, ever found him a dutiful, and an obedient son: but his pride was not to be conquered, and Mrs. Swift finding her son inflexible, hastened back to *Leicester*, where she continued till her death" (*Remarks on the Life and Writings of Dr. Jonathan Swift*, p. 33). These stories seem to have been invented out of whole cloth, perhaps stimulated by Swift's peeved attitude towards his sister during the 1730s. Swift assumed that class rankings should govern a society, but he did not characteristically look down on others simply because of their class.

32 "From Swift's settlement in *Dublin* as Dean of St. *Patrick*'s, his choice of companions in general shewed him of a very depraved taste" (Orrery, *Remarks on the Life and Writings of Dr. Jonathan Swift*, pp. 67-68).

33 Orrery, *Remarks on the Life and Writings of Dr. Jonathan Swift*, p. 19.

Swift's aim in his satire: "In those tracts, where he tries to make us uneasy with ourselves, and unhappy in our present existence, *there*, I must yield him up entirely to censure."[34] Orrery is the first commentator on Swift to assume that Swift was a 'misanthrope.'[35] We have been digging out of several Orrery-built holes since 1752.

I would like to insert a few words here about Patrick Delany's 1754 *Observations* upon Lord Orrery's *Remarks*, because Delany met Swift at least 15 years earlier than any of Swift's young biographers. Unlike Orrery, Deane Swift, and Sheridan, Delany lived with Swift weekly if not daily for twenty years; and he was not quite as young as they were (he met Swift in 1718 when he was 32 and Swift was 50). First of all, Delany celebrates with utter confidence and conviction Swift's public admirability.[36] Delany's comments and evidence persuade me that Swift was more admirable than he is generally assumed to have been, but, following in Orrery's footsteps, we usually seem to believe that it is a sign of mental toughness to emphasize Swift's faults rather than that admirability.

Delany does *not* agree, and he had plenty of experience with Swift to base this opinion on, that Swift was avaricious.[37] Nor that he was vulnerable to adulation.[38] Nor that he was excessively ambitious.[39] Nor that he disliked his sister.[40] Nor that he learned his use of scurrilous language by mixing with the poor.[41] Nor that he chose ill Irish friends.[42] Nor that Temple was Swift's father.[43] Nor that his religion was less than fully sincere.[44] Delany is, though wrong on the publication date of *Cadenus and Vanessa*,[45] a seemingly reliable witness of the tension between Esther Vanhomrigh and Esther Johnson. Delany consistently found Swift's poems better than Orrery thought them.[46]

34 Orrery, *Remarks on the Life and Writings of Dr. Jonathan Swift*, p. 325.
35 Swift was not afraid to face squarely the underside of human behaviour, but he was by no means a hater of people. He wrote to try to work with us.
36 Patrick Delany, *Observations upon Lord Orrery's Remarks on the Life and Writings of Dr. Jonathan Swift* (London: W. Reeve, 1754), p. 30.
37 Delany, *Observations upon Lord Orrery's Remarks*, p. 4.
38 Delany, *Observations upon Lord Orrery's Remarks*, pp. 15, 18.
39 Delany, *Observations upon Lord Orrery's Remarks*, p. 30.
40 Delany, *Observations upon Lord Orrery's Remarks*, p. 71.
41 Delany, *Observations upon Lord Orrery's Remarks*, p. 73. Delany thought Swift learned it from Pope. I think he learned it at school.
42 Delany, *Observations upon Lord Orrery's Remarks*, pp. 90-91.
43 Delany, *Observations upon Lord Orrery's Remarks*, p. 73.
44 Delany, *Observations upon Lord Orrery's Remarks*, p. 44.
45 Delany assumes that *Cadenus and Vanessa* appeared before Esther Vanhomrigh died in 1723, not as it did in 1726 (*Observations upon Lord Orrery's Remarks*, p. 57).
46 Delany, *Observations upon Lord Orrery's Remarks*, p. 135.

He agreed that Swift was rough on company in his last years, but he draws an important distinction: "I have heard the Dean often charged with ill-nature: indeed I cannot remember any one instance of that kind."[47] He found, contrary to the usual interpretation, Swift a very conscientious manager of St Patrick's vicars choral.[48] And alone of Swift's early biographers, Delany recognized and emphasized how important becoming historiographer was to Swift – "no man was better fitted for any employment, than he was, for that"[49] – a crucial insight because it enables us to free Swift from being seen as merely a satirist.

Delany, though, has also misled us in several areas where he does not seem to have had full information. He did not know any more about Swift's early life than Orrery did, writing to Orrery: "Your account of SWIFT's birth, parentage, and education, is so just, that, I believe, nothing is to be added to it."[50] Delany was uncertain about Esther Johnson's birth and mixed up about it.[51] He also gave a significant boost to Orrery's speculation that Swift had married Esther Johnson by writing, though he was not sure, "Your account of his marriage, is, I am satisfied, true."[52] Delany reinforced Orrery's insinuation that Swift was responsible for Esther Johnson's death: "Her chagrin, and sickness ... followed soon, and sensibly increased after [the publication of *Cadenus and Vanessa*]."[53] Delany praises Swift for allowing Esther Johnson, whom he assumed to be Swift's wife, to make her own will (though the fact that she made her own will is, on the contrary, evidence against her having been his wife).[54]

From reading Delany's many religious writings, particularly his defences of the Biblical King David's moral character, Delany appears to have been sincere, but seriously naïve, so it is not surprising that he basically agrees with Orrery about *Gulliver's Travels* being too critical of human nature[55] and that Swift was a misanthrope.[56]

47 Delany, *Observations upon Lord Orrery's Remarks*, p. 188.

48 Delany, *Observations upon Lord Orrery's Remarks*, p. 189.

49 Delany, *Observations upon Lord Orrery's Remarks*, p. 86.

50 Delany, *Observations upon Lord Orrery's Remarks*, p. 48.

51 Delany writes, "Mrs. JOHNSTON, and Mrs. DINGLEY, were both relations to Sir WILLIAM TEMPLE ... Mrs. JOHNSTON then was not the daughter of Sir WILLIAM'S menial servant; at least if she was, that servant was his relation" (*Observations upon Lord Orrery's Remarks*, p. 54).

52 Delany, *Observations upon Lord Orrery's Remarks*, pp. 52-53.

53 Delany, *Observations upon Lord Orrery's Remarks*, p. 59. It is not clear whether Delany here was assuming that *Cadenus and Vanessa* was published in 1723 or in 1726.

54 Delany, *Observations upon Lord Orrery's Remarks*, p. 288.

55 Delany, *Observations upon Lord Orrery's Remarks*, pp. 138, 161, 171.

56 Delany, *Observations upon Lord Orrery's Remarks*, p. 176.

In 1755, a year after Delany and three years after Orrery, Deane Swift entered the biographical fray. Deane Swift's helpfulness as a biographer was considerable. He was impressed with Swift's mother, and offers plausible evidence for his admiration: Abigail Swift, he writes, was

> a woman greatly beloved and esteemed by all the family of the SWIFTS. Her conversation was so extreamly polite, chearful and agreeable even to the young and sprightly that some of the family, who paid her a visit near fifty years ago at Leicester, speak of her to this day with the greatest affection. I am told she was of a generous and hospitable nature, that she was very exact in all the duties of religion, and paid her attendance at the publick worship generally twice a day ... that her chief amusements were needle-work and reading, and that she was equally fond of both her children, notwithstanding some disagreements[57] that subsisted between them.[58]

Deane also is in sympathy with Swift's choice most often to walk when he travelled during his 20s:

> His company in those flights were, I believe, all sorts of people which he met in towns and villages where he chanced to refresh himself; some chat for an hour, and again to the fields. His imagination was always alive, and perhaps beyond all others he had a power to conciliate his ideas to the several capacities of all [the] human race, and at the same time catch entertainment to himself from every species of understanding.[59]

Deane followed eighteenth-century convention in placing Swift's "Mrs Harris's Petition" in the category of "low humour," but he clearly enjoyed and admired the poem. He recognized the greatness of *A Tale of a Tub*, "this great and mighty bulwark of our glorious reformation."[60] He showed excellent taste also in praising Swift's several works of 1708:

> We may observe the genius of Dr. Swift to break forth upon us in the year 1708 with such an astonishing blaze of humour, politicks, religion, patriotism, wit and poetry; that if the world had been totally unacquainted with all his former reputation, the productions of that one year would have been highly sufficient to have established his fame unto all eternity.[61]

---

57 Deane Swift's choice to characterize the difficulties between Swift and his sister Jane as "disagreements" seems more in keeping with the surviving evidence than does the stubborn and complete separation between them that is usually assumed.

58 Deane Swift, *An Essay upon the Life, Writings, and Character, of Dr. Jonathan Swift* (London: Charles Bathurst, 1755), pp. 22-23.

59 Deane Swift, *An Essay upon the Life, Writings, and Character*, p. 100.

60 Deane Swift, *An Essay upon the Life, Writings, and Character*, p. 32.

61 Deane Swift, *An Essay upon the Life, Writings, and Character*, p. 131.

More particularly, he enthused,

> The *Argument against abolishing* CHRISTIANITY, which is the production of the same year, is according to the best of my judgment the most delicate, refined, compleat, unvaried piece of irony, from the beginning to the end, that ever was written since the creation of the world.[62]

Many people since Deane Swift have not been able to see as clearly as he did the excellence of Swift's political writings:

> These are a course of writings not to be considered in the light of *occasional pamphlets*, or little paultry *journals* thrown into the world by some *hackney jade* in the defence of CORRUPTION, and to serve the iniquitous designs of a party. No, these writings are to be considered, and read over and over again, as lectures of true unprejudiced constitutional politicks.[63]

And Deane was savvy about Swift's political principles: "[The principles of a moderate Whig, as articulated in his *Letter from a Member of the House of Commons in Ireland to a Member of the House of Commons in England*] were the political principles of Dr. SWIFT, from which I am persuaded that he never once swerved throughout his whole life."[64]

On the other hand, Deane Swift sounds like a lunatic whenever an issue related to the Swift family comes up in his biography. Orrery casually wrote that Swift was the greatest luminary in his family. Deane Swift had not even reached page 3 of his biography before he expressed his anger at Orrery for the supposedly critical light in which that remark placed the Swifts: "I am wholly at a loss to conceive, what invidious spirit, enemy to candor, friendship, and benevolence, could have instigated one of our modern criticks to asperse the remains of an old, faithful, and loyal family at so unmerciful a rate."[65]

Though an Anglophile himself, Deane Swift thoroughly admired Swift's defence of Ireland against the exploitation of England.[66] He had mixed feelings

---

62 Deane Swift, *An Essay upon the Life, Writings, and Character*, p. 135.

63 Deane Swift, *An Essay upon the Life, Writings, and Character*, p. 150.

64 Deane Swift, *An Essay upon the Life, Writings, and Character*, p. 130. See also Downie, *Jonathan Swift: Political Writer*, pp. ix-x.

65 Deane Swift, *An Essay upon the Life, Writings, and Character*, p. 2. Deane Swift introduces into his biography gratuitous praise of the Swift family as a whole, as when he quotes [or invents a quote from] a wholly unnecessary Bishop Sheridan, talking with Swift about the authorship of *A Tale of a Tub*: "Oh, Mr. SWIFT ... I have had a long acquaintance with your uncles, and an old friendship for all your family" (*An Essay upon the Life, Writings, and Character*, pp. 122-23).

66 Deane Swift, *An Essay upon the Life, Writings, and Character*, p. 198.

about *Gulliver's Travels*, but he saw values in it that Orrery did not see.[67] He also valued *A Modest Proposal* more than Orrery did.[68] He understood the purpose of Swift's poetry, and by implication, of his publications in general: Swift, he wrote,

> is not to be considered in the light of a professed poet; the multitude of his writings on various subjects both in verse and prose being an evident demonstration, that he was superior to any particular course of learning. He was born to be the encourager of virtue, and the terror of the wicked. He never sate musing in his elbow chair upon new subjects, for the exercise of his genius, and the advancement of his fame; but writ occasionally to please and to reform the world, as either politicks or humour gave the spur to his faculties.[69]

Deane was not swayed either by the need to make Esther Johnson and Esther Vanhomrigh opposites, and so seems to give a much fairer assessment of the latter: "I have been assured, that Miss VANHOMRIGH was in her general converse with the world, as far from encouraging any stile of address, inconsistent with the rules of honour and good-breeding, as any woman alive ... Her only misfortune was, that she had a passion for Dr. SWIFT, which was not to be conquered."[70]

Along with these strengths, though, Deane Swift, too, has been a major misleader. He assumed that what Swift wrote about his own life was literal truth. He calls Swift's autobiographical notes "a paper of instructions for any one, that should think it worth his leisure to employ himself in that kind of writing."[71] He takes literally Swift's account of his grandfather, Revd Thomas Swift, for example, in the improbable words that he was "plundered two and fifty times" during the Civil Wars. He also takes literally Swift's remark that his father purchased a pension for his wife upon their marriage: "She had a small annuity of twenty pounds a year, which her husband had purchased for her in *England* immediately after his marriage."[72] And in Deane's account, his own grandfather, Swift's uncle Godwin, on very flimsy evidence, sails right to the top of the heroes who made Swift's life possible.

67 Deane Swift, *An Essay upon the Life, Writings, and Character*, pp. 182, 207, 218, 225.

68 Deane Swift, *An Essay upon the Life, Writings, and Character*, p. 204.

69 Deane Swift, *An Essay upon the Life, Writings, and Character*, p. 226.

70 Deane Swift, *An Essay upon the Life, Writings, and Character*, p. 264.

71 Deane Swift, *An Essay upon the Life, Writings, and Character*, p. 7n.

72 Deane Swift, *An Essay upon the Life, Writings, and Character*, p. 23. Deane seems not to have asked himself how Swift's impecunious father would have had this money. A 20-pound per year pension for a young woman would have cost at least 400 pounds in 1665.

Also, Deane misleads us by idealizing Esther Johnson as Stella, naming Swift's letters to Esther Johnson and Rebecca Dingley in 1710-13 *The Journal to Stella*. Deane did not know either Esther Johnson or Esther Vanhomrigh, so all his evidence about them is from Swift's *Bon Mots de Stella* and from Swift's poetry.[73] Without proof, he believed Orrery that Swift and Esther Johnson were married. "That she was married to Dr. SWIFT in or about the year 1716 I am thoroughly persuaded,"[74] he writes. He adduces as a reason for Swift not acknowledging this "marriage" a very unlikely one, that Esther was "a wife ... very meanly extracted."[75] Such a resort to class superiority was characteristic of Deane but not of Jonathan. Deane never doubts Orrery's explanation of Sir William Temple's bequest of a thousand pounds to Esther Johnson "as an acknowledgment of her father's just and faithful services."[76] He surmises that, when Swift returned to Ireland in 1714, Esther Johnson was depressed by his unwillingness to marry, so, he writes, unconvincingly,

> *it is not unreasonable to imagine* that SWIFT, thoroughly and sincerely her friend, and almost her lover, was unable to endure the least abatement in her chearfulness and vivacity: and therefore to raise her spirits, and to secure the fame of her innocence from all possibility of reproach, resolved to gratify her with the consciousness of being his *legal* wife.[77]

He adds that this is "certainly the reason that he ever married her at all." All this is imagination. Deane's evidence that Swift and Esther Johnson married is utterly useless.[78]

Because he shared Orrery's social-class prejudices, Deane also accepts at face value the Earl's assessment of a supposed quarrel between Swift and his sister Jane over her marrying Joseph Fenton: "Neither can I blame the Doctor for his behaviour in this particular," Deane writes, "because how reputable soever trade is beginning to be in *Ireland* at this time, it is certain that fifty or sixty years ago it was in the utmost contempt."[79] Again, Deane attributes to Swift his *own* feelings.

---

73 Deane Swift, *An Essay upon the Life, Writings, and Character*, p. 80.

74 Deane Swift, *An Essay upon the Life, Writings, and Character*, p. 92.

75 Deane Swift, *An Essay upon the Life, Writings, and Character*, pp. 84-85.

76 Deane Swift, *An Essay upon the Life, Writings, and Character*, p. 85. For rhetorical emphasis, Deane has expanded Orrery's "faithful services" (*Remarks on the Life and Writings of Dr. Jonathan Swift*, p. 22) to "just and faithful services."

77 Deane Swift, *An Essay upon the Life, Writings, and Character*, p. 95; my emphasis.

78 Deane Swift, *An Essay upon the Life, Writings, and Character*, p. 94.

79 Deane Swift, *An Essay upon the Life, Writings, and Character*, p. 103.

Finally, Deane Swift has misled us by being the first critic to assume in Swift's mind a link between the Yahoos and the Irish poor. When Swift arrived in Ireland in 1714, Deane reports, "he was frequently pointed at and abused by several of the meaner shopkeepers, mechanicks and other base fellows without name or occupation. These abominable wretches like their brethren the YAHOOS, would oftentimes scrape the kennels with their nasty claws to throw dirt and filth at him as he passed through the city."[80] But in *Gulliver's Travels* it is evident that Swift designed the Yahoos as a satire most pertinently on the upper, not the lower classes. When Swift takes up ministers of state in Book Four, he finds them far worse than the bulk of Mankind: "In most Herds there was a Sort of ruling *Yahoo* (as among us there is generally some leading or principal Stag in a Park), who was always more *deformed* in Body, and *mischievous in Disposition*, than any of the rest."[81] But many later commentators have attributed to Jonathan Swift Deane's prejudice here.

Thomas Sheridan's character seems to have been genial, though he was a bit too much in awe of his godfather (Swift). He opens his biography of Swift with a shameless compliment, borrowing his epigraph – *Detur Dignissimo* [let it be given to the worthiest] – from Swift's *Tale of a Tub*. He writes in the first page of his Dedication that "In the following history [that is, his biography] SWIFT has been represented as a man of the most disinterested principles, regardless of self, and constantly employed in doing good to others."[82] This is patently not true.

Sheridan's biography has all the polish and sense of completeness that readers like in a biography, and it has many strengths. Most notably, Sheridan was the first biographer to see the point of Book Four of *Gulliver's Travels*: "It was ... necessary to give this creature [the Yahoos] the human form, in order to bring the lesson home to man, by having the vicious part of his nature reflected back to him from one in his own shape; for in the form of any other creature, he would not think himself at all concerned in it."[83] Sheridan's testimony concerning Swift's late-life peevishness is invaluable because it was first hand, corroborated by other sources, and shows that Swift's own testimony increasingly throughout the 1730s is not very credible: "It was his custom to try their [people meeting him for the first time] tempers and disposition, by some abrupt question that bore the appearance of rudeness. If this were well

80 Deane Swift, *An Essay upon the Life, Writings, and Character*, p. 183. This is language that Deane Swift would use, but not, I think, Jonathan.

81 *Gulliver's Travels*, in *Prose Works*, XI, 262 (IV, vii, 13).

82 Sheridan, *The Life of the Rev. Dr. Jonathan Swift*, sig. A1r.

83 Sheridan, *The Life of the Rev. Dr. Jonathan Swift*, pp. 505-6.

taken, and answered with good humour, he afterwards made amends by his civilities."[84] Sheridan also describes a final quarrel between Tom Sheridan, Sr, and Swift in 1738 that seems plausible, given Swift's mental condition by that year.[85] Sheridan, though, was clearly irritated that his father was not taken seriously by either Orrery or Deane Swift, and in response he gives his father several notable good qualities, plausible ones, such as the care he took for Esther Johnson in her last years, but also less plausible ones, such as pairing Swift and Sheridan as "two men of genius, who had a great similarity both of disposition and talents."[86]

Sheridan's misleading comments in his biography of Swift consist primarily of his telling plausible stories of which we have to question the veracity because he so consistently adds an effective narrative twist to a story that we now realize he had read elsewhere. Like Swift's other young men, Sheridan uses the language of Swift's autobiographical notes and treats Swift's comments as if they were facts.[87] Typical of Sheridan's method is the way he embellishes the story of Swift's being stolen away by his nurse. Here is Sheridan's version:

> When he was but a year old, he was, without the knowledge of his mother or relations, stolen away by his nurse, and carried to Whitehaven; which place she was under a necessity of visiting, on account of the illness of a relation, from whom she expected a legacy; and, as is usual among Irish nurses, she bore such an affection to the child, that she could not think of going without him. There he continued for almost three years; and she took such care of him, that he had learned to spell, and could read any chapter in the Bible before he was five years old.[88]

Adding "as is usual among Irish nurses ... she could not think of going without him," Sheridan gives the story more heart by giving the nurse a nationality and ascribing to her a supposed national trait.

Likewise, Sheridan assumes the veracity of many of Orrery's and Deane Swift's inferences. Without offering any evidence, for example, he posits that "the expence of [Swift's] education [was] defrayed by his uncle Godwin Swift."[89] And of Swift's time at Trinity College, he invents the detail that "[Godwin Swift], being father of a numerous offspring by four wives, was under a necessity of reducing the stipend allowed to his nephew for his support at the University, as

84 Sheridan, *The Life of the Rev. Dr. Jonathan Swift*, p. 409.
85 Sheridan, *The Life of the Rev. Dr. Jonathan Swift*, p. 392.
86 Sheridan, *The Life of the Rev. Dr. Jonathan Swift*, p. 370.
87 Sheridan, *The Life of the Rev. Dr. Jonathan Swift*, p. 1.
88 Sheridan, *The Life of the Rev. Dr. Jonathan Swift*, p. 2.
89 Sheridan, *The Life of the Rev. Dr. Jonathan Swift*, p. 2.

low as possible."[90] Sheridan assumes that Swift was ungrateful to all his uncles who had, he assumes, supported him: "He never afterwards could think with patience of his uncle Godwin, nor could heartily forgive the neglect shewn him during that time by his other relations."[91] If the ingratitude Sheridan adds here to Swift's biographical story were true, Sheridan's unqualified admiration of Swift would hardly be justified.

Reinforcing an assumption made by Orrery, Sheridan projects a young Swift into his biography that he could only have inferred from some of Swift's late-life tendencies. While at school, Sheridan writes, Swift "scorned to take up with those of a lower class, or to be obliged to those of a higher. He lived therefore much alone."[92] And he assumes that applying to Sir William Temple for the position of secretary was "grating … to the proud spirit of Swift."[93] While both of these assumptions are possible, no evidence survives that supports them. Sheridan sums up Swift's youth dramatically: "The recluseness of his life had rendered him little known; and a temper naturally splenetic, sowered by the misery of his situation, did not qualify him much for making personal friends."[94] This view of Swift gives a cause-effect logic to Sheridan's biography: "It is to those very circumstances, probably [– the want of money, want of learning, want of friends –] that the world owes, *a Swift*."[95]

So Sheridan either consciously or unconsciously added in these projections concerning Swift's childhood to make his overall story of Swift's life more coherent. We have no evidence that would lead us to think that Swift lacked either money or learning or friends as a young man. The surviving evidence, admittedly meager, suggests that Swift had enough money (though not keeping-up-with-the-Joneses money), plenty of learning (if not exactly what his teachers wanted him to learn), and several friends. Young Jonathan made and kept friends readily throughout his life, though the loss or destruction of his letters in his early years do not allow us to enumerate too many of his early friends other than the Waring brothers, John Jones, William Congreve, Dillon Ashe, and Tom Davys (Mary Davys's husband).[96]

More particularly, ever in search of coherence and plausibility in his biography, Sheridan added to stories that did not seem quite complete: "Sir William Temple had bequeathed to Mrs. Johnson a legacy of a thousand pounds, in

90 Sheridan, *The Life of the Rev. Dr. Jonathan Swift*, p. 2.
91 Sheridan, *The Life of the Rev. Dr. Jonathan Swift*, p. 3.
92 Sheridan, *The Life of the Rev. Dr. Jonathan Swift*, p. 6.
93 Sheridan, *The Life of the Rev. Dr. Jonathan Swift*, p. 12.
94 Sheridan, *The Life of the Rev. Dr. Jonathan Swift*, p. 8.
95 Sheridan, *The Life of the Rev. Dr. Jonathan Swift*, p. 9.
96 *Correspondence*, ed. Woolley, I, 151.

consideration of her father's faithful services, and her own rising merits."[97] Since Sheridan was not convinced by Orrery's hint that Esther Johnson might have been Temple's illegitimate child,[98] Sheridan invented "her own rising merits." In fact, Sheridan frequently invented stories when he needed them, as in his account of the Duchess of Somerset's response to Swift's attack on her in "The Windsor Prophecy": "The Duchess ... went in person to the Queen, and, throwing herself on her knees, entreated, with tears in her eyes, that she would not give the Bishoprick to Swift."[99] The Duchess died in 1722, Sheridan was born only in 1719, and he cites no source for this (melo)dramatic description.

Sheridan added significantly to the Esther Johnson versus Esther Vanhomrigh lore. First, prompted by Swift's own description of his temperament – "my cold temper" – in his 1692 letter to Revd John Kendall, Sheridan gave credence to an inclination among later biographers to think of Swift as asexual: "[Swift] seems to have been of a very cold habit, and little spurred on by any impulse of desire."[100] Swift's meaning seems to have been not that he was asexual but that he was judgmental.[101] Focusing rather on sexuality, Sheridan repeated Orrery's claim, often reiterated since, that Swift and Esther Johnson never conversed "but in the presence of a third person."[102] But Sheridan gave more credence to Orrery's claim by adding, as if he had been a witness, "which was usually her companion Mrs. Dingley."[103] Sheridan's account of Swift's marriage to Stella, which he believed to have taken place, came from Elizabeth Sican, certainly a good friend of Swift during the 1730s, but a young child when the marriage supposedly took place in 1716, and still a youth (we do not know the year of her birth) when Esther Johnson died. She is not likely to have been a well-informed witness.

Furthermore, Sheridan claimed an unnamed source, "a common friend to both,"[104] for his account of Swift's and Esther Johnson's thoughts about a possible marriage. If Elizabeth Sican was not this "source," Sheridan's father, also Thomas Sheridan, perhaps was: the younger Sheridan relates a supposed conversation in which Esther Johnson expresses to "the common friend" her hopes

---

97 Sheridan, *The Life of the Rev. Dr. Jonathan Swift*, p. 35.

98 Sheridan, *The Life of the Rev. Dr. Jonathan Swift*, p. 367.

99 Sheridan, *The Life of the Rev. Dr. Jonathan Swift*, p. 95.

100 Sheridan, *The Life of the Rev. Dr. Jonathan Swift*, p. 285.

101 Hannah More, for example, wrote in 1777 about a book she had been given, "a slowness to applaud betrays a cold temper or an envious spirit" (William Roberts, *Memoirs of the Life of Mrs. Hannah More*, 2nd ed., 4 vols [London: R. B. Seeley and W. Burnside, 1839], I, 47).

102 Sheridan, *The Life of the Rev. Dr. Jonathan Swift*, p. 296.

103 Sheridan, *The Life of the Rev. Dr. Jonathan Swift*, p. 296.

104 Sheridan, *The Life of the Rev. Dr. Jonathan Swift*, p. 321.

for a marriage.[105] Such a conversation would have had to occur before 1716, when Esther and Swift allegedly married, but the older Sheridan did not know Swift until 1718, two years after the alleged marriage. Although Sheridan sounds confident, quotes liberally, and gives details, he is unlikely to have known anything substantive on this issue.[106] All the lines of argument Sheridan offers – Esther Johnson's concern for her reputation, Esther Johnson's jealousy of Esther Vanhomrigh, Swift's insistence on the necessity of a more solid financial standing to marry – were readily available to Sheridan, so he could use them to make up a plausible story.

Sheridan's discussion of the 'marriage' climaxes in a great story, which unfortunately is not likely to contain any grain of truth. Orrery had written, without evidence:

> [Esther Vanhomrigh] often pressed [Swift] to marry her. His answers were rather turns of wit than positive denials; till at last, being unable to sustain her weight of misery any longer, she writ a very tender epistle to [him] insisting peremptorily upon as serious an answer, and an immediate acceptance, or absolute refusal of her, as his wife. His reply was delivered by his own hand. He brought it with him when he made his final visit at *Selbridge*: and throwing down the letter upon her table, with great passion hastened back to his horse, carrying in his countenance the frowns of anger and indignation.[107]

Sheridan revised Orrery's story of Swift's supposed ride to Celbridge by making Esther Vanhomrigh's first concern whether or not Swift and Esther Johnson were married, and by claiming that Esther Vanhomrigh wrote not to Swift, as Orrery had asserted, but to Esther Johnson herself. Then Sheridan adds persuasive-sounding circumstantial details: Esther Johnson "inclosed the note she

105 Sheridan, *The Life of the Rev. Dr. Jonathan Swift*, p. 321.

106 Sheridan acknowledges that "the only unequivocal proof remaining of the ceremony's having passed between them arises from Mrs. Johnson's declaration of it, in the presence of Dr. Sheridan" (p. 366). Sheridan is using his father here to dare us to disbelieve him. But I do not believe. First, the testimony of Jane Brent and Rebecca Dingley against the marriage should outweigh that of Orrery, Deane Swift, and Sheridan for it, because Mrs Brent and Mrs Dingley knew Swift, and knew him during the time that the Swift/Esther Johnson/Esther Vanhomrigh drama was playing out, infinitely better than Swift's young biographers did. Second, *if* Swift and Esther Johnson were married, Swift's sexual and emotional behaviour with Esther Vanhomrigh in the early 1720s would have been reprehensible, and not merely disloyal. Neither Swift's character nor his concern for the reputation of the Church of Ireland would, I think, have allowed him to act so callously. I believe Sheridan *wanted* a Swift/Esther Johnson marriage to be true, and *wanted* his father to be a key witness to its truth, and had the storytelling ability to convince others of what he had already convinced himself.

107 Orrery, *Remarks on the Life and Writings of Dr. Jonathan Swift*, p. 115.

had received from Miss Vanhomrigh to Swift. After which, she immediately went out of town without seeing him, or coming to any explanation, and retired in great resentment to Mr. Forde's country-seat at Wood-Park."[108] The rest is high drama: "Exasperated to the highest degree, [Swift] gave way to the first transports of his passion, and immediately rid to Celbridge ... He then flung a paper on the table, and immediately returned to his horse. The violent agitation of her mind threw her into a fever, which in a short time put a period to her existence."[109] Esther Johnson "retired" to Wood-Park in March 1723. But March 1723 is an implausible date for this supposed incident. By that month, Esther Vanhomrigh was already dying of tuberculosis, and she was staying in Turnstile Alley in Dublin, not at Celbridge. Yet Sheridan's storytelling is so compelling that readers find his account, despite its implausibility, difficult to dismiss.

Sheridan then retails another dramatic story concerning Esther Johnson's death to match the drama of his and Orrery's ride-to-Celbridge story about Esther Vanhomrigh's death. According to Sheridan's story, not hinted at by any earlier biographer, Esther Johnson, dying, and in the presence of Thomas Sheridan, Sr, asked Swift to acknowledge their marriage. "Swift made no reply, but turning on his heel, walked silently out of the room, nor ever saw her afterwards during the few days she lived."[110] From all we know of Swift and Esther Johnson neither the walking out nor the refusal to see her seems plausible. Sheridan seems to have written this story to account for Esther Johnson making a will that did not bequeath the bulk of her estate to Swift: "Roused by indignation, she inveighed against [Swift's] cruelty in the bitterest terms; and sending for a lawyer, made her will, bequeathing her fortune by her own name to charitable uses."[111] But there is no need for such a story to account for Esther Johnson's will, which included Swift in very trusting ways, and gave, as Swift would certainly approve, the bulk of her estate to charity after making it available to her mother and her not-well-off sister Anne for the duration of their lives.

108 Sheridan, *The Life of the Rev. Dr. Jonathan Swift*, p. 330.

109 Sheridan, *The Life of the Rev. Dr. Jonathan Swift*, pp. 330-31. What witness could there have been for this event?

110 Sheridan, *The Life of the Rev. Dr. Jonathan Swift*, p. 361.

111 Sheridan, *The Life of the Rev. Dr. Jonathan Swift*, pp. 361-62. Oddly, Sheridan ignores his story here only a few pages later when he cites a 15 July 1726 letter from Swift to Worrall encouraging Esther Johnson to leave her fortune to charity (p. 367).

Immediately after this story, Sheridan makes his father a hero:

> During the few days [Esther Johnson] lived after this, Dr. Sheridan gave her constant attendance, and was in the chamber when she breathed her last. His grief for her loss was not perhaps inferior to the Dean's. He admired her above all human beings, and loved her with a devotion as pure as that which we would pay to Angels. She, on her part, had early singled him out from all the Dean's acquaintance, as her confidential friend.[112]

Sheridan's comment honours his father: "No wonder therefore if the Doctor's [Sheridan's] humanity was shocked at the last scene which he saw pass between her and the Dean, and which affected him so much, that it was a long time before he [and Swift] could be thoroughly reconciled."[113] They did, though, jointly start *The Intelligencer* within four months.

In his biography, Sheridan is surprisingly frank about Swift's sexual urges, which of course he cannot have known:

> It will be hardly credible, that … [passing] many hours alone with a young and charming woman, who loved him to adoration, [Swift and Esther Vanhomrigh] should not, in some unguarded moment, have given way to the frailty of human nature. And yet extraordinary as it may appear, there are many strong reasons to believe that this never was the case.[114]

By way of explanation, Sheridan added that "Swift, having lived to such an advanced time of life in a state of continence, and a constant habit of suppressing his desires, at last lost the power of gratifying them: a case by no means singular, as more than one instance of the kind has fallen within my knowledge."[115] Sheridan has no evidence here but a hunch based on his own limited experience:

> And I think there is one strong argument of his never having entered into any commerce of that sort with Vanessa, that it is hardly credible he should have refrained, in that case, from a similar gratification with Stella, who was possessed of greater personal charms, and was more an object of desire, than the other.[116]

Rather than assume Swift's platonic love for Esther Johnson as a given, as Sheridan does here, to argue deductively that Swift's love for Esther Vanhomrigh

112 Sheridan, *The Life of the Rev. Dr. Jonathan Swift*, p. 362.
113 Sheridan, *The Life of the Rev. Dr. Jonathan Swift*, pp. 362-63.
114 Sheridan, *The Life of the Rev. Dr. Jonathan Swift*, p. 338.
115 Sheridan, *The Life of the Rev. Dr. Jonathan Swift*, p. 340.
116 Sheridan, *The Life of the Rev. Dr. Jonathan Swift*, p. 340.

was also platonic, I think we should frankly open the question, given the frequent sexual flirtation in Swift's 1710-13 letters to Esther Johnson, of whether Swift had between 1700 and 1710 a sometime sexual relation with her. Sheridan wisely concludes his discussion of Swift's mixed relationship with Esther Johnson and Esther Vanhomrigh, "I have dwelt the longer on this point, because much of the moral part of Swift's character depends on it."[117] That is why we are still so seriously debating these questions.

Given our susceptibility to several of these young biographers' inferences, scholars of Swift need to find more evidence for the years when evidence is scarce. Irvin Ehrenpreis did this impressively when his investigation of Swift's school record at Trinity showed that Swift's performance was far from a disgrace and in fact well above average. It is difficult to find new evidence about Swift by this point, but we need to try, in the spirit of Ehrenpreis, to chip away at the certainties of Orrery, Deane Swift, and Sheridan.

One key issue, where I hope we will be open to re-examining our assumptions, is our almost universal use of Swift's poetic names, Stella and Vanessa, to refer to the women Esther Johnson and Esther Vanhomrigh. We have been seduced by the romance in these names, and we have perhaps allowed ourselves to use them for 270 years in part because both women were named Esther, and it seems too complicated to try to distinguish them using their real names. But Swift used neither "Stella" nor "Vanessa" consistently to refer to these women (though "Stella" had considerable staying power from 1719 to 1728). Swift's nickname for the young Esther Vanhomrigh was not Vanessa, but "the brat." His nicknames for her from 1720 to 1722, when their letters to each other suggest that they were carrying on a sexual affair, were "Skinage"[118] and "Governor Huff." We are given the impression by almost all biographers (and critics) that Swift called Esther Johnson "Stella" all his life, in large part because Deane Swift decided to title his publication of Swift's letters to her from 1710-13 the *Journal to Stella*. But Swift's first recorded use of that name is his 1719 poem for her birthday. Swift most often addressed his journal letters to "MD" ("my dears"), MC ("mes cheris"?), or ME ("mes enfants"?). He never addressed Esther Johnson in his "journal" letters as "Stella." Deane Swift edited the more than half of Swift's letters to Esther Johnson, which he received from the

117 Sheridan, *The Life of the Rev. Dr. Jonathan Swift*, p. 341.

118 David Woolley suggests that the name is possibly a reference to Hessy being skinny by 1720 (*Correspondence*, ed. Woolley, II, 341n5). Later, at Market Hill, he gave a similar nickname to Lady Anne Acheson (see James Woolley, "Swift's 'Skinnibonia': A New Poem from Lady Acheson's Manuscript," *Reading Swift: Papers from The Fifth Münster Symposium on Jonathan Swift*, ed. Hermann J. Real [Munich: Wilhelm Fink, 2008], pp. 310-42).

Dean's cousin and housekeeper, his mother-in-law Martha Whiteway,[119] but he edited very unhelpfully: "To avoid perplexing the reader," he wrote in his 1768 edition of these letters, "it was thought more advisable to use the word *Presto* for Swift."[120] He also inserted "Stella" in place of any term that Swift used for Esther Johnson. The letters Deane Swift used have since been lost, so we cannot check to find out which names Swift actually used. Following Deane Swift's lead, Thomas Sheridan, when in 1784 he published the full set of journal letters that we now have, titled them *Dr. Swift's Journal to Stella*, the title by which they are still unfortunately known. The letters after February 1712, that is, the letters that Sheridan had but Deane Swift did not, still survive, and we see in them Swift's frequent use of "Ppt" or "saucebox" for Esther Johnson and "Pdfr" [possibly, poor dear friend] for himself. Judging from what Swift called Esther Johnson in the original letters that survive, this collection should be called *The Journal to Saucebox*, or *The Journal to Poppet*.[121] Both poppet and saucebox give us a more accurate sense of how Swift felt about Esther Johnson at the time he wrote this journal than does the name Stella, his retrospective, late-life name for her.

We could safely call Esther Johnson Hetty. She was called Tetty as a preteenager at Moor Park, and Hetty at Moor Park from about the time that she was 16.[122] Lady Giffard calls her Hetty in a 1697 letter,[123] confirmed by John Geree, who in his 1757 article for *The Gentleman's Magazine* writes that she "was usually called in the family, Miss *Hetty*."[124] And on a receipt Swift signed for Esther Johnson's and Rebecca Dingley's mourning clothes in January 1699, now in Yale's Beinecke Library, he wrote on the back, "Bill for Mrs. Dingley & Hetty."[125] So Swift called Esther Johnson Hetty, and so, safely, I think, can we,

---

119 *Journal to Stella*, ed. Abigail Williams (Cambridge: Cambridge University Press, 2008), pp. lxxii-lxxvi.

120 Deane Swift, *Letters Written by the Late Dr. Jonathan Swift, DD, Dean of St. Patrick's Dublin*, 6 vols (London: Bathurst, 1768), IV, 5n.

121 Or *The Journal to the Saucy Monkeys* or *The Journal to the Dear Rogues* or *The Journal to the Young Women* or *The Journal to the Brave Boys*. 9 February 1712 is the first *Journal* letter unedited by Deane Swift.

122 *Correspondence*, ed. Woolley, I, 129-30 and n1.

123 Lady Giffard writes to the Duchess of Somerset on 30 December [1697]: "I make use of my cousin Dingley whenever I am in want, Hetty's [Esther Johnson's] place [as principal servant to Lady Giffard] being the height of her [Dingley's] ambition" (Longe, *Martha Lady Giffard*, p. 215).

124 [John Geree]," Anecdotes of Dean Swift and Miss Johnson," *The Gentleman's Magazine*, 27 (November 1757), 487-91 (p. 488); reprinted in *The Lives of Jonathan Swift*, ed. Cook, III, 552-57.

125 Moor Park Papers, Beinecke Library, Osborn Collection, fb 182. This document has not been brought to bear on Swift's biography before.

distinguishing Swift's most intimate female friends as Hessy and Hetty. Having done that, we can look through a clearer lens both at the characters of Hetty and Hessy, and at the character that Swift himself showed in his attempts to manage these two intimate but conflicting friendships.

Newly applied evidence also re-colours our acceptance of Deane Swift's assertions that his grandfather Godwin served as Swift's principal support in his youth, and should lead us to question whether Swift was culpably ungrateful to Godwin and his other relatives. Swift's paternal grandmother, Elizabeth Dryden Swift, has been largely ignored in imagining who might have supported young Jonathan before he became linked with Sir William Temple. Her husband Thomas died in 1658, and all Swift's biographers seem to have implicitly assumed that she died with him. But Elizabeth Swift was an energetic woman both before and after her husband's death. In Bruno Ryves's *Mercurius Rusticus*, she is portrayed as at least as brave as her husband in response to the terrors of the English Civil Wars. And Swift's grandfather's imprisonment in Raglan Castle in the early 1650s, as well as his death in 1658, left his wife Elizabeth to help set the career paths of their sons. Godwin and Thomas completed their educations during the 1650s while their father was in prison. William started at Gray's Inn just days before his father died. Adam was too young (15) at the time of his father's death to have acquired any legal education by that time. So the educations of all four – Godwin, Thomas, William, and Adam – were either exclusively, or at least primarily, supervised by Elizabeth Swift, Swift's grandmother.

In his autobiographical account, *Family of Swift*, Swift noted that his grandfather during the Civil Wars "was deprived of ... his Church livings ... and his estate [was] sequestered."[126] But despite the depredation that the Swifts suffered during the war, Thomas Swift's will indicates that, when he died in 1658, his family was still financially comfortable.[127] His lands, his substantial home, and his clerical living worth £100 per year had been restored to him before he died. Deane Swift in his *Essay* estimated that Revd Swift's total income, including land and inheritance, was "about four hundred pounds a year,"[128] an amount that fits well with the support, primarily annuities for their daughters and education for their sons, that Thomas and his widow Elizabeth provided for their family.

126 *Prose Works*, V, 190.

127 Ehrenpreis, *Mr Swift*, I, 268.

128 Deane Swift, *An Essay upon the Life, Writings, and Character*, p. 11. Deane Swift sometimes invents rather than researches his details, but as an heir, following his grandfather and father, to the Goodrich estate, he may have had good reason to have known this amount that he states so confidently.

Conventionally, Revd Swift left his estate to his wife Elizabeth, naming Godwin, his eldest son, his executor. His will savours of the farm. He specifies leaving his "bacon beefe, butter, cheese, wheate, rye, barley, mault, and beere of all sorts to my deare and welbeloved wife." He left to Godwin "all the rest of [his] personall estate,"[129] noting that his surviving four daughters and five sons, Jonathan Sr among them, have had "their seuerall porcons [portions] ... already paid or secured to them." The portions "paid," most logically, must have been to the older Godwin, Dryden, and Thomas to cover the cost (roughly £100 per year for room, board, fees, and travel)[130] of their Oxford or Gray's Inn educations. The portions "secured" (that is, set aside) would explain how William and Adam could afford a Gray's Inn education after their father's death, and probably also the annuity given to Jonathan's wife Abigail when they married, since Jonathan had not used his "portion" for an education. These "portions," and the fact that Revd Thomas's wife Elizabeth lived long enough to oversee their distribution, helped, I believe, not only the Revd Thomas Swift's children, but his grandchildren, among them, Jonathan Jr, get off to a solid start in life.

Swift's childhood was enhanced by the sometime presence of his "granddame." Since his maternal grandmother, Elizabeth Imins Erick, died in 1663, four years before he was born, his frequent references to his "granddame" in his letters and published works must all be to his father's mother, Elizabeth Dryden Swift, from Goodrich. Widowed in 1658, Elizabeth was alive at least until 1680 when Swift was 13, and possibly for several years beyond that. He could have known her through a childhood trip or trips to Goodrich. More likely, though, she lived regularly in either the William or Godwin Swift household in Dublin. From surviving Herefordshire Hearth Tax Records and Exchequer Port Book records,[131] we can reliably infer that Elizabeth Swift was living on her husband's estate at Goodrich in 1665, seven years after her husband's death, that

129 The Goodrich home and land remained in the Swift family for more than 100 years. In 1738, Jonathan wrote in his autobiographical account, "The house is above an hundred years old and still in good repair, inhabited by a Tenant of the female line, but the Landlord [is] a young Gentleman [Deane Swift, who] lives upon his own estate in Ireland [Castle Rickard]" (*Prose Works*, V, 188).

130 William Nicolson, Bishop of Carlisle and then Derry, kept detailed records of the expenses of his son Joseph. Queen's College, Oxford, between 1707 and 1712, cost him nearly £500, or roughly £100 per year (*The London Diaries of William Nicolson, Bishop of Carlisle, 1702-1718*, eds Clyve Jones and Geoffrey Holmes [Oxford: Clarendon, 1985], p. 55).

131 The Herefordshire Hearth Tax rolls suggest that Elizabeth Swift left her home in Goodrich sometime between 1665 and 1673. In the 1665 Herefordshire Hearth Tax rolls, "Widow Swift, 4 hearths" is in the list (Hearth Tax Rolls, Herefordshire Record Office). In the 1673 Herefordshire Hearth Tax rolls, we find instead "Thomas Vaughan for Mr. Swift's house." Vaughan had married Swift's aunt Elizabeth.

she left the family home, allowing one of her daughters, also named Elizabeth, to live in it, sometime between 1665 and 1673, and that she was living in Ireland in 1680.[132] That places her probably in Ireland between 1670 and 1680 and possibly beyond – we do not have a date for her death – during at least the years when young Jonathan was growing from 3 to 13, and plausibly perhaps until he was 23. In later life, Swift remembered his grandmother as a reliable sage. He recalls her folk wisdom and other habits six times in his correspondence and in his poetry:

To Esther Johnson, he wrote in 1713, "My Grandmother used to say, More of your Lining, and less of your dining."[133]

To Knightley Chetwode, he wrote in 1715, "My Grandmother used to say that good Feeding never brings good Footing."[134]

To Charles Ford, in 1721, he wrote, "I find there is less trusting in Friends than even our Grandmothers warn us again[st]."[135]

In his 1724 poem, "The Answer to Dr. Delany," Swift remembered that when his grandmother heard something she did not like, it

> made my Grand-Dame always stuff-her-Ears,
> Both Right and Left, as Fellow-sufferers. (ll. 39-40)

132 In the 1680 Chester shipping records, we find several shipments of cattle in the name of Elizabeth Swift: 1) "15 June 1680 Elizabeth Swift ind [indigena] Ir Sheep 1£ 5s 2d – In the Happy returne [name of the ship] pd"; 2) "[presumably also 15 June 1680] Elizabeth Swift ind [indigena]: 106 Ir sheepe – In the Happy Returne pd". 3) "21 June [1680] Elizabeth Swift ind 42 Ir. Cattle, 40 Sheepe – In the Lamb of Chester, Richard Innsworth, Master a Dublin 5£ 11s 2d"; 4) "July 6 [1680] Elizabeth Swift ind 49 Ir cattle, 337 sheepe and other goods 6£ 11s 2d – In the Welcome pd"; 5) "July 6 [1680] Elizabeth Swift ind 96 Ir sheepe – In the Darien Swan pd 1£ 2s 9 1/2 d" (*Controller's Chester Port Rolls*, Christmas 1679 to Christmas 1680, TNA E190, 1343/12. The National Archive, UK). Swift's memories of his Grandmother's sayings, the hearth tax records, and these shipping records suggest that some time between 1665 and 1673 Elizabeth Swift left Goodrich for Dublin, that she lived with either William or Godwin Swift, and that her name was used for the 1680 shipments in order to pay the lower customs duties that indigenous residents were entitled to. Elizabeth was presumably helping to stock the family's Goodrich farm now managed by her daughter and son-in-law, Thomas and Elizabeth Vaughan. The English Cattle Acts forbidding the importation of Irish cattle into England were suspended in 1679 and renewed in 1681, leaving a small window in 1680 that the Swifts took advantage of.

133 *The Journal to Stella*, ed. Abigail Williams, p. 502.

134 *Correspondence*, ed. Woolley, II, 119.

135 *Correspondence*, ed. Woolley, II, 371.

Grandmother Swift also finds a place in "The Bubble," his poem upon the South Sea project (1720):

> The Sea is richer than the Land,
> I heard it from my Grannam's Mouth,
> Which now I clearly understand,
> For by the Sea she meant the *South*. (ll. 97-100)

Even as late as "A Character, Panegyric, and Description of the Legion Club" of 1736, Swift reinforces his point that the wickedness of Parliament is proportional to its proximity to the Church,

> Making good my Grandame's Jest,
> *Near the Church* – you know the rest. (ll. 7-8)[136]

All these examples imply that Swift recalled frequent contact with his grandmother and not just an occasional visit. This is the tough, slightly cynical, courageous, and spirited woman whom we first met in Ryves's account of the Civil Wars in *Mercurius Rusticus*.

The donor of Abigail Swift's annuity has been a mystery, and the source of much speculation, since both of Abigail's parents were dead when she married, and her husband Jonathan possessed no apparent means.[137] But the wills of Swift's grandfather Thomas, with its mention of paid and secured portions, and of his cousin Willoughby, who writes that his grandfather "Thomas Swift of Hereford Clergyman settled a small Estate of thirty-one pounds per Ann ... as a Joynture on my Mother ... and on her issue," and that Willoughby in turn had settled on his daughter Honoria a "portion promised with her in marriage,"[138] imply that the likeliest source of this annuity was Abigail's mother-in-law, Jonathan Jr's grandmother, Elizabeth Swift, who had already supervised the education of her sons William and Adam, and who, perhaps with the assistance of her son Godwin, was managing the portions "secured" by her husband for his children.[139] And if Swift's grandmother managed most of the money

136 Quotations are from *Poems*, ed. Williams. Rogers takes "Near the church and far from God" for the proverb that Swift alludes to here, an appropriate proverb from the lips of the knowing wife of a clergyman (*Poems*, ed. Rogers, p. 892).

137 Deane Swift follows Swift in assuring us that Abigail's husband bought this annuity (*An Essay upon the Life, Writings, and Character*, p. 23).

138 PRO London: Will of Willoughby Swift "of the County of Hereford," 1715, Folio 57, p. 146.

139 Deane Swift, as usual, gives the credit to his grandfather Godwin: "If it should be questioned, how came the Doctor's sister to be worth 300 l. when the Doctor himself was not worth a groat until after the death of Sir William Temple, I answer, the same generous

for his education, we do not need to regard Jonathan's seeming ungratefulness to his uncles quite so dramatically as the fundamental character trait that we often do.

Young men do not generally distinguish carefully between facts and inferences. They are so confident that their inferences are true that they forget the inferences' origins in sometimes only a single fact. In our case, the fifth Earl of Orrery's, Deane Swift's, and Thomas Sheridan's inferences, masquerading as facts, have, I believe, much too strongly coloured the water in our biographical well. *Pace* Orrery, Deane Swift, and Thomas Sheridan, Jonathan Swift may well have had his mother's support and presence through much of his youth; may not have associated love and distance; may have been supported throughout his youth by his paternal grandmother; may not have been supported primarily by his Uncle Godwin at any time; may have been a humorous, congenial young man; may have liked his sister Jane well into their adulthood; may have been consistently on good terms with his uncles excepting Godwin; may not ever have married Esther Johnson; may have called his two Esther friends Hessy and Hetty; may have regarded Hetty at least from 1700 to 1713 as a mischievous saucebox; may have enjoyed a sexual relationship with both Hetty and Hessy; may not have treated either Hessy or Hetty badly in their last days; and may not have been a misanthrope. How would these possibilities, I would say even probabilities, affect the way we interpret his works?

benefactors, the family of the Swift's who had supported and educated her brother until he was seven and twenty, made up this little fortune among them to push her into the world, as they had been equally beneficent to her from the days of her infancy" (*An Essay upon the Life, Writings, and Character*, p. 102). But it seems at least equally likely that Jane Swift's 300-pound dowry, like that mentioned in Willoughby Swift's will and that I assume paid for the education of Jonathan, came from the "portions" that Revd Thomas Swift made available to his grandchildren in his will, perhaps with Swift's uncles serving as executors of them after Elizabeth Swift's death.

J. A. Downie
Goldsmiths' College, University of London

The Biographer as Historian

Abstract. In *Gulliver's Travels*, Swift offered a cynical account of how history comes to be written. Yet in his own attempts at writing memoirs and history, he claimed "to write with the utmost impartiality … as a faithful historian." Contemporaries were not so sure, Chesterfield describing Swift's *History of the Four Last Years of the Queen* as "a party pamphlet, founded on the lie of the day." One of the problems with Swift's accounts of events was that most of the information he was relaying to his readers as factual was second-hand at best. This would appear to raise serious issues for Swift's biographers and critics. Propagandists are under no obligation to be factually accurate, let alone tell the truth. Almost all of the evidence for his influence with the ministers originates from Swift himself. In such circumstances, it is incumbent upon biographers to acquire detailed knowledge of the primary sources for themselves rather than merely relying upon the available secondary sources for their understanding of the political and social contexts of the age in which Swift lived.

My old supervisor, mentor, and friend, W. A. Speck – Bill Speck to everyone who knew him – would have been standing here today had it not been for a freak accident in February. Several speakers have already mentioned Bill, but I would like to add a few words of my own. I remember first seeing Bill as if it were yesterday, even though it was in October 1970. He had spent a year at Yale working on Volume VII of the *Poems on Affairs of State* with another of our old friends, Frank Ellis. (Bill's name would have appeared as editor of the volume along with Frank's on the title page had Frank not insisted in his Introduction that Tory and Whig were irrelevant to the politics of Queen Anne's reign, whereas Bill had just published a version of his Oxford DPhil thesis with the title, *Tory and Whig: The Struggle in the Constituencies.*) So I had not seen Bill at any point during my first year reading History at Newcastle. The door of the lecture room opened and in walked this young man – Bill was 32 at the time – dressed in a leather jacket and stripy trousers with longish hair and a Zapata moustache – very fashionable in 1970. He proceeded to sit on the edge of the desk, throwing a stick of chalk up and down as he talked conversationally about various theoretical approaches to the study of history and their bearing on the seventeenth and eighteenth centuries, walking to the blackboard from time to time to write something down. He was quite a revelation. Little wonder, then, that I ended up taking his special option, England in the Reign of Queen Anne. And the rest, as they say, is history. I have spent my career following in Bill's footsteps. At the very first Münster Symposium in 1984, Bill, appropriately enough, gave

 | DOI:10.30965/9783846763971_003

a paper on "Swift and the Historian." As he had returned to work on the great Dean around the time of the tercentenary of the death of Queen Anne, he was going to give a paper this year called "'Swift and the Historian' Revisited." After Bill's death, our convenors asked me if I would give a paper in his stead. I am not competent to tackle Bill's topic head-on, but I wanted to offer something related to it. Hence the title of my paper, "The Biographer as Historian."

Everybody knows how, in Glubbdubdrib, Gulliver became "disgusted with modern History":

> For having strictly examined all the Persons of greatest Name in the Courts of Princes for an Hundred Years past, I found how the World had been misled by prostitute Writers, to ascribe the greatest Exploits in War to Cowards, the wisest Counsel to Fools, Sincerity to Flatterers, *Roman* Virtue to Betrayers of their Country, Piety to Atheists, Chastity to Sodomites, Truth to Informers. How many innocent and excellent Persons had been condemned to Death or Banishment, by the practising of great Ministers upon the Corruption of Judges, and the Malice of Factions. How many Villains had been exalted to the highest Places of Trust, Power, Dignity, and Profit: How great a Share in the Motions and Events of Courts, Councils, and Senates might be challenged by Bawds, Whores, Pimps, Parasites, and Buffoons: How low an Opinion I had of human Wisdom and Integrity, when I was truly informed of the Springs and Motives of great Enterprizes and Revolutions in the World, and of the contemptible Accidents to which they owed their Success.[1]

Swift (like Sterne) has been described as a deconstructionist *avant la lettre*, and certainly this cynical account of how history comes to be written calls into question the possibility of objective or even factually accurate accounts of past events, although, as we have rightly been reminded, Swift's "attitudes towards history" were "not static." After 1714, Ashley Marshall argues, he "felt that history had become – so the *Travels* suggest – dishonest, misleading, and amoral."[2] Yet Swift would have been more likely to have subscribed to the view of Professor Binns, the history teacher in J. K. Rowling's Harry Potter books – "'My subject is History of Magic,' he [explained] in his dry, wheezy voice. 'I deal with *facts*, Miss Granger, not myths and legends'"[3] – rather than to the opinion of the founding father of microhistory, Carlo Ginzburg, who, after reflecting in his

1 Jonathan Swift, *Gulliver's Travels*, ed. David Womersley (Cambridge: Cambridge University Press, 2012), pp. 298-99 (III, viii, 5).

2 Ashley Marshall, *Swift and History: Politics and the English Past* (Cambridge: Cambridge University Press, 2015), p. 219.

3 J. K. Rowling, *Harry Potter and the Chamber of Secrets* (London: Bloomsbury Publishing, 1999), p. 158.

most recent book, *Threads and Traces: True False Fictive* (2012), on the nature of evidence in the wake of post-structuralists and postmodernists, concludes that "historical narratives speak to us less about reality than they do about whoever has constructed them."[4] Of course, Professor Ginzburg had no inkling that we were about to enter the post-truth era when he wrote these words, but in the early twenty-first century literary critics – even crusty ones – have largely come to accept that texts do not have meanings, but that texts have meanings assigned to them by individual readers.

Patently, there was a powerful personal dimension to Gulliver's account as far as Swift was concerned, which appears to be borne out by his own professed aim "to write with the utmost impartiality … as a faithful historian"[5] in works like *Memoirs, Relating to That Change which Happened in the Queen's Ministry in the Year 1710*, *An Enquiry into the Behaviour of the Queen's Last Ministry*, and particularly in the Preface to the misleadingly entitled *History of the Four Last Years of the Queen*, written in the 1730s, in which he insisted that

> it was very well understood some years before her Majesty's death, how the new King would act immediately upon his entrance in the choice of those (and those alone) whom he resolved to trust; and consequently what reports would industriously be raised, as well as spread, to expose the proceedings of her Majesty herself, as well as of her servants; who have been ever since blasted as enemies to the present establishment, by the most ignorant and malicious among mankind.[6]

It was to counter the reports of "those miserable pamphleteers, or their patrons," that Swift was so anxious for the *History of the Four Last Years* to appear in print, despite the manifest lack of enthusiasm shown by Oxford and Bolingbroke at the time he was writing it, as well as by Oxford's son and his erstwhile undersecretary, Erasmus Lewis, in the 1720s and 1730s. In addition to anticipating the objection of future biographers and critics that "Swift's lengthy character sketches [of contemporary politicians] in Book One undermine any real sense of objectivity,"[7] Lewis wryly observed that despite Swift's insistence that, as "a witness of almost every step they made in the course of" Queen Anne's last ministry, he "must have been very unfortunate not to be better

4 Carlo Ginzburg, *Threads and Traces: True False Fictive*, trans. Anne C. Tedeschi and John Tedeschi (Berkeley, Los Angeles, London: University of California Press, 2012), p. 3.

5 *Prose Works*, VII, xxxiv.

6 *Prose Works*, VII, xxxiii.

7 Ashley Marshall, "'*Swift*'s rhapsodical Tory-book': The Aims and Motives of *The History of the Four Last Years of the Queen*," *Reading Swift: Papers from The Sixth Münster Symposium on Jonathan Swift*, eds Kirsten Juhas, Hermann J. Real, and Sandra Simon (Munich: Wilhelm Fink, 2013), pp. 197-223 (207).

informed than those miserable pamphleteers,"[8] he was not privy to everything relating to the transactions of which he was purporting to give an accurate account. This was of particular relevance, according to Lewis, to "the transactions with Mr Buys [which] might have been represented in a more advantageous light, and more to the Honour of that Administration, and undoubtedly they would have been so by your pen, had you been master of all the facts."[9]

And there's the rub. Despite his repeated claims to have been the recipient of inside information which enabled him to write authoritatively about "passages, which the curious of another age would be glad to know the secret springs of"[10] – a metaphor he used both in the passage from *Gulliver's Travels* quoted at the beginning of this essay and in the *Memoirs, Relating to That Change* – Swift was apparently kept in the dark about some of the Ministry's more dubious proceedings. "I know very well it is your intention to do honour to the then treasurer," Lewis acknowledged. "Lord Oxford knows it: all his family and friends know it; but it is to be done with great circumspection. It is now too late to publish a pamphlet, and too early to publish a history."[11] This has not of course escaped the attention of biographers and critics. In one of his letters, the Earl of Chesterfield called Swift's *History* "a party pamphlet, founded on the lie of the day, which, as Lord Bolingbroke who had read it often assured me, was coined and delivered out to him, to write *Examiners*, and other political papers upon. Swift took these hints *de la meilleure foi du monde*, and thought them materials for history."[12] This chimes in with the cutting comments of Orrery:

> He was elated with the appearance of enjoying ministerial confidence. He enjoyed the shadow: the substance was detained from him. He was employed, not trusted; and at the same time he imagined himself a subtile diver, who dextrously shot down into the profoundest regions of politics, he was suffered only to sound the shallows nearest the shore, and was scarce admitted to descend below the froth at the top. Perhaps the deeper bottoms were too muddy for his inspection.[13]

---

8 *Prose Works*, VII, xxxiii-xxxiv.

9 *Correspondence*, ed. Woolley, IV, 513.

10 *Memoirs* in *Prose Works*, VIII, 108.

11 *Correspondence*, ed. Woolley, IV, 465-66.

12 *The Letters of Philip Dormer Stanhope, 4th Earl of Chesterfield*, ed. Bonamy Dobrée, 6 vols (London: Eyre and Spottiswoode, 1932), V, 2303-4.

13 John Boyle, fifth Earl of Orrery, *Remarks on the Life and Writings of Dr. Jonathan Swift, Dean of St. Patrick's, Dublin* (London: A. Millar, 1752), pp. 47-48.

I have previously drawn attention to Orrery's tone, and to his motives in writing about Swift in this way.[14] As Orrery himself acknowledges at the beginning of his *Remarks*, he only knew Swift "in the decline of life." Why, therefore, should he wish to denigrate the memory of a man whose "friendship" (he assured his son) "was an honour to [him]?" But Orrery's observation that he "was employed, not trusted" accords both with what Lewis writes about Swift not being "master of all the facts," and Chesterfield's suggestion that the *History of the Four Last Years* was "founded on the lie of the day."

Interestingly, in the opening paragraph of the *Memoirs, Relating to That Change*, Swift himself raises the question of the extent to which he was actually involved in policy-making. One of the problems with Swift's accounts of events, as he freely admits in the *Memoirs*, is that most of the information he was relaying to his readers as factual was second-hand at best, and even then he confessed that he had been thwarted from being able to give "a particular account of every circumstance and passage during that whole transaction" by the "negligence" of "the Queen, the Earl of Oxford, and [his] Lady Masham," and that it was for this reason that he could "give but an imperfect account of the first springs of that great change at court, after the trial of Doctor Sacheverel, *[his] memory not serving [him] to retain all the facts related to [him]*, but what [he] remember[s][he] shall set down."[15]

If what Swift intimates about not knowing "*all the facts*" appears strangely similar to what Erasmus Lewis alleged in relation to the *History of the Four Last Years*, what I find most striking is the reason given by Swift for writing the *Memoirs, Relating to That Change* in the first place. Far from attempting "impartial" history, Swift freely acknowledged that his request for information proceeded not "from curiosity, or the ambition of knowing and publishing important secrets; but, from a sincere honest design of justifying the Queen, in the measures she then took, and after pursued, against a load of scandal which would certainly be thrown on her memory, with some appearance of truth."[16] Swift, in other words, wished to write an apology. A similar point might be made about the *History of the Four Last Years*. As Swift put it himself in 1738: "My chief Design in this History was with the utmost Truth and Zeal to defend the Proceedings of that blessed Queen and her Ministry, *as well as my self*."[17]

14 J. A. Downie, "Swift and the Oxford Ministry: New Evidence," *Swift Studies*, 1 (1986), 2-8.

15 *Prose Works*, VIII, 109-10; my emphasis.

16 *Prose Works*, VIII, 109.

17 Mrs Whiteway and Swift to Orrery, [2 February 1737-8], *Correspondence*, ed. Woolley, IV, 494; my emphasis.

Considerations such as these would appear to raise serious issues for Swift's biographers and critics. Propagandists are under no obligation to be factually accurate, let alone to tell the truth. On the contrary, as the example of *The Conduct of the Allies* perfectly illustrates, it can be argued that successful propagandists have succeeded precisely because they pandered to the prejudices of their target readers. Swift's role in the Oxford ministry is a contentious issue nevertheless: just how much did he know? And how is the biographer to decide? Most of the evidence for his influence with the ministers originates with Swift himself, especially in his letters to Esther Johnson and Rebecca Dingley, as well as the *Memoirs*, the *Enquiry*, and the *History of the Four Last Years*, in which he repeatedly refers not only to "the time [when] [he] was either trusted or employed,"[18] but also to his "endeavours, for above two years, to reconcile" Oxford and Bolingbroke.[19] If this implies a little naivety on Swift's part, it corresponds with the hostile testimony of some of his contemporaries. "They laugh at you," Steele bluntly told him in 1713, "if they make you believe your interposition has kept me thus long in office."[20] To this might be added the malicious portrait of Swift as "the principal man of talk and business ... act[ing] as a master of requests" at Windsor, penned later on in the same year by White Kennett.[21] Pieces of documentary evidence such as these would seem to support what Chesterfield, Orrery, and others have insinuated, suggesting that there was a significant discrepancy between what Swift believed or understood at the time he was involved with the Oxford ministry, and what was really going on during the Queen's four last years. In these circumstances, the biographer, like the historian, has no alternative but to draw those "modest inferences about personal relationships" which, according to Park Honan, are "incumbent upon a biographer."[22]

Patently, the tasks of the biographer and the historian often intersect. In the search for details of Swift's early life, for instance, the biographer uses the tools of the historian to dig in the archives to uncover as much documentary evidence as possible. "As we all know," Arthur E. Case pointed out in his surmise on Swift's supposed ingratitude towards his Uncle Godwin, "the factual material dealing with Swift's early life is scanty, and conjecture has had to be called upon to fill gaps." "There can be no quarrel with conjecture so long as it is not labelled as fact," Case continued. "Unfortunately, some conjectures

18 *Prose Works*, VIII, 108.

19 *Prose Works*, VII, xxxvi; see also *Prose Works*, VIII, 132.

20 *Correspondence*, ed. Woolley, I, 487.

21 *Correspondence*, ed. Williams, V, 228-29; see also G. V. Bennett, *White Kennett, 1660-1728: Bishop of Peterborough* (London: S.P.C.K., 1957), pp. 261-62.

22 Park Honan, *Christopher Marlowe: Poet & Spy* (Oxford: Oxford University Press, 2005), p. 1.

about Swift have been repeated so often that their conjectural nature has been forgotten."[23] In his magisterial biography of Swift, Irvin Ehrenpreis purposely set out to "eliminate fables."[24] Several recent biographers, from David Nokes onwards, have seen fit to resuscitate some of those old, exploded traditions, thus creating more of a stir in bookish circles by suggesting sensational aspects to Swift's life which were almost certainly fictitious. "Selection and arrangement are essential parts of the biographer's art, and of larger import than the crowded attempt to leave nothing unsaid," Harold Williams sagely observed in his essay on Swift's early biographers: "How many biographers in striving to relate all that a man did failed to show what he was."[25]

While issues of interpretation are inevitably raised by the scanty factual material of Swift's early life, these are relatively straightforward, it seems to me, compared with the problems posed by his relations with the most prominent political figures of his day. For instance, one either accepts or rejects the story that Swift was abducted and taken to Whitehaven in Cumberland by his wet nurse "when he was a year old … where he continued for almost three years."[26] True, there is the added complication that Swift himself appears uncertain about how long he stayed at Whitehaven, for of course he would be reliant on second-hand testimony for the dates, and Swift's memory was increasingly fallible in his declining years. But that is not of huge import in my opinion. What *is* dangerous, as Case points out, is when those writing about Swift's early life represent their conjectures as fact, as Denis Johnston did in his *In Search of Swift*. Based on what he called inferences drawn from his examination of the Black Book of the King's Inns, Johnston insisted that Swift's father "*could* not have been"[27] Jonathan Swift senior, the Steward of the King's Inns, because the latter's hand does not appear in the Black Book after 16 November 1666. I am unable to corroborate either this assertion or Johnston's insistence that, "with one exception,"[28] the minutes in the Black Book were in the hand of Jonathan Swift, Sr until 16 November 1666, for the simple reason that no authenticated example of his handwriting is known. What Johnston does not make clear, moreover, is that there are no entries in the Black Book between 16 November

23 Arthur E. Case, "Swift's Supposed Ingratitude toward his Uncle Godwin: A Surmise," in *Pope and his Contemporaries: Essays Presented to George Sherburn*, eds James L. Clifford and Louis A. Landa (Oxford: Clarendon Press, 1949), pp. 129-34 (129-30).

24 Ehrenpreis, *Mr Swift*, p. ix.

25 Harold Williams, "Swift's Early Biographers," in *Pope and his Contemporaries*, eds Clifford and Landa, pp. 114-28 (114).

26 *Prose Works*, V, 192.

27 Denis Johnston, *In Search of Swift* (Dublin: Hodges Figgis, 1959), p. 69.

28 Johnston, *In Search of Swift*, p. 51.

1666 and April 1667 when Abigail Swift, the widow of "the late Steward," presented her petition for assistance in collecting £120 in arrears due to her late husband.[29] In sum, Johnston drew conclusions that cannot be substantiated from the Black Book of the King's Inns to support a thesis about Swift's parentage which cannot be documented.[30]

While the scanty facts about Swift's early life present comparatively few issues of interpretation, the matter is much more complicated when Swift's accounts are themselves primary sources of some importance for the most momentous political events of the day. In such circumstances, it is incumbent upon biographers to acquire detailed knowledge of the available primary sources for themselves rather than merely relying upon the available secondary sources for their understanding of the political and social contexts of the age in which he lived. Despite its subtitle, "The Man, his Works, *and the Age*," perhaps the least satisfactory part of Irvin Ehrenpreis's biography is his grasp of the age, particularly the political context, and especially the politics of the period. This can be detected in a number of ways, but the key indicator is his reliance on the thesis, drawn from Namier, put forward by Robert Walcott in 1956, that, during the years when Swift was intimate with leading English politicians, British politics were dominated not by Tory and Whig, but by family connections. Thus we find sentences such as these:

> In the 1701 House of Commons all the organized 'Whig' cliques together amounted to about eighty, if we exclude men normally attached to the court; while the Nottingham-Seymour-Harley connections totalled less than a hundred. Yet the members who did not belong to an organized group (apart from the government interest) numbered something like 250. Among those outside Parliament the tendency to feel unaffiliated was even stronger.[31]

Unfortunately, the second volume of Ehrenpreis's biography was first published in 1967 – the same year as J. H. Plumb's Ford lectures, *The Growth of Political Stability in England*, and Geoffrey Holmes's authoritative *British Politics in the Age of Anne*. As Bill Speck brilliantly put it in his Oxford DPhil thesis: "The slender branches of the family trees, so carefully cultivated by Walcott, will not bear the weight of the political fruit which he seeks to graft upon them."[32]

---

29 The Black Book of the King's Inns, fols 208 and 209.

30 Interestingly, neither Nokes nor Glendenning nor Damrosch nor Stubbs refers to the Black Book. Ehrenpreis refers to it twice, silently modernizing the text when he quotes from it.

31 Ehrenpreis, *Dr Swift*, p. 253.

32 W. A. Speck, "The House of Commons, 1702-14: A Study in Political Organization" (unpublished Oxford DPhil thesis, 1965), p. 21.

It was no coincidence that Walcott elected to focus on the complex politics of 1701 in his monograph, *English Politics in the 'Early' Eighteenth Century*, because there were not one but two general elections in this utterly untypical year. As it was also the year in which Swift wrote and published his first political pamphlet, 1701 provides one of the best instances of the tasks of the biographer, the critic, and the historian colliding. Since the publication of Frank Ellis's scholarly edition of *A Discourse of the Contests and Dissentions* in 1967, a number of scholars have attempted to elucidate aspects of Swift's rhetoric, including his manipulation of the classical sources upon which he based his argument "from history." More recently, in an essay with the significant title, "Situating Swift's Politics in 1701," the historian Mark Goldie implicitly takes Swiftians to task for "tend[ing] to examine the *Discourse* diachronically, within the frame of its author's career-long tergiversatory dialogue with Whiggism and Toryism." Adopting what he calls a synchronic approach, Goldie sets out to consider the *Dialogue* "in relation to Whig and Tory arguments at the moment of its composition."[33] This is undoubtedly the correct procedure to take if the purpose of the exercise is to identify the polemical strategy adopted by Swift in the *Discourse* but, as is indicated by his conclusion that it "remains a perplexing work, since it supports the Whigs *in unexpected ways*,"[34] a number of Goldie's assumptions raise complications of a biographical nature, particularly his conclusion that "while Swift ran his colours up the Junto's mast, his *Discourse* could not satisfactorily be colligated with the stance shared by Somers, Defoe, and Locke. Accordingly, the Whiggism of the *Discourse* was decidedly distinctive."[35]

In order to relate the *Discourse* to arguments which were current "at the moment of its composition," we need to establish when it was written; we cannot simply assume that Swift was responding in some way to the arguments of the many writers who participated in the paper war of 1701, or even that he was aware of them. "We know very little of [Swift's] personal life during this 1701 trip," Eugene Hammond points out in his recent biography.[36] Infuriatingly, the 1700/1 account book, which was in the possession of Dr Lyon in 1765 and of Dr Tuke of St Stephen's Green in 1811, is no longer extant, and all we know from Lyon's preliminaries to Hawkesworth's biography of Swift is that "In April Swift

33 Mark Goldie, "Situating Swift's Politics in 1701," *Politics and Literature in the Age of Swift: English and Irish Perspectives*, ed. Claude Rawson (Cambridge: Cambridge University Press, 2010), pp. 31-51 (32).

34 Goldie, "Situating Swift's Politics in 1701," p. 42, my emphasis.

35 Goldie, "Situating Swift's Politics in 1701," p. 47.

36 Eugene Hammond, *Jonathan Swift: Irish Blow-In* (Newark, Delaware: University of Delaware Press, 2016), p. 152.

went to London; return[d] to Irel[d] Sep[t] following."[37] That Swift was in Ireland when "the Hott party in the House of Commons" began to pursue the Duke of Portland and William's former ministers with a view to impeachment is significant. In the paragraphs leading up to the famous passage in the *Memoirs, Relating to That Change* in which he described how he "first began to trouble [him]self with the difference between the principles of Whig and Tory," Swift explained how he came to write the *Discourse*:

> I had dealt very little with politics, either in writing or acting, till about a year before the late King William's death; when, returning with the Earl of Berkeley from Ireland, and falling upon the subject of the five great Lords [actually there were only four – Portland, Somers, Halifax and Orford], who were then impeached for high crimes and misdemeanors, by the House of Commons, I happened to say, that the same manner of proceeding, *at least as it appeared to me from the views we had of it in Ireland*, had ruined the liberties of Athens and Rome, and that it might be easy to prove it *from history*. Soon after I went to London; and, in a few weeks, drew up a discourse.[38]

If analysed carefully, this passage is of great interest for the biographer. According to *The Flying Post*,[39] Berkeley set sail for England from Dublin on 9 April 1701. Frank Ellis asserts, without any documentation, that "Swift arrived in London in the entourage of Lord Berkeley"[40] on 15 April. Presumably, when Swift wrote, "Soon after I went to London; and, in a few weeks, drew up a discourse," he was referring to the weeks immediately following the impeachments of Somers and Halifax on 14 April. By contrast, Irvin Ehrenpreis (followed by David Nokes) posited that "Swift worked *through the summer of 1701* to compose a defence of the four lords,"[41] after the *Discourse* was advertised as "To morrow will be published" in *The Flying Post* for 21-23 October.

Why is this significant? If Swift did write his *Discourse* immediately after he arrived in London in the middle of April, it means he would have been writing it during the weeks when "the Hott party in the House of Commons" upped the ante by depriving William of £100,000 of his already inadequate civil

37 Fol. 36 of the preliminaries, quoted in *The Account Books of Jonathan Swift*, eds Paul V. Thompson and Dorothy Jay Thompson (Newark, Delaware: University of Delaware Press, and London: Scolar Press, 1984), pp. xiii-xiv.

38 *Prose Works*, VIII, 119; my emphases.

39 *Flying Post*, 22 April 1701.

40 Jonathan Swift, *A Discourse of the Contests and Dissentions between the Nobles and the Commons in Athens and Rome*, ed. Frank H. Ellis (Oxford: Clarendon Press, 1967), p. 49.

41 Ehrenpreis, *Dr Swift*, p. 47 (my emphasis); David Nokes, *Jonathan Swift, a Hypocrite Reversed: A Critical Biography* (Oxford: Oxford University Press, 1985), p. 54.

list on 5 May, when the Kentish Petition was presented to the Commons on 8 May, and when Defoe delivered the Legion-Letter to Harley, as Speaker of the Commons, on 14 May. Even more significantly, Swift would have been writing it when the Commons finally exhibited fourteen articles against Somers and sent them up to the Lords on 19 May. These were the weeks when Swift might have felt a defence of the impeached lords was required: on 19 June, Somers was acquitted by the Lords by 55 votes to 33 when the Commons failed to appear to prosecute their case. William prorogued Parliament on 24 June, and dissolved it on 11 November – barely nine months after it had first assembled.

After the impeachment proceedings had come to an abrupt halt in the middle of June 1701, there would have been no pressing reason for Swift to write in defence of the four lords. This would seem to throw into doubt Goldie's attempt to consider the *Discourse* "in relation to Whig and Tory arguments at the moment of its composition," because none of the pamphlets he compares and contrasts with Swift's had been published by the end of June 1701. Although he concludes that "Swift ran his colours up the Junto's mast," at one point Goldie argues that "his *Discourse* was far from endorsing the Somers-Defoe position,"[42] at another he goes on to suggest that it "reads as if Swift was unaware of the Junto party line."[43] Since Swift was not introduced to Somers and Halifax until his visit to London in 1702, and seeing that he wrote his pamphlet before the publication of Somers's *Jura Populi Anglicani* or Defoe's *History of the Kentish Petition*, this is scarcely surprising. Swift almost certainly wrote the *Discourse* in blissful ignorance of what Goldie calls "the Somers-Defoe position." (There is no evidence, either, that Defoe was linked to Somers at this, or indeed at any other time.) "The Parties are every day writing and printing against one another with great bitterness," the Secretary of State, James Vernon, informed the Duke of Shrewsbury at the beginning of September, "and the chiefs seem to have a hand in it."[44] But according to John Lyon, Swift returned to Ireland in September, just as the paper war was intensifying.

I have chosen to focus on 1701 because scholars can learn from the various attempts by biographers, critics, and historians to locate Swift's *Discourse* with accuracy in the turmoil of those febrile months when Swift was in London, but it applies *mutatis mutandis* to other periods of his life, too. If historians really want to situate Swift's politics, whether in 1701, 1714, or 1727, they have

42 Goldie, "Situating Swift's Politics in 1701," p. 42.

43 Goldie, "Situating Swift's Politics in 1701," p. 42.

44 *Letters Illustrative of the Reign of William III from 1696 to 1708: Addressed to the Duke of Shrewsbury by James Vernon*, ed. G. P. R. James, 3 vols (London: Colburn, 1841), III, 155-56.

to be thoroughly acquainted with the details of his life. If, on the other hand, biographers – and critics – want to do what Frank Ellis announced as the aim of his introduction to his edition of the *Discourse* – "to represent certain political and literary events of 1697-1701 as Swift saw them"[45] – then they have to be aware of the complex politics at work in 1701, including understanding why William turned to Harley and his "New Country Party" allies in the summer of 1700, and what was behind the political manoeuvrings in the Parliament which assembled on 6 February 1701 and which proceeded to pass the Act of Settlement, before Harley lost control of the Commons. Only then will they be in a position to make those "modest inferences ... incumbent upon the biographer" without which life-writing could not be attempted. This is the proper province of the biographer, even if it appears an exercise fraught with difficulty. It is also a requirement of the historicist critic.

In the analysis offered in the *Discourse*, Swift is concerned about the rise of what he calls the "*Tyranny of the Commons*." Maintaining that "nothing is more dangerous or unwise than to give way to the *first Steps* of Popular Encroachments,"[46] he repeatedly reflects on what he describes as the "late Proceedings of the Commons," or "the late publick Proceedings among us."[47] True, in the added fifth chapter he attempts, not entirely convincingly, to widen the scope of his analysis. But up to this point, his argument is specifically relevant to the weeks between the impeachments of Somers and Halifax on 14 April and the collapse of the case on 19 June. Swift, then, was writing his pamphlet at the time that "the Hott party in the House of Commons" was getting out of hand. As one contemporary observed about the attempt to deprive the King of £100,000 of his civil list:

> This incident has put our Ministry into a very great disorder, as tending much to the diminution of their Credit with the king, since they have so little authority with their party as not to be able to restrain them from doing unreasonable & Extravagant things only to lessen the king, & it is not doubted but it will put the King upon em playing the Whiggs again, as they are usually called.[48]

45 Swift, *A Discourse of the Contests and Dissentions between the Nobles and the Commons in Athens and Rome*, ed. Ellis, p. 14.

46 Swift, *A Discourse of the Contests and Dissentions between the Nobles and the Commons in Athens and Rome*, ed. Ellis, p. 115.

47 Swift, *A Discourse of the Contests and Dissentions between the Nobles and the Commons in Athens and Rome*, ed. Ellis, pp. 125, 116.

48 British Library Add. MS 7074, fol. 15: John Ellis to George Stepney, 6 May 1701.

Harley blamed the dissolution of Parliament later in the year on his failure to prevent the impeachments. William turned back to the Whigs because of Harley's failure to control "the Hott party in the House of Commons," actually informing him, according to his own account, "Mr. Speaker, your Project of the Succession has done me no good." "O silly, silly," Harley reports Lord Sunderland as saying at the time: "Had they left alone Lord Portland and the Civil List, they might have hanged the other three in a Garret."[49]

49 British Library Add. MS 70272, unfoliated: Harley's "Large Account: Revolution & Succession."

BIBLIOGRAPHICAL AND TEXTUAL STUDIES

Andrew Carpenter and James Woolley
University College, Dublin, and *Lafayette College*

Faulkner's *Volume II. Containing the Author's Poetical Works*: A New Uncancelled Copy

Abstract. A unique uncancelled copy of Faulkner's 1735 edition of Swift's poems was deliberately assembled, at some point after 1735, to preserve the texts that were to have been jettisoned or expurgated. A fresh analysis confirms that the cancellations were designed primarily to avoid re-publishing personal satire and to limit Faulkner's exposure to prosecution or other governmental interference.

George Faulkner's 1735 octavo edition of Swift's poems, Volume II of *The Works of* J. S, *D. D, D. S. P. D.*, is by far the most significant collection of Swift's poems published in his lifetime. It is also one of the most extensively cancelled of all eighteenth-century books. In its completely uncancelled state, the volume is rare. Though the existence of cancels in the ordinary copies had long been known, no uncancelled copy was known before 1967, when Margaret Weedon reported the acquisition of an uncancelled copy by the English Faculty Library of the University of Oxford.[1] Here, in three notes, we report the discovery of a new and unique uncancelled copy and assess its significance.

1. Discovery
by Andrew Carpenter

Like many Swiftians, I had been intrigued by the story Margaret Weedon told and had hoped that perhaps I might come upon another uncancelled copy

1 "An Uncancelled Copy of the First Collected Edition of Swift's Poems," *Library*, 5th ser., 22 (1967), 44-56. Herman Teerink had reported evidence of cancellation in *A Bibliography of the Writings in Prose and Verse of Jonathan Swift, D.D.* (The Hague: Nijhoff, 1937), p. 31. Important recent discussions of Faulkner's edition include James McLaverty, "Naming and Shaming in the Poetry of Pope and Swift," in *Swift's Travels: Eighteenth-Century British Satire and its Legacy*, eds Nicholas Hudson and Aaron Santesso (Cambridge: Cambridge University Press, 2008), pp. 160-75 (169-73); Stephen Karian, *Jonathan Swift in Print and Manuscript* (Cambridge: Cambridge University Press, 2010), pp. 30-43; Ashley Marshall, "The '1735' Faulkner Edition of Swift's *Works*," *The Library*, 7th ser., 14 (2013), 154-98; and James McLaverty, "George Faulkner and Swift's Collected Works," in *Jonathan Swift and the Eighteenth-Century Book*, eds Paddy Bullard and James McLaverty (Cambridge: Cambridge University Press, 2013), pp. 154-75.

 | DOI:10.30965/9783846763971_004

of Volume II; but for many years, every Volume II that I handled contained the normal cancels. Until 2015. In the spring of 2015, I was visiting the Dublin bookseller Éamonn de Búrca[2] who, like many booksellers, keeps odd volumes in the hopes that in time he will be able to make up complete sets for rebinding and sale.

Éamonn de Búrca was generous enough to allow me to spend time among the sundry incomplete sets and odd volumes in the back room, where I came across, lurking at the bottom of a pile, three of the four volumes of the Faulkner 1735 octavo printing. Volume I was missing – which was lucky since, had it been there, the set would have been sold long before I set eyes on it; the other three volumes appeared to be in uniform eighteenth-century bindings.

I noticed several odd things about Volume II of this incomplete set. In a typical set of the 1735 *Works*, Volume II is the fattest of the four, partly because of stubs left when the leaves to be cancelled – the *cancellanda* – were cut out, but this copy seemed to be even fatter than usual. It contained a surprising number of blank leaves: blank sheets were bound in where the contents leaves should be, and blank sheets were also bound in at the end of the book. Most surprisingly, in several sheets at the end of the book, poems or parts of poems were pasted over with blank paper or with passages from other poems. The signatures and pagination were also irregular, and the book contained many more leaves than the normal Volume II.

I purchased the three volumes.

2. The Printing and Cancelling
by James Woolley

In Faulkner's *Dublin Journal* on 10 February 1733, he announced his four-volume octavo edition of Swift's works, seeking subscribers.[3] Printing seems to have been well advanced by 3 November 1733, when he announced that "there are almost 3 Volumes finished," of which the poems volume would have been one. After many delays, the first three volumes were published on 27 November 1734 (all with 1735 title pages), with Volume IV added on 6 January 1735.[4]

2 De Búrca Rare Books, Blackrock, Co. Dublin.

3 This informative advertisement, dated 9 February 1733 and frequently reprinted during the first several months of 1733, is edited in *Prose Works*, XIV, 42-43.

4 These dates come from Faulkner's extensive series of advertisements in the *Dublin Journal* and in his other publications 1733-35. I am drawing here on research done for the Swift Poems Project, particularly by the late A. C. Elias, Jr.

Since 1967, when Margaret Weedon reported on the uncancelled copy in the English Faculty Library, three other uncancelled copies had come to light: two of them, one at Yale and one in the Gilbert Collection of the Dublin Public Library, are large-paper copies, neither preserving the replacement leaves.[5] By contrast, the Carpenter copy, like the English Faculty Library copy, is on ordinary paper, and it preserves most of the replacement leaves.

In cancelling, one or more leaves in a volume are removed and replaced by other leaves.[6] If a book includes cancels, one can deduce that the compositor and printer were required to make changes after printing had been finished. The changes might be authorial or editorial and the reasons many and varied: sometimes the author had second thoughts or wanted to insert notes, sometimes the bookseller might fear political or legal consequences that might follow the issue of the original text. Typically, the binder, who did the cancelling, discarded the *cancellanda*. Since this cancelling was an intentional act, the cancelled leaves, if they survived, could provide valuable material evidence about the history of the text and the intentions of its author or publisher.

On 30 August 1734, Swift told Edward, the second Earl of Oxford, "I have put [Faulkner] under some Difficultyes by ordering certain Things to be struck out after they were printed, which some friends had given him. This hath delayed his work, and as I hear, given him much trouble and difficulty to adjust."[7] The cancelling occurred, so far as is known, almost entirely in Volume II.[8] Cancellation on the scale undertaken in Volume II was expensive, primarily because of the waste of large amounts of paper, paper costs being as significant a factor as labour costs in the total expense of producing an eighteenth-century book.[9] A printer would presumably not willingly incur such costs except for an urgent reason. Comparison of the *cancellanda* with their replacements makes clear that Faulkner's massive cancelling operation was not undertaken to correct ordinary errors or infelicities that might have been discovered in proofreading. Faulkner speaks of having such proofreading sessions with

5 English Faculty Library acc. no. 29165 (= XL77 1735); Yale Ik Sw55 C735 v.7; Dublin Public Libraries, Gilbert 16E (16), v.2. Copies preserving only one or two of the *cancellanda* are in the collections of Trinity College Cambridge (THE ROTHSCHILD LIBRARY 2151), Harvard (*EC7. Sw551.B735w(B), v.2), and James Woolley.

6 The classic work on the subject is R. W. Chapman, *Cancels* (London: Constable, 1930).

7 *Correspondence*, ed. Woolley, III, 753.

8 Minor cancelling is observable in Volume IV (TEERINK AND SCOUTEN, p. 27); the possibility of whole-sheet cancels in the four volumes cannot be ruled out, though its cost makes it improbable.

9 Philip Gaskell calculates that in the eighteenth century, paper costs were "about 50 per cent" of total book production costs (*A New Introduction to Bibliography*, corrected reprint [Oxford: Clarendon Press, 1974], p. 177).

Swift, and proofreading may well have resulted in revisions *before* printing was carried out.[10] The cancelling, by contrast, occurred *after* all 1152 copies of the book had been printed.[11] The following list shows what poems were "struck out" and what poems replaced them, as well as which poems were expurgated:

Cancels in Swift, *Works*, octavo (Dublin: Faulkner, 1735), Vol. II

The octavo Vol. II ends on p. 480; the duodecimo Vol. II (which lacks cancels) ends on p. 363.

pp. 207-20 "Mad Mullinix and Timothy," Swift's lampoon on the Irish politician Richard Tighe, was cancelled and replaced by "Joan Cudgels Ned," "The Run upon the Bankers," "Stella at Wood Park," "A Receipt to Restore Stella's Youth," and "To Quilca" (all these poems except "The Run upon the Bankers" being previously unpublished). "Mad Mullinix and Timothy" was first published in 1728 in the *Intelligencer* and was reprinted, with some excisions, in the 1732 volume of the Swift-Pope *Miscellanies*.

pp. 281-93 "An Epistle to a Lady," previously published, was probably most offensive for its derogatory innuendo that George II was a "Monkey," a "strutting, chatt'ring Vermin." It was cancelled and replaced by "A Panegyrick on the Dean in the Person of a Lady in the North."[12]

pp. 298-99 "An Epigram on Fasting" was cancelled and replaced by "Clever Tom Clinch Going to be Hanged." The "Epigram on Fasting" was previously unpublished, as was "Clever Tom Clinch."

pp. 343-46 "The Author upon Himself" (previously unpublished) was expurgated to soften its abuse of the Duchess of Somerset, whom Swift blamed for blocking his appointment to an English deanery in 1713. The uncancelled state's first line is "By an old red-Pate murd'ring Hag pursu'd;" the expurgated state's first line is easily identified: "By an ——— ——— ——— pursu'd."

p. 358 The headnote of "An Excellent New Song on a Seditious Pamphlet" was expurgated. This poem was Swift's 1720 satire on Judge William Whitshed's prosecution of the Dublin printer Edward Waters for publishing Swift's *A Proposal for the Universal Use of Irish Manufacture*. The

---

10 In later editions of his *Works of Swift*, Faulkner claimed that Swift had required him to attend him in the Deanery every morning while the *Works* were going through the press; in fact, says Faulkner, "he corrected every Sheet of the first seven Volumes that were published in his Life Time, desiring the Editor [Faulkner himself] to write Notes" ("To the Reader," *Volume I. of the Author's Works*, 18° [Dublin: Faulkner, 1762], p. vii). Karian casts doubt on Faulkner's claims that Swift read proof (*Jonathan Swift in Print and Manuscript*, pp. 36-42).

11 The figure is calculated by McLaverty, "George Faulkner and Swift's Collected Works," p. 160.

12 *Poems*, ed. Williams, II, 364; McLaverty makes this point about the offensiveness of "An Epistle to a Lady" ("Naming and Shaming in the Poetry of Pope and Swift," p. 171).

poem was previously unpublished. In the headnote, the uncancelled state calls Whitshed "*that infamous Wretch*," whereas the cancelled state does not; the effect of this and other changes is that the headnote is "no longer a personal satirical attack; it is a complaint about injustice."[13]

pp. 372-79 "Traulus: The First Part" and "Traulus: The Second Part," lampoons on Lord Allen, were cancelled and replaced by "A Pastoral Dialogue between Richmond-Lodge and Marble-Hill" and "On the Five Ladies at Sots Hole." The "Traulus" poems had been privately published in 1730. The two replacement poems were previously unpublished.

pp. 417-24 "To Mr. Gay," previously unpublished, was expurgated to soften references to Walpole, both in the text and the footnotes, and "The Hardship Put upon Ladies" was added on p. 417; the uncancelled state lacks "The Hardship."

pp. 479-80 The "Carbery Rocks" translation by William Dunkin appears on a cancel leaf even in the uncancelled copies; that is, the original leaf is not known to exist in any copy, suggesting that this was the earliest cancellation in the volume. The cancel, leaf 2I1, is signed at the bottom "Ii"; presumably the uncancelled version (which would have been leaf 2H8) would have been unsigned. The likely explanations for the cancel are either that an earlier unsatisfactory translation by some other poet was replaced by Dunkin's, or that after being set in type, Dunkin's translation required revision and was replaced with the cancel leaf signed "Ii."

In summary, five poems were deleted: "Mad Mullinix and Timothy," "An Epistle to a Lady," "An Epigram on Fasting," and the two "Traulus" poems; several others were softened. There were ten replacement poems: "Joan Cudgels Ned," "The Run upon the Bankers," "Stella at Wood Park," "A Receipt to Restore Stella's Youth," "To Quilca," "A Panegyric on the Dean in the Person of a Lady in the North," "Clever Tom Clinch Going to Be Hanged," "A Pastoral Dialogue between Richmond-Lodge and Marble-Hill," "On the Five Ladies at Sots Hole," and "The Hardship Put upon Ladies." It is clear that these ten were chosen at least in part for their length: they served to fill holes left by the cancellations. Whether any or all of these ten had been initially considered and judged not worthy of inclusion is an open question. Some interesting poems – "The Run upon the Bankers," "A Panegyric on the Dean," "A Pastoral Dialogue," to name three – would probably have remained unpublished in Swift's lifetime, and perhaps forever, were it not for this extensive cancelling. The extent of Swift's responsibility for the cancellation and the choice of replacements is uncertain and may have varied from instance to instance.

13 McLaverty, "Naming and Shaming in the Poetry of Pope and Swift," p. 172.

In October 1733, when work on the Swift edition had already begun, Faulkner had been taken into custody by the Irish House of Commons for publishing an abstract of Swift's inflammatory *Considerations upon Two Bills ... Relating to the Clergy of Ireland.*[14] Then in London during January 1734, the publishers of *An Epistle to a Lady*, which had come out in November 1733, were prosecuted; those arrested included Matthew Pilkington and Mary Barber.[15] Faulkner departed for London on 16 February 1734, at least in part to seek additional works by Swift.[16] In March 1734, the *Political State of Great Britain* reported that in Dublin, in late January, "several Printers and Publishers ... [had been] taken into Custody for printing and publishing a Poem, called, *The Rapsody on Poetry*, the same being deemed to be a scurrilous and s[c]andalous Libel." Whether these printers and publishers included Faulkner seems unlikely, since he did not publish the Dublin edition; but obviously in this climate, it would have been foolhardy for him to publish *An Epistle to a Lady*, and it is probable that that poem was cancelled from his Swift edition, and the expurgated poems expurgated, in the spring of 1734, once he had returned from London on 21 May.[17] The poems cancelled for ethical reasons could conceivably have been removed several months earlier.

Swift's claim that the poems excised from Volume II had been at least partly supplied to Faulkner by Swift's friends and not by Swift himself has been supported by Stephen Karian. He argues that Swift became "actively engaged" in the preparation of Volume II only "quite late" – that is, at the time the cancelling occurred and not during some putative proof-correction process: "If Swift had been reading proof, then he probably would have made the decision to exclude these poems at a much earlier time such that there would be no surviving evidence of cancelled leaves."[18]

James McLaverty has suggested that such poems seemed beneath the dignity of a collected works.[19] "An Epigram on Fasting," with its joke about religious fasting, may have seemed unworthy of a member of the clergy. The epigram

14 *Prose Works*, XII, xxxviii.

15 John Irwin Fischer, "The Government's Response to Swift's *An Epistle to a Lady*," *Philological Quarterly*, 65 (1986), 39-59.

16 Ehrenpreis, *Dean Swift*, p. 785.

17 Ehrenpreis, *Dean Swift*, p. 785.

18 Karian, *Jonathan Swift in Print and Manuscript*, p. 40. These comments are broadly supported by Karian's pages on Faulkner's edition of Swift's works, pp. 30-43. Weedon, without the benefit of Karian's evidence and arguments, believes it at least as likely that Swift himself, rather than his friends, chose what to include and later changed his mind about some of the flagrant personal abuse in the lampoons on Richard Tighe and Lord Allen (Weedon, "An Uncancelled Copy of the First Collected Edition of Swift's Poems," p. 54).

19 McLaverty, "George Faulkner and Swift's Collected Works," p. 166.

purports to be a translation from the French and therefore ridicules Roman Catholic fasting; at that time, fasting was apparently not zealously practised within the Anglican community.[20] In 1746, in a preface to Volume VIII of Swift's works, Faulkner, while in general seeking to publish as many of Swift's uncollected works as possible, declined to publish, he said, "a few satyrical Pieces on particular Persons; who, notwithstanding they had highly provoked him, yet were pardoned by him afterwards: And the Author laid repeated Commands on his Printer, never to publish such Pieces of private Resentment."[21] This point, I strongly suspect, is at the heart of the ethical exclusions, and it supports an inference that Swift actively intervened in Faulkner's edition only late: had these "commands" been delivered earlier, before the poems of "private Resentment" were printed, Faulkner would not have wasted time and money printing them. In the interval between Swift's "Traulus" lampoons on Lord Allen in 1730 and Faulkner's cancellations in the collected *Works of* J. S, *D. D, D. S. P. D.* in 1734, it would appear that Swift resolved to move to the moral high ground. It was during this interval that he drafted "Verses on the Death of Dr. Swift," in which the supposed "impartial" observer is made to claim that "Malice never was his Aim; / He lash'd the Vice but spar'd the Name."[22] Swift evidently found complete fidelity to that claim to be beyond him, but these cancellations were in the spirit of sparing the name, even though Swift had not literally named Richard Tighe in "Mad Mullinix and Timothy" or Lord Allen in the "Traulus" poems. In short, the expurgation of the uncancelled Volume II had two different purposes and perhaps also two different occasions: it was designed both to preserve Swift's ethical character as a satirist and to shield Faulkner from prosecution or other governmental harassment. Although, as Ashley Marshall has pointed out, the cancellation did not eliminate Swift's anti-Walpole references, it lessened them.[23]

---

20 *Poems*, ed. Williams, III, 948-49. A contemporary Anglican authority said that fasting did not require substituting fish for meat but only "forbearing those Pleasures, and Varieties of Meats, and Drinks, and Diversions, which we may at other Times Innocently enjoy" (*The Clergy-Man's Vade Mecum*, 2nd ed. [1707], p. 158).

21 "The Preface by the Dublin Bookseller," *Volume VIII. of the Author's Works*, 12° (Dublin: Faulkner, 1746), sig. a3v.

22 *Poems*, ed. Williams, II, 571, ll. 459-690.

23 Marshall, "The '1735' Faulkner Edition of Swift's *Works*," pp. 168-70.

3. The New Copy
by Andrew Carpenter and James Woolley

Margaret Weedon concluded that the English Faculty Library copy resulted from a binder's mistake – that he was given the sheets of the book and the sheets of cancels and simply put a binding on the whole thing rather than performing the cancellation.[24] The preservation of both the *cancellanda* and the replacement leaves was probably an accident in the English Faculty Library copy, but in the Carpenter copy it is obvious that the preservation of the *cancellanda* was deliberate. The Yale and Gilbert (Dublin Public Library) copies probably remained uncancelled because their binders had no access to the sheets of cancels; the Gilbert copy, at least, was clearly assembled very late, since it has a 1763 title page. But the Carpenter copy results not from any binder's error but from the deliberate wish of the purchaser to preserve, in full legible texts, both the cancelled and unexpurgated poems and the newly added poems. To this end, the expurgated versions were discarded and the sheets of cancels had their redundant bits pasted over; it is important to note that the over-pasting, either with blank paper or with other parts of the cancels, does not constitute slip-cancellation: the pasting was not part of Faulkner's preparation of the edition for publication.[25] In one or two instances, leaves have been cut apart and reassembled so as to provide coherent readable texts of all poems, old and new.

Before these pasted-over sheets of cancels, the poem "Prometheus" – which is normally in Volume IV of the set – is inserted, paginated 385 and signed Cc as in Volume IV, but following p. 480 of Volume II. ("Prometheus" is also moved into a copy of Volume II now at Cornell.[26]) In Volume IV, "Prometheus" is normally inserted as an afterthought on a two-leaf gathering that follows "*FINIS*." on what was to have been the last page, p. 384. The poem is introduced with a note: "After these Works were printed off, upon examining the Poetical Volume, we found the following Poem omitted, which we have thought proper to insert here." This seems to mean not merely that the "Poetical Volume" had been "printed off" by the time "Prometheus" was remembered but that it had been gathered, stitched, and bound, so that it was then too late to insert a two-leaf cancel gathering there. In Volume IV of the set to which the Carpenter

24 Weedon, "An Uncancelled Copy of the First Collected Edition of Swift's Poems," p. 46.

25 See Sarah Werner, "Correcting with Cancel Slips," *The Collation* (Washington: Folger Shakespeare Library, 2015, <http://collation.folger.edu/2015/04/correcting-with-cancel-slips/>, accessed 15 March 2018).

26 Cornell University Library PR3720.D35 v.4.

uncancelled copy of Volume II belongs, this two-leaf gathering is missing, so it seems almost certain that the binder chose, or was directed, to move that bifolium into Volume II. The fact that Volume IV was still being worked on after Volume II was published shows that the Carpenter copy was assembled after Volume IV was finished in January 1735. That is, what we have here is not a pre-publication copy or a publisher's mock-up or draft but rather a specially prepared post-publication copy.

In the Carpenter Volume II, the four blank leaves (two ProPatria halfsheets with horizontal chains) standing where a table of contents should be were probably intended for a manuscript table of contents. The uncancelled state of the book seems never to have had a title page or table of contents, which would have been printed last, and the table for the ordinary cancelled version would not have represented this copy accurately at all.

The frontispiece normally present is absent, but a stub visible between gatherings B and C probably was once cognate with the frontispiece. In the normal copy, the frontispiece stub is visible between gatherings *A* and B, but the four-leaf *A* gathering, consisting of the title page, the "Advertisement" leaf, and a two-leaf table of contents, had had its table of contents cancelled (and perhaps by that time replaced by the blank leaves, or perhaps not), so the frontispiece was probably wrapped around the more substantial gathering B, with the stub appearing between leaves B8 and C1.

The blank leaves at the very end of the book were not guillotined with the rest of the book but added as an afterthought after binding. These leaves were perhaps intended for manuscript additions of then unpublished poems or unpublished passages, notably the extra lines of "On Poetry: A Rhapsody." A copy of the cancelled volume at the Huntington has extra pages inserted for manuscript transcripts of "An Epistle to a Lady" and the extra lines of "On Poetry: A Rhapsody,"[27] but a purchaser of the uncancelled volume would not have needed a transcript of "An Epistle to a Lady," and the passages of "On Poetry" would not require nearly as much blank space as these added leaves provide. A copy of Faulkner's 12° Volume II of 1735 uses leaves tipped in for manuscript texts of the extra lines of "On Poetry: A Rhapsody" as well as the two poems Delany engraved on window panes of St Patrick's Deanery (beginning "Are the guests of this house still doomed to be cheated" and "A bard on whom Phoebus his spirit bestowed").[28] Thus the notion of providing leaves for additional poems or lines was not novel, but in this copy, the blank leaves remained blank.

27 Huntington Library 81494, v.2.

28 University of Michigan Library Hubbard Imaginary Voyages PR3721.F26 1735 v.2.

It would be pleasant to report that the book's original owner annotated it with comments on the texts that were to have been cancelled. But the book contains no reader's marks of any kind, nor is there any indication that subsequent owners had an appreciation of the volume's uniqueness.

The binding, though not fancy, is not one of the sorts of publisher's binding commonly seen on ordinary sets of the "1735" Faulkner edition of Swift's *Works*.[29] Scholars of Irish bindings we have consulted believe that the books were bound in Dublin, though it is hard to assign a definite date to the bindings. If the set was bound in the 1740s or later, it is quite possible that the contents were assembled from sheets remaining in Faulkner's warehouse after he had already published his 1737 edition of Volume II and perhaps also his 1744 edition.

In 1736, Richard Tighe died. In 1742, Swift was declared mentally incompetent. In 1745, Joshua, Lord Allen, Sir Robert Walpole, and Swift all died. The Duchess of Somerset and William Whitshed were long dead. With the passage of time, Faulkner probably became willing to cooperate with an interested customer who wanted to preserve the original texts of the "1735" edition, even though most of those texts were never restored in Faulkner's reprints of Volume II. We hope that it may yet be possible to establish the dating of the binding and to identify the binder from the binder's tools used in the spine decoration and on the outer edges of the boards. The spines of the Carpenter set are somewhat abraded, but one of the spine compartments from Volume III is reasonably well preserved (Figure 3.1). The only other use of any of these particular binding tools that we have so far found occurs in a copy of *Justini historiarum ex Trogo Pompeio libri XLIV* (Dublin: Grierson, 1727), in the collection of Philip Maddock, MD. One spine compartment of the Maddock volume, also illustrated in Figure 3.1, shows the corner tools with greater clarity than does the Carpenter volume.[30] The fact that the corner tools are identical in both compartments encourages us to conjecture that the Carpenter Volume II and the Maddock Justinus were bound by the same Dublin binder.

What we *can* say with confidence is that the owner of the Carpenter Volume II was aware that interesting poems had been cancelled from or expurgated in Volume II as published and wanted to save them in their best (that is, unexpurgated) state. It remains likely that the English Faculty Library's uncancelled copy resulted from a binder's error. Although we have not attempted

29 See Stuart Bennett, *Trade Bookbinding in the British Isles, 1660-1800* (New Castle: Oak Knoll, 2004), pp. 41, 43, 116, and 118.

30 We are grateful to Dr Maddock for examining the Carpenter volumes and for providing the photographs for Figure 3.1.

FIGURE 3.1 Left: a spine compartment from Volume III of the set to which the uncancelled Volume II of Swift's "1735" *Works* belongs (collection of Andrew Carpenter).
Centre: a spine compartment from the Grierson edition of Justinus (collection of Philip Maddock, MD).
Far right: corner tools used in the two compartments, isolated to facilitate comparison: Swift above, Justinus below. (The rule shown is in centimetres.)

(and Weedon did not attempt) to date that copy from its binding, she says that it has the bookplate of "W. Godley," probably denoting "The Revd. Mr. William Godley," who is listed among the subscribers in Volume I. This fact tends to confirm that the English Faculty Library copy was one of those issued to subscribers in 1734 and that it therefore, unlike the Carpenter copy, resulted from a binder's error rather than having been deliberately assembled to preserve the *cancellanda*.[31]

The intentional character of the Carpenter volume gives some insight into an interested albeit unknown eighteenth-century reader of Swift's poems. Otherwise, the main implications of our findings are these: first, that the Volume II cancellations and expurgations were done for two main reasons: to avoid re-publishing personal satire, particularly in a volume whose authorship would be only barely concealed in the initials "*J. S*, D. D. D. S. P. D." and to reduce Faulkner's exposure to prosecution or government interference; second, that at least a few people in Dublin were aware that the cancelling suppressed significant texts that were worth preserving; and third, that at least in the case

31 Weedon, "An Uncancelled Copy of the First Collected Edition of Swift's Poems," p. 45.

of the Carpenter volume, Faulkner did not make the suppressed *cancellanda* available until later, and that the extent of Faulkner's agency in making the *cancellanda* available, either in the Carpenter volume or any of the other uncancelled copies, remains undetermined.

We are eager to see whether additional uncancelled copies can now be discovered, and if so whether they also preserve the replacement leaves and any other signs showing when and why they came to be assembled and sold. The list of cancels above ("Cancels in Swift, *Works*, octavo [Dublin: Faulkner, 1735]), Vol. II") is designed to facilitate a quick check of any copy of the 8° Volume II for the possible presence of uncancelled leaves. Since partially uncancelled copies have been found, it is necessary to check each of the eight groups of cancel leaves. We would be delighted to hear of the discovery of additional uncancelled or partially uncancelled volumes.[32] We would be equally delighted to learn of any other bindings exhibiting the binder's tools shown in Figure 3.1.

32 Via email to woolleyj@lafayette.edu. The Swift Poems Project has examined only about 40 of the estimated 1150 copies printed; many of the others probably survive in libraries or in private collections.

James E. May
Lancaster, Pennsylvania

False and Incomplete Imprints in Swift's Dublin, 1710-35

Abstract. This paper examines the varying fullness of Dublin imprints employed by printers during the period 1710-35, identifying printers with particular attention to cut printers' ornaments, increasingly employed after 1710, typographical practices, and other sorts of evidence helpful in identifying where, when, and by whom books were printed. It reveals that Dublin printers of the period, because they often published what they printed (much more often than did London printers), usually acknowledged their work in imprints. It assesses the relative frequency of real, false, and incomplete imprints and examines the diverse motives for false and incomplete imprints. They were employed by printers and publishers for many reasons besides hiding their identities to avoid recrimination from authors, the public, and publishers as well as from church and governmental authorities. Identifying silent and hidden printers by mastering ornament stocks and typographical fingerprints provides solid information on collaboration and division within the book trade. Particular attention is given to imprints employed in controversies during 1713, 1723, and 1733 and to the practices of printer-publisher George Faulkner, whose early false and incomplete imprints are listed in an appendix.

I wish to examine false and incomplete Dublin imprints dated 1710-35, going beyond the usual explanation that Dublin printers sought thereby to hide their identities. How many editions lack imprints (colophons included) or contain therein misrepresentations of the conventional information? What were the diverse motives determining the nature and extent to which printers and publishers identified themselves? These questions can now be addressed with the aid of M[ary] Pollard's *Dictionary of Members of the Dublin Book Trade, 1550-1800* (2000), the *English Short Title Catalogue* (ESTC), and The Eighteenth Century Collection Online (ECCO).[1] Little research has examined cut ornaments to establish what particular Dublin printers produced.[2] A good command of imprints real, false, and incomplete and the motives for using

1 M[ary] Pollard's *Dictionary of Members of the Dublin Book Trade, 1550-1800: Based on the Records of the Guild of St Luke the Evangelist Dublin* (London: Bibliographical Society, 2000). Also consulted was H. Teerink's *A Bibliography of the Writings of Jonathan Swift*, 2nd ed., rev. Arthur H. Scouten (Philadelphia: University of Pennsylvania Press, 1963).

2 One bright exception is James Woolley's "Sarah Harding as Swift's Printer," in *Walking Naboth's Vineyard*, eds Christopher Fox and Brenda Tooley (Notre Dame, Indiana: University of Notre Dame Press, 1995), pp. 164-77, with a bibliography of Harding's editions.

 | DOI:10.30965/9783846763971_005

such can help identify not only who printed and published items, but sometimes who wrote them, and also contributes to our understanding of the relationship between members of the book trades and their relations with authors, readers, and the larger religious and political cultural forces. Identifying silent and hidden printers by mastering ornament stocks and typographical fingerprints provides solid information on collaborative relations between printers and between printers and publishers. The ESTC contains no shared imprints linking Samuel Fairbrother with Aaron Rhames or George Grierson, yet Fairbrother borrowed many ornaments from both. It fails to link Sarah Hyde and George Faulkner as more than two of many co-publishers of works printed by others, but Faulkner borrowed many of Hyde's ornaments and co-printed at least one work with her.

The effort to identify printers with the evidence of cut ornaments is greatly facilitated by ECCO, which boasts 180,000 titles. These include digitized, searchable facsimiles of 3,167 items from the ESTC's 5,079 records of items printed in Dublin 1710-35 (about sixty per cent). Cut ornaments are uncommon during the first five to ten years of the period, but then their use grows substantially. Individual pieces have to be tracked over the years, for they shift ownership and appearance. They were frequently borrowed. Thus, one must ask whether the proposed borrower owned or lacked the type of ornament in question, such as folio headpieces or duodecimo ornamental initials. (Some printers relied on factotums and did not own any cut initials, such as James Carson, S. Powell, and E. Sandys.) Also, is the proposed borrower known to have borrowed ornaments, and from the owner of the piece? Are there any known relations between the two, if only their printing for the same publisher, and are they on the same side of any socio-political divides? Cut ornaments can suggest and sometimes confirm where and when a work was printed and by whom. They allow us to reject some conjectures in the ESTC about the place of publication, such as "London" in T145876 for *Some Considerations upon the Late Attempt to Repeal the Test Act* (London: Printed for H. Clements, and sold by J. Hyde, Bookseller in Dublin, 1719), as the pamphlet has Rhames's ornaments. Ornament evidence greatly increases the number of editions that the ESTC indicates were printed by a particular printer, thus adding four records (T201611, N3724, T177397, T178987) to the six for James Hoey in 1734. For editions without mention of printers, ornaments often reveal which publishers depended on which presses, as Robert Owen relied on the Hyde-Dobson press, and, for those with multiple printer-publishers in the imprint, which did the printing, as John Hyde, not Grierson, printed Philip Frowde's *The Fall of Saguntum* (Dublin: Printed "for" both, 1727), N31660.

In addition, identifying printers requires various typographical considerations, including the quality of type and rules, and the typographical style, such as on the title page. Early in the period 1710-35, some Dublin printers had no solid rules suited to small formats, relying on rules of pieces; thus, an edition with a title-page rule of seven or eight shorter quad-length pieces might be the work of a printer like Carter but not of Rhames or Powell, who might have a rule of pieces in the text but rarely on a title page. Short on rules, Carter often used single-ruled frames around titles, instead of the standard double-ruled. Double-ruled frames and black letter continued to be used on title pages by some older printers in the 1730s when they were abandoned by those new to the trade. In 31 works by Sarah Hyde dated 1730-34, eight have double-ruled frames, including the eight-volume Plutarch and the four-volume *Don Quixote*, and 14 have black letter, including the Plutarch; by contrast, in 26 works printed by Richard Reilly from the end of 1734 through 1736, only one has a double-ruled frame and none has black letter. There are a few other typographical peculiarities for particular presses. For instance, the use of a rule over a date in Roman numerals is good evidence that *Tythes No Gospel Ordinance* by William Morris ("Re-Printed in the Year MDCC X"), N13706, was printed by Rhames, who uses a rule over roman dates at this time, such as in Matthew French, *An Answer to J. B.'s Ordination Sermon* (Rhames, MDCCIX), T69988; Charles Leslie's *A Short and Easie Method with the Deists* (Rhames, for J. Pepyat, MDCCIX), T175183; and Edward Drury, *A Discourse Occasioned by Mr. Boyse's Ordination Sermon* (Rhames, for J. Hyde, MDCCIX), T69986. Assuming *Tythes No Gospel Ordinance* is a Dublin edition (ESTC gives "[Dublin?]"), the typography suits Rhames: the text has solid rules, reducing the number of contenders in Dublin. That typographical evidence is joined to other considerations: it had never been printed in Ireland, nor in Britain since 1680, and the subject of tithes was then controversial in Dublin. Other revealing typographical features include the choice of format (whether 8vo in 8s or 4s, 12mo in 12s or 6s, for instance, sometimes reflecting the shop's type stock), and the consistency of details in the skeleton (for example, whether half the gatherings' leaves are signed). Also, damaged type-pieces, improper alterations in font size or between roman and italic, and the lack of solid rules all exclude the best Dublin presses and generally suggest printing outside London during our period.

Of particular importance to Swift studies, typography can help identify George Faulkner's printing. At least in Faulkner's first decade, his presswork was neither good nor creative; he produced many short octavo pamphlets in half-sheets that were typically signed only on the first leaf of a gathering (with the first gathering unsigned); he was prone to errors in signing and pagination;

he used a limited selection of cut ornaments, many unattractive, which he supplemented with borrowed ornaments; his rules in octavos are usually formed of about 15 short pieces closely fitted (in reproductions often looking like solid rules); he relied heavily on the same few cast pieces for recurrent designs, like a cast block with floral lines often joined on title pages to form a square or in rows forming a downward triangle or the widely-owned circle-oval-circle casting bounded by a rule on one side. Less definitive preferences include pagination in parentheses, arabic numerals in dates, and a large roman "FINIS."

Typographical features are helpful in distinguishing Faulkner's printing from Sarah Hyde's in 1729-32, when Faulkner frequently borrowed ornaments from Hyde. This is a difficult but important question because Swift had work printed by both. John Hyde had been variously employed by Swift for years, such as handling the Irish leg of the London subscription edition of Matthew Prior's poems in 1718 and printing the first Irish *Gulliver's Travels* and probably the first and revised editions of *Cadenus and Vanessa*; when he died (17 November 1728), his wife Sarah, the daughter of master-printer Joseph Ray, continued printing with her husband's partner Eliphal Dobson, Jr, but also by and for herself. She would be entrusted by Swift with printing *On Poetry: A Rapsody* (1734). Faulkner and Hoey had good relations with Sarah Hyde, hiring her in 1729 to co-print one work (discussed below) and to print James Thomson's *Britannia* ("Printed for" Faulkner and Hoey, 1729), T161393; all three ornaments present in the latter belong to the Hyde-Dobson press, and the title page employs solid rules. Hyde printed little in the first year of her widowhood, and perhaps these jobs were consigned to support her. In this context, consider *A Letter from a Certain Great Man to Caleb D'Anvers ... relating to the Vienna Treaty* (n. p.: "Printed in the Year, 1731"), N19475, 8vo, 8 pp., which has Hyde's framed headpiece of a man with a beard wearing a beret, facing right, in an oval with a fruit basket above, flanked by angels blowing inward horns with draped flags; 29 × 81 mm. The title page of *A Letter* has rules of short pieces and a square design of four cast blocks. The Hyde-Dobson press had a good inventory of solid rules from 1725, and no rules of short pieces appear on the title pages of 21 1730-32 editions examined of the Hyde-Dobson press (none in the many on ECCO including those for Robert Owen that mention no printer), and only one (*A Letter to a Member of Parliament* [n.p., 1732], N19543) has a square design of four cast pieces and that differing. However, Faulkner principally used rules of short pieces on his title pages until late 1731. Of 22 editions by Faulkner in 1731 on ECCO, solid rules appear on the title page of only five works.[3] In addition,

3 Solid rules appear on the 1731 title pages of James Darcy's *Love and Ambition*, [ESTC] N39, 12mo; George Lillo's *The London Merchant*, T169725, 12mo; Henry Fielding's *The Tragedy of*

Faulkner uses the same title-page ornament: the square design formed of four cast blocks that potentially create a () shape with four circles within occurs in seven 1731 editions with Faulkner's imprint; and the same cast block is also used in diminishing rows to form a triangular tailpiece.[4]

The framed headpiece of a man facing right in *A Letter* raises the question whether Faulkner also printed *Memoirs of Capt. John Creichton*, edited or co-written by Swift (n. p.: "Printed in the Year, 1731"), T113807. The headpiece appears on p. 9, and the title-page ornament is Hyde's tailpiece of a lion walking right. Both ornaments were acquired by Hyde and Dobson from Rhames in late 1724 or early 1725; both appear in Hyde's printing in years before and after 1731; indeed, the headpiece appears in Swift's *On Poetry: A Rapsody* ("Re-printed, by and for S. Hyde ... 1734"), T446. The *Memoirs* has five solid rules (four in double rules) on the title page, but over the preface on A2 the two rules are 12-16 short pieces locked tightly together as in many Faulkner editions. The Hydes, as often as not, used double solid rules on title pages (in at least 12 editions in 1730-32). As noted, most of Faulkner's title pages in 1731 have rules of pieces; only one of the few with solid rules has two double rules as in the *Memoirs*: Henry Fielding's *The Tragedy of Tragedies*, T225881, dating it "[1731?]." Faulkner will also use a double solid rule above the imprints in two 1732 editions (Pope's *Of Taste*, T5706, 4to; and Gilbert West's *Stowe: The Gardens*, T123975, 8vo). The strongest evidence that Faulkner printed *Memoirs* is that it is an octavo in fours with only $1 signed, Faulkner's usual practice but not Hyde's. Hyde gathers octavos more often in 8s than 4s (unlike Faulkner), signing to the second or third leaf only; in one 1731 octavo in fours (A-H^4), she signs half the leaves consistently (*Some Thoughts concerning Government in General* by A. D. ["by

Tragedies, T225881, 8vo; Lord Hervey's *A Reply to the Late Lord B---ke's Final Answer*, T175994, 8vo; and [probably] *Calista: An Opera*, T187738, 8vo. Besides many works by "Faulkner" dated 1731 with rules of short pieces, seven of the attributed works dated 1731 in the Appendix do as well.

4 The square design is on the title pages of William Arnall's *The Detection of the Infamous Answer ... by Francis Walsingham* (T164880); Bolingbroke's *The Craftsman's Vindication of his Two Hor.ble* [*sic*] *Patrons*, by Caleb D'Anvers (T118984); Sir John Browne's *Reflections upon the Present Unhappy Circumstances of Ireland* (T150012), 8vo; Richard Helsham's *A Letter from ******, MD* (N20307), 8vo; Lord Hervey's *Remarks on the Craftsman's Vindication of his two Hon.ble Patrons in ... May 22, 1731* (T118714); (with two squares side by side) Lord Hervey's *A Reply to the Late Lord B---ke's Final Answer* (T175994); and James Miller's *Harlequin-Horace* (T36014). The same cast block is used to create a triangle with rows of 4-3-2-1 in *A Poem to the Memory of Mrs. Oldfield* (T62651), 8vo. Downward triangles with three to five rows of these pieces are common on title pages or as tailpieces in 1730-32 works with Faulkner's imprint or attributable to him, such as Swift's *To Doctor D-L---Y, on the Libels* (Dublin, 1730), T51103; *Advice to the Ladies of Great-Britain* (London: for the Author, 1730), T164684; and Swift's *Traulus: The Second Part* (no place, 1730), with variant states: T196710 and T449.

and for S. Hyde"]), T65114. Also, the *Memoirs* has an arabic date, much the more common form in Faulkner than in Hyde: of 55 items by Faulkner dated 1730-31, only 8 of 55 have roman numerals (including one misdated "MDCCXXI" [T181858]), but, for Hyde, 7 of 16 dated 1730-32 do. Hyde's ornaments appear in earlier work claimed by Faulkner, such as Matthew Pilkington's *Poems on Several Occasions* ("Printed by George Faulkner," 1730), T123124. Faulkner seems to have printed the whole of Pilkington, even though most of the ornaments belonged to Hyde, for several of Faulkner's are used repeatedly early, middle, and late, and some gatherings have ornaments owned by both printers. (Hyde never borrowed ornaments for octavos.) Most tellingly, this octavo in fours has only the first leaf of gatherings signed and a pagination blunder fitting Faulkner more than Hyde. However, aside from this instance I find no 1730-33 publications printed "by" Faulkner with the headpiece and title-page ornaments in Creichton's *Memoirs*, though Faulkner throughout 1731 had the same small ornament stock that he had in 1728 and he borrowed other Hyde ornaments in 1731 (such as the triangular tailpiece of cupid shooting left, found in Bolingbroke's *The Craftsman's Vindication of his Hor.ble [sic] Patrons* [Faulkner, 1731] and his *A Final Answer to the Remarks on the Craftsman's Vindication* ["R. Francklin, 1731"], T118984 and T182946). If we assume Faulkner did print the work, we must wonder whether Swift chose these ornaments or whether those involved wanted the work to appear as if printed by Hyde. The case for Hyde's printing is strengthened by her having, in conjunction with Dobson, more status and experience in the Dublin trade, being more likely to print and publish a book successfully than Faulkner, but Hyde does not list Creichton in her book-lists, such as the two-page advertisement at the end of *On Poetry: A Rapsody* (nor does Faulkner). It is also possible that the work was co-printed, with Hyde printing at least the first half-sheet with the ornaments.

An earlier edition offers an example of co-printing sorted out with attention to ornaments and typography: Samuel Johnson's *Hurlothrumbo: or, The Super-Natural*, with the imprint "London: Printed for the Author and, Dublin: Re-printed by James Hoey, and George Faulkner, at the Pamphlet-Shop," 1729, T36870, 8vo: *A*^{4} B-H^4, with gathering E signed with an asterisk (called a cancel by ESTC). It contains on A3 Faulkner's (formerly Harding's) headpiece of a fruit basket over putto flanked by a leafy vine ending in roses and on B1 Faulkner's headpiece of two linked fruit horns (with identifying break to bottom inside rule at centre); later it has three Hyde ornaments: on G2/43 an unframed headpiece with a six-petal flower flanked by pine cones and then peacocks; H3/53 a headpiece with fountain and four putti (left frame shaved at bottom as in Edward Synge's *Catholick Christianity* ["for R. Owen," 1729], T28899); and H4 the tailpiece on the title page of Creichton's *Memoirs*. The

Hoey-Faulkner press produced half-sheets A-E, with only the first leaf signed and with the recto running title "*The* SUPER-NATURAL." The Hyde-Dobson press printed F-H with the first two leaves of gatherings signed and the running title "*The* SUPER-NATURAL."

An important piece of physical evidence that cannot be obtained without examining copies involves the paperstock. The watermark allows one to know that Powell's second printing of Edward Young's *The Merchant* ("1730"), T172103, occurred in "1742" or thereafter. Dublin editions are much more frequently printed on paper with grapes watermarks and French countermarks than are English editions. The presence of a grapes watermark in a "third edition" of Sir Thomas Burnet's *The Necessity of Impeaching the Late Ministry: In a Letter to the Earl of Hallifax* suggests Dublin printing. It is a 24-page octavo with the imprint "London: Printed by W. Wilkins; and Sold by J. Roberts in Warwick-Lane, 1715," T211064. There is an authorized "third edition" with the same imprint but with 37 pages like three other London editions, all four of which exist in many copies with locations indicating they are not Irish editions. The false "third edition" is only held by Trinity College Dublin and the House of Lords; the only edition like it in pagination and imprint is another likely Dublin printing with a false Wilkins imprint, a duplicate "fourth" edition, T218050, also only at two locations with one being in Dublin.

As this example suggests, the publication record is often indicative, perhaps showing, as in the above case, no Dublin editions for a popular work yet duplicate edition numbers for a London edition. A case in point is this incomplete imprint probably printed in Dublin: Defoe, *The True-Born Englishman* (n.p.: "Printed in the Year MDCCXIII"), T70658, 8vo: A-B^8 [$2-4 signed], 32 pp. Although the only extant copies are at the Boston Public Library and the British Library, the absence of any Dublin edition since its appearance in 1700 until Samuel Fuller's in 1728 raises suspicion – and Fuller's is also a 32-page octavo (Dublin reprints often copied earlier Dublin reprints). That Fuller published another edition in 1730 argues a local appetite for the satire. Here we recognize two considerations for provenance: subject and author. One expects a Dublin origin for a work on Trinity College or Dublin politics or by a local minor poet. References in works by Dubliners or in Dublin newspapers can also point the finger.

Another flag for false imprints involves the locations of copies, which the ESTC greatly facilitates. If the majority of copies in the British Isles are in Ireland, one should suspect Irish printing regardless of the imprint. Searches on the ESTC with multiple Irish locations have helped me locate many false "London" printings. A related consideration, used frequently by David Foxon, is what a copy is bound with. For example, Foxon conjectures a Dublin printing for an edition of Abel Evans's *The Apparition* (n. p.: "Printed in the Year MDCCX"), T174610, known to him only in two copies in American libraries, because one copy "is bound in a collection of Dublin tracts" (E525). In this case, I withhold a decision until seeing the paperstock, for there are no Irish locations and the edition is well printed in a style suiting a London edition. Of course, bookplates and manuscript annotations on extant copies could also be telling.

Inaccuracies in imprints also send up a red flag. The misspelling of John Baker's name as "Barker" points to a possible Dublin reprint with false imprint. *The Tories Defeated: or, The Doctor almost Turn'd Christian* (on Henry Sacheverell) was published with the imprint "London: Printed for J. Baker, at the Black-Boy in Pater-Noster-Row, 1713," N27642, and then it was reprinted with the same imprint but for the misspelling "Barker," N27644, an edition with two of five locations in the British Isles being in Dublin. A better example might be the unusual spelling of the imprint "by and for S. Hide" in *A Protestant's Resolution: Shewing his Reasons Why He will not be a Papist* (1734), T14173, with the proper spelling in the final leaf's advertisement of books published by "S. Hyde, widow." The Hydes never printed a book with the spelling "Hide." The sole ornament, on p. 46, is a tailpiece of spread-winged eagle facing left on an "I"-shaped pedestal, appearing on the title pages of works printed "by Theo. Jones" as early as 1735 (for example, Robert Dodsley's *The Toy-Shop*, T51497). However, sometimes it is the accuracy of information transcribed in a reprint that suggests a Dublin printing, such as the copying of the London price on a reprint that is smaller and shorter and should sell for less.

Before launching into general observations on Dublin imprints, I should stress that my observations are based on the sketchy bibliographical record offered by the ESTC. Many unrecorded items are held by libraries and individuals that did not report holdings to the project. Much that was printed is nowhere extant. Very little popular literature, such as short devotional materials, especially for Catholics, chapbooks, slip ballads and the like, is recorded for Dublin 1710-35. The fragility of the bibliographical record is suggested by how few copies have luckily survived: of 138 extant Dublin printings in 1723, there survive but a single copy of 40 items, only two copies of 21 items, and only three of 21 items. Thus, 82 of 138 records, 60 per cent of known publications, exist in three or fewer copies. Over half a dozen serious and lengthy books are among these unique or nearly unique items. Accordingly, our knowledge of the book trade is also spotty, further reduced by the loss of manuscript records, such as the Guild of St Luke's apprenticeship book for the years before 1741.[5] In consequence, there are numerous publishers named in a single Dublin imprint that

5 Pollard, *Dictionary of Members of the Dublin Book Trade*, p. xxx.

may be misspellings or false fronts. The ESTC has single publication records for John Crossby (T217486), Richard Dixon (T232100, undated, blundering the active printer Richard Dickson's name), Margaret Ffookes (T117914), John Haite (N4398), P. K. in 1723 (T193615), Tim. Donnovan or Donovan (T165608), J. Mason (T4976), Theophilis Musgrove (T196928), and others. The Mason record, for the undated *The Little Beau's Lamentation: For the Loss of Miss C---t*, is one of seven poems from 1726-28 making fun of Patrick Walsh as the "little Beau," most of which are slips employing unique fictional publishers' imprints (such as "John Little" in "Christ-Church-Lane, 1727," T41095, and "John Toybow, in Sheep-street, opposite the Bulls-head," 1728, T5165, FOXON S463). Moreover, whether or when an actual individual operated a press is often uncertain. The ESTC records four plays in 1730 with imprints claiming they were "printed by T[homas] Lawler" (T215599, T169343, N52081, and N30065), but there is reason to doubt that he, though apprenticed to Rhames, printed them, for at least one (T169343) has Hyde's ornaments and the only other records for him indicate that Powell and C. Hussey printed them in 1732 and 1733 (T175169 and T169400).

Few false "London" imprints were printed in Dublin, decidedly fewer than were printed in Edinburgh. The ESTC identifies from David Foxon's *English Verse, 1701-1750* far more false Edinburgh imprints than Dublin imprints during Swift's years. The Dublin trade in 1715-35 made little if any effort to send its printing to London surreptitiously. I cannot find then a good parallel to the 1767 edition of Edward Young's *The Complaint: or, Night-Thoughts* printed "Cork: Printed by and for W. Flyn, and for J. Ferrar, in Limerick," T165426, that was shipped to England with the imprint "London: Printed and Sold by all the Booksellers in Great-Britain, M.DCC.LXVII," T27226 (no copies of the latter issue are in Irish libraries). The ESTC may give the impression that there are relatively more false "London" imprints employed by Dublin printers than in fact exist because often Dublin printers began their imprints with the formula "London printed" followed by the statement "Dublin reprinted" or "sold by" and a Dublin publisher's name and address without the word "Dublin." For instance, ESTC N9027 indicates "The imprint is false; printed in Dublin" for *The Duke of Anjou's Succession Further Consider'd, as to the Danger that may arise from it to Europe ... Part II.* with the imprint "London: Re-printed at the Back of Dick's Coffee-House in Skinner-Row, and are to be Sold by Jacob Milner Bookseller in Essex-Street, 1701." There is nothing false in this imprint. Dozens of London editions in the same period record a work's origin by beginning the imprint with "Dublin printed" or "Printed at Dublin." However, a few Dublin imprints omit "Dublin" to suggest a London provenance, such as "London: Printed for A. Baldwin and M. G. [Matthew Gunne] at Essex-Street-Gate, 1711," on an edition of Francis Hare's *The History of the Management of the War*

(T53820). As here, sometimes Dublin work was falsely passed off as printed in London for a public "having an Opinion that Books are better printed in England than here," as printer John Brocas admitted when questioned about reprinting the title page of the London edition of *An Impartial Account of the Life and Actions of James the Second* in 1701.[6] More often, to add value Dublin publishers called attention to the work's origins in London by implying such with the simple phrase "Reprinted by" or by noting "London printed." Indeed, the word "Reprinted" can suggest an item was printed outside London, such as in *Christianity no Creature of the State* ("Re-printed in the Year, MDCCXVII"), N15031, which ESTC conjectures was printed in Dublin, citing John Robert Moore (*A Checklist of the Writings of Daniel Defoe*, 1960), who attributed it to Daniel Defoe (the typography and copy locations support Dublin provenance).

Although early in the period 1710-35 Dublin printers often began imprints with reference to London publication, the percentage of Dublin imprints including reference to prior London publication declines in 1720s and 1730s. In 1713, at least 19 of the Dublin imprints (*c.*160 records) mention an earlier publication in London, and in nine cases the London publisher; the formula is used by Cornelius Carter, Francis Dickson, Elizabeth Ray, and Edward Waters only. This practice declines over the next two decades. In 1723, only eight Dublin works (of *c.*142 records) refer to earlier London publication, and none mention a London publisher. In 1733, although 34 Dublin items (of *c.*236 records) refer to earlier London publication, only one London publisher is mentioned, A. Dodd, in an edition by Christopher Dickson. For the phrase "Reprinted in Dublin," ESTC has 75 per cent fewer imprints in 1731-40 than in 1711-20. However, in the first two decades of the century, it is so common that the phrasing was even used for Dublin productions never printed in London, such as *Some Pious Resolutions of the Whiggs in the Irish House of Commons* ("Dublin: Reprinted [by Francis Dickson], 1713-14"), T49333.

And it should be noted that there are also editions with false "Dublin" imprints. An example is the "A Dublin, M.DCC.XXI." imprint of *Les Trois justaucorps*, the adaptation of *A Tale of a Tub* by René Macé, T89998, which Teerink thought was printed by Thomas Johnson in The Hague.[7] In some cases, the title pages copy the Dublin editions' reprinted, and no effort is made to pass the reprints off as the originals, such as *Hibernia Sacra* of Sir James Ware ("Dublinii, Typis JOHANNIS CROOK, Typographi Regii, & Lugduni Batavorum [Leiden], apud Joh: du Vivie, MDCCXVII"), T63319 (still treated as a Dublin edition by the ESTC). In other cases, the foreign printer wished to claim the authority

6 Pollard, *Dictionary of Members of the Dublin Book Trade*, pp. 395-96.

7 Teerink and Scouten, pp. 178-79, #262.

of publication in Ireland, such as in *Le Génie anglois, ou histoire abrégée des révolutions*, with "Dublin" imprint "chez Jaques Pepiat," 1723, T40708, signed $1-7 and recognized in the ESTC as probably printed in Holland (most copies are located outside the British Isles). Many London editions employed false "Dublin" imprints, such as William King's *A Letter from Mr. Lewis O Neil to Peregrine O Donald, Esq; with Mr. O Donald's Answer* ("Dublin: Printed in the Year MDCCXXXIV"), N19581, with the title page bearing James Bettenham of London's small tailpiece of a standing figure of justice, ponytail blowing to left, sword in left hand and scales in right; found on c2v of Volume I of Samuel Jebb's *De vita & rebus gestis* (London: J. Woodman and D. Lyon, 1725; with colophon "Typis J. Bettenham" on I, 622), T95522. Curiously, King's *The Toast: An Epic Poem* was printed in London with the false claim "Dublin: Printed in the Year, MDCCXXXII" (N13480 and N13481; Foxon K79 and K80). The genuine Dublin edition, also dated 1732 and without publisher's name, T62885, has a single cut ornament, on p. 10, belonging to James Carson, who placed it on the title pages of at least three works, including *Death: A Poem* (by and for J. Carson and Syl. Pepyat, 1731), N331, and Bezaleel Morrice's *The Country-House* (by and for J. Carson, 1735), N1114. As in *Le Génie anglois*, one finds imprints falsely including the name of Dublin publishers, particularly of George Faulkner, who was evidently associated with Swift. Thus, the London publishers used the phrasing "Reprinted from the Dublin Edition, for G. F. and sold by A. Dodd" when reprinting Swift's *The Presbyterians Plea of Merit* [1733] (T90339) and the anonymous *A Vindication of the Protestant Dissenters, from the Aspersions Cast upon Them* [1734] (T89555). Although the first work was previously printed by Faulkner (Dublin, 1733, T92255), the second was "by S. Powell" and argues for the repeal of the Test Act and against Swift's and Faulkner's positions. Besides the stated place of publication, there can also be a false claim regarding the origin of the material, such as in *The Secret History of an Old Shoe*, a satire on Walpole and others, asserting "Dublin, Printed: London, Reprinted by J. Dickenson ... 1734" (T53809).

The Dublin trade printed a number of editions that have separate London issues, in at least three cases for Theodore Sanders, active in Little Britain from 1719 to 1748. Most of these give Dublin as the place of printing and so are treated as Dublin imprints in the ESTC, but there are harder-to-detect issues not referencing Dublin. Among those is *The Life of the Late Victorious and Illustrious Prince, John Duke of Marlborough*, by an "impartial hand" ("London: Printed for Theodore Sanders, at the Bell in Little Britain," 1723), N19099, 8vo, *c.*350 pp. (no copies in Irish locations). Not noted by the ESTC, this book, with a list of subscribers, was also issued as "Dublin: Printed by E. Waters, for Thomas Thornton, and William Smith, 1723," T169125. Most Dublin books reissued in London are learned, such as Caleb Threlkeld, *Synopsis stirpium Hibernicarum*, printed by S. Powell for three Dublin publishers in 1726 (T210828), then reissued separately in 1727 as "Dublin: Printed by S. Powell, for the Author, and are to be sold by T. Sanders in Little Britain," T99225. Similarly, a year after the Dublin publication of *The History of the Lives and Reigns of the Kings of Scotland* (John Harding for the author, 1722), T79534, it was reissued as *The History of the Kingdom of Scotland* with the imprint "Dublin: Printed for the Author, and are to be Sold by T. Sanders," N17890 (no extant copies in Ireland). And Rhames, who printed more London separate issues at this time than other Dublin printers, produced in the same year as his edition for the Dobsons a separate London issue of Edward Hunt's *An Abridgment of all the Statutes in Ireland* (Dublin: Printed by A. Rhames, for William Churchill, London, 1718), N43111. Other editions by Rhames with separate Dublin and London issues include Thomas Burgh, *A Method to Determine the Areas of Right-Lined Figures Universally*, 1724, for J. Hyde in Dublin (N4023) and for Richard Wilkins in London (T144039); and William Nicolson, Bishop of Derry, *The Irish Historical Library*, 1724, for R. Owen in Dublin (T57518) and for W. Taylor in London (T57517), and, with a joint Dublin-London imprint, *Desid. Erasmi Roterodami Colloquia Familiaria*, 1712, for J. Churchill in London and E. Dobson in Dublin (T138075).

The most minimal imprint will include at least a date and place where printed, employing something like the formula "Dublin: Printed in the Year." Yet it is surprising how many publications fail to offer a date. Some printers seemed to prefer leaving out the date: over half the ESTC records for Thomas Walsh lack the date (8 of 13) as do a third of those for Nicholas Hussey, Sarah Harding's second husband (5 of 12). Frequently location and date are implicit in the title (as in news and proclamation broadsides with drop-head titles and datelines) and thus might not be expected from an imprint. Sometimes, identifying information is included in a frontispiece, which can function like an engraved title page, and an imprimatur or license to print can also provide information left otherwise understood. Some items were not printed for sale and so needed no imprint, such as short announcements and proclamations, like three leaflets against the requirement to swear oaths issued by the Quaker meeting houses in 1723, and also poems by wealthy individuals, like Knightley Chetwode's *Advice to a Young Lady* (T498537, noting [1714]), which can be dated from a reference in a letter by Jonathan Swift.[8]

A complete imprint, in addition to date and place of publication, will normally name the publishers (required by law in England), both whoever by financing printing costs exercises some editorial control and the distributing

8 *Correspondence*, ed. Woolley, II, 482-83n, n5. David Woolley dates it December 1723.

publisher, who sells to the public. The controlling publisher could well be the author or editor, such as Swift for several posthumous works of Sir William Temple; the distributing publisher could be the author as well. The address of the distributor is also conventional, presumably more so in a city of larger size (more useful in London than in Dublin). In some cases, but not usually, the printer(s) are noted in imprints, particularly when the same agent is both printer and publisher. While this information conventionally appears on a title page, in short works with drop-head titles, it would be expected at the end of the text in a colophon. During our period, there are occasions when printers employ an imprint for publishing information and then a colophon identifying themselves (London printer James Bettenham frequently does such). Even pamphlets will sometimes have both an imprint and a colophon with duplicate information, and a work could be reissued by adding a secondary imprint, something Carter does to a pamphlet printed by Thomas Hume with the dateline title *Custom-House, Dublin. March the 12th, 1725-6*. The original colophon set to the page-width of the lines above it on p. 4 reads "Dublin: Printed by Thomas Hume, at the Custom-House-Printing-House, in Essex-Street, 1726," but on p. 1, in a manner unconventional in a four-page folio, Carter has added before the catchword "Dublin: Printed by C. C. 1725-6." ESTC N56357 wrongly lists it as if printed by Carter, but Carter, printing little longer than a funeral broadside at this time (and that in shabby type), had become an unprofessional tradesman who in early 1727 would counterfeit Thomas Walsh's *The Castle Courant.*[9]

Generally speaking, "false" and "incomplete" are applied to three expected details in an imprint: location, publisher, and date, during the period 1700-40 in Dublin we conventionally find a fourth detail, the printer. Although we do not speak of a London imprint stating publisher but not printer as incomplete, Dublin printers of the period so frequently designate themselves, sometimes adding a different seller, that we might expect to learn both from the imprint. For the years 1710-34, out of 4,868 ESTC records for Dublin, 2,790 (57 per cent) have "printed by" in the imprint, but only 381 (under eight per cent) have "printed for;" whereas, of the 42,784 records for London books in that period, 7,067 (17 per cent) have "printed by," and 19,904 (47 per cent) have "printed for." I can use my own count for certain years. In 1723, of 138 printed items that are not newspapers, "Printed for" precedes an author once and a bookseller 15 times (11 per cent), including two unexamined editions "for" Grierson, which he may have printed. In these 138 items, the formula "printed by" or the equivalent ("ex officina Georgii Grierson" and "at the Rein Deer") occurs in 115, that is, for 83 per cent of the items. In 1713, over 75 per cent of what is printed has no

9 See ESTC P1620 and Pollard, *Dictionary of Members of the Dublin Book Trade*, pp. 93 and 586.

publisher other than the printer; only about 22 of the 162 records indicate the work was printed for someone other than the printer. Only eight Dublin imprints in 1713 have the formula "Printed for" and the publisher's name without mentioning the printer. "Printed by" is so frequently the formula that it was used at times incorrectly in place of "Printed for."

In the 1720s, the supremacy of the printers seems greater than it actually was because of several developments. One is that Grierson began printing his own books in 1720, as did John Hyde and Eliphal Dobson, Jr, in 1725, and thus we have "printed by" imprints when we would otherwise have had "printed for." Second, around 1721, John Chantry, formerly of the London book trade, begins to publish books without his imprint, books with imprints stating "Printed by" such printers as William Helme, Pressick Rider and Thomas Harbin, S. Powell, Elizabeth Sadleir, and, especially, J[ames] Watts, without any mention of Chantry, but sometimes with a youthful co-publisher like Patrick Dugan or Joseph Leathley as seller or indicating Chantry's address: "sold opposite the Watch-House on the North-Side of College Green" in 1724-27 and thereafter to 1732 "at the Corner of Sycomore Alley at Dame's Street." Chantry listed a substantial number of his publications at the end of Thomas Otway's *The History and Fall of Caius Marius* ("Printed by J. Watts, and sold opposite the Watch-House, the North-side of College Green," 1725), N17442, and the list includes Thomas Wood's *An Institute of the Laws of England*, published as "Printed by J. Watts, and sold opposite the Watch-House," 1724 [1725], T118567, a folio of almost 700 pages priced over a pound – not a book that young Watts could have afforded to print. Chantry's many advertisements in *The Dublin Gazette* include, on 8-11 August 1724, the proposal for "An Institute of the Laws of England ... containing one hundred and eighty Sheets on good Paper and new Letter ... at sixteen Shillings in Sheets ... Subscriptions ... taken in and Proposals and Specimens are given gratis at the Undertaker, Mr. John Chantry's House, opposite the Watch-House on the North-side of College-Green." Chantry gave progress reports until the work was distributed in April.

With Dublin books more than London books, to discover the printer is to discover the publisher or at least approach him, for the two functions were more often shared by the same individual and, when they were not, ideological and familial relations bound printers and publishers more than in London. Political and religious divisions ruled out certain printers from a publisher's choice, particularly in years of great division (the unity within the trade during the Wood's patent struggle, 1724-25, was atypical). By contrast, in London at this time, Edmund Curll might contract work with over a dozen printers from across the political spectrum. But George Risk and John Hyde usually turned, respectively, to the presses of S. Powell and A. Rhames, and, after Grierson started printing in 1720, George Ewing often had Grierson, his brother-in-law, print his work. In divisive years such as 1713, 1723, and 1733, Tory publications were predictably printed by Carter, Faulkner, Daniel Tompson, or Waters. Whig publications had more options.

By my count, of the 236 Dublin items from 1733, 20 have no imprint or colophon, and 35 have "Printed in the Year" or similar incomplete imprint or colophon. And to these 55 can be added several false "London" imprints (Swift's *The Life and Genuine Character* [Faulkner] and Whitehead's *The State Dunces* satire [Powell]), bringing the total to 57. Thus, well over twenty per cent lack the usual seller and/or address information. By comparison, if we use ESTC figures, in 1733, only 58 of 1,661 London publications and 11 of 140 Edinburgh publications have "Printed in the year" imprints. (Searching exact phrase in ESTC's "anywhere" field is more inclusive than in "publisher," which gives 27 fewer records for Dublin.) The absence of booksellers' names is in part due to the topical nature of what is published in 1733, a quarrelsome year. Of the 57, at least 34 involve political and religious controversy, bawdiness, scatology, or Roman Catholicism. Over a dozen involve the potential repeal by Parliament of the Test Act, and many involve elections (at least ten), particularly of Swift's friend, Lord Mayor Humphry French. (There would have been fewer incomplete imprints in 1733 were Swift not in Dublin.) Many were broadsides sold on streets like newspapers. They had dozens of sellers perhaps and no principal shop of sale. Of 55 items without seller in 1733, 40 are one sheet or less. Only one, *A Manual of Prayers and Other Christian Devotions*, T122613, is over two sheets long; it is a thick Catholic devotional book, and this holds true in 1723, when the lengthiest work without place or printer is the Roman Catholic *The Sinners Guide* by the Portuguese Dominican Father Luis de Granada (N36292), last printed (without place) in 1702 (T121453). In any longer work, the main reason for the absence of identifying imprints was to avoid adverse consequences, real or imagined.

What we see in 1733 are controversial works that have imprints calling attention to the printer-publisher or concealing his identity. The printers are less anonymous than the authors. In general, setting aside broadcasted sheets, one supposes some items without imprints or with false imprints are such to avoid offense and thus recrimination from, first, authors; second, the government and the powerful in church, commerce, and the aristocracy; third, the consuming public; and fourth, others in the Guild of St Luke's and the book trade in general. Regarding authors, clearly a printer or publisher did not want to lose consignments from a bishop or minister potentially offering work, such as Edward Synge or Joseph Boyse. Also, he did not want to cross some authors even if he never would receive work from them. For instance, Jonathan Smedley's *An Hue and Cry after Dr. S---t* (1714) has no early eighteenth-century Dublin imprints. There are eight editions with the London publisher J. Roberts's imprint in 1714, including two "third editions," one 23 pages with Roberts's advertisement on p. [24] and one 15-page octavo almost certainly a Dublin edition with false imprint. The latter (N7222) adds "the Examiner," to the title before "Dr. S---t" as do a 15-page "sixth edition" ("for J. Roberts"), T190890, found only at Trinity College, Dublin, and a 1727 reprint ("London: Printed in the Year"), T100942, both being likely Dublin editions.

In a society divided by religious and political factions, not surprisingly, most printers and publishers took care not to identify themselves with either side of major divisions within the public. In 1733, most printers, led by George Faulkner, printed against Dissenters and for the Test, and very few, most especially Samuel Powell, published for the repeal of the Test. Publications on the Test Act frequently lack full imprints for various reasons. In some cases, no address was needed, for they were broadsides sold on the streets by mercuries. Two reasons also apply to why most publications on the Test were anonymous. First, pamphlets for or against the repeal might stir ill will against the seller by the opposite side. And, second, the printer-publisher's name, as might the author's, could telegraph the position in the tract, and one might thus leave out that information for the same reason one chose a title that did not reveal the position, as in *The Test Act Considered in a Political Light*, a broadside against the repeal, only indicating "Printed in the Year 1733" (T7748). However, given how tribal and partisan the public can be, it is not surprising that George Faulkner in particular wished to be associated with forces for keeping the Test Act. He published with his imprint at least seven items against the repeal, though almost all were short enough for broadside distribution without any imprint. Several have titles not declaring their conclusions, such as *The Case of the Test Considered, with Respect to Ireland* (T73913), 8vo, 15 pp; *The History of the Test Act*, 8vo, 28 pp, variously attributed to Bishops Thomas Sherlock and Edmund Gibson (N8125); and two editions of Swift's *The Presbyterians Plea of Merit; in order to Take off the Test, Impartially Examined* (T1823 and N20458). But others with Faulkner's imprint are clearly partisan:

The Dispute Adjusted, about the Proper Time of Applying for a Repeal of the Corporation and Test Acts: By Shewing that no Time is Proper. By ... [Edmund Gibson], *Bishop of London. To which are added ... Some Queries relating thereto.* [that is to the Test] *By the Reverend Dr. J.S.D.S.P.D.* (T75446), 8vo, 37 [3] pp.;

The Natural Impossibility of Better-Uniting Protestants and Securing the Constitution ... by Repealing the Test (T4849), 8vo, 32 pp.;

Plain Reasons against the Repeal of the Test-Act (T73917), 8vo, 15 pp.; and

The Tables Turned against the Presbyterians: or, Reasons against the Repeal of the Sacramental Test (T87761), folio, 2 pp.

Faulkner does not use his imprint in several other anti-repeal publications. One is Swift's *A Letter from a Member of the House of Commons in Ireland, to a Member of the House of Commons in England, concerning the Sacramental Test. Written in the Year 1708* (Dublin: Printed in the year 1733), N19756, TEERINK AND SCOUTEN 512A, a 24-page octavo, which Teerink noted was reissued in the same typesetting in Volume IV of the 1735 *Works of J.S, D.D, D.S.P.D.*[10] The absence of Faulkner's imprint may have been required by Swift to reduce attribution of the work to himself, by now identified with Faulkner. Faulkner also did not use his imprint on broadsides with Swift's "queries" in *Dispute Adjusted*, hawked on the streets, nor did he in the satiric Scots-dialect poem *The Grunters' Request, to Take off the Test*, an octavo half-sheet with 3 pp. of glossary (1733, T166406).

Other pieces with printers' own names include the anonymous *Some Considerations Humbly Offer'd upon the Present Attempt of the Dissenters, to Obtain a Repeal of the Test Act* "Printed by Anne Crooke" (T73919); and the periodical printed by Hoey, *The Correspondent*, attacking Dissenters as well as defending the Test (P6192), with material in issues 3-4 attributed to Swift (but doubted by TEERINK AND SCOUTEN, p. 360, #736). Sarah Hyde printed without imprint Bishop Edward Synge's *Postscript* (T221196) to *A Peaceable and Friendly Address to the Non-conformists Treating the Test*, 1697 (R184783), reprinted by Faulkner in 1732 (T85524), leading to Synge's 4-page postscript dated 21 November 1733.

Several printers can be identified as publishing tracts for repeal. In printing an argument for repeal that criticizes one of Faulkner's publications, Rhames left his name off, as did the author: [Wm. Harris], *Remarks on the History of the Test. In which Some Mistakes are Corrected* (Dublin: "Printed for J. Mc. Cleland ... in Sycamore-Alley, 1733"), T168871, with ornaments on the title page and A2 owned by Rhames. This critic of *The History of the Test Act* (Faulkner, 1733), N8125, stresses several commonplaces in arguments for the repeal: the Dissenters made a sacrifice in accepting the Test as an effort to protect Protestants from Papacy; former parliamentary discussions of bills show there was an expectation that a time would come when the Test would be lifted; and the present threat from the Deists is good reason to repeal the Test, which weakens Protestantism and the state (p. 23).

10 TEERINK AND SCOUTEN, p. 264.

Samuel Powell, who took control of his family's press in or before 1731, stands out as a supporter of the repeal. He was an earnest man who would later print and publish a great many tracts for John Wesley, making himself instrumental in Wesley's mission beginning in 1747. The Powell press was less dependent on the public than most other printers, its principal clients being publishers. Ornaments reveal Powell printed the pro-repeal *An Inquiry into the Propriety of Applying to Parliament, for the Repeal of the Corporation and Test Acts: In a Letter to Samuel Holden, Esq*; ("London Printed, and Dublin Re-printed for J. Smith and W. Bruce," 1733), N16990. The headpiece of an open book on A2 had been Hyde's until 1731 but was repeatedly used by Powell in 1733, and the factotum had been used by the Powells since at least 1726. In 1733, Powell printed at least five pro-repeal publications for himself, without sellers:

A Letter from a Gentleman in the Country to a Member of Parliament in the City, T180935, 8vo, 16 pp. The anonymous author purports to be a member of the Established Church who lives where "these People [Dissenters] are most numerous" (p. 3), and he believes the Test Act is uncharitable. He refutes the claim that repealing the Test "will bring in great Numbers of Scotch Presbyterians and English Dissenters upon us" (p. 14);

The Reasonableness of Repealing the Sacramental Test Consider'd: In Answer to Some Late Pamphlets, Particularly to The Dispute Adjusted, and The History of the Test-Act, N26364, 8vo, 56 pp.;

Reasons for the Repeal of the Sacramental Test, a five-part serial with continuous pagination, parts 3 and 5 with "Printed by S. Powell," T20924;

A Vindication of the Protestant Dissenters, from the Aspersions Cast upon them in a Late Pamphlet, intitled, The Presbyterians Plea of Merit ... To which are added, Some Remarks upon a Paper, call'd, The Correspondent (T92255), 8vo, 48 pp., an anonymous reply to Hoey's periodical and Swift; and

The Case of the Episcopal Dissenters in Scotland, and that of the Dissenters in Ireland Compar'd [a defence of Dissenters], T120244, 8vo, 20 pp.

In addition, Powell may well have printed (given its position and the quality of its typography) *The Case of the Protestant Dissenters of Ireland with respect to the Sacramental Test Humbly Represented to the Legislature* (no imprint), T87114, [2]-p folio, which argues for repeal with the common topic that Dissenters played an important role in the revolution.

Powell's public association with the case for repeal may have led him to leave off his imprint on a moderate tract opposing the repeal: *Three Letters on the Following Questions, concerning the Repeal of the Test. I. Hath the Church a Right to Exclude ...*, second edition ("Dublin: Printed in the Year, 1733"), T1991. The anonymous author concludes that "the Sacramental Test ... ought to be insisted upon" (p. 21). Powell's ornaments here include his commonly used headpiece with four ships in a line at centre right and rowboat to left (as on p. 3 of Walter Chamberlaine's *The Three Travellers: A Tale* [S. Powell, for T. Thornton, 1733], T484).

Among the 1733 imprints, one suspects fear of recrimination led to incomplete imprints on several sorts of material offending much of the public, such as the bawdy and the scatological. The first is exemplified in Faulkner's not putting his imprint on *St. Patrick's Well* (T160349), a bawdy poem in a half-sheet octavo about the speaker's getting lucky; the second, in the puerile verses *On Miss Vane's F--t* [*Fart*] (T215883). Dublin publications cite earlier London imprints for sexual material (perhaps owing in part to Edmund Curll's publications), and London publications often refer to earlier Dublin publication in scatological materials, frequently associated with Swift. In many cases, such as *Human Ordure, Botanically Considered* ("Printed at Dublin: And Reprinted at London, for F. Coggan," [1733]), T128223, the earlier Dublin printing actually occurred (by S. Powell for J. Watson, 1733), T36734 – though the Dublin edition does not attribute authorship to Swift as does the London – but in others the claim seems false, as in *A Turd Is as Good for a Sow as a Pancake* ("Dublin, Printed: London, Re-printed for J. Roberts," 1732), T226383. Presumably, *The Benefit of Farting* and *The Wonderful Wonder of Wonders*, published in 1722 separately and sometimes in combination with *Miscellanies Written by Jonathan Swift, D.D.* (TEERINK AND SCOUTEN 19), helped associate excremental humor with Swift. The publication record shows that *Benefit* and *Wonderful* were more popularly received in London than Dublin.

One obvious sort of publication threatening recrimination by the public as well as Church and State involves religious materials, particularly Roman Catholic. The publication of Catholic devotional literature frequently led to the arrest of printer and publisher during the early eighteenth century. Thus the absence of even place from the 1733 Dublin edition of the popularly reprinted (and evolving) classic *A Manual of Prayers*. An earlier attempt to publish it had led to five or more arrests: Pollard notes that in November 1708 James Malone, his apprentice and fellow Catholic Luke Dowling, the Protestant Peter Lawrence and Patrick Murtagh along with printers Carter and Waters were taken into custody for "suspition of Printing and Vending Popish Prayer-Books."[11] She notes Lawrence turned state's evidence, as did Waters later in February 1709. The "defendants stated that *Manual of devout prayers* had been sold for last 20 years 'without having been taken notice of by the government'" (citing J. T. Gilbert, *History of Dublin*, I, 179-80, quoting Exchequer records). Malone and company were fined a huge sum, 300 marks, later reduced to five according

---

11 Pollard, *Dictionary of Members of the Dublin Book Trade*, p. 396.

to Gilbert. Certainly, it was true that the *Manual* had been sold in Ireland previously, often in Continental editions, and it was openly published by the Catholic bookseller Thomas Meighan in London by 1728. Meighan published a library of Catholic materials that would have led to prosecution in Dublin. This 1733 duodecimo of over 500 pages is very well printed with cut ornaments appearing in other Dublin editions. Pollard identified in it a cut factotum and a headpiece employed in Otway's *The Orphan* "Printed by C[hristopher] Hussey, for T. Lawler, 1733" (T169400; the "C" in the imprint has since been pulled off the sole copy by the removal of tape). This is the only imprint with "C. Hussey" as printer in the ESTC. However, the *Manual* is certainly a Dublin printing of 1733, which the ESTC until recently failed to notice, giving it to R. Cross, a publisher active 1763-1800, due to inserted plates with his name. That factotum, unframed with a book over the opening, a reader in bed on the left, and a candle to the right, was used repeatedly in 1735 by Theophilus Jones, including in Congreve's *The Double-Dealer* (by Jones, for Risk, Ewing, and Smith), T10000. Also, the headpiece on A2 had been employed by William-Shaw Anburey in *A Letter to the Revd. Joseph Boyse* ("sold by" G. Ewing, *et al.*, 1727), T205485. Another Catholic book printed in Dublin without place or publisher is Luis de Granada's *The Sinners Guide* (1723), N36292, probably printed in Dublin since two of three extant copies are in Ireland and since it was reissued by Catholic bookseller Ignatius Kelly in 1740 with a new title page bearing an ornament owned by S. Powell. The Catholics were not the only oppressed denomination: Quakers faced prejudicial publications and had to rely on a subset of active printers (the Rays, for a time Quakers, the Sadleirs, Fairbrother, William Wilmot, and Quakers Samuel Fuller and Isaac Jackson).

Even before Dean Swift exerted much authority in Dublin, there was civil discord encouraging incomplete imprints. In 1713, tensions between the Tory privy council and the Whig aldermen bubbled over in disputes about by-laws for electing the mayor and then in a rancorous election of representatives to Parliament, which Whig candidates Ben Burton and John Forster won in November.[12] During this period, when Tories were called "Papists" and Whigs, "Commonwealth men," loyalist printers like Waters and Carter battled Whigs like John Whalley and Francis Dickson. The best contemporary history of the year is *A Long History of a Short Session of a Certain Parliament in a Certain Kingdom*, attributed to Richard Helsham and Patrick Delany, with a 1714 imprint lacking place and publisher, T2069. When reprinted in London over a decade later, that incomplete imprint was repeated (T1888). The Dublin 1714 edi-

12 See David Dickson, *Dublin: The Making of a Capital City* (London: Profile Books, 2015 [2014]), p. 131.

tion lacks cut ornaments and offers a challenging case of attribution. Whalley reported in his newspaper that the work was printed by "one Dring, who call'd himself Thompson, a Jacobite, who ... fled for England."[13] The evidence confirms that it was printed by Daniel Tompson, who printed at least one other item for Delany that year, probably two. The same double-row of cast flowers over the preface of *A Long History* is employed over the preface of both *The Life of Aristides*, attributed to Delany (T814), and of Thomas Sheridan's *An Easy Introduction of Grammar in English* (T90538), both printed by Tompson in 1714. All appear to have in "Preface" a "P" where the loop does not reach the ascender. As in *A Long History*, Tompson's 1714 printings tend to employ rules of short pieces and are signed consistently on half the leaves of a gathering. Also, in *A Long History*, the Sheridan, and Tompson's 1714 printing of Peter Browne's *A Second Part of Drinking in Remembrance of the Dead* (T83991), prefaces occur in gatherings signed with symbols, an asterisk in *A Long History* and a dagger in the other two. (Waters could be a candidate, but he relies on solid rules, not rules of pieces.)

By my count, 44 of the roughly 166 extant Dublin publications in 1713 involve the municipal and parliamentary elections in Dublin; that is, well over a quarter of the extant publications involve the elections and the dispute between the Tory administration and the Commons. Most are less than a sheet in length; most have no imprint. Nineteen of the 36 editions or issues that I identify as printed by Waters in 1713 concern Dublin elections. Waters is one of the very few to associate himself with the Tory side in the dispute. For instance, of 11 items returned by the ESTC with a search of "aldermen" in 1713, only three by Waters give any printer's or seller's name. Waters prints without his name or place such pieces as *An Argument Made before the Lords-Justices and Council, concerning the Dispute between the Lord-Mayor and Aldermen*, a 14-p. 4to ("Printed in the Year, 1713"; with N15916 wrongly calling it "[London]" – there are ten copies in Ireland and none in the UK); and *A Letter from a Whig in Town to his Friend a Whig in the Country: Containing a Full Account of the Two Late Elections Made of New Lord Mayors*, lacking an imprint (T79207). Both those pamphlets are identifiable as printed by Waters from their use of his unframed ornamental "I" (14 × 14 mm) with branches of leaves radiating from the centre to the corners, found in four other items in 1713 with Waters's name in the imprints. Carter, the printer of several newspapers by Edward Lloyd and their publisher after Lloyd fled, also boldly put his imprint on Tory publications, such as Swift's *Some Advice Humbly Offer'd to the Members of*

13 Pollard, *Dictionary of Members of the Dublin Book Trade*, p. 570, quoting Whalley's *News-Letter*, 1 February 1716.

the October Club (N43969), the numbers of *The Examiner* as well as *An Answer to the Observations upon the State of the Nation. In January 1712/3* (N15104), drawn from *Examiner*, no 17 (27 February 1713); *The Honor & Prerogative of the Queen's Majesty Vindicated and Defended against the Unexampled Insolence of the Author of the Guardian* (N475044); and *The Oxford-Scholar's Answer to the Bishop of Sarum's New Preface* ("London: Printed, and re-printed in Dublin, by C. C."; T101407). Like Waters, Carter was a candidate for printing something anti-Whig without a complete imprint, such as *The R-----r's SPEFCH* [sic on ECCO] *at Mr. B---se's Convinticle* [sic] *The Women and Children Being Withdrawn, by Order of Mr. B-----se* (no imprint), a satirical mock address that is wrongly characterized by ESTC T212769 as by John Forster, the Dublin Recorder. Forster, the purported speaker, a Whig candidate, asks for the support of Reverend Boyse's congregation. He boasts of having "broken every Trust Repos'd in me for your sake," that is, the Dissenters' sake, asking, "Did not I then Refuse to undertake the *Church's Cause*?" (p. 1). The front page of this broadside has the unframed factotum with seven flowers, tulips at top and sides and multi-petal flowers at corners, that Carter employed in *The Humble Address of ... the Lords Spiritual and Temporal in Parliament Assembled Presented to Her Majesty, on Tuesday the Eleventh Day of December, 1711*, with his address if not name in its colophon: "at the Old Post-Office in Fish-shamble-Street. 1711" (T202697). Fidelity to party is apparent in Carter's publishing William King's *A Vindication of the Reverend Dr. Henry Sacheverell* in 1711 (T193236 and T200566) and Sacheverell's *A Sermon Preach'd before the Sons of the Clergy, at their Anniversary Meeting in the Cathedral-church of St. Paul* [10 December 1713] in 1714 (N37571), and Waters's publishing in 1713 two Sacheverell sermons (*The Christian Triumph*, N52415, and *False Notions of Liberty*, T177790), along with a broadside of verses attacking Sacheverell's Whig prosecutors (*The Pack of Bear-Dogs*, T170292).

In attributing publications of this period, one must bear in mind that most printers were not in the Tory camp. The Powells, Rhames, the Rays and their successor Fairbrother, Elizabeth Sadleir, and Edwin [Ann] Sandys were moderates sympathetic to groups like Dissenters, Quakers, and others outside the Tory camp and bore allegiance to the pre-Tory political establishment. Carson's 1715-16 imprints give his address as at the "Sign of King George." Joseph Ray had his press appropriated when James II took over Dublin. John Whalley, who had not forgotten that he was forced to flee the island in 1689, was vehemently anti-Papist, promoting a five-pound bounty on Catholic priests and every year attacking Catholicism in his almanac *Advice to the Stars*. In its 1699 volume, Whalley writes that he intends "every year to handle some one particular of the Romish Superstitions ... until I have prov'd that the Protestant (and not the

Romish) is the true visible Church" (p. 2). Whalley was a lightning rod for publications by Carter especially, who had printed the 1698 volume of Whalley's almanac the year before Whalley began printing it. Carter, for instance, in 1714 wrote and printed *Advice from the Stars, in a Letter to the Pretending Doctor, Whaley* (T208056). Francis Dickson, who joined in the combat over the elections and printed much for the city, published several anti-Catholic and anti-Tory pieces, including *Advice to the Romish Catholick Priests of Ireland, to Take Speedily the Oath of Abjuration* ("Printed by F. D. and sold at the Union on Cork-Hill," 1713), N55251, and *The Report of the Committee, in Relation to Edward Lloyd* ("by Francis Dickson," 1713), T7746, a 4-page folio on the House of Commons' investigation of a Tory journalist. The election disputes aggravated the division over a secondary topic in 1713-14, the negotiations leading to the Peace of Utrecht (and spin-offs such as the treatment of the Duke of Marlborough).

Although incomplete imprints are common in controversies dividing the trade, Dublin printers in 1710-35 do not appear to have often hid their identities behind false imprints from other members of the trade. Because Dublin printers were for the most part publishers, and because the guild had no monopoly and the trade was usually not cohesive (1724-25 being a rare period of amicable relations), printers often competed with each other for the market not only in newspapers but in other publications. Every year, several or more competing editions of the same work appeared from multiple publishers. There are competing editions of six titles in 1712 (Waters competes for five of these titles), six in 1713, eight or nine in 1714, and the pattern continues: eight of 117 editions/issues in 1717 (Thomas Hume competes for six titles) and seven in 1729. This may seem to involve only a few editions, but the totals are significant against the totals of Dublin editions, such as, for example, 119 in 1720 with 12 in competition. In 1713, when there were 13 editions of six titles (three presses compete for Bishop Peter Browne's *Of Drinking to the Memory of the Dead*: Carter, Waters, and Rhames for Pepyat), only two of the editions lack the printer's or seller's name. Waters was particularly aggressive and forthright in 1711-19, but perhaps only once with a fellow Tory. Hume was, too, in 1714-28 and frequently competed with fellow Whigs. Religious tracts and plays are among the types of publication in competition, the latter more surprisingly since they were longer works, thus greater investments. Faulkner and Waters competed over several poems, including *The Life and Genuine Character of the Rev. Dr. S---t, D.S.P.D.*: Waters in a cheaper 12-page octavo under his own name (TEERINK AND SCOUTEN 729; ESTC T450; FOXON S886); Faulkner, to judge from cut ornaments, in a 20-page octavo with false imprint "London ... for J. Roberts in Warwick-Lane" (TEERINK AND SCOUTEN 728; ESTC N19162; FOXON S885). Faulkner had perhaps left the door open by using a false London imprint. Faulkner and Waters threw elbows in 1740 over Samuel Wesley the Elder's *The Battle of the Sexes*, both in octavos of 32 pages with their own imprints. Evidently, Faulkner brought out an edition (T58889; FOXON W338) while Waters was preparing his own (T215691; FOXON W340), leading Waters to add on the last recto a criticism of Faulkner's text for "several alterations" and insisting "the publick would rather see this poem as it was wrote by the author."

Even though Hume had previously printed several works for Grierson, there was a nasty competition between them in 1723 over *A Report from the Committee Appointed by Order of the House of Commons to Examine Christopher Layer*. Hume's edition, a 74-page folio, is apparently not in the ESTC and is confused with a London folio on ECCO. The same report was published "for G. Grierson, E. Dobson, R. Owen, and G. Ewing, MDCCXXIII," in [2] 76 pp. (ESTC T212871, describing it as House of Commons' "Proceedings 1723-04-23"). Hume had two other folio pamphlets on the treason investigation and trial of Layer, and thus much invested. On his edition's title page, Hume has an advertisement presumably addressing Grierson and company: "Whereas some malicious Persons, with a Design of doing me Prejudice, have industriously insinuated to the Publick, that I don't resolve to publish the latter Part of Layer's Tryal; these are therefore to advertise that the said Tryal shall be compleatly finish'd and publish'd on Wednesday, and this Report on Friday next at farthest" (transcribed from Huntington copy, shelfmark 356324). The text suggests that the title page was posted about town as an advertisement.

Hume felt he had the right to be angry, but in some cases printers seem to have expected hardball competition. In 1729, Waters admitted to reprinting a fellow Tory printer's text of *A Hue and Cry after the Letter to the Lord-Mayor*, with the notice "I have taken the above scurvy letter exactly from Mrs. Hussey, alias [Sarah] Harding's print" (T5318). The Dublin trade was too small of a community for printers easily to print rival editions without recognition – certainly cut ornaments would have led to recognition. A printer mainly printing his own publications could cross an established publisher. The Rein Deer, a minor press specializing in chapbooks and short homiletic materials, repeatedly printed cheaper copies of the Church of Ireland's *A Form of Prayer* liturgies assigned by the Church to the King's Printer, Andrew Crooke. A good example involving an unidentified third printer is *A Form of Prayer and Thanksgiving to Be Used in All Churches ... on the Twenty Fifth Day of April 1723*: Crooke printed the authorized version in two-sheets quarto (T223140); the Rein Deer, in an octavo half-sheet, for the "Poor ... at Half-pence a Piece" (T183077); and another produced an octavo half-sheet with no imprint, though possibly cut off the sole copy (T212989). Similarly, the London intruder Andrew Hinde, during a brief stay in Dublin, challenged Crooke (T183085) for the sale of *A Form of Prayer and Thanksgiving* [16 June 1713] ("Bublin [sic]: Printed by A. Hinde"), N61511. One unlikely exception to the general avoidance of bogus names for competing Dublin editions involves a false imprint on an edition of Allan Ramsay's *The Tea-Table Miscellany*. Powell printed an edition for G. Risk in 1729, T179146, 8vo, pp. 342, and what looks like a rival edition has the imprint "Dublin: Printed for E. Smith, and Sold by the Booksellers of Great-Britain and Ireland," 1729, T62905, 3 vols, 12mo with continuous pagination to p. 334. Regarding "Smith" (a suspicious name for starters), Pollard asks "fictitious?"[14] and that seems certain: this is the only instance of "Booksellers of Great-Britain and Ireland" in a Dublin imprint before 1751; of five extant copies, none are in Ireland (one of two in Britain is in Edinburgh); I have not seen the tailpiece on I.A2v in a Dublin book; and publishing a work in three roughly 100-page volumes with continuous pagination and volume signatures is rarely if ever seen then in Dublin.

Although Carter printed several newspaper issues with Thomas Walsh's imprint,[15] in 1710-35, a Dublin printer very rarely used another's imprint to represent himself falsely. We do not find the practice that is common among Edinburgh or London pirates of adding value by claiming to be Jacob Tonson or another distinguished printer or publisher. We do not find materials clearly beneath the standards of an Aaron Rhames claiming to have been printed by "Rhames." When a printer or publisher is falsely listed by a printer either to add value or avoid recrimination, usually a London publisher is noted. An analogous instance involves a Belfast printer in 1722 probably avoiding trouble by claiming that a work was published in "Dublin: Printed by John Brocas": *An Answer to a Paper Lately Printed ... Entituled, An Impartial Enquiry into the Personal Persuasion alias Self-Conceit or Vanity of Dr. Ferguson Publisher, and Mr. James Kilpatrick*. Brocas had died a dozen years earlier, and ESTC N63993 notes this work replies to the controversial broadside by William Dugud: *Some Remarks on the Declaration of the Synod Assembled in Belfast* [Belfast, 1721], T160230.

Some benign or deceit-free considerations led to false and incomplete imprints. A surprising number of imprints unintentionally have incorrect dates due to blunders, which suggests comparable errors in names. The dead often live on in imprints. Although widows Jane Dobson, Sarah Harding, Jane Jones, Sarah Hyde, Alice Reilly, and Margaret Rhames used their own initials on taking over presses, some widows continued to use their husbands' names in

14 Pollard, *Dictionary of Members of the Dublin Book Trade*, p. 531.
15 Pollard, *Dictionary of Members of the Dublin Book Trade*, p. 586.

the address, as did Deborah Powell and Ann Sandys, who always employed "S. Powell" and "Edwin [or "E."] Sandys." Clearly, brevity is a consideration: if three printers had a hand in printing the sheets, no more than one is likely to be noted. In cases of shared printing, whoever printed the title might defer the honour to his colleague or name himself as the printer, as occurred in Francis Beaumont and John Fletcher's *The Prophetess: or, The History of Dioclesian*, with the imprint "Printed by S. Powell, for James Hoey," 1735, T175073. In this octavo (A-C^8 G-I^4), Powell's ornaments are found at the start of the work, such as his headpiece of a nude goddess in a sea-chariot headed to right; but on pp. 70 and 71 appear Hoey's landscape headpiece with a hunter chasing a stag to the right and his tailpiece of a savage with a club. The signatures and running titles indicate the division of labour: Powell produced gatherings in eight employing the running title "*The* Prophetess," and then Hoey printed G-I in fours with the running title "*The* PROPHETESS." Unless Powell's larger share decided the matter, perhaps Hoey wished to name the pre-eminent press in 1735 to add value or he deferred to the Powell press's seniority. However, occasionally when a young printer was assisted by a master printer, the junior may have taken full credit for the publication, which probably happened with *The History of the Lives and Reigns of the Kings of Scotland* "Printed by John Harding for the author [unnamed], 1722," T79534, for its cut ornaments were elsewhere and sometimes earlier employed by Elizabeth Sadleir, a much superior printer (who may have been Harding's mother-in-law).[16] When it was better or safer for distribution, presumably some printers and publishers put down another's name in the imprint even if they published it and sold it from their shops, as Curll frequently placed John Morphew's and James Roberts's addresses in his publications. Catholics probably resorted to this practice in Dublin. When several paid for and many would sell an edition, the "London" imprint must have prevented envy and suited many venues of sale. Also, it was easier to produce an incomplete "Printed in the Year" imprint than to work up a crowded imprint with several different fonts, and probably on occasion the press did not know what the client wanted in the imprint.

Sometimes, a false name was given for the publisher (or an author) with recognition of the falsity essential for the humour or satirical effect. Pollard records one such imprint (not in the ESTC): "Printed by Joseph Meanwell," 1725, in *Solid Reasons Humbly Offer'd for Castrating Physicians*.[17] This practice occurs often with names adding sexual or vulgar connotations. Thus the bogus London imprint of *Kick Him, Jenny: A Merry Tale*, 1733, is "Printed for Roger Clevercock"

16 Pollard, *Dictionary of Members of the Dublin Book Trade*, p. 275.

17 Pollard, *Dictionary of Members of the Dublin Book Trade*, p. 404.

(N68882); the Dublin reprint repeats that and adds "Dublin: Re-printed for Dorothy Kilcock, near Lucas's Coffee-House on Cork-Hill, 1734" (T174970). One of the better known fictional imprints as employed in some London and Dublin editions of *The Benefit of Farting Explain'd* is "Long-Fart: Printed by Simon Bumbubbard, at the Sign of the Wind-Mill opposite Twattling-Street," 1722, with the addition in the Dublin edition of "and Sold by Edward Hamilton, at the Corner of Christ's Church Lane, MDCCXXII" (T120408) – with a two-bird tailpiece on A2v used by James Carson in editions from 1721 to at least 1744. There may be humour in saying that a loco-pornographic work by Thomas Stetzer, *A Merry Allegorico-Botanico-Badinical Piece*, describing sexual anatomy ("arbor vitæ") is printed for "the Company of Gardeners" ("London" [Dublin], 1734), T105784. In these cases, the imprint characterizes the subject and sets the tone of the work. At times, a real person named in the imprint is the target of satire, such as in *A Character of Don Sacheverellio, Knight of the Firebrand; in a Letter to Isaac Bickerstaff, Esq*; by "John Distaff," with the false "Dublin" imprint: "Dublin: Printed and sold by Francis Higgins, Bookmaker; and to be had of A. Baldwin, in London" [1710]. Francis Higgins, for a time prebend of Christ-Church Dublin, was repeatedly criticized and prosecuted in 1707-1712.

Frequently, imprints are false because the printer copied the original's title verbatim. A Dublin broadside might have the colophon "London: Printed in the Year, 1728," simply because that was there on the printer's copy. It was true: the ballad was published then in London (an example is *A New Ballad Inscripe'd [sic] to Polly Peachum ... by the Author of Leheup's Ballad*, T4399). Powell reprinted Young's *The Merchant* (the subtitle actually of *Imperium Pelagi*) in 1730 for Risk, Ewing, and Smith, and, over ten years later when they needed another edition for their nonce *Works* of Young, the press reprinted it with the same date (T172103). Thomas Ruddiman in Edinburgh reprinted John Hervey's *A New C---t Ballad*, on the change of the Ministry in January 1742, with the false imprint "Dublin: Printed by James Stone, in High-Street" because that was the imprint on the original, which Foxon thinks was printed in London (FOXON H160 and H159; ESTC T39817 and T39816, respectively). Sometimes, an earlier imprint was transcribed to state a historical fact. Hugh Speke did this in *Some Memoirs of the Most Remarkable Passages and Transactions on the Late Happy Revolution in 1688 ... By way of Answer to a Late Pamphlet or Libel Intituled, A Diary ... from September the 24th 1688, to the Coronation of King William, April 11th 1689*, which has the imprint "Printed in Dublin, Ireland, in 1709" (this 8vo has three units, all signed "A": pp. [2], 5 [7], 8). ESTC T14301 notes that the pamphlet was published in London in 1713. Indeed, it was, as the running title to the middle section indicates, but what is reproduced at the start is a 1709 dedication to Thomas Earl of Wharton in *Some Memoirs* ("Dublin: Printed, and are to be sold by the Booksellers, MDCCIX"), T49304. Following the dedication praising Wharton for service, Speke on A4v retracts the eulogy: "I am heartily sorry ... that ever I writ the foregoing Lines, seeing the said Earl's Actions ... here in Ireland," for, he writes, he was "deceived" (dated "Printed in Dublin, Jan. 1710").

Some false imprints involve "Printed by" statements in which the printer named is only the publisher, who had another actually print the item, as is apparent from cut ornaments in the work. These false imprints occurred when a master printer with a big press, like Powell or Rhames, printed for another printer, as those two did for Hoey, Hyde-Dobson, Faulkner, Grierson, and the Pepyats. Presumably, the frequent use of the "Printed by" formula encouraged these misleading imprints. Also, the designated printer sometimes was the official "printer" to an institution like the city, encouraging the "printed by" formula. This happens in some imprints for Sylvanus Pepyat, such as *An Abridgment of the Statute ... for the better Regulating the Work-House* ("Printed by Sylvanus Pepyat, in Skinner-Row, Printer to the Hon. City of Dublin, 1728"), T120265, with the ornaments and typography of S. Powell. That same year, Powell is acknowledged as printing for Pepyat and Thomas Benson *The Treacherous Confident*, T128713. Pepyat had a press: by 1729, he printed some short texts for the city, and by 1731, he acquired some ornaments once owned by Hume, but his products were crude, and as late as 1735 he turned to Richard Reilly to print two works on the city's water supply, which have both Reilly's ornaments and his competence: *An Essay toward Supplying the City of Dublin with Water*, T3349; and Gabriel Stokes's *A Scheme for Effectually Supplying Every Part of the City of Dublin with Pipe-water*, T3348, both with the imprint "Printed by Syl. Pepyat, Printer to the Honourable City of *Dublin*," 1735. Grierson was printing good work within a year of setting up a press in 1720, yet in 1726, during the period he printed Shakespeare's plays, he had S. Powell print *The Poems of Shakespear* ("Printed by and for George Grierson ... and for George Ewing," 1726), T197426. Here the distinction between the roles of Grierson and Ewing makes this a false imprint.

Under pressure to complete an edition while their presses were tied up, some Dublin printers would, like their London counterparts, turn the printing of some sheets over to another. The best instances of this involve editions by the most eminent Dublin printers, Powell and Rhames, both with large ornament stocks, where both shops printed sheets but only one's name appears in the imprint. Swift's *Travels* printed "by S. P. for G. Risk, G. Ewing, and W. Smith," 1727, T208193, has Rhames's ornaments in the prelims and Book Three. Also, in Volume I of Chevalier Ramsay's *The Travels of Cyrus* (by Powell, for Risk, Ewing, and Smith, 1728), T176329, 2 vols, the ornaments indicate that B-F^{12} G^{6}

were printed by Rhames (Powell printed Volume II but only Volume I's prelims, A^{12} and b^{6}). When labour is neatly divided between volumes, as often as not, all printers are recognized. For instance, *The Thousand and One Days* translated by Ambrose Philips (for Risk, Ewing, and Smith, 1727), N498275, credits Rhames for printing Volumes I and III and Wilmot for Volume II.

Of course, false imprints were used to avoid arrest for sedition or libel; even the libel of a fellow of Trinity College could lead to prosecution (it ruined Anburey and Watts in 1730).[18] Not surprisingly, false and incomplete imprints were frequently employed by Waters, who had more trouble with the government than any other printer during the dozen years beginning with his arrest in November 1708: he was investigated or prosecuted again in 1712, 1714, 1715, and 1720, the last occasion for Swift's *Proposal for the Universal Use of Irish Manufacture*.[19] I have identified more false imprints by Waters during his most prolific years as a printer-publisher, 1710-15, because he then used cut ornaments more than his peers. Waters's title-page ornament of a bearded face like an elf's, inside a diamond-shaped shield with the sides rising upward as arms, 39 × 36 mm, identifies him as the printer of *The Speech of the Lord Haversham's Ghost* ("London: Printed in the Year, MDCCX"), T133848, repeating the London imprint of this defence of the Duke of Marlborough; Defoe's *The Secret History of the October Club* ("London Printed for *A. Baldwin*, 1711"), T172333, altering the London original, which lacked seller or noted "J. Baker;" and *The Declaration of an Honest Church-man, Relating to the Times* ("London: Printed for M. Gunne at Essex-Street-Gate, 1711"), T195686, reprinting a 1710 pamphlet sold by Morphew. Waters's large tailpiece of a striped phoenix helps to identify him as the printer of *The Memorial of the Church of England* ("Printed in the Flourishing Year of the *Church*, 1711"), T173531 and T176086, a controversial text repeatedly printed in London 1705-6 without a publisher's name; and the sole edition of *A Familiar Answer to a Familiar Letter* ("London: Printed in the Year, 1720"), T86028, Foxon F53, satirical verse replying to Jonathan Smedley's *A Familiar Epistle to his Excellency Charles Earl of Sunderland* (1720), N1475. Usually Waters repeated "London" from the original, but in the last instance, sometimes attributed to Swift, he used it for the first edition.

As Waters resorted to Baldwin's name, Dublin printers often took London publishers' names. In 1710-35, the most common bogus names in London imprints, "Moor," "More," and "Moore,"[20] are never used with a Dublin location,

---

18 Pollard, *Dictionary of Members of the Dublin Book Trade*, p. 599.

19 Pollard, *Dictionary of Members of the Dublin Book Trade*, pp. 589-90.

20 Michael Treadwell discusses "Moore" and other false imprints in "On False and Misleading Imprints in the London Book Trade, 1660-1750," *Fakes & Frauds: Varieties of Deception in*

but the most common form, "A. Moore," is used with false "London" locations in at least seven Dublin printings by Faulkner (including Faulkner and Hoey) and one by Hoey solo (a "T[homas] Moore" publishes in Dublin from 1730). Faulkner, printing with Hoey, first employed the Moore imprint for the only edition of *A True State of the Present Affairs of Limerick: Shewing the Rise and Progress of the Disputes in that City with Some Remarks on the Dangerous Consequences which must Attend the Investing Military Men with the Civil Power of Corporations* ("London: Printed for A. Moore, near St. Paul's, 1726"), T177229, with Faulkner's headpiece of a pile of military trophies flanked by exiting putti blowing horns, one of his two main headpieces through 1731. Faulkner heavily relied on it in editions with genuine and false imprints even though it was identifiably damaged in the left and right frames – as if he intended it to be a coded shop-sign. Also, some Faulkner publications without imprints, including several attributed to Swift, are reprinted in London with the "A. Moore" imprint: *A Libel on Dr. D---ny, and a Certain Great Lord* ("Printed at Dublin: and Re-printed at London, for A. Moore," 1730), N19497, and *A Satire on Dr. D---ny. By Dr. Sw--t* ("Printed at Dublin: and Re-printed at London, for A. Moore," 1730), T447. One wonders if Faulkner (and even Swift) profited from any of these publications.

During his first decade as a printer, Faulkner printed more false imprints than any of his peers; in this respect, he is Dublin's equivalent of Edmund Curll. For those dated 1726 and 1729 to early 1730 (times Faulkner was in London), Hoey deserves credit as well (Hoey's name comes first in eight of eleven 1730 imprints that he and Faulkner produced prior to their break-up in early May), and later Hoey published false imprints of his own. Faulkner's false and incomplete imprints to 1735 are listed in an appendix, which may suggest diverse reasons that Dublin printers employed such imprints. Besides using "Moore" and "London" without a publisher, sometimes he employed the names of actual London publishers, as in Bolingbroke's *A Final Answer to the Remarks on the Craftsman's Vindication*, seventh edition ("London: Printed by

Print and Manuscript, eds Robin Myers and Michael Harris (New Castle, Delaware: Oak Knoll Press, 2006 [1989]), pp. 29-46 (41-43). "Moore" exemplifies what Treadwell calls a "stock" false name, one "widely established as false" (p. 41), his four other overlapping categories of false names are "commonplace names, deformed names, disguised names, [and] real names" (p. 37). See also Andrew Benjamin Bricker, "Who Was 'A. Moore'? The Attribution of Eighteenth-Century Publications with False and Misleading Imprints," *Papers of the Bibliographical Society of America*, 110 (2016), 181-214. After a general discussion of false imprints, Bricker identifies through cut ornaments specific London printers of imprints with "A. Moore" and suggests that Thomas Read reserved certain cut ornaments for his hidden imprints to avoid detection (pp. 207-8), something that Faulkner and others in Dublin did not do.

and for R. Francklin," 1731), T182946, with a booklist for "George Faulkner" on D3v-D4; reissued as an eighth edition with the same imprint and advertisement (N31532); and *The Natural History of the Arbor Vitæ: or, The Tree of Life, Versify'd and Explain'd* ("London: Printed for J. Wilkinson, near Charing-Cross; and sold by the Booksellers of London and Westminster," n.d.), ESTC T101980 and FOXON N8 suggesting "[1732?]." Both works have Faulkner's headpiece of military trophies and two exiting putti and Hyde's triangular tailpiece of a cupid shooting a bow to the left, employed by Hyde and Dobson repeatedly in 1730-32 (such as on p. 232 of Volume VIII of *Plutarch's Lives in Eight Volumes*, 1730, N20528). Faulkner reprinted Swift's *The Life and Genuine Character of the Rev. Dr. S-----t D.S.P.D.* using the imprint of the first, folio edition: "London: Printed for J. Roberts," 1733, N19162. Faulkner's use of incomplete and false imprints declines after 1733, though his ornaments identify a few during the late 1730s: *The Man of Honour ... To which is added, The Curious Females* ("London Printed: And sold by the Booksellers of London and Westminster. M D XXXVII" [sic: presumably for 1737]), T132829; Joseph Trapp's *The Royal Sin: or, Adultery Rebuked* ("London: Printed and sold by J. Huggonson, in Chancery-Lane," 1738), T119040; and James Miller's *The Great Man's Answer to Are These Things So?* ("London: Printed for T. Cooper at the Globe in Paternoster-Row," 1740), T131910.

There are a handful of instances in which other Dublin printers around 1730 used false "London" imprints, but in some cases, where any risk was involved, they may have been printing work to be sold by Faulkner. One such edition with Powell's ornaments is *The Observations on the Treaty of Seville Examined* ("London: Printed for R. Francklin ... 1730"), N10859. Although M. Pollard records no brushes with the law for the Powell press, their ornaments are in some anti-ministerial pieces at this time, such as the Pope-attribution *The History of the Norfolk Steward Continued* (Dublin: *s.n.*, 1728), N1488. Perhaps these works were printed for others in the trade, as were 80 per cent of Powell productions through 1740. Powell's ornaments are also found in *The State Dunces* attributed to Paul Whitehead, with the false "London" imprint for "W. Dickenson in Witch-Street," 1733, T434 (the original London imprint may also be false). Powell's role is disclosed by the sole ornament, on A2: a cityscape headpiece with street and buildings in the foreground and a sun at the horizon in the back, 25 × 71 mm, used in multiple Powell printings that year (for instance, B1 of Capt. Downes, *All Vows Kept* ["by S. Powell, for P. Crampton"], T56243). Faulkner employed Powell often enough to suspect that Faulkner published *The State Dunces*. Powell was the initial printer of *The London and Dublin Magazine* (P2810), January 1734, sold by, and within a year printed by, Faulkner, and all the cut ornaments are Powell's in *Critical Remarks upon Gulliver's Travels; Particularly his Voyage to the Houyhnhms* [*sic*] *Country ... By Doctor Bentley* ("Printed at Cambridge ...

and now Reprinted in Dublin, by Geo. Faulkner," 1735), N2074. One other false imprint by Powell reminds us that the London imprint could be copied without any desire to avoid trouble. Powell printed an "eleventh edition" of *The Spectator* in eight volumes "for P. Crampton" in 1735, indicating so in the imprints of Volumes I-V and VIII; but Volumes VI and VII have the imprint: "London: Printed for J. Tonson, at Shakespear's-Head, over-against Katharine-street in the Strand. 1729," T230781. Transcribing that imprint of Tonson's 1729 edition (numbered the "tenth" in Volumes II-VIII), T98542, was akin to Powell's employing for a title-page vignette his version of the oval-framed ornament portraying Shakespeare that also appears on the title pages of Tonson's edition of *The Spectator*. Here, as in Faulkner's printing of Bolingbroke's *The Final Answer* with an advertisement for his books, is another false imprint not apparently intended to dissemble so much as to maintain fidelity with the original.

Appendix: Some Hidden and False-Imprint Editions by George Faulkner, 1726-35[21]

– Noailles, Louis-Antoine de. *The Mandate of his Eminence the Lord Cardinal D'Noailles, Archbishop of Paris. On the Subject of a Miracle ... on the 31st of May, 1725* (n. p.: "Printed in the Year 1726"), T171513, 4to in twos, 38 pp; solid rules; on tp is GF's fountain tailp, 24 × 34 mm [same as tp of Ch. Forman's *A Letter to ... Sir Robert Sutton* (GF and Hoey, 1728), T178064]; on p. 3 is an unframed orn. "L," shading on right, surrounded by leaves, cup flower centre left.

– *A True State of the Present Affairs of Limerick* ("London: Printed for A. Moore, near St. Paul's, 1726"), T177229, 8vo, 81 [1]; as ESTC notes, with p. 3 GF's hdp of military trophies flanked by exiting putti with horns and also a crown factotum (same as p. 3 of J. S. Kusser's *Heaven Invaded* [Faulkner, {1727}], T188412).

– *A Comical Dialogue between Parson Mag---e, and J---th--n B---ll, Quaker* (no imprint), T232206, 2-p. folio; sole copy at Trinity College dated "1727" in MS; on p. 1 is an unframed

21 By or in early 1733, Faulkner acquired a number of cut ornaments formerly used by William Bowyer, which are referenced below by their numbers in K. I. D. Maslen, *The Bowyer Ornament Stock* (Oxford: Oxford Bibliographical Society; Bodleian Library, 1973). Hereafter cited as MASLEN. Maslen puts the total Faulkner obtained at ten and suggests the transfer occurred in the late 1720s to early 1730s (p. 4), but I have seen none in Faulkner's works before the 1730s.

Titles are almost all shortened, as are some imprints; some authors noted are but attributions in the ESTC. Abbreviations include: "P" [in bold print] at the left margin standing for "possibly printed by Faulkner." Other abbreviations include "advt" for "advertisement," "GF" for Faulkner, "hdp" for "headpiece," "hft" for "half title," "orn." for "ornament" or "ornamental," "tp" for "title page," "tailp" for "tailpiece."

orn. "T" with leafy branches flanking [same as A2 of *A Letter to the Revd. Mr. Stephen Radcliffe, M.A.* (see the next item)].

– *A Letter to the Revd. Mr. Stephen Radcliffe, M.A. Vicar of Naas, on the Subject of his Letter and Reply to Mr. Synge's Sermon and Vindication ... By an Anonimous Author* ("Dublin: Printed in the Year, 1727"), T179570; dated "Dublin, January the 12th, 1726-7" (p. 37); on A2 is GF's hdp of two fruit horns with inside bottom framing rule cut at centre (38 mm over) and with nick at 43 over on the top rule (damage absent in Powell's variant cut; same as B1 of Christopher Bullock's *Woman's Revenge* [GF and J. Hoey, 1728]), T200738, and GF's orn. "T" with leafy branches.

– Shippen, William. *A Speech against Sir R____ W____'s Proposal, for Increasing the Civil List Revenue, as it was Spoken in the House of Commons, July 3. 1727* (no imprint), T232205 giving [Dublin: *s.n.*, 1727], folio broadside; on p. 1: orn. "I" used on p. **1 of *Fraud Detected* (Faulkner, 1725), T001864, and p. 1 of *Seasonable Reflections Address'd to the Citizens of Dublin* by Capt. Gulliver ("Faulkner," 1727), T224535, folio. On p. 2 is advt for "A Sermon Preach'd at the Coronation of King George II. and ... October 11, 1727. By ... John [Potter], Lord Bishop of Oxford" and "A Letter to W---- S----, Esq; In Answer to the above Speech." The first item was published with GF's imprint; the second is untraced but presumably reprints *A Letter to W___ S___ Esq;* by "Manlius" (L. T. Warner, 1727), giving date as 6 October 1727, N20759. GF printed another edition of Shippen's speech with his imprint in 1727, T193584.

– *Dr. Anthony's Nocturnal Ramble with Comical and Moral Remarks on a Lew'd House* (no colophon, *c.*1727: 1726-1731 is the date range for nine or more broadsides and slips without colophon featuring Dr Anthony's comments in prose or verse), T232140, folio broadside. With GF's fountain tailp on verso [same as that on the tp of *A Letter to Robert Sutton* (GF and J. Hoey, 1728), T178064, and on p. 81 of *A True State of the Present Affairs of Limerick* (A. Moore, 1726)]. This work (T232140) typographically resembles Doctor Anthony's *Epidemical Pills: or, An Antidote against the Scurvy Consumption and Drunkenness* (no imprint), T232156, 1 p. folio without cut orn.

– *The Church too Hard for the State: or, The Knight Overthrow. A Poem* ("London: Printed in the Year, 1729"), T98148; on p. 3: GF's hdp of two linked fruit horns with break in inner bottom rule.

– *A Brief History of the Restauration. Published from Original Letters, and other Royal Authorities*, by a "Person of Honour" ("London: Printed, and *Dublin* Re-Printed in the Year MDCCXXIX"), N15458; 8vo, 15 [1]; with three orns of GF, including hdp of two linked fruit horns; advt on p. 16 for GF's books sold at the "Pamphlet-shop in Skinner-Row." The omission of publishers' names is odd since this is the sole edition of the title in ESTC.

– Gay, John. *Polly: An Opera* ("London: Printed for the Author," n.d. [probably 1729]); N11852, giving "London" (yet both copies in British Isles are in Ireland); 8vo: *A*^{8} B-E^8 F^4 [$1-2 (+E3, E4; -F2) signed]; pp. 3-4 misnumbered "4" and "3;" preliminaries end on A6/ix;

A6v paginated "1," with uneven numbers thereafter on rectos, thus p. 6 on B1 and p. 22 on C1; on p. v: tailp with "I"-shaped flower vase with six round flowers inside a frame, flanked by long-stem flowers (borrowed?); p. 1: GF's hdp of two linked fruit horns; p. 76: GF's tailp of cupid shooting left with flanking fruit horns, the right side higher (same as p. 16 of John Potter's *Sermon Preach'd at the Coronation* [11 October 1727] [Hoey and Faulkner, 1727], N22985).
– Johnson, Samuel. *Hurlothrumbo: or, The Super-Natural* ("London: Printed for the Author and, Dublin: Re-printed by James Hoey, and George Faulkner," 1729), T36870, 8vo; as discussed in the text above, partly printed by the Hyde-Dobson press.
P – *Advice to the Ladies of Great-Britain* ("London: Printed for the Author; and to be sold by the Booksellers, and several Pamphlet-sellers, 1730"), T164684, FOXON A94 noting [D] presumably because copies located are in Irish libraries or American ones with strong Irish collections. *Advice* has no cut orns but has typography typical of GF's work: unsigned octavo half-sheet; several simple triangular designs of rows 3-2-1 of the same cast piece (tp and tailp) used in many 1730 pamphlets by GF; hdp of two rows of cast square blocks with circle-oval-circle pieces top and bottom of those two rows; rules of short pieces (*c.*15) closely set; pagination in (); and large roman "FINIS" on p. 8.
– Blackwell, James, "Operator for the Feet" (pseud.). *A Friendly Apology for a Certain Justice of Peace; by Way of Defence of H____y H____n, Esq*; (n. p.: "Printed in the Year MDCCXXX."), T40236; FOXON B270; 8vo [unsigned]: 7 [1] pp.; tp rules of short pieces; large roman "FINIS;" on p. [3] GF's hdp of military trophies flanked by exiting putti and p. 7 GF's ugly, tilted tailp with scrollwork arch around flower [both are in James Delacour's *The Progress of Beauty* (Faulkner, 1732), T176712].
– [Delany, Patrick, anon.]. *The Pheasant and the Lark: A Fable* ("Dublin: Printed in the Year MDCCXXX"), T42218; FOXON D203; 8vo [unsigned]: 8 pp. with p. 2 in () and pp. 3-8 in [] (p. 6 with only left bracket in ECCO copy); tp with rules of pieces and GF's tailp of cupid shooting bow to left; p. 3 GF's hdp of military trophies flanked by exiting putti; roman "FINIS" modest sized.
– [Delany, Patrick, anon.]. *The Pheasant and the Lark: A Fable*. "The Second Edition with Editions" [sic] ("Dublin: Printed in the Year MDCCXXX"), N11363; FOXON D204; unsigned octavo half-sheet; tp rules of short pieces; p. 3: GF's hdp of two linked fruit horns.
– *The Fatigues of a Great Man: or, The Plague of Serving One's Country. A Satire* ("London: Printed for A. Dodd, and sold by Booksellers of London and Westminster, 1730"), T215600; FOXON F77, only identifying printing in Dublin; p. 2 GF's hdp of two linked flower horns.
– Gulliver, Martin (pseudonym). *A Letter from Martin-Gulliver to George Faulkner, Printer* (n. p.: "Printed in the Year MDCCXXX"), N5581, place from FOXON G317; 8vo, 8 pp. With no cut orns, but GF's typography: tp with downward triangle of cast pieces and rules of short pieces; pagination in (); large roman "FINIS"; hdp of cast pieces:

two rows of blocks inside of circle-oval-circle with "!" between cast pieces [the design resembles that in Swift's *A Libel on D-- D-----*, 1730, N5046, and closer still to that on A2 of Theophilus Cibber's *Patie and Peggy* (Faulkner, 1730), T119877]; also the first "T" in "LETTER" on tp is damaged identically to that on tp of *Letter to his Excellency Mr. Ulrick D'Ypres* (Faulkner, n.d. [1731, year of London publication]), T84343: the "T" has almost no upper left serif and has an excessively long upper right serif.

– [Hervey, John, attributed to]. *A Satyr, in the Manner of Persius: In a Dialogue between the Poet and his Friend. By a Certain English Nobleman* ("London: Printed, and Sold by the Booksellers of London and Westminster, 1730"), T118801; 8vo, 15 [1] pp.; FOXON H161.5, noting printed in Dublin and Hervey the "likely" author; first edition [not printed in London until 1739]; tp rules of short pieces; on p. 3 GF's hdp of two linked fruit horns and p. 15 GF's tailp of cupid shooting bow left; roman "FINIS."

– Lloyd, John. *A Satyr on the Times, and Some of the Modern Plays ... By John Lloyd, M.A. Minister of Gilden Sutton in Cheshire, and Author of The Art of Politicks, &c ....* (n.p.: "Printed in the Year MDCCXXX"), T113668, 8vo, 15 [1] pp.; FOXON L207; p. 5: GF's hdp of military trophies flanked by exiting putti. Has GF deliberately misrepresented Lloyd as author of James Bramston's *The Art of Politicks* and is that related to the choice of a false imprint?

– *Observations on the Inconveniencies [sic] that Might Have Happened to the Publick ... [by] Passing of the Said Bill* ("Dublin: Printed in the Year MDCCXXX"), T185769, attributing printing to Faulkner and Hoey; 8vo: 15 [1] pp., pagination in () but 8-9 and 11-13 in []; on A2 GF's hdp of two linked fruit horns.

– Poekrich, Richard. *The Temple-Oge Ballad* ("Rathfarnam: Printed, at the Cherry-Tree, MDCCXXX"), T49943; FOXON P516, claiming "possibly printed" by GF and Hoey "who used this address" [but the address is nowhere else in ESTC]; 8vo half-sheet unsigned; tp with GF's ugly, tilted tailp of scrollwork arch over flower; p. 3: GF's hdp of military trophies flanked by exiting putti; large roman "FINIS."

– Swift. *An Epistle upon an Epistle from a Certain Doctor to a Certain Great Lord: Being a Christmas-Box for D. D---ny* ("Dublin: Printed in the Year 1730"), N856, 8vo, 8 pp.; on p. 3 GF's hdp of two linked fruit horns.

P – Swift. *Lady A____S____N Weary of the Dean* (colophon without place between rules of short pieces: "Printed in the Year MDCCXXX"), T197390; FOXON S868, giving [Dublin]; one-page, two-column folio broadside without cut orns; advt under colophon: "Just publish'd, A View of the Irish Bar, in a Character of the Lawyers."

– Swift. *A Libel on D-- D------ , and a Certain Great Lord* (no place: "Printed in the Year MDCCXXX"), N5046; FOXON S877, noting 4to: *A*^{4} B^2; TEERINK AND SCOUTEN 689A; tp with GF's ugly, tilted tailp of scrollwork arch over flower; on p. 3: orn. unframed "D," shaded on right; with leaves all round with horizontal shading; vine growing up left side.

– Swift. *A Libel on D--- D---, and a Certain Great Lord* (n. p.: "Printed in the Year 1730"), T40860, ascribing printing to GF on authority of Trinity College's catalogue; 8vo,

8 pp; FOXON S878, noting on p. 2 variant states with hdp and another with cast pieces; TEERINK AND SCOUTEN 688; paper with same shield watermark found in *Observations on the Inconveniencies* (no place [GF] 1730). FOXON S879 (TEERINK AND SCOUTEN 687) is another edition, unexamined, with imprint: "[Dublin?] Printed Anno 1730" (only at University of Pennsylvania).

– Swift. *To Doctor D-L---Y, on the Libels Writ against him* ("London: Printed. And, Dublin Reprinted in the Year MDCCXXX"), T51103; FOXON S913; 8vo: A[8]; 16 pp.; with hft between rules of short pieces; tp orn: GF's ugly tailp with tilted scrollwork arch over flower; on p. 5 GF's hdp of military trophies flanked by exiting putti; on p. 16 large roman "FINIS" and then tailp of cast pieces in rows of three, two, one.

– Swift. *Traulus: The First Part. In a Dialogue between Tom and Robin* (n. p.: "Printed in the Year MDCCXXX"), T705; FOXON S914; TEERINK AND SCOUTEN 699. Tp with rules of short pieces and downward triangle of three rows with 3-2-1 cast blocks [same design and cast piece as on p. 16 of preceding item, T51103]; on p. 3 cast devices as hdp including that piece on tp; on p. 8, first line ends "wou'd."

– Swift. *Traulus: The First Part* (title and imprint as the preceding), T196708; FOXON S915; TEERINK AND SCOUTEN 699. Different settings (and different but similar hdp designs) from preceding: p. 8, first line ends "wo'ud."

– Swift. *Traulus: The Second Part* (no place: "Printed in the Year MDCCXXX"), tp with rules of short pieces and downward triangular design of square cast blocks: 5-4-3-2-1; 8vo, pp. 7 [1, called a blank in TEERINK AND SCOUTEN 699]. Apparently, one edition in two states illustrated by two copies on ECCO linked to T449 (BL, C.136.aa.1 [16]) and T196710 (BL, Ashley 1834): The T449 (FOXON S916) has GF's hdp of military trophies flanked by exiting putti; T196710 (FOXON S917) has GF's hdp of two linked fruit horns.

P – [Swift?] *A View of the Irish Bar: To the Free-Mason's Tune, Come Let us Prepare, &c.* ("Dublin: Printed in the Year, 1729-30"), T50778; folio broadside; FOXON V94; advertised as "Just publish'd" at the bottom of *Lady A____S____N Weary of the Dean* (no place: *s.n.*, 1730).

– Swift. *A Vindication of his Ex----y the Lord C---, from the Charge of Favouring None but Toryes, High-Church-men, and Jacobites* ("London: Printed, and Dublin Re-Printed in the Year MDCCXXX"), T73031; TEERINK AND SCOUTEN 698; 8vo: pp. [2, hft], 37, [1]; tp with rules of short pieces and GF's tp orn. of cupid shooting bow to left; large roman "FINIS."

– *The Whole Tryal of Richard Lyddel, Esq; at His Majesty's Court of Common-Pleas ... for Carrying on a Criminal Conversation with the Late Lady Abergavenny, on Monday the 16th of February, 1729/30* ("London: Printed for A. Moore, near St. Paul's, and Sold by the Booksellers of London and Westminster, 1730"), T118900, 8vo: 23 [1]; tp rules of short pieces; on p. 23 is GF's ugly triangular tailp with scrollwork arch over flower.

P – *The Band: Inscrib'd to the Gentlemen of the Long Robe* (n. p.: "Printed by A. Moore, in the year, 1731"); folio broadside; ESTC T5185 wrongly claims that there is an A. Moore active on Castle Street in 1726-29 (in 1726, Faulkner is on Pembroke Court, Castle Street); FOXON B53, noting that provenance of the two known copies (at BL and Cambridge) is Irish as is the subject: "the reintroduction to Ireland of the fashion of lawyers wearing bands." Not seen, but probably by GF since Faulkner and Hoey are alone known to use the Moore imprint in Dublin at this time.

– Bolingbroke, *A Final Answer to the Remarks on the Craftsman's Vindication; and to All the Libels ... Mentioned in the Craftsman of the 22d of May*, 7th ed. ("London: Printed by and for R. Francklin," 1731), T182946, 8vo: *A*^{4} B-C^4 D^2 [$1 signed]; 29 [*3*] pp.; booklist of works sold by Faulkner on D2-D2v; on p. 5 GF's hdp of military trophies flanked by exiting putti; on p. 29 Hyde's triangular tailp of cupid shooting bow left, arrow inclining slightly upward (same as p. 20 *The Craftsman's Vindication of his Two Hor.ble [sic] Patrons* [Faulkner, 1731], T118984), presumably borrowed from the Hyde-Dobson press. Note the appearance of GF's identifiable hdp and booklist in a work with a false London imprint.

P – Creichton, John [with Swift]. *Memoirs of Capt. John Creichton* (n. p.: "Printed in the Year, 1731), T113807; small 8vo: *A*^{4} B-X^4 Y^2 [apparently Y2 is final blank; $1 alone signed]; pp. *1-9* 10-169 *170-72*. As discussed above in the text, possibly printed by GF despite Hyde's orns.

P – *The Duel: A Poem. Inscribed to the Rt. Hon. W---- P-----Y, Esq*; ("London: Printed by A. Moore, near St. Paul's, 1731"), T163345, 8vo [unsigned], 8 pp.; ESTC gives place of publication as London, citing FOXON D493; no cut orns. The typography is typical of GF's: tp with square of four cast blocks (same as that on tp of *Sir Robert Brass*, in orientation and probably in pieces, and the same design and materials used in at least seven GF imprints in 1730); the hdp design common in GF: double-row of the same blocks with circle-ellipse-circle cast pieces above and below; all rules are of short pieces; paginated in (); on p. 8 large roman "FINIS."

– *The Famous History of Will Towzer, the Yorkshire Attorney: With Some Remarks on the Management of the Affairs of the Crown-Inn ... To which is added, A Letter to Francis Walsingham, Esq*; (n. p.: "Printed in the Year MDCCXXXI" [1731]), ESTC T224067 noting apparently an attack on William Pulteney; no cut orns but with typography typical of GF: rules of short pieces; 8vo: *A*^{4} B^4 with only B1/9 signed; 16 pp. in (); roman "FINIS" on p. 16; advertised with books "printed and sold by George Faulkner" (priced 3d.) in *The Whole of the Proceedings in the Arches-Court of Canterbury* (1732), T219000.

– *A Letter from a Certain Great Man to Caleb D'Anvers ... Relating to the Vienna Treaty* (no place: "Printed in the Year, 1731"), N19475, unsigned 8vo, 8 pp.; as discussed in the text, this edition was likely printed by GF despite the presence of Hyde's hdp of bearded man facing right.

P – Pilkington, Matthew. *An Infallible Scheme to Pay the Publick Debt of this Nation* (n. p.: "Printed in the Year 1731"), N29237, unsigned 8vo: [apparently *A*^{8}]: 16 pp. in (); two solid rules on tp and over HT; with same tp typography as GF's *Scheme of the*

Proportions which the Protestants of Ireland (n. p.: *s. n.*, 1731/2), T87712, with GF's tp orn. of cupid shooting bow to left. Pilkington published his *Poems* with Faulkner in 1730.
– *Reasons for Regulating the Coin, and Reducing the Interest: With a Scheme for Paying Part of the National Debt without Burthening Ireland* (no place: "Printed in the Year, 1731"), N26391, locating it as [Dublin] but wrongly giving 12mo; 8vo in fours: *A*^{4} B-C^4 [$1 signed]; 23 [1] pp. in (); tp rules of short pieces; on A2 is framed hdp of fruit basket over a putto [same as p. 3 of *The Case of Mr. P----- Fully Stated, and Considered* (Faulkner, 1731), T186688]; italic "*FINIS*."
– *Reflections on the National Debt: With Reasons for Reducing the Legal Interest* (n. p.: "Printed in the Year 1731"), T83367, unsigned 8vo, 16 pp. in (); hft with GF's commonly used cast block in rows; tp rules of at least several pieces; on p. 5 GF's hdp of military trophies flanked by exiting putti; p. 16 GF's ugly tailp with scrollwork arch over flower; large italic "*FINIS*."
– *Sir Robert Brass: or, The Intrigues, Serious and Amorous, of the Knight of the Blazing-Star. In Hudibrastick Verse* ("London: Printed by A. Moore, and Sold by the Booksellers of Town and Country, 1731"), N23306, Foxon S476, noting a state with "Intrgues" on tp; 8vo: *A*^{4} B-C^4 [$1 signed]; 24 pp. in (); all rules of short pieces; on p. 24 of GF's tailp of Venus headed right in chariot pulled by two sparrows [same as tp orn. of *The Tryal of Richard Franklin* (Faulkner, 1732), T216825]; Foxon notes advertised by GF in *Bœoticorum liber* (Faulkner, 1732), N15383.
– Walpole, Horatio, Baron. *The Case of the Hessian Forces, in the Pay of Great-Britain ... In Answer to a Late Pamphlet, Intitled, Considerations on the Present State of Affairs, &c. By Caleb D'Anvers* ("London: Printed by R. Francklin, in Russel-Street, Covent-Garden, 1731"), N26753, 8vo: *A*^{4} B-C^4 D^2 [$1 signed]; 28 pp. in (); tp rules of short pieces; on A2 GF's hdp of military trophies flanked by exiting putti. The imprint copies that of R. Francklin's two editions or issues, one dated 1731 (T20198) and one undated (N14590).
– Younge, William, Sir. *Sedition and Defamation Display'd* ("London: Printed for J. Roberts, near the Oxford-Arms in Warwick-Lane, MDCCXXXI"), N21627; 8vo: *A*^{4} B-D^4 [$1 signed]; pp. [2], i-iv, [1] 2-25 [1] in (); tp with rules of short pieces and downward triangle of four rows of cast blocks; on A2 GF's hdp of military trophies flanked by two exiting putti; on A3 tailp of Venus in chariot pulled right by sparrows; on A4 GF's hdp of two linked fruit horns; on p. 25 GF's ugly, tilted tailp with scrollwork arch over flower; on p. 26 list of books "sold by George Faulkner."
– *The English Impostor Detected: or, The History of the Life and Fumigation of the Renown'd Mr. J------ T-----, Occulist* ("Dublin: Printed in the Year M, DCC, XXXII"), T104204, unsigned 8vo: pp. *1-3* 4-16 in (); sole orn. on p. [3] is GF's boarhunt to right with shaved top-left corner.
P – *A Letter to a Certain Great Lord, concerning the Present State of the Church with Some Advice ... By an Old Christian* (n. p.: "Printed in the Year 1732"), N19550, unsigned 8vo: pp. 15 [1] in (); mostly solid rules on tp and over HT.

– *The Natural History of the Arbor Vitæ: or, The Tree of Life; Versify'd and Explain'd. Addressed to the Ladies, by a Member of a Society of Gardeners* ("London: Printed for J. Wilkinson, near Charing-Cross; and sold by the Booksellers of London and Westminster" [n.d., probably 1732]), T101980; unsigned 8vo: 15 [1] pp. in (); versification of Thomas Stretzer's work of same name; FOXON N7, noting advt for London edition (with same imprint, N40557) in *Daily Journal*, 17 June 1732; Foxon does not recognize this edition as Faulkner's, but A3/5 has GF's hdp of military trophies flanked by exiting putti.
– *The Remonstrance: A Poem, to his G******** the D****** of D*********** ("London: Printed. And, | Dublin Re-printed in the Year Mdccxxxii."), T83108, unsigned 8vo: 16 pp. in (); GF's commonly used design of two squares of four cast blocks on tp; p. 5: GF's hdp of military trophies flanked by putti.
– *Scheme of the Proportions which the Protestants of Ireland May Probably Bear to the Papists; Humbly Offer'd to the Publick* (n. p.: "Printed in the Year, 1731-2"), T87712; 8vo [A4v/8 signed "B"]: *1-2* 3-16 in (); tp with GF's tailp of cupid shooting bow to left.
– *A Serious Proposal for the Entire Destruction of Popery in Ireland* (n. p.: "Printed in the Year MDCCXXXII"), T207270, 8vo [unsigned]; pp. *1-3* 4-15 *16*; tp with solid rules; on p. 3 GF's hdp of boar-hunt to the right with top-left corner shaved [same hdp on p. 5 of Patrick Delany's *The Present State of Learning* (Faulkner, 1732), T103381]; ECCO repeats the error only recently corrected on ESTC, that "Ornaments are those used by Stephen Powell."
P – [Swift]. *Considerations upon Two Bills Sent down from the R---- H---- the H----- of L------ to the H-----ble H----- of C----- Relating to the Clergy of I***********d* ("London: Printed for A. Moore, near St. Paul's, and Sold by the Booksellers of Westminster and Southwark, 1732"), dated "Dublin Feb. 24. 1731-2;" 8vo: *A*^{4} B-E^4 F^2 (-F2); ECCO copy lacks p. 3 (possibly with hdp); T73914, noting attribution to Swift. With GF's typography: signed $1 only; title page with rules of short pieces and square design of four cast blocks in the same grouping (failing to form the customary () shape) as found on tp of Charles Johnson's *The Cobler of Preston* (Faulkner, 1732; T30861); paginated in () with many in italic; on 42 large roman "FINIS." A portion of the text was reprinted as *A Proposal for an Act of Parliament, to Pay off the Debt of the Nation* probably by Faulkner in 1732, T219081 (see below).
– [Swift]. *Examination of Certain Abuses, Corruptions, and Enormities in the City of Dublin* ("Dublin: Printed in the Year 1732"), T81147; TEERINK AND SCOUTEN 718. 8vo: *A*^{4} B-C^4 D^2 [$1 signed]; pp. [*3*] 4-27 [1] in (). Tp with solid rules and rectangular design of four rows of cast piece circle-oval-circle; large roman "FINIS;" listed in GF's booklist on E2v of *The Whole of the Proceedings in the Arches-Court* (1732), T219000, and advt in Swift's *A Proposal for an Act of Parliament* (see next item).
– [Swift]. *A Proposal for an Act of Parliament, to Pay off the Debt of the Nation, without Taxing the Subject ... By A----- P-----, Esq;* ("Dublin: Printed in the Year M, DCC, XXXII"),

T219081; unsigned 8vo; 15 [1] pp. in (); TEERINK AND SCOUTEN 717A, noting it was previously published within *Considerations upon Two Bills* (London: Moore, 1732; T73914); with hft; on A3/5 GF's hdp of boar-hunt to right with top-left corner shaved; on p. 15 two squares of same four cast blocks often used by GF for squares; on p. [16] advt for *An Examination of Certain Abuses* (see previous item). ESTC N46521 is another record (possibly a duplicate) for the same title, also referenced as TEERINK AND SCOUTEN 717A.

– *The Grunters' Request, to Take off the Test: A Poem* (n. p.: "Printed in the Year 1733"), T166406; unsigned 8vo; pp. [2] 1-6 with italic () on 2-6; solid tp rules; FOXON G307, recognizing Faulkner as printer, presumably from orns, including tp orn. of heads of dogs faced outward, back to back, formerly Bowyer's (MASLEN #124); p. 5: GF's hdp of boar-hunt to the right; p. 6: sunface over pedestal with face of Indian with feather headdress; italic "*FINIS*."

– Knightley, John. *Postscript, to Ballycastle Collieries* (no imprint but dated "Ormond Key, 29th of March, 1733"), T228637, supplementing *Ballycastle Collieries Set in their Proper Light* (Faulkner, 1733), T94274.

– Madden, Samuel. *A Letter concerning the Necessity of Learning for the Priesthood* ("Dublin: Printed for Thomas Thornton," 1733), T70694, with several orns formerly Bowyer's, including on tp: tailp with heads of two dogs faced outward (MASLEN #124), and p. 3: hdp of seated angel or man facing right with anchor (MASLEN #58) [same as p. 3 of *Ballycastle Collieries* (Faulkner, 1733), T94274]. GF rarely printed for another as here for Thornton.

– *St. Patrick's Well: A Tale* ("Dublin: Printed in the Year M DCC XXXIII"), T160349, unsigned 8vo; pp. *1-2* 3-7 *8* in (); solid rules; italic "*FINIS*"; tp orn. of heads of two dogs (MASLEN #124); p. 3 hdp with plant in oval flanked by demons faced out (MASLEN #33).

P – [Swift?]. *Advice to the Freemen and Freeholders of the City of Dublin, in their Choice of a Representative in the Ensuing Election* (colophon under solid rule: n. p.: "Printed in the Year, 1733"), T196128, 2-p folio; p. 1 with two rows of cast blocks with floral design (that principally used by GF 1730-1732). Eugene Hammond attributes the work to Swift in *Jonathan Swift: Our Dean* (Newark: University of Delaware Press, 2016, p. 650), noting Swift's admiration for French. ESTC notes that "T166287 [*A Great Deal More Seasonable Advice*] may be a sequel by the same author."

P – [Swift?]. *A Great Deal More Seasonable Advice to the Freemen and Freeholders of the City of Dublin, concerning the Choice of a Member to Represent them in Parliament* (colophon under solid rule: no place: "Printed in the Year 1733"), T166287, [2]-p folio; with reference to the preceding item (T196128).

– Swift. *A Letter from a Member of the House of Commons in Ireland, to a Member of the House of Commons in England, concerning the Sacramental Test. Written in the Year 1708* (n. p.: "Printed in the Year, 1733"), N19756, quoting TEERINK AND SCOUTEN 512A

on this being largely the "same printing [typesetting]" as that "in *The Works of J.S, D.D, D.S.P.D. in four Volumes*, Dublin 1735, v. 4."
– Swift. *The Life and Genuine Character of the Rev. Dr. S---t, D.S.P.D.* ("London: Printed for J. Roberts in Warwick-Lane, and sold by the Booksellers, &c. 1733"), N19162; FOXON S885; TEERINK AND SCOUTEN 728; tp with solid rules; A2 with rows of the cast block common in GF; and cut orns: tp: tailp of phoenix facing upward to left with sunface above, under scrollwork arch extending from fruit horn on left and flower horn on right, with motto on banner at base, variant of a Bowyer orn. (MASLEN #120); B1/9: GF's unframed hdp of crown flanked by roses whose stem forms an inward C-curl and then by thistles on a stem from centre; formerly Bowyer's orn. (MASLEN #26) [same as A2 of *A Dissertation upon Parties* (Faulkner, 1735), N8886]; p. 20: tailp of flower flanked by a "V" of long-stemed flowers, tied with ribbon floating below (MASLEN #123) [same as p. 138 of *The Cupid* (Faulkner and Hoey, 1737), T189242].
– [Swift]. *Some Queries upon the Demand of the Presbyterians* (n. p.: Printed in the Year, 1733), T49349, TEERINK AND SCOUTEN 725, noting that it repeats the ideas in Swift's *Quœries Wrote by Dr. J. Swift, in the Year 1732* (no imprint: probably published in 1733), T46160, giving "[1732]"and citing TEERINK AND SCOUTEN 726; as noted above, GF reprinted the queries with the attribution to Swift in Edmund Gibson's *The Dispute Adjusted* (Faulkner, 1733), T75446.
– *The Knight and the Prelate: A New Ballad ... To which is added, An Epistle from a Gentleman at Twickenham to a Nobleman at St. James's* ("London: Printed in the YEAR MDCCXXXIV"), T66768; 8vo: A-C^4, pp. 23 [1]; "An Epistle" has the same imprint as A1; on A2/3 GF's boarhunt hdp; on B2v/12 is tailp with torso of an Indian in headdress (Maslen #121) used in Bramston's *The Man of Taste* (GF, 1733), T62656, on p. 19.
– *Observations upon the Case of Holding Ecclesiastical Benefices* ("[Dublin:] Printed in the Year 1735"), T185644, 8vo: *A*^{4} B-C^4 [$1 signed], 24 pp. in (); on p. 3 GF's hdp with a round urn, formerly Bowyer's (MASLEN #49) [same as that on p. [1] in James Miller's *Seasonable Reproof: A Satire* (Faulkner, 1736), N21635]; p. 24: GF's tailp of six roses on crossed stems, with two thistles at top and one on each side.[22]

22 In 2018, over half a dozen other false and incomplete Faulkner imprints have been discovered, several with "R. Franklin" imprints. These will be listed in a future article on Faulkner's booklists.

Dirk F. Passmann and Hermann J. Real
Westfälische Wilhelms-Universität, Münster

Annotating J. S. Swift's Reading at Moor Park in 1697/8

Nothing dates as fast as ahistoricity.
TIMOTHY CHAPPEL, *Times Literary Supplement*

Abstract. Although Swift was an avid, and adversarial, reader at all times of his life, three major reading periods stand out in his career: the first when at Trinity College the young Jonathan, tired of the curricular tedium there, began to neglect his "Academical Studyes" and "turned himself to reading History and Poetry;" the second when, as Sir William Temple's secretary at Moor Park in the latter half of the 1690s, the newly ordained clergyman "devoted eight hours a day to the prosecution of his studies," and the third in the early 1720s when the mature Dean having embarked on the composition of *Gulliver's Travels* interspersed his masterpiece with the fruits of much reading.

At Moor Park, from January 1696 to January 1697, Swift "kept an Account one Year of the Books he read." This 'Account,' a total of thirty-seven titles by thirty-six authors, survives in a transcript made by the Revd John Lyon and bound in at the beginning of Lyon's copy of John Hawkesworth's *Life of the Revd Jonathan Swift, D.D.* The authors here present a list of the identified titles in a basic bibliographical format and with descriptive labels as to language, subject, and scope. They conclude that Lyon's 'Account,' allegedly a transcript of Swift's holograph, is actually an inflated list containing titles presumably not read at Moor Park in 1697/8 but added at some later stage.

1

Throughout his life, the Dean of St Patrick's, Dublin, THE Dean, was a reader of books. Later in life, as his income increased, he also became a collector and, later still, a donor of books, but during the whole of his career, he was a reader, avid and regular, consistent, comprehensive, and preoccupied with carefully chosen areas; in fact, it is probably no exaggeration to say that Swift was a physical manifestation of reading.[1] In a section of his *Thoughts on Various Subjects* presumably taken down by Sheridan from Swift's telling, he visualized himself

1 For more of the details, see Hermann J. Real, "Swift as Bookman: Reader, Collector, and Donor," *Material Moments in Book Cultures: Essays in Honour of Gabriele Müller-Oberhäuser*, eds Simon Rosenberg and Sandra Simon (Frankfurt on Main: Peter Lang Edition, 2014), pp. 211-32.

 | DOI:10.30965/9783846763971_006

as an interlocutor who engaged in surrogate dialogue with books, material objects, it is true, but living opposite numbers nonetheless: "When I am reading a Book, whether wise or silly, it seemeth to me to be alive and talking to me."[2]

Swift's passion for reading began early, we may say with confidence while still at Trinity College and before "taking his degree of Batchlor" in February 1686. In his autobiographical fragment, *Family of Swift* (*c.*1728), the old Dean recalls, the young Jonathan, tired of the curricular tedium there,[3] began to neglect his "Academical Studyes, for [some parts of] which he had no great relish by Nature," and "turned himself to reading History and Poetry."[4] We do not know what authors and titles Jonathan read at this stage but may presume that, since he thought his 'turn to reading' worth mentioning, it was on a large scale. Some ten years later, patterns laid down in youth repeating themselves in the life of the adult, the newly ordained clergyman, since the early summer of 1696 safely ensconced back at Moor Park as Sir William Temple's secretary, embarked on what has become widely known as another great reading period. Early biographers like Thomas Sheridan, the Dean's future biographer and editor, report that during this time of "almost four years," lasting from May 1696 until Temple's death in January 1699,[5] Swift "devoted eight hours a day ... to the prosecution of his studies."[6] Sheridan's predecessor Patrick Delany even dated the beginning of these rigorously systematic studies from the time of Swift's Oxford M.A. in July 1692: "He had often been heard to say, that from the time of his taking this degree, he studied at least eight hours a day, one with another, for seven years."[7] Of course, it is doubtful whether we may take this statement on trust. Delany was relying on oral, potentially untrustworthy, anecdotal hearsay. "Seven years" – from Oxford to the death of Temple – is a long time, and while it is not at odds with the biographical chronologies of the two men, it stands to reason whether Swift would at all times have found the resources necessary to satisfy his ostensibly omnivorous appetite for reading.

It is equally remarkable that Swift does not seem to have been a relaxed reader as a rule, one who would settle down in a comfortable armchair thoroughly

2 *Prose Works*, IV, 253, 300.

3 Ehrenpreis, *Mr Swift*, pp. 43-77; see also Kirsten Juhas and Hermann J. Real, "'The Falsity of that Definition animal rationale': Philosophical Foundations of Swift's 'Misanthropy,'" *The Eighteenth-Century Intelligencer*, 29, no 1 (2015), 16-30.

4 *Prose Works*, V, 192.

5 Ehrenpreis, *Mr Swift*, p. 257.

6 *The Life of the Rev. Dr Jonathan Swift, Dean of St Patrick's, Dublin* (Dublin: Luke White, 1785), p. 22.

7 *Correspondence*, ed. Woolley, I, 117n3; Patrick Delany, *Observations upon Lord Orrery's Remarks on the Life and Writings of Dr. Jonathan Swift* (London: W. Reeve and A. Linde, 1754), p. 50.

determined to enjoy himself. While he may have done that, too, more often than not, the act of reading for Swift was arduous and laborious, occasionally also repetitive, requiring him to sit down, perhaps at his much treasured escritoire,[8] and demanding the taking of notes,[9] usually full of concentration if at times impaired by rage and resentment.[10] At Moor Park, in the 1690s, when Swift did not yet own the books that absorbed him, he would "abstract" them, jotting down memorabilia into a commonplace book, his private record of what he took to be meaningful excerpts.[11] Some of these florilegia were still extant in 1755; we have Deane Swift's word for it that, at the moment of writing, he had "a demonstration lying before [him]."[12] Later in life, by the time the Dean was about to embark on the composition of *Gulliver's Travels*, he would read, in fact "reread," the bulky tomes of Herodotus' *Historiarum libri IX*[13] and *The Historie of the Civill Warres of France* by the Italian historian Enrico Caterino Davila (1576-1631),[14] not to mention the three folio volumes of Clarendon's *History of the Rebellion and Civil Wars in England* of 1707, which towards the end of his life he claimed to have "finished" no less than four times.[15] To an extent, it is correct to claim that "Swift wrote and researched *Gulliver's Travels* similarly to the way he wrote and researched *A Tale of a Tub*: he drafted both for several years before publishing, and then interspersed much reading with revising his drafts."[16] And to crown it all, by 1729, he had even ploughed through the formidable Cardinal Baronius (1538-1607), librarian of the Vatican, whose

8 Swift treasured his escritoire, a present from the Countess of Orkney "made to the donor's design" in 1712, to the end (*Correspondence*, ed. Woolley, I, 452 and n1, 613 and n1).

9 For a complete list of Swift's own copies, including the annotated ones, and their current locations, see Dirk F. Passmann, "Jonathan Swift as a Book-Collector: With a Checklist of Swift Association Copies," *Swift Studies*, 27 (2012), 7-68.

10 See, for example, *Prose Works*, V, 247-51, 257-62, 266-94.

11 See also "Textual and Historical Introduction," *A Tritical Essay upon the Faculties of the Mind*, ed. Hermann J. Real, with the assistance of Kirsten Juhas, Dirk F. Passmann, and Sandra Simon (Online.Swift/Ehrenpreis Centre for Swift Studies, Münster, November 2011, updated August 2016 <http://www.online-swift.de/tritical_essay.html>).

12 *An Essay upon the Life, Writings, and Character, of Dr Jonathan Swift* (London, 1755), p. 276.

13 See the "Judicium de Herodoto post longum tempus relecto," *Prose Works*, V, 243; PASSMANN AND VIENKEN II, 840-41.

14 Hermann J. Real and Heinz J. Vienken, "'A Pretty Mixture': Books from Swift's Library at Abbotsford House," *Bulletin of the John Rylands University Library of Manchester*, 67 (1984), 522-43; PASSMANN AND VIENKEN I, 500-8.

15 *Prose Works*, V, 295; PASSMANN AND VIENKEN II, 940-55.

16 Eugene Hammond, *Jonathan Swift: Our Dean* (Newark: University of Delaware Press, 2016), p. 197. See also Myrddin Jones, "A Living Treasury of Knowledge and Wisdom: Some Comments on Swift's Attitude to the Writing of History," *Durham University Journal*, 67 (1974), 180-88.

Annales ecclesiastici, the Catholic rejoinder to Illyricus Flacius' Protestant *Historia ecclesiastica*, better known as the *Magdeburg Centuries*, he owned in a twelve-volume set, all of which he claimed to have read, an excruciating total of 6,500 pages in Latin and in spite of a withering verdict on the Cardinal.[17] As the owner of these titles, Swift now no longer bothered to jot down what he took to be significant into the commonplace books of his earlier years but liberally sprinkled annotations in the margins – glosses, notes, and comments of a wide variety, repeatedly with a sarcastic, ironical bite, frequently lending a cutting edge to his judgements on historical personages and events, and ranging from the correction of factual errors to alternative explanations and interpretations as well as from the rebuttal of political arguments and theological doctrines to downright denunciation and ferocious fulmination.[18] It is good advice to bear in mind in reading Swift's reading that the Dean was not only an avid reader but also an adversarial one.[19]

2

Back in the latter half of the 1690s, we are on less firm ground, appearances notwithstanding. "When he was at Moor-park," Thomas Sheridan declared in *The Life of the Rev. Dr Jonathan Swift* of 1784, "he kept an Acc^{t} one Year of the Books he read in the following manner:

> From Jan:7. 1696/7
> Lord Herbert's Harry 8. f$^{ol.}$
> *Sleidan*'s Com̄ent: abstracted f$^{ol.}$
> Council of *Trent* abstr: f$^{ol.}$
> *Virgil, bis*

17 *Correspondence*, ed. Woolley, III, 231 and n8; PASSMANN AND VIENKEN I, 152-61; see also Real, "Swift as Bookman," p. 212 and n8.

18 See the selection "Marginalia" in *Prose Works*, V, 241-320. Of course, many of these reading practices are common annotation strategies between 1700 and 1750, and while they may give useful insight into specific mental processes at specific times, the question always remains to what creative and functional uses Swift put them in his writing (see also Stephen Colclough, "Diversities of Reading Practice, 1695-1770," *Consuming Texts: Readers and Reading Communities, 1695-1870* [Houndmills, Basingstoke, Hampshire: Palgrave Macmillan, 2007], pp. 64-87 [78-81]).

19 See Brean S. Hammond, "Swift's Reading," *Reading Swift: Papers from The Fourth Münster Symposium on Jonathan Swift*, eds Hermann J. Real and Helgard Stöver-Leidig (Munich: Wilhelm Fink, 2003), pp. 133-46; reprinted in *The Cambridge Companion to Jonathan Swift*, ed. Christopher Fox (Cambridge: Cambridge University Press, 2003), pp. 73-86.

Horace, 9 [*recte* 3] volumes
Sr *W. Temple*'s Memoirs
—— Introduction
Camden's Elisabeth
Prince *Arthur*
Histoire de *Chypre*
Voyage de *Syam*
Voiture
Memoires de *Maurier*
Lucius Florus, ter
Colliers Essays 2 volumes
Count *Gabalis*
Sr *John Davis* of the Soul
Conformité de Religion, &c
Dialogues de Morts, 2 vol:
Lucretius, ter
Histoire de Mr *Constance*
Histoire *d'Æthiopie*
Histoire de *Cotes* de &c
Diodorus Siculus, abstr: f^{o}
Cyprian & *Irenæus* abstr: f^{o}
Voyage de *Maroc* &c
Ælian, 1st Vol:
Homer, Iliad & Odyss.
Cicero's Epistles
Bernier's Grand Mogol 2 Vol:
Burnet's Hist: of Reform: f^{o}
Petronius Arbiter
Oevres Melées 5 Vol:
From Jan: 7th 1697/8
Thucydides by *Hobbes* f$^{ol.}$ abstracted
Theophrasti Characteres
Vossius de Sybillinis
No farther Acc^{t} remains of his Studys at this time.[20]

Although Sheridan suggests that he saw Swift's holograph – after all, he declared that the document was "preserved in his own hand-writing" – the original appears to be no longer extant; if it is, its present location is unknown. The 'Account' survives in a transcript made by the Revd John Lyon, Prebendary

20 *The Life of the Rev. Dr Jonathan Swift*, p. 22. See also Jonathan Swift, *A Tale of a Tub, to which is added, The Battle of the Books, and the Mechanical Operation of the Spirit*, eds A. C. Guthkelch and D. Nichol Smith, 2nd ed. (Oxford: Clarendon Press, 1958), pp. lv-lvi; and *Jonathan Swift, "The Battle of the Books": eine historisch-kritische Ausgabe mit literarhistorischer Einleitung und Kommentar*, ed. Hermann Josef Real (Berlin and New York: Walter de Gruyter, 1978), pp. 128-29.

of St Patrick's and devoted and conscientious manager of the Dean's affairs in his last years.[21] The transcript is bound in at the beginning of Lyon's copy of the Dublin edition of John Hawkesworth's *Life of the Revd Jonathan Swift, D.D.* (1755),[22] which he annotated and which is part of the Victoria and Albert Museum's Forster Collection today.[23] It was subsequently reduplicated in a second interleaved copy of Hawkesworth's *Life*, "in the same edition used by Lyon, with almost all of Lyon's known corrections and additions painstakingly copied in," which has only recently resurfaced and has been acquired by the University of Pennsylvania Library.[24]

Assuming that we have succeeded in identifying the thirty-seven items with any degree of certainty – their authors and titles as well as their editions and languages – and hoping, no doubt vainly, that we have managed to sidestep uncounted bibliographical pitfalls, some preliminary statistics is revealing. Here is our list of the identified titles, in a rather elementary bibliographical format, with a few descriptive labels as to language, subject, and scope:

Herbert, Edward, Baron Herbert of Cherbury. *The Life and Raigne of King Henry the Eighth*. London: E. G. for Thomas Whitaker, 1649 (PASSMANN AND VIENKEN II, 824-30).
English / History / 575 pp.[25]

Sleidanus, Johannes, *nom de plume* of Johannes Philippson, son of Philipp, at Schleiden, Eifel. *Commentariorvm de statv religionis & reipvblicæ, Carolo Quinto Cæsare, libri XXVI*. Strasbourg: Theodosius Rihelius, 1576.
Commentariorvm de statv religionis & re pvblicæ Carolo V Cæsare libri XXVI. Frankfurt: J. Th. Schönwetter, 1610.
A Famouse Cronicle of oure Time Called Sleidanes Commentaries, concerning the State of Religion and Commonwealth, during the Raigne of the Emperour Charles the Fift ... Translated out of Latin into Englishe by [*John Daws*]. London: by John Daye for Abraham Veale and Nicholas England, 1560.
Latin / History / 805 pp.

21 *Correspondence*, ed. Woolley, IV, 352 and nn1,3, 595 and n1; I, 266n2; II, 634n3. The most meticulous and fullest account is by A. C. Elias, Jr, "Swift's *Don Quixote*, Dunkin's *Virgil Travesty*, and Other New Intelligence: John Lyon's 'Materials for a Life of Dr. Swift,' 1765," *Swift Studies*, 13 (1998), 27-104 (pp. 28-32, 37-40).

22 TEERINK AND SCOUTEN 1344.

23 No 579, shelfmark 48.D.39.

24 Elias, "Swift's *Don Quixote*, Dunkin's *Virgil Travesty*, and Other New Intelligence: John Lyon's 'Materials for a Life of Dr. Swift,' 1765," p. 29.

25 This and all subsequent figures refer to the actual pagination of the books, the numbering of usually non-paginated but frequently elaborate indices not being included.

Soave, Pietro, Polano, pseudonym of Pietro Sarpi. *The History of the Council of Trent, Containing Eight Books ... Whereunto is added, The Life of the Learned Author, and The History of the Inquisition.* London: John Macock for Samuel Mearne, *et al.*, 1676 (PASSMANN AND VIENKEN III, 1704-5).

English, translated from the Italian / History / **769** pp., plus 52 pages of letters by various correspondents and 64 pages of *The History of the Inquisition.*

Virgilius Maro, Publius. *Publii Virgilii Maronis Bucolica, Georgica et Æneis, ad optimorum exemplarium fidem recensita.* Cambridge: Jacob Tonson, 1701 (PASSMANN AND VIENKEN III, 1916-17).

Latin / Poetry / **686** pp., ll. **13,251** / **26,502.**

Horatius Flaccus, Quintus. *Qvintvs Horativs Flaccvs: accedunt nunc Danielis Heinsii De satyra Horatiana libri duo*, 3 'vols' (in one) (Leiden: Elzevir, 1629) (PASSMANN AND VIENKEN II, 905).

Latin / Poetry / 239 pp., 250 pp., 296 pp. / 785 pp. / ll. **7760.**

Temple, Sir William. *Memoirs of What Past in Christendom, from the War Begun 1672 to the Peace Concluded 1679.* London: by R. R. for Ric Chiswell, 1692 (PASSMANN AND VIENKEN III, 1805).

English / History / **392** pp.

Temple, Sir William. *An Introduction to the History of England* (London: Richard Simpson and Ralf Simpson, 1695) (PASSMANN AND VIENKEN III, 1805).

English / History / **320** pp.

Camden, William. *Rerum Anglicanarvm et Hibernicarvm annales regnante Elisabetha.* Leiden: Elzevir, 1639 (PASSMANN AND VIENKEN I, 336).

Latin / History / **856** pp.

Blackmore, Sir Richard. *Prince Arthur: An Heroick Poem, in Ten Books.* London: Awnsham and John Churchil, 1695 (PASSMANN AND VIENKEN I, 235-36).

English / Poetry / **296** pp. / ll. *c.***9,700.**

Graziani, Antonio Maria. *Histoire de la guerre de Chypre: écrite en latin par Antoine Maria Gratiani, evesque d'Amelia, et traduite en François par Monsieur Le Peletier, prieur de Saint-Gemme.* Paris: André Pralard, 1685; republished in two volumes at Lyon, 1686.

French / History / **414** pp.

Tachard, Guy. *Voyage de Siam des Pêres Jésuites, envoyez par le Roy aux Indes et à la Chine: avec leurs observations astronomiques, et leurs remarques de physique, de géographie, d'hydrographie, et d'histoire.* Paris: Arnould Seneuze et Daniel Horthemels, 1686; reprinted at Amsterdam by Pierre Mortier in 1687 and 1689, and translated into English shortly after under the title *A Relation of the Voyage to Siam Performed by Six Jesuits, Sent by the French King to the Indies and China in the Year 1685: With their Astrological Observations and their Remarks of Natural Philosophy, Geography, Hydrography and History* (London: by T. B. for A. Churchil, 1688).

French / History and Travel / **423** pp.

Choisy, François-Timoléon de, abbé de Balleroy. *Journal du voyage de Siam, fait en M.DC.LXXXV et M.DC.LXXXVI*. Paris: Sebastien Mabre-Cramoisy, 1687; followed by a second edition by the same publisher in the same year and reissued at Paris by Antoine Dezallier in 1690.

Voiture, Vincent de. *Les Œvvres de Monsievr de Voitvre*. 6th ed. (Paris: Avgvstin Covrbé, 1660) (PASSMANN AND VIENKEN I, 336-37).
French / Letters / Poetry / **758** pp.

Aubery du Maurier, Louis. *Mémoires pour servir à l'histoire de Hollande et des autres Provinces-Unies*. Paris: Jean Villette, 1687 (PASSMANN AND VIENKEN I, 107).
French / History / **484** pp.

Florus, Publius Annius. *Rerum Romanarum epitome interpretatione et notis illustravit Anna Tanaquilli Fabri filia*. Paris: F. Léonard, 1674 (PASSMANN AND VIENKEN I, 636-37).
Latin / History / **205** pp. / **605** pp.

Collier, Jeremy. *Essays upon Several Moral Subjects*, 2nd ed., 2 vols (London: R. Sare and H. Hindmarsh, 1697) (ESTC R24276).
English / Essays / **420** pp.

Montfaucon, Nicolas-Pierre-Henri de, Abbé de Villars. *The Count de Gabalis: or, Conferences about Secret Sciences*. London: by Th. James for Robert Harford, [1680] (ESTC R226487).[26]
English / French / Occultism / **128** pp.

Davies, Sir John. *The Original, Nature, and Immortality of the Soul: A Poem. With an Introduction concerning Human Knowledge*. London: W. Rogers, 1697 (ESTC R14959).[27]
English / Poetry / **55** pp.

Estienne, Henri. *L'Introdvction av traité de la conformité des merueilles anciennes auec les modernes: ov, Traité preparatif à l'Apologie pour Herodote*. [Zurich]: Guillaume de Marescs, 1580 (PASSMANN AND VIENKEN I, 586-87).
French / Satire / **656** pp.

---

26 The use of English *Count* rather than *Comte* in "Count *Gabalis*" suggests that Swift read one of the English translations, of which there were at least two different editions in 1680, rather than the French original, *Le Comte de Gabalis: ou, Entretiens sur les sciences secrètes*, first published in Paris by Claude Barbin in 1670.

27 Swift presumably read this edition, marked in his account "Sr *John Davis* of the Soul," shortly after its publication in May 1697, a reissue of Davies's philosophical poem *Nosce teipsum*, first published in 1599. The reissue was edited by Nahum Tate, who also provided a four-page introductory essay, in heroic couplets, "Upon the Present Corrupted State of Poetry." The poem itself consists of two 'elegies,' "Of Humane Knowledge: or, An Account of Man" (pp. 1-6), and "Of the Soul of Man, and the Original, Nature and Immortality thereof" (pp. 7-55), and had already appeared in 1688 under the variant title *Nosce teipsum: or, The Delphick Oracle Expounded, as a Looking-Glass for the Soul* (ESTC R171693); this may also have been the edition Swift read.

Le Bovier de Fontenelle, Bernard. *Nouveaux dialogues des morts.* Amsterdam: Antoine Schelte, 1694 (PASSMANN AND VIENKEN II, 1055-60).[28]
French / Essays / **356** pp.

Lucretius Carus, Titus. *Titi Lucretii Cari De rerum natura libri sex: quibus additæ sunt conjecturæ & emendationes Tan. Fabri cum notulis perpetuis.* Cambridge: by John Hayes for W. Morden, 1675 (PASSMANN AND VIENKEN II, 1122).
Latin / Poetry / **454** pp., ll. **11,756** / **35,268.**

Orléans, Pierre Joseph d'. *Histoire de M. Constance, Premier Ministre du Roy de Siam, et de la dernière révolution de cet estat.* Tours: Philbert Masson, and Paris: Daniel Horthemels, 1690; 2nd ed. (Paris: Daniel Horthemels, 1692).
French / History / **244** pp.

Ludolf, Hiob. *Nouvelle histoire d'Abissinie ou d'Ethiopie.* Paris: A. Cellier, 1684.
French / History and Travel / **275** pp.

Coste, Hilarion de. *Histoire catholique: ou sont descrites les vies, faicts, et actions héroiques & signalées des hommes & dames illustres, qui par leur pieté ou saincteté de vie se sont rendus recommendables dans les XVI & XVII siècles.* Paris: Pierre Chevalier, 1625.
French / History / **801** pp.

Coste, Pierre. *Histoire de Louis de Bourbon II. du nom, Prince de Condé, Premier Prince du Sang.* Cologne: F***, 1693; 2nd ed., revised, corrected and augmented by the author (Cologne: F****, 1695); translated from the first edition into English by Nahum Tate under the title *The Life of Lewis of Bourbon, Late Prince of Condé ... with Many Curious Remarks on the Transactions of Europe for the Last Sixty Years* (London: Tim Goodwin, 1693 [ESTC R21621]).[29]
French / History / **581** pp.

---

28 The 'Account' of Swift's reading notes "Dialogues des morts, 2 vol." No edition with this title is listed in any catalogue of Swift's library, and it is therefore likely to refer to one of at least three editions of Fontenelle's *Nouveaux dialogues des morts* Swift owned. All of these are subdivided into three 'parts' (*I: Dialogues de morts anciens*; *II: Dialogues de morts anciens avec les modernes*; *III: Dialogues de morts modernes*), but none is bound in two 'volumes.' The explanation probably is that Swift only read the first two 'parts' of *Nouveaux dialogues*, which were more germane to his purposes while he was embroiled in the *querelle* that led up to *The Battle of the Books*.

29 What author and title "Histoire de Cotes de &c" exactly refers to is probably the greatest enigma of Lyon's 'Account.' If it is correct to assume, as it seems natural to do, that "Cotes" is a phonetic spelling of the French surname "Coste," there are two titles to choose from, both of which are indicative of Swift's voracious interest in history and historiography. Hilarion's *Histoire catholique* presents material that Swift would have found valuable while he was preoccupied with *A Tale of a Tub*; it also contains biographical information on historical personalities for whom Swift had a high (dis)regard, such as Thomas More and Ignatius of Loyola as well as Queen Mary and Queen Elizabeth of England; finally, there is a reference to the burning of Frère Jean Forest, to which he alludes in *A Serious Poem on William Wood* (*Poems*, ed. Williams, I, 334, ll. 21-22), not to mention the

Diodorus Siculus. *Diod. Siculi Bibliothecæ Historicæ libri XV: … His accesserunt eclogæ seu fragmenta, ex libris quibusdam auctoris, qui desiderantur. Omnia cum interpretatione Latina … ac temporum annotatione illustrata … Studio et labore Laurentii Rhodomani Cherusci.* 2 vols (in 1) (Hanau: Typis Wechelianis, apud Claudium Marnium et haeredes Ioannis Aubrii, 1604).
The Historical Library of Diodorus the Sicilian: In Fifteen Books … To which are added, The Fragments of Diodorus that are Found in the Bibliotheca of Photius. Made English by G. Booth. London: by Edward Jones for Awnsham and John Churchil, 1700 (ESTC R15327).
Greek / English / History / **799** pp.

Cyprian, Saint. *Sancti Cæcilii Cypriani opera recognita & illustrata per Ioannem Oxoniensem episcopum* [John Fell]. Oxford: Sheldonian Theatre, 1687.[30]
Latin / Theology and Ecclesiastical History / Letters / **579** pp.

Irenaeus, Saint. *Sancti Irenæi Lugdunensis episcopi & martyris, Adversus Valentini & similium Gnosticorum hæreses libri quinque.* Paris, 1675.[31]
Latin / Ecclesiastical History / **569** pp.

Fréjus, Roland. *Relation d'vn voyage fait en 1666 aux royaumes de Maroc et de Fez.* Paris: Gervais Clouzier, 1682; first published by the same printer under a different title in Paris, 1670, and translated into English only a year later (London: W. Godbid, 1671).
French / Travel / **286** pp.

---

inflated apparatus of paratexts complete with dedicatory and recommendatory poems, prefaces, tables of contents, and approbations by the learned ridiculed in the *Tale*. On the other hand, a striking phrase like "Prince du Sang" from the *Histoire de Louis de Bourbon* by Locke's friend Pierre Coste, which also contains a survey of seventeenth-century European history of particular interest to Swift, points towards its English translation, "Prince of the Blood," in Gulliver's Voyage to Lilliput (*Prose Works*, XI, 30 [I, ii, 3]).

30 The edition Swift presumably used is the magnificent first edition of St Cyprian's complete works printed in England, edited by the Bishop of Oxford, John Fell (1625-86), and published at the University Press in folio in November 1682 (ARBER I, 512). St Cyprian's writings, mainly short and popular treatises and letters, would have been of interest to Swift while he was at work on *A Tale of a Tub*, not only because of the Father's stand against the papacy but also because of the affinity of some of their themes, such as the unity of the church ("De unitate ecclesiæ") and the character of zeal and envy ("De zelo et livore") (pp. 104-20; 221-28).

31 Swift "abstracted" St Irenaeus in a folio edition of the bishop's chief work, but we do not know which edition he used. This important variorum edition, complete with a life of the Saint as well as scholia and annotations and chronologically close to Swift, had been published at Paris in 1675. The words allegedly used in Gnostic ritual, which constitute one of the epigraphs on the title page of *A Tale of a Tub*, are quoted from St Irenaeus (see *A Tale of a Tub and Other Works*, ed. Marcus Walsh [Cambridge: Cambridge University Press, 2010], p. 316).

Aelian, Claudius. *Clavdii Æliani varia historia Tanaqvillvs Faber emendauit*. Saumur: Jean Lesnier, 1668 (PASSMANN AND VIENKEN I, 15-16).
Latin / Greek / History / **428** pp.

Homer. *Homeri quae extant omnia*. Basle: S. Henricpetri, 1606 (PASSMANN AND VIENKEN II, 890-93).
Greek / Latin / Poetry / **I, 427** pp. / ll. **15,693;** II, **340** pp. / ll. **12,110.**

Cicero, Marcus Tullius. *M. Tullii Ciceronis epistolarum ad T. Pomponium Atticum libri XVI*. Lyon: I. Pillehotte, 1589 (PASSMANN AND VIENKEN I, 414).
Latin / Letters / **768** pp.

Bernier, François. *Voyages ... contenant la description des états du Grand Mogol*. 2 vols (Amsterdam: Paul Marret, 1699 [PASSMANN AND VIENKEN I, 190-91]).
French / History and Travel / **383** pp.
Histoire de la derniere revolution des estats du Grand Mogol. 2 vols (bound in one) (Paris: Claude Barbin, 1671 [PASSMANN AND VIENKEN I, 190]).
French / History and Travel / **678** pp.
Suite des Memoires ... sur l'Empire du Grand Mogol. 2 vols (Paris: Claude Barbin, 1671).
French / History and Travel / I, **178** pp.; II, **296** pp.

Burnet, Gilbert. *The History of the Reformation of the Church of England, in Two Parts: The First Part of the Progress Made in it during the Reign of K. Henry the VIII*, 2nd ed. (London: by T. H. for Richard Chiswell, 1681) (ESTC R19796).
The History of the Reformation of the Church of England: The Second Part of the Progress Made in it till the Settlement of it in the Beginning of Q. Elizabeth's Reign. London: by T. H. for Richard Chiswell, 1681 (ESTC R29152).
English / History / I, **744** pp.; II, **837** pp. (**1581** pp.)

Petronius Arbiter, Titus. *Petronii Arbitri Satyricon: cum notis & observationibus variorum*, ed. Joannes a Wower (Leiden: F. Rapheling, 1596) (PASSMANN AND VIENKEN III, 1407-9).
Latin / Menippean Satire / **394** pp.

Marguetel de Saint-Denis, Charles, seigneur de Saint-Évremont. *Œuvres meslées: nouvelles impressions augmentée de plusieurs pièces curieuses*. 4 vols (Paris: Claude Barbin, 1693) (PASSMANN AND VIENKEN II, 1190-92).[32]

32 Which edition, and which parts, of Saint-Évremont's *Œuvres melées* Swift read at Moor Park remains a matter of speculation. The entry in Lyon's transcript confusingly states: "Oevres Melées 5 Vol." This cannot refer to either of the two sets Swift owned (PASSMANN AND VIENKEN II, 1190-96). The pre-1697 one consists of only four volumes (bound in two), while his seven-volume set (Cologne: P. Marteau, 1708) postdates the chronology of his reading. Under the circumstances, the entry in the 'Account' seems to refer to an additional odd volume V, from another unidentified multi-volume set (possibly *Oeuvres meslées*, 5 vols [Paris: Claude Barbin, 1690-94]). Whether it means that Swift only read this fifth volume or the complete set of five remains unclear.

French / Letters / Moral Essays / I-IV, **1154** pp.; V, **266** pp.
From Jan: 7th 1697/8

Hobbes, Thomas. *The History of the Grecian War, in Eight Books, Written by Thucydides: Faithfully Translated from the Original.* 2nd ed. (London: Andrew Clark for Charles Harper, 1676).
English / Greek / History / **358** pp.

La Bruyère, Jean de. *Les Caractères de Théophraste traduit du Grec, avec les caractères ou les moeurs de ce siècle.* 3 vols (Paris: Estienne Michallet, 1697) (Passmann and Vienken II, 1016-17).
French / Character Types / **878** pp.

Vossius, Isaac. *De Sibyllinis aliisque quæ Christi natalem præcessere oraculis: accredit ejusdem responsio ad objectiones nuperæ criticæ sacræ* (Oxford: Sheldonian Theatre, 1680) (Passmann and Vienken III, 1945).[33]
Latin / Old-Testament and Classical Prophecy / 104; 59; **163** pp.

From this list, the following conclusions may be drawn:
first, of the thirty-seven titles (by thirty-six authors), twenty-three resurface in the various catalogues of Swift's library at one stage or another (1715, 1742, 1745). Although all of them have been reliably identified, it is dangerous to conclude that the titles Swift professes to have read in 1697/8 were identical with those that subsequently appear in any of his library catalogues. Currently, next to nothing is known about the growth of Swift's library, and he may have read books at Moor Park in the late 1690s (by implication, borrowing them from Sir William Temple's library), which he acquired, or purchased himself, only later in life, for whatever reasons. A case in point is Claudius Aelianus, the Greek rhetorician and writer on miscellaneous subjects (*c.*170-235 AD). According to Lyon's 'Account,' Swift read "*Ælian*, 1st Vol:" in 1697/8. Straightforward though it seems, the entry is confusing and raises a number of problems. For one, Swift cannot have read his own copy of the *Historical Miscellanies* since the date and price of purchase recorded in his handwriting on the title page confirm that he acquired it as late as 1711 (The Rothschild Library 2305). For another, even if Swift read Aelian in an edition owned by Sir William Temple, it is difficult to account for "1st Vol." No pre-1697 edition of *Varia historia*, no matter whether in Greek and Latin or in English translation, consists of two (or more) 'volumes'

33 Vossius' *De Sibyllinis* is something like the 'odd one out' among the titles Swift read in 1697/8. From Swift's "formal inscription of ownership," later cancelled, we know that the volume was a gift from Sir William Temple (A. C. Elias, Jr, *Swift at Moor Park: Problems in Biography and Criticism* [Philadelphia: The University of Pennsylvania Press, 1982], pp. 103, 109-10 and nn), and his protégé may simply have felt obliged to dip into his patron's donation.

so that "1st Vol" does not seem to make sense. The explanation could be that, in jotting down Aelian into his list, Swift misremembered that the Saumur 1668 edition rather than consisting of two *volumes* consisted of two *parts*. While the first part comprises the first seven books of this anecdotal collection, supplemented by the editor's emendations, the second part, which comprises Books VIII to XIV, is introduced by a divisional title and a new pagination. In that case, Swift would have read Books I to VII only.

A similar, albeit not quite identical, case is François Bernier's *Suite des Memoires … sur l'Empire du Grand Mogol*, published by Claude Barbin in two volumes at Paris in 1671. A marginal note in *A Discourse concerning the Mechanical Operation of the Spirit*, which comments on "the **Jauguis*, or enlightned Saints of *India*, [who] see all their Visions, by Help of an acquired straining and pressure of the Eyes," sends readers to "**Bernier, Mem. de Mogol*." This gloss at first misled us into assuming that it referred to Bernier's two-volume *Voyages … contenant la description des états du Grand Mogol* of 1699, which Swift owned but which was published a year *after* Lyon's 'Account' claims Swift read it. Thus, in 1697/8, Swift seemed to have read an earlier title by Bernier, *Histoire de la derniere revolution des estats du Grand Mogol*. According to several references to this volume in Temple's essays, this edition was in Sir William's library,[34] and Swift may have availed himself of it. But then, this earlier *Histoire de la derniere revolution des estats du Grand Mogol* does not contain any reference to the Yogis. This in fact is found in Bernier's *Suite des Memoires … sur l'Empire du Grand Mogol*, also published in Paris in two volumes in 1671, as partly suggested by Swift's marginal gloss and partly by Lyon's entry ("*Bernier*'s Grand Mogol 2 Vol:").[35]

Second, in addition to his native English, Swift read Latin and French, both ostensibly with ease.[36] Among the thirty-seven titles in Lyon's 'Account,' thirteen

---

34 See Jutta Winnefeld, "'Beauty without Order': Temple's Essays *Upon the Gardens of Epicurus* und *Of Heroick Virtue*," doctoral dissertation, Westfälische Wilhelms-Universität, Münster, 1980, pp. 123, 185, and *passim*.

35 *A Tale of a Tub, to which is added, The Battle of the Books, and the Mechanical Operation of the Spirit*, eds Guthkelch and Nichol Smith, p. 271n1. See also *A Discourse concerning the Mechanical Operation of the Spirit*, ed. Hermann Josef Real, with the assistance of Janika Bischof, Kirsten Juhas, Dirk F. Passmann, Eva Schaten, and Sandra Simon (Online.Swift/ Ehrenpreis Centre for Swift Studies, Münster, July 2016, updated September 2017 <http://www.online-swift.de/mechanical_operation.note.mech_108.html>).

36 For Swift's knowledge of French, see *Correspondence*, ed. Woolley, I, 101, 231n2, 509n7; II, 109-10 and n, 304-5 and n6, and *passim*. For his proficiency in French during his time at Moor Park, see also Archibald E. Irwin, "Swift as Translator of the French of Sir William Temple and his Correspondents," *Studies in English Literature, 1500-1900*, 6 (1966), 483-98. Against Irwin's findings, Temple's judgement of Swift as having "some french" in his

are in French, while twelve, possibly eleven, are in Latin, depending on the fact whether Swift read Sleidan's *Commentaries* in English translation rather than in the original Latin. In other words, out of a total of thirty-seven, twenty-five were in a foreign language. But there is more than meets the eye.

Third, at first sight, Lyon's 'Account' shows Swift to have read rather indiscriminately, but this impression is misleading. While there are thematically coherent sections on *Satire*, both ancient and modern,[37] on *Letters* and *Letter-Writing*, also ancient and modern,[38] as well as the *Essay*, both as a literary exercise and a study in character-type,[39] there is a clear predominance of *Poetry*

recommendatory letter to Sir Robert Southwell (*Correspondence*, ed. Woolley, I, 101) seems somewhat ungenerous (see also Eugene Hammond, *Jonathan Swift: Irish Blow-In* [Newark: University of Delaware Press, 2016], p. 77). For Swift as a Latinist, see *Correspondence*, ed. Woolley, I, 101, 111; III, 397-98 and nn.

37 See Titus Petronius Arbiter, *Petronii Arbitri Satyricon: cum notis & observationibus variorum*, ed. Joannes a Wower (Leiden: F. Rapheling, 1596), and Henri Estienne, *L'Introdvction av traité de la conformité des merueilles anciennes auec les modernes: ov, Traité preparatif à l'Apologie pour Herodote* ([Zurich]: Guillaume de Marescs, 1580). Estienne's *Introdvction*, jotted down in Lyon's 'Account' as "Conformité de Religion, &c.," a repository of all forms of trickery and deceit as practised by doctors, lawyers, and clergymen would have been of the greatest interest to Swift while being embarked on the numerous 'corruptions' of the Catholic Church in *A Tale of a Tub*, such as the invocation of saints, the worship of images, and the trade in relics.

38 Marcus Tullius Cicero, M. *Tullii Ciceronis epistolarum ad T. Pomponium Atticum libri XVI* (Lyon: I. Pillehotte, 1589). The note, "*Cicero*'s Epistles," is annoyingly vague, and whether it refers to the whole voluminous corpus of Cicero's *Letters to Atticus* and *Letters to Friends*, including the correspondence to Brutus and his brother Quintus, remains unclear. So does the question whether Swift read Cicero's epistles in an individual edition from his library shelves, or in either of the *Opera omnia* sets which he owned, in four and nine volumes, respectively (provided that he had already purchased either, or both, of the *Opera omnia* sets). We do know, however, that in 1693 Swift bought a French edition of the *Letters to Atticus*, annotated by the distinguished scholar Dionysius Lambinus, among others. This seems to have been the only individual edition of Cicero's *Epistles* he owned in 1697/8, and its title notwithstanding, it also contains the *Epistulae ad Quintum fratrem* and the *Epistulae ad Brutum*. If Swift had also read by then the *Epistulae ad familiares*, the first quotation of which is recorded only a few years later, he would have had to fall back on one of his *Opera omnia* sets.

A second author in this category is Vincent de Voiture, *Les Œvvres de Monsievr de Voitvre*, 6th ed. (Paris: Avgvstin Covrbé, 1660). Again, Swift's reference to his reading "Voiture" is tantalizingly imprecise. If the remarks he left in his correspondence on Voiture as a writer of letters are anything to go by, he was more interested in the Frenchman's letters and art of letter-writing (*Correspondence*, ed. Woolley, III, 284 and n1; IV, 203 and n2) than in the *Poësies* and *Métamorphoses*, bound together with the correspondence.

39 See Jeremy Collier, *Essays upon Several Moral Subjects*, 2nd ed., 2 vols (London: R. Sare and H. Hindmarsh, 1697), and Jean de La Bruyère, *Les Caractères de Théophraste traduit du Grec, avec les caractères ou les moeurs de ce siècle*, 3 vols (Paris: Estienne Michallet, 1697).

and *History* as well as *History* in tandem with *Travel*, followed by Fathers and historians of the Church. What seems most remarkable about Swift's choice of titles is not only the spectrum of themes and approaches but also the variety and diversity of events and aspects, bearing witness to an embracing inquisitiveness, open-mindedness, and desire for 'alterity.'

Fourth, Swift's mark in Latin at the terminal examinations at Trinity College, Easter 1685, was "bene" (as it was in Greek, for that matter),[40] and the sheer amount of his classical reading at Moor Park in 1697/8 bears this out – to an unrealized, and perhaps even implausible, degree. Lyon's 'Account' testifies to Swift's reading an immortal triad of Roman poets of whom he each had several editions on his shelves and for whom he retained a particular regard throughout his life – Horace, Virgil, and Lucretius.[41] Whereas Swift studied Horace 'only' once during this single year, he read Virgil "twice [*bis*]" and Lucretius "three times [*ter*]."[42] We do not know which editions, either from his own library or from that of Sir William, Swift used, but we assume that he read all three poets in Latin and not in translation, such as those by John Dryden or Thomas Creech, of which he was also aware.[43]

Fifth, we assume *Horace, Virgil*, and *Lucretius* to mean that Swift read the whole of Horace, the whole of Virgil, and the whole of Lucretius; more precisely, the *Odes, Epodes*, and *Carmen saeculare* as well as the *Satires, Epistles*, and *Ars poetica* by Horace (all told, 7,760 lines of verse); the *Bucolica, Georgica*, and *Aeneis* by Virgil (not to mention the apocryphal *Appendix Vergiliana* often included in editions of the poet; in numbers, 13,251 lines of verse), and the six books of *De rerum natura* by Lucretius (in numbers, 22,248 lines). Given the fact that differences between the various editions of the texts tend to be minimal, we arrive at the total of *c.*43,259 lines of Latin verse ostensibly read by Jonathan during the course of one single year. And that does not yet allow any time for the other thirty-four titles still on Swift's reading list, among them, Homer's *Iliad* and *Odyssey*, which he probably read in the Basle 1606 folio edition by the French humanist-scholar Jean de Sponde, printed with Homer's Greek and de Sponde's Latin verse rendering in parallel columns (15,693 lines of *The Iliad*, 12,110 of *The Odyssey*, all told ll. 27,803) as well as the *c.*9,700

40 Ehrenpreis, *Mr Swift*, p. 279.

41 For the details, see PASSMANN AND VIENKEN II, 905-12, 1122-26, and III, 1913-23.

42 Swift belonged to that camp of readers who annotated their Latin books in Latin and their French ones in French (H. J. Jackson, *Marginalia: Readers Writing in Books* [New Haven and London: Yale University Press, 2001], p. 89).

43 See Hugh MacDonald, *John Dryden: A Bibliography of Early Editions and of Drydeniana* (London: Dawsons, 1966 [1939]), pp. 56-59 (33a-d); Cosmo Alexander Gordon, *A Bibliography of Lucretius* (London: Rupert Hart-Davis, 1962), pp. 169-77 (331-331D).

humdrum couplets of Blackmore's *Prince Arthur*. We confess that, as we were noting these sobering facts, a nagging suspicion arose whether Lyon's 'Account' of Swift's reading at Moor Park in 1697/8 may be invested with the kind of trust and reliance that one, perhaps all too instinctively, wishes to accord it. If one does take the record on trust, Swift read 80,762 Latin and English lines of verse in a single year. In practical terms, this means that Temple's secretary would have had to read some 269 lines per day and 34 lines per hour provided one assumes that he ploughed on stolidly, and with the most rigorous discipline, for 300 days per annum and eight hours per diem; in the case of 250 days per annum and eight hours per diem, this figure rises to 323 lines per day and 40 lines per hour; in the case of 200 days per annum and eight hours per diem, it approximates 403 lines per day and 50 lines per hour.

Sixth, suspicion is further fuelled by an equally quantitative analysis of Swift's preoccupation with history and historiography. In fact, of the thirty-seven titles recorded in Lyon's 'Account,' no less than half – eighteen – deal with matters of history. Of the seven "abstracted," or excerpted, authors, all seven are historiographers; none of these he is known to have given away later in life. The histories Swift studied were ancient and modern, religious and secular, Greek and Roman, English, Dutch, and French, German and Italian, Mongolian, Chinese, and Siamese as well as Moroccan and Ethiopian.

More particularly, among Greek historiographers, Swift immersed himself in one of four editions of Thomas Hobbes's translation of Thucydides' *History of the Grecian Wars*,[44] which is eminent for its combination of factual accuracy with the search for causality (358 pages) as well as the massive world history, in fifteen books, by the Greek-writing Sicilian Diodorus, whose *Bibliothēkē historikē*, despite its character of an uncritical compilation, is a mine of information on classical mythology and religion, ancient geography and the chronology of the wars from Troy to Alexander the Great on to Julius Caesar. Both Hobbes's Thucydides and Diodorus apparently mattered to Swift; both carry the addendum "abstracted." Surprisingly, among Roman historians, Swift studied not any of the more powerful writers like Sallust, Livy, and Tacitus, who all became favourites only later in life,[45] but Florus' epitome of Roman history,

---

44 Which of four editions available to him before 1698 Swift read (see Hugh MacDonald and Mary Hargreaves, *Thomas Hobbes: A Bibliography* [London: The Bibliographical Society, 1952], pp. 1-3 [nos 1-4]) is unknown. The one chronologically closest to him was the second edition of 1676, "much Corrected and Amended." It was dedicated to Hobbes's patron Sir William Cavendish, Earl of Devonshire, and accompanied by a preface to the readers (sigs b3r-b4v), the life and history of Thucydides (sigs a1r-b2v) as well as an elaborate geographical index (sigs b3r-e2v). Swift would remember his early reading of Thucydides as late as 1726 in *Gulliver's Travels* (Ehrenpreis, *Mr Swift*, p. 68 and n41).

45 Passmann and Vienken II, 1089-92; III, 1634-37, 1784-90.

from the reign of the kings up to the age of Augustus, no less than three times in a single year (205 / 615 pages). Which of at least three Florus editions in his library he used is unknown. A remark in *The Publick Spirit of the Whigs* (1714), according to which Lucius Florus was the author of a "*Roman* History wherein Lads are instructed," suggests that Swift may have been having the 1674 Paris *ad usum Delphini* edition in mind.

Seventh, in English historiography, Swift focused on the Reformation, its origins, course, and largely baneful after-effects. He started off with Lord Herbert of Cherbury's *Life and Raigne of King Henry the Eighth* of 1649 (575 pages), the first title in Lyon's 'Account' and probably the one most ferociously annotated,[46] following this up with William Camden's annals of the reign of 'Good Queen Bess,' *Rerum Anglicanarvm et Hibernicarvm annales regnante Elisabetha* of 1639 (856 pages), which he would have found a valuable quarry for the *Discourse concerning the Mechanical Operation of the Spirit*, as he is likely to have considered Gilbert Burnet's two impressive folio volumes of *The History of the Reformation of the Church of England,* here called "Parts," a substantial source for *A Tale of a Tub* (I and II, 1581 pp.), its controversial status and his personal reservations against the Bishop of Salisbury notwithstanding.[47] The same may safely be said of the Continental historian of the Reformation, Johannes Philippson, better known as Sleidanus, from his birthplace Schleiden, in the Eifel mountains. Swift "abstracted" a 'folio' edition of Sleidan's *Commentaries* early in 1697. Regrettably, the reference to Sleidan's *Commentaries* is not specific enough as to decide whether Swift availed himself of an edition in the Latin original, first published in 1555 in folio (469 leaves), republished in 1576, and reprinted in a "corrected" edition in 1610, for example; whether he read the work in an English translation, the first of which came out in 1560, and whether, in case he did use an English translation, this edition also contained the Continuation by Edmund Bohun, first published chronologically close to Swift in 1689 (*The General History of the Reformation of the Church from the Errors and Corruptions of the Church of Rome, Begun in Germany by Martin Luther, with the Progress thereof in All Parts of Christendom from the Year 1517 to the Year 1556* [London: by Edward Jones for Abel Swalle and Henry Bonwicke, 1689]).

Eighth, another thematic focus in addition to *Poetry* and *History* is *Travel*, often in combination with the history of the various exotic countries Swift 'visited' as a reader. One example among several is the "Histoire d'*Æthiopie*,"

---

46 PASSMANN AND VIENKEN II, 824-30. See also the same authors' more detailed essay "That 'Hellish Dog of a King': Jonathan Swift and Henry VIII," in *Henry VIII in History, Historiography, and Literature*, ed. Uwe Baumann (Frankfurt on Main: Peter Lang, 1992), pp. 241-79.

47 See Ehrenpreis, *Dr Swift*, pp. 84-90.

originally published in Latin under the title *Historia Æthiopica, sive brevis & succincta* by the oriental scholar Hiob Ludolf, a lifelong student of Ethiopia (Frankfurt: J. D. Zunner, 1681). It was translated into English by Milton's godson and protégé John Phillips in 1682 and two years later also into French, albeit revised and restructured as well as adorned by plates showing the plants and animals of Ethiopia. The inscription on the label of this French version and its running title are identical with the bibliographical description Swift remembered when jotting it down, *Histoire d'Ethiopie.*

A second example is the "Voyage de *Siam*," for which there are two contenders: François-Timoléon de Choisy, Abbé de Balleroy, *Journal du voyage de Siam, fait en M.DC.LXXXV et M.DC.LXXXVI* (Paris: Sebastien Mabre-Cramoisy, 1687), and the Jesuit Guy Tachard's *Voyage de Siam des Pêres Jésuites, envoyez par le Roy aux Indes et à la Chine: avec leurs observations astronomiques, et leurs remarques de physique, de géographie, d'hydrographie, et d'histoire*, first published at Paris by Arnould Seneuze et Daniel Horthemels in 1686, and reprinted at Amsterdam by Pierre Mortier in 1687 and 1689. Closer analysis reveals that Father Tachard's account, which not only stressed the religious aspects of the embassy, but also drew on the writings of earlier Jesuit missionaries, made an impact on Swift's memory, leaving him a more likely candidate than the Abbé de Choisy. Not only is the reference to "the Reverend Fathers the *Eastern* Missionaries" in *A Tale of a Tub* a translation of "*Pêres Jésuites*" from Tachard's title, several scenes, themes, and motifs are also reminiscent of *Gulliver's Travels*.[48]

Our third example in this section is of supplemental interest: Pierre Joseph d'Orléans, *Histoire de M. Constance, Premier Ministre du Roy de Siam, et de la dernière révolution de cet estat*, first published at Tours by Philbert Masson, and simultaneously in Paris by Daniel Horthemels in 1690, with a second edition following two years later (Paris: Daniel Horthemels, 1692). Swift owned this prolific French historian's *Histoire des révolutions d'Angleterre* of 1695 (PASSMANN AND VIENKEN II, 1344), but there is no evidence that he read any of the three volumes. Conversely, he did read the *Histoire de M. Constance*, a biography of Constance Phaulkon, born Konstantinos Gerakis (1647-88), which he did not own, presumably in a copy from Sir William Temple's library. Phaulkon was a Greek adventurer who became prime minister of Siam, and the story of his life supplemented Swift's interest in the voyages of the Jesuit missionaries to Siam

48 See *A Tale of a Tub and Other Works*, ed. Walsh, pp. 68, 387; Dirk Friedrich Passmann, *"Full of Improbable Lies": "Gulliver's Travels" und die Reiseliteratur vor 1726* (Frankfurt: Peter Lang, 1987), pp. 299-306.

undertaken at about the same time. This reading is reflected in a reference to "that Noble *Jesuit*" in the Conclusion to *A Tale of a Tub*.[49]

Further cases in point are:

Fréjus, Roland. *Relation d'vn voyage fait en 1666 aux royaumes de Maroc et de Fez*. Paris: Gervais Clouzier, 1682; first published by the same printer under a different title in Paris, 1670, and translated into English only a year later (London: W. Godbid, 1671). The identification of "Voyage de *Maroc*" with Fréjus's account is not entirely certain; if Swift read it, he presumably read the French original.

Graziani, Antonio Maria. *Histoire de la guerre de Chypre: écrite en Latin par Antoine Maria Gratiani, evesque d'Amelia, et traduite en François par Monsieur Le Peletier, prieur de Saint-Gemme*, first published at Paris in 1685, and republished in two volumes at Lyon in 1686, is referred to, in Lyon's 'Account,' by "Histoire de *Chypre*," a title vaguely descriptive rather than bibliographically precise. The French translation is of a Latin original, *De bello Cyprio libri V*, first published at Rome in 1624 and later in the century translated into French and English, both translators apparently "[departing] widely from the Latin original" (*The History of the War of Cyprus, Written Originally in Latin* [London: J. Rawlins and Randal Taylor, 1687]). The likelihood that Swift did read Graziani, who is one of several candidates, is chiefly based on the arresting typographical evidence of the title page: he jotted down the words highlighted by bold capitals, "Histoire de *Chypre*."[50]

Ninth, during this great reading period at Moor Park, Swift was at work on his first stroke of genius, *A Tale of a Tub*. One would expect him to have cast his net wide, eager to fill his commonplace books with material demonstrating "the numerous and gross Corruptions in Religion and Learning," all the more so if these 'Corruptions' stuck out starkly against the 'perfection' of the Church of England, which the *Tale*, according to its Apology added in 1710, purports to celebrate. In his *Essay upon the Life, Writings, and Character, of Dr Jonathan Swift*, Deane Swift described the reading experience that was to compose the lattice of ideas and relationships in this "Satyr ... useful and diverting."[51] Defending his relative against the aspersions of the Earl of Orrery, Deane extolled "the course of ecclesiastical history" and the Fathers of the Church Swift went through in 1697/8: "And yet I cannot help declaring upon this occasion, that I have a demonstration lying before me this very instant ... It is a book of extracts from St. CYPRIAN and St. IRENÆUS." "He has not marked in this

49 *A Tale of a Tub and Other Works*, ed. Walsh, pp. 134, 462.

50 For reasons of space, we cannot discuss in the same detail all titles which Swift read at Moor Park in 1697/8, and which fall under this thematic section.

51 *A Tale of a Tub and Other Works*, ed. Walsh, pp. 5, 6; italics inverted.

book," Deane continues, "when he began to read St. CYPRIAN; but the day, on which he completed his extract, was *Nov.* 19, 1697, and the day following he began to read St. IRENÆUS, and finished his extract from that early father, *Dec.* 12, 1697." In other words, the extent of Swift's interest in Irenaeus (and possibly in Cyprian, too) is indicated by the fact that he laboured almost a whole month over it. The bishop's detailed attack on Gnosticism, particularly in his chief work *Adversus omnes haereses*, would have been of the greatest interest to Swift while he was himself indulging in satiric attacks on Gnosticism and heretics in *A Tale of a Tub*.[52] Last but not least, Deane goes on to assure us, "in the preceding part of the same year [1697], he took some very copious extracts from SLEIDAN's commentaries, and from *Padre* PAOLO's History of the council of *Trent*, which are also at present lying upon my table" (p. 276). While these excerpts were still in Deane Swift's possession in 1755, they have since disappeared, occasioning what is perhaps a sobering conclusion: all our efforts to shed a better light on the composition of a masterpiece still as challenging as *A Tale of a Tub* will tend to be but efforts of interpreting ourselves.

This state of affairs is being exacerbated by two 'minor' problems:
first, it is difficult to account for Swift's interest in the two Fathers in the first place, to identify the *spiritus rectores* that attracted him to them; neither figures in contemporary lists with suggestions for reading in the field of theology, such as Thomas Barlow's *De studio theologiæ: or, Directions for the Choice of Books in the Study of Divinity*.[53] Second, more importantly, it is entirely unclear how Swift managed to secure an edition of St Cyprian and St Irenaeus at Moor Park in 1697/8; neither was in his own library at any stage of his career nor, to the best of our knowledge, in that of Sir William Temple.[54] Third, it is equally

52 See Dirk F. Passmann and Hermann J. Real, "*Fiat Nox: A Tale of a Tub* and the Biblical Account of Genesis under Erasure," *The Enlightenment by Night: Essays on After-Dark Culture in the Long Eighteenth Century*, eds Serge Soupel, Kevin L. Cope, and Alexander Pettit (New York: AMS, 2010), pp. 431-49 (448-49).

53 Thomas Barlow, *De studio theologiæ: or, Directions for the Choice of Books in the Study of Divinity*, ed. William Offley (Oxford: L. Lichfield, 1700); Thomas Bray, *Proposals to the Reverend Parochial Clergy ... for Promoting Lending Libraries* (London: William Hawes, 1698). The selection of topics for disputations, "the most distinctive feature of the academic course of this period," was to some extent based on "the works of the Fathers," but whether St Cyprian and St Irenaeus were among the ones chosen is unknown (Constantia Maxwell, *A History of Trinity College Dublin* [Dublin: The University Press, 1946], pp. 50-53).

54 See, in addition to Ehrenpreis, *Mr Swift*, pp. 286-87, PASSMANN AND VIENKEN IV, 185-215, who have systematically 'reconstructed' the evidence chiefly assembled in the two Münster doctoral dissertations by Jutta Winnefeld ("'Beauty without Order': Temple's Essays *Upon the Gardens of Epicurus* und *Of Heroick Virtue*") and Martin Kämper (*Sir William Temples Essays "Upon Ancient and Modern Learning" und "Of Poetry": eine historisch-kritische Ausgabe mit Einleitug und Kommentar* [Frankfurt am Main: Peter Lang,

unclear who among his acquaintances and friends could have lent Swift the editions he excerpted; we have been unable to think of any. Finally, to go by what we know of Swift's movements, Jonathan never left Moor Park for any extended period of time between January 1697 and January 1698, so that he never seems to have had an opportunity to read, let alone "abstract," the two Fathers of the Church.[55] Alternatively, it is tempting as well as logical to assume that he studied them in the detail that his florilegia suggest at an earlier phase of his career – from 1692 to 1694 while preparing for holy orders, when most of the reading for his ordination occurred,[56] earlier when at Oxford in June and July of 1692 to take his M.A.,[57] and subsequently, from January 1695 till the spring of 1696, at Kilroot, even though this impoverished and destitute Presbyterian prebend is perhaps the least likely place.[58] Given the fact that the edition Swift presumably used was the magnificent first edition of St Cyprian's complete works edited by the Bishop of Oxford, John Fell (1625-86), and published at the University Press in folio in November 1682 (ARBER I, 512), Oxford seems a better guess than any. Later, while he was at work on *A Tale of a Tub*, St Cyprian's writings, mainly short and popular treatises and letters, would have become of interest to Swift not only because of the Father's stand against the papacy but also because of the affinity of some of their themes, such as the unity, or schism, of the church ("De unitate ecclesiæ") and the character of zeal and envy ("De zelo et livore") (pp. 104-20; 221-28).

What is more, there is additional evidence accompanying Swift's reading of Lucretius and Diodorus the Sicilian to suggest that he did not read them when he said he did in 1697/8 but only a year or two later.

Swift allegedly read Lucretius three times in 1697/8. If this assumption is correct, he may have used the Cambridge text of 1675, edited by Tanneguy Lefèvre (always provided that he did not resort to an unidentified edition from Temple's library). However, we do not know at what stage he acquired the Cambridge text, and it is therefore of interest to note that Swift owned a second edition of

1995]) as well as earlier authorities on Temple (Homer E. Woodbridge, *Sir William Temple: The Man and his Work* [New York: The Modern Language Association of America, and London: Oxford University Press, 1940], and A. C. Elias, Jr, *Swift at Moor Park: Problems in Biography and Criticism* [Philadelphia: The University of Pennsylvania Press, 1983]).

55 See Paul V. Thompson, "A Jonathan Swift Daybook," typescript, Ehrenpreis Centre for Swift Studies, Münster (EC 2196), s.v. 1697 and 1698.

56 *Correspondence*, ed. Woolley, I, 104 and n6, 120-21, 122n2. See also Phillip Harth, *Swift and Anglican Rationalism: The Religious Background of "A Tale of a Tub"* (Chicago and London: The University of Chicago Press, 1961), pp. 158-61.

57 *Correspondence*, ed. Woolley, I, 116 and n3.

58 See Ehrenpreis, *Mr Swift*, pp. 150-65 (162-65); Louis A. Landa, *Swift and the Church of Ireland* (Oxford: Clarendon Press, 1954), pp. 8-24.

De rerum natura, printed at Amsterdam in 1631.[59] This he purchased in April of 1699, a year *after*, it is true, but, remarkably, it bears traces of his rather careful reading; an observation that opens up a new option: Swift used for his reading of Lucretius not the 1675 Cambridge edition but the Amsterdam school text of 1631, with the implicit consequence that Lyon's 'Account' records titles that it should not.

The second case in point is Diodorus the Sicilian, ostensibly "abstracted" by Swift in 1697/8 and an authority often invoked in early satires like *A Discourse concerning the Mechanical Operation of the Spirit* (1704) and *A Discourse of the Contests and Dissentions* (1701).[60] Diodorus was never in Swift's library at any stage, so Temple's secretary once again needed to avail himself of any of the pre-1697 editions in his patron's library, such as the massive two-volume *Bibliothecæ Historicæ libri XV*, an edition of the complete Greek text published with a Latin prose paraphrase and a commentary by the German philologist and historian Lorenz Rhodoman (1546-1606) in the town of Hanau in 1604: "*Omnia cum interpretatione Latina ... ac temporum annotatione illustrata ... Studio et labore Laurentii Rhodomani Cherusci.*" However, there is evidence hard to rebut that, in *A Discourse of the Contests and Dissentions* of 1701, Swift relied not on any of these humanist editions, which may, or may not, have been in Sir William's library, but on the English translation of Diodorus by George Booth, *The Historical Library of Diodorus the Sicilian*, published in two equally massive volumes in London in 1700, two or three years after 1697/8. The point here is not so much that Swift in 1701 repeated Booth's errors, which from the scholarly point of view may indeed be scandalous,[61] but the hypothesis this chronology necessitates: the assumption that Swift within the short period of two to three years used two different, equally heavy and unwieldy tomes of the *Bibliothēkē historikē*; more particularly, that he should have resorted to a new edition in 1701 after having mined the same author in another edition with considerable labour three years earlier. We find that hard to believe, inferring instead that Swift rather took hold of the Booth rendering from the very beginning.

The upshot of this hypothesis (for which, admittedly, there is no evidence but suspicion) is obvious: Lyon's 'Account,' allegedly a transcript of Swift's holograph, is an *inflated* list containing titles not read during what has been widely called Jonathan's great reading period at Moor Park in 1697/8 *but added*

---

59 PASSMANN AND VIENKEN II, 1122; Passmann, "Jonathan Swift as a Book Collector," pp. 48-49; *Prose Works*, V, xxxi and n5.

60 *Prose Works*, I, 186, 187, 199, 209, and 225.

61 *A Discourse of the Contests and Dissentions between the Nobles and the Commons in Athens and Rome*, ed. Frank H. Ellis (Oxford: Clarendon Press, 1967), pp. 130 and 161.

at some later stage. Of course, this leaves us with the most vexing problem to find out *which* of these titles were added at a later stage. Neither do we know *when exactly* Swift, who was notoriously unreliable with numbers, compiled his 'Account,' nor do we know in what way the compilation took place, successively (recording the titles as, or soon after, they were read) or haphazardly (recording the titles as they entered his head whenever he took them down). Unlike the 1715 inventory of Swift's library, which was drawn up by himself and whose hands as well as quills and inks allow more or less educated guesses on addenda, the 'Account' only survives in Lyon's transcript. The very fact that almost all of the titles are vaguely descriptive rather than bibliographically precise – Voyage de *Siam*, *Histoire d'Ethiopie*, Histoire de *Chypre* – makes us surmise that Swift's list (and, by implication, Lyon's transcript) is rooted in recollection by hindsight, and that, consequently, it is as reliable and trustworthy as recollections by hindsight tend to be.

Suspicion hardens when, once again, we look at the numbers, the sheer quantity of what Swift claims to have read at Moor Park in 1697/8. Soldiering on with determination and discipline, Jonathan, we learnt, grappled with **80,762** Latin and English lines of verse in a single year. But this is a far cry from the sum total. Adding up the page numbers of the works in prose – the thematically coherent sections on *Satire, Letters* and *Letter-Writing*, the *Essay* and *Characters, History* and *History* in tandem with *Travel*, not to forget the Fathers and historians of the Church he is said to have tackled at the same time – we arrive at the total of some **16,700** pages. In practical terms, this means that Jonathan would have had to read some **53** pages per day and **6.6** pages per hour provided one assumes that he ploughed on stolidly, and with the most rigorous discipline, for 300 days per annum and eight hours per diem; in the case of 250 days per annum and eight hours per diem, this figure rises to **64** pages per day and **8** pages per hour; in the case of 200 days per annum and eight hours per diem, it approximates **80** pages per day and **10** pages per hour. We doubt that this is possible, all the more so in the light of the evidence that, apart from the recorded titles in Lyon's 'Account,' Swift is bound to have additionally read unrecorded ones, ever since he had embarked on the composition of that erudite triad of *A Tale of a Tub, The Battle of the Books*, and the *Discourse concerning the Mechanical Operation of the Spirit*, whose genesis at least partly intersected with his great reading period at Moor Park in 1697/8.[62] Here, bulky tomes like Archbishop Tillotson's sermons easily spring to mind[63] or the flood

62 On the genesis of the triad, see *A Tale of a Tub and Other Works*, ed. Walsh, pp. xxxvi-xxxix.

63 PASSMANN AND VIENKEN III, 1858-60; see also Harth, *Swift and Anglican Rationalism: The Religious Background of "A Tale of a Tub"*, pp. 36-40, 44-49, 55-57, and *passim*.

of publications, both books and pamphlets, originating during the controversy about the authenticity of the letters of Phalaris and its polemical aftermath, to mention only a few.[64]

3

These are the facts, or at least some of the facts, but the facts are less 'factual' than we would like them to be, to a large extent due to the bibliographical imprecision of Lyon's 'Account.' As a result, we can never be *quite* sure about the authors and titles Swift claims to have read: neither have we been able to ascertain with any degree of certainty their languages and editions nor their years of publication and the parts Swift did read. And this is not to ignore what is, perhaps, the most exasperating feature of all, the disappearance, or even loss, of the excerpts from his commonplace books; a loss which, as long as they do not resurface, is bound to hamper all future efforts to shed a better light on the orientation and intent of a masterpiece still as challenging as *A Tale of a Tub*. Its appearance notwithstanding, the account of Swift's reading at Moor Park in 1697/8 while no doubt partly illuminating does not abolish our ignorance entirely. We realize we have said this before, but it is a thought which bears repeating.

In conclusion, we beg not to be misunderstood. We are still intentionalists, and we intend to remain so, we still uphold, and practise, the Münster 'methodology' of mining the quarry of Swift's library and reading in trying to come to grips with the problems of annotation posed by his texts, and we have no intention of discouraging our fellow-Swiftians from following that principle and, indeed, from disseminating it more widely. What we intend, however, is to advocate caution by urging fellow-scholars to resist facile and simplistic certainties. Our man, we remember, loved to play games, he loved to play at hide-and-seek, and he was thrilled to see his readers spending their time in finding out his meaning; in short, he tended to take playfulness seriously, or rather seriousness playfully. It is no coincidence that some circles still regard him as the 'enigmatic' Dean. Even so, the principle still holds.

64 See *The Battle of the Books*, ed. Hermann J. Real, with the assistance of Kirsten Juhas, Dirk F. Passmann, and Sandra Simon (Online.Swift/Ehrenpreis Centre for Swift Studies, Münster, October 2011, updated September 2017 <http://www.online-swift.de/battleofthebooks.html>).

EARLY SATIRES

Rebecca Ferguson
University of Wales, Trinity Saint David, Lampeter

His Hob-Nailed Shoes: Time as a Creature and Reformation Polemic in Swift's *A Tale of a Tub*

Abstract. This article examines the nature of Time as an anthropomorphic and emblematic entity in the early sections of *A Tale of a Tub*, most notably in relation to the "Dedication to Prince Posterity." While tracing the contextual history (mythic and literary, graphic and emblematic) which bears upon Swift's representation of the figure of Time, the essay opens up two new and significant contexts for the narrator's combat with his avowed enemy: firstly, certain visual representations of Time which depict him as a victim of assault, and secondly, a range of references in Swift's text which draw upon Reformation polemic and represent Time in the role of Catholic antagonist and Antichrist. These allusions not only widen our sense of what the *Tale*'s narrator believes he is fighting, but show how Swift is drawing together both his ludic reflections on Ancient and Modern learning and his pointed satire on "Abuses in Religion."

Time, and the agonistic struggle against Time's tyrannies, are a key concern of the modern narrator in Swift's *A Tale of a Tub*, most obviously in the early parts of the text: the "Epistle Dedicatory, to His Royal Highness Prince Posterity," which makes up one of a number of formal openings to the work, and Section I ("The Introduction") which shortly follows it.[1] In the first of these, the narrator's extended complaints express craven resentment, mounting to despair, at Time and his many outrages; Time is the professed enemy of modern authors, whose works he destroys and consigns to oblivion, and besides – as we progressively learn from the *Tale* – the Moderns have little knowledge, judgement, or finesse when it comes to Chronos and his cognate order, chronology. It does not help matters that the narrator has a weak memory, a fault to which he openly admits. In "The Introduction," by contrast, he boasts of the defeat – or at least the severe drubbing – of Time at the hands of the vengeful "Writers of and for *GRUB-STREET*;" this has been achieved, he proclaims, through their copious productions such as "Westminster *Drolleries, Delightful Tales, Compleat Jesters*, and the like" (p. 40).

1 References to the *Tale* are taken throughout from *A Tale of a Tub and Other Works*, ed. Marcus Walsh (Cambridge: Cambridge University Press, 2010) and will be given in parentheses within the text.

 | DOI:10.30965/9783846763971_007

In both of these accounts, many readers of our own age – like Swift's contemporaries – may readily identify the features by which the emblematic and personified figure of Father Time is known: the "Dedication" draws attention to his "large and terrible Scythe," "the Length and Strength, the Sharpness and Hardness of his *Nails* and *Teeth*" (p. 21), while in the countering passage from the "Introduction" we are told how the Moderns have "in these latter Ages so nobly triumph'd over *Time*; have clipt his Wings, pared his Nails, filed his Teeth, turn'd back his Hour-Glass, blunted his Scythe, and drawn the Hob-Nails out of his Shoes" (p. 40). The hob-nailed shoes – like the injurious nails – are an apparent novelty in the received image of Time, and I will give closer attention to these, along with the litany of Time's assaults, the significance of his "baneful abominable *Breath*" (p. 21), and the narrator's invectives at his arrogation of power later in my discussion. Aside from these dislikeable features, however, the Tubster's enemy presents the standard set of attributes: he has wings because he flies so swiftly, and his scythe and hour-glass are held in common with Death, since they cut down the living and warn us of our limited time on earth. His teeth are reminders not only of his damaging powers, but of the long-established entanglement of his name and history with the identity of Saturn (*chronos* being the Greek word for time and later "the personification of time,"[2] and *Kronus* [or Kronos] the Greek name of the god whom the Romans named Saturn, the *ur*-patriarch who devours his own children).[3] This fortuitous

2 See Samuel L. Macey, *Patriarchs of Time: Dualism in Saturn-Cronus, Father Time, the Watchmaker God, and Father Christmas* (Athens, Georgia, and London: The University of Georgia Press, 1987), p. 42, and Kristen Lippincott, "Timely Secrets," *Apollo*, 151, no 455 (2000), 24-29; Lippincott observes that it was the "encyclopaedists, commentators and grammarians writing during the early centuries of the middle ages" who were principally responsible for developing the now-familiar iconographic formulae for Time. Macey refers specifically to Swift's passage on defeating time as evidence that "Father Time still remained an emblem in the consciousness of eighteenth-century Englishmen" (p. 62). For a detailed contextual analysis of the handling of Time within the early pages of the *Tale*, see Sabine Baltes, "Father Time: The Emblematic and Iconographic Context of 'The Epistle Dedicatory to His Royal Highness Prince Posterity' in Swift's *Tale*," *Swift Studies*, 20 (2005), 41-50. Baltes notes the importance to both Catholic and Protestant writers of the adage that "Truth is the daughter of Time" (pp. 43-48), and underlines the contradictions implied by Swift's adaptation of this "by making Posterity the ward of Time" (p. 46).

3 See particularly Erwin Panofsky, *Studies in Iconology* (New York: Harper and Row, 1962 [1939]), pp. 69-91 (70-75), and the comments on his discussion by Edith Wilks Dolnikowski: "Although there was no god of time in the earliest Greek pantheon ... by the fourth century BCE *Kronos*' name had been changed to *Chronos* and he was widely considered to be both a Titan and the god of time ... The association of Chronos with Kronos has had a considerable influence on artistic expressions of time in western Art. Panofsky observes that Father Time is usually depicted as an old man with a scythe because Kronos, originally a god of agriculture, had those characteristics" (*Thomas Bradwardine: A View of Time and a Vision of Eternity in*

synthesis was long recognized by mythographers, and is noted in seventeenth- and eighteenth-century observations on the subject.[4] Ovid's phrase "Tempus edax rerum," "Time, devourer of [all] things,"[5] underlines the conflation, and much later classicized images of Kronos the Titan, along with Saturn the planet, accentuate the monstrosity of his child-slaughter.[6] The striking visual rendition of Time gnawing at a statue in the frontispiece of François Perrier's *Segmenta nobilium signorum et statuarum* of 1638 amplifies the ruinous force of his teeth – which are also referenced in the work's extended title – while the torso, shorn of its limbs, inevitably connotes the savagery of Kronos (Figure 6.1).[7] Similarly, in Swift's "Epistle Dedicatory," the narrator's complaint against Time's murdering infant texts in their cradles is in part an extension of the Saturnian reputation for infanticide.

Fourteenth-Century Thought [Leiden: Brill, 1995], p. 15n2). Panofsky's exclusive focus on Time as Kronos in fifteenth-century illustrations of Petrarch's *Trionfi* (1351) has, however, been criticized by Simona Cohen, who points out that there were many illustrations which "bore no relationship to the nude Saturn devouring a child or holding a scythe" (*Transformations of Time and Temporality in Medieval and Renaissance Art* [Leiden and Boston: Brill, 2014], p. 127).

4 Petro Bentio, in *Roma proprio triumphans nomine* (Paris: E. Couterot, 1654), comments: "Saturnus autem Mythologis Tempus est, imò Temporis autor: Graecè enim dicitur Κρονος, quam proprium est Temporis vocabulum [Saturn represents time or the author of time in mythology; in Greek he is called Kronos, as the word that signifies time]" (p. 82). See also Andrew Tooke, *The Pantheon of the Heathen Gods and Illustrious Heroes ... Written by Fra[nçois] Pomey* (London: Charles Harper, 1698), s.v. "Saturn": "That by *Saturn* is meant *Time*, is plain from his Greek Name ... which by one letter only is different from [the Greek word], *time*. Thus *Saturn* is painted devouring his Children and vomiting them up again; as indeed Time devours and consumes all things which it hath produced" (p. 165).

5 Ovid, *Metamorphoses*, XV, 234. Later in the same final book of the *Metamorphoses*, Ovid seems to allude to his own earlier words in concluding "Iamque opus exegi, quod nec Iovis ira nec ignis / nec poterit ferrum nec edax abolere vetustas [And now my work is done, which neither the wrath of Jove, nor fire, nor sword, nor the gnawing tooth of time shall ever be able to undo]" (ll. 871-72). The translation is that by Frank Justus Miller, *Ovid, Metamorphoses*, 2 vols (London: William Heinemann, and Cambridge, Massachusetts: Harvard University Press, 1956-58), II, 426-27.

6 The fearsome image of Saturn is highlighted in an engraving dated 1586, taken from a series depicting "Statues of Bacchus and the Seven Planets" by Philips Galle; Saturn here wields a scythe directly at a dangling infant gripped in his other hand, as if to lacerate or behead it (British Museum no 1862,0712.308). Another print from a series of months of the year, dated 1698, depicts Saturn – representing the end of December – grasping and devouring a child (BM no 1904,0711.14). Rubens completed a striking painting of him sinking his teeth into an infant's breast (1636; Prado Museum, Madrid) and an accomplished sketch of the same subject is attributed to Charles Le Brun (undated; BM no Ff,4.43).

7 The full title of Perrier's volume of Roman remains is *Segmenta nobilium signorum et statuarum quae temporis dentem invidium evasere* (Paris, 1638), clearly referencing the "envious tooth of Time" as a metonym for ruin.

FIGURE 6.1 François Perrier, Frontispiece to *Segmenta nobilium signorum et statuarum* (Paris, 1638).
Etching. British Museum Department of Prints and Drawings no 1895,1031.27.

Within this broadly classical field of reference, the narrator's unpersuasive boast that the Moderns, identified as the Grub Street hacks, have latterly "*triumph'd*" over Time (my italics) suggests most immediately the military triumphs staged by the Romans, designed as a public display of a vanquished enemy. The reader might equally think of other developments of the "triumph": Petrarch's celebrated *Trionfi*, including the "Trionfo del Tempo,"[8] or the long history of literary, iconographic, and spectacular 'Triumphs' celebrating victories – some worldly and political, others metaphysical, moral, spiritual or allegorical – of one antagonist, or set of antagonists, over another.[9] Throughout the seventeenth century, Lord Mayor's Day in London offered a notable opportunity for such pageants, and they remained very popular up to the early eighteenth century.[10] In Swift's passage, however, the ancient military triumphs

8 In Petrarch's sequence, one allegorical figure defeats another, and there is no final immortality even for the greatest works of human art; although Death is overcome by Fame, Time in his turn defeats Fame, and in the Christian perspective Eternity finally triumphs over Time.

9 Two instances among Protestant texts, for example, are John Foxe's apocalyptic play *Christus Triumphans* (1556), in *Two Latin Comedies by John Foxe the Martyrologist*, ed. and trans. John Hazel Smith (London: Cornell, 1973); and Andrew Willet, *Ecclesia triumphans: that is, The Joy of the English Church, for the Happie Coronation of the Most Virtuous and Pious Prince, Iames [I] … Defendour of the Faith, &c.* (Cambridge and London: John Legat, 1603). In the latter title, "triumphans" has accentuated significance, in so far as the Church Triumphant is itself a Roman Catholic designation for the souls of the faithful in heaven, here appropriated to the cause of the Protestant Church in England. Daniel Featley, Protestant author of *The Romish Fisher Cavght and Held in his Owne Net: or, A True Relation of the Protestant Conference and Popish Difference. A Iustification of the One, and Refutation of the Other* (London: by H. L. for Robert Milbourne, 1624), predicts that after this disputation "I well knew, and foretold … that whatsoeuer the issue of the combate were, Master Deane of Carlile [Dr White] and my selfe, should be notwithstanding conquered *in effigie*, and led in triumph in many a Pageant at *Doway, Bruxels, Rhemes*, and *Rome*" (sig.п3v).

10 Pageants for Lord Mayor's Day were held in London – though not consistently – from the sixteenth through to the early years of the eighteenth century; they were conceived above all as "triumphs," presenting a display of civic and political power to patriotic citizens. See, for example, Thomas Dekker, *Troia-Nova Triumphans: London Triumphing, or the Solemne, Magnificent, and Memorable Receiving of that Worthy Gentleman, Sir John Swinnerton, Knight, into the City of London* (London: Nicholas Okes, 1612), and particularly Dekker's introductory passage extolling the delight and appropriateness of Triumphs for these occasions. In Dekker's schema, the key figures set in opposition to each other are Envy and Fame. The 1672 celebrations were also entitled "London Triumphant," those of 1687 "London's Triumph, or the Goldsmith's Jubilee," and those of 1691 (drawn up by Elkanah Settle) "The Triumphs of London." For a fuller description of the records for each year's display, see Frederick William Fairholt, *Lord Mayors' Pageants: Being Collections towards a History of These Annual Celebrations, with Specimens of the Descriptive Pamphlets Published by the City Poets* (London: T. Richards, 1843), Parts 1-2.

are more specifically suggested by Time's appearance in his distinctive footwear, his "hob-nailed shoes."[11] These are surely the *caligae* of the Roman soldier, against which Juvenal warns the reader twice in his satires, and which Dryden translates in both instances by the phrase "Hob-nail'd Shoos;" they are damaging enough to crush a victim's feet or leave bloody imprints on a hapless citizen's legs.[12] In wearing them, Time appears not only as a militant figure, but as a gracelessly aggressive one, liable to trample on others or strike at their shins like Juvenal's loutish soldiers. Regarding the other assaults that the narrator brags of having made on Time, "Par[ing] his nails" is a phrase that familiarly meant "disempowering,"[13] while "clipping the wings" has the same commonplace meaning; at the same time, it plays with deeper irony on the widespread topos of Time himself clipping the wings of Cupid (Figure 6.2). Representations of this allegorical subject abound in visual art of the seventeenth century,[14] and

11 So far as I can determine, visual representations of Time always show him barefoot.

12 *The Satires of Decimus Junius Juvenalis: Translated into English Verse, by Mr. Dryden and Several Other Eminent Hands* (London: Jacob Tonson, 1693). Satire III (ll. 392-99) complains of how the walker is crushed, pressed, tripped, elbowed, and begrimed in the city crowds, while "some Rogue-Souldier, with his Hob-nail'd Shoos, / Indents his Legs behind in bloody rows" (p. 48). Satire XVI (ll. 34-39) advises the citizen not to enter into legal complaints against soldiers, who can wreak bitter revenge on one's legs:

But would'st Thou Friend who hast two Legs alone,
(Which Heav'n be Prais'd, Thou yet may'st call Thy own)
Would'st Thou to run the Gantlet These expose
To a whole Company of Hob-nail'd Shoos?
Sure the good Breeding of Wise Citizens
Shou'd teach 'em more good Nature to their Shins. (p. 312)

A note on the latter passage explains: "*Hob nail'd Shoos*. The *Roman* Souldiers wore Plates of Iron under their Shoos, or stuck them with Nails; as Countrymen do now" (p. 315).

13 *A Tale of a Tub and Other Works*, ed. Walsh, p. 353n41. See also William Winstanley, *The Protestant Almanack for the Year from the Incarnation of Iesus Christ, 1669* (Cambridge, 1669), "Epistle Dedicatory," where the reason for the Pope's not having excommunicated kings or princes for some time is said to be that "The Pope's Nails were paired [*sic*], and his Teeth knock'd out" (sig. A3r).

14 See Otto van Veen, *Amorum Emblemata* (Antwerp: Henricus Swingenius, 1608), pp. 236-37, Pierre Mignard, "Time Clipping Cupid's Wings" (1694) (Denver Art Museum), Francesco Furini's early seventeenth-century painting of the same subject, Johan Heinrich Schönfeld's "Allegory of Time (Chronos and Eros)" from the 1630s (Galleria Nazionale d'Arte Antica, Rome), and a work described as being from the "Circle of Charles Le Brun," "Chronos Clipping Cupid's Wings in the Presence of Venus and Mars" (listed in Blouin's Art Sales Index, and now in private hands). Schönfeld's painting shows a particularly radical shearing of the two wings in their entirety, with Mercury delivering one of them to the hand of Chronos and dropping the other at his feet. Constantijn Huygens, Jr, who maintained a constant presence in London during the years of 1688-97 (the period of the War of the Grand Alliance), also owned a striking painting of "Saturn Clipping the

FIGURE 6.2 François Perrier, *Time Clipping Cupid's Wings* (1632-33).
Etched print. British Museum Department of Prints and Drawings no 1874,0808.969.

the disarming of Cupid by either his mother[15] or Time also has an extended literary history; indeed the rhetoric of the Tubster's boast of thrashing Time, in which he lists the weapons he has wrecked, closely echoes that of Venus' demand for vengeance against Cupid in Apuleius' *The Golden Ass*:

> How shall I repress this beast? … to her [Sobriety] must I have recourse for help … who may correct thee sharply, take away thy quiver, deprive thee of thy arrowes, unbend thy bow, quench thy fire, and which is more subdue thy body with punishment and when that I have rased and cut off this thy haire … and when I have clipped thy wing … then shall I think to have revenged myself sufficiently for the injury which thou hast done.[16]

While the irony of Swift's reversed-role depiction of Time being subjected to the violence he traditionally practises may appear as a new and witty conception, it is not in fact unique; at least two visual renditions of that subject had appeared in Simon Vouet's paintings "Father Time Overcome by Love, Hope and Beauty" (1627) and "Saturn [or Father Time] Conquered by Amor, Venus and Hope" (1645/6).[17] The second of these was reproduced as an etching

---

Wings of Cupid" by Van Dyck, to which he refers in his diary entry for 20 February 1691; see Rudolf M. Dekker, *Family, Culture, and Society in the Diary of Constantijn Huygens, Jr., Secretary to Stadholder-King William of Orange* (Leiden: Brill, 2013), p. 86. Concerning Lord Devonshire's request to buy this painting, and Huygens's refusal to sell it, Dekker remarks that "Huygens was not an art dealer and did not want to part with this highlight of his collection" (p. 80).

15 Examples include Andrea Alciato's "Cupid Punished," in *Emblematum libellus* (Venice, 1546; the first edition of the second group of Alciato's emblems) and Charles Le Brun, "Venus and Minerva Clipping Cupid's Wings," *c.*1655 (Museo de Arte de Ponce).

16 Apuleius' text dates from the late second century AD; the passage cited is taken from *The Golden Asse of Lucius Apuleius: Translated out of Latin by William Adlington Anno 1566* ([n.p.]: Simpkin, *et al.*, 1925 [1922]). A similar scenario and similar rhetoric appear again in Petrarch's *Trionfi* ("The Triumph of Chastity"), where Laura's chastity defeats Amor, or earthly love, on whom she and other virtuous heroines revenge themselves by completely disarming him:

> *Lucrece* came
> On her right hand: *Penelope* was by,
> Those broke his bow, and made his arrowes ly
> Split on the ground, and pull'd his plumes away
> From off his wings …
> it griev'd Love much to go
> Anothers prisoner, expos'd to scorne,
> Who to command whole Empires seemed borne

(*The Triumphs of Love: Chastitie, Death. Translated out of Petrarch by* [*Mistress*] *Anna Hume* [Edinburgh: Evan Tyler, 1644], pp. 64, 66).

17 We cannot be certain that the titles specifying "Father Time" or "Saturn" were of Vouet's choosing, especially when the attributes of the two are so nearly interchangeable. I think

by Michel Dorigny in the 1640s,[18] and – most suggestively when we consider the period of the *Tale*'s composition – another mezzotint version was produced by John Smith between 1680 and 1690 (Figure 6.3).[19] Both of Vouet's compositions show the antagonists tearing at Saturn's or Time's wings and pulling his hair, while his hourglass and scythe lie useless near his feet;[20] in the earlier of the two, Cupid is energetically pulling out Time's feathers with his teeth, leaving the plumes strewn on the ground, while Hope is swinging her anchor at his head. It is entirely possible that Swift had seen Smith's mezzotint of Vouet's later painting, but this has to remain a matter of speculation;[21] part of its importance is that here Time meets his fate at the hands of theological agents, Hope being one and – if we connect Amor or Love with the frequent emblematic presentation of this figure as *amor divinus* – another.[22]

Thus far, I have focused chiefly on classical and vernacular analogues for Swift's rendition of Time's attributes and the physical counter-assault on Time. There is, however, another cultural context for his representation, one which seems most apparent in the "Dedication to … Prince Posterity," but which may also connect suggestively with the figuration of Time from Section I of the *Tale*. Within the exaggerated pleas and lamentations of the "Dedication," it is difficult not to hear parodic echoes of both the arguments and discursive terms of Reformation polemic. To begin with, on the broadest front, the accusations against Time's tyranny, his excising the Moderns' texts from the annals of literature and his destruction of the books' bodies, above all the interposition of his "*insolent*" (p. 21) self between the authors and their hoped-for

---

it can be assumed, from the presence of Hope as an ecclesiastical virtue, that Time is the subject in both paintings.

18 An album of prints based on Vouet's works is held in the British Museum Department of Prints and Drawings, Museum no 1841,1211.39; Dorigny's print also appears as Museum no X,6.65.

19 British Museum Department of Prints and Drawings, Museum no 1876,1111.41; another copy of this print is in the National Portrait Gallery, London; NPG D11749.

20 The two paintings are respectively in the Prado Museum, Madrid, and the Musée du Berry, Bourges (France).

21 Another print after Bernard Picart, representing Cupid clipping Time's wings and entitled "L'Amour enchaine le Tems," is in the British Museum (no 1914,0214.256). The date of this image is estimated to be between 1705 and 1713. On the theme of *Amor Vincit Tempus*, see also Macey, *Patriarchs of Time*, p. 61.

22 On the graphic representation of *amor divinus*, see Els Stronks, *Negotiating Differences: Word, Image and Religion in the Dutch Republic* (Leiden: Brill, 2011), p. 60, and John Manning, *The Emblem* (London: Reaktion, 2002), p. 166. The Catholic emblem book of Otto Vaenius, *Amoris Divini Emblemata* (Antwerp: Martinus Nutius and Joannes Meursius, 1615) is one important example of this development from Eros (Cupid) to Divine Love.

FIGURE 6.3 John Smith, "Love, Hope, and Beauty, All together strive," after the engraving by Michel Dorigny of Simon Vouet, "Father Time Conquered by Amor, Venus and Hope" (1645/6).
Mezzotint, 1680-1690. The text accompanying Dorigny's print identifies the figure under attack as Saturn – mistakenly, in my view – but the verses below Smith's mezzotint clearly indicate Time as the 'old Fugitive.'

life in Posterity, all evoke long-standing Protestant denunciations of Rome.[23] The Moderns cannot gain the ear of Posterity (akin to God, or Immortality, or simply other Christian souls) because Time, like the Roman Church and the Pope himself, stands in as an obstructive intercessor. Other more specific analogues chime with the details of the Tubster's language and imagery. Time is said to have "usurped the *Priesthood*" (p. 22 [italics reversed]);[24] he has maliciously brought to nothing the "*never-dying* Works" of the Moderns,

23 The argument may be applied to souls which are damned by the corrupted Roman faith, and equally to books per se. See Richard Baxter, *Church-History of the Government of Bishops and their Councils Abbreviated … and a True Account of the Most Troubling Controversies and Heresies till the Reformation* (London: John Kidgell, 1680): "We may conjecture at former times by our own: We see now, that among the most Reformed Churches, too often the most worldly part are uppermost … it's they that make the noise, are the noted part that carry the name, and that Histories write of. A few men got into places of power, seem to be all the Church, or Nation … They may give Laws; They may have the power of Press and Pulpit, so that nothing shall be published but what they will" (p. 18, §43). Baxter's argument is that certain Reformed Churches have come to behave just as the Romanists have done in abusing their powers and censoring all written and spoken opposition.

24 Not only is the term "Priesthood" telling, but the Pope's "usurping" of powers (over other Bishops, Emperors, or Kings, nations and the conscience of the believer) is a habitual charge in Protestant invective. See Baxter, *Church-History of the Government of Bishops and their Councils Abbreviated*, pp. 189, 358 ("*the presumptuous usurpations of the Pope*"), and John Favour, *Antiquitie Triumphing over Noveltie: Whereby it Is Proved that Antiquitie Is a True and Certaine Note of the Christian Catholicke [ie. Reformed] Church and Verity, against All New and Upstart Heresies Advancing themselves against the Religious Honour of Old Rome* (London: Richard Field, 1619), where the Pope is said to have achieved domination by "first a claim of superioritie, then a title of universalitie, then an usurpation of powerfull regalitie, at last a possession of tyrannicall supremacie" (p. 370). The virulently anti-Catholic Bishop Thomas Barlow also inveighs against "*Papal Usurpations*, and Anti-monarchical practices," pronouncing that "the Original Error, from which the rest follow, is that vast Supremacy, which the Pope … Usurps over Kings," and that he persecutes all those who oppose his "Usurp'd Greatness and Worldly Interest" (*Popery: or, The Principles and Positions Approved by the Church of Rome* [London: T. Newcomb, 1679], pp. 4, 53, 94). See also John Williams, *Christianity Abused by the Church of Rome, and Popery Shewed to Be a Corruption of it* (London: Walter Kettilby, 1679), p. 3: "Our Saviour expressly cautions the Apostles against any such Usurpation" as the Pope's claim to be Christ's Vicar or head of the Church; Edward Welchman, *A Dialogue betwixt a Protestant Minister and a Romish Priest: Wherein Is Shew'd that the Church of Rome Is Not the Only True Church*, 3rd ed. (London: Joseph Downing, 1723): "I am sure [the Catholic believers] sin by such an absolute *subjection* of their *Faith* to you, and so do you too, in Usurping such a *Dominion* over it" (p. 13); and [anonymous], *Questions and Answers concerning the Two Religions, viz. that of the Church of England, and … the Church of Rome* (London: Joseph Downing, 1724): "The Superiority [the Roman Church] claims is nothing but Usurpation" … "As the throwing off the Power of the Pope of *Rome*, was one Part of the Reformation; so … we did not throw off Obedience to a lawful Sovereign, but Subjection to an Usurpation" (pp. 25, 36).

which – it is strongly implied – he has contrived to make disappear, just as the Catholics had striven to do with the texts and records of all reputed "hereticks" and Protestants,[25] so that they are "devoted to unavoidable Death" and barred from "*Immortality*" (pp. 21-22).[26] He is an "*insolent*" (p. 21)[27] who stands in the way of the "glorious Tryals" (p. 20)[28] that enlightened Posterity might otherwise make in perusing the works of the Moderns, and has promoted himself with "an unparallel'd Ambition and Avarice" (p. 22); whatever his other villainies, "Avarice" is not a vice of which Time generally stands accused, whereas in

25 A standard argumentative challenge put to Protestants concerned the existence or "visibility" of their tenets prior to Luther's time; to this it was generally countered that almost all of the written history was either owned or manipulated by their oppressors. See Matthew Poole, *A Dialogue between a Popish Priest and an English Protestant: Wherein the Principal Points and Arguments of Both Religions Are Truly Proposed, and Fully Examined* (London: T. R., 1672): "That little that was written, was written by men of the times, who would not do their Enemies that honour and right to put them into their Histories ... such Book or Books in which they were recorded, might either be lost by the injury of time, or suppressed by the tyranny of your Predecessors [the Romanists], who made it their business ... that the name and remembrance of true Christians might be blotted out of the earth" (pp. 48-49).

26 The phrases suggest not only the silencing of texts, but the Catholics' responsibility for leading countless souls to damnation.

27 See John Foxe, *Actes and Monuments of Matters Most Speciall and Memorable, Happening in the Church: With a Universall Historie of the Same*, 2 vols (London: Company of Stationers, 1610), I, 1174 ("the insolencie, wrong and violence on the popes part"), and the English translation of Pierre du Moulin's *The Papal Tyranny, as it Was Exercised over England for Some Ages: Represented by the Late Reverend Doctor Peter Du Moulin* (London: H. Brome, 1674): "It was a principal Engine of the Pope to bring Kings under his Feet, for him to tread upon their Necks, and to prey upon *England* with the highest Insolency" (sig. B1r).

28 The phrase "glorious Tryals" connotes martyrdom and/or agonistic spiritual revelation, while it was often claimed that the Pope feared above all things the exposure of Catholics to Protestant literature. Matthew Poole observes to an imaginary Papist counterpart that "the Controversies between your Church and ours, are by Gods blessing ... brought to this pass, that I am perswaded there is nothing wanting to the Conviction of divers of you, but a free and diligent perusal of their [Protestants'] Books ... This your Priests knowing, it is their great design to keep you from looking into them" (*A Dialogue between a Popish Priest, and an English Protestant* ["To the People of the Romish Church"], sig. A1r). In John Jewel's core defence of the Church of England, the Romanists are accused of distorting everything that the Protestants put forward: "These folke falsely accuse and slaunder all our doings ... and for malice doo so misconstrue and deprave all our sayings & doings, as though it were impossible, that any thing could be rightly spoken or done by us ... They neither truly nor sincerely ... but darkly and craftily charge and batter us with lyes, and doo abuse the blindnesse and fondnesse of the people, together with the ignorance of Princes, to cause us to be hated" (*The Apologie of the Church of England* [London: J. R. for Thomas Chard, 1600], pp. 15-16).

Protestant polemic both ambition and monstrous greed are constantly underlined as core vices of the Papacy.[29] In addition, Time acts as the "*Governour*" of Posterity (a term repeated five times, and always set in italics), arrogating total power to himself in that role and taking care "to keep [Posterity] in almost an universal Ignorance of our Studies, which it is Your inherent Birth-right to inspect" (p. 20). "*Governour*" appears, in this context, a significant term in so far as the Pope's claim to hold the position of Governor was a central issue for the Reformists; it was repeatedly pointed out that, in the unfolding course of impositions which led to the Pope's arrogated power as Supreme Head of the Church, he had proclaimed himself to be a Governor over fellow Bishops, as well as assuming authority over secular Emperors, Kings, and Princes,[30] and all

29 See William Guild, *Anti-Christ Pointed and Painted out in his True Colours: or, The Pope of Rome Proven to Bee that Man of Sinne and Sonne of Perdition, Fore-Prophesied in Scripture* (Aberdeen: James Brown, 1655), p. 43: "This beast [the Roman Church represented in the Pope] did arise out of the earth, as being hatched out of earthlie avarice and ambition, as Gregorie [the Great] speaketh of *Antichrist*, calling him therefore, *The King of Pryde, who by usurping the Title of Universall Bishop would exalt Himself like Lucifer above all his fellow Angels*." Samuel Mason (a convert from Rome to the Church of England) testifies that "the covetousness of the Bishop[s] of *Rome* for these several hundred of years past have increased more than ordinary: First their covetousness caused them to forget God ... Secondly, it hath caused them to accept of the earthly pleasures of this world, [and] ... to assume to themselves the Titles due to Emperors, Kings and Princes;" John Nalson and Robert Ware, *Foxes and Firebrands: or, A Specimen of the Danger and Harmony of Popery and Separation*, 2nd ed. (Dublin: Joseph Ray, 1682), pp. 17-18. Compare Foxe, *Acts and Monuments*, 9th ed., 3 vols (London: Company of Stationers, 1684), I, 3, condemning the "pomp and pride ... riches and superfluity ... avarice insatiable, ambition intolerable" of the Roman Church, and John Jewel, *An Epistle Written by the Reverend Father in God John Jewel ... to Seignor Scipio, a Venetian Gentleman* (London: T. H. for Richard Chiswell, 1685), pp. 153, 163, censuring "the Avarice and Insolence of the Court of Rome" (p. 163) and the Pope as "an Ambitious Covetous Proud Man" (p. 177). Thomas Harris characterizes popery as "a Mixture of Ambition and Covetousness ... Her chief Object is to aggrandise its [sic] own Faction, and to secure to herself the Riches and Government of the whole Earth" (*Popery and Slavery Display'd: Containing the Character of Popery, and a Relation of Popish Cruelties*, 3rd ed. [London: C. Corbett and T. Harris, 1745], pp. 4, 8; chiefly drawn from the translated works of Bartolomé de las Casas, 1484-1566).

30 Jewel's *Apologie* delivers an extended and emphatic complaint at the Papacy's assigning sole power of judgement in religious matters to itself, having "aforehand condemned us with out judgement," thereby excluding "Princes" (secular monarchs) from having any role or education in such matters (see pp. 243-85). Consequently, princes no longer "understand the state of their owne *Churches*" (p. 258), and "through their owne lack of understanding, and through their owne blindness these [Papists] have them fast yoked, & in their danger" (p. 276). In contrast, the Old Testament patriarchs and prophets were often also "Civill Magistrate[s]" like Moses (pp. 264-65), and the early Christian churches settled difficulties through "Counsels of Free Citties, as of *Carthage* under *Cyprian*" (p. 287). A particular sore point for Protestant commentators was the exclusion of

professed Christians. For obvious reasons, that title was resisted and resented by many English Protestant commentators, especially those with strong monarchist loyalties;[31] indeed, the word "Princes" (as in Swift's "Prince Posterity") was very commonly used to signify secular rulers generally.[32] The Latin word "gubernator" featured notably in an address which was considered to be one of the earliest and more egregious cases of blasphemy concerning the Pope, the oration of Christopher Marcellus to Julius II in 1512:

> Cura denique, ut salutem quam dedisti nobis, & vitam & spiritum non amittamus. Tu enim Pastor. Tu medicus. Tu gubernator. Tu cultor. Tu denique alter Deus in terries [Take care that we do not lose that salvation, that life and breath which you have given us. You are our shepherd. You our physician. You our governor. You our husbandman. You are, finally, another God upon earth].[33]

---

reformist secular rulers, "*Christian kings* and good *Princes*," from the Convocation of the Council of Trent (Jewel, *The Apologie of the Church of England*, pp. 258-59).

31 Thomas Barlow thunders: "That *England* is a *Monarchy*, the *Crown Imperial*, and our Kings SUPREME Governors, and SOLE SUPREME Governors of this Realm, and all other Dominions, will (I believe, I am sure it should) be granted ... In our Oath of Supremacy we Swear, that the King is, the ONELY SUPREME *Governor*. SUPREME, so none (not the Pope) above Him" (*Popery*, p. 4). See also Harris, *Popery and Slavery Display'd*, berating the Pope's claim to be a governor above the "*Protestant* Prince or Govenor" (p. 71); and Jewel, *The Apologie of the Church of England*, p. 44: "There can bee no one mortall creature, which is able to comprehend, or conceive in his minde the Universall Church, that is to wit, all the parts of the world, much lesse able rightly, and duely to put them in order, and to governe them."

32 As two examples among many, see John Savage, *Rome's Conviction: or, A Vindication of the Original Institution of Christianity, in Opposition to the Many Usurpations of the Church of Rome, and their Frequent Violation of Divine Right* (London: G. Kunholt, 1683), pp. 7-8: "A considerable part of this sublunary World, are wrought into a belief, That the Church of *Rome* is the only Oracle of the Universe, whose Doctrine is always true ... how many Kings and Princes are swayed by this perswasion? ... Princes have commonly Divines, Preachers, and Confessors of their own Subjects and Nations, to whose conduct they presume they may safely trust the regulating of their Consciences;" and Guild, *Anti-Christ Pointed and Painted out*, p. 83: "The Pope exalteth himself above all Princes or Magistrates."

33 The address was delivered at the fourth session of the Fifth Lateran Council, which commenced in 1512; I have followed the punctuation of the transcript published separately as *Christophori Marcelli ... In quarta Lateranen[sis] Concilii Sessione Habita Oratio. IIII Idus Decembris M.D.XII* (I Mazochium, 1513). It is recorded in its full context in the decretal records, and in many replications of these, including *Acta Conciliorum et Epistolae Decretales, ac Constitutiones Summorum Pontificum; ab anno MCCCCXXXVIII ad annum MDXLIX* (Paris: Ex Typographia Regia, 1714). The whole passage as cited above is repeated as proof of Papal "*Pride*" and "*Insolence*" by Richard Baxter in *The Successive Visibility of the Church of which the Protestants Are the Soundest Members* (London: R. W. for Nevil Simmons, 1660), pp. 178, 181-82. The translation is mine.

Although the words "Deus in terris" may seem the most outrageous of these, the Nonconformist Richard Baxter, writing in 1660, stresses that Julius repudiated none of the laudatory terms, and fixes on the word "Governour" as a title that is as glaringly impious as the culminating claim: "Brethren, as such, are no subjects: and therefore if the Pope Rule men, but as Brethren, he rules them not by Governing authority at all."[34] Again, Baxter accosts his antagonist, the Catholic William Johnson, on the viability of that term:

> Is not the very life of the Cause between you and us, whether the Pope be the Universal Head of the Church, vice Christi. & vicarius Christi? Are not these the most common titles the Papists give them, and that they take unto themselves? Nay look back in your own papers here pag. 6 [35] whether you say not that they are [Instituted Governours in Christs place of his whole Visible Church]."[36]

Another of Swift's references to papal insolence is the Tubster's seemingly ordinary complaint against the "Sharpness and Hardness" of Time's "*Teeth* and *Nails*." To a reader acquainted with Reformation literature, this might well be a reminder of one of Pope Gregory VII's more overweening declarations, delivered at the time of the Castilian crisis in 1080, when one of his legates in Spain had returned a scandalizing report to him on affairs in that country.[37]

---

34 Baxter, *The Successive Visibility of the Church*, pp. 176-77. Baxter cites "*Binnius pag.* 562, 563, 564" as his own source (p. 182), and views the address as further evidence that the successive Popes represent Antichrist. He harangues his Catholic adversary: "If you say that the Pope accepteth not this; I answer that it was in an oration spoken in a Generall Council, in his presence, without contradiction, yea by his own command, as the Oratour professeth" (p. 182).

35 The page reference is clearly to Johnson's own notes.

36 Baxter, *The Successive Visibility of the Church*, p. 177. Italics and square brackets in original; the square brackets indicate Baxter's quoting of Johnson's exact words. Compare Jewel, *The Apologie of the Church of England*, p. 176, citing Bernard of Clairvaux's words in chastising Papal corruption of the Scriptures: "'What then shall I say heere, ô yee principall posts [pillars] of religion, ô ye Archgovernors of Christes Church: is this that your reverence which yee give to Gods Word?'" and his attack on the Pope's and Cardinals' arrogance: "For it is a common saying with them, that, *If Christ him selfe, or the Apostles were alive againe, they could neither better, nor more Godly governe Gods Church, then it is at this present Governed by them*" (p. 212).

37 The legate was one Cardinal Richard; for the context of the episode, see H. E. J. Cowdry, *Pope Gregory VII, 1073-1085* (Oxford: Clarendon Press, 1998), pp. 476-78, and Walter Ullmann, *The Growth of Papal Government in the Middle Ages: The Ideological Relation of Clerical to Lay Power*, 2nd ed. (London: Methuen, 1962), pp. 304-5. This was one of the first instances of papal or sacerdotal power being exercised through force against a secular leader, and Ullmann notes: "In this category of repression by police action will soon come also the persecution of heretics" (p. 305). Gregory VII was a particular object of scorn and opprobrium for many Reformists; Thomas Barlow refers to him as "that Prodigy of

Gregory sends word via Hugh, Abbot of Cluny, that if the people will not depose their king[38] for his offences, he himself will not find it too heavy a task to come over with a force and impose hard and sharp punishment.[39] Again, the episode and the missive's phrasing drew the attention of Richard Baxter in his *Church-History of the Government of Bishops and their Councils* (1680), where he translates the Pope's threatening words as follows:

> For we think meet to signifie to him by you, that we will excommunicate him if ... he correct not his fault, and will solicite all the faithful in the parts of *Spain* to his confusion: And if they be not obedient to my command, I will not think much to travel into *Spain* my self, and there to endeavor *dura et aspera, Things hard and sharp against him* as an enemy of the Christian religion.

Baxter added to this passage: "O brave Pope! had not these men a notable Knack or hap that could sit and talk down Emperors, and Kings, and subdue and dispose of Kingdoms, by sitting at home and talking big, and telling them that St. *Peter* was angry with them?"[40] It is important to underline that this episode cemented the reality of the powers set down in or around 1075 through the *Dictatus Papae*, whereby the universal jurisdiction of the Bishop of Rome was proclaimed. From this time, the Pope asserted his precedence over secular rulers, assumed the right to absolve subjects of their duty of allegiance to kings

wickedness and Papal Tyranny" (*Popery*, p. 11), while Pierre du Moulin comments: "The height of the Popes Power and Glory, and together the depth, and as it were the midnight of the darkest ignorance, was from the year 1073 upon which *Gregory* the VII. entred into the Papal See, and the year 1517 when *Leo* the X ... began to sell Heaven for ready money" (*The Papal Tyranny, as it Was Exercised over England for Some Ages*, p. 2). A prefatory account in the ninth edition of Foxe's *Book of Martyrs* (1684) remarks that the "time of Antichrist, and loosing of Satan, or desolation of the Church" encompassed a period "in which ... both Doctrine and sincerity of Life was utterly almost extinguished: namely, in the chief Heads and Rulers of this West Church, through the means of the *Roman* Bishops, especially counting from *Gregory* the seventh, called *Hildebrand, Innocentius* the third, and Friers which with him crept in" (*Acts and Monuments*, I, 1). See also Guild, *Anti-Christ Pointed and Painted out*, pp. 81-82.

38 Alphonso VI.

39 The Latin words of the letter are: "Qui si minus praeceptioni nostrae obedirent, non gravem existimaremus laborem nos ad Hispaniam proficisci et adversum eum, quemadmodum Christianae religionis inimicum, dura et aspera moliri." Cited in Ullmann, *The Growth of Papal Government in the Middle Ages*, p. 304n3.

40 Baxter, *Church-History of the Government of Bishops and their Councils Abbreviated*, p. 360, §52.

and princes who incurred his displeasure, and claimed an exclusive right to adopt imperial insignia.[41]

In addition to these anti-Catholic allusions, Swift's "Dedication" highlights Time's role as a tyrant who not only destroys texts but martyrs them: "Unhappy Infants, many of them barbarously destroyed, before they have so much as learnt their *Mother-Tongue* to beg for Pity. Some he stifles in their Cradles ... Some he flays alive, others he tears Limb from Limb" (pp. 21-22).[42] The detail

41 Henry Jones, in *A Sermon of Antichrist, Preached at Christ-Church, Dublin, Nov. 12, 1676* (London: Nathaniel Ponder, 1679), notes that "in this *Gregory* 7. is by *Popish* writers that glory given, that he was *Imperii Pontificii fundator*; others his Predecessours attempted the reaching at temporal power, but [it] was not till now attained" (p. 13).

42 Swift was surely aware of records concerning the fate of the Waldensians and their infants in a campaign of persecution in 1488; among other sources, details are recounted in Clarke's *A Generall Martyrologie Containing a Collection of all the Greatest Persecutions which Have Befallen the Church of Christ from the Creation to our Present Times* (London: A. M. for Thomas Underhill and John Rothwell, 1651). Clarke's narrative states:

> But when [the troops] came to the valley, they found no inhabitants; for they were all retired into their Caves in the high mountains, having carried their little children ... with them. Then did this cruel Lieutenant cause much wood to be laid to the mouths of the caves, and set it on fire, so that some were choaked with smoak; others burnt with the fire ... and if any stirred out, they were presently slain by the souldiers.
>
> In this Persecution, there were found within the Caves, *four hundred infants stifled in their cradles*, or in the arms of their dead mothers" (*Generall Martyrologie*, 2nd ed. [London: Thomas Radcliffe, 1660], p. 113 [my italics]).

In the margin of the text against these passages, the words "Barbarous cruelties" appear, perhaps replicated in Swift's phrase "barbarously destroyed," although such phrases had common currency in relation to atrocities generally. I have not found any parallel detail on the infants' fate in Foxe's accounts of this group, although he mentions the use of smoke to murder the Waldensians in hiding; nor is the episode covered in Morland's *History of the Evangelical Churches of the Valleys of Piemont* (see below), but the account quoted above appears almost verbatim in the translated French text of Jean Paul Perrin, *Luthers Fore-Runners: or, A Cloud of Witnesses, Deposing for the Protestant Faith. Gathered together in the Historie of the Waldenses, who for Divers Hundred Yeares before Luther Successively Opposed Popery ... Translated out of the French by Samson Lennard* (London: Richard Field, John Beale, *et al.*, 1624), Book 2, Chapter 1, pp. 32-33.

The third edition of Clarke's *Martyrologie* (1677) also includes a series of memorable woodcuts, within which Figure 6 (opposite p. 125) shows at the top left "Som [Waldensians] smothered in Caves on ye mountains," showing the fire and smoke at the mouth of the cave, with a fourth image of bodies being dismembered and legs and arms scattered about. The Waldensians were particularly important to the Reformers' accounts of their cause, as an example of an enduring pre-Reformation sect which consistently refused to conform to Rome despite repeated campaigns against them, including those of the mid-seventeenth century; they are cited as evidence of the pre-history of Protestantism by Poole (*A Dialogue between a Popish Priest and an English Protestant*, p. 50), and the more contemporary persecutions are highlighted in Clarke, "A Narrative of the bloody cruelties which were exercised against the Protestants of the Valleys of *Piemont* during of these sufferings, most distinctively the mass stifling of infants, may well be derived from the Dissenter Samuel Clarke's *Generall Martyrologie*, first printed in 1651 and later adorned with illustrations, although Clarke's account of the smothering of several hundred Waldensian children who are described as being "stifled in their cradles" in 1488 is repeated in other works concerning this pre-Reformation denomination (Figure 6.4). Swift himself owned a particularly important illustrated text on the Waldensians (*History of the Evangelical Churches of the Valleys of Piemont*) compiled by Sir Samuel Morland, an ambassador who was centrally involved in the negotiations for their defence in the mid-seventeenth century.[43] "The value of the *History* as propaganda was

the heat of the late Massacre in *April, Anno 1665*," in his *Generall Martyrologie* (1660), pp. 418-31, John Milton's sonnet 18, "On the Late Massacre in Piedmont" (1655), and the accounts of the 1655 massacre and related transactions in Samuel Morland's *The History of the Evangelical Churches of the Valleys of Piemont: Containing a Most Exact Geographical Description of the Place, and a Faithfull Account of the Doctrine, Life, and Persecutions of the Ancient Inhabitants; together with a Most Naked and Punctual Relation of the Late Bloudy Massacre, 1655* (London: by Henry Hills for Adoniram Byfield, 1658), Books II-IV [pp. 189-709]). Clarke indicates that he derived his information concerning the Waldensians' history from Perrin, *Luthers Fore-Runners* – see "Preface," sig. A2r-v and Book 2, Chapter 1 of that work – and from Anthony Cade's *A Justification of the Church of England* (London: G. Purslowe and J. Beale for George Lathum, 1630), which shows that their status and persecutions were well known prior to Morland's comprehensive work. Regarding their earlier history, Thankfull Owen declared that "The barbarous Murders of the *Albigenses* and *Waldenses* remain a lasting Monument of unparallel'd Popish Cruelty," noting that the Inquisitor Reinerius conceded in his report on them that they were in fact very righteous people, "*only they speak evil of the Roman church and clergy*" (*A True and Lively Representation of Popery, Showing that Popery Is only New-Modell'd Paganism* [London: R. Everingham, 1679], p. 79). See also [anonymous], *A Short Refutation of the Principal Errors of the Church of Rome: Whereby a Protestant of a Mean and Ordinary Capacity May Be Enabled to Defend his Religion against the Most Subtle Papist* (London: J. Downing, 1722), p. 22, and Welchman, *A Dialogue betwixt a Protestant Minister and a Romish Priest*, pp. 38-39: "And were I at a Loss for an Answer to that idle Question, *Where was your Religion before* Luther? Those *poor Christians* would furnish me with a very *good one*; and I might say, It was in the *Valleys* of *Piedmont*."

43 Morland, *History of the Evangelical Churches of the Valleys of Piemont* (PASSMANN AND VIENKEN II, 1292-93). Other details that may connect with Swift's text include Morland's opening comments (recalling Psalm 83:4) on the persecutors' efforts to blot out the memory of their enemies: "They said to one another, come and let us cut them off from being a people, that so their name may be had no more in remembrance" ("Authors Epistle Dedicatory"); see Swift's allusion to Deuteronomy 32:26 in the *Tale* (p. 22): "I enquired after them among Readers and Booksellers, but I enquired in vain, the *Memorial of them was lost among Men, their Place was no more to be found.*" The tearing of children limb from limb (*Tale*, p. 22) also features prominently in Morland's narrative and images (*History of the Evangelical Churches of the Valleys of Piemont*, p. 349), recounting and illustrating how soldiers pursuing a woman with a "young sucking Childe" "having found

FIGURE 6.4 Samuel Morland's *History of the Evangelical Churches of the Valleys of Piemont*, 1658, p. 346, "Children torn in pieces limb-meal".

immense," and it "drew on a wider documentary base than almost any other similar tract," with many of the manuscripts supporting its evidence being lodged in the University Library at Cambridge;[44] the enduring series of persecutions which the Waldensians endured and survived, and their evident purity of faith, represented an ideal model for post-Reformation Protestants. While they form only a part of the compilation, the details of the rebellious Christians' martyrdom were, of course, of central importance to the work, and certain more graphic atrocities are illustrated in finely-worked engravings.

the Infant in the Cradle, in a most Salvage manner took it out, and pull'd it into four pieces or quarters," and p. 346, depicting the three children of Giovanni Andrea Michialin "torn in pieces limb-meal," with another bisected with a sword. The latter episode was notorious enough to find its way into George Fox's *The Arraignment of Popery Being a Short Collection, Taken out of the Chronicles, and Other Books of the State of the Church* (London: *s. n.*, 1667), p. 97: "Another woman had three children torn into pieces, tearing them by the legs one from another." Grim accounts of the flaying of Waldensian victims are also illustrated and described both in Morland (see p. 355 concerning one Paolo Garnier, who was allegedly maimed and "stript [of his skin] alive") and in other accounts of the massacres in Piedmont; see Jean Léger, *Histoire générale des églises évangéliques des vallées de Piémont ou Vaudoises* (Leyden: Jean le Carpentier, 1669 [Passmann and Vienken II, 1063-64]) and Thomas Harris, *Popery and Slavery Display'd*, pp. 28, 30.

44 Passmann and Vienken II, 1293.

Further sustaining the theme of martyrdom, Swift's narrator poignantly demands to know the specific and longer-term fates of the Moderns' books: "Were they drowned by *Purges* or martyred by *Pipes?*", "Who has annihilated them?" and "Is their very Essence destroyed?" (p. 21).[45] Again evoking the countless grim forms of martyrdom detailed in Foxe's *Acts and Monuments*,[46] Clarke's *Martyrologie*,[47] and countless other texts including Morland's, he laments that "Books, like Men their Authors, have no more than one Way of coming into the World, but there are ten Thousand to go out of it, and return no more" (p. 23). Most significantly, in his protest against the works having been sunk into "the Abyss of Things," he highlights a torture that was notoriously associated with the Spanish Inquisition, and declares that Time-the-tormentor carries responsibility for its outcome: "The Fault is in Him, who tied Weights so

45 The jest about the sordid fates of unwanted texts was a well-established one (see *Tale*, p. 333n5, and Pope's later reference to "the martyrdom of jakes and fire" in the 1742 *Dunciad*, I, 144; *The Dunciad in Four Books*, ed. Valerie Rumbold [Harlow: Longman, 1999], p. 119), but here the theme of martyrdom is more strongly grounded and developed. On the Tubster's question of whether the texts' "very Essence" is destroyed, there were significant concerns among Protestant writers over whether the souls of right-thinking ancestors misled in their faith by the Catholic Church were necessarily lost. John Favour suggests that, although we cannot know their fates, "I for my part make no doubt, but honest and devout men, though in some points carried away with the sway of time, so questioned [on the core tenets of Christian faith], truly answering, faithfully beleeving, and so dying, might be saved, and so without doubt in the most ignorant ages many were" (*Antiquitie Triumphing over Noveltie*, p. 486; see also pp. 481, 484, and 487-96). Favour deplores the extreme Romanist view "*that whosever doth not hold all and every point of the Catholicke faith entirely, shall perish eternally*," and declares that "We [Protestants] are not so peremptorie, so rigorous, so comfortlesse, so mercilesse" (pp. 491-92). See also Welchman, *A Dialogue betwixt a Protestant Minister and a Romish Priest*, pp. 25-26: "I do not absolutely deny that *Salvation* is to be had in your Church ... I am not for *damning* more than needs must; how far infinite Mercy may extend it self, even to *honest Heathens*, I know not."

46 John Foxe, *Actes and Monuments of Matters Most Speciall and Memorable Happening in the Church*, 2 vols (London: Company of Stationers, 1610). This is the edition that Swift had in his library (PASSMANN AND VIENKEN II, 642-43). Indignation at Catholic persecutions was fuelled also by much later accounts of martyrdom, for example, the campaigns against the Waldensians mentioned above, or those detailed in Huguenot publications such as Jean Claude, *An Account of the Persecutions and Oppressions of the Protestants in France* (London: John Norris, 1686). See also *Speculum Papismi: or, A Looking-Glasse for Papists, Wherein they May See their Own Sweet Faces*, the Second Part of *The Protestant Almanack for ... 1669* (Cambridge, 1669), which promises "a short Scheme of the various Tortures and Cruelties exercised upon the Innocent Protestants, by the Ever-Bloody-PAPISTS."

47 See details in note 42 above. Clarke's Nonconformist (Presbyterian) religious affiliation is firmly indicated by lines from a prefatory poem addressed to him in the 1660 edition of his *Martyrologie*: "I quake to hear what Saints in former daies / Ne're shook to feel, so they might win the Baies. / They conquer'd all; Their patient disposition, / O'recame both Pope, and *Spanish* Inquisition" (sig. [a4v]).

heavy to their Heels, as to depress them to the Center" (p. 21). This practice of racking an accused heretic's body by hoisting the victim aloft and attaching progressively-increased weights to the heels was frequently described as being exercised against dissidents and Protestants, and the crime was aggravated by the torturers' customary declaration that if lasting injuries or death should ensue, these were the victim's own fault (since he or she had either refused to confess or was deemed to have made an incomplete confession).[48] A hair-raising account of the weights-and-pulleys torture derived from Raimundo Gonzálea de Montes' testimony is repeated almost verbatim in Clarke's *Martyrologie*, and again in a pamphlet of 1680 attributed to Richard Dugdale, which formed part of Robert Harley's library collection; other sources present more summary details of the same procedures.[49] The extreme brutality

48 Lu Ann Homza, in her anthology of contemporary sources on the Inquisition, includes a translation of the directions recorded for the case of Maria Gonzalez: "Then their reverences [the Inquisitors] went to the torture room and admonished Maria Gonzalez to declare the truth about what she had said ... For it was imperative for their reverences to know the entire truth, and they assured her that if she should receive death, a wound, or the loss of some limb during the torture, it would be her own fault, because their intention was nothing more than to know the entire truth about what she had said in her confessions" (*The Spanish Inquisition, 1478-1614: An Anthology of Sources* [Indianapolis and Cambridge: Hackett, 2006], pp. 55-56; see also the editor's note 12 [p. 55]). The practice of laying blame on the victim in advance of the actual torture is also described in Philip a Limborch's *Historia Inquisitionis* (Amsterdam: H. Wetstenium, 1692), II, iv, 29. For a translation of the passage, see Philip van Limborch, *The History of the Inquisition ... Translated into English by Samuel Chandler*, 2 vols (London: J. Gray, 1731), II, 218: "The Judges also usually protest, that if the Criminal should happen to die under his Torture, or by reason of it, or should suffer the Loss of any of his Limbs, 'tis not to be imputed to them, but to the Criminal himself." In the case of Isaac Orobio, accused of being a Jew, this declaration is duly applied prior to his torments (II, 221). For a similar observation on how the Tribunal lays fault on the victim, see Luke Beaulieu, *The Holy Inquisition: Wherein Is Represented What Is the Religion of the Church of Rome, and how they Are Dealt with that Dissent from it* (London: Joanna Brome, 1681), pp. 134-35; p. 138 gives an account of the weights and pulleys torture itself.

49 See Raimundo Gonzálea de Montes, *A Full, Ample and Punctuall Discovery of the Barbarous, Bloudy, and Inhumane Practises of the Spanish Inquisition against Protestants ... Manifested in their Proceedings against Sundry Particular Persons, as well English as Others, upon whom they Have Executed their Diabolicall Tyrannie ... First Written in Latin by Reginaldus Gonsaluius Montanus*, 2nd ed., trans. Vincent Skinner (London: John Bellamy, 1625), pp. 48-49, and Clarke's *Martyrologie*, 3rd ed. (1677), p. 165. Dugdale's clearly plagiarized description is entitled *A Narrative of Unheard-of Popish Cruelties towards Protestants beyond Seas: or, A New Account of the Bloody Spanish Inquisition* (London: John Hancock, 1680); reprinted in *The Harleian Miscellany*, eds William Oldys and Thomas Park, 10 vols (London: John White and John Murray; and John Harding, 1808-11), VII, 103-21. The text of the latter reads: "Both hands and thumbs are fastened to a pulley, which hangs on the gibbet: then they put great and heavy bolts on his heels, and hang upon those bolts between

of the treatment appears to have been one important weapon in the armoury of the Reformists, and this is hardly surprising. It is equally notable that the breath with which Time stifles his infant martyrs or sends them into mortal convulsions is described in the *Tale* as "baneful ... Enemy to Life *and Matter*, infectious and corrupting" (my italics) – these are the fatal properties commonly attributed to the basilisk or cockatrice, which was often invoked in Protestant religious discourse as a cipher of spiritual evil.[50] Pliny and others

his feet certain weights of iron, and so hoist him or her up from the ground ... Having hung thus a good while, they command him to be let down, and twice so much weight to be fastened to his heels, and so hoisted up again." Compare Thomas Harris, *Popery and Slavery Display'd*, pp. 39-40: "When the Prisoner is first hoisted from the Ground, an Hour-glass is turned up, which (if not prevented by such a Confession of his Heresies, as the Inquisitor ... expects) must run out before he can be taken down." A woodcut image of an Inquisition victim with huge weights tied to his ankles forms one of a set of four illustrations prefacing James Salgado, *The Slaughter-house: or, A Brief Description of the ...: Spanish Inquisition ... In which is Laid open, the Tyranny, Insolence, Perfidiousness, and Barbarous Cruelty of that Tribunal* (London: William Marshall, 1683), sig. A4 (Figure 6.5).

50 There is properly a distinction between the basilisk (a kind of serpent, deriving from classical accounts) and the cockatrice, which need not be elaborated here; both, in addition to a fatal stare, were believed to have fatal breath. For a full account of the former, see Laurence E. Breiner, "The Basilisk," in *Mythical and Fabulous Creatures: A Source Book and Research Guide*, ed. Malcolm South (New York, Westport, Connecticut, and London: Greenwood, 1987), pp. 113-22; he explains the early belief that "Should it blow upon any other animal, without even biting it, its victim dies" (p. 113). Pliny states that the basilisk "killeth all trees and shrubs not onely that he toucheth, but also that hee breatheth upon ... so venimous and deadly he is," and asserts that it destroys the very ground (*The Historie of the World: Commonly called, The Naturall History of C. Plinius Secundus*, trans. Philemon Holland, 2nd ed., 2 vols [London: Adam Islip, 1634], I, 206 [Book VIII, Chapter xxi]). Swift owned the 1635 Elzevir edition of *Historiae naturalis libri XXXVII* in three volumes (see for VIII, xxi, I, 423-25 [PASSMANN AND VIENKEN II, 1459-61]). Lucan's *Pharsalia*, of which Swift had four editions in his library (PASSMANN AND VIENKEN II, 1107-8), likewise claims that the basilisk's breath brings death before it bites (IX, 724-26, in *Pharsalia*, ed. Thomas Farnaby [Amsterdam: Jean Blaeu, 1665], p. 276). See also Solinus, *The Excellent and Pleasant Worke of Julius Solinus Polyhistor Contayning the Noble Actions of Humaine Creatures, the Secretes and Providence of Nature*, trans. Arthur Golding (London: I. Charlewoode, 1587), Chapter XXXIX, which describes the creature under the name of 'Cockatrice' but as a serpent "wyth as it were a little myter, proportioned in lynes on his heade. Hee is given to the utter destruction not onely of man and beast, or whatsoever hath life, but also even of the earth it selfe ... To be short, he destroyeth hearbs, kylleth Trees, and infecteth the very aire ... with his pestilent breath." The term "cockatrice" is used in the King James Bible, and thus Edward Topsell argues that the creature must exist since Scripture refers to it; he notes that "his breath and poison [are] mortall to all manner of Beasts," while "We do read that in *Rome*, in the days of Pope *Leo* the fourth, there was a Cockatrice found in a Vault of a Church or Chappel ... whose pestiferous breath had infected the air round about, whereby great mortality followed in *Rome*" (*The History of Serpents and Four-Footed Beasts* [London: E. Cotes, 1658], pp. 679, 678). Thomas Browne questions whether basilisk and cockatrice are the same, and whether the latter

FIGURE 6.5
James Salgado, *The Slaughter-House: or, A Brief Description of the ... Spanish Inquisition* (London: William Marshall, 1683), sig. A4.

even exists, but he also takes pains to account for the efficacy of its poison being conveyed through the air rather than through bodily contact (*Pseudodoxia Epidemica*, ed. Robin Robbins, 2 vols [Oxford: Clarendon Press, 1981], I, 181-86; II, 808-13 [Book III, Chapter 7, "Of the Basilisk"]). Compare Alexander Ross, *Arcana Microcosmi* (London: Thomas Newcombe, 1652), Book 2 ("The Second Book of the strange diseases and Accidents of MANS Body"), Chapter 3, which describes a snake's power of fascination as proceeding from "some malignant vapour, breath, or spirit from the eye or mouth" and supports this theory "by the story of the Basilisk killing with his look or breath rather, at a distance" (p. 110).

Particularly in the context of the King James Version of Isaiah 59:5, basilisk and cockatrice often appeared as diabolic creatures (Breiner, "The Basilisk," p. 115), associated with Satan or the Antichrist; see Rudolf Wittkower, *Allegory and the Migration of Symbols* (London: Thames and Hudson, 1977), p. 79. They were thus readily available to Protestant polemicists as signifiers of Catholic duplicity and political threat. Alison Margaret Conway cites the satiric representation of Charles II's French mistress, Louise de Kérouaille, as a Catholic basilisk, "The Commons hater, and false France's Friend," in *The Protestant Whore: Courtesan Narrative and Religious Controversy in England, 1680-1750* (Toronto, Buffalo, London: University of Toronto Press, 2010), pp. 31-32. The Laudian bishops who were believed to be traducing the Church of England are likewise attacked state that the basilisk's breath is so baneful that it can destroy the earth and burst rocks apart,[51] and one may detect its lair by the burnt ground around it; in Swift's phrasing, Time's breath is "abominable,"[52] a word which, especially in this context, resonates with Reformation prophecy and polemic drawing on the visions of Daniel and St John and the many references to "abominations" in the Bible.[53] It was common for many Protestant Christian exegetes, as with

in an anonymous pamphlet of 1644 which describes Matthew Wren as a "right Basilisk," Richard Mountague [who had died in 1641] as "a Roman Basilisk" and Francis White as "a dangerous Basilisk," "one whose poisonous breath infected the sanctity of the Sabbath ... and writ whole volumes in defence of Arch Arminians" (*A Nest of Perfidious Vipers: or, The Second Part of the Parliament's Calendar of Black Saints* [London: G. Bishop, 1644], in *The Harleian Miscellany*, eds Oldys and Park, V, 434-36 [p. 436]). The basilisk was sometimes identified with the horned viper or Cerastes, featured in the anti-Papal image and verses of *The Pope's Pyramides* (London: Printed in Shoe Lane, 1620) (BM 1992-1-25-16), itself based on a Dutch print (*Piramide Papistique*) of 1599 by Hendrick Hondius. This depicts a pyramidal entangled mass of smaller serpents within the body of one great one, a composite of the Roman Church; the first of the accompanying verses compares Rome to a serpent which "all the world infecteth, farre and nigh, / Like the *Cerastes*, threatning speedy death, / If unawares we come within her breath." For a full discussion of these two prints, see Helen Pierce, *Unseemly Pictures: Graphic Satire and Politics in Early Modern England* (New Haven and London: Yale University Press, 2008), pp. 48-49; as Pierce also demonstrates, the hatching of cockatrice's eggs was another graphic device drawn from Isaiah 59:5, and denoting Catholic plots and subterfuge (pp. 61-64).

51 See Pliny, note 50 above.

52 Possibly, Swift is also alluding to Catholic rituals of sanctifying with the breath, including breathing on infants at baptism. Jewel's *The Apologie of the Church of England* expresses incredulity at the idea that St Peter, as the supposed Apostolic founder of the Roman Church, ever "Consecrated with his holy Breath, *Oyle, Waxe, Wooll, Belles, Chalices, Churches*, and *Alters*" (p. 301); on the practice of the Priest consecrating holy water in the font by breathing on it, and blowing three times upon the infant at baptism, see Alexander Ross, Henrick van Haestens, and John Davies, *Pansébeia: or, A View of all Religions in the World* (1653), 2nd ed. (London: T. C. for John Saywell, 1655), p.461, and Fox, *The Arraignment of Popery*, p. 40.

53 "Abomination[s]" and the adjective "abominable" are incessantly invoked in anti-Catholic writings and sermons, with the biblical focus especially on Daniel 9:26-27 and 11:31, Matthew 24:15-16, and Revelation 17:4; these scriptural admonitions were applied particularly to the iniquities of successive Popes and the Roman Church. See the sermon preached by John Tillotson on 31 January 1688, "*Being the Day Appointed for a Publick Thanksgiving to Almighty God for Having Made His Highness the Prince of Orange the Glorious Instrument of the Great Deliverance of this Kingdom from Popery and Arbitrary Power* (London: Brabazon Aylmer and William Rogers, 1689), p. 15: "*Should we again break thy Commandments, and again join in affinity with the People of these abominations* [the Romanists], *wouldest thou not be angry with us till thou hadst consumed us?*" Baxter's *Church-History of the Government of Bishops and their Councils Abbreviated*, p. 252, §133, refers to "[the] abominable Pride and Vanity" of the Catholic Church, and Jewel's *The Apologie of the Church of England* to the "abhominable naughtiness" of Rome

the Waldensians before them,[54] to identify the terrible fourth beast appearing in the Book of Daniel 7:19-21 with the all-powerful Roman empire[55] – in fact, the dream and prophecies of Daniel came to have a significant and positive place in the eschatology of the tenth-century Roman Church, long before the Reformation[56] – and for innumerable Reformist interpreters the ominous little

---

(p. 118) manifested in the Catholics' endorsement of "Voluptuousnes, Adultery, Ribaudry, Whoredome, Murthering of Kin, Incest, and others [sic] more abhominable partes" (p. 112). Compare also Harris, *Popery and Slavery Display'd*, p. 74: "Let us pray for the Ruin and Downfal of the *Papal* Antichrist, as that which God hath cursed ... and therefore should be here kept out and cast away as an abominable Thing," and Poole, *A Dialogue between a Popish Priest and an English Protestant*, p. 86, claiming that Protestants refer themselves to the Scriptures and "to the Fathers for the first six hundred years, till your abominations had leavened the world, according to what was foretold, *Rev.* 13.8."

54 Morland, *History of the Evangelical Churches of the Valleys of Piemont*, I, 143-44. The Waldensian view as summarized here is that Antichrist does not consist in one identifiable figure, but is an "assembled congregation" [the Roman Church], "that which is called *Antichrist*, or *Babylon*, or the *fourth Beast*, or the *Whore*, or the *Man of Sin*, the *Son of perdition*."

55 The verses concerning the fourth beast run as follows in Daniel 7:19-21:

> 19: Then I would know the truth of the fourth beast, which was diverse from all the others, exceeding dreadful, whose teeth were of iron, and his nails of brass; which devoured, brake in pieces, and stamped the residue with his feet;
> 20: And of the ten horns that were in his head, and of the other which came up, before whom three [horns] fell; even of that horn that had eyes, and a mouth that spake very great things, whose look was more stout than his fellows.
> 21: I beheld, and the same horn made war with the saints, and prevailed against them. (King James Version)

One obvious reason for identifying this beast as the ancient Roman empire is the reference in the dream itself (Daniel 7:7 and 7:19) to its monstrous iron teeth and trampling feet, and to its power as "dreadful and terrible, and strong exceedingly." This extravagant power may, however, be extended to the dominance of the succeeding, Christian Roman empire (the see of the Popes); see, in addition to note 56 below, W. Stanford Reid, "The Four Monarchies of Daniel in Reformation Historiography," *Historical Reflections*, 8, no 1 (1981), 115-23. Martin Luther produced commentaries on both the Book of Daniel (1521 and 1530) and Revelations, describing the Pope's conduct as "the abomination and stench of which Christ speaks in Matthew 24:15" and declaring that he "has set up his own law for God's law and his own priesthood for Christ's priesthood, and thus set abomination in the holy place" (*Luther's Works*, eds Jaroslav Pelikan and Helmutt T. Lehmann, 55 vols [St Louis: Concordia, and Philadelphia: Fortress, 1955-86], XXXI, 393, and XXXVI, 218). John Calvin likewise commented extensively on the Book of Daniel.

56 Ullmann, writing of the reign of Otto I in the tenth century AD, observes:

> The Ottonian acknowledgement of the Donation of Constantine was the implicit confirmation of the papal point of view that the Roman empire was at the disposal of the pope, by virtue of Constantine's action.
>
> And, so it was held, this Roman empire could never perish: that empire which is, according to tenth-century conceptions, the idolized political manifestation of

horn with eyes and a mouth that appears on the head of that beast, supplanting three of its former ten horns, signified the upstart tyranny of the Pope, who would pronounce blasphemies, multiply spiritual abominations, and bring kingdoms under his yoke.[57] The fourth beast represented the Fourth Kingdom, and in the prophecies of Daniel 7:9-10, as Henry More comments, "the fourth Kingdome necessarily is understood ... to reach at least to the first point of that time of Judgment" referred to also in Revelation.[58]

Likewise, the beast of Revelation 13:11 was constantly identified with the Pope by Reformists, and the Hussites' holding to that belief is presented by Daniel Featley in 1624 as the true reason for the Church's persecution of them from the fourteenth century onwards: "What was it so inflamed the Pope against the *Hussites* ... It was that article of the *Hussites*, gathered out of their writings by *Alanus*. *Papa est bestia de qua habetur in Apocalypsi, 12* [*recte* Revelation

> Christianity, must be defended against [the Eastern emperor] who arrogates to himself the title "emperor of the Romans." This, so it was held, was the proper interpretation of the prophecy of Daniel [7:14]: the four empires of this prophecy were the Assyrian-Babylonian, the Persian, the Greek and the Roman empires. This fourth kingdom "shall be diverse from all kingdoms and shall devour the whole earth and shall tread it down and break it to pieces" (Daniel 7:23). Already widely current in the middle of the ninth century, this eschatological interpretation of the biblical prophecy furnished a strong ideological ferment in the tenth century as also in later times. In a way, this eschatology was a spiritualized teleology of history. (*The Growth of Papal Government in the Middle Ages*, p. 234)

See also pp. 237-38 of this study on the perceived continuity of the "imperium Romanum" or "Caesarianum" or "Octavianum" with the (Roman) Christian empire.

57 Examples of such expositions are legion, and are reflected in almanacs as well as innumerable treatises, tracts, and sermons in seventeenth- and eighteenth-century Britain; for extensive commentary on the former, see Bernard Capp, *English Almanacs, 1500-1800: Astrology and the Popular Press* (Ithaca, New York: Cornell, 1979), especially pp. 165-69 and 212-81; some other studies are cited in note 59 below. Robert Collis notes that the French Huguenot Pierre Jurieu anticipated "the destruction of the Roman Church and the beginning of the millennium between 1710 and 1715;" "These dates were based on the calculation that the reign of the Antichrist began in AD 450 or 455 and that 1260 years would pass until the advent of the millennium" (*The Petrine Instauration: Religion, Esotericism, and Science at the Court of Peter the Great, 1689-1725* [Leiden: Brill, 2011], p. 197). See also Hillel Schwartz, *The French Prophets: The History of a Millenarian Group in Eighteenth-Century England* (Berkeley: University of California Press, 1980), pp. 37-38: "England in 1706 was no stranger to prophecy or to millennial speculation ... In 1706, according to Thomas Beverly, the world was seven years along the apocalyptic finish to time ... For Bishop William Lloyd, vicar William Allen, mathematician William Whiston, the world in 1706 had yet a little respite before the end – some ten, twenty or thirty years at most" (p. 37).

58 Henry More, *A Plain and Continued Exposition of the Several Prophecies or Divine Visions of the Prophet Daniel, which Have or May Concern the People of God* (London: by M.F. for Walter Kettilby, 1681), p. 262.

13]. *Datum est ei, bellum facere cum sanctis.* The Pope is the beast, whereof it is said in the 12. of the *Reuelation*; It is *granted* to him (the beast) *to warre with the Saints*."[59] Ecclesiastical Rome is the Beast, the Man of Sin and the infamous Babylon which glorifies the scarlet-clad Whore with her cup of abominations. It was particularly important to many Protestant exegetes to insist on this identification as referring to the Rome of the present, against other interpretations that protected the contemporary Roman church by suppositions or evasions; thus Matthew Poole declared to his Catholic disputant:

> That the worshippers of the *Babylonish* Beast, *Rev.* 13. and 14. are in a damnable condition, you all grant, and it is affirmed by God himself, *Rev.* 14.8, 9,10,11. And that *Rome* is that *Babylon*, the most and Learnedest of your Doctors agree, only some of them pretend it is *Rome Heathen* as it was; and others, that it is *Rome Jewish*, as it shall be in the end of the world; both which conceits are fully refuted by divers of our Authors.[60]

It need hardly be added that these scriptural texts were especially significant for nonconformist groups in Swift's time, particularly those who expected the Apocalypse very imminently.[61]

As to his own interest in such expositions, Swift's library contained two theological works by the Cambridge Platonist Henry More, a staunch Anglican whose close and scholarly commentaries on Daniel and Revelation were central to his Protestant profession. Both of these volumes – *A Plain and*

59 Featley, "The Fifth Assertion," *The Romish Fisher Caught and Held in his Owne Net*, sig. Q4*r-v. See also Featley, p. 85. Other polemical writers frequently noted that those of the Roman faith – including Petrarch and Girolamo Savonarola – had hinted that the Pope was Antichrist; see Jewel, *An Epistle Written ... to Signor Scipio*, pp. 177-79.

60 Poole, *A Dialogue between a Popish Priest and an English Protestant*, p. 5.

61 There is a huge body of scholarship on millenarianism in Britain, especially that which flourished in the seventeenth century. On the persistence of millenarian thinking well into the late seventeenth and early eighteenth centuries, see Margaret C. Jacob, "Millenarianism and Science in the Late Seventeenth Century," *Journal of the History of Ideas*, 37 (1976), 335-41; Pat Rogers, "Apocalypse Then: Pope and the Prophets of Dulness," in *Orthodoxy and Heresy in Eighteenth-Century Society: Essays from the DeBartolo Conference*, eds Regina Hewitt and Pat Rogers (Lewisburg: Bucknell University Press, 2002), pp. 112-33; William Johnston, *Revelation Restored: The Apocalypse in Later Seventeenth-Century England* (Woodbridge: Boydell, 2011); and *The Millenarian Turn: Millenarian Contexts of Science, Politics, and Everyday Anglo-American Life in the Seventeenth and Eighteenth Centuries*, eds James E. Force and Richard H. Popkin (Dordrecht, Boston, London: Kluwer Academic Publishers, 2010). Ronald Paulson, in *Hogarth's Harlot: Sacred Parody in Enlightenment England* (Baltimore: Johns Hopkins University Press, 2003), explores the persistence of seventeenth-century radical sectarian influences into the visual as well as literary domains.

Continued Exposition of the Several Prophecies or Divine Visions of the Prophet Daniel, which Have or May Concern the People of God (1681)[62] and *Paralipomena Prophetica: Containing Several Supplements and Defences of Dr. Henry More his Expositions of the Prophet Daniel and the Apocalypse* (1685)[63] – strenuously uphold the identification of the Papacy with both the ten-horned Beast of Daniel and the Beast of Revelation 13:11. More's many other works in this exegetical domain include the thoroughgoing *An Illustration of those Two Abstruse Books in Holy Scripture, The Book of Daniel, and the Revelation of S. John, by Continued Brief, but Clear Notes, from Chapter to Chapter, and from Verse to Verse* (1685),[64] designed presumably for readers less minutely learned in theology, and as comprehensive as the title promises. Within the latter, More follows various predecessors in arguing that the Beast in Daniel which had "great iron teeth" and nails of brass, and which stamped upon whatever it had not already devoured, must signify the Roman Empire both in its pagan *and* its later (degenerated) Christian guises; both empires advance or embody the campaign of Antichrist on earth. The fourth Beast of Daniel's vision is a prophetic analogue of the Beast referred to in Revelation 17:8, mysteriously described there as "*the Beast that was, and is not, and yet is.*"[65] Glossing Daniel 7:19-20, More writes:

---

62 Passmann and Vienken II, 1283.

63 *Paralipomena Prophetica: Containing Several Supplements and Defences of Dr. Henry More his Expositions of the Prophet Daniel and the Apocalypse* (London: Walter Kettilby, 1685) (Passmann and Vienken II, 1284).

64 More, *An Illustration of those Two Abstruse Books in Holy Scripture* (London: M. Flesher for Walter Kettilby, 1685). See particularly pp. 70-86 and 284-86. Among his other works, More also expounded his views on the Book of Daniel and Revelations in *Apocalypsis Apocalypseos: or, The Revelation of St. John the Divine Unveiled* (1680) and *Synopsis Prophetica: or, The Second Part of the Enquiry into the Mystery of Iniquity* (1664).

65 See More, *A Plain and Continued Exposition of the Several Prophecies or Divine Visions of the Prophet Daniel*, p. 256; More explains "that this Beast [representing the "Roman Kingdome"] once healed, or in such a condition, that it may be said of him that he is *the Beast that was, and is not, and yet is*, (which is when he is become *Pagano Christian*) is this Empire actually divided into ten Kingdomes, and that together with this Division the Empire began to relapse gradually into Idolatry by the Agency and Guidance of the *Two-horned Beast* or the *Whore*, whom I have also shewed to be Synchronal to the healed Beast, or *the Beast that was, and is not, and yet is*." In other words, "there is a Coincidence at least of time, if not of affairs, or complication of natures ... betwixt this *little Horn* in Daniel and those three Synchronals, the *restored Beast*, the *Whore*, and the *Two-horned Beast*" (p. 257), and Antichrist is "very expresly foretold in this Vision of the *little Horn* which ... did fabricate *Imperium in Imperio* ... erecting an *Ecclesiastick* Antichristian Empire within the *Civil* ... in opposition to the true Empire or Kingdome of Christ" (pp. 260-61). Henry Jones identifies the Beast which has been wounded with a sword (Rev. 13:12-15) with the last Emperor of the old Roman Empire, Romulus Augustulus (reigned

> And as this Kingdom is typified, *chapt.* 2. [of Daniel] by the iron legs of the Image [in Nebuchadnezzar's dream], so the strength of it here is set out by its great *iron teeth*. Both import that it is *strong exceedingly*. For so is that metal. And the courage, cruelty and exceeding largeness of the *Roman* Empire must needs make it *dreadfull* and *terrible*. And for the enormous cruelty of this Empire, which was found so salvage that no one *species* of wild Beast could sufficiently set out the direfulness thereof while *Pagan* and *Paganochristian*, the horrid persecution of the Primitive Christians, and that no less of the *Evangelici* under the *Papacy*, is too ample and astonishing a monument.[66]

The trampling fourth Beast of Daniel – by far the most important of Daniel's visions, in More's exegesis – is also seen as specifically prophetic of the Pope in so far as the latter had thus displayed his power over earthly rulers, forcing them "in publick Assemblies to sit at his feet, and if they will not be dutifull enough, to be troad upon by his feet, as *Frederick Barbarossa* was served by Pope *Alexander* the Third ... treading upon his neck in sight of the people," in a "barbarous insultation over the Emperour."[67] Regarding the similar Beast of

475-76), who is succeeded in his powers by the Papacy who gave the Beast life again (*A Sermon of Antichrist*, p. 15).

66 More, *An Illustration of those Two Abstruse Books in Holy Scripture*, pp. 77-78. In his *A Plain and Continued Exposition of the Several Prophecies or Divine Visions of the Prophet Daniel*, More expresses high disgust at Calvin's applying and limiting the relevant verses in Daniel to ancient Rome; even the two Jesuit commentators with whom More engages in the *Exposition*, together with the ancient Fathers, "ingenuously confess, that Antichrist is prefigured in those parts of the Visions ... But Calvin not allowing so much as that they are Predictions of Antichrist, but bounding the Vision in the seventh Chapter, and ... that in the Eleventh, upon the first coming of Christ, and interpreting things concerning the *Pagan Roman* Empire, his Expositions are so childishly argute and whisling, so dilute, shallow and slubbering, so preposterous, forced and confused ... that *Calvin* is not at all like *Calvin* in this performance." As to Hugo Grotius, he is "so nasute on the behalf of the Church of *Rome*, that foreseeing if the fourth Beast were the Roman Empire, it would infallibly fall to the share of the Pope to be the *little Horn* with eyes and a mouth ... that is to say, to be Antichrist, he to befriend the Papacy denies, against the authority of all Antiquity, or against the Roman [Catholic] Interpreters themselves, that the fourth Beast is the Roman Empire" (p. xviii).

67 More, *An Illustration of those Two Abstruse Books in Holy Scripture*, p. 83. More refers again to how the little horn of the Beast (the Pope) subdues and supplants the powers of the three other horns symbolizing certain kings, including "lastly, the Emperours of *Germany*, whom from the days of *Henry* the fourth he excommunicated, deposed and trampled under his feet." The metaphor of being trodden underfoot by Catholic power was quite a common one in Protestant writings of the seventeenth century (p. 85). Compare Henry Jones, *A Sermon of Antichrist*, inveighing once more against Gregory VII: "*Particularly, as to* Gregory the 7th or Hildebrand, *of whom* Eberardus in Aventinus *thus speaketh*[:] *Hildebrand* one hundred and seventy years since, was the first, who under colour of Religion laid the foundation of *Antichrists Empire*. Those Babylonian Priests

Revelation, there is ultimately a Satanic or "Draconick" union of purpose between them, "For the old Serpent was at the bottom of all the doings that turned the Christian *Roman* Empire into a Beast again, which is here described. Whose seven Heads and ten Horns shew him to be the *Roman* Empire."[68] More's emphasis on the continuity between pagan and Catholic Christian Rome, and the uniting of both in the character of Antichrist, could not be more clearly and firmly stated than in the marginal summary in his "Preface to the Reader" in the *Plain and Continued Exposition*:

> The great importance of proving the fourth Kingdome in *Daniel* to be the *Roman*, for making good the opinion of the ancient Fathers that the times of the *little Horn with eyes* are the times of Antichrist &c. and consequently the Times of *Antichrist* the Times of the Papacy.[69]

Declaring his absolute conviction on this point, he later proclaims: "Whether the Pope be not the Antichrist and the Papal Hierarchy understood in all those

---

would reign alone, an equal they cannot endure, they cease not to trample all under foot; *they sit in the Temple of God*, and are exalted above all that is worshiped ... many say that *Gregory* is Antichrist" ("To the Reader," sig. B2r); and see also Welchman, *A Dialogue betwixt a Protestant Minister and a Romish Priest*, p. 20: "The *Supremacy* of the Pope was condemn'd, even by the Pope, *viz. Gregory the Great*, toward the latter end of the *Sixth* Century, as a piece of *devillish* Pride, trampling upon the Necks of all the other *Bishops* in the World."

68 More, *An Illustration of those Two Abstruse Books in Holy Scripture*, p. 286. The conviction that pagan Rome was, in fact, nobler and morally better than the Papacy is clearly stated in the verses of the anonymous "R.W. D.D." in *An Exclamation against Popery: or, A Broad-Side against Rome. Occasioned by His Majesty's Last Gracious Speech* (Nov. 14th, 1678):

What! is the *Eagle* from the *Mitre* flown?
Is there of Caesar nothing left in *Rome*?
Must that Renowned City, here-to-fore
Fam'd for her Vertues, well as for her Pow'r;
Instead of *Consuls*, Vagabonds imploy? (p. 1r)

69 P. xliv; bold print in original. More's commentary on the same page goes further in its detail, connecting up Daniel Chapters 7 and 11 with 2 Thessalonians 2:1-12 and Revelation Chapters 13 and 17, all of which allegedly refer to the times of the Papacy, and he refers the reader to his *Synopsis Prophetica* (Book II, Chapter 21) for yet more verification: "So that if the Pope with his Hierarchy be they [all the abominable agents or visions of these biblical sources] ... it is evident, that the *Papal* Polity or Hierarchy is ... the *very Antichrist* properly so called, which the Church in the times of the Apostles was so solicitous about, they not knowing how near his coming might be ... though they were assured out of the Prophecies of *Daniel*, that, when he did come, he would prove horribly bad ... his tyranny and salvage cruelty against them [true Christians] being unutterable" (*A Plain and Continued Exposition of the Several Prophecies or Divine Visions of the Prophet Daniel*, p. xlvi).

Prophecies in *John* and *Daniel* which the Ancient Fathers and Primitive Writers understood of Antichrist … these things I profess are as clear to me as any point in all Theology and Philosophy, Geometry itself being not excepted."[70]

If there is, as surely appears, an abiding strain of Protestant and sectarian polemic at work in Swift's references,[71] it is in one sense fully to be expected that Time will be involved in the argument; Time is, as Augustine argued, a creature in the sense that it was made at the time of Creation and will end with the destruction of this world,[72] and Time is key to the interpretation of the scriptural revelations.[73] Eschatological and millenarian readings of the Bible are pre-eminently concerned not only with the calculation of time spans and with the identity, advent, and fall of Antichrist, but with the time for the ending of Time; and if we view Swift's Tubster as a kind of itinerant Dissenting preacher,[74] among his other mountebank roles, one rationale for his brag that the residents of Grub Street have "turn'd back [Time's] Hour-Glass" may be that his brethren have boldly set down the temporal order for the fulfilment of prophecies, or even tried to set backwards certain natural outcomes of time to fit in with their own predictions. For example, the "French Prophet" John Lacy accounted for the failed resurrection of his follower Thomas Emes in May of 1708 by arguing that the crowd which gathered was too large and hostile, and that in such circumstances "all acts of devotion are obstructed, and even suspended till a more seasonable time."[75] Swift's satirical prophecy on

70 *A Plain and Continued Exposition of the Several Prophecies or Divine Visions of the Prophet Daniel*, p. lxxxv.

71 It is obvious, of course, that such polemic informs the satire of the *Tale* as a whole; see Hugh Ormsby-Lennon, *Hey Presto! Swift and the Quacks* (Newark: University of Delaware Press, 2011), pp. 212-13.

72 Augustine, *The Confessions*, trans. Maria Boulding (New York: New City Press, 1997), XI (pp. 284-311), and *De Genesi ad litteram* (*On the Literal Interpretation of Genesis*), c.AD 415, trans. John Hammond Taylor (Mahwah, New Jersey: Paulist Press, 1982).

73 For an excellent summary discussion of the interpretation of Time in the framework of Christianity and other belief systems, see Hillel Schwartz, "Sacred Time," in *The Encyclopaedia of Religion*, eds Lindsay Jones, *et al.*, 15 vols (Gale Virtual Reference Library: Macmillan Reference USA, 2005), XII, 7986-97. Schwartz highlights the central importance of Time to those Protestant circles debating "the chronology of grace or redemption," and notes that in this context "the Sacred demands the upper case, as if the Sacred were a book. Among religions that rely upon Scripture, Sacred time seems bound up with language and with efforts towards the permanent inscription of truths."

74 See Ormsby-Lennon, *Hey Presto!* pp. 27-49. As this scholar and others have noted, Grub Street and the area around it was known as a centre of dissenting groups as well as for housing "scribblers" of all kinds; see also Sharon Achinstein, *Literature and Dissent in Milton's England* (Cambridge: Cambridge University Press, 2003), p. 116.

75 Lacy's foretelling of the resurrection of Emes, supposed to take place on 25 May 1708, was followed up by a pamphlet, *Esquire Lacy's Reasons why Doctor Emes Was Not Raised from*

this outcome was presented in Isaac Bickerstaff's *Predictions for the Year 1708*, where he notes that the month of June would be "distinguished ... by the utter dispersing of those ridiculous deluded Enthusiasts, commonly called the prophets."[76] But in the case of the *Tale*'s narrator and his protestations, there remains this unexpected dimension: Time appears not to be directed by any higher authority (God) but is instead positively *identified* with the abuses of papal authority. The narrator's proclamations seem to gesture, albeit rather helplessly, towards the much-desired defeat of Antichrist, not as an outcome of time but conceiving of Time as if he *were* the Antichrist himself. Along with Time's classical characteristics, we may see evident connections with the fourth Beast of Daniel's dream, devouring, tearing, and trampling, and this Beast may be identified both with the pagan Roman empire and the Papal Roman empire as its malign inheritor. While Henry More's comments make perhaps the most strongly-stated claim for that continuity, it was a repeated theme both of earlier Reformation argument and of polemical literature closer to Swift's time. For example, in his highly popular sermon *The Midnight Cry*, dating from the early 1690s, the Anglican preacher John Mason refers to the Pope's having taken over "the Fag-end of the Roman Empire,"[77] and Daniel Featley's *The Romish Fisher*

---

the Dead (1708), reprinted in *The Harleian Miscellany*, eds Oldys and Park, VII, 195-96. Lacy also pronounced in this pamphlet that "if it was lawful for the apostles and Christ himself to avoid the fury of their wicked and unbelieving adversaries; we hope no man can reasonably blame us for deferring the accomplishment of the said intended miracle" (p. 195). For fuller accounts of this circle, see Hillel Schwartz, *The French Prophets: The History of a Millenarian Group in Eighteenth-Century England* (Berkeley and Los Angeles: University of California Press, 1980) and Lionel Laborie, *Enlightening Enthusiasm: Prophecy and Religious Experience in Early Eighteenth-Century England* (Manchester: Manchester University Press, 2015). Another instance of deferred miracles which may very well have been known to Swift, and which was the subject of several publications in 1694, is the case of John Mason, Rector of Water-Stratford and leader of the Church of Philadelphia. Mason not only declared that he had seen the prophecies of Revelation 22 enacted and that the Second Coming – to take place in Water-Stratford in that year – was about to occur "as Lightning," but allegedly pronounced he had been promised "That he should see Christ here," without dying. After his death, this was said to be fulfilled by his reported vision of the person of Christ. See Mason, *The Angels Oath, Time is no Longer ... A Prophecy from Mr. Mason's People at Water-Stratford* (London: Printed for the Author, 1694) and [anonymous], *The Present State of Mr. Mason's Followers* ([1694]), which notes that "instead of Breaking, as 'twas expected upon Mr. *Mason*'s death, they Continue still together, and are resolved so to do, fully perswading themselves that they shall see the full issue of their expectations, according to the aforesaid scheme laid down by Mr. Mason" (p. 10).

76 *Prose Works*, II, 139-50.

77 John Mason, *The Midnight-Cry: A Sermon Preached on the Parable of the Ten Virgins ... by J.M. M.A. Rector of W[ater-Stratford] in the County of B[uckinghamshire]*, 5th ed. (London: Nathanael Ranew, 1694) takes up the text of Matthew 24 and 29-30 on the tribulation to

Cavght repeats the same observation: "Now all the world seeth, that the Papacie is built vpon the ruines of the Romane Empire, and at this day possesseth the seat thereof."[78] In fact, it was argued, the Papacy had created a still more powerful empire out of Rome than the old had been.[79] Thus the hob-nailed shoes conferred upon Time by Swift's Tubster appear entirely consistent with both Roman *caligae* and the trampling feet of papal might. In the annals of oppression, Reformers and Protestant martyrologists argued that just as the heathen Romans persecuted the early Christians, after the lapse of some centuries the Church of Rome had renewed the operation. Martin Luther preached that "we [in the Roman Church] are doing just like the Jews, we deny and persecute the Word of God, kill the Christians who confess and preach this Gospel, as at the first the Romans, and afterwards to the present day, the Pope, bishops, princes, monks and priests do;"[80] while George Fox's *The Arraignment of Popery* (1667)

---

come and comments: "This is an Overthrow of an Empire, which is of the fourth Great Empire [the Papal Empire, the Pope's having the Fag-end of the Roman Empire]" (Square brackets in original). John Favour also compares the levels of corruption in ancient Rome and in the see of Rome, stating that the lives of Catiline, Nero, and Heliogabalus are all outdone by the "monstrously wicked" litany of the Pope's misdeeds (*Antiquitie Triumphing over Noveltie*, p. 398).

78 *The Romish Fisher Cavght and Held in his Owne Net*, p. 84. See also p. 85: "That Prophecie, *Reuel. 13.11* ... agreeth to the Papacie and Pope, who ... carrieth himselfe like a Dragon in the Church, and he exerciseth also the power of the first Beast, to weet, the Romane Empire, described in the first verse, by seuen heads and ten hornes, because, as the first Beast, the Romane Empire, by power and temporal authority, so the Pope, by policie and spirituall iurisdiction, ruleth ouer a great part of the world." Compare Thomas Mason and John Foxe, "The Epistle Unto the Reader," *Christs Victorie over Sathans Tyrannie* (London: George Eld and Ralph Blower, 1615): "The abominable desolations of *Nebuchadnezzar*, and of *Titus* and *Vespasian* of the materiall Temples were but prophecies of the Papists abominable desolations of Gods Saints" (sig. A7r). Likewise, according to William Guild, in *Anti-Christ Pointed and Painted out*, the Pope rose to become the eighth head in sovereignty over Rome, "who arose thereto by the decay of the Roman Empyre" (p. 56); however, "*Rome* Heathen under imperiall governement procured [the] subjection of nations to her by force and martiall coaction, but *Rome* as shee is described by Iohn to be the Seate of Antichrist, and under papall governement procured subjection of nations to her by fraud and Whoorish allurements" (p. 66); "she is guiltie of no lesse sinnes, but rather greater, nor ever she was guiltie of in the time of the old Roman Emperours" (p. 73).

79 Henry Jones, *A Sermon of Antichrist*, states: "I shall ... add a little touching the *greatness of this* 7th *Head, or Government of Rome, the Papacy*, And that *it falls not short of the Greatness of the former Emperours of Rome*, according to the Estimate made of both by the *Romanists*" (p. 15); "On which thus St. *Chrysostom: when the Empire of* Rome *is dissolved or removed*, Antichrist *shall invade that vacant place, and snatch at the Empire both of God and Man* (Chrystostom in 2. Thess. 2. Hom. 4)" (p. 16).

80 Luther, "Sermon for the Twenty-Fifth Sunday after Trinity: Matthew 24:15-28," from Luther's Church Postil; first published 1525, in *The Sermons of Martin Luther*, trans. and

promises in its title "*A Relation of their Cruelties* [the Papists] *they Acted after the Pope got up ... New Rome Having Proved like Old.*" Encompassing both cases, the Tubster represents Time as a vicious yet powerful dotard, a monster who brutally crushes all the Moderns, favouring only the legacy of the Ancients[81] as he falsely purports to look after the interests of Posterity (p. 20).

This last point may perhaps explain why Swift (through his narrator) has chosen to cast Time as an oppressive Roman figure and indeed the Antichrist, in so far as the realm of theological and ecclesiastical dispute presented a distinctive aspect of the battle over "Ancient" and "Modern." The quarrel on this foundation was important not only to the well-documented cultural and intellectual combat between Temple and Wotton, but in a different way to the extended Reformation struggle over the foundations of Christian belief and practice. One of the key weapons on the Romanists' side was the claim that they represented Antiquity or the ancient Church, with its unassailable authority deriving from the Apostles and St Peter himself, and that the Roman Church stood as the divinely appointed guardian of tradition. There was just one, all-encompassing Catholic Church, and no other with any true foundation or history. According to that view, opposition to Rome proceeded from "modern," or novel and heretical, delusions, and after all this must have been a strongly persuasive argument in the eyes of many Christians steeped in the old ways and precepts of the faith.[82] On the other side, Protestants were schooled to counter that pre-emptive claim, and in such works as John Favour's *Antiquitie Triumphing over Noveltie* (1619)[83] – the title of which misleadingly suggests a justification of

ed. John Nicholas Lenker, 8 vols (Grand Rapids, Michigan: Baker Book House, 1983), V, 364-78 (p. 369).

81 *A Tale of a Tub and Other Works*, ed. Walsh, pp. 20-21: "I know very well, that when *Your Highness* shall come to riper Years, and have gone through the Learning of Antiquity, you will be too curious to neglect inquiring into the Authors of the very age before You."

82 See Jewel, *The Apologie of the Church of England*, p. 187: "For this is a high bragge, they have ever made, howe that all *Antiquity*, and a *Continuall Consent* of all ages dooth make on their side: and that all our cases bee but *New*, and yester dayes work, & untill these few late yeeres were never heard of." The Roman priest in Matthew Poole's *Dialogue* states: "Another Argument against your Church and way, is taken from the Novelty of it; As for our Religion, it hath had possession in the world ever since the Apostles days; but you are of Yesterday, and know nothing; your Religion is an upstart Religion, never heard of in the world till *Luthers* days" (p. 27). Henry Jones, *A Sermon of Antichrist*, declares: "Popery and that Church doth pass for Catholick, Antient, Holy, and the very way to Salvation. *Whereby not few have been seduced and drawn away from the Truth professed ... who hear of nothing to the contrary*" (sig. B4).

83 John Favour, *Antiquitie Triumphing over Noveltie* (London: Richard Field, 1619). Another work with a comparable title is William Prynne's *Truth Triumphing over Falshood,*

Rome – the premises are reversed to show that it is Protestants who are reclaiming the purity of the true faith as practiced by the early Christians, while the Church of Rome has corrupted it with unsanctioned novelties which began to take root around 600 AD.[84] "Nothing," declares Favour in the first of his chapter headings, "is more dangerous to the Christian Catholique Church,[85] then the usurped pretence of Antiquity, and the false imputation of Noveltie, whereby the truth of God is deluded, and error supported among the children of unbeleefe, within the bosom of the seemingly visible Church."[86] The Romanists use this "to cover the deceipt of their infoysted Novelties" and, what is worse, to "wickedly obtrude the name of *Antiquitie* against all reformation."[87] The arguments on both sides would certainly be familiar to any cleric such as Swift,[88] and are rehearsed at length in Daniel Featley's *The Romish Fisher Cavght and*

Antiquitie over Noveltie ... In Refutation of Mr. Iohn Goodwins Innocencies Triumph ... and of All Anti-Monarchicall, Anti-Parliamentall, Anti-Synodicall, and Anarchicall Paradoxes of Papists, Prelates, Anabaptists, Arminians, Socinians, Brownists, or Independents (London: John Dawson, 1645).

84 The ecclesiastical history of Foxe's *Book of Martyrs* describes the first "suffering time of the Church" when Christians were widely martyred as encompassing the first three centuries AD, and the next three hundred years as "the flourishing time of the Church" (*Acts and Monuments* [1684], I, 1). In this overview, there follows another three hundred years of comparatively moderate or tolerable "declining or backsliding," which persists "until the loosing out of Satan, which was about the thousandth year after the ceasing of Persecution," that is, around 1300. This "time of Antichrist" fulfils key prophecies in the Book of Daniel and Revelations, instigated especially by the corruptions of the Popes from Gregory VII onwards. The Reformation represents both the purging of the Church and the revelation of Antichrist in his true identity. On the oft-repeated argument that the Protestant Church had the true claim to antiquity, while the Roman Church was "New," see *A Short Refutation of the Principal Errors of the Church of Rome*, p. 55, and Welchman, *A Dialogue betwixt a Protestant Minister and a Romish Priest*, pp. 17-20.

85 By "Christian Catholique," Favour means the Protestant churches.

86 Favour, *Antiquitie Triumphing over Noveltie*, p. 1. In the same passage, he terms this "the vaine blast of pretended Antiquitie" and "the visard of Antiquity."

87 Favour, *Antiquitie Triumphing over Noveltie*, pp. 1, 4.

88 See Baxter, *The Successive Visibility of the Church*, p. 881: "*Their Papall Religion* ... is that which is controverted: They affirm I. the *Right*. 2. The *Antiquity* of it: We deny both;" Foxe, *Book of Martyrs* (1684), I, 2: "Wherefore, whosoever shall have hereafter to do with any adversaries, about the Antiquity or Authority of the Church of *Rome*, let him here well consider when and how, the Title, Jurisdiction and Corruption of Doctrine in the Popes See [arose]. And so shall he see, that the Church of *Rome*, as it is now governed ... never descended from the Primitive Age of the Apostles, or from their Succession;" and Jewel, *The Apologie of the Church of England*, p. 27: "[The Romanists] shall manifestly see, how all these titles of Antiquitie, whereof they boast so much, are quite shaken out of theyr hands."

Held in his Owne Net (1624). The author explains how one Master Bugges, a Protestant, became deeply anxious that the antiquity of the Roman church endorsed its claim to be the only legitimate Christian faith, and that he was at risk of dying as a heretic; this occasioned a thoroughgoing debate which was held in June 1623 and recounted (with an emphatic slant towards Protestant convictions) in Featley's volume. The supposed lack of evidence for the long-term existence of Protestantism – or to put it differently, for the Reformed churches' creeds being adopted by pre-Reformation Christians, and for the opposition of such believers to Roman articles of faith – was a crux of the dispute. The challenge presented by Bugges's Jesuit admonishers, including the Catholic John Fisher [John Percy], was that "it could not bee prooued by all the Protestants in the Kingdome, that they had any Church before *Luther*;" accordingly this contingent "perseuered still in questioning him, Where his Church was before *Luther*?" and demanded evidence naming such "visible" Protestants as could be "shewed and prooued out of good Authors."[89] This is not, I think, an issue remote from the early matter of Swift's *Tale*; it is quite striking that the conundrum faced by the *Tale*'s narrator presents an important parallel with Featley's case. In the former, Time destroys the Moderns' works and will then ("for I am well informed of his Designs" [p. 21]) silence Posterity's enquiry concerning them by demanding to know "where they are? and what is become of them? and pretend it a Demonstration that there never were any, because they are not then to be found" (p. 21). In the latter, Featley's initial defence "Are all visible mens names upon Record? Are all the Records that were in former times, now to bee produced?" is seized upon by the Catholic contingent: "Heer divers of Master *Fishers* company, called, *Names, names, names*." Featley wins the day, however, by setting out a history of early and latter-day reformers with their names – in effect re-enacting the same task as John Foxe had so comprehensively undertaken before him[90] – and by denouncing the ploys of his adversaries:

89 This demand is clearly seen by Featley as a serious challenge, since "the Priests and Jesuites doe daily cast out papers, and disperse them in secret: in which they vaunt, that no Protestant Minister dareth encounter them in this point" (*The Romish Fisher Cavght and Held in His Owne Net*, sigs B1r-4v).

90 *The Romish Fisher Cavght and Held in His Owne Net*, "Touching the Names of visible Protestants in all Ages," especially the sections headed "The second Assertion" and "The third Assertion," sigs P3-Q2*. Foxe defends the Reformers against the same accusations arising from Catholics: "'What (say they)? where was this Church of yours before these fifty years?'" (*Acts and Monuments* [1684], I, 3), affirming that the Protestants' Church preceded theirs in its authenticity and precepts. His volumes repeatedly highlight the extirpation of books and alleged heretics as a flagrantly tyrannical policy, "Forsomuch as

> Heere see the craft of Satan, and malice of Antichrist and his Ministers: they waste the flock of Christ with bloudy slaughters, and require of us, Where are those of our brethren whom they have slaine? They traduce us for paucity, whom they by their massacres have brought to so small a number. They upbraid us with those maymes, and skarres which themselves have given us, and put us to produce those evidences which themselves have burned and made away.[91]

The parallel is not of course exact, since Swift's Modern makes no claim at all to be the true preserver of Antiquity, and his own efforts to name texts which presently exist are both plaintive and feeble. None the less, his protest at their anticipated disappearance carries some resonance (parodic or otherwise) when we are reminded of the dictatorial power of the Romanists and their guile in keeping "Posterity" well away from the writings of heretics.[92] Even in

---

it is and hath alwaies been the common guise and practise of the popes church to extinct, condemne and abolish all good books and holesome treatises of learned men, under a false pretence of errors and heresies, whereof examples abundantlie may appeare in this historie" ([1610], II, 1135). He sets down in full the words of the Proclamation of July 1546 ordering the books of Coverdale, Tindal and others to be burned (II, 1135), and those of "The railing Bull of Pope Leo against Luther": "We forbid under the incurring of all and singular the penalties afore expressed in so doing, that no man presume by anie manner of waie ... to reade, holde, preach, praise, print, publish or defend ... the saide books and writings ... to the intent that his memorie may utterlie be rooted out from the fellowship of Christian people, or rather with fire to consume them, as is before declared" ([1610], II, 1169).

91 *The Romish Fisher Cavght and Held in His Owne Net*, "The Eighth Assertion," sigs N8-O1. Featley's outrage is expressed again under the heading "The Fifth Assertion" when he presents the accession of Hildebrand (Pope Gregory VII) as so "transcendent" for the abusive power of the Roman Church that it is astonishing that any resistance to papal authority was voiced at all: "It is rather to be maruailed, that wee haue any who haue displayed the abominations of the *Whore* of *Babylon*." "Set the Pope or Church of Rome out in her colours, and shee will make you a *light* of the Church, by burning you at a stake" (sig. Q3*v). As to books and annals, he continues by noting that "*For some hundreds of yeeres, the chiefe Records and Monuments of the Westerne Church haue been in the hands of our Romish aduersaries, who haue partly burned them, partly corrupted them, and partly kept them from vs* ... our aduersaries take away from vs, or make away from vs our records; and then they *non*-sute vs, for want of euidence" (sig. Q4*v). Concerning the persons of heretics, and specifically the Waldensians, Perrin's *Luthers Fore-runners* declares "they have been cruelly condemned to death, banished, sacked, burnt, cursed, and persecuted with violence of armes ... Without reason then is it demanded, where the Church was in these ages long past" ("Preface," sig. A3).

92 Featley writes that "*Auentine* brandeth Pope *Hildebrand* [Gregory VII] with the marke of a corrupter of Chronicles, and a razer out of them the things that were done ... If we might haue accesse to the Popes Library, we doubt not, but that wee should finde many more bookes written, both in Latine and Greek, against the Pope" ... "so hee that hath but

the reign of James II, the King gave orders for the English translation of Jean Claude's account of the persecution of Protestants in France[93] to be burned as "an infamous libel," thus attempting to negate the credibility of the events and remove any record of them. The appeal of Swift's Hack against the partiality of Time also echoes those of Protestant works such as Favour's; Favour laments that under the power of Rome, "our cause is prejudiced, our credits empaired, and our persons condemned unto temporall, our soules unto eternall condemnation," and that "we ... have already felt, and have good cause yet to feare manifold, unsufferable and intollerable grievances, from that ignorant, passionate, partiall, and unrighteous Judge [the Bishop of Rome]" (p. 582).

However incongruous it may seem to place such weighty issues as papal oppression, martyrdom, and the foundations of the Church side by side with Swift's essentially light-spirited, satirical voicing of the Modern's opening complaints against Time, the intertextual connections between the two subjects have a cumulative potency and persuasiveness. Although the links with theological and ecclesiastical discourse are not sustained throughout the "Dedication to Prince Posterity," they form a significant prelude to Swift's development, in the *Tale* as a whole, of intricate and witty connections between what we may now think of as the "literary" domain and the realms of religious dispute and historiography. Both of these – most especially the latter – formed the basis of the hugely expanded print culture within which the *Tale*'s Moderns forage for a living; and it should also be no surprise to find, once again, the identity of a dissenting Christian underlying (or interwoven with) that of the wounded, subjected, and carping narrator in the Tale's "Dedication." Above all, as a preacher within the Anglican establishment in Ireland, Swift is not simply engaged in parody of the dissenting enthusiast's obsessions concerning the Catholic threat and Catholic legacy; he must have drawn extensively on his own theological training and reading to touch on some of the key Reformation arguments concerning papal authority, as well as on the more obsessive (or

halfe an eie, may see, that the Romanists, in their *Indices expurgatorij*, blot out all sorts of Authors, whatsoeuer liketh them not, or any way makes against them" (sig. R*1r-v). See also Favour, *Antiquitie Triumphing over Noveltie*, pp. 354-55.

93 Jean Claude, *An Account of the Persecutions and Oppressions of the Protestants in France* (London: J. Norris, 1686). Steve Pincus points out that many British Catholics at this time were themselves opposed to the excesses of French Catholicism under Louis XIV and to the perceived excesses of James; see "The European Catholic Context of the Revolution of 1688-89: Gallicanism, Innocent XI, and Catholic Opposition," in *Shaping the Stuart World, 1603-1714: The Atlantic Connection*, eds Allan I. Macinnes and Arthur H. Williamson (Leiden and Boston: Brill, 2006), pp. 79-114 (101).

repetitious) dogmas and revelatory projections of dissenting Protestantism. I would not be so rash as to propose that he had read all or even many of the works cited in this article (his opinion of Richard Baxter, for example, was not high, although his having an opinion at all suggests that he had looked at some of Baxter's work);[94] but his allusions to so many of the episodes and issues raised in a range of Protestant literature suggest a familiarity with controversies that none the less enrich and enliven his satire.

94 See Swift's marginal note, inscribed in his copy of Gilbert Burnet's *History of his Own Times, 1724-34*, p. 180. To Burnet's comment that Baxter was "A man of great piety, and if he had not meddled in too many things, would have been esteemed one of the learned men of the age: he writ near 200 books," Swift has added: "Very sad [poor] ones" (*Prose Works*, V, 270).

Rudolf Freiburg
Friedrich-Alexander-Universität, Erlangen-Nürnberg

"These you distil in *balneo Mariæ*": Swift's Use of Alchemy in *A Tale of a Tub*

Abstract. Alchemy is a highly complex and paradoxical 'system' of thought. On the one hand, it ushers in the new Age of the Enlightenment, since it refutes scholastic philosophy and develops an experimental attitude towards nature and reality, with which many members of the New Science – among them, Isaac Newton and Robert Boyle – could easily sympathize. On the other hand, alchemy reveals the contours of an idiosyncratic doctrine based on a melange of myths, biblical quotations, vulgar errors, and speculations. With its endeavour to produce gold (*chrysopoeia*), its belief in immortality, and its search for the philosopher's stone, alchemy builds castles in the air, which in the eyes of many eighteenth-century philosophers were absurd. It is precisely this grotesque aura of alchemy that interests a satirist like Jonathan Swift. Although he detested alchemy and its garrulous representatives such as Artephius, Thomas Vaughan, and Elias Ashmole, he was fascinated by the preposterous ideas of these 'occult writers.' In his most brilliant satire, *A Tale of a Tub* (1704), Swift imitated the language and thought of both alchemists and Rosicrucians in order to explode 'gross corruptions' in religion and learning. Whereas Swift lavishes abuse on Peter, the representative of Catholicism, and Jack, the spokesman of Puritanism, whom he associates with alchemical learning, he widely spares Martin, the representative of Anglicanism, who has been regarded as the satirical norm. This paper shows that alchemy is a strong force in the field of semantic gravitation.

1. Introduction: The Paradoxes of Alchemy

When I asked Julian Barnes about his attitude towards God in an interview in 1999, he gave me an answer which was to be repeated in his meditation on mortality, *Nothing to Be Frightened of* (2008) a decade later: "I don't believe in God, but I miss him."[1] Reading Jonathan Swift's *A Tale of a Tub* (1704) again this year, I found that Barnes's paradoxical aphorism offered itself as an appropriate appraisal of Swift's use of alchemy in his most difficult satire: Swift, it is clear from the start, does not believe in alchemy, but 'he misses it.' The theme of 'alchemy' permeates the *Tale* to such a degree that it is impossible to deny

1 See Rudolf Freiburg, "'Novels Come out of Life Not Theory': An Interview with Julian Barnes," in *"Do you consider yourself a postmodern author?": Interviews with Contemporary English Writers*, eds Rudolf Freiburg and Jan Schnitker (Münster: LIT, 1999), pp. 39-66 (56), and Julian Barnes, *Nothing to be Frightened of* (London: Jonathan Cape, 2008), p. 1.

 | DOI:10.30965/9783846763971_008

Swift's fascination for this specimen of esoteric learning. On the one hand, for Swift, alchemy is a clearly defined satirical target, which enabled the later Dean of St Patrick's to lavish as much abuse upon it, as he liked; on the other hand, alchemy is the integral part of a highly colourful and mystic world view which gives the *Tale* a poetic touch: alchemy provides precisely that linguistic charm and stylistic bathos which transforms the harsh attacks on religion and learning into a *tour de force* through human insanities, and it permits Swift to present even the most absurd ideas in a beautiful shape: "Pretty! in amber to observe the forms of ... dirt," as Alexander Pope once put it in his "Epistle to Dr Arbuthnot" (1735).[2] As is so often the case with Swift, the reader faces an intriguing paradox: Swift seems to be deeply immersed in precisely that system he intends to attack;[3] the *Tale*'s persona reveals a mindset characterized by superstition, Cabbalism, Neoplatonism, Paracelsianism, and Rosicrucianism that was scorned by Swift and his patron Sir William Temple. But the authenticity of the persona's occult style, which is almost indistinguishable from the writings of Thomas Vaughan, Artephius, and Paracelsus also proves that Swift was well familiar with alchemy and esoteric thinking:[4]

> During the seventeenth century belief in more esoteric doctrines appeared to wane, or was at least driven underground. The relationship between natural science and esoterica was undoubtedly complex. A new historiography of alchemy and chemistry has shown that the two disciplines are not readily distinguishable, and that scientists practised both disciplines concurrently.[5]

---

2 Alexander Pope, "Epistle to Dr. Arbuthnot: or, Prologue to the Satires," in Alexander Pope, *Collected Poems*, ed. Bonamy Dobrée (London: Dent, 1975 [1924]), p. 257, ll. 169-70.

3 See Miriam Kosh Starkman, "Philosophy, Old and New, Bright and Dark," *Swift's Satire on Learning in "A Tale of a Tub"* (New York: Octagon Books, 1968 [1950]), pp. 23-63 (63): "Swift thought with the mind of a philosopher and attacked philosophy. He wrote as dialectically as any metaphysician and attacked metaphysics. He celebrated the power of Reason and attacked man's rationalism. In his immense erudition he attacked intellectualism. In his overwhelming pride as a creature of God he attacked man's pride. Were he not so devout a Christian, he could not have been so militant a moralist; were he not so militant a moralist he could not have been so devastating a satirist of the madness and depravity of 'frail man', 'sole arbiter of truth, in endless error hurled.'"

4 For the manifold influences on Swift and the extraordinary significance of Nicolas de Montfaucon de Villar's *Le Comte de Gabalis: ou, Entretiens sur les sciences secrètes* (Paris, 1671) and Louis Moréri's *Great Historical, Geographical, and Poetical Dictionary* (1694), see Brean Hammond, "Swift's Reading," *The Cambridge Companion to Jonathan Swift*, ed. Christopher Fox (Cambridge: Cambridge University Press, 2003), pp. 73-86 (79). In his library, Swift had books on occult philosophy by Henricus Cornelius Agrippa and Paracelsus (PASSMANN AND VIENKEN I, 28-32 and 259-68).

5 Marcus Walsh, "Introduction," *A Tale of a Tub and Other Works*, ed. Marcus Walsh (Cambridge: Cambridge University Press, 2010), pp. xxxi-xc (lxxii).

Arcane learning, one could maintain, is an integral element of the prevailing world view of the late seventeenth century. Like a Baconian idol, it shapes ideas to such a degree that they might be looked upon as a kind of *a priori* categories in the perception of the world,[6] as lingering intellectual gravitational forces bending even such an alert mind as that of Isaac Newton.[7] Members of the highest echelons of society practised alchemy, and paragons of the Enlightenment like René Descartes and Robert Boyle were not immune to the enticement of occult learning. (Admittedly, Boyle is usually regarded as the 'scientist' who, with the publication of *The Sceptical Chymist* of 1661, bid farewell to alchemy and ushered in the age of modern chemistry, but then, he was keen to find the philosopher's stone.[8]) As is well known, Newton, who paradoxically "belonged to the pre-Newtonian world,"[9] followed suit. Not only did he write a commentary on the Emerald Table,[10] his biographers also conjecture that his mental breakdown in 1693 was caused by intense experimentation with mercury.[11] A fascinating melange, consisting of clear scientific ideas and dubious alchemical notions simultaneously, shaped the thinking of many members of the Royal Society, among them, Elias Ashmole,[12] Thomas Henshaw, Sir Robert Paston, and Christopher Wren.[13] In a world in which the cultures of arcane learning and modern science interfere, it is the satirist whose metier paradoxically

6 For Bacon's doctrine of the idols, see Wolfgang Krohn, *Francis Bacon* (München: Verlag C. H. Beck, 1987), pp. 93-107.

7 Newton, throughout his life, never lost his interest in alchemy; he spent a fortune on the purchase of alchemical instruments and studied occult writings; he was "not only a secret alchemist but, in the breadth of his knowledge and his experimentation, the peerless alchemist of Europe" (James Gleick, *Isaac Newton* [London and New York: Fourth Estate, 2003], p. 101).

8 In order to get access to the arcana of alchemy, Boyle even sent many gifts to Georges Pierre des Clozets, "who claimed to be the agent of the 'Patriarch of Antioch,' leader of a society of alchemical members," whom Boyle wanted to join (Lisa Jardine, *Ingenious Pursuits: Building the Scientific Revolution* [London: Little Brown, 1999], pp. 325-31 [330]).

9 Gleick, *Isaac Newton*, p. 102.

10 See B. J. T. Dobbs, "Newton's *Commentary* on the *Emerald Tablet* of Hermes Trismegistus: Its Scientific and Theological Significance," *Hermeticism and the Renaissance: Intellectual History and the Occult in Early Modern Europe*, eds Ingrid Merkel and Allen G. Debus (Washington: Folger Books; London and Toronto: Associated University Presses, 1988), pp. 182-91.

11 See Jardine, *Ingenious Pursuits*, p. 331.

12 See also Robert M. Schuler, "Some Spiritual Alchemies of Seventeenth-Century England," *Journal of the History of Ideas*, 41 (1980), 293-318 (p. 294).

13 The attempt to find the 'longitude at sea' is a good example of this interference between alchemical procedures and science; see Rudolf Freiburg, "'Our never failing guide, the Watch': der 'Längengrad' in der englischen Literatur und Kultur des achtzehnten Jahrhunderts," *Zwischen Literatur und Naturwissenschaft: Debatten –*

resembles that of the alchemist. Like Paracelsus in his *Ars spagyrica*,[14] the satirist tries to separate the gross matter of superstition (the *caput mortuum* in alchemy) from the finer ingredients of scientific truth. The satirist looks for the ultimate truth or the norm, just as the alchemist searches for the philosopher's stone or the touchstone. Both see themselves as physicians intending to heal diseases of the body and the mind. Both accentuate the binary opposition of 'matter' and 'spirit', and both try to 'conjunct' (*coniunctio*) opposites like 'male' and 'female.' Thus, the satirist's language heavily leans on alchemical lore. And due to its almost impenetrable aura of darkness, which makes Swift's 'mock book' so difficult to read,[15] it is closely linked to classical works of occultism such as the legendary *Tabula Smaragdina* (6th century), the *Anthroposophia Theomagica* (1650), the *Fama Fraternitatis* (1614), *The Chymical Wedding* (1616), or the *Theatrum Chemicum* (1602). All these texts present hermeneutical riddles to their clientele, all of them may be looked upon as epitomes of radical hermeticism allowing only a small coterie of neophytes to enter their secret worlds. In these esoteric texts, obscurity was a kind of protection,[16] to prevent a mass audience from learning the secret messages of the elitist texts.[17] The world of "hermetic semiosis,"[18] of ambivalence, and semantic pluralism, is also a hallmark of the *Tale*, in which Swift was

> the spurious guardian of textual secrets and magical sub-texts which he mirrored in his own writings ... he perpetuated the very obscurantism he sought to condemn: excelled in erudition while attacking the erudite and, in giving vent to his iconoclastic impulses, embraced the supremely iconic. But far from creating

Probleme – Visionen, eds Rudolf Freiburg, Christine Lubkoll, and Harald Neumeyer (Berlin and Boston: Walter de Gruyter, 2017), pp. 33-62.

14 See Claus Priesner, "Über die Wirklichkeit des Okkulten: Naturmagie und Alchemie in der Frühen Neuzeit," *Diskurse der Gelehrtenkultur in der Frühen Neuzeit: ein Handbuch*, ed. Herbert Jaumann (Berlin and New York: Walter de Gruyter, 2011), pp. 305-45 (313).

15 See also Walsh, "Introduction," *A Tale of a Tub and Other Works*, ed. Walsh, p. xxxiii.

16 See Gerhard Eis, "Von der Rede und dem Schweigen der Alchemisten," *Vor und nach Paracelsus: Untersuchungen über Hohenheims Traditionsverbundenheit und Nachrichten über seine Anhänger* (Stuttgart: Gustav Fischer, 1965), pp. 51-73.

17 See also Stanton J. Linden, "Alchemical Art and the Renaissance Emblem," *Secret Texts: The Literature of Secret Societies*, eds Marie Mulvey Roberts and Hugh Ormsby-Lennon (New York: AMS, 1995), pp. 7-23 (7-8).

18 For Umberto Eco's formula of "hermetic semiosis," see Petra Feuerstein-Herz and Stefan Laube, "Zur Einführung," *Goldenes Wissen: die Alchemie – Substanzen, Synthesen, Symbolik*, eds Petra Feuerstein-Herz and Stefan Laube (Wiesbaden: Harrassowitz, 2016 [2014]), pp. 13-17 [16]).

> a broom-stick for his own back, Swift was, in fact, playing the obscurantists at their own game.[19]

Seen from this perspective, the *balneum Mariæ* addressed in the title of this essay serves as an appropriate metaphor for the structure of the *Tale*: the *bain-marie*, or 'Mary's Bath,' is "a double-hulled pot used for warming components slowly and evenly. The outer pot is subjected to direct heat and is filled with a liquid, usually water, into which the second, inner pot is placed. The substance to be heated is placed inside the second vessel."[20] The bipartite structure of the *Tale*, consisting of paratexts and allegory, resembles the structure of this instrument.

2. Allusions to Alchemy in the *Tale*

In his "Apology," Swift leaves no doubt that he set out to lambaste the "*gross Corruptions*" of religion and learning,[21] but right from the start, the messages and the meaning of the *Tale* are concealed behind a veil of obscurity, inconsistency, and eccentricity. The reader is made to stumble through a maze of paratextual passages, not untypical of seventeenth-century texts in general,[22] but in Swift's case a clear attempt to imitate the adept's difficult approach to arcane wisdom. According to the alchemical and Rosicrucian predilection for the number 'seven,' one would expect as many preambles, but Swift presents only 'six', a number regarded as the most productive in Cabbalah: the "Apology," "The Dedication to Lord Somers," "The Bookseller to the Reader," "The Epistle Dedicatory to His Royal Highness, Prince Posterity," and finally "The Preface" are likely to bewilder anyone who enters the world of the *Tale* for the first time, since they seemingly lack order and coherence. The reader's mind 'rotates' like a tub thrown into high water; any attempt to cling to this tub sets it in motion again. Just as in the grand narratives of alchemy, these preliminary texts are intended to fend off any person not dignified enough to learn the arcana. To be

19 Marie Mulvey Roberts, "Science, Magic and Masonry: Swift's Secret Texts," *Secret Texts*, eds Roberts and Ormsby-Lennon, p. 97.

20 Jordan Stratford, *A Dictionary of Western Alchemy* (Wheaton, Illinois: Theosophical Publishing House, 2011), p. 13.

21 See Swift, "Apology," in *A Tale of a Tub and Other Works*, ed. Walsh, pp. 5-15 (5). All further quotations from Swift's *Tale* refer to this edition and are given in parentheses within the text.

22 See also Ehrenpreis, *Mr Swift*, pp. 204-15 (204-5), who sees these paratexts as "elaborate arrangements" which are "bestowed on books whose content did not deserve them."

sure, the amorphous structure of the book could be explained with a reference to the etymology of satire as *satura lanx*; but in the *Tale* the lack of coherence is also reminiscent of the techniques of alchemical writers, such as the Pseudo-Geber in his *Summa perfectionis magisterii* (13th century),[23] who intentionally jumbles the individual chapters of his occult text in order to render its understanding more difficult.[24] Moreover, the obscurity of Swift's *Tale* echoes the world of many freak-shows and Paracelsian bombastic promises of self-appointed (miracle) healers, quacks, and barkers,[25] and it is meant to provoke the reader's curiosity. On a more primitive hermeneutical level, it promises to let him in on a secret; on a more advanced level of understanding, it creates a *jeu d'esprit* for the truly enlightened.

Swift is no stickler for alchemical terminology in his *Tale*; when it serves his satirical intentions, he imitates the common virtuoso's language meticulously, only to deviate from both the jargon and the logic of arcane learning a moment later; it is a specific 'satirical licence' which Swift claims – just as he did when he imitated nautical terminology in *Gulliver's Travels* (1726). He ironically addresses readers who are eager not to miss a subtle allusion that might enable them to create the *opus magnum*, the great alchemical work, and perhaps to find the philosopher's stone themselves. Wild conjectures about hidden meanings in the *Tale* are provoked by the partly garrulous, partly solemn 'tubman,' whose interest it is to keep the tale rotating, since in alchemy 'rotation' is said to be a successful device to transform matter into spirit and to bring down the *quinta essentia* from heaven.[26] The tubman himself could be seen as a reference to Tubal-Cain, "the biblical father of metallurgy, mentioned in Genesis

23 For the tremendous influence the ideas of Geber (721-815) or Abu Musa Jabir, ibn Hayyan al-Azdi, had on Western alchemy, see *A Dictionary of Western Alchemy*, ed. Stratford, p. 36.

24 See Volkhard Wels, "Die Tradierung alchemischen Wissens bei Michael Maier, Andreas Libavius und Oswald Croll," *Natur – Religion – Medien: Transformationen frühneuzeitlichen Wissens*, eds Thorsten Burkard, *et al.* (Berlin Akademie Verlag, 2013), pp. 63-85 (66).

25 The best introduction into this fantastic world of mountebanks, quacks, and imposters is to be found in Hugh Ormsby-Lennon, *Hey Presto! Swift and the Quacks* (Newark: University of Delaware Press, 2011); for Swift's and Johann Burkhard Mencke's endeavours to warn against this popular culture of superstition, false learning, and Rosicrucian hubris in healing, see Chapter 6 "Aping the Medicine Show: Mencken, Salmon, Yworth" (pp. 133-71).

26 For the principle of 'rotation' in alchemy, see Alexander Roob, "Einleitung: das hermetische Museum," *Das hermetische Museum: Alchemie & Mystik* (Köln: Taschen, 2006 [1996]), pp. 8-33 (30-31); see also Thomas Vaughan, *Magia Adamica: or, The Antiquitie of Magic* (London: by T. W. for H. Blunden, 1650), p. 7; now available in *The Works of Thomas Vaughan*, eds Alan Rudrum and Jennifer Drake-Brockman (Oxford: Clarendon Press, 1984), p. 153.

4:22."[27] Swift was writing his tract at a time when his contemporaries were fascinated with the devices of *cryptologia* and *cryptographia*, sophisticated methods to conceal the intended meaning from an uninspired audience:

> The gods and nature would not themselves have hidden so many things from us, if they had intended them for common understandings, or that others should treat of them, after an easie and perspicuous way: Hence was it that the learned men of former times were so generally inclined, to involve all their Learning, in obscure and mysterious expressions.[28]

Secret messages were concealed in candles or (following the example of Herodotus and Aulus Gellius) they were tattooed on the skin of a person's skull before he let his hair grow again.[29] John Wilkins, a passionate teacher of cryptography, recommends that that "which is written with the water of putrified Willow, of the distilled Juice of Glow-Worms, will not be visible but in the dark, as *Porta* affirms from his own experience."[30] Swift, as we know from his *Journal to Stella* (1766), was fond of linguistic games such as "inversions," "transmutation," "diminution," and "augmentation,"[31] and since alchemy and arcane learning worked with secret codes of language, the very title *A Tale of a Tub* could be identified as an anagram meaning 'But a foe [of the] elate,"[32] that is, of the enthusiast, or inspired *adeptus*, of both arcane learning and religion. Such a process of deciphering would probably qualify for one of the 9,743 persons, the "current number of *Wits* in this Island," potential members of the Academy, which among many other schools ("a large *Pederastick* School;" "The School of *Salivation*") also comprises a "*Spelling* School" (pp. 41-42).

Especially in his "Preface," Swift conditions his reader to become aware of the potential arcane messages hidden in the *sanctum* of his *Tale* (p. 33); he issues ironical instructions how to interpret his text, and in this way follows the time-honoured tradition of arcane writings.[33] In a well-known alchemical text

27 *A Dictionary of Western Alchemy*, ed. Stratford, p. 84.

28 John Wilkins, *Mercury: or, The Secret and Swift Messenger, Shewing How a Man May with Privacy and Speed Communicate his Thoughts to a Friend at Any Distance* (London: Richard Baldwin, 1694), p. 16.

29 Wilkins, *Mercury: or, The Secret and Swift Messenger*, pp. 29-31.

30 Wilkins, *Mercury: or, The Secret and Swift Messenger*, p. 42.

31 Wilkins, *Mercury: or, The Secret and Swift Messenger*, p. 21.

32 Wordplays like this are "ubiquitous in alchemical literature" (*A Dictionary of Western Alchemy*, ed. Stratford, p. xxiii).

33 The quack's claims about the frequency of the letter 'O' (p. 187) and his suggestions for mathematical operations (multiplication and division) do not make any sense; see Douglas Duhaime, "Pseudo-Cryptography in Jonathan Swift's *Tale of a Tub*"

of the thirteenth century, the *Rosarium Philosophorum*, this hermeneutical advice may be found:

> Wherever we have spoken openly, we have (actually) said nothing. But where we have written down something as a coded text and in images, there we have veiled the truth.[34]

This advice recurs in this instruction in the *Tale*:

> There are certain common Privileges of a Writer, the Benefit whereof, I hope, there will be no Reason to doubt; Particularly, that where I am not understood, it shall be concluded, that something very useful and profound is coucht underneath, And again, that whatever word or Sentence is Printed in a different Character, shall be judged to contain something extraordinary either of *Wit* or *Sublime*. (p. 29)

'Satirical licence' allows Swift to impress his audience with a pseudo-learned technique of name-dropping. Many depictions in the *Tale* reveal the contours of a mind deeply immersed in alchemy. The description of the "Modern Theatre" in "The Introduction" associates "weighty Matter" with the alchemist's materials of "Lead" and "Gold" and interprets communication in the theatre as a process of "refinement" and "distillation" (p. 39), and the same is true of the Hack's description of the pulpits in the context of a "Physico-logical Scheme of Oratorial Receptacles or Machines;" in other words, "tools" that serve the purpose to transcend the level of gross matter (p. 39). It is no coincidence that the Hack uses the word "exalt" here (p. 39), a technical term pilfered from the alchemist's dictionary, a kind of 'sublimation' which has the power to draw all things unto it.[35] And the "Ladder," finally, is one of the most popular images in alchemy and serves to symbolize the connections between the material and the spiritual world (p. 40). These descriptions are accompanied by hermeneutic instructions to regard all things as polysemic entries into the "Book of

(<http://douglasduhaime.com/blog/pseudo-cryptography-in-jonathan-swifts-tale-of-a-tub>, accessed 22 January 2017).

34 "Wo immer wir offen gesprochen haben, haben wir (eigentlich) nichts gesagt. Aber wo wir etwas verschlüsselt und in Bildern niedergeschrieben haben, dort haben wir die Wahrheit verhüllt;" quoted from Roob, "Einleitung," *Das hermetische Museum*, p. 31. According to Samuel Butler, hermetic philosophers use spectacles with which they revert their object and "turn the wrong End of [the] sentences upwards and make them look like sense;" here quoted from J. Andrew Mendelsohn, "Alchemy and Politics in England, 1649-1665," *Past and Present*, 135 (1992), 30-78 (p. 78).

35 See *A Dictionary of Western Alchemy*, ed. Stratford, p. 31.

Nature,"[36] which can only be appropriately interpreted by readers aware of all the literal, typological, tropological, and anagogical connotations of a word.[37] The irony cannot be overlooked here, because the pulpits employ a kind of alchemical process of distillation by focusing not on matter but on something that is spiritual per se from the beginning: "*Sense*" and "*Human Reason*":

> Now this Physico-logical Scheme of Oratorial Receptacles or Machines, contains a great Mystery, being a Type, a Sign, an Emblem, a Shadow, a Symbol, bearing Analogy to the spacious Commonwealth of Writers, and to those Methods by which they must exalt themselves to a certain Eminency above the inferiour World. By the *Pulpit* are adumbrated the Writings of our *Modern Saints* in *Great Britain*, as they have spiritualized and refined them from the Dross and Grossness of *Sense* and *Human Reason*. (p. 39)

The subsequent allusions to Saturn, the God of "Time and Chronology" and an important force in alchemical processes, refer to the alchemist's dream of controlling time: the "clipping of Saturn's wings," the "paring of his Nails," and the "filing of his teeth" symbolize the alchemist's intention to abolish the laws of chronology (p. 40), to achieve in a few hours something for which nature needs ages, particularly *chrysopoeia*,[38] the production of gold. The "Illustrious Fraternity" may clearly be seen as an allusion to the Rosicrucian Fraternity (p. 40),[39] which held out the promise of immortality,[40] and their *spiritus rector* Christian Rosenkreuz, who was said to have conquered time and lived for

36 See Thomas Vaughan, *The Fame and Confession of the Fraternity R.C., Commonly, of the Rosie Cross, with a Praefece Annexed thereto, and a Short Declaration of their Physicall Work* (London: Giles Calvert, 1652), p. 47: "Although that great Book of *Nature* stand[s] open to all Men, yet there are but few that can read and understand the Same."

37 See Hugh Ormsby-Lennon, "Nature's Mystic Book: Renaissance Arcanum into Restoration Cant," in *Secret Texts*, eds Roberts and Ormsby-Lennon, pp. 24-96.

38 See *A Dictionary of Western Alchemy*, ed. Stratford, p. 19.

39 Such a group never existed in Germany; it is a "legend without historical evidence" (Paul Arnold, "Descartes und die Rosenkreuzer," *Antaios*, 1 [1959], 227-45 [p. 229]). Nevertheless, this non-existing group exerted an enormous influence on Germany. See W. Beeler, "Johann Valentin Andreae," *Dictionary of Literary Biography, 164: German Baroque Writers, 1580-1660*, ed. James Hardin (Detroit and London: Bruccoli Clark Lyman, 1996), pp. 13-19 (17): "The effect of the Rosicrucian texts was remarkable: soon after their appearance Germany was inundated with publications related to the Rosicrucian Society."

40 See also Beeler, "Johann Valentin Andreae," p. 16: "Wehre es nicht ein köstlich Ding, daß du köndtest alle Stunde also leben als wenn du von Anfang der Welt bißher gelebet hettest, und noch ferner biß ans Ende derselben leben solltest? [Would it not be a delightful thing if you were to have lived all hours from the beginning of the world until now and moreover were to continue to live till its end]?"

more than 100 years.[41] The members of the Rosicrucian Society tried to remain completely invisible.[42] The alchemical conditioning of the reader in "The Introduction" comes to the fore in the passage in which the Hack laments that the productions of his "Society" are no longer understood adequately:

> But the greatest Maim given to that general Reception, which the Writings of our Society have formerly received ... hath been a superficial Vein among many Readers of the present Age, who will by no means be persuaded to inspect beyond the Surface and the Rind of Things; whereas *Wisdom* is a *Fox*, who after long hunting, will at last cost you the Pains to dig out: 'Tis a *Cheese*, which by how much the richer, has the thicker, the homelier, and the courser Coat; and whereof to a judicious Palate, the *Maggots* are the best. 'Tis a *Sack-Posset*, wherein the deeper you go, you will find it the sweeter. *Wisdom* is a *Hen*, whose *Cackling* we must value and consider, because it is attended with an *Egg*; But then, lastly, 'tis a *Nut*, which unless you chuse with Judgment, may cost you a Tooth, and pay you with nothing but a *Worm*. (pp. 41-42)

All these images express the relationship between the outward appearance of a thing and its essence, but again Swift is here referring to the alchemist's opinion that all true things are veiled and enshrouded. Swift's method consists of employing images frequently used by alchemy; clearly, "he found value in alchemical ideas and images as an imaginative force."[43] The 'fox' usually symbolizes sulphur in alchemical texts,[44] but here it could also be interpreted as a reference to the Quaker George Fox, who was a connoisseur of "mystical birdsong."[45] The 'hen' evokes thoughts of black magic, with the 'egg' being not only an alchemical "digesting flask,"[46] or an "Athanor," an "egg-shaped vessel,"[47] but also the result of alchemical endeavours to produce the philosopher's

41 See Everett F. Bleiler, "Johann Valentin Andreae, Fantasist and Utopist," *Science Fiction Studies*, 35, no 1 (2008), 1-30 (p. 2).

42 For the relationship between the Rosicrucians and the 'Invisible College,' to which eminent figures such as Samuel Hartlib, John Drury, and Johann Comenius belonged, see Roberts, "Science, Magic and Masonry: Swift's Secret Texts," in *Secret Texts*, eds Roberts and Ormsby-Lennon, pp. 102-3; see also Frances A. Yates, *The Rosicrucian Enlightenment* (London and Boston: Routledge and Kegan Paul, 1972), pp. 182-83.

43 See Gregory Lynall, "Swift's 'Poetical Chymistry': Alchemy and Allusion in the Verse," *The Review of English Studies*, NS, 63, no 26 (2011), 588-607 (p. 607).

44 See Roob, *Das hermetische Museum*, pp. 300-1.

45 For George Fox as a representative of the mystic interpretation of "Adam's living library," see Hugh Ormsby-Lennon, "Rosicrucian Linguistics: Twilight of a Renaissance Tradition," *Hermeticism and the Renaissance*, eds Merkel and Debus, pp. 311-41 (320-23).

46 See "The Chymistry of Isaac Newton" (<http://webapp1.dlib.indiana.edu/newton/reference/glossary.do>, s.v., accessed 21 February 2018).

47 For further uses of the egg in alchemy, see Mark Haeffner, *Dictionary of Alchemy: From Maria Prophetissa to Isaac Newton* (San Francisco: Harper Collins Publishers, 1994 [1991]), pp. 82-85.

stone, a veritable reason for Rosicrucians to feel proud.[48] In Thomas Vaughan's *Magia Adamica* (1650), the hen and the egg are even associated with the Holy Ghost:

> The *Holy Spirit* moving upon the *Chaos*, which *Action* some *Divines* compare to the *Incubation* of a *Hen* upon her *Eggs*, did together with his *Heat* communicat other *manifold Influences* to the *Matter*.[49]

The 'nut' has always been a symbol of riddles; it was not only used in "Salomon's *Song of Songs*" (300 BC) and in Shakespeare's *Hamlet* (1602), but also inspired the tale of the nut Krakatuk in E. T. A. Hoffmann's alchemical fairy tale *Nußknacker und Mausekönig* (1816),[50] and Joyce made use of it as late as in *Finnegan's Wake* (1939).[51] In Cabbalistic contexts, the term "to mount into the depth of the nut" means to meditate upon the theme of 'Nothing,' a meditation with which the *Tale* concludes with the Hack setting out on an "Experiment very frequent among Modern Authors; which is to *write upon Nothing*" (p. 135). Likewise, the 'maggot' has many meanings in the eighteenth century, including "whim," "quirk," and "obsession,"[52] and it also turns up in iatrochemical contexts.[53] The 'cheese,' finally, may be a compliment that Swift as a critic of alchemy pays to his predecessor Erasmus who, in *De generatione et corruptione*, had harshly attacked both the doctrines and logic of alchemists.[54] The reference to 'Sack-Possets' may allude to Thomas Vaughan's *Magia Adamica*, where the "dark author" meditates about the role of women in alchemy.[55]

---

48 See Bleiler, "Johann Valentin Andreae, Fantasist and Utopist," p. 14: "We stood around this egg with joy, just as if we had laid it ourselves."

49 Thomas Vaughan, "To the Reader," *Magia Adamica*, in *The Works of Thomas Vaughan*, eds Rudrum and Drake-Brockman, p. 148.

50 For an alchemical interpretation of this fairy tale, see Harald Neumeyer, "Wie eine Naturwissenschaft zum Märchen wird: die Alchemie-Debatte der Aufklärung und ihre literarischen Folgen," in *Zwischen Literatur und Naturwissenschaft*, eds Freiburg, *et al.*, pp. 63-84 (75).

51 See Roob, *Das hermetische Museum*, p. 264.

52 See John Fowles, "Prologue," *A Maggot* (London and Sidney: Pan Books, 1985), pp. 5-6 (5).

53 William R. Newman, *Atoms and Alchemy: Chymystry and the Experimental Origins of the Scientific Revolution* (Chicago and London: University of Chicago Press, 2006), p. 146.

54 See Newman, *Atoms and Alchemy*, pp. 48-49. Swift highly appreciated Erasmus and Thomas Morus because they – like himself – tried to make their readers think for themselves; see also Eugene Hammond, *Jonathan Swift: Irish Blow-In* (Newark: University of Delaware Press, 2016), p. 226.

55 See Thomas Vaughan, *Magia Adamica*, in *The Works of Thomas Vaughan*, eds Rudrum and Drake-Brockman, p. 220. For the influence Vaughan had on Swift's *Tale*, see Walsh, "Introduction," *A Tale of a Tub and Other Works*, ed. Walsh, pp. lxxii-lxxiii.

3. Alchemy and Religion

By praising the achievements of alchemy, the Hack prepares the very 'scandal in disguise' Pope speaks of in his "First Epistle of the Second Book of Horace."[56] Beyond the Hack's encomium on alchemy Swift reveals an abyss of irony, suggesting that the hermetical doctrines are as hollow and empty as Christian Rosenkreuz's grave. The aura of alchemy thus strengthens the very field of semantic gravity,[57] by which lofty concepts of thought and ideology are rigorously pulled 'down to earth' again. The bare suspicion that the representatives of a philosophical system sympathize with the hermeticism of alchemy suffices to render them absurd; no one is supposed to take esoteric learning seriously. The moment religion and learning merge with alchemy, they are in extreme danger of losing both their identity and their reputation. In his attack on alchemy and Rosicrucianism, Swift obviously endorsed his admired patron, Sir William Temple, who had written in *Some Thoughts upon Reviewing the Essay on Antient and Modern Learning* (1701):

> I have always look'd upon alchymy in natural philosophy, to be like enthusiasm in divinity, and to have troubled the world much to the same purpose. And I should as soon fall into the study of the Rosycrucian philosophy, and expect to meet a *nymph* or a *sylph*, for a wife or a mistress, as with the elixir for my health, or philosopher's stone for my fortune.[58]

Like the Earl of Shaftesbury,[59] Swift looked upon Rosicrucianism as an extreme form of religious superstition. In his *Tale*, he derided both Catholicism and Puritanism from the normative perspective of Anglican orthodoxy.[60] However, if these two can be associated with the absurdities of alchemy and Rosicrucianism, implicit symbols of religious enthusiasm, as Temple maintained, they are entirely at the satirist's mercy.

Peter, the authoritarian representative of staunch Catholicism in the *Tale*, becomes Swift's first victim. His decision to turn "*Projector* and *Virtuoso*" (p. 68) associates him with alchemy. Among his "Discoveries, Projects and Machines"

---

56 "Praise undeserved is scandal in disguise;" see Alexander Pope, "The First Epistle of Second Book of Horace," in Pope, *Collected Poems*, ed. Dobrée, p. 303, l. 413.

57 See Joseph Bentley, "Semantic Gravitation: An Essay on Satiric Reduction," *Modern Language Quarterly*, 30 (1969), 3-19.

58 Here quoted from Ehrenpreis, "A Tale of a Tub (I)," *Mr Swift*, pp. 185-203 (198).

59 See A. Owen Aldridge, "Shaftesbury, Rosicrucianism and Links with Voltaire," *Canadian Review of Comparative Literature / Revue Canadienne de Littérature Comparée*, 23, no 2 (1998), 393-401 (p. 393).

60 See Starkman, "Philosophy, Old and New, Bright and Dark," p. 34.

(p. 68), such as the "Whispering Office" (p. 69) and the "Office of Ensurance" (p. 70), there are also those that refer to the world of alchemy: his "Sovereign Remedy for the Worms" (p. 69), the "Universal Pickle" (p. 70), and the "*Powder Pimperlim pimp*" (p. 70) may be identified as references to Sir Kenelm Digby's "*sympathetic powder*,"[61] to the alchemist's endeavour to find a Paracelsian panacea based on thaumaturgy and magic,[62] and also to the Rosicrucian ambition to heal all kinds of diseases. This esoteric mode of alchemy is redolent of the false promises of quacks and barkers, such as William Salmon, who offered "powders, plasters, salves, and drugs."[63] Peter's remedy "places him squarely within the mainstream of Restoration mountebankery."[64]

But the parallels between Catholicism and alchemy do not end here. One of the most essential elements of Catholicism is its belief in transubstantiation, the belief that in the Eucharist bread is turned into Christ's body and wine into his blood. For a satirist, the allurement to detect alchemical traces in this process is obvious. The practical alchemist, libelled as a mere "puffer" by the philosophers,[65] tries to transmute cheap metals into gold, while the esoteric alchemist tries to transform the human being into a mystic one by '*exantlation.*' To the utter astonishment of his Anglican and Puritan brothers, Peter transforms his "brown Loaf" of 'bread' (p. 74) into 'beef', which has the properties of an alchemical *quintessence*:

> *Bread*, says he, *Dear Brothers, is the Staff of Life; in which Bread is contained*, inclusivé, *the Quintessence of Beef, Mutton, Veal, Venison, Partridge, Plum-pudding, and Custard: And to render all compleat, there is intermingled a due Quantity of Water,*

---

61 The powder of 'pimperlimpimp' is an onomatopoetical word imitating the sounds of the chemist's pestle when he mixes his remedies in a mortar; see Arthur Conrad Ernsting, *Nucleus totius medicinae quinque partitus: Pars I. continet lexicon & dispensatorium pharmaceuticum; oder, Der volnkommene und allezeit fertige Apothecker*, I (Braunschweig: Meißner, 1741), 610; see also Clement Hawes, "Jonathan Swift and the Philosopher's Stone," *"The first wit of the age": Essays on Swift and his Contemporaries in Honour of Hermann J. Real*, eds Kirsten Juhas, Patrick Müller, and Mascha Hansen (Frankfurt on Main: Peter Lang, 2013), pp. 135-48 (140).

62 See Lucien Braun, "Magie bei Paracelsus," *Nova Acta Paracelsia*, 17 (2003), 17-27 (pp. 19-20).

63 See Hugh Ormsby-Lennon, "Universal Improvement of Mankind," in *Hey Presto!*, pp. 71-91 (79); for the 'worm-powder,' see pp. 84-85.

64 Hugh Ormsby-Lennon, "*Classis*? Under the Stage Itinerant," *Swift, the Enigmatic Dean: Festschrift for Hermann Josef Real*, eds Rudolf Freiburg, Arno Löffler, and Wolfgang Zach (Tübingen: Stauffenburg, 1998), pp. 173-99 (193).

65 See Schuler, "Some Spiritual Alchemies of Seventeenth-Century England," p. 311. Vaughan calls these persons who are only interested in producing gold and securing money "false *Alchimists*;" see also Vaughan, *The Fame and Confession of the Fraternity of R:C: Commonly of the Rosie Cross*, pp. 30, 52.

> *whose Crudities are also corrected by Yeast or Barm, thro' which means it becomes a wholesome fermented Liquor, diffused thro' the* Mass *of the Bread.* (p. 74)

Peter's insistence on the truth of the alchemical transformation of bread into beef finally causes the schism between him, and Martin and Jack; the Anglican and the Puritan brothers tend to trust their eyes. But it is not only the transformation from one form of matter into another that qualifies Peter as religious 'alchemist.' As Gregory Lynall has shown,[66] in the *Tale* "alchemical hermeneutic" is often used as a metaphor for illegitimate forms of interpretation and exegesis;[67] Peter follows the practice of alchemists to distort the meaning of texts:

> Not only did alchemists intentionally shroud their own works in symbolism, they also sought to discover the occult significance of non-alchemical texts by using cabbalistic or Rosicrucian formulae in their hermeneutical methods; a tendency to '*squeeze out a dangerous Meaning that was never thought on*' (p. 8).[68]

In Peter's attempt to interpret his father's will, the stratagems of Neoplatonic thought, Cabbalistic exegesis, alchemical obsession with secret meaning, and Rosicrucian predilection for literal-numerical anagrams are merged. Peter does not even try to understand a sentence as it is written down in his father's testament, but subjects it to a process of alchemical analysis, dissecting the scriptural matter before putting it together again in an arbitrary and idiosyncratic way. His alchemical anatomy of the literal '*corpus*' of his father's will is a ruthless vivisection of the living spirit. With his own interest in "shapes," "types," "symbols," "allegories," and "mystical numbers," Peter could doubtless become a member of the 'Rosicrucian Fraternity.' In Johann Valentin Andreae's *Chymische Hochzeit*, for instance, the protagonist faces an *Ænigma de Nomine*, a riddle made up of letters and numbers:

> My Name contains five and fifty, and yet hath only eight letters, the third is the third part of the fifth, which added to the sixth will produce a Number, whose root shall exceed the third it self by just the first, and it is the half of the fourth. Now the fifth and the seventh are equal, the Last and the first are also equal, and

66 Gregory Lynall, "'An Author *bonæ notæ*, and an *Adeptus*': Swift's Alchemical Satire and Satiric Alchemy in *A Tale of a Tub*," *Swift Studies*, 24 (2009), 27-45.

67 See Lynall, "'An Author *bonæ notæ*, and an *Adeptus*': Swift's Alchemical Satire and Satiric Alchemy in *A Tale of a Tub*," p. 32.

68 Lynall, "'An Author *bonæ notæ*, and an *Adeptus*': Swift's Alchemical Satire and Satiric Alchemy in *A Tale of a Tub*," p. 30.

> make with the second as much as the sixth hath, which contains just four more than the third tripl'd. Now tell me, my Lord, how am I called?[69]

The solution of the riddle is the word "alchemy."[70] Accompanied by three individual methods, the attempt to interpret the testament, according to the principles of "*totidem verbis*," "*totidem syllabis*," and "*totidem literis*" (p. 54) is reminiscent of the cabbalistic methods *Notarikon*, *Temurah*, and *Gematria*.[71] With these tricks, Peter gains more and more power to control the exegesis of the text; finally, he disregards the text completely and establishes a new mode of oral authority (the distinction between "*Nuncupatory* and *scriptory* wills") (p. 55). For Swift, alchemy was tantamount to *hubris*.

As he emphasized in his "Apology," Swift intended to "Celebrate the Church of England as the most perfect of all others in Discipline and Doctrine" (p. 6),[72] Martin comes forward as the physical manifestation of the satirical norm;[73] this is probably why Swift does not criticize him by portraying him as a disciple of alchemy. Although Martin's behaviour is not blameless when he first enters the scene, his further development leads him to a sober attitude towards life, preventing him from any of the imbecilities so characteristic of his brothers. "Humility and learning, by the *Tale*'s lights, are the best guides to the conduct of life," as one of Swift's more recent biographers sums up the "core intellectual point" in the Tale.[74]

By contrast, Jack, the representative of Puritanism, is not averse to the allurements of alchemy. Although he breaks away from Peter and tries to develop a religious culture of his own, towards the end of the *Tale* he is presented as just another, perhaps more radical, 'alchemical-Catholic-Puritan' enthusiast permanently confused with Peter by friends who encounter him. Since the

69 Christian Rosenkreuz, *The Hermetick Romance: or, The Chymical Wedding*, trans. E. Foxcroft (London: A. Sowle, 1690), p. 91.

70 For detailed guidance how to solve the riddle, see Bleiler, "Johann Valentin Andreae, Fantasist and Utopist," p. 10.

71 These methods were widely used in alchemy; see Haeffner, *Dictionary of Alchemy*, pp. 51-52.

72 For a concise survey of the religious contexts of the *Tale*, see Walsh, "Introduction," *A Tale of a Tub and Other Works*, ed. Walsh, pp. lviii-lxviii.

73 See Hammond, *Jonathan Swift*, p. 225: "Swift took the Christianity as practiced by the Church of England as a reliable guide to an ethical life, and more important (though more strange to us), as an essential intellectual and moral authority in a well-run state."

74 Hammond, *Jonathan Swift*, pp. 194-95. Hammond refutes Irvin Ehrenpreis who regarded Martin as "the weakest ingredient of the Tale;" according to Hammond, Martin had to remain unimpressive, since a religious code of ethics is not compatible with heroism and grandeur (p. 209).

publication of Samuel Butler's *Hudibras* (1663), the famous mock-heroic poem that influenced the composition of the *Tale* profoundly, the close connection between Puritanism, radicalism, enthusiasm, and alchemy was well known.[75] The arcane learning of Sidrophel, the astrologist, adds to the context of ridiculousness by which the Puritan enthusiasts are characterized. The Hack shows himself convinced that Jack's story will not be taken literally, but that it will reveal hidden meanings for those who are able to understand; about the events in Jack's life he remarks:

> Nor do I at all question, but they will furnish Plenty of noble Matter for such, whose converting Imaginations dispose them to reduce all Things into *Types*; who can make *Shadows*, no thanks to the Sun; and then mold them into Substances, no thanks to Philosophy; whose peculiar Talent lies in fixing Tropes and Allegories to the *Letter*, and refining what is Literal into Figure and Mystery. (p. 123)

Imagination works as an alchemical esemplastic force, transforming things into types, according to the doctrine of biblical typology, and creating substances out of shadows.

Of course, Swift here, as in his *Discourse concerning the Mechanical Operation of the Spirit* (1704), also uses the traditional attacks against Puritanism – the association of enthusiasm with madness, the absurd belief in exaggerated inspiration and illumination, illustrated by the burning candle swallowed by Jack, the preposterous belief in providence – but these attacks are even intensified by aligning Jack with the Brotherhood of alchemists and Rosicrucians. Just like Henry More in his *Enthusiasmus Triumphatus* (1662),[76] Swift pokes fun at the self-proclaimed prophets who detect meaning in everything. Similarly, Johann Valentin Andreae, who had suffered from his father's demonic obsession with alchemy, an obsession that left him and his family impoverished, and who wrote the *Chymical Wedding* as a *ludibrium*,[77] Swift ridicules the Puritans' desire to see secrets where none are to be detected. Jack's reading habits seem to have been spoilt by too an intense reception of the *Fama Fraternitatis* (1614)

---

75 The idea is that alchemy, astrology, and enthusiasm are closely linked to political radicalism; for an analysis and correction of this idea, see Mendelsohn, "Alchemy and Politics in England 1649-1665," pp. 30-78.

76 N. J. C. Andreasen, "Swift's Satire on the Occult in *A Tale of a Tub*," *Texas Studies in Literature and Language*, 5 (1963), 410-21 (pp. 412-13).

77 For the ambiguous meaning of *ludibrium*, see Bernd Steinbrink, "Die Hochzeit von Himmel und Erde: die Rosenkreuzer-Schriften und die Sozialutopie Johann Valentin Andreaes," *Literatur ist Utopie*, ed. Gert Ueding (Frankfurt am Main: Suhrkamp, 1978), pp. 131-58 (143).

and the *Confessio Fraternitatis* (1615), 'sacred texts,' which, briefly after their publication, were met with a passionate reception, not only in Germany but also in France and England.[78] The Hack,[79] and Jack, too, could be looked upon as dedicated followers of Rosicrucianism; they are transformed into those mountebanks who pestered London at this time and made their living by imposture:[80]

> Yet he began to entertain a Fancy, that the Matter was *deeper* and *darker*, and therefore must needs have a great deal more of Mystery at the bottom. *Gentlemen,* said he, *I will prove this very Skin of Parchment to be Meat, Drink, and Cloth, to be the Philosopher's Stone, and the Universal Medicine.* (p. 123)

In a quasi-inverted alchemical process, Jack reduces the spirit of the text to its material basis, behind which he then looks out for hidden meanings.

If the reader thinks that absurdity has now reached its apex, he is in for a surprise; the next step towards grotesqueness is the glorious system of the Aeolists, a sect which Jack is said to have founded. Aeolism is the system in which the satire on religion is fused with that of learning.

4. Alchemy and Learning

The *Tale* is both a satire on religion and a satire on learning, written in the "anti-genre of the Menippean vein,"[81] and for Swift, alchemy as a subcategory of 'learning' is another of those "happy occasions" that allow him "to exercise his intellectual muscles."[82] But the relationship between alchemy and learning is at least as complex as that between alchemy and religion. As is well known, all discussions of the role of learning in the late seventeenth and early eighteenth centuries take place in the context of an intellectual fray, the *Querelle*

78 See Bleiler, "Johann Valentin Andreae, Fantasist and Utopist," p. 3; besides Bacon and Newton, René Descartes was fascinated with the prospects of Rosicrucianism (Arnold, "Descartes und die Rosenkreuzer," pp. 227-45). For the reception of Rosicrucianism in England, see Thomas Willard, "*De furore Britannico*: The Rosicrucian Manifestos in Britain," *Aries: Journal for the Study of Western Esotericism*, 14 (2014), 32-61.

79 See Philip Pinkus, "*A Tale of a Tub* and the Rosy Cross," *The Journal of English and Germanic Philology*, 59 (1960), 669-79: "Surely one might conclude that the hack also is Rosicrucian" (p. 671).

80 See Hugh Ormsby-Lennon, "Aping the Medicine Show: Mencken, Salmon, Yworth," *Hey Presto!*, p. 145.

81 See Walsh, "Introduction," *A Tale of a Tub and Other Works*, ed. Walsh, p. lv.

82 Ehrenpreis, *Mr Swift*, p. 206.

des Anciens et des Modernes.[83] Sir William Temple, Jonathan Swift, William Wotton, and Richard Bentley are the most relevant participants in this fight, and their positions can easily be identified by reading their contributions to this dispute. But alchemy does not really fit into the bipolarity of the *Querelle*. A paradoxical ambiguity characterizes alchemy. With its origin in ancient Egypt (alchemy was derived "from Arabic *al-kemi* referring to black, fertile ground,"[84] and it includes the meaning of *chymeia*, which means "cast metal"),[85] its philosophical heritage harks back to Hermes Trismegistos, Jewish Cabbalism, Elias and Mary the Jewess.[86] With its impressive line of renowned representatives – among them, Avicenna and Raimundus Lullus – alchemy boasts of a prestigious pedigree comparable to that of the classics; it is even older than Aesop's fables and the controversial letters of Phalaris.[87] In this respect, alchemy could be looked upon as a renowned representative of the Ancient World, to be respected because of its age.

Reading texts by Jacob Boehme, Paracelsus, Thomas Vaughan, Elias Ashmole and the leading representatives of Rosicrucianism, one is amazed to find philosophical ideas these alchemists share with the spokesmen of Modernism. Paracelsus refused to imitate the Ancients,[88] and, as another *Elias artista*, he tried to reconcile alchemy with soteriology.[89] The Rosicrucian texts, for example, set out to demand religious and intellectual freedom; with their attacks on popery and arbitrary power as well as their ruthless abuse lavished on the "*gross Corruptions*" of Roman Catholicism, they could even induce Swift to

83 See Hermann Josef Real, "Literarhistorische Einleitung," *Jonathan Swift, The Battle of the Books: eine historisch-kritische Ausgabe mit literarhistorischer Einleitung und Kommentar* (Berlin and New York: Walter de Gruyter, 1978), pp. xv-xxxv. See also Joseph M. Levine, *The Battle of the Books: History and Literature in the Augustan Age* (Ithaca and London: Cornell University Press, 1991).

84 Stratford, *A Dictionary of Western Alchemy*, p. 7.

85 Priesner, "Über die Wirklichkeit des Okkulten: Naturmagie und Alchemie in der Frühen Neuzeit," p. 309; see also Florian Ebeling, "Ägypten als Heimat der Alchemie," *Goldenes Wissen*, eds Feuerstein-Herz and Laube, pp. 23-34; these doctrines reveal an intense Platonic influence (p. 24).

86 Mary the Jewess is also referred to as Maria Prophetissa (Haeffner, *Dictionary of Alchemy*, pp. 139-40).

87 See Real, "Literarhistorische Einleitung," pp. xxvii-xxii.

88 See Braun, "Magie bei Paracelsus," p. 23.

89 See also Michael Lorber, "Alchemie, *Elias artista* und die Machbarkeit von Wissen in der Frühen Neuzeit," *Natur – Religion – Medien*, eds Burkard, *et al.*, pp. 87-113, who interprets alchemy in general and the work or Paracelsus in particular as the "proto-history of scientific experimentation" (p. 89).

sympathize with them.[90] Both the fictitious Christian Rosenkreuz and Vaughan do not tire to condemn the devastating consequences of the thoughtless use of syllogisms in philosophy, which – for them – puts fetters on the human mind. They bear an inveterate hatred against Aristotle, taunted as a "blinde beast" by Vaughan.[91] Aristotle's philosophy is but "noise," and his scholastic interpreters produce nothing but "Philosophy of *meer* words;"[92] and they are denigrated as brainless followers who "lick up a *vomit*" of the Stagyrite.[93] Irrespective of the rude style, whole passages of these tracts sound as if they had been written by Sir Francis Bacon, who, in his *The Advancement of Learning* (1605), had also attacked the *ipse-dixit*-doctrine of Aristotle and the slavish intellectual obedience of his scholastic followers.[94] Some of these attacks of Rosicrucian provenience seem to modify Bacon's doctrine of the idols, with which the Lord Chancellor intended to free mankind from that notorious "self-imposed nonage." And just like Bacon recommends the institutionalization of science with his conception of "Salomon's House" in his utopia *New Atlantis* (1627),[95] Rosicrucian ideas contributed to a systematization of scientific activities.[96] One is led to assume that with these approaches to natural philosophy, alchemists and Rosicrucian thinkers helped usher in the age of science and modernism; that is probably why they became interesting to later representatives of contemporary science like Newton and Boyle.[97] Alchemical confessions also contain the acceptance of natural experiments,[98] those *experimenta fructifera*,

---

90 See Vaughan, *The Fame and Confession of the Fraternity of R:C: Commonly of the Rosie Cross* (London: by J. M. for Giles Calvert, 1652), p. 43.

91 Vaughan, *Magia Adamica*, in *The Works of Thomas Vaughan*, eds Rudrum and Drake-Brockman, p. 202; see also pp. 151, 166, 194.

92 Vaughan, *The Fame and Confession of the Fraternity of R:C: Commonly of the Rosie Cross*, in *The Works of Thomas Vaughan*, eds Rudrum and Drake-Brockman, p. 483.

93 Thomas Vaughan, *Anthroposophia Theomagica: or, A Discourse of the Nature of Man and his State after Death, Grounded on his Creator's Proto-Chimistry and Verifi'd by a Practicall Examination of Principles in the Great World* (London: by T. W. for H. Blunden, 1650), in *The Works of Thomas Vaughan*, eds Rudrum and Drake-Brockman, p. 53. See also p. 201.

94 For aspects of Rosicrucianism in Bacon's work, especially in his *New Atlantis* (1627), see Yates, *The Rosicrucian Enlightenment*, pp. 119-29.

95 See Francis Bacon, *The Advancement of Learning and New Atlantis* (1605), ed. Arthur Johnston (Oxford: Clarendon Press, 1974), pp. 239-47.

96 See Karin Johannisson, "Magic, Science, and Institutionalization in the Seventeenth and Eighteenth Centuries," *Hermeticism and the Renaissance*, eds Merkel and Debus, pp. 251-61.

97 This does not mean, as Yates maintains, that the Royal Society "was an outgrowth of the brotherhood;" for a correction of Yates's ideas, see Ormsby-Lennon, "Rosicrucian Linguistics," *Hermeticism and the Renaissance*, eds Merkel and Debus, p. 316.

98 According to Boyle, these experiments, however, should not "inrich mens purses, but their brains," as he claims in his apology for alchemy; see Robert Boyle, "An Historical

which Bacon recommended alongside the *experimenta lucifera*.[99] Although Bacon criticized the shortcomings of alchemy,[100] he did not completely despise its values:

> And yet surely to alchemy this right is due, that it may be compared to the husbandman whereof Aesop makes the fable; that, when he died, told his sons that he had left unto them gold buried under ground in his vineyard; and they digged over all the ground, and gold they found none; but by reason of their stirring and digging the mould about the roots of their vines, they had a great vintage the year following: so assuredly the search and stir to make gold hath brought to light a great number of good and fruitful inventions and experiments, as well for the disclosing of nature as for the use of man's life.[101]

Whereas they share the scientists' refutation of Aristotelian thinking and the use of syllogisms, the dark authors fight against the sciences at the same time. Agrippa,[102] Paracelsus, John Dee, and Thomas Vaughan disdain science as a form of intellectual poverty. Alchemy is not as easy a target for satirists as one might imagine; on the one hand, it certainly reveals the mechanical operations of bewildered minds, who would resort to biblical authority whenever they were at a loss to prove a thesis; on the other hand, their attitude towards nature is immune against those errors collected by Sir Thomas Browne in his *Pseudodoxia Epidemica* (1646). A satirist who attacks alchemy might find himself proven wrong by the achievements of a discipline that is about to transform itself into a new field of genuine scientific research. While it may have been easy to attack Newton,[103] he nevertheless detected the laws of gravitation. Alchemy "was at the heart of the thought and method of these pioneers

---

Account of a Degradation of Gold Made by an Anti-Elixir: A Strange Chymical Narrative," *The Alchemy Reader: From Hermes Trismegistus to Isaac Newton*, ed. Stanton J. Linden (Cambridge: Cambridge University Press, 2003), pp. 234-42 (236).

99 See Hermann Josef Real and Heinz J. Vienken, *Jonathan Swift: Gulliver's Travels* (München: Fink, 1984), p. 89.

100 Bacon was of the opinion that Aristotelian learning and alchemy both served the same purpose: "*populus vult decipi*;" see Bacon, "Of Tribute: Praise of Knowledge": "All the philosophy of nature which is now received, is either the philosophy of the Grecians, or that other of the alchemists ... The one is gathered out of a few vulgar observations, and the other out of a few experiments of a furnace. The one never faileth to multiply words, and the other ever faileth to multiply gold" (here quoted from Gleick, *Isaac Newton*, p. 52).

101 Bacon, *The Advancement of Learning and New Atlantis*, ed. Johnston, p. 31.

102 See Priesner, "Über die Wirklichkeit des Okkulten: Naturmagie und Alchemie in der Frühen Neuzeit," p. 316.

103 For the reasons Swift had to attack Newton, see also Douglas Duhaime, "Swift, Natural Theology, and the Crisis of Newton's Chronology," *Swift Studies*, 29 (2014), 24-41.

of modern science" such as Boyle,[104] and while it was tempting to deride him, his experiments with air laid the ground for modern chemistry. From the perspective of the history of ideas, alchemy is a most interesting field of studies. Its experimental approach to the world has much in common with astronomy and physics as well as anatomy and chemistry, those developing branches of later modern science. Alchemical experiments – though to no avail frequently – blaze the trail for a world view based on empiricism, thus revealing the obsoleteness of traditional ideas. Modern science distinguishes itself from alchemical thought in that it accepts this existential provocation, whereas alchemy tries to complement its own findings with magic and mysticism. In occultism, astronomy has to be accompanied by astrology, alchemy has to be embedded into a context of animism, medicine has to be reconciled with the world of animal spirits. The fear of a general disenchantment with the world keeps the occult alchemist alive and kicking. Natural science increases the power of man, it is true, but there he is no longer at home in the charming world of magic and hermeticism. Thus alchemy accompanies modern science as a paradoxical by-product, a psycho-logical device to alleviate fears and to soothe the pain that comes with the insight into nature's secrets. Bacon separated theology from natural science in order to sidestep charges of blasphemy and atheism. Alchemists prefer the blend of a quasi-scientific approach with the comforts of a religious, holistic, Christian, and mystical world view.

The pivotal centre of the alchemical universe is the philosopher's stone; it not only promises omniscience, but also reveals close affinities with Christian theology: in alchemical texts, the stone is interpreted as a synecdoche for Christ and a symbol of his resurrection:

> By the Magicall or Prospective Stone it is possible to discover any person in what part of the world soever, although never so secretly concealed or hid; in chambers, closets, or cavernes of the Earth: for there it makes a strict inquisition. In a word, it fairely presents to your view even the whole world, wherein to behold, heare, or see your desire. Nay more, it enables man to understand the language of the creatures, as the chirping of birds, lowing of beasts, &c., to convey a spirit into an image, which by observing the influence of heavenly bodies, shall become a true oracle; And yet this as E. A. assures you, is not any wayes necromanticall or devilish; but easy, wonderous easy, natural and honest.

> That there is a gift of prophesie hid in the Red-stone, Racis [Rhazes] will tell you; for thereby (saith he) philosophers have foretold things to come: And Petrus Bonus avers, that they did prophesie, not only generally but specially; having a fore-knowledge of the Resurrection, Incarnation of Christ, Day of Judgement,

104 Linden, "Introduction," *The Alchemy Reader*, pp. 1-23 (1).

> and that the world should be consumed with fire: and this not otherwise, then from the insight of their operations.[105]

Another fantasy of alchemical omnipotence is the idea of the 'universal book,' the epitome of all epitomes, the literary quintessence of everything that has ever been written or thought. This is an attractive idea: instead of spoiling one's eyes by eons of studying in dusty libraries, the meta-book promises instant enlightenment and knowledge about everything.[106] It is the dream of adolescent polymaths who want to enjoy reputation without having to shoulder the burden of spending hours on end with recondite learning and arid logic. Instead, these 'scholars' reveal "A Liberal Art, that costs no pains / Of Study, Industry, or Brains."[107] This meta-book is the equivalent of the panacea in medicine or the philosopher's stone in occultism, it is the *lutum sapientiae*.[108] One could even imagine that this book would no longer have to be read, but that, in an act of bibliophagy, it might be swallowed like a pill containing the complete knowledge of Mankind. This dream of the universal book plays an eminent role in the Rosicrucian utopia of a better life, as presented in Vaughan's translation:

> Were it not a precious thing, that you could so read in one onely book, and withal by reading understand, and remember all that, which in all other books (which heretofore have been, and are now, and hereafter shal come out) hath been, is, and shal be learned, and found out of them?[109]

The Hack, too, bewails "that no famous *Modern* hath ever yet attempted an universal System in a small portable Volume, of all Things that are to be Known, or Believed, or Imagined, or Practised in Life" (p. 82). In alchemy and

---

105 Elias Ashmole, "The Prolegomena to the *Theatrum Chemicum Britannicum*," *The Alchemy Reader*, ed. Linden, pp. 222-33 (228-29).

106 See also Pinkus, "*A Tale of a Tub* and the Rosy Cross," p. 679.

107 See Samuel Butler, *Hudibras: Written in the Time of the Late Wars*, ed. A. R. Waller (Cambridge: Cambridge University Press, 1905), p. 15, ll. 473-90.

108 *Lutum sapientiae* is "the bottling of wisdom, a euphemism for alchemy itself" (Stratford, *A Dictionary of Western Alchemy*, p. 53).

109 Thomas Vaughan, *The Fame and Confession of the Fraternity of R:C: Commonly of the Rosie Cross*, pp. 39-40. See also the original text in *Fama Fraternitatis: oder, Entdeckung der Brüderschafft des löblichen Ordens des Rosen Kreuzes, beneben der Confession, oder Bekantnus derselben Fraternitet an alle Gelehrte und Häupter in Europa geschrieben, auch etlichen Responsionen von Haselmeyern und anderen gelehrten Leuten auff die Famam gestellet* (Dantzig: Andrea Hünefeldt, 1615), pp. 61-62: "Were es nicht ein köstlich Ding / daß du also lesen köndtest in einem Buch / daß Du zugleich alles was in allen Büchern die jemals gewesen / noch seyn / oder kommen und außgehen werden / zu finden gewesen / noch gefunden wird / unnd jemals mag gefunden werden / lesen / verstehen und behalten möchtest?"

in Rosicrucianism, this universal meta-book is more a philosophical concept than a physical object; like the philosopher's stone, it is something that only those who do not need it any longer would finally achieve; it is the ultimate goal of the *adeptus*, the final *telos*, he can reach. All alchemical books distance themselves from the disdainful intention just to produce gold,[110] their genuine endeavour is to transcend the limits of average knowledge and scholarship. The philosopher's stone is the outward marker of a person who is no longer dependent on its magic, someone who has transformed himself into a mystic being congenial to the wisdom of the highest spirits. It is typical of Swift that he takes this symbol literally, employing the recipes of alchemy itself on the attempt to produce it. Here is the Swiftian 'transmutation' of the alchemical concept into a satirical object of ridicule:

> YOU take fair correct Copies, well bound in Calfs Skin, and Lettered at the Back, of all Modern Bodies of Arts and Sciences whatsoever, and in what Language you please. These you distil in *balneo Mariæ*, infusing *Quintessence of Poppy Q.S.* together with three Pints of *Lethe*, to be had from the Apothecaries. You cleanse away carefully the *Sordes* and *Caput mortuum*, letting all that is volatile evaporate. You preserve only the first Running, which is again to be distilled seventeen times, till what remains will amount of about two Drams. This you keep in a Glass Viol *Hermetically* sealed, for one and twenty Days. Then you begin your Catholick Treatise, taking every Morning fasting, (first shaking the Viol) three Drops of this *Elixir*, snuffing it strongly up your Nose. It will dilate it self about the Brain (where there is any) in fourteen Minutes, and you immediately perceive in your Head an infinite Number of *Abstracts, Summaries, Compendiums, Extracts, Collections, Medulla's, Excerpta quaedam's, Florilegia's* and the like, all disposed into great Order, and reducible upon Paper. (p. 82; italics reversed)

This sounds like the Struldbruggs' secret diet for old age and universal knowledge, no matter in what language it was presented; it is an absurd recipe for preparing a substantial meal for the voracious brain of a modern scholar who quickly wants to acquire knowledge for which he does not have to work. The passage is teeming with alchemical innuendos: The calf skins may allude to the Golden Fleece,[111] a kind of precious parchment, to which alchemists entrusted their most secret wisdom; the distillation describes the alchemical process of producing *quintessences*,[112] the *balneum Mariæ* is the *bain-marie* with its

110 The Rosicrucians, especially, disdain any form of 'making gold;' they regard it as a mere '*parergon*;' see *Fama Fraternitatis*, pp. 47-48, and *Confession, oder Bekantnus derselben Fraternitet*, p. 81.

111 See Antoine Faivre, *The Golden Fleece and Alchemy* (Albany: State University of New York Press, 1993).

112 See Stratford, *A Dictionary of Western Alchemy*, p. 70.

allusion to Mary the Jewess, who was considered to have been the first alchemist, of course, but it also refers to "praeternatural fire," needed to gain the necessary heat for transmutations, as, for instance, described by Artephius in his *Sacred Book* (c.1150).[113] *Sordes* and *caput mortuum* are the waste products of alchemical processes, remaining at the bottom of the *balneum*, after the transformations have been concluded. The 21 days are the product of 3 by 7,[114] thus playing with the Rosicrucians' predilection for this number, the Elixir like the *quintessence* express pre-states of the goal of the philosopher's stone, the acme of omnipotence.[115] The elixir refers to the alchemist's "medical powder."[116]

Up to this point, the passage could be reprinted in any alchemical book and would probably find as many disciples as Johann Valentin Andreae's famous *ludibrium* did. But the alert reader stumbles over the end of the quotation. All of a sudden, the alchemist turns into a literary person, a kind of mock Grub-Street writer who recommends the use of those literary forms which Swift and the culture of traditional learning condemned. Abstracts, summaries, extracts, excerpts, and *florilegia* are the tools of those alchemical writers who produce books by a kind of literary 'mechanical operation of the spirit;' they have perfected the art to scrounge ideas from books, and without using their own brains, to copy them into another. And the drops of elixir, which dilate about the brain, are strongly reminiscent of Swift's own ideas of madness as described in his "Digression concerning Madness" in the *Tale* (pp. 105-21). The association is clear: alchemical wisdom is tantamount to madness.

113 See Artephius, *The Secret Book*, Chapter 6: "Work therefore with it, and you shall obtain from it what you desire, for it is the spirit and soul of sol and luna; it is the oil, the dissolving water, the fountain, the Balneum Mariae, the praeternatural fire, the moist fire, the secret, hidden and invisible fire" (<http://www.levity.com/alchemy/artephiu.html>, accessed 21 February 2018). See also Vaughan's *Magia Adamica*: "For a Cloze, I must tell thee, the Philosophers call'd this *Fire* their *Balneum*, but it is *Balneum Naturæ*, a Naturall Bath, not an *Artificall* one" (*The Works of Thomas Vaughan*, eds Rudrum and Drake-Brockman, p. 221).

114 See also William Bragg Ewald, "The Author of *A Tale of a Tub: Parody*," *The Masks of Jonathan Swift* (Oxford: Basil Blackwell, 1954), pp. 13-26 (17): "The cryptic references to the magic numbers – seven, nine, and their multiple, sixty-three; to alchemy; to the mysterious words and the Latin phrase from Irenaeus's *Contra Haereses*; and to the error of Philaletes (a pseudonym of Thomas Vaughan) mark this passage as humorous imitation of the occultists."

115 See also Hawes, "Jonathan Swift and the Philosopher's Stone," p. 138: "His target – aptly summed up in the symbol of the philosopher's stone – is better understood in terms of the occultist fantasies of omniscience and omnipotence that emerged as the not-quite-hidden underbelly of the early Royal Society."

116 Stratford, *A Dictionary of Western Alchemy*, p. 31.

5. Religion, Learning, and the Alchemical Notion of Wind

"Much in *A Tale of a Tub* is of air, and much is of madness, and all is of a marvellous method."[117] If any doubt should remain about the parallels between alchemical learning and madness, Swift dismisses it with a sneer. In Section VIII, the centre of his satire, the philosophy of Aeolism is described; here, the worlds of religion and learning are fused together and ridiculed. The *tertium comparationis* between religion and learning is nothing less than the alchemical and Rosicrucian obsession with wind. The Hack resorts to a technique which Butler had already employed in his *Hudibras* in order to satirize the Puritan knight when characterizing him as a connoisseur of logic and analytics based on the false premises of syllogisms. Although even a superficial glance at the productions of the Rosicrucians suffices to prove that they and their alchemist followers were extremely critical of Aristotelianism and syllogistic reasoning, Swift makes the Hack use a syllogism, which for the purposes of this study could be slightly altered: "Words are but Wind; and Learning *and Religion* are nothing but Words; Ergo, *Learning and Religion are* nothing but Wind" (see p. 100; my italics).

In the middle of the seventeenth century, the topic of 'wind' was 'in the air.' Experiments with air were integral parts of the Royal Society's scientific programme. Robert Hooke, Robert Boyle, Christiaan Huygens, and Denis Papin worked together in order to construct an air-pump with which the effects of the artificially created vacuum could be studied.[118] Due to the difficult task, these experiments often failed and caused considerable mockery on the recipients' side. Boyle wanted to know if the growth of plants was influenced by the lack of air, while the London public cruelly amused itself observing animals die when "Mr. Boyle's Pneumatic Engine" was started.[119] After an air pump had been constructed big enough for a man to enter it, Hooke volunteered to experiment on himself; fortunately he survived the experiment feeling only giddy and suffering from a pain in his ears.[120] In Book Three of *Gulliver's Travels*, Swift refers to these rather atrocious experiments in pneumatology letting a dog die through a virtuoso's air pump, a "large Pair of Bellows" with which the poor animal was inflated.[121]

---

117 Starkman, "Philosophy, Old and New, Bright and Dark," p. 25.

118 See also Hawes, "Jonathan Swift and the Philosopher's Stone," p. 146.

119 Jardine, *Ingenious Pursuits*, p. 54.

120 See Jardine, *Ingenious Pursuits*, pp. 42-89 (50-65).

121 See Jonathan Swift, *Gulliver's Travels*, ed. Paul Turner (Oxford: Oxford University Press, 1971), pp. 181-82 (III, v, 11).

The bellows are not only a symbol of scientific pneumatology, they also belong to the alchemist's standard equipment in his laboratory. And in alchemy, air, too, plays a considerable role.[122] Many alchemists took their own metier to be an imitation of divine cosmology;[123] they felt entitled "to recreate the first six days in alembics and furnaces, with mercury, Sulphur and salt" and to "play God in the laboratory."[124] Alchemy is "God's created handmaid,"[125] or "God's midwife;"[126] the earthly alchemist tries to copy the highest alchemist, God.[127] Birth, growth, adolescence, maturity, decay, and death are forms of the alchemical transformation of the human body, which the divine alchemist has planned from the beginning when he breathed life into an inanimate lump of clay. In mysticism, air and wind are forces of creation, symbolizing 'breath,' the divine principle of life. According to Hermes Trismegistus, alchemical truth was born in the womb of the wind.[128] Wind makes nature appear to be alive, it symbolizes the animistic ontology of existence typical of occultism, no matter if it appears in human beings,[129] animals, plants, or even stones. For Paracelsus, the *limus terrae* was animated by God's breath;[130] aether is the air breathed by the Gods,[131] wind often represents *ruach*,[132] the spirit of God.[133] Because of the philosophy of wind, the Rosicrucians are often compared with the "Brahmins of India;"[134] in their writings they represent the presence of divinity by describing sudden breezes and strong winds, as, for example, at the beginning

122 For the role of 'air' in Swift's literary work, see also Gregory Lynall, "Swift's Pneumatics, Fanatics, and Satiric Mechanics," *Swift Studies*, 29 (2014), 6-23.

123 See Dane T. Daniel, "Medieval Alchemy and Paracelsus' Theology: Pseudo-Lull's *Testamentum* and Paracelsus' *Astronomia Magna*," *Nova Acta Paracelsica*, NF, 22/23 (2008-9), 121-35 (p. 125).

124 Mendelsohn, "Alchemy and Politics in England, 1649-1665," pp. 40-42.

125 See, for example, Thomas Tymme, "Dedication to Joseph Quercetanus's *The Practise of Chymicall, and Hermetical Physicke*" (1605); quoted from J. Linden, *Darke Hierogliphicks: Alchemy in English Literature from Chaucer to the Restoration* (Lexington: The University Press of Kentucky, 1996), p. 6.

126 See Steinbrink, "Die Hochzeit von Himmel und Erde: die Rosenkreuzer-Schriften und die Sozialutopie Johann Valentin Andreaes," p. 151.

127 God is regarded as the true and reliable alchemist; his antagonist is Satan, the "false Chymist" (Linden, *Darke Hierogliphicks*, p. 217).

128 See Stratford, *A Dictionary of Western Alchemy*, p. 40.

129 See Roob, "Einleitung," *Das hermetische Museum*, p. 18.

130 See Daniel, "Medieval Alchemy and Paracelsus' Theology: Pseudo-Lull's *Testamentum* and Paracelsus' *Astronomia Magna*," p. 127.

131 See Stratford, *A Dictionary of Western Alchemy*, p. 4.

132 See Robert Fludd, "The Mosaicall Philosophy," *The Alchemy Reader*, ed. Linden, pp. 191-98 (196).

133 See Bleiler, "Johann Valentin Andreae, Fantasist and Utopist," p. 8.

134 See Willard, "*De furore Britannico*: The Rosicrucian Manifestos in Britain," p. 45.

of the *Chymical Wedding*.[135] As "secretaries of nature" (a role which the *Tale*'s Hack adopts), the Rosicrucians revere wind. Their English admirer, Vaughan, keeps on praising wind or air in his writings. For him, air is the "*Vitall Cœlestial Breath*," the "*Magicians Backdoor*," the "Animal Oyl," or the "*Mare Rerum invisibilium*." "Air" is an hybrid substance, no longer a mere "element": "This is no Element, but a certain miraculous *Hermaphrodit*, the *Cœment* of two *worlds*, and a Medley of Extremes."[136]

Perhaps Swift accepted the idea of a divine breath, which is associated with the creation of human beings (Genesis), but he definitely refuted the apotheosis of wind. Employing his satiric programme of radical reductionism, he pulls down to earth what seems too lofty and sublime to be true. Section VIII is a consistent attack on the adherents of the 'religion of wind.' Like a medieval scholar, he analyses the properties of 'wind,' but unlike his alchemical and Rosicrucian opponents, he does not recognize any superior or metaphysical meaning in these qualities but reinterprets them as sheer phenomena of 'uninspired' materialism. In his view, the four winds, which the Aeolists expect with their mouths wide open because they need it for their inspiration, achieve nothing at all; they simply inflate the Aeolist priests, puff them up and turn them into ridiculous oversized figures, reminiscent of *Alazon*, whose fate was sealed by *Eironos*' needle.

The Aeolists' love of the windy region of Lapland serves Swift as another occasion for ridicule: Lapland was a favourite subject often discussed by the Royal Society; Laplanders were looked upon as a tribe capable of mastering the wind, they even sold wind by 'bottling' it in special tubes (p. 104).[137] As so often, Swift resorts to the forces of scatology to deconstruct false notions of inspiration. In his description of Aeolism, the sublime air of allegedly divine origin witnesses a satirical transformation that leaves nothing but totally disillusioned forms of *caput mortuum*. The satirical alchemist Swift transforms inspiration into flatulence and belching, the Rosicrucians' tendency to transcend the body by meditation and contemplation in their endeavour to become airy substances

---

135 For the role of 'wind' in Rosicrucianism, see also Arnold, "Descartes und die Rosenkreuzer," pp. 235-36.

136 See Vaughan, *Anthroposophia Theomagica: or, A Discourse of the Nature of Man and his State after Death*, pp. 19-20, in *The Works of Thomas Vaughan*, eds Rudrum and Drake-Brockman, pp. 55, 65.

137 See Ann Talbot, "Locke and the Lapland Witches," *"The Great Ocean of Knowledge": The Influence of Travel Literature on the Works of John Locke* (Leiden and Boston: Brill, 2010), pp. 45-62 (50); Dirk F. Passmann and Hermann J. Real, "Barbarism, Witchcraft, and Devil-Worship: Cock-and-Bull Stories from Several Remote Nations. of the World," *Swift Studies*, 23 (2008), 94-110 (pp. 104-7).

themselves is countered by point-blank allusions to sexuality and obscenity: the spiritual is turned into the carnal. In a further satirical-alchemical transmutation, by which Swift demonstrates his own mercurial sardonic mind, the sublime winds of alchemical provenience become mere "vapours,"[138] *effluvia* of a rather nasty kind. Swift combines elements of alchemy with both humoral pathology and faculty psychology, when his satirical pneumatology focuses on the human abdomen. The winds mutate into vapours caused by the processes of physical putrefaction,[139] subsequently ascending to the brain where they cause lunacy.[140] By perverting the metaphysical alchemico-Rosicrucian doctrine of wind into a mechanical-physical operation of the digesting body, that is, by interpreting it as the influences of physiological dysfunctions that end in insanity, Swift presents a devastating comment on the principles of contemporary 'enthusiasm,' which was mainly associated with Puritanism. Thus it is clear that Jack is the creator and most dedicated follower of this 'mad religion,' whose adherents believe in 'inspiration,' 'inward light,' and 'seeing best when one is blind.'

(Corrupted) religion, (arcane) learning, Rosicrucianism, science, and alchemy are strange bedfellows, it is true, but they have a lot in common: Since religion is divine learning, and learning is tantamount to words, and words tantamount to wind, religion and learning of this kind are nothing but wind. Swift suggests that these end in nothing, not the 'nothing' of philosophical speculation, or the perfect state of absence described by the Sefiroth, but 'nothing' signifying total irrelevancy. He criticizes those systems of thought that "fall back upon the primitive stages of occidental philosophy."[141] These share "a common foundation – a tendency to ignore or abuse reason, to declare independence from the *consensus gentium* or tradition":[142]

> To Swift, the Baconian natural history, the philosopher's stone, and the *magnum opus*, equally represented mechanical efforts to reach God's mystery, and were equally ridiculous. In *A Tale of a Tub*, the method to create the 'universal system in a small portable volume' (Section V) is both a Royal Society experiment and a Rosicrucian nostrum. The many allusions in the *Tale* to the *magnum opus*

138 See also Starkman, "Philosophy, Old and New, Bright and Dark," pp. 28-30.

139 For the special role 'putrefaction' plays in the doctrines of Theophrastus Bombastus of Hohenheim, see Paracelsus, "Of the Nature of Things and Paracelsus his Aurora," *The Alchemy Reader*, ed. Linden, pp. 151-69 (158-59).

140 See Ehrenpreis, *Mr Swift*, pp. 216-25 (221).

141 Hermann Josef Real, "Nachwort," *Jonathan Swift, Ein Tonnenmärchen*, trans. Ulrich Horstmann (Stuttgart: Reclam, 1994), pp. 273-84 (279).

142 Andreasen, "Swift's Satire on the Occult in *A Tale of a Tub*," p. 415.

> have Royal Society as well as Rosicrucian overtones. Ultimately Rosicrucianism becomes a caricature of the Royal Society and its methods. By deliberately confusing the two groups Swift can impose on the Royal Society all the baggage of the Rosicrucians: cabalism, occultism, mysticism, magic, religious, fanaticism, all these become the property of the virtuosos and the learned philosophers of the *Tale of a Tub* world.[143]

After analysing the role of alchemy in *A Tale of a Tub*, a number of questions remain. More particularly, it is unclear why Swift focuses on dark authors and Rosicrucian philosophers at a time when their influence had long ceased to be a major force in intellectual life:

> Writing alchemical satire at a time when the hermetic philosophy had been almost universally rejected, at least publicly, it is apparent that Swift found an intellectual potency in the representational power of alchemy. From a number of sources, some of them encyclopaedic, and very few of them identified, Swift had knowledge of many of alchemy's authorities, methods, both practical and hermeneutic, and modes of writing. The appropriation of these alchemical ideas gave Swift the imaginative potential to explore questions which for him were more important and fundamental, allowing him to think in a different way and to view his targets through an alternative satiric lens.[144]

6. Conclusion in Which Nothing is Concluded

In fact, at the end, the *Tale* looks as if Swift reanimated a lifeless intellectual system of thought in order to kill it again. Maybe the dark influence of arcane learning was rather to be 'felt' than to be read, that it infiltrated minds like a poison which could not be detected until it was too late. This would explain why Swift attacked both alchemy and the science as it was practised by the members of the Royal Society. Swift thought that too many members of that prestigious circle were still deeply immersed in arcane learning, as especially Newton's example proves. In this case, Swift's satire would have tried to work like a homeopathic remedy: it would alert the body's immune system to fight against the imminent disease before it could turn into an epidemic.[145] Both

143 Pinkus, "*A Tale of a Tub* and the Rosy Cross," p. 675.

144 Lynall, "'An Author *bonæ notæ*, and an *Adeptus*': Swift's Alchemical Satire and Satiric Alchemy in *A Tale of a Tub*," p. 45.

145 For this homeopathic theory of satire, see Fredric V. Bogel, *The Difference Satire Makes: Rhetoric and Reading from Jonson to Byron* (Ithaca and London: Cornell University Press, 2001).

the world of Anglicanism and the Royal Society had to be protected against the childhood diseases like alchemy and Rosicrucianism. The satirical alchemist Swift created his own *opus magnum*, a panacea in order to cure the epidemic of madness. The answer for this – and for many other riddles in the *Tale* – is, as the Nobel Prize winner of 2016 would say, 'blowing in the wind.'

POETRY AND MUSIC

Moyra Haslett
Queen's University Belfast

"With brisk merry lays": Songs on the Wood's Halfpence Affair

Abstract. This essay considers the eighteen songs on the Wood's Halfpence affair which have survived, the vast majority of which celebrate "the Drapier" and respond directly to Swift's *Drapier's Letters*. Close readings of these songs, paying particular attention both to song texts and tunes, illustrate how apparently loyal songs could be used in the service of political opposition. The essay argues that recalling these popular songs is an important context for the Wood's Halfpence affair and for the shaping of Swift's reputation in Ireland. It also reminds us of the pervasiveness of music in the cultural life of Dublin, a context which is important for studies of Swift's poetry, irrespective of the question of Swift's own musicality.

That Swift was not himself musical, or especially interested in music, has been noted by many scholars, and in support of their claims are Swift's own references, to his understanding music "like a Muscovite," for example (an opaque phrase, but hardly positive),[1] or his reluctance to allow members of the choir to rehearse for Handel's *Messiah*.[2] On the contrary side, others have reminded us of the care Swift took with regard to the Cathedral choir or of his connections

* I would like to thank in particular Ingrid Lennon-Presby of the Beinecke Library and Professor Aileen Douglas of Trinity College, Dublin, whose timely scanning and photocopying of many of these ballads permitted me to complete an early draft of this paper.

1 See Hermann J. Real, "The 'Musical' Muscovite: A Presto Hemisemidemiquaver," *The Eighteenth-Century Intelligencer*, 20, no 3 (2006), 29-32.

2 Swift to Edward Harley, 9 February 1720, *Correspondence*, ed. Woolley, II, 323. See also "The Dean to Himself on St Cecilia's Day," *Poems*, ed. Williams, II, 521-22, in which he claims to know "no more than an ass" of music; and Swift's comment to Lady Carteret: "I know nothing of musick, madam; I would not give a farthing for all the musick in the universe. For my own part, I would rather say my prayers without it" (quoted in Patrick Delany, *Observations upon Lord Orrery's Remarks on the Life and Writings of Dr. Jonathan Swift* [London: W. Reeve and A. Linde, 1754], p. 192). Contemporary comments corroborate this. Pope describes Swift as a swan which does not sing (*Mr Pope's Literary Correspondence for Thirty Years, from 1704 to 1734* [London: E. Curll, 1735], p. 112); Patrick Delany writes that "Swift had no skill in musick, nor ear for its beauties" (*Observations*, p. 190), and Deane Swift that Swift "rather hated than loved music" (*Letters, Written by the Late Jonathan Swift*, ed. Deane Swift, 3 vols [Dublin: J. Williams, 1768], II, 44).

 | DOI:10.30965/9783846763971_009

with the Irish harpist Turlough Carolan (Toirdhealbhach Ó Cearbhalláin).[3] This paper addresses the broad topic of Swift and music from a different angle, because it reads the ballads which circulated in Swift's time as, first and foremost, songs, and when we recall the pervasive singing of ballads in early eighteenth-century Dublin, then music assumes a new significance for our understanding of Swift.

Many of Swift's poems reveal a knowledge of the rhythms of street ballads; several are ballads whose tune-settings are specifically signalled in their full titles; and there may be as many as 34 songs ascribed to Swift in his own lifetime. Although the vast majority of these ascriptions are almost certainly false, it remains significant that Swift was associated so closely with this culture in the view of his contemporaries.[4] In addition to these, several poems attributed to Swift inspired new musical settings shortly after their first publication: *A Modern Love Song*, for example, which appeared in a song sheet around the same time as the first printing of the text (1733), and musical settings for five poems purportedly by Swift were included in a collection of catches, glees, and canons published in 1757.[5] The circulation of popular music in Swift's Dublin is

3 For considerations of Swift and music, see David B. Kesterson, "Swift and Music," *Texas Studies in Literature and Language*, 11 (1969), 687-94; Frank Llewelyn Harrison, "Music, Poetry and Polity in the Age of Swift," *Eighteenth-Century Ireland / Iris an dá chultúr*, 1 (1986), 37-63; Arno Löffler, "'Suit Your Words to Your Musick Well': Swift and the Poetic Harmonists," *Swift, the Enigmatic Dean: Festschrift for Hermann Josef Real*, eds Rudolf Freiburg, Arno Löffler, and Wolfgang Zach; with the assistance of Jan Schnitker (Tübingen: Stauffenburg, 1998), pp. 99-112; Joseph McMinn, *Jonathan Swift and the Arts* (Newark: University of Delaware Press, 2010); Andrew Carpenter, "Swift and Song," *The Oxford Handbook of Irish Song, 1100-1850* (forthcoming). For Swift and Carolan, see, additionally, Andrew Carpenter and Alan Harrison, "Swift's 'O'Rourke's Feast' and Sheridan's 'Letter': Early Transcripts by Anthony Raymond," *Proceedings of The First Münster Symposium on Jonathan Swift*, eds Hermann J. Real and Heinz J. Vienken (Munich: Wilhelm Fink, 1985), pp. 27-46.

4 Songs either by Swift or attributed to him are set to the tunes of "Grim King of the Ghosts," "Cut-Purse" (twice), "The King Shall Enjoy his Own Again," "Packington's Pound" (three times), "Ye Commons and Peers," "Derry down," "Youth youth," "Chivie Chase," "I'll tell thee Dick," and "London is a fine town." See also John Sitter's comment: "The tetrameter line" (favoured by Swift) "is closer to the meter of ballads (alternating tetrameter and trimeter) and other popular songs than is the heroic line" (*The Cambridge Introduction to Eighteenth-Century Poetry* [Cambridge: Cambridge University Press, 2012], p. 50).

5 "A Love Song in the Modern Taste. The Words by Dean Swift. Set by Mr Butler" (London, c.1733), reproduced at <http://www.irishsongproject.qub.ac.uk/song/135> (accessed 19 September 2017); William Hayes, *Catches, Glees and Canons, for Three, Four and Five Voices* ([Oxford]: printed for the author, 1757), includes song settings for the following texts which are claimed to be by Swift: "Verses Made for Women who Cry Apples, &c." (pp. 4-7); "An Epigram on Wood's Brass-Money" ("Carteret was welcomed to the shore") (p. 8); "The Power of Time" ("If neither Brass nor Marble can withstand") (p. 9); "The Hardship Put upon the Ladies" ("Poor

also testified by a close comparison of some musical scores: amidst the Italian-aria-sounding coloratura of Swift's satirical "Cantata," with music by John Echlin, there emerges a glimpse of a popular tune, which had become known as "the Irish Jigg" or the "Irish trot" (see Figure 8.1 and Figure 8.2).[6]

Swift particularly knew the power that a well-known tune would bring to a political message. In 1720, following the prosecution of Edward Waters for publishing Swift's *Proposal for the Universal Use of Irish Manufacture*, a song written to urge the wearing of Irish cloth gave the arguments of the pamphlet popular expression, the link made obvious even in its title: *An Excellent New Song on a Seditious Pamphlet.* In composing the song, Swift used one of the best-known ballad tunes of his day, Packington's Pound.[7] It is not surprising that the same tune would be used for one of the songs on the Wood's Halfpence affair. This essay focuses on these songs in particular, although in doing so it hopes to illuminate aspects of Swift and music beyond the particular example of that controversy.

Ladies, tho' their Bus'ness be to play") (p. 16); and "Joan Cudgels Ned" (p. 16). See <http://imslp.org/wiki/Catches,_Glees_and_Canons_(Hayes,_William)>, accessed 19 September 2017. For a further example of a song, more certainly by Swift, see "Ye Commons and Peers / Pray Lend me your Ears" on the battle of Audenarde (11 July 1708). This was published in *Poetical Miscellanies*, 6th Part (1709), and appeared in the same year in *Wit and Mirth: or, Pills to Purge Melancholy*, 6 vols (London: by W. Pearson for J. Tonson, 1719-20), IV, 331, with music by Richard Leveridge. The tune then adopted the title "Ye Commons and Peers," although the song had previously been issued in broadside form as "Jack Frenchman's Lamentation: An Excellent New Song, To the Tune of *I'll tell thee Dick*" (1708). See Claude M. Simpson, *The British Broadside Ballad and its Music* (New Brunswick, New Jersey: Rutgers University Press, 1966), pp. 801-3.

6 The quotation of the popular tune at this point in the "Cantata" is perhaps inspired by a comic pun on "Fiddle stick," / "Fiddle." The tune was first published as that of "My bonny dear Shonny" (published three times in 1683 and reprinted in 1710). Later, the tune became known as "the Irish Jigg," and was increasingly associated with bawdy, rather than political, texts. "Irish Jigg" itself became a comically euphemistic term for sex. The song was included in *The Beggar's Opera* under the name of the "Irish Trot" (Air 36). For further details of this song, see <http://www.irishsongproject.qub.ac.uk/song/75> (accessed 19 September 2017).

7 *An Excellent New Song on a Seditious Pamphlet. To the Tune of Packington's Pound. Written in the Year 1720.* The text of the song was first published in Faulkner's *Works* of Swift, 4 vols (Dublin, 1735), II, 358. See also *Poems*, ed. Williams, I, 236-38. For a second example of the inflammatory potential of a popular song, see the accounts of the dispute between supporters of William Connolly and Viscount Midleton when the latter sang an anti-Connolly ballad ("Sir Owen MacHugh") at the Smock-Alley theatre in January 1724; see David Hayton, "Two Ballads on the County Westmeath By-Election of 1723," *Eighteenth-Century Ireland / Iris an dá chultúr*, 4 (1989), 7-30; and the same author's *The Anglo-Irish Experience, 1680-1730: Religion, Identity and Patriotism* (Woodbridge: Boydell Press, 2012), p. 31.

FIGURE 8.1 "A Cantata" music: Source: *The Works of Jonathan Swift, D.D, D.S.P.D.* (Dublin: Faulkner, 1741-46), Vol. VIII (1746).
By permission of The Board of Trinity College, Dublin. OLS L-11-407 (detail)

FIGURE 8.2 "The Irish Jig: or, The Night Ramble" (London, *c.*1710).

In 1725, when the affair of Wood's Halfpence had been resolved with the revocation of Wood's coinage, George Faulkner published the first collected edition of Swift's *Drapier's Letters* and included in that edition five songs in praise of the Drapier, under the collective title "Songs Sung at the Drapier's Club in Truck Street Dublin" (see Figure 8.3).[8] Although the title page claimed that these had "never before" been printed, we know that at least two of these five songs had appeared in Dublin broadside form, and – such is the ephemeral nature of broadsides – the remaining three may also have been published in broadsides. The Preface to *Fraud Detected*, described on the title page as a statement which will explain "the Usefulness of the Whole," duly turns to the closing sections of its collection:

> *Prometheus* [Swift's poem on the Wood's Halfpence affair] is a Master-Piece; and tho' the Liberty and Learning of *Rome* and *Athens* expired together; yet the Genius of poor *Ireland* arose when *its Liberty was almost set, and was resolved to expire like the* Swan, *in a* Song. (Preface, p. v)

The simile is typically hyperbolic. Unlike the swan, Ireland as a country could not be said to have only sung at this moment of political crisis. Even early colonial writers had felt they had to concede the musicality of the Irish: Gerald of Wales (Giraldus Cambrensis), for example, praised Irish harpers in a work which otherwise characterized the Irish as barbaric, the *Topographia Hiberniæ* (1188).[9] And many songs – purportedly "Irish Songs" – had appeared in print since at least 1683.[10] But the cluster of songs which were published in little over

8 *Fraud Detected: or, The Hibernian Patriot, Containing All the Drapier's Letters to the People of Ireland, on Words, Coinage etc ... Also a New Poem to the Drapier and Songs Sung at the Drapier's Club in Thick Street, Dublin, Never before Printed* (Dublin: George Faulkner, 1725). The collection printed the five *Drapier's Letters* which had been published separately by John Harding in 1724; two further *Letters* would first be published in Faulkner's *Works* (1735).

9 This praise is quoted in a footnote to "Verses Occasioned by the Sudden Drying Up of St Patrick's Well near Trinity College, Dublin in 1726," see Jonathan Swift, *Works*, 11 vols (Dublin, 1762), X, 269-75 (p. 270, note c). Joseph McMinn suggests that this may be "one of the very few occasions in Irish literary history where an author has used Cambrensis, not to continue the propagandistic campaign against Irish barbarism but, on the contrary, to pay tribute to Irish cultural distinction" (*Jonathan Swift and the Arts*, p. 17). For the widespread knowledge of Cambrensis' comments in the eighteenth century, see Barra Boydell, "'Whatever has a *Foreign* Tone / We like much better than our own': Irish Music and Anglo-Irish Identity in the Eighteenth Century," in *Music and Identity in Ireland and Beyond*, eds Mark Fitzgerald and John O'Flynn (Farnham: Ashgate, 2014), pp. 19-38 (20-21).

10 At least 17 songs, purportedly 'Irish,' had been printed at this point, not counting the many Williamite ballads of the 1690s and other songs which do not identify themselves as 'Irish.' See "My Bonny dear Shonny" (London, 1683); "A New Song Set by Mr Leveridge, Sung att

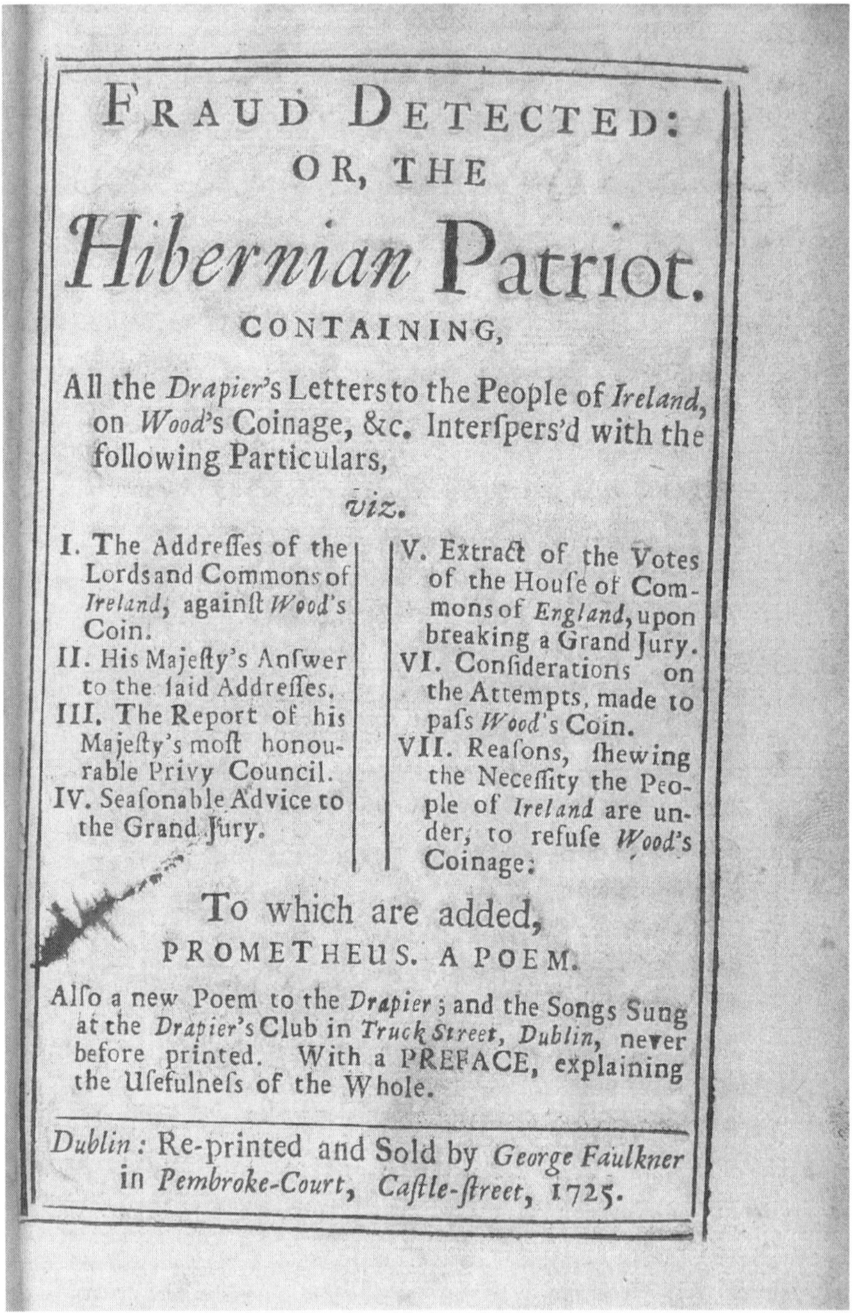
FRAUD DETECTED:
OR, THE
Hibernian Patriot.
CONTAINING,
All the *Drapier's* Letters to the People of *Ireland*, on *Wood's* Coinage, &c. Interſpers'd with the following Particulars,
viz.

I. The Addreſſes of the Lords and Commons of *Ireland*, againſt *Wood's* Coin.
II. His Majeſty's Anſwer to the ſaid Addreſſes.
III. The Report of his Majeſty's moſt honourable Privy Council.
IV. Seaſonable Advice to the Grand Jury.
V. Extract of the Votes of the Houſe of Commons of *England*, upon breaking a Grand Jury.
VI. Conſiderations on the Attempts, made to paſs *Wood's* Coin.
VII. Reaſons, ſhewing the Neceſſity the People of *Ireland* are under, to refuſe *Wood's* Coinage;

To which are added,
PROMETHEUS. A POEM.
Alſo a new Poem to the *Drapier*; and the Songs Sung at the *Drapier's* Club in *Truck Street*, *Dublin*, never before printed. With a PREFACE, explaining the Uſefulneſs of the Whole.

Dublin: Re-printed and Sold by *George Faulkner* in *Pembroke-Court*, *Caſtle-ſtreet*, 1725.

FIGURE 8.3 Title page of *Fraud Detected: or, The Hibernian Patriot* (Dublin: G. Faulkner, 1725). Beinecke Rare Book and Manuscript Library, Yale University. NZ Z725s one year in Dublin (1724-25) was unprecedented. While Williamite ballads of the 1690s repeatedly returned to an Irish theme or character (the English Broadside Ballad Archive collects 41 such ballads), these were all London-printed songs, and their Irish dimension was what we might call an accident of history, when European politics hung in the balance as events unfolded in Ireland. Other miscellaneous 'Irish' songs were also published in London, as, of course, was entirely typical of print culture more generally at this time. But the outpouring of printed pamphlets, letters, poems, and songs from Dublin printers in 1724 and 1725 was extraordinary. As many as one hundred printed items concerning, or at the very least referring to, the Wood's Halfpence affair were published in Dublin.[11] Mindful that the distinction between poetry and song is often impossible to make, I have compiled a bibliography of eighteen songs which have survived from this period concerning the affair of Wood's Halfpence (see Appendix). All identify themselves as "songs" or indicate that they are to be sung, by the inclusion of a reference to a specific tune, a refrain or chorus. A definitive list will never be possible (the irony of historiography being that often the most popular and pervasive elements of a culture are

---

the Theatre in Dublin" (London, 1700, "Marinda's Face like Cupid's Bow"); "Mac Ballor" (London, 1707, "If a Woful Sad Ditty to Know thou Art Witty Man"); "The Irish Hallaloo" (London, 1707, "Instead of our Buildings and Castles so Brave"); "The Irish Disappointment" (London, [1710], "Once I Lov'd a Lady"); "The Irish Jig: or, The Night Ramble" (London, [1710], "One Night in my Ramble I Chanc'd to See"); "The Irish Howl" (London, [1710], "Remember Damon you Did Tell"); "A Song Set by Mr Leveridge" (London, [1710], "One Sunday after Mass"); "A New Song ... Sung at ye Theatre in Dublin" (London, [1710], "Thus Damon Knock't at Celia's Door"); "A New Song ... Sung at ye Theatre in Dublin" (London, [1710], "When Sawney first Did Woe me"); "The New Kilmainham Ballad: To the Tune of, Ye Commons and Peers" ([Dublin], 1711, "At a Sessions of late"); "Shein sheis shuus lum" (London, 1714-15); "An Irish Wooing" (London, 1719-20, "*Dermot* Lov'd *Sheela* Well and Strove her Heart to Gain"); "The Tipling Philosophers, Set by Mr Leveridge and Sung at the Theatre in Dublin" (Dublin, 1720, "Diogenes Surly and Proud"); "An Irish Song" (London, 1720, "Hub ub ub boo"); "The Original Black Joke, Sent from Dublin" (London, *c.*1720); "Plaracanarorka, Let All Men Remember" (Dublin, 1724, "Let All Men Remember").

11 See Bryan Coleborne, "Jonathan Swift and the Voices of Irish Protest against Wood's Halfpence," *Monash Swift Papers*, eds Clive T. Probyn and Bryan Coleborne, 1 (1988), 67-86 (pp. 68-69); the same author's "The Problem of 'Blue-Skin's Ballad,'" in *An Index of Civilisation: Studies of Printing and Publishing History in Honour of Keith Maslen*, eds R. Harvey, W. Kirsop, and B. J. McMullin (Monash University: Centre for Bibliographical and Textual Studies, 1993), pp. 129-136 (131); and Clive T. Probyn, "Jonathan Swift at the Sign of the Drapier," *Reading Swift: Papers from The Third Münster Symposium on Jonathan Swift*, eds Hermann J. Real and Helgard Stöver-Leidig (Munich: Wilhelm Fink, 1998), pp. 225-37. Sabine Baltes-Ellermann has collated and transcribed over 130 such pieces in *Jonathan Swift's Allies: The Wood's Halfpence Controversy in Ireland, 1724-25*, ed. Sabine Baltes-Ellermann, 2nd rev. ed. (Frankfurt on Main: Peter Lang, 2017).

those which escape the historian's eye). But the list of eighteen titles is at least useful in indicating what might lie beyond that which we can now map.

The songs were published within roughly an eighteen-month period; all appeared first as broadside sheets; and all, or possibly all but one, were first published in Dublin (with at least five published by John Harding, the publisher of the *Drapier's Letters*).[12] It is possible to give approximate dates to some of the songs according to key events, such as the first pamphlet and broadside attacks on Wood (summer of 1723), the first Drapier's letter (March 1724), the active boycotting of the coin (August 1724), Harding's arrest for printing the fourth Drapier's letter, and Judge Whitshed's dismissal of the first jury in his trial (November 1724). The songs in the bibliography can thus be given in approximate chronological order. For the editors of the Cambridge edition of Swift's poetry, none of these can be confidently attributed to Swift, although at least four of the poems were ascribed to Swift in printings before 1746.[13] It is likely that one is by Swift's close friend, Thomas Sheridan, and several other poems were ascribed to specific writers in *The Hibernian Patriot* (1730).[14] Most writers, of course, were, and remain, anonymous.

The eighteen songs represent a collection of poems linked together by common themes, attitudes, tones, and styles. However, with only one slight exception, the songs do not borrow or quote from each other, so that as complete songs each is unique in terms of its text.[15] The song by Thomas Sheridan, for example, is more 'literary' than others: in the first verse, we are already singing about the "Egregious hazards run" (Song 12). And this song is also politically more daring than many of the others, with verses 10-11 openly singing of

---

12 It is a relatively safe guess that the three songs for which the only surviving copy is in *Fraud Detected* (1725) were also originally printed as broadsides, as was also that of *Will. Wood's Petition* (Song 15). There is some debate as to whether the Dublin broadside *Blue-Skin's Ballad* preceded the song's first London printing (see Coleborne, "The Problem of 'Blue-Skin's Ballad'").

13 I am grateful to James Woolley and Stephen Karian for confirming that none of these songs will be ascribed to Swift in the forthcoming Cambridge edition. For contemporary ascriptions, we might note: Song 1 (in *Whartoniana*, 1727), 5 (in *Whartoniana*, 1727), 11 (in Swift, *Miscellanies*, 1733), and 15 (in Faulkner 1746; Swift's *Miscellanies*, 1746; and Deane Swift 1755). Songs 4, 11, and 13 were printed as by Swift in Scott's 1814 edition.

14 Sheridan is first identified as the author of "The Drapier's Ballad" in *The Hibernian Patriot: Being a Collection of the Drapier's Letters to the People of Ireland* (London: A. Moore, 1730), and this ascription is accepted by Sheridan's modern editor; see *The Poems of Thomas Sheridan*, ed. Robert Hogan (Newark: University of Delaware Press, and London and Toronto: Associated University Presses, 1994), pp. 134-37, 324-25. *The Hibernian Patriot* names [Robert] Witheral and Charles Shadwell as the authors of Songs 1 and 2, respectively.

15 A number of lines and verses are shared only in Songs 1 and 2.

freedom and liberty (Figure 8.4). But we would expect to find a degree of convention in these songs, and common elements can easily be identified. All inveigh against Wood personally and the imposition of the "trash" of his coinage upon Ireland, and all but two praise and celebrate the Drapier's efforts in defeating him. (The two exceptions are concerned with the trial of John Harding, the publisher of the Drapier's letters.) One song ventriloquizes Wood's own voice, but allows him, of course, to damn himself. Although Sheridan's song stresses the importance of liberty and freedom to Ireland, most of the songs articulate loyalty to the King, although some of the songs may be more 'conspicuously' or performatively loyal than genuinely so. The songs are clearly part of a male homosocial culture of convivial drinking; several songs exhort their singers (or listeners) as fellow "boys," and there are a couple of bawdy touches: *Ireland's Warning* (Song 1) invokes the simile of a fine lady and her "mange," and *An Excellent New Song upon the Late Grand-Jury* (Song 11) sings of the dairy-maid who gave away her virginity for free. Unsurprisingly, over half of the songs might be defined as 'drinking songs' which culminate in toasts, particularly to the Drapier, but sometimes to both the Drapier and King George I.

That the songs attempt to fashion a sense of collective identity is obvious. Those listening are invited to raise a glass and join in the song. Many of the songs feature a burden or a chorus, which extends an invitation to those listening. Five of the songs use the same burden, "Which nobody can deny," which, as a phrase in itself, with its commonplace coercion, is a wonderfully apt distillation of club-identity as process.[16] And, although the setting of the song is not always noted, in the cases in which a tune is referred to, these are obviously familiar, popular tunes: "Packington's Pound," "The London Prentice," "O London is a fine town," "Randel a Barnaby," "Lillibulero," "Which nobody can deny" (a shortened form of "Greensleeves"), and "The Apprentices' Song." All of these tunes are easily recoverable to us in works such as *Wit and Mirth: or, Pills to Purge Melancholy* (1719-20 edition) or the engraved prints of the second London edition of Gay's *The Beggar's Opera* (1728).[17] Many were of very long standing: "Packington's Pound" has been dated as early as 1596 and was among

16 See Songs 1, 2, 10, 11, and 16. All of these songs can be sung to the shortened form of the tune "Greensleeves," a tune which became known as "Which nobody can deny" (Simpson, *The British Broadside Ballad*, pp. 277-78).

17 Only one tune remains obscure: that of "We have catcht you in the nick," which is named as the tune for *An Excellent New Song Made by a Lover of his Country* (Song 3). I have also not been able to find a notated copy of the drinking song "Randel a Barnaby" (the tune for Song 14), though the English collector Joseph Ritson records the lyrics in his 1802 collection, *The North County Chorister.*

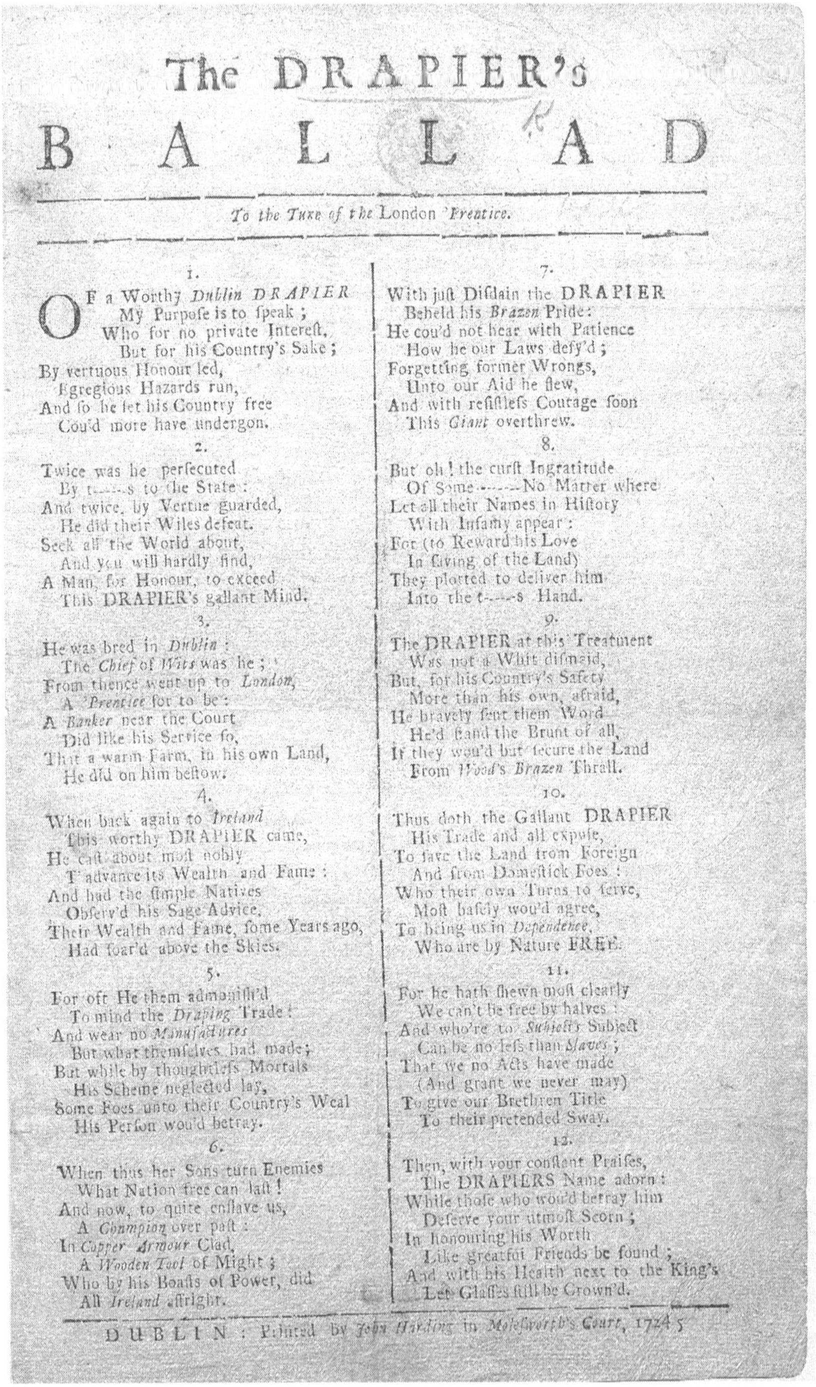

The DRAPIER's BALLAD

To the Tune of the London *'Prentice.*

1.

Of a Worthy *Dublin* DRAPIER
  My Purpoſe is to ſpeak ;
Who for no private Intereſt,
  But for his Country's Sake ;
By vertuous Honour led,
  Egregious Hazards run,
And ſo he ſet his Country free
  Cou'd more have undergon.

2.

Twice was he perſecuted
  By t-----s to the State :
And twice, by Vertue guarded,
  He did their Wiles defeat.
Seek all the World about,
  And you will hardly find,
A Man, for Honour, to exceed
  This DRAPIER's gallant Mind.

3.

He was bred in *Dublin* :
  The *Chief* of *Wits* was he ;
From thence went up to *London*,
  A *'Prentice* for to be :
A *Banker* near the Court
  Did like his Service ſo,
That a warm Farm, in his own Land,
  He did on him beſtow.

4.

When back again to *Ireland*
  This worthy DRAPIER came,
He caſt about moſt nobly
  T' advance its Wealth and Fame :
And had the ſimple Natives
  Obſerv'd his Sage Advice,
Their Wealth and Fame, ſome Years ago,
  Had ſoar'd above the Skies.

5.

For oft He them admoniſh'd
  To mind the *Draping* Trade :
And wear no *Manufactures*
  But what themſelves had made;
But while by thoughtleſs Mortals
  His Scheme neglected lay,
Some Foes unto their Country's Weal
  His Perſon wou'd betray.

6.

When thus her Sons turn Enemies
  What Nation free can laſt !
And now, to quite enſlave us,
  A *Champion* over paſt :
In *Copper Armour* Clad,
  A *Wooden Tool* of Might ;
Who by his Boaſts of Power, did
  All *Ireland* affright.

7.

With juſt Diſdain the DRAPIER
  Beheld his *Brazen* Pride :
He cou'd not bear with Patience
  How he our Laws defy'd ;
Forgetting former Wrongs,
  Unto our Aid he flew,
And with reſiſtleſs Courage ſoon
  This *Giant* overthrew.

8.

But oh ! the curſt Ingratitude
  Of Some -------No Matter where
Let all their Names in Hiſtory
  With Infamy appear :
For (to Reward his Love
  In ſaving of the Land)
They plotted to deliver him
  Into the t-----s Hand.

9.

The DRAPIER at this Treatment
  Was not a Whit diſmaid,
But, for his Country's Safety
  More than his own, afraid,
He bravely ſent them Word
  He'd ſtand the Brunt of all,
If they wou'd but ſecure the Land
  From *Wood's Brazen* Thrall.

10.

Thus doth the Gallant DRAPIER
  His Trade and all expoſe,
To ſave the Land from Foreign
  And from Domeſtick Foes :
Who their own Turns to ſerve,
  Moſt baſely wou'd agree,
To bring us in *Dependence*,
  Who are by Nature FREE.

11.

For he hath ſhewn moſt clearly
  We can't be free by halves :
And who're to *Subject's* Subject
  Can be no leſs than *Slaves* ;
That we no Acts have made
  (And grant we never may)
To give our Brethren Title
  To their pretended Sway.

12.

Then, with your conſtant Praiſes,
  The DRAPIERS Name adorn :
While thoſe who wou'd betray him
  Deſerve your utmoſt Scorn ;
In honouring his Worth
  Like greatful Friends be found ;
And with his Health next to the King's
  Let Glaſſes ſtill be Crown'd.

DUBLIN : Printed by *John Harding* in *Moleſworth's Court*, 1724 5

FIGURE 8.4 [Thomas Sheridan], *The Drapier's Ballad. To the Tune of the London 'Prentice* (Dublin: J. Harding, 1724-25).

the most popular song airs in seventeenth-century England.[18] "O London is a fine town" has been dated as early as 1614.[19] "Lillibulero's" circulation in Ireland hardly needs explanation. (The tune was used for at least seven Williamite ballads in the 1690s, with the most famous of these settings – "Ho brother Teague, dost hear the decree / Lilliburlero bullen a-la" – said to have circulated in 40,000 copies among William's supporters. That song's author, Thomas Wharton, famously boasted that it had driven James II out of three kingdoms.[20]) Even the Freemason song "The Entred Apprentice" was available in print. Contrary to our modern sense of Freemasonry as a secret society, Freemasonry in the early eighteenth century authorized hundreds of print titles and inspired a huge range of parodies and satiric attacks. These were published from the early 1720s onwards, in both London and Dublin. The tune of the "Entred Apprentice's Song" was printed in James Anderson's expensive quarto edition of *The Constitutions of the Free-Masons* (London, 1723). And George Faulkner printed

---

18 See Simpson, *The British Broadside Ballad*, p. 565, and Christopher Marsh, *Music and Society in Early Modern England* (Cambridge: Cambridge University Press, 2010), p. 236.

19 *Popular Music of the Olden Time: A Collection of Ancient Songs, Ballads and Dance Tunes, Illustrative of the National Music of English*, ed. William Chappell, 2 vols (London: Cramer, Beale, and Chappell, 1857-59), I, 218.

20 The seven Williamite ballads are: [Thomas Wharton], *A New Song* ([London: *s. n.*, 1688]), "Ho brother Teague, dost hear the decree, Lil-li burlero bullen a – la;" [Thomas Wharton], *Second Part of Lill-li burlero bullen a-la* ([London: *s. n.*] 1688 [i.e. 1689]), "There was an old prophesie found in a bogg;" [Thomas Wharton], *Second Part of Lill-li burlero bullen a-la* ([London: *s. n.*, 1689]), "By love my dear Morish vat makes de sho'shad;" *The Protestants Delight: or, An Health to his Highness the Prince of Orange, and the Rest of the Royal Family. Tune of, Lilli Burlero* ([London]: J. C., [1689]), "Come all ye Protestant lads in the land;" *Englands Hopes: or, Look to't Teague, Being a Preparative Beaten, against the French and Irish Rebells. To the Tune of, Ise often for my Jeny Strove: or, Lilli borlero* ([London]: Printed for J. C., 1689), "French and Irish now beware;" *Teague and Sawney: or, The Unfortunate Success of a Dear-Joys Devotion by St Patrick's Cross. Being Transform'd into the Deel's Whirligig. To the Tune of Lili bolero* ([London]: C. G. [1690]), "You that love mirth, give ear to my song;" *The Reading Skirmish: or, The Bloody Irish Routed by the Victorious Dutch. Five Hundred Papishes Came there, to Make a Final End of All the Town, in Time of Prayer, but God did them Defend. To the Tune of, Lilli Bolero* [1689], "We came into brave Reading by night." The tune was included in a 1686 instruction book for the recorder: Robert Carr, *The Delightful Companion*, 2nd ed. (1686), [sig. F_3] untitled melody; see <http://www.irishsongproject.qub.ac.uk/song/183> (accessed 19 September 2017). Anthony Heywood has traced an early notation of the tune in a book of metrical psalms set to old folk tunes of the Low Countries (*Souter Liederkens* [Antwerp, 1540]); see his "Is Lilliburlero an Old Dutch Folk Tune?" *English Dance and Song*, 61, no 1 (1999), 4. See also Brendan Ó Buachalla, "Lillibulero: The New Irish Song," *Familia: Ulster Genealogical Review*, 2, no 7 (1991), 47-69, and James Porter, "The Cultural Expropriation of 'Lillibulero,'" *Scottish Studies Review*, 5, no 1 (2004), 19-32.

a cheap single-sheet version of the texts of the two main Freemason songs in Dublin, possibly in 1725.[21]

The songs themselves often pay tribute to the solidarity of Dublin's citizens. Encouraged to accept the coin, to betray the Drapier, and to bend to the pressure of the Judge in the trial of John Harding, they stood fast. And the songs work to strengthen and confirm that cohesion. A number of them hint at Swift's identity in puns or hidden clues, and these allusions clearly serve to bind the singers and audience together in knowing alliance.[22] Many of the songs record the various trades, guilds, and friendly societies who combined to support and protect the Drapier. In one of the earliest of the songs, *Ireland's Warning* (probably issued in spring 1724), a soldier finds himself unable to pay the prices asked by the tapster and the baker, and fights with the butcher at market while the farmer finds his rent, offered in Wood's halfpence, refused by the squire. The song, in exploring the effects of the depreciation of coins on "this Man, and that Man, and all Men," also notes how beggars are reduced to the lice on their bodies, as farthings are now worthless. But despite this gesture, the song, like the others, remains firmly addressed to the shopmen, tradesmen, and farmers, who are all exhorted to read the Drapier's pamphlet.

The frequent references to various kinds of tradesmen in the songs underscore the significance of the trade guilds in the Wood's Halfpence affair. In late August 1724, a number of guilds published declarations against Wood's halfpence, stating publicly that their members would boycott the coin.[23] And the following song commemorates the publication of these declarations: *An Excellent New Song upon the Declarations of the Several Corporations of the City of Dublin, against Wood's Half-pence, To the Tune of London is a fine Town &c.* (Song 4). The tune is comprised of a short 8-bar melody sung repeatedly (see Figure 8.5). The broadsheet prints 34 verses and alternating choruses, but the song could continue indefinitely, especially as the tune itself ends incon-

21 See James Anderson, *The Constitutions of the Free-Masons: Containing the History, Charges, Regulations, &c. of that Most Ancient and Right Worshipful Fraternity. For the Use of the Lodges* (London: by William Hunter for John Senex and John Hooke, 1723), p. 90; and *The Enter'd Prentices Song [and] The Fellow Crafts Song* (Dublin: George Faulkner [ESTC 1725-1727]).

22 For example, Sheridan's Drapier's song (Song 12) alludes to Swift's earlier pamphlet, *Proposal for the Universal Use of Irish Manufacture* (1720) in verse v: "For oft He them admonish'd / To mind the *Draping* Trade, / And wear no *Manufactures* / But what *themselves had made*;" and "The Drapier Anatomiz'd" (Song 8) hints at Swift's identity in singing of how he has done more "*Than All of his Cloath* / Or of any, whatever Persuasion." The Proclamation against the author of the Drapier's *Letter to the Whole People of Ireland* remained in force until April 1725.

23 *Jonathan Swift's Allies*, ed. Baltes-Ellermann, pp. 223-28.

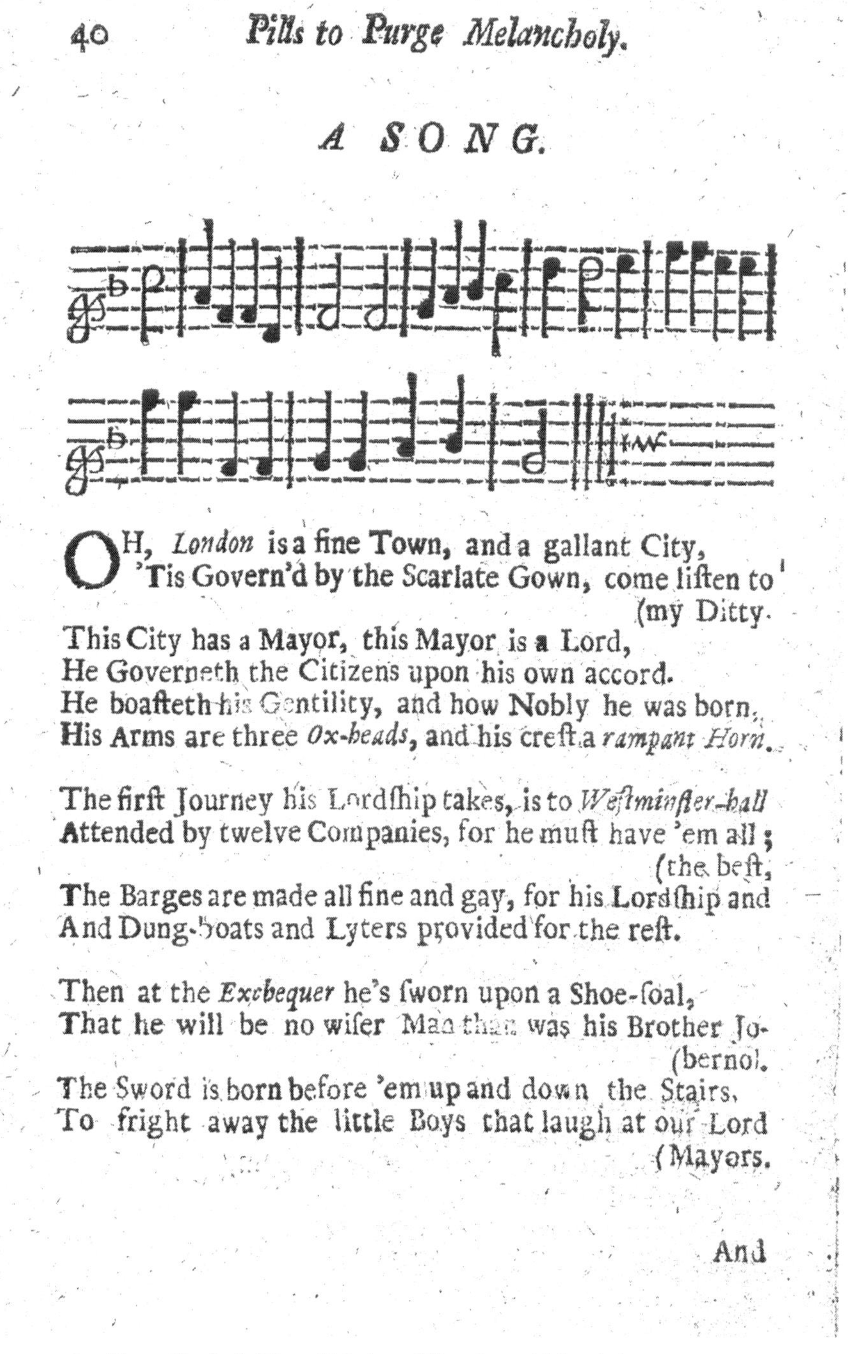

40 *Pills to Purge Melancholy.*

A SONG.

OH, *London* is a fine Town, and a gallant City,
'Tis Govern'd by the Scarlate Gown, come liſten to (my Ditty.
This City has a Mayor, this Mayor is a Lord,
He Governeth the Citizens upon his own accord.
He boaſteth his Gentility, and how Nobly he was born,
His Arms are three *Ox-heads*, and his creſt a *rampant Horn*.

The firſt Journey his Lordſhip takes, is to *Weſtminſter-hall*
Attended by twelve Companies, for he muſt have 'em all;
The Barges are made all fine and gay, for his Lordſhip and (the beſt,
And Dung-boats and Lyters provided for the reſt.

Then at the *Exchequer* he's ſworn upon a Shoe-ſoal,
That he will be no wiſer Man than was his Brother Jo- (bernol.
The Sword is born before 'em up and down the Stairs,
To fright away the little Boys that laugh at our Lord (Mayors.

And

FIGURE 8.5 Henry Playford, *Wit and Mirth: or, Pills to Purge Melancholy* (London, 1707).

clusively on the 6th note of the key. This allows for a long list of tradesmen, a veritable virtual procession of bankers, brewers, tailors, clothiers, shoemakers, chandlers, butchers, bakers, tinkers, carpenters, joiners. (It is highly unlikely that tinkers formed themselves into a guild, of course, let alone published a declaration, although a declaration, probably fictitious, by beggars was published in one Dublin newspaper.[24]) The song relishes its catalogue of the serried ranks of tradesmen lining up to condemn and defeat William Wood. Similarly, *The Donore Ballad* (Song 7) has various groups come to look at the painting of the Drapier above a tavern in Truck Street: shopkeepers, weavers, tailors, brewers, bakers, joiners, carpenters, surgeons, barbers, turners, skinners, curriers, butchers, flying-stationers. The ballad ends "Pray come buy My Ballad and merrily Sing," which suggests that the roll call may be an astute commercial tactic.[25] Single-sheet broadside ballads, of course, were the cheapest form of print and typically sold for a penny or two.

Beyond the groups of specific trades and guilds are the supporters of the Drapier, who explicitly fashioned a club identity in four of the songs. The first of these takes the title "A New Song Sung at the Club at Mr Taplin's. The Sign of the Drapier's Head in Truck-Street." All four were included in *Fraud Detected*, where they joined the song written by Thomas Sheridan. These songs are among the few extant references to the existence of this Club, and, if we believe that the songs convey something of what happened in Truck-Street in 1724, then these gentlemen met weekly at Taplin's tavern, to sing with their host and toast the Drapier. The inclusion of Latin tags in the publications, which are linked to the Club, suggests a highly literate audience and reminds us that ballads are not only enjoyed by the relatively poor.[26] Truck-Street itself is just off the lower Coombe, about a seven-minute walk from St Patrick's

---

24 A "Declaration of the Beggars, Lame and Blind, Halt and Maimed, both Male and Female, in and about the City of Dublin" was published in the *Dublin Impartial News Letter* (12 September 1724); reprinted in *Jonathan Swift's Allies*, ed. Baltes-Ellermann, pp. 230-31.

25 See Christopher Marsh on how ballads in early modern England often catalogued dozens of different social and occupational categories, so as to "shape and shadow" their audience (*Music and Song in Early Modern England*, p. 271). Song 14 also ends in this way.

26 That the Club meets weekly is suggested in Song IV of *Fraud Detected*, which concludes: "Thus, ye Sons of Pleasure, / Who at TAPLIN's weekly sing, / In alternate measure / Loudly let him ring." A later poem by a "Member of the Club" is a loose adaptation of an Horatian Ode (Book I, Ode ii): *A Congratulatory Poem on Dean Swift's Return to Town. By a Member of the Club, Held at Mr Taplin's in Truck-Street, October 7th, 1725* (Dublin: C. C., 1725). The same poem suggests that Taplin is the main singer, with the assembled company joining in with the chorus. Other references to Taplin are found in the broadside poem, *A Poem on the Drapier's Birth-Day, Being November the 30th* (Dublin, 1725). These references do not, however, rule out the possibility that the existence of the Club was fictitious.

Cathedral and lies just outside the city liberties. (Now called Brabazon Street, adjacent streets have since been renamed Weaver's Court and Weaver's Street.)

Of the eighteen songs, half are identified with a specific tune in the broadsides. That others are not identified is not surprising; indeed, not naming the specific tune would become increasingly common in the printing of broadside ballads, as this permitted singers to choose different tunes for their performances. However, a further five songs include the refrain "Which nobody can deny" and can be sung to the tune of that name.[27] And the song identified as being sung to the tune of the "Entered Apprentice's Song" was first published in broadside form with another song, whose text is rhythmically identical, so that both these songs may well have been sung to the same tune. If we accept these hypotheses, we have plausible tune titles for thirteen of the eighteen songs.[28]

All of these tunes are ones which we would think of as 'English' tunes, and several carried specifically anti-Jacobite connotations: "Lillibulero," most obviously, here used as the setting for a song which refers specifically to the campaign against Wood as "the Protestant cause;" and the tune "O London is a fine town," which had recently been used for a song celebrating the 1715 Jacobite defeat, as is evident in its chorus: "Ye *Whiggs* and eke you *Tories* give Ear to what I Sing, / For it is about the *Chevalier* that *silly Wou-d-be-king.*"[29] Thus, a consideration of the songs of the Wood's Halfpence affair appears to confirm that the controversy rallied only the middling ranks of the English-speaking, Protestant population of Dublin. But there are a couple of further points to note which complicate this conclusion, or at least suggest it is not the entire story.

The only melody printed in connection with the Wood's Halfpence affair links the campaign, curiously, with an interest in Gaelic Irish music. Probably designed to be played on the harp, the tune was printed in *A Collection of the Most Celebrated Irish Tunes, Proper for the Violin, German Flute or Hautboy*, under the title "Sq^{r} Woodes's Lamentation on ye Refusall of his HALF PENCE." This 1724 publication is the earliest-known printed collection of Irish music,

27 See note 15 above. Some tunes, such as "Chevy Chase," could be used to accompany songs in common ballad metre.

28 The exceptions here are Songs 5, 7, 15, 17, and 18, which may well be singable to tunes known to be current at this time.

29 See "The Right and True History of Perkin, To the Tune of, ---- O London is a fine Town," in *A Collection of State Songs, Poems, &c. that have been Publish'd since the Rebellion, and Sung in the Several Mug-Houses in the Cities of London and Westminster, &c.* (London: for Andrew and William Bell, *et al.*, 1716), pp. 83-89. The song specifically attacks the Earl of Mar.

containing the first recorded compositions by Turlough Carolan and giving us an unrivalled glimpse of music in Dublin in the late seventeenth and early eighteenth centuries. In the words of its modern editor, Nicholas Carolan, it is "the earliest single body of Irish music to emerge from some nine to ten thousand years of music making in the country." "Squire Wood's Lamentation" stands out in the collection because of its striking topicality, and because its inclusion alongside Gaelic and Jacobite tunes raises questions not only about the performers and audiences for these tunes, but also about the cultural and political dynamics of the Wood's Halfpence affair itself. Nicholas Carolan notes that "it is likely to be of some significance that the collection appeared in the same year as the first four of Swift's *Drapier's Letters* and in a somewhat fevered period of early eighteenth-century colonial nationalism." [30]

The collection's focus on 'Irish' tunes is not the 'Irish' of colonial stereotype, of which there had certainly been quite a few examples in printed song, as in other texts, since the 1680s.[31] A number of its tune titles celebrate Jacobitism or patrons drawn from Gaelic and Old English families, although several recent commentators have noted how it presents its native Irish airs in an Italianate style, so as to appeal to the tastes of the Anglo-Irish.[32] Appearing to corroborate this interpretation is the inclusion of the tune "Squire Wood's Lamentation," with its obvious appeal to the 'Protestant' interest in Dublin. Taking this diverse array of influences into account ("Gaelic Irish," "Anglophone" and "Italian"), Nicholas Carolan concludes that the collection appears, on internal evidence, to be targeted at an audience of interested musicians, whose curiosity for tunes may have outweighed any easy partisanship (p. 35).

Donal O'Sullivan tentatively attributed "Squire Wood's Lamentation" to Carolan and thought it newly composed during the controversy.[33] However,

---

30 John and William Neal, *A Collection of the Most Celebrated Irish Tunes Proper for the Violin, German Flute or Hautboy, Dublin 1724*, ed. Nicholas Carolan (Dublin: ITMA, 2010 [1986]), pp. 29, 37. The only known copy of this book to survive is that owned by Edward Bunting, now in Special Collections in Queen's University Belfast. Subsequent quotations from Carolan's edition will be cited in parentheses within the text.

31 See, for example, the comic love song sung by an Irish barber which begins "Wid me Strings of shmall Cats-Guts am I come / And a Harp made of Wood," in *Teagueland Jests: or, Bogg-Witticisms in Two Parts* (London: *s.n.*, 1690), pp. 119-20.

32 See Leith Davis, *Music, Postcolonialism and Gender* (Notre Dame: University of Notre Dame Press, 2006), p. 31; and Barra Boydell, "'Whatever has a *Foreign* Tone / We like much better than our own': Irish Music and Anglo-Irish Identity in the Eighteenth Century," (p. 28).

33 Petrie's manuscript collection also included the tune as "Wood's Lamentation, by Carolan;" see Donal O'Sullivan, *Carolan: The Life, Times, and Music of an Irish Harper* (London: Taylor and Francis, 2001 [1958]), p. 303.

the melody is almost identical with a dance tune which appears in John Young's *A Collection of Original Scotch Tunes for the Violin* (London, c.1700) as "An Irish Tune."[34] The tune is thus likely to have been a familiar one, which took on an association with the Wood's affair quite quickly into the controversy. (Newspaper advertisements allow us to date the publication of the collection before August 1724.) Its inclusion within a compilation of explicitly Irish, Gaelic tunes suggests what has been termed the "double inscription" of music in Ireland, its particular ability to register the complexities of cultural encounter. Music's inherently hybrid character can cross and unsettle the boundaries and polarities upon which colonialism and nationalism both rely.[35]

It is thus noteworthy that the songs on the Wood's Halfpence affair do not exemplify some of the more sectarian elements which were evident in several pamphlets of the time, such as the ones which argued that William Wood was Catholic.[36] If we compare the song tunes used for the Williamite ballads with those identified for the Wood's Halfpence ballads, there is an overlap with only one tune, "Lillibulero."[37] And although the song set to Lillibulero (Song 6)

---

34 This tune is included in Aloys Fleischmann, Mícheál Ó Súilleabháin, Paul McGettrick, eds, *Sources of Irish Traditional Music c.1600-1855*, 2 vols (New York and London: Garland, 1998), I, 41, no 206, but is not connected there to the "Squire Woods" tune. *Sources* does include a cross reference between the Neals' published "Squire Wood's Lamentation" and a dance tune ("Love is the Cause of my Mourning") in Henry Playford, *A Collection of Original Scotch Tunes (Full of the Highland Humours) for the Violin: Being the First of this Kind yet Printed. Several Being in the Compass of the Flute*, 2nd ed. (London, 1701), I, 42, no 213.

35 See Leith Davis, *Music, Postcolonialism and Gender, passim.*

36 One pamphlet claimed that Wood was a Jesuit in disguise and another argued that he and his associates were "Papists;" see *A Letter from a Quaker-Mercht to Will. Wood Hard-Ware-Man* (Dublin, 1724), p. 14, and *The Fifth and Last Letter to the People of Ireland in Reference to Wood and his Brass* (Dublin, 1724), p. 12. The exceptional songs are "An Excellent New Ballad against Wood's Half-pence, &c. To the tune of, Lillibolero &c." (discussed further above) and "An Excellent New Song Made by a Lover of his Country; against Wood's Brass Half Pence. To the tune, We have catcht you in the nick" ([Dublin], 1724). This song at one point turns anti-Jacobite (but not explicitly anti-Catholic): "Remember well the *Brass* that fell, / At the Battle of the *Boyn*." See also James Ward's essay which traces how indebted the language and imagery of the Drapier's letters are to the Williamite wars and the Revolution settlement ("Brass Money and Wooden Shoes: Transmuting Anti-Catholic Rhetoric in Swift's Drapier's Letters," *Eighteenth-Century Ireland / Iris an dá chultúr*, 25 [2010], 82-97).

37 Tunes identified for the Williamite ballads are "March Boys, March Boys," "Hey Boys up we go," "Lay of your Pleading," "Liggan Water" / "Logan water," "Billy and Mally," "My Life and my Death," "Sawny will ne're be my Love again," "The Orange," "The Spinning Wheel," "The French Dancing-Master: or, The Soldiers Departure," "Valiant Jockey" and – the most popular settings – "Lillibulero" and "Let Caesar Live Long." Tunes identified for the Wood's Halfpence songs are "Packington's Pound," "We have catcht you in the nick," "Randel a

refers openly to the "Protestant cause," in other respects it is among the more subversive of the songs. There is no toast to the King here, instead – to quote the song itself – there is a "*Hope* that the KING is our Friend," and the suggestion that a monument ought to be raised to the Drapier recalls the fairly recent erection of a bronze statue to George I on a pier at Essex Bridge (1722).[38] If King George had a statue, there was no reason why the Drapier, who had done so much (more) for Ireland, should not have one.[39] Here the tune, with its consciously Williamite and loyal resonances, may have helped to 'inoculate' the text from the suspicion of disloyalty.

The same song refers to Wood becoming a "Munster crack" if the Irish send back the coin. This proverbial phrase occurs in "Irish Eloquence" (possibly written by Swift in the mid-1730s) as the comic put-down for someone who is a braggart, liar, or crazed. But the same phrase had been used of the Duchess of Kendal in a satirical broadside poem printed in the early 1720s, alluding to her Irish peerage title, Duchess of Munster.[40] She became particularly famous in Ireland, of course, for her involvement in the Wood's affair, having sold the patent to produce coinage in Ireland to William Wood for a reported £10,000 in 1722. This is the only known song or ballad of the period that alludes so

---

Barnaby," "London is a fine town," "Which nobody can deny," "London Prentice," and "Lillibulero."

38 *Correspondence*, ed. Woolley, II, 431 and n4.

39 I am grateful to my colleague Professor David Hayton for suggesting this reading of the ballad. On the politicization of Dublin's royal statues, see David Hayton, "An Image War: Representations of Monarchy in Early Eighteenth-Century Ireland," *Ourselves Alone? Religion, Society and Politics in Eighteenth- and Nineteenth-Century Ireland: Essays Presented to S. J. Connolly*, eds D. W. Hayton and Andrew Holmes (Dublin: Four Courts Press, 2016), pp. 20-41. Robin Usher interprets the siting of the statue at Essex Bridge as signifying the connection between the Crown and commerce, with the Custom House immediately to its right and trading ships moored by its steps. He also quotes from Swift's letter to Robert Cope of 9 October 1722 in which Swift mocks the statue of George I as a "brazen image;" see Robin Usher, *Protestant Dublin, 1660-1760: Architecture and Iconography* (Basingstoke: Palgrave, 2012), pp. 111-16. See also Swift's reference to the statue as costing £30,000 in the second Drapier's letter, *A Letter to John Harding* (Dublin: John Harding, 1724), p. 11. Several other songs called for a statue to the Drapier to be raised (Songs 4 and 16, or in the case of Song 9, a monument), as did the broadside poem, *A Letter from Aminadab Firebrass, Quaker Merchant, to M. B. Drapier* (Dublin: John Harding, [1724]), in *Jonathan Swift's Allies*, ed. Baltes-Ellermann, pp. 374-75.

40 *The Lady's Case: or, A Letter from an Injur'd Wife beyond Sea to a Munster Crack.* The only copy of the broadside poem known to have survived is in the National Archives in London. ESTC tentatively suggests a London 1720 printing. The gloss of "crack" in "Irish Eloquence" is that offered in *Swift's Irish Writings: Selected Prose and Poetry*, eds Carole Fabricant and Robert Mahony (Basingstoke: Palgrave, 2010), p. 185.

daringly to the Duchess of Kendal.[41] That it is sung to the tune of the most famously loyalist song of its day, Lillibulero, puts the connotations generated by its (safely loyalist) tune and (riskily daring) text into productive tension.

In the ballad set to the tune of "Which nobody can deny" (Song 2), the supporters of Wood's Halfpence sing in ironic jubilation of the new coin and in so doing drop their guard as crypto-Jacobites: "Ye *Britains* let *Kettles* and *Warming* Pans Ring" (an obvious allusion to the smears surrounding the legitimacy of the Pretender). It is they who scandalously sing of Wood's Halfpence as "*His Majesty's Treasure*." "Disloyalty" (connecting the coin with the King's authority) is articulated through the voice of Wood's supporters, but the association between King and coin remains. The song satirizes Jacobitism and the supporters of Wood, but through that satire also articulates a critique of George I.[42] And in many of the other songs, toasts to the King and to the Drapier work to place them at least on level terms and sometimes, it is implied, in terms more flattering to Swift. (In one broadsheet poem, for example, Swift and George I share the honours of a final toast, but only after Swift has been praised in such fulsome terms as "What's *Great* or *Good*, is bounded all in YOU."[43])

The song tunes themselves also demonstrate an ability to transcend usual affiliations and boundaries and to represent possibilities of political complexity. Ballads were sung to pre-existing tunes, and thus these tunes had the potential to shake the moorings of past association. "Packington's Pound" – a popular 'English' tune since 1596 – had been used in a 1665 Dublin-printed ballad which celebrated the victory of James, Duke of York, at Lowestoft. "O London is a fine town" had been parodied in a Dublin broadside on the unveiling of the statue to King George I on a pier erected at Essex Bridge (1722). The air of "The London Prentice," which was used for Sheridan's "The Drapier's Ballad," had originally accompanied a bawdy ballad of the prentice and his lover with the refrain of "Blow the candle out."[44] Even "Lillibulero" had been used in an anti-Williamite response in the 1690s: under the title "A New Song

41 Swift's poem "Prometheus," however, does glance at the Duchess of Kendal in one line: "(*Venus* was Brib'd to let it pass)" (*Poems*, ed. Williams, I, 345, l. 40).

42 See John Robert Moore's brief reading of the ballad which claimed only that the song is anti-Hanoverian in animus ("An Unrecorded Drapier Poem," *The Yearbook of English Studies*, 2 [1972], 115-17).

43 *A Congratulatory Poem on Dean Swift's Return to Town: By a Member of the Club Held at Mr Taplin's in Truck-Street, October, 7th, 1725* (Dublin, 1725) in *Jonathan Swift's Allies*, ed. Baltes-Ellermann, pp. 511-13. Note also the ending of Song 12: "And with his Health, next to the King's / Let Glasses still be Crown'd."

44 *The Royal Victory: Obtained, with the Providence of Almighty God, against the Dutch Fleet, June the second, 1665* (Dublin, [1665]), "Let England, and Ireland, and Scotland rejoice;" *Upon the Fringes, Commonly so Call'd by the Vulgar* (Dublin, 1722), "O Dublin is a fine Town

upon the Hogen Mogen," this version mockingly ventriloquized the colloquialisms of the Dutch, rather than the Irish, and sang of how "your Orange we'll squeeze."[45] And later accounts of the sacking of Kilbroggan depicted three pipers of James's army playing "Lillibulero" as well as the more obviously Jacobite songs "When the King Enjoys His Own Again" and "The Humours of Bandon," as the army pillaged the church.[46] Later, "Lillibulero" would be used as the setting for a song in *The Beggar's Opera* (Act III, Air iv) in which friendship is cynically re-envisioned as self-interest, and the tune would be used in at least eleven further ballad operas and printed in many popular miscellanies of song, with only a few of these carrying the anti-Catholic connotations of the famous Williamite versions of the 1690s.[47] The ability of tunes to circulate widely should thus be understood in two senses: that of being learned by many listeners but also in being applied to various song texts. Both of these unsettle easy or inherent interpretations of meaning or intent.

Changes within Gaelic literature also suggest that an openness to cultural transfer may have been newly possible, with a particularly heightened mobility of song texts and tunes. In the early eighteenth century, a new generation of Irish-language authors began to write for a larger and more socially diverse audience than had been the case of their predecessors in the bardic tradition: "The changing tone and content of the literature was accompanied by an important change in form as scribes increasingly associated poems with the airs of popular tunes, a practice that was unknown in the seventeenth century but which began to appear in the manuscripts in the 1720-40 period."[48] Scribes in this period often competed as to who could compile or compose most versions of song. Such developments point to a situation in which many tunes might be assigned to one song text, and many song texts to one tune. Although this

---

and a Gallant City," "The London Prentice," in *Wit and Mirth: or, Pills to Purge Melancholy*, VI, 342-43.

45 See Simpson, *The British Broadside Ballad*, pp. 449 and 452n6; James Porter, "The Cultural Expropriation of 'Lillibulero,'" p. 21; and James Hogg, *The Jacobite Relics of Scotland: Being the Songs, Airs and Legends of the Adherents of the House of Stuart*, ed. Murray Pittock, 2 vols (Edinburgh: Edinburgh University Press, 2012), I, 481. Pittock's note includes additional examples of the tune as setting for Jacobite airs: "Vox Clero" (dated 1689) and *The Yellow Sash: or, H – R BESHIT* (London, 1743).

46 George Bennett, *The History of Bandon and the Principal Towns in the West Riding of County Cork* (Cork, 1869), p. 287.

47 See Porter, "The Cultural Expropriation of 'Lillibulero,'" pp. 22-23.

48 Vincent Morley, "The Popular Influence of *Foras Feasa ar Éirinn* from the Seventeenth to the Nineteenth Century," *Irish and English: Essays on the Irish Linguistic and Cultural Frontier, 1600-1900*, eds James Kelly and Ciarán Mac Murchaidh (Dublin: Four Courts Press, 2012), pp. 96-115 (114).

makes tracing definitive song traditions more difficult, it suggests that song culture – always hybrid – was becoming ever more fluid, complex, and braided. With the Jacobite threat receding, the time may have been opportune for a relaxation of musical division, for both formal and historical reasons.

The ubiquity of the Wood's affair in the musical culture of 1724 and 1725 is confirmed in a number of poems to Swift, which refer to the importance of song in the Drapier's campaign to defeat William Wood.[49] And in an article in the *Dublin Weekly Journal* (17 July 1725), James Arbuckle complained of how ballads had been allowed to interfere in politics, "the Affairs of the Nation set to a Tune."[50] Because these songs belong to a particular moment, they were not reprinted in the song books of the mid- and late century, and many of these broadsides survive in only one or two copies, with five broadsides held uniquely in the holdings of the Beinecke Library, Yale University. The five songs collected together in 1725 by Faulkner were the exception to this, printed in collected editions of Swift's works, several of which reserved a particular section for "Ballad and Song," where they confirmed the identity of Swift as Irish patriot. There are certainly a number of significant echoes and parallels between the songs and the Drapier's letters.[51] And the songs undoubtedly helped create a popular response to the Drapier's letters and to protect Swift's identity when he was under threat.

Beyond the Wood's Halfpence affair, the existence of these ballads helped to establish and confirm Dublin as a flourishing centre of print in the 1720s;

---

49 See *An Express from Parnassus, to the Reverend Dr Jonathan Swift, Dean of St Patrick's* [Dublin: *s.n.*, 1724] and *A Congratulatory Poem on Dean Swift's Return to Town: By a Member of the Club Held at Mr Taplin's in Truck-Street, October 7th 1725* (Dublin, 1725); reprinted in *Jonathan Swift's Allies*, ed. Baltes-Ellermann, pp. 506-8, 511-12.

50 Arbuckle, writing under the pseudonym of *Hibernicus*, also notes that this practice is now "pretty much laid aside" (James Arbuckle, *A Collection of Letters and Essays on Several Subjects, Lately Publish'd in the Dublin Journal*, 2 vols [London: J. Darby and T. Browne, *et al.*, 1729], I, 134; originally *The Dublin Journal*, 16 [17 July 1725]). See also Swift's own comment: "I begin to grow weary of my Office as a Writer; and could heartily wish it were devolved upon my *Brethren*, the Makers of *Songs* and *Ballads*, who perhaps are the best qualified at present to gather up the Gleanings of this Controversy" (*A Letter to the Right Honourable the Lord Viscount Molesworth. By M. B. Drapier* (Dublin: J. Harding, [1724], p. 20).

51 There are particularly strong parallels between *A Letter to the Tradesmen, Shop-Keepers, Farmers, and Common People in General, of the Kingdom of Ireland* and Songs 1 and 2. Wood's Irish collaborators are called "vipers" in the second Drapier's letter addressed to Harding ([Dublin, 1724], p. 13) and in Song 3. The songs also exhort their listeners to read the letters. For example, *Ireland's Warning* ends "Ye Shop-Men and Trades-Men and Farmers go read it. / For I think in my Soul at this time that you need it, / Or I Gad if you don't there's an End of your Credit."

they fostered among the guilds and journeymen societies in particular a sense of common identity and shared purpose, and this confidence would manifest itself in a wide range of guild-related publications, including many poems, which were printed in Dublin between 1725 and 1730. They offer a glimpse of an oral, musical culture which was a key part of Swift's Dublin and thus of his early reception. Swift, we remember, never claimed to be musical. One of the birthday poems addressed to him depicts the infant Swift being endowed with various gifts from the gods: Apollo gives him the gift of music but is so enthusiastic about doing so that he accidentally damages the hearing of the young boy. Despite this, Swift maintains a musicality in his poetry, the poem argues.[52] No matter whether Swift could whistle a tune or was tone-deaf, however, the culture of the Dublin in which he lived was one which was imbued with the music of song and popular balladry.

In a recording commissioned for the Irish Song Project at Queen's University Belfast, the Dublin singer Ian Lynch sings the ballad which begins "With brisk merry Lays / We'll sing to the Praise / Of that honest Patriot, the DRAPIER" (Song 9). Since the ballad was sold as being sung to the tune of the "Apprentices Song in Massonary," we can trace this to a tune first printed in the 1714 edition of *Wit and Mirth: or, Pills to Purge Melancholy*.[53] Once we have listened to the song several times, as potential buyers in 1725 would have done as ballad-sellers advertised their broadsheets by singing their tunes, it becomes almost impossible to read the text without hearing the tune setting. Ballads easily dismissed as 'doggerel' or hack-work take on a new vitality when sung, and the tunes contribute as much to their meanings as the texts. Where these songs have survived, then, and where we can recover the specific tunes to which we know they were set, these should be remembered as songs, with all the historical resonances and interpretative implications which singing their music brings to our understanding, and enjoyment, of them.

52 *A Poem Delivered to the Reverend Doctor Swift, Dean of St Patrick's, Dublin: By a Young Nobleman, November 30, 1725, Being the Dean's Birth-Day* (Dublin, 1725). This was printed as a broadsheet poem; Hogan attributes it to Thomas Sheridan in his *The Poems of Sheridan*, pp. 157-59 and 340-41.

53 See <http://www.irishsongproject.qub.ac.uk/recordings> and <http://www.irishsongproject.qub.ac.uk/song/136> (accessed 19 September 2017).

Bibliography of Songs on the Halfpence Affair (1724-25)

The texts of these ballads are reprinted in *Jonathan Swift's Allies: The Wood's Halfpence Controversy in Ireland, 1724-1725*, ed. Sabine Baltes-Ellermann, 2nd rev. ed. (Frankfurt on Main: Peter Lang, 2017).

1) *Ireland's Warning, Being an Excellent New Song, upon Wood's Base Half-Pence. To the Tune of Packington's Pound* (Dublin: John Harding, [1724]). Broadside. First line: "YE People of *Ireland*, both *Country* and *City*" (FOXON I66).

2) *An Excellent New Ballad upon the New Half-Pence. To the Tune of, Which No Body Can Deny* (Dublin: J. Harding, [1724]). First line: "YOU Subjects of *Ireland* come all and Rejoice" (FOXON E570).

3) *An Excellent New Song Made by a Lover of his Country; against Wood's Brass Half-Pence. To the Tune, We have catcht you in the nick* ([Dublin, 1724]). First line: "Last Week as I was Walking" (FOXON E588).

4) *An Excellent New Song upon the Declarations of the several Corporations of the City of Dublin, against Wood's Half-Pence. To the Tune of, London is a fine town &c.* ([Dublin, 1724]). Broadside. First line: "O DUBLIN is a fine Town / And a Gallant City" (FOXON E593).

5) *An Excellent New Song upon His Grace our Good Lord Archbishop of Dublin. By Honest Jo. One of His Grace's Farmers in Fingal: To the Tune of ----* (Dublin: J. Harding, 1724). Broadside. First line: "I Sing not of the *Draper*'s Praise" (FOXON S846).

6) *An Excellent New Ballad against Wood's Half-Pence, &c. To the Tune of, Lillibolero &c.* (Dublin: J. Harding, 1724). First line: "NOW *Woods* and his Half-pence are all gone to Pot" (FOXON E541.5).

7) *The Donore Ballad: Inscrib'd to the Praise of the Worthy M. B. Drapier. Written on the Occasion of Putting up his Head in Truck-Street* (Dublin: C. Carter, 1724-25). Broadside. First line: "YE Loving *Hibernians* come listen a while" (FOXON D403).

8) and 9) *The Drapier Anatomiz'd: A Song* [and] *A New Song Sung at the Club at Mr. Taplin's, the Sign of the Drapier's Head in Truck-Street. To the Tune of the Apprentices Song in Massonry* (Dublin, 1724). Broadside. First lines: "THE DRAPIER I Swear" and "WITH brisk merry Lays / We'll sing to the Praise" (FOXON D428).

10) *An Excellent New Ballad upon the Present Gr[a]nd Jury* (Dublin, 1724). Broadside. First line: "NO Thanks to OUR *FOES*, our cause it is clear" (FOXON E571).

11) *An Excellent New Song upon the Late Grand-Jury [who Threw out the Bill against Harding, the Printer. By Jonathan Swift? Dean of St Patrick's]* (Dublin:

[J. Harding], 1724). Broadside. First line: "POOR *Monsieur* his Conscience preserv'd for a Year" (FOXON E594).

12) [Thomas Sheridan], *The Drapier's Ballad. To the Tune of the London Prentice* (Dublin: J. Harding, 1724-25). Broadside. First lines: "Of a Worthy *Dublin* DRAPIER / My Purpose is to speak" (FOXON S406).

13) *Blue-Skin's Ballad. To the Tune of Packington's Pound* ([Dublin], 1724-25). Broadside. First line: "Ye Fellows of Newgate whose Fingers are nice." Final verse on Wood and the Drapier (FOXON N288).

14) *An Excellent New Song Call'd the Irishman's Joy, for the Downfall of Woods and his Brass Half-Pence & Farthings. To the Tune of Randel a Barnaby &c.* ([Dublin, 1724]). Broadside. First line: "My Dear Loving Country-men listen a while" (FOXON E583.5).

15) *Will. Wood's Petition to the People of Ireland, Being An Excellent New Song, Supposed to be Made and Sung in the Streets of Dublin, by William Wood, Iron-monger and Half-Penny-monger* (1725). Broadside – no copies survive. First line: "My dear *Irish* Fokes. / Come leave off your Jokes."

16) – 18) 3 of the 5 songs in *Fraud Detected* (Dublin, 1725) do not survive in broadsheet:

Song I (= 10 above). First lines: "With brisk merry Lays / We'll sing to the Praise."

Song II. First line: "Since the Drapier's set up, and *Wood* is cry'd down."

Song III (= 12 above) First lines: "Of a worthy *Dublin Drapier* / My purpose is to speak."

Song IV. First lines: "Now we're free by nature / Let us all our power exert." Refrain: *Fill Bumpers*, &c.

Song V. First lines: "When *WOOD* had like t'have taken root / And canker'd all the Nation."

Also

A Collection of the Most Celebrated Irish Tunes, Proper for the Violin, German Flute or Hautboy (Dublin: John and William Neal, [1724]), "Sq.r Woodes's Lamentation on ye Refusall of his HALF PENCE."

Daniel Cook
University of Dundee

Swift after Horace

Abstract. Despite his career-long interest in Horace, Swift did not write formal "imitations" in the extensive manner in which Dryden or Pope did. This might in part explain the relative neglect of his Horatian poems in Swift studies and in surveys of literary translation of the period. In many of these poems, such as "The First Ode of the Second Book Paraphrased," "Part of the Seventh Epistle of the First Book of Horace Imitated," "Horace, Lib 2, Sat 6. Part of it Imitated," "To the Earl of Oxford … out of Horace," and "Toland's Invitation to Dismal … Imitated from Horace," Swift deals with parts, not wholes. In "Horace, Book I, Ode XIV," by contrast, he engrafts onto the original striking new material, including a primer for his implied readership. While earlier critics have examined Swift's Horatian poems in terms of the theory and practice of literary translation, this essay shifts the focus onto the translator rather than the translation, the persona rather than the paraphrased. Thus, it works towards a larger study of Swift's appropriative poetics beyond formal imitation.

1

Swift's letters are filled with quotations from Horace.[1] He owned at least four editions of Horace's *Opera*, among them, Daniel Heinsius' Elzevir edition of 1629 and James Talbot's Cambridge edition of 1699, as well as – later in life – John Pine's superbly engraved Horace (1733-37), to which he subscribed.[2] He also knew Thomas Creech's 1684 rendering into English verse and Charles Carthy's *A Translation of the Second Book of Horace's Epistles* (1731).[3] And Swift kept imitating Horace, in fits and starts – beginning in 1712 with "Toland's Invitation to Dismal" (a witty adaptation of Horace's *Epistles*, I, v) through to "Part of the Ninth Ode of the Fourth Book of Horace" in 1720 or 1721. Beyond that, in 1726, he produced a sort of interpolated version of *Odes*, I, xiv ("O Navis, referent in mare te novi / Fluctus") for a modern Irish readership. In 1729 or 1730, he loosely paraphrased a large part of the first poem of the Second Book of Horace's *Satires* in his own "A Dialogue between an Eminent Lawyer and Dr Swift, Dean of St Patrick's" (the first poem in Pope's *Imitations of Horace*,

1 See, in addition to Passmann and Vienken II, 908-12, *Correspondence*, ed. Woolley, v: The Index, 256-57.
2 Passmann and Vienken II, 905-7.
3 *Poems*, ed. Williams, III, 666.

 | DOI:10.30965/9783846763971_010

in contrast, is more faithful to the original). He abandoned a partial imitation of one of Horace's most famous poems, "Hoc erat in votis" (*Satires*, II, vi), though it eventually appeared in print in 1727 with some additions from Pope. "Traulus: The First Part in a Dialogue between Tom and Robin" (1730), among other works, follows Horace in the broadest sense. "On Noisy Tom," a late lampoon written against Sir Thomas Prendergast in 1736, stems from a small passage in Horace's *Satires*, I, vi. Swift paraphrased *Satires*, I, x – "Ridicule has greater Pow'r / To reform the World, than Sour" – in "An Epistle to a Lady, Who Desired the Author to Make Verses on Her, in the Heroick Stile" (1728),[4] within a much larger panegyric-libel on the Government. One of Horace's most influential epistles, *Ars poetica*, is casually reworked, along with a wide array of other classical and modern sources, in one of Swift's longest poems, *On Poetry: A Rhapsody* (1733).

His career-long interest in Horace notwithstanding, Swift did not write formal "imitations" in the extensive manner Dryden or Pope did. This might in part explain the relative neglect of his Horatian poems in Swift studies and in surveys of literary translation of the period. In many of these poems, Swift deals with parts, not wholes. While earlier critics have examined Swift's Horatian poems in terms of the theory and practice of literary translation,[5] this essay shifts the focus onto the translator rather than the translation, the persona rather than the paraphrased. In my reading of the 1726 imitation of Horace's *Odes*, I, xiv, for instance, I demonstrate the creative invasiveness of Swift's approach to his inherited material. He hijacks the most public and venerable of forms, the Horatian ode, in order to scrutinize – cynically, it turns out – his own standing as the Hibernian Patriot exiled, as it were, in his home country. Swift, post-Drapier, here includes substantial interpolations that mark out a deliberate misapplication of the original poem to modern politics. Set against other translations – most notably Creech's popular version[6] – Swift's imitation of this ode seems interventional, even impulsive, and far from merely occasional. In other

4 *Poems*, ed. Williams, II, 636, ll. 199-200. Unless otherwise noted, subsequent references are to this edition and are given in parentheses within the text.

5 William Kupersmith, *Versions of Roman Satire in the Earlier Eighteenth Century* (Newark, Delaware: University of Delaware Press, 2007), pp. 32-52. See also the same author's "William Diaper and Two Others Imitate Swift Imitating Horace," *Swift Studies*, 10 (1995), 26-36, and "Swift and 'Harley, the Nation's Great Support': *Horace, Epistle VII, Book I: Imitated and Addressed to the Earl of Oxford*," *Swift Studies*, 1 (1986), 39-45; as well as Niall Rudd, *The Common Spring: Essays on Latin and English Poetry* (Bristol: Bristol Phoenix Press, 2005), pp. 143-60; and M. Elaine Dolan Brown, "The Poet's Mask: Swift, Horace, and Steele in 'The First Ode of the Second Book of Horace Paraphrased,'" *Swift Studies*, 5 (1990), 3-10.

6 Thomas Creech, *The Odes, Satyrs, and Epistles of Horace: Done into English* (London: Jacob Tonson, 1684). On Creech as a successful translator of the classics, see Hermann J. Real,

words, I wish to reconsider how familiar metaphors work in and frame Swift's poetry. The whole poem is gratuitously littered with ornamental similes, after all. I want to outline Swift's appropriative poetics (or the art of "stealing hints," as he called it) beyond formal imitation.

Instead of addressing all of Swift's Horatian poems wholescale, I will turn my attention more narrowly to the political urgency of the odes and epistles rather than, say, the metapoetry of *On Poetry*, or other themes. In passing, that is, I want to say something about Swift's choice of poetic form as a vehicle for his position-taking in the late 1720s. Before that, we will turn to Swift's work for the Tory administration between 1710 and 1714. In the Horatian poems produced between these years, Swift not only steals hints but lifts entire phrases from Richard Steele, with whom he was involved in a rapid-fire pamphlet war, leaving behind but not fully abandoning the premises of the original works. In fact, he revelled in the agitated imitation of seemingly redundant or unlikely modes. In order to make sense of Swift's mockery of the ambitions of his rival in the odes and epistles of the 1710s, the reader needs to be aware of the contrastive allusions made to the historian Gaius Asinius Pollio (76 BC-AD 4), among other things. In "Horace, Book I, Ode XIV," moreover, the "Inscription" at the opening functions as a sort of primer for the reader, namely, an address to Swift's audience in specific ways and in a particular register. At the same time, for the more informed reader the well-worn Ship of State metaphor gains new life precisely because of its staleness.

2

Embroiled in a series of pamphlet wars with the Whig party's mouthpiece, Richard Steele, in the 1710s, Swift turned not to the spiky urbanite Juvenal but to the gentler Horace as his guide in poetry. Even so, Swift's odes are nevertheless interventional as much as they are merely occasional – as knowingly wounding as readily as they are reactive. Making a show of discreetly dashing out proper names, "*T—l—nd's* Invitation to *DISMAL*, to Dine with the CALVES-HEAD Club," a one-page broadside first printed in the summer of 1712, brutally lampoons the Whigs and their supporters.[7] The Earl of Nottingham ("Dismal," on account of his swarthy appearance), a prominent High Church

Untersuchungen zur Lukrez-Übersetzung von Thomas Creech (Bad Homburg, Berlin, Zürich: Gehlen, 1970). For Creech's translation of Horace, see pp. 23-24.

7 The Dublin broadsheet makes even more of a show of dashing out the names: many of the dashes there, especially in the last third of the poem, look noticeably elongated.

Tory, had entered into an agreement with members of the opposition to support their resistance to peace at Dunkirk if they assisted him in passing his Occasional Conformity Bill then coming yet again before Parliament.[8] The fictive Nottingham, in the company of a gathering largely made up of a gallery of caricatured Whigs, engages in a sort of mock-Eucharist dinner undertaken at the semi-mythical republican Calves' Head Club.

Swift sharpened the satire by making the secretary the well-known deist John Toland. Steeped in religious (or, more to the point, irreligious) iconography, the piece forms an ironic part of a long and noble tradition of invitation poetry, from Alcaeus to Horace, and beyond. More specifically, as the subheading makes clear, "Toland's Invitation" is "*Imitated from* Horace, *Epist. 5. Lib I.*" – Ben Jonson's "Inviting a Friend to Supper" (1616) remains the most famous English reworking of what is a relatively benign epistle.[9] Where Jonson largely regurgitates the gentle sentiments of Horace's original, Swift delivers (to borrow Leonard Moskovit's phrase) a "purposeful revision" in a modern setting. Instead of Caesar's birthday, they commemorate the anniversary of Charles I's death. Instead of genial conversation ("sermone benigno," p. 344, l. 11), Toland promises talk of "*what Fools call Treason*" (I, 163, l. 16). A celebration of private hospitality becomes a mockery of political jockeying behind closed doors. By associating Nottingham's opposition to occasional conformity with Whiggish threats to the Established Church (as Swift understood it), Swift might even have sought to revise his prior attempts to justify the Bill under the guidance of Lord Somers, an English Whig. The mock-epistle affords the author room to recalibrate his career as a political poet, now that he is writing for the administration under Robert Harley, the first Earl of Oxford.

As "Toland's Invitation" is a political poem written to the moment, how important is its nominal connection with Horace's epistle? We might also consider whether relying on the original as a sort of familiar shorthand, Swift could have got to his unheroic lampoon more quickly, more economically. He certainly suggested that readers' awareness of the original would enhance their enjoyment of his imitation. "Have Y seen Toland's Invitation to Dismal?" he asked his young correspondent, Esther Johnson. "How do Y like it? but it is an

8 Eugene Hammond, *Jonathan Swift: Irish Blow-In* (Newark: University of Delaware Press, 2016), pp. 186-87.

9 Aside from some grammatical alterations (additional semi-colons, or colons in place of commas) and some revisions ("Sollicitis" in place of "Solicitis," for example), the broadsheet as printed in *Poems*, ed. Williams (I, 162-66) follows the 1699 Tonson edition of Horace's *Opera*, ed. Talbot, which Swift owned. Unless otherwise noted, subsequent references to Horace are taken from the Talbot edition.

Imitation of Horace, and perhaps Y don't understand Horace."[10] To this end, the broadside crams almost the entire Latin original onto the bottom of the page (rather than interlaying it with the new poem, or placing extracts more suggestively in the margins). Superficially at least, Swift from the outset mimics Horace's address to his guest, Torquatus:

> Si potes archiacis conviva recumbere lectis,
> Nec modica cœnare times olus omne patella;
> Supremo te sole domi, Torquate, manebo. (p. 344, ll. 1-3)[11]

Swift goes with a brisker if slightly flabbier, and a noticeably more exacerbated, opening:

> If, dearest *DISMAL*, you for once can Dine
> Upon a single Dish, and Tavern Wine,
> *T—l—nd* to you this Invitation sends,
> To eat the *CALVES-HEAD* with your trusty Friends. (I, 162, ll. 1-4)

The conditional tense (Si, If) remains, but the guest gains prominence through the word order and black-letter appearance of his name on the page.[12] More than that, the would-be guest is marked out as someone who does not usually choose, or is unable, to dine with his "trusty Friends," a redundant, ominous phrasing that corrupts Horace's convivial tone. If readers knew their Horace, they would recall that Torquatus was later praised, in *Odes*, IV, vii, as a man of piety and eloquence. By contrast, Swift had already attacked Nottingham's lack of piety in "An Excellent New Song, Being the Intended *SPEECH of a Famous Orator against Peace*" and in his prose satires – and he extends that here in "Toland's Invitation."[13] The poem is perhaps better understood as a kind of pseudo-imitation of Horace, *Epistles*, I, v – not quite a parody or even a pastiche, but a work that by design does not fully commit to the original. Elements

---

10 *Journal to Stella: Letters to Esther and Rebecca Dingley, 1710-1713*, ed. Abigail Williams (Cambridge: Cambridge University Press, 2013), pp. 433-34.

11 The Latin text follows that given on the broadsheet. H. Rushton Fairclough translates: "If you can recline at my table on couches made by Archias, and are not afraid of 'a dinner of herbs' only, from a modest dish, I shall expect you, Torquatus, at my house at sunset" (Horace, *Satires, Epistles, and Ars Poetica* [Cambridge, Massachusetts: Harvard University Press, and London: William Heinemann, 1999 {1926}], pp. 281-83 [281]).

12 This technique is also used in Swift's prose attacks on Nottingham and others, such as in *A Dialogue upon Dunkirk* and *A Hue and Cry after Dismal*.

13 For a discussion of Swift's "purposive defamation" of rivals as Harley's chief propagandist, see Ashley Marshall, *Swift and History: Politics and the English Past* (Cambridge: Cambridge University Press, 2015), pp. 183-86.

of the poem can be enjoyed on different levels, whether it is the immediacy of the slapstick rhymes or a readerly investment in the intertextual back and forth between two prominent propagandists.

A general understanding of the importance placed on good hospitality in the original (or "entertainment perfect" in Jonson's version) helps the reader to appreciate more immediately the tenor of Swift's satire (the moral depravity of the Whigs). But in effect, "Toland's Invitation" extends into verse a campaign the author had long been waging in *The Examiner*, where he had charged that the Whigs have "a Design of destroying the *Establish'd Church*" and are "Enemies to Monarchy," arguing that "the Regard they bear to our *Monarchy*, hath appeared by their open ridiculing the Martyrdom of *King Charles the First*, in their Calves-head Clubs, their common Discourses and their Pamphlets."[14] An awareness of the relentless savaging of Nottingham conducted by Swift and other Tory propagandists gives extra heft to the blunt portrayal of Dismal's cross-party scheming. But, to be sure, Swift shoves his ill-feeling towards his subject into an unequivocal couplet:

> Suspend a while your vain ambitious Hopes,
> Leave hunting after Bribes, forget your Tropes. (I, 162, ll. 5-6)

These lines add political saliency to the less aggressive original ("Mitte leves spes, & certamina divitiarum [Dismiss airy hopes and the struggle for wealth]," p. 344, l. 8)[15] in what amounts to a momentary distraction from the ultimate focus of the satire. Swift suddenly injects into Horace's work a description of the grisly revelry of the Calves' Head Club, in which "our latest *Proselyte*, shalt share":

> When We, by proper Signs and Symbols tell,
> How, by *Brave Hands*, the *Royal TRAYTOR* fell;
> The Meat shall represent the *TYRANT*'s Head,
> The Wine, his Blood, *our Predecessors* shed:
> Whilst an *alluding* Hymn some Artist sings,
> We toast Confusion to the Race of Kings:
> At Monarchy we nobly shew our Spight,
> And talk *what Fools call Treason* all the Night. (I, 162-63, ll. 9-16)

14 *Swift vs. Mainwaring: "The Examiner" and "The Medley"*, ed. Frank H. Ellis (Oxford: Clarendon Press, 1985), pp. 399-400. See also Peter J. Schakel, *The Poetry of Jonathan Swift: Allusion and the Development of a Poetic Style* (Madison, Wisconsin: The University of Wisconsin Press, 1978), p. 64.

15 Unless otherwise indicated, the English prose translations accompanying Horace's Latin are from the Loeb library edition by H. Rushton Fairclough (see note 11).

Not only does this passage forthrightly target the Whigs' irreligiousness, as Swift understands it, it also brilliantly sets the poem up for an extensive bout of naming and shaming, a departure from Horace's more general truths about social drinking:

> Quid non ebrietas designat? operta recludit,
> Spes jubet esse ratas, ad prœlia trudit inertem,
> Solicitis animis onus eximit, addocet artes.
> Fecundi calices quem non fecere disertum?
> Contracta quem non in paupertate solutum? (pp. 344-45, ll. 16-20)
> [What a miracle cannot the wine-cup work! It unlocks secrets, bids hopes be fulfilled, thrusts the coward into the field, takes the load from anxious hearts, teaches new arts. The flowing bowl – whom has it not made eloquent? Whom has it not made free even amid pinching poverty?]

Swift wants us to look at the faces, if not quite the names, of the Earl of Godolphin and other men pinched beneath the nib of his pen:

> Who, by Disgraces or ill Fortune sunk,
> Feels not his Soul enliven'd when he's Drunk?
> Wine can clear up *G—d—lph—n*'s cloudy Face,
> And fill *J—ck Sm—th* with Hopes to keep his Place;
> By Force of Wine ev'n *Sc—rb—r—w* is Brave,
> *Hal—* grows more Pert, and *S—mm—rs* not so Grave:
> Wine can give *P—rt—d* Wit, and *Cl—v—nd* Sense,
> *M—t—g—e* Learning, *B—lt—n* Eloquence:
> *Ch—ly*, when Drunk, can never lose his *Wand*,
> And *L—nc—n* then imagines he has Land. (I, 163-64, ll. 17-26)

"Toland's Invitation" then snaps back into the format of Horace's epistle, thereby exposing the crassness of the modern dinner party by way of contrast. Horace stresses his obligations as a host ("Hæc ego procurare & idoneus imperor, & non / Invitus [Here is what I charge myself to provide – and able and willing I am]," p. 345, ll. 21-22): clean tables, plates, and napkins. Swift's Toland says similarly, "My Province is, to see that all be right, / Glasses and Linnen clean, and Pewter bright" (I, 165, ll. 27-28). Horace will be discreet ("ne fidos inter amicos / Sit, qui dicta foras eliminet [that there be none to carry abroad what is said among faithful friends]," p. 345, ll. 24-25), as will Toland, though Toland takes a more aggressive stance on his enemies: "From our *Mysterious Club* to keep out Spies, / And *Tories* (dress'd like Waiters) in Disguise" (I, 165, ll. 29-30). Again, Swift lards up the outline of the original with bespoke political shaming. "Men you love" (I, 165, l. 32) – men Swift hated – are briefly mentioned, again under the pretence of dashed-out names (Sunderland, Ormond, Richmond, and Hampden). But it is Thomas Wharton, "the most universal villain" Swift ever knew, who takes pride of place among the grotesques at the conclusion of the poem. Lord Lieutenant of Ireland, for a time, and an outspoken opponent of the Tory government under Queen Anne, Wharton felt the sting of Swift's pen in *The Examiner*, in (to use the author's own words) "a damned libellous pamphlet," *A Short Character of His Ex. T. E. of W.* (1710), of which 2,000 copies were sold on the day of publication, and in *A Letter of Thanks from My Lord Wharton to the Lord Bishop of St. Asaph* (1712), in which Swift impersonated him with devilish glee, among other works.[16] Here, in "Toland's Invitation," Wharton takes on the small role played by Sabinus in the original: a womanizer. But where Horace favours a fairly innocuous word to describe the object of Sabinus' desire (*puella*, the common Latin word for "girl," often with the connotation of "girlfriend"), Swift seizes the opportunity to smear Wharton's character yet further ("*Wh—n*, unless prevented by a Whore, / Will hardly fail," I, 166, ll. 35-36).[17] *A Short Character* had already labelled Wharton "a Presbyterian in Politics, and an Atheist in Religion," although, the pamphlet continues, "he chuseth at present to whore with a Papist."[18] "Light love" in Horace has taken on a seedier association in "Toland's Invitation" for readers attuned to the conflation of debauchery and politics in Swift's character sketches of the modern Whigs.[19] "Mens Characters are best known from their Actions," after all, as Swift wrote in *A Short Character*.[20] Arguably the most influential Whig in Anne's reign, Wharton embodied the flagrant irreligiousness Swift and other prominent Irish churchmen associated with that party.

Not content with the spread of his attack, Swift adds another figure of fun: Heneage Finch, the Baron of Guernsey and younger brother of the Earl of Nottingham.[21] At the end of Horace's epistle, the host entreats the hard-working Torquatus to give a client the slip so that he can attend their genial evening. Similarly, returning to his main invitee, Nottingham, Swift's Toland

16 See Christopher Robbins, "'The Most Universal Villain I Ever Knew': Jonathan Swift and the Earl of Wharton," *Eighteenth-Century Ireland*, 18 (2003), 24-38. Swift's comments on the libellous pamphlet come from the *Journal to Stella*, ed. Abigail Williams, p. 83 (8 December 1710). See also Christopher Robbins, *The Earl of Wharton and Whig Party Politics, 1679-1715* (Lampeter: The Edwin Mellen Press, 1991), pp. 227-59.

17 Thomas Creech renders *puella* as "dearer Miss" in his 1684 translation (*The Odes, Satyrs, and Epistles of Horace*, p. 487). Fairclough has "goodlier girl" (*Satires, Epistles, and Ars Poetica*, p. 283).

18 *Prose Works*, III, 179.

19 Schakel, *The Poetry of Jonathan Swift*, p. 66.

20 *Prose Works*, III, 178.

21 See Henry Horwitz, *Revolution Politicks: The Career of Daniel Finch, second Earl of Nottingham, 1647-1730* (Cambridge: Cambridge University Press, 1968), *passim*.

asks him to escape from his brother, whom he associates with High Church principles ("He'll teaze you with King *Charles* and Bishop *Laud*, / Or make you Fast, and carry you to Prayers," I, 166, ll. 42-43). The irony of the advice – with an abrupt reference to Charles I's concerns about his misplaced faith in the uncompromising Archbishop of Canterbury, William Laud, at the end of his reign – finally undermines the words of the narrator, John Toland. Toland, a controversial author whose books the Government had publicly burned, was, of course, already a dubious host. An ambitious orator, Wharton has also been silenced – cavorting has distracted him from his other favourite hobby: the art of political lying (again, in Swift's words). A private poem about gentlemanly hospitality has become, through various sleights of hand, an uncompromising attack on the English Whigs and their unreliable spokesmen. Not merely an unheroic inversion of Horace's gentle epistle (though clearly it is that, too), Swift's poem functions as a pseudo-imitation that simultaneously expands the nominal original at specific junctures and pulls in Swift's ongoing pamphleteering against the Government's (and the ambitious churchman's) enemies. In a sense, "Toland's Invitation" is a companion piece to "An Excellent New Song, Being the *Intended SPEECH of a Famous Orator against Peace*," which circulated the day before Nottingham addressed the House of Lords in late 1711.[22]

Impersonating Toland in the later poem, in "An Excellent New Song" Swift instead dons the persona of a fictive Nottingham. Whereas the mock-epistle invites the apostate Tory into a Whig scene, "An Excellent New Song" puts him centre-stage, in Parliament, and lets him speak at length. Before he even opens his mouth, however, Swift blunts Nottingham's authority: the framing narrator stresses the subject's desperation ("AN Orator *dismal* of *Nottinghamshire* … Out of Zeal for his Country, and *want of a Place*, / Is come up," I, 142, ll. 1-4) and lazy authorship ("He has vamp't an old Speech," I, 143, l. 5). The Speech itself is full of farcical flatulence ("her G—let a F—t," I, 143, l. 18), inconsistency ("I alter'd my Note," I, 144, l. 39), and strained puns on his own name ("while I'm *Not in game*," ll. 4, 26, 34). A man that, in the words of Wharton, would "save England," Nottingham had already been portrayed as an ineffectual speaker in "An Excellent New Song." Another companion piece, "Peace and Dunkirk," a ballad composed to an old Cavalier tune latterly taken up by the Jacobites ("*The King shall enjoy his own again*") in the summer of 1712, similarly portrays the prominent agitators as frustrated, inarticulate losers: "And *DISMAL* double-*DISMAL* looks; / *Whar—n* can only Swear by Fits," I, 168, ll. 12-13). Along with the Whigs he sought for support, Dismal has been "laughed off the

22 *Journal to Stella*, ed. Abigail Williams, p. 339 and n18.

stage," as Michael Foot once put it so memorably.[23] No matter whether silent participation at a republican club or a calamitous speech among politicians, Swift's impersonations of his enemies could take any form. Horace proved to be a reliable if unlikely helpmate.

In "Part of the Seventh Epistle of the First Book of Horace Imitated," Swift took half of the original as the basis of a self-serving story about himself. Although the new poem was only fitfully tied to the original, early printings indicated in footnotes extensive verbal parallels between the texts. Comprising a series of brief stories, Horace's epistle politely refuses any further work for his patron Maecenas, the addressee of the poem, on account of his own ailing health and need for personal independence. The last tale, concerning Philippus and Volteius Mena, is taken up by Swift. Intrigued by a modest peddler named Mena, Horace's Philippus invites him to his lavish home. Mena, though grateful for the attention, soon wants to return to his former life ("vitæ me redde priori," p. 354, l. 95). Swift's Harley ("the Nation's great Support," I, 170, l. 1) is similarly fascinated with "Dr. *S—t:* / A Clergyman of special Note" (I, 171, ll. 26-27) who "Went where he pleas'd, said what he thought" (I, 171, l. 33). Unlike the happy and contented Mena, this Swift is a frustrated satirist ("since he could not spend his Fire, / He now intended to Retire," I, 172, ll. 45-46) set to take up a position in the Church of Ireland – "Doctor, you shall be a *Dean*," Harley tells him; "You need but cross the *Irish* Seas, / To live in Plenty, Power and Ease" (I, 173, ll. 88, 91-92).

A lengthy vision of what being the Dean of St Patrick's Cathedral will entail takes up a sixteen-line passage ("Suppose him, now, a *Dean* compleat, / Devoutly lolling in his Seat," I, 174, ll. 97-98) before the fictive Swift rushes to Harley's home and begs a "Truce, good MY LORD, I beg a Truce!" – "Pray leave me where you found me first" (I, 175, ll. 130, 138). By implication, Swift – this version, at least – will return to his old life. But the resolution is ambiguous since it remains unclear whether he will return to the savage political libels he had been writing ("Had giv'n the *Faction* many a Wound, / And Libell'd all the *Junta* round," I, 171, ll. 37-38) or, frustrated by the apparent suppression of libels, retire as intended. Like Horace's Mena, Swift's Swift wants his independence, but the latter's independence is tied up with his propagandist ambitions. Mena wants to return to his humble friends; Swift wants to return to the men of wit. A gentle reworking of Horace's original story amplifies Swift's thwarted ambitions.

Swift resorted to similar authorial tricks when attempting to bring down the Whig politician and propagandist Richard Steele in "The First Ode of the

23 Michael Foot, *The Pen and the Sword: Jonathan Swift and the Power of the Press* (London: Collins, 1984 [1957]), p. 321.

Second Book of Horace Paraphrased." Writing towards the end of Harley's reign in government, Swift again turns to Horace. As in "Toland's Invitation" and "Part of the Seventh Epistle," though in a choppier manner, Horace's poem literally becomes a part of Swift's text as relevant quotations litter the foot of the page. At the same time, the poem participates in a literary quarrel that had first occurred between the rival pamphleteers in the pages of *The Examiner* (Swift) and *The Guardian* (Steele) in May 1713. In September appeared Steele's *The Importance of Dunkirk Considered*, to which Swift retorted aggressively a little over a month later with *The Importance of the Guardian Considered*.[24] Meanwhile, from late October onward, Steele kept announcing in *The Englishman* the appearance of a forthcoming pamphlet on the impending Hanoverian succession to Anne's reign. Swift seized the opportunity to mock his rival's feeble delay. "The First Ode" came out in the first week of the new year, 1714, almost a fortnight before *The Crisis* finally appeared. Swift did not let the feud lie: his destructive rejoinder to that pamphlet, *The Publick Spirit of the Whigs*, came out in late February.[25]

Just as in the prose attacks on Steele, Swift's poem discusses Steele's standing as an author. Indeed, here Swift lumps together two of the Whig party's chief propagandists, Steele and Gilbert Burnet, whom he had frequently damned as bad writers (in *The Importance of the Guardian Considered* and in "A Preface to the Bishop of Sarum's Introduction," respectively, and elsewhere).[26] The opening is gleefully gossipy:

> *DICK*, thour't resolv'd, as I am told,
> Some strange *Arcana* to unfold,
> And with the help of *Buckley's* Pen
> To vamp the *good Old Cause* again,
> Which thou (such *Bur—t*'s shrewd Advice is)
> Must furbish up and Nickname *CRISIS*. (I, 180, ll. 1-6)

Swift's Steele resorts to vamping old material, an authorial sin also committed by Wharton as a parliamentary speechwriter in "An Excellent New Song." Swift later mocked Steele, in *The Publick Spirit of the Whigs*, for bulking out his pamphlet with redundant reprinted matter, and for being inelegant ("He has a confused Remembrance of Words since he left the University, but has lost half their Meaning, and puts them together with no Regard but to their Cadence").[27]

---

24 *English Political Writings, 1711-1714: The Conduct of the Allies and Other Works*, eds Bertrand A. Goldgar and Ian Gadd (Cambridge: Cambridge University Press, 2008), pp. 34-35.

25 *English Political Writings, 1711-1714*, eds Goldgar and Gadd, pp. 37-39.

26 *English Political Writings, 1711-1714*, eds Goldgar and Gadd, p. 35.

27 *English Political Writings, 1711-1714*, eds Goldgar and Gadd, p. 248.

At the same time, the poem brazenly repurposes Steele's own material. The 'paraphrase' of Horace's ode to his friend Pollio, a tragedian and historian, to put it another way, is a cypher for Swift's larger obsessions with the role of authors in politics.

Affecting to adapt a celebratory ode by one of the most widely imitated ancients, one whose name appears prominently stretched out in the middle of the front page of the original London publication (HORACE), "The First Ode" mimics the works of a faltering modern, whose name is feebly dashed out beneath (*Richard St—le*, Esq.).[28] One of Swift's readers has speculated that, in his ode, Horace praised his subject in language taken from Pollio's now lost *Historiae*.[29] Swift certainly adopts this approach, lifting out ugly phrases from *The Englishman* and forcing them into comical rhymes for derisory effect. In fact, some of the phrases were nabbed by Steele from *The Examiner*, and so, more accurately, Swift snatches them back. One example is "*plenipoes*," crude slang for the diplomats (plenipotentiaries) who had carried through the delicate peace negotiations at Utrecht. Swift loathed the abbreviation, as he made clear in a sarcastic article for *The Tatler* in September 1710 – a journal edited by Steele, lest we forget:

> Thus we cram one Syllable, and cut off the rest; as the Owl fattened her Mice after she had bit off their Legs, to prevent them from running away; and if ours be the same Reason for maiming of Words, it will certainly answer the End, for I am sure no other Nation will desire to borrow them. Some Words are hitherto but fairly split; and therefore only in their Way to Perfection; as *Incog.* and *Plenipo's*: But in a short Time, it is to be hoped, they will be further docked to *Inc* and *Plen.* This Reflection had made me, of late Years, very impatient for a Peace; which I believe would save the Lives of many brave Words, as well as Men.[30]

Swift's poem now associates the maiming of words with Steele, an agitator against peace; neither the English language nor human lives are safe. The truncated but not quite monosyllabic word "*Plenipo's*" is wrenched into the conclusion of a brisk couplet:

28 In fact, Horace's name appears twice on the 1713 printing by A. Dodd: in the title of the poem and beneath a slightly altered quotation taken from *Satires* (I, vi). Swift's name is absent.

29 Dolan Brown, "The Poet's Mask: Swift, Horace, and Steele in 'The First Ode of the Second Book of Horace Paraphrased,'" p. 5.

30 *The Tatler*, no 230 (28 September 1710), in *Prose Works*, II, 173-77 (pp. 175-76); annotated in *The Tatler*, ed. Donald F. Bond, 3 vols (Oxford: Clarendon Press, 1987), III, 190-96.

> Thou'lt rail devoutly at the *Peace*,
> And all its secret *Causes* trace ...
> Of *Tricks*, the Lord of *Ox—d* knows,
> And *Errors* of our *Plenipoes*. (I, 180-81, ll. 15-20)

At the outset of the 36th issue of *The Englishman* (26 December 1713), Steele quotes a lengthy passage from a recent essay in *The Examiner* (18-21 December 1713), in which the phrase had been used in quite an aggressive way ("*There is a Pretender* [... whose] *Envoys and Plenipoes come over publickly, and hold Conferences of a military Nature for the supporting and enlarging of his Interests*"). Rather than respond in his own voice, Steele returns to a familiar character from *The Guardian*, Nestor Ironside, who scorns what he perceives to be a failed attempt by *The Examiner* to depict the Duke of Marlborough as a greedy warmonger:

> And this indiscreet Writer, instead of giving Terrors and Apprehensions of Danger from the Coming and Going of his Plenipoes, as he calls them, administers great Delight to all true *Englishmen*, that so able and loyal a Subject of Her Majesty is situated so, as to make proper Observations for the Good and Service of his Queen and Country. [31]

Swift's poem, published within a fortnight, responds to this critique by turning to a noted, successful defamer of the exiled Marlborough, the incumbent first minister, Robert Harley: appropriation here entails the acquisition of new authority. Indeed, Steele's railing devoutly, zealously, against peace makes a mockery of Horace's original, in which Pollio studiously outlines the "belli ... causas" (p. 54, l. 2) in order to comment on the devastating effect of civil strife.

In fact, before it can appear in print, Steele's new writing, *The Crisis*, is preempted by Swift in terms that mock the likely style and redundant content: "Thou pompously wilt let us know / What all the World knew long ago" (I, 180, ll. 7-8). Further accentuating Steele's pretentiousness, Swift draws attention to his own ironic borrowings from *The Englishman* and *The Tatler* (as noted in the marginal references):

> Thou'lt tell of *Leagues* among the Great
> Portending ruin to our State,
> And of that dreadful **coup d'eclat*,   * *Vide Englishman*, No. 36.
> Which has afforded thee much Chat. (I, 181, ll. 21-24)

31 *The Englishman*, no 36 (26 December 1713), in *The Englishman: A Political Journal by Richard Steele*, ed. Rae Blanchard (Oxford: Clarendon Press, 1955), pp. 144-48 (147).

Mischievously, Swift now attributes to Steele a clunky phrase (*coup d'eclat*, a great feat) that he had first used, sarcastically, in the same *Examiner* essay quoted at length in Steele's *Englishman*. By responding so rapidly, so economically, and with such attentiveness to language, Swift gained the upper hand in the authorial paper wars. Rhyming *coup d'eclat* with such a bathetic word, *chat*, dramatically ridicules the inelegant rival in his 'own' words, before he has even uttered them. Chat and chat Steele might, he has already been defeated (in Swift's mind). Taken together, these verbal jabs help Swift to undermine his rival's suitability to the pacey life of political commentary. As he writes in *The Importance of the Guardian Considered*, "What shadow of a Pretence has [Steele] to offer his crude Thoughts in Matters of State?"[32] Really, it is low comedy in which Steele excels, according to Swift, in another telling contrast with Horace's Pollio, who is associated with the "severæ Musa tragœdiæ [stern tragic Muse]," p. 55, l. 9).[33] Swift addresses Steele:

> Thou must no longer deal in *Farce*,
> Nor pump to cobble wicked Verse;
> Untill thou shalt have eas'd thy Conscience,
> Of Spleen, of Politicks and Nonsense,
> And when thou'st bid adieu to Cares,
> And settled *Europe's Grand* Affairs,
> 'Twill then, perhaps, be worth thy while
> For *Drury-lane* to shape thy Stile. (I, 181, ll. 35-42)

At this point, as signalled by a gossipy marginal note ("*This is said to be the Plot of a Comedy with which Mr.* St—le *has long threatned the Town*") and quotation marks, Swift audaciously mimics in miniature Steele's unreleased theatrical work:

> To make a pair of Jolly Fellows,
> The Son and Father, join to tell us,
> How Sons may safely disobey,
> And Fathers never shou'd say nay,
> By which wise Conduct they grow Friends
> At last—and so the Story ends. (I, 181, ll. 43-48)

If that is indeed where "the Story ends" for Steele – which it does not – that amounts to a sad reversal of his former glories in the verbal arts (Swift, sarcastically, is referring to Steele's claim, in the character of Bickerstaff for *The*

---

32 *English Political Writings, 1711-1714*, eds Goldgar and Gadd, p. 230.

33 Schakel usefully itemizes telling contrasts between Swift's Steele and Horace's Pollio (*The Poetry of Jonathan Swift*, pp. 66-71).

Tatler, that "[he was] adept in astrological speculations"): "When first I knew thee, *Dick*, thou wert / Renown'd for Skill in *Faustus* Art" (I, 182, ll. 49-50).[34] Abandoning the world of books, Steele gained election to Parliament for Stockbridge in the summer of 1713:

> But now the *Senate* (if things *hit*
> And thou at *Stockbridge* wert not *bit*)
> Must feel thy Eloquence and Fire,
> Approve thy Schemes, thy Wit admire,
> Thee with *Immortal Honours* crown,
> Whilst *Patr'ot-like* thou'lt strut and frown. (I, 182, ll. 59-64)

The politician struts across Swift's page as nothing more than a vainglorious clown ("Methinks I see thee, spruce and fine, / With Coat embroider'd richly shine, / And dazzle all the *Idol-Faces*," I, 182, ll. 73-75). Though praising Steele's eloquence and wit, Swift drowns out his rival's voice ("Methinks I hear thee loud, as Trumpet, / As Bagpipe shrill," I, 182, ll. 71-72). Abruptly, having lampooned Steele at length, Swift turns back to speaking Steele's words before they appear for real:

> Now manfully thou'lt run a Tilt
> "On *Popes*, for all the Blood they've spilt,
> For Massacres, and Racks, and Flames,
> For Lands enrich'd by crimson Streams,
> For Inquisitions taught by *Spain*,
> Of which the Christian World complain." (I, 183, ll. 93-98)

Swift brilliantly blends Horace's stark account of civil war ("Quis non Latino sanguine pinguior / Campus sepulcris impia prœlia / Testatur, auditumque Medis / Hesperiæ sonitum ruinæ?," p. 56, ll. 29-32[35]) with Steele's alarmist view of modern politics. The effect is a curious one: does the unlikely merger undermine the grim glory of the original ode or more straightforwardly lampoon the propaganda of the Whig pamphlets?

Before we can settle on the answer, Swift suddenly changes course again: this time he enters into a blokish conversation with Steele, steering him away from the affairs of the nation. Turning back to the ode to Pollio, his nominal

34 *The Tatler*, ed. Bond, II, 452 (no 174, 20 May 1710).

35 Niall Rudd translates: "What plain has not been enriched with Latin blood, bearing witness by its graves to our unholy battles, and to the crash of Westland's downfall, which has been heard by the Medes?" (*Horace: Odes and Epodes* [Cambridge, Massachusetts, and London: Harvard University Press, 2012 {2004}], pp. 96-99). Prose translations of Horace's odes are taken from this edition.

source, Swift splices the humility of Horace's speaker ("Sed ne relictis, Musa procax [But steady, my impertinent Muse!]," p. 56, l. 37) with an old dig at his rival ("You mistake your Talent, whenever you meddle with Matters of *State*," an early contributor wrote in *The Examiner*[36]) in terms that again scorn the fitness of the Moderns:

> Thy *Genius* has perhaps a knack
> At trudging in a beaten Track,
> But is for *State-Affairs* as fit,
> As mine for Politicks and Wit. (I, 183, ll. 103-6)

The taunt is especially snide as Swift capitalizes on his former friend's heavy drinking habits, something to which he had, unkindly, referred in *The Importance of the Guardian Considered* a year previously ("He hath no Invention, nor is Master of a tolerable Style; his chief Talent is Humour ... for after the first Bottle he is no disagreeable Companion").[37] Unfit for the grotto – a place of poetry in the ancient world – Swift and Steele have to make do with a claustrophobic tavern peopled with the likes of Tom D'Urfey, Ambrose Philips, John Dennis, and other hack writers:

> Then let us both in time grow wise,
> Nor higher, than our Talents, rise,
> To some snug Cellar let's repair
> From Dunns and Debts, and drown our Care;
> Now quaff of honest Ale a Quart,
> Now venture at a Pint of Port,
> With which inspir'd we'll club each Night
> Some tender Sonnet to indite,
> And with *Tom D'Urf—y, Phill-ps, D—nnis,*
> Immortalize our *Dolls* and *Jenneys*. (I, 184, ll. 107-16)

Such a bathetic ending brings a comic relief to the quarrel long waged in print. Indeed, it reads like a willing stalemate, as though Swift had grown weary of the fight. But the relief is only temporary, of course. Once *The Crisis* finally appeared, Swift quickly retaliated with *The Publick Spirit of the Whigs*, the last major work he published in defence of the Harley ministry. Even within the confines of the poem, in which Swift has voiced Steele (on two extended occasions) and delimited the output of the hacks (as would-be love poets), the rapprochement is a sacrificial ruse. And, on the theme of forthcoming authorship,

36 *The Examiner*, no 5 (24-31 August 1710). Swift's first article for this newspaper is dated 2 November.

37 *English Political Writings, 1711-1714*, eds Goldgar and Gadd, pp. 220-21.

the conclusion is ambiguous. Readers will ask themselves if these men will collaborate, as Swift had been doing with the Scriblerians, or if they will compete with each other. As late as April 1714, Swift still pursued the position of Historiographer Royal, and so the comparative figure, Pollio, a noted historian as well as a tragedian, stands in for both Swift and Steele.[38] Momentarily reduced to an anticlimactic chat between a failed historian and a failed dramatist, the textual war was not set to end anytime soon.

In these years, Horace also proved to be a genial model for Swift. "To the Earl of Oxford, Late Lord Treasurer" takes off the second poem in the Third Book of the *Odes*; "Part of the Ninth Ode of the Fourth Book of Horace" adopts the final half of the poem referenced directly in the title. Fairly faithful to the originals, these two pieces do not lean on the readers' knowledge of Horace to anywhere near the same extent as the Steele poems do. Omitting the first twelve lines of the second poem in the Third Book of Horace's *Odes*, "To the Earl of Oxford" gets straight to the military virtues outlined in the primary text. Horace's iconic line "Dulce & decorum est pro patria mori [It is sweet and fitting to die for one's country]" (p. 91, l. 13) becomes in Swift's poem a slogan of sorts for the imprisoned former minister ("HOW blest is he, who for his Country dies," I, 210, l. 1). For men in Harley's position, "faithful Silence" will have "a sure Reward" (I, 210, l. 15) – a direct transposition of Horace's "Est & fideli tuta silentio / Merces [There is also a sure reward for loyal silence]," (p. 92, ll. 25-26). "Part of the Ninth Ode" is addressed to William King, the Archbishop of Dublin. "I hear you are likely to be the sole opposer of the bank," Swift wrote to him, referring to the proposal for the establishment of a National Bank in Ireland. (Swift associated such a scheme with opportunistic stockjobbers.)[39] Virtually tracing over the lines of Horace's ode ("Ne forte credas," p. 165, l. 1), Swift nevertheless flattens out its irony. A propagandist in effect, Horace staunchly praises a favourite of Augustus, Marcus Lollius, against whom accusations of avarice were routinely levelled. Swift, by contrast, praises King expressly for his opposition to the greed of the Whigs: "Your Hand alone from Gold abstains, / Which drags the slavish World in Chains," I, 243, ll. 13-14). Horace writes:

> non ego te meis
> Chartis inornatum sileri,
> Totve tuos patiar labores
> Impune, Lolli, carpere lividas

38 See Ehrenpreis, *Dr Swift*, pp. 746-48.

39 F. G. Hall, *The Bank of Ireland, 1783-1946* (Dublin: Hodges Figgis, and Oxford: B. H. Blackwell, 1949), pp. 21-22, 25-28; Sean Moore, "Satiric Norms, Swift's Financial Satires and the Bank of Ireland Controversy of 1720-1," *Eighteenth-Century Ireland*, 17 (2002), 26-56.

> Obliviones.
> [I shall not pass you over in silence, unhonoured by my pages; nor shall I allow jealous oblivion to erode your countless exploits, Lollius, without fighting back]. (p. 167, ll. 30-34)

Swift has, similarly:

> never shall the Muse endure
> To let your Virtues lye obscure,
> Or suffer Envy to conceal
> Your Labours for the Publick Weal. (I, 242-43, ll. 3-6)

The heroism outlined in both of Horace's odes is bent with little labour towards the actions of Swift's modern figures. Horace's praising persona becomes Swift's demanding poet ("To the Earl of Oxford": "He who betrays his Friend, shall never be / Under one Roof, or in one Ship with me," I, 210, ll. 17-18).

3

Written during or (more likely) in the immediate aftermath of Swift's pamphleteering as the Drapier in the mid-1720s, "Horace, Book I, Ode XIV" explores the author's dwindling reputation as the Hibernian Patriot unable, or perhaps unwilling, to lead his people. Swift alternates between close paraphrase of Horace's original and interpolated applications of the passages to the present state of Ireland, which are largely introduced with explicit verbal markers: *like, thus, as,* and *so*.[40] Swift's opening proem ("The Inscription"), too, shows a great detail of self-awareness of its position in a notable classical tradition of post-war displacement:

> *Thou, fixt of old, be now the moving Land?*
> *Altho' the Metaphor be worn and stale*
> *Betwixt a State, and Vessel under Sail;*
> *Let me suppose thee for a Ship a-while,*
> *And thus address thee in the Sailor Stile.* (III, 770, ll. 4-8)

For one reader, Swift's ambitious use of this well-known Horatian ode suggests that he viewed it here as an ideal "vehicle for rallying Irish patriotism in its

40 Jens Martin Gurr, "'Let me suppose thee for a ship a-while': Nautical Metaphors and Contemporary Politics in Eighteenth-Century Translations of Horace's Ode, I, xiv," *Swift Studies*, 20 (2005), 70-81.

resistance to British colonialist oppression."[41] But Horace's ode seems utterly unsuitable for the speaker's purposes in a post-heroic age, which is partly its point. In a manuscript variation, incidentally, Swift has the line "Alow [*sic*] me one old Simile to Steal," which further suggests the disconnection between the borrowed form of the poem and its uneasy, unconfident patriotic register. Swift's emphasis on the staleness of the metaphor in the first printing (a small octavo pamphlet issued in Dublin) (FOXON S859) better fits the poem's internal conflict and larger sense of national estrangement. Swift's description of Ireland is in equal measure sympathetic ("*Poor floating Isle*," l. 1) and dismissive ("*the Land of Slaves*," l. 2).

Horace begins more immediately with an address to the imperilled vessel, "O Navis, referent in mare te novi / Fluctus" (p. 22, ll. 1-2). His apparently patriotic speaker clamours for a peaceful resolution to civil unrest ("o quid agis? fortiter occupa / Portum," p. 22, ll. 2-3). In Swift's version, the speaker is resigned to failure. More stress is laid on the ineptitude of the ship itself, for one thing; the casual use of the word *some* when seeking a neighbouring port reveals a defeated desperation. The depiction of the winds as "giddy" and the treatment of the ship as mere sport ("ludibrium" in Horace, p. 23, l. 16) accentuates the overwhelming danger faced by the disadvantaged subject:

> UNHAPPY Ship, thou art return'd in Vain:
> New Waves shall drive thee to the Deep again.
> Look to thy Self, and be no more the Sport
> Of giddy Winds, but make some friendly Port. (III, 770, ll. 9-12)

In effect, the poem has begun again – it has two beginnings: the primer and the poem proper. Although largely following the original much more closely, Creech's 'Englished' Horace similarly stresses at greater length the "violent fury" of the choppy oceans: "And" – it begins that abruptly (whereas Swift has two beginnings, Creech does not truly have one):

> And shall the raging Waves again
> Bear Thee back into the Main!
> Oh what dost do! put close to shore,
> And never trust the Ocean more:
> Thy Oars are gon, and Southern blasts
> Have rent thy Sails, and torn thy Masts;
> Nor without tackling can'st thou brave
> The violent fury of the Wave:

41 Carole Fabricant, "Swift the Irishman," *The Cambridge Companion to Jonathan Swift*, ed. Christopher Fox (Cambridge: Cambridge University Press, 2003), pp. 48-72 (68).

Thy Stern is gone, thy Gods are lost,
And thou hast none to hear thy cry,
When thou on dangerous Shelves art tost,
When Billows rage, and Winds are high.[42]

Creech's lines offer a semblance of hope, should the cautious advice be followed. Even the peril appears to be temporary if relentless, particularly in the anaphoric "When" in the final two lines. And his blunt phrasing "thy Gods are lost" mimics Horace closely ("Non Di, quos iterum pressa voces malo," p. 23, l. 10), whereas Swift expands on this, heaping blame on the nation:

A larger Sacrifice in Vain you vow;
There's not a Pow'r above will help you now:
A Nation thus, who oft Heav'ns Call neglects,
In Vain from injur'd Heav'n Relief expects. (III, 771, ll. 33-36)

In Horace's ode, moreover, the speaker stands on the shore, lamenting the perilous state of his desired one ("Nuper solicitum quæ mihi tædium, / Nunc desiderium, curaque non levis," p. 23, ll. 17-18), which Creech renders as "my grief and fear, / And now my fresh and present Care" (p. 22, ll. 23-24). Although similarly concerned for the ship's safety, Swift's speaker by contrast is firmly, nauseously, trapped on-board:

Weary and Sea-sick when in thee confin'd,
Now, for thy Safety Cares distract my Mind,
As those who long have stood the Storms of State,
Retire, yet still bemoan their Country's Fate.
Beware, and when you hear the Surges roar,
Avoid the Rocks on *Britain*'s angry Shore:
They lye, alas, too easy to be found,
For thee alone they lye the Island round. (III, 772, ll. 57-64)

That final couplet, the discomfiting conclusion of the poem, offers little relief for the imperilled ship of state or the now isolated speaker. At once he wishes the country to remain the same – "Dear Vessel, still be to thy Steerage just, / Nor, change thy Course with ev'ry sudden Gust" (III, 771, ll. 53-54) – yet acknowledges that change has been imposed upon it. In particular, an overriding theme of the poem is the displacement of patriotic allies in favour of government cronies. One prominent man who had endured the political "Storms of State," Viscount Midleton, had resigned from his position as Lord Chancellor in 1725,

42 Creech, *The Odes, Satyrs, and Epistles of Horace*, p. 21, ll. 1-12. Subsequent references are to this edition.

and was replaced by the Englishman Richard West. Another of the lost "faithful Counsellors" (III, 770, l. 14) was Thomas Lindsay, Archbishop of Armagh and Primate of all Ireland until his recent death in 1724. He was replaced by another Englishman, Hugh Boulter, a devoted supporter of George I and the Whig administration.[43] For all of their mutual support, though, the speaker separates himself from "those who long have stood the Storms of State," and even Ireland is left to its own devices ("For thee alone they lye the Island round"). Or, rather, Ireland has been taken over by "supple Patriots of the modern Sort, / Who turn with ev'ry Gale that blows from Court" (III, 771, ll. 55-56). The speaker's love for his country has been damaged by political upheaval.

Against the turncoat politicians, the speaker, in one critic's reading, embeds a prophetic warning that increases in emotional intensity as Swift departs from his source: "Thy Mast, which like some aged Patriot stood / The single Pillar for his Country's Good, / To lead thee, as a Staff directs the Blind" (III, 770, ll. 15-17). For this critic, the prophetic warning of the poem coheres with the Drapier's attempts to lead his countrymen out of dependence: "to let you see, that by the Laws of GOD, of NATURE, of NATIONS, and of your own Country, you ARE and OUGHT to be as FREE a People as your Brethren in *England*."[44] But this is to ignore the impending destruction of the mast that "cracks by yon rough *Eastern* Wind" (III, 770, l. 18), a possible reference to another departing ally, the chronically ageing Archbishop King. And the symbolism of the imperilled ship at large, along with the nauseated (or unseated) speaker at the heart of the poem, could plausibly be said to articulate Swift's longstanding feeling of isolation within his home country.

We need look no further than Swift's polite refusal to sanction Pope's opinion of him as a patriot in the conventional sense: "what I do is owing to perfect rage and resentment, and the mortifying sight of slavery, folly, and baseness about me, among which I am forc'd to live."[45] Cynically, one might view Swift's prophetic patriotism as a sham. More generously, one might consider his description of his own 'confinement' on the "Poor floating Isle" as a humbling, foundational component of his emergent patriotic disquiet. Within this purview, the poem could be read as a defeatist, even fatalist, resignation to the fact that Ireland is doomed to fall on "*Britain*'s angry Shore" (III, 772, l. 62).

43 In addition to DIB, I, 670-73, see *Correspondence*, ed. Woolley, II, 621-22, and *passim*. See also George Thomas Stokes, "William King, and his Contemporaries, Boulter and Swift," *Some Worthies of the Irish Church: Lectures Delivered in the Divinity School of the University of Dublin*, ed. Hugh Jackson Lawler (London: Hodder and Stoughton, 1900), pp. 272-81.

44 See Schakel, *The Poetry of Jonathan Swift*, pp. 161-64, quoting from *The Letter to the Whole People of Ireland* in *Prose Works*, X, 63.

45 Swift to Alexander Pope, 1 June 1728, *Correspondence*, ed. Woolley, III, 184.

After all, the formal Union between the English and Scottish parliaments threatened to obstruct the Irish from ever gaining positions of true power: "When the strong Cords of Union once are Broke. / Torn by a sudden Tempest is thy Sail, / Expanded to invite a milder Gale" (III, 770, ll. 23-24). By sanctioning the Union of Parliaments, in this view, Queen Anne had irrecoverably compromised Ireland's power. The poem openly alludes to the recent Declaratory Act of 1720 that had further exacerbated Ireland's situation as a depending, "Captive" kingdom. Or rather, the politicians have taken the independent kingdom by force, callously overlooking the sacrifices the English in Ireland had made during the Williamite wars of 1688-89: "an Empress, now a Captive grown, / She saved *Britannia*'s Right, and lost her own" (III, 771, ll. 45-46). In a manuscript variation, "*Britannia's* Right" is rendered as "Europes Liberty," suggesting that Swift sought to stress more emphatically the rupture between the Kingdoms of England and Ireland rather than, say, the Continental conflict between Protestants and Catholics.

4

In "Horace, Book I, Ode XIV," the speaker's attention is turned specifically to his "Nation" and "Country," a further indication of Swift's emergent patriotism in print. For all of his efforts, though, the pamphleteering priest is unable to rescue the "sinking Nation," as we see in this extended interpolation:

> As when some Writer in a public Cause,
> His Pen to save a sinking Nation draws,
> While all is Calm, his Arguments prevail,
> The People's Voice expand[s] his Paper Sail;
> 'Till Pow'r, discharging all her stormy Bags,
> Flutters the feeble Pamphlet into Rags.
> The Nation scar'd, the Author doom'd to Death,
> Who fondly put his Trust in pop'lar Breath. (III, 770-71, ll. 25-32)

Swift readdresses the issue of the diminishing value of his Hibernian pamphlets with similar imagery in a slightly later self-homage poem, "Drapier's Hill":

> When none the DRAPIER's Praise shall sing;
> His Signs aloft no longer swing;
> His Medals and his Prints forgotten,
> And all his Handkerchiefs are rotten;
> His famous LETTERS made waste Paper. (III, 875, ll. 13-17)

The Drapier's rotting pamphlets in such poems resemble the "Ships decay'd" in which "no Mariner confides, / Lur'd by the gilded Stern, and painted Sides" (III, 771, ll. 47-48). More broadly, the ruling classes favour the superficial trappings ("They on the Gold Brocades and Satins rav'd," III, 771, l. 51), wilfully blinding themselves to their own subjugation or, at least, the confinement of their countrymen and women ("And quite forgot their Country was enslav'd," III, 771, l. 52). Such pointed criticism adds new momentum to Horace's subtler critique of the state's elitist assumptions. As in Horace's original, the Irish ship is made of noble wood, a symbol of its imperial strength metonymically contrasted against the patriot's waste paper: "thy Descent is from the *British* Oak" (III, 771, l. 38; Pontic pine, for Horace [p. 23, l. 11]). But if we put the focus on the translator rather than the translated text, in Swift's post-Drapier period, we should be more attentive to his fictive failures (pamphlets turned into rags, to use his image) – he appears to have given up on his project.

Moreover, Horace queries the stability of power as a sailor's natural fear will override any arbitrary reverence for ancestry ("Jactes & genus, & nomen inutile: / Nil pictis timidus navita puppibus / Fidit [Although ... you boast of your lineage and name, such things are of no avail; the terrified sailor puts no trust in painted sterns]," p. 23, ll. 13-14). Swift follows suit ("'Twill not avail ... when your Name and Family you boast, / From Fleets triumphant," III, 771, ll. 37-40), similarly undermining the conventional definition of a country's strength in merely martial terms. Military victories dwindle onto the pages of the history books. For all of their fame, even the "Sons descended from the *British* Line," "whose Valour still remains / On *French* Records for twenty long Campains" (III, 771, ll. 42-44) will be lost "when thy strong Sides are broke" (III, 771, l. 37). Where Creech has "fearful Seaman" (p. 21, l. 17), a close approximation of Horace's "timidus navita" (p. 23, l. 14), Swift hints that the spiritual demise of the nation goes hand in hand with a diminished patriotic feeling among the general populace devoid of emotional loyalty to the state ("In Ships decay'd no Mariner confides"). The rampaging winds – the "stormy Bags" – of the new rulers utterly defeat the "pop'lar Breath" (III, 771, l. 32) of the people. Infiltrating the primary text, Swift makes strategic use of its stale metaphors in his jaded take on Anglo-Irish politics. Indeed, Swift freely raided the familiar works of the Latin satirist: "Toland's Invitation to Dismal," "The First Ode of the Second Book of Horace Paraphras'd," and "Part of the Seventh Epistle of the First Book of Horace Imitated" are just three other Horatian poems written in like manner. But as the titles alone suggest, these are fragments.

Swift had also attempted, back in 1714, a fairly close but heavily abridged imitation of the sixth poem in the Second Book of Horace's *Satires* ("Horace, *Lib.* 2. *Sat.* 6. Part of it Imitated"). Evidently unsatisfied with his work, he abandoned it.[46] In the version belatedly published in the 1727 *Miscellanies*, we witness the worn-out satirist seeking retirement in a comfortable setting:

I Often wish'd, that I had clear
For Life, six hundred Pounds a Year,
A handsome House to lodge a Friend,
A River at my Garden's End,
A Terras Walk, and half a Rood
Of Land set out to plant a Wood. (I, 198, ll. 1-6)

Pope wanted to refashion the poem in 1737, having incited a mutual friend, Charles Bathurst, into asking Swift if he intended to finish it himself.[47] Swift declined, freeing Pope to publish what he had probably composed already. Aside from an interpolation near the beginning of the poem, Pope's most substantial addition to Swift's version occurs after a closing death wish buried in the penultimate line masquerading as a triumph in retreat

Thus in a Sea of Folly tost,
My choicest Hours of Life are lost:
Yet always wishing to retreat;
Oh, could I see my Country Seat.
There leaning near a gentle Brook,
Sleep, or peruse some antient Book;
And there in sweet Oblivion drown
Those Cares that haunt the Court and Town. (I, 202, ll. 105-12)

Here Swift ended his partial imitation, stopping short of the town-mouse fable delivered by Horace's characters, and skipping ahead to a world-wearied preference for country life. At this point, Pope (so we presume) engrafted eighty-eight additional lines, supplying the missing allegory. Endeavouring to "hit [Swift's] style exactly" (so he later claimed), Pope had the country mouse deliver a modern political plea in terms reminiscent of Cowley's famous rendering: "Give me again my hollow Tree! / A Crust of Bread, and Liberty!"[48] For

46 *Poems*, ed. Williams, I, 197-202. "I have done the Imitation of Hoc erat in votis," he wrote to Charles Ford on 3 August 1714. "Tis pretty well, and will serve in some scurvy Miscellany." Four days later, he conceded that "it is not yet sufficiently corrected to my Mind, thô I have labored it much" (*Correspondence*, ed. Woolley, II, 45, 60). The poem first appeared in print in the 1727 *Miscellanies*, and was also included in the second volume of Faulkner's 1735 edition of *Works*.

47 For a discussion of Pope's role in the revisions of the poem, see Dustin Griffin, *Swift and Pope: Satirists in Dialogue* (Cambridge: Cambridge University Press, 2010), pp. 207-9.

48 Griffin, *Swift and Pope*, p. 208. Having used Williams's edition of Swift's poems for the first 112 lines (those attributed to Swift), I have taken the rest of the poem from *The Poems*

Cowley, hard-fought peace would more than suffice, but for Pope's Swift (in the guise of the Hibernian Patriot), personal (and national) liberty had particular if slightly delayed resonance after the *Drapier's Letters* appeared. Swift's version of *Odes*, I, xiv more emphatically turns against the original. Even the outwardly imitative odes and epistles, more broadly, rely on aggressive appropriation, a technique we are accustomed to celebrating in his pamphlets. Reading the pamphlets and poems together suggests that Swift's authorship thrived best not when imitating popular models but when writing to the moment in a sort of sham spontaneity.

of Alexander Pope, ed. John Butt (London: Methuen, 1973 [1963]), pp. 659-64. On Pope's Swiftian continuations, see John M. Aden, *Something like Horace: Studies in the Art and Allusion of Pope's Horatian Satires* (Nashville, Tennessee: Vanderbilt University Press, 1969 [1962]), pp. 85-105, Frank Stack, *Pope and Horace: Studies in Imitation* (Cambridge: Cambridge University Press, 1985), pp. 222-44, and Peter J. Schakel, "'Friends Side by Side': Theme, Structure, and Influence in the Swift-Pope *Miscellanies* of 1727," *Reading Swift: Papers from The Second Münster Symposium on Jonathan Swift*, eds Richard H. Rodino and Hermann J. Real, with the assistance of Helgard Stöver-Leidig (Munich: Wilhelm Fink, 1993), pp. 103-12 (110-12).

GULLIVER'S TRAVELS

Norbert Col
Université de Bretagne-Sud

True-to-Life History? What the Dead Say in *Gulliver's Travels*, or: Sensational Disclosures (Gulliver Tells All)

Abstract. Although Gulliver's stay in Glubbdubdrib ostensibly grants access to the truth, truth remains one of the episode's most vexing issues. Not only is the Voyage to Glubbdubdrib a *parti-pris* piece in Swift's politico-literary arsenal against Whiggery; it also abides by the jocular conventions of the *Dialogues of the Dead*, a fact which undercuts the purported veracity of what Gulliver is imparted: learning from the dead may simply result in more illusions. Indeed, what Gulliver discovers is a variety of political histories which finally boil down to a *reductio ad fornicationem*, even *ad prostitutionem*, and which do not rise above those very 'anecdotes' that are the 'hallmark' of faulty history. Thus, Gulliver's 'restoration' of historical truth suggests that history rests on thin air and that, especially when it serves the practical purposes of politics, it is no better than "obscene necromancy."

Over two centuries after Swift, another Irish poet, Patrick Kavanagh, published his "Sensational Disclosures! (Kavanagh tells all)," an alleged "megaton bomb," in fact, a controlled damp squib in "the poetry war." The poem, claiming to "expose all the guilty men," only yields the gloom, glee, and self-mockery of one who "could swallow without dodgery / Ted Hughes' menagerie" and "often spat forth / Lions of more wrath."[1] Petty settlements of poetic accounts are not everything, though. Recounting elsewhere an argument between the Duffys and the McCabes over a plot of land in County Monaghan at the time of "the Munich bother," Kavanagh concludes: "Homer's ghost came whispering to my mind / He said: I made the Iliad from such / A local row. Gods make their own importance."[2] So does Gulliver encounter Homer's ghost, and something of Kavanagh's alleged "sensational disclosures" transpires in "a Whisper from a Ghost, who shall be nameless," about those commentators who "had so horribly misrepresented the Meaning" of their superiors.[3] Their grievous errors

1 Patrick Kavanagh, "Sensational Disclosures! (Kavanagh tells all)," *Collected Poems* (London: Martin Brian and O'Keeffe, 1977 [1972]), pp. 188-90.

2 Kavanagh, "Epic," *Collected Poems*, p. 136.

3 All references to *Gulliver's Travels* are from the edition by Allan Ingram (Peterborough, Ontario: Broadview, 2012) and will be given in parentheses within the text. Here, p. 252 (III, viii, 1).

 | DOI:10.30965/9783846763971_011

may have been interred with their bones, but why should the informant ghost be anonymous, since the dead "would certainly tell me Truth; for Lying was a Talent of no Use in the lower World" (p. 249 [III, vii, 6])? The truth, indeed, but humans, apart from Gulliver, are not, it seems, fit receivers of the whole of it, as if their controversies might embarrass the supposedly safe source from the "lower World." Accordingly, Swift's sensationalism, not much removed from Kavanagh's "lions of wrath," embarrassingly recalls Christ's own words, "neither will they be persuaded, though one rose from the dead" (Luke 16:31).

Swift travelled a dangerous road amidst his biblical echoes. Buried "with their Heads directly downwards," the Lilliputian dead are properly positioned to "rise again" when "the Earth (which they conceive to be flat) will turn upside down," a residual superstition scorned by "the Learned among them" yet perpetuated "in compliance to the vulgar" (p. 104 [I, vi, 3]). The oblique satire of literal readings of the resurrection (the selection of "eleven," not twelve, "thousand moons" is fussy enough) elicited Orrery's objections to placing "the resurrection (one of the most encouraging principles of the Christian religion) in a ridiculous, and contemptible light."[4] A twenty-first century reader likewise remarks that "the ghost of Swift's alleged irreligion still hovers over contemporary critical discourse;" at the same time, this reader admits the Dean's veiled orthodoxy: "Not being the most serious of divines sometimes leads to being mythologized out of recognition."[5] For another critic, Swift satirized "literal-mindedness in the observation of religious ceremonies" and "certain practices among some of the peoples of whom he had read."[6] Conversely, the Voyage to Brobdingnag has little on the metaphysics of death,[7] merely narrating, as it

---

4 John Boyle, fifth Earl of Cork and Orrery, "Letter XI," *Remarks on the Life and Writings of Dr. Jonathan Swift*, ed. João Fróes (Newark: University of Delaware Press, and London: Associated University Presses, 2000), pp. 175-83 (180); reprinted in Swift, *Gulliver's Travels*, ed. Ingram, p. 445.

5 Nathalie Zimpfer, "Swift and Religion: From Myth to Reality," *Swift Studies*, 24 (2009), 46-69 (pp. 47, 69). One can also read with profit, all from *Swift Studies*, 14 (1999), Michael DePorte, "Phillip Harth's *Swift and Anglican Rationalism*: A Retrospective and Evaluation," pp. 5-6; Peter J. Schakel, "The Context of Phillip Harth's *Swift and Anglican Rationalism*," pp. 7-12; Michael J. Conlon, "*Swift and Anglican Rationalism*: A Retrospective View," pp. 13-20; Marcus Walsh, "*Swift and Anglican Rationalism* and the Grounds of Interpretation," pp. 21-28; and Phillip Harth, "Recent Religious History and *A Tale of a Tub*," pp. 29-36; see also Zimpfer, "From 'Rabelais in his Senses' to the 'Father of Black Humour': Notes on Jonathan Swift's Critical Reception in France," *Swift Studies*, 23 (2008), 80-93 (see pp. 85-86 on the contemporary reception of *A Tale of a Tub* in England as an attack on Christianity).

6 *Gulliver's Travels*, ed. Ingram, p. 104n. See Dirk F. Passmann, "Jean de Thevenot and Burials in Lilliput," *Notes and Queries*, 231 (1986), 50-51.

7 At the most Gulliver says, on his capture by a giant: "All I ventured was to raise mine Eyes towards the Sun" (p. 137 [II, i, 6]). "Towards the Sun," not towards Heaven: Gulliver's faith seems to be somewhat tepid.

does, those situations in which Gulliver's life is in danger or those, more sinister to his moral character, in which he boasts of the arts of war (a boast which he repeats in Houyhnhnmland [pp. 183-84, 303 {II, vii, 3-4; IV, v, 7}]). In the latter voyage, the lines about the widowed mare, behaving "chearfully" after her husband's death that very morning, yet dying "about three Months after" (p. 331 [IV, ix, 323]), can either be taken at face value or as a suggestion that the detachment of stoicism is inapplicable,[8] thus buttressing Swift's Christian orthodoxy.

Book Three, which, "although placed third ... was written last,"[9] has numerous and rewarding investigations into death. A Lagado dog fatally bursts during an experiment for a cure of "the Cholick," "and we left the Doctor endeavouring to recover him by the same Operation" (p. 234 [III, v, 11]), a depressing variation on the resurrection of the Lilliputian departed. In the Struldbrugg passage (pp. 265-69 [III, x, 7-17]), death is cryptically confirmed by the epistemological impossibility of imagining, and thus positing, immortality.[10] Ultimately, this episode, with its stress on amnesia, challenges that belief in the ancient constitution that Swift wielded against the New Whiggism of Walpole and his satellites.[11] In between Lagado and the Struldbruggs, Gulliver's stay in Glubbdubdrib, otherwise "the Island of *Sorcerers* or *Magicians*" (p. 247 [III, vii, 3]), confirms Swift's cryptical undermining of his political standpoints. Prima facie, the séance overturns official history and suggests a Tory/Jacobite alternative.[12] Though Gulliver is offered true-to-life history, one is tempted to

---

8 Swift, *Thoughts on Various Subjects*, in *Prose Works*, I, 244: "The Stoical Scheme of supplying our Wants, by lopping off our Desires, is like cutting off our Feet when we want Shoes."

9 J. A. Downie, *Jonathan Swift: Political Writer* (London: Routledge and Kegan Paul, 1984), p. 281.

10 Norbert Col, "The Struldbruggs and History," *Swift Studies*, 26 (2011), 108-19 (pp. 110-11). See also Paul-Gabriel Boucé, "Death in *Gulliver's Travels*: The Struldbruggs Revisited," *Swift, the Enigmatic Dean: Festschrift for Hermann Josef Real*, eds Rudolf Freiburg, Arno Löffler, and Wolfgang Zach (Tübingen: Stauffenburg, 1998), pp. 1-13. Incidentally, Tithonus, Aurora's husband, was granted immortality but Aurora neglected to ask for everlasting youth, which brings Tithonus close to the Struldbruggs, though the latter are not even so fortunate as to be changed into cicadas, as Tithonus eventually, and mercifully so, was.

11 Col, "The Struldbruggs and History," pp. 114-16. On Whiggism, see J. G. A. Pocock, *Virtue, Commerce, and History* (Cambridge: Cambridge University Press, 1991 [1985]). Downie regards Swift as an Old Whig, while the present essay tilts him more towards the crypto-Jacobitism identified in Ian Higgins's *Swift's Politics: A Study in Disaffection* (Cambridge: Cambridge University Press, 1994).

12 Nothing exceptional about that, since the *Dialogues of the Dead* participated in an "oblique discourse which was more acceptable than direct exposure" (Michel Henrichot, "Réflexions sur les dialogues des morts à l'Âge classique," *Les Représentations de la mort*, ed. Bernard-Marie Garreau [Rennes: Presses Universitaires de Rennes, 2002], pp. 127-41 [140]). For obvious reasons, Swift provided a scanty alternative political history: the offhanded dismissal of the Atterbury trial (III, vi, 236-37) was about as far as he could safely

opt for 'true-to-death' and the endless queries raised by the inversion of the set phrase, which ultimately opens onto an incrimination of historical truth as such.[13]

Indeed, truth is one of the most vexed issues in *Gulliver's Travels*: "*Nec si miserum Fortuna Sinone / Finxit, vanum etiam mendacemque improba finget*" – "Though Fortune has made Sinon miserable, she will not also make him false and a liar."[14] But Sinon, so the credulous Trojans learnt by their own destruction, was just another *splendidus mendax*, and Gulliver's belief in an "Essence" of "*Falshood*," just as there is one of "*Truth*" (p. 306 [IV, v, 16]), is paltry theology.[15] Conversely, Swift's own "contrary views" and "ambiguities" did not lead him into "Pontius Pilate's relativistic trap, 'What is truth'?"[16] which is tantamount to regarding Gulliver's inroads into divinity as the butt of authorial criticism. Accordingly, the veracity question in Glubbdubdrib is exposed to the general possibility of Swiftian irony, and the genre of the *Dialogues of the Dead* shows death, a mere "convention" permitting the confrontation of "interlocutors who could not have conversed in this world,"[17] as of little concern. The Governor of Glubbdubdrib has a proviso whereby Gulliver's "Questions must be confined within the Compass of the Times they [the dead] lived in" (p. 249 [III, vii, 6]). However, such demands are loosely observed, as with the "*Sextumvirate*" of Brutus, "his ancestor *Junius, Socrates, Epaminondas, Cato* the Younger, Sir *Thomas More*" (p. 251 [III, vii, 10]) and, further down, those other "time-riders,"[18] Homer, Didymus, and Eustathius, then Aristotle, Descartes, and Gassendi, whose discussion apparently results in Aristotle's victory, since the two Moderns do not seem to participate in the resumption of the exchange between Gulliver and Aristotle (pp. 252-53 [III, viii, 1]). The touch of vanity in Aristotle also suggests that Swift's use of the veracity convention, in

go. On such precautions, see Col, "Oblique Writing in Time of 'Moderate' Persecution: The Example of *Gulliver's Travels*," *Swift Studies*, 28 (2013), 96-114.

13 The *Travels* bring together "the various acceptations of history" at the time, namely "the historians' history, with its chronology and claims to veracity, history as imaginary narrative, let it be presented as truthful or not, and history as observation" (Jean Viviès, *Revenir/Devenir: Gulliver ou l'autre voyage* [Paris: Éditions Rue d'Ulm/Presses de l'École normale supérieure, 2016], p. 115). The latter feature, evocative as it is of Pliny the Elder, does not relate to the present study.

14 Virgil, *Aeneid*, II, 79-80, in *Gulliver's Travels*, ed. Ingram, p. 348 and n3 (IV, xii).

15 Norbert Col, "Langage et information dans *Gulliver's Travels*," *Mentalities/Mentalités*, 16, nos 1-2 (2001), 89-98 (pp. 91-92).

16 Loftus Jestin, "*Splendide Mendax*: Purposeful Misprision, Determinant Irony, in *Gulliver's Travels*," *Swift Studies*, 14 (1999), 99-114 (p. 107).

17 Henrichot, "Réflexions sur les dialogues des morts à l'Âge classique," pp. 127, 129.

18 Boucé, "Death in *Gulliver's Travels*: The Struldbruggs Revisited," p. 7.

combination with his general scorn of the Moderns,[19] does not preclude the possibility that the dead Ancients still succumb to the customary pride among alive-and-kicking humans. Just as strikingly, the *Dialogues of the Dead* were a jocular genre, as shown by Fontenelle's Pluto attempting to restore order in his pandemonium,[20] which may be paralleled by the Governor's ineffective injunctions. Swift's own deadpan seriousness, addressing lofty issues ranging from history to epistemology and contemporary politics, accordingly calls for more than a few pinches of salt.

It has to be added that the Glubbdubdrib passage is not, *stricto sensu*, a *Dialogue of the Dead*: this series of conversations between Gulliver and certain departed people is, in keeping with the tenor of the *Travels*, filtered through the retrospective quality of indirect speech.[21] Moreover, although both the *Odyssey* and the *Aeneid* share with the *Travels* the use of conversations *with* the dead, not dialogues *of* the dead, Gulliver does not ask for his defunct relatives (whose memories never burden him) nor his "good master Master *Bates*" (pp. 63-64 [I, i, 1-3]), to whom, irrespective of the question whether one accepts the pun or dismisses it, he owed so much.[22] Unsentimental Gulliver, as against Ulysses or Aeneas,[23] may not actually *speak* the truth about himself, though he lets it slip through various interstices. Elsewhere, Gulliver perfunctorily

19 To Alain Bony, Swift's shafts at Descartes and Gassendi enable him to bypass Locke, who inspired him with "ambivalent sentiments" given his rationalism and perverse epistemology, and Newton. Swift regarded the latter as an enemy who, given his position at the head of the Mint, was at the origins of the Wood affair. Newton's system also permitted to dispense with God ("Swift et la 'philosophie,'" *Bulletin de la société d'études anglo-américaines des XVIIe et XVIIIe siècles*, 58 [2004], 235-57 [pp. 249, 252, 255]).

20 Henrichot, "Réflexions sur les dialogues des morts à l'Âge classique," p. 139. See Fontenelle, *Nouveaux dialogues des morts* (1683), ed. Jean Dagen (Paris: Marcel Didier, 1971). Fénelon's serious *Dialogue entre Confucius et Socrate* (written between 1692 and 1695) was a maverick piece; see Charles Coutel, "Fénelon entre Confucius et Socrate," *L'Esprit oriental: un regard occidental*, eds Michael Hearn and Li Xiaohong (Paris: You Feng, 2012), pp. 67-72 (69).

21 For brief occurrences of direct speech in the *Travels*, see the King of Brobdingnag's outburst against English politics (pp. 181-82 [II, vi, 18]) or Gulliver's account of lawyers and judges (pp. 304-6 [IV, v, 10-17]). Fontenelle's "Jugement de Pluton" was also written in indirect speech (Henrichot, "Réflexions sur les dialogues des morts à l'Âge classique," p. 139).

22 On the issue of the pun, see Christopher Fox, "The Myth of Narcissus in Swift's *Travels*," *Eighteenth-Century Studies*, 20 (1986-87), 17-33, and Paul-Gabriel Boucé, "Gulliver's Master Bates Once Again," *Bulletin de la société d'études anglo-américaines des XVIIe et XVIIIe Siècles*, 55 (2002), 85-95.

23 Georges Kliebenstein remarks that Ulysses fails on three occasions to embrace his mother's shade (*Odyssey*, XI, 206) and Aeneas that of his wife in a dream (*Aeneid*, II, 792-93), then his father's in the netherworld (*Aeneid*, VI, 700-1). Gulliver also evokes the Roman ritual of *conclamatio* in which the dead were called thrice to make sure that they were

mentions his longing for his wife and children, but goes back to sea as soon as possible (his longest stay back home is a bare five months, in between the third and fourth voyages).[24] Ostensibly, this is prompted by practical, financial demands, and one might stretch the point that a heavy heart does not enlarge on what grieves most. However, Gulliver's asking for the illustrious dead alone accords with his permanent insistence that he mixed with those at the top and was bitterly disappointed with them. In Glubbdubdrib, though, his frustration is of another nature. It originates in what Gulliver comes to learn, but he never challenges his sources, and this blind spot of his may well point to an unidentified biblical substratum.

It is often argued that the conventional location of the *Dialogues of the Dead* in the ancient world warded off criticism from established Christianity.[25] The point does not need to be challenged, but Holy Writ, where raising the dead violates God's commands, strikes quite another note. Most relevant is Saul's plea that the witch of Endor should "bring vp" Samuel "vnto [him]." The witch initially demurs, invoking the king's earlier persecution of "wizards" in keeping with Exodus 22:18, "Thou shalt not suffer a witch to live." Her mind is set at rest by the still anonymous Saul, then she recognizes him (how so is a moot point, with its own supernatural intimations) when Samuel appears, only to be reassured once more by the guilty king, who then learns about his impending death in battle against the Philistines (1 Samuel 28:3-25).[26]

Witchcraft relates to rebellion, and Saul's fate seems already sealed in an earlier chapter when Samuel, then still alive, brackets the king's sparing of Agag, king of the Amalekites, with "rebellion," "the sin of witchcraft," "stubbornness," and "iniquity and idolatry;" rejection of "the word of the LORD" has led the latter to reject Saul "from *being* king" (1 Samuel 15:23), a proleptic indication of the revelation at Endor. Rebellion also connects with a lack of faith, since Saul died for not keeping "the word of the LORD" and "asking *counsel* of *one that had*

really departed; see *Figures du destin stendhalien* (Paris: Presses Sorbonne Nouvelle, 2004), p. 333 and n. Obviously, *conclamatio* would be of no use in Glubbdubdrib.

24 See also Allan Ingram, "Gulliver's Travails: Labour and Self-Loathing in Several Remote Nations of the World," *"The first wit of the age": Essays on Swift and his Contemporaries in Honour of Hermann J. Real*, eds Kirsten Juhas, Patrick Müller, and Mascha Hansen (Frankfurt on Main: Peter Lang, 2013), pp. 257-68 (258).

25 Henrichot, "Réflexions sur les dialogues des morts à l'Âge classique," p. 133.

26 Without entering into the various fortunes of the episode, from Augustine and Aquinas to Luther and Calvin, one ought to remember that Hobbes denied the witch the gift of prophecy, since there is no evidence "that God commanded the raising" of the "Phantasme of Samuel": he "onely guided that Imposture to be a means of Sauls terror and discouragement, and by consequent, of the discomfiture, by which he fell" (*Leviathan* [1651], ed. C. B. Macpherson [Harmondsworth: Penguin, 1985 {1968}], p. 458 [III, xxxvi]).

a familiar spirit, to enquire *of it*" instead of "the LORD" (1 Chronicles 10:13-14). Later on, "witchcraft" is one of "the works of the flesh" (Galatians 5:19-20), and Saint Paul's warning against "the man of sin ... whose coming is after the working of Satan, with all power and signs, and lying wonders" (2 Thessalonians 2:3, 9), remotely relates Satan to the feats of Pharaoh's magicians before they were defeated by Moses (Exodus 7 and 8), which disturbingly intermingles truth and falsehood.

The question now is what we have to think of Gulliver's participation in a séance, otherwise his entering the realm of Satan, "prince of the power of the air" and agent of "disobedience" (Ephesians 2:2).[27] Gulliver's "lower World" (p. 249 [III, vii, 6]) may agree with that of the Ancients more than with Christianity's Hell or Old Testament depictions since no Saul-like punishment befalls him, and the supernatural chill of Endor merely runs through the frightful aspect of the guards as a remote echo of the dangers surrounding a visit to the dead in Homer and Virgil. Even so, Gulliver's initial "horror" is at odds with that homely atmosphere where, under certain conditions, the Governor of Glubbdubdrib can command "service" from the dead, to which Gulliver becomes accustomed (p. 249 [III, vii, 4]). Swift's uneven combination of Ancient and Christian traditions, together with his echoes of the playful *Dialogues of the Dead* from Antiquity to the seventeenth century, allows Gulliver both to learn safely from the dead, which squares with the Ancients, and also to be faced with a much less trustworthy account than the one imparted to Saul. He is not told about his own death since he merely asks about that past which seems to be the sole field of Glubbdubdribban expertise; but there are so many tricks in Satan's bag of lies that Gulliver may not be the better off in his search for historical truth,[28] as if the *Travels* confirmed the remark that "*A Tale of a Tub*, as a religious allegory of the history of the Christian (Catholic and universal) church, was not a tale of the progressive self-revelation of the Divine Light but a chronicle of the descent of Night on Christianity,"[29] or that more general insight into "the

27 See Dirk F. Passmann and Hermann J. Real, "Barbarism, Witchcraft, and Devil Worship: Cock-and-Bull Stories from Several Remote Nations of the World," *Swift Studies*, 23 (2008), 94-110 (p. 104).

28 On a perfectly contemporary perception of Satan, see Yannick Deschamps, "Daniel Defoe et le Prince des Ténèbres: le pouvoir du Diable et ses limites dans *The Political History of the Devil* (1726)," *La Nuit dans l'Angleterre des Lumières*, ed. Suzy Halimi (Paris: Presses Sorbonne Nouvelle, 2008), pp. 205-23.

29 Passmann and Real, "Barbarism, Witchcraft, and Devil Worship," p. 108.

triumph of Dulness" over the human mind as encapsulated in Pope's "Universal Darkness buries All."[30]

The atmosphere is, initially, somewhat sedate, even 'conventional.' Alexander the Great's tale of his own death silently confirms Plutarch's rejection of the tradition that he was poisoned.[31] Slightly more controversial is the account of Hannibal, who claims that "he had not a Drop of Vinegar in his Camp" (p. 250 [III, vii, 8]), as against Livy and Juvenal, while Polybius, the earliest surviving source, says nothing about it,[32] and Gulliver builds up his own originality by taking Polybius' silence to unsubstantiated conclusions. Later, Orrery provided little of significance: "Hannibal seems to have been summoned with no other view than to censure Livy the historian." Another, anonymous gloss connects Hannibal with Alexander, stressing how "ridiculous" "those destroyers of the human race [are], when stripped of their royalty and command, as well as their ability to perpetrate any further mischief."[33] Clearly, there is not much of sensationalism here, nor in the opening paragraphs of the following chapter. Lucian's *True History* already granted the traditionally blind poet, Homer, the "most quick and piercing" eyes, also mentioned by Gulliver; yet there is no evidence, even in that jocular tradition, backing Gulliver's description of Aristotle as a "stooped" figure with "Hair lank and thin" and a "hollow" voice (p. 252 [III, viii, 1]),[34] a reminder that the reader must permanently be on the alert. This specifically applies to that incrimination of the present day which is the real gist of Gulliver's findings from the dead, as if things came to life, if one may, with the more political side of the matter, which reaches far beyond the jocose contemporary *Dialogues of the Dead*.

This is indicated, though paradoxically so, by the more or less remote world liberally providing names, such as Alexander, Hannibal, Aristotle, Brutus, and others, down to Thomas More, while the more recent world is a nameless host of ghosts. Of course, such anonymity is meant to cover the burning topicality of contemporary satire, but it also performs a function similar to the "impersonality and abstractedness" which "seem to remove the critic from his argument,"

30 Alexander Pope, *The Dunciad*, ed. James Sutherland, 3rd ed. (London: Methuen, and New Haven: Yale University Press, 1963), p. 409 (IV, l. 656). See Gerald J. Butler, "Our Own Service in the Empire Pope's *Dunciad* Predicts," *Great Expectations: Futurity in the Long Eighteenth Century*, eds Mascha Hansen and Jürgen Klein (Frankfurt on Main: Peter Lang, 2012), pp. 291-303 (302).

31 *Gulliver's Travels*, ed. Ingram, p. 249n2.

32 See *Gulliver's Travels*, ed. Paul Turner (Oxford: Oxford University Press, 1994), pp. 188, 342.

33 *The Works of Dr Jonathan Swift, Dean of St Patrick's, Dublin*, 8 vols (Edinburgh: A. Donaldson, 1761), IV, 186n (Teerink and Scouten 96).

34 *Gulliver's Travels*, ed. Ingram, p. 252n.

as a result of which "his insights … seem to spring directly from reality."[35] Such impersonality is compounded by Swift's sustained use of the passive voice, generally obfuscating agents or dismissing them to irrelevance. A case in point is the informant ghost, which ultimately undercuts Gulliver's credentials as restorer of history, even if it agrees with both apparently innocuous contemporary commonplaces and their potential for subversion. Indeed, the ancient world, though comparatively safe material, was also one of virtuous tyrannicide, as exemplified by Caesar's falling in, out of a belated sense of public duty, with his murderer, Marcus Junius Brutus: "The greatest Actions of his own [Caesar's] Life were not equal by many Degrees to the Glory of taking it away" (p. 250 [III, vii, 10]). Evocative though this is of Fontenelle's knack for staging the most unlikely amicable conversations in the netherworld, such as that between Cortez and Montezuma,[36] its gist is its compatibility with 'Country' thinking. Tyrannicide was part and parcel of formal education, excepting an isolated Hobbes who indicted the subversive seedbed.[37] In the 1720s, celebrating tyrannicide also tallied with a nexus of crypto-Jacobite propaganda that praised Ravaillac, as in Swift's earlier *Tale of a Tub* (1704), and implied that assassinating William III would not have been immoral.[38] This made classical echoes, unassailable as such, dangerously serviceable to the most heated of all topical concerns. To one critic, the "Roman republican, regicidal radicalism" in the *Travels* was not "an anachronistic Old or True Whig political stance as is supposed in Swift studies," but evoked "the Jacobite velleities of a disaffected High Churchman whose loyalty to the settlement founded upon the Revolution could be radically ambiguous."[39]

Indeed, four-square Gulliver swiftly turns to the heart of the matter: "I was chiefly disgusted with modern History," he avers (p. 255 [III, viii, 5]) before specifying, in the slyest form of *praeteritio*, that "present times" are not addressed: "I would be sure to give no Offence even to Foreigners (for I hope the Reader need not be told that I do not in the least intend my own Country in what I say upon this Occasion)" (p. 256 [III, viii, 7]). However, that very immediate history that he claims to shun is inevitably affected by what may be most central to the wheels and cogs of human conduct. Indictment of "prostitute Writers" (p. 255 [III, viii, 5]) exposes the contamination of politics by errant

35 Irvin Ehrenpreis, "The Wholeness of History: Social Theory and Literary Criticism," *Swift Studies*, 19 (2004), 5-16 (p. 11). The original lecture was given in 1982 (see Real's editorial note [p. 5]).

36 Henrichot, "Réflexions sur les dialogues des morts à l'Âge classique," p. 135.

37 Hobbes, *Leviathan*, ed. Macpherson, pp. 369-70 (II, xxix).

38 Higgins, *Swift's Politics*, pp. 64-66, 69, 71, 74.

39 Higgins, *Swift's Politics*, p. 66.

sexuality. Obviously, should the adjective, "prostitute," be an isolated instance in the lexical field, little needs to be said about the betrayal of one's duties as a historian, that mere synonym of treachery, disloyalty, untruthfulness. This is implied by the term-by-term oppositions attributing "the greatest Exploits in War to Cowards, the wisest Counsel to Fools, Sincerity to Flatterers, *Roman* Virtue to Betrayers of their Country, Piety to Atheists, Chastity to Sodomites, Truth to Informers" (p. 255 [III, viii, 5]), where pretence clashes with reality. But it is not amiss to scrutinize the several elements in Swift's enumerations,[40] since they generally include a telling odd one out.

One of these catalogues tackles the "Interruption of Lineages," which connotes errant sexuality, "by Pages, Lacqueys, Valets, Coachmen, Gamesters, Fidlers, Players, Captains, and Pick-pockets" (p. 255 [III, viii, 4]), with "captains," supposedly a nobler line of duty, calling for investigation. Not much light is shed by the brief accounts of those sea captains whom Gulliver encounters, with Don Pedro de Mendez, who occupies by far the largest space, hardly qualifying for membership in such a slighted crew. The faintest of all possible echoes might be of Locke's report, after José de Acosta, of Brazilians and "*many other Nations, which have no certain Kings, but as occasion is offered in Peace or War, they choose their Captains as they please,*"[41] as if Swift endorsed political mutability in accordance with that Whig bugbear, Locke. It is also tempting to remember the fanciful titles, including that of "Captain," with which Irish and other highwaymen, many of them inclining to Jacobitism, graced themselves, possibly implying that Swift himself was not above Jacobite sympathies.[42] If so, the Lockean echo could be trusted to dispel suspicion. The most plausible explanation bears on the indictment of standing armies, in keeping with Swift's 'Country' misgivings, whereby "Captain" comes alongside other mercenary callings and their association with crime, including sexual offences. Gulliver's scorn of the Lorbrulgrud militia shows him as a Court Whig, hence the butt of Swiftian satire (p. 188 [II, vii, 11]).[43] In Glubbdubdrib, however, the political

40 Clement Hawes insists on "the unruly energy of catalogues" in *Gulliver's Travels*, adding: "Few things, as François Rabelais had brilliantly shown, are potentially funnier than lists" ("Cousins Sympson and Simson: Gulliverian Intertextuality," *Swift Studies*, 19 [2004], 49-71 [p. 60]).

41 John Locke, *Second Treatise of Government*, 1689, in *Two Treatises of Government*, ed. Peter Laslett (Cambridge: Cambridge University Press, 1960), p. 335 (viii, §102). Locke used Edward Grimestone's translation of Acosta (1604).

42 Brean S. Hammond and Nicholas Seager, "Jonathan Swift's Historical Novel, *The Memoirs of Capt. John Creichton* (1731)," *Swift Studies*, 24 (2009), 70-87. Creichton was a Jacobite (p. 80). See, however, J. A. Downie, "Swift and Jacobitism," *ELH*, 64 (1997), 887-901.

43 However, the size of the militia matches that of a standing army, thus blurring topical criticism. See Col, "Oblique Writing in Time of 'Moderate' Persecution: The Example of *Gulliver's Travels*," p. 105.

dimension is allowed freely to fuse with sexuality. That the latter's pervasiveness should make it safe material is another matter.

Another enumeration handles "how great a Share in the Motions and Events of Courts, Councils, and Senates might be challenged by Bawds, Whores, Pimps, Parasites, and Buffoons" (p. 255 [III, viii, 5]), with "Buffoons" as the odd one out. Since the profession of a court jester had not been revived by Charles II after the Interregnum, Gulliver seems to point to the disconnection of politics from whatever reminded rulers of their finiteness, if jocularly so: there simply remain the practical arts of sexual promotion and low entertainment. Similarly, a pyramid of vitiated politics describes how "a Whore can govern the Back-stairs, the Back-stairs a Council, and the Council a Senate" (p. 256 [III, viii, 6]). Besides referring to those stairs used by servants, "Back-stairs" could also mean secret political influence.[44] The mechanical rationality of sexuality provides Gulliver with a moralist's account of the world and enables him, of all men, to identify "the true Causes of many great Events that have surprized the World" (p. 256 [III, viii, 6]).

The first set of oppositions can now be reverted to, pointing as it does to the central conjunction of sodomy and politics, otherwise of individual and community. The jibe at "Chastity to Sodomites" hints at contemporary punishments, including the potentially lethal pillory. "Prostitute Writers," presumably writing for the sake of male patrons and sharing in some guilt by association, ought to be similarly pilloried. One cannot help remembering Swift's scorn for Defoe's stint in the pillory in 1703,[45] even though the connection is tenuous at best. "Some confessed, they owed their Greatness and Wealth to Sodomy," and, it must be added, "Incest" (p. 256 [III, viii, 7]); another instance concerns the frustrated Roman officer who was not preferred to the ship that he regarded as his by right, and whose own ship was "given to a favourite Page of *Publicola* the Vice-Admiral" (pp. 257-58 [III, viii, 9]). Even if sodomy covered all forms of "sexual acts that were regarded as unnatural,"[46] meaning that crimes like "sodomy" or "buggery" were, "as it were, sex-, age- and even species-*neutral* offenses,"[47] such deviant intromission into either

44 Edmund Burke, *Thoughts on the Cause of the Present Discontents* (1770), in *The Works of the Right Honourable Edmund Burke* (London: George Bell and Sons, 1907-10), I, 316.

45 See *A Letter concerning the Sacramental Test* (1709), in *Prose Works*, II, 113 and n: "The Fellow that was *pilloryed*, I have forgot his Name." On the pillory as a deterrent for subversive writers, see Hermann J. Real, "'A Printer brave enough to Venture His Eares': Defoe, Swift, and the Pillory," *Swift Studies*, 25 (2010), 165-66.

46 *Gulliver's Travels*, ed. Ingram, p. 255n2.

47 Martin Bunzl, *Real History: Reflections on Historical Practice* (London and New York: Routledge, 1997), p. 59, drawing from Jeffrey Weeks, *Sex, Politics and Society* (London: Longman, 1989).

male, female, or animal carried unmistakable political and religious implications. Initially a weapon in the Puritans' rhetorical arsenal against James I as well as Charles I and the Established Church, sodomy was then harnessed by Restoration Royalists, including John Dryden, in a wholesale incrimination of Dissenters and Whigs, and even assuming them to worship Satan's anus.[48] That "Chastity to Sodomites" should closely follow on the heels of "Piety to Atheists" confirms Swift's gleeful sensationalism where the (wrong) end of the telescope is voyeuristically applied to the unidentified prone object of contemporary and immediate history.

Obviously, there is a spate of readings positing that Swift was only concerned with a general satire of Mankind,[49] but such standpoints do not really accord with the furore that attended publication and the amusement, even at Court, partly owing to the book's pointed allusions.[50] Indictment of post-1688 Britain appears when Gulliver asks about those who, as his own reading taught him, did "some great Services to Princes and States" (p. 257 [III, viii, 8]). He learns two things from the would-be helpful dead: first, that those "Names were to be found on no Record" (p. 257 [III, viii, 8]) thus proving human history wrong; second, that some of those who had been highly deserving according to traditional historiography were in fact known "as the vilest Rogues and Traitors" (p. 257 [III, viii, 8]), which again nullifies human history, just as does the following information about those servants of the public good who had been committed to the dust heap of history since Gulliver "had never once heard of them" (p. 257 [III, viii, 8]). What follows – "They all appeared with dejected Looks, and in the meanest Habit; most of them telling [Gulliver] that they died in Poverty and Disgrace, and the rest on a Scaffold or a Gibbet" (p. 257 [III, viii, 8]) – not only recalls More's fate but also that of William Sancroft, who lost his archbishopric for refusing to acknowledge William of Orange as King of England. This provides a link with the ups and downs of human history; of note is that the netherworld, for example, strangely echoes changing human outlooks since none among the "*Sextumvirate*" rises in dejection. Implicitly, More

---

48 Ronald Paulson, "Burke's Sublime and the Representation of Revolution," *Culture and Politics from Puritanism to the Enlightenment*, ed. Perez Zagorin (Berkeley: University of California Press, 1980), pp. 241-69 (249); Paul Hammond, "Titus Oates and 'Sodomy,'" *Culture and Society in Britain, 1660-1800*, ed. Jeremy Black (Manchester: Manchester University Press, 1997), pp. 85-101.

49 See Simon Varey's discussion, "Exemplary History and the Political Satire of *Gulliver's Travels*," *The Genres of "Gulliver's Travels"*, ed. Frederik N. Smith (Newark: University of Delaware Press, and London and Toronto: Associated University Presses, 1990), pp. 39-55. A recent assertion along this line is Viviès, *Revenir/Devenir*, p. 50.

50 Downie, *Jonathan Swift*, p. 289; protection came from Henrietta Howard and Princess Caroline (Higgins, *Swift's Politics*, p. 155).

triumphs over Henry VIII who, though previously eulogized as a Protestant hero, had come to acquire a bad name, even with that staunch Whig, Gilbert Burnet, given his confiscation of Church property.[51] As a result, instead of rectifying human prejudices, the dead in Glubbdubdrib stick to the evolution of human outlooks. This may even suggest that, some day, Tory and Jacobite grievances will be recognized as legitimate: William III, then George I, tilted both Church hierarchy and the Lords to serve the exclusive promotion of Whigs in some *ad hoc* repetition of Henry VIII's earlier inglorious moves,[52] but this is just propaganda, or history made serviceable to present-day preoccupations.

There are additional ambiguities surrounding the "*Sextumvirate*" itself. One Publius Valerius, later Publicola, fought alongside Lucius Junius Brutus against the Tarquins at the time of Lucretia's rape and the foundation of the Republic. His name is not numbered among the "*Sextumvirate*" but it emerges through that "*Publicola* the Vice-Admiral" who scandalously promoted his "favourite Page" (pp. 257-58 [III, viii, 9]). The emotional account of the anonymous, gallant officer's heroism and humility, loss of his only son in action and later frustrations[53] is also bound to expose 'modern history' as a web of incompetence and sexual politics. Publicola has been identified as Lucius Gellius Publicola,[54] who was accused of incest with his stepmother, was pro-republican after Caesar's assassination, then betrayed Marcus Junius Brutus and rallied around Octavian and Mark Antony. When the latter two waged war against each other, he sided with Antony and allegedly died during the battle of Actium (31 BC). Mention of that page evokes the real-life accusation of incest, but Publicola's erroneous connection with Octavian, not Antony, may flesh out the earlier allusion to "an Admiral, that for want of proper Intelligence ... beat the Enemy to whom he intended to betray the Fleet" (p. 256 [III, viii, 6]).[55] That was just, so the story went, Edward Russell's conduct previous to the Battle of Barfleur, then the Hogue. One of the Immortal Seven who invited William against James II, Russell (later first Earl of Orford) was reported to have contemplated defection

51 Bernard Cottret, *Henri VIII: le pouvoir par la force* (Paris: Payot, 1999), p. 14. See also Dirk F. Passmann and Heinz J. Vienken, "That 'Hellish Dog of a King': Jonathan Swift and Henry VIII," *Henry VIII in History, Historiography, and Literature*, ed. Uwe Baumann (Frankfurt on Main: Peter Lang, 1992), pp. 241-79.

52 F. P. Lock, *Swift's Tory Politics* (London: Duckworth, 1983), p. 178.

53 Though in more lurid colours, they belong to the same mood as the hermit's life story in Samuel Johnson's *Rasselas* (1759).

54 *Gulliver's Travels*, ed. Ingram, p. 258n.

55 The immediately preceding lines are: "A General confessed in my Presence, that he got a Victory purely by the Force of Cowardice and Ill conduct" (p. 256 [III, viii, 6]). It would be tempting, though unsubstantiated, to think of Marlborough.

to his former king should the Dutch reinforcements not join him in time,[56] and the foggy circumstances may account for Swift's "want of proper Intelligence." If Russell could have taken either side and yet managed to save his career under William, then there is no reason why Lucius Gellius Publicola should not have done the same, matching, though shamefully so, the earlier, and nobler, Publicola's momentary reversals of fortune. Worse still, William himself, that seafarer of 5 November 1688, had at least one "favourite Page" in the person of Arnold Joost van Keppel, whom he later made first Earl of Albemarle and who was "implicated in a homosexual scandal in the late 1690s."[57]

Such far-fetched interpretations, partly based on common anti-William slurs, agree with the more general purposes of Swift's oblique writing under the threat of prosecution, even though his use of the name, Publicola, may simply be the expression of pure delight in antiphrasis. That the paragraph about the officer should follow the general onslaught on "a very modern Period" (p. 256 [III, viii, 7]) signals similar frustrations in the post-Glorious Revolution era, illustrating a reader's reminder that Swift believed in the universality of human nature and in cyclical history.[58] Similarly, those "many parallel Cases in other Countries" (p. 258 [III, viii, 10]) universalize Swift's points about Britain at the same time his fussy delicacy makes his "own Country" the real butt of exposure.

However, interrogating Swift's cautious slurs and just as cautious cover-ups might distract attention from the historiographical import of the passage. He makes Gulliver take to task "the Roguery and Ignorance of those who pretend to write *Anecdotes*, or secret History" and challenges those historians who claim to restore the truth and "have the perpetual Misfortune to be mistaken" (pp. 255-56 [III, viii, 6]). Their accounts teem with sensational information about, say, kings and poison – while Gulliver knows better from Alexander himself – but mostly Gulliver explodes that ancient tradition where raw narratives were enlivened and dramatized by conversations (even if with an eye to plausibility). In this incrimination of "anecdotes," Swift was also targeting Gilbert Burnet's posthumous *History of his Own Time* (published from 1724)[59] –

---

56 Lock, *Swift's Tory Politics*, p. 121; *Gulliver's Travels*, ed. Ingram, p. 256n.

57 Daniel MacLachlan, *An Essay upon Improving and Adding to the Strength of Great Britain and Ireland, by Fornication* (1735), ed. Janine Barchas, in *Eighteenth-Century British Erotica*, Part II, Vol. I, eds Alexander Pettit and Patrick Spedding (London: Pickering and Chatto, 2004), 521.

58 Varey, "Exemplary History and the Political Satire of *Gulliver's Travels*," pp. 41-42.

59 Hammond and Seager, "Jonathan Swift's Historical Novel, *The Memoirs of Capt. John Creichton* (1731)," p. 79: "Reading Burnet rendered Swift sceptical of any naive view that written history was a record of truth based on objective fact." Ingram agrees: "Swift

that Burnet who had been promoted to a bishopric for supporting William and whose *History* boosted his part in the Revolution in a similarly unverifiable manner – as one of "anecdotes." For instance, Burnet posed as a go-between reconciling diffident William and submissive Mary, the latter accepting that "when she became queen her husband must be invested for life with full regal rights" since "the laws of God," subjecting wife to husband, should supersede those of England.[60]

Now, information from a séance is "secret History" par excellence, and most of it boils down to a *reductio adfornicationem*, even *adprostitutionem*. Writers of "secret History" may have been deluding themselves and, most certainly, their readers, but Gulliver's redressing boast can hardly be more reliable. Of course, his alleged "true Causes" provide the titbits that have always made enjoyable reading, including a moralist's ambiguities, but his sweeping pronouncements that money, ambition, and sex rule the world hardly need the props of supernatural confirmation. Similarly, his distinction between "*Infirmities*," such as "Panderism," to which it is "reasonable" to give "due Allowance," trivial and widespread as they are, against the unforgivable ones such as "the prostituting of their own Wives and Daughters" (p. 256 [III, viii, 7]), sounds like a casuist's attempt to differentiate between ordinary, professional "Panderism" and the more sinister devotion of a self-pusher. It may be a token of Gulliver's grim sanity to devise such rungs but, again, supernatural information, while adding weight to ordinary rumour, endangers by such proximity its very superiority as supernatural. Consequently, Gulliver's communication with the "lower World" derives from the bitter frustrations of mere mortals claiming that they know better than the official truths poured onto them.

The real question no longer concerns Gulliver as Swift's political mouthpiece on topical issues but his inability to grasp epistemological issues. His paradoxical achievement is that he helps Swift deflate his Country, or Tory, or crypto-Jacobite positions in the same manner as he does in the Struldbrugg episode, where the immortals' amnesia undermines belief in an immemorial, unwritten constitution. History is just a matter of conflicting *doxas* and is built on thin air alone. An indignant Gulliver is both in the right and vaingloriously myopic, a fact which sheds light on Swift's subtle undercutting of opposition propaganda. Political commitment is a strictly irrational activity that one may be welcome to engage in, but that one should also guard against since it

regarded Burnet's work as made up of gossip, scandals, and anecdotes" (*Gulliver's Travels*, ed. Ingram, p. 255n).

60 Lucile Pinkham, *William III and the Respectable Revolution: The Part Played by William of Orange in the Revolution of 1688* (Cambridge: Harvard University Press, 1954), p. 20.

leads to disregard of the truth at the very moment one boasts of mastering it. It may come to be known in some better world, but that the netherworld of Glubbdubdrib should largely take its cue from the whims and fads among the living seriously casts doubt on the very possibility of attaining the ultimate truth.

The last two paragraphs return to what had been lost sight of, namely "modern History" and, specifically, Britain. In keeping with sexual politics, pre-eminence is given to "the Pox," which has "altered every Lineament of an *English* Countenance" and "shortened the Size of Bodies" (p. 258 [III, viii, 11]), in a resumption of Gulliver's more general remarks about the true provenance of hereditary features. Even that is open to suspicion, vaguely evocative as it is of Nicolas Henrion's account of the reduction of human bodies since Adam.[61] So has the "true Spirit of Liberty" (p. 259 [III, viii, 12]) been lost, in agreement with Country claims, though in such a general manner that Swift's dangerous allusions and mock Publicolan scholarship can easily be put down to the misrepresentation of history coming from that gull, Gulliver himself. What we call independent conjecture are just figments of our imagination. In this, while apparently providing for opposition tastes and expectations, Swift's epistemological points cut Gulliver down to size. The dead converse before him or with him, but there is hardly any re-enactment of their deeds; nothing, for instance, resembling the performance of the actors' re-enacting the murder of Hamlet's father. This performance let the cat out of the bag, but the "words, words, words" of the dead, by courtesy of *Hamlet* (II, 2), have no greater significance than hearsay in the Glubbdubdrib episode.

The epistemological consequences are dramatic. Gulliver's boasted restoration of history does not reach beyond the "practical" history, or "retrospective politics," otherwise "obscene necromancy," pinpointed by Michael Oakeshott.[62] Another reader aptly stresses the contrast between Gulliver's discovery that "most modern history conceals and distorts the truth" and his earlier myopia in Brobdingnag.[63] But the subtext is that any restoration of history is a blind alley. Swift may have hated "secret History" and approved of moral and

---

61 Nicolas Henrion, *Une eschelle chronologique de la difference des tailles humaines depuis la création du monde jusqu'à Jésus Christ* (1718). See William A. Eddy, *Gulliver's Travels: A Critical Study* (New York: Russell and Russell, 1963 [1923]), p. 123. Henrion's book never saw the light of day and is only remembered, putatively, by Gros de Boze's brief summary (Antoine Schnapper, "Persistance des géants," *Annales: Économies, Sociétés, Civilisations*, no 1 [1986], 177-200 [pp. 191-92]).

62 Michael Oakeshott, "The Activity of Being an Historian" (1958), in *Rationalism in Politics and Other Essays*, rev. ed. (Indianapolis: Liberty Press, 1991), pp. 151-83 (181).

63 Varey, "Exemplary History and the Political Satire of *Gulliver's Travels*," p. 47.

exemplary history,[64] but Gulliver's pompous move from one *doxa* to just another, or from an alleged "true history" to "a fable,"[65] simply reveals the general illusions Humankind permanently suffers from. In this, Swift's combination of universality and topicality illustrates the moralist's awareness of Man's finiteness and inability to think things out *sub specie aeternitatis*. If only the dead had remained silent: practitioners in "*the Thing which was not*," they leave us "worse than in Ignorance," to quote those other victims of illusion, Gulliver's cherished Houyhnhnms (p. 296 [IV, iv, 1]) – possibly Swift's oblique recognition that Christianity alone is of value because its ultimate disclosure cannot be communicated to us.

64 Françoise Lapraz-Severino, *Relativité et communication dans les "Voyages de Gulliver" de Jonathan Swift* (Paris: Didier Érudition, 1988), p. 501.

65 See Flavio Gregori's account of Gianni Celati's *Finzoni occidental* (Torino: Einaudi, 1975) in his "The Italian Reception of Swift," *The Reception of Jonathan Swift in Europe*, ed. Hermann J. Real (London: Bloomsbury, 2013 [2005]), pp. 17-56 (50).

Allan Ingram
University of Northumbria at Newcastle

Travels with Horses: Swift, "Bolingbroke" and "Stay-behind's mare"

Abstract. Swift is best known, where horses are concerned, for his creation of the Houyhnhnms in Gulliver's Fourth Voyage. But, at a time when the horse was a major feature of everyday life in most parts of the world, Swift was hardly using something remote from his and others' experience. He was also familiar with works of equine management, including Gervase Markham and such classical texts as Xenophon. Swift had a high regard both for the animal itself and for those who knew how to treat it properly. This essay looks at Swift's prior dealings with horses, from his retirement to Dublin following the death of the Queen in 1714.

These dealings were far from satisfactory. His time in Ireland until the creation of the Houyhnhnms had been a catalogue of promising horses becoming unpromising, mistrust of horse-dealers, and the incompetence his own grooms and servants in dealing with horses. When he began to write the Fourth Voyage, he had a long period of dissatisfaction and disgruntlement behind him, mainly with the management of horses by those who should have known better, and of increasingly impatient aspiration for a good horse. The stage was set for Houyhnhnmland.

To begin, not with *Gulliver's Travels*, but with a poem, here is one that has a horse in it – and a very splendid horse, too. This is "The Grand Question debated WHETHER *Hamilton's Bawn* should be turned into a *Barrack* or a *Malt House*," from 1729. It involves a debate between Sir Arthur Acheson and his wife Lady Anne, who take opposite sides of the question, as to whether the building, owned by Sir Arthur, should become a barracks or a malt-house, she for the former, he, on the grounds of potential financial profitability, the latter. It is one of the Market Hill poems, composed during Swift's long visits there in the wake of the death of Stella and in the course of his intense friendship with Lady Anne Acheson.[1] The speaker here, and for most of the poem, however, is the maid, "*Hannah*," who powerfully (and rather impertinently, given her lowly rank in the household) sides with her ladyship, and in doing so paints a vivid and imaginative picture of "the *Captain*" arriving on horseback "At the Head of his Troop, with Trumpet and Drum":

1 See James Woolley, "Swift's 'Skinnibonia': A New Poem from Lady Acheson's Manuscript," *Reading Swift: Papers from The Fifth Münster Symposium on Jonathan Swift*, ed. Hermann J. Real (Munich: Wilhelm Fink, 2008), pp. 309-42 (329-39).

 | DOI:10.30965/9783846763971_012

> See, now comes the *Captain* all dawb'd with gold Lace:
> O law! the sweet Gentleman! look in his Face;
> And see how he rides like a Lord of the Land,
> With the fine flaming Sword that he holds in his Hand;
> And his Horse, the dear *Creter*, it prances and rears,
> With Ribbins in Knots, at its Tail and its Ears:
> At last comes the Troop, by the Word of Command
> Drawn up in our Court; when the *Captain* cries, STAND.
> Your *Ladyship* lifts up the Sash to be seen,
> (For sure, I had *dizen'd* you out like a *Queen*:)
> The *Captain*, to shew he is proud of the Favour,
> Looks up to your Window, and cocks up his Beaver.
> (His Beaver is cock'd; pray, Madam, mark that,
> For, a *Captain* of Horse never takes off his Hat;
> Because he has never a Hand that is idle;
> For, the Right holds the Sword, and the Left holds the Bridle,)
> Then flourishes thrice his Sword in the Air,
> As a Compliment due to a Lady so fair;
> How I tremble to think of the Blood it hath spilt!
> Then he low'rs down the Point, and kisses the Hilt.[2]

Swift has put this imaginative description into the mouth of a garrulous and, one would have thought, unknowing lady's maid, complete with its military manners and equine detail, someone who quite clearly combines her rank's supposed fascination with the figure of the glamorous and brave soldier with an awareness of the horsemanship necessary for both the Captain's figure and his effective operation. Such awareness should have been more at home coming from Sir Arthur himself, who has the knightly rank to support it. The Dean, meanwhile, whose opinion of horses and horsemanship this actually is, is reduced to not even a walk-on role. He and his clerical kind are a topic for mockery at the imagined dinner table conversation ("'But, Z[ound]s, by their Looks, they never keep Lent,"' says the Captain [l. 146]), and is only heard from off-stage at the end – "Till she heard the *Dean* call, *Will your Ladyship walk?*" (l. 180), which produces from her Ladyship the firm instruction to "*Hannah*": "For your Life, not a Word of the Matter, I charge ye" (l. 189). As Lady Anne, who clearly knows the Dean of old, adds:

> But the *Dean*, if this Secret shou'd come to his Ears,
> Will never have done with his Gibes and his Jeers. (ll. 187-88)

2 *Poems*, ed. Williams, III, 870-71, ll. 93-112. All quotations are from this edition and will appear within parentheses in the text.

The supreme irony of the scene, then, amongst the many adjacent ironies, is that Hannah's opinion of horsemanship and the handling of horses is exactly Swift's own, albeit his role in the poem is as a self-obsessed sponger whose stock-in-trade is tiresome mockery of the woman he is obsessed with. Swift, as several writers on the topic have pointed out,[3] was himself an excellent horseman with firm opinions, rooted in real knowledge and experience, of dealing with horses, from their purchase to their feed, their ailments and their handling. Unlike "*Hannah*," who might not even have been literate, he had read, indeed owned, some of the most authoritative works on farriery, and on horsemanship, from Xenophon to Gervase Markham (1568-1637), whose *Master-Piece Containing All Knowledge Belonging to the Smith, Farrier, or Horse-Leach, Touching the Curing of All Diseases in Horses* had been compiled from his own and a wide range of sources and was first printed in 1610. Swift's library included one of the many editions (seventeen between 1610 and 1710, by one authoritative source) published over the next century.[4] The work contained, certainly, a multitude of details about day-to-day care for horses, about which Swift was very knowledgeable and very concerned, but Markham also had things to say about the temperaments, humours, and spirits of horses, about what constitutes a well-shaped horse, and about how to ensure loyalty in your animal, how to "make a Horse to follow his Master."[5] Of the horse's shape, for example, he begins his second book with general advice to the farrier about equine proportion, the "true and well-formed Body":

> I think it meetest that I begin with the true proportion and measure which is required in every Member of a well-shaped Horse, that the careful Farrier thereby understanding how, and in what fashion every Lineament should be placed, or what proportion and quantity they do contain, he may at no time through ignorance either dismember or disgrace the same: as I have many times seen simple Farriers do.[6]

---

3 See Ehrenpreis, *Dean Swift*, pp. 431-32; Michael DePorte, "Swift's Horses of Instruction," *Reading Swift: Papers from The Second Münster Symposium on Jonathan Swift*, eds Richard H. Rodino and Hermann J. Real, with the assistance of Helgard Stöver-Leidig (Munich: Wilhelm Fink, 1993), pp. 199-211; Hermann J. Real, "Swift Horsing Around: or, The Madness of Reason," "*... that I wished myself a horse": The Horse as Representative of Cultural Change in Systems of Thought*, ed. Sonja Fielitz (Heidelberg: Winter, 2015), pp. 61-81.

4 Passmann and Vienken II, 1197-98.

5 It is unknown which of the editions published between 1610 and 1720, when Swift embarked on the composition of *Gulliver's Travels*, was in his library. Quotations are from the Ehrenpreis Centre edition of Gervase Markham, *Markham's Master-Piece* (London: Thomas Passenger, 1675), p. 381.

6 *Markham's Masterpiece*, p. 160.

The horse, in other words, is capable of physical perfection – and "*the Perfection of Nature*," we must remember, is what we are told is the etymological derivation for "Houyhnhnm" in Part Four of *Gulliver's Travels*.[7] For Markham, it is the responsibility of those who care for horses to recognize this capacity and to preserve it, rather than to amend or spoil it. Equally, there are important points to observe when buying a horse, if one is to supply oneself with the best possible mount: "a comely well proportioned Head, with an out looking eye, good well raised shoulders, and a thick large breast, broad brawn, large and broad flat Leggs, short Pasterns, and little feet." Age and temperament, too, are key factors in making a wise purchase: "Put your hand before his Eyes, to know if he see well, look into his Mouth for his age: if he be past eight years old, feel all down the strunt of his Tayl with your hand, and … if it have any rough knobs towards the end, buy him not, for his good dayes are past;" while "If he turn up the white of his Eye, or lay his Ear to his Neck when he is ridden, he is a sullen Jade, and full of naughty qualities."[8] Throughout his book, too, Markham is very ready to castigate those who work with horses for not being aware of the kind of knowledge and expertise he here regards as essential: it is "Ignorance," "Sloth," and "Folly," for example, that prevents people from discerning, or mistaking, the many "sorts of Fevers" he has described in detail; it was "the Ignorance of our old Farriers" that prevented their recognizing the disease "Foundring;" the "*greedy Worm*" similarly goes unmarked because "most of our Horse Masters being of great ignorance, hold it a special vertue to see a Horse eat eagerly;" again, a horse may be wounded "by the ignorance of any unskilful Farrier that letteth him Blood;" and he speaks, finally, in his "Postscript" of those "many illiterate Farriers, who are not Book-learned, and therefore have no more knowledge than Horses themselves, but are subject through their Ignorance to run into many gross Errors."[9] In short, it is often the incompetence of those who should know better that is responsible for the ailments, suffering, and even deaths of horses.

Markham's Preface, or rather his "Admonition to the Reader," sets the minutely detailed knowledge and advice that follows in a context of obligation and fitness that Swift clearly appreciated: "I can give the Reader," Markham declares,

> no better a Reason to persuade him to read my Book, than to shew him the real use of Horses, well managed, according to the Rules of Horsemanship … and a

7 Jonathan Swift, *Gulliver's Travels*, ed. Allan Ingram (Peterborough, Ontario: Broadview, 2012), p. 291 and n2.

8 *Markham's Masterpiece*, p. 154.

9 *Markham's Masterpiece*, pp. 92, 94, 408.

> great pity it is, that such an excellent Beast should anyway miscarry for want of knowing his natural Diseases, and the Cure thereof.
>
> I have now made the Souldier and all others, Masters of Art in the Cures of their Horses, if Farriers be failing to advise and consider with them: For it is a Knowledge fit for a Gentleman, both in Peace and War, to be able to cure the Diseases incident to his Horses.[10]

Soldiers, like the Captain; gentlemen, like Sir Arthur; and, we take it, reading between the lines of "The Great Debate," deans like Swift himself, should be allowed no excuses if they fail to be as much masters of horses as they are of riding and of equine deportment.

If we look back, beyond Markham, to his acknowledged predecessor Xenophon (and Swift owned two editions of his surviving works, *Quæ exstant opera*, both in Greek and Latin),[11] we find even more stress on a gentleman's responsibilities as an owner and rider of horses. Xenophon certainly pays attention to the groom's education, including how to avoid creating sores with the halter, how to fit the muzzle, and of course the sequence and method of grooming,[12] but ultimately it all comes back to the owner and user, rather than his employee, because it is first and foremost "the mark of a good horseman … to see that his groom, like himself, is instructed in the way in which he should treat the horse [videtur etiam nobis viri equestris esse, vt equisonem edoctum habeat, quomodo cum equo sit agendum]."[13] Successive chapters deal with buying the horse, the proper build and proportions of the horse, training an unbroken colt, the placing and arrangement of the stable, and exercise and feeding. Such matters, though, are addressed not, as in Markham, partly to farriers and grooms, but wholly to the master, the one who will ride the horse, doubtlessly, in the period in which Xenophon was writing, ride him to war, and who will also, where appropriate, need to appear to his best advantage in the saddle. A good proportion of the text, too, is devoted to horsemanship, from mounting ("When he has made his spring in order to mount, he should

---

10 *Markham's Masterpiece*, sig. a3r.

11 PASSMANN AND VIENKEN III, 1985-86.

12 Xenophon, "On the Art of Horsemanship [De re equestri]," in *Scripta minora*, trans. E. C. Marchant (Cambridge, Massachusetts, and London: Harvard University Press, 1968 [1925]), pp. 313-21. Subsequent quotations are from this edition and will be given within parentheses in the text. The Latin quotations accompanying the English translation reproduce the prose paraphrase in the Ehrenpreis Centre copy of the 1625 Paris edition of Xenophon's complete works, which was one of the two editions in Swift's library (see note 11). Readers are thus given the chance to read the same text the Dean is bound to have read.

13 Xenophon, "On the Art of Horsemanship," p. 317 (p. 938D [V, 1]).

raise his body with his left hand, while at the same time he helps himself up by stretching out his right; for by mounting in this way he will not present an awkward appearance even from behind by bending his leg [posteaquam ad conscensum se leuiorem reddiderit, sinistra corpus subleuet; simul dextram extendens, se sustollat. Nam ita conscendens, ne quidem à tergo deforme spectaculum exhibebit]"),[14] to posture once mounted ("We would not have him sit as if he were on a chair, but as though he were standing upright with his legs astride [non laudamus sessionem, qualis est in sella; sed eam, quæ cruribus diuaricatis equitem velut erigit]"),[15] to handling as a rider ("The exercise that we recommend is the one called the ring, since it accustoms the horse to turn on both jaws [eam vero laudamus equorum agitationem, quæ pedicæ nomen habet. Nam adsuefacit equos, vt ab vtraque maxillarum parte convertantvr]"),[16] and finally to dismounting ("When the time has come to dismount, the rider must never dismount among other horses or near a group of people or outside the riding-ground; but let the place where the horse is forced to work be the place where he also receives his reward of ease [vbi iam descendendi tempus erit, non hoc fiat inter equos, nec iuxta cœtum aliquem hominum, nec extra spatium agitationis: sed quo loco laborem equus perferre cogitur, ibidem & requiete potiatur]").[17] Most notably, though, not least for Swift's "Great Debate," or rather for Hannah's imagination, is what Xenophon then goes on to say about style. There is the "proud and stately style," the secret of which is the handling of the bit, which should be used first to seem to restrain the horse while also driving him forwards, and then suddenly slackened off:

> But if, when he is thus excited, you give him the bit, then, mistaking the looseness of the bit for a deliverance from restraint, he bounds forward for very joy with a proud bearing and supple legs, exultant, imitating exactly in every way the graces that he displays before horses. And those who watch the horse when he is like that call him well-bred, a willing worker, worth riding, mettlesome, magnificent, and declare his appearance to be at once pleasing and fiery. [At si quis equo sic excitato frænum concesserit, ibi præ gaudio, ob laxitatem se lupis liberatum existimet, glorioso quodam gestu, cruribusque mollibus exsultabundus fertur, & in omnibus exprimit elegantiam illam, cum qua solet equos alios adire. Ac talem qui spectant equum, & liberalem adpellant, & spontaneum, & equestrem, & animosum, & fastuosum, simulque iucundum & terribilem adspectu.] [18]

14 Xenophon, "On the Art of Horsemanship," p. 329 (942B [VII, 2]).
15 Xenophon, "On the Art of Horsemanship," p. 329 (942D [VII, 5]).
16 Xenophon, "On the Art of Horsemanship," p. 333 (943C [VII, 13]).
17 Xenophon, "On the Art of Horsemanship," p. 335 (944B [VII, 19]).
18 Xenophon, "On the Art of Horsemanship," p. 353 (950A [X, 16-17]).

A horse owned "for parade [equo ad pompas idoneo]," equally, should have "plenty of spirit and a strong body [existere prius animum in eo magnum, & robustum corpus]," but again by dextrous use of the bit he can be made by the skilful rider to raise himself to show his "belly and sheath" so that "he may appear to the onlookers to be doing willingly the finest things that a horse can do [hæc vero quum facit, frænum ei remittendum est; vt quæ pulcherrima præstantur ab equo, & faciat lubens, & ita facere iudicio spectatorum existimetur]."[19] If the owner is commander of a troop or regiment of cavalry, moreover, warns Xenophon, "he must not make it his object to be the one brilliant figure, but must attach much more importance to making the whole troop behind him worth looking at [quod si contingat alicui, talem equum nancto, vel tribunatus, vel equitum magisterium; non hoc dumtaxat eniti debet, vt solus ipse sit splendidus, sed multo magis vt comitatum vniversum spectatu dignum exhibeat]."[20] Xenophon concludes:

> If a man buys his horses well, trains them so that they can stand work, and uses them properly in the training for war, in the exhibition rides and on the battle-fields, what is there then to hinder him from making horses more valuable than they are when he takes them over, and why should he not be the owner of famous horses, and also become famous himself for his horsemanship, provided no divine power prevents? [Si denique feliciter equum aliquis emerit, ad laborum tolerantiam educarit, eodem recte tum in exercitiis ad actiones bellicas, tum in agitationibus ad ostentationem comparatis, & in prœliorum certaminibus vtatur: quid huic obstare possit amplius, quominus equos pretij maioris efficat, quam eos acceperit; ac tum probatos habeat, tum ipse rei equestris gloria floreat, nisi diuinitus impediatur?][21]

Or, to bring things up to Swift's own time, the interposition of some men.

Donna Landry, in her *Noble Brutes: How Eastern Horses Transformed English Culture*, cites Xenophon on the relation between horse and rider, the nobility of one shared with the other, and vice versa. She takes the argument an important stage further, though, by drawing attention to the traditional symbolic significance of that relationship, quoting Sir Philip Sidney's *Arcadia*, where he makes the key suggestion "that it seemed, as he borrowed the horse's body, so he lent the horse his mind." Landry comments:

> The art of horsemanship as an exercise in negotiation rather than coercion could hardly be more persuasively described. In "riding the great horse" in the manège or indoor school, such a sympathetic form of communication was meant to

19 Xenophon, "On the Art of Horsemanship," pp. 353 (950C [XI, 3]).
20 Xenophon, "On the Art of Horsemanship," p. 357 (951B [XI, 10-11]).
21 Xenophon, "On the Art of Horsemanship," pp. 357-59 (951D-E [XI, 13]).

> develop between horse and rider that it would be as if some peculiar osmosis had occurred. The horse would have allowed his body to be "borrowed" by the rider, and the rider in turn would have "lent" his mind to the horse. The rider commands, expresses "sovereignty," but by commuting the horse's will into the virtue of a beautiful performance. This exhibition of the horse's intrinsic beauty and nobility can only be achieved through sympathetic or empathetic rather than violent means.[22]

And she broadens the nature of this symbolic potential:

> In short, horses were property. Yet horses were also powerfully symbolic. To ride a horse well was to possess the virtues necessary for social authority and even political rule. Commanding a horse required both technical skills and an ability to reason with a creature that embodied the passions but showed signs of being capable of a degree of reason. Indeed, in the later seventeenth and early eighteenth centuries the horse began to figure as an idealized version of the human self.[23]

The horse, more specifically, as Michael DePorte reminds us,[24] has long stood not just as an exemplar of animal beauty and proportion, or indeed of the human self, but as a metaphor for imagination and, more specifically, for poetic inspiration. Horses, for example, "are an especially potent symbol of poetic genius in *The Battle of the Books*, where an essential part of the unflattering comparison of Moderns to Ancients has to do with horseflesh" – the bulky but ill-conditioned mounts of Moderns like Davenant and Dryden as opposed to the vigorous and fiery horses of Homer, Lucan, and Virgil, who alone as riders are capable of handling such creatures.[25] In harmony with its rider, then, the perfect coordination between man and beast, the horse had come to represent the proper balance between reason and imagination. Swift, in "The Great Debate" and in innumerable other instances in his works, is drawing on, and playing with, and of course undermining, this familiar figure, appropriately for someone with so deep an appreciation of a good horse.

However, for a man so alert to everything to do with horses, including their metaphoric values, and, as he frequently wrote to Stella and to others, to the

22 Donna Landry, *Noble Brutes: How Eastern Horses Transformed English Culture* (Baltimore: The Johns Hopkins University Press, 2009), pp. 26-27. The reference to Sir Philip Sidney is from Book Two and can be found in *The Countess of Pembroke's Arcadia* (1590), ed. Ernest A. Baker (London: George Routledge and Sons, 1907) p. 148. I am indebted to Leigh Wetherall-Dickson for drawing Landry's work to my attention.

23 Landry, *Noble Brutes*, p. 16.

24 DePorte, "Swift's Horses of Instruction," pp. 199-211.

25 DePorte, "Swift's Horses of Instruction," p. 203.

health benefits of riding, Swift for a critical part of his life had extremely bad luck with his own horses. The period in question was from his return to Ireland in 1714 on the death of Queen Anne, and it lasted for over seven years, up to and including the writing of much of *Gulliver's Travels*, though we can see it beginning even earlier, as he travels to Holyhead in the summer of 1713 on his way to Dublin to be installed as Dean of St Patrick's. He writes to Stella on 6 June, from Chester:

> Having not used riding these 3 years, made me terribly weary; yet I resolve on Monday to sett out for Holyhead, weary as I am ... I will come when God Pleases, perhaps I may be with you in a week: I will be 3 days going to Holyhead; I cannot ride faster; say [what you] will. I am upon Stay-behind's mare.[26]

Here the fault would seem, to Swift's mind, to be in both rider, through lack of recent practice, and in horse, from simply being not a particularly speedy horse: the very antithesis, perhaps, of Hannah's Captain and his "dear *Creter*." If Swift and "Stay-behind's mare" are to be representative of the perfect coordination between man and beast, then it is a very sad comment on both of them.

Swift's horse problems began in earnest, though, with his permanent return to Dublin in late August 1714. One horse that he had brought with him from England in 1713, was "Bolingbroke," so called, it is assumed, because he was a gift from the Viscount. (Indeed, Michael DePorte suggests that "by naming his horse 'Bolingbroke'" he would be able to "exercise the authority he would have liked to exercise over his mercurial friend."[27]) The horse had been in Dublin for the past year. David Woolley, in fact, believes that "Bolingbroke" and "Stay-behind's mare" are one and the same, notwithstanding the obvious gender difference: perhaps in referring to a male horse as a "mare," Swift in this case would be deliberately compounding the "Stay-behind" insult. Certainly, Vanessa wrote from London to Swift on 6 June 1713, as he was riding to Chester, asking "how does Bolinbroke performe."[28] Presumably, therefore, "Bolingbroke" had been a good mount once, but accidents prevented him from being so any longer. Swift writes on 27 September 1714 that his "English horse was so ill I was forced to send him to Grass." This is no doubt connected to the additional problems he was having in finding both hay for feeding his horses and a good and reliable groom to look after them. In the same letter (to Knightley Chetwode), Swift

---

26 Jonathan Swift, *Journal to Stella*, ed. Harold Williams, 2 vols (Oxford: Clarendon Press, 1948), II, 670-71.

27 DePorte, "Swift's Horses of Instruction," p. 206.

28 *Correspondence*, ed. Woolley, I, 502 and n5. All further quotations are from this edition and appear in parentheses within the text.

complains that "I want a stock of Hay, and I cannot get any … I can neither get Hay nor Horse, and the Season of the former is going" (*Correspondence*, II, 83), while on 6 October, also to Chetwode, he complains of his groom: "I have got in Hay; but my Groom offended against the very letter of a Proverb, and stackt it in a rainy day, so that it is now smoaking like a Chimny." "My Stable," he adds, "is a very Hospitall for sick Horses" (II, 85). This, perhaps, is the same "Scotch groom" who, as Swift informs Chetwode on 20 October, "ran away from [him] ten days ago & robbed [him] & several of the neighbourhood" (II, 89). "Bolingbroke" was eventually passed on to Archdeacon Thomas Walls, the Master of the Free School of St Patrick's and a friend of Swift,[29] but not before he had been involved in an episode that was as outrageous, to a man who took horses as seriously as Swift did, as it was absurd – though the horse, disappointing as he might have become by this time, was entirely blameless.

This was the well-known drunken ride which, as Swift described to Walls the following day, took place on Sunday, 26 December 1714. Swift was riding with Tom, his footman, on "Bolingbroke," and Will, his then groom, from Dublin to Belcamp, a little to the north of the city, across the ferry over the Liffey and along the Strand. Swift writes:

> I was forced to come back to the Deanry for something I had forgot. It was near 3 before I crosst the Ferry. There Tom and the Groom waited, and my Horses were standing at a Shop where Brandy is sold: at the door of it, I used to take Horse. I observed the 2 Loobyes put on my Cloak the wrong side outwards, and I found Will was drunk: I rode on, and found Tom did not come up, I stayd, he galloped up; I chid him, he answered foolishly, he was drunk as a Dog, tottered on his Horse, could not keep the way, sometimes into the sea, then back to me, swore he was not drunk. I bid him keep on, lasht him as well as I could, then he vowed he was drunk, fell a crying, came back every moment to me. I bid him keep on, at last with galloping and turning backwards & forwards Bolingbroke grew mad, & threw him down, I came up, & called a Boy and Man to get the Horse from him, he resisted us all 3, was stark mad with drink, at last we got the Bridle from him, the Boy mounted, and away we rode, Tom following after us; What became of him I know not, I fancyed he would reel hither.[30] (*Correspondence*, II, 105-6)

Significantly, it is Will, the groom, who is dismissed, while Tom, as Woolley suggests, "was ultimately forgiven" (II, 106n2). The behaviour of each was foolish, but in the case of a groom, one assumes, Swift considered it intolerable for

29 See *Correspondence*, ed. Woolley, II, 154 and n1.

30 See also Ehrenpreis, *Dean Swift*, pp. 34-35.

him to have been drunk with responsibility for creatures as valuable and as important as horses.

Swift's groom problems, clearly, were severe. His horse problems also continued unabated. "I am here at the Fair," he wrote from Trim to Walls in June 1715, "to buy a Horse, but cannot succeed" (II, 128). He complains in December 1716 that one of his horses has been so "lamed" by Gillespy, his steward, that "it will be never good for any thing" (II, 197-98), and declares a week or so later, again to Walls, that he needs to find "another Horse" (II, 208). At Trim, by the end of the following month, he writes that "My Horses [are] the Drs" – that is, Dr Anthony Raymond, the Rector of Trim (II, 222). He is still unable to obtain decent horses of his own in February 1719, writing to Charles Ford: "This whole Kingdom will not afford me the medicine of an unfoundred trotting Horse" (II, 290), though by May, in Laracor, he has "bought a Horse," but "at a great Price" (II, 301). A year later, however, he again complains – and summarizes:

> I hunted four years for horses, gave 26*l*. for one of three years and a half old, have been eighteen months training him, and when he just grew fit to ride, behold my groom gives him a strain in the shoulder, he is rowelled, and gone to grass.

He adds, in frustration, "Shew me a misfortune greater in its kind" (II, 333). The same complaint, amplified and extended, follows in June 1721:

> I have been 7 years getting a Horse and have lost 100ll by buying without Success. Sheridan has got his Horses again – and I recovered one that my Servt had lost – Every body can get Horses but I. (II, 383)

By October, he is speaking of his "weak horses" (II, 401), and in January 1722 laments that he is "as much at a loss for one as ever, and so I fear shall continue till my riding days are over" (II, 411). Swift, clearly, would have concurred with the sentiment expressed by Nathaniel Harley, uncle to Edward, the future second Earl, and a merchant in Aleppo, who was a main figure in the introduction of the Arabian horse into Britain. Harley wrote to his brother in 1705: "Next to choosing a Wife for a man, The most difficult thing is to please him with a Horse."[31]

From 1714 to 1721, from sluggish horses, to drunken grooms; from grooms and stewards (to say nothing of farriers and "Horse-Masters") who lame or strain previously good horses, to soaking wet hay and sick mounts; from grooms that

31 Nathaniel Harley to Edward 'Auditor' Harley, 29 December 1705, British Library, Add. MSS 70143, 179v. Cited by Landry, *Noble Brutes*, p. 107.

turn thief, to markets bereft of decent horses at a decent price; finally, frustrated, angry, losing faith in both the availability of his (and Hannah's) admired animals and the utter incapacity of the men who were supposed to assume responsibility for them, Swift was ready to write Part Four of *Gulliver's Travels*, the very consummation of his feelings and experience of horses over the time he had been back in Ireland. "The most important thing about Houyhnhnms as horses," Michael DePorte writes, "is also the most obvious: they are horses without riders."[32] To go further, they are without grooms, drunken or otherwise, without stewards, indeed without Mankind at all: they simply do not need us. Not only does this underline Gulliver's and our complete redundancy in Houyhnhnmland, but it also draws unavoidable attention to how much we, in Swift's time at least, needed the horse, be it in contemporary Ireland, or England, or in fictitious Lilliput, Brobdingnag, and still-to-be-written Laputa, in all of which the relation to horses is just as in the world outside the pages of the book. In none of these worlds could man exist without the horse, but in Houyhnhnmland Humankind is quite irrelevant. It is seen by the Houyhnhnms themselves as on a level with the Yahoos, indeed as being virtually indistinguishable from Yahoos, whose possible extermination, of course, is debated by the Houyhnhnm General Assembly (IV, ix, 3). The Houyhnhnm Master cannot even see how a creature such as Gulliver is able to exist, having no physical characteristics that are worth anything in terms of survival, let alone be capable of exercising control over the horses of his native land. In fact, from the Houyhnhnm perspective, Mankind has no point at all. If Part Four, then, effectively demolishes any inclination we have to see the man/horse relationship as a metaphor for perfect human/animal coordination, or for ideal beauty, or for poetic inspiration (and we must remember the excellence Gulliver claims for Houyhnhnm poetry),[33] it also counters, as has been argued, our assumption that Man is in any way the custodian of reason.[34] Indeed, with this in mind, and with hindsight of the whole voyage, perhaps the most damning statement in Part Four of this damning book is Gulliver's opening remark to the first two Houyhnhnms he encounters, made in the desperation of trying to deduce where on earth he is and what on earth is going on:

> Upon the Strength of this Reasoning, I ventured to address them in the following Manner: Gentlemen, if you be Conjurers, as I have good Cause to believe, you can understand any Language; therefore I make bold to let your Worships

32 DePorte, "Swift's Horses of Instruction," p. 204.

33 See DePorte, "Swift's Horses of Instruction," p. 206.

34 Real, "Swift Horsing Around: or, The Madness of Reason," pp. 13-18.

> know, that I am a poor distressed *Englishman*, driven by his Misfortunes upon your Coast; and I entreat one of you, to let me ride upon his Back, as if he were a real Horse, to some House or Village, where I can be relieved. In return of which Favour, I will make you a Present of this Knife and Bracelet.[35]

Few more inappropriate openings could be imagined, and few worse attempts to exercise the human capacity for reason.

He is, of course, politely ignored.

35 *Gulliver's Travels*, ed. Ingram, pp. 282-83 (IV, i, 8).

Florian Klaeger
Universität Bayreuth

Thalesian Lessons: Mad Astronomers in British Fiction of the Long Eighteenth Century

Abstract. Taking its cue from the representation of astronomy in Book Three of *Gulliver's Travels* and versions of Thales of Miletus' stargazing accident circulating in eighteenth-century England, this essay examines 'mad' astronomers in fictions of the long eighteenth century. In Margaret Cavendish's *The Blazing World*, Swift's Voyage to Laputa, Charlotte Lennox's *The Female Quixote*, Dr Johnson's *Rasselas*, and Mary Shelley's *The Last Man*, it explores the links that stargazers establish between reason, represented by the practice of astronomy as a 'pure' observational science, and the imagination, represented by madness and fiction. Either overly cerebral or motivated by the most basic drives, fictional astronomers hold up for consideration various kinds of madness that offer insight into the developing relationship between science and the imagination, and in particular the legitimacy and dangers of fictionalizing.

The Academy of Lagado represents, in Allan Ingram's penetrating analysis, an anatomy of mental illness in that it "not only distinguishes" but actually classifies madness, "room from room, experiment from experiment, obsession from obsession": "This is madness isolated, identified and pinned down to single meaning: Gulliver and reader move between delusions, resisting the seduction of each in turn, passing on secure in seeing each insanity safely contained within the mental space appropriate for it."[1] Concerning the episode's attitude towards science, Gregory Lynall has shown that the satire in the Academy is not merely concerned with "making a distinction between pure and applied disciplines, or between abstraction and common sense," but that for Swift, the practical application of "the new sciences" always entails "political, social, and moral choices" examined in this episode.[2] By juxtaposing these two points, we can see that one dimension of this episode – the focus on science and its application – aims at opening up discourse (from science to politics, society, and morals); the other – the focus on madness – shows how, to a chilling effect, discourse is closed down (from exuberance and variety to taxonomy and

1 Allan Ingram and Michelle Faubert, *Cultural Constructions of Madness in Eighteenth-Century Writing: Representing the Insane* (Houndmills, Basingstoke, Hampshire: Palgrave Macmillan, 2005), p. 13.

2 Gregory Lynall, *Swift and Science: The Satire, Politics, and Theology of Natural Knowledge, 1690-1730* (Houndmills, Basingstoke, Hampshire: Palgrave Macmillan, 2012), p. 109.

 | DOI:10.30965/9783846763971_013

pathology). Both Ingram and Lynall have also contextualized the catalogue of mad scientific pursuits in the Academy: in biographical terms by reference to Swift's friend and 'longitude lunatic' Joseph Beaumont, who took his own life around the time of the composition of *Gulliver's Travels*,[3] and in intertextual terms by reference to the contemporary medical discourse on madness and poetic representations of visits to Bethlehem Royal Hospital (also known as Bethlem Royal Hospital or Bedlam).[4] In eighteenth-century satire in general, as Allan Ingram has written, madness is often employed "for its capacity to reveal a moral meaning":

> The eighteenth century's obsession with madness was not, in fact, simply the desire to silence the alternative discourses of unreason. Behind the impulse to restrain was a very real fear of the terrifying proximity of insanity. The satirists' preoccupation with the difference between outside and inside easily translates into the pressing need to distinguish between sane and insane. The novelists' interests in narrative and character are attempts to find meaning and consistency in human consciousness and identity.[5]

Discussing the Scriblerians' treatment of longitude projectors – a specific kind of mad scientist, one might say – Lynall has written that "their writings reflected and shaped intellectual, moral and cultural questions ... concerning the validation and commodification of technological improvement" and that the "cultural prominence of longitude proposals also gave the Scriblerians license to pursue their own projecting imaginations, inhabiting the project-genre parodically for satiric, but also whimsical purposes."[6] It is these kinds of intersection and mutual appropriation between meaning-making in the domains of science and literature that I want to trace in the following by using Laputa as a key example. Its occupants are, by far, not the only contemplators of the heavens in eighteenth-century fiction to be mentally disturbed, and I want to explore the links such fictional 'mad' stargazers construct between reason, represented by the practice of astronomy as a 'pure' observational science, and the imagination, represented by lunacy and fiction. It appears that stargazing, as

3 See, in addition to Lynall, *Swift and Science*, pp. 92-93, Gregory Lynall, "Scriblerian Projections of Longitude: Arbuthnot, Swift, and the Agency of Satire in a Culture of Invention," *Journal of Literature and Science*, 7, no 2 (2014), 1-18.

4 See Ingram and Faubert, *Cultural Constructions of Madness in Eighteenth-Century Writing*, p. 13. See also Michael V. DePorte, *Nightmares and Hobbyhorses: Swift, Sterne, and Augustan Ideas of Madness* (San Marino: The Huntington Library, 1974), pp. 3-53 (3-6).

5 Allan Ingram, *The Madhouse of Language: Writing and Reading Madness in the Eighteenth Century* (London and New York: Routledge, 1991), p. 12.

6 Lynall, "Scriblerian Projections of Longitude: Arbuthnot, Swift, and the Agency of Satire in a Culture of Invention," p. 12.

a practice that exposes the mind to danger through the contemplation of specific objects or ideas, is connected with 'errors of the imagination' that induce, or signal, some kind of madness. So the question is what kinds of madness we encounter in astronomers, and what reasons are offered for them: Does astronomical observation make people mad, or do individuals prone to madness choose to practice astronomy? How is the proximity between this 'science' and madness constructed and functionalized? In particular, what uses does this kind of madness linked to the imagination have in fiction? Is there a metafictional element to the mad astronomer as a character?

The three domains of madness, astronomy, and poetry entertained strong mutual bonds in eighteenth-century Britain: the mad astronomer in the final plate of Hogarth's *Rake's Progress* (original 1735, revised 1763) has justly been described as "the century's most abiding image of insanity in confinement."[7] According to the conventional classical idea of the *furor poeticus*, there was a particular proximity between the poet and the lunatic.[8] What is more, the task of the eighteenth-century fiction writer has been described as being "a *scientist of the interior self* who penetrated the psyche's entrails: a Newton of the mind, as it were, dissecting human nature ... with the same precision as the natural philosopher charting the physical world."[9] Fictional observers of earth's 'outside,' and of other worlds, raise questions about the interplay between the object of observation and its observer which apply not only to the

7 Ingram and Faubert, *Cultural Constructions of Madness in Eighteenth-Century Writing*, p. 177.

8 Porter traces the commonplace first and foremost to the *Symposium*, where "Plato had imagined the poet as a man filled with 'afflatus' (the divine breath) or 'divine fury'" (Roy Porter, *Mind-Forg'd Manacles: A History of Madness in England from the Restoration to the Regency* [London: Penguin, 1987], p. 21). Another *locus classicus* for the link between madness and poetry is Plutarch's dialogue on love, which differentiates between "a certain Madness transmitted from the Body to the Soul, proceeding from a malignant Mixture of ill Humours, or a noxious Vapour, or rather pernicious Spirit, that possesses the Heart; which Madness is a rugged and terrible Disease" and a "sort of *Enthusiasm*, which is proper to the Muses, which possessing an even temper'd and placid Soul, excites and rouses up the Gifts of Poetry and Music" (Plutarch, *Plutarch's Morals ... Translated from the Greek, by Several Hands*, 5 vols [London: W. Taylor, 1718], IV, 277-78). Perhaps the best-known native re-statement is Theseus' in *A Midsummer Night's Dream*: "The lunatic, the lover, and the poet / Are of imagination all compact ... / The poet's eye, in a fine frenzy rolling, / Doth glance from heaven to earth, from earth to heaven; / And as imagination bodies forth / The forms of things unknown, the poet's pen / Turns them to shapes, and gives to airy nothing / A local habitation and a name" (William Shakespeare, *A Midsummer Night's Dream*, ed. Sukanta Chaudhuri [London and New York: Bloomsbury Arden Shakespeare, 2017], 5.1.7-8, 12-17).

9 George S. Rousseau, "Science, Culture, and the Imagination: Enlightenment Configurations," in *Eighteenth-Century Science*, The Cambridge History of Science, ed. Roy Porter (Cambridge: Cambridge University Press, 2003), pp. 762-99 (770-71).

reader of the sidereal text, but also to readers and writers of the psyche in and through fiction. The telescope *and* the pen appear as instruments that reduce the distance between man and nature, but at the same time, they threaten to distort reality in the process of representation to a degree that threatens sanity. In this spirit, I am interested in the parallels between judgements passed on the sanity of astronomers and of poets, and the attitudes these judgements express towards the imagination.

1. Madness and Poetry

The eighteenth century conceptualized madness as "an extremely broad sociocultural category"[10] encompassing a range of troubles from mental to physical causes and from the classic melancholic to the violent raver, as emblematized by the two famous figures over the gate to Bedlam, created by Colley Cibber's father in the late seventeenth century. "All agreed that it was of the essence of lunacy to be visible, and known by its appearance," Roy Porter writes. "Madness advertised itself in a proliferation of symptoms, in gait, in physiognomy, in weird demeanour and habits."[11] The precise nature of how mind and body interacted in madness was a matter of much debate.[12] As William Battie (1703-76), one of the most influential writers on the subject in the eighteenth century, commented, there were two "species" of madness that differed by their causes:

> The first is solely owing to an internal disorder of the nervous substance: the second is likewise owing to the same nervous substance being indeed in like manner disordered, but disordered *ab extra*; and therefore is chiefly to be attributed to some remote and accidental cause. The first species, until a better name can be found, may be called *Original*, the second may be called *Consequential Madness*.[13]

Battie was thus interested primarily in the physical, that is, bodily, causes of consequential madness, and the term 'lunacy' itself signalled such an outside influence in describing "a disease whose distemper followeth the course of the Moon [that works] distempers both in body and mind" (as John Swan put it in

10 Porter, *Mind-Forg'd Manacles*, p. x.
11 Porter, *Mind-forg'd Manacles*, p. 35.
12 Porter, *Mind-forg'd Manacles*, especially pp. 55-61 and 123-32.
13 William Battie, *A Treatise on Madness* (London: J. Whiston, and B. White, 1758), pp. 43-44.

1698).[14] Others focused on ideas, the imagination, and fancy for bringing about troubles of mind. For John Locke, madmen have not

> lost the Faculty of Reasoning: but having joined together some *Ideas* very wrongly, they mistake them for Truths; and they err as Men do, that argue right from wrong Principles. For by the violence of their Imaginations, having taken their Fancies for Realities, they make right deductions from them.[15]

Accordingly, Richard Baxter (1615-91), in *The Signs and Causes of Melancholy* of 1716, distinguished between those "who are *rationally sorrowful for Sin*," and those in whom "the Imagination, Fantasie or Thinking Faculty is ... Crazed or Diseased" and who suffer from true melancholy, "this Diseased Craziness, Hurt or Error of *the Imagination*, and consequently of the Understanding."[16] John Haslam (1764-1844), the apothecary of Bedlam, argued in 1798 that madness was "*a disease of ideas*," with no "corporeal remedies for it,"

> and that to endeavour to convince madmen of their errors, by reasoning, is folly in those who attempt it, since there is always in madness the firmest conviction of the truth of what is false, and which the clearest and most circumstantial evidence cannot remove.[17]

This is disturbing in that the resources of reason are mustered against reason itself (in Locke) or at least exposed as powerless against reason, and as tools of "folly" themselves (in Haslam). In scholars particularly, errors of the imagination could be disastrous. In 1729, Bedlam doctor Nicholas Robinson (1697-1775) described how

> PERSONS, of the greatest natural Parts, of the finest Genius's, and most elevated Imaginations, are often observ'd, in their Flights, to start into Madness [when, as] the aspiring Soul is pursuing some lofty Thought, soaring to an uncommon Height, and teeming with the grand Discovery, the Impulses prove too strong

---

14 John Swan, *Speculum mundi: or, A Glass Representing the Face of the World Shewing Both that it Did Begin, and Must also End, the Manner how, and Time when, Being Largely Examined. The Whole of Which May Be Fitly Called an Hexameron*, 4th ed. (London: by W. R. for W. Whitwood, 1698), p. 300.

15 John Locke, *An Essay concerning Human Understanding* (1690), ed. Peter H. Nidditch (Oxford: Clarendon Press, 1975), p. 161 (II, xi, § 13). See also Ingram, *The Madhouse of Language*, p. 10.

16 Quoted from *Patterns of Madness in the Eighteenth Century: A Reader*, ed. Allan Ingram (Liverpool: Liverpool University Press, 1998), p. 43.

17 John Haslam, *Observations on Insanity: With Practical Remarks on the Disease, and an Account of the Morbid Appearances on Dissection* (London: F. and C. Rivington, 1798), pp. 105-6.

FIGURE 12.1
William Hogarth, *A Rake's Progress*, Plate 8 (1735).
HARRIS BRISBANE DICK FUND, METROPOLITAN MUSEUM OF ART. <HTTPS://METMUSEUM.ORG/ART/COLLECTION/SEARCH/403276>

> for the feeble Brain to support, the Intenseness of Thought disconcerts the tender Fibres, and the whole Magazine of most beautiful Ideas are shatter'd, and jumbled into the greatest and most irregular Confusion, by the Force of the labouring Imagination.[18]

Thus, an excess of imaginative work could excite the brain to produce an overload that destroys the objects of contemplation and creates discord from concord. This, perhaps, is the kind of madness represented by Hogarth's Bedlam astronomer (above).

In Tom Rakewell's final destination in Bedlam asylum, we see, among "three figures obsessed with measurement," an astronomer "squinting through a rolled-up sheet of paper" next to a longitude projector and a mad tailor, isolated by their madness and rendered incapable of human interaction.[19] The plate is inscribed with an apostrophe to madness, the "Chaos of the Brain" and "Tyranny of Fancy's Reign":

18 Nicholas Robinson, *A New System of the Spleen, Vapours, and Hypochondriack Melancholy: Wherein All the Decays of the Nerves, and Lownesses of the Spirits are Mechanically Accounted for. To which is subjoin'd, A Discourse upon the Nature, Cause, and Cure, of Melancholy, Madness, and Lunacy* (London: Printed for A. Bettesworth, W. Innys, and C. Rivington, 1729), p. 244; reprinted in *Patterns of Madness in the Eighteenth Century*, ed. Ingram, p. 81.

19 Ingram and Faubert, *Cultural Constructions of Madness in Eighteenth-Century Writing*, p. 179.

Mechanic Fancy; that can build
Vast Labyrinths, & Mazes wild,
With Rule disjointed, Shapeless Measure,
Fill'd with Horror, fill'd with Pleasure!
Shapes of Horror, that wou'd even
Cast Doubt of Mercy upon Heaven.

The phrasing recalls Pope's *Essay on Man*, and it makes a similar point about the dangers of overestimating the human powers of measuring and reasoning. Roy Porter has commented on the immense influence of this representation, arguing that "subsequent pictures of Bedlam then mirrored Hogarth, and art commented on art not life."[20] Indeed, this influence extends beyond the pictorial to poetry; in the 1776 "Bedlam: A Poem" we read of "a Sage, immers'd in Thought profound" who "points his Course reverted to the Skies":

His ready Fancy still supplies the Means,
Forces his Tools and fixes his Machines;
Erects his Sluices and his Mounds sustains,
And whirls perpetual Windmills in his Brains.
All Problems, have his lively Thoughts subdu'd,
Measur'd the Stars, and found the Longitude;
And squar'd the Circle and the Tides explain'd.[21]

Similarly, in Henry Mackenzie's *Man of Feeling* (1771), the visitor to Bethlem encounters a "maniac" who "had once been a very celebrated mathematician" but had fallen "a sacrifice ... to the theory of comets; for, after having, with infinite labour, formed a table on the conjectures of Sir Isaac Newton, he was disappointed in the return of one of those luminaries, and was very soon after obliged to be placed here [in Bethlem] by his friends."[22]

While these instances illustrate the nexus between astronomy and lunacy, the proximity between the solitary genius's imagination and poetry is rendered in a visit to Bedlam in George Lyttelton's *Letters from a Persian in England* (1735), which reveals an inmate "who had been bred to Merchandize, but being of too lively an Imagination for the Dulness of Trade, he applied himself to Poetry, and neglecting his other Business, was soon reduced to the State I saw him in" in the asylum. This former merchant-turned-poet has a plan for leaving behind his miserable state,

20 Porter, *Mind-forg'd Manacles*, p. 37.

21 G. Fitzgerald, *Bedlam: A Poem* (London: Printed for the Author, 1776), pp. 14, 16.

22 Henry Mackenzie, *The Man of Feeling* (London: T. Cadell, 1771), pp. 55-56.

> for this lucky Confinement having given him more Leisure for Study, he had quitted Poetry, and taken to the Mathematicks, by the means of which he had found out the Longitude, and expected to obtain a great Reward which the Government promised to the Discoverer.[23]

It is implied that the man is committed to confinement as a poet, and as his lunacy escalates further, he is turned into a longitude projector whose work links astronomy and geometry. The preoccupation with astronomy is here sought out by a mind already disturbed by "too lively an Imagination." The scientist shared the poet's obligation "that imagination should not be wayward, idiosyncratic and visionary but should abide by the solid information of the senses and be tempered by judgement."[24] The relationship between the two spheres is potentially mutual: astronomy can breed lunacy, and lunacy seeks an outlet in astronomy. James Carkesse, the late-seventeenth-century poet and "patient extraordinary" of Bethlem, in his *Lucida intervalla*, makes ample use of the trope of the 'lunatic poet,' for example, when he has a physician in Bethlem state that "Unless the *Moon* assist him, I well know it, / *Apollo* never singly made a *Poet.*"[25]

2. Four Versions of Thales

The idea of the stargazer as an impractical theorist, social outcast, and object of ridicule has had a long history.[26] The meanings ascribed to it over the past two millennia may be explored in an anecdote from the life of Thales of Miletus, recounted by Plato, Diogenes Laertius, and others, of the philosopher falling into a ditch while gazing at the stars during a nocturnal walk. In eighteenth-century Britain, we encounter the story in Thomas Stanley's *History of Philosophy*:

---

23 George Lyttelton, *Letters from a Persian in England to his Friend at Ispahan*, 4th ed. (Dublin: by M. Rhames for R. Gunne, *et al.*, 1735), p. 10.

24 Roy Porter, *A Social History of Madness: The World through the Eyes of the Insane* (New York: Weidenfeld and Nicolson, 1988), p. 62.

25 James Carkesse, *Lucida intervalla: Containing Divers Miscellaneous Poems, Written at Finsbury and Bethlem by the Doctors Patient Extraordinary* (London, 1679), Augustan Reprint Society, nos 195-96, ed. Michael V. DePorte (Los Angeles: William Andrews Clark Memorial Library, 1979), p. 27.

26 See Hans Blumenberg, *The Laughter of the Thracian Woman: A Protohistory of Theory* (1987), New Directions in German Studies, no 11 (New York: Bloomsbury Academic, 2015). Originally published in German under the title *Das Lachen der Thrakerin: eine Urgeschichte der Theorie* (Frankfurt am Main: Suhrkamp, 1987). The four anecdotes discussed here are all taken from this volume.

> *Thales* being earnestly addicted to Astrology became obnoxious to the Censure of some Persons. *As he was led abroad one night by an old Woman*, his Maid (a *Thracian*), *to look upon the Stars, he fell into a Ditch* (wherein she purposely led him) *to whom as he complained*, Thales, *said she, do you think, when you cannot see these things that are at your feet, that you can understand the Heavens?*

Underlined passages indicate Stanley's additions to the original story from Diogenes Laertius (in italics in the original). Through these transformations, the astronomer ('astrology' here being used as a synonym) is said to have been disliked and was being tricked; the maid is presented as deceitful. Stanley also relates the second part of the anecdote:

> He was also for preferring this Study before Wealth, reproved by some Friends, not without Reproach to the Science, as conferring no advantage on its professors; whereupon he thus vindicated himself and the Art from that Aspersion. *When they upbraided him*, saith Aristotle, *with his Poverty, as if Philosophy were unprofitable, it is said, that he by Astrology, foreseeing the plenty of Olives that would be that year ... bought up all the places for Oyl at* Miletus *and* Chios, *which he did with little Money, there being no other chapman at that time to raise the price; and when the time came that many were sought for in hast, he setting what rates on them he pleased, by this means got together much Mony.*

Thus, Thales vindicates himself and astronomy and proves "*that it was easie for Philosophers to be Rich, if they would themselves, but that Wealth was not their aim.*"[27] Stanley excuses the stargazer by stressing the deceitful agency of others and his agency both in producing profit and in renouncing it. The astronomer's practice is *seen* as useless, but this only discredits those who "censure" him. They represent a society hostile to 'philosophy' or science which has no immediately evident profit. The science, on the other hand, represents knowledge for its own sake.

A second transformation of the story is found in Samuel Richardson's *Aesop's Fables* (1740) in the fable of "The Astrologer Admonish'd" (where 'astrology' has acquired its modern sense to mean something different from 'astronomy'):

> A certain stargazer had the misfortune, in the very middle of his celestial observations, to stumble into a very deep ditch; and while he was scrabbling to get out, friend, says a sober fellow passing by, make a right use of your present misfortunes; and, for the future, pray let the stars go on quietly in their courses,

---

27 All quotations are from Thomas Stanley, *The History of Philosophy: Containing the Lives, Opinions, Actions, and Discourses of the Philosophers of Every Sect*, 3rd ed. (London: W. Battersby, *et al.*, 1701), p. 11 (I, Chapter VIII, Section 5). See also Diogenes Laertius, *De vitis, dogmatibus, et apophthegmatibus clarorum philosophorum libri X*, ed. Marcus Meibomius, 2 vols (Amsterdam: Hendrik Wetstein, 1692), I, 21, 34.

FIGURE 12.2 'Astrologer admonish'd', in Samuel Richardson's edition of *Aesop's Fables*. THE BODLEIAN LIBRARIES, THE UNIVERSITY OF OXFORD, SHELFMARK DOUCE A 421, ILLUSTRATION FACING P. 57.

> and do you look a little better to the ditches; for is it not strange, that you should tell other people their fortune, and know nothing of your own?

Richardson comments in no uncertain terms: "*This Fable is a just Rebuke to such as neglect their own Concerns to pry into those of other People*," and an added "Reflection" attacks "the impudent Pretensions of Fortune-tellers, Gypsies, Wizards, and such-like, who so much impose on the Credulity of the Weak and Ignorant, as well in Town as Country, especially in the latter."[28] The stargazer here serves as the prototype, not of those who neglect worldly affairs but of those who meddle in the affairs of others with fraudulent intent. As in Stanley, there is poetic justice, but here the stargazer is not vindicated but punished.

---

28 All quotations are from Samuel Richardson, *Æsop's Fables: With Instructive Morals and Reflections, Abstracted from All Party Considerations, Adapted to All Capacities, and Design'd to Promote Religion, Morality, and Universal Benevolence* (London: J. Osborn, 1740), in Samuel Richardson, *Early Works*, ed. Alexander Pettit (Cambridge: Cambridge University Press, 2012), p. 191 (no 76).

His occupation stands, not for 'pure science' but impure deceit.[29] The "impudent Pretensions" are not only wholly irrational, but wilfully dishonest "arbitrary fictions." The penchant for irrationality and fiction, however, is not to be found in the stargazer but in his customers. Where Stanley's astronomer exposed society's disregard for 'pure' reason and noble philosophy, Richardson's astrologer exposes its gullibility by pseudo-science.

Hans Blumenberg identified a further treatment of the anecdote. Kant, in *Dreams of a Spirit-Seer* (1766), relates a similar episode about Tycho Brahe, who supposedly undertook to find the shortest route for a nightly coach-ride by the stars and was reproached by his coachman: "My dear master, you may have a thorough understanding of the heavens, but here on earth you are a fool." Kant's point in recounting this episode is aimed against those who claim to have the metaphysical gift of transcending mundane experience by communicating with spirits, granting them visions of the 'other world.' He argues that those "who with such application and absorption train their metaphysical telescopes on those remote regions and find themselves able to report wonders from those distant places" might, by "someone of sound understanding but little tact," be given the reply Tycho received. Kant holds that "intuitive knowledge of the *other* world can only ever be attained here by forfeiting something of that understanding which one needs for this *present* world."[30] This is a very different view from Stanley's and Richardson's: there is such a thing as misguided science which disregards the importance of the material world. The astronomer's telescope and its objects serve as metaphors of metaphysical pursuits that, for all Tycho's greatness, cannot produce universally useful results in this world. This is a third potential attitude one may take towards the unworldly stargazer: one that is critical of astronomy as the paradigmatic theoretical science even without deceitful intent. The astronomer is impractical and, worse, does not realize it. The thrust of this critique aims at the scientists' inability to discern the limits of their expertise, and perhaps more generally, to tell useful from useless, reliable from unreliable knowledge. In commenting on a quotation from Pope's *Essay on Man*, Kant had earlier wondered in the *Universal Natural History and Theory of the Heavens* (1755): "Who can show us the border where well-founded probability ends and arbitrary fictions begin?"[31] Ultimately, he

---

29 Blumenberg, *The Laughter of the Thracian Woman*, pp. 90-91.

30 Quotations are from Immanuel Kant, *Theoretical Philosophy, 1755-1770*, eds David Walford and Ralf Meerbote (Cambridge: Cambridge University Press, 2002), pp. 328-29.

31 Kant comments here on the passage from Pope, "Vast chain of being, which from God began, / Natures æthereal, human, angel, man, / Beast, bird, fish, insect! what no eye can see, / No glass can reach! from Infinite to thee; / From thee to Nothing!" (*An Essay on Man*, ed. Maynard Mack [London: Methuen, and New Haven: Yale University Press, 1964], I,

upturns this claim for immanent knowledge in the *Critique of Pure Reason*, where it is not the reality of the mundane but the sublime incomprehensibility of the heavens that brings home the limits of human understanding:[32]

> The observations and calculations of astronomers have taught us much that is worthy of admiration, but most important, probably, is that they have exposed for us the abyss of our ignorance, which without this information human reason could never have imagined to be so great; reflection on this ignorance has to produce a great alteration in the determination of the final aims of the use of our reason.[33]

This is a fourth attitude towards astronomical speculation, one making the astronomer realize "the fragility of the ground we stand on,"[34] both literally and metaphorically. The relation between the mundane and the cosmic not only dwarfs the mundane, but also the contemplators by rendering them aware of the minuteness both of themselves and of their powers of apprehension. In view of "the abyss of our ignorance," the human self-image is put into humbling perspective, the line between "well-founded probability" and "arbitrary fictions" is dangerously blurred, and the view of philosophy at large is "greatly altered." It is easy for us to see that this way madness might lie.

This single little anecdote alone reveals a range of possible attitudes towards what stargazing could do to people's *compositio mentis*, and how contemporaries might respond to individuals thus disposed. Now is the time to turn to instances of 'mad' stargazing in more extended fictions: *The Blazing World*, *Gulliver's Travels*, *The Female Quixote*, and *Rasselas*, and, by way of conclusion, Mary Shelley's *The Last Man*.

2.1. *The Blazing World*

In Margaret Cavendish's 1666 scientific utopia *The Description of a New World, Called the Blazing World*, a lady from our world travels by ship to another, which is populated by various beast-men; there she marries the Emperor and directs the affairs of the realm. This plot involves reviewing the activities of scientific companies, including that of the bear-men, "experimental philosophers," who produce telescopes for the bird-men astronomers. The Empress is upset at the

ll. 237-41). For further discussion, see Justus Fetscher, "*Vielleicht*: über eine Minimalfigur kosmologischer Imagination zwischen Milton und Kant," *Modern Language Notes*, 125, no 3 (2010), 511-35 (pp. 525-28).

32 Blumenberg, *The Laughter of the Thracian Woman*, p. 89.

33 Immanuel Kant, *Critique of Pure Reason*, trans. Paul Guyer and Allen W. Wood (Cambridge: Cambridge University Press, 1998), p. 555 [A575/B603; AA III 387].

34 Blumenberg, *The Laughter of the Thracian Woman*, p. 89.

failure of these instruments to produce clear insight: she sees them rather as "false informers" who, "instead of discovering the truth, delude your senses."[35] Hence, she bans them, to the chagrin of the bear-men:

> The bear-men replied, that it was not the fault of their glasses which caused such differences in their opinions, but the sensitive motions in their optic organs did not move alike, nor were their rational judgments always regular: To which the Empress answered, that if their glasses were true informers, they would rectify their irregular sense and reason; but, said she, nature has made your sense and reason more regular than art has your glasses, for they are mere deluders, and will never lead you to the knowledge of truth; wherefore I command you again to break them; for you may observe the progressive motions of celestial bodies with your natural eyes better than through artificial glasses.

This statement is remarkable for the faith it expresses in the powers of the senses and of reason, although the Empress is warned by those who use the instruments that the fault lies with the observer, not the device. Ideally, she says, the instrument should improve on the faculties of the observer, whereas in fact it deludes them. The bear-men take the position we have seen in Kant's *Critique*, of stargazing as revealing the depths of our ignorance and the limitations of our senses. Their response to this predicament, however, is surprising: they proceed to plead with the Empress to let them keep their telescopes,

> for, said they, we take more delight in artificial delusions than in natural truths. Besides, we shall want employments for our senses, and subjects for arguments; were there nothing but truth, and no falsehood, there would be no occasion for to dispute, and by this means we should want the aim and pleasure of our endeavours in confuting and contradicting each other; neither would one man be thought wiser than another, but all would either be alike knowing and wise, or all would be fools; wherefore we most humbly beseech your Imperial Majesty to spare our glasses, which are our only delight, and as dear to us as our lives.

In full awareness of the faulty nature of their deluded insight, the bear-men still prefer it over natural truths, delusion being more delightful and affording more food for disputation. Thus, willful delusion and the disputations it spawns offer a means of distinguishing between the wise and the foolish – a distinction that in this satire emerges as a construct made in full awareness of its arbitrariness. The Empress suffers the bear-men, fools that they are, and

35 All quotations are from Margaret Cavendish, *The Blazing World and Other Writings*, ed. Kate Lilley (London: Penguin, 1994), pp. 141-42.

allows them to keep their telescopes, "but upon condition, that their disputes and quarrels should remain within their schools, and cause no factions or disturbances in state, or government" (p. 142). She isolates them and sees to it that their silly disputes do not spill over into the rational government she is setting up. The bear-men seem mad in that they deliberately work from wrong principles, as Locke might put it – and the only response is to separate them from sane society.

2.2. *Gulliver's Travels*

Cavendish's attitude towards the social construction of madness recalls the *Tale*'s assessment of "the great Introducers of new Schemes in Philosophy": "It is plain," Swift argues, "that several of the chief among them, both *Antient* and *Modern*, were usually mistaken by their Adversaries, and indeed, by all, except their own Followers, to have been Persons Crazed, or out of their Wits." He compares the acceptability of opinions and behaviours to musical notes, which, if in tune with those of others, will sound pleasing, and if out of tune will produce discord: "For if you chance to jar the String among those who are either above or below your own Height, instead of subscribing to your Doctrine, they will tie you fast, call you Mad, and feed you with Bread and Water."[36] What counts as sanity is relative, and the isolation of scholars from their social surroundings can easily make them appear insane. The phrasing, "if you *chance* to jar" suggests a degree of contingency to who or what is considered mad or authoritative.[37]

Swift's Laputians are brazenly Thalesian in their disregard of the material and social environment and in their dependence on flappers to save them from the "manifest danger of falling down every Precipice, and bouncing [their] Heads against every Post."[38] When Gulliver signals that he can do without a flapper, the Laputians deduce "a very mean Opinion of [his] Understanding" (p. 149 [III, ii, 3]). Satiric inversion turns theorizing into the social norm and combines the attitudes we saw in Stanley's version and Kant's Tycho episode, but here it is not the astronomer who is derided by society, but a society of

36 *A Tale of a Tub and Other Works*, ed. Marcus Walsh (Cambridge: Cambridge University Press, 2010), pp. 107-8.

37 Stargazers were aware of this danger: "The astrologer Ebenezer Sibly, it was claimed, had written 'in the very language of Bedlam' – an attack echoed in the astronomer William Herschel's prediction that some would think him 'fit for Bedlam' for his stellar theories" (Porter, *Mind-forg'd Manacles*, p. 26).

38 *Gulliver's Travels* [1726], ed. Robert DeMaria (London and New York: Penguin, 2001), pp. 148-49 (III, ii, 3). Further references are to this edition and will be given in parentheses within the text.

astronomers who look down (literally, from their flying island) upon those of a more practical mindset. This hyperbole only serves to emphasize their impracticability and moral myopia. Remarkably, Swift never comments on *why* astronomy, mathematics, and music should be so popular among the Laputians – within the narrative, they are self-evidently autotelic.

For all their impracticability, the Laputian scholars are said to be "wholly strangers" to "Imagination, Fancy, and Invention" (p. 152 [III, ii, 11]), but the imagination does find an outlet in their attitude towards the heavens. As Gulliver reports, they are plagued by "continual Disquietudes, never enjoying a Minute's Peace of Mind." Because they evidently cannot imagine that the celestial phenomena should not be 'about them,' that is, concern them in some way, they worry that, among other celestial catastrophes,

> the Earth very narrowly escaped a brush from the Tail of the last Comet, which would have infallibly reduced it to Ashes; and that the next, which they have calculated for one and Thirty Years hence, will probably destroy us. (p. 153 [III, ii, 13])

It has been extensively documented that this is a parody of contemporary fears linked with the return of Halley's Comet, indeed projected to occur in 1758, thirty-two years in the future from 1726.[39] This comet was seen by many – and not only millenarian Whistonites[40] – as heralding a time of revolution and change. In Halley's new scheme,

> other comets engaged in the destruction, the renovation, and the transformation of celestial bodies; and during the course of the eighteenth century, they became ensconced as active agents in an array of evolutionary cosmogonies. In this way, the traditional comet lore, so often scoffed at as irrational and superstitious, and so often claimed to have died in the wake of Newton's and Halley's proof of comet periodicity, was in fact given new life by Halley's and Newton's theories.[41]

This phenomenon is not, however, a sign that irrationalism and superstition gained 'scientific' credentials – rather, the science that raised such fears was discredited and tainted by association with religious enthusiasm and political revolution. Nicolson and Mohler observe that science actually feeds this

39 Sara Schechner Genuth, *Comets, Popular Culture, and the Birth of Modern Cosmology* (Princeton: Princeton University Press, 1997), pp. 174-77.

40 On Whistonianism, see George S. Rousseau, "'Wicked Whiston' and the Scriblerians: Another Ancients-Modern Controversy," *Studies in Eighteenth-Century Culture*, 17 (1987), 17-44, and Lynall, *Swift and Science*, pp. 120-40.

41 Genuth, *Comets, Popular Culture, and the Birth of Modern Cosmology*, p. 177.

lunacy in that the Laputians' "dread ... of a comet is greater than had been their ancestors', for their fear is more profoundly rooted in contemporary science."[42] Method augments madness. Swift presents the degree of this fear with acerbic hyperbole:

> They are so perpetually alarmed with the Apprehensions of these and the like impending Dangers, that they can neither sleep quietly in their Beds, nor have any relish for the common Pleasures or Amusements of Life. When they meet an Acquaintance in the Morning, the first Question is about ... what hopes they have to avoid the stroke of the approaching Comet. (p. 153 [III, ii, 14])

We may compare these symptoms with those identified for the "Spleenetick" man in Nicholas Robinson's *New System*: "He starts in his Sleep, and often awakes from his Slumbers, terribly affrighted with the Horrors of his Dreams." Such men

> are subject to very impertinent and groundless Fears, that render Life not only uneasy to themselves, but greatly perplexing to all their Friends about them. Sometimes they fancy they are just going to die, and call for their Relations and Neighbours, in as formal a Manner, as if they were immediately about to expire.[43]

The splenetic lives in an irrational world of fictions that become reality through their interaction with others on whom they impose these fictions. Their 'fancy' takes manifest shape. Crucially, Swift concludes his discussion of the Laputians' comet conversations by likening them to the delight boys take in "terrible stories of Spirits and Hobgoblins, which they greedily listen to, and dare not go to Bed for fear" (pp. 153-54 [III, ii, 14]). Where there is no outlet for fancy, the imagination will haunt man in some other way. Swift thus employs the analogy between 'reading into the stars' and the production of poetic meaning to valorize the imaginative faculty: without it (that is also, without finding a suitable outlet for it), people will fall victim to delusions and over-interpretation. This creative faculty makes the difference between the Laputians' wild conjectures and the laudable pursuit of insight that Swift describes in his *Thoughts on Various Subjects* (1727):

> The Motions of the Sun and Moon; in short, the whole System of the Universe, as far as Philosophers have been able to discover and observe, are in the utmost

---

42 Marjorie H. Nicolson and Nora M. Mohler, "The Scientific Background of Swift's 'Voyage to Laputa,'" *Annals of Science*, 2 (1937), 299-334 (p. 310).

43 Robinson, *A New System of the Spleen, Vapours, and Hypochondriack Melancholy*, pp. 208, 209.

> Degree of Regularity and Perfection: But wherever God hath left to Man the power of interposing a Remedy by Thought or Labour, there he hath placed Things in a State of Imperfection, on purpose to stir up human Industry; without which Life would stagnate, or indeed rather could not subsist at all: *Curis acuens mortalia corda.*[44]

In spite of Newton's celebrated discovery of laws that hold true throughout the universe, Swift here returns to a dual world system of the 'perfect' sidereal and the imperfect sublunary. In that system, there is room for divine purpose and intention – the world is fitted to the human predicament of *cura* (care) in that it encourages us to strive for perfection but prevents us from reaching it 'below.'[45] As Gregory Lynall has argued, this passage articulates Swift's concern that "appropriations of the new natural philosophy," such as William Whiston's, "were fostering new or variant forms of superstitious credulity, rather than extinguishing unenlightened views of the cosmos."[46] Hence, perhaps, the Houyhnhnms' alternative: their 'rational' astronomy extends only to the observation of sun and moon (p. 251 [IV, ix, 6]). They are wholly on the side of Cavendish's Empress in their rejection of scientific 'opinion,' because, as they say, "*Reason* taught us to affirm or deny only where we are certain" (p. 246 [IV, viii, 9]). This degree of certitude is available to the naked horse-eye.

---

44 *Prose Works*, IV, 245. For a commentary, see *Thoughts on Various Subjects*, eds Hermann J. Real, *et al.* (Online.Swift/Ehrenpreis Centre for Swift Studies, Münster, November 2011, updated August 2016, <http://www.online-swift.de/thoughtsonvarious.note.thou_062.html>). See also Douglas Lane Patey, "Swift's Satire on 'Science' and the Structure of *Gulliver's Travels*," *ELH*, 58 (1991), 809-39 (p. 832). The quotation is from Virgil's *Georgics*, where Jupiter is said to "whet the hearts of mortals with care."

45 On care as a concept, see Blumenberg, *The Laughter of the Thracian Woman*, pp. 123-25. George Rousseau argues that the Scriblerians "were not erudite in matters mathematical or astronomic, but their intuition informed them that in every movement in the skies there could not be portents of imminent catastrophe. In this sense the Scriblerians were of the party of the Moderns – more discriminating, less superstitious – and eventually recognized to what degree cometary Whiston was no more prophetic than they were. For them the best of times was just beginning" (Rousseau, "'Wicked Whiston' and the Scriblerians," p. 41). The more traditional ridicule of astrologers speaks from Swift's premature "Elegy on Mr. Partridge," the "*cobbler, starmonger*, and *quack*" ("An Elegy on Mr. Partridge, the Almanac-maker, who died on the 29th of this Instant *March*, 1708," in *Major Works*, eds Angus Ross and David Woolley [Oxford and New York: Oxford University Press, 2008], pp. 205-8). In the present context, Gulliver himself is, of course, here as elsewhere characterized by a lack of imagination: he, along with the "sequacious herd" in England, is the butt of the joke when he observes that the Laputians' apprehensions about the stars have "Causes which very little affect the rest of Mortals" – he simply does not think in cosmic dimensions and cannot imagine that anybody else does (*Gulliver's Travels*, ed. DeMaria, p. 153 [III, ii, 13]).

46 Lynall, *Swift and Science*, pp. 90-91.

2.3. *The Female Quixote*

A short and marginal passage in Charlotte Lennox's *The Female Quixote* (1752) lends an illuminating twist to the association between astronomy and lunacy in *Gulliver's Travels*. Whereas the Laputians try to exorcize fiction and find themselves haunted by it, Lennox's deluded protagonist Arabella believes in the reality of romance to such a quixotic extent that she is deemed a fool by many of her acquaintances. At a relatively early point in the novel, her cousin Miss Glanville declares that she will as soon believe Arabella's 'romance' interpretation of events as that "the Moon is made of a Cream Cheese." Arabella's initial response is in keeping with her naïvety, as she takes the cliché seriously, that is, reads it literally:

> Is it possible, Miss, said *Arabella*, that you can offer such an Affront to my Understanding, as to suppose, I would argue upon such a ridiculous System; and compare the Second glorious Luminary of the Heavens to so unworthy a Resemblance? I have taken some Pains to contemplate the heavenly Bodies; and, by Reading and Observation, am able to comprehend some Part of their Excellence: Therefore it is not probable, I should descend to such trivial Comparisons; and liken a planet, which, haply, is not much less than our Earth, to a thing so inconsiderable, as that you name –

Arabella's pedantry shows that she has difficulty differentiating between figurative language (and hence, fiction) and its referent (that is, reality). However, when her cousin replies, she exposes the depth of her own, much greater, ignorance:

> Pardon me, dear Cousin, interrupted Miss *Glanville*, laughing louder than before, if I divert myself a little with the Extravagance of your Notions. Really, I think, you have no Reason to be angry, if I supposed you might make a Comparison between the Moon and a Cream Cheese; since you say, that same Moon, which don't appear broader than your Gardener's Face, is not much less than the whole World: Why, certainly, I have more Reason to trust my own Eyes, than such whimsical Notions as these.
>
> *Arabella*, unwilling to expose her Cousin's Ignorance, by a longer Dispute upon this Subject, begged her to let it drop for the present.[47]

Although she is severely deluded otherwise (and repeatedly suspected of 'madness' and 'lunacy'),[48] Arabella is reasonable enough not to trust her senses in the same way as the ignorant Miss Glanville; and she is kind enough not to

---

47 Charlotte Lennox, *The Female Quixote: or, The Adventures of Arabella* (1752), ed. Margaret Dalziel (London, New York, Toronto: Oxford University Press, 1970), pp. 142-43.

48 Lennox, *The Female Quixote*, ed. Dalziel, pp. 339, 366 and 368.

mock her ignorance.[49] Evidently, delusion and credulity about fiction do not necessarily entail astronomical 'misreadings,' nor does worldliness or a familiarity with metaphorical language protect from them. Ridiculing the insights of astronomers can thus illustrate an epistemological foolishness, while ontological foolishness (that cannot tell fact from fiction) may occur alongside epistemological reason. This is the precondition for Arabella's 'redemption' at the end of the novel (in a chapter often attributed to Samuel Johnson) – unlike the Laputians, she does come to see that she had been misguided by "the Blaze of Enthusiastic Bravery."[50]

2.4. *Rasselas*

As *Rasselas* explores, through its questing princely protagonist, the nature of happiness in a fallen world, Johnson presents a complex attitude towards the nature and purpose of fiction through an episode focusing on an astronomer who has lost his wits by the contemplation of the heavens and by the excessive exercise of his imagination prompted by this activity. Imlac, the poet, recalls his meeting with the astronomer, who holds by conventional wisdom that "to man is permitted the contemplation of the skies, but the practice of virtue is commanded."[51] This notion of the proper object of study poses a problem in that the two have become interlinked in the astronomer's mind: his many years of study have led him to the fantastical belief that he can control the weather. So absorbed has he become in the object of his study that he has implicated himself in it psychologically, through delusion: having observed the heavenly phenomena, he convinces himself that they are subject to his will (pp. 144-45). He acknowledges that there were times he suspected himself of madness (p. 147), and that there is no proof for his skill – yet "it is sufficient," he says, "that I feel this power" (p. 147). This misunderstanding entails a moral quandary: should he use his power to privilege certain regions of the earth? "I have," he protests,

> diligently considered the position of the earth and sun, and formed innumerable schemes in which I changed their situation. I have sometimes turned aside the axis of the earth, and sometimes varied the ecliptick of the sun: but I have found it impossible to make a disposition by which the world may be advantaged; what one region gains, another loses by an imaginable alteration, even

49 See Mary Patricia Martin, "'High and Noble Adventures': Reading the Novel in *The Female Quixote*," *Novel*, 31 (1997), 45-62 (pp. 54-55).

50 Lennox, *The Female Quixote*, ed. Dalziel, p. 381.

51 Samuel Johnson, *The History of Rasselas, Prince of Abyssinia* (1759), ed. Gwin J. Kolb (New Haven and London: Yale University Press, 1990), p. 143. All further references are to this edition and will be given in parentheses within the text.

> without considering the distant parts of the solar system with which we are unacquainted. (p. 148)

Johnson presents the astronomer's predicament as madness with a method to it – indeed, the madness seems to have been *caused* by an unreasonable surfeit of method. As Imlac comments, "Few can attain this man's knowledge, and few practise his virtues; but all may suffer his calamity. Of the uncertainties of our present state, the most dreadful and alarming is the uncertain continuance of reason" (p. 149).[52] What began as a 'reasonable' pursuit of knowledge has escalated into an excess of fancy.

When the princess and her maid Pekuah mock the astronomer, however (p. 149), this prompts an unexpected second dissertation from Imlac which contrasts with his first, "Upon Poetry," in Chapter X (pp. 38-45). This time, the old poet feels compelled by the fate of the astronomer to hold forth on "the dangerous prevalence of imagination," which he presents as a result of excessive self-absorption: "To indulge the power of fiction, and send imagination out upon the wing, is often the sport of those who delight too much in silent speculation." The lonely scholar will tend to project his own desires onto the object of his study:

> He then expatiates in boundless futurity, and culls from all imaginable conditions that which for the present moment he should most desire, amuses his desires with impossible enjoyments, and confers upon his pride unattainable dominion. The mind dances from scene to scene, unites all pleasures in all combinations, and riots in delights which nature and fortune, with all their bounty, cannot bestow.
> In time ... the reign of fancy is confirmed; she grows first imperious, and in time despotick. Then fictions begin to operate as realities, false opinions fasten upon the mind, and life passes in dreams of rapture or of anguish. (pp. 150-52)

Imlac likens the process of fictionalizing to a frenzied procedure by which the self-absorbed scholar becomes the anthropic centre, ruler, and telos of the system he observes. The fictions of the erring mind will suggest that escape from reality is possible, and thus goad the mind into despotic subjection to fiction's own allures. This is not only the effect of the astronomer's madness, it is also the conventional charge against novels that Johnson himself shared: where they encounter untrained minds, the products of the imagination can

52 The latter sentence was to become the motto for Haslam's *Observations on Insanity* (1798) (see note 17).

tragically mislead.[53] The inexperience of novel readers in the ways of the world is mirrored by the astronomer's social isolation; both fall victim to the "reign of fancy." Where we "send imagination out upon the wing," we must beware where it goes, and the "wing" is powerful enough to take the unwary reader far from the path of virtue.

The travellers try to help the astronomer by weaning him from his cosmic preoccupations and leading him towards "sublunary pleasures" (p. 160), and his new social involvement brings him to realize that he was deluded: "I have chosen wrong. I have passed my time in study without experience; in the attainment of sciences which can, for the most part, be but remotely useful to mankind" (p. 161).[54] This turn not only discredits the astronomer's activities in natural philosophy, but also the moral implications he wrongly imputed to them. Having lost the ability to tell the difference between reality and illusion (p. 161), the astronomer is cured by the travellers, who themselves come to see this difference for the first time in the process – returning the astronomer to earth also lets them find the way towards the world of experience.[55] The only guard against the astronomer's melancholy is sociability (pp. 161-62). Still, the conflation of the astronomer and the poet is compounded in the book's vexing "conclusion, in which nothing is concluded" (pp. 175-76): as all the other travellers make their 'choices of life' – for a religious life, for the pursuit of knowledge, for earthly power – only the poet and the astronomer are "contented to be driven along the stream of life without directing their course to any particular port" (p. 176). The striking comparison between mad astronomer and poet is only made possible by a dissociation between mind and world under the empiricist paradigm: *Rasselas* proposes that to believe in the coalescence

53 Samuel Johnson, *The Rambler*, no 4, Saturday, 31 March 1750, in *The Yale Edition of the Works of Samuel Johnson*, III, eds W. J. Bate and Albrecht B. Strauss (New Haven and London: Yale University Press, 1969), 19-25.

54 This matches Johnson's own view, expressed in the "Life of Milton," that "the knowledge of external nature, and the sciences which that knowledge requires or includes, are not the great or the frequent business of the human mind." Johnson objects to those who "are turning off attention from life to nature. They seem to think, that we are placed here to watch the growth of plants, or the motions of the stars. Socrates was rather of the opinion, that what we had to learn was, how to do good, and avoid evil." Hence, it comes as no surprise that Johnson should approve of the treatment of astronomy in *Paradise Lost*: "Raphael's reproof of Adam's curiosity after the planetary motions, with the answer returned by Adam, may be confidently opposed to any rule of life which any poet has delivered" (Samuel Johnson, *The Lives of the Most Eminent English Poets; with Critical Observations on their Works*, ed. Roger Lonsdale, 4 vols [Oxford: Clarendon Press, 2006], I, 248-49, 282-92).

55 Leonard Orr, "The Structural and Thematic Importance of the Astronomer in *Rasselas*," *Recovering Literature: A Journal of Contextualist Criticism*, 9 (1981), 15-21.

of words and things is madness, to "indulge the power of fiction" is to risk violating common sense. This is a Thalesian lesson with a twist, in that the astronomer does renounce his art and its delusions and affirm the value of the mundane and social. For the poet, this has unwelcome consequences,

> because the modern writer cannot now assert the truth-value of those imaginary worlds which he invents and controls unless he also concedes that they are, in fact, only imaginary. He must accept a difference, which the astronomer has learned to accept, between his pleasing fictions, his verbal self-delusion, and the 'actual nature of things.' If the writer allows himself to be deceived by the coherence of his text he joins the Mad Astronomer, yet if he denies the authority of his writing he yields forever its power to recover the truth.[56]

2.5. *The Last Man*

Written after the deaths of both Percy Bysshe Shelley and Byron, *The Last Man* (1826) has often been viewed as Mary Shelley's sorrowful engagement with the artistic and political creeds of these men, as well as with the ideology of Romanticism at large. The Byronic figure of Raymond, who conquers Constantinople only to unleash the fatal plague on the world, represents boundless overreaching and transgressing the borders of the imaginable. Its sensational title apart, *The Last Man*'s epistemology is established from the very beginning of the narrative as concerned with extremes of perception, relation, and interpretation.[57] Surely, the most innovative and chilling aspect of the novel is its description of the plague's effect on the world; as the human population of the planet is wiped out within a few years, nothing else changes. Humanity does end with a whimper, not a bang, as the narrator Verney notes with indignation:

> Nature was the same, as when she was the kind mother of the human race; now, childless and forlorn, her fertility was a mockery; her loveliness a mask for deformity. Why should the breeze gently stir the trees, man felt not its refreshment?

56 C. H. Knoblauch, "Coherence Betrayed: Samuel Johnson and the 'Prose of the World,'" *boundary*, 27, no 2 (1979), 235-60 (p. 256).

57 Shelley's 'last man' was, on the novel's publication in 1826, already part of a vogue: a series of similar narratives had appeared in previous years, and Shelley positioned her novel in relation to them. See the survey of the genre and Shelley's novel in it in Steven Goldsmith, "Of Gender, Plague, and Apocalypse: Mary Shelley's *Last Man*," *Yale Journal of Criticism*, 4 (1990), 129-73 (pp. 132-38); see also Jane Blumberg, *Mary Shelley's Early Novels: "This Child of Imagination and Misery"* (Houndmills, Basingstoke, Hampshire: Macmillan, 1993), pp. 119-24.

> Why did dark night adorn herself with stars – man saw them not? Why are there fruits, or flowers, or streams, man is not here to enjoy them?[58]

Verney personifies narcissistic anthropicism in its purest form, asking why the stars should even shine if there is no human spectator to see them. He feels insulted and humiliated by what appears to be the all-too-clear message of the plague: Humankind is a flimsy and insignificant part of creation, its absence no more remarkable than that of a "field of corn blighted in the ear" (p. 398). The narrator's anthropic exasperation escalates dramatically as the novel proceeds, building up to an outburst that is difficult to read as anything but madness. Lamenting that "the species of man must perish; his frame of exquisite workmanship; the wondrous mechanism of his senses; the noble proportion of his godlike limbs; his mind, the throned king of these; must perish," Verney asks:

> Will the earth still keep her place among the planets; will she still journey with unmarked regularity round the sun; will the seasons change, the trees adorn themselves with leaves, and flowers shed their fragrance, in solitude? Will the mountains remain unmoved, and streams still keep a downward course towards the vast abyss; will the tides rise and fall, and the winds fan universal nature; will beasts pasture, birds fly, and fishes swim, when man, the lord, possessor, perceiver, and recorder of all these things, has passed away, as though he had never been? O, what mockery is this! (pp. 412-13)

The praise of Humankind's fine physical and intellectual properties is offset by the evident ease with which the species was eliminated, and with the immense narcissism with which Verney wonders whether the planet still deserves its place in the solar system, now that it is no longer graced with human inhabitants. Crucially, the source of his "internal voice" remains enigmatic, its authority questionable – is this view of humankind's doom a result of Verney's madness, or should it be taken seriously?

Besides Verney's explicit professions of faith in an anthropic universe, the novel also includes a deluded, if not entirely mad astronomer who clearly recalls Johnson's *Rasselas* and Swift's Laputians. While Shelley's stargazer, Merrival, does not believe that he has any influence on the objects he observes, he is so preoccupied with them as to forget all earthly responsibilities that arise from his family's suffering under the pandemic:

---

58 Mary Wollstonecraft Shelley, *The Last Man* (1826), ed. Morton D. Paley (Oxford and New York: Oxford University Press, 2008), p. 329. All further references are to this edition and will be given in parentheses within the text.

> His astronomical theories absorbed him; calculations were scrawled with coal on the bare walls of his garret: a hard-earned guinea, or an article of dress, was exchanged for a book without remorse; he neither heard his children cry, nor observed his companion's emaciated form, and the excess of calamity was merely to him as the occurrence of a cloudy night, when he would have given his right hand to observe a celestial phenomenon. His wife was one of those wondrous beings, to be found only among women, with affections not to be diminished by misfortune. Her mind was divided between boundless admiration for her husband, and tender anxiety for her children – she waited on him, worked for them, and never complained, though care rendered her life one long-drawn, melancholy dream. (p. 289)

The practice of astronomy is, quite conventionally, presented as otherworldly and 'theoretical;' it is also gendered as masculine through the contrast between the astronomer's single-mindedness and his wife's care for others.[59]

The astronomer is first introduced not as a mere obsessive, but as a ridiculously otherworldly theorist, in the same passage that also introduces the spreading of the plague from Constantinople. In a debate with the materialist Ryland, whom the narrator almost consistently disagrees with, Merrival suggests that an earthly paradise is a mere hundred thousand years away, when the coincidence of the "pole of the earth ... with the pole of the ecliptic" will produce "an eternal spring ... and earth become a paradise." As the company proceeds to discuss the prevention of the plague,

> Merrival did not join in this conversation; drawing near Idris, he proceeded to assure her that the joyful prospect of an earthly paradise after an hundred thousand years, was clouded to him by the knowledge that in a certain period of time after, an earthly hell or purgatory would occur, when the ecliptic and equator would be at right angles. (pp. 220-21)

The humour is reminiscent of the Thalesian satire in *Gulliver's Travels* and at the astronomer's expense; so evidently do his concerns clash with those of the present. Yet they are also made to serve as the source of figurative language, as Ryland concludes that "it is as wise to discuss the probability of a visitation of the plague in our well-governed metropolis, as to calculate the centuries which must escape before we can grow pine-apples here in the open air" (p. 221). Ryland's low estimation of Merrival testifies to his own lack of imagination; as

59 This recalls the relationship between William Herschel and his sister Caroline, who would sometimes literally have to feed him during lengthy observation sessions and who did in fact give up her ambition of becoming a singer to assist him in his calling (Michael A. Hoskins, *Discoverers of the Universe: William and Caroline Herschel* [Princeton: Princeton University Press, 2011], p. 39). It is unlikely, however, that Mary Shelley was aware of this.

the reader is well aware, the plague will reach London, and it will bring to an end the good government of England. Stargazing, and the reflection about the place of Humankind in the universe, is presented as an alternative epistemology whose lesson – Humankind is at the mercy of forces beyond its control – is indisputable. It is this conflict between the contingent, its realization and acceptance, and its expression, that *The Last Man* explores with an ultimately resigned attitude.

As the plague proceeds to claim human lives across the world, Merrival remains blissfully preoccupied with his inquiry into the future shifts of the earth's axis. The narrator recalls that his own reaction was not unlike Ryland's, dismissive and condescending with a hint of ridicule. Even the virtuous Idris cannot suppress a smile as Merrival presents a paper to her, although all around them people are dying of the plague:

> Though not apt to forget the precipice of time on which she stood, yet I could perceive that she was amused for a moment, by the contrast between the contracted view we had so long taken of human life, and the seven league strides with which Merrival paced a coming eternity. (p. 290)

In a very broad sense, the astronomer's epistemology is actually reassuring. While humanity may be at the brink of destruction, Merrival's spirit of scientific enquiry allows him and his audience to take a wider perspective: the insignificance of human life and even of humanity, which is always implicit in astronomical time frames, offers a sense of continuity and calm, making the preoccupation with present human suffering seem a "contracted view." Cruelly, however, Idris's amusement is dispelled in the very next lines by the news that her own child, Evelyn, is sick with a fever. Taking the long view is incompatible with social human existence, as Merrival's disregard for his family also documents. However, he does not retain his aloof attitude either. When he loses his own family to the plague, he falls into a "delirium of excessive grief" resembling another kind of madness. Only at the personal loss does he feel "the system of universal nature which he had so long studied and adored, slide from under him," and he curses God:

> His accent of bitter scorn thrilled me – 'Do not tempt me to speak,' he continued, 'my words would scare you – in an universe of cowards I dare think – among the church-yard tombs – among the victims of His merciless tyranny I dare reproach the Supreme Evil ... I do not fear His hell, for I have it here; I do not desire His heaven, let me but die and be laid beside them; let me but, when I lie dead, feel my flesh as it moulders, mingle with theirs. Promise,' and he raised himself painfully, and seized my arm, 'promise to bury me with them.' (pp. 305-6)

Merrival himself is forced to adopt a "contracted view" of human life, and he quickly dies, "embracing the sod" on the graves of his family, his gaze now averted from the heavens, his awareness of the body in marked contrast to his former disregard of physical comfort, either his own or his family's. Where Merrival had been mildly disturbed at the prospect of "earthly hell" in several hundred thousand years' time, he now rages about finding hell on earth through the loss of his loved ones. Hence, his own "long view" is discredited, its seeming epistemological advantages exploded by the encounter with suffering and contingency, which it cannot alleviate or counter.

As the narrator reminisces about the final days with his friends, he recalls their difficulties in finding anything they dared read, since too many works of literature seemed to bring to their minds "combinations and emotions never more to be experienced by us":

> Metaphysical disquisition; fiction, which wandering from all reality, lost itself in self-created errors; poets of times so far gone by, that to read of them was as to read of Atlantis and Utopia; or such as referred to nature only, and the workings of one particular mind; but most of all, talk, varied and ever new, beguiled our hours. (p. 431)

Literature as a means of communication and of establishing human rapport has acquired a negative function, since it *suggests* a human community for which the survivors can no longer hope. Fiction that is its own single object and purpose is a good distraction from reality, and similarly, Verney's own narrative later functions for him "as an opiate; while it described my beloved friends, fresh with life and glowing with hope, active assistants on the scene, I was soothed" (p. 267). Crucially, this soothing function of fiction is entirely independent of readers – being the Last Man, Verney does not have, and could never have, any readers. Hence, he bids "Farewell to the arts ... farewell to poetry and deep philosophy, for man's imagination is cold, and his enquiring mind can no longer expatiate on the wonders of life, for 'there is no work, nor device, nor knowledge, nor wisdom in the grave, whither thou goest!'" (p. 321) However, in the face of this pathetic lament, Verney's narrative practice reveals that "composition can perform a function independent of readers; it has value independent of the 'transaction' that takes place between an author and a reader."[60]

60 Samantha Webb, "Reading the End of the World: *The Last Man*, History, and the Agency of Romantic Authorship," *Mary Shelley in her Times*, eds Betty T. Bennett and Stuart Curran (Baltimore: Johns Hopkins University Press, 2000), pp. 119-33 (127).

3. Conclusion

For all the criticism that Michel Foucault's writings on madness have had to endure, one of his conclusions still bears consideration. Foucault argues that there is a shift, in "the second half of the eighteenth century," when

> madness was no longer recognized in what brings man closer to an immemorial fall or an indefinitely present animality; it was, on the contrary, situated in those distances man takes in regard to himself, to his world, to all that is offered by the immediacy of nature ... madness was possible because of everything which, in man's life and development, is a break with the immediate.[61]

The fictional astronomers considered above seem to sit on either side of this divide – they *are* overly cerebral, devoted to distancing themselves through speculation from the world and its immediate concerns. At the same time, they do not have to be half-bears to show recognizably 'base' instincts, notably for domination over others.

The Laputians appear mad to Gulliver (and the reader) because they choose the otherworldly over the mundane and useful. That is the classic argument against Thales, but what is more, they do not hold a sound balance between imagination and reason, and they ignore the scientist's moral obligation to use his art for good, and to know its limitations. In Cavendish, the verdict of madness against the bear-men is based on their self-condemning admission that they prefer delusions over fiction; they purposefully delude themselves, and their shared delusion has social causes and effects. In Johnson, Imlac states that the astronomer misinterprets signs and has concluded wrongly from his observations; and the astronomer – much like Shelley's Merrival – comes to conclude that the mundane matters more. The bear-men and the Laputians do not see their own madness; Johnson's and Shelley's astronomers eventually do, although Merrival's insight only precipitates his further descent into another kind.

Madness emerges, from the representation and evaluation of these astronomers, as relative – in Cavendish and Swift, 'sane' society shuns the astronomers, and the astronomers, society. In both, it is ultimately the reader who imputes madness to them. Lennox suggests that a disregard of astronomy can constitute a kind of foolishness in otherwise worldly people, while knowledge of astronomical matters does not necessarily indicate soundness of mind or prevent social ostracism. In Johnson, and to some extent in Shelley, madness

61 Michel Foucault, *Madness and Civilization: A History of Insanity in the Age of Reason* (1961), trans. Richard Howard (New York: Random House, 1988), p. 220.

actually arises from the sublime object of observation, whereas in Cavendish and Swift the conclusion that someone should be seen as 'mad' arises rather from their social context. Astronomers behave ridiculously and impractically, or they are simply misunderstood. The 'distancing' that Foucault speaks of, however, is evident as the astronomer is used, in the Thales anecdotes and in fiction, as a representative of someone who disregards the immediate in favour of the delights of fancy's delusions. In all instances, astronomer-characters also offer commentary on the legitimacy of fiction: Cavendish gives her bear-men's madness licence, as long as it remains inconsequential; Swift's Laputians show how the imagination will assert itself against repression; Johnson's astronomer is crushed by his delusions of responsibility; Lennox's Arabella shows, even before she sees the error of her ways, that an understanding of science and a misunderstanding of fiction are not mutually exclusive and need not preclude social competence; Shelley's astronomer is pulled from blissful oblivion into the painful awareness of his own impotence. If there is an ethical point to Swift's astronomers, it is surely right to see it in the responsibility for the practical applicability of science; in Johnson and Lennox, it is about the dangers of the imagination and of reading; and in Shelley, it is about the relative importance of 'abstract,' timeless science and immediate personal relationships subject to contingency.

PHILOSOPHICAL AND RELIGIOUS ISSUES

David Alvarez and Patrick Müller
DePauw University, Greencastle and Dresden

Anatomies of Unbelief: Clandestine Dialogues between Swift and Shaftesbury

Abstract. As satirists of religious enthusiasm, Swift and the third Earl of Shaftesbury sometimes were confused with one another in the eighteenth century. Their politics and understandings of religion, however, made them each other's satirical target. This essay argues that, in order to understand the partisan dialogue between Shaftesbury and Swift, it is necessary to grasp its clandestine nature. Only very close readings of the two writers' texts unveil their hidden allusions to each other; in fact, these were part of a strategic game of rhetorical hide-and-seek. In the light of this premise, new interpretations of both Shaftesbury and Swift are being offered, showing that their intellectual duel was far more than a footnote in the struggle between Whigs and Tories. Rather, this clandestine dialogue reveals the broader lines of their political and religious battle.

1. Introduction[1]

On the face of it, two men could not have been more different in character, temper, and their most cherished ideals than Jonathan Swift and Anthony Ashley Cooper, third Earl of Shaftesbury (1671-1713). However, in the intellectual climate of the 1700s, it was possible to think that the author of the decade's most notorious literary *succès de scandale, A Tale of a Tub*, had a few years later also written *A Letter concerning Enthusiasm.* In terms of literary tone – especially their practice of religious satire – it seems that contemporaries detected many similarities between two men who were instrumental in shaping the ideologies of Whigs and Tories in this age of political contention. The question is how this was possible when the agendas of these two titanic writers were ostensibly worlds apart: the one an Irish clergyman turned energetic campaigner for the

1 The authors wish to express their gratitude to that most knowledgeable of all Shaftesbury scholars, Dr Christine Jackson-Holzberg, Munich, for her invaluable assistance in preparing this essay.

 | DOI:10.30965/9783846763971_014

Harley administration, the other a staunch believer in Whig principles[2] who came to be regarded as the "Oracle of Deism" after his premature death in 1713.[3]

Based on these observations, our reading of some of Swift's and Shaftesbury's texts might have to be readjusted; indeed, the antagonism between these two giants was far more pronounced than has hitherto been recognized. In fact, we would like to suggest that there was an extended, clandestine dialogue between the two men in some of their texts published between 1704 and 1714, a dialogue that helps us understand the importance of religion for both the politics of the day and for the practice of satire. Apart from open, partisan hostility, clandestinity was an important stylistic strategy;[4] rhetorical figures of indeterminacy were used to veil authorial intent, and hidden allusions were employed to attack other writers who were meant to remain anonymous for reasons of decency or caution. Besides opening up new contexts, the evidence that is produced here draws heavily on the work of other scholars. Admittedly, some of this 'evidence' is based on rhetorical analogies that could easily be contested. However, to bolster our argument we would like to point out that there is a common thrust underlying the various arrows shot by both writers: the role of religion in personal lives, society, and the State.

Moreover, the relationship between these iconic figures reveals a great deal about the importance and inner mechanisms of literary circles as well as about partisan techniques of composition in early eighteenth-century England. Many

---

2 Both men, however, continuously professed to converse with men from both parties and that they were willing to compromise. Such claims help explain some of the intricacies encountered here.

3 In Elisha Smith's *The Cure of Deism: or, The Mediatorial Scheme by Jesus Christ the Only True Religion. In Answer to the Objections Started, and to the Very Imperfect Account of the Religion of Nature, and of Christianity, Given by the Two Oracles of Deism, the Author of Christianity as Old as the Creation; and the Author of the Characteristicks*, 2 vols (London: W. Innys and R. Manby, 1737).

4 For general introductions, see, for example, Margaret C. Jacob, "The Clandestine Universe of the Early Eighteenth Century" (<http://www.pierre-marteau.com/c/jacob/clandestine.html>, accessed 3 June 2017), and Leo Strauss, "Persecution and the Art of Writing," *Persecution and the Art of Writing* (Chicago and London: University of Chicago Press, 1980 [1952]), pp. 22-37. For Swift and Shaftesbury, see Lawrence E. Klein, *Shaftesbury and the Culture of Politeness: Moral Discourse and Cultural Politics in Early Eighteenth-Century England* (Cambridge: Cambridge University Press, 1994), pp. 181-83; John Sitter, *Arguments of Augustan Wit* (Cambridge: Cambridge University Press, 1991), pp. 132-37; James Noggle, *The Skeptical Sublime: Aesthetic Ideology in Pope and the Tory Satirists* (Oxford: Oxford University Press, 2001), pp. 91-96; and Ronald Paulson, *Don Quixote in England: The Aesthetics of Laughter* (Baltimore: The Johns Hopkins University Press, 1998), pp. 121-31. See also James Pratt's thoughts on "Shaftesbury and Swift (or Shaftesbury *as* Swift)" (<http://spectacledavenger.blogspot.de/2015/08/a-tale-of-tub.html>, accessed 4 June 2017).

of the texts circulated in manuscript form before they were published; some of them were radically rethought and reworked after inception.[5] The surviving library catalogues of both Swift and Shaftesbury suggest that they were oblivious to each other. Yet while Shaftesbury's works do not appear to have been in Swift's library at all, we know from the Earl's correspondence that he received and read texts written by Swift after his library catalogue had been compiled in 1709.[6] Like almost everyone else, he had read *A Tale of a Tub*, and he was to prove an especially close reader of Swift's *Proposal for Correcting, Improving, and Ascertaining the English Tongue* (1712). Swift had read at least Shaftesbury's *Letter concerning Enthusiasm* and *Miscellaneous Reflections*. However, there is more than meets the eye, and the devils that the two men saw in each other are indeed hidden in the details of their texts.

2. A Not So Modest Proposal: The Clandestine Rhetoric of Swift and Shaftesbury

Any assessment of the relationship between the two men will at some point have to refer to Shaftesbury's vicious attack on Swift in a letter to Pierre Coste, written in Naples on 25 July 1712:

> Witness the prevalency and first Success of that detestable Writing of that most detestable Author of the *Tale of a Tub*, whose Manners, Life and prostitute Pen and Tongue are indeed exactly answerable to the Irregularity, Obscenity,

5 For the circulation of Swift's manuscripts, see Stephen Karian, "Manuscript Circulation through 1714," *Jonathan Swift in Print and Manuscript* (Cambridge: Cambridge University Press, 2010), pp. 44-71. For the circulation of manuscripts in general, as a form of "scribal" publication, see Harold Love, *Scribal Publication in Seventeenth-Century England* (Oxford: Clarendon Press, 1993).

6 See <http://www.dozenten.anglistik.phil.uni-erlangen.de/shaftesbury/rr_engfrit.html>, accessed 31 May 2017. In 1985, Pickering and Chatto sold a copy of William Wotton's *Reflections upon Ancient and Modern Learning, to which is now Added a Defense thereof, in Answer to the Objections of Sir W. Temple with Observations upon the Tale of a Tub* (London: Tim. Goodwin, 1705), extracted from Shaftesbury's library, the remnants of which survive at the family's ancestral seat, St Giles's House in Dorset (see <http://www.dozenten.anglistik.phil.uni-erlangen.de/shaftesbury/rr_christies.html>, accessed 17 June 2016). For the books relating to Swift sent to Shaftesbury in Naples, see Patrick Müller, "Mapping a Tory's 'prostitute Pen and Tongue': Satire, Criticism, and the Political Dimension of Shaftesbury's Aversion to Swift," *"The first wit of the age": Essays on Swift and his Contemporaries in Honour of Hermann J. Real*, eds Kirsten Juhas, Patrick Müller, and Mascha Hansen (Frankfurt: Peter Lang, 2013), pp. 297-314 (306). Moreover, the library catalogue contains [John Oldmixon], *The History of Addresses: By one Very Near a Kin to the Author of the Tale of a Tub* (London, 1709); see <http://www.dozenten.anglistik.phil.uni-erlangen.de/shaftesbury/rr_engfrit.html>, accessed 27 June 2017.

> Profaneness and fulsomeness of his false Wit and scurrilous Style and Humor. Yet You know how this extraordinary Work pleas'd even our great Philosophers themselves; and how few of those who dislik'd it dar'd declare against it.[7]

Shaftesbury's uncharacteristically vituperative language, an attack on both Swift's life and writings, reveals a deep animosity. Something that has been overlooked so far is an interesting chronological coincidence and a passage in Swift's *Proposal for Correcting, Improving, and Ascertaining the English Tongue* which helps us understand the Earl's anger. The *Proposal*, published on 17 May 1712, was sent to Shaftesbury, then in Naples, soon after publication. He was still very much interested in reading about partisan politics in England, with a clear bias for anything Swift and those who commented on him had to offer.[8] In the *Proposal* itself, he would inevitably have stumbled across the following passage:

> SEVERAL young Men at the Universities, terribly possessed with the fear of Pedantry ... think all Politeness to consist in reading the daily Trash sent down to them ... This they call *knowing the World*, and *reading Men and Manners*. Thus furnished they come up to Town, reckon all their Errors for Accomplishments, borrow the newest Sett of Phrases, and if they take a Pen into their Hands, all the odd Words they have picked up in a Coffee House ... are produced as Flowers of Style, and the Orthography refined to the utmost ... To this we owe that strange Race of Wits, who tell us, they Write to the *Humour of the Age*: And I wish I could say, these quaint Fopperies were wholly absent from graver Subjects.[9]

---

7 Shaftesbury to Pierre Coste, 25 July 1712 (TNA: PRO 30/24/23/9, fol. 131r), due to be published in a forthcoming volume (*Correspondence* III 5) of the *Standard Edition: Complete Works, Selected Letters and Posthumous Writings*, eds Wolfram Benda, *et al.* (Stuttgart-Bad Cannstatt: frommann-holzboog, 1981-2017). All references to the Earl's writings will be to this edition. The treatises are: *Soliloquy: or, Advice to an Author* and *Letter concerning Enthusiasm* (I, 1); *Miscellaneous Reflections* (I, 2); *Sensus Communis* and *Instructions* to the printer for the second edition of *Characteristicks* (I, 3); *Ainsworth Correspondence* (II, 4). Unless otherwise indicated, we give the versions of the texts published individually by Shaftesbury before 1711 (the year when he collected them in *Characteristicks*; references in square brackets are to this edition) since these were the only texts Swift could have referred to in his own writings up to 1711 (with the exception of the *Proposal for Correcting, Improving, and Ascertaining the English Tongue* as well as the Earl's *Miscellaneous Reflections*, which was the only treatise he wrote specifically for inclusion in *Characteristicks*).

8 For the chronology, see Müller, "Mapping a Tory's 'prostitute Pen and Tongue': Satire, Criticism, and the Political Dimension of Shaftesbury's Aversion to Swift," pp. 305-6.

9 *A Proposal for Correcting, Improving, and Ascertaining the English Tongue* (London: Benjamin Tooke, 1712), pp. 24-25. See also Swift's complaints about Anglican preachers who are "full fraught with Admiration of our Town Politeness" and "*understand Men and Manners*" ("Tatler, no 230," *Parodies, Hoaxes, Mock Treatises: Polite Conversation, Directions to Servants and Other Works*, ed. Valerie Rumbold [Cambridge: Cambridge University Press, 2013],

These lines constitute, most obviously so, unfavourable reflections on the author of *Characteristicks on Men, Manners, Opinions, Times*, published in 1711.[10] This curious philosophical work, which consists of three neatly structured tomes, contains various attacks against "*Pedantry* and *Bigotry*" ("Mill-stones able to sink the best Book;" *Sensus Communis*, p. 26 [67]). Above all, it outlined a cultural programme based on the concept of "politeness."[11] By publishing *Characteristicks*, Shaftesbury aimed to wrest away from Tories and High-Churchmen their "Soveraignty in Arts & Sciences, their Presidentship in Letters, their Alma-Mater's and Academical virtues, which have been acknowleg'd and taken for granted" and instead reveal them "not as Corrupters merely of Morals & Publick Principles; but the very Reverse or Antipodes of Good Breeding, Schollership, Behaviour, Sense & Manners."[12] The polished style of Shaftesbury was one of the features that caught the attention of early readers, and it was this stylistic adroitness, marked by his experiments in literary form and celebration of raillery, which was meant as an antidote to the "current Humour *of* the Times" based on "the irregular fancy of the World" (*Soliloquy*, p. 178).[13]

In their efforts to diagnose and cure the "current Humour *of* the Times," we are here drawn right into the middle of the dialogue between Swift and Shaftesbury: in the *Tale*, the bookseller mentions that "*our present Writers*" often fit texts "to the Humour *of* the Age."[14] Both writers sought to provide antidotes to the present age,[15] and yet both apparently saw the antidotes of

---

pp. 89-103 [101-2]). Published on 28 September 1710, this is probably a reference to two famous passages in *Soliloquy* (first published in June 1710), which define poetry in a classical vein as "*an Imitation* chiefly of Men and Manners," the true poet being a master in "describ[ing] both *Men* and *Manners*" (pp. 94-96 and 108-10). It thus offers, *in nuce*, the same criticism later to be specified in the *Proposal*.

10 For another possible cross-reference between the *Proposal* (pp. 6-7) and *Soliloquy*, p. 130 [223], see <http://spectacledavenger.blogspot.de/2015/08/a-tale-of-tub.html>, accessed 4 June 2017.

11 A comprehensive survey is found in Klein's seminal study *Shaftesbury and the Culture of Politeness*, *passim*.

12 Shaftesbury to Somers, 30 March 1711 (TNA: PRO 30/24/22/4, fols 355-56).

13 We believe that Swift was chief among the "modern Authors" attacked in this passage. The characterization of "our *Writers* as unshapen still and monstrous in their Works" clearly anticipates the language of the Coste-letter (p. 178); see also the remark that "*the Bookseller* [makes] *the Author*" (p. 180).

14 Jonathan Swift, *A Tale of a Tub and Other Works*, ed. Marcus Walsh (Cambridge: Cambridge University Press, 2010), p. 19.

15 An expression Swift also used in "The Sentiments of a Church-of-England Man with Respect to Religion and Government," *Miscellanies in Prose and Verse* (London: John Morphew, 1711), pp. 95-151 (115) in the context of Whiggish attacks against the High Church

the other as part of the problem. Shaftesbury seems to refer to this passage in the section from *Soliloquy*, and now it was Swift's turn in the *Proposal* to tell Shaftesbury that his cultural programme of Whig politeness had failed spectacularly; instead, all that he had achieved was to bring the "quaint Fopperies" of the town to prospective clergymen at England's universities who, unfortunately, adopted these in their writings on "graver Subjects," just as the Earl had done in *Characteristicks*.[16]

In this way, it seems, Shaftesbury's thought had infected and corrupted the minds of those being educated for work in the Church. Given the view Swift seems to have had of the ideas presented throughout *Characteristicks*, few things could have been more repellent to him. In fact, the veiled attack in the *Proposal* is even more poignant upon closer inspection: the Earl's express aim had been to liberate "Lady" philosophy from the confines of academic "Colleges and Cells" (*Moralists*, p. 24 [184]) and to re-establish her, as Shaftesbury added in the 1714 edition of *Characteristicks*, on the "publick *Stage*" as a tool for refining the minds of prospective statesmen (*Moralists*, p. 24 [184]). According to Swift, however, a fine example of the knowledge which "young Men at the Universities" gain from the trash of the town and coffee houses is that they care more about "Orthography refined to the utmost" than about the meaning of the words they parrot and prettify. Style triumphs over substance, foppery over serious consideration of graver political and religious matters.[17]

These hidden references help us understand the nature of the 'dialogue' between Shaftesbury and Swift. The two never attacked each other openly. Rather, they would reflect on each other's ideas by way of short quotations or indirect allusions: the passage from the *Proposal* is replete with Shaftesburian

clergy: "THEREFORE a *Church of England* Man abhors the Humor of the Age in delighting to fling Scandals upon the Clergy in general; which ... casts an Ignominy upon the Kingdom that it doth not deserve." This text might well be regarded as a companion piece to the anti-Shaftesburian *Argument against Abolishing Christianity* (see Section IV below). Both were said to have been written in 1708.

16 In December 1711, roughly half a year after the publication of *Characteristicks*, Shaftesbury's friend Sir John Cropley wrote to James Stanhope claiming that "Characteristicks has a wonderfull reputation Oxford dos not encounter it & all ye foreign universities exstol it" (Kent History and Library Centre, Maidstone; Stanhope of Chevening Manuscripts, CKS U1590 C9/31). The Earl's letter to Michael Ainsworth of 3 June 1709 shows that *The Moralists* was also read in Oxford (*Ainsworth Correspondence*, p. 403). John Toland spent two years (1694/5) at Oxford.

17 See "The Sentiments of a Church-of-England Man," pp. 112-13, where the Whigs are accused of "insult[ing] the *Universities* as Poisoned Fountains, and Corrupters of Youth." Swift's persona concludes that the Whigs had "encouraged or connived ... Intemperance of Speech, and Virulence of Pen, in the worst and most prostitute of the Party," most probably the freethinkers.

vocabulary and references to the style of *Characteristicks*, just as the Earl's own *Soliloquy* is at times rife with obvious allusions to Swift's work. The allusive character of these clandestine methods makes it difficult to produce indubitable evidence. Nonetheless, Shaftesbury had certainly read Swift's *Proposal*. On 1 September 1712, in a letter sent to his friend Thomas Micklethwaite to be passed on to his printer John Darby without the more personal remarks, he sarcastically referred to "the new Reformer of Language and Witt, (Doctor *Swift*)" (*Instructions*, p. 238).[18] Shaftesbury criticized Swift, who while he complains particularly about the "Multiplication of Monosyllables, can afford to come out with them by Dozens, and by Twentys in a String ... in so short a Piece; which he might so easily have polish'd" (*Instructions*, pp. 238-40). Since he was counting syllables, Shaftesbury, that great enemy of pedantry, seems to have read the text rather closely.

Based on such references, one could argue that two great artists and stylists, tuned to even the most oblivious linguistic niceties, had found an encrypted prose which could only be understood by a close circle of adepts. But why would they go to such lengths? The available evidence will eventually enable us to show that both men represented certain 'types' for each other. For Swift, Shaftesbury was the snobbish, elitist freethinker and, consequently, an enemy of the Church only a Whig could turn into, whereas the former was for the latter the epitome of the High Church clergyman whose morose temper turned him into an enemy of decency, good-breeding, liberty, and, consequently, of a cultural renovation in England. This helps us explain why both of them actually saw the necessity to refer to each other's writings intermittently: despite their public reputations as leading satirists of religion, each of them embodied for the other the most dangerous religious tendencies of the time.

18 For evidence that Shaftesbury owned and read the second edition of the *Proposal*, see Clive T. Probyn, "Jonathan Swift, the Third Earl of Shaftesbury, and the Monosyllable," *Swift Studies*, 22 (2007), 97-101 (pp. 99-100). However, Probyn does not realize that the passage he quotes to prove his argumentation (on p. 25 of the *Proposal*) contains direct references to Shaftesbury. Dating the rise of "harsh and unharmonious" monosyllables to "the Time of the Restoration," Swift links the loss of a polite style to post-Civil War politics. Shaftesbury contests such a history of style by linking its progress to Whig political liberty. His instructions to Darby to adhere to a strict limit of "*Nine* consecutive Monosyllables" also playfully allude to his own strictures on their use in *Miscellaneous Reflections*. Shaftesbury's criticisms of Swift's monosyllables and other stylistic infelicities show that the latter cannot rise to a polite style (he is "a *Prose*-Author, who attempts to write politely;" p. 310 [265]) – even when he knows its characteristics.

3. There is No Politics without Religion, and: Does the "Digression concerning Madness" Satirize the *Inquiry*?

In identifying Shaftesbury as a danger for contemporary churchmen, Swift's *Proposal* placed the Earl squarely in the camp of the Deists or freethinkers. In this context, it is first of all important to look at the way Swift himself used such terminology. In the *Argument against Abolishing Christianity*, we find him chastise "the Atheists, Deists, Socinians, Anti-Trinitarians, and other subdivisions of free-thinkers."[19] It seems, then, that he could not be bothered with any terminological niceties: the tribe of the freethinkers was for him the body of the Hydra rearing ever so many ugly heads. The truly Deist writers of the time, John Toland, whom Swift calls "the great oracle of Antichristians" in the *Argument*, and Matthew Tindal, who is accused of having been "reconciled to the Romish faith," were for Swift the propagandist "free-thinkers" patronized by the Whigs, who were in turn to be blamed for "the trumpery" published by their protégés.[20]

As he was to write in *Examiner*, no 39, "We accuse [the Whigs] of the public encouragement and patronage to Tindal, Toland, and other atheistical writers."[21] This accusation is significant as it provides the foundation for a more detailed investigation of the rift between Shaftesbury and Swift, one which at the same time epitomizes the divide between Whigs and Tories.

Of course, Shaftesbury came to be regarded as one of the paradigmatic Deist writers himself as the eighteenth century progressed. He would, however, have begged to differ, for he saw profound discrepancies between his own Cudworthian 'Theism' and the atheistic tendencies he detected in contemporary Deist writers.[22] Be that as it may, any reader of Swift and Shaftesbury knows that the realms of the political and the religious, both undergoing momentous shifts at the time, were disciplines not to be divided. It has been argued that the term 'religion' should be regarded as an object of political

19 *An Argument to Prove that the Abolishing of Christianity in England, May as Things Stand now, Be Attended with some Inconveniencies, and perhaps not Produce those many Good Effects Proposed thereby*, in *Jonathan Swift: Major Works*, eds Angus Ross and David Woolley (Oxford and New York: Oxford University Press, 1984), pp. 217-27 (225).

20 *An Argument against Abolishing Christianity*, in *Jonathan Swift*, eds Ross and Woolley, pp. 225-26. In fact, Shaftesbury was among the patrons from whom Tindal received financial aid (see *Ainsworth Correspondence*, p. 403,6n [455]).

21 3 May 1711 (*Prose Works*, III, 142). For another comparison between the principles of Whigs, Dissenters, and freethinkers, see "The Sentiments of a Church-of-England Man," pp. 100-1.

22 For an in-depth investigation, see Patrick Müller, "A Pious Heathen: Shaftesbury's Enlightened Critique of Religion and the Question of Deism," forthcoming.

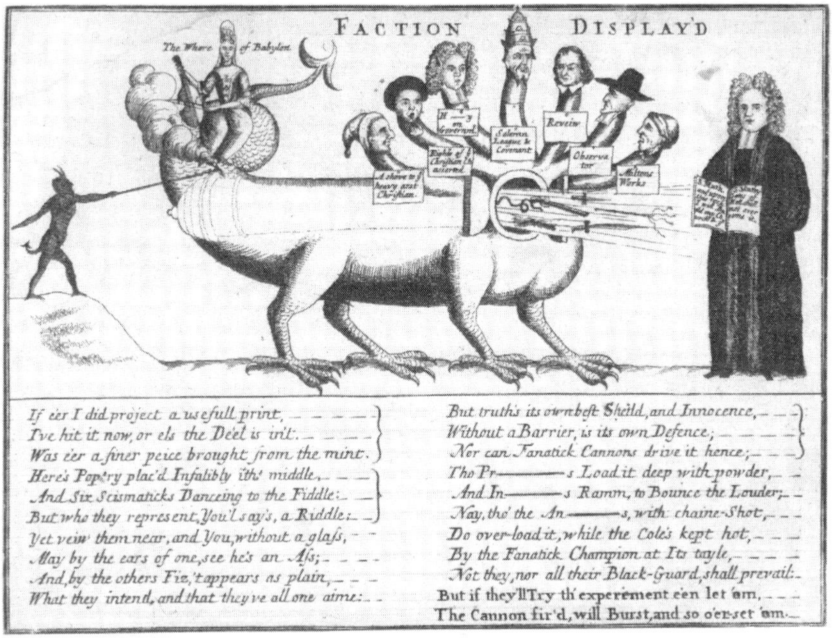

FIGURE 13.1 *Faction Display'd*

Note: Swift's verbal description bears striking resemblances to satirical prints published at the time in the context of the Sacheverell affair; see this broadsheet here (BM Satires 1508) and also BM Satires 1502. *Faction Display'd* (whose title refers to a 1705 poem of the same name attributed to Defoe) shows, among others, Tindal (as the author of *Rights of the Christian Church Asserted*) and Toland (as author of the "Life of Milton," which prefaced his edition of Milton's *Works*) as two of seven heads of an atheistical beast.

analysis; in fact, the eighteenth century saw religion being transformed, partly by a political project.[23] Branding Toland and Tindal "atheistical writers" patronized by the Whigs, and hailing Lord Somers as a "*Deist*" and "*Socinian*"

23 See Klein, *Shaftesbury and the Culture of Politeness*, p. 9. See also Talal Asad in Craig Martin, "*Genealogies of Religion*, Twenty Years On: An Interview with Talal Asad," *Bulletin for the Study of Religion*, 43 (2014), 12-17 (p. 13): "My problem with 'universal definitions of religion,' therefore, has been that by insisting on a universal essence they divert us from asking questions about what the definition includes and what it excludes, how, by whom, for what purpose." Swift remarked, in "The Sentiments of a Church-of-England Man," that "the Extreams of *Whig* and *Tory* seem with little Justice to have drawn Religion into their Controversies, wherein they have small Concern" (p. 102).

intimately acquainted with Toland's writings in *Examiner*, no 26,[24] Swift paradigmatically reflects this amalgamation of religion and party politics, despite his repeated statements that he could not care less about the differences between Whig and Tory.[25] As a clergyman, he of course believed in the State's "right to require specific religious observances."[26] He was more concerned with and about religious doctrine, and in how far adherence to the Established Church was necessary for keeping England free from civil disorder.[27] For many Tories, accusing the Whigs of undermining the Anglican Church was a propagandistic tool meant to expose the other party's thirst for contention, their deplorable lack of the intellectual discipline required to keep peace in the country.[28] In a nutshell, while Swift was more concerned with the institutional aspects of religion, Shaftesbury's focus was on both individual spirituality and the individual's right *not* to exercise certain religious observances. In this respect, the Earl was of course a freethinker himself. As early as 1701, he wrote to Pierre Des Maizeaux: "I have a generall Acquaintance (as you very well know) with most of our Modern Authors & free-Writers, severall of whome I have a particular influence over."[29] However, just as with the Deists (a term he, like Swift, might have used interchangeably with free-thinking), he came to regard

24 *Prose Works*, III, 142. For the semantic spectrum of the terms "Deism" and "Socinianism," see the Online.Swift commentary on the *Apology: An Apology for the, &c*, eds Hermann J. Real, *et al.* (Online.Swift/Ehrenpreis Centre for Swift Studies, Münster, February 2013, updated September 2017, <http://www.online-swift.de/apology.note.apol_007.html>, accessed 17 January 2018).

25 See "The Sentiments of a Church-of-England Man," where we find the claim that "I converse in full Freedom with many considerable Men of both Parties" (p. 98).

26 See the introduction to *An Argument against Abolishing Christianity*, in *Jonathan Swift*, eds Ross and Woolley, p. 641.

27 In "The Sentiments of a Church-of-England Man," "*Occasional Conformity*" is called "an Evil in it self" (pp. 107-8) and Swift's persona points out the "Danger to the Publick Peace" consequent upon the debate. Moreover, "any great separation from the Established Worship ... may be an Occasion of endangering the Publick Peace" (p. 119). The Tory critic Mary Astell argues similarly against Shaftesbury in *Bart'lemy Fair: or, An Enquiry after Wit, in which Due Respect is Had to a Letter concerning Enthusiasm, to my Lord* *** (London: R. Wilkin, 1709), pp. 23-25, 110-11.

28 See "The Sentiments of a Church-of-England Man," where the Deist freethinkers, under "the shelter of some popular Principles in Politicks and Religion, undermine the Foundations of all Piety and Virtue" (p. 117). The argument then points out the dangers of these practices for "the Publick Peace" (see preceding footnote).

29 5 August 1701 (British Library, Add. MSS 4288, fol. 98r). At this time, Shaftesbury occasionally supported, for example, William Stephens, whose 1701 sermon before the Commons caused considerable controversy. For Stephens, see J. A. Downie, "William Stephens and the *Letter to the Author of the Memorial of the State of England* Reconsidered," *Bulletin of the Institute of Historical Research*, 50 (1977), 253-59.

the freethinkers as a misguided set of writers who "now a days have espousd those Principles wch Mr *Hobbs* set afoot in this last Age."[30]

At this point, it is time to introduce one of the key differences between Swift and Shaftesbury as thinkers and writers.[31] In the Earl's case, there was almost always a constructive appeal in his thought. In free-thinking, enthusiasm, and 'Deism,' for example, he saw two sides of a coin. The polished face of the free-thinking coin is shown in *Miscellaneous Reflections* (written in late 1710), in which Shaftesbury outlines "the noblest of Characters (that of a *Free-Thinker*)" (p. 366 [311]) as that of a reasonable philosopher who champions liberty, whereas those High Church (and, by implication, Tory) divines for whom "*a* LIBERTY in *Thought* and *Action*, implies Debauch, Corruption, and Depravity" (p. 358 [305]) are branded as agents of tyranny and persecution.[32] For him, High Church Anglicans represented the "peremptory institutionalism of Peter [Catholicism]" in Swift's *Tale*; at the same time, Shaftesbury stood for "the anarchic, egotistical individualism of Jack [radical personal belief]."[33] Indeed, Shaftesbury's own religion can best be described as that of a 'pious heathen,'[34] who believed in a benevolent deity caring more about the sincerity of individual expressions of faith and ethical behaviour (without a Deity meting out rewards or punishments) in everyday life and privacy than about institutional intrusion in matters of faith.[35] For Swift, such professions must have reeked of dissent.

While Shaftesbury's attitude towards Deism was ambivalent, the same holds true for his treatment of enthusiasm. Together with *The Moralists* (January 1709), his *Letter concerning Enthusiasm* (1708) constitutes a comprehensive philosophical treatment of both the aberrations and the individual uses of

30 The problems Shaftesbury saw were their denial of natural order and, as he told Ainsworth, the ethical relativism these writers espoused, which "threw all *Order* & *Vertue* out of ye World, & made ye Very Ideas of these (wch are ye same as those of *God*) *unnatural* & without foundation in our Minds" (*Ainsworth Correspondence*, p. 403).

31 These could be attributed to their different ideas about the nature of satire (also discussed below): Juvenalian in Swift, Horatian in Shaftesbury (see Müller, "Mapping a Tory's 'prostitute Pen and Tongue': Satire, Criticism, and the Political Dimension of Shaftesbury's Aversion to Swift," pp. 307-8, and Barbara Schmidt-Haberkamp, "Shaftesbury's Concept of Ridicule as an Antecedent to Scriblerian Satire," *Swift Studies*, 17 [2002], 125-34).

32 This connection is also made in "The Sentiments of a Church-of-England Man": "Thus, the Atheists, Libertines, Despisers of Religion and Revelation in general, that is to say, all those who usually pass under the name of *Free-Thinkers*, do properly join with the [Whigs]" (pp. 100-1).

33 See the introduction to Jonathan Swift, *A Tale of a Tub and Other Works*, eds Angus Ross and David Woolley (Oxford and New York: Oxford University Press, 1991 [1986]), p. x.

34 We are indebted to Professor Friedrich A. Uehlein for this phrase.

35 See the introspective yet enthusiastic "Prayer" in SE II,6 (532-41).

enthusiasm, propounding a Whig defence of tolerance against the Tory spirit of persecution. Both texts can be read as a Whig reply to Swift's *Tale* (which is not to say that *we* read this as a Tory text) and its "attack [on] the force of individualistic religion as 'zeal' or 'enthusiasm,' and to ascribe it to pride, that 'sufficiency' which [Sir William] Temple saw as the root of political dissidence and intellectual arrogance."[36] At the same time, these texts, especially *The Moralists*, in which we find Shaftesbury define and embrace a reformed kind of enthusiasm, must have represented exactly these tendencies for Swift.

The "Digression concerning Madness" has been read as an extended satire *cum* parody of the 1699 edition of Shaftesbury's *Inquiry concerning Virtue in Two Discourses* as a principal instance of the modern aberrations of learning.[37] While a good deal of what this critic has to say about both the publication history and the philosophical background of the *Inquiry* is questionable, the textual evidence he produces to support his general argument is at least sometimes compelling. The question that is left unanswered, though, is exactly *why* Swift might have thought it worthwhile to satirize a book which had not left much of a trace upon publication. One answer is that he was killing two birds with one stone: Shaftesbury himself and, by implication, John Toland. That implies, however, that we may take for granted Toland's involvement in both the composition and the publication of the *Inquiry*,[38] or that the stories about Toland's publishing the book surreptitiously were common lore in contemporary literary circles. This is too far of a stretch, since the evidence we have is much too meagre. Moreover, the rhetorical analogies between the *Tale* and the *Inquiry*, based on the musical and anatomical metaphors of both texts, were simply stock-in-trade used by many contemporary writers.[39]

---

36 See Swift, *A Tale of a Tub and Other Works*, eds Ross and Woolley, pp. x-xi.

37 See Kenneth Craven, "Shaftesbury: Virtue Trampled," *Jonathan Swift and the Millennium of Madness: The Information Age in Swift's "A Tale of a Tub"* (Leiden: E. J. Brill, 1992), pp. 85-108. Louis A. Landa argues that Swift's sermon "On the Testimony of Conscience" takes issue with the *Inquiry* (*Prose Works*, IX, 114).

38 A. B. Worden's suggestion that Toland's editorial interference was far more substantial than hitherto supposed can neither be proved nor discarded (see his edition of Edmund Ludlow's *A Voyce from the Watch Tower, Part Five: 1660-1662* [London: Royal Historical Society, 1978], pp. 24, 28-29).

39 Criticism of Craven's theses along these lines can be found in Alfred Owen Aldridge, "Jonathan Swift's Message for Moderns," *Modern Age*, 37 (1995), 170-75 (p. 174). Hugh Ormsby-Lennon's interpretation of Shaftesbury's dedicatory letter to Somers accompanying the *Letter concerning Enthusiasm* (TNA: PRO 30/24/22/4, fols 312-13) exemplifies the interpretative intricacies mentioned above all too well: Ormsby-Lennon thinks that the reference "Writ in Jack's Hand" added above the letter refers to Swift's Jack in the *Tale*;

In order to understand how far Shaftesbury could have stood for "*The Establishment of New Empires by Conquest: The Advance and Progress of New Schemes in Philosophy; and the contriving, as well as the propagating of New Religions*,"[40] it might be useful to broaden the scope of Swift's satirical objects. For this purpose, it is worthwhile to consider the circles the two men moved in at the time when both the *Tale* and the *Inquiry* were composed and published. When Swift finished the first version of the *Tale* in 1697/8, he was at Moor Park. Sir William Temple was, as is well-known,[41] an eminent critic of the first Earl of Shaftesbury's religious politics, and it was Swift who made this criticism eventually public in Temple's *Memoirs* in 1709. In the late seventeenth century, Shaftesbury himself was MP for Poole, and he was closely associated with the Commonwealthmen of the time (including John Trenchard, Walter Moyle, Robert Molesworth, Andrew Fletcher, and, interestingly, Robert Harley). Moreover, he encouraged Toland to edit and publish republican texts by Algernon Sidney, John Milton, and James Harrington.[42]

Moreover, Shaftesbury and Swift both knew Charles Davenant, the former definitely by the mid-1690s, and the latter probably likewise. Swift's cousin Thomas was related to the Davenants on his mother's side, and Swift was later helpful in securing a post for Charles's son Henry Davenant.[43] We know for certain that Shaftesbury's *Inquiry* circulated in manuscript form before it was published in late 1698, Henry Day, author of the only explicit criticism of the *Inquiry*, "having formerly had a sight of the *MS*, tho yet ignorant of the author."[44] It has been claimed that Shaftesbury and Charles Davenant collaborated on the

---

this is more probably, however, the Earl's amanuensis John Howard (see "Swift's Spirit Reconjured: das Dong-an-sich," *Swift Studies*, 3 [1988], 9-78 [p. 67]).

40 *A Tale of a Tub and Other Works*, ed. Walsh, p. 105.

41 See Müller, "Mapping a Tory's 'prostitute Pen and Tongue': Satire, Criticism, and the Political Dimension of Shaftesbury's Aversion to Swift," p. 304.

42 For details, see Patrick Müller, "'An equal Commonwealth': Lord Ashley and the Republican Project of the Late 1690s," *Shaping Enlightenment Politics: The Social and Political Impact of the First and Third Earls of Shaftesbury*, ed. Patrick Müller (Berlin: Peter Lang, 2018), pp. 115-33. For more information on these Commonwealthmen, see Caroline Robbins, *The Eighteenth-Century Commonwealthmen: Studies in the Transmission, Development and Circumstance of English Liberal Thought from the Restoration of Charles II until the War with the Thirteen Colonies* (Cambridge, Massachusetts: Harvard University Press, 1961).

43 See *Correspondence*, ed. Woolley, I, 543-44 and n1.

44 [Henry Day], *Free Thoughts in Defence of a Future State, as Discoverable by Natural Reason, and Stript of All Superstitious Appendages: Demonstrating against the Nominal Deists that the Consideration of Future Advantages is a Just Motive to Virtue; of Future Loss and Misery, a Powerful and Becoming Restraint of Vice. With Occasional Remarks on a Book Intituled, "An Inquiry Concerning Virtue," and a Refutation of the Reviv'd Hylozoicism of Democritus and Leucippus* (London: Daniel Brown and Andrew Bell, 1700), p. 20.

Inquiry, although the evidence we have for this is weak.[45] However, in theory, it does remain possible that Swift saw the manuscript before publication. In his 1701 *Discourse of the Contests and Dissensions between the Nobles and Commons in Athens and Rome*, Swift took to task Charles Davenant's notion of a "balance of power" as spelled out in the *Essays* of the same year.[46]

Of course, Shaftesbury also knew Lord Somers, the man who, as Swift claimed later on, introduced him to "the difference between the principles of Whig and Tory"[47] after having read and admired the *Discourse of the Contests and Dissensions*, which prompted him to seek Swift's acquaintance.[48] Somers did own the *Inquiry*,[49] and it is not at all unlikely that the Irish clergyman was introduced to the text, and maybe even its author, at Somers's London home in the early 1700s.[50] It is exactly the two men's relationship to Somers which is significant: the views on religion of the man whom Swift would later openly vilify as a "Socinian" and "Deist" must have been suspicious to him right from the start. By the time Swift met Somers, Shaftesbury was already associated with the Deist camp for those who knew that he was the author of the *Inquiry* (those being a very select few). The title of Day's reply to the *Inquiry* immediately associated Shaftesbury's thinking, which radically severed ethics from religion, with those people Swift would later diagnose as the religious cancer of the body politic;[51] it must have irritated Swift to find Somers associated with such heterodoxies. It is this complex background that helps us explain why the two men chose to enter their game of literary hide-and-seek, beginning with Swift's reading of the *Inquiry* and oblique inclusion of it in the "Digression concerning Madness": what Swift possibly found in the Earl's text was a heterodox anthropology, one which undermined religion's traditional moral prerogative

45 See Müller, "'An equal Commonwealth': Lord Ashley and the Republican Project of the Late 1690s," p. 127.

46 See Ehrenpreis, *Dr Swift*, pp. 54-55.

47 "Memoirs Relating to that Change which Happened in the Queen's Ministry," *Prose Works*, VIII, 120.

48 See William Lewis Sachse, *Lord Somers: A Political Portrait* (Manchester: Manchester University Press, and Madison, Wisconsin: University of Wisconsin Press, 1975), p. 200.

49 See British Library, Add. MSS 40751, fol. 17r. In fact, the catalogue lists two copies of the *Inquiry*.

50 For the relationship between Swift and Somers at that time, see *Correspondence*, ed. Woolley, I, 147 and n4, 208n5, 257n, n1, 258n4.

51 In early responses to the *Tale*, the author was often depicted as a Deist; see Frank T. Boyle "Profane and Debauched *Deist*: Swift in the Contemporary Response to *A Tale of a Tub*," *Eighteenth-Century Ireland*, 3 (1988), 25-38.

based on the notion of a future state,[52] a move not least designed to undermine John Locke's arguments for the usefulness of the doctrine of futurity in *Reasonableness of Christianity* (1695), which is why Locke's friend William Popple wrote an unpublished reply to Shaftesbury's treatise.[53]

Instinctively, Swift would also have understood (or even discussed with Somers) the veiled political overtones of the *Inquiry*, which presents a Whiggish, moralizing version of the divine-right theory in which the English "commonwealth" is supervised by a benign monarch.[54] The two historical examples Swift produces at the beginning of the "Digression" in order to show the hypocritical causes of human behaviour are French Catholic monarchs, and the context evoked by these examples is that of "Universal Monarchy."[55] At the time Swift wrote the *Tale*, Shaftesbury and his associates were very much concerned to fend off the peril of re-Catholicization, which was of course associated with absolutism. Here, Swift would have remembered Temple's criticism of the first Earl, whose aggressive crusade against 'popery' is the principal subject of the *Memoirs*. In Swift's able hands, the text satirizes both the French monarchs' cruel, ideologically charged practices and the craze about "universal monarchy" among the Whigs as a primary source of frenzied exaggerations. In the third Earl, Swift might have seen a philosophical version of the delusions the grandson had imbibed from that towering political figure, his grandfather. Only someone "whose Fortunes and Dispositions have placed him in a convenient Station to enjoy the Fruits of this noble Art ... to sodder and patch up the Flaws and Imperfections of Nature" could be

> a Man truly wise, cream[ing] off Nature, leaving the Sower and the Dregs, for Philosophy and Reason to lap up. This is the sublime and refined Point of Felicity, called, *the Possession of being well deceived*; The Serene Peaceful State of being a Fool among Knaves.[56]

It is tempting to read these lines as a characterization of Shaftesbury and the ideas he had put forth in the *Inquiry*: the aristocrat gone philosopher, a man

52 For an introduction to the debate and Swift's own position, see Hermann J. Real, "'An horrid Vision': Jonathan Swift's '(On) the Day of Judgement,'" *Swift and his Contexts*, eds John Irwin Fischer, Hermann J. Real, and James Woolley (New York: AMS Press, 1989), pp. 65-96.

53 See British Library, Add. MSS 8888, c. 269.

54 See Patrick Müller "Rewriting the Divine Right Theory for the Whigs: The Political Implications of Shaftesbury's Attack on the Doctrine of Futurity in his *Characteristicks*," *Great Expectations: Futurity in the Long Eighteenth Century*, eds Mascha Hansen and Jürgen Klein (Frankfurt: Peter Lang, 2012), pp. 67-88.

55 *A Tale of a Tub and Other Works*, ed. Walsh, pp. 106-7.

56 *A Tale of a Tub and Other Works*, ed. Walsh, p. 112.

without a care in the world, indulging in lofty ideas of human nature meant to support a benevolently governed, peaceful utopia.[57] We would like to suggest, however, that the scope of the attack is much broader: it blends criticism of the several tendencies Swift found in modern learning, including the Deists' reliance on Epicurean materialism designed to undermine the Christian religion as well as Anglican authority, and Shaftesburian optimism about human nature, meant to question Christian morality and coupled with a political agenda. All these tendencies unwittingly shake the very premise on which they are based, namely the pretence of reasonable enquiry into received truths. The *Tale* exposes these innovations as outpourings of ideologically overcharged individuals, often young men privileged by their inherited social status, and Shaftesbury could well have been one example of this species. Just like the image of the freethinker, we have here a many-headed Hydra rather than a single, identifiable satirical object. While the Hydra is a beautiful, attractive monster, Swift's satire exposes the distortions of its face and the ideas the beast produced as madness, delusion, and frenzy: in his satirical cosmos, the commonwealth appears to be an anarchic intellectual battleground that sees disoriented individuals fumble for elusive points of reference, which inevitably leads them to steer the wrong course. The upshot, it seems, is that only a sane religion provides the moral compass necessary to restore order and peace in the commonwealth. And that was for Swift, of course, Anglicanism (if not necessarily for the *Tale*'s narrator, the Hack).

Consequently, rather than being the sole target of the "Digression," Shaftesbury could be just one among many. His express aim, stated at the outset of the *Inquiry*, to overturn received notions concerning the primacy of religion in ethics introduced a new, unorthodox anthropology and was, as such, one of the "new Schemes in Philosophy" or "new Systems"[58] that the Hack deems worth alluding to in his tour de force through the aberrations of learning. To sum up, saying that Swift unveiled "Shaftesbury's seductive moral philosophy that lulls the modern world into believing that wayward humans … are somehow gaining on the vicious natures that give resonance to the *Tale*'s nasty satiric voice"[59] accords the *Inquiry* too much prominence. It is not least, and quite generally, the Deists' deluded ravings that Swift is taking to task, hypotheses which were already fraught with the Whig connotations that he would later so blatantly demolish for his Tory propaganda. The people he met and the texts he read after meeting Somers might well have prompted him to add

57 Craven, "Shaftesbury: Virtue Trampled," pp. 98-99.

58 *A Tale of a Tub and Other Works*, ed. Walsh, p. 107.

59 Craven, "Shaftesbury: Virtue Trampled," p. 108.

a few spices to the "Digression" designed to pepper his criticism of the latest ideological blend of philosophy, theological speculation, and political theory which he found dangerous.

4. The Shaftesburian Context of Swift's *Argument* and Some Repercussions

By the time Swift penned *An Argument against Abolishing Christianity*, the evidence that the two men were involved with each other had become much more substantial. In order to understand the real anti-Shaftesburian thrust of the *Argument*, it is, however, necessary to have a look at Swift's techniques of composition and Shaftesbury's publications at the time. In 1708, the Earl published (his own initial intentions notwithstanding) the 'infamous' *Letter concerning Enthusiasm*, a book which circulated well before publication and was frequently attributed to Swift.[60] Indeed, we believe that it was the *Letter* that prompted Swift to write the *Argument*.[61] There is no reason, as the 1711 *Miscellanies* tells us, to assume that he did not compose the bulk of the *Argument* in 1708. Yet there are obviously traces of later additions, that is, of techniques of composition which can also be found in the *Tale*. After the publication of the *Letter*, Shaftesbury published, in quick succession, *The Moralists* (January 1709), *Sensus Communis* (May 1709), and *Soliloquy* (June 1710). As we will show, there are references to the first two of these texts in the *Argument*, whereas *Soliloquy*, as we have seen, attacks the *Tale* and resounds in the *Proposal*.

Some of the material Swift used for the *Argument* could well have been overheard at conversations described by Shaftesbury, probably the epitome of the "polite free-thinker,"[62] in his letter to Somers written in March 1708:

> He was in Company at Table with some Divines & University-Men who, upon the Turn of the Discourse towards Bookish Matters, took occasion to rail at several Pieces y^{t} had of late been writ; some in an open way barefac'd-ly (they said)

60 See Müller, "Mapping a Tory's 'prostitute Pen and Tongue': Satire, Criticism, and the Political Dimension of Shaftesbury's Aversion to Swift," pp. 302-3.

61 See Robert Phiddian, "The *Argument* as an Essay in Shaftesburian Ridicule," *Swift's Parody* (Cambridge: Cambridge University Press, 1995), pp. 86-94. We do, however, disagree with some of the conclusions Phiddian draws from this premise, arguing that "what we have here is a text claimable for radically different (and essentially antagonistic) ideologies" (p. 93), an "anarchic" text useful for Swift's career at the time (transitioning from Whig to Tory).

62 *An Argument against Abolishing Christianity*, in *Jonathan Swift*, eds Ross and Woolley, p. 222.

> against Religion; others pretendedly for it: but in so Burlesque a Manner as overthrew It more effectually.[63]

It seems that such conversations were commonplace at the time: Shaftesbury mentions, apart from "the Author of *ye Tale of a Tub*," the free-thinking quatrumvirate "*Toland, Tindal, C—s*, Asgil" – in the *Argument*, these become "Asgil, Tindal, Toland, Coward."[64]

The description of Swift's text as a parody of anti-clerical Whig-speak[65] fits nicely with the 'clandestine nature' of the back and forth between Swift and Shaftesbury, and we would like to highlight some passages that seem to allude more directly to Shaftesbury's particular form of anti-clerical Whig-speak. These allusions contest the Earl's claims about the emancipatory and ennobling power of wit and raillery, insist on connecting Church and State (no Church, no Monarchy), and reveal how the definitions of religion in each writer also define their political positions.

In *Sensus Communis: An Essay on the Freedom of Wit and Humor*, Shaftesbury argues that political oppression and religious persecution give rise to satire:

> If Men are forbid to speak their Minds seriously on certain Subjects, they will do it ironically. If they are forbid to speak at all upon such Subjects; or if they find it really dangerous for 'em to do so; they will then redouble their Disguise, involve themselves in Mysteriousness, and talk so as hardly to be understood, or at least not plainly interpreted, by those who are dispos'd to do 'em a Mischief. And thus Raillery is brought more in fashion, and runs into an Extreme. 'Tis the persecuting Spirit has rais'd the bantering one: And want of Liberty may account for want of a true Politeness, and for the Corruption or wrong Use of Pleasantry and Humour. (p. 32)

Shaftesbury connects "the bantering" spirit and irony with the lack of free expression. If people are forbidden from speaking their minds, then they will express themselves through wit and irony. And if such "Raillery ... runs into an Extreme," the fault lies not in the practice of satire but in those who prohibit freedom: the more persecution, the more extreme the practice of irony, until such "want of Liberty" makes "true politeness" impossible. Excessive wit – bad satire – is the result of an oppressive Church and State. Or, as Shaftesbury

63 TNA: PRO 30/24/22/4, fols 312-13.

64 *An Argument against Abolishing Christianity*, in *Jonathan Swift*, eds Ross and Woolley, p. 219.

65 Ian Higgins, "*An Argument against Abolishing Christianity* and its Contexts," *Reading Swift: Papers from The Fifth Münster Symposium on Jonathan Swift*, ed. Hermann J. Real (Munich: Wilhelm Fink, 2008), pp. 203-23.

writes elsewhere in *Sensus Communis*, "The higher the Slavery, the more exquisite the Buffoonery" (p. 32).

Swift's parody of Shaftesbury identifies the cause of dangerous wit not in political or church authorities but in "Great wits" themselves, who

> love to be free with the highest objects, and if they cannot be allowed a God to revile or renounce, they will speak evil of dignities, abuse the government, and reflect upon the ministry, which I am sure few will deny to be of much more pernicious consequence, according to the saying of Tiberius, *Deorum offensa diis curae.*

Freedom for Swift's "Great wits" is acting on the impulse to attack "the highest objects." Here Swift shows that raillery is not the result of a "persecuting spirit" but is instead merely a matter of unthinking fashion and pride. Swift reverses the terms: instead of finding the source of "bantering" in oppressive church and state power, he locates it in the pretensions of subversive wits. The Latin tag – "Insults to the gods are the gods' concerns" – can be read as supporting the claim that religion is useful for distracting wits from political concerns, since religious insults are of concern only to the Church. But the passage also suggests that "Great wits" are unlikely to limit their criticism of "the highest objects" to religious topics: insults to religion will also include attacks on the state.

As Swift explains at the end of this same paragraph, a military officer guilty of blasphemy should not be suspected of going "so far as to raise a mutiny ... for surely, the commander of an English army is like to be but ill obeyed whose soldiers fear and reverence him as little as they do a Deity."[66] The passage ostensibly urges that blasphemy is inconsequential to military and civil order, but it is actually a form of disorder: obedience requires "fear and reverence" of a deity. Swift seems intent on showing that criticism of the Church and State go hand in hand, and that what will weaken the one will also weaken the other. He repeatedly argues that without Christianity freethinkers would attack the State instead of just the Church, but the point of such observations is to show that in attacking the Church they also attack the State.[67]

Swift also displays his intimacy with the Earl's *Letter* in the *Argument*, as he mocks Shaftesbury's claims that it is "necessary ... to give way to this Distemper

66 *An Argument against Abolishing Christianity*, in *Jonathan Swift*, eds Ross and Woolley, p. 219.

67 *An Argument against Abolishing Christianity*, in *Jonathan Swift*, eds Ross and Woolley, p. 224. See also the conclusion of Swift's *Abstract of Mr. C____ns's Discourse of Free-Thinking* (1713), in *Prose Works*, IV, 25-50.

of Enthusiasm" and that every nation has its own variety of it: "The *Lymphatici* of the *Latins* were the *Nympholepti* of the *Greeks*." Indeed, "All Nations have their *Lymphaticks* of some kind or another; and all Churches (Heathen as well as Christian) have had their Complaints against Fanaticism" (pp. 366-68). For Shaftesbury, the "Distemper" of enthusiasm – an excessively fearful or exuberant religiosity – must be given vent or it will threaten the social order (and in this passage, he treats Christianity as just one more version of "religion"). The State should thus allow its people enough freedom to work out their religious enthusiasm, which Shaftesbury believes can be regulated through the social practice of raillery instead of the sovereign power of the State.

Swift likewise declares in the *Argument* that "There is a portion of enthusiasm assigned to every nation, which, if it hath not proper objects to work on, will burst out and set all into a flame." This seems a clear response to claims like Shaftesbury's, but Swift defines "a portion of enthusiasm" in terms of "the spirit of opposition" a "darling inclination of mankind" that has nothing to do with religion but instead is based on taking "a pride and merit" in distinction.[68] For Swift, enthusiasm has no religious element but is always a deluded ethical and dangerous political impulse. Accordingly, giving greater "liberty of conscience" will do nothing to solve this problem, since the problem for Swift is not "religious."

And yet for both writers, satire is the solution to the problem of enthusiasm. In Swift's case, however, satire should not target "religion" in the sense of exuberant spiritual practices and claims but rather the ethical disorders in individuals (pride) leading to religious and political disorder. Shaftesbury's practice of raillery is another example of such pride, and Swift's satire targets it to argue that "free-thinking Whig" satire is neither politically neutral nor ethically improving to its practitioners. Raillery does not enable a public to regulate itself; instead, the moral authority of the Church aided by the power of the State is required to maintain social and political order.

Shaftesbury, however, frequently enthuses about politeness as a practice that is ethically ennobling and that both depends on and supports liberty: "All Politeness is owing to Liberty. We polish one another, and rub off our Corners and rough sides by this amicable Collision" (*Sensus Communis*, p. 22). Polite conversation makes us better people by smoothing off our unsociable rough edges and liberating us from errors of reasoning created by various forms of rhetorical "imposture." Swift, however, represents such conversation as actually promoting moral blindness and as inescapably contaminated by the

68 *An Argument against Abolishing Christianity*, in *Jonathan Swift*, eds Ross and Woolley, p. 224.

"imposture" it claims to liberate us from. He points, for example, to the benefits of clergy participating in such polite conversation:

> I am very sensible how much the gentlemen of wit and pleasure are apt to murmur, and be choqued at the sight of so many daggled-tail parsons that happen to fall in their way, and offend their eyes, [but] … what an advantage and felicity it is for great wits to be always provided with objects of scorn and contempt, in order to exercise and improve their talents and divert their spleen from falling on each other or on themselves; especially when all this may be done without the least imaginable danger to their persons.[69]

The benefits for "gentlemen" of the clergy's continued existence include the pleasures of superiority. Far from figures of "imposture," Swift's "daggled-tail parsons" have no power but are instead simply objects of ridicule. Indeed, the force of "imposture" belongs entirely to "the gentlemen of wit and pleasure." The "talents" that they develop are reduced to pride and, as the last phrase highlights, cowardice. Ridiculing parsons, Swift suggests, is a safe way for wits to achieve distinction – not least because it saves them from being the object of ridicule by other wits or of thinking about their own faults. There is no risk that polite raillery will either physically endanger its practitioners or improve them: satire is an invitation to enjoy the faults of others.[70]

In the *Argument against Abolishing Christianity*, Shaftesbury is accorded a special place among the freethinkers: "And therefore the free-thinkers consider it as a sort of edifice, wherein all the parts have such a mutual dependence on each other that if you happen to pull out one single nail, the whole fabric must fall to the ground."[71] This passage is as close as it gets in Swift to an almost verbatim reference, this time from *The Moralists*' vision of cosmic harmony:

> Thus in contemplating all on Earth, we must of necessity view *All in One*, as holding to one common Stock. Thus too in the System of the bigger World. See there the mutual Dependency of Things; the Relation of one to another … And know … that by this you will be oblig'd to own the UNIVERSAL SYSTEM, and coherent Scheme of Things … For who, till he had well survey'd this universal

69 *An Argument against Abolishing Christianity*, in *Jonathan Swift*, eds Ross and Woolley, p. 224.

70 As Swift writes in the preface to *The Battle of the Books*: "Satyr is a sort of *Glass*, wherein Beholders do generally discover every body's Face but their Own; which is the chief Reason for that kind of Reception it meets in the World, and that so very few are offended with it" (*A Tale of a Tub and Other Works*, ed. Walsh, p. 142 [italics inverted]).

71 *An Argument against Abolishing Christianity*, in *Jonathan Swift*, eds Ross and Woolley, p. 226.

> Scene, cou'd have believ'd *a Union* thus demonstrable, by such numerous and powerful Instances of mutual Correspondency and Relation.[72]

The passage in the *Argument* proceeds to show that the real aim of the free-thinkers is "freedom of action,"[73] that is to say, acting without the restraints put on them by the Christian religion – in short, libertinism. Shaftesbury, in providing the cosmic philosophical background and justification for those atheist tendencies, has obviously already become the 'Oracle of Deism,' the Promethean forethinker and architect of that "edifice"[74] in which those who wish to abolish Christianity find shelter and of necessity turn into debauched, immoral knaves. And this argument closes the circle which had begun with the opening lines of the *Inquiry* (and Swift's possible perusal of, and reaction to, them): the radical separation between religion and morality is bound to issue in moral anarchy.

In keeping with this, Swift's obviously well-calculated use of the terms "nominal Christianity," "nominal religion," and "nominal faith"[75] could very well refer to Shaftesbury's distinction between "real" and "nominal" Theists in *The Moralists*, in the course of which Theocles claims "that 'tis alone the Province of Philosophy to prove what Revelation at most does but suppose."[76] It is not unlikely that Shaftesbury was referring back to Day's criticism of the *Inquiry* (which is identified in the title of Day's book as the work of a "*Nominal Deist*") when using the term. Swift would almost certainly have stumbled across the passage in which Theocles projects Philocles' ingenuity "to reject our modern *Deism*, and challenge those who assume a Name to which their Philosophy can never in the least intitle 'em."[77] As a lover of paradox, this must have constituted for Swift one of the most profound paradoxes of the time: the free-thinking Deist Shaftesbury disavowing allegiance with that school whose principal professor he was.

At the same time, Swift's persona gives the argument a malignant twist. The condensation of arguments, in the context of "two young gentlemen of

72 *The Moralists, a Philosophical Rhapsody: Being a Recital of Certain Conversations upon Natural and Moral Subjects* (London: John Wyat, 1709), pp. 102-3.

73 *An Argument against Abolishing Christianity*, in *Jonathan Swift*, eds Ross and Woolley, p. 226.

74 Theocles talks about himself as a "Builder" who wishes to "lay such a Foundation" as is sufficient "to bear the Structure" of his thought (*The Moralists*, p. 85). The context is Shaftesbury's attempt to prove a divine providence.

75 *An Argument against Abolishing Christianity*, in *Jonathan Swift*, eds Ross and Woolley, pp. 218-20.

76 *The Moralists*, p. 85.

77 *The Moralists*, p. 84.

real hopes" lately "broke for blasphemy," from the *Letter* and *Sensus Communis* (one to be spelled out more explicitly in *Miscellaneous Reflections*, pp. 112-14 [86-87]) in the expression "if persecution once begins, no man alive knows how far it may reach or where it will end" constitutes, together with the remark that all the splenetic abuse of the clergy could be exercised "without the least imaginable danger to their persons,"[78] a clear intimation that it might be worth punishing the vilifiers of Christianity. Hiding behind masks of raillery, free thought, and wit, these writers do not liberate the mind; rather, they fall victim to their own spleen, and should be judged accordingly.

The Examiner provides an interesting example of how Swift could have reimagined Shaftesbury's view of satire, which was based on exactly such religious premises. Without wanting to employ the inapposite image of Swift as a misanthropist here, it is nevertheless appropriate to point out how far ideas about the depravity of humanity as they expressed themselves in his satire were, for Shaftesbury, the hub of the problem. In *Examiner*, no 28 (15 February 1711), Swift, under the guise of the familiar pose of impartiality,[79] published two letters, one by a Whig and another by a Tory, accusing Mr Examiner of bias. In Swift, the Tory is level-headed and committed to a fair exchange of arguments, whereas the Whig's prose is morose, fraught with aggression and the usual Whig batteries against "*Popery* and *Slavery*, and *Arbitrary Power*."[80] This is exactly the opposite image of Tory versus Whig satire characteristic of *Miscellaneous Reflections*, written in late 1710 and early 1711, but also of *Sensus Communis*, which was by and large composed in reply to criticisms of Shaftesbury's endorsement of "the *Freedom of Raillery* ... against serious Extravagances and spleenitick Humours" (*Letter concerning Enthusiasm*, p. 330) from a Tory perspective.[81] In *Sensus Communis*, the Earl defined raillery in terms of its use in "an ideal Whig community"[82] – in the *Examiner*, the Whig appears to be, in the Earl's own terms, "extravagantly morose and ill-humour'd" (*Letter concerning Enthusiasm*, p. 352).

78 *An Argument against Abolishing Christianity*, in *Jonathan Swift*, eds Ross and Woolley, pp. 219, 224.

79 See David Nokes, *Jonathan Swift, a Hypocrite Reversed: A Critical Biography* (Oxford: Oxford University Press, 1985), p. 123.

80 *The Examiners for the Year 1711, to which is prefix'd, A Letter to the Examiner* (London: John Morphew and A. Dodd, 1712), p. 88. See also the reference in no 27 to "MORALISTS" who "make two kinds of Avarice" (p. 82).

81 See, above all, Mary Astell's *Bart'lemy Fair*.

82 Ronald Paulson, *Don Quixote in England*, p. 119.

In January 1713, Swift composed and published the mock *Abstract of Mr. C____ns's Discourse of Free-Thinking*,[83] the title page of which quoted two passages from *Characteristicks* (one from the *Letter*, another from *Miscellaneous Reflections*), again emphasizing the Earl's intimate connection with the Deist and, by implication, atheist writers of the time. Anthony Collins was an intimate acquaintance of Shaftesbury's, a fact which will not have escaped Swift. His assessment of Collins was damning, and the Shaftesburian context evoked by Collins's quotes of *Characteristicks* will have confirmed Swift's opinion that its author was the godfather of the freethinkers.

5. Why Was the Dialogue between Shaftesbury and Swift Clandestine?

In order to understand why Swift and Shaftesbury chose to fight their intellectual battles under the guise of a rhetoric fraught with allusions, it is once again worthwhile to consider the circles they moved in. Much has been said about Swift's relationship to Somers; whatever its manifold and meandering highs and lows may have been, one thing seems to be clear: Shaftesbury thought Swift's treatment of Somers in the dedication to the *Tale* and, above all, in the *Examiner* indecent at best.[84] He was by no means prepared to accept that his friend's name should be thus defiled in public, least of all by a man whose status did not entitle him to such indiscretions. Interestingly and importantly, the *Proposal for Correcting, Improving, and Ascertaining the English Tongue* was addressed to Robert Harley, that astute political manager whose support Swift sought at the time he was writing *The Examiner* and the *Proposal*. In 1714, the year after Shaftesbury's death and that of the publication of the second edition of *Characteristicks*, Toland, never one to be picky in his choice of weapons, would savagely denounce Swift as "that profligate *Divine*, who, prostituting his sacred Function, has sold himself for Hire to Iniquity, vilely turning State-Buffoon to a couple of the greatest State-mountebanks in the World. O poor *Ireland*!"[85] The mountebanks were, of course, Harley and Bolingbroke.

Shaftesbury knew Harley well, having followed his fall from grace with the Whigs in the early 1700s. In 1702, we find him blame Harley in strong terms for

83 See Eugene Hammond, *Jonathan Swift: Irish Blow-In* (Newark: University of Delaware Press, 2016), p. 620.

84 See Müller, "Mapping a Tory's 'prostitute Pen and Tongue': Satire, Criticism, and the Political Dimension of Shaftesbury's Aversion to Swift," p. 305.

85 John Toland, *The Grand Mystery Laid Open: Namely by Dividing of the Protestants to Weaken the Hanover Succession, and by Defeating the Succession, to Extirpate the Protestant Religion* (London: Ferd. Burleigh, 1714), p. 5.

what he regarded as an (almost) unpardonable instance of ideological corruption: for the Earl, it was Harley "& He alone that wounds us, for all the Strength of the Tories or Church Party is nothing but by that Force wch he brings over to them from our Side." Consequently, Harley had lost all "Reputation & Trust amongst" the Whigs.[86] However, at that point, Shaftesbury still believed him capable of redemption. Of greater interest, however, is the "Breach" that Shaftesbury claimed would finally have come about in 1712 had he himself still been in England and involved in politics: nothing in previous years had induced him to 'violate' his friendship with Harley, but now, in a letter written a week after the one to Coste in which he had so unequivocally voiced his opinion about Swift, he announced that the time had come to part ways.[87] Shaftesbury was certainly in the know about the Harley-Swift connection, and this is how the Irish clergyman was neatly brought into the political picture, too.

The year before, there had already been an incident which helps explain how far the Tories regarded Whig penmen as a real threat and why Shaftesbury is likely to have regarded the breach with Harley as irrevocable. The *Post Boy* for 24 July 1711 reports that the State Lottery was in search of a printer, and in it John Darby, printer of *Characteristicks*, appears in an unsavoury light from a Tory, High-Church perspective:

> *John Darby*, an *Anabaptist*, whose sole Merit and Pretensions are, having printed TINDAL's *Rights of the Christian Church*; TOLAND's *Christianity not Mysterious*; Sydney *of Government*; and HARRINGTON's *Oceana*: The Tendency of which Books are to destroy *Monarchy* and *Episcopacy*; as also a Weekly-Paper, call'd *The Medley*, writ to asperse and reflect on the Right Honourable the Lord Treasurer, and the present Ministry; which has been presented by the *Grand-Jury* of *Oxford*, as a scandalous and seditious Pamphlet.[88]

---

86 Shaftesbury to Benjamin Furly, 27 February 1702 (TNA: PRO 30/24/20/57, fols 139r-40v). Harley may even have been involved, along with Shaftesbury, in Toland's 1700 edition of Harrington (see Justin Champion, *Republican Learning: John Toland and the Crisis of Christian Culture, 1696-1722* [Manchester: Manchester University Press, 2003], p. 99). Harley's "old Whig principles" are outlined in J. A. Downie, *Jonathan Swift: Political Writer* (London: Routledge and Kegan Paul, 1984), p. 137. For Harley's propagandistic activities in general, see J. A. Downie, *Robert Harley and the Press: Propaganda and Public Opinion in the Age of Swift and Defoe* (Cambridge: Cambridge University Press, 1979).

87 See Shaftesbury to Micklethwaite, 2 August 1712, NS (TNA: PRO 30/24/23/9, fols 132-133): "I may justly congratulate with You, and with my self, that I am under such an Incapacity of acting in publick Affairs at such a Season when the Consequence woud in all likelihood be a total Breach with those old Friends, and particularly that *Great-one* with whom no Power of Courts or Partys, no private Obligations or Disobligations to Ministrys, coud ever make me violate an old Friendship which I held from my earlyest Youth for *him* and *his*."

88 *High-Church Aphorisms, Written by Those Twin-Brothers in Scandal, the Author of the Examiner, and Modest Abel* ([London], 1711), sig. A1v. The Deist and Republican classics

In fact, Lord High Treasurer Harley and the Tory government saw to it that Darby was committed to Newgate in October of the same year for having printed pamphlets by those authors Swift seems to have regarded as the minions of their aristocratic oracle, Shaftesbury, and the Republican pamphlets in which, ironically, Harley himself might have been involved in his early, Whig years. It seems that Henry St John, then Secretary of State for the Northern Department and not yet Viscount Bolingbroke, was the driving force behind the apprehension of fourteen booksellers, printers, and publishers whose 'crime' consisted in disseminating pamphlets which would voice views opposed to the Tory, High-Church establishment.[89] As the author of *Characteristicks*, the Whig ideology of which had the potential of arousing orthodox and Tory opposition, the Earl would have been far from pleased with this move of the Harley administration, which for him was yet another indication of the Tories' dangerous blend of ecclesiastical policy and politics.

Just how far the propagandistically loaded Harley-Swift connection haunted Shaftesbury's imagination may be seen in a letter written to Somers on 30 March 1711, sent along with the first volume of *Characteristicks*:

> It woud be the highest advantage to a certain Party, that Your Ld^{p} shoud stir a step out of y^{r} Character, or seem to act ag^{t} them in any other Capacity than that in wch you have hitherto mov'd. For as in a Ship that goes with Wind & Tide & carrys us prosperously & to heart's content, we hear nothing but *Steady*! *Steady*! So is it with your *Character*. And so woud I have it continue: That no noise may be heard from any side but that of *Steady*! – Let others tack or shift their Sails as occasion serves. 'Tis Joy to me to see you hold the helm[90] thus steady as you still do. Even now amidst the Storm tis Joy to me to remember that there was once a Time when *one* Pilot alone advis'd putting off to Sea, & sav'd us from riding securely in a Calm, upon a Coast where if we had remain'd ever so little, we must inevitably have perish'd. How naturally every Man loves his Pilot when he is himself abroad wth all his goods & effe<c>ts depending in a manner on head or hand is easily understood. For my own part I have learnt almost from the moment of my Birth to embark my self with the Publick, & to have no other Bottom than that alone. How tender therefore I naturally am of my Pilot, y^{r} Lord^{sp} may easily imagine. And tho as an Enthusiast, I coud readily cast myself away & be a *Jonas* for the advantage of the Ship; yet I can truly boast that I am more sparing of *the Pilot* than any one in the Vessel. And for that reason I have within the Space of a Twelve month been strong in my resentment ag^{t} those of the Crew who mutiny

---

mentioned in this note are all advertised in *Books Sold by John Darby in Bartholomew-Close, London* ([London], [1717]) and they all are, of course, important for the contexts of *Characteristicks*.

89 See also William E. Alderman, "English Editions of Shaftesbury's *Characteristics*," *Papers of the Bibliographical Society of America*, 61 (1967), 315-34 (pp. 320-21).

90 This image is frequently used in Swift's *Discourse of the Contests and Dissentions between the Nobles and the Commons in Athens and Rome* (see *Prose Works*, I, 220).

> because their *Pilot*, taking his proper Measures, & working in his own way, is not at every Turn ready upon the Deck to do common Drudgery, & expose himself equally in every Capacity besides.[91]

This passage, juxtaposing Somers's steadiness of character with Harley's political fickleness, blends classical and biblical imagery with references to the frontispiece of *A Tale of a Tub* and its author in an attack on the Earl of Oxford's administration; "*Jonas*" Swift's ruthless treatment of Somers in the *Examiner* for 1 February may well have been the trigger for the manifold innuendos to the political daily business we find here.

In the iconographic engraving for the *Inquiry*, which he designed for the second edition of *Characteristicks* (published posthumously 1714/5), Shaftesbury returned to this imagery: the biblical-Hobbesian-Swiftian Leviathan turns out to be the ultimate threat to the enlightened, classically-minded commonwealth he envisaged.

Shaftesbury himself would never have thought it appropriate to attack political enemies openly, not least because this would have contradicted his view of satire as well as his ideas of politeness and etiquette.[92] However, it remains to be explained why Swift, who was never shy in conducting personal vitriolic attack, spared Shaftesbury. In the *Instructions* sent to Micklethwaite on 1 September 1712, we find Shaftesbury's last stand in the perpetual duel he was fighting with the Tories, not least of all through Swift. It is worth having a look at this rather interesting statement, which has the Earl reflect on the fate of the first edition of *Characteristicks* and its impact on party politics:

> 'Tis plain how the smallest Work which comes abroad is now-a-days canvass'd and nois'd about, by Friends, Enemys, Examiners, and Criticks. 'Tis plain again how strongly this very Work it-self was attack'd when only the *Letter of Enth.*, its little finger, first appear'd. The Body at last follow'd, and shew'd it self daringly, in the very worst time. Open Defyance was bid to the whole Party and opposite Tribe. And what ensu'd? – Perfect Stillness and Quiet – ... the Word was *Hush*! – "The Author has a Name and Character. He is not yet made desperate. His being falln upon and forc'd to declare himself, may urge such a Spirit as his to make mad Work. Whereas if we contain ourselves, and let him alone, he will either be wholly quiet, or at least go no further than those tollerably decent Bounds which reach not the Vulgar. And for this he has in a manner given us his Word." (*Instructions*, pp. 246-48)

91 TNA: PRO 30/24/22/4, fols 355-56.

92 Shaftesbury had initially planned to dedicate *Characteristicks* to his Whig friend Somers, but again political considerations constrained him from doing so. See Müller, "Mapping a Tory's 'prostitute Pen and Tongue': Satire, Criticism, and the Political Dimension of Shaftesbury's Aversion to Swift," p. 301.

FIGURE 13.2 Frontispiece to *A Tale of a Tub*

FIGURE 13.3 Detail from an engraving for the *Inquiry* (1714/5)

Indeed, Shaftesbury had "a Name and Character," but so did Somers (whom, however, Swift bore a personal grudge). Yet the Earl's self-confidence in these lines seems to be well founded. Swift obviously regarded him as a cunning free-thinking Prometheus whose flame should not be brought to the "Vulgar" but only to the initiated reader well-versed in the game of decoding neat literary allusions. To have made the works of this corrupter of prospective clergymen more prominent than they already were would have been dangerous.

In the first paragraph above, Swift, Mr Examiner, is granted the accolade of being neither friend nor foe nor mere "Critick," but a category of his own. His vitriolic attack in the Coste-letter and the pedantic counting of monosyllables in the *Proposal for Correcting, Improving, and Ascertaining the English Tongue* notwithstanding, Shaftesbury realized how shrewdly Swift manipulated the public with his claims of impartiality. Moreover, there would have been no need for him to attack Swift personally since he represented everything that the Earl abhorred and attacked in his texts: he detested the vulgar satire and vulgar manners of a man he regarded as a turncoat and dangerous representative of the High Church spirit.

6. Conclusions

The clandestine dialogue between Swift and Shaftesbury is not surprising because each represented to the other the antithesis of his own views about the role of religion in personal lives, society, and the State. They were obvious targets for one another. Although their contemporaries found it easy to confuse them because both satirized religion and enthusiasm, their practice and theory of religious satire are very different. Swift and Shaftesbury diverge in their understanding of the "humor of the age": for Swift, it is the empty style and phrasings of both religious enthusiasts and the libertine "town fop;" for Shaftesbury, it is the oppressive oratorical imposture of the Court and High-Church Anglicans. Shaftesbury's religious satire aims to puncture the rhetorical imposture, gravity, and fear-mongering of High-Church Tories, being at pains to liberate readers and restore the public's capacity to reason. For Swift, likewise, satire is a tool for liberation, but his target is self-authorizing enthusiasm and the town's polite practice of raillery itself. He often uses satire as a form of reader entrapment, in which readers themselves become satiric objects, partly in an attempt to enlighten them about the power of satiric form to manipulate. For Swift, Shaftesbury is thus dangerously deluded, since the Earl does not acknowledge satire's power to seduce, but instead conceives of it as purely a practice of liberty that cultivates rationality and autonomy. Although Shaftesbury decries rhetorical "imposture," for Swift, the Earl's wit is just another form of it. Moreover, because it is cut off from the ethical and intellectual resources of Anglicanism, Shaftesbury's raillery is dangerously naïve about its ability to develop ethical individuals and maintain social and political order. Satire for Swift is no substitute for institutionalized religion.[93]

And yet, with its cultivation of intensely self-reflective readers, who are aware of the dangers of manipulation by raillery and town cant, Swift's satirical practice nonetheless promotes an individualistic understanding of religion. Both Shaftesbury's conceptualization of religion in terms of the sincerity of

---

93 Sophie Gee argues similarly about Swift's use of the essay form: "It enabled him to depict minds in disrepair and to make the case that neither individuals nor the essay as a form had the power or the authority to correct internal turmoil. In his view, such authority resided elsewhere: in divine sovereignty and its temporal manifestations in kingdoms, monarchs, and established churches" ("'Such Opinions Cannot Cohere': Swift's Inwardness," *Republics of Letters: A Journal for the Study of Knowledge, Politics, and the Arts*, 4.1, <http://arcade.stanford.edu/rofl/such-opinions-cannot-cohere-swifts-inwardness>, accessed 9 June 2017). For Swift's understanding of, and commitment to, institutional religion, see Roger D. Lund, "Swift's Sermons, 'Public Conscience,' and the Privatization of Religion," *Prose Studies: History, Theory, Criticism*, 18 (1996), 150-74.

individual expressions of faith and ethical behaviour and Swift's self-reflective practice of satire support the same way of thinking about religion. Despite their differences, their satires promote a taken-for-granted understanding of religion as a matter of privatized belief and choice. Both, therefore, ultimately contribute to ushering in our secular age. If their anatomies of unbelief reveal their individual religious stance, their rhetorical anatomies of each other connect those stances to politics. Swift came to regard Shaftesbury as a dangerous oracle of free-thinking and Deism, whereas the Earl saw in the Irish clergyman the epitome of "Polemick *Divinity*; *or the* Writing *Church-Militant*" (*Miscellaneous Reflections*, p. 30 [9]), an ill-natured, self-serving satyr whose only wish was to mock his readers.

FIGURE 13.4
Detail from the engraving designed for *Miscellaneous Reflections*

Marcus Walsh
University of Liverpool

Swift, the Church, and Religion: The Sermons, the *Tale*, and the Critics

Abstract. Focusing on the sermons and *A Tale of a Tub*, this essay argues that certain recent critical arguments for religious heterodoxy, or self-contradiction, in Swift's writings are inappropriately influenced by modern political, social, and religious views, by a lack of attention to Swift's informing contexts, and by modern hermeneutic assumptions and methods. Swift's writings, ironic and indirect (the *Tale*) as well as non-ironic and direct (the sermons), are like other literary works essentially determinate though complex and plural in meaning at the local, propositional, level. Larger-scale understandings of these works need to be consistent with those local meanings. Modern allegations of the heterodoxy or conflicted nature of the sermons and *Tale* may be refuted by attention to their determinate propositional meanings.

Jonathan Swift represented himself as an orthodox and faithful son of the Church of England. He insisted that the fundamentals of the Church's polity and doctrine "both were deduced from Christ and his Apostles, and the Instructions of the purest and earliest Ages."[1] In the Apology written for the 1710 *Tale of a Tub*, he famously affirmed that the work "Celebrates the Church of *England* as the most perfect of all others in Discipline and Doctrine, it advances no Opinion they reject, nor condemns any they receive."[2] Swift's self-description has been broadly accepted by such scholars as Louis Landa, who speaks of Swift's "conservative adherence to simple and indisputable orthodoxy as he conceived it," and Donald Greene, who describes him as "just one … of the vast majority of important English writers, thinkers, and artists of the century" who were "professing, often devout Christians." Nathalie Zimpfer, in an essay published more recently, has cogently set out the "reality" of Swift's religious positions, in contrast with the "myth" of Swift's heterodoxy which began in his own lifetime and has lingered, with a more or less healthy life, for the three centuries since.[3]

1 *Remarks upon a Book, Intitled, The Rights of the Christian Church Asserted*, in *Prose Works*, II, 78-79.

2 Jonathan Swift, *A Tale of a Tub and Other Works*, ed. Marcus Walsh (Cambridge: Cambridge University Press, 2010), p. 6 (italics converted).

3 Louis Landa, Introduction to the Sermons, *Prose Works*, IX, 101; Greene, "The Via Media in an Age of Revolution: Anglicanism in the Eighteenth Century," *The Varied Pattern: Studies in the*

 | DOI:10.30965/9783846763971_015

In academia, there has been over the last two or three decades a lingering tendency to prefer or, I would argue, to construct, a 'Swift' altogether more in tune with ideals that we all nowadays share: social equality, the distribution of wealth, religious toleration, and freedom of speech. (I am aware that I beg a number of questions in making that statement.) Carole Fabricant, for example, is troubled by what she describes as Swift's conservative attribution of "an inflated value to quiet and stability in the realm," and not unreasonably seeks evidence of "Swift's capacity to speak to contemporary struggles and concerns;" more problematically, she seeks to rescue him from what she calls "the paralytic grip of criticisms that artificially freeze Swift in time."[4] There has been a concerted attempt to represent Swift as heterodox (rather than uninterestingly orthodox) in religion, whether as anti-Trinitarian, freethinking, or even as pagan.[5] The Swift who appears, on the *prima facie* evidence of what he wrote, to have believed in a conservative politics and a conformist religion, is found unsatisfactory, failing as he does to live up to our own ideals. So, we have recently been told, the Swift who proposed giving badges to Dublin's deserving poor "exerts few charms."[6] Many critics of Swift, in fact, adopt some variation of a common discursive logic. They begin by postulating or desiderating a modern liberal Swift. Having done this, they blame Swift for failing, in his writings, to consist with that preferred modern version. In so blaming Swift, they cite abundant textual evidence of his lamentably contemporaneous and rebarbative views.[7] They then necessarily derive from this position a radically conflicted Swift, compromised by false consciousness, whose theology and politics are unstable like his satire. Such critical strategies would require us to reject as untrustworthy, or wholly to disregard, a good deal of unhelpful evidence from Swift's works; to assume from the outset that ironic writing is radically and necessarily unstable; and to place no reliance on such of his writings as the sermons as were written straight, unironically, *in propria persona*.

Eighteenth Century, eds Peter Hughes and David Williams (Toronto: A. M. Hakkert, 1971), pp. 297-320 (300); Zimpfer, "Swift and Religion: From Myth to Reality," *Swift Studies*, 24 (2009), 46-69.

4 Carole Fabricant, *Swift's Landscape* (Notre Dame and London: University of Notre Dame Press, 1995), pp. x, xxv.

5 See, for example, Todd C. Parker, "'The Idlest Trifling Stuff that ever was Writ': or, Why Swift Hated his Sermons," *Swift as Priest and Satirist*, ed. Todd C. Parker (Newark: University of Delaware Press, 2009), pp. 58-71 (61); Sarah Ellenzweig, *The Fringes of Belief: English Literature, Ancient Heresy, and the Politics of Freethinking, 1660-1760* (Stanford, California: Stanford University Press, 2008), p. 83.

6 Parker, "'The Idlest Trifling Stuff that ever was Writ': or, Why Swift Hated his Sermons," p. 58.

7 For example, Fabricant, *Swift's Landscape*, pp. xxv-xxvi.

We should not seek, or expect to find, a charming and agreeable Swift. The Swift who was born in 1667 was a man of his time, not ours. He grew up of course and wrote at a time when the consequences of both political and religious dissent could credibly and reasonably be regarded, on the basis of recent experience, as dangerous. Political and religious conservatism, the stability of a settled state, was for Swift, as for John Dryden, a stated highest good. There was no thought of pleasing us when he was writing *A Tale of a Tub*, or *Gulliver's Travels*, or *The Presbyterians Plea of Merit*. Criticism that seeks to understand him in his own moment is not by any necessary tendency paralytic or refrigerating. Like other forms of humanist scholarship, it seeks not to accommodate the past to ourselves, but to help us understand ourselves and the world better by delineating the precise differences of other times and other places. We can delineate those differences more fully and more safely by reading with appropriate seriousness the writings he left, and resisting the temptation to elide or translate what we find inconvenient. In what follows I shall attempt to continue the defence of an orthodox Swift by describing and addressing what seem to me some familiar, ideologically-driven misreadings.

Few of Swift's writings have seemed more inconvenient to many modern critics than his sermons, not least because they state so straightforwardly and uncompromisingly views that are less liberal, less egalitarian, less ecumenical than many would wish to associate with him. There has been, following the familiar logic outlined, an attempt to rule the sermons out of the evidential record by arguing that Swift did not himself take them seriously, and indeed that he looked upon them with something approaching contempt. Louis Landa, in the Introduction to the Sermons in the *Prose Works*, provides a balanced survey of the evidence for Swift's estimation of his homiletic writings, concluding that "we may well view with suspicion Swift's slighting remarks and receive cautiously any presumption that he was entirely indifferent to his own sermons."[8] Todd Parker, with less caution, asks "why are the sermons so offensive to Swift?"[9] Robert Mahony accepts as a "fact" that Swift had "little regard

---

8 *Prose Works*, IX, 99. Swift sent Dr Sheridan a package of his sermons, probably 35 in number, with a characteristically dismissive covering note: "*Here are a bundle of my own sermons; you may have them if you please: they may be of use to you, they have never been of any to me*" (John Boyle, Earl of Orrery, *Remarks on the Life and Writings of Dr. Jonathan Swift, Dean of St. Patrick's, Dublin* [London: A. Millar, 1752], p. 289). Walter Harte reported that Swift sent eleven of the sermons, stitched together, in a black leather case, to Pope; see *Prose Works*, IX, 100.

9 Parker, "'The Idlest Trifling Stuff that ever was Writ': or, Why Swift Hated his Sermons," p. 60.

for his sermons."[10] The main evidence provided for the view that Swift thought little of his sermons is his letter to his successor at Kilroot, the Reverend John Winder, dated 13 January 1698/9, in which Winder is discouraged from making use of the sermons Swift had left behind him:

> Those sermons … will utterly disgrace You, unless you have so much credit that whatever comes from You will pass. They were what I was firmly resolved to burn and especially some of them the idlest trifling stuff that ever was writt, calculated for a Church without Company or a roof.[11]

This understandable modesty topos was written by a novice clergyman who had barely passed the age of thirty, in respect of early sermons written at a remote rural parish, which he did not want another clergyman to steal. The letter tells us nothing convincing about his attitude to sermons written and delivered in the city of Dublin twenty and thirty years later, in the course of his professional duties as a senior churchman, in a church which had both a company and a roof. There is no reason to think that Swift did not take sufficiently seriously the sermons he delivered as Dean of St Patrick's, or that they do not represent, however lacking they may be in desirable charm, originality or radicalism, serious statements of his own understandings of Christian doctrine and behaviour.

Swift's sermon "On the Trinity" is a characterizing statement of his theological position. Its hermeneutic methodology is deliberately stripped and simple. It is written in plain terms, so as to be comprehensible even, as Swift puts it, to "the most Ignorant" among his audience.[12] This statement should not be taken as Swiftian disdain for his audience; it was for Swift and his contemporaries a normal and widely shared view of the proper level of the effective sermon. Swift's Trinity sermon is not a work of indirection or irony; it is to be taken at face value. It locates revelation unequivocally in Scripture. It identifies from the beginning those who have argued against the Scripture-derived Church doctrine of the Trinity, as "Enemies to all Revealed Religion." It offers to ordinary capacities a summary of the Trinity doctrine so far as they need to understand it. It insists that the doctrine is clearly and plainly expressed in Scripture, even though the word 'Trinity' itself

10 Robert Mahony, "Certainty and Irony in Swift: Faith and the Indeterminate," *Swift as Priest and Satirist*, ed. Parker, pp. 37-57 (38).

11 *Correspondence*, ed. Woolley, I, 138.

12 *Prose Works*, IX, 159.

> is indeed not in Scripture, but was a Term of Art invented in the earlier Times to express the Doctrine by a single Word, for the Sake of Brevity and Convenience. The Doctrine then, as delivered in Holy Scripture, although not exactly in the same Words, is very short, and amounts only to this, That the Father, the Son and the Holy Ghost, are each of them God, and yet that there is but One God.[13]

This last statement has, however, seemed at best a prevarication and a self-deception to more than one recent commentator. Todd Parker remarks that

> the Trinity thus becomes a function of readerly intention ... it is the interpretive act that brings the Trinity ... into being ... as such ... The doctrine of the Trinity is an approximation ... of a meaning from scripture that cannot be localized in any particular verse. The "term of Art" that signifies the Trinity is, then, a signified without local signifiers, and its adequacy to the doctrine it symbolizes depends ... on the skill of those readers "of an earlier Time to express, the Doctrine by a single word."[14]

Parker's language as well as his argument here is deconstructive, and both his language and his argument operate according to hermeneutical assumptions foreign to Swift. The concept of the Trinity that Swift states is not brought into being by an "interpretive act," "a signified without local signifiers." It is rather a paraphrasing inference from the multiple moments of textual evidence, each thought of as plain in itself, provided by Scripture. For Swift the doctrine of the Trinity is effectively and fully delivered in Scripture, even though the word 'Trinity' itself was "invented" – that is, *found, discovered* – "in the earlier Times" – that is, by the Church Fathers. That the doctrine as a whole is not explicitly stated in a single scriptural locus is of no great consequence for Swift. Swift finds in Scripture plain though multiple statements in support of the Church's doctrine:

> I see it plainly declared in Scripture, that there is but one God; and yet I find our Saviour ... saying *He and his Father are one*; and, *before Abraham was, I am*. I read, that the Disciples worshipped him: That *Thomas* said to him, *My Lord and my God*. And, Saint *John*, Chap. 1st, *In the Beginning was the Word, and the Word was with God, and the Word was God*. I read likewise that the Holy Ghost bestowed the Gift of Tongues, and the Power of working Miracles.[15]

---

13 *Prose Works*, IX, 160.

14 Parker, "'The Idlest Trifling Stuff that ever was Writ': or, Why Swift Hated his Sermons," pp. 64-65.

15 *Prose Works*, IX, 161.

Swift's rhetoric itself, the reiterated "I see it plainly declared," "I read," "I read," insists to his audience that the mystery he seeks to explain to them is communicated through plain and multiple texts of Scripture. This is a deliberately simple version of Anglican hermeneutics, and no doubt in itself a deliberate rhetorical strategy.[16] It is ostentatiously not an elaborated "interpretive act." Its signifieds are based, precisely, upon "local signifiers."

Scripture emphatically is the authority on which Swift's theology is based. This sermon preaches "the Doctrine of the Trinity, as it is positively affirmed in Scripture." Mysteries are to be believed so far, and only in so far, as they are "taught and commanded in Holy Writ."[17] It is true that Swift wrote and uttered these words for and in the pulpit, with the authority of a Dean guiding his congregation. A number of modern Swift scholars have argued that, for Swift, "faith is not restricted absolutely to Scripture, but extends to the interpretive authority of the Church."[18] However, Swift did not in his sermons understand and represent "the interpretive authority of the Church" in such a way. The English Church claimed not to make doctrine, but to derive doctrine from the divine revelation made through Scripture. Clearly, Scripture is a text to be interpreted, but Anglicans of course believed and regularly argued that (in Hooker's words) "of things necessary to all men's salvation ... they are in Scripture plain and easy to be understood,"[19] and safely therefore comprehensible to ordinary readers. Evidently, in such mysteries as the Trinity, Swift's congregation required instruction, but that instruction rests on Scripture: "It can never be said, that we preach Mysteries without Warrant from Holy Scripture." The Roman Church, in clear contrast, has, as Swift put it, "enriched herself by trading in Mysteries, for which they have not the least Authority from Scripture ... such as *Transubstantiation, Worshipping of Images, Indulgences* for *Sins, Purgatory*, and *Masses* for the *Dead*."[20] These of course are doctrinal claims made by Brother Peter in *A Tale of a Tub*, and enforced in that work by the absolute spiritual authority of excommunication and the irresistible secular authority of Peter's dragoons.[21] Peter locks up Scripture, the primary evidence of revelation, in a

16 Nathalie Zimpfer, "The Paradoxical Rhetoric of Swift's Homiletics," *Reading Swift: Papers from The Sixth Münster Symposium on Jonathan Swift*, eds Kirsten Juhas, Hermann J. Real, and Sandra Simon (Munich: Wilhelm Fink, 2013), pp. 265-82.

17 *Prose Works*, IX, 162.

18 For example, Mahony, "Certainty and Irony in Swift: Faith and the Indeterminate," p. 40.

19 *The Works of Mr Richard Hooker ... Vindicating the Church of England as Truly Christian and Duly Reformed* (London: J. Best for Andrew Crook, 1662), pp. 30-31 (I, xiv). This edition was in Swift's library (Passmann and Vienken I, 899-900).

20 *Prose Works*, IX, 162, 163.

21 Swift, *A Tale of a Tub and Other Works*, ed. Walsh, pp. 76, 78.

strong-box; Swift's congregation, like Martin and Jack, have access to the word of Scripture itself.

In guiding his congregation, Swift understood himself to be not a judge or dictator of scriptural meaning, but a teacher. This distinction between the roles and authority of judge and teacher is crucial.[22] Like other Anglican clergymen, he claimed no absolute authority from the gown. Hooker had written more than a century earlier that the Anglican priest has the authority of a guide and instructor, who teaches what the words of Scripture mean, and who is worthy of his congregation's credit:

> Whatsoever we believe concerning salvation by Christ, although the Scripture be therein the ground of our belief; yet the authority of many is, if we mark it, the key which openeth the door of entrance into the knowledge of the Scripture. The Scripture could not teach us the things that are of God, unless we did credit men who have taught us that the words of Scripture do signify those things.[23]

In its essentials, this would be a normative understanding amongst Church of England polemicists. John Tillotson, Archbishop of Canterbury, for example, asserts that

> God hath appointed Guides and Teachers for us in matters of Religion, and if we will be contented to be instructed by them in those necessary Articles and Duties of Religion, which are plainly contained in Scripture; and to be counselled and directed by them in things that are more doubtful and difficult, I do not see why we might not do well enough without any infallible Judge or Guide.

Where the guidance of Scripture is plain, "no Guide or Judge can in reason claim that Authority over men, as to oblige them to believe or do the contrary; no, tho he pretend to Infallibility."[24] Here of course Tillotson's target is the overriding interpretative authority claimed by the Church of Peter. The Church of England preacher, for Tillotson as for Hooker, has an authority derived from, and dependent on, his wisdom and learning. Congregations do well to respond to that rather different kind of authority: "When men are once come to this, to think themselves wiser than their Teachers, and to despise and cast

22 I have developed this argument at greater length in "Profession and Authority: The Interpretation of the Bible in the Seventeenth and Eighteenth Centuries," *Literature and Theology*, 9 (1995), 383-98.

23 *The Works of Mr Richard Hooker*, p. 52 (II, vii).

24 John Tillotson, *Works ... Containing Fifty-Four Sermons and Discourses, on Several Occasions*, 3rd ed. (London: B. Aylmer and W. Rogers, 1701), p. 232 (Sermon 21). This edition was in Swift's library (PASSMANN AND VIENKEN III, 1858-60).

off their Guides, no wonder if *then* they go astray."[25] William Sherlock, Dean of St Paul's, in his *Discourse concerning a Judge of Controversies in Matters of Religion* (1686), similarly insists on the distinction between judge and teacher, and understands in the same way the different authority of the two roles: "To teach and instruct, and to determine as a Judge, are two very different things; the first reserves to us a liberty of judging; the second determines us to believe the Dictates of our Judge."[26]

This standard distinction is implicit everywhere in Swift, and explicit in several places. So, in his parodic Abstract of *Mr. Collins's Discourse of Free-Thinking* (1713), he makes the freethinker "conclude, that there ought to be no such Thing in the World as Priests, Teachers, or Guides, for instructing ignorant People in Religion; but that every Man ought to *think freely* for himself."[27] More straightforwardly, in his sermon "On False Witness," Swift defines the gradient of authority, from the scriptural revelation, through the priest as guide, to the individual Christian reader: "Next to the Word of God, and the Advice of Teachers, every Man's Conscience strictly examined will be his best Director."[28] Swift's word is "Advice;" not judgement, or dictation.

This gradient of authority underlies, and is often explicit in, those of Swift's sermons which have seemed particularly obnoxious to modern readers, dealing with subordination in society, the practical exercise of charity, and the Irish poor, particularly the sermons "On Mutual Subjection," "On the Poor Man's Contentment," and "Causes of the Wretched Condition of Ireland." Of the first of these, one critic remarks that "Swift aims his indignation here at the poor for aspiring to sin above their station, and yet this too is presumably the Swift whose heart was lacerated by social injustice."[29] One might suggest that the savage indignation that lacerated Swift's heart was provoked by other views of social injustice and the liberty of men than ours. More to the point, Swift's views on social subordination were conventional enough amongst Anglican thinkers of his time, and indeed of earlier and later times, and scarcely amount to a surprise or a paradox. The argument has been made convincingly by earlier Swift scholars,[30] and needs no repetition. What does need to be insisted on is

25 Tillotson, *Works*, p. 449 (Sermon 38).

26 William Sherlock, *A Discourse concerning a Judge of Controversies in Matters of Religion* (London: Robert Clavell, 1686), p. 47.

27 *Prose Works*, IV, 34-35.

28 *Prose Works*, IX, 188.

29 Parker, "'The Idlest Trifling Stuff that ever was Writ': or, Why Swift Hated his Sermons," p. 58.

30 See, among others, Louis Landa, "Jonathan Swift and Charity," *Journal of English and Germanic Philology*, 44 (1945), 337-50.

the repeated, emphatic, necessary connection that Swift makes, in his sermons and elsewhere, between Christian belief as revealed in the text of Scripture, and the morality that he preaches – however difficult that morality, and some of the social and political views with which it is associated, may seem to us. The coupling of the words "truth" and "duty," of "faith" and "duty," of "revelation" and "morality," is one of the most distinct features of his theological writings, and of his sermons in particular. In *The Sentiments of a Church-of-England Man* (1708), Swift asserts that the claimed belief of many in God and "revealed Religion" is "practically" contradicted by "the Immorality of their Lives."[31] In "A Sermon upon the Excellency of Christianity," he found that the "defects in morals" of the ancient pagan philosophers were the mere and necessary consequences of "want of a support by revelation from God."[32] That revelation, it needs to be re-emphasized, is, for Swift as for other Church of England men, always scriptural. Swift's sermons like other sermons are a teacher's comments upon a text. "On Mutual Subjection," for example, is based on 1 Peter 5:5, and begins with the words: "The Apostle having in many Parts of this Epistle given Directions to Christians concerning the Duty of Subjection or Obedience to Superiors." We may not much like Swift's notions of subjection or obedience; but for him they were duties that arose necessarily from "the Doctrine of the Text."[33] Moral cleanliness, for Swift, is not next to godliness, but a central aspect of godliness. His arguments for the moral life, for virtue, courtesy, obedience, and civility, are based on scriptural revelation. They are, to speak generally, part of his orthodox Arminianism, often unstated because profoundly internalized. More particularly, they are a crucial part of the beliefs of churchmen of his time: "This fast union of morality and religion" (in Melvyn New's words) "is one of the marks of Latitudinarian Anglicanism."[34] In theology, if not in politics, Swift was essentially at one with the legacy of Tillotson and his fellow latitude men.

We can deny Swift a theology only by demanding that the theology he stated was other than it was, or by assuming that an orthodox theology can be no theology at all, or by insisting that true belief must be an internal and personal rather than an external and public matter. These demands and assumptions and insistences are modern, or, from Swift's perspective, heterodox. They are foreign to Swift and his orthodox contemporaries. Swift had read his

31 *Prose Works*, II, 4.

32 *Prose Works*, IX, 247.

33 *Prose Works*, IX, 141, 144.

34 Melvyn New, *Lawrence Sterne as Satirist: A Reading of "Tristram Shandy"* (Gainesville, Florida: University of Florida Press, 1969), p. 15.

Bible rather closely, and had prepared for the priesthood with some care. He knew the orthodox positions of Anglicanism, and had no difficulty articulating those positions. He did so on the basis of his understanding that revelation came from Scripture; that Scripture was interpretable, offering us "plain, easy Directions;"[35] and that it was the duty of the preacher to communicate that revelation, from those plain directions, in comprehensible language. It is in his sermons, as we would expect, that Swift most fully and straightforwardly undertakes and carries out what he understands to be his duty.

It is not, however, Swift's sermons only which have been the subject of misreading by a tendency in modern criticism. Evidently, texts such as *A Tale of a Tub* and *Gulliver's Travels*, amongst others, are allegorical in method, figurative in discourse, ironic in mode, various and often fugitive in speaking voice. Such productions have been properly open to diverse critical readings at the level of the work as a whole. Many of those readings may be valid (have truth value), within the possible meaning horizons of these texts.[36] Some of those readings, I shall argue, cannot be valid.

Some assumptions underlying what follows: All pieces of writing are made up, normally, of sentences, in syntactical form.[37] Those sentences are, in the sense that they express meanings, propositions. They are as propositions generally comprehensible, and communicable. They are constructed of shareable lexis, shareable syntactical structure, shareable reference. They have a textual and an extra-textual context which guides understanding. The meanings of those sentences, however complex and multiple and difficult, are in principle determinate. Without determinacy of meaning, as E. D. Hirsch puts it, "there can be no knowledge in interpretation, nor any knowledge in the many humanistic disciplines based upon textual interpretation."[38] Determinacy does not imply or require simplicity or singularity; determinate meanings may be, and in literary works typically are, complex and multiple, but they are at the same time bounded.[39] 'Literary' writings, and most especially the

35 Swift, *A Tale of a Tub and Other Works*, ed. Walsh, p. 123.

36 See E. D. Hirsch's discussion of the Husserlian concept of the meaning "horizon," and its effect in setting the boundaries of implication, in *Validity in Interpretation* (New Haven and London: Yale University Press, 1967), pp. 221-24.

37 "Normally" allows for numerous non-syntactical tendencies common long before modernism or post-modernism, for example in the lists of Homer or Rabelais or Swift, or the "Chough's language" used to hoodwink Parolles in the fourth Act of *All's Well that End's Well*, or the significations of paratextual elements in both literary and non-literary texts.

38 *The Aims of Interpretation* (Chicago and London: The University of Chicago Press, 1976), p. 3.

39 See also Hirsch, *Validity in Interpretation*, pp. 44-45: "Undoubtedly, most verbal meanings are imprecise and ambiguous, and to call them such is to acknowledge their

writings of Jonathan Swift, of course notoriously raise issues of fictionality, voice, and figuration: allegory, narrative, parody, personation, irony, metaphor. Largely because of such properties, philosophers from Plato onwards have denied imaginative literature's claim to truth, and many have explicitly denied that literature can achieve the specifically propositional rigour of a genuine discipline.[40] John Locke, much to the present purpose, credibly insists that "by the *Philosophical Use* of Words, I mean such an use of them, as may serve ... to express, in general Propositions, certain and undoubted Truths, which the Mind may ... be satisfied with, in its search after true Knowledge."[41] Locke does not find such usage in literary writing. Some modern philosophers of language and theorists of literature argue, however, that, in the words of the Liverpool philosopher Richard Gaskin, "the referential content of a work of literature ... will take a propositional form, and can, if true, be an object of propositional knowledge."[42] This is a challengeable position but a defensible one, both logically and ethically.[43]

The relation between the meaning of a work as a whole and the meanings of the propositions it contains is complex, and has long and notoriously been a central issue for hermeneutic theory. Schleiermacher provides this statement of the hermeneutic circle:

---

determinacy ... An ambiguous meaning has a boundary like any other verbal meaning ... Determinacy ... means self-identity ... Without it neither communication nor validity in interpretation would be possible."

40 In an important and persuasive recent discussion, Susan Haack denies that literature can claim to adopt "the attitude of disinterested truth seeking" characteristic of philosophy and the natural and physical sciences, but allows "that literary works may make, or convey, true claims ... and in a perfectly ordinary sense of 'true.'" Haack's argument is about 'literature' as such (she is fully aware that philosophy – notably the writings of Locke – may be literary in character); it need not be thought to threaten the distinct but connected claim that literary criticism, and *a fortiori* literary scholarship, like other disciplines of knowledge, may and should aspire to "disinterested truth seeking" ("Reading in a Literary Spirit," in Haack's *Manifesto of a Passionate Moderate: Unfashionable Essays* [Chicago and London: University of Chicago Press, 1998], pp. 48-68 [49, 59]; see also "'Dry Truth and Real Knowledge': Epistemologies of Metaphor and Metaphors of Epistemology," *Manifesto of a Passionate Moderate*, pp. 69-89).

41 John Locke, *Essay concerning Human Understanding*, ed. Peter H. Nidditch (Oxford: Clarendon Press, 1979), p. 476 (III, ix, 3).

42 Richard Gaskin, *Language Truth and Literature: A Defence of Literary Humanism* (Oxford: Oxford University Press, 2013), p. 94.

43 I discuss this argument at greater length in an essay entitled "Mimesis and Understanding in Samuel Johnson's Notes to Shakespeare (1765)," *The Age of Johnson*, forthcoming.

> Complete knowledge always involves an apparent circle, that each part can be understood only out of the whole to which it belongs, and vice versa. All knowledge which is scientific must be constructed in this way.[44]

Without interrogating the contested history of the hermeneutic circle, let me assert that, as a methodology, it is defensible in principle and viable in practice.[45] History of course shows that it is possible to offer a variety of readings of any complex and challenging work of literature. Some of those will be legitimately "deduceable from the Text" (to steal a phrase from the *Tale of a Tub* itself).[46] At the level of the work, what makes some readings legitimate and others not? For the purpose of my present argument, I make the limited assertion that interpretations of the text as a whole which either do not resort to the evidence of the propositions which make up that work, or which are based on flawed readings of the individual propositions which make up that work, cannot have truth value. Such readings may accord with favoured, prior, ideological positions, but they cannot count as knowledge. As Gerald Graff has put it, "the subjectivity of [interpretative] vision is a fact about its genesis, not about the adequacy of its truth claim."[47] Interpretations are hypotheses. Worthwhile hypotheses may be strengthened by confirming evidence, and falsified by contrary evidence. All empirical enquiry risks confirmation bias, and empirical enquiry conducted according to strongly held ideological positions is no doubt particularly liable to confirmation bias.[48]

Some recent work on Swift has in my view been compromised by such perspectivism, by confirmation bias, by local (and, it follows, by larger-scale)

44 F. D. E. Schleiermacher, *Hermeneutics: The Handwritten Manuscripts*, ed. Heinz Kimmerle, trans. James Duke and Jack Forstman (Missoula, Montana: Scholars Press, 1977), quoted from Kurt Mueller-Vollmer, ed., *The Hermeneutics Reader* (Oxford: Blackwell, 1986), p. 84.

45 Schleiermacher's account of the circle of hermeneutics is a recognizable and credible account of the process of editorial explication in particular.

46 Swift, *A Tale of a Tub and Other Works*, ed. Walsh, p. 119.

47 Gerald Graff, *Literature against Itself: Literary Ideas in Modern Society* (Chicago and London: The University of Chicago Press, 1979), p. 200.

48 I make an exception here for "the ideology of truth," as being, in E. D. Hirsch's words, "structurally different from any other political ideology." Hirsch argues that "under other political ideologies, we desire and sometimes pre-determine a particular result. Under the ideology of truth, our desire for a particular result is subordinated to our desire to be right. Our orientation is a posteriori, not a priori. We decide after the fact, not before the fact" (E. D. Hirsch, Jr, "The Politics of Theories of Interpretation," *Critical Inquiry*, 9 [1982], 235-47 [pp. 235-36]).

interpretative hypotheses which are false on the evidence, and compromised too by a refusal to surrender falsified hypotheses.[49] I shall offer three examples.

My first example, however, no doubt not a unique exception to the rule, is of a darling hypothesis, apparently supported by good evidence, which proved to be false, but which the scholar concerned rejected when the evidence proved to be mistaken. Everything is ideological, and in this case, too, there is an ideological tendency, but the critic concerned might claim to be pursuing the ideology of truth. This scholar, working on Swift's "On the Trinity," was intrigued by the passage in which Swift tells us that the doctrine of the Trinity, though not explicitly set out in Scripture, may be assembled or collected from clear though separate statements:

> I see it plainly declared in Scripture, that there is but one God; and yet I find our Saviour ... saying *He and his Father are one*; and, *before Abraham was, I am*. I read, that the Disciples worshipped him: That *Thomas* said to him, *My Lord and my God*. And, Saint *John*, Chap. 1st, *In the Beginning was the Word, and the Word was with God, and the Word was God*. I read likewise that the Holy Ghost bestowed the Gift of Tongues, and the Power of working Miracles.[50]

This scholar was thrilled to discover an apparent statement of just such a hermeneutic principle and methodology, in a discussion of the Scripture doctrine of the Trinity, in Richard Hooker's *Of the Lawes of Ecclesiastical Politie*:

> There hath been some doubt ... whether *containing in Scripture*, do import express setting down in plain terms, or else *comprehending* in such sort, that by reason we may from thence conclude all things which are necessary. Against the former of these two constructions instance hath sundry ways been given. For our belief in the Trinity, the Co-eternity of the Son of God with his Father, the proceeding of the Spirit from the Father and the Son ... the necessity whereof is by none denied, are notwithstanding in Scripture nowhere to be found by express literal mention, only deduced they are out of Scripture by collection. This kinde of comprehension in Scripture [is] therefore received.[51]

Our scholar had never found any similar statement of a principle of collection or assembly in his readings in Anglican hermeneutics, and was deeply satisfied to find such compelling authority for Swift's statement. He naturally wished to strengthen his hypothesis by seeking further instances and development of

49 For instance, the hypothesis that Swift wrote "The History of Martin." See Marcus Walsh, "Si vulgus vult decipi, decipiatur," *The Eighteenth Century: Theory and Interpretation*, 56 (2015), 392-96.

50 *Prose Works*, IX, 161.

51 *The Works of Mr Richard Hooker*, pp. 30-31 (I, xiv).

this idea of textual 'collection' in Hooker. And indeed, Hooker uses the word 'collection' very frequently. Investigation revealed, however, that Hooker consistently uses this word not to mean the gathering or assembly of multiple concurring though separate textual places, but rather to mean deduction, inference, of meaning from a single textual place. OED confirms this older, rarer, technical sense.[52] Chastened, our scholar abandoned his darling hypothesis. His ignorance of this special sense of "collection," and of its use by Hooker throughout the *Lawes*, is not at all to his credit, nor yet is his recycling of this episode of infamy on this occasion. Something, however, is to be said for his decision to acknowledge the hypothesis as falsified, and to drop it from his paper.

My second example is from a recent critic, part of whose purpose is to demonstrate the hypothesis, common enough in discussions of the sermons, that Swift was heterodox or pagan in religion. From that critic's extended analysis, I select their response to this passage, describing a scene of devotion from the *Discourse concerning the Mechanical Operation of the Spirit*:

> You perceive the Vapors to ascend very fast ... the Preacher ... begins a loud Hum, which pierces you quite thro'; This is immediately returned by the Audience, and you find your self prompted to imitate them, by a meer spontaneous Impulse.[53]

According to this critic, Swift suggests "in this passage that the mechanical operation of the spirit is encouraged by the clergy, who take advantage of and exploit the people's natural vulnerability to superstition."[54] However, Swift makes explicit, both in the quoted sentences and in the sentences of its immediate textual context, that he here describes not an orthodox Anglican congregation, but "an Assembly of Modern Saints." The "Preacher" is not an Anglican clergyman, but one of "our *British* [spiritual] *Workmen*." Like the Tub-Preacher depicted in the plate in Section I, he wears the two-part black and white cap of the Presbyterian preacher, and holds forth, to a behatted audience. The "Assembly" is identified as Presbyterian, or possibly Quaker, by the "Hum" of the preacher, and the artificial turning inwards of the eyes of the congregation. In this passage, as throughout the *Tub* volume, Swift attacks belief in individual inspiration by the Spirit, representing it as an internal, mechanical, and

---

52 OED, *n*. 5. "The action of inferring or deducing; an inference, deduction, conclusion. *Obs*. [<Latin *collectio*.]" OED gives examples dated from 1529 to 1705, including Milton, *The Doctrine and Discipline of Divorce*, 15: "Wrong collections have been hitherto made out of those words by modern Divines."

53 Swift, *A Tale of a Tub and Other Works*, ed. Walsh, p. 176.

54 Ellenzweig, *The Fringes of Belief*, p. 106.

delusory operation. Swift distinguishes explicitly here between understanding the Spirit as a genuine "supernatural Assistance, approaching from without," and the deluded Saints' belief in a spirit "proceeding entirely from within."[55] (The distinction is articulated by a persona, in indirect and ironic terms, but here, as often in the *Tale*, the direction of the irony is sufficiently clear.) Swift's satirical point is not (as this critic goes on, by a logical leap, to claim) "that the spirit is a fiction,"[56] but that the enthusiastic preacher and assembly he describes and, fairly or unfairly, mocks rely on a purely internal inspiration, "a meer spontaneous impulse," and defend themselves from the "Approaches" of the true divine Spirit, the cloven tongues of the Holy Ghost,[57] by their headwear. Here, in fact, a particular passage, and the propositions within it, have been misread; and that more local misreading, informed by this critic's prior thesis, leads to a larger misinterpretation of the work.

My third example is from a distinguished critic who, writing in 1998, might be taken as representative of hermeneutic positions and assumptions not uncommon at that date, and still somewhat persistent. This critic begins his essay on the *Tale of a Tub* with the familiar claim that "Swift's satire is a semantic *perpetuum mobile* ... it never allows what critics call a 'standard interpretation' ... the very history of reader-response-criticism imitates its object's dynamics by refusing any definitive interpretations."[58] I would with respect disagree with such formulations on principle: the image of the "semantic *perpetuum mobile*" is a sceptical *reductio* of the possibility of determinable meaning; the notion of "standard" or "definitive" interpretation is a straw man of no very definite shape (a determinate interpretation, like any other hypothesis, cannot claim to be either "standard" or "definitive"); and that readers have offered many interpretations does not logically entail that they have offered many valid interpretations. My main concern again, however, is with an apparently characteristic response of such a mode of criticism to the propositions which make up the *Tale*. For instance, the brothers begin by interpreting the Will by a method of which Swift and other Anglican theorists approved, *totidem verbis*

55 Swift, *A Tale of a Tub and Other Works*, ed. Walsh, pp. 174-76. For commentary, see pp. 515-16.

56 Ellenzweig, *The Fringes of Belief*, p. 111.

57 Later in his life, Swift explicitly insisted that the Pentecostal visitation was genuine, in terms consistent with this passage in the *Tale*: "The Holy Ghost bestowed the Gift of Tongues ... such as could be done by the Inspiration of God alone" ("On the Trinity," *Prose Works*, IX, 161).

58 Rudolf Freiburg, "Enlightened Darkness: The Treatment of Arcane Learning in Jonathan Swift's *A Tale of a Tub*," *Swift, the Enigmatic Dean: Festschrift for Hermann Josef Real*, eds Rudolf Freiburg, Arno Löffler, and Wolfgang Zach (Tübingen: Stauffenburg, 1998), pp. 47-69 (47). Further references will be given in parentheses within the text.

(that is, propositionally). That method, however, does not meet the brotherly readers' requirements for change in their coats, that is, in their religion. Here the "*Book-learned*" brother advocates interpretation of the Will *totidem syllabis* or *totidem literis*. Our third, modern, critic remarks:

> Swift ... here touches the basis of Christian belief, demonstrating that the whole church may be based on doctrines which themselves are mere products of arbitrary interpretations of so called holy texts. By subjecting the Testament, that is the Bible, to the teleology [*sic.*; *recte* <to theology>?] of a strictly profane kind, both religious lore and homiletic tradition are severely chastised. (p. 59)

At this pre-Reformation moment, the brothers, as yet effectively undifferentiated, are all no doubt implicated. But the hermeneutic scam is that of Peter (as he will shortly be named), and it parodies modes of interpretation practised in the pre-Reformation Church to justify abuses here represented as specifically Roman Catholic. It is not clear how the entire post-Reformation Christian Church, and particularly the Church of England, could be a "mere product" of these particular and historical modes of interpretation. Swift does not endorse "arbitrary interpretations" in the *Tale*, and indeed sets out a very different hermeneutics in the "Apology" particularly; Swift's position in the *Tale* on this issue is entirely consonant with that generally held and set out within the Church of England, of which Swift professed himself a loyal member.[59] Moreover, to which "holy texts" does our critic refer, and by whom are these holy texts "so called"? Again, our critic alleges "the connection between Protestantism, Catholicism and Puritanism on the one hand and the enigmatic learning of cabala, Gnosticism, Rosicrucianism and alchemy on the other," and asserts that

> the three great religions are infiltrated by arcane learning to different degrees; Protestantism comes off best, but on the whole the harsh criticism that Swift here launches on the "errors" in religion in general can hardly be overlooked. (pp. 56-57)

This conclusion seems open to question. Swift's tale of the three brothers is an allegory of course; but it is nevertheless an allegory, like other allegories, made up of determinate, propositional, statements. As the two younger brothers attain individuality in the course of the *Tale*, Martin is associated decisively with Luther, and the Church of England; and Jack, much more variously and extensively, and equally specifically, with a large number of historical

59 I have belaboured this point in "Text, 'Text,' and Swift's *A Tale of a Tub*," *Modern Language Review*, 85 (1990), 290-303.

manifestations of sectarian Protestantism: Anabaptists, Gueuses, Huguenots, Familists, Ranters, Muggletonians, Presbyterians, Independents, Quakers.[60] Martin and Jack are distinct. To generalize the three brothers as representatives of "the three great religions," and especially to generalize Martin and Jack as "Protestantism" and "Puritanism," enables a move (representative of the hermeneutic procedure here adopted) from the identification of Swift's satire on specific tendencies in Jack as well as Peter, in (mostly Calvinist) Protestant dissent and in the Roman Church, to the allegation that Swift's target is "religion in general." If that allegation is to stick, it would be necessary to demonstrate how and where, in the propositions offered in the *Tale*, Martin – the English Church – is implicated in this part of Swift's satire. In his 1705 *Observations* on the *Tale*, William Wotton similarly asserted that the *Tale*-teller was guilty of an attack on all religion, driven by "his contemptible Opinion of every Thing which is called Christianity." Our critic offers essentially the same response to the *Tale* as William Wotton, and like Wotton's his argument falls, in my view, on *interpretative* grounds.[61]

Led by some modern theoretical assumptions, and by some modern cultural and political preferences, such criticism risks generating a version of Swift and Swift's thinking false to the texts he wrote. It must be legitimate for a modern reader to find some of the social and doctrinal positions stated in Swift's sermons rebarbative and unacceptable; it is not legitimate on those grounds to make those sermons say something other than they do, to claim they are incoherent or necessarily conflicted, and to represent them as marginal. It is legitimate to find in any one of the complex propositions in the *Tale* a plurality of determinate, and determinable meanings. It is legitimate to disagree with some or all of those plural determinate meanings and the positions they articulate (and for us as modern readers this is often not only a credible but a necessary option). It is legitimate to argue for almost any number of readings of the *Tale* (or of *Hamlet*, or of *Mansfield Park*) as a whole text, on the basis of the complex interrelations of the plurality of determinate meanings

60 Particularly, in *Tale*, Section VI. I offer evidence for these interpretations in Swift, *A Tale of a Tub and Other Works*, ed. Walsh, pp. lxii-lxvi, 407-11.

61 William Wotton, *Reflections upon Ancient and Modern Learning … With Observations upon the Tale of a Tub*, 3rd ed. (1705); reprinted in Swift, *A Tale of a Tub and Other Works*, ed. Walsh, p. 224. In an essay entitled "Against Hypocrisy and Dissent" (forthcoming in *The Oxford Handbook of Eighteenth-Century Satire*, ed. Paddy Bullard [Oxford: Oxford University Press, 2019]), I offer a longer discussion of Wotton's response, as consistent with the widespread contemporaneous sense of scandal provoked by the *Tale*, but as unconvincing in its interpretative argument that the *Tale* attacks all Christianity. Wotton's *Observations* nevertheless remain the most sustained and methodologically credible attack on the orthodoxy of Swift's *Tale*.

of those complex propositions. It is not legitimate to mistake the terms of those propositions, or to misunderstand or misrepresent, or merely to assert, the relations of subjects and predicates within those propositions. It is not, I have particularly attempted to show, legitimate to argue for, or to assert, readings of the whole text based on such misprisions, or assertions, of the propositions it contains. The interpretation of complex and distant texts is a challenging discipline, and error is a normal and inevitable part of that discipline. We all live in glass houses; it is always possible to make, in Hooker's sense of the term, "wrong Collections." Nevertheless, perhaps especially at a time when truth in public discourse is at a premium, and perhaps especially in the case of Swift, there is an argument to be made for our best fidelity to the utterances of the authors we study.

Melinda Alliker Rabb
Brown University, Providence

Swift, Defoe, Civil War, and the Meaning of (Bare) Life

Abstract. The English Civil Wars had profound effects on eighteenth-century literature, yet the manifestations of those effects often are indirect. This essay argues that works by Jonathan Swift and Daniel Defoe displace the trauma of that internal conflict – a conflict that destroyed bodies and beliefs – onto fictions that at first appear not to be about war. Readings of texts including *Gulliver's Travels, The Drapier's Letters, The Journal of the Plague Year*, and *Robinson Crusoe* are framed by first-hand accounts of military experiences during the Wars, such as preparing, fighting, and surviving battle or siege, and by concepts such as sovereignty, the state of exception, and bare life. Civil war raised fundamental questions about the value of life, epitomized in the practice of granting no quarter. Both Swift and Defoe find ways to examine the political and moral dilemma of who is empowered to decide if a life is worth living.

In *The Writing of the Disaster*, Maurice Blanchot says that [disaster] "is related to forgetfulness": it "is the unknown name for that in thought itself which dissuades us from thinking of it;" it "is the limit of writing."[1] The English Civil Wars were an unprecedented disaster. It took several generations to confront and to process events that shaped, in both subtle and obvious ways, the imaginations of Jonathan Swift, Daniel Defoe, and other of their contemporaries. We, as twenty-first-century readers living in a time of global civil war, may be particularly well situated to reconsider the inevitable limits of both thought and representation, then and now. The expression "civil wars" is, of course, an oxymoron whose implicit aporia defies resolution. "Civil" means courteous, polite, obliging, designating a community, state, or body politic as a whole, but "war" means hostile, contentious, violent, designating divided and opposing forces. All civil wars belong to a category of conflict in which enemies and friends, attackers and neighbours, are not simply opposing but interconnected, and can be difficult to distinguish.

1 Maurice Blanchot, *The Writing of the Disaster* [*L'Ecriture du désastre*], trans. Ann Smock (Lincoln and London: University of Nebraska Press, 1995), pp. 3, 5, 7. Further citations are from this edition and will be given in parentheses within the text.

 | DOI:10.30965/9783846763971_016

The soldier Edmund Ludlow published memoirs that Swift and Defoe (both of whose works are central to this essay) owned and knew.[2] Ludlow describes an encounter on the battlefield. He recognizes a comrade: "Observing one Mr. *William Neale*, who was of my Acquaintance, and formerly my School-fellow, I called to him, telling him, that I was sorry to see him there … he retreated towards his Party, where … he called me to come on, which I did." Ludlow trusts his childhood companion: "But he retreated again till he came within the shelter of their Foot, and one with him dismounting, fired a Musquet at me loaded with a brace of Bullets, of which one went into the Belly of my Horse, the other struck upon my Breast-plate, within half an Inch of the bottom of it."[3] A mere half-inch of metal saves Ludlow from death. Other combatants would describe comparable incidents and ask: "Whose Blood stains the Walls of our Towns, and defiles our Land? Is it not all English?"[4]

Defoe revisits this problem seven decades later in one of the rare explicit fictionalizations of the Civil Wars, *Memoirs of a Cavalier* (1720). Defoe's protagonist, a seasoned veteran of the Thirty Years War, and a soldier not given to strong emotion or deep introspection, is nevertheless moved to speak of his "unaccountable sadness" when he "saw [him]self at the cutting the throats of my friends, and indeed some of my near relations":

> I found a strange secret and unaccountable sadness upon my spirits to see this acting in my own native country. It grieved me to the heart, even in the rout of our enemies, to see the slaughter of them … to hear a man cry for quarter in English, moved me to a compassion which I had never been used.

Shared language, culture, and personal history cause him momentary confusion in the midst of fighting:

> and when I heard a soldier cry, "O God, I am shot," I looked behind me to see which of my own Troop was fallen … My old comrades … were some *with* us and some *against* us, as their opinions happened to differ.[5]

---

2 Passmann and Vienken II, 1134-35; Daniel Defoe, *Memoirs of a Cavalier*, ed. N. H. Keeble in *The Novels of Daniel Defoe*, eds W. R. Owens and P. N. Furbank, 10 vols (Pickering and Chatto, 2008), IV, 14.

3 *Memoirs of Edmund Ludlow Esq; Lieutenant General of the Horse, Commander in Chief of the Forces in Ireland, One of the Council of State, and a Member of the Parliament which Began on November 3, 1640*, 2 vols ([London], 1698), I, 118.

4 Bulstrode Whitelocke, *Memorials of the English Affairs: or, An Historical Account of what Passed from the Beginning of the Reign of King Charles the First to King Charles the Second* (London: Nathaniel Ponder, 1682), p. 80; italics inverted.

5 Defoe, *Memoirs of a Cavalier*, ed. Keeble, IV, 148. The ambiguous, difficult-to-place tone of this passage seems to resonate with Swift's account of dismemberment – the flayed woman

Perhaps even more than Defoe, Swift "was haunted by the cultural memory of the seventeenth-century war," as David Oakleaf argues, which had "radically transformed the communities to which he was most deeply attached" and from which they were still recovering. Explicit, graphic descriptions of the actual conflict are rare in his work, yet "the brutal fact of war was central to all of [his] writing."[6]

Detachment, Blanchot writes, is "a sign of the disaster" (p. 9). Detachment can be an attitude or a corporeal condition. Representations of injured men in the aftermath of the Civil Wars participate in a process of displacement, not only the physical displacement of body parts, but also the indirection and transference through which texts negotiate ideas difficult to confront whole and entire. Eighteenth-century literature has many examples of dismembered, damaged men. Aphra Behn's royal slave mutilated in *Oroonoko*, Delarivier Manley's Osman exploded from a cannon in *The Royal Mischief*, John Dryden's ironic swordsman severing a head so deftly that it remains in place, Swift's Gulliver describing bodies dropping in pieces from the clouds, Defoe's Crusoe discovering cannibalized limbs on the beach of his island, Alexander Pope's male sylph Ariel cleft in twain, scattered carcasses fed on by vultures in Samuel Johnson's *Idler*, the damaged groin of Laurence Sterne's Uncle Toby in *Tristram Shandy*, and Tobias Smollett's scalped, disfigured Lieutenant Lismahago in *Humphry Clinker* – these men, among others, are implicitly or explicitly connected to historic trauma.[7]

Indirection and avoidance are powerful human responses to trauma. At the Restoration of monarchy, Charles II – whose father suffered the era's most famous bodily detachment – issued the Act of Indemnity and Oblivion to discourage revivals of what he obliquely euphemized as "the late distractions" and "the occasions thereof."[8] Edward Hyde, Earl of Clarendon's *History of the Rebellion and Civil Wars in England* (which Swift read and reread)[9] also demurs: "But We are rather desirous to draw a Veil over all the Calamities, that have proceeded from this Cause; as well because the impression those mistakes have

---

and dissected beau in *A Tale of a Tub* – at which the narrator can "hardly believe, how much it altered [their] Person[s] for the worse" (*A Tale of a Tub and Other Works*, ed. Marcus Walsh [Cambridge: Cambridge University Press, 2010], p. 112). I do not suggest that Defoe's Cavalier is ironic, merely that his attitude seems inappropriate.

6 David Oakleaf, *A Political Biography of Jonathan Swift* (London: Pickering and Chatto, 2008), p. 11.

7 See Melinda Alliker Rabb, "Parting Shots: Eighteenth-Century Displacements of the Male Body at War," *ELH*, 78 (2011), 103-35.

8 *English Historical Documents, 1660-1714*, ed. Andrew Browning (London: Eyre and Spottiswoode, 1966), p. 164.

9 Passmann and Vienken II, 940-87.

made, and the marks they have left behind them."[10] Jeremy Taylor, author of *Holy Living and Holy Dying*, was captured in a storm at Cardigan Castle where 350 soldiers were slain, a crisis that might well have informed his thought, but he alludes only once to this disturbing event in all of his writings.[11] Yet the human imagination could hardly ignore thousands (20,000 in the Thomason Collection) of parliamentary reports, newspapers, and personal memoirs of the seventeenth-century wars that record "the cutting off of privy members, ears, fingers, and hands," of "legs and arms flying apace," of guts lying on the ground, of bowels and brains flying in men's faces, of a body mangled beyond recognition save for an identifying mole on the neck, of bits and pieces that defy imagining. Explicit narratives like Defoe's *Memoirs of a Cavalier* are surprisingly more circumspect about the war-torn body than representations in which memory is "refigured and refracted in the literary imagination," and displaced onto remote regions,[12] like Gulliver's Houyhnhnmland or Crusoe's island, or onto seemingly unrelated events, like a coinage patent or an outbreak of plague.

Here is an example of displacement. *Memoirs of a Cavalier* narrates events from the end of the Thirty Years War to the surrender to Fairfax, and we might expect a narrative of horrors. But the Cavalier is oddly immune to physical suffering. The real soldier Ludlow remembers constant hunger, and even when provisions arrive, he "could scarce eat it, my jaws for want of use having almost lost their natural facility."[13] Yet the Cavalier enjoys "four or five great pieces of bacon, as many of beef ... two or three loaves, and a large leather bottle of liquor."[14] Defoe transfers the problem of hunger to a remote island in the Caribbean. Crusoe is preoccupied with food production in the first volume; in the second, desperately ravenous people try to pull raw meat out of a boiling pot, but starvation prevents their bodies from accepting food. By the third volume, Crusoe explicitly articulates the underlying connection between his adventures and the civil wars. Years of travel lead him home to contemplate the "separations and schisms among us, more than there are in any other nation in the world ... [They] were all here during the bloody intestine wars in the

10 Edward Hyde, Earl of Clarendon, *The History of the Rebellion and Civil Wars in England, Begun in the Year 1641*, 3 vols (Oxford: at the Theatre, 1707), I, VI; italics inverted.

11 Charles Carlton, *Going to the Wars: The Experience of the British Civil Wars, 1638-1651* (London and New York: Routledge, 1994), p. 344.

12 *The English Civil Wars in the Literary Imagination*, eds Claude J. Summers and Ted-Larry Pebworth (Columbia and London: University of Missouri Press, 1999).

13 Ludlow, *Memoirs*, I, 45.

14 Defoe, *Memoirs of a Cavalier*, ed. Keeble, IV, 180.

years 1640 to 1656 ... [The] difficult question which still remains before us ... is, what remedy can we apply to this malady?"[15]

The present essay will combine two approaches to the question of displaced trauma of the Civil Wars in the work of Swift and Defoe. First, embodiment theory provides a conceptual frame within which to assess the tensions between the cultural investment in the intact male body, its actual vulnerability, its dis-integration in war, and the ensuing corporeal fantasies of that body in the eighteenth century. Second, theories of biopolitics and sovereignty support more extensive analysis of questions of agency, specifically the tensions between two distinct ways in which the effects of war are measured in and on bodies, besides their actual dismemberment: chance and choice. On the one hand, personal danger may result from chance, contingency, and accident, but on the other, trauma may result from choice, deliberation, and decision. *Gulliver's Travels* offers a ready example of this distinction. For Swift, chance violence escapes a certain kind of onus. The events that initiate Gulliver's physical abandonment and vulnerability on each of his voyages occur in a meaningful sequence, beginning with utter chance and ending in conscious choice. He washes up on the shores of Lilliput because a storm, an unplanned act of nature, causes shipwreck; he is stranded in Brobdingnag because the crew flees in fear at the sight of the giants, an instinctive act of human nature; the surprise attack by pirates, an external assault, brings him to Laputa; but finally, mutiny, a planned conspiracy and overthrow of command from within the ship's population, a choice to wage deliberate civil war or rebellion, banishes Gulliver to Houyhnhnmland.[16]

2

The Civil Wars' legacy of broken and exposed bodies owed much to chance. From the beginning, according to Bulstrode Whitelocke, things seemed out of control: "We have insensibly slid into this beginning of a Civil War, by one unexpected Accident after another, as waves of the sea, which have brought us this far: and we scarce know how, but ... We are now come to the question

15 Defoe, *Serious Reflections during the Life and Surprising Adventures of Robinson Crusoe*, ed. G. A. Starr, in *The Novels of Daniel Defoe*, eds Owens and Furbank, III, 162-63.

16 Jonathan Swift, *Gulliver's Travels*, ed. David Womersley (Cambridge: Cambridge University Press, 2012), pp. 33 (I, i, 5), 122 (II, i, 4), 221-22 (III, i, 9-10), 332 (IV, i, 2-3).

of raising forces."[17] Once forces are raised, "one unexpected accident after another" took deadly tolls. Three common liabilities were gunpowder, disease, and weather.

In *The Soldier's Grammar* (1643), Gervase Markham claims: "Now in these moderne and latter times, wherein the Inuention of Shott and Powder is founde out ... the danger, Sodainnesse, and Violence of the Fire is knowne."[18] Negligence, inexperience, and technically inaccurate weapons made accidents frequent and dramatic. After the battle of Newbury, "upon the heath, lay a whole file of men, six deep, with their heads all struck off with one cannon shot of ours."[19] One careless moment could change everything. While inspecting plunder after the capture of Hoghton Tower, a soldier lit his pipe, blowing up the arsenal, himself, and sixty other men. Whitelocke reports that the Earl of Haddington "and twenty more Knights and a Gentleman in an instant were all slain by an accident of Fire, which blew up the Magazine of Powder in a Vault, and they were killed by the Stones which flew."[20] John Milton and Swift would be fervent – in *Paradise Lost* and *Gulliver's Travels* – on the subject of gunpowder as the work of the devil and as the indictment of humankind.[21] A popular Civil Wars ballad, "The Maunding Soldier, or the Fruit of War is Beggary," less eloquently claims:

> Twice through the Bulke I have been shot,
> My braines have boyled like a Pot:
> I haue at lest these dozen times,
> Been blowne up by those roguish Mines.[22]

When explosives did not kill, they confused. In battle, Richard Atkyns recalls, "the air was so darkened by the smoke of the powder, that ... there was no light seen, but what the fire of the volleys of shot gave ... I knew not wither to go, nor what to do." The smoke clears at Powick Bridge like an eerie dream: "Ours gave

17 Whitelocke, *Memorials of the English Affairs*, p. 58.

18 Gervase Markham, *The Souldiers Grammar: Containing the High, Necessarie, and Most Curious Rules of the Art Militarie* (London: William Shifford, 1626), p. 10.

19 John Gwyn, *The Military Memoirs*, ed. Norman Tucker (London: Longmans, 1967), p. 53.

20 Whitelocke, *Memorials of the English Affairs*, p. 34.

21 See John Milton, *Paradise Lost*, ed. Alastair Fowler (London and New York: Longman, 1971), pp. 191 (IV, 17-18), 333-34 (VI, 498-515); *Gulliver's Travels*, ed. Womersley, pp. 191-92 (II, vii, 7, 3).

22 Martin Parker, *The Maunding Souldier: or, The Fruits of Warre is Beggery* (London: F. Groue, [1656]).

fire, and then theirs gave fire ... But all of a sudden we found all the troops on both sides of us melted away."[23]

Diary entries and memoirs record nature's random acts of sabotage:

> Incessant rain flooded the mines during the sieges of York and Gloucester.
>
> The winter is already come and our lying in the field hath lost us more than have been taken away either by the sword or the bullet.
>
> From as clear a sunshine day as could be seen, there fell a sudden mist, that we could not see ten yards off.
>
> The unceasing winds next morning soon dried up our ... wet clothes [that] we lay pickled in all night.[24]

So many deaths occurred from disease, say medical historians, that "it would not be unreasonable to assume that the Civil Wars produced slightly more indirect deaths than direct ones."[25] Dirty water, typhoid fever, malnutrition, dysentery, and bubonic plague were rife. Of Ireland, Colonel Richard Lawrence wrote: "The plague and famine [have] swept away whole counties that a man might travel twenty or thirty miles and not see a living creature."[26] Unexpected events worked havoc on both armies: bridges collapse as troops are crossing; floors gave way as councils were meeting – stories of accidents are so plentiful that the neat lines, geometric shapes, and abstract symbols that replace bodies in printed battle plans seem egregiously naïve in the face of lived disorder.

Sir Richard Bulstrode recalls the self-absorbed aggression activated by the frenzied fighting at Edgehill: "In a battle, the next man can hardly make a true relation of the actions of him that is next to him; for in such a Hurry and smoke of a Set Field, a man takes notice of nothing but what relates to his own safety."[27] This sounds a lot like what Hobbes will call war – "where every man is Enemy to every man," when "men live without other security, than what their own strength, and their own invention shall furnish them withal."[28] However, Bulstrode's disorganized "Hurry and smoke" permits a degree of exoneration for acts of cruelty and slaughter. Hobbes's phrase, "what ... their own invention shall furnish them withal" shifts the onus onto what are conscious decisions.

---

23 Richard Atkyns, *Military Memoirs: The Civil War*, ed. Peter Young (London: Longmans, 1967), p. 19; *An Account of Powick Bridge by a Trooper in Captain Nathaniel Fiennes's Troop* (1642), p. 10.

24 Carlton, *Going to the Wars*, p. 105; Gwyn, *Military Memoirs*, ed. Tucker, p. 52.

25 *The Impact of the English Civil War*, ed. John Morrill (London: Collins and Brown, 1991), p. 20.

26 Carlton, *Going to the Wars*, p. 213.

27 Quoted in Carlton, *Going to the Wars*, p. 129.

28 Thomas Hobbes, *Leviathan*, ed. Noel Malcolm, 3 vols (Oxford: Clarendon Press, 2012), II, 192.

3

Against the backdrop of so much that is unplanned, then, deliberate acts appear all the more distinct – acts that followed the heat of battle or siege, when the matter of winners and losers was no longer in question – when troops were not stunned by explosives, blinded by smoke, upset by sudden storms, or incapacitated by illness. Decisive acts were the purview of the victors who could choose the manner in which they would treat their victims and captives. The disturbing realities of these decisions were extensively reported. And even if reports were partisan and distorted, they constitute a kind of reality that later generations would inherit.

Two crucial choices are documented over and over in accounts of war – the choice to strip bodies, and especially the decision to grant no quarter – a practice eventually designated a war crime by the Lieber Code of 1863 and by the 1949 Geneva Conventions, specifying that "a person who is recognized or who, in the circumstances, should be recognized to be *hors de combat*, shall not be made the object of attack."[29] Blanchot says that the disaster is related to forgetfulness (p. 3). If there was one thing most needful to forget about the seventeenth-century conflict, it was the atrocity of no quarter – the victor's decision, after the heat of battle, to execute or otherwise eliminate soldiers and prisoners, "in the power of an adverse party" or "expressing intentions to surrender" or "rendered unconscious or otherwise incapacitated by wounds or sickness." The question becomes not simply the cohesive or fractured condition of the body, but whether that body contains a life worth saving. Here, the theoretical frame shifts to questions of abandonment, states of exception, and bare life. Broken and summarily executed men – a king or a nameless foot soldier – raise new questions about sovereignty and power. It was the burden of eighteenth-century literature to come to terms with this aspect of the paradigm-shifting conflict of the preceding generation.

What can provide perspective on these horrors and on their displacement into literature? Here are two pairs of first-person accounts – the first set refers to stripping of prisoners; the other, to choosing no quarter:

29 The Lieber Code was prepared by Francis Lieber and promulgated as General Orders No 100 by President Abraham Lincoln, 24 April 1863 (<Avalon.law.yale.edu/19th_century/lieber.asp>, accessed 5 November 2018). Each of the four Geneva Conventions of 1949 defines the elimination of defenseless soldiers as a war crime. Legal scholars consider the most authoritative definition of no quarter to be in Additional Protocol I to the Geneva Conventions, Articles 40 and 41 (1977), from which the quoted phrases in this paragraph are taken (<https://ihl-databases.icrc.org/applic/ihl/ihl.nsf/vwTreaties1949.xsp>, accessed 31 October 2018).

> First: [The sight of the naked] broken helpless prisoners was too much for many of the victors ... so dirty and dejected as was rare to see ... none of them, except some few of their officers, did look any of us in the face.
> Second: [W]hile we were waiting ... our nakedness was brought home to us; we really had nothing now except our bare bodies ... all we possessed, literally, was our naked existence.

> First: [H]e ordered all of the officers to be [killed], every tenth man shot, and the rest sent to [labour in] Barbados.
> Second: His right hand was lifted, and with the forefinger of that hand he pointed ... to the right or to the left ... but far more frequently to the left ... Someone whispered ... that to be sent to the right would mean work.

In each pair, the first passage is from a civil wars diary.[30] The second passage is from Viktor Frankl's account of his years in Auschwitz.[31] The resonance between these passages draws attention to the work of philosophers and theorists (like Blanchot, and Giorgio Agamben) concerned with the concept of abandoned life, and with the violence that underpins social and political order in the modern world, who have reacted to the atrocities of the twentieth century – totalitarianism, the camp, and holocaust – but who have also rooted their thinking in the post-English Civil Wars ideas of Thomas Hobbes's *Leviathan*, a text whose importance they share with Defoe and Swift.

The work of these philosophers centres on the concept of decision, beginning with the famous definition of the sovereign as "he who decides upon the state of exception."[32] The connection between the sovereign and abandoned life is a complicated one, expressed in metaphors of threshold and liminality. Michel Foucault explains the emergence of biopolitics in the late seventeenth and eighteenth centuries as the effect of power to organize and control bodies and lives through disciplining institutions (like the clinic, the prison), a defining modern development.[33] But for Agamben, the modern state and its expanding network of regulatory institutions nevertheless retain the vestiges

---

30 Richard Symonds, *Diary of the Marches of the Royal Army during the Great Civil War*, ed. Charles Edward Long (London: Camden Society, 1859), p. 66; *State Papers Collected by Edward Earl of Clarendon Commencing from the Year 1621, Containing Materials from which his History of the Great Rebellion was Composed*, 3 vols, eds R. Scrope and T. Monkhouse (London: Camden Society, 1859), II, 22.

31 Victor E. Frankl, *Man's Search for Meaning* (Boston: Beacon Press, 2006 [1959]), pp. 15, 12.

32 Giorgio Agamben (*State of Exception*, trans. Kevin Attell [Chicago: University of Chicago Press, 2003], p. 1) rethinks the definition of the sovereign articulated by Carl Schmitt, *Politische Theologie: vier Kapitel zur Lehre von der Souveränität* (München und Leipzig: von Duncker und Humblot, 1922).

33 Michel Foucault, *The History of Sexuality, Volume I: An Introduction*, trans. Robert Hurley (New York: Pantheon Books, 1978), 140-41.

of their earlier monarchal foundations, what he refers to as "the essential continuity between the state of exception and sovereignty":

> He who has been banned is not, in fact, simply set outside the law and made indifferent to it but rather abandoned by it, that is, exposed and threatened on the threshold in which life and law, outside and inside, become indistinguishable.[34]

The trial of Charles I epitomized the conflation of sovereign and bare life before the law, and the paradox of inclusion/exclusion that binds the empowered and the disempowered. Parliament could endorse the stamp of royal authority as legitimate while charging treason against the King "as a man."[35] We know how central the "whole Tryall, and ... Death" of the "Royal Martyr" was to Swift's historical imagination, to his preoccupation with the Civil Wars, and to his belief that the execution of the king marked a watershed in the English constitution, which had been "so shattered and crazy almost ever since."[36] Agamben connects the state of exception to civil war: "It is difficult even to arrive at a definition of the term [exception] given its position at the limits between politics and law ... The state of exception constitutes a 'point of imbalance' ... that is situated – like civil war, insurrection, and resistance – in an 'ambiguous, uncertain, borderline fringe.'"[37] I want to take Agamben's thought to the plight of the soldier (and his displacement in eighteenth-century texts).

"It was common throughout the [civil] war," historian Michael Braddick writes, "for the fallen to be stripped, so that in the morning the field was

34 Agamben, *State of Exception*, trans. Attell, p. 1.

35 Giorgio Agamben cites the beheading of Louis XVI of France, not Charles I of England, but the point is the same: "The enormity of the rupture ... consisted not in the fact that a monarch was killed but in the fact that he was submitted to a trial and executed after having been condemned to capital punishment ... In modern constitutions, a trace of the unsacrificeability of the sovereign's life still survives in the principle according to which the head of state cannot be submitted to an ordinary legal trial" (*Homo Sacer: Sovereign Power and Bare Life*, trans. Daniel Heller-Roazen [Stanford: Stanford University Press, 1998], pp. 102-3).

36 Hermann J. Real, "A New Letter from Swift: His Answer to the Earl of Strafford, 29 March 1735, Recovered," *Swift Studies*, 18 (2003), 20-25. See also S. J. Connolly, "The Church of Ireland and the Royal Martyr: Regicide and Revolution in Anglican Political Thought, c.1660-c.1745," *Journal of Ecclesiastical History*, 54 (2003), 484-506, and Howard D. Weinbrot, "Swift's Thirtieth of January Sermon: Politics, the Pulpit, and the Choice of Strife," *Reading Swift: Papers from The Fifth Münster Symposium on Jonathan Swift*, ed. Hermann J. Real (Munich: Wilhelm Fink, 2008), pp. 225-44; *Gulliver's Travels*, ed. Womersley, pp. 470-73.

37 Agamben here (*State of Exception*, trans. Attell, p. 1) cites Alessandro Fontana, *Du droit de résistance au devoir d'insurrection*, in *Le Droit de resistance*, ed. Jean-Claude Zancarini (Paris: ENS, 1999), p. 16.

covered with naked corpses."[38] This action resonates with Agamben's provocative metaphor of "bare life," referring to the woundable, expendable body not, as in Hobbes's state of nature, simply natural reproductive life, the *zoe* of Aristotle, nor fully *bios*, a good life within a meaningful political order. Bare life is damaged life, bereft of political significance and subjected to "unlimited exposure to violation, which does not count as a crime."[39] The *homo sacer* – the man who can be killed but not sacrificed – describes the defeated soldier or prisoner, whose death can no longer be a meaningful sacrifice because the justification for his personal fighting no longer exists, or at least he is now excluded from its attainment.

Stripping warriors has ancient precedents. In the *Iliad*, valuable armour was a victorious warrior's plunder, a part of the heroic code. In Book VI, Nestor promises the Achaeans the looting of the Trojan bodies (VI, ll. 66-71), and Glaucis cannot prevent the stripping of Sarpedon in Book XVI (XVI, ll. 477-526). In contrast, Simeon Ashe remembers nothing heroic at Marston Moor: "In the morning there was a mortifying object to behold, when the naked bodies of thousands lay upon the ground and not altogether dead." In Scotland, troops "forced well-dressed men to strip naked before hacking them to death." More often, there was little in the way of beautiful armaments or accoutrements to plunder as prizes. At Cirencester, men were "hazed ... stripped and bound together." A cavalry witness at Lostwithiel wrote: "No tongue can express the barbarous usage of our men by the Enemy. They stripped many stark naked." Like dismemberment, stripping dehumanized and effaced identity: "The field was covered with the dead, yet no one could tell to what party they belonged." Historian Charles Carlton writes: "After a few days, once ... the dead had been stripped and tossed aside, they resembled the pathetically white matchsticks shown on films of liberated concentration camps."[40]

Peter Brooks has contended that "in patriarchal societies, the male body is ostensibly deproblematized, decathected as an object of curiosity or of representation, and concomitantly more thoroughly hidden." He continues: "There is an apparent paradox here: if the male body ... becomes the norm ... one might expect [it] to be more openly displayed and discussed ... [But] the gaze is 'phallic,' its object is not ... Despite ... the attention paid to viewing woman naked, the paternal phallus may be the ultimate taboo object of our culture."[41]

38 Michael Braddick, *God's Fury, England's Fire: A New History of the English Civil Wars* (London: Penguin, 2009), p. 246.

39 Agamben, *Homo Sacer*, trans. Heller-Roazen, p. 10.

40 Carlton, *Going to the Wars*, p. 146.

41 Peter Brooks, *Body Work: Objects of Desire in Modern Narrative* (Cambridge, Massachusetts, and London: Harvard University Press, 1993), p. 15. The figure of the cuckold, from this

Civil War documents challenge this assertion; men are far more exposed than the theory of the gaze would suggest.[42] Against the idea of the intact clothed patriarch, uniformed and armed, are reports that violate Brooks's ultimate taboo. Clarendon describes just such a scene of the father's nakedness after Edgehill when Royalists "return'd to the field to view the dead Bodies ... where they found many not yet dead of their wounds, but lying stripp'd among the dead; among whom ... young Mr *Scroop* brought off his Father, Sr *Gervas Scroop*; who ... had faln with sixteen wounds in his body and head; and had layen stripp'd among the dead, from that time, which was about three in the afternoon on *Sunday*, all that cold night, all *Monday*, and *Monday* night, and till *Tuesday* evening, for it was so late before his Son found him."[43] The symbolic importance, yet the fragility of the intact patriarch, arouses deep ambivalence in Restoration and eighteenth-century texts. Rochester's aristocratic rakes have imperfect enjoyments. In the famous phallic handshake scene of Behn's *Love Letters between a Nobleman and his Sister*, Count Beralti's paternal organ is exposed to the amusement of his daughter Sylvia and his regicide son-in-law Philander; in Sterne's *Tristram Shandy*, Uncle Toby's compromised paternal organ is kept discreetly within his red plush breeches. Both Gulliver and Crusoe fear the exposure of their own nakedness. All of these (and other) examples embody displaced anxiety about political authority and social order.

Although Defoe's *Memoirs of a Cavalier* is an explicit narrative of the Civil Wars, it avoids scenes of stripping corpses. Defoe's Cavalier keeps his clothes and even has an eye for fashion; when he confronts Scottish soldiers, he notices the "oddness and barbarity of their Garb and Arms." He dons costumes for a masquerade: "We were disguised like country ploughman; we got at a Farmer's house ... clothes of all sorts ... thus dressing myself up a la Paisant, with a white cap on my head, and a fork on my shoulder, and one of my comrades in the Farmer's Wife's russet gown and petticoat ... the other [decked out] with an old crutch like a lame man."[44]

essay's perspective, can be understood as a figure of displacement. Analysed by Sedgwick to demonstrate that adultery is a homosocial phenomenon, an act of aggression between men for whom the woman is merely the conduit of their relationship, cuckoldry has traditionally been symbolized by the cuckoo and the stag's horns. See Eve Kosofsky Sedgwick, *Between Men: English Literature and Male Homosocial Desire* (New York: Columbia University Press, 1985).

42 It seems historically significant that the word "phallus" enters English in the seventeenth century and signifies a cultural need to recast a male body part as a corporeal image of abstract power.

43 Clarendon, *History of the Rebellion*, II, 43.

44 Defoe, *Memoirs of a Cavalier*, ed. Keeble, IV, 179.

Instead, anxiety over male nudity is displaced onto Crusoe, who famously admits, "I could not go quite naked; no, tho' I had been inclined to it, which I was not, nor could I abide the thoughts of it, tho' I was all alone." Critics have variously explained Crusoe's urgent rejection of even the slightest impulse to undress. His European skin may be too delicate. An English or Christian sense of propriety or shame inhibits him. He needs to display colonial and racist superiority towards his savage and bestial subjects, who are, as Derrida points out, naked without knowing it.[45] These anthropocentric and ethnocentric explanations have merit. Yet Crusoe's angst about his bare body – not abiding the thought of it – is also linked to memories we know he carries of the Civil Wars; he explicitly voices these memories in Volume Three, where stripped bodies were abandoned as his has been abandoned on the island. For 26 years, he exists outside English law, confined against his will, and excluded from the sovereign power that might give his life order and meaning. At the same time, he *is* the sovereign power over his island, his kingdom as he calls it. Simultaneously prisoner and monarch, both inside and outside the law, he wears a pastiche of garments approximating European style but contrived from local materials, both royal robes and prison uniform, camouflaging the sign of his bareness and abandonment.

A Journal of the Plague Year reworks this problem differently. Early in the narrative, the Saddler thinks of Civil Wars soldiers: "Those who had been in the Armies in the War which had not been many years past."[46] Near the end, his thoughts return to the Civil Wars: "It was not the least of our misfortunes, that with our Infection, when it ceased, there did not cease the Spirit of Strife and Contention, Slander and Reproach, which was really the great Troubler of the Nation's Peace before; it was said to be the Remains of the Old Animosities, which had so lately involv'd us all in Blood and Disorder." Within these framing memories, the Saddler sees heaps, cartloads, and pits-full of naked human bodies. The Saddler says that he "at least expected that [plague victims] would have been decently laid in ... [but] bodies ... some ... wrapt up in Linen sheets, some in Rugs, some little other than naked, or so loose, that what covering they had, fell from them, in the shooting out of the Cart, and they fell quite naked among the rest." The disfiguring marks of plague – a disease that no one could control – perturb him less than the deliberate decision of "undaunted

45 Jacques Derrida, "The Animal That Therefore I am (More to Follow)," *Critical Inquiry*, 28 (2002), p. 373. For a review and discussion of perspectives on Crusoe's nakedness, see R. John Williams, "Naked Creatures: Robinson Crusoe, the Beast, and the Sovereign," *Comparative Critical Studies*, 2, no 3 (2005), 337-48 (pp. 337-40).

46 Defoe, *A Journal of the Plague Year*, ed. John Mullan, in *The Novels of Daniel Defoe*, eds Owens and Furbank, VII, 31, 201.

Creatures ... [who did not] fail to search [the] Pockets, and sometimes strip off [the] clothes" of the victims.[47]

Swift's Gulliver, like Crusoe, is abandoned, especially on his final voyage when his crew mutinies and banishes their "mini-sovereign" – from the little kingdom of his ship.[48] Like Crusoe, he is a solitary clothed man with a deep aversion to stripping in a world of naked creatures. No wonder his account of the mutiny includes the seemingly frivolous detail that they "[let] me put on my best suit of cloaths." But unlike Crusoe's circumstance, Gulliver is not alone. He is surrounded by the nakedness of "perfect human figures" who inhabit a nation in which sovereignty is neither marked by royal robes nor embodied in human form. Clothes are merely a unique act of subterfuge by a foreign Yahoo, not superiority but an indictment in the eyes of Houyhnhnms who would never think of concealing, as they put it, "what Nature had given."[49]

The Yahoos exemplify the liminal condition of bare life: the Houyhnhnms ban them from legal membership in the state. While Yahoos lack an absolute sovereign of their own to maintain order through a founding violence, yet they display some rudimentary behaviours that gesture at sovereignty/ordering institutions: "In most Herds ... a Sort of ruling *Yahoo* ... *deformed* in Body and *mischievous in Disposition*" tries and fails to prevent aggression or to control the threat of what the Houyhnhnm Master learns to call "a *Civil War* among themselves."[50] The more a clothed Gulliver tries to be included in the Houyhnhnm polis, the more intensely the reader feels his simultaneous inclusion/exclusion from Yahoo bare life. When his clothes wear out, he makes new coverings for his body – some out of Yahoo skins, a detail that has bothered more than one reader. What could be a better sign of the paradox of inclusion/exclusion? Every time he puts on his shoes, his own Yahoo skin is technically separate from, but also enclosed within, more Yahoo skin.[51] And as for piles of naked dead, as in the *Journal of the Plague Year*, although Swift does not lead Gulliver directly to the edge of a pit or into a field where heaps of naked corpses lie, we know that somewhere in Houyhnhnmland such mass graves must exist after the Houyhnhnms decided to conduct a "general hunting" of the Yahoos.[52] Perhaps Swift had read the parliamentary record from 1646 de-

47 Defoe, *A Journal of the Plague Year*, ed. Mullan, in *The Novels of Daniel Defoe*, eds Owens and Furbank, VII, 71, 84.

48 Srinivas Aravamudan, "Subjects/Sovereigns/Rogues," *Eighteenth-Century Studies*, 40 (2007), 457-65 (p. 461).

49 *Gulliver's Travels*, ed. Womersley, p. 351 (IV, iii, 8).

50 *Gulliver's Travels*, ed. Womersley, p. 391 (IV, vii, 6), 394 (IV, vii, 13).

51 *Gulliver's Travels*, ed. Womersley, pp. 394, 391, and 416 (IV, x, 1).

52 *Gulliver's Travels*, ed. Womersley, p. 409 (IV, ix, 2).

scribing an ambush during the Civil Wars: "We had a gallant hunting of them from place to place over the hills."[53]

A Modest Proposal also envisions vast piles of naked dead: 120,000 human carcasses annually put to the knife rivals anything in the Great Pit of the *Journal of the Plague Year*. Infant's flesh just dropped from its dam conveniently requires no stripping. The proposer's speculation that Irish teenagers might supply want of venison cites the obscene precedent of a Formosan woman whose stripped "plump" body was sold by joints from the gibbet from which she had been hung.[54] The Proposer repeats the term 'carcass' – the outward shell of bare life, an unclothed shape emptied of meaning. *The Drapier's Letters*, too, encourage visions of masses of bodies violently laid bare. The Drapier, in response to Walpole's reputed threat "to make [the Irish] swallow his Coin in Fire-balls,"[55] calculates the entire population of the kingdom, ingesting seventeen bite-size portions of gunpowder apiece, thus capable of setting off, from within their naked selves, a million and a half singed corpses.

4

Finally, to arrive at the most difficult issue, the decision to grant 'no quarter' or to cull a few survivors for forced labour or enslavement, takes us from the wounding and exposure of the body to the question of its right to live – and, if it is to be killed, whether that death endows the body with meaning or disposes of the body emptied of significance.

There are some vivid moments in the records of the Civil Wars when the sanctity of life and body and the exertions made to preserve it are as unforgettable and as haunting as the reckless slaughters. The Royalist surgeon Richard Wiseman tells the story of a soldier under Colonel John Arundel who was shot in the face: "He fell down, and in the retreat was carried off amongst the dead, and laid down in an empty house ... in the morning early, the Colonel marching by that house heard a knocking against the door. Some of the officers ... lookt in, and saw this man standing by the door without eye, face, nose, or mouth." Wiseman hardly knows where to begin: "One part of the jaw hung down by his throat ... I saw the brain working under the lacerated scalp on both sides between his ears and brows. I could not see any advantage that he could have

53 Carlton, *Going to the Wars*, p. 233.

54 *Prose Works*, XII, 113.

55 Quoted from *The Drapier's Letters to the People of Ireland against Receiving Wood's Halfpence*, ed. Herbert Davis (Oxford: Clarendon Press, 1965 [1935]), pp. xli, 86.

by my dressing ... I helpt him to clear his throat, where was remaining the root of his tongue." Wiseman and companions manage to pour milk down the soldier's throat – in order to sustain him as long as possible.[56] One thinks of the welcome relief of Defoe's story of the sleeping piper tossed in among the dead in the *Journal of the Plague Year*, the surprise discovery that life persists – "*Lord Bless us. There's somebody in the cart not quite dead!*" – and the comic quality of his rescue: "*You are in the Dead-Cart and we are a going to bury you. But I an't dead tho', am I?* ... and he went about his business."[57] Even Gulliver's foreign captors and mutinous crew spare the life they easily could destroy.

But many – too many – Civil Wars eye-witnesses report decisions to deny life by granting no quarter, and to choose a small group for hard labour. After the 1641 rebellion, "killing of Irish prisoners became routine." In 1644, Parliament passed an ordinance that "no quarter should be offered to Irishmen or papists born in Ireland."[58] But the practice was widely employed by and against Royalists and Parliamentarians: "Covenanters butchered a hundred of the garrison at Asiog Castle ... who surrendered on promise of quarter." At Abbotsbury, Sir Anthony Ashley Cooper recalls, "and then they cried for quarter, but ... I gave command that there should be none given." At Cirencester, "they without quarter killed all they overtook."[59] At Leicester, Captain Richard Symonds reports "no quarter given to any."[60] Lord Byron said, "I put them all to the sword, which I find the best way to proceed." At Lincoln's garrison, a Parliamentary soldier recalls, Royalists "cried out for quarter, saying that they were poor [conscripts]. We slew fifty of them." At Barthomley Church, the story is the same: "Nothing was heard but 'Kill dead! Kill dead!'"[61]

Although Defoe's Cavalier has one uncharacteristically poignant moment of emotion when he heard men "cry for quarter in English," he lapses back into equivocation: "I cannot deny but ... sometimes the Prince gave a liberty to some cruelties," yet "this war was managed with as much Humanity on both sides as could be expected." He does not struggle over the decision to spare or take a life because "Exigences and Necessities oblige us to do things which at other times we would not do." Of the siege of Leicester, he claims

56 This episode is described in Richard Wiseman, *Several Chirurgical Treatises* (London, 1686), pp. 402-20, and is cited in Stephen Bull, "*The Furie of the Ordnance*": *Artillery in the English Civil Wars* (Woodbridge: The Boydell Press, 2008), p. 31.

57 Defoe, *A Journal of the Plague Year*, ed. Mullan, in *The Novels of Daniel Defoe*, eds Owens and Furbank, VII, 93.

58 Braddick, *God's Fury, England's Fire*, p. 318.

59 Carlton, *Going to the Wars*, pp. 123, 172-73, 174.

60 Carlton, *Going to the Wars*, p. 177.

61 *The Impact of the English Civil War*, ed. Morrill, pp. 19, 30.

"they demanded quarter, which our Foot at first refused them ... till at last they threw down their arms ... and then I can testify that fair Quarter was given them." And afterwards, Fairfax offers honourable terms of surrender: "For my own part I went home fully contented."[62]

Despite the Cavalier's complacence, the practice of no quarter exposes the dangers of a world retaining the sovereign's right to impose the ban and to kill with impunity – but also reliant on biopolitical means of controlling bodies. Who gets to decide – and on the basis of what do they decide – if lives are expendable? What happens in exceptional situations of crisis or emergency when sovereign power to maintain 'good life' is suspended or dispersed – or when the institutions that replace it malfunction? At the end of the Civil Wars, in April 1648, Whitelocke wrote in his diary of the problematic redistribution of sovereign power:

> Such is the uncertainty of worldly affairs, when the Parliament & their Army had subdued their common enemy, then they quarreled among themselves, the Army against the Army ... so that they were in continual perplexities and dangers ... The Soldiers were generally against any kind of Monarchy, though every one of them was a Monarch in his Regiment or company.[63]

Unlike the Cavalier, Crusoe thinks in terms of abandoned life and sovereign power, even when deliberating the fate of inanimate objects, like his well-known deliberation over money: "O Drug! Said I aloud, what art though good for ... go to the Bottom as a Creature whose Life is not worth saving. However, upon Second Thoughts, I took it away." He is less benevolent towards the island cats – members of what he calls "[his] family" – when he came to be "so pester'd ... that [he] was forc'd to kill them like Vermine or wild Beasts, and to drive them from [his] house as much as possible."[64] Defoe also displaces the issues raised by "no Quarter" and civil war onto the *Journal of the Plague Year*, in which the Saddler reproaches the court, law, and religion for "abandoning the people in their danger" and in which the plague metaphorically becomes a hostile troop with explosive weapons: "a formidable Enemy ... arm'd with Terrors, that every Man is not sufficiently fortified to resist, or prepar'd to stand the Shock against."[65] Like Civil War combatants who were neighbours and

62 Defoe, *Memoirs of a Cavalier*, ed. Keeble, in *The Novels of Daniel Defoe*, eds Owens and Furbank, IV, 150, 151, 168, 222.

63 Whitelocke, *Memorials of the English Affairs*, p. 212.

64 Defoe, *The Life and Strange Surprising Adventures of Robinson Crusoe*, ed. W. R. Owens, in *The Novels of Daniel Defoe*, eds Owens and Furbank, I, 91, 133.

65 Defoe, *A Journal of the Plague Year*, ed. Mullan, in *The Novels of Daniel Defoe*, eds Owens and Furbank, VII, 201.

family members, Londoners often cannot tell friend from foe, healthy from sick. As in war, morbidity often is a matter of chance, since no one knows how or why or when the affliction will strike.

But additional loss of life results from decision, not disease – "the shutting up of houses thus by force, and restraining, or rather imprisoning people in their own houses" – the problem over which the Saddler constantly worries: "If family's could have sent out the one sick person or retired themselves from the house they had all been preserved; whereas, when upon one, or more, sickening in a family the house has been shut up, the whole family have perished." A new kind of enforcement army of twenty thousand men must be formed "for it was said, that at one time, ten thousand houses shut up, and every house had two watchmen to guard it."[66] In the absence of a king who has fled London, biopolitical forces in the city work pretty well to organize bodies – citizens have food, the carts circulate only at night, and so on – with the crucial exception of the complex system of watchmen, aldermen, searchers, and constables, caught up in shutting houses and deciding that a life is not worth saving.

Selective killing of one's own and the moral dilemma of its justification was a legacy of the Civil Wars that was difficult to confront directly. In *The Shortest Way with the Dissenters* (1702), Defoe attempted irony. The language of the proposal to kill Dissenters recalls the demeaning nakedness and bestialization of captured enemy troops. Accounts describe soldiers held in sheep pens in market squares, tethered together like cattle, and, as one surviving soldier remembers of Cirencester, people watched "to see us drove along more like hogs or horses than men."[67] Thus Defoe's Church-of-England persona proclaims "the Time of Mercy is over" for Dissenters: "Shall any Law be given to such wild Creatures: Some Beasts are for Sport, and the Huntsmen give them advantages of Ground; but some are knocked on Head by all possible ways of Violence and Surprize ... they are to be rooted out of this Nation." He ironically invokes the sovereign state of exception to control the dissenting population by culling its leaders: "There is no doubt but the Supreme Authority of a Nation has in its self, a Power, *and a Right to that Power*, to execute the Laws upon any Part of that Nation it governs ... I am not supposing that all the Dissenters in *England*

66 Defoe, *A Journal of the Plague Year*, ed. Mullan, in *The Novels of Daniel Defoe*, eds Owens and Furbank, VII, 80.

67 Lucy Hutchinson, *Memoirs of the Life of Colonel Hutchinson*, ed. N. H. Keeble (London: J. M. Dent, 1995), p. 125; R. Andrewes, *A Perfect Declaration of the Barbarous and Cruell Practises Committed by Prince Robert, the Cavalliers, and Others in his Majesties Army* (London: Fr. Coule, 1642), Thomason E242 [33], sig. A3; *An Exact Relation of the Proceedings of the Cavaleers at Cicester* (London: Iohn Damm, 1643), Thomason E3695a, sig. A3.

shou'd be Hang'd or Banish'd ... if a few of the Ring-leaders suffer."[68] These extermination fantasies, which have their origin in the realities of the war, resonate with Swift as well.

Swift's Drapier explains the practical need to spare some lives for a workforce that will prepare the explosive coins for a million and a half Irish to swallow: "To administer this Dose, there cannot be conveniently Fewer than Fifty thousand *Operators*, allowing one *Operator* to every Thirty, which, considering the *Squeamishness* of some Stomachs and the *Peevishness* of *Young Children*, is but reasonable."[69] The Modest Proposer also invokes the sovereign decision, calculating that "of the Hundred and Twenty Thousand Children ... Twenty thousand may be reserved for Breed; whereof only one Fourth Part to be Males."[70]

Swift narrates another episode of population control of what Houyhnhnms deem "wild Creatures" and "Beasts" to be slaughtered and culled for hard labour. Houyhnhnms, for whom everything is always already clear, need to make very few decisions. They have only one ongoing debate whether Yahoo lives are worth saving. Like Cromwell's troops granting no quarter but sparing a few for work in the Barbados, they "[made] a general Hunting, and at last enclosed the whole Herd [of Yahoos/humans] ... every *Houyhnhnm* kept two young Ones ... using them for Draught and Carriage."[71] Claude Rawson, in his study of Swift, genocide, and barbarism, argues that Swift's loathing for mass slaughter and genocidal atrocities informed satirical extermination fantasies like Gulliver's Fourth Voyage and *A Modest Proposal*. He analyses contexts that are historical (Ireland and the Wild Irish; Nazi Germany and the Jews), classical (Thucydides and the Helots in Sparta), colonial (the Amerindians), and Biblical (Noah, Abraham, Lot). And he touches on the issue of unclear divisions within populations when he observes that hostile parties (specifically the Irish and English) "are preoccupied with their differences from one another precisely because ... they are, racially and otherwise, very similar."[72] It is possible to add another context that is closer to home – the civil conflict about which Swift knew and cared so much.

68 Defoe, *The Shortest Way with the Dissenters: or, Proposals for the Establishment of the Church* (London, 1702), in *Political and Economic Writings of Daniel Defoe*, 8 vols, eds W. R. Owens and P. N. Furbank (London: Pickering and Chatto, 2000), III, 98, 106.

69 *The Drapier's Letters to the People of Ireland*, ed. Davis, p. 86.

70 *Prose Works*, XII, 111.

71 *Gulliver's Travels*, ed. Womersley, p. 409 (IV, ix, 2).

72 Claude Rawson, *God, Gulliver, and Genocide: Barbarism and the European Imagination, 1492-1945* (Oxford: Oxford University Press, 2001), p. 10.

A passage from the first two editions of *Gulliver's Travels*, which would be omitted after 1735, adds a detail to the travestied story about the genesis of the Yahoos. Two of them, so the story is told, appeared on a mountaintop in Houyhnhnmland "from whence the Opinion is, that the Race of those Brutes hath descended." The omitted passage suggests that Swift may have been thinking of civil conflict because Gulliver notices that the faces of these hateful creatures also remind him of countrymen back home: "the [original pair] ... may have been English, which indeed I was apt to suspect from the Lineaments of their Posterity's Countenances."[73] Swift did not need to look far to find examples of atrocities committed by creatures who look like one another. In writing *A Modest Proposal*, he would not have needed to look further than Colchester where, according to a Civil Wars memoir, a soldier observed a woman with a starving infant begging for food: "God damn me! That child would make a good meal well boiled."[74] And even if Swift grants the power of determining the state of exception to the nonhuman form of horses in the Fourth Book of his *Travels*, he emphasizes the degree to which his human protagonist would like to make himself indistinguishable from his decisive equine sovereign. Gulliver famously tries to do everything possible to look, sound, move, and behave like a horse. At the same time, he inevitably does everything that looks, sounds, moves, and behaves like a Yahoo. His complacent reporting of the slaughter of the Yahoos – no quarter granted to all but a few – may be the ultimate measure of the moral confusion to which the *Travels* have led readers since their publication.[75]

A passage in Frankl's *Man's Search for Meaning* sheds a glimmer of light on Gulliver's homecoming and the ever-contentious ending of his travels. Frankl discusses the danger for the survivor, one who had directly confronted the disaster, of complete alienation from Humankind because the disaster is caused not by chance – an earthquake or epidemic – but by the decision to turn against one's own, as Ludlow's schoolfellow turns against him. Frankl writes,

> Apart from the moral deformity ... there were two other fundamental experiences which threatened to damage the character of the liberated prisoner: bitterness and disillusionment when he returned to his former life ... one's fellow man (whose superficiality and lack of feeling was so disgusting that one finally felt like creeping into a hole and neither hearing or seeing human beings any more) but ... [also] that he could suffer still more, and still more intensely.[76]

---

73 *Gulliver's Travels*, ed. Womersley, pp. 442, 718.
74 Carlton, *Going to the Wars*, p. 324.
75 *Gulliver's Travels*, ed. Womersley, p. 409 (IV, ix, 2).
76 Frankl, *Man's Search for Meaning*, pp. 91-92.

And here is Gulliver: "I had no Commerce with the Master, or any of his Men; but, pretending I was sick kept close in my Cabbin ... My Wife and Family received me ... the Sight of them filled me only with Hatred, Disgust and Contempt; and the more, by reflecting on the near Alliance I had with them." He hopes if possible [to spend fewer hours in the stable and] "to habituate myself by Time to tolerate the Sight of a human Creature."[77]

I cannot imagine that Frankl or Swift or Defoe or other eighteenth-century writers knew of greater indictments than the camp and no quarter. It was the burden of eighteenth-century literature to come to terms with the paradigm-shifting conflict of the preceding generation. These writers sought language for what Blanchot called "that in thought itself which dissuades us from thinking of it" (p. 5), leaving later generations to decide if they will venture to look beyond "the limit of writing."

77 *Gulliver's Travels*, ed. Womersley, pp. 433-34 (IV, xi, 16-17), 443 (IV, xii, 11).

POLITICAL PROBLEMS

Stephen Karian
University of Missouri

Lost Works by Swift and the Ballad of January 1712

Abstract. Identifying "lost" works by Swift has been an active scholarly pursuit since the late eighteenth century. John Nichols was the first Swift editor to compile a list of works that Swift was known to have written but that had not been located. Since Nichols, many major discoveries have been made, though many works remain lost. This essay attempts to identify one of these, the collaboratively composed ballad Swift mentions in the *Journal to Stella* on 4 January 1712. Drawing on a range of inferences and contextual evidence, it argues that this ballad is *An Excellent New Song Call'd the Trusty and True English-man*. If persuasive, this essay expands the poetic canons not only of Swift but also of John Arbuthnot, the principal author of the January 1712 ballad.

One of the most tantalizing challenges of literary scholarship is identifying and locating works by major writers that for all practical purposes have been declared "lost." In the case of Swift, the concerted effort to recover his lost works began during his lifetime with the endeavours of, among others, his friend Charles Ford and his Dublin bookseller George Faulkner. Ford attempted to preserve portions of *Gulliver's Travels* that were censored in Benjamin Motte's London edition, and he maintained a sizeable collection of Swift's writings from the last four years of Queen Anne's reign. In both instances, Ford was far better informed than Swift was about the whereabouts of these texts.[1] Faulkner, after publishing four volumes of Swift's *Works* in Dublin in 1734-35, continued to acquire more and more works, genuine and spurious, such that by 1772 he had expanded his edition to twenty volumes.

But the first true hero in this quest for lost Swift works is the indefatigable printer, bookseller, editor, collector, antiquarian, and book historian John Nichols (1745-1826). As early as age seventeen, Nichols immersed himself in Swift, assisting his master William Bowyer the younger with the thirteenth and fourteenth octavo volumes of Swift's *Works*, published in 1762. Nichols most

* I am grateful to my University of Missouri research assistants for their help with various tasks related to this essay: Erin Niederberger, Juliette Paul, and Sarah Judd. I also thank James McLaverty for checking two poems in the Bodleian Library.

1 See the letters between Swift and Ford in *Correspondence*, ed. Woolley, III, 66-68, 692-93, 698-99, and 707-9; and Daniel Cook and James Woolley, "Charles Ford's Library: New Light on Swift and Arbuthnot," *Swift Studies*, 32 (2017), 9-44.

 | DOI:10.30965/9783846763971_017

likely compiled the index in the fourteenth volume, the very first index of Swift's writings.[2] Over the next twelve years, Nichols continued to study Swift for the purpose of editing and publishing his writings. By 1774, he had discovered that many of Swift's previously published writings were not in the quarto and octavo volumes of the London edition. Nichols remedied this situation in 1775 by editing and co-publishing a seventeenth octavo volume of Swift's *Works*, which supplemented the sixteen volumes of the John Hawkesworth / Deane Swift edition. Nichols appended to this volume an expanded index to Swift's works and letters.[3] He continued his Swiftian labours in 1776, with his *Supplement to Swift's Works*, presented as the twenty-fourth octavo volume of the London edition. Here for the first time appears a list of works known to be by Swift that had not yet been found.[4] Nichols offered an expanded list in *Miscellaneous Pieces in Prose and Verse* (1789).[5]

Nichols was not without editorial faults. He inserted a number of dubious Swift attributions into the canon, and scholars have been questioning them ever since. But Nichols's industry and energy are undeniable. He printed from original editions and manuscripts whenever possible, corrected the texts when he believed they were in error, and wrote numerous annotations. His full contribution to the study of Swift can be assessed only by poring over his many volumes: his supplement volumes of the 1770s, his two-volume edition of Swift's poems for *The Works of the English Poets* (1779), and his nineteen-volume

2 According to TEERINK AND SCOUTEN, p. 81, Nichols was responsible for this index in the fourteenth volume (TEERINK AND SCOUTEN 90, vol. 14 [p. 96]). This claim is plausible given Nichols's account in his *Illustrations of the Literary History of the Eighteenth Century*, 8 vols (London: Nichols and Bentley, 1817-58), V, 391.

3 TEERINK AND SCOUTEN 88, vol. 17 (p. 90). See Nichols's "Advertisement," dated 25 March 1775, on pp. v-x. This seventeenth octavo volume corresponds to the ninth quarto volume of this edition, TEERINK AND SCOUTEN 87, vol. 9 (p. 86).

4 TEERINK AND SCOUTEN 88 (p. 91). See Nichols's "Advertisement," dated 1 August 1776, on pp. v-x, which concludes with the list of lost works. Nichols published a revised version of this list in the *Gentleman's Magazine*, 47 (June 1777), 260-61, and added further comments in the *Gentleman's Magazine* that September (pp. 419-21) and November (pp. 531-32), as well as November 1778 (pp. 521-23).

5 See pp. [v]-vi. On Nichols's involvement with this volume, see *The Works of the Rev. Jonathan Swift, D.D.*, 19 vols (1808), I, lx-lxi, and John Irwin Fischer, "Swift's Early Odes, Dan Jackson's Nose, and 'The Character of Sir Robert Walpole': Some Documentary Problems," *Reading Swift: Papers from The Second Münster Symposium on Jonathan Swift*, eds Richard H. Rodino and Hermann J. Real, with the assistance of Helgard Stöver-Leidig (Munich: Wilhelm Fink, 1993), pp. 225-43 (231-35).

edition of Swift's works, first published in 1801, revised in 1803, and revised again in 1808.[6]

Despite Nichols's best efforts, he could not locate some of Swift's works. In fact, some of the items in Nichols's lists were not found before the twentieth century:

It's Out at Last: or, French Correspondence Clear as the Sun (1712), found by Hamilton Lavers-Smith;[7]
A Hue and Cry after Dismal (1712), noted by Harold Williams;[8]
the punning ballad on the 1710 Westminster election, identified by C. F. Main and George P. Mayhew as *A Dialogue between Captain Tom and Sir Henry Dutton Colt*;[9]
A Dialogue upon Dunkirk: Between a Whig and a Tory (1712), conclusively identified by David Woolley;[10] and
A Letter to the Bishop of Killala, identified by Ian Higgins.[11]

6 On Nichols as the editor of the Swift volumes in *The Works of the English Poets*, see *The Works of the Rev. Jonathan Swift, D.D.* (1808), I, xlv. Many notes in the Second Volume of *The Works of the English Poets* are initialed "N." For assessments of Nichols as an editor and collector of Swift, see his self-assessment in *Illustrations of the Literary History of the Eighteenth Century*, V, 391-97, as well as Martin W. Maner, "An Eighteenth-Century Editor at Work: John Nichols and Jonathan Swift," *Papers of the Bibliographical Society of America*, 70 (1976), 481-99, and Daniel Cook, "*Labor ipse voluptas*: John Nichols's Swiftiana," *From Compositors to Collectors: Essays on Book-Trade History*, eds John Hinks and Matthew Day (New Castle, Delaware, and London: Oak Knoll Press and The British Library, 2012), pp. 43-62. For broader surveys, see Albert H. Smith, "John Nichols, Printer and Publisher," *The Library*, 5th ser., 18 (1963), 169-90; Julian Pooley, "The Papers of the Nichols Family and Business: New Discoveries and the Work of the Nichols Archive Project," *The Library*, 7th ser., 2 (2001), 10-52; and Pooley, "'A Laborious and Truly Useful Gentleman': Mapping the Networks of John Nichols (1745-1826), Printer, Antiquary, and Biographer," *Journal for Eighteenth-Century Studies*, 38 (2015), 497-509.

7 Hamilton Lavers-Smith, "Swift's Political Tracts," *The Athenaeum*, no 3915 (8 November 1902), 619-20.

8 Harold Williams, "*A Hue and Cry after Dismal*," *Review of English Studies*, 6 (1930), 195-96.

9 C. F. Main, "Defoe, Swift and Captain Tom," *Harvard Library Bulletin*, 11 (1957), 71-79, and George P. Mayhew, "Swift's Political 'Conversion' and His 'Lost' Ballad on the Westminster Election of 1710," *Bulletin of the John Rylands Library*, 53 (1971), 397-427.

10 David Woolley, "*A Dialogue upon Dunkirk* (1712) and Swift's '7 penny Papers,'" *Reading Swift: Papers from The Second Münster Symposium on Jonathan Swift*, eds Rodino and Real, pp. 215-23.

11 This item is mentioned in the *Journal to Stella* on 17 October 1710; see *Journal to Stella: Letters to Esther Johnson and Rebecca Dingley, 1710-1713*, ed. Abigail Williams (Cambridge: Cambridge University Press, 2013), p. 42n59. *A Letter to the Bishop of Killala* is scheduled to appear in Ian Higgins's volume *Writings on Religion and the Church to 1714* as part of *The Cambridge Edition of the Works of Jonathan Swift*.

Nonetheless, there remain works that we know Swift wrote that have not yet been identified or located. Here is a list of twelve such items for his career up through 1714:

"Letters to Elisa," possibly from 1689 and mentioned in Swift's 13 January 1699 letter to John Winder;[12]
The Ramble, written to a young lady in Ireland and mentioned in Swift's 3 May 1692 letter to his cousin Thomas;[13]
a translation of book six of Virgil's *Aeneid*, mentioned in the same letter to his cousin;
The Poet, a Pindaric ode quoted in Swift's 1693 poem to William Congreve;[14]
a pamphlet on the 1704 Occasional Conformity bill, apparently finished after the Parliamentary vote but never published, and mentioned in Swift's 3 February 1704 letter to William Tisdall;[15]
Conjectures on the Thoughts of Posterity about me, mentioned in a proposed list of contents for the volume that became Swift's 1711 *Miscellanies in Prose and Verse*;[16]
On the Present Taste of Reading, also mentioned in the proposed list for the 1711 *Miscellanies*;
The Writer of Plays, most likely a poem, listed in the 10 April 1710 Stationers' Company register entry for the 1711 *Miscellanies*;
the ballad mentioned in the *Journal to Stella* on 24 November 1711;[17]
"some other verses" mentioned in the *Journal to Stella* on 23 December 1711;[18]
the ballad mentioned in the *Journal to Stella* on 4 January 1712; and
Dunkirk Still in the Hands of the French, one of Swift's "penny papers," advertised in the *Examiner* on 17 July 1712.[19]

My goal in this essay is to reduce this list of twelve to eleven by identifying the penultimate item, the ballad mentioned in the *Journal to Stella* on 4 January 1712. All we know for certain about this ballad is what Swift wrote to Esther Johnson and Rebecca Dingley: "I was in the city to-day, and dined with my

12 *Correspondence*, ed. Woolley, I, 138-39. See also Eugene Hammond, *Jonathan Swift: Irish Blow-In* (Newark: University of Delaware Press, 2016), pp. 52-53.

13 *Correspondence*, ed. Woolley, I, 111.

14 *Poems*, ed. Williams, I, 49-50.

15 *Correspondence*, ed. Woolley, I, 151.

16 Swift's original list does not survive, but we have the Reverend John Lyon's transcript in his interleaved and annotated copy of John Hawkesworth's biography of Swift, *The Life of the Revd. Jonathan Swift, D.D.* (Dublin: S. Cotter, 1755), National Art Library, Victoria and Albert Museum, MS Forster 579 (48.D.39), leaf between pages 36 and 37. This list is transcribed in Ehrenpreis, *Dr Swift*, pp. 768-69.

17 *Journal to Stella*, ed. Abigail Williams, p. 330.

18 *Journal to Stella*, ed. Abigail Williams, p. 351.

19 This advertisement indicates that it was in fact published. Most of the other items in this list seem not to have been published, thus making their recovery all the less likely.

printer, and gave him a ballad made by several hands, I know not whom. I believe lord treasurer had a finger in it; I added three stanzas; I suppose Dr. Arbuthnot had the greatest share."[20] At first glance, these two sentences tell us very little. But upon closer inspection, they tell us a great deal.

Swift's reference to "[his] printer" clearly indicates John Barber. Swift mentions Barber by name only once in the *Journal to Stella*, but his *Account Books* and other sources show that Barber is the person Swift frequently calls "[his] printer."[21] Swift had recently spent a lot of time working with Barber, who printed multiple editions of *The Conduct of the Allies* (1711). Yet Barber's name never appeared in the imprints of Swift's works. Those printings either include no name at all or that of the trade publisher John Morphew.[22] We would therefore expect that this ballad was printed by Barber in London but that its imprint has either no name or Morphew's name.

In calling this poem a "ballad," Swift is using that term either in a broad way or in a narrow way. When he discussed the punning "ballad" on the 1710 Westminster election, he seems to have used the term in a broad way to indicate its bibliographical format as a half-sheet poem.[23] So it is possible that Swift is using the term "ballad" in that broad way, in which case we would expect this poem to be a half-sheet or possibly a full-sheet printing. But the reference to stanzas suggests that Swift is using the term in a narrow way, which would also mean that this poem is based on a song or imitates a song structure.

Swift indicates that it was a collaboratively written ballad, a ballad "made by several hands, [he knows] not whom." But then he goes on to indicate that John Arbuthnot was the primary author, and that Swift, Lord Treasurer Oxford, and others contributed to it. The mystery implied by "[he knows] not whom" strongly suggests that this ballad was published, anonymously or pseudonymously.

---

20 *Journal to Stella*, ed. Abigail Williams, pp. 359-60.

21 The one mention is on 29 July 1711 (*Journal to Stella*, ed. Abigail Williams, p. 251). See also Paul V. Thompson and Dorothy Jay Thompson, *The Account Books of Jonathan Swift* (Newark: University of Delaware Press, 1984), p. l; *English Political Writings, 1711-1714: The Conduct of the Allies and Other Works*, eds Bertrand A. Goldgar and Ian Gadd (Cambridge: Cambridge University Press, 2008), pp. 328-30; and my *Jonathan Swift in Print and Manuscript* (Cambridge: Cambridge University Press, 2010), pp. 17-19 and especially 210-11n13.

22 For further discussion of this pattern, see the important article by Michael Treadwell, "Swift's Relations with the London Book Trade to 1714," *Author/Publisher Relations during the Eighteenth and Nineteenth Centuries*, eds Robin Myers and Michael Harris (Oxford: Oxford Polytechnic Press, 1983), pp. 1-36 (18-26).

23 *Journal to Stella*, ed. Abigail Williams, pp. 31 (7 October 1710), 44 (20 October), and 60 (8 November).

And because multiple authors worked on the poem, but apparently not in a closely cooperative way, it probably lacks a continuous narrative.

Swift also indicates how much each author wrote, hinting at the ballad's minimum length. Because Swift added three stanzas and because Arbuthnot wrote "the greatest share," Arbuthnot had to have written at least four stanzas, and possibly more. Swift implies that Oxford wrote at least one stanza, so this poem has at least eight stanzas in total.

Another important clue is the date of Swift's remark: 4 January 1712. This date's significance is best explained by briefly reviewing the events of the preceding month. On 7 December 1711, the Parliamentary session began, and the main topic at hand was the Ministry's plan to end the War of the Spanish Succession. The publication of Swift's *Conduct of the Allies* was timed to precede the Parliamentary session and to build support for Oxford's peace policy. This policy was immediately under threat in the House of Lords because the Earl of Nottingham – the man Swift satirized as "Dismal" – moved his "No peace without Spain" amendment. That is, Nottingham argued that there should be no peace as long as Spain remained in France's sphere of influence. Deserting his fellow Tories to join with the Whigs, Nottingham demanded that the Spanish throne be taken from Philip V, the grandson of Louis XIV of France, and given to the Austrian Archduke Charles.

Nottingham's successful motion was a major setback for the Oxford Ministry. As December wore on, Swift became despondent and quite critical of Oxford's handling of the situation. But things turned around dramatically at the end of December, when the Queen created twelve new peers, thus ensuring the success of the peace policy, and dismissed the Duke of Marlborough from his offices over his improper handling of funds and contracts related to the war. We should therefore expect that this ballad written by Arbuthnot, Swift, and Oxford would be not only a piece of pro-Ministry propaganda, but also an especially optimistic one, perhaps one that gloated about the Ministry's recent change of fortune for the better.

One final clue about this ballad is that Swift never alludes to it again, which suggests that it was not frequently reprinted, that it was not imitated, and that it did not prompt any responses. In the *Journal to Stella*, Swift gleefully boasted about his successful publications such as *A Description of a City Shower* or *The Virtues of Sid Hamet the Magician's Rod*. The absence of any subsequent reference to this ballad almost certainly means that it made little impact at the time.

So to summarize the probable traits of this ballad: it was printed by John Barber in London as a half-sheet or a broadside; its imprint contains either no name or that of John Morphew; it was published anonymously or pseudonymously; it is based on a tune or uses a song structure; it has at least eight stanzas; its contents are discontinuous; it promotes the Ministry's peace policy from an optimistic perspective in early January 1712; and it did not make a strong impact on contemporary readers.

Before proceeding further, I should acknowledge three assumptions I have made in my efforts to identify this ballad:

First, that this ballad was in fact printed, which seems a safe assumption because Swift states that he gave it to his printer.

Second, that at least one copy of this ballad has survived. We know that in some cases no copy of early eighteenth-century printings has survived, among them, many ephemeral publications, including ballads. So the assumption that at least one copy of this ballad has survived may turn out to be incorrect.

Third, that a copy of this ballad has been catalogued in either the Eighteenth-Century Short-Title Catalogue (ESTC) or D. F. Foxon's catalogue of *English Verse, 1701-1750*. Mentioning both sources is necessary because even though ESTC is an ongoing project and Foxon's catalogue was published over forty years ago, there are still items in Foxon but not in ESTC.

Operating from these three assumptions and bearing in mind the probable qualities of this ballad, I have conducted a thorough search of verse publications that can be dated to 1711 or 1712. I included publications with the year 1711 in the imprint in case the ballad was dated according to the year beginning on 25 March rather than 1 January. Of the over 300 separately published poems that can be dated to those years, the vast majority are poor candidates and can be dismissed, whether because of the imprint, the likely date of publication, the lack of a stanza form, or the poem's political content or lack thereof.[24] Of those examined, only two are remotely plausible candidates.

One is *The Truth's Come Out at Last: or, The Downfall of a Great Favourite. Tune of, O brave Popery* (1711, ESTC n014195, mentioned in FOXON, I, 827). This ballad gloats over Marlborough's dismissal, which is portrayed as a recent event. The Queen's letter of dismissal was delivered to Marlborough on 29 December 1711, Marlborough replied on 30 December, and Swift reported a rumour about his dismissal on 31 December and confirmed that rumour on 1 January.[25] This ballad was most likely written on 1 January at the earliest and in principle could be the ballad Swift mentions on 4 January. But its sole focus on Marlborough is

24 At the time of submitting this article, I was unable to examine *Beelzebub's Advice to his Club at the Devil* (no year, Foxon B159), which is possibly not a ballad.

25 For these dates, see Edward Gregg, *Queen Anne* (London: Routledge and Kegan Paul, 1980), pp. 348-49, and *Journal to Stella*, ed. Abigail Williams, p. 358.

an argument against its candidacy. Swift's denigration of Marlborough is well known, but it had its limits, as he suggested on 1 January 1712:

> I confess my belief, that [Marlborough] has not one good quality in the world besides that of a general, and even that I have heard denied by several great soldiers. But we have had constant success in arms while he commanded. Opinion is a mighty matter in war, and I doubt but the French think it impossible to conquer an army that he leads, and our soldiers think the same; and how far this step may encourage the French to play tricks with us, no man knows. I do not love to see personal resentment mix with publick affairs.[26]

Though this final sentence is disingenuous, the passage as a whole resonates with Swift's remarks elsewhere about Marlborough, such as "although I love him not, I dislike his being out."[27] It is thus unlikely that on 4 January 1712 Swift would have contributed three stanzas to a poem whose sole purpose was to attack Marlborough.

The other candidate is *An Excellent New Song Call'd the Trusty and True English-man* (no year, Foxon E584 and E585). Ample contextual evidence suggests that this is the ballad Swift describes on 4 January 1712 (see the Appendix for the text of this poem). In the course of promoting the Ministry's peace policy and celebrating the recent turn of events for the better, it refers to all major political events since the opening of the Parliamentary session on 7 December 1711. This ballad was written after Marlborough was dismissed, and after the twelve new peers were announced on 31 December.[28] It was written before 5 January, when after many delays, Prince Eugene of Savoy, general for Emperor Charles VI and Marlborough's second-in-command for the Allied forces, arrived in England.[29] The ballad's twenty stanzas could be re-arranged with no

26 *Journal to Stella*, ed. Abigail Williams, p. 358.

27 *Journal to Stella*, ed. Abigail Williams, pp. 364-65 (8 January 1712). See also p. 375 (25 January).

28 The final ten peers of the twelve were listed in the *London Gazette* of 1 January 1712 in a news item dated 31 December. The elevations of Lords Compton and Bruce had already occurred. Swift learned of the creation of the twelve peers on the evening of 29 December (*Journal to Stella*, ed. Abigail Williams, p. 356). For further details, see Clyve Jones, "Lord Oxford's Jury: The Political and Social Context of the Creation of the Twelve Peers, 1711-12," *Parliamentary History*, 24 Supplement (2005), 9-42 (pp. 18-19).

29 As early as 10 December 1711, Eugene was expected to travel to England (*British Mercury*). On 11 December, a Postscript to the *Evening Post* states that in a few days he will set out for England, though his visit was delayed again and again. On 16 December, Swift writes that "Prince Eugene, who was expected here some days ago, we are now told, will not come at all" (*Journal to Stella*, ed. Abigail Williams, p. 347). Eugene finally arrived in London on 5 January 1712, the day after Swift mentions the ballad in the *Journal to Stella*; see *Evening*

loss to its import. Other than the one reprinting, it does not appear to have generated any response from contemporaries.

Only a few scholars have even mentioned *The Trusty and True English-man*. In his 1892 biography of Arbuthnot, George A. Aitken tentatively nominated it as the January 1712 ballad.[30] With greater confidence though without citing any evidence, F. Elrington Ball made the same identification.[31] Harold Williams, however, disagreed, stating in his edition that the poem's style "hardly commends any part of it as Swift's."[32] Williams followed C. H. Firth in thinking that the "ballad made by several hands" was *A Fable of the Widow and her Cat*, a satire on Marlborough.[33] But *A Fable* seems to have been published on 16 January 1712 or soon thereafter.[34] The ballad Swift mentions on 4 January was given to the printer that day and must have been published almost immediately. Furthermore, *A Fable* generated many poetic responses, whereas the January 1712 ballad apparently did not.[35]

Post (5 January), *The Supplement* (7 January), the *Evening Post* (8 January), and the *Journal to Stella* (6 January; *Journal to Stella*, ed. Abigail Williams, p. 361).

30 George A. Aitken, *The Life and Works of John Arbuthnot* (Oxford: Clarendon Press, 1892), pp. 42-43.

31 F. Elrington Ball, *Swift's Verse: An Essay* (London: Murray, 1929), pp. 125-26.

32 *Poems*, ed. Williams, III, 1097.

33 *Poems*, ed. Williams, I, 151-52, and see C. H. Firth, "Two Poems Attributed to Prior," *Review of English Studies*, 1 (1925), 456-58.

34 Evidence for this date comes from multiple sources: Narcissus Luttrell's date of 16 January 1712 on his FOXON F14 copy of *A Fable* (Newberry Library, Case 6A 159, no 84); the poem advertised as "this Day is publish'd" in the *Post-Boy* on 19 January; the ROTHSCHILD LIBRARY copy of FOXON F14 (Trinity College Cambridge Library, ROTHSCHILD LIBRARY 2203; RW. 70.39) annotated with 22 January 1711 (=1712); and the poem's transcription in a 24 January 1711 (=1712) letter from John Thomas to a Mr Davis (Longleat House, Thynne Papers, vol. 26, ff. 204-5).

Even less plausibly, John Nichols stated that the January 1712 ballad was Swift's poem "Corinna." But see my essay "Who Was Swift's 'Corinna'?" *Reading Swift: Papers from The Sixth Münster Symposium on Jonathan Swift*, eds Kirsten Juhas, Hermann J. Real, and Sandra Simon (Munich: Wilhelm Fink, 2013), pp. 417-31 (419).

35 Responses to *A Fable* include: *As Bob as a Robin: or, All's Well that Ends Well* (FOXON A335); *A Dialogue between the Miller and his Dogg* (FOXON D269); *The Fable of the Cocks and Ganders* (FOXON F5); *A Fable of the Housewife and her Cock* (FOXON F8); *The Fable of the Lyon and the Fox* (FOXON F9); *The Fable of the Shepherd and his Dog, in Answer to The Fable of the Widow and her Cat* (FOXON F10); *The Grand Enquiry: or, What's to Be Done with him?* (FOXON G243 and G244); *'Tis Pity they Shou'd Be Parted: or, The Fable of the Bear and the Fox* (FOXON T316; and T317 under the title *Where's your Impeachment Now? Or, the D— Safe Delivery*); *The Tr—us Treaty: Exemplified in the Fable of the Wolves and Sheep* (FOXON T535); and *When the Cat's Away, the Mice May Play. A Fable Humbly Inscrib'd to Dr. Swift* (FOXON W384).

Beyond a stylistic judgement, Williams rejected *The Trusty and True English-man* because the British Library copy of the poem, previously owned by the contemporary collector Narcissus Luttrell, contains the date 2 January. Because James M. Osborn has argued that Luttrell recorded dates of publication rather than dates of purchase, this piece of evidence would seem to exclude *The Trusty and True English-man* as the ballad that Swift handed to Barber on 4 January.[36]

But Luttrell's dates should not be treated as incontrovertible facts for dates of publication. Having compared his dates of poems with advertised dates of publication that Foxon cites, I have found dozens of differences, including more than four dozen instances in which Foxon cites a publication date at least two days later than Luttrell's date. More tellingly, I have found three dozen instances in which Foxon cites a publication date at least two days prior to Luttrell's date. It is possible that there are other advertised dates that Foxon did not locate, and it is also possible that some of these advertised dates are incorrect. But these discrepancies suggest that Luttrell's date of *The Trusty and True English-man* need not be treated as an unassailable piece of evidence. Therefore, *The Trusty and True English-man* deserves another look as the collaboratively written ballad of 4 January.

The poem deals with all major political developments since the opening of the Parliamentary session on 7 December. These include Nottingham's opposition to the Ministry announced at the outset of the session as well as Nottingham's bill against occasional conformity (lines 86-88), introduced on 15 December, passed on 20 December, and given the royal assent on 22 December. The poem seems to glance at the Duke of Hamilton case (line 102), debated in the Lords on 20 December. James Hamilton, the Scottish fourth Duke of Hamilton, had been created a peer of Great Britain in September 1711 as Duke of Brandon, and when Parliament convened in December, he sought to sit in the Lords in his own right and not as one of the sixteen elected Scottish peers. The Whigs rejected Hamilton's patent to sit as a peer of Great Britain to prevent the Ministry from expanding its influence by enlarging Scottish representation in the Lords.[37] The poem also alludes to the investigation into allega-

36 The Luttrell copy of *The Trusty and True English-man* at the British Library is 162.m.70 (13), and is described in Stephen Parks, *The Luttrell File: Narcissus Luttrell's Dates on Contemporary Pamphlets, 1678-1730* (New Haven: Beinecke Library, 1999), p. 60 (item 1027). Osborn discusses Luttrell's dates as dates of publication in "Reflections on Narcissus Luttrell (1657-1732)," *The Book Collector*, 6 (Spring 1957), 15-27 (p. 22; p. 10 in the repaginated version in Parks, *The Luttrell File*).

37 See G. S. Holmes, "The Hamilton Affair of 1711-1712: A Crisis in Anglo-Scottish Relations," *English Historical Review*, 77 (1962), 257-82.

tions of corruption by the Duke of Marlborough (lines 79-83), which occupied the Commons on 21 and 22 December. The poem exults in the Queen's creation of twelve new peers (line 138) and looks ahead to the arrival of Prince Eugene (lines 121-25).

Further evidence that *The Trusty and True English-man* is the 4 January ballad derives from the poem's many parallels to the two main works of Tory propaganda concerning the war: Swift's *Conduct of the Allies*, published on 27 November 1711, and Arbuthnot's five *John Bull* pamphlets, published between March and July 1712.[38] The poem's praise of the "Trusty and True Englishman" resonates with Arbuthnot's portrayal of John Bull. The attacks on opponents to the peace, both foreign and domestic, are perfectly congruent with similar charges made by both Arbuthnot and Swift. Here I am referring to attacks on the Holy Roman Emperor for his ingratitude (line 9), the Dutch for their deception and failure to carry their burden of the war (line 10), Marlborough for his corruption, Nottingham for his dark complexion and political treachery, and the Whigs for being intellectually and temperamentally aligned with the regicides of 1649 (line 130).[39] The poem laments the effects the war has had on England, including the loss of life in battles, even victorious battles, and the damage to the economy, resulting in poverty and high taxation.[40] The poem hints that the English will become "Beggars" (line 53), which reflects Swift's fear as expressed in *The Conduct of the Allies* that if the war continued, England would be reduced "to a state of Beggary."[41]

Swift wrote in the *Journal to Stella* that Oxford "had a finger in" the poem. He is possibly referring to lines 86-88, which scoff at the Protestant Dissenters' alliance with the Whigs: "Poor deluded Dissenters / You are sold like Debentures, / By the *Junto* made over by Deeds and Indentures." This comment is quite similar to a statement in a letter that Swift wrote in Oxford's name on 21 December 1711, which refers to the Dissenters as "poor deluded creatures, that have for

38 For dates of publication, see *English Political Writings, 1711-1714*, eds Goldgar and Gadd, p. 342, and John Arbuthnot, *The History of John Bull*, eds Alan W. Bower and Robert A. Erickson (Oxford: Clarendon Press, 1976), p. xvii.

39 On the Holy Roman Emperor, see *The History of John Bull*, pp. 40-41; on the Dutch, see *The History of John Bull*, p. 33, and *The Conduct of the Allies* in *English Political Writings, 1711-1714*, eds Goldgar and Gadd, p. 62; on the Whigs, see Swift's *Examiner* 36 (5 April 1711), 37 (12 April), and 40 (3 May), in Jonathan Swift and Arthur Mainwaring, *Swift vs. Mainwaring: "The Examiner" and "The Medley"*, ed. Frank H. Ellis (Oxford: Clarendon Press, 1985), pp. 345, 356-57, and 399-401.

40 On the economic effects on England, including the view that the Allies were not contributing their fair share, see *The History of John Bull*, pp. 10-11, 18, 38, 58, passages that bear comparison to lines 19, 30-34, 48, and 58-60 of the poem.

41 *English Political Writings, 1711-1714*, eds Goldgar and Gadd, p. 94; see also p. 97.

seventeen years been acting against all their principles."[42] Both comments refer to the recent bargain that the Whigs had struck with Nottingham to support his bill against occasional conformity in order to secure his opposition to the peace.[43]

Swift wrote that he "added three stanzas" to the poem. He most likely added the last three, which contain the poem's most up-to-date references, the creation of the twelve new peers and the pending visit from Prince Eugene. One of the stanzas comments critically about the political stance of a group of English bishops, a topic that would have been of great interest to Swift. In doing so, the poem makes a connection between modern Whigs and the Dissenters who abolished the Established Church and the monarchy in the 1640s. This is a connection that Swift had often made in his *Examiner* essays of the previous year.[44] Furthermore, the handling of metre and rhyme in these stanzas is more expert than in much of the poem, and their meaning is more lucidly expressed. The *Dundr'heads / Hundreds* rhyme (lines 124-25) demonstrates the ingenuity often found in Swift's comic rhymes.

Although *An Excellent New Song Call'd the Trusty and True English-man* appears to have had no discernible impact on contemporaries, we do know of one who owned a copy: the Earl of Oxford himself. Two nineteenth-century book catalogues list a volume Oxford owned that contained about forty poems, most in half-sheets. One of them was *The Trusty and True English-man*.[45] The current whereabouts of this volume are unknown. Its contents not surprisingly reflect the outlook of Oxford and his Ministry, and include five of Swift's separately published poems from 1710 to 1713, namely *A Dialogue between Captain Tom and Sir Henry Dutton Colt, The Windsor Prophecy, The Fable of Midas, Toland's Invitation to Dismal*, and *Part of the Seventh Epistle of the First Book of Horace Imitated*, which Swift addressed to Oxford.[46] If Oxford contributed, however slightly, to *The Trusty and True English-man*, then it is not surprising that he would have kept a copy.

---

42 "Oxford" to John Shower, 21 December 1711, *Correspondence*, ed. Woolley, I, 403.

43 See Henry Horwitz, *Revolution Politicks: The Career of Daniel Finch, Second Earl of Nottingham, 1647-1730* (Cambridge: Cambridge University Press, 1968), pp. 231-34.

44 See note 39 above.

45 Thomas Thorpe, *A Catalogue of Very Choice, Rare, and Valuable Books in Various Languages and in All Classes of Literature* (1839), part III, p. 238 (item 1968), and *Catalogue of the Exceedingly Choice and Valuable Library of the Late William Knight, Esq., F.S.A.* (a Sotheby's auction catalogue) (1847), p. 79 (item 883).

46 Absent from this volume are *The Virtues of Sid Hamet the Magician's Rod* (which Oxford admired), *An Excellent New Song Being the Intended Speech of a Famous Orator against Peace* (Swift's first attack on Nottingham and a poem Oxford requested), and *Peace and Dunkirk*.

The existence of Oxford's volume does not of itself show that *An Excellent New Song Call'd the Trusty and True English-man* is the January 1712 ballad. But the available evidence in its totality points to this poem as the most likely candidate among all surviving poems that I have examined. Barring future discoveries, I think we can cross off another item from our list of previously lost works by Swift.

Appendix

The text of this poem is based on the FOXON E584 copy at the University of Leeds, Brotherton Library, Lt q SWI. I am grateful to the Ehrenpreis Centre for providing me with a reproduction of this copy. The Leeds copy has the latest and most correct state of this edition. The only emendation for the text below is at line 99; the Leeds copy does not have a period after "&c".

An Excellent new Song,
CALL'D
The Trusty and True English-man.

POOR *England*'s Condition
By Sons of Perdition,
Never was more in danger, thro' *Whiggish* Ambition;
And yet you will see,
That saved she will be,
By *English* Men Trusty and True.
In spight of Designers, and Court-Underminers
Black Dismal, *and* Coventry *blue.*

From *High-German* Threats,
And *Low-Dutch* Deceits,
And fear of the *French* after twenty Defeats:
Brave Lads make a Stand,
And rescue your Land,
Like *Englishmen* Trusty and True.
In spight, &c.

The *Austrian* Race,
And *M———h*'s Grace,
Declare it's too early to think of a Peace:
But our poor *Common-weal*,
From them does Appeal
To *English*-men Trusty and True.
In spight, &c.

We have Warr'd twenty Years,
As it plainly appears,
The *Dutch* for good Towns, We for Whimsies and Fears:
But you may be assur'd,
All this will be cur'd
By *English*-men Trusty and True.
In spight, &c.

Our Riches are gone,
Our Trade is undone,
The Nation is mortgag'd, for Money at Loan:
In such Losses and Dangers,
We'll trust no more Strangers,
But *English*-men, Trusty and True.
In spight, &c.

Thus our dismal Distress,
Our Allies would redress,
Who got little by War, by Peace shall get less:
But, thank God, there are some,
Whose Hearts are at Home,
All *English*-men Trusty and True.
In spight, &c.

Our Force to employ,
Our Land to destroy,
To make a poor *German*, a *Spanish* Vice-Roy:
For such must we bleed,
Tax our Beef and our Bread?
No, say *English*-men Trusty and True.
In spight, &c.

The Freedom we boast,
Is too near being lost,
For Beggars and Slaves live on the same Coast.
From none can the Nation,
Expect Preservation,
But *English*-men Trusty and True.
But not from Designers, &c.

Poor *England*'s drawn dry,
By each petty Ally,
She gives both the Ware, and the Money to buy:
Then let us esteem
Such as would her redeem,
As *English*-men Trusty and True.
In spight, &c.

A Curse on their Care,
Who would Foreigners spare,
And lay on our Backs, what falls to their share:
Be they never so Martial,
I'm sure they are partial,
'Gainst *English*-men Trusty and True.
But favour Designers, &c.

When the Ass is sunk in,
Quite up to the Chin,
The Horse gets at last, both the Load and the Skin:
Then it will be too late,
To complain of our Fate,
To *English-men* Trusty and True.
Betray'd by Designers, &c.

Poor Soldiers take heed,
How you're brought into need,
By short'ning your Pay, and shaving your Bread:
Who deals so by you,
Is worse than a *Jew*;
Not an *English*-man Trusty and True.
But favours Designers, &c.

Poor deluded Dissenters,
You are sold like Debentures,
By the *Junto* made over by Deeds and Indentures;
You are ty'd Back to Back
By *N———m*'s Black,
Not by *English*-men Trusty and True;
For you join'd with Designers, &c.

Such as own no Right,
But their Will and their Might,
What Black is to Day, to Morrow is White:
They renounce their Opinion,
When it thwarts their Dominion,
Not like *English*-men Trusty and True:
But more like, &c.

With the *Scotch* they unite,
When they think to get by't,
But when the Noose pinches they strive to unty't:
For War they are hearty,
For it favours their Party,
Not like *English*-men Trusty and True:
But more like, &c.

They would call the *Pretender*,
Or the mad King at *Bender*,
Or the Devil, to pull down our Church's Defender:
But the Projects too plain,
We'll not trust them again,
But *English*-men Trusty and True:
In spight of, &c.

H———r be wise,
And open thine Eyes,
Discard the false *Junto*, their Intriegues and their Lies:
For those that have got 'em,
Find 'em not sound at bottom,
Like *English*-men Trusty and True:
But more like, &c.

If little *Eugene*
Comes here to get *Spain*,
We'll send him as wise as he comes back again;
Tho' a parcel of Dund'rheads
Should meet him by Hundreds,
Not like English-men Trusty and True.
But more like, &c.

What a shame to the Gown,
To see Prelates bow down
To those who would tread both on Mitre and Crown:
Eleven out of Fourteen,
Seduc'd by Whigs Courting!
Are they English-men Trusty and True?
Or more like, &c.

The twelve Peers of *France*,
Are fam'd in Romance,
Who their Country's Honour so high did advance:
But our *British* Twelve Peers,
Are worth Fifty of theirs,
For they are English-men Trusty and True.
In Spight of Designers, and Court-Underminers,
Black Dismal, *and* Coventry *blue.*

Ashley Marshall
University of Nevada, Reno

Swift, Oldisworth, and the Politics of *The Examiner*, 1710-14

Abstract. In 1710-11, Jonathan Swift penned thirty-three issues of the Tory *Examiner*, the leading ministerial paper at the end of Queen Anne's reign. This essay revisits the story of Swift's instalment as Mr Examiner and his stepping down from that role. Scholars have argued that Swift served as Mr Examiner at the request of Robert Harley, who wanted him to moderate the paper's High Tory tone, and that as the paper began to move back toward the political right, Harley dismissed Swift. Critics have had little to say about the pre- and post-Swift phases of *The Examiner*, but reading Swift's contribution within the context of the whole enterprise raises questions about these long-standing assumptions of Harley's management of the paper. *The Examiner* of later 1711-14, moreover, functions as a complement to Swift's polemical contributions to ministerial defence and Tory unity. The notion that Harley was responsible for removing Swift turns out to seem implausible. There are excellent reasons to see *The Examiner* as the more radically Tory Henry St John's project – and thus to rethink Swift's complicated and obscure relationship with the Ministry during the last years of Queen Anne's reign.

Between 2 November 1710 and 14 June 1711, Jonathan Swift contributed thirty-three weekly issues of *The Examiner*, a ministerial journal that most contemporaries understood "to be writ by the Direction, and under the Eye of some Great Persons who sit at the helm of Affairs."[1] Queen Anne had changed her ministry in August 1710, and one of *The Examiner*'s principal aims was to defend the new leaders (Robert Harley and Henry St John) and lambaste the old (the Whig junto led by Sidney Godolphin and the Duke of Marlborough). That Swift was writing at the Ministry's "Direction" is undeniable, but the position of Mr Examiner vis-à-vis the administration was not an uncomplicated one. Scholars have stressed the fundamental disagreements between Harley and St John about what the Government's objectives and policies should be. Harley called for moderation and was determined to achieve shared governance between Whigs and Tories; St John pushed for more radically High-Tory measures and the exclusion of all Whigs. Mr Examiner, critics have argued, had to be either Harley's or St John's man. As W. A. Speck concludes, this conflict is what

1 John Gay, *The Present State of Wit, in a Letter to a Friend in the Country* (London, 1711), p. 9. Thirty-two of Swift's contributions are solo; another was co-authored with Delarivier Manley.

 | DOI:10.30965/9783846763971_018

ultimately led to Swift's decision not to carry on in this capacity: "*The Examiner* began to justify St. John's proceedings more than Harley's until Swift came to realize that he was caught in the firing line between the rival ministers, and stopped contributing … when the end of the Parliamentary session gave him a convenient excuse."[2] J. A. Downie has more explicitly attributed Swift's abandonment of the examining role to Harley, who dismissed him when the paper became too much a vehicle for St John's extremism.[3]

Is this a fair representation of what happened with Swift and *The Examiner*? In what follows, I want to revisit the common story about Swift's instalment as Mr Examiner and his stepping down from that role. The bulk of my discussion will be devoted to an analysis of *The Examiner* in its entirety – that is, the paper that existed before Swift took over and ran (with a brief lapse) for three years after he ceased being the sole author. Scholars have had singularly little to say about the pre- and post-Swift phases of *The Examiner*, despite the fact that Swift evidently continued to participate – perhaps even direct – the journal between December 1711 and July 1714. Leo Damrosch's succinct dismissal reflects the general attitude: the paper was "carried on for a while, not very well, by others."[4] Part of my objective is to re-read Swift's *Examiner* within the context of the paper as a whole, which turns out to be helpful in assessing the politics of Swift's contributions. Such a re-reading also raises questions about the nature of Harley's involvement in the management of *The Examiner*.

By way of conclusion, I shall also briefly consider the place of *The Examiner* within the culture of partisan journalism in the last four years of Anne's reign. *The Examiner* was the object of especially sharp criticism from opposition writers; the frequency and bitterness of the complaints about it are exceptional. Though Swift's role in the paper has bestowed upon it a special importance among scholars, the distinctiveness of its contemporary reception has received little comment. Most broadly, I wish to make the case for engaging with the whole of *The Examiner*, and for appreciating Swift's collaboration with St John on the paper, which continued after he ceased to be sole author. How did *The Examiner* evolve, and what does Swift's evolving role in it tell us about both his and the paper's relationship to the Harley ministry?

2 W. A. Speck, "*The Examiner* Re-Examined," *Prose Studies*, 16 (1993), 34-43 (p. 34 [special issue of the journal, *Telling People What to Think: Early Eighteenth-Century Periodicals from "The Review" to "The Rambler"*, eds J. A. Downie and Thomas N. Corns]).

3 J. A. Downie, *Robert Harley and the Press: Propaganda and Public Opinion in the Age of Swift and Defoe* (Cambridge: Cambridge University Press, 1979), pp. 135-37.

4 Leo Damrosch, *Jonathan Swift: His Life and his World* (New Haven and London: Yale University Press, 2013), p. 210.

1. "Very Great *Hands* have *Fingers* in it": The Rise and Fall of *The Examiner*

The Examiner launched on 3 August 1710, five days before the Earl of Godolphin was dismissed from his post as Lord High Treasurer. Godolphin's fellow Whig, the Earl of Sunderland, had been sacked in June, and though the Whig ministry's removal was not complete until September, by early August the Tory *Examiner* was already anticipating a major turnover. The inaugural issue addresses the Queen's right to select her ministers, and mocks the notion that the Whig Marlborough will refuse to serve as general upon such a change. Authorship of numbers one through 13 is difficult to establish with any precision, but Dr William King, Francis Atterbury, Dr John Freind, Matthew Prior, Delarivier Manley, and St John himself were involved in the enterprise at the outset.

The Examiner was, from the first, a potent vehicle of Tory propaganda, as the Whig response makes clear. In John Oldmixon's telling, "The old Ministry [Godolphin's] saw it was absolutely necessary to set up a Paper in Opposition to the *Examiner*, to dispel the Mists it cast before the Peoples Eyes." To that end, Arthur Mainwaring recruited Joseph Addison for *The Whig-Examiner*, which began on 14 September 1710 and ended a month later. Mainwaring then decided on "a new Paper with a new Title, the sole Business of which should be to watch the Motions of the *Examiner*, and guard against the ill Effects of them."[5] The first issue of *The Medley* appeared on 5 October. In other words, *The Whig-Examiner* lived and died, and *The Medley* was well launched, before the Irish vicar took up his quill as Mr Examiner. Frank H. Ellis's edition of *The Medley* and *The Examiner* opens with Swift's first issue, and then prints *The Medley*'s response, giving a somewhat misleading impression. Swift was enlisted to oppose Mainwaring, not the other way around.[6]

Was *The Examiner* Harley's or St John's brainchild? Scholars disagree. Ellis suggests that Harley "recruited" King to undertake the venture but was dissatisfied by the ultra-Tory nature of the early contributions.[7] David Nokes attributes *The Examiner* initially to St John, but he maintains that "Harley was anxious"

5 John Oldmixon, *Memoirs of the Press, Historical and Political, for Thirty Years Past, from 1710 to 1740* (London: T. Cox, 1742), pp. 8, 9.

6 A good account of Mainwaring is to be had in Frank H. Ellis, "Arthur Mainwaring as Reader of Swift's *Examiner*," *The Yearbook of English Studies*, 11 (1981), 49-66.

7 Introduction, *Swift vs. Mainwaring: "The Examiner" and "The Medley"*, ed. Frank H. Ellis (Oxford: Clarendon Press, 1985), pp. xxiv-xxv. All quotations from Swift's contributions to *The Examiner* are taken from this edition and are given in parentheses within the text. A version of Ellis's Introduction also appears as "'A Quill worn to the Pith in the Service of the

for the paper to "express his own, rather than his Secretary's views,"[8] and he hoped to use Swift as his mouthpiece. On the last point, Nokes is in agreement with other Swiftians, who assume that by involving Swift Harley was looking to establish the paper as "his." The Lord Treasurer wished to use the paper to advance a more moderate platform, the story goes, and so he enlisted the Irish vicar, someone "whose understanding of Harley's propaganda needs was almost clairvoyant."[9] Downie goes further, hypothesizing that "the original authors, including St John, were not consulted" about Swift's appointment as Mr Examiner.[10]

We have precious little contemporary comment about the establishment of the paper. The most extensive is John Oldmixon's retrospective account, which suggests Swift's early involvement and describes St John as one of "the *Harleians*" who collectively launched *The Examiner*.[11] Swift and St John evidently did not meet until 11 November, when the two of them dined with Harley, Erasmus Lewis, and Freind,[12] though this need not necessarily mean that both Swift and St John were not already engaged with the paper. On 10 October, Swift had written to Archbishop King about Harley's warm reception of him, adding, "He says, Mr. Secretary *St. John* desire[s] to be acquainted with me, and that he will bring us together."[13] Exactly how and why Swift became involved specifically with *The Examiner* we can only speculate. In the *Memoirs* written after Queen Anne's death, Swift recounted Harley's telling him, in the fall of 1710, that "the Queen was resolved to employ none but those who were friends to the constitution of church and state," and that the Ministry's "great difficulty lay in the want of some good pen, to keep up the spirit raised in the people, to

State': Swift's *Examiner*," in *Proceedings of The First Münster Symposium on Jonathan Swift*, eds Hermann J. Real and Heinz J. Vienken (Munich: Wilhelm Fink, 1985), pp. 73-82.

8 David Nokes, *Jonathan Swift, a Hypocrite Reversed: A Critical Biography* (Oxford: Oxford University Press, 1985), p. 122. Downie likewise suggests that St John "sponsored the launching of the ultra-tory *Examiner*, and he gave the paper a purpose in his *Letter to the Examiner*" (*Robert Harley and the Press*, p. 122).

9 Ellis, Introduction, *Swift vs. Mainwaring*, ed. Ellis, p. xxxi.

10 Downie, *Robert Harley and the Press*, p. 127.

11 John Oldmixon, *The History of England, during the Reigns of King William and Queen Mary, Queen Anne, King George I* (London: Thomas Cox, Richard Ford, and Richard Hett, 1735), p. 456.

12 In the *Journal to Stella* for 7 October 1710, Swift reports that Harley told him "he must bring Mr. St. John and me acquainted" (p. 30). On 11 November, he reports what appears to be their first meeting (p. 64). All references to the *Journal* are to Abigail Williams's edition (Cambridge: Cambridge University Press, 2013), and are given in parentheses within the text.

13 *Correspondence*, ed. Woolley, I, 302 and n5.

assert the principles, and justify the proceedings of the new ministers."[14] Here Swift identifies Harley as the man responsible for his recruitment, but throughout the *Memoirs*, he takes pains to overemphasize his connection with Harley and to de-emphasize St John, and for good reason. At the time of composition, the new king had arrived, and the Whigs were looking for High Tory blood; that Swift wanted to decouple himself from the more extreme St John was eminently reasonable. In any case, that Harley enlisted him to moderate the tone of the paper is plausible, though what moderation Swift managed to achieve was always limited, and he soon abandoned it.[15] Another explanation is that *The Examiner* continued to be St John's enterprise despite the change of hands, and that Harley introduced Swift to St John as "their" new man, not his own. After all, as of November 1710, the split between the Ministers had not happened; H. T. Dickinson places St John's rejection of Harley's moderate policies in the early months of 1711.[16]

Swift evidently enjoyed his seven months as Mr Examiner, and his stepping down from the post has puzzled scholars. His last solo issue was 7 June 1711, where he not very compellingly waxes triumphal: "And now I conceive the main Design I had in writing these Papers, is fully executed. A great Majority of the Nation is at length thorowly convinc'd, that the Qu[een] proceeded with the highest Wisdom, in changing Her Ministry and Parliament" (p. 470). Swift claims that his "main Design" has been "fully executed," but most Swiftians have presumed this to be insincere. They tend to explain his resignation as a compulsory rather than voluntary act: Swift had fallen more and more under the influence of the hot-headed St John, swinging the paper to the political right; Harley was displeased, and took action.[17] But the essay that seems most likely to have upset Harley appeared three months before Swift stepped aside. In *The Examiner* for 15 March, Swift recounted the stabbing of Harley by a French refugee, the Marquis de Guiscard. Problematically, Mr Examiner reported that Guiscard had "confessed in *Newgate*, that his chief Design was against Mr. *Secretary St. John*" – a lie, the source of which was almost certainly St John himself, emerging as a rival to the Lord Treasurer and resentful of his

---

14 *Memoirs, Relating to That Change which Happened ... in the Year 1710*, in *Prose Works*, VIII, 123.

15 See W. A. Speck, "*The Examiner* Examined: Swift's Tory Pamphleteering," *Focus: Swift*, ed. C. J. Rawson (London: Sphere, 1971), pp. 138-54. See also Speck's "*The Examiner* Re-Examined."

16 H. T. Dickinson, *Bolingbroke* (London: Constable, 1970), pp. 76-78.

17 Downie, *Robert Harley and the Press*, p. 135.

celebrity in the wake of the stabbing.[18] Swift's naïve falsehood, critics plausibly suggest, must have frustrated Harley, who was none too eager to share the victim's spotlight with his ministerial adversary. Because of this particular occasion, and because of the generally increasing Toryism of *The Examiner*, historians have concluded that Harley had had enough. "Swift had been told," Downie, among others, asserts, "that if he intended to write without consulting the general policies of the government, then his services were no longer required."[19]

Scholars assume that Swift was unhappy about giving up his role, and that may have been true. In the *Journal to Stella* for 7 June, he foretold the abrupt depreciation of the periodical:

> As for the *Examiner*, I have heard a whisper, that after that of this day, which tells what this parliament has done, you will hardly find them so good. I prophecy they will be trash for the future; and methinks in this day's *Examiner* the author talks doubtfully, as if he would write no more, so that if they go on, they may probably be by some other hand, which in my opinion is a thousand pities; but who can help it? (p. 225)

But reading tone is not necessarily easy here. It remains unclear whether Swift is voicing serious alarm about the fate of the paper or whether he is being playfully self-aggrandizing, disingenuously distancing himself from the venture. If he did feel pushed out, then the distinct lack of *ex post facto* complaint is remarkably uncharacteristic. Swift does not tend to be reticent about his life's disappointments, especially when he feels wounded by those in power.

The unfortunate reality is that we have no record of any conversation between Harley and Swift about *The Examiner*. We do not know what if any part Harley played in Swift's relinquishment of the role, or what else might have compelled Swift to bow out. What we do know is that Swift and Manley co-authored the 14 June issue, and then she carried the paper on for six weeks; it temporarily lapsed after issue no 52, but was revived in December 1711 by William Oldisworth. The last issue appeared on 26 July 1714, which unfortunately deprives us of Mr Examiner's commentary on both Harley's fall from power (he was officially removed on 27 July) and Anne's death on 1 August.[20]

---

18 Swift's quotation is *Swift vs. Mainwaring*, ed. Ellis, p. 303. See Ellis's notes to ll. 110 and 113-24 on St John's fabrications about this episode. As Irvin Ehrenpreis observes, "Harley was unlikely to feel consoled for his near-murder by an assurance that the intended victim was his hated rival" (*Dr Swift*, p. 470).

19 Downie, *Robert Harley and the Press*, p. 137.

20 The paper was briefly revived at the beginning of George I's reign, but suppressed. As Brian Cowan explains, "Warrants were issued for the arrest of the publishers and the

The Examiner, in other words, ends at roughly the same time Swift too was going quiet, at least in the realm of public pronouncement. To the content of the paper across these authorship changes we now need to turn.

2. The Political Evolution of *The Examiner*

For our purposes, *The Examiner* can be divided into three obvious phases: pre-Swift, Swift, and "post"-Swift. The standard accounts of Swift's instalment and then dismissal as Mr Examiner presume some ideological and/or tonal shift between the first and second, and between the second and third, of those phases: something changed when Swift took over, and, by implication, something else happened when he quit. Virtually no ink has been spilled on the contents of *The Examiner* before and after Swift, and the untested assumption has been that Swift's contributions are distinct from those of his predecessors and successors, and not only in qualitative terms. But is this in fact the case?

2.1. The Examiner*'s Consistent Themes and Attitudes*

The Examiner no 1 includes a prefatory announcement of the journal's principal aim: "*I meet with a great Variety of Papers, neither so Correct, so Moral, nor so Loyal as they ought to be*," and "*Some of these Papers I intend to* Examine." This statement anticipates the antagonistic nature of the new weekly, which Addison sharply observed "wou'd have been more properly entitled the *Executioner*,"[21] but does little to signal the actual content of the subsequent issues. What themes were established in the early weeks of this venture?

Ideologically, the paper was decidedly High Tory, and aggressively so. Many contemporary papers eschewed overt commentary about the basis of power, sticking to reportage or insinuating rather than declaiming, but not *The Examiner*. Issue no 3 anticipates a parliamentary and ministerial upheaval: Oldmixon explains that the "weekly Libel" was initiated principally "in order to prepare the Way for this astonishing Change in the Ministry."[22] The defence of the change is a defence of the prerogative, and no 3 reproaches those who, though asserting "*Friendship* and *Fidelity* to the *Chief Ministers*," forget their

author of the paper, and by May 1715 the crackdown had reached the coffeehouses who supplied the *Examiner* to their customers" (*The Social Life of Coffee: The Emergence of the British Coffeehouse* [New Haven and London: Yale University Press, 2005], p. 219). I have seen only one issue, dated 14 September 1715.

21 *The Whig-Examiner*, no 1; *The Medleys for the Year 1711: To which are prefix'd, The Five Whig-Examiners* (London: John Darby, 1712), pp. 9-10.

22 Oldmixon, *The History of England*, p. 456.

"Duty to the *Crown*." In the upcoming election, landowners are encouraged to choose those "Men that hold Her Majesty's Hereditary Right" over "those who plainly deny it to Her" (no 10). The writers call for obedience from subjects, caution against revolution, and affirm that "*Hereditary Right* ... is *Fundamental* to our *Constitution*" (no 9). No 13 rebukes those who have "Condemn'd, Curs'd, Exploded and Ridicul'd" the doctrine of non-resistance, and passionately objects to the "precarious Principle ... *That the Good of the People is the ONLY End of Government*." Authority comes from God, not from the people, and when "Subjects [become] the Governours," government ceases to exist. The political philosophy of the paper as Swift inherited it is authoritarian, conservative, and nostalgic – adjectives all highly applicable to Swift's own contributions.

Much of the attitude established in the early issues turns out to be consistent across the life of *The Examiner*. The hostility towards the Dutch introduced in no 4 – they "treat *England* as if we were a Feudatory Kingdom" – persists throughout Swift's tenure and beyond. So do the intolerance of Protestant dissenters and the rejection of the association of "high church" with "popery" and the Pretender. From inception to termination, *The Examiner* defends the royal prerogative against encroachments from below, and characterizes the Whigs as a routed party practiced in "the Art of *Political Lying*."[23] A desire to unite the Tories and divide the Whigs is evident throughout the duration of the paper. There are some changes, to which we will return, but in general there is marked consistency of political outlook.

The Examiner's attitude towards power is anti-populist and anti-resistance. In no 13, the last before Swift took over, the author concludes, "I suppose the Authority of Governors to be deriv'd only from *God*; which I am sensible will never be granted by those who place the Original of it in the *People*." In no 9, Mr Examiner had asserted divine right, while cagily qualifying his claim: "It is manifest that the Power and Authority of Governors is *from God* ... But *indefeisible* [*sic*] or *inalienable* Right is quite another Thing." Ellis has suggested that the non-denial of indefeasibility contributed to Harley's decision to replace the original authors of *The Examiner* with Swift,[24] but in his third contribution, Swift appears if anything to go further than his predecessor:

23 Swift uses this phrase in no 15 (p. 20); Oldisworth uses it as well in *The Examiner* of 7 February 1712. All citations of Oldisworth's *Examiner* will be to the volume number and issue number; the 7 February issue is II, 10 (volume 2, no 10). The second volume begins when Oldisworth revives the paper (6 December 1711); the last issue is VI, 19. Subsequent references to Oldisworth's *Examiner* will give volume and issue number.

24 Ellis, Introduction, *Swift vs. Mainwaring*, ed. Ellis, p. xxv.

> 'Tis as plain as the Words of an Act of Parliament can make it, That her present Majesty is Heir to the Survivor of the late King and Queen her Sister. Is not that an *Hereditary Right*? What need we explain it any further? ... Suppose we go further, and examine the Word *Indefeasible*, with which some Writers of late have made themselves so merry: I confess it is hard to conceive, how any Law which the supream Power makes, may not by the same Power be repeal'd: So that I shall not determine, whether the Queen's Right be *indefeasible* or no. But this I will maintain, that whoever affirms it so, is not guilty of a Crime. For in that Settlement of the Crown after the Revolution, where Her present Majesty is named in Remainder, there are (as near as I can remember) these remarkable Words, *To which we bind our selves and our Posterity* for ever. Lawyers may explain this, or call them words of Form, as they please: And Reasoners may argue that such an Obligation is against the very Nature of Government; but a plain Reader, who takes the Words in their natural Meaning, may be excus'd, in thinking a Right so confirm'd, is *indefeasible*. (pp. 41-42)

Mr Examiner seems in no doubt that those who promulgate indefeasibility are completely within their rights; he is sanctioning, in other words, a political philosophy based on non-resistance. His attitude towards the "Reasoners" who advocate a more contractual idea of power is not admiring. I must respectfully disagree with David Oakleaf: Swift did not "dismiss" the notion of passive obedience "as pedantry."[25] Defending those who presume indefeasibility is not the same thing as preaching passive obedience, but we are a long way, here, from reducing High Tory convictions to foolish and slavish dogma. Throughout his *Examiner*, Swift treats the prerogatives of the prince as sacred, and his attack on the Whigs has everything to do with their having "no very great Veneration for *Crowned Heads*" (p. 345).[26] He may moderate the High Tory tone of the early *Examiners*, at least for a little while, but the fundamental outlook does not change.

The authoritarian tendencies of Swift's *Examiners* endured long after his official involvement with the paper had ended. Oldisworth is explicit in his rejection of Whig ideology: he takes for granted that "the *Queen* is Supream over all Orders of the Realm," and upbraids the Whigs for "mak[ing] *Obedience* the Duty of the Sovereign" (III, 16).[27] Swift and Oldisworth likewise share the view that freedom is a perilous concept. Although it would become a buzzword for inalienable personal rights later in Swift's career, as of 1710-14 "liberty" represents

25 David Oakleaf, *A Political Biography of Jonathan Swift* (London: Pickering and Chatto, 2008), p. 111.

26 I have made this argument at length in *Swift and History: Politics and the English Past* (Cambridge: Cambridge University Press, 2015), especially pp. 181-91.

27 The only article-length study of Oldisworth is Robert J. Allen, "William Oldisworth: 'The Author of *The Examiner*,'" *Philological Quarterly*, 26 (1947), 159-80.

something menacing. In *Examiner* no 37, he cautioned against those (Whigs) who operate according to "false Notions about *Liberty*" (p. 360), and in no 32, he presented "Liberty" as "*the Daughter of* Oppression," responsible not only for arts and learning but also for faction and unrest (p. 285). In February 1712, Oldisworth would attest that the "Word ... has more Witchcraft in it ... than it has real Charms." Although "Liberty is ... an invaluable Blessing," especially in its "true *English* or true *Roman*" sense, the Whigs have perverted it, using the battle cry of freedom "to introduce a Tyranny of the worst sort, and to share the Bulk of Power among themselves" (III, 27). Like Swift in the *Discourse of the Contests and Dissensions*,[28] Oldisworth depicts Julius Caesar as the symbol of tyranny achieved "by Popular Arts," tyranny arrived at when "The Power of the People to dictate to the *Senate* [is] openly Asserted and Encouraged" (III, 47).

Oldisworth was as staunchly conservative as Swift, perhaps even more so. He brands the Whigs irreverent innovators rather than upholders of the sacred constitution: "How can we think it possible, that any *Briton*, who is tolerably acquainted with the Nature, Antiquity, Coherence, and durable Excellency of his own Constitution, should presume to mend it by a Model so full of Absurdities?" (III, 27) His history of "*Modern Whiggery*" (27 July 1713) is sneering: Whigs were once upon a time powerless Puritans, but the "*Jesuits*" "took care to Infuse into [them] several pernicious Notions, relating to the Rights of Nature, the Subjection of Governors, and the Power of the Subject, on purpose to make this little One a Thorn in the Sides of the Nation." The Whigs became politicized, working "against the Power and Person of their Sovereign" in "the Name of *Republican*[s]." Only around the time of the Revolution do Whigs "declar[e] for Monarchy, but such a Monarchy, so restrained and limited, as to make the Sovereign the Creature and Servant of the People." This account is meant to demonstrate a singular lack of principle: the Whigs have "Turn'd, and Tack'd, and Chang'd to fine Purpose," and "can no more call themselves a *Party* ... than a *Chaos* is a *World*, or a *heap of Ruins* a *compleat Piece of Architecture*." But Oldisworth also associates them with a dangerous and destabilizing form of government, precisely because they "never could be reconcil'd to the *Regal Power*" (IV, 21). The Whigs, with no respect for authority, "Cavil at

28 When Caesar appears in the *Discourse*, he does so as a man who "by [his] Credit with the People" attempted to "pull ... down the *Nobles*." In his most anti-populist work, Swift writes of Caesar's (dangerous) "Arts of pleasing the People," and of his "publick and avowed Pretensions for beginning the Civil-War," which "were to restore the Tribunes and the People, oppressed (as he pretended) by the *Nobles*." And, he continues, the consequences of Caesar's rise were dire: the "entire Subversion of the *Roman* Liberty and Constitution, was altogether owing to those Measures which had broke the Ballance between the *Patricians* and *Plebeians*" (*Prose Works*, I, 219, 221).

the *Original* of *Government*, and Perplex and Confound the first Principles of *Policy*" (V, 40). In ideological terms, Swift's *Examiner* and Oldisworth's are of a piece, though the latter outdoes the former in the frequency and extensiveness of his arguments about power and authority. Oldisworth called his contributions "Essays on Government,"[29] and indeed the last Mr Examiner is committed to offering a political philosophy – yet another tendency that marks him as more St John's man than Harley's.

One major component of the battle between *The Examiner* and the rival *Medley*, as their editor has explained,[30] concerns interpretation of 1688, and Swift is not the only Mr Examiner to voice ambivalence about that climactic event. In his first *Examiner*, Swift describes the "Nobility and Gentry" who orchestrated the Revolution as "true Lovers of their Country" who were compelled "to yield to those Breaches in the Succession of the Crown ... out of a regard to the Necessity of the Kingdom" (p. 5). Swift's assessment of 1688, then, is that it was perhaps necessary but still a "Breach," and one not to be lightly replicated. The earlier authors of *The Examiner* reached a similar conclusion in no 9: "About twenty Years since, we had a *Revolution* in *England*, which had some *very good Consequences*, and some *not so good*: Therefore we must *now* talk, write, and think of nothing else."[31] He goes on to observe, sardonically, that "One *Revolution* had the luck to do good; therefore *Revolution* for *Revolution's sake* is extremely desirable." Oldisworth likewise cites the events of 1688-89 as introducing a lamentable new political reality: "Since the *Revolution*, there seems to have been a studied Design carry'd on for many Years to deprive the Crown, not only of the Art, but even the Power of Preferring" (III, 15).

From Swift and Manley to Oldisworth, the position of *The Examiner* continues to be polarizing, fiercely antagonistic to the Whigs and supportive of the High-Church landed gentry. The elitist contempt is familiar to readers of Swift's *Examiner*: "I have often heard it made a wonder, how an obscure Sort of Men, dissenting from the Establishment both in Church and State, should, in little more than half an Age, become so Rich, so Numerous, yet so Obnoxious to the true Interest of their Country" (II, 1).[32] Oldisworth scolds "the *Mutinous*

---

29 *The Examiner*, 9 February 1713 (III, 23).

30 See Ellis, Introduction, *Swift vs. Mainwaring*, ed. Ellis, p. xxi.

31 The language of this critique is echoed in Swift's 1721 epistolary *apologia*: "The Prince of Orange's expedition" might have been justified by "the publick good," but "in the consequences it produced some very bad effects, which are likely to stick long enough by us" (*Correspondence*, ed. Woolley, II, 360).

32 In *Examiner* no 15, for example, Swift reflects unhappily that, "We have seen a great part of the Nation's Mony got into the Hands of those, who by their Birth, Education and Merit, could pretend no higher than to wear our Liveries" (p. 25). Swift clearly shares St John's

Party" of Whigs, "with their limited Politicks, or very much extended Knavery" (II, 23). He also continues the old attack on the Godolphin-Marlborough junto: any rational man knows that "the Insolence of the late Men in Power to the Q[uee]n was such, as was never offered to any Crowned Head before," that "a General for Life [Marlborough] was intended," and that "the Prerogative ... was openly struck at" (II, 44). As he observes in the next issue, "EVERY time I reflect upon the Conduct of the late Ministry, still I discover more Abuses." The ministerial change is by this point two years past, but the anti-Junto offensive is going strong. More generally, Mr Examiner reckons "The Conduct of the *Whigs*" to be "very surprizing and unaccountable," full of "Clamour and Malice" (III, 10). "Father *Time*" is, we are told, obviously "a most inveterate *Tory*; for he has detected more Iniquities of the People called *Whigs*, than all the honest Zeal of their Inspectors could possibly pry into" (III, 17). Whigs are virtually sub-human, the "Insects and Venomous Reptiles of the *Political World*" (IV, 1).

Many of the fundamental convictions of Mr Examiner, then, seem consistent, but there are changes over the life of this paper. We need now to ask what the nature of the relationship between Swift's contributions and the rest of the *Examiner* is, what happened when he took over, what happened when he stepped down, how the paper's voice evolved, and how that evolution corresponded to changes in political circumstances.

2.2. *From St John's Tories to Harley's Swift?*

Swift assumed the role of Mr Examiner in early November 1710, immediately after the Tory rout of the Whigs in the October General Election. The election results were not a surprise: by the spring, the majority of Anne's subjects were increasingly weary of the expensive, seemingly interminable war that Whig leadership was keen to continue. Oppressive taxes, the bloodbath of Malplaquet, and the bill for the naturalization of foreign Protestants all intensified the anti-Whig sentiment. By the time Swift took up his pen, the Tories found themselves in the unfamiliar position of being the people's choice. How did he respond to this new political climate, and what changes did his takeover produce?

The partisanship of Swift's contributions, as we have seen, corresponds fairly closely to that of the preceding numbers. According to the standard explanation, Swift was assigned to this position in order to restore some degree of moderation to the paper, to neutralize the High-Church polemics of the preceding issues. In his inaugural number, Swift's Mr Examiner does indeed

prejudice, his "deep-rooted ... hostility to the moneyed interest" (Dickinson, *Bolingbroke*, p. 80).

signal a change: he apologizes for having, "for some Weeks past ... been forc'd in [his] own Defence, to follow a Proceeding that [he has] so much condemn'd in others" (p. 1). The audience is evidently to assume continuity of voice: the author of no 14 does not introduce himself as new, merely as mildly repentant. His apology seems to be more for manner than for content, since he does not recant any of the previous positions. In any case, the following sentence highlights the grudging nature of this self-criticism: "Several of my Acquaintance among the declining Party, are grown so insufferably Peevish and Splenatick ... and represent the State of Things in such formidable Idea's, that I find my self dispos'd to share in their Afflictions, though I know them to be groundless and Imaginary." For his "peevishness," then, the opposition has itself to blame. Significantly, Swift maintains the language of the early *Examiners*, characterizing the Whigs as "the declining Party" (p. 1), and insinuating that they are masters of the art of political lying. He complains unequivocally about "the Malice of a ruin'd Party," meant "to render the Queen and Her Administration odious, and to inflame the Nation" (p. 3). That said, the tone of no 14 is much calmer and more reasonable than the previous issues; Swift does not sustain the accusatory indignation with which the pre-Swift *Examiner* had closed.

The essays written by King, St John, and others are emotional, indignant, defensive; the attitude towards anyone who dares question the Queen's right to make a ministerial change is judgmental and unapologetic. Swift is not without judgment, even from the get-go, and he does not tend towards apology, but he is more conciliatory in his language. Initially, he seems to be trying to give the appearance of explaining Anne's decision in rational terms: "It was the most prudent Course imaginable in the Queen, to lay hold of the Dispositions of the People for changing the Parliament and Ministry at this Juncture" (p. 9). He repeatedly assures his readers that he is attempting to achieve a *via media*, that he wishes to avoid "entring into the Violences of either Party;" he can go so far in that direction as to describe the "two parties" as "both pretend[ing] a mighty Zeal for our Religion and Government, only they disagree about the Means" (p. 34). Swift's position at the outset of his *Examiner* is not as aggressively High Church, appealing more broadly to the landed gentry, lamenting "that *Power*, which according to the old Maxim, was us'd to follow *Land*, is now gone over to *Money*" (pp. 4-5).[33]

Swift's moderation, then, is mostly a matter of broadening his audience, from the rigidly High Tory to all Tories (and "Old" Whigs, whom he treats as

33 As Downie rightly notes, "Swift was to try to reconcile the country gentlemen to the real nature of the regime envisaged by the prime minister" (*Robert Harley and the Press*, p. 128).

essentially Tories). On one occasion, he appears to challenge both the warmongering, freethinking Whigs as well as the highest-flying Tories. In no 16, he denounces the Whig *Review* and radical Whig *Observator*, and brands the Jacobite Charles Leslie's *Rehearsal* "yet more pernicious" (p. 35). Swift criticizes the extreme Tory position here, but in fact he seems merely to be paying lip service to moderation. He has nothing of substance to say against Leslie, and his position towards the high-flyers is not disparaging, even if he momentarily adopts a more moderate Tory stance. He maintains the legitimacy of the "church in danger" cry so common among High Tories, and he depicts Sacheverell as "a faithful Subject" whose loyalty has been branded disaffection (p. 39).

At no point does Swift kowtow to the Whigs, and – *pace* J. A. Downie – neither does he peddle the same propaganda as we find in Simon Clement's Harleyite *Faults on Both Sides* (1710). That pamphlet attempts "to mediate between the parties," demonstrating "that both parties were partly to blame for inciting conflict in the nation."[34] The furthest Swift goes in this direction is to announce a desire to "converse in equal Freedom with the deserving Men of both Parties," but within a handful of paragraphs he hails the change at Court necessary to end the (Whig-favoured) war, complains about the "Malice of a ruin'd Party," laments that the moneyed class has gained on the landed, voices ambivalence about 1688, and casts aspersions on Godolphin's fiscal practices.[35] Mr Examiner does say once that his aim is "to let the remote and uninstructed part of the Nation see, that they have been misled on both sides" (p. 36), but Swift's unsustained attempt at the rhetoric of moderation could not have fooled the Whigs, and did not. His first issue (no 14) is provocative and polarizing, in a skilfully non-inflammatory way, perhaps, but courting potential Whigs was never Swift's game. Neither was criticizing the Tories. *Faults on Both Sides* describes "the Generality of the *Tories*" as "a looser and less thoughtful sort of People, who look no further than the Outside of things, and take up with Notions they don't understand" (p. 46). Swift would never sanction or adopt such a position. If Harley was afraid that the "tory resurrection was in danger of becoming a rout," and wished to enlist some moderate Whigs in support of the new ministry, *The Examiner* was not the paper meant to help smooth the way.[36]

34 Downie, *Robert Harley and the Press*, p. 119.

35 *Swift vs. Mainwaring*, ed. Ellis, pp. 1, 3, 5, 6.

36 The quotation is Downie, *Robert Harley and the Press*, p. 128. Swift leaves no doubt of how he divides his countrymen: "In *Them* it is humble and loyal to reflect upon the Q[ueen] and the Ministry," but "in *Us* it is insolent to defend Her Majesty and Her Choice" (*Swift vs. Mainwaring*, ed. Ellis, p. 165).

In his seminal work on *The Examiner*, W. A. Speck noted that Harley must have disliked the original *Examiner*'s treatment of the war and of England's allies: it ran the risk of "alarm[ing] the allies against his ministry," expressing lack of support for continuing the war and frustration with the Dutch for providing less than England and standing to gain more.[37] Swift softens the tone, but in his first issue he reiterates much of the message: the allies are not "upon the same Foot with us," and "the greatest part of the Money circulates among" the Continental powers, "whereas ours crosses the Sea … and every Penny of it … is so much lost to the Nation for ever." The bottom line, for the new Mr Examiner, is clear: the Queen needed to "extricate[e] … Her self, as soon as possible, out of the Pupilage of those who found their Accounts only in perpetuating the War" (pp. 8, 9). Swift's manner is more indirect, but his argument still intimates that the Ministry is not wholly in league with the allies.

Swift's position is, in fact, not so very different from that of St John in *A Letter to the Examiner* (1710), which was, scholars agree, written to guide the authors of the early issues. St John assumes the role of counsellor: "These are the Things, Sir, that deserve to pass under your Pen" (p. 16). In the *Letter*, St John deals extensively with the mismanagement of the war and with the inordinate dependence of the allies upon English men and money: "We engag'd as *Confederates*, but we have been made to proceed as *Principals*" (p. 6). This tone, coolly rational rather than severe, resembles that of issue no 14 (Swift's) more than that of the preceding numbers: "From hence it appears probable enough, that if the War continue much longer on the present Foot" (p. 9). St John proceeds, like Swift, to praise the Queen and voice concern about the disloyal opposition who seek "to *Limit* the *Allegiance* of the Subject" (p. 14). St John is not aggressively denunciatory, not fiery hot; rather, he is regretful, lamenting the state of affairs and hoping that the situation can be set right. Reading the *Letter* alongside Swift's early contributions to *The Examiner*, one finds continuity, and still more reason to suspect that Swift was not imposed upon St John by Harley, or brought in to replace and silence the secretary.

Swift's adoption of a more conciliatory tone perhaps reflects, to some extent, an unusual political reality. When he took over *The Examiner*, the Tories appeared to be the strong party, with good prospects under Anne and with considerable popular support. On 1 February 1711, he gloated about "a Flourishing Ministry, in full Credit with the Q[uee]n, and belov'd by the People" (p. 211), and throughout his *Examiner*, he swore the Tories to be the choice of the majority. The "truest way of judging the Dispositions of the People," he contended, "is by computing the County-Elections; and in these, 'tis manifest that five

37 Speck, "*The Examiner* Examined," p. 145.

in six are entirely for the present Measures" (p. 181). Lee Horsley has argued that, in his *Examiner* essays, Swift "appropriated Whig arguments in defense of Toryism," and that "it was Swift who took most advantage of the opportunity to present the Tories as a national party."[38] Perhaps the shift we see from the pre-Swift phase of *The Examiner* to the Swift phase has something to do with the Tory leadership's desire to capitalize on this new popularity, to build the party's base. Swift's persona, unlike that of the earlier essays, is that of a fairly moderate Tory gentleman, one duly antagonistic towards the Whig faction but neither too little nor too much a conservative churchman. If this is the case, we need not assume that Harley installed Swift as a block to St John's High Tory initiatives. Uniting the Tories against the Whigs – as Swift does in *The Examiner* – was more St John's strategy than it was his rival's. By the spring of 1711, says Dickinson, St John was almost monomaniacally driven by "his concern for the welfare and the future prospects of the Tory party," impatient with Harley's leniency towards the Whigs, and "frantic ... to keep the Tories together and in power."[39]

The crux here is that, though scholars believe that Swift was increasingly doing St John's bidding, there is some possibility that as Mr Examiner he was *always* doing St John's bidding.[40] Significantly, St John's rejection of Harleyite moderation has been located not in the autumn of 1710 but in the early months of 1711, meaning that the Secretary's own trajectory, vis-à-vis moderation, roughly corresponds with that of Mr Examiner's. "The more [St John] saw Harley's ... moderation alienating the Tory rank and file, the more he was tempted" to join the rebellion.[41] Swift, to be sure, never actually rebelled against Harley; the closest he comes is in his identification of St John as Guiscard's intended victim. But he does ultimately use *The Examiner* on behalf of principles that are not Harley's, and not only at the end of his tenure as sole author. That said, Swift genuinely admired Harley, and he evidently preferred to unite Harley and St John rather than diminish the former for the latter. What this means is that we need to allow for the possibility that St John was behind Swift's resignation, that he whispered in Swift's ear that *The Examiner* should change hands. In any case, the paper continued to be aggressively Tory under Oldisworth, and arguably even more so.

38 Lee Horsley, "*Vox Populi* in the Political Literature of 1710," *Huntington Library Quarterly*, 38 (1975), 335-53 (pp. 345, 339).

39 Dickinson, *Bolingbroke*, p. 80.

40 Speck concludes that Swift gradually revealed himself to be "temperamentally ... more sympathetic to the views of the Secretary" ("*The Examiner* Examined," p. 152).

41 Dickinson, *Bolingbroke*, p. 78.

2.3. *Swift's "Constant Drudge": Oldisworth as Mr Examiner*

The premise has been that Swift was removed from his examining role because he was tending too far to the right. If that was the cause for Swift's dismissal, then we might reasonably expect the post-Swift *Examiner* once more to swing towards the political centre, or at least to shift meaningfully in either tone or content. We shall see if this is what happened.

Swift's immediate successor was not Oldisworth but Delarivier Manley, who collaborated with him on the 14 June issue and then contributed five more issues; her last was 26 July 1711. Manley's essays are comparatively dull; they continue the attack on the Whigs and on the late ministry, but without Swift's sharpness and sense of urgency. Manley's authorship does, however, raise an interesting question. If Swift was removed because Harley was uncomfortable with the paper's shift back to the political right, why would Harley then instal Manley, who was probably involved in the early, ultra-Tory *Examiner*? Soliciting Manley's pen sounds more like the work of St John and Swift than of the Lord Treasurer. In any case, the paper suspended publication in late July and lay dormant for three and a half months. What brings it back to life, and what is the relationship between Oldisworth's *Examiner* and Swift's?

The first of the new *Examiner* papers appeared on 6 December 1711, and the timing is significant. As Oldisworth announces, in a swaggering opening paragraph, he was reviving the journal "upon the Second Meeting of the present Parliament," and he invited his "*Old Adversaries*" to "prepare their Pen and Ink" to contend with him. On 7 December, Parliament sat, and the Whigs scored a major victory against the Ministry. Harley and St John had secretly negotiated a peace treaty with France, which would end England's involvement in the War of the Spanish Succession, but which made what the Whigs believed to be outrageous concessions to the French. From the Whig point of view, the treaty represented a betrayal of England's allies and did not require the Spanish throne to be entirely restored to the house of Austria. The Whig cry of "No peace without Spain" represented an ultimatum, and on 7 December, the Earl of Nottingham carried a vote to that effect in the House of Lords. In the *Journal to Stella*, Swift wrote almost desperately of the "melancholy" turn of events. Nottingham's motion was "carried by the Whigs by about six voices: and this has happened entirely by my lord treasurer's neglect, who did not take timely care to make up all his strength, although every one of us gave him caution enough." Swift describes the "No peace without Spain" vote as "a mighty blow and loss of reputation to lord treasurer," portending that it "may end in his ruin" (p. 340). Swift remained on edge for the rest of the month; on 29 December, he writes giddily, "we are all safe; the queen has made no less than twelve lords to have a majority" (p. 356). Anne's constitutionally dubious manoeuvre saved the Tory peace – allowing the Ministry to proceed with their treating, despite Spain – but only heightened the controversy surrounding the negotiations. For our purposes, the key is that Swift was apprehensive about the parliamentary session, and that the revival of *The Examiner* was manifestly about cultivating support for the outcomes that both Swift and St John favoured.

The major difference between Oldisworth's *Examiner* and Swift's is not fundamental political outlook but focus and subject matter. Swift had written almost exclusively of domestic circumstances, with occasional references to the war and its costs; for Oldisworth, the peace is the principal concern. He is relentless in his defence of the Ministry's treaty, and in his criticism of the war-mongering Whigs and of England's ungrateful allies. Throughout the winter, he assures readers that "Care [has been] taken for every Particular proposed by the several Powers in the Grand Alliance" (II, 4), and laments that the English "might have been a *Rich*, a *Peaceful*, and a *Happy* People, which glorious State they voluntarily exchanged for *Poverty, War*, and *Desolation*" (p. 12). He blames the Whigs for their "Warlike Spirit" (p. 14), and reflects on the bittersweet nature of Marlborough's success: he "hath … been Victorious, but for whom? we are poorer at the end of a ten Years successful War, than we could have been by being only fairly Beaten" (p. 9). Oldisworth highlights the human cost of war (lingering on images of "Men with their Limbs shot off, lying upon the Field" [p. 20]), but his particular gripe is with the fiscal irresponsibility of those who would have England continue to fight.

That Oldisworth advertises, cites, and concurs with, Swift's *Conduct of the Allies* (published in November 1710) is not surprising. On 20 March 1712, he maintains flatly that, "whatever hath been charged upon the Allies, by the Author of the *Examiner*, of *The Conduct*, &c., or any other reasonable Writer, might be proved, beyond all Contradiction." Echoing *The Conduct*, Oldisworth voices outraged incredulity at the exorbitant share England has had to bear, and he attributes any "Disunion of our Allies" to the negligence of the Dutch, by whose "Behaviour they have forced our Nation to shew their Weakness and Inability to support any longer the Burden of the War" (II, 30). The arguments and conclusions correspond to those of Swift, and as Mr Examiner Oldisworth is capable of sounding a good deal like his distinguished predecessor: "AMONG a thousand popular Expressions which have lately been very much used, and very little understood; that of a *Separate Peace* is none of the most Inconsiderable … Are these Gentlemen … really of the Opinion, that when we entered into the War, we obliged our selves never to make Peace, unless when the *Dutch* should be pleased to give us leave?" (p. 42). By July 1712, in the wake of a French victory at Denain that effectively ended Dutch resistance to the Tory peace, the great majority of Anne's subjects were eagerly anticipating peace.

Oldisworth's papers reflect this change: talk of the treaty becomes much less prominent, and he carries out instead a broader indictment of the Whigs. A Tory in religion as well as politics, he targets the freethinkers in general and Anthony Collins in particular (III, 12), and curses the Whigs for "their excessive want of Faith in matters of Religion" (III, 13). He deems the Whigs to be vile in "every Article of their Infidel No-Creed" (IV, 22), recalling Swift's earlier description in *The Examiner* of that group as "a very odd mixture of Mankind," having been "forced to enlarge their Bottom by taking in every Heterodox Professor either in Religion or Government" (p. 314). If we expect the post-Swift *Examiner* to move more towards the political centre, we must be disconcerted by Oldisworth's relentless polarization: "The only true material Distinction of Persons with regard to the Church, is that of its real *Friends*, and its real *Enemies*." The former are "*for*," the latter "*against* their own Native Country" (II, 37). From summer 1712 to summer 1713, Oldisworth disparages Whig populism, Whig hypocrisy, Whig irreligion, Whig history as written by Bishop Burnet, and in general the absurd and pernicious nature of "*Whig-Logick*" (III, 30). By the spring of 1713, he is sparring with Richard Steele, whose *Englishman* (October 1713 - February 1714) was principally devoted to challenging *The Examiner* and to neutralizing High-Church propaganda.

The point here is not to provide an exhaustive analysis of Oldisworth's *Examiner*, but to observe that it represents an effective complement to Swift's coterminous polemics. What Oldisworth's tenure as Mr Examiner makes crystal clear is that Swift was not dismissed so that the paper would sound like someone other than Swift. That Harley removed him in order to re-establish a moderate Tory mouthpiece is highly implausible given the directions in which the paper went after Oldisworth took over, and given that Swift stayed intimately involved with it. As Swift suggested in the *Journal to Stella*, he and St John were instrumental in the revival of *The Examiner*: on 5 December 1711, he announced, "I have got an under spur-leather [Oldisworth] to write an *Examiner* again, and the secretary and I will now and then send hints." If Harley had ordered Swift to step down, Swift and St John would hardly have continued to dictate the contents of the paper. Other explanations for his abandonment of the role are more plausible, including the one he himself proffers: he had become recognizable as Mr Examiner,[42] and ideally the new persona would be "a little upon the Grubstreet, to be a match for [Whig] writers" (pp. 338-39). Conceivably, Swift simply wanted to turn to other kinds of work, to serve the Ministry through his polemical poetry and pamphleteering. Another possibil-

42 In *The Present State of Wit*, Gay had named Swift as the author and listed Atterbury and Prior as his primary assistants (p. 10).

ity is that he was unsettled by the growing rivalry between Harley and St John. There is some chance that *The Examiner* was suffering an identity crisis: its *raison d'être* had been to defend the ministerial change, and by the summer of 1711 that subject could have seemed thoroughly exhausted. Writing in the fall of 1714, Swift explained his decision in vague, evasive, and disingenuous terms: "My stile being soon discovered, and having contracted a great number of enemies, I let [the paper] fall into other hands, who held it up in some manner till her Majesty's death."[43]

Whatever made Swift step down, the notion of a "post-Swift" *Examiner* is misleading. We have no reason to assume that his involvement in the paper ended, and the politics of *The Examiner* were sufficiently consistent from its Swift to its Oldisworth phase that contemporaries continued to connect it with him. Oldmixon would later suggest that Swift, too, was involved in "the First *Examiner*,"[44] suggesting either that the vicar was part of the project from its beginning or that Oldmixon made no distinction between the first and second phases of the paper. The latter seems most probable. Steele never ceased to associate *The Examiner* with Swift, and he made a game out of insinuating Swift's authorship.[45] The anonymous author of *The Publick Spirit of the Tories* (1714) described Swift as "Supervisor to that Weekly Lampoon upon Honesty, the *Examiner*." Oldisworth ("Timothy") is merely "a constant Drudge," whose "Master is labouring in the Vineyard, like an honest Parson, with two or three Friends, and only steps in to help when *Timothy* is at a Loss."[46] In 1735, Oldmixon would record that, "The common Drudge for [the paper] was one *Oldesworth*, an obscure Person; but Mess. *St. John, Swift*, and *Prior*, were Fellow-Labourers in supporting it."[47]

Swift and Oldisworth were seen as allied Tory tools – usually as St John's Tory tools – and though Swift might not have approved of all of his successor's efforts, the content of the paper continued to be what we can safely call 'Swiftian' in many important respects. Oldisworth's *Examiner* represents not a break from but an extension of Swift's, albeit one written in evolving political circumstances and therefore with different emphases and concerns.

43 *Memoirs*, in *Prose Works*, VIII, 124.

44 Oldmixon, *The History of England*, p. 456.

45 Charles A. Knight discusses this at some length in *A Political Biography of Richard Steele* (London: Pickering and Chatto, 2009), pp. 117-19.

46 *The Publick Spirit of the Tories, Manifested in the Case of the Irish Dean, and his Man Timothy* (London: J. Roberts, 1714), pp. 6, 9.

47 Oldmixon, *The History of England*, p. 456.

2.4. *Swift, Oldisworth, and the Tories*

An important context for Swift's and Oldisworth's *Examiner* was what was happening (1711-14) within the Ministry and within the Tory party more broadly. Both Swift and Oldisworth were keen to serve the Tory party, and to varying degrees they each reflected on the tensions within that party. To contemplate the Tory divisions, it is necessary to consider the rivalry between the moderate, Whig-courting, Old Whig Harley and the hot-headed High Church St John, to examine the attitude of Swift's *Examiner* to the Ministry as well as Oldisworth's response as the fissures became more apparent in 1712-14.

A theme of Swift's *Examiner* was that the "Old Whigs" were politically more congruent with his Tories than with the new Whigs, and one has to wonder whether he was – ineffectively – trying to build a bridge between Harley and St John and their respective followers. On 22 March, he professed, "I am not sensible of any material Difference there is between those who call themselves the *Old Whigs*, and a great majority of the present *Tories*" (p. 314), and earlier he had made a similar point: if one examines not an extremist but "a reasonable honest Man of either side, upon those Opinions in Religion and Government, which both Parties daily buffet each other about, he shall hardly find one material Point in difference between them" (p. 37). The impression created by this middle-ground-finding passage is that the ideological differences between two parties – Tories and *proper* Whigs – are not profound. What does Mr Examiner gain by establishing continuity between present-day Toryism and pre-1688 Whiggism? Perhaps, he was trying to augment the legitimacy of the Tory party, or at least to make it more appealing to conservative Whigs, who might wish to dissociate themselves from the modern fanatics sharing their name. Oldisworth would make a similar argument in the later *Examiner*, inviting "the *Old Whigs* [to] consider, how far these degenerate Wretches are gone off from the best Principles of their Forefathers" (III, 2). Later, he addresses the "*Remnant* among the *Whigs* ... who profess to follow their Forefathers," urging them to acknowledge that the "Men, call'd *Tories*" have "answer'd all the great Ends, which even an *Old Whig* could propose for the Security and Repose of the State" (IV, 23).

Swift, like Oldisworth, is clearly trying to make the case that the real successors to the Old Whigs are not the new Whigs but their Tory "rivals." He is waxing moderate, highlighting the reasonableness and widespread currency of a set of conservative, traditional, core ideals, while also trying to divide (and conquer) the Whigs. Mr Examiner's nemesis took exception to this tendency and highlighted its malicious intent. In *Medley* no 18, Mainwaring and Oldmixon complained that *The Examiner* "will, like the rest of the Faction, confound *Whig* and *Tory*, by dividing the Whigs into *Old* and *Modern*; a wicked Distinction invented by their Enemies to ruin those by *Divisions*, they cou'd never have contended with without them" (p. 205). Defoe had raised a similar objection in the *Review* for 26 November 1709: the Tories hope "to make an irreconcilable Breach among the *Whigs*" by introducing "these foolish Distinctions of *Old* Whigs and *New* Whigs," and Mr Review regrets "that these Distinctions have prevail'd so far, and that some are so warm upon the Division, that they cannot see the Hand that divides it."[48]

Swift's objective was straightforward: split the Whigs, unite the Tories. On 1 March, he admits that the Tories are not all like-minded – "*some* are thought too warm and zealous; *others* too cool and remiss" – but grumbles that "these Divisions are industriously fomented by the discarded Faction" (p. 273). He implicitly warns the Tories to stand together: the "Discontent" of those out of power is "apt to breed Differences among those who are in Possession," and the Tories must resist squabbling and pulling apart (p. 274). Over the course of Swift's tenure in the examining role, the divisions within the Tory party became increasingly apparent, and he was anxiously aware of them. The most important conflict was between St John's October Club – High-Church country Tories – and Harley, whom they considered too moderate, too willing to pay court to the Whigs. Harley was in turn suspicious of St John's intensity and extremism. Swift was worrying about these tensions by early 1711. In the *Journal to Stella* for 18 February, he reports that, "We are plagued here with an October Club," and stresses the divide between the Ministry ("for gentler measures") and "the other Tories," who want "more violent" policies (pp. 145, 146). On 27 April, he expresses his apprehension that Harley and his allies "take things ill of Mr. St. John, and by some hints given me from another hand that I deal with, I am afraid the secretary will not stand long." He resolves to "tell [St John] my opinion, and beg him to set himself right, else the consequences may be very bad" (p. 194). By the spring, Harley had regained some of his popularity, and St John had failed to rally the Tory backbenchers against his rival. The rumours that he "would be fortunate to survive as Secretary of State" had clearly reached Swift.[49]

By the end of his reign as Mr Examiner, Swift was evidently seeking, however lamely, to unite the Ministers and the Tories. In the 24 May issue, he appears to be trying to persuade the High-Church interest that Harley is serving them as well: "The Clergy, and whoever else have a true Concern for the Constitution of the Church, cannot but be highly pleas'd with one Prospect in this new Scene of Publick Affairs" (p. 440). Two weeks later, he praises Harley for his effective

48 *Defoe's Review*, ed. John McVeagh (London: Pickering and Chatto, 2003-11), VI, 504, 506.

49 Dickinson, *Bolingbroke*, p. 83.

debt-control measures and for having "obtain'd of Her Majesty a remission of the First Fruits and Tenths to the Clergy of *Ireland*." That last point is clearly meant to endear Harley to men of the October variety; in this *Examiner*, Swift's last, he highlights "my Lord High Treasurer's Concern for Religion" (p. 468). Swift was genuinely frightened when Harley was attacked, and fretted mightily over his recovery; when Harley had previously been indisposed, Swift wrote to Stella, "pray God preserve his health, every thing depends upon it" (p. 154). Perhaps, he also recognized that Harley still held the reins of power; we know from the *Journal* that he was cognizant of St John's precarious position. This sense of conflict between them, or his own ambivalence about with whom to stand, could very well have played a part in Swift's decision to give up *The Examiner*, in which case we would have a resignation, not a dismissal.

Oldisworth was every bit as alarmed as Swift about the state of the Tory party. In January 1714, he praises the "Cause" of the Tories, but targets those among them who "set up against their own Friends." Any Tory who, "at this time of Day especially, endeavours at any thing that may Divide his own Party, or create Misunderstandings between them, takes the shortest, the surest, and the only way to Ruin them" (V, 11). A few weeks later, he complains that "*Quarrels at Court*" are "Judgments ... upon the *Ministry*," and concludes that any "*Tory*, who wishes to Displace any one but a *Whig*, is really a *Whig* of the worst sort" (V, 15). His sentiments are obviously a good deal closer to those of St John than to those of Harley. On 14 May, Mr Examiner takes the present ministry to task for "a plain notorious Mistake in their Conduct" – to wit, that they "have not yet alter'd their gentle Treatment of their Adversaries" (p. 48). In his emphatic rejection of the Whigs, and in his desire to consolidate Tory power, Oldisworth is a fellow traveller of St John's and Swift's. In Swift's response to the collapse of the Tory party (*c.*1712-16), he cited his frustration with Tory passivity: "I have been told, that for two Years past it hath been the Politicks of that Party to let every thing go as it would, without interposing."[50] Oldisworth, writing before the crisis of Anne's death, tried to cultivate a sense of Tory concord: "I remember the Time, when the *Tories* at the Helm, were but a handful of Men, in comparison of the *Whigs*; and yet how Weighty was that *little Body?* What a glorious Stand did they make? ... Such was the Power of Concord and Unanimity" (VI, 2).

That Oldisworth was St John's man is very difficult to deny, and his joining the Scottish Jacobites in 1715 distances him from Harley and Harley's cause only further. Swift, at least as Mr Examiner, was also St John's man, and not just

50 *Correspondence*, ed. Woolley, II, 285. See my "'*fuimus Torys*': Swift and Regime Change, 1714-1718," *Studies in Philology*, 112 (2015), 537-74.

gradually or eventually. At the outset of his examining, he had no need to think of himself as either one politician's or another's, but when the choice needed to be made, he followed the Secretary. Swift's personal dealings with, and his relationship to, his ministerial masters is also important to our speculations about his decision to abandon the role of Mr Examiner.

2.5. *Swift, St John, and Harley*

Our best insight into these connections is the *Journal to Stella*, always, of course, with the caveat that Swift is every bit as playful and elusive in these intimate letters as he is revealing. From December 1710 throughout the spring and early summer of 1711, Swift makes frequent reference to visiting with St John, and the two seem to get along swimmingly. In his encounters with Harley, by contrast, one senses some strain. On 12 December, he reports having been "at the secretary's office" (p. 85). Two days later: "I went to-day to the court of requests ... in hopes to dine with Mr. Harley," but was told that Harley "did not dine at home," so "met with Mr. secretary St. John, and went home and dined with him, where he told me of a good bite" (p. 90). On 22 December, obviously somewhat irked by Harley's constant unavailability, Swift announces, "I am going now to Mr. Harley's Levee on purpose to vex him; I'll say I had no other way of seeing him, &c" (p. 96). Four days later: "I called at Mr. Harley's, who was not within" (p. 101). On 29 December, he recounts an evening with Harley and St John, explaining that after the Lord Treasurer left, the other two spent another hour together: "I took the secretary aside, and complained to him of Mr. Harley, that he had got the queen to grant the First-Fruits, promised to bring me to her, and get her letter to the bishops in Ireland; but the last part he had not done in six weeks, and I was in danger to lose reputation, &c" (p. 103). Though Swift would attribute the First Fruits success to Harley, here he seems to esteem St John a more helpful ally, and two days later he comments that St John "has promised to [get results] in a very few days" (p. 104). On 2 January, St John tells Swift "that the warrant was now drawn, in order for a patent for the First-Fruits ... he assures me 'tis granted and done, and past all dispute, and desires I will not be in any pain at all" (p. 109).

Swift's proximity to St John is clear. Scholars have suggested that both ministers "had a happy knack of avoiding the scrounging Doctor,"[51] but in the *Journal* only Harley's evasiveness is on display. On 5 January, Swift reports, "Mr. secretary St. John sent for me this morning so early that I was forced to go without shaving" (p. 112), and two days later, something similar: "Mr. secretary St. John sent for me this morning in all haste; but I would not lose my shaving"

51 Downie, *Robert Harley and the Press*, p. 131.

(p. 115). The next day Swift announces that he "promised to be with Mr. secretary St. John," but he decides not to oblige; he goes two days later instead (p. 116). On the twelfth, Swift was again "upon some business with Mr. secretary," who "made me promise to dine with him, which otherwise I would have done with Mr. Harley, whom I have not been with these ten days" (p. 118). Swift would be responsible for *The Examiner* for another five months, and yet he already seems fairly distant from his ostensible master. On 25 January, he spends the morning with St John upon "some business" again (p. 130), and yet once more a week later (p. 131). On 4 February, Swift explains that "Mr. Harley reproached me the last time I saw him, that to please me he would be reconciled to Steele, and had promised and appointed to see him, and that Steele never came." The same day he says St John has promised to find a place for Swift's young friend, William Harrison (p. 133). The following night he visited with Harley from six until eleven, and then vowed to Stella, "henceforth I will chuse to visit him in the evenings, and dine with him no more if I can help it. It breaks all my measures, and hurts my health" (p. 134). "It breaks all my measures" might simply be a reflection of their late-night revelling, of a piece with "hurts my health," though on 6 February Swift expresses deeper frustration with the Lord Treasurer. "Mr. Harley desired I would dine with him," he writes, "but I refused him, for I fell out with him yesterday, and will not see him again till he makes me amends" (pp. 134-35).

The falling out had to do with Harley's offering Swift a bank note for £50, a sizeable sum that the vicar evidently refused. Following other scholars, Abigail Williams explains, "Swift was outraged, and refused to visit Harley until ten days later,"[52] but this is not wholly accurate. On 12 February (six days later), he reports sending "Mr. Harley into the house to call the secretary, to let him know I would not dine with him if he dined late" (p. 142). He ended up spending the evening with St John, and perhaps his using Harley as a go-between was meant as a passive-aggressive rebuke, but he did see Harley. On the 15th, he again contemplated and half-attempted to connect with Harley: "I went to the court of requests, thinking if Mr. Harley dined early, to go with him," but others "invited me to dine with them, and away we went" (p. 143). The next day, he and Harley "made up our quarrel;" the following night he dined with Harley and St John together (p. 144), but on the 18th and the 26th, and again on 4 March, he is with St John, not Harley. The 22 April letter explains that "the secretary ... has engaged me for every Sunday" (p. 190). There is a definite trend in this socializing, and, if the *Journal* is to be trusted, in his talking politics and doing 'business' with St John.

---

52 *Journal to Stella*, ed. Abigail Williams, p. 135n14.

His growing distance from Harley seems difficult to deny, between the long gaps in contact and the miscellaneous tensions and reproaches. On 9 February – three days after the £50 incident – Swift tells Stella, with obvious disappointment, that

> Mr. Harley of late has said nothing of presenting me to the queen: – I was overseen [mistaken] when I mentioned it to you. He has such a weight of affairs on him, that he cannot mind all; but he talk'd of it three or four times to me, long before I dropt it to you. (p. 138)

One has to wonder whether the bank note represented an attempt to pull Swift back from St John, a kind of unofficial patronage meant to cultivate loyalty. Whatever Harley's motivations, the *Journal* makes clear that Swift remained much more closely connected to St John, at this point, and that he tended to view the Secretary as a more reliable benefactor. His *Examiner* is more and more in line with St John's politics; he spends more and more time in St John's company; and he and St John appear to have been involved in the continuation of the paper under Oldisworth. This raises the question: what is the evidence suggesting Harley's responsibility for Swift's removal as Mr Examiner?

3. Mr Examiner among the Journalists

The Examiner was enormously influential, a paper that incited the creation of rival journals and fuelled considerable controversy. Addison's *Whig-Examiner* and *The Medley* (authored primarily by Mainwaring with assistance from Oldmixon and Steele) began in response to the pre-Swift *Examiner*; Steele's *Englishman* made Oldisworth's *Examiner* a major target.[53] Anonymous Whig pamphleteers and journalists heaped scorn upon what Mainwaring and Steele called an "*Orthodox* Libel" and a "*Protected* Paper."[54] Opposition commentators voiced much exasperation with the paper, and Steele expressed a sense of piqued futility: "THERE is no Possibility of applying any Remedy to the Evils which this Rascal commits twice a Week."[55] Why the fuss over *The Examiner*, and what can we learn from its critics?

---

53 For more on Steele and Mr Examiner, see my "Steele's Rhetorical Duel with the Authors of *The Examiner*," *Swift Studies*, 34 (2019), forthcoming.

54 *The Medley*, in *Swift vs. Mainwaring*, ed. Ellis, pp. 281, 282 (no 23, which was a collaborative effort); throughout the paper, he denounces "such Scriblers as *Abel* and his Brother" (p. 349).

55 Steele, *The Englishman: Being the Sequel of the "Guardian"* (London: Sam. Buckley, 1714), p. 86. Further quotations are from this edition and are given in parentheses within the text.

Modern scholars have stressed the Harleyite dimension of Swift's *Examiner*, at least in its beginnings, an emphasis helped by associating the paper with Defoe's Whiggish *Review*. Critics are fond of quoting the Whig historian Oldmixon, who in 1715 would reflect that "*Foe* and *Swift* [were] fellow Labourers, in the Service of the *White-Staff*."[56] This association may be challenged,[57] but in any case Oldmixon's pairing is anomalous. The coupling almost all writers make is between Swift and Abel Roper, the editor of the thrice-weekly *Post-Boy*. On 25 September 1712, Oldisworth points out that, "It hath been a very frequent Topick of Wit, among my Brother-Authors of the *Whig* Party, to couple honest *Abel* my Fellow-Labourer and Me together." Oldisworth's observation is accurate. The author of *High-Church Aphorisms* (1711) targeted Mr Examiner and his brother Abel as "Two Political Lyars," twin "*UNDERTAKERS*" who bury "People's *Reputations*" (p. 1). The same language recurs in *Bouchain: In a Dialogue between the Late Medley and Examiner* (published September 1711, after Swift's tenure had ended), the author (possibly Francis Hare) has Mr Examiner refer to "[his] Fellow-Labourer *Abel*" (p. 17). *The Flying-Post* for 3 February 1713 – like Steele, continuing to associate *The Examiner* with Swift – challenges "*Abel* and his Brother the *Examiner*." The Whig paper mocks those Tories who "want nothing but the Sanction of *Abel* and the *Examiner* to publish [anything] as *Gospel*." The connection between *The Examiner* and *The Post-Boy* is one Swift himself announces, proudly, in the *Journal to Stella*: "Roper is my humble Slave" (p. 412). He also contributed to *The Post-Boy*.[58] The point here is that contemporaries emphasized the High-Tory nature of *The Examiner* by linking it with the *Post-Boy*, a paper that has been justly described as "a tool of Bolingbroke, who wrote pieces to be inserted in it and directed many others."[59] Perhaps Oldmixon was trying to damage Defoe by dubbing him a fellow traveller of Mr Examiner's – but in any case, taking his partisan swipe as representative of contemporary judgements is problematic.

Obviously, the Whigs disliked *The Examiner*'s ideological commitments, taking exception to its High-Tory, anti-populist position. In *The Englishman* no 46

56 [John Oldmixon], *The Life and Posthumous Works of Arthur Maynwaring, Esq*; (London: A. Bell, W. Taylor, and J. Baker, 1715), p. 276.

57 Marshall, "Robert Harley and the Politics of Daniel Defoe's *Review*, 1710-1713," forthcoming in *1650-1850*.

58 See *Journal to Stella*, ed. Abigail Williams: "I have been drawi[n]g up a Paragraph for t[h]e Post boy, to be out to morrow, and as malicious as possible, and very proper for Abel Roper th[e] Printer of it" (p. 460).

59 Henry L. Snyder, "The Circulation of Newspapers in the Reign of Queen Anne," *The Library*, 5th ser., 23 (1968), 206-35 (p. 211). In the *Observator* for 10 January 1711, Ridpath linked the *Examiner* to an even higher-flying paper, *The Rehearsal* (referring to Mr Examiner's "Brother *Lesley*").

(first series), Steele asserts that "The true Basis of Government, is the Affection of those who are subject to it," and accuses Mr Examiner and his ilk of seeking "to abate the Warmth of this [principle]" and thus "to destroy the Constitution" (p. 295). *The Medley*, too, challenged its rival's arguments about the basis of power, from the beginning attempting to devalue the core principles contemporaries associated with *The Examiner*. In *Medley* no 3, Mainwaring alludes to "a great deal of Bustle about the *Hereditary*, &c.," deprecating the "dangerous" doctrine promulgated by the Examiner and his "Fellow-Labourers."[60] The cross examinations of *The Examiner* make plain that contemporaries *always* understood it to be a polarizing, High-Church paper alarmingly capable of disseminating ultra-conservative dogma. If they connected the "weekly Libel" with Harleyite moderation, no trace of that association remains.[61]

But objections to *The Examiner* were about more than ideology. As Heinz-Joachim Müllenbrock suggests, "the Examiner's arrogant self-assurance was often denounced by his adversaries," and his paper "became the leading opinion-journal, setting the pace for public debate and relegating the other papers in the Tory interest to a subsidiary role."[62] *The Examiner* does seem to have been uniquely upsetting. Whig critics frequently use words like "libelous," "impudent," "scurrilous," "dull," and "false." Mr Examiner's treatment of Marlborough was, for the Whigs, unconscionable; his remarks on Godolphin, Wharton, and Somers represented the kind of personalized abuse that did not belong in print, at least not in the form of political journalism. The author of *High-Church Aphorisms* includes an epitaph on the late Mr Examiner, one which mimics the defamatory language associated with the paper: "*Thus Insects, that from Dunghills rise, / And are to flies prefer'd, / Descend soon after their Demise, / To their Original a Turd.*"[63] The same author looks back to the original *Examiner*, making no distinction between the pre-Swift and Swift phases of the journal: "*He was to maul the Whigs*. Scandal was the only Thing he pretended to; and knowing he had very little good to say of his Masters that employ'd him, he could do no less than promise to write a great deal of Ill of their Opponents"

60 *The Medley*, in *The Medleys for the Year 1711*, p. 27.

61 Those who connect Harley with the politics of *The Examiner* tend to be trying to brand him more of a High Tory than an Old Whig. This is certainly true for Steele, who generally expresses hostility to Oxford's treatment of Marlborough and who assumes that *The Examiner* is written "under Oxford's direct control" (Knight, *A Political Biography*, p. 141).

62 Heinz-Joachim Müllenbrock, "Swift as a Political Essayist: The Strained Medium," *Reading Swift: Papers from The Second Münster Symposium on Jonathan Swift*, eds Richard H. Rodino and Hermann J. Real, with the assistance of Helgard Stöver-Leidig (Munich: Wilhelm Fink, 1993), pp. 151-58 (157-58).

63 This quotation is at the end of the epitaph, on the last page of prefatory matter.

(p. 3). He goes on to complain that *The Examiner* uses "the only Language that they take pleasure in reading" (p. 13), a language of insolence and contempt. In *Medley* no 23, Mainwaring and Steele had similarly disparaged Swift for passing "Ribaldry ... for Wit," for being "foul-mouth'd" and "scurrilous in an extraordinary degree" (p. 280). To be sure, Swift and the Tories in turn accuse the Whigs of similar impertinence, but the degree of disapprobation with Mr Examiner's audacity is conspicuous. Even the high-flying *Rehearsal* does not warrant so much censure.

What especially infuriates Whig writers is the fact that this "libel" is not only permitted but even endorsed by the Ministry. The author of *Essays Divine, Moral, and Political* (1714) scorns Mr Examiner as "*a Creature of Power, a Spaniel that Fetches and Carries at the Command of his Master*" (p. v).[64] In *The Publick Spirit of the Tories*, the writer marvels at the fact that such a virulent paper "should meet with a Toleration under so excellent a Government" (p. 10), and expresses the country's expectation "that the *Examiner* shou'd be silenced" (p. 12). The pamphleteer behind *Two Letters concerning the Author of the Examiner* (1713) indirectly counsels the Ministry "to bring that Wretch to open Shame and Punishment." Their "Forbearance" is what "has given Occasion to some unthinking Persons to suspect them for the Encouragers, nay the Patrons of this Wretch" (p. 21).[65] This is a constant theme of anti-*Examiner* polemic. In *The Englishman* for 7 November 1713, Steele grumbles that the "unexampled Licence" of "loose Papers" such as this one signifies a more general "Corruption" at Court. Mr Examiner "transgress[es] the Rules of Decency ... with respect to Persons distinguished by high Stations," and, what is worse, Steele supposes the paper to be "supported by a Peer of the Realm" (pp. 96-97).[66] In no 42 of 9 January 1714, Steele includes a "letter" addressed to the Englishman, urging him to "attack" the Examiner: he should not be allowed to take such "indecent Liberty ... with Great Men out of Power," and "if he has any Encouragement from [the Ministry] to demean himself as he does, 'tis illegal and criminal"

64 The *Essays* is obviously targeting Swift throughout, and its author clearly associates him with *The Examiner*, even though this volume appears three years after Swift ceased to be "Mr Examiner."

65 The author of *Two Letters* also highlights the paradoxical nature of Mr Examiner's anonymity, wondering why "he should pretend all along to write for the Ministry, and at the same time labour as much to lie concealed, as if he were set on to assassinate them" (p. 5). For further complaints about *The Examiner*'s being written at the direction of the Ministry, see *Reflections upon the Examiner's Scandalous Peace* (London: A. Baldwin, 1711), p. 3, and *A Letter to the Examiner, Suggesting Proper Heads for Vindicating his Masters* (London: J. Moore, 1714), p. 4.

66 Gay makes this point as well, and goes further: the paper is "look'd on as a sort of publick Notice which way [the Ministers] are steering us" (*The Present State of Wit*, p. 9).

(pp. 273-74). Oldmixon would later reflect similarly, though he specifically faults St John for allowing *The Examiner* to be so egregious. Mainwaring, he recalls, "had a very mean Opinion not only of Mr. *St. John*'s Honesty, but of his Capacity ... and, with very great Indignation, observ'd how he suffer'd the best Men in the Nation to be bely'd, and vilify'd in his *Libel*." And, he continues, Mainwaring "never doubted Mr. *St. John*'s being a main Promoter of that detestable Libel."[67]

Whig writers also attested, unhappily, to the journal's potency. *The Examiner* was from its beginning viewed as toxic. In his *History of England*, Oldmixon describes a conversation with Mainwaring about this new paper: "He began with Complaints of the Villainy and Insolence of the *Examiner*, saying, *It did a World of Mischief*."[68] The Whig answerers, however, did nothing to diminish the journal's effectiveness, which remained considerable well after Swift ceased to be sole author. In *The Englishman* for 15 February 1714, Steele coldly pronounces *The Examiner* to be one of the "Oracles of Policy" (pp. 381-82). The 1715 *Letter to the Examiner*, a Whig polemic, singles out Mr Examiner as a crucial disseminator of Tory opinion: "This is the Man on whom they lay so great a stress; this is him from whom they pick their Argument, whom they quote, whom they refer to: His Papers are sent into every Corner of the Kingdom, received as Oracles" (p. 12). This author links the paper with Oldisworth (p. 17), but also cites his "Master, the *Irish* Dean" (p. 20), presumably hoping that both men will be in difficulties in the new reign, and keen to publicize their utility to the treasonous ministry of Harley and St John.

The critical consensus has been that *The Examiner* was less interesting and less important after Swift 'left' the paper (which never happened). Damrosch's casual dismissal – "carried on for a while, not very well, by others" – is only the most explicit statement of a long-standing assumption. This notion, however, is wrong. Swift continued to pull the strings, to some degree and in some fashion, and contemporaries continued to connect him with the venture. *The Examiner* also remained a powerful Tory outlet, one with which the Whigs continued to do fierce battle and about which they sharply complained well after Anne's death.

The middle phase of *The Examiner*, from November 1710 to June 1711, is, as critics have always argued, different from what preceded and followed, though

67 Oldmixon, *The History of England*, p. 456.

68 Oldmixon, *The History of England*, p. 456. Keith Feiling describes the paper as "the life of Tory politics during the first half of 1711." It "was read aloud to village congregations by country clergy" (*A History of the Tory Party, 1640-1714* [Oxford: Clarendon Press, 1970 {1924}], p. 429). Feiling, like most scholars, focuses solely on the Swift phase of *The Examiner*.

the differences have been significantly overstated, and the presumption that Harley was responsible for removing Swift turns out to seem implausible. This standard explanation also tends to ignore other changes in circumstances. When Swift took control of *The Examiner*, the Tories had just won a massive majority in the general election; that he tried to be less polarizing, and to cultivate the notion of a popular Tory party is not astonishing, and it might or might not have had anything to do with Harley's preferences. Swift stepped down in the summer of 1711, but he was involved in its revival and three-year long continuation, and Oldisworth's *Examiner* looks enough like Swift's, so that contemporaries seemed unaware of any operational change. *The Examiner* of later 1711-14, moreover, functions as a complement to Swift's polemical contributions to ministerial defence and Tory unity. The phases of *The Examiner* would seem to have as much to do with the changing needs of the Tory party as they do with Harley's attempt to wrest control from St John. *The Examiner* never paid court to the Whigs, not for a day, and contemporaries never took it to be anything other than High Tory, a paper with a "great ... Reputation among *Churchmen*."[69] If Swift were assigned by Harley "to take the wind out of tory sails,"[70] then we can only conclude that he failed. And if Harley removed him because the paper had fallen under St John's influence, the installation of first Manley and then the Jacobite Oldisworth is utterly inexplicable. There is, in point of fact, very little solid evidence connecting Harley to the management of *The Examiner* – nothing like what we have to associate him with the inception of the *Review*. We have, on the contrary, excellent reasons to see *The Examiner* as St John's project, and thus to rethink Swift's complicated and frustratingly obscure relationship with the Ministry during the fraught last years of Queen Anne's reign.[71]

69 *The Thoughts of a Tory Author, concerning the Press* (London: A. Baldwin, 1712), p. 3.

70 Downie, *Robert Harley and the Press*, p. 135.

71 For advice on earlier drafts of this essay, I am grateful to Rob Hume and Ron Paulson.

CHRISTOPHER J. FAUSKE
Salem State University

The Quietude of Establishment: On Jonathan Swift, the Irish House of Lords, and the Established Church

> I regard the establishment [of the Church] as a nonsense in philosophy and theology and as impracticable in every other way ... nothing to do with religion and everything to do with shoring up a particular concept of national life.
>
> DONALD SOPER[1]

ABSTRACT. Throughout Jonathan Swift's life and writings there can be found a consistent and principled adherence to the idea that the church is a divine creation functioning as best it can in a political state. Swift's writings and the topics upon which he chose to say nothing or little all demonstrate an understanding that, finally, the church could have an authority outside the state and that the church-state compact was a negotiated, revocable contract rather than an inviolable natural state. In making this case, the essay particularly considers the "Ode to Dr William Sancroft," the *Letter concerning the Sacramental Test, Some Arguments against Enlarging the Power of Bishops*, and the nature of Swift's comments on the Irish House of Lords in general.

Before he became Dean of St Patrick's, Dublin, Jonathan Swift had been vicar of the united parishes of Kilroot, Ballynure, and Templecorran, with their almost non-existent congregations and their three churches in various stages of disrepair, only the one at Templecorran being even remotely usable. Surrounded by Presbyterians, Swift could almost look across the water to the Rhins of Galloway and see Scotland, where the 'saviour' of the Irish Protestants, William of Orange, now William III of England and therefore also King of Scotland and of Ireland, had done nothing to preserve the Episcopal Church, whose bishops had unanimously chosen to respect their oath to James VII. To the south of Kilroot were the united dioceses of Kilmore and Ardagh, whose diocesan, William Sheridan (1636-1711), was Ireland's only Nonjuror bishop.[2]

* This essay expands on the paper presented at the Seventh Münster Symposium by incorporating some remarks made the previous week at the celebration of Swift's 350th birthday held at Trinity College, Dublin.

1 Donald Oliver Soper, Baron Soper, interviewed by Walter Schwarz, "Lord of the Soapbox," *The Guardian*, 28 January 1993; reprinted in *The Bedside Guardian 42* (London: Fourth Estate, 1993), p. 106 (ellipsis in original).

2 *Correspondence*, ed. Woolley, IV, 37n3; see also DIB, s.v. "Sheridan, William."

 | DOI:10.30965/9783846763971_019

Once he was Dean, Swift lived close by William King, Archbishop of Dublin, the senior Irish-born cleric of the Church of Ireland.[3] King, along with Samuel Foley (1655-95), later briefly Bishop of Down and Connor,[4] had been one of the two inexperienced and relatively junior clerics left in charge of the Church of Ireland in Dublin after senior clergy fled when James made the city the headquarters of his campaign against William of Orange.[5] Assessing the situation, King had considered what a Jacobite victory would mean for his church if bishoprics were left unfilled as a result of the monarch's refusal to nominate successors to vacancies. We "ought to keep up their succession [and] break the correspondence between the church and state," he wrote.[6] Should such a rupture come to pass, King envisioned drawing comfort from knowing that the Church of Ireland would be in a similar position to "the primitive Christians ... under the heathen emperors."[7]

Swift, of course, would use the era of the "heathen emperors" to great effect in his brilliant savaging of *Mr. Collins's Discourse of Free-thinking*:

> [*Varro*] says ... there are many Things false in Religion ... *Which the Vulgar ought not to know, but it is Expedient they should believe*. In this last he indeed discovers the whole Secret of a Statesman and Politician, by denying the Vulgar the Priviledge of *Free-thinking* ...
>
> The Grave and Wise *Cato* the Censor ... [wondered how one priest could] forbear laughing when he [saw] another ... This shews that *Cato* understood the whole Mystery of the *Roman* Religion, *as by Law Established*. I beg you Sir, not to overlook these last Words, *Religion as by Law Established*.[8]

---

3 See Christopher Fauske, *A Political Biography of William King* (London: Pickering and Chatto, 2011), pp. 11-46.

4 In addition to DIB, s.v. "Foley, Samuel," see Richard Mant, *History of the Church of Ireland* (London: John W. Parker, 1840), pp. 43-44, and K. Theodore Hoppen, *The Common Scientist in the Seventeenth Century: A Study of the Dublin Philosophical Society, 1683-1708* (Charlottesville, Virginia: The University Press of Virginia, 1970), pp. 38-39.

5 See J. G. Simms, *Jacobite Ireland, 1685-91* (London: Routledge and Kegan Paul, and Toronto: University of Toronto Press, 1969), pp. 62-66, 84-85, 95-100, and *passim*; see also the essays by James McGuire and Harman Murtagh in *Kings on Conflict: The Revolutionary War in Ireland and its Aftermath, 1689-1750*, ed. W. A. Maguire (Belfast: The Blackstaff Press, 1990), pp. 45-57, 61-91.

6 Quoted in Andrew Carpenter, "William King and the Threats to the Church of Ireland during the Reign of James II," *Irish Historical Studies*, 18 (1972), 22-28 (p. 25).

7 Quoted in Carpenter, "William King and the Threats to the Church of Ireland," p. 25.

8 Jonathan Swift, *Mr. C---ns's Discourse of Free-thinking, Put into Plain English, by Way of Abstract, for the Use of the Poor* (London: John Morphew, 1713), in *Prose Works*, IV, 27-48 (p. 43).

The emphasis Swift places here on those "last Words, *Religion as by Law Established*" was not accidental.

The actions of the Scottish bishops and of Sheridan, as well as the analysis of King and Foley, clearly indicated a strong strain of thought within establishment clergy that the church-state compact was not, ultimately, an inviolable requirement of divine law but a political creation, and Swift's remarks on various occasions indicate he was well aware of this train of thought. There was, however, one potentially crucial difference between the position of the Scottish bishops and Sheridan and that contemplated by King. The Scots, Sheridan, and, indeed, all the British Nonjurors had lost state sanction by refusing oaths of loyalty rather than by acting pre-emptively, as King had considered might be necessary.

A little more than 250 years later, Eivind Berggrav, Bishop of Oslo at the time of the German occupation, wrote a letter on behalf of all Norwegian bishops announcing their individual and unanimous resignations from governmental responsibilities, which they had previously held it their duty to perform in accordance with several articles in The Hague Conventions explicating the expected conduct of civil administrators in an occupied country. While continuing to exercise their official duties during the first 20 months of the occupation, the bishops had consistently asserted their demand that both the German authorities and Vidkun Quisling's government behave with respect for the law and the place of the church in it. When it became clear that those demands were being ignored, Berggrav's statement of action and justification was clear:

> The Spiritual calling which has been ordained to me at the altar of God remains mine, by God and by right ... [But] the moment has arrived in which we must follow our convictions, and maintain the right of the Church against the injustice of the State. The form of the State may change ... [but] woe to us if we were not to obey God more than man.[9]

The views of the Archbishop with whom he had so complex a relationship and those of a later Norwegian bishop essentially mirror the view of Jonathan Swift about the political nature of the church-state compact.

Soon after King had envisioned the possible separation of the Church of Ireland from the Irish state, Swift was in England working on a poem remarkable

9 Eivind Berggrav, "Letter of Resignation Sent by Each Bishop to the Minister for Church and Education, 24 February 1942," Appendix 3, *With God in the Darkness by Eivind Berggrav, and Other Papers Illustrating the Norwegian Church Conflict*, eds George Bell and H. M. Adams (London: Hodder and Stoughton, 1943), pp. 90-93 (93). The significance of this resignation of state functions was not trivial as Berggrav had earlier been instrumental in arguing that the non-military functions of the Norwegian state should continue under German occupation.

for its idealism in the face of political reality. The "Ode to Dr William Sancroft, Late Lord Archbishop of Canterbury" was, Swift reported, written at the request of Francis Turner, the Nonjuror bishop of Ely.[10] "Dr Sancroft [is] a gentleman I admire at a degree more than I can express," he told his cousin Tom Swift on 3 May 1692, when the likelihood of a Jacobite victory in either England or Ireland had been reduced to zero.[11] The poem was unpublished in Swift's lifetime and the adjective "late" in front of Sancroft's title was apparently added by an editor prior to its 1789 publication, more likely referring not to Sancroft's dispossession but to the fact that he was dead. For Swift, Sancroft remained archbishop *de jure* if not *de facto*. Indeed, Swift would revere Sancroft's memory throughout his life, and one of the most strident notes among his numerous marginalia is his rejection of Gilbert Burnet's accusation that during James II's reign Sancroft "lay silent at Lambeth ... of such a timorous temper and so set on the enriching his nephew, that he shewed no sort of courage." This was, Swift wrote, a calumny as "false as hell."[12]

Sixteen years later, writing the 1708 *Letter concerning the Sacramental Test* attacking the proposed repeal of the Test Act in Ireland, Swift directly confronted the government he was then lobbying for the remission of the First Fruits and Twentieth Parts.[13] Withering sarcasm aside, Swift was clear that his main concern was the preservation of the Church of Ireland in the face of political attack from within the status quo, as, for example, when he remarked upon

> an honest *Bell-weather** of our House (you have him now in *England*, I wish you could keep him there) [who] had the Impudence, some Years ago, in Parliament Time, to shake my Lord Bishop of *Killaloo* by his Lawn Sleeve, and tell him in a threatening Manner, *That he hoped to live to see the Day, when there should not be one of his Order in the Kingdom*.[14]

---

10 "Ode to Dr William Sancroft," *Poems*, ed. Rogers, pp. 60-67 and 609-11.

11 Swift to Thomas Swift, 3 May 1692, *Correspondence*, ed. Woolley, I, 110.

12 *Prose Works*, V, 285.

13 Swift's *Correspondence* is studded with references to this mission on behalf of the Church of Ireland; see V: The Index, s.v. See also, in addition to Ehrenpreis, *Dr Swift*, pp. 225-29, Christopher Fauske, *Jonathan Swift and the Church of Ireland, 1710-1724* (Dublin: Irish Academic Press, 2002), pp. 27-33, and John Irwin Fischer, "Learning '*David*'s Lesson': Some New Information concerning the Remission of First Fruits and Twentieth Parts in Ireland," *Swift Studies*, 1 (1986), 15-23.

14 *Prose Works*, II, 109-26 (p. 117). The bellwether is presumed to have been Alan Broderick, Speaker of the Irish House of Commons. The Bishop of Killaloe was Thomas Lindsay, later Primate of All Ireland (Mant, *History of the Church of Ireland*, pp. 262-63, 267-68, 407-8; DIB, V, 509-10).

Unlike the *Argument to Prove that the Abolishing of Christianity in England May … Be Attended with Some Inconveniences* published earlier that year,[15] the *Letter concerning the Sacramental Test* is not about manners nor about doctrine, but about something far more critical: the very nature of church-state relations; and it takes as its starting point the position that the church is more important than the state, which should go about its secular business as it sees fit, but only so far as that business does not threaten the well-being of the church.

Consider the 1723 tract offering *Some Arguments against Enlarging the Power of Bishops, in Letting of Leases.*[16] This pamphlet achieved the remarkable effect of causing William Nicolson, the most strident of the English administration's advocates among the Church of Ireland bishops, to suggest that the work be "allow'd to atone for a multitude of [Swift's] bypast Transgressions."[17] Swift was opposing a bill proposed by the Irish House of Commons to align Irish law with English and Welsh law, which allowed bishops to make an immediate profit by offering extended leases of their land with a large down payment, while limiting the amount by which rent could later be increased. One example in a tract that stands out among Swift's works for its hard-headed, coolly reasoned logic is the retelling of an observation by, of all people, Gilbert Burnet, that "the Liberty which Bishops in *England* have of Letting Leases for Lives, would … be one Day the Ruin of Episcopacy."[18]

Such was Swift's great concern for the foundations of his church that one of his very first attempts at writing was a defence of the most notable of all the Nonjuror bishops. Later, in the midst of lobbying for significant financial relief in aid of his impoverished church, he turned his vitriol on the very government that could grant that relief, and, later still, he co-opted the insight of a man he despised to demonstrate the wisdom of the entire Irish bench of bishops in acting, almost uniquely, as one in opposing a bill popular with the bulk of the lay patrons of his church. When he had to choose, Swift did so with precision and certainty; and he always chose church over state.

So precise was Swift's analysis that he understood, too, that, while not always the case, the Church of Ireland as a political proposition often had one last bastion on its side in Ireland.

---

15 *Prose Works*, II, 26-39.

16 *Prose Works*, IX, 43-60.

17 William Nicolson, Bishop of Derry, to William Wake, Archbishop of Canterbury, quoted in Louis A. Landa, *Swift and the Church of Ireland* (Oxford: Clarendon Press, 1954), p. 99.

18 *Some Arguments against Enlarging the Power of Bishops*, in *Prose Works*, IX, 52.

Not long after his installation as Dean of St Patrick's, Dublin, Swift described himself as "obscurely here alone / Where [he was] neither lov'd nor known."[19] "At my first coming" to be installed, he had written, "I thought I should have dyed with Discontent."[20] Swift was not being entirely disingenuous in either case. Years later, he would write to Robert Harley, Earl of Oxford, "I have the fewest acquaintance[s] in this kingdom of any man who is condemned to live in it. I am hated mortally by every creature in power."[21] Given these sentiments, and even allowing for a significant degree of dissembling, it is hardly surprising that the Dean would on occasion lace his opinion on matters of public debate with a vitriol not fully justified by the facts. Yet there was one part of the Irish political establishment about which, more often than not, he essentially held his tongue: the Irish House of Lords.

It was the Upper House that could, and did, at times act as an institution to protect and promote the welfare of the church-state compact, a role recent history had shown both the Crown and the Irish House of Commons were all too happy to forsake. While in London in 1711 enmeshed in Tory politics, Swift had heard from a correspondent in Ireland:

> Perhaps it will not be ungrateful to you, to know our session of Parliament ended on Friday last. We threw out, in the House of Lords, two bills ... and voted an address, in opposition to the Commons address about Revolution principles. We likewise burned Mr. Stoughton's sermon ... After this, we burned Mr. Boyse's book of A Scriptural Bishop; and some *Observators* ... I forgot to tell you, we agreed to another address against Dissenting ministers, and their twelve hundred pounds per annum.[22]

That was the House of Lords acting as Swift – and others – thought it should, as a check upon those with 'revolutionary principles,' Dissenters, and the otherwise dissolute.

When the Upper House failed in that role Swift did not spare it, but even then he generally reserved his criticism for the private sphere as in his scathing letter to Charles Ford after passage in Westminster of the Act for the Better Securing the Dependency of the Kingdom of Ireland on the Crown of Great Britain, better known to all as the Declaratory Act.[23] He prefaced his comments to Ford on the bill with the observation that he believed himself "not

19 "In Sickness," *Poems*, ed. Williams, I, 203.
20 Swift to Esther Vanhomrigh, 8 July 1713, *Correspondence*, ed. Woolley, I, 513.
21 Swift to Robert Harley, Earl of Oxford, 28 April 1730, *Correspondence*, ed. Woolley, III, 305.
22 Archbishop King to Swift, 10 November 1711, *Correspondence*, ed. Woolley, I, 393.
23 An Act for the Better Securing the Dependency of the Kingdom of Ireland on the Crown of Great Britain (6 Geo. I, c. 5).

guilty of too much veneration for the Irish H – of L[ord]s."[24] But he had not too little veneration, either. One might put this down to some sort of snobbery: relative silence over the House of Lords, withering scorn, more often than not, about the Commons. But something far more significant was at work, an ideal of the state constitution as it should have worked and, in his mind at least, still on occasion did.

Swift venerated one English monarch above all others, that sometime saint of the Church of England, Charles, King and Martyr.[25] Whatever his thoughts on the historical accuracy of the matter, Swift embraced the propaganda value of the idea that "Had Charles been willing to abandon the Church, and give up Episcopacy, he might have saved his throne and his life. But on this point Charles stood firm; for this he died, and by dying saved it for the future."[26] That

24 Swift to Charles Ford, 4 April 1720, *Correspondence*, ed. Woolley, II, 327.

25 I make no attempt to judge the various current and historical claims as to Charles's exact status following the 1660 convocations of Canterbury and York, which canonized "Charles, King and Martyr" (see, among others, S. J. Connolly, "The Church of Ireland and the Royal Martyr: Regicide and Revolution in Anglican Political Thought, *c.*1660-*c.*1745," *Journal of Ecclesiastical History*, 54 [2003], 484-506; Howard D. Weinbrot, "Swift's Thirtieth of January Sermon: Politics, the Pulpit, and the Choice of Strife," *Reading Swift: Papers from The Fifth Münster Symposium on Jonathan Swift*, ed. Hermann J. Real [Munich: Wilhelm Fink, 2008], pp. 225-44). Services for Charles on his prayer day, 30 January, were not one of the required state services although often assumed to be, and were authorized by royal proclamation issued at the start of each monarch's reign from Charles II to Victoria. With the omission of thc state services from the 1859 printing of the Book of Common Prayer (an action taken without the consent of Convocation) the observance of the day, already in decline, plunged further.

Just as an individual's take on Luke 14:23 offers some insight into his attitude towards Dissenters, so one indication of a cleric's sympathies can be found in his perspective in a sermon preached upon the subject of the martyrdom of King Charles I. For more on the subject, see Andrew Lacey, *The Cult of King Charles the Martyr* (Woodbridge: Boydell Press, 2003). For some indication of the sentiment of those faithful in their observation of the martyrdom, see the web page of The Society of King Charles the Martyr, "which has a history dating back to the 19th century … The origins of the Society can be traced back more specifically to when the Feast of S. Charles was unjustly removed [from] the Kalendar of The Prayer Book. The Society was founded in 1894 as 'a Church Defence Union under the banner of the Martyr-King' and its initial prime objective was 'intercessory prayer for the defence of the Church of England against the attacks of her enemies.' Since its founding the work and objectives of the Society have broadened into a wider devotional society with its continuance in the tradition of Catholic Anglicanism" (<http://skcm.org/about-skcm/>, accessed 23 April 2017).

26 Creighton Mandell, "Laud's Position in the History of the Early English Church," *Archbishop Laud Commemoration, 1895: Lectures on Archbishop Laud, together with a Bibliography of Laudian Literature and the Laudian Exhibition Catalogue*, ed. William Edward Collins (London: Allhallows Barking, 1895), pp. 3-26 (25).

this claim ignores Charles's offer to suspend episcopacy in England in return for Scottish military assistance mattered not to later proponents of Charles's virtuous integrity.[27]

It had been the English House of Commons that had fermented the civil war that led to regicide. They

> had first turned the bishops out of the House of Lords; in a few years after, they murdered their King; then immediately abolished the whole House of Lords; and so, at last, obtained their wishes, of having a government of the people, and a new religion, both after the manner of Geneva, without a king, a bishop, or a nobleman; and this they blasphemously called, the kingdom of Christ and his saints.[28]

Swift was clear that because

> the children of the murdered Prince were forced to fly, for the safety of their lives, to foreign countries … one of them, at least, I mean King James II, was seduced to Popery; which ended in the loss of his kingdoms, the misery and desolation of this country, and a long and expensive war abroad. Our deliverance was owing to the valour and conduct of the late King; and therefore, we ought to remember him with gratitude, but not mingled with blasphemy or idolatry. It was happy that his interests and ours were the same … But, as a house thrown down by a storm is seldom rebuilt without some change in the foundation; so it hath happened, that since the late Revolution, men have sate much looser in the true fundamentals both of religion and government, and factions have been more violent, treacherous, and malicious than ever, men running naturally from one extreme into another; and, for private ends, taking up those very opinions professed by the leaders in that rebellion, which carried the blessed Martyr to the scaffold.[29]

The exceptions were the Irish-born bishops of the Church of Ireland, all of whom sat in the Irish House of Lords, from whence they conducted a variety of holding actions designed to prevent or delay any further depredations of establishment rights. That on occasion they had enough allies among the Irish

27 It is, as they say, complicated. Charles had earlier sought to re-impose episcopacy on Scotland, expanding on the minor concessions James I/VI had secured for Scottish episcopalianism. However, "in forming his Scottish policies, Charles relied on anglicized Scots, such as the Marquis of Hamilton and the Earl of Lennox … In doing so he fatally damaged the already weak institution of Scottish episcopacy by yoking it to a hated alien form of worship" (Charles Carlton, *Charles I: The Personal Monarch*, 2nd ed. [London: Routledge, 1995], p. 195).

28 Swift, "A Sermon upon the Martyrdom of K. Charles I," *Prose Works*, IX, 219-31 (p. 223).

29 Swift, "A Sermon upon the Martyrdom of K. Charles I," *Prose Works*, IX, 224.

lay peers,[30] or, more often than Swift cared to admit, among the English-born bishops, made it critical for him not to undermine the credibility of the House of Lords as a whole, as he was willing to do that of the House of Commons, composed of those who would "Tear the Bible all to Pieces," who were "Footman, Traytor, vile Seducer, / Perjur'd Rebel, brib'd Accuser" and "Sprung from Papists and a Regicide."[31]

Ironically, given the execution of Archbishop William Laud, the cult of Charles, King and Martyr, was essentially Laudian in character and distinctly High Church. The Church of Ireland still enjoyed protections granted by Charles I, many of which had been lost by the Church of England in the aftermath of 1688. In the period of his great silence in Dublin before the appearance of the *Proposal for the Universal Use of Irish Manufacture* (1720), Swift had written to Bolingbroke, reminding him to "Think upon Lord Bacon, Williams, Strafford, Laud, Clarendon, Shaftesbury, the last Duke of Buckingham ... All great geniuses in their several ways, [who], if they had not been so great, would have been less unfortunate."[32] Swift, of course, included Harley and Bolingbroke himself in that list, but the inclusion of Laud in a roll call of names not typically linked with his was surely no accident, and it could hardly have been designed to flatter in a conventional manner Bolingbroke, whose religious leanings were such that Samuel Johnson famously defined irony thus, "A mode of speech in which the meaning is contrary to the words: as, *Bolingbroke was a holy man.*"[33]

As Dean, Swift increased the frequency of Holy Communion in his cathedral and encouraged other practices Laud had advocated in order to distinguish the Church from an encroaching Presbyterianism. As Laud had done, he staunchly defended the requirement that those holding civil office had to conform to the Established Church and that the proper test of this was to be found in more than the occasional taking of communion.[34]

In Swift's surviving sermons, we find evidence of this Laudian bent, as in his remarks *On Brotherly Love*, a sermon probably preached in response to

---

30 Sources on the composition, attendance, and voting habits of the Irish Houses of Parliament in this period are numerous and diverse. Robert E. Burns provides a useful introductory study in his *Irish Parliamentary Politics in the Eighteenth Century*, 2 vols (Washington, DC: The Catholic University of America Press, 1989-90).

31 "A Character, Panegyric, and Description of the Legion Club," *Poems*, ed. Williams, III, 827-39 (pp. 831-32).

32 Swift to Viscount Bolingbroke, 19 December 1719, *Correspondence*, ed. Woolley, II, 316.

33 Samuel Johnson, *A Dictionary of the English Language*, 2 vols (London: J. and P. Knapton, *et al.*, 1755), I, s.v. "Irony."

34 *Prose Works*, II, 102-3; VII, 16, 18, 21.

John Evans, the Bishop of Meath, who in the commemoration service on 5 November 1717 had articulated a broadly latitudinarian position that included that great anathema of Church of Ireland purists, recognizing marriages performed by Dissenting ministers. Swift responded to Evans's sermon with something close to fury:

> This Nation of ours hath for an Hundred Years past, been infested by two Enemies, the Papists and Fanaticks, who, each in their Turns, filled it with Blood and Slaughter, and for a Time destroyed both the Church and Government. The Memory of these Events hath put all true Protestants equally upon their Guard against both these Adversaries, who, by Consequence, do equally hate us.[35]

One other great failing of the State towards the Church of Ireland, as Swift saw it, was the repeated failure after 1713 to issue a writ of Convocation along with the writ of Parliament. The Convocations of 1709 and 1713 had been futile and marred by infighting. That of 1711 occupied itself with attacks upon Dissenting doctrine and practice, with an expression of concern about popery tacked on at the end almost as a pro forma matter.[36] With Convocation a dead issue after 1714, although he continued to protest at it not being summoned, Swift also saw in the Irish House of Lords the last repository of Church of Ireland self-governance. Individual bishops he would, on occasion, castigate, and with Bishop Evans he would never make peace,[37] but as a corporate body and as an interest group in Parliament, Swift was enormously reluctant to attack them. It was, however, not just as a matter of politics that Swift was quiet about the bishops; there was a deeper principle underlying his position.

For Swift, the separation of the Nonjurors from the main body of the church was to be regretted, but it was significant that they had withdrawn themselves from the fray, maintaining, essentially, a silent observation of a common faith, using the same creed, the same prayer book, the same calendar as the Established Church, differing only in their view of the relationship between the Crown and the Church. They had also gone quietly from their livings, renouncing their incomes without appeal to Court, Parliament, or the mob. The Nonjurors had retired; they had not sought revolution. Significantly, too, as the Nonjuring bishops began to die and the survivors decided to preserve

35 *Prose Works*, IX, 169-79 (p. 172).

36 David Hayton, "High Churchmen in the Irish Convocation," *Reading Swift: Papers from The Third Münster Symposium on Jonathan Swift*, eds Hermann J. Real and Helgard Stöver-Leidig (Munich: Wilhelm Fink, 1998), pp. 117-40.

37 See *Correspondence*, ed. Woolley, II, 306 and n2, 381 and n2; Ehrenpreis, *Dean Swift*, pp. 49-58.

episcopal succession by appointing new bishops, the two bishops selected to continue the unbroken line of succession from St Peter took the titles of Bishop of Thetford and Bishop of Ipswich, both sees created by the Suffragan Bishops Act 1534 (26 Hen 8 c 14) but unfilled since the sixteenth century, underlining the fact that the Nonjurors were not outwardly challenging the existing church.

But in 1713 matters changed. George Hickes, the former Dean of Worcester, who had been consecrated Bishop of Thetford, was the last surviving Nonjuror bishop. Rather than allow the episcopal succession to end with him, he travelled north and persuaded two of the bishops of the non-established Episcopal Church in Scotland to join him in consecrating a new generation of Nonjuror bishops. For many, this represented a fundamental shift in tone. Hickes and Thomas Wagstaffe, Nonjuring Bishop of Ipswich, had been consecrated by bishops who had been approved by the then-monarch as head of the Church. Hickes and the two Scottish bishops had not themselves been subject to royal approval, and their actions marked a transition from passive disobedience to active resistance, from silent withdrawal to outright schism. King's proposal about continuing the succession of bishops in the event of James winning the struggle against William would, of course, have led in time to the same situation, as had happened in Scotland as the first generation of non-establishment bishops died out. But, crucially, at the same time as Hickes travelled north, debate began within the remaining Nonjuror movement about changing doctrinal and liturgical practices to move the group closer either to Roman Catholicism or to Eastern Orthodoxy, depending on the proposal. By the time of the failure of the 1715 rising, the last vestige of establishment sympathy for the newer expressions of the Nonjury movement had passed.[38]

In late 1716, Swift reported to King of news reaching Dublin of "a Parcel of obscure Zealots in London, who, as we hear, are setting up a new Church of England by themselves … it seems to be a Complication of as much Folly, Madness, Hypocrisy, and Mistake, as ever was offered to the World."[39] In response, King excoriated the position of Hickes and his cohort, who held, the Archbishop wrote, that

38 For more on the Nonjurors, see Ernest Gordon Rupp, *Religion in England, 1688-1791* (Oxford: Clarendon Press, 1986), pp. 5-28. Among other useful works for placing the Nonjurors in context are G. V. Bennett, *The Tory Crisis in Church and State, 1688-1730: The Career of Francis Atterbury, Bishop of Rochester* (Oxford: Clarendon Press, 1975), and John William Charles Wand, *The High Church Schism* (New York: Morehouse-Gorham, and London: The Faith Press, 1951).

39 Swift to Archbishop King, 13 November 1716, *Correspondence*, ed. Woolley, II, 187.

> all persons owe allegiance to the pretender under pain of damnation …
> … That the revolution is founded on the doctrine that Resistance is lawfull, & that B may be deprived by meer lay power, wch are Heresyes …
> … That w^{n} a Kingdom is conquered by a greater power, the subjects are not to make the best conditions with the conqueror they can, but rather suffer all their throats to be cut, than own him.[40]

Plainly, Hickes's position was Jacobite and had moved far beyond the position taken by Sancroft, Sheridan, and the other first-generation Nonjurors.

King's remarks on Hickes contrast with his attitude towards Sheridan, whose refusal to recognize William and Mary as *de jure* monarchs would later earn him praise from Richard Mant, an English-born cleric who became Bishop of Down, Connor, and Dromore and a passionate defender of the Church of Ireland's self-proclaimed historical identity. Sheridan, Mant wrote, in terms that echo those Swift had used about Sancroft, "retaliated the injuries inflicted on him from his late sovereign [James] by a faithful and immoveable allegiance."[41] The Bishop of Kilmore and Ardagh left Ireland upon his refusal to take the oaths and retired to London, where he lived in increasing penury and, most importantly, in political silence. His poverty was relieved occasionally by the efforts of Church of Ireland bishops. In February 1704, for example, King wrote to Bartholomew Vigors, Bishop of Ferns, reporting: "Bishop Sheridan has been with me: he is exceeding poor and crazy. It is not fit one of our order should be exposed to begging. I hope the lords the bishops will remember him, as they did last year: pray subscribe for me 10*l.* as I did before."[42] The continued use of the title and the recognition of Sheridan as "one of our order" are testament to the understanding of those who had shepherded the Church of Ireland through the years of James that the principled alternative to an at times uncomfortable passive obedience was not outright resistance but passive disobedience.

Sheridan's actions, and post-withdrawal-to-London silence, had an impact that likely surpassed expectations. A 1697 attempt in the Irish parliament to impose an oath of abjuration renouncing the Stuart claims to the throne (as was already on the books in England and Wales, and in Scotland) was virulently opposed by all four archbishops of the Church of Ireland. It was Sheridan's courage that seems to have motivated this surprisingly principled stand: "These prelates," one historian writes, "were men who cared for the moral nature of

40 Archbishop King to Swift, 2 November 1716, *Correspondence*, ed. Woolley, II, 191.

41 Richard Mant, *History of the Church of Ireland, II: From the Revolution to the Union of the Churches of England and Ireland, January 1, 1801* (London: John W. Parker, 1840), p. 28.

42 Mant, *History of the Church of Ireland*, II, 29.

the Church, and ... the non-juring movement was a powerful witness to this nature."[43]

For both King, who had supported Sheridan financially, and for Swift, who had so admired Sancroft, the first-generation Nonjurors were men of principle, quiet witnesses to their own conscience. The second-generation were rebels, seeking through agitation and propaganda to disrupt the status quo. Indeed, one might look to the post-World War II British Labour politician Tony Benn (1925-2014) for clarification of the difference between Sheridan and Hickes, between the man of faith and the advocate of change: "A faith is something you die for; a doctrine is something you kill for. There is all the difference in the world."[44]

The Church of Ireland had largely avoided the Nonjuror disruption, but its hold on the levers of power in Ireland was otherwise shakier than in England, and so it was, Swift held, vital for the Church to preserve a united front. The Dean had his disputes with the vicars choral.[45] The vicar of Laracor had disputes with his superior. But he kept these arguments in-house, however vociferous and doctrinaire his language might have been. The 'Irish patriot' issued anguished pleas on behalf of a variety of constituencies, and he condemned all manner of Irish House of Commons or British parliamentary undertakings, but about measures in the Irish House of Lords he generally either held his tongue or, when he could, spoke in support of the bishops' position, as in the 1723 *Arguments against Enlarging the Power of Bishops*.

Swift's opening gambit in the tract is not just rhetorical; it captures the heart of his appreciation of the role which the Irish House of Lords was the last to practice: "Those ... who profess themselves Members of the Church established, and under the Apostolical Government of Bishops, do desire the Continuance and Transmission of [that church] to Posterity, at least, in as good a Condition as it is at present."[46]

The Irish House of Commons Swift had less time for, and his indignation and contempt reached its peak with his attack upon "a Building large and lofty, / Not a Bow-shot from the College, / Half the Globe from Sense and

43 Robert H. Murray, "The Church and the Revolution," *History of the Church of Ireland from the Earliest Times to the Present Day*, ed. Walter Alison Phillips, 3 vols (London: Oxford University Press, 1933), III, 165.

44 Tony Benn, the Rt Hon., MP, BBC Television, 11 April 1989 [most likely *Newsnight*, 22:20, BBC Two], cited in Michael Holmes, *Dying to Know* ([London], 2005), p. 25.

45 See *Correspondence*, ed. Woolley, I, 576 and n; II, 83 and n, 116n1.

46 *Some Arguments against Enlarging the Power of Bishops*, in *Prose Works*, IX, 45.

Knowledge."[47] This outburst was triggered by the latest step in the ongoing series of legislative raids by "Rural Squires, that Kingdom's Bane,"

> Biennial Squires, to Market brought;
> Who sell their Souls and Votes for Naught;
> The Nation stript go joyful back,
> To rob the Church, their Tenants rack.[48]

From 1714 onwards, Swift took enormous pains to protect and extend the privileges of the Dean of St Patrick's.[49] It is easy to presume that such energy came as a result of his frustration over closed political opportunities, but that is to miss the point: What the Church was, how it should conduct itself, the very nature of its visible expression was something both critical and removed from matters of State. The clinching evidence for this might best be found in the 1732 broadside that offers an example of the exception proving the rule, the *Considerations upon Two Bills Sent down from the R— H— the H— of L— to the H—ble H— of C—— relating to the Clergy of I**********d*, whose fabulous title hiatuses are worth reproducing at least once.[50] If taken at face value, this polemic could be said to be addressing two of the key concerns of Irish clerics: a lack of glebes and manses for parish clergy and the number of clerics holding multiple livings – Swift himself had served three parishes when vicar of Kilroot, and as vicar of Laracor he held *in commendam* the rectory of Agher and the vicarage of Rathbeggan. Indeed, the tract is utterly unironic throughout, and the attack upon the two bills lays out a clear account of the financial state of the Church of Ireland, noting that "[I]t is well known and allowed, that the Clergy, round the Kingdom [of Ireland] think themselves well treated, if they lose only one single Third of their legal Demands" of tithes.[51]

But all arguments moral and social aside, the heart of Swift's point in his *Considerations upon Two Bills* was that the proposal violated not just one of the most basic precepts of parliamentary law but, more importantly, that it traduced the most fundamental precept of church government:

> An Act of Parliament for setling or selling an Estate in a private Family, is never passed, until all Parties give Consent. But in the present Case the whole Body of the *Clergy* is, as themselves apprehend, determined to utter Ruin, without

47 "A Character, Panegyric, and Description of the Legion Club," *Poems*, ed. Williams, III, 827-39 (p. 829).

48 "Verses on the Death of Dr. Swift," *Poems*, ed. Williams, II, 571.

49 See *Correspondence*, ed. Woolley, II, 159n3, 159-60, 365-66 and n5, and *passim*.

50 *Prose Works*, XII, 189-202.

51 *Prose Works*, XII, 195.

> once expecting or asking their Opinion; and this a Scheme contrived only by one Part of the Convocation, while the other Part, which has been chosen in the usual Forms, wants only the regal Permission to assemble, and consult about the Affairs of the Church, as their Predecessors have always done in former Ages.[52]

In the normal course of affairs, Swift could have waited until the Irish House of Commons took up the bill, at which point he would have been free to lambaste once again those "footmen, traitors, vile seducers, perjured rebels, and bribed accusers sprung from papists and a regicide,"[53] who comprised the Lower House. Or he could have held his peace. But in this case, he was willing to attack the Irish House of Lords because he saw its actions as specifically intruding upon clerical matters that should be settled in-house by Convocation.

Henry VIII had robbed the church;[54] Charles I had died for it; Charles II had overlooked it; James II had forsaken it; William III had neglected it; Anne had cherished it, but too late and for too little time; and George I ignored it. In Ireland, more often than not, the one remaining bulwark against further depredation was the House of Lords. To attack that House, except *in extremis*, was to undermine the last defensive structure of the church-state compact. Winston Churchill once observed that he was "not a pillar of the church but a buttress – [he supported] it from the outside."[55] The Dean of St Patrick's, as good with words as was Churchill, and as careful of them, would have understood the metaphor precisely, and it explains his relationship with the Irish House of Lords, itself a buttress for the embattled Church of Ireland.

52 *Prose Works*, XII, 199-200.

53 See the quote associated with note 12 for the source of this paraphrase.

54 For a consideration of Swift's opinion on Henry VIII and what that might indicate about his understanding of religious authority, see Christopher Fauske, "Secular Dean or Religious Secularist," a paper presented on 8 June 2017 at the celebration of Swift's 350th birthday, Trinity College, Dublin, 8 June 2017 (<https://www.academia.edu/33716994/Secular_Dean_or_Religious_Secularist>, accessed 5 November 2018). See also, for further criticism, PASSMANN AND VIENKEN II, 824-31.

55 Cited in Roy Jenkins, *Churchill: A Biography* (London: Plume, 2002), p. 49n.

IRELAND

Sabine Baltes-Ellermann
Hürth

"Yr Lemmons They Say are Good": Swift on Fruit, Provisions, and the Condition of Ireland

Abstract. Swift's correspondence, account books, and occasional verse are interspersed with various allusions to fruit. The Dean may be observed thanking some acquaintance for presents of fruit, applauding its fine quality. He receives invitations to dinner or country visits which promise the enjoyment of particular dainties. Now and then, he makes delighted as well as disappointed comments on the anticipated fruit harvest in his garden. His account books record purchases not only of oranges, cherries, raspberries, and raisins, but also of fruit-related groceries like sugar and brandy. Thus we obtain an impression of the various ways in which fruit was consumed and preserved given the limited options of refrigeration. Besides, references to fruit fall into a context of widespread gardening activity and also bear witness to the keen interest among the Irish landed class in gustatory novelties. Home-grown fruit also had important commercial value on domestic markets and gradually became the object of interest to those dedicated to the improvement of the country's agricultural and economic situation.

1. Introduction

An entry in Swift's account book for 13 March 1735 reads: "Oranges 1 ll – 8s – 6d,"[1] which was an impressive amount of money spent on a single commodity. Besides, two of Swift's most memorable quotes involve a reference to fruit. A letter to Vanessa of 1711 closes with an enigmatic farewell over which biographers and critics alike have puzzled: "Adieu till we meet over a Pott of Coffee, or an Orange and Sugar in the Sluttery."[2] Quite apart from whatever innuendo may be contained in it, the sentence suggests that an orange in those days was

1 *The Account Books of Jonathan Swift*, eds Paul V. Thompson and Dorothy Jay Thompson (Newark: University of Delaware Press, and London: Scolar Press, 1984), p. 250.

2 Swift to Esther Vanhomrigh, 18 December 1711, *Correspondence*, ed. Woolley, I, 399. For a discussion of this sentence and its various interpretations, see Hermann J. Real, "Confessions of a Coffee Drinker: or, How Coffee Became Sex(y)," *The Eighteenth-Century Intelligencer*, 24, no 3 (2010), 6-13. For a while, Swift was a passionate coffee drinker, and expenses for coffee occur with great frequency in the extant account books before 1718. His taste for the drink seems to have diminished, however, for by 1728 he declared coffee to be "unwholesome" ("An Answer to a Paper Called a Memorial of the Poor Inhabitants, Tradesmen and Labourers of the Kingdom of Ireland," *Prose Works*, XII, 20).

 | DOI:10.30965/9783846763971_020

a special treat, and we will see later that Swift was partial to this kind of fruit.[3] Even so, like some of his contemporaries, he did not consider fresh fruit in general as wholesome as later generations would find it: He professed himself certain that the explanation for his recurrent bouts of deafness and vertigo lay in a surfeit of apples during his time as Sir William Temple's secretary: "I got my Giddyness by eating a hundred golden pippins at a time, at Richmond."[4]

A closer look at Swift's correspondence reveals not only a considerable number of specific references to his eating habits, but also his views on the growing and preserving of fruit.[5] His account books, too, give an idea of what purchases he made and what kind of fruit he favoured. The Dean's keen enjoyment of fruit becomes clearer to modern understanding when one considers that plants had a stronger flavour in the past, which may better explain the deep satisfaction of the eaters at the relish of very simple foods.[6] We also find that invitations to dinner in Swift's correspondence as well as the occasional verse which shuttled back and forth among his friends sometimes explicitly refer to fruit. These suggest that both fruit-growing and fruit-tasting were part of a wider social pattern and central to rituals of sociability and various forms of conviviality. If anything, such references refute the stereotype that the eighteenth-century Irish gentry were practically living off nothing but meat and claret.[7] Besides, fruit was central to the development of 'taste' and fashion in the early eighteenth century, as well as the object of scientific interest and

---

3 Vanessa, in turn, hoped for Swift to find a similar refreshment while he was travelling in 1713: "It is impossible to tell you how often I have wished you a cupe of coffee and an orange at your Inn" (Esther Vanhomrigh to Swift, 6 June 1713, *Correspondence*, ed. Woolley, I, 502).

4 Swift to Mrs Howard, 19 August 1727, *Correspondence*, ed. Woolley, III, 120. "Golden pippins" were an apple variety recommended by Temple in his essay "Upon the Gardens of Epicurus," which Swift prepared for publication in 1690 (London: by T. M. for Ri. and Ra. Simpson, 1690). To Mrs Pendarves, he underlined again: "I got a giddiness by raw fruit when I was a lad in England, which I never could be wholly rid of" (29 January 1736, *Correspondence*, ed. Woolley, IV, 256-57).

5 Building my argument on contexts where fruit did mean fruit, I decline to engage in any speculation about risqué innuendo in any of the quoted references.

6 Joan Thirsk, *Food in Early Modern England: Phases, Fads, Fashions, 1500-1760* (London: Hambledon Continuum, 2007), p. xv. The author adds that "contemporary literature conveys a strong impression that we have lost some of the sensitivity to flavours our forebears possessed, for we do not experience so many subtleties in the same food items as did people in the past."

7 The stereotype of the meat-eating and claret-drinking Irishman was not entirely unfounded. The Irish gentry ate prodigious quantities of meat, which accounted for an average of one-third of their food expenses. The most common varieties of meat eaten were beef and mutton (L. A. Clarkson and E. Margaret Crawford, *Feast and Famine: Food and Nutrition in Ireland, 1500-1920* [Oxford: Oxford University Press, 2001], pp. 36, 38).

horticultural experiment. So while a focus on the Dean's preference of fruit may be of interest in that it contributes another piece to the mosaic of Swift the private man, we may also draw some conclusions about the status of fruit in Irish society and its significance for the economy in his time.

2. Growing Fruit

Swift had a keen, well-documented interest in gardening: Not only did he frequently comment on the projects of his friends and acquaintances,[8] he also embarked on improving his little glebe at Laracor with enthusiasm when he took up his duties as vicar in 1700, landscaping it and planting a garden with cherry and apple trees. During his London years, he regularly referred to the place with nostalgia and occasionally yearned for the produce of his fruit trees: "Oh, that we were at Laracor this fine day! ... I was a-dreamed last night that I eat ripe cherries."[9] When, in 1721, he acquired a plot of three acres in Dublin, situated two hundred yards south of the Deanery, which he named Naboth's Vineyard, he planted fruit trees, "which included peach, nectarine, pear and, of course, his beloved apples. These trees were arranged along the south wall of the garden, which was specially bricked for the retention of heat."[10] Praising the apples which he grew in his "little garden," Swift told Chetwode, "I pretend to

8 See Swift to Chetwode, 5 December 1721: "I hope you are grown regular in your Plantations, and have got some skill to know where and what Trees to place, and how to make them grow" (*Correspondence*, ed. Woolley, II, 404); Swift to Daniel Jackson, 26 March 1722: "In what Condition are your Gardens and Forest Trees? ... Is any new work to begin this Summer?" (II, 418); Swift to Chetwode, 12 February 1723: "Do you find that your Trees thrive, and your drained Bog gets a new coat?" (II, 448). Yet he also scolded Patrick Delany for his frenetic gardening activities at Delville, where he was constantly "at vast Expences / In Whims, Parterres, Canals and Fences" ("An Epistle upon an Epistle from a Certain Doctor to a Certain Great Lord: Being a Christmas-Box for D. D—ny," *Poems*, ed. Williams, II, 477, ll. 61-62). Scholarly works focusing on Swift's attitude to gardens are, for example, Joseph McMinn, *Jonathan Swift and the Arts* (Newark: University of Delaware Press, 2010), pp. 51-80; Edward Malins and the Knight of Glin, "Landscape Gardening by Jonathan Swift and his Friends in Ireland," *Garden History*, 2, no 1 (1973), 69-93. See also Sabine Baltes-Ellermann, "Boundless Wit in Confined Spaces: The Occasional Poems on Gaulstown House, Delville, and Quilca by Swift and his Friends in the 1720s," *Infinity and Beyond / L'Infini et au-delà, Actes du Colloque in Memoriam Paul-Gabriel Boucé, 25-26 juin 2014*, ed. Elizabeth Durot-Boucé (Rennes: TIR, 2014), pp. 79-103.

9 *Journal to Stella: Letters to Esther Johnson and Rebecca Dingley, 1710-1713*, ed. Abigail Williams (Cambridge: Cambridge University Press, 2013), p. 166.

10 McMinn, *Jonathan Swift and the Arts*, p. 61.

have the finest paradise Stockes of this age in Ireland."[11] He also prided himself on his connoisseurship of fruit and was always ready to appreciate the quality of his friends' produce. In September 1724, he thanked Chetwode for a present of fruit: "Y^{r} Bergamot Pears are excellent, and the Orange Bergamots much be[tter] than those about this Town. Your Apples are very fair and good of their kind, and y^{r} Peaches and Nectarins as good as we could expect from the Year."[12] Likewise, Swift forwarded the praise of others: "Y^{r} Lemmons they say are good," he told Archdeacon Walls in 1717.[13] The topic of fruit would at times provide a piece of news in itself that was worth relating to one's correspondents: "A Gentleman here [at Trim] shewd us the Finest large Oranges with Teats (the Ladyes know what I mean) that ever I saw, for 12 pence a dozen."[14]

Fruit, it seems, was a recurrent topic of conversation and often something to enthuse about. This becomes understandable when considering that some fruit seems exotic for a latitude such as Dublin. Yet "the cultivation of these delights, often under glass, was actually quite common in Ireland, and we know that several of Swift's friends and neighbours were industriously … growing a wide range of fruit."[15] Prosperous townspeople gardened as fervently as the country gentry, for large urban plots in the residential areas not only provided an escape from an increasingly crowded and malodorous city, but also gave the affluent the illusion of leading "a country-life in town" as well as abundant space to propagate and innovate.[16] As with the current fashion for landscaping one's garden, there was a competitive edge to the ability of growing tasty fruit or exotic varieties, which were often the result of laborious gardening experiments. Sir John Temple, for one, grew a wide range of fruit at Palmerstown, including apricots, figs, grapes, nectarines, peaches, and strawberries. "By the

11 Swift to Chetwode, 14 February 1727, *Correspondence*, ed. Woolley, III, 73.

12 Swift to Chetwode, 22 September 1724, *Correspondence*, ed. Woolley, II, 522. According to a contemporary definition, a "Bergamot" was "a Pear of a delicious Taste" (Nathan Bailey, *An Universal Etymological English Dictionary* [1721] [Hildesheim and New York: Georg Olms, 1969], s.v.), whereas "Orange Bergamots" were the fruit of "a tree of the orange and lemon kind (*Citrus bergamia*)," from the rind of which "a fragrant oil is prepared" (OED online, s.v.).

13 Swift to Walls, 13 January 1717, *Correspondence*, ed. Woolley, II, 217.

14 Swift to Walls, 28 January 1717, *Correspondence*, ed. Woolley, II, 221. As oranges did not yet have the smooth exterior they usually have nowadays, Swift is probably referring to the nubbly texture of the peel.

15 McMinn, *Jonathan Swift and the Arts*, p. 61.

16 Swift to Bolingbroke, 14 September 1714, *Correspondence*, ed. Woolley, II, 79; Toby Barnard, *Making the Grand Figure: Lives and Possessions in Ireland, 1641-1770* (New Haven and London: Yale University Press, 2004), p. 202. John Rocque's map entitled "Exact Survey of the City and Suburbs of Dublin" (1756) shows numerous plots dotted with trees.

1680s, it was oranges which dominated his ambitions," which he probably grew under glass, "watching their progress with a parent's anxious pride."[17] In 1714, Archbishop King received gifts of fruit from Lord Fitzwilliam's Mount Merrion property, which included melons, peaches, apricots, and almonds.[18] Bishop Edward Synge took a keen interest in his gardens and hothouse in Roscommon, where he grew apricots, grapes, melons, nectarines, pears, and strawberries.[19] Patrick Delany, likewise, was a dedicated gardener on his small estate at Delville: "Round the house was a small *parterre* on which he successfully grew orange trees, and on the north-west side was a kitchen garden with a wall of good fruit."[20] Such walls, usually south-facing and made of brick, worked as a reservoir of warmth and helped to grow delicate fruit like peaches, apricots, and figs, especially if the trees were planted directly against the walls in esplaniers. Robert Molesworth, too, grew cherries and Bergamot pears against the walls around the parterre garden, the bowling green, and even against the house itself, at Breckdenston.[21] Across the Irish Sea, Alexander Pope's fruit garden at Twickenham produced peaches, figs, nectarines, and mulberries, including melons and pineapples,[22] and despite his bodily infirmities, Pope took a practical interest. Rather than leave such work to his gardener, he recounted to Swift how he cut himself while pruning a plum tree.[23]

By travel or through gifts from fellow-cultivators, people constantly discovered new varieties of fruit that were the result of regional differences in climate

17 Toby Barnard, *Irish Protestants: Ascents and Descents, 1641-1770* (Dublin: Four Courts Press, 2004), p. 232.

18 Barnard, *Making the Grand Figure*, p. 209.

19 Clarkson and Crawford, *Feast and Famine*, p. 48. Silver strawberry dishes, made in early eighteenth-century Ireland, bear testimony to the popularity of the fruit (Barnard, *Irish Protestants*, p. 218).

20 Malins and Glin, "Landscape Gardening by Jonathan Swift and his Friends in Ireland," p. 74. Presumably, the orange trees adorning the parterre were grown in pots, so that they could be moved to a sheltered place during cold weather.

21 Vandra Costello, *Irish Demesne Landscapes, 1660-1740* (Dublin: Four Courts Press, 2015), pp. 84-85. Sir William Temple explained that such constructions were indispensable, "the best Fruits not ripening without the Advantage of Walls or Palisades, by Reflection of the faint Heat we receive from the Sun" ("Upon the Gardens of Epicurus," *The Works of Sir William Temple, Bart*, 2 vols [London: A. Churchill, *et al.*, 1720], I, 181). Swift, however, discovered that his garden wall offered no sufficient protection against northeasterly winds; see Swift to Pope, 20 April 1731, *Correspondence*, ed. Woolley, III, 383-84.

22 See Swift to Sheridan, 12 August 1727, *Correspondence*, ed. Woolley, III, 115; Pope to Swift, 25 March 1736, *Correspondence*, ed. Woolley, IV, 278.

23 Pope to Swift, 17 February 1727, *Correspondence*, ed. Woolley, III, 76.

and soil.[24] Returning to Ireland in October 1727, Swift carried with him "a sample of English Apples" as a souvenir,[25] and it is tempting to imagine him ordering his gardener to plant the pips in Naboth's Vineyard. The interest in growing exotic fruit was partly owing to botanists who roamed the world in search of plants, partly to a widening commercial world in which seeds and plants were shipped back from the colonies and the tropics by enterprising merchants.[26] Such expeditions were sometimes sponsored by wealthy *aficionados* who "hoped to popularize the finds among their dull neighbours."[27] Some fruit growers gave away seeds or cuttings to favoured persons who shared the giver's botanical enthusiasm, whereas others of a more enterprising mind established their own nurseries.[28] Bills and private accounts testify to a growing number of commercial nurserymen, whose services were eagerly sought. Their advertisements for seeds, plants, and trees in provincial newspapers suggest that "the craze for gardening and growing fruit and vegetables extended well beyond the boundaries of the upper classes."[29] The passion for gardening also caused a burgeoning of specialist publications: "Dublin printers were extremely busy with the profitable business of producing guides for gardeners."[30] Swift, for his part, owned Richard Bradley's popular gardening manual *New Improvements of Planting and Gardening, both Philosophical and Practical* (1720), which "would have guided him – and his gardeners – through the horticultural calendar over the four seasons."[31] Bradley supplied detailed advice about the planting of fruit

24 See Richard Bradley, *New Improvements of Planting and Gardening, both Philosophical and Practical*, 4th ed. (Dublin: George Grierson, 1720), p. 14: "To set down the several various Names of *Apples*, would be a Work almost impossible, seeing how many various kinds are yearly produced from the Kernels in almost every County in *England*; and where they happen to prove good, either for making *Cyder* or Table-use, have Names given them according to the mind of the Person that rais'd them."

25 Gay and Pope to Swift, 22 October 1727, *Correspondence*, ed. Woolley, III, 135.

26 Barnard, *Irish Protestants*, p. 209.

27 Barnard, *Making the Grand Figure*, p. 191; see also Costello, *Irish Demesne Landscapes*, pp. 22-23.

28 Barnard, *Making the Grand Figure*, p. 215; Costello, *Irish Demesne Landscapes*, pp. 120-23.

29 Clarkson and Crawford, *Feast and Famine*, pp. 49-50. An early eighteenth-century advertisement sheet, entitled *A Catalogue of Garden Seeds and Flower Roots*, displayed the impressive scale and variety of stock in John Johnson's shop on Cork Hill in Dublin. Under the category "*Fruit-Trees*," Johnson offered "divers sorts" of apples, pears, plums, cherries, quinces, figs, grapes, walnuts, peaches, apricots, nectarines, strawberries, raspberries, mulberries, as well as "*Dutch* Goosberrys, the scarlet smooth, and scarlet hairy, and the large green hairy" (reprinted in Barnard, *Making the Grand Figure*, p. 214).

30 McMinn, *Jonathan Swift and the Arts*, p. 64.

31 McMinn, *Jonathan Swift and the Arts*, p. 64; see also PASSMANN AND VIENKEN I, 281-82. Given the payments to gardeners recorded in Swift's surviving account books for the years

trees and offered "copperplate illustrations for several horticultural challenges, notably that for the proper construction of glass-houses for delicate fruits."[32] Whereas such books provided both botanical knowledge and practical advice, new ideas were also bound to spread by corresponding on the subject with friends and acquaintances as well as by observing the innovations undertaken by one's neighbours. Besides, gentlemen would doubtless exchange views and discuss their latest projects in convivial gatherings, particularly over the dinner table.

3. Consuming Fruit

Although he could at times enjoy the modest produce of his garden or received gifts of fruit from friends and acquaintances, being for most of his life a city dweller, Swift's food supplies were chiefly the result of purchase: he had to rely on local markets to satisfy his domestic wants. In his surviving account books, items such as oranges, apples, cherries, and raspberries stand out prominently by being listed under the heading "Extr^{dys}" [extraordinaries]. However, although fruit frequently appeared on eighteenth-century dinner tables as part of the dessert course, when Swift was entertaining, his expenses are rendered only in total and give no clue as to whether fruits (or vegetables) were usually part of the menu. In fact, in his correspondence and in the occasional poems exchanged with his learned friends only meat and wine are mentioned as constituent parts of a good dinner.[33] By contrast, in "Quilca House to the

1718 and 1735, "it is almost certain that, whenever financially possible, he ... employ[ed] gardeners at St Patrick's" (p. 66).

32 McMinn, *Jonathan Swift and the Arts*, p. 66. Philip Miller's *The Gardeners Dictionary*, too, first published in London in 1731, but soon reprinted by Stephen Powell in Dublin in 1732, was extremely popular and eagerly consulted by improvers (see Barnard, *Making the Grand Figure*, p. 209). It has also been pointed out that "clergymen and gardening seems to have become something of a niche-market for publishers at this time, as evidenced, for example, by Grierson's 1719 edition of John Laurences's popular gardening manual *The Clergyman's Recreation, Shewing the Pleasure and Profit of the Art of Gardening* (1714)" (McMinn, *Jonathan Swift and the Arts*, p. 63n30).

33 Private recipe books, bills and accounts, however, provide ample documentation that there was both demand for, and availability of, fresh vegetables and herbs. We are also given an idea of the most common vegetables in Sheridan's poem "To the Dean, when in England, in 1726," which refers to his meagre (or non-existent) crop of cabbages, turnips, carrots, parsnips, green peas, and green sprouts (*The Poems of Thomas Sheridan*, ed. Robert Hogan [Newark: University of Delaware Press, and London and Toronto: Associated University Presses, 1994], p. 164, ll. 45-47). In *An Examination of Certain Abuses, Corruptions, and Enormities in the City of Dublin*, Swift mentions the cries of street-traders

Dean," Henry Brooke directs Swift's attention to a particular manifestation of Sheridan's consistent and unstinting hospitality: "The best of mutton you have eat / An apple-pie, too, was a treat."[34] Similarly, in "Mighty Thomas, A Solemn Senatus I Call," Patrick Delany invites Matthew Pilkington to Delville and announces a special bill of fare:

> I've mutton for you, sir; and as for the ladies,
> As friend Virgil has it, I've *aliud mercedis*;
> For Letty, one filbert, whereon to regale;
> And a peach for pale Constance to make a full meal;
> And for your cruel part, who take pleasure in blood,
> I have that of the grape, which is ten times as good.[35]

While principally teasing the ladies for being fastidious eaters (and perhaps Mrs Pilkington on account of her diminutive stature), this list of dainties is still noteworthy for its itemization of fruit, underlining as it does the exquisiteness of the repast: peaches were the pride of the ambitious gardener, whereas filberts (a kind of hazelnut) were a valuable and sought-after commodity that was imported from Turkey, Italy, and Spain.[36]

---

vending celery and turnips (see *Prose Works*, XII, 230). Revealing, too, are the drawings by Hugh Douglas Hamilton (*The Cries of Dublin: Drawn from the Life by Hugh Douglas Hamilton, 1760*, ed. William Laffan [Dublin: Irish Georgian Society, 2003]), among whose subjects we find sellers of herbs and watercress (p. 61), peas (p. 81), onions, root vegetables and (presumably) lettuce (p. 101) and turnips (p. 149).

34 *The Poems of Thomas Sheridan*, ed. Hogan, p. 149, ll. 23-24. The apple pie was probably not intended as a dessert, but was rather part of the "sweet course," which was served as part of the second meat course (Thirsk, *Food in Early Modern England*, p. 148). See also the sumptuous menu offered by Mrs Delany in 1747: The first course consisted of "fish – beefstakes – soup – rabbit and onions – Fillet Veal;" the second course comprised "Turkey Pout – salmon grilde – pickled salmon – quails – little Terrene Peas – Cream – Mushrooms – Apple Pye – Crab – Leveret – Cheese-cakes" (quoted from Clarkson and Crawford, *Feast and Famine*, p. 38). The dessert course is again revealing for its lavish choice of fruit: Mrs Delany offered blancmange, cherries, Dutch cheese, raspberries and cream, sweetmeats and jelly, strawberries and cream, almond cream, currants and gooseberries, and orange butter (J. L. McCracken, "The Social Structure and Social Life, 1714-60," *A New History of Ireland*, eds T. W. Moody and W. E. Vaughan, 9 vols [Oxford: Oxford University Press, 1986], IV, 47).

35 *The Poems of Patrick Delany, Comprising also Poems about him by Jonathan Swift, Thomas Sheridan, and Other Friends and Enemies*, eds Robert Hogan and Donald C. Mell (Newark: University of Delaware Press, 2006), p. 170, ll. 5-10. Pilkington's nickname was "Tom Thumb" because of his diminutive size; see *Memoirs of Laetitia Pilkington*, ed. A. C. Elias, Jr, 2 vols (Athens, Georgia, and London: University of Georgia Press, 1997), I, 283.

36 Julie Berger Hochstrasser, *Still Life and Trade in the Dutch Golden Age* (New Haven and London: Yale University Press, 2007), p. 82.

While apples were among the most popular fruit consumed by the gentry in Ireland,[37] many kinds of fruit were actually luxury goods. Among the prosperous, the results of successful cultivation attempts were proudly presented to friends and acquaintances for tasting trials at the dinner table. "The best sorts" of apples and pears, it was said, "serve as the last course for the table in most men's houses of account, where, if they grow any rare or exotic fruit, it is then set forth to be seen and tasted."[38] Exotic delicacies imported from far away were intended to impress visitors and to display one's own refined taste. Accordingly, "traders and manufacturers vied to proffer novelties [as] consumers sought the new."[39] To a certain extent, this enthusiasm for fresh food experiences was determined by the price tag. Some people thought nothing was good unless it was dear, and growers tended to obey market forces.[40] This prestige also explains why fruit is found as an object in paintings to adorn grand houses, an artistic influence that probably came from the Low Countries.[41] Sometimes, such representations were artfully charged with meaning, yet often painters captivated their audiences solely with lavish depictions of shiny fruit that had no allegorical function at all. Some fruit was even considered to be a suitable present for royalty: Sir Thomas Hanmer used to send grapes from his vineyard to Queen Caroline each year as a gift.[42] Similarly, relating in "An Apology to the Lady Carteret" how the vicereine condescended to visit his garden and "eat

---

37 In England, too, "apples reached the kitchen in most quantity, as apple pies were so often named as everybody's fare, and they were relatively easily stored" (Thirsk, *Food in Early Modern England*, p. 152). See also Bradley, *New Improvements of Planting and Gardening*, p. 14: "There is no kind of Fruit better known in *England* than the *Apple*, or more generally cultivated. It is of that Use, that I hold it almost impossible for the *English* to live without it, whether it be employ'd for that excellent Drink we call *Cyder*, or for the many Dainties, which are made of it in the Kitchen: In short, were all other Fruits wanting to us, *Apples* would make us amends."

38 John Parkinson, *Paradisi in sole* ([London], 1629), p. 588, quoted from Barnard, *Irish Protestants*, p. 223.

39 T. C. Barnard, "Hamilton's 'Cries of Dublin': The Society and Economy of Mid-Eighteenth-Century Dublin," *The Cries of Dublin*, ed. Laffan, p. 28.

40 Thirsk, *Food in Early Modern England*, p. 119.

41 Joan Thirsk points out that still-life painting "became a rich branch of art that is beginning to be studied more deliberately by historians, though they have yet to link it with current horticultural and food history, rather than emphasizing the classical associations and the moralizing and sexual connotations of fruit and vegetables" (*Food in Early Modern England*, pp. 294-95). The dynamics between still-life painting and economic activity is the subject of Julie Berger Hochstrasser's richly illustrated book *Still Life and Trade in the Dutch Golden Age*. By depicting fruit from the Mediterranean, she concludes, "the Dutch displayed yet another colourful dimension of the vigour of their trading prowess" (p. 82).

42 Malins and Glin, "Landscape Gardening by Jonathan Swift and his Friends in Ireland," p. 78.

some Fruit," presumably freshly picked, Patrick Delany boasted of the quality of his garden products and his virtuosity as gardener.[43]

At the same time, Delany's poem reflects an intellectual tendency in the eighteenth century that campaigned for simpler diets, with fruit as the central ingredient. His claim to treat Lady Carteret to a meal without "Pride, or vain Magnificence" in the form of freshly picked fruit is supplemented by the assertion that "to Stomachs clog'd with costly Fare / Simplicity alone is rare."[44] Moderation and restraint had always been the shibboleths of those with religious scruples towards luxury and ostentation; yet now a preoccupation with physical well-being made some declare that "nothing conduce[d] more to *Health* and *Long Life*, than *Abstinence* and *plain Food*."[45] Sir William Temple, in his essay "Of Health and Long Life," had already argued in favour of "Simplicity of Diet, rather Fruits and Plants than Flesh, which easier corrupts," and he had invoked the longevity of both biblical and indigenous tribes as evidence for this view.[46] Besides health-related recommendations of this kind, there was the influence of the classical tradition, most notably the ideals of rural retreat, pastoral simplicity, and frugal diet.[47] Presumably, however, there was a good deal of affectation and self-indulgence in the celebration of rustic simplicity, and considering social pressures and fashion dictates, one suspects that people did not always practise what they preached. Even so, many started to appreciate the health benefits of fruit, thus reappraising earlier opinion, which had tended to condemn the consumption of fresh fruit as potentially harmful.[48] Sir

43 *Poems*, ed. Williams, II, 378, l. 88; James Woolley, "The Canon of Swift's Poems: The Case of 'An Apology to the Lady Carteret,'" *Reading Swift: Papers from The Second Münster Symposium on Jonathan Swift*, eds Richard H. Rodino and Hermann J. Real, with the assistance of Helgard Stöver-Leidig (Munich: Wilhelm Fink, 1993), p. 256. For the attribution of the poem to Delany, see pp. 248-57.

44 *Poems*, ed. Williams, II, 378, ll. 102, 105-6.

45 George Cheyne, *An Essay of Health and Long Life*, 6th ed. (Dublin: W. Wilmot, 1725), p. 38.

46 *The Works of Sir William Temple*, I, 275.

47 See, for instance, Virgil, *Eclogues*, I; Horace, *Satires*, II, ii.

48 The physician Thomas Cogan (*c.*1545-1607) "dismissed apples as 'unwholesome' and liable to 'breed winde in the second digestion' ... Cogan had advice about figs too: they were blamed for the spread of lice. Anthony Wood's notes reveal that fevers sweeping Oxford in the 1670s were commonly put down to the consumption of fruit" (Emily Cockayne, *Hubbub: Filth, Noise and Stench in England, 1600-1770* [New Haven and London: Yale University Press, 2007], p. 94. Quotations are from Thomas Cogan, *The Haven of Health: Chiefly Gathered for the Comfort of Students, and Consequently of All those that Have a Care of their Health*, 4th ed. [London: Anne Griffin, 1636], pp. 100, 110; *The Life and Times of Anthony à Wood, Antiquary, of Oxford, 1632-1695, Described by himself*, ed. Andrew Clark, 5 vols [Oxford: Clarendon Press, 1891-1900], II, 198, 253). More realistically, overeating was condemned for causing sickness, although some people deemed raw pears to be poison, while others took the 'precaution' to eat brown bread to countermand the diseases caused by eating fruit raw (Thirsk, *Food in Early Modern England*, p. 298). Sir William Temple

William Temple recommended the copious eating of fruit before and after every meal:

> For all Illnesses of Stomach, or Indigestions …, to which my whole Family has been much subject, as well as many of my Acquaintance … I have never found any thing of much or certain Effect, besides the eating of *Strawberries*, common *Cherries*, white *Figs*, soft *Peaches*, or *Grapes*, before every Meal, during their Seasons; and when those are past, *Apples* after Meals; but all must be very ripe … and the usual Quantity is about forty *Cherries*, without swallowing either Skin or Stone.[49]

By contrast, Swift's love of fruit continued to be tainted by dread, since he was convinced that fruit had been the cause of his headaches and dizzy spells, although he was never specific as to what kind had caused his latest bout of discomfort. In September 1712, for instance, he relates: "I have eat mighty little Fruit, yet I impute my disorder to that little, and shall henceforth wholly forbear it."[50] A year earlier, he had been more careful: "I durst not eat any fruit, but one fig … I envy people maunching and maunching peaches and grapes, and I not daring to eat a bit."[51] In 1727, during his stay with Alexander Pope at Twickenham, his old complaint recurred: "I have been this ten Days inclining to my old Disease of Giddiness, a little Tottering … Cyder and Champagne and Fruit have been the Cause."[52] Six weeks later, Swift was still unwell and resolved to be abstinent in his diet, despite the temptations of Pope's fruit garden: "I will be very Temperate; and in the midst of Peaches, Figs, Nectarins, and Mulberries, I touch not a bit."[53]

By contrast, expenses for citrus fruit appear in Swift's account books relatively often. Before settling in Dublin, he bought oranges only in small quantities, paying no more than 6d or 7d at a time, but in the 1730s he recorded several large purchases, which at one time peaked with the steep sum of £1 14s 6d. In fact, historians have attested to a considerable consumption of oranges and lemons in Ireland.[54] Consignments from importers were eagerly snapped up, because they made attractive presents,[55] and it helped that the price of both oranges and lemons fell throughout the century with imports from Bermuda

rather blamed "ill or unripe Fruit" to be the cause of "so many untimely Deaths, or so much Sickness about Autumn, in all great Cities where 'tis greedily sold as well as eaten" ("Upon the Gardens of Epicurus," *The Works of Sir William Temple*, I, 189).

49 "Of Health and Long Life," *The Works of Sir William Temple*, I, 286-87.

50 *Journal to Stella*, ed. Abigail Williams, p. 444.

51 *Journal to Stella*, ed. Abigail Williams, p. 271.

52 Swift to Sheridan, 1 July 1727, *Correspondence*, ed. Woolley, III, 103.

53 Swift to Sheridan, 12 August 1727, *Correspondence*, ed. Woolley, III, 115.

54 Clarkson and Crawford, *Feast and Famine*, p. 48.

55 Barnard, *Irish Protestants*, p. 218.

as well as from the Mediterranean.[56] Whereas "ordinary folk in London were seen munching them in the streets,"[57] in Dublin, too, oranges were widely sold by street vendors, and especially in theatres as refreshments for the audience. Swift's remark that, while staying at Trim, he was shown "the Finest large Oranges with Teats ... that ever I saw, for 12 pence a dozen" indicates the relatively modest price even outside the metropolis.[58]

Citrus fruit was not only enjoyed for its own taste, but was also used to create unique flavour sensations in combination with other foodstuffs. Lemon juice, for instance, was one of the most popular flavourings: it was added to alcoholic drinks, especially rum. In a poetic invitation to Swift, Thomas Sheridan proposed to round off their sumptuous dinner as follows: "A quart of rum with juice of lemon, / Which we'll tope off like any seamen."[59] Lemons and oranges were likewise used as a condiment for meat dishes and to add juice to sauces. On another occasion, Sheridan invited Swift to "An excellent loin of fat veal to be roasted, / With lemons, and butter, and sippets well toasted."[60] In "Verses Made for Women who Cry Apples etc." Swift has his speaker advertise her ware with reference to its various uses:

> Come, buy my fine Oranges, Sauce for your Veal,
> And charming when squeez'd in a Pot of brown Ale.
> Well roasted, with Sugar and Wine in a Cup,
> They'll make a sweet Bishop when Gentlefolks sup. [61]

No doubt these creations put in an appearance at Deanery dinners.

Dried fruit like prunes, currants, and dates, too, were used to flavour meat dishes, but also found their way into sweet pastries and cake.[62] Besides, "*Candy'd Peel*" and "a Drop ... / Of *Orange-Water* for Perfuming-sake" were

56 William Laffan and Brendan Rooney, "Oranges and Lemons," *The Cries of Dublin*, ed. Laffan, p. 86.

57 Thirsk, *Food in Early Modern England*, p. 136.

58 Swift to Walls, 28 January 1717, *Correspondence*, ed. Woolley, II, 221.

59 Thomas Sheridan, "The Invitation," *The Poems of Thomas Sheridan*, ed. Hogan, p. 112, ll. 33-34.

60 Thomas Sheridan, "An Invitation to Dinner, from Doctor Sheridan to Doctor Swift. Written in the Year MDCCXXVII," *The Poems of Thomas Sheridan*, ed. Hogan, p. 166, ll. 7-8. A "sippet" is "a small piece of toasted or fried bread, usually served in soup or broth, or with meat, or used for dipping into gravy, etc.; a small sop" (OED online, s.v.).

61 *Poems*, ed. Williams, III, 953, ll. 1-4. "Sweet Bishop" was wine spiced with sugar, oranges, or lemons (Laffan and Rooney, "Oranges and Lemons," p. 86).

62 Thirsk, *Food in Early Modern England*, p. 104. There is evidence that shipments of such delicacies had found their way into Ireland since the sixteenth century; see Clarkson and Crawford, *Feast and Famine*, pp. 17, 21.

considered to add the finishing touches to an apple pie.[63] Swift took particular pride in the quality of his "Deanery Puddings," which consisted chiefly of suet and (probably dried) plums.[64] He recorded purchases of raisins, spending 8d on "Honey & Rozin" in June 1733, and 1s 6d on "Meat [and] Raisins" in December 1735.[65] Dried fruit would similarly have enhanced the attractions of gingerbread, one of Swift's regular indulgences.[66]

4. Preserving Fruit

Fruit was vulnerable to damage and quick to decay. Hence, expert storage became an important domestic task. Whereas a gentleman's manor sometimes boasted an ice house, apples could be kept reasonably fresh for months when stored in barrels in dry sand or cushioned in straw.[67] Contemporaries devised a "trick for keeping the grapes till Christmas, by packing them in layers in a barrel of dry clean sand, sealed tight."[68] Vendors of fruit faced an even greater challenge as they needed to present their wares in an attractive condition, even if they could not always offer the freshest specimen:

> Orange sellers were thought to freshen their wares by polishing them or by boiling and puffing them up, leeching their juice away in the process. Small conical basket punnets, available on deposit from the street vendors, afforded delicate soft summer fruits some protection. [Matthew] Bramble complained about the 'pallid contaminated mash, which they call strawberries, soiled and tossed by greasy paws through twenty baskets crusted with dirt.'[69]

Besides, the practice of giving fruit as gifts to friends and acquaintances demanded forethought and careful planning for safe transportation. Most importantly, fruit needed to be kept cool and softly cushioned, and required speedy arrival at its destination. When Swift thanked Chetwode for a present of fruit,

63 [Leonard Welsted], "Apple-Pye: A Poem," *Epistles, Odes &c. Written on Several Subjects* (London, 1724), p. 72 (FOXON B418).

64 Swift to Lord Castle-Durrow, 24 December 1736, *Correspondence*, ed. Woolley, IV, 375-76.

65 *Account Books*, eds Thompson and Thompson, pp. lxxxii, 218.

66 Clarkson and Crawford, *Feast and Famine*, p. 43. See *Account Books*, eds Thompson and Thompson, pp. 9, 11, 170-72, 175, 178, 179, 183-85, 223, 245, 250, 255, 260.

67 Barnard, *Irish Protestants*, p. 218; Thirsk, *Food in Early Modern England*, p. 300. On ice houses, see Costello, *Irish Demesne Landscapes*, pp. 69-70.

68 Thirsk, *Food in Early Modern England*, p. 74.

69 Cockayne, *Hubbub*, p. 94. She refers to Sean Shesgreen, *The Criers and Hawkers of London: Engravings and Drawings of Marcellus Laroon* (Aldershot: Scolar Press, 1990), pp. 84, 138, and quotes Tobias Smollett, *The Expedition of Humphry Clinker*, 3 vols (London, 1771), II, 10.

he informed him that the peaches and nectarines had been too delicate to arrive in good condition: "But it is too great a Journy for such nice Fruit, and they are apt to take the Tast of the Moss."[70] In this case, the soft bedding had actually worked to spoil the gift. In late 1727, Swift asked his London friends to remind Sir Spencer Compton of "his promise of giving me 3 or 4 Marseill's Figs, and some of his most early grapes, and do you get them put into boxes with Earth, and send them to Whitehall, and let them be kept cool and I will send for them."[71] To his annoyance, his intended gift for the Achesons, his hosts at Market Hill, had arrived in unsatisfactory condition: "You are a bad packer of bad Grapes," he chided his vicar John Worrall in September 1728.[72] Likewise, Sheridan's present of fruit and vegetables from Cavan apparently did not survive the journey unharmed: "The only Defect of them all," the Dean wrote with characteristic sardonic humour, "were, that they wanted Colour, Sight, and Smell; yet as to the last, we both acknowledged them all to exhale a general Fustiness, which however did much resemble that of your Cavan Air."[73]

In the country, the seasons still prescribed what kinds of fruit were available, although constructions like brick walls and glass houses made the cultivation of delicate fruit easier and less dependent on a volatile climate. Besides, as ways of preserving fruit became more and more sophisticated, seasonal gluts could be managed and summer fruit could even be enjoyed in winter.[74] Contemporary recipe books were concerned with "conserving vegetables and fruits so that they could be enjoyed out of season, and candying with sugar ... was becoming ever more common since sugar was so freely available in the market and people were developing a taste for sweet things."[75] Swift, too, did not consume fruit only in its natural fresh state, judging from several references in his correspondence and hints thrown in the occasional verse. He claimed to have a special recipe for preserving oranges which involved "keep[ing] them in some warm place within the smell of a fire, till they grow dry."[76] Perhaps he had obtained it from the person to whom he paid 17s 8½d for "Orang[e]s preserv^{d}" on 30 March 1733.[77] This recipe was eagerly coveted by Lord Orrery,

70 Swift to Chetwode, 22 September 1724, *Correspondence*, ed. Woolley, II, 522.
71 Swift to Gay and Pope, 23 November 1727, *Correspondence*, ed. Woolley, III, 142.
72 Swift to Worrall, 28 September 1728, *Correspondence*, ed. Woolley, III, 199.
73 Swift to Sheridan, 10 July 1736, *Correspondence*, ed. Woolley, IV, 331.
74 Thirsk, *Food in Early Modern England*, p. 94.
75 Thirsk, *Food in Early Modern England*, p. 81; see also Regina Sexton, "Food and Culinary Cultures in Pre-Famine Ireland," *Food and Drink in Ireland*, eds Elizabeth FitzPatrick and James Kelly (Dublin: Royal Irish Academy, 2016), pp. 274-75.
76 Swift to Unknown Lady, 24 March 1736, *Correspondence*, ed. Woolley, IV, 276.
77 *Account Books*, eds Thompson and Thompson, p. 213.

who bolstered his request for a copy with judicious praise: "Certainly the best Oranges (I mean preserv'd ones …) are the produce of your Table."[78] In Swift's surviving account books, the large payments for oranges in the spring of 1735 suggest bulk purchases intended for preserving,[79] and "it can be reasonably assumed that the *lost* accounts for the intervening years testified similarly."[80] In fact, judging from the frequency of the purchases, preserving fruit in Swift's household went along with a considerable use of sugar. Sometimes these commodities are listed together, such as "Ras^{bry} & Sug^{r}" in August 1733. Hence, Swift's remark to eat "an Orange and Sugar in the Sluttery" may indicate fruit that had been preserved in sugar syrup or candied, or – more prosaically – steeped in sugar to soften a taste that may have been somewhat sour.[81] Swift also appears to have spoiled Vanessa's sister Mary with occasional presents in the form of sugar plums.[82] Such delicacies acquired connotations that came down to posterity as proverbial. A ballad of 1724 referring to attempts of influencing the Dublin Grand Jury claims that their compliance could not be bought for "a Sweet *Sugar-Plumb*, with *Honey* and *Spice*."[83] Although evoking the image of a sticky sweet, "sugar and honey" was a contemporary slang expression for money, whereas "plumb" denoted a fortune.[84] Likewise, another ballad on the same theme referred to "a Sweet Sugar Plumb, which you put in a Posset,"[85] which in turn informs of another way fruit was being consumed.

Both fresh and conserved fruit provided a filling for pies and puddings. When staying at Quilca, Swift allegedly lectured Mrs Sheridan on her ways of preparing "conserves and pastry."[86] Besides, fruit could be bottled and sterilized in

78 Orrery to Swift, March 1740, *Correspondence*, ed. Woolley, IV, 610. A few weeks later, Orrery thanked Mrs Whiteway "for the Receipt of the Oranges and the Directions to make them so good" (12 May 1740, *Correspondence*, ed. Woolley, IV, 618).

79 He recorded £1 14s 6d for oranges on 14 February 1735, and again £1 8s 6d on 3 March 1735 (*Account Books*, eds Thompson and Thompson, p. 250).

80 *Correspondence*, ed. Woolley, IV, 276, Headnote.

81 Swift to Esther Vanhomrigh, 18 December 1711, *Correspondence*, ed. Woolley, I, 399; *Account Books*, eds Thompson and Thompson, p. 223. There were two different varieties of orange, one sweet and one sour, although they did not differ in appearance (Hochstrasser, *Still Life and Trade in the Dutch Golden Age*, pp. 75-77).

82 Swift to Mrs Vanhomrigh, 6 June 1713, *Correspondence*, ed. Woolley, I, 504.

83 *An Excellent New Ballad upon the Present Gr[a]nd Jury* (Dublin, 1724).

84 Eric Partridge, *A Dictionary of Slang and Unconventional English*, 2 vols, 5th ed. (London: Routledge and Kegan Paul, 1961), I, 846, 641, s.v.

85 *An Excellent New Song upon the Late Grand-Jury* (Dublin, 1724 [FOXON E594]). "Posset," according to a contemporary definition, was "Milk turn'd with Ale" (Bailey, *An Universal Etymological English Dictionary*, s.v.). The OED online elaborates: "A drink made from hot milk curdled with ale, wine, or other liquor, flavoured with sugar, herbs, spices, etc." (s.v.).

86 *The Poems of Thomas Sheridan*, ed. Hogan, p. 149, ll. 31-34.

the oven, although steeping it in alcohol was apparently another favourite. In 1715, Swift wrote to Chetwode: "Give my Service to [your wife], and desire her to let you know what quantity of Cherryes she has for Brandy; you may steep them in just enough to keep them alive, and I will send you some very good if I can."[87] Apparently, Mrs Chetwode continued to provide Swift with this delicacy for years. In 1724, Swift assured his 'friend': "Y^r^ Cherry Brandy I depend on the goodness of, but would not suffer it to be tasted till another Time."[88] Occasional purchases of brandy are also documented in Swift's account books, sometimes explicitly for cherries and raspberries.[89] Alternatively, as apple, pear, and cherry trees were common in the more settled parts of Ireland, fruit was turned into cider and perry or even into vinegar, all of which, however, required a relatively large harvest.[90] In fact, apple cider experienced a surge in popularity, being transformed from a poor countryman's taste to a modish urban and upper-class drink.[91] Inviting Swift to dinner, Sheridan offered "as fine cyder as ever I drank at a tavern," ignorant of Swift's suspicion that the drink was one of the causes for his attacks of giddiness.[92] On the whole, the Dean professed to prefer wine anyway: "My chief support is French wine, which ... I drink a bottle to my self every day."[93]

87 Swift to Chetwode, 2 August 1715, *Correspondence*, ed. Woolley, II, 141.

88 Swift to Chetwode, 22 September 1724, *Correspondence*, ed. Woolley, II, 522.

89 *Account Books*, eds Thompson and Thompson, p. 255.

90 Barnard, *Irish Protestants*, p. 232; Thirsk, *Food in Early Modern England*, p. 147. A contemporary recipe for orange wine, too, required at least 50 oranges to be added to a syrup made from 6 gallons of water and 12 pounds of sugar; see the manuscript reproduced in Madeline Shanahan, "'Whipt with a twig rod': Irish Manuscript Recipe Books as Sources for the Study of Culinary Material Culture, *c.*1660 to 1830," *Food and Drink in Ireland*, eds FitzPatrick and Kelly, p. 204.

91 Thirsk, *Food in Early Modern England*, p. 18; Barnard, *Irish Protestants*, pp. 214-15. This renaissance is also reflected by the popularity of John Evelyn's treatise *Pomona: or, An Appendix concerning Fruit-Trees in relation to Cider, the Making and Several Ways of Ordering it*, 4th ed. (London, 1706), or John Philips's publication *Cyder: A Poem in Two Books* (Dublin: Edwin Sandys, 1715).

92 Sheridan to Swift, 28 June 1734, *Correspondence*, ed. Woolley, III, 741 (translation of Sheridan's pseudo-Latin); Swift to Sheridan, 1 July 1727, *Correspondence*, ed. Woolley, III, 103. By contrast, Ralph Austin's *A Treatise on Fruit-Trees* (Oxford, 1653) proposed that cider and perry were drinks that ensured health and long life (Thirsk, *Food in Early Modern England*, p. 101).

93 Swift to John Barber, 21 March 1735, *Correspondence*, ed. Woolley, IV, 62. By that time he stressed that he drank wine chiefly for medical reasons: "I drink a bottle of French wine myself every day, though I love it not; but it is the onely thing that keeps me out of pain" (Swift to John Arbuthnot, *c.*12-15 November 1734, *Correspondence*, ed. Woolley, IV, 15); "Wine is good for me, and I drink a Bottle to my own share every day, to bring some heat into my Stomach" (Swift to John Barber, 3 September 1735, *Correspondence*, ed. Woolley,

5. Fruit and the Condition of Ireland

Examining Swift's attitudes to fruit, we have so far investigated a gentleman's personal taste, that of a member of a social group in which gardening only partly occurred out of a need for basic food supply, and in which eating and drinking were directed to satisfying more senses than hunger.[94] It may therefore come as a surprise that, despite his obvious appreciation of fruit, not only for its taste but also as a yardstick for Ireland's degree of civilization, one searches in vain for any proposal in Swift's tracts on the Irish economy for the growing of fruit or the manufacture of fruit products, such as cider or vinegar. Instead, the only instances when the Dean mentions fruit occur in entirely different contexts. At one time, he evokes the image of a humble country vicar whose apples are in danger of getting stolen. Expressly referring to this as an English example, as his real target is the deplorable condition of the Irish clergy, Swift suggests by implication that such a rural setting was not to be found in Ireland.[95] Elsewhere, he makes the satiric proposal to turn all Ireland to grazing, to the effect that "the industrious Shepherd and Cow-herd may sit ... under his own Blackberry Bush, and his own Potatoe-Bed, whereby this happy Island will become a new *Arcadia*."[96] By contrast, his public writings of the 1720s and 1730s are predominantly concerned with the lack of effective husbandry in Ireland and the urgent need for a sustained cultivation of staple foods.[97] "There is not an older or more uncontroverted maxim in the politics of all wise nations," he declared, "than that of encouraging agriculture."[98] Hence, it was deplorable that "even Ale and Potatoes [were] imported from *England*, as well as Corn."[99] The Dean also pressed the Irish Parliament to consider "the

IV, 172). See also Michael DePorte, "*Vinum daemonum*: Swift and the Grape," *Swift Studies*, 12 (1997), 56-68.

94 Clarkson and Crawford, *Feast and Famine*, p. 5.

95 "On the Bill for the Clergy's Residing on their Livings," *Prose Works*, XII, 182.

96 "The Answer to the *Craftsman*," *Prose Works*, XII, 176.

97 Although the rural population faced periodic crises of subsistence, the 1720s were a decade of particular economic difficulties, as the effects of chronically low grain prices were exacerbated by successive harvest failures; see S. J. Connolly, *Religion, Law, and Power: The Making of Protestant Ireland, 1660-1760* (Oxford: Oxford University Press, 1992), pp. 41, 47-48; L. M. Cullen, *An Economic History of Ireland since 1660*, 2nd ed. (London: B. T. Batsford, 1987), p. 50.

98 "An Answer to Several Letters Sent me from Unknown Hands," *Prose Works*, XII, 89.

99 "A Short View of the State of Ireland," *Prose Works*, XII, 9. "Corn" is here used as a collective term for cereal plants or crops (see OED online, s.v.).

cultivating our own Soil, encouraging *Agriculture* … that we might not be under the Necessity of sending for *Corn* … from *England*."[100]

One reason for Swift to disregard fruit cultivation as an efficient economic measure may have been the volatile climate, which he did not always find conducive to a plentiful crop: "Our fruit is all destroyed with the long spring north-east winds," he complained in 1732, "and I shall have the tenth part of my last year's fruit."[101] While staying at Sheridan's place at Quilca in very bad weather, Swift thought gloomily of his garden in Dublin: "I am told there is very little Fruit in the Kingdom, and that I have but 20 Apples where I expected 500."[102] His early cultivation efforts at Laracor, too, were at times thwarted by inclement weather: "I am here quarrelling with the frosty weather, for spoiling my poor half dozen of Blossoms," he told Dean Stearne in April 1710.[103] Likewise, when in "An Apology to the Lady Carteret" the vicereine visited Patrick Delany to enjoy the produce of his garden, it was a breezy day and her Ladyship was uncomfortable outdoors, owing to "the scorching Sun" that was offset by the "chilling Air."[104]

While it is true that the country's harvests were at times affected by wet and cold weather, it appears that various kinds of home-grown fruit like apples and pears were usually in plentiful supply. A drawing by Hugh Douglas Hamilton of a street vendor in Dublin later in the century shows her surrounded by wicker baskets filled to their brims,[105] and the gradual renaissance of cider implies that apple harvests were sufficiently large.[106] In fact, there are a number of inconsistencies in Swift's frequently asserted view that Ireland was a country devoid

100 "An Humble Address to Both Houses of Parliament," *The Drapier's Letters to the People of Ireland against Receiving Wood's Halfpence*, ed. Herbert Davis (Oxford: Clarendon Press, 1965), p. 172. The country was not entirely dependent on grain imports; rather, it "remained more than self-sufficient in its main food cereal, oats … and although [it] had become a net importer of wheat, domestic production accounted for a high proportion of consumption even in a bad year" (Cullen, *An Economic History of Ireland since 1660*, p. 68).

101 Swift to Dean Brandreth, 30 June 1732, *Correspondence*, ed. Woolley, III, 495.

102 Swift to Chetwode, 19 July 1725, *Correspondence*, ed. Woolley, II, 573.

103 Swift to Dean Stearne, 17 April 1710, *Correspondence*, ed. Woolley, I, 279.

104 *Poems*, ed. Williams, II, p. 378, l. 122; Woolley, "The Canon of Swift's Poems: The Case of 'An Apology to the Lady Carteret,'" p. 248.

105 See William Laffan and Brendan Rooney, "Apples and Pears," *The Cries of Dublin*, ed. Laffan, p. 116.

106 Arthur Young was impressed by the apple harvest for cider production in Co. Clare: "I never beheld trees so loaden with apples as in Sir Lucius O'Brien's orchard; it amazed me that they did not break under the immense load which bowed down the branches. He expected a hogshead a tree from several" (*A Tour in Ireland with General Observations on the Present State of that Kingdom*, 2 vols [Dublin: George Bonham, 1780], I, 466).

of hope with regard to successful cultivation.[107] A case in point is Sheridan's place in Cavan, about which the Dean constantly grumbled, exaggerating its disorderly condition and even painting it as emblematic of the dismal state of the country.[108] However, while staying in London in 1727, he confessed to his friend: "[I] long to eat your Fruit, for I dare eat none here."[109] So it appears that Sheridan's gardens and orchards did produce acceptable crops after all. In July 1735, Sheridan tried to entice a reluctant Swift to visit him in the country by enumerating various culinary delights and continued: "Such fruit! ... such rasp-berries! such bilberries! ... were never yet seen in any one country yet!"[110] Similarly, in June and July 1736, he boasted of a plentiful harvest of strawberries and sent the Dean a list of the victuals on offer at his place, such as raspberries, gooseberries, currants, and even oranges, not to mention a wide range of meats and vegetables.[111] Although this proof of Sheridan's successful cultivation efforts and the gifts he sent to the Deanery should have assuaged Swift's criticism, the Dean would still reply with characteristic grumpiness that he believed "nothing of [Sheridan's] Garden Improvements."[112] Yet when it suited his argument, he would equally downplay Ireland's shortcomings or go so far as to claim a degree of superiority. Trying to entice his friends Pope and Gay to visit him in Dublin, he claimed: "As to Ireland, the Air of this House is good, and of the Kingdom very good, but the best fruits fall short a little. All things to Eat and drink except very few, better th[a]n in London."[113] Likewise, when staying at Market Hill in 1728, he told Lord Oxford that even up north, "Codlins

107 His view was certainly influenced by the uneven state of agriculture in the country, as "areas of intense cultivation alternated with stretches of common and waste" (Connolly, *Religion, Law, and Power*, p. 42).

108 See Baltes-Ellermann, "Boundless Wit in Confined Spaces: The Occasional Poems on Gaulstown House, Delville, and Quilca by Swift and his Friends in the 1720s," pp. 93-98.

109 Swift to Sheridan, 24 June 1727, *Correspondence*, ed. Woolley, III, 101.

110 Sheridan to Swift, 16 July 1735, *Correspondence*, ed. Woolley, IV, 144.

111 Sheridan to Swift, 3 June and 6 July 1736, *Correspondence*, ed. Woolley, IV, 309, 327-28.

112 Swift to Sheridan, 5 June 1736, *Correspondence*, ed. Woolley, IV, 313. Swift's continual lecturing of his friend was an ironic means of showing his fondness for Sheridan, but he probably also feared that any favourable report might weaken the force of his argument of Ireland's unfortunate condition: It was unacceptable, he asserted, that "because there may be a Dozen Families in this Town, able to entertain their *English* Friends in a generous Manner at their Tables; their Guests, upon their Return to *England*, shall report, that we wallow in Riches and Luxury" ("A Short View of the State of Ireland," *Prose Works*, XII, 12). The pamphlet was a reaction to the publication of John Browne's *Seasonable Remarks on Trade*, which had painted a rosy picture of Ireland's economic future; see James Kelly, "Jonathan Swift and the Irish Economy in the 1720s," *Eighteenth-Century Ireland*, 6 [1991], 7-36 [pp. 20, 23-24]).

113 Swift to Pope and Gay, 23 November 1727, *Correspondence*, ed. Woolley, III, 141.

will sometimes grow ripe, provided it will be a favorable season."[114] This positive impression was shared by strangers to the country. In September 1729, Chetwode informed Swift that he had just had a visitor "of some figure and distinction" who "gorged himself with what he calld better fruit than he eat in England or abroad."[115]

While there is plenty of evidence relating to the fruit gardens and orchards of the Irish social elite, not only in letters, diaries, and account books but also on contemporary maps and in structural remains, the relevance of fruit cultivation within the Irish economy at large is difficult to fathom. Travellers and surveyors usually focused on the production and consumption of staples like meat, potatoes, cereals, and dairy products, and mentioned fruit only in passing, if at all.[116] This overall scarcity of references suggests that fruit was not a topic of interest to economists, who rather looked out for sources of commercial value (like grain) or of nutritional value (like potatoes). One of the few pamphlets arguing in favour of promoting orchards in Ireland conceded that this was merely a side issue in the larger debate on the promotion of husbandry.[117] Official attempts to encourage economic improvement disregarded fruit trees in the various legislative initiatives relating to the promotion of tree-planting.[118]

---

114 Swift to the Earl of Oxford, 21 September 1728, *Correspondence*, ed. Woolley, III, 197. Codlins were a "variety of apple, in shape elongated and rather tapering towards the eye" (OED online, s.v.).

115 Chetwode to Swift, 10 September 1729, *Correspondence*, ed. Woolley, III, 250.

116 Surveying the countryside in the early 1680s, William Molyneux related that land in County Wexford had been improved and now yielded "all sorts of ... corn, grain, orchards, fruits, sweet herbs." Roads in eastern Ulster were lined with "houses, little orchards and gardens," and he identified there a "preference for fruit trees good cider being sold here for 30s the hogshead" (quoted from Clarkson and Crawford, *Feast and Famine*, p. 16). By contrast, Sir William Petty did not mention any fruit, but rather asserted that the typical diet of the poorer country dwellers consisted of milk, bread cakes, potatoes, eggs, butter as well as meat like "hen or rabbet" or shellfish in coastal regions ("A New Anatomy of Ireland [1672]," *Tracts Chiefly Relating to Ireland* [London: Boulter Grierson, 1769], p. 355). Several decades later, a pamphlet arguing for the extension of tillage, too, calculated the food requirements of a farmer's family as chiefly comprising cereals, potatoes, buttermilk, cheese, butter, meat, eggs, as well as "the produce of the garden" (probably pulses and vegetables) (Philip Skelton, *The Necessity of Tillage and Granaries: In a Letter to a Member of Parliament Living in the County of ----* [Dublin, 1741], pp. 9-11).

117 Samuel Madden, *Reflections and Resolutions Proper for the Gentlemen of Ireland* (Dublin: by R. Reilly for George Ewing, 1738), p. 153 (mispaginated as "145").

118 William J. Smyth, "The Greening of Ireland: Tenant Tree-Planting in the Eighteenth and Nineteenth Centuries," *Irish Forestry* 54, no 1 (1997), 70. An exception was the *Act to Encourage the Improvement of Barren and Waste Land and Bogs, and Planting of Timber Trees and Orchards*, passed in 1731 (5 Geo. II, c. 9), which decreed that tenants planting apple or pear trees were to be rewarded with a shilling for every "bearing and profitable"

However, the terms of the leases among tenant farmers sometimes stipulated the planting and tending of fruit trees, and benevolent proprietors furnished saplings from their own nurseries.[119] Besides, an eminent historian has identified several regions where orchards for cider-making were common, although these were "far fewer on the homesteads of families below the rather ambiguous status of minor gentry or gentlemen farmers."[120] Hence, it appears once more that fruit cultivation depended very much on social class as well as on the area of residence within Ireland. Especially in the western regions, problems of soil and exposure as well as the absence of a solid tenant farming class militated against tree-planting.[121] As a result, the classic image associated with the British Isles of the small farmer's cottage adorned with an apple tree was rarely to be encountered.[122] Rather, for those living close to subsistence level, such as the large number of cottiers and labourers, nutritious food like potatoes as well as those kinds of vegetable that could be grown from their seeds in virtually all kinds of soil were of primary importance. Meanwhile, the chances of finding wild fruit in the forests and hedgerows were rather slim, because owing to more than a century of exploitation and upheaval, there was still a widespread scarcity of hedgerows and woodland in Ireland.[123] Also, the radical redefinition of property rights that had taken place in the sixteenth and

---

tree at the expiration of the lease (*The Statutes at Large, Passed in the Parliaments Held in Ireland: From the Third Year of Edward the Second, A.D. 1310, to the First Year of George the Third, A. D. 1761 Inclusive*, 8 vols [Dublin: Boulter Grierson, 1765], V, 515).

119 See Barnard, *Making the Grand Figure*, pp. 191, 196; Smyth, "The Greening of Ireland: Tenant Tree-Planting in the Eighteenth and Nineteenth Centuries," p. 58, as well as the examples in Costello, *Irish Demesne Landscapes*, p. 87n77.

120 L. M. Cullen, *The Emergence of Modern Ireland, 1600-1900* (New York: Holmes and Meier, 1981), p. 168. The regions of most intense concentration of orchards, Cullen says, were those of "strong pre-1641 colonization of English settlers, where landowners and tenants introduced their homeland style of agriculture," that is, of the cider-rich south of England (p. 167).

121 Smyth, "The Greening of Ireland: Tenant Tree-Planting in the Eighteenth and Nineteenth Centuries," p. 61.

122 I am indebted to Professor Andrew Carpenter for this vital information.

123 McCracken, "The Social Structure and Social Life, 1714-60," pp. 42-43. The destruction of woodland had begun with the increasing settlement of the country and was quickened by the demand for timber and by the rapid growth of the iron industry in the seventeenth century (Cullen, *An Economic History of Ireland since 1660*, p. 8). Besides, during times of trouble, trees had been felled to prevent miscreants from hiding in them (Barnard, *Making the Grand Figure*, p. 194). Although the Irish Parliament now legislated to encourage tree-planting, Swift's assessment was less than sanguine: "All the acts for encouraging plantations of forest-trees are, I am told, extremely defective ... the hedges generally miscarry ... merely for want of common skill and care." He likewise predicted the futility of proposing to landlords "to oblige all tenants and cottagers to plant ash or elm before their

seventeenth centuries had imposed a body of English property law which extinguished customary use rights like gleaning or access to common land.[124]

On the other hand, the gardens and orchards of the grand estates and large farms provided work for a variety of people, not only for a bevy of gardeners and under-gardeners, but also seasonal work for unskilled labourers, such as weeding and picking, down to jobs for children, such as scaring away birds.[125] These locals may occasionally have received a share of the harvest surplus or been given cuttings or seeds from the demesne. The gardeners were sometimes allowed to sell what was not needed at the master's table as an addition to their wages (with some of them choosing to do so without permission).[126] There is also evidence of contracts by which enterprising outsiders were permitted to harvest fruit from country farms or from the demesnes of absentee landlords.[127] Finally, servants delivering gifts of fruit to some honoured neighbour could expect to supplement their earnings with handsome tips.[128]

Fruit, then, possessed commercial value and played a vital part as a marketable commodity in a domestic context. While excess produce from the landlord's demesne was usually sent to market for sale, rent obligations, especially in times of low grain prices, ensured that farmers, too, tended to sell any produce that was not needed for subsistence.[129] Sales opportunities offered themselves on local fairs and in provincial towns. In Dublin, country dwellers selling the produce of their gardens or orchards were a common feature, either in the city streets or at Ormond Market, which was located on the quay at the south side of Ormond Bridge. Fruit could likewise be obtained from individual street vendors, who hawked imported goods like oranges and lemons in the street

cabbins, and round their potatoe-gardens" ("An Answer to Several Letters Sent me from Unknown Hands," *Prose Works*, XII, 88).

124 Connolly, *Religion, Law, and Power*, p. 55; Raymond D. Crotty, *Irish Agricultural Production, its Volume and Structure* (Cork: Cork University Press, 1966), pp. 6-8. Yet whether, especially in times of want, such property rights were always respected (or, in turn, forcibly pressed by the landlord) is another matter; see, for instance, Lord Molesworth's complaint in *Some Considerations for the Promoting of Agriculture and Employing the Poor* (Dublin: George Grierson, 1723), pp. 32-33.

125 Barnard, *Making the Grand Figure*, p. 208. This was important because underemployment, especially among the cottiers and labourers, was one of the causes of extensive rural poverty (Cullen, *An Economic History of Ireland since 1660*, p. 64).

126 Barnard, *Making the Grand Figure*, p. 219; Costello, *Irish Demesne Landscapes*, pp. 41-42.

127 See Barnard, *Making the Grand Figure*, p. 219.

128 Barnard, *Making the Grand Figure*, p. 199.

129 Connolly, *Religion, Law, and Power*, p. 54; Cullen, *An Economic History of Ireland since 1660*, p. 47.

or sold them door-to-door. Swift depicted poor street hawkers selling apples, plums, pears, and oranges in his "Verses Made for Women who Cry Apples":

APPLES.
COME buy my fine Wares,
Plumbs, Apples and Pears,
A hundred a Penny,
In Conscience too many,
Come, will you have any;
My Children are seven,
I wish them in Heaven,
My Husband's a Sot,
With his Pipe and his Pot,
Not a Farthing will gain 'em,
And I must maintain 'em.[130]

Using dramatic impersonation rather than authorial comment, Swift relies on the speaker for an illustration of her doleful world. Asserting Swift's compassion and charity towards people in need,[131] Delany related to Lord Orrery how the Dean used to go and see poor women, some of whom "sold plumbs," and also made the odd small purchase from these vendors.[132] However, judging from Hamilton's drawings, street sellers of fruit in Dublin were not necessarily of the poorer kind. The orange vendor, for instance, is depicted wearing good quality shoes with raised heels;[133] the woman selling gingerbread and apples appears to possess the paraphernalia of her trade, displaying her wares in two large baskets placed on low stools; the couple selling apples and pears are depicted perching behind three baskets of different size, which are either placed on a stool or before a trestle table. This array of equipment suggests that they have a cart for transportation at their disposal. In fact, Dublin being a teeming and prosperous city, "these street traders survived and thrived because there was a growing demand among the respectable and modest rather than from a

130 *Poems*, ed. Williams, III, 951-52, ll. 1-11.

131 See *Account Books*, eds Thompson and Thompson, p. cxxxvi.

132 Patrick Delany, *Observations upon Lord Orrery's Remarks on the Life and Writings of Dr. Jonathan Swift* (London: W. Reeve and A. Linde, 1754), p. 131. He continues: "If any of their ware were such, as he could possibly make use of, or pretend to make use of, he always bought some: and paid for every half-penny-worth, at least sixpence: and for every penny-worth, a shilling" (pp. 132-33). Besides, Swift's accounts for 1734 record a Christmas gift of 1s 1d to an "Apple wom^{n}" (*Account Books*, eds Thompson and Thompson, p. 265).

133 Laffan and Rooney, "Oranges and Lemons," p. 86. This, of course, was also the result of a vibrant trade with cast-off clothes.

few rich establishments."[134] For those with some capital, fruit selling could also expand into a small-scale business venture: One of Hamilton's drawings shows a woman offering "saucer pies," a common refreshment made of two pieces of pastry with a filling, often apple.[135]

On the whole, vending home-grown fruit on domestic markets was a seasonal business, precisely because it did not keep overly long, unless the seller possessed the means to store or preserve it. Arguably, for the same reason, fruit carried only a limited potential as trading goods. The mainstay of the Irish economy was the export of a narrow range of basic products, such as grain, beef, butter, and wool. Among these, grain was easy to store for a long period of time, and perishable goods like beef and butter could be transported in barrels and preserved in salt. Most fruit was vulnerable to damage when transported over long distances and, even when of greater durability, required expert storage, which was bound to inflate transportation costs. Besides, all of Europe being agricultural and largely self-sufficient,[136] foreign markets seem to have been indifferent to imports of any such commodities from Ireland. No economic account, contemporary or modern, suggests that the produce of Irish orchards, either fresh, dried, or processed, played any part in the export statistics. By contrast, there was a steady flow of imports of fruit that needed a milder climate, such as oranges, lemons, raisins, figs, and almonds, which were usually shipped from Spain, Portugal, France, or Morocco.[137] Swift, as was his wont, ironically pleaded for countermeasures:

> I heartily wish a Law were enacted, under severe Penalties, against drinking any *Punch* at all: For, nothing is easier, than to prove a disaffected Liquor. The chief Ingredients, which are *Brandy, Oranges*, and *Lemons*, are all sent us from *Popish* Countries; and nothing remains of *Protestant* Growth, but *Sugar* and *Water*.[138]

---

134 Barnard, "The Society and Economy of Mid-Eighteenth-Century Dublin," *The Cries of Dublin*, ed. Laffan, p. 28. Sales opportunities improved as the city's population expanded from 45,000 in 1685 to 92,000 in 1725 (Connolly, *Religion, Law, and Power*, p. 44).

135 William Laffan and Brendan Rooney, "Ginger Bread and Apples," *The Cries of Dublin*, ed. Laffan, p. 168.

136 Cullen, *An Economic History of Ireland since 1660*, pp. 9, 26.

137 See, for instance, Clarkson and Crawford, *Feast and Famine*, p. 51, Table 3.5. Some still-life paintings depicting fruit give us an idea of the containers in which they were probably transported; see, for example, the painting entitled *Still Life with Oranges and Walnuts* (1772) by Luis Meléndez in the National Gallery, London.

138 "An Examination of Certain Abuses, Corruptions, and Enormities in the City of Dublin," *Prose Works*, XII, 224.

However, although he constantly derided the volume of foreign imports, Swift was not averse to enjoying foreign delicacies himself. What is more, contemporary proposals to raise the duties on these and related luxury goods to increase the revenue roused the Dean's disapproval: "If you should lay an additional duty of one penny a pound on raisins, or sugar, the revenue, instead of rising, would certainly sink; and the consequence would be, to lessen the number of plum-puddings, and ruin the confectioner."[139] One wonders whether he was in jest when he defended such luxuries as necessities; after all, their demand was probably inelastic in that price increases would not have greatly depressed consumption. Yet, significantly, Swift not only claimed that taxation would have serious repercussions on domestic business activity, but went as far as to insinuate that such a measure would undermine fashion and refinement among the Irish gentry and even threaten British cultural influence.[140]

6. Conclusion

Fruit had a different relevance for different parts of Irish society in the eighteenth century, and its impact was closely linked to the development of fashion and commercialization. For some, it was a highly valued (and sometimes highly priced) commodity with important social implications; for others, it was chiefly of commercial significance as a seasonal supplement to, or a primary source of, their cash income.

The various comments by Swift and his friends testify to a central position of fruit in the lives of the Irish gentry, which was hardly different from that in England.[141] To a great extent, this was the result of a carefully maintained identification with English ways and manners including the social obligations of a well-kept table and a carefully tended garden. Among the prosperous, fruit was not simply a garden produce to meet the household's victualling requirements but the object of competitive cultivation, which emerged from "a deep scientific curiosity about botany ... plus a fashion for gardening and display ... It was

139 "A Proposal that all the Ladies and Women of Ireland should appear constantly in Irish Manufactures," *Prose Works*, XII, 125.

140 In fact, puddings and pies evolved as icons of British food identity throughout the eighteenth century, while increased attention to sweet dishes and desserts led to a rise in status of domestic and commercial confectioners (see Sexton, "Food and Culinary Cultures in Pre-Famine Ireland," pp. 282-83).

141 This is confirmed by contemporary recipe books; see the analysis by Shanahan, "'Whipt with a twig rod': Irish Manuscript Recipe Books as Sources for the Study of Culinary Material Culture," pp. 187-205.

all enlivened and empowered by … the publication of books, and diverse other contacts with foreign food cultures."[142] In their desire to emulate English ways and fashions, the Irish gentry had to work harder than their neighbours, as they had to deal with the challenges posed by Ireland's climatic conditions, the quality of the soil, and not least the scarcity of a skilled workforce.[143] Hence, the pleasure generated by the successful growing of tasty or even exotic fruit infused garden owners with particular pride, and the result was judiciously presented to friends and visitors.

Swift was as ardent a lover of fruit as any of his contemporaries, even if this partiality was tinged with the fear of side-effects on his physical well-being. To be sure, he was among the fortunate who did not have to economize to satisfy their taste for fruit. Although home-grown apples and pears had an established place on domestic markets, and although the range and volume of imported fruit like oranges and lemons increased, dietary extravagances did not reach the population at large. If they had sufficient means, people living in market centres might enjoy a taste of such delicacies, just as they were the most likely to benefit from the surpluses of the rich man's estate sent into town for sale. Yet on the whole, most fruit retained the status of a luxury. This view is borne out by Swift's private account books, where purchases of fruit (oranges, lemons, cherries, raspberries, and raisins) appear as separate items and are listed under the heading "Extr^{dys}" – just as the entries for sugar, gingerbread, and brandy. It is also implied in Swift's ironical comparison of the cravings of his countrymen for imported "Extravagancies" like "Flanders Lace … Italian or Indian Silks, Tea, Coffee, Chocolate" to those of "the beggar [who] could not eat his Veal without Oranges."[144] It is even suggested by the proverbial use of a term like "plum," which in certain contexts denoted a fortune.

Given the fact that orchards were an integral part of both grand estates and tenant farms, it is still remarkable that none of Swift's tracts on the condition of Ireland contains any reference to the economic potential of fruit cultivation; nor do his account books give a hint that he encouraged the systematic growing of fruit among his parishioners.[145] Moreover, although the growing and selling of fruit was providing work for a wide range of people, the Dean did apparently not consider it to have the potential to compensate the widespread underemployment which he frequently blamed on the neglect of agricultural

---

142 Thirsk, *Food in Early Modern England*, p. 294.

143 Those who could afford it employed expert gardeners from England or the Continent (see Barnard, *Irish Protestants*, pp. 227-28).

144 "Answer to Several Letters from Unknown Persons," *Prose Works*, XII, 79-80.

145 The produce of his tithe lands were chiefly grain, hay, and wool (see *Account Books*, eds Thompson and Thompson, pp. xcvi-xcvii).

production. Indeed, it is not known whether he supported the Dublin Society's proposal in the late 1730s for the planting of fruit trees to encourage the manufacture of cider: "Were Orchards more generally planted among us," one of them argued, "we might soon have Cyder enough, not only for the common use for our own Tables, but for Inns and Alehouses."[146]

In fact, Swift preferred not to waste his time on discussing any practical schemes; on the contrary, he had become chronically impatient with "idle and visionary" projects "for preserving this Kingdom from utter ruin," and declared himself weary of "so many crude Proposals in letters sent me from unknown hands."[147] His attitude was that of a moralist, who focused on highlighting public grievances and on lecturing those whom he held responsible for the well-being of the Irish economy. Despite his pervading pessimism, he claimed that Ireland was "capable of producing all Things necessary, and most Things convenient for Life, sufficient for the Support of four Times the Number of its Inhabitants."[148] Therefore, he vigorously denounced those landlords who "by *penal Clauses*, absolutely prohibit[ed] their Tenants from Plowing" and kept exhorting the elite to live up to their responsibilities and encourage planting and tillage.[149] His most acerbic scorn was reserved for the absentee landlords who squandered their fortunes abroad, neglected their estates, and were thus chiefly responsible for "the depopulating of the Kingdom, the leaving of so many Parts of it wild and uncultivated."[150] Swift constantly nagged his friend Charles Ford to look after his Irish estate: "If you had told me you began to take a Relish in planting and improving the Scene, I should begin to have favorable Thoughts of Y[ou]r Conversion."[151] It may appear inconsistent with this critical

---

146 Madden, *Reflections and Resolutions Proper for the Gentlemen of Ireland*, p. 70. The Dublin Society was a group of public-spirited gentlemen who intended to improve the country's agricultural and economic situation.

147 "A Letter to the Archbishop of Dublin, concerning the Weavers," *Prose Works*, XII, 66. Elsewhere, he declared: "There is hardly a scheme proposed for improving the trade of this Kingdom, which doth not manifestly shew the Stupidity and ignorance of the Proposer" ("An Answer to Several Letters Sent me from Unknown Hands. Written in the Year 1729," XII, 79).

148 "Causes for the Wretched Condition of Ireland," *Prose Works*, IX, 199.

149 "A Proposal for the Universal Use of Irish Manufacture," *Prose Works*, IX, 15.

150 "An Humble Address to Both Houses of Parliament," *The Drapier's Letters*, ed. Davis, p. 159.

151 Swift to Ford, 12 November 1708, *Correspondence*, ed. Woolley, II, 217. There were quite a few, however, who took their duties seriously and devoted their energies to improving their estate and experimenting with new crops and methods; see the examples in Barnard, *Making the Grand Figure*, pp. 188-225. Swift did give someone credit for being an exemplary landlord: Staying at Sir Robert Cope's place at Loughgall, he declared: "The People, the Churches and the Plantations make me think I am in England" (Swift to Ford, 22 July 1722, *Correspondence*, ed. Woolley, II, 427).

attitude, therefore, that he did not frown upon those who, by lavishing both their attention and their funds on the choice produce of their gardens and greenhouses, were (literally) indulging their appetites. After all, next to blaming them for negligence, the Dean habitually berated his compatriots for what he considered extravagance and taste for luxuries. Even good and intimate friends like Sheridan and Delany received their share of (admittedly comic) exposure, the one for the incompetent management of his estate, the other for his pretentious gardening projects.[152] Yet like others, Swift apparently saw no contradiction between relishing the fruits of the earth and the advancement of the public good. However much the Irish nobility and gentry might satisfy their ambition and craving for pleasure by growing rare or exotic fruit, they hardly deserved to be scolded, because they were, after all, cultivating the soil, investing into their property, promoting a spirit of emulation among friends and dependants, and thus acting in the service of their country.[153]

152 See *Poems*, ed. Williams, II, 476-78, ll. 59-88; III, 1035, ll. 1-12; *Prose Works*, V, 219-21; Baltes-Ellermann, "Boundless Wit in Confined Spaces: The Occasional Poems on Gaulstown House, Delville, and Quilca by Swift and his Friends in the 1720s," pp. 90-91, 94-98.

153 See Baltes-Ellermann, "Boundless Wit in Confined Spaces: The Occasional Poems on Gaulstown House, Delville, and Quilca by Swift and his Friends in the 1720s," pp. 100-1. Although gardening enthusiasts chiefly added to the pleasures of the table among their own rank, "seeming indulgences could be justified for their wider applications. Trials might in time improve yields, set standards for neighbours and tenants, raise rents and alleviate shortages of staple foods" (Barnard, *Making the Grand Figure*, pp. 218-19). One problem, however, was that these garden devotees projected on others the very pleasure which they derived from their activities. It was difficult to convince those of the benefit of such improvements who did not own the plot (p. 224).

D. W. Hayton
Ulster University

Swift and the Politics of Dublin, 1727-33

Abstract. Swift's involvement in Dublin corporation politics in 1733, in publishing adjurations to common councilmen to vote for Eaton Stannard as Recorder and Humphrey French for Lord Mayor, was unprecedented. It reflects his extraordinary popularity and the status he had acquired as a political oracle. The background to these two short works has not hitherto been investigated. Evidence from the Dublin corporation records and newspaper reports as well as printed pamphlets and broadsheets shows a city in crisis. Severe economic problems, resulting in social dislocation and a breakdown in public order, combined with the corporation's own record of incompetence, had undermined the standing of the city's Aldermen and broken down the consensus politics of the period 1715-*c*.26. Factionalism within the guilds, the common council and the Court of Aldermen created a febrile atmosphere in which every municipal election was fiercely contested. Swift did not engage with these local issues, however, couching his response instead in the traditional terms of a national political discourse of patriotism and corruption.

During 1733, Swift twice intervened directly in Dublin civic politics, publishing papers which called upon inhabitants to cast their votes for particular candidates, first in an election for the Recordership and then for a by-election in the parliamentary constituency. On the face of it, making a direct appeal of this kind to the city electorate would seem a perfectly natural thing for him to have done. After all, the *Drapier's Letters* had elevated him to heroic status with the Dublin populace, so much so that political interests of every stripe claimed his favour; indeed, the allegation that one candidate in a parliamentary by-election, Alderman James Somerville, had previously urged the prosecution of the Drapier, was sufficiently alarming for Somerville's supporters to rush into print to protest their candidate's innocence.[1] Furthermore, Swift was witnessing at close quarters the dire condition of the city. In the early 1730s, the neighbourhood of the deanery swarmed with the casualties of Dublin's collapsing social fabric: ruined tradesmen and unemployed artisans, ragged beggars fleeing from starvation in the countryside, the throng of prostitutes who roamed the streets at night, and, not least, violent gangs like the "Kevan Bail" who, when they were not hacking each other to pieces, assaulted passing gentlemen and collegians, and fought pitched battles with the constables. Swift had already written about

1 *Dublin Intelligence*, 30 September, 11, 14 October 1729; *October 11, 1729: To the Worthy Freemen and Freeholders of this City* ([Dublin, 1729]).

 | DOI:10.30965/9783846763971_021

the problem of urban poverty and the influx of vagrants, although primarily as an instance of the demise of traditional social norms and the degeneration of the Irish landed gentry, who were no longer prepared to assume their proper responsibilities for the dispensation of charity.[2] He had also taken a keen interest in the economic plight of the weavers in the Liberties, though again his primary focus was on what he saw as the underlying cause, the malign consequences of Ireland's constitutional subordination to Westminster. These were long-standing concerns. But they had issued in political writings of a general nature and had not previously driven him to try to influence the outcome of elections in the city. To understand why he should have involved himself directly in the civic politics of Dublin in 1733 requires first and foremost that we understand what was going on in the capital at the time, and, despite the considerable attention that has been paid by scholars to Dublin's history, the pattern of events in the late 1720s and early 1730s remains tantalizingly unclear.

Eighteenth-century Dublin has been written about extensively, and in particular Jacqueline Hill and Sean Murphy have done much to elucidate the nature and dynamics of the city's political life.[3] But the various narratives that are available have little to say about the 1720s and 1730s. Customarily, the story jumps several decades, from the bitter party struggles of Whig and Tory factions among the city Aldermen in Queen Anne's reign to the appearance of a different kind of political agitation in the 1740s, the campaigns of the popular tribune, Charles Lucas. This leap requires the reader to ignore the work of scholars like Bryan Coleborne, who have traced the emergence of a lively political culture in the capital, centring on the proliferation of cheap print, long

2 See, for example, *A Modest Proposal for Preventing the Children of Poor People from Being a Burden to their Parents or Country; and for Making them Beneficial to the Publick* (Dublin: S. Harding, 1729), in *Irish Political Writings after 1725: A Modest Proposal and Other Works*, eds D. W. Hayton and Adam Rounce (Cambridge: Cambridge University Press, 2018), pp. 154, 159; *A Proposal for Giving Badges to the Beggars in All the Parishes of Dublin* (Dublin: George Faulkner, 1737), in *Irish Political Writings after 1725*, eds Hayton and Rounce, p. 312.

3 Jacqueline Hill, *From Patriots to Unionists: Dublin Civic Politics and Irish Protestant Patriotism, 1660-1840* (Oxford: Clarendon Press, 1997); and the same author's "Corporate Values in Hanoverian Edinburgh and Dublin," *Conflict, Identity, and Economic Development: Ireland and Scotland, 1600-1939*, eds S. J. Connolly, R. A. Houston, and R. A. Morris (Preston: Carnegie Publishing, 1995), pp. 114-24; Sean Murphy, "Charles Lucas and the Dublin Election of 1748-1749," *Parliamentary History*, 2 (1983), 93-111; and all of the following titles by the same author: "The Corporation of Dublin, 1660-1760," *Dublin Historical Record*, 38 (1984), 22-35; "Municipal Politics and Popular Disturbances, 1660-1800," *Dublin through the Ages*, ed. Art Cosgrove (Dublin: College Press, 1988), pp. 77-92; "Charles Lucas, Catholicism and Nationalism," *Eighteenth-Century Ireland*, 8 (1993), 83-102. See also, in general, David Dickson, *Dublin: The Making of a Capital City* (London: Profile Books, 2014), Chapter 3.

before Lucas's arrival in the spotlight.[4] This neglect of the decades immediately following the Hanoverian Succession seems to reflect a broader assumption made by previous generations of historians, that once a Whig ascendancy had been firmly established in Ireland in 1714, all life was squeezed out of electoral politics. Skirmishes in the Irish parliament, it was thought, no longer had much, if any, relevance to the 'political nation' at large. Thus, even in a city the size of Dublin, racked by serious economic and social problems and with a vibrant market in printed matter, the control of the Whig oligarchy was not challenged until Lucas and James Digges Latouche took up the cause of municipal reform in 1742 on behalf of the ordinary freemen against the aldermanic elite.

According to this traditional interpretation, the Irish electoral system became increasingly sclerotic after 1714, dominated by the landed class: parliamentary seats – contested only rarely – were at the disposal of patrons, to the extent that they were bought and sold as a species of property.[5] More recently, however, detailed local investigations by Toby Barnard, David Fleming, and others have shown that in some boroughs – small towns like Kinsale and Youghal in County Cork, Dungarvan in County Waterford, or Navan in County Meath, and more substantial urban centres like Limerick and Sligo – voters could not be taken for granted, and ruling interests were occasionally overturned; moreover, in these boroughs there were real political conflicts, over real issues, some of them local and specific, others of a national character.[6] It seems reasonable

4 Bryan Coleborne, "Jonathan Swift and the Dunces of Dublin," doctoral dissertation, National University of Ireland, 1982; and the same author's "The Dublin Grub Street: The Documentary Evidence in the Case of John Browne," *Swift Studies*, 2 (1987), 12-24. See also James Kelly, "Political Publishing, 1550-1700," *The Oxford History of the Irish Book, III: The Irish Book in English, 1550-1800*, eds Raymond Gillespie and Andrew Hadfield (Oxford: Oxford University Press, 2006), 216-24; Toby Barnard, *Brought to Book: Print in Ireland, 1680-1784* (Dublin: Four Courts Press, 2017), Chapter 2.

5 Edward Porritt and Annie G. Porritt, *The Unreformed House of Commons: Parliamentary Representation Before 1832*, 2 vols (Cambridge: Cambridge University Press, 1909), II, 295-366; J. L. McCracken, "Irish Parliamentary Elections, 1727-68," *Irish Historical Studies*, 5 (1946-47), 209-30; and the same author's "The Political Structure, 1714-60," *A New History of Ireland, IV: Eighteenth-Century Ireland, 1691-1800*, eds T. W. Moody and W. E. Vaughan (Oxford: Clarendon Press, 1986), 72-76; Edith M. Johnston, *Great Britain and Ireland 1760-1800: A Study in Political Administration* (Edinburgh: Oliver and Boyd, 1963), pp. 118-78; A. P. W. Malcomson, "'The Parliamentary Traffic of this Country,'" *Penal Era and Golden Age: Essays in Irish History, 1690-1800*, eds Thomas Bartlett and D. W. Hayton (Belfast: Ulster Historical Foundation, 1979), pp. 137-61.

6 T. C. Barnard, "Considering the Inconsiderable: Electors, Patrons and Irish Elections, 1659-1761," *Parliamentary History*, 20 (2001), 106-27; D. A. Fleming, "Patriots and Politics in Navan, 1753-5," *Irish Historical Studies*, 36 (2008-9), 502-21; the same author's *Politics and Provincial People: Sligo and Limerick, 1691-1761* (Manchester: Manchester University Press, 2010), Chapters 1-2. See also D. W. Hayton, "Voters, Patrons and Parties: Parliamentary Elections in Ireland,

to consider whether Dublin might have shared in this development, especially since evidence suggests an unusual level of political activity after 1727 in both the corporation and the parliamentary constituency.

To take the parliamentary constituency first. George I's death in 1727 precipitated a general election in Ireland – until the passage of the Octennial Act in 1768 this was the only circumstance in which a dissolution was imperative – and in a poll which began in October and lasted for three weeks, the freemen and freeholders of Dublin city chose Alderman Samuel Burton (1687-1733) and William Howard (*c.*1680-1727), younger brother of the Church of Ireland Bishop of Killala. It was a three-cornered contest, the defeated candidate being Swift's friend, Alderman John Stoyte (*c.*1660-1729), who was said to have had the Dean's backing. The total number of voters, between 1,500 and 2,000, was relatively small by English standards – London in this period had well over 7,000 voters and Westminster over 8,000[7] – but the election was strenuously fought, with a great deal of competitive entertainment for the voters, and thus unusually expensive for Ireland, costing as much as £1,500 at a time when election expenses were usually tallied in the low hundreds.[8]

By accident of circumstance, there were three further elections within the next six years. In January 1728, Dubliners went to the polls following the sudden death of William Howard (and in passing it is worth noting that Howard's father reported that his funeral cortege had been attended by "vast crowds," which suggests an unusual degree of popular mourning for the loss of a young man whose public career could scarcely be described as distinguished).[9] This time, Stoyte was successful, by a narrow margin, in an election in which over 2,700 votes were cast.[10] We hear nothing of Swift being involved, though he must have been gratified by the result. Unfortunately, Stoyte himself died not long afterwards, and within a year the seat was again contested, this time by two Aldermen, James Somerville (the alleged enemy of the Drapier) and a former

---

*c.*1692-1727," *Partisan Politics, Principle and Reform in Parliament and the Constituencies, 1689-1880: Essays in Memory of John A. Phillips*, eds Clyve Jones, Philip Salmon, and R. W. Davis (Edinburgh: Edinburgh University Press, 2005), pp. 44-70.

7 Romney Sedgwick, *The House of Commons, 1715-54*, 2 vols (London: H.M.S.O., 1970), I, 279-80, 285-86.

8 Archbishop King to Edward Southwell, 3 October 1727 (Trinity College, Dublin, King papers, MS 750/9, p. 28); *Daily Journal*, 28 October 1727; *Mist's Weekly Journal*, 18 November 1727; Hugh Howard to Bishop Howard, 27 February 1727/8 (National Library of Ireland, Wicklow papers, MS 38,598/3).

9 Bishop Howard to Hugh Howard, 6 January 1727[/8] (NLI, MS 38,598/4). The crush was so bad that "some had like to have been killed."

10 *Dublin Intelligence*, 27 January 1727/8; *Daily Journal*, 13 February 1728; *Mist's Weekly Journal*, 17 February 1728.

lord mayor, Sir Peter Verdoen. Originally, there had been two other candidates, one of them Swift's friend Sir William Fownes (1672-1735), but both withdrew when polling began, leaving Somerville to register a comparatively easy victory.[11] The high mortality of the Dublin MPs continued with Burton's sudden death in the summer of 1733, which necessitated yet another by-election. Once more both candidates were Aldermen: the outgoing lord mayor, Humphrey French (1680-1736), and a highly ambitious merchant, John Macarell (*c*.1695-1757), who had been appointed to a government office in 1732, as registrar of the barracks, had only just acquired his alderman's gown, and hoped to enhance his employability still further through a seat in the Commons.[12] In the early stages of the campaign, Swift published his broadsheet *Advice to the Free-Men of the City of Dublin in the Choice of a Member to Represent them in Parliament*, which made the case for French, as a disinterested patriot, as opposed to Macarell, a man in the employ, and presumably at the disposal of, Government.[13] Whether frightened off by the Dean's intervention, or intimidated by French's popularity, Macarell decided to leave the field discreetly, and French was opposed at the poll by his own successor as lord mayor, Thomas Howe. French made a very public point of spending nothing on treating the electors, while Howe used his own money and also the resources of his office, exploiting the occasion of the King's birthday, which fell during polling, to arrange for the roasting of an ox and the distribution of free ale to the inhabitants of the Liberties, at the corporation's expense.[14] Nonetheless, he was comprehensively outvoted, and threw in the towel before the true margin of his defeat could become apparent.[15]

The temptation to dismiss this flurry of electioneering as the outcome of a chapter of actuarial accidents does not survive a scrutiny of the corporation records which, as we shall see, reveal a governing body in turmoil. Hitherto, municipal office in Dublin had not been contested territory. The Aldermen formed a classic self-perpetuating oligarchy, recruiting new members by voting on candidates proposed by the lord mayor from members of the Common Council. Membership of the Common Council was in turn closely controlled by the Aldermen; the 140-strong 'commons' comprised 48 'sheriffs' peers,'

---

11 *Dublin Intelligence*, 7 October 1729; *Daily Journal*, 11 October 1729; *Dublin Weekly Journal*, 25 October 1729.

12 Edith Mary Johnston-Liik, *History of the Irish Parliament, 1692-1800: Commons, Constituencies and Statutes*, 6 vols (Belfast: Ulster Historical Foundation, 2002), V, 151-52.

13 *Advice to the Free-Men of the City of Dublin in the Choice of a Member to Represent Them in Parliament* [Dublin, 1733] in *Irish Political Writings after 1725*, eds Hayton and Rounce, pp. 279-87.

14 *Daily Courant*, 7 November 1733.

15 *Fog's Weekly Journal*, 10 November 1733.

selected by a committee of Aldermen, and 92 'numbers,' chosen from the trade guilds: here again, Aldermen voted on a slate of candidates nominated by each guild master, and the fact that many of the guilds were dominated by senior municipal figures represented a double aldermanic lock on admission.[16] It almost goes without saying that the common councilmen were all Protestant; Catholics could not become full guild members, having to be content with a subordinate status as "quarter brothers."[17] At the same time, there was nothing to prevent Protestant Dissenters from becoming Freemen, Common Councilmen, or Aldermen, if they were prepared to conform 'occasionally,' as most Dublin Presbyterians were. In theory, and for almost all the time in practice, the hold of the aldermen over city government was unshakable. Since the prolonged dispute over the lord mayoralty in 1711-14, when a handful of Tory Aldermen, supported by the Irish Privy Council, had attempted to cram the election of a Tory Lord Mayor down the throats of their unwilling colleagues, there had been no visible cracks in the adamantine edifice of aldermanic consensus.[18]

Things began to change, however, after the 1727 general election, and to change quickly and dramatically. In April 1727, Humphrey French, later to be a controversial and divisive figure, was elected as an Alderman with the usual lack of opposition.[19] But the atmosphere soon became poisonous. A replacement for the deceased John Stoyte on the Court of Aldermen was only agreed after five mayoral nominations had been rejected, and it took eight attempts to secure the promotion of James Somerville (the supposed enemy of the Drapier) to a second vacancy.[20] Ultimately, these elections were still made *nem. con.*, without a formal vote, even if the winnowing process proved to be long drawn out. But things went a step further in 1730, when the Aldermen had to vote between three candidates, and there was a second poll in 1731, when the Barracks Registrar, John Macarell, finally secured his aldermanic seat after

16 Hill, *From Patriots to Unionists*, pp. 43-44.

17 Maureen Wall, "The Catholics of the Towns and the Quarterage Dispute in Eighteenth-Century Ireland," *Catholic Ireland in the Eighteenth Century: Collected Essays of Maureen Wall*, ed. Gerard O'Brien (Dublin: Geography Publications, 1989), pp. 61-72.

18 C. M. Flanagan, "'A Merely Local Dispute?' Partisan Politics and the Dublin Mayoral Dispute of 1709-1715," doctoral dissertation, University of Notre Dame, 1983; Hill, *From Patriots to Unionists*, Chapter 2.

19 Dublin Corporation "Monday book," 17 April 1727 (Dublin City Archives [henceforth DCA], G/102/05, p. 79).

20 *Calendar of the Ancient Records of Dublin*, eds J. T. Gilbert and R. M. Gilbert, 17 vols (Dublin: Joseph Dollard, 1889-1921) (henceforth *CARD*), 8, 427-28, 430-32; "Monday book," 22 July 1727, 16 May 1728 (DCA, G/102/05, pp. 90-91, 95-96).

several unsuccessful attempts.[21] In between, there were still a few unanimous and apparently uncontested elections to the aldermanship but on those occasions only just over half the Aldermen were present, which might indicate absenteeism on the part of a dissatisfied minority. There are other signs, too, that the corporate body was deeply troubled: the unprecedented sight of a contested election for the office of Coroner, and the unilateral decision of the Lord Mayor in 1731 to change the manner of choosing Common Councilmen by arrogating the choice to himself, a ruling reversed the following year by Humphrey French when he took up the mayoral office.[22] French, incidentally, had been chosen Lord Mayor *nem. con.*, but in an election attended by no more than 13 of the 24 Aldermen.[23] Finally, in the spring of 1733, before French was returned to Parliament that autumn, there was a disputed election for the position of Recorder of Dublin, who was the corporation's principal legal adviser and a city magistrate in his own right. Swift published *Some Considerations Humbly Offered to the Right Honourable the Lord-Mayor, the Court of Aldermen, and Common Council of the Honourable City of Dublin, in the Choice of a Recorder* to promote the candidature of a lawyer friend, the "patriot" MP Eaton Stannard (1685-1755), who was eventually chosen at the second attempt, in a contest which in many respects served as a dry run for the parliamentary by-election.[24]

Clearly, there was something very significant happening here, the equivalent of a grinding of tectonic plates to devastate what had previously appeared to be a tranquil political landscape. But it is difficult to be certain of the nature of the process and its underlying cause, since we have to rely on the bare bones of the corporation's records, supplemented by newspaper reports, broadsheets, and the occasional pamphlet. There are no surviving letters from Aldermen or other political figures with connections in the city which would explain the background. Swift's correspondence gives no hint of anything beyond a simple struggle between political virtue and political corruption. What follows must therefore be to a large extent conjectural, a hypothesis based primarily on circumstantial evidence.

The simplest, and most obvious, explanation would be that the conflict within the corporation derived from friction between individual Aldermen or groups of Aldermen: a ramification of personal animosities. This would be perfectly natural in any small closed group. But personal friendships and personal

21 "Monday book," 7 February 1729[/30], 19 January 1730[/1] (DCA, G/102/05, pp. 107, 116).

22 "Monday book," 9 April 1730, 21 April, 19 December 1732 (DCA, G/102/05, pp. 108, 127, 130).

23 "Monday book," 21 April 1732 (DCA, G/102/05, p. 128).

24 "Monday book," 21 April 1732 (DCA, G/102/05, p. 128); *Pue's Occurrences*, 13-17 February 1733; *Daily Courant*, 1 March 1733; *Daily Journal*, 1 March 1733.

antipathies cannot provide the whole answer. For one thing, we are still left with the problem of why there should have been such a rapid deterioration of interpersonal relations among the corporate elite in 1728-30, and why this acrimony could not be contained within the Court of Aldermen but spilled over into parliamentary elections and print culture. It also leaves out of account the various social contexts, in the city and in the country at large: the economic downturn and its repercussions; and the arguments about politics and policy raging in Parliament and the press. Certainly, some of those writing for or against particular candidates explored these issues and tried to relate the contests in Dublin to the broader political scene.

For Swift, everything could be traced back to one primary cause: Ireland's constitutional malaise. He argued the paramount importance of supporting those who would take a 'patriotic' stance in the House of Commons. His appeals to the Dublin electors to give their votes to Humphrey French in the parliamentary by-election of 1733 were based on French's incorruptibility, in contrast to the all-too-obvious corruptibility of the placeman, Macarell. "My dear citizens," Swift wrote,

> How is it possible you can conceive, that any person who holds an office of some hundred pounds a year, which may be taken from him whenever power shall think fit, will if he should be chosen a member for any city, do the least thing when he sits in the House, that he knows or fears may be displeasing to those who gave him, or continue him in that office.[25]

French, by contrast, was a candidate of unmatched personal probity: "He hath shown more virtue, more activity, more skill, in one year's government of the city, than a hundred years can equal."[26] Moreover, he was a man of independent means, without attachment to any interest but that of the public. Earlier, in 1733, Swift had taken a similar line in his recommendation of Eaton Stannard for the Dublin Recordership. Stannard's opponent was John Forbes, an Alderman's son whom John Stoyte had beaten in the parliamentary by-election of 1728, and Swift had to counter the argument of Forbes's supporters that it was better to have a Recorder with strong connections to the corporation and to the city's commerce. On the contrary, Swift argued, what was most important was the candidate's political virtue and whether, as Stannard

25 *Advice to the Free-Men of the City of Dublin in the Choice of a Member to Represent them in Parliament* [Dublin, 1733], in *Irish Political Writings after 1725*, eds Hayton and Rounce, p. 282.

26 *Advice to the Free-Men of the City of Dublin in the Choice of a Member to Represent them in Parliament* [Dublin, 1733], in *Irish Political Writings after 1725*, eds Hayton and Rounce, pp. 286-7.

had already shown himself, "he be a man of courage; not to be drawn from his duty by the frowns or menaces of power, nor capable to be corrupted by allurements or bribes?"[27]

Swift's emphasis on the overriding importance of political virtue found echoes in some other quarters. A broadsheet in support of Stannard's bid for the Recordership praised not only his abilities but his "exemplary life, with respect to religion and morals," his disinterested devotion to advancing the well-being of ordinary citizens, and his love of liberty, while later in the year another print linked the election of Stannard "for his merit" to the necessity of returning French to Parliament "for his steady and intrepid virtue."[28] Eulogies on French's character emphasized personal integrity, and this theme was picked up in newspaper reports of the election, with French's ostentatious refusal to bribe voters contrasted with the lavish expenditure of his opponents.[29] To focus on a candidate's superior personal qualities was of course a rhetorical trope, but it may have meant something more if extended into the area of political principle and parliamentary action. Swift's advocacy of Stannard and French rested on the idea that they would both exercise independent judgement, and not be suborned by the Castle to act against the interests of Ireland. In other words, they were 'patriots' in the very specific sense adopted by oppositionists in the Irish House of Commons, defending the liberty of the subject, upholding the right of Irish Protestants to be governed only by laws to which they had given consent through their representatives, and seeking to advance the economic interests of the country against English exploitation.

27 *Some Considerations Humbly Offered to the Right Honourable the Lord-Mayor, the Court of Aldermen, and Common Council of the Honourable City of Dublin, in the Choice of a Recorder* ([Dublin, 1733]), in *Irish Political Writings after 1725*, eds Hayton and Rounce, p. 272.

28 *A Great Deal More Seasonable Advice to the Freemen and Freeholders of the City of Dublin, concerning the Choice of a Member to Represent them in Parliament* ([Dublin, 1733]). The same point was made in relation to Stannard in *An Address Humbly Offered to the Mature Consideration of the Right Honourable the Lord-Mayor, Aldermen, Common Council, and Citizens of the City of Dublin* (Dublin, 1733).

29 *Advice to the Freemen and Freeholders of the City of Dublin; in their Choice of a Representative in the Ensuing Election* ([Dublin], 1733); *Astraea's Congratulation: An Ode upon Alderman Humphry French Being Elected Representative for the City of Dublin, on Account of his Wise and Just Administration during his Late Mayoralty* ([Dublin], 1733 [Foxon A364]); *A Full Vindication of the Behaviour of Humphry French, late Lord-Mayor of Dublin: Addressed to the Citizens* ([Dublin, 1733]); *Fog's Weekly Journal*, 10 November 1733; *London Evening Post*, 10 November 1733.

Swift was not the only person to use the term "patriot" when praising his favoured candidates,[30] but the precise meaning of the term in the context of electoral canvassing is by no means clear. Indeed, it may not have carried any particular freight at all but simply have been a customary compliment to a candidate that he had the interests of his country and his countrymen at heart. In this sense, any right-thinking person was a 'patriot,' just as all men professed to cherish liberty and practise virtue. The problem with seeing the conflicts within the corporation more specifically as a manifestation of the opposition between 'Court' and 'Country' (or 'patriot') interests is that this imposes too much solidity on the notion of a Court-Country polarity in Irish politics. Certainly, there were 'patriot' back-benchers in the Irish House of Commons who raised popular issues, and in every session there were heated debates, but there was no formed 'patriot' opposition. Instead, the key elements of the political structure of the Commons were factions headed by prominent politicians and incorporating family-based connections, principally the 'old corps' of Speaker Conolly, eventually taken over by Brabazon Ponsonby, and the "Munster squadron" once headed by Lord Midleton and since inherited by Henry Boyle, which had come over from opposition to government in 1733.[31] Where a 'party' division can be detected in disputed elections in this period, what we often see is no more than a local manifestation of factional rivalries – Conolly against Brodrick in County Westmeath in 1724, for example, or Boyle against Ponsonby in Clonmel in 1733.[32]

There was, however, one recognizable form of party, as opposed to factional politics which does seem to have appeared with some regularity in parliamentary constituencies; not Court against Country but Whig against Tory. In Queen Anne's reign, many Irish parliamentary boroughs had witnessed battles between identifiable Whig and Tory interests. This included Dublin, where the 1713 parliamentary election ended in a riot, the calling out of troops, and at least one fatality.[33] But the Whig triumph in the 1715 general election was followed by the inevitable exodus of the more moderate, or career-conscious, Tories: men like Francis Bernard, Marmaduke Coghill, Sir Richard Levinge,

30 See, for example, another broadsheet in support of Humphrey French: *Error in Choice: or, A Mistake on the Right Side* ([Dublin, 1733]).

31 D. W. Hayton, *Ruling Ireland, 1685-1742: Politics, Politicians and Parties* (Woodbridge: The Boydell Press, 2004), pp. 123-24, 217-35, 243-44, 247-48, 250-51, 252-54, 260-70.

32 D. W. Hayton, "Two Ballads on the County Westmeath By-Election of 1723," *Eighteenth-Century Ireland*, 4 (1989), 7-30; William Taylor to [the Earl of Egmont], 11 December 1733 (British Library, Add. MS 46984, pp. 214-15).

33 J. G. Simms, "The Irish Parliament of 1713," *Historical Studies IV*, ed. G. A. Hayes-McCoy (London: Bowes and Bowes, 1963), pp. 82-92 (85-86).

and Agmondisham Vesey took office and crossed the floor of the House of Commons. By 1727, only a small rump of diehards remained.[34] While Toryism was gradually disappearing in Parliament, there are signs from the mid-1720s onwards that Tory interests in the constituencies were beginning to revive. Tories – including some suspected Jacobites – who had been forcibly removed from the corporation of Galway by Act of Parliament in 1717 were returning to municipal office by 1725.[35] Toby Barnard has discovered that the old Tory grouping in Youghal was also recovering its strength, albeit under an assumed name, and David Fleming has observed similar developments in Limerick.[36] It is harder to recognize such a process happening in Dublin, since there is little continuity in personnel. Sir William Fownes seems to have been the only Tory Alderman from 1714 still in office in 1727. But although the court of Aldermen in Dublin had always been overwhelmingly Whig, there had been a substantial Tory element among the common council before 1714, and it seems unlikely that this had wholly evaporated.[37]

Fragments of evidence suggest a possible Tory revival in the city in the late 1720s. The Dissenting interest in city politics re-emerged with the election of a Presbyterian, Joseph Kane, as Lord Mayor in 1726, and his assumption of office may have provoked a reaction from churchmen, or at least provided a grievance, long before Walpole's ministry tried to secure a repeal of the Sacramental Test.[38] In the various parliamentary elections which followed the death of George I, there were repeated accusations that Dissenting ministers were mobilizing the freemen in their congregations to vote for particular candidates. In the 1727 general election, it was William Howard (despite the fact that his brother was a bishop) who was said to have been the beneficiary of the Nonconformist vote; and the following year, Dissenters supported John Forbes, who later became Stannard's opponent for the Recordership.[39] At the next by-election, to replace Alderman Stoyte, there was no talk of Dissenting voters, but of the two candidates who stood the poll, Sir Peter Verdoen seems to have

34 Hayton, *Ruling Ireland, 1685-1742*, pp. 119, 122.

35 Hayton, "Voters, Patrons and Parties: Parliamentary Elections in Ireland, *c.*1692-1727," p. 66.

36 Barnard, "Considering the Inconsiderable: Electors, Patrons and Irish Elections, 1659-1761," pp. 118-19; Fleming, *Politics and Provincial People*, pp. 72-77.

37 *A Station List for the City of Dublin for the Year Commencing, 1711* [Dublin, 1711].

38 J. R. Hill, "Dublin Corporation, Protestant Dissent, and Politics, 1660-1800," *The Politics of Irish Dissent, 1650-1800*, ed. Kevin Herlihy (Dublin: Four Courts Press, 1997), pp. 32-33.

39 T. C. Barnard, "The Government and Irish Dissent, 1704-1780," *Politics of Irish Dissent*, ed. Herlihy, pp. 24-25; *Letters of Marmaduke Coghill, 1722-1738*, ed. D. W. Hayton (Dublin: Irish Manuscripts Commission, 2005), p. 46.

been a Tory in Queen Anne's reign, and was publicly presented as a stalwart of the Established Church.[40]

Swift was quick to deny that party in the Whig and Tory sense still existed in Ireland: by the late 1720s all talk of 'Tory' conspiracy emanated from the fevered brains of Whigs like Richard Tighe, determined to blackguard their opponents as Jacobites.[41] Even though the controversy over the Sacramental Test in 1731-34 reawakened anti-Presbyterian sentiment, the Dean and those who, like him, came to the defence of the Established church, could not afford to present themselves as High Churchmen. Nonetheless, a modest Tory resurgence was taking place. Across the country, a number of candidates in the 1727 general election stood on an avowedly Tory platform.[42] Dublin was not obviously part of this process; indeed, Verdoen was the only parliamentary candidate in the years 1727-33 who could conceivably have been labelled as a Tory. Stoyte had always been a strong Whig, even though after his death he was eulogized as a staunch churchman,[43] and the same was true of Humphrey French and Eaton Stannard. Indeed, one of French's supporters made a point of recalling his brave refusal to bend the knee to the Tory ministry in 1711-14.[44] None of this deterred 'honest churchmen' among the voters. In French's case, the undergraduates of Trinity, whose Tory allegiances were an open secret, pledged their support for him as Dublin's MP, and published their views in a printed address.[45] Elsewhere, his election was welcomed across the Irish Sea by the Tory news-writer Nathaniel Mist as providing an example for English voters to follow.[46]

But in this respect, as in so many others, Dublin needs to be treated separately from Irish provincial towns, where political structures and issues were very different. Dublin dwarfed all other Irish conurbations in size, combining in a unique way the functions of a seat of government, a manufacturing and

40 *A Station List for the City of Dublin for the Year Commencing, 1711* [Dublin, 1711]; *Dublin Intelligence*, 11 October 1729.

41 See, for example, *A Vindication of His Excellency the Lord Carteret, from the Charge of Favouring None but Toryes, High-Churchmen, and Jacobites* (Dublin, 1730), in *Irish Political Writings after 1725*, eds Hayton and Rounce, p. 197.

42 Richard Holmes, "English Whigs and Irish Patriots; Archbishop Boulter and the Politics of Party in Hanoverian Ireland," *Eighteenth-Century Ireland*, 31 (2016), 88-89.

43 *An Elegy on the Much Lamented Death of Alderman John Stoyte* (Dublin, 1728) (Foxon E248).

44 *A Great Deal More Seasonable Advice to the Freemen and Freeholders of the City of Dublin, concerning the Choice of a Member to Represent them in Parliament* ([Dublin, 1733]).

45 *Daily Courant*, 7 November 1733; *Address to Humphry French Esq; Late Lord Mayor of the City of Dublin from the Hon. Senate of Trinity College, Dublin* (Dublin, [1733]).

46 *Fog's Weekly Journal*, 10 November 1733.

trading hub, and a magnet for polite society. The most obvious comparison is not with regional capitals in Ireland like Cork, Galway, or Limerick, but with cities of similar size and importance in England, and it is in the civic Toryism of London and places like Norwich, Bristol, and Newcastle that we can find a key to understanding developments in Dublin after 1727. Tories in these English cities had re-configured themselves since *c.*1700 as radical challengers to the domination of corporate governance by Whig commercial elites.[47] By 1730, London Tories were casting themselves as the representatives of honest small traders against a corrupt and engrossing Whig oligarchy.

There are hints that something similar was happening in Dublin. In their elections in 1733, both Stannard and French seem to have relied on the backing of the Common Council against opponents representing a majority of the Aldermen. The support given by the common council to Stannard over Forbes for the Recordership is obvious from the process itself: it was the refusal of the Common Council to accept a unanimous vote of the Aldermen for Forbes which forced a second vote and Stannard's return.[48] As for French's election as an MP, a broadsheet published at the time of the poll stated that "It is notorious that the majority of the aldermen of this city, oppose his election to a seat in parliament, while the commons, almost to a man, are determined in his favour."[49] Other materials published in his support specifically targeted "you of the lower degree of people, who in the most sensible manner have experienced his goodness."[50] There is also some suggestive, though by no means conclusive, evidence in the behaviour of the guilds in relation to the parliamentary election. In the early stages of campaigning, several declared for Macarell, feasting him and admitting him to guild membership, indicating perhaps that the masters favoured his candidacy, but nearer the poll the same compliment was paid to French, which might indicate a response to pressure from rank-and-file freemen.[51]

Why should there have been tension between the Aldermen and the "commons"? The first place to look for an answer is in the low public esteem in

47 Gary Stuart De Krey, *A Fractured Society: The Politics of London in the First Age of Party, 1688-1715* (Oxford: Clarendon Press, 1985), Chapter V; Alfred James Henderson, *London and the National Government, 1721-1742: A Study of City Politics and the Walpole Administration* (Durham, North Carolina: Duke University Press, 1945); Nicholas Rogers, *Whigs and Cities: Popular Politics in the Age of Walpole and Pitt* (Oxford: Clarendon Press, 1989).

48 *Daily Courant*, 1 March 1733.

49 *A Full Vindication of the Behaviour of Humphry French, late Lord-Mayor of Dublin: Addressed to the Citizens* ([Dublin, 1733]).

50 *A Little More Advice to the People of Dublin* ([Dublin], 1733).

51 *Faulkner's Dublin Journal*, 31 July-4 August, 7-11, 14-18 August, 8-11 September 1733.

which the Aldermen were held. Small tradesmen, craftsmen, and journeymen who were enduring economic hardship as a consequence of the collapse of the city's economic infrastructure naturally focused their resentment on the wealthy merchants who seemed to be prospering at their expense: the "engrossers" and "forestallers" cornering markets in basic household commodities, food and fuel, and jacking up prices as far as they could; and the bankers, whose failures seemed to heap suffering on everyone except themselves.[52] Aldermen were routinely lampooned in the press for their greed and dishonesty. According to James Arbuckle, "A *Hog* would lose but little of his Nature, and nothing at all of his Stomach, in becoming an Alderman."[53] Even the financial misfortunes of individual aldermen became fodder for satirists: one "scandalous paper" in 1729 made fun of the hapless Alderman Henry Burrows, a bankrupt who had been obliged to appeal to his colleagues for money to provide for himself and his family.[54]

Public disgust at the moral dereliction of Dublin's civic leaders intensified as evidence began to emerge of incompetence and corruption at the highest level of the corporation. The most serious revelations came as a consequence of parliamentary inquiries in the autumn of 1729 into law and order in the capital, which exposed systematic corruption in the administration of justice, centring on the dubious figure of John Hawkins, Keeper of the Newgate and Marshalsea prisons, and an Irish version of Jonathan Wild. The city constables, some of whom were directly under Hawkins's control, and others of whom looked to his leadership, were behaving little better than the criminal gangs they were supposed to suppress. The first reaction of the aldermen to the revelations of Hawkins's criminality was to ignore the evidence, before they were embarrassed into a volte-face and the removal of Hawkins from office.[55]

Worse was to follow, as the Irish Parliament arrested two Aldermen and the city Coroner for soliciting bribes to drop prosecutions.[56] The collapse of public

52 [Hugh Howard] to Bishop Howard, 6 February 1730/1 (NLI, MS 38,598/7).

53 [James Arbuckle], *A Collection of Letters and Essays on Several Subjects, Lately Publish'd in the Dublin Journal*, 2 vols (London: J. Darby and T. Browne, *et al.*, 1729), II, 196. See also *A Hue and Cry after a C[it]y M[agistra]te* (Dublin, [1733]).

54 *Dublin Intelligence*, 12 July 1729, 14 April 1730; *Dublin Weekly Journal*, 30 August 1729; *CARD*, VII, 461, 465, 488-89; VIII, 61-63.

55 *The Journals of the House of Commons of the Kingdom of Ireland*, 2nd ed., 19 vols (Dublin, 1753-76), V, 668, 708 (henceforth *C. J. Ire.*); *CARD*, VII, 467, 472, 477; Neal Garnham, "The Short Career of Paul Farrell: A Brief Consideration of Law Enforcement in Eighteenth-Century Ireland," *Eighteenth-Century Ireland*, 11 (1996), 46-52; Timothy D. Watt, "The Corruption of the Law and Popular Violence: The Crisis of Order in Dublin, 1729," *Irish Historical Studies*, 39 (2014-15), 8-23.

56 *C. J. Ire.*, V, 733-35; *Historical Register*, 15 (1730), 112-28.

trust in the civic elite was exacerbated by the economic crisis which began in 1726. Shortages in the supply of basic foodstuffs coincided with a slump in trade. Protests against high food prices, sometimes ending in riots, were directed against profiteering merchants who were exploiting bread shortages to raise their prices.[57] There were also tensions between journeymen and their masters, and episodes of ritualized violence – "colting" – against imported cheap labour, which resulted in the Irish Parliament passing a statute "to prevent unlawful combinations of workmen, artificers, and labourers."[58] The raw materials for a populist political campaign were present in abundance. Moreover, the intense, and ultimately successful, press campaign against Wood's Halfpence only a few years before may have begun the process of politicizing the city's population, especially the distressed weavers in the Liberties, of all people the most severely affected by English discriminatory legislation, and a class of men who had come to look to the Drapier as their deliverer from Westminster's tyranny.

Into this morass of poverty and disorder stepped Humphrey French, who in the year of his lord mayoralty, 1732-33, made a reputation as the representative of the interests of the 'middling sort' of citizens for whom times had recently become so very much harder, the kind of people represented by the guild freemen on the Dublin Common Council, and by the members of various journeymen's associations – essentially friendly societies – which had looked to Swift as a public advocate.[59] French represented their concerns almost perfectly, with a mayoral policy which combined acts of personal philanthropy, paternalist involvement in the market-place and a tough approach on issues of law and order. He visited the city's markets regularly, intervening directly to alleviate food shortages by confiscating "unmerchantable provisions" from bakers and other retailers and distributing it among the poor; spent his own money in releasing debtors from the Marshalsea; tried to deal with abuses in city government, and organized a rescue package with leading merchants to

57 *C. J. Ire.*, V. 709; *A Poem Occasion'd by the Lord Mayor's Reducing the Price of Coals, &c.* (Dublin, 1729 [Foxon P559]); Neal Garnham, *The Courts, Crime and the Criminal Law in Ireland, 1692-1760* (Blackrock, Co. Dublin: Irish Academic Press, 1996), pp. 198-99.

58 *Dublin Intelligence*, 14, 28 July 1731; *The Poor Man's Case Consider'd: or, A Pill for Colts and Cure for the Publick, Being the Address of All and Singular the Journeymen of the City of Dublin* (Dublin, 1732); Mel Doyle, "The Dublin Guilds and Journeymen's Clubs," *Saothar: Journal of the Irish Labour History Society*, 3 (1977), 6-14.

59 *The Lamentation of the Poor of the City of Dublin after the Late Lord Mayor, with a Word of Advice to the Freemen, &c. of Said City* ([Dublin], 1733); Patrick Walsh, "Club Life in Late Seventeenth- and Early Eighteenth-Century Ireland: In Search of an Associational World, c.1680-c.1730," *Clubs and Societies in Eighteenth-Century Ireland*, eds James Kelly and Martyn J. Powell (Dublin: Four Courts Press, 2010), pp. 36-49 (44-48).

guarantee the capital of investors when a run on the banks seemed imminent.[60] Interestingly, in this respect he may have been following a lead given a few years earlier by another 'patriot' Lord Mayor and parliamentary candidate, the Tory Sir Peter Verdoen, who also seems to have engaged in acts of personal philanthropy, made efforts to regulate the city's gaols, and took direct action to reduce the price of coal.[61] But in French's case, this paternalistic impulse ran alongside a campaign against criminal and riotous behaviour, combining moral reform with the reimposition of social order. He personally led a reorganized city constabulary in putting down disturbances, raiding brothels, and arresting huge numbers of destitute vagrants, with whom he filled the workhouse and the new bridewell.[62] The distressed tradesmen who formed his natural constituency responded with tributes that had not been given to other lord mayors, the corporation of shoemakers making him a present of plate, for example, and the city's Common Council paying for his portrait to be painted.[63] So popular was French's interventionist style that Thomas Howe, on succeeding to the mayoralty, and with at least one eye on the forthcoming parliamentary election, deliberately followed suit, visiting the market to check on the quality and price of the bread being sold, and, as winter began to bite, fixing the price of coal to prevent profiteering.[64]

What may have been happening in Dublin in 1733 is something much more interesting than the personalized virtue-politics that we find in Swift's writings. In response to a sharp economic downturn, and a major crisis in public order, the Protestant artisan class seems to have lost faith in their civic institutions. The corporation itself underwent a major political upheaval, with the consensus presided over by Whig Aldermen ever since 1714 coming under

60 *Pue's Occurrences*, 31 October-4 November 1732, 23-27 January, 14-18 August, 22-25, 25-29 September 1733; *Faulkner's Dublin Journal*, 14-18 August, 8-11, 22-25 September 1733. See also *The Lamentation of the Poor of the City of Dublin after the Late Lord Mayor, with a Word of Advice to the Freemen, &c. of Said City* ([Dublin], 1733); *A Full Vindication of Humphrey French, Late Lord Mayor of the City of Dublin* ([Dublin], 1733).

61 *An Elegy on the Much Lamented Death of Alderman Peter Verdoen, Kt.* ([Dublin: E. Waters, 1731] [Foxon E265]); *Faulkner's Dublin Journal*, 21-25 April 1730; *A Poem Occasion'd by the Lord Mayor's Reducing the Price of Coals, &c.* (Dublin, 1729). See also Watt, "The Corruption of the Law and Popular Violence: The Crisis of Order in Dublin, 1729," p. 13.

62 *Pue's Occurrences*, 5-9, 14-18, 25-28 November 1732.

63 *Pue's Occurrences*, 29 May-2 June 1733; *Daily Journal*, 3 July 1733; *St James's Evening Post*, 27 October 1733; *Address of the Society of Yellows, to Alderman Humphry French, Late Lord Mayor of the City of Dublin* ([Dublin], 1733).

64 *Faulkner's Dublin Journal*, 6-9 October 1733, 15-19 January 1733[/4]. See also *Daily Journal*, 5 November 1733, which, in describing the election contest between French and Howe, noted that Howe was "endeavouring to excel" French in the care he was taking for the well-being of the city.

serious strain. It looks very much as if conflicts within the Court of Aldermen reflected a movement among the city's freemen in the Common Council and the guilds, to challenge the oligarchy which had failed them. Underlying this defiance of oligarchy may have been a modest revival of Tory sentiment, but a rather different kind of Toryism than the High Churchmanship of the first decade of the century, more akin to the civic radicalism of contemporary English urban politics. And the challenge was being led, not by a populist agitator like Lucas, but by a paternalist Alderman whose concern was to improve the working of civic institutions and reintroduce a moral order rather than remodel the system of city government to make it more representative.

By contrast, Swift's contribution to Dublin civic politics depicted a traditional struggle to maintain the moral uprightness and political independence of the true patriot against the corrupting power of place and pension, rather than the kind of crusade on which Humphrey French was embarked, to cleanse civic government and relieve the distress of the poor: the ultimate objective for Swift was to cure the underlying faults of the Irish political system, rather than alleviate the suffering of the citizens. So he did not do justice to the kind of politics that French and others represented. He must have been well aware of the underlying Toryism which coloured Dublin civic patriotism, but chose not to draw attention to it because this would have been a tactical error. What is more striking is the incompleteness of his engagement with the real problems affecting the Dublin freemen whose votes he sought to influence. He lamented the collapse of the woollen manufacture but primarily as an example of English misrule; he lent money to poor tradesmen but did not advocate any systematic programme to alleviate debt; and he worried over the problem of beggars on the streets but seems to have paid little attention to the high level of violence. In one pamphlet, he alluded briefly to the crisis of order and the failure of civic institutions, but having begun his *Examination of Certain Abuses, Corruptions, and Enormities in the City of Dublin* in 1732 with a comment on the defective nature of policing in the city, he quickly moved on to an altogether more flippant discussion of the supposed treasonableness of street-sellers' cries, and the emblems visible on tavern-signs.[65] Elsewhere, his sardonic comments in verse on the murderous activities of the "jolly boys" of the "Kevan Bail" and the brutality of industrial disputes bordered on the insouciant.[66] He was engaged with Dublin politics, at this critical point in the history of the city, but the angle of engagement was oblique.

---

65 *An Examination of Certain Abuses, Corruptions, and Enormities in the City of Dublin* (Dublin, 1732), in *Irish Political Writings after 1725*, eds Hayton and Rounce, pp. 240-63.

66 *Poems*, ed. Williams, III, 814-17. See also *Faulkner's Dublin Journal*, 7-11 October 1729.

Jonathan Pritchard
London

Dubliners: Swift and his Neighbours

In memory of Donna Perry

Abstract. For the last thirty years of his life, in his capacity as the Dean of St Patrick's Cathedral, Jonathan Swift lived in a small, populous, and largely independent district of Dublin. Beyond the jurisdiction of the civic and ecclesiastical authorities, the Liberty of St Patrick's was in some part a realm unto itself, and Swift was its sovereign. His dealings with his many neighbours have, however, attracted little scholarly attention. This essay accordingly offers a literary-historical survey of the quarter and its residents. Following a brief overview of how Swift conceptualized the condition of being a neighbour, it describes the privileges of his office, the built environment of the franchise that was his charge, and the kinds of person who lodged there. The second half of the essay introduces some of the Dean's more prominent neighbours, four individuals with whom he had disputes of various kinds. For all the provocations of those amongst whom he lived, his vis-à-vis with his neighbours can finally be seen to have been a source of considerable personal contentment.

Six months after he had been installed as the Dean of St Patrick's Cathedral, Dublin, Jonathan Swift learnt that his vicars choral intended to sign a lease which would beggar their successors in office. Having departed for London after the ceremony, the new dean must have seemed far removed from Dublin affairs. Swift nonetheless reacted to the initiative by insisting on his authority. "I desire you will let the Vicars know," he instructed his deputy, John Worrall (d.1751),

> that I shall to the utmost resent their presuming to make any Lease without the consent of the Dean and Chapter, which they are bound to have by their own Subscriptions. Let them know further, that I am very well instructed in my own Power both from the late Dean, and from Dr Synge; and that I will immediatly deprive every Man of them who consents to any Lease without the Approbation aforesaid, and shall think the Church well ridd of such men who to gratify their unreasonable Avarice would starve their Successors.[1]

The considerable distance at which he wrote did not diminish his anger. It may even have intensified it. At the financial expense of future vicars choral, the incumbents intended to lease a tract of land near St Stephen's Green in Dublin

1 Swift to John Worrall, 31 December 1713, *Correspondence*, ed. Woolley, I, 576.

 | DOI:10.30965/9783846763971_022

to James Hamilton (*c*.1661-1734), sixth Earl of Abercorn, the renewal of which contract lay in the gift of the Dean and Chapter. The letter is interesting for a number of reasons. In the first place, it demonstrates that Swift expected his authority to be upheld. The message also emphasizes the importance he placed on continuity in clerical office, his sense of historical precedent, and on guarding his and his canons' prerogatives. And it also serves as an early *terminus a quo* for the struggles he would endure for much of his decanal career.[2]

Such disputes become more vivid when we recall that some of Swift's colleagues were also his neighbours in the precinct of St Patrick's. Indeed, a proportion of his working life after he had returned to Dublin, and some of his literary activities, were concerned with problems arising from the misfortunes of, or from disputes with, those amongst whom he lived. The many individual episodes that collectively typify his dealings with his neighbours do not seem, however, to have caught the attention of literary scholars. Although Christopher Fauske has observed that the consequences of economic hardship were visible "whenever [Swift] ventured out of his front door," "every time he walked through the Liberties surrounding St Patrick's Cathedral," and Leo Damrosch has described his subject as a "reluctant Dubliner," Swift's vis-à-vis with his neighbours has yet to be addressed at any length.[3] This might come as a surprise. The idea of neighbourliness amplifies the tenor of one of the most celebrated passages in his correspondence. "Since you will now be so much better employd when you think of the World give it one lash the more at my Request," he wrote to Alexander Pope; "principally I hate and detest that animal called man, although I hartily love John, Peter, Thomas and so forth."[4] The conurbation of which he was a citizen was crowded with that animal called man, but he administered his cathedral amidst neighbours he could name.

This essay accordingly surveys the literary-historical terrain. It is a largely Irish, and more specifically Dublin, undertaking. In none of the places in England in which he stayed for an extended period (at Moor Park, for example, or in Twickenham) can Swift be thought to have been an active neighbour in

2 For problems with the singing men at the very end of his life, see "Two Drafts of Swift's Order to the Chapter of St. Patrick's concerning the Conduct of the Vicars Choral" (both 1742), in *Correspondence*, ed. Williams, V, 266-68.

3 Christopher J. Fauske, *Jonathan Swift and the Church of Ireland, 1710-1724* (Dublin and Portland, Oregon: Irish Academic Press, 2002), pp. 73, 83; Leo Damrosch, *Jonathan Swift: His Life and his World* (New Haven and London: Yale University Press, 2013), pp. 267-85; see further pp. 415-16. The phenomenon has also attracted historiographical interest; see Alexandra Walsham, *Charitable Hatred: Tolerance and Intolerance in England, 1500-1700* (Manchester: Manchester University Press, 2006); and Emily Cockayne, *Cheek by Jowl: A History of Neighbours* (London: The Bodley Head, 2012).

4 Swift to Alexander Pope, 29 September 1725, *Correspondence*, ed. Woolley, II, 606-7.

any biographically interesting sense (where *neighbour* is not the same thing as paid employee, retainer, or house guest).[5] Nor does it treat of his acquaintance in rural Ireland, of the many individuals mentioned in socially promiscuous letters and verse.[6] A final exclusion concerns literary figures who lived elsewhere in the capital and in its hinterland. They, too, have been well covered in the secondary literature.[7] What remains from setting to one side the foreign, the provincial, and the suburban, in fine, is the most populous of the places Swift called home. The municipally independent Liberty of St Patrick's was his allodium for the last three decades of his life and the district which did most to vivify his understanding of the idea.

1. The Word and its Senses

In its morphology, *neighbour* is obviously a Germanic term, found in Old English in the first tranche of a bewildering variety of spellings over more than ten centuries of verbal and literary expression. All the cognate forms denoting socially achieved developments of the concept (such as *neighbourhood* or *neighbourly*) are understandably first attested centuries later. Nor do there seem to have been any specifically Irish English senses of the word, meaning in this context idioms adapted from, or informed by, the Gaelic vernacular. The noun is qualified, in fact, by an Irish loan in "A Dialogue in Hybernian Stile between A, and B" and – cited here – "Irish Eloquence" (both *c.*1732-34), in which Swift mocks the idiolect of the Protestant soldiers and adventurers who had planted Leinster and Munster, settlers "of the sourest Leven, and the meanest birth," as he characterized them.[8] "His Neighbor Squire Dolt is a meer Buddough," the purportedly epistolary author of the latter work writes, where

5 From a critical perspective, note the riparian gossip of "A Pastoral Dialogue between Richmond-Lodge and Marble-Hill" (1727; published 1735), in *Poems*, ed. Williams, II, 407-11.

6 See, for example, Swift to John Stearne, 17 April 1710, *Correspondence*, ed. Woolley, I, 279; Swift to Esther Vanhomrigh, 8 July 1713, I, 514; and Swift, "A Panegyrick on the D—n, in the Person of a Lady in the North" (1730; published 1735), in *Poems*, ed. Williams, III, 886-97. Of great help in this regard are the Biographical Dictionary in Swift, *Poems*, ed. Rogers, pp. 907-42; and Richard Haworth, "Jonathan Swift and the Geography of Laracor," *Swift Studies*, 24 (2009), 7-26.

7 Representative here are C. G. Ó Háinle, "Neighbors in Eighteenth Century Dublin: Jonathan Swift and Seán Ó Neachtain," *Éire-Ireland*, 21, no 4 (1986), 106-21; and A. C. Elias, Jr, "*Senatus Consultum*: Revising Verse in Swift's Dublin Circle, 1729-1735," *Reading Swift: Papers from The Third Münster Symposium on Jonathan Swift*, eds Hermann J. Real and Helgard Stöver-Leidig (Munich: Wilhelm Fink, 1998), pp. 249-67.

8 Swift to Pope, 10 January 1721, *Correspondence*, ed. Woolley, II, 359.

the last term is a borrowing of the Irish *bodach*, a churl or boor.[9] Neither the root word nor any of its cognates was informed by the verbal manner of the land of his birth.

Of the several senses that were available to Swift and his contemporaries, three seem recurringly important. The first remains the most familiar in modern discourse: "A person who lives near or next to another" (*OED*, third edition, sense 1a). Thus the Drapier identifies his first constituency as "[his] Neighbours the *Butchers*, and *Bakers*, and *Brewers*, and the rest."[10] This is the kind of person also found in meditations on Swift's calling. "Every man, as a member of the commonwealth, ought to be content with the possession of his own opinion in private, without perplexing his neighbour or disturbing the public."[11] And in the clergyman's mind, residential proximity had a pastoral consequence: neighbours are often synonymous with parishioners, and neighbourhoods with parishes.[12] The epitome of such associations, "A Quiet Life and a Good Name," might thus be expected to exemplify an ideal of considerate, reciprocating neighbourliness. But it does not. Long believed to versify Thomas Sheridan's marital travails, Swift's most vividly realized description of parish life is strikingly ironic:

Will went again to visit Dick
And entring in the very nick,
He saw Virago Nell belabor
With Dick's own Staff his Peacefull Neighbor.

What is worse, "A Quiet Life" concludes with one of the more dramatic instances of a community's self-policing: "The Prentices procur'd a Riding / To act his Patience, and her chiding." The boys of the parish lay on a skimmington to guy the couple who are the subject of the poem.[13] Swift was fully alive to the demands of the established social order.

---

9 *Parodies, Hoaxes, Mock Treatises: "Polite Conversation," "Directions to Servants," and Other Works*, ed. Valerie Rumbold (Cambridge: Cambridge University Press, 2013), pp. 531-32.

10 Swift, *A Letter to the Shop-Keepers, Tradesmen, Farmers, and Common-People of Ireland* (1724), in *Prose Works*, X, 7.

11 Swift, "Thoughts on Religion" (published 1765), in *Prose Works*, IX, 261. The distinction between neighbours and the public recurs in the sermon *On Mutual Subjection* (published 1744), in *Prose Works*, IX, 141-49 (pp. 146-47).

12 [Swift], William Harrison's *Tatler*, no 5 (23-27 January 171[1]), in *Parodies, Hoaxes, Mock Treatises*, ed. Rumbold, pp. 113-14; *Directions to Servants* (published 1745), p. 509.

13 Swift, "A Quiet Life, and a Good Name" (1719; published 1735), ll. 19-22, 53-54, in *Poems*, ed. Williams, I, 220-21. The standard account of the phenomenon remains E. P. Thompson, "Rough Music" (1972), revised in *Customs in Common* (London: The Merlin Press, 1991), pp. 467-538.

The second sense is more expansive, in the contexts in which he wrote both topographically more removed and socio-economically narrower: "A person who lives in an adjoining or not far distant town, district, or country" (2a). Squire Dolt, in other words – or "*Gatherall* of the Peak," the Derbyshire gentleman whose estate abuts Sir John Linger's property, or "our neighb'ring dull Divines," "our neighb'ring Friends," and "The Neighbours who come here to dine" mentioned in the poems associated with Market Hill and "the neighbourhood round."[14] By extension, this sense also comprehends "a country, district … that borders or is next to another." Often found in the plural, this further shade of meaning is illustrated in the *OED* by an extract from the *Argument against Abolishing Christianity*: "His People would be more scandalized at our Infidelity, than our Christian Neighbours."[15] Figurative applications of this sense can also be found in Swift's poetry. His verse epistle "To Mr Gay" (1730), written under the misapprehension that his friend had accepted a place as steward to the Duke of Queensberry, treats of "how to deal with Servants, Tenants and Neighboring Squires," the author explained, "which [he took] to be Courtiers, Parl[ia]m[en]t and Princes in Alliance, and so the Parallell goes on."[16] That application features often enough in Swift's prose, both in terms or conceptually (he writes of how Danes and Saxons were ancestrally "nigh neighbours," of contemporary "neighbouring Crowns," and of "Princes whose Dominions lie contiguous"),[17] to remind us that he had much to say one way and another, in one form or another, about the geopolitics of Christendom.[18] A dozen years later, as Swift returned to affairs of state from the other side of the Irish Sea, England would regularly feature as the island's overbearing and faithless neighbour.

---

14 Swift, *A Treatise on Polite Conversation* (1738), in *Parodies, Hoaxes, Mock Treatises*, ed. Rumbold, p. 392; "A Panegyrick on the D—n," *Poems*, ed. Williams, III, 888-91, ll. 64, 81, 135; "My Lady's Lamentation and Complaint against the Dean" (1728; published 1765), III, 858, l. 212.

15 Swift, *An Argument to Prove, that the Abolishing of Christianity in England, May, as Things Now Stand, Be Attended with Some Inconveniencies* (1708), in *Prose Works*, II, 38.

16 Swift to Gay and Catherine Douglas, née Hyde, Duchess of Queensberry, 13 March 1731, *Correspondence*, ed. Woolley, III, 368; the interpolations are editorial.

17 Swift, "An Abstract of the History of England" (published 1765), in *Prose Works*, V, 5; *A Tale of a Tub* (published 1710), in *A Tale of a Tub and Other Works*, ed. Marcus Walsh (Cambridge: Cambridge University Press, 2010), p. 106; *The Conduct of the Allies* (1711), in *English Political Writings, 1711-1714*, eds Bertrand A. Goldgar and Ian Gadd (Cambridge: Cambridge University Press, 2008), p. 105.

18 On which, see Matthew Charles Gertken, "Jonathan Swift, Sir William Temple and the International Balance of Power," doctoral dissertation, The University of Texas at Austin, 2013, available online at <http://hdl.handle.net/2152/23023> (accessed 1 October 2017).

The third sense of the term appears to confound further discussion. Under this definition stands everyone who has ever lived or ever will do. Echoing biblical passages teaching responsibility towards others, such as the parable of the Good Samaritan (Luke 10:25-37), the noun means simply "a fellow human" (1b). Samuel Johnson's gloss is conceptually narrower, but still helpful: "[In divinity.] One partaking of the same nature, and therefore entitled to good offices."[19] That is how the translators of the Apostle Paul employed the word in Romans 13:9 ("and if there be any other commandment, it is briefly comprehended in this saying, namely, Thou shalt love thy neighbour as thyself"), and the notion of encompassing fellowship informs Swift's "Politicall" sermon on *Brotherly Love*, after its own vituperatively denominational fashion,[20] as also his exhortations *On False Witness, On Mutual Subjection*, and on *Doing Good*.[21]

But the homilies were unusual in Swift's œuvre in being inherently dramatic. He was a preacher. Much in his sermons is conscious of the circumstances of utterance, the physical environment of the cathedral in which he was speaking.[22] His exordium to the lecture *On the Trinity*, for instance, expresses the bathetic hope that in his treatment of the topos, "the most Ignorant among you may return home better informed of your Duty in this great Point, than probably you are at present."[23] In this context, the term *neighbour* also had a local referent. "You who are my Hearers," as he described those who gathered in the sight of God (and he is said to have attracted large numbers to hear him

19 "Neighbour," sense 5, in Samuel Johnson, *A Dictionary of the English Language*, 2 vols (London, 1755), II, s.v.

20 Swift, *On Brotherly Love* (1717; published 1754), *Prose Works*, IX, 171-79. The clergyman wrote "Politicall" on the title page of the autograph; see Herbert Davis, "The Manuscript of Swift's Sermon on Brotherly Love," *Pope and his Contemporaries: Essays Presented to George Sherburn*, eds James L. Clifford and Louis A. Landa (Oxford: Clarendon Press, 1949), pp. 147-58 (153).

21 *On False Witness* (published 1762), in *Prose Works*, IX, 180-89; *On Mutual Subjection*, IX, 141-49; *Doing Good* (1724; published 1765), IX, 232-40.

22 According to its title page, *On Brotherly Love* was "Preached in St. Patrick's Church; On December 1st, 1717." The tenors of *Doing Good* and *Causes of the Wretched Condition of Ireland* evoke delivery in a metropolitan setting; *On Mutual Subjection* seems to have been read in the Cathedral in 1718 (C. P. Daw, "Swift's 'Strange Sermon,'" *Huntington Library Quarterly*, 38 [1974-75], 225-36); and *Upon the Martyrdom of King Charles I* was "Preached at St. Patrick's, Dublin, January 30, 1725/6," *Prose Works*, IX, 219.

23 *On the Trinity* (published 1744), in *Prose Works*, IX, 159-68 (p. 159); and see further the drily self-conscious introduction to *Upon Sleeping in Church* (published 1762), in *Prose Works*, IX, 210-18.

preach every fifth Sunday), were neighbours both in the biblical sense, and in the more immediate sense of residents of the Liberty of St Patrick's.[24]

2. The Deanery of St Patrick's

Not that Swift was often enamoured of his congregations. The Dean of St Patrick's typically thought little of those who assembled in his cathedral – "the Rabble," as he described them in the *Holyhead Journal*, albeit in the recollection of a dream.[25] He was a more considerable person by far. The wounded *amour propre* of the English House of Commons helps us to place him in the degrees of churchmen. Following a stirringly radical sermon on the anniversary of Charles I's execution read by William Stephens (1649/50-1718), the Rector of Sutton in Surrey, in 1700, the lower English house voted to invite only deans or doctors of divinity to preach thenceforth.[26] As Lady Acheson (d.1737) is imagined to say: "Envy must own, you understand your / Precedence, and support your Grandeur: / Nor, of your Rank will bate an Ace, / Except to give D---n *D—l* place."[27] This was a reference to "that abominable puppy and Poet" Richard Daniel (1680/1-1739), "the greatest Puppy and vilest Poet alive," who served as an accommodatingly Hanoverian Dean of Armagh till 1731 before his promotion to the same – but more valuable – office at Down Cathedral.[28]

"Precedence," "Grandeur," "Rank." Despite his protests elsewhere, and taking the literary context into account ("in the Person of a Lady in the North," the title of the poem concludes), these are not terms inflected with an absolute irony. Swift denigrated the capacities of the deans of Irish cathedrals in a letter to the Duke of Dorset (1688-1765), the Lord Lieutenant. "Be not allarmed at the Word *Deanry*, nor imagine it a Dignity like those we have in England," he reassured, "For, except three or four, the rest have neither Power nor Land as Deans and Chapters."[29] There was some truth in this. In his manuscript response to a bill of residence proposed by Edward Tenison (1673-1735), Bishop

24 *Prose Works*, IX, 154 and 181; William Monck Mason, *The History and Antiquities of the Collegiate and Cathedral Church of St Patrick, near Dublin* (Dublin: Folds, 1820), p. 420, note w.

25 Swift, "Holyhead Journal, 1727," in *Prose Works*, V, 205.

26 Howard D. Weinbrot, *Literature, Religion, and the Evolution of Culture, 1660-1780* (Baltimore: The Johns Hopkins University Press, 2013), p. 106.

27 "A Panegyrick on the D—n," in *Poems*, ed. Williams, III, 888, ll. 45-48.

28 Swift to Charles Ford, 20 September 1728, *Correspondence*, ed. Woolley, III, 196; Swift to Edward Harley, second Earl of Oxford and Earl Mortimer, 21 September 1728, III, 198.

29 Swift to Lionel Cranfield Sackville, Duke of Dorset, [30 December 1735], *Correspondence*, ed. Woolley, IV, 248-49.

of Ossory and "*Baboon* of *K[ilkenn]y*" (the latter dignity was unofficial), Swift mentions Down, Derry, and Raphoe as being "the only opulent Deanries in the whole Kingdom."[30] The fourth position worth its name was undoubtedly that of St Patrick's, however, "the best deanery in Ireland" in the view of the twentieth-century Church of Ireland's official history, and "then – as now – the most important deanery in Ireland" in a more recent estimate.[31] The office Swift held was no mere consolation for the several bishoprics in which he was disappointed.

A number of reasons explain why the Dean of St Patrick's was invariably a respected figure in the Church. In the first place, although Armagh was the senior province of the communion, Dublin was the capital of the kingdom. What is more, the establishment that was Swift's charge imposed itself on the capital. The grandest church in the island, 300 feet (91 metres) from west to east, St Patrick's was comparable in size to smaller British cathedrals such as Bristol, Glasgow, Lichfield, and St Davids.[32] Its bells tolled regularly.[33] A final consideration was that its leading prebendary enjoyed significant clerical powers. "The Dean has great prerogatives," Swift explained, appealing to "constant immemorial custom":

> He visits the Chapter as Ordinary, and the Archbishop only visits by the Dean. The Dean can suspend and sequester any member, and punishes all crimes except heresy, and one or two more reserved for the Archbishop. No lease can be let without him. He holds a court-leet in his district, and is exempt from the Lord Mayor, &c. No Chapter can be called but by him, and he dissolves them at pleasure. He disposes absolutely of the Petty Canons and Vicars Choral places. All the Dignitaries, &c. swear canonical obedience to him.[34]

30 Swift, "On the Irish Bishops" (1732), *Poems*, ed. Williams, III, 803, l. 10; "On the Bill for the Clergy's Residing on their Livings" (1732; published 1789), in *Prose Works*, XII, 185.

31 D. A. Chart, "Close Alliance of Church and State, 1702-1760," *History of the Church of Ireland: From the Earliest Times to the Present Day*, ed. Walter Alison Phillips, 3 vols (London: Oxford University Press, 1933-34), III, 175-241 (p. 190); A. P. W. Malcomson, *Archbishop Charles Agar: Churchmanship and Politics in Ireland, 1760-1810* (Dublin: Four Courts Press, 2002), p. 465.

32 Christine Casey, *Dublin: The City within the Grand and Royal Canals and the Circular Road with the Phoenix Park*, The Buildings of Ireland (New Haven and London: Yale University Press, 2005), pp. 19-20.

33 Toby Barnard, "St Patrick's Cathedral in the Age of Swift, 1690-1745," *St Patrick's Cathedral, Dublin: A History*, eds John Crawford and Raymond Gillespie (Dublin: Four Courts Press, 2009), pp. 197-218 (203-4).

34 Swift to Bishop Atterbury, 18 April 1716, *Correspondence*, ed. Woolley, II, 159-60.

Self-interested though this summary is, the incumbent was undeniably also a commanding figure in the temporal realm. From John Comin (d.1212), Archbishop of Dublin and the founder of the collegiate church that was the antecedent of the Cathedral, and from later patrons and instruments ("subsequent Grants and Confirmations of Popes, Parlmts, Kings, and Arch-Bishops"[35]), the Dean and Chapter received certain rights that freed them not only from much – but by no means all – of the metropolitan's oversight but also, and perhaps more importantly, from the corporate jurisdiction of the city. Those privileges were defined in *Dignitas Decani*, a bound collection of copies of charters and other documents still held in the Cathedral archives, and a volume to which Swift would refer in a dispute with a neighbour.[36] As the Dean of St Patrick's, his clerical and temporal powers were as broad as their physical compass was narrow.

3. The Liberty of St Patrick's

For his authority was limited only by its reach. His writ was confined to the modest tract demarcated as the Liberty of St Patrick ("Patricks Close" was the common contemporary name), one of several districts that were independent of Dublin's governing body. Insisting on their ancient customs, precedents, and rights, and thus regularly holding their own courts leet to oversee matters such as the welfare of the disadvantaged, public hygiene, weights and measures, and the orderly running of alehouses, they greatly complicated governance of the capital.[37] Their number exacerbated *ancien-régime* perplexity. The other franchises were the Archbishop's Liberty of St Sepulchre; the Liberty of Thomas Court and Donore, a possession of the Earls of Meath to the south-west of the intramural city and where the conurbation's textile industries were concentrated; the Liberty of Christ Church, a one-acre block in which stood Dublin's other – in fact, its senior – cathedral; and the Manor of Kilmainham, beyond the municipality's western boundary.[38] On 1 August every third year, the

35 Swift to Robert Mossom, 14 February 1721, *Correspondence*, ed. Woolley, II, 365.

36 Reproduced in Newport B. White, ed., *The "Dignitas Decani" of St Patrick's Cathedral, Dublin* (Dublin: Stationery Office, 1957). On the increasing contemporary interest in such muniments, see further Toby Barnard, "John Lyon and Irish Antiquarianism in the Time of Swift," *Reading Swift: Papers from The Fifth Münster Symposium on Jonathan Swift*, ed. Hermann J. Real (Munich: Wilhelm Fink, 2008), pp. 245-54.

37 Barnard, "St Patrick's Cathedral in the Age of Swift," p. 208.

38 Kenneth Milne, *The Dublin Liberties, 1600-1850*, Maynooth Studies in Local History, 82 (Dublin: Four Courts Press, 2009).

several limits were effectively recognized when the civic authorities "rode the franchises," a ceremony akin to the parochial custom of beating the bounds.[39]

The likelihood of, and opportunity for, conflict between the Dean and the Archbishop were increased by the fact that the Liberty of St Patrick's lay within – it was physically surrounded by – the Liberty of St Sepulchre's. "This is to welcome you to my neighbourhood at St. Sepulchers," William King (1650-1729) pointedly greeted the new Dean – even as he wrote from Chester to London.[40] (They had known each other, of course, and had corresponded, for years beforehand.) In Ireland, they would scarcely be physically closer. King and Swift were neighbours over the wall that marked the boundary between their respective demesnes, the palace garden lying within the Archbishop's Liberty and the half-acre Deanery garden lying within Patrick's Close. That same wall almost certainly precluded chatty neighbourliness. We should imagine the two plots divided by an imposing structure: gardens had historically been enclosed by a substantial curtain, and would long remain so.[41] The wall surrounding Naboth's Vineyard, Swift's one-acre paddock which lay a couple of hundred yards south of the Deanery, was "eight or nine Feet high;" that surrounding a late Ascendancy garden in Leinster – with which J. M. Synge (1871-1909) may have had in mind an appurtenance of Glanmore Castle or of Castle Kevin – was "seven or eight feet high."[42] Numerous further examples might be cited. However enthusiastic Swift was as a horticulturalist,[43] he is likely to have seen his most immediate neighbour in settings rather more formal than that of their adjoining gardens.

Elsewhere, the metes and bounds were much less visible. In a number of places, the line dividing the two ecclesiastical manors ran down the centre

39 See the excerpt from "The Cavalcade: A Poem on the Riding the Franchises" ([1716]), *Verse in English from Eighteenth-Century Ireland*, ed. Andrew Carpenter (Cork: Cork University Press, 1998), pp. 103-7.

40 Archbishop King to Swift, 16 May 1713, *Correspondence*, ed. Woolley, I, 484.

41 Paula Henderson, *The Tudor House and Garden: Architecture and Landscape in the Sixteenth and Early Seventeenth Centuries* (New Haven and London: Yale University Press, 2005), pp. 145, 256n13.

42 *Dr Swift's Will* (1740; published 1745), in *Prose Works*, XIII, 156. On his difficulties with the building of the wall, which was – eventually, in his opinion – "the best in *Ireland*," see further *Memoirs of Laetitia Pilkington*, ed. A. C. Elias, Jr, 2 vols (Athens and London: The University of Georgia Press, 1997), I, 35. J. M. Synge's description of "A Landlord's Garden in County Wicklow" (published 1907) can be found in his *Collected Works*, ed. Robin Skelton, 4 vols (London: Oxford University Press, 1962-68), II, 230-33 (p. 230).

43 Joseph McMinn, "The Gardener in the Deanery," *Swift, the Enigmatic Dean: Festschrift for Hermann Josef Real*, eds Rudolf Freiburg, Arno Löffler, and Wolfgang Zach (Tübingen: Stauffenburg, 1998), pp. 127-35.

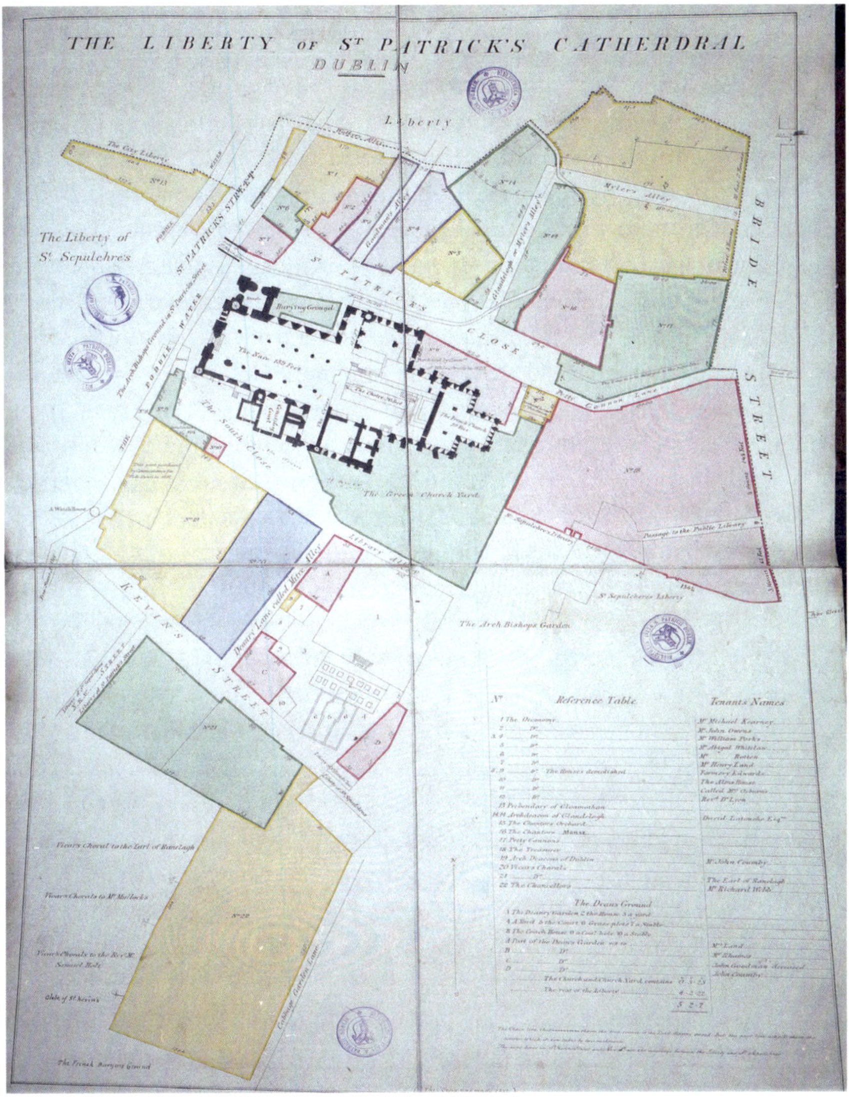

FIGURE 21.1 A nineteenth-century copy of Roger Kendrick, *The Liberty of St Patrick's Cathedral, Dublin* (1754). Note that the map is oriented north-north-west; as it stands, the Cathedral is aligned due east and west.

THE IMAGE IS KINDLY SUPPLIED BY THE IRISH HISTORIC TOWNS ATLAS PROJECT, ROYAL IRISH ACADEMY, AND IS REPRODUCED WITH THE KIND PERMISSION OF MARSH'S LIBRARY, DUBLIN.

of a road. A textual perambulation of those bounds may thus be helpful (see Figure 21.1, the map of the precinct drawn by Roger Kendrick [d.1778], the City Surveyor). Starting at the Cathedral's west door, the verge of the Liberty extended north along St Patrick's Street, before turning east through the maze-like quarter that lay to the north of St Patrick's Close, and which included Walker's Alley and "Glandelogh or Myler's Alley." Issuing in Bride Street, the boundary then continued south-east down that thoroughfare as far as the junction with Peter's Street, where it turned west to skirt Marsh's Library, before aligning itself almost due south to divide the prelates' gardens, to negotiate a jog in crossing Kevin Street, and to range down the western side of Cabbage Garden Lane. From the bottom of that cul-de-sac, the boundary zigzagged its way north-west, between individual parcels and via New Street and Kevin Street, to the Cross Poddle, the road junction named after the tributary of the River Liffey that was, at this point, barely subterranean. Not forgetting an isolated, narrowly elongated parcel that stretched from the western side of St Patrick's Street to Francis Street and which was the property of the Prebendary of Clonmethan, the Liberty covered a little over five acres.

What kind of built environment was to be found within the franchise? The capital city of brick and stone to which Swift returned to assume his office, home to a minimum of *c.*80,000 persons, was different both in degree and in kind from the impoverished, plague-ravaged, and largely timber-framed provincial centre of his birth and earliest years, when the population had amounted to a minimum of *c.*50,000.[44] (In seventeenth-century Dublin estate papers, "a stone house is always cited as a landmark precisely because it is unusual."[45]) After the alarms and excursions of the House of Stuart's contested reign, political stability, economic recovery, and consequent immigration from all parts of the British Isles resulted in metropolitan expansion beyond the walls of the medieval town and its suburbs. Those walls were gradually removed between *c.*1690 and *c.*1730. Prestigious developments such as the Aungier and Dawson estates south of the Liffey (beginning in 1660 and in 1705, respectively), and the

---

44 The figures cited should be treated with caution. See variously R. A. Butlin, "The Population of Dublin in the Late Seventeenth Century," *Irish Geography*, 5, no 2 (1965), 51-66; David Dickson, "The Demographic Implications of Dublin's Growth, 1650-1850," *Urban Population Development in Western Europe from the Late-Eighteenth to the Early-Twentieth Century*, eds Richard Lawton and Robert Lee (Liverpool: Liverpool University Press, 1989), pp. 178-89; and Patrick Fagan, "The Population of Dublin in the Eighteenth Century with Particular Reference to the Proportions of Protestants and Catholics," *Eighteenth-Century Ireland*, 6 (1991), 121-56.

45 Robin Usher, *Protestant Dublin, 1660-1760: Architecture and Iconography* (Basingstoke: Palgrave Macmillan, 2012), p. 171.

Jervis and Gardiner estates to the north (1674 and *c.*1720), precincts laid out often in symmetrical plan, had begun to provide commodious accommodation for the mercantile and professional classes, landowners, and office-holders in the viceroy's train.[46] And the Deanery had recently been rebuilt along similarly generous lines, "a vast unfurnished house" large enough to host chapter meetings and dinners, but so grand that at first Swift lived in only a small part of it and never quite lost the feeling that he was rattling around.[47]

At least the residence conformed to the dignity of his office. The contrast with the rest of the neighbourhood was stark, for the Liberty was one of the oldest and remained one of the poorest quarters of the conurbation, a low-lying district that much earlier, during the period of Hiberno-Norse settlement, had been insulated by branches of the River Poddle. In subsequent Anglo-Norman sources, the church John Comin chose for his own foundation was known as St Patrick *de insula*, and for centuries thereafter, the cathedral and "the Precincts of the Cathedral ... which are called the Liberty of St. Patrick's," were occasionally flooded by the river or by heavy rainfall.[48] The canton defined by the antiquary John Lyon (1710-90) comprehended

> the two Closes of the Church, on each Side, and such parts of the adjoyning Streets as now contain the whole Compass of the Ground antiently assigned for Houses & Gardens to the Dean, Dignitarys, Prebendarys, Minor Canons, Vicars Choral & Choristers, beside the common Estate called the Oeconomy.[49]

That the gardens of the various members of the Cathedral had been "*antiently* assigned" bears (my) emphasis. Horticulture and recreation had succumbed

---

46 The best account of the development of the capital remains Nuala T. Burke, "Dublin 1600-1800: A Study in Urban Morphogenesis," doctoral thesis, Trinity College, Dublin, 1972, available online at <http://hdl.handle.net/2262/40108> (accessed 1 October 2017). The growth of the metropolis is illustrated in H. B. Clarke, *Dublin: Part I, to 1610*, Irish Historic Towns Atlas, 11 (Dublin: Royal Irish Academy, 2002); and Colm Lennon, *Dublin: Part II, 1610 to 1756*, Irish Historic Towns Atlas, 19 (Dublin: Royal Irish Academy, 2008).

47 Swift to Pope, 28 June 1715, *Correspondence*, ed. Woolley, II, 133; Swift to John Boyle, fifth Earl of Orrery, [20 April 1733], III, 629; Swift to Thomas Sheridan, [22 May 1736], IV, 303.

48 Cited in A. C. Elias, Jr, "Swift's *Don Quixote*, Dunkin's *Virgil Travesty*, and Other New Intelligence: John Lyon's 'Materials for a Life of Dr. Swift,' 1765," *Swift Studies*, 13 (1998), 27-104 (p. 94). Flooding occurred in 1687, in 1701 (Monck Mason, *The History and Antiquities of the Collegiate and Cathedral Church of St Patrick*, pp. 205, 217), in 1726 (M. Pollard, "Who's for Prison? Publishing Swift in Dublin," *Swift Studies*, 14 [1999], 37-49 [p. 38]), in 1778 (Monck Mason, p. 449), in 1835 and in 1882 (Damrosch, *Jonathan Swift*, pp. 471-72).

49 Elias, "Swift's *Don Quixote*, Dunkin's *Virgil Travesty*, and Other New Intelligence," pp. 94-95. And see further Thomas Drew, "Surroundings of the Cathedral Church of St Patrick de Insula, Dublin," *Journal of the Royal Society of Antiquaries of Ireland*, 5th ser., 1 (1891), 426-32.

to residential and industrial development, and the demesne continued to suffer from in-filling, as can be inferred from Swift's bequest to his cousin and housekeeper, Martha Whiteway (1690-1768), of "[his] Lease of forty Years of *Goodman*'s Holding, for which [he received] Ten Pounds *per Annum*; which are two Houses, or more lately built."[50] Throughout his period of office, the district was as crowded as the Deanery was empty.

To add to the physical impoverishment of the sept were the misfortunes of many of its residents. A more industrial quarter than that surrounding Christ Church, the Liberty was home to a number of Protestant weavers. Many were French, a different kind of sept, Huguenots who had been encouraged to settle in Ireland during the course of Swift's life. Indeed, since 1665 the Lady Chapel at the east end of St Patrick's had been devoted to those Calvinists who were prepared to conform to Anglican sacramentalism; they amounted to about one-third of Dublin's Huguenot population. The Dean kept his distance. Suspicious of those he regarded as spreading disrespect for orthodoxy and church authority, Swift tried to have "nothing to do with the[m] further than sometimes reading or gabbling with the French clergy who come to me about business of their Church."[51] (More welcome, perhaps, despite his reservations over the management of the institution, was the first Keeper of Marsh's Library, a neighbour as close as the archbishops of Dublin, the Huguenot physician and scholar Élie Bouhéreau [1643-1719].) Demand for the ware of those employed in the cloth trades nonetheless declined during periods of national economic hardship, and the artisans of the neighbourhood were amongst those who suffered most in the 1720s and 1740s.

The misery visited upon the weavers in those years compounded the abiding poverty of the manor. In theory, Swift distinguished between sturdy beggars who were drawn to the capital in the spring and summer months and the deserving poor of the Liberty and its environs. The scheme to compel mendicants to wear "Badge[s], marked and numbered," about which he preached in 1725 and which he revisited in a tract of 1737, was intended to confine the indigent to beg within their own parishes.[52] "Unquestionably he felt that his

---

50 *Dr Swift's Will*, in *Prose Works*, XIII, 153.

51 Swift, Introduction to *A Treatise on Polite Conversation* (1738), in *Parodies, Hoaxes, Mock Treatises*, ed. Rumbold, p. 280; Swift to Knightley Chetwode, 5 December 1721, *Correspondence*, ed. Woolley, II, 404 (the elision is mine); Ruth Whelan, "Sanctified by the Word: The Huguenots and Anglican Liturgy," *Propagating the Word of Irish Dissent, 1650-1800*, ed. Kevin Herlihy (Dublin: Four Courts Press, 1998), pp. 74-94.

52 Swift, *Causes of the Wretched Condition of Ireland* (*post* 1715; published 1762), in *Prose Works*, IX, 207; and *A Proposal for Giving Badges to the Beggars in All the Parishes of Dublin* (1737), in *Prose Works*, XIII, 131-40.

first obligation was to the small tradesmen and weavers who lived in the vicinity of the Cathedral and in the adjacent liberties."[53] And within his own demesne, he succeeded. "There was no such thing as a vagrant, or unbadged beggar seen about his cathedral," Patrick Delany claimed.[54] In practice, however, Swift tried to alleviate want where he saw it. Consistent with his unsmilingly brisk Christian sympathy, he regularly bought small goods from a seraglio of elderly and infirm women scattered throughout the city, and closer to home dispensed coppers to those who crowded the door of the Cathedral after service, and sixpence to "the lame old Man that sells Ginger-bread at the Corner, because he tries to do something, and does not beg."[55] Similarly deserving were a small number of the Liberty's "most ancient and orderly widows," who lived in an almshouse Swift built within the precinct, and the pupils of no fewer than three charity schools, one of which he helped to found in 1716.[56]

Artisans, widows, and schoolchildren were not the only residents of Patrick's Close. In the particular circumstances of the Liberty, certain other neighbours were unavoidable. The Dean was the landlord of several fellow clerics and members of the Cathedral staff, including Henry Land (d.1757), the obliging sexton, who held the tenancy of a house in the narrow thoroughfare known as Mitre Alley ("Deanry Lane called Mitre Alley," as it appears on Kendrick's map).[57] They all shared the area, moreover, with the dearly departed. Quite apart from the eminent lying inside St Patrick's, a variety of persons had been interred in the graveyard north of the Deanery garden. The memorials that marked their burial were an inconvenience. In "removing Tomb stones" to plant elm trees there, coeval with the introduction of elm trees into the Deanery garden, Swift "disturbed the Dead, and angered the Living."[58] And a final group may have been consequent upon neighbours we have just met. Latterly the Dean had to contend with "Soldiers drumming through my Liberty twice a day, and going to a Barrack the Governmt hath placed just under my Nose" – meaning troops

53 Louis A. Landa, "Jonathan Swift and Charity," *Journal of English and Germanic Philology*, 44 (1945), 337-50 (p. 339).

54 Patrick Delany, *Observations upon Lord Orrery's Remarks on the Life and Writings of Dr Jonathan Swift* (London: W. Reeve and A. Linde, 1754), p. 9.

55 *Memoirs of Laetitia Pilkington*, ed. Elias, I, 27, 35.

56 Delany, *Observations upon Lord Orrery's Remarks*, p. 8; Landa, "Jonathan Swift and Charity," pp. 340-41, 342 and n32.

57 *Dr Swift's Will*, in *Prose Works*, XIII, 153; Louis A. Landa, "Swift's Deanery Income: A New Document," *Pope and his Contemporaries*, eds Clifford and Landa, pp. 159-70 (165-66); Martha Whiteway to Swift, 2 December 1735, *Correspondence*, ed. Woolley, IV, 242-43.

58 Swift to Knightley Chetwode, 5 December 1721, *Correspondence*, ed. Woolley, II, 404; Monck Mason, *The History and Antiquities of the Collegiate and Cathedral Church of St Patrick*, "Additional Notes and Illustrations," note "A" ([xlix]-lxiii).

garrisoned in Kevin Street "*to suppress Riots.*"[59] This was almost certainly a reference to the first of a long-running series of disturbances between "Ormond boys," who were mainly Catholic butchers from Oxmantown, north of the Liffey, and "Liberty boys," Protestant weavers from the neighbouring Coombe.[60]

Over almost all these groups Swift came to exercise a proprietorial concern. "I walk the streets in peace, without being justled, nor ever without a thousand blessings from my friends the Vulgar," he told Pope after twenty years in office:

> I am Lord Mayor of 120 houses. I am absolute Lord of the greatest Cathedral in the Kingdom: am at peace with the neighboring Princes the Lord Mayor of the City, and the A. Bp. of Dublin, only the latter, like the K. of France sometimes attempts encroachments on my Dominions, as old Lewis did upon Lorrain.[61]

The following sentence deprecates the passage as "railery," but we shall hear more presently about encroachments of the kind. (Note, too, that the vehicle of his simile has recourse to what were still unresolved geopolitical contentions.) Three years later, Swift expressed himself in even grander, sovereign terms:

> My Realm extends to 120 Houses, whose Inhabitants constitute the Bulk of my Subjects; my Grand Jury is my House of Commons, and My Chapter the House of Lords: I must proceed no further because My Arts of Governing are Secrets of State.[62]

The cohesion between the two passages is striking. That he was able to give a precise figure for the number of properties naturally quantifies the size of the Liberty. "To perform this work in every house where the parishes are very populous," he had written in disputing Charles M'Carthy's "walking brief" (a form of charitable extortion), "consisting sometimes here in town of 900 or 1000 houses, would take up the space of a year."[63] The accuracy of his

---

59 Swift to the Rev. Thomas Sheridan, [15-16 June 1735], *Correspondence*, ed. Woolley, IV, 122 and 124n9.

60 On which and whom, see James Kelly, *The Liberty and Ormond Boys: Factional Riot in Eighteenth-Century Dublin*, Maynooth Studies in Local History, 64 (Dublin: Four Courts Press, 2005).

61 Swift to Pope, 8 July 1733, *Correspondence*, ed. Woolley, III, 663. He mentions similar public acclaim from his "lower friends" in a later message to Pope, 9 February 173[7], IV, 386.

62 Swift to William Flower, Lord Castle-Durrow, [24 December 1736], *Correspondence*, ed. Woolley, IV, 375.

63 Swift, "The Humble Representation of the Clergy of the City of Dublin" (1724; published 1765), in *Prose Works*, V, 88. The M'Carthy affair is discussed in Ehrenpreis, *Dean Swift*, pp. 341-45.

enumeration – neither 100 nor 150 but "120 Houses" – also indicates that his temporal possessions were well documented. If he needed to defend the Liberty in law, he would do so with cadastral precision. Small though it may have been in physical and demographic terms, Swift cherished his domain.

The extracts also suggest that Patrick's Close enjoyed a distinct religious and socio-cultural identity. This was unusual. What lay beyond the bounds of the franchise had long been a largely characterless confusion of streets and lanes. Only during Swift's life did change come to Dublin's ecclesiological landscape. Beginning in the last decades of the seventeenth century, increasing administrative demands on parish vestries (such as night-time policing, moral regulation, and tax collection), and beginning in the first decades of the eighteenth century, a determined programme of church building (initiated by William King, who was particularly grieved by the absence of steeples, likening the city to "a Cow without horns"), served to create self-identifying parishes seemingly for the first time.[64] In finding their various dispositions, however, such parishes merely emulated the quiddities of the precinct the Dean was pleased to call his own. No quarter of the Irish capital was more distinctive than the Liberty of St Patrick's, and no quarter's distinctiveness was more carefully policed than that of the Liberty under Swift's hold.

4. An Archbishop for a Neighbour: William King

The vigour with which Swift defended his temporal privileges was matched by the exasperation of the two archbishops of Dublin with whom he served. The prelate who held that position was Swift's physically closest neighbour and, by virtue of their respective rights, the neighbour with whom Swift was most likely to disagree.

Disagree with both archbishops he certainly did. To take their incumbencies in turn, Swift's relationship with King gradually became – through periods of principled dispute and occasional incomprehension – tolerably good. It did not begin well. (Six months later, his relationship with the vicars choral would not begin well.) The Archbishop had early attempted to assert his authority – in the letter in which he welcomed Swift to "[his] neighbourhood at

64 Usher, *Protestant Dublin, 1660-1760*, pp. 49-50; King to John Forster, 20 November 1716, cited in Edward McParland, *Public Architecture in Ireland 1680-1760* (New Haven and London: Yale University Press, 2001), p. 45. McParland identifies the recipient as Lord Chief Justice Forster (p. 216n161); John Forster (1668-1720) served, in fact, as Chief Justice of the Common Pleas for Ireland, a different office.

St. Sepulchers" – by mentioning a scheme dear to his own heart. John Stearne (1660-1745), the foregoing Dean and King's coadjutant, had proposed to raise a distinguishing spire over Minot's Tower, the Cathedral's flat-roofed, fourteenth-century belfry:

> which kind of ornament is much wanting in Dublin, he has left your Œconomy clear and 200ll in bank for this purpose. The Steeple is 120 feet high, 21 feet in the clear wide where the spire is to stand. the design was to build it of brick, 120 feet high ... But we have no workman that understands any thing of the matter. I believe you may be acquainted with several that are conversant with such kind of work, and if you would discourse some of them, and push on the work as soon as settled, it might be of use to you, and give the people there an advantageous notion of you, *dimidium facti, qui bene capit habet*.[65]

Swift was unimpressed with his predecessor's ambition and unmoved by King's exhortation, a rendering of Horace's *Epistles*, I, ii, 40: "Half-finish'd is the Work, if well-begun," in George Ogle's imitation.[66] The likely outlay was also a dissuasive. "I am apt to think it will cost more than is imagined," the new Dean prevaricated; "and, I am confident, that no Bricks made in that Part of Ireland, will bear being exposed so much to the Air."[67] Not before 1749 – four years after Stearne's death as the diocesan of Clogher, who bequeathed £1,000 for the project – was an octagonal spire a little over 100 feet (30 metres) high added to the tower, to a design by the celebrated Irish architect and builder George Semple (*c.*1700-82), and in granite, not brick.

The episode of the spire was predictably local. In matters of doctrine and ministry throughout the Church of Ireland, such as prayer, music, and the celebration of the Lord's Supper, the two men were often in accord.[68] Their responses to affairs in the temporal realm were similarly congruous. By the 1720s, as Swift began to think about, and to articulate, Ireland's constitutional and economic plight, he found an ally in King, even as they differed over strategy and method. They largely concurred over 6 Geo. I, c. 5, the Declaratory Act (1719), which spelt out the legislative supremacy of Westminster; over Whitehall's policy of filling Irish benefices with clergymen from Britain; over the question of a national bank; and over how best to alleviate hunger and disease in their capital. Both offered financial support to weavers impoverished as a result of

65 *Correspondence*, ed. Woolley, I, 485.

66 George Ogle, *The Second Epistle of the First Book of Horace Imitated* (London: R. Dodsley, 1738), p. 11 (Foxon O104).

67 Swift to Archbishop King, 23 May 1713, *Correspondence*, ed. Woolley, I, 490.

68 On King's churchmanship, see his *A Discourse concerning the Inventions of Men in the Worship of God* (Dublin, 1694).

the "South-sea, and the Ruin of the Kingdom, and scarcity of money."[69] And "Dub[lin] and his dean" was the cohesive phrase John Evans (*c.*1652-1724), the Welsh-born, Oxford-educated and decidedly political Bishop of Meath, employed in describing their concerted opposition to Wood's Halfpenny patent.[70] Collaborating in that regard encouraged "a spirit of union among us," Swift conceded, "at least in this point, in the midst of all our former divisions."[71]

Those former divisions may have been the exercise of their local prerogatives, church politics writ small. Less than a year after he had taken up residence in the shadow of St Patrick's, the Dean reflected that "[his] amusements are defending [his] ... dominions against the Arch-Bishop, and endeavouring to reduce my rebellious Choir."[72] The following years were troubled, furthermore, by King's success in placing his clients in the Cathedral hierarchy, and Swift's corresponding failure to advance his friends (the head of the Chapter disposing of only "the Petty Canons and Vicars Choral places").[73] And the Dean's final exeat provoked a quarrel over attendance. At his visitation in 1727, King demanded a proxy for the absentee – "a thing wholly new and unheard of," Swift replied from England, "let the consequences be what they will, I shall never comply with it."[74] He even prepared for litigation, declaring that he would spend "a hundred or two Pounds, rather than be enslav'd, or betray a Right which [he did] not value Three-pence, but [his] Successors may," a sum that had increased to "two or three Hundred Pounds" a week later.[75] The matter fell thereafter, and their relationship soon returned to well-tempered mutual esteem, but the episode can be seen to be of exemplary importance. In the short term, it was almost certainly the occasion of efforts to gather and to secure the documentary record of the Cathedral's governance.[76] And in the longer view, it helps us understand how Swift beheld his office. "I will set no unworthy

69 Swift to Esther Vanhomrigh, 15 October 1720, *Correspondence*, ed. Woolley, II, 348. See, for example, Swift to the Rev. John Worrall, 30 July 1721, II, 392.

70 Cited in Philip O'Regan, *Archbishop William King of Dublin (1650-1729) and the Constitution in Church and State* (Dublin: Four Courts Press, 2000), p. 304; the interpolation is O'Regan's. And see further E. D. Evans, "'A Man of the World': John Evans, Bishop of Meath, 1716-24," *Journal of Welsh Religious History*, NS, 4 (2004), 1-28.

71 *Doing Good*, in *Prose Works*, IX, 236. See also *Jonathan Swift's Allies: The Wood's Halfpence Controversy in Ireland, 1724-25*, ed. Sabine Baltes-Ellermann, 2nd rev. ed. (Frankfurt on Main: Peter Lang, 2017), *passim*.

72 Swift to Pope, 28 June 1715, *Correspondence*, ed. Woolley, II, 133.

73 Ehrenpreis, *Dean Swift*, pp. 40-49.

74 Swift to Archbishop King, 18 May 1727, *Correspondence*, ed. Woolley, III, 87.

75 Swift to the Rev. Thomas Sheridan, 24 June 1727, *Correspondence*, ed. Woolley, III, 101; Swift to the Rev. Thomas Sheridan, 1 July 1727, III, 104.

76 *The "Dignitas Decani" of St Patrick's Cathedral, Dublin*, ed. White, pp. viii-ix.

examples for my successors to follow," he concludes the letter of principled refusal to his neighbour.[77]

5. Richard Bettesworth's Threats

Amongst the more unusual examples Swift set his successors – noteworthy even in an age in which sudden violence was unremarkable – was how to defend oneself from physical attack. Riding along the strand between Dublin and Howth in the winter of 1715-16, he was run into a ditch by the chaise of Cadwallader Blayney (1693-1732), seventh Lord Blayney, who then threatened him with a loaded pistol. The Dean talked him down, and the event went unpunished. And the year after Blayney's death, Swift had words with, following his mocking words for, Richard Bettesworth (1689-1741). A Serjeant-at-Law and a prominent Member of Parliament for Midleton in County Cork, Bettesworth had noisily supported both a bill to commute the tithe on hemp (a measure that would deprive the clergy of a fraction of their income), and the repeal of the Test Act.[78] Neither proposal was welcomed by Swift, who was stirred by the counsellor to include him in a typically anonymous attack on Ulster's Scottish Presbyterians:

> Thus at the Bar that Booby *Bettesworth*,
> Tho' Half a Crown o'er-pays his Sweat's Worth;
> Who knows in Law, nor Text, nor Margent,
> Calls *Singleton* his Brother Serjeant.[79]

A promptingly multisyllabled proper noun was one of Swift's greatest verbal delights, but also, in this case, the fatal Cleopatra that all but identified him as the author of the poem. The subsequent reference to Henry Singleton (1682-1759), Bettesworth's superior as Prime Serjeant and a good but not particularly intimate friend of Swift, was conclusive.

77 *Correspondence*, ed. Woolley, III, 88; Louis A. Landa, *Swift and the Church of Ireland* (Oxford: Clarendon Press, 1954), pp. 92-93.

78 There were three such serjeants-at-law in Ireland, a superior order of barrister. For his parliamentary career, see Edith Mary Johnston-Liik, *History of the Irish Parliament, 1692-1800: Commons, Constituencies and Statutes*, 6 vols (Belfast: Ulster Historical Foundation, 2002), III, 179-80.

79 Swift, "On the Words – Brother Protestants, and Fellow Christians, so Familiarly Used by the Advocates for the Repeal of the Test Act in Ireland, 1733" (published 1734), in *Poems*, ed. Williams, III, 812, ll. 25-28.

Having recognized the culprit, the parliamentarian threatened violence. "On Monday last week, towards evening, there came to the Deanry one Mr. Bettesworth," Swift relates,

> who, being told by the servants that I was gone to a friend's house, went thither to enquire for me, and was admitted into the street-parlour. I left my company in the back room, and went to him ... When he began to grow over-warm and eloquent, I called in the gentleman of the house, from the room adjoining; and the Serjeant, going on with less turbulence, went away. He had a footman in the hall during all his talk, who was to have opened the door for one or more fellows, as he hath since reported; and, likewise, that he had a sharp knife in his pocket, ready to stab or maim me.[80]

In following Swift to John Worrall's house, Bettesworth retraced his steps, for the Dean's vicar lodged a few doors down from the aggrieved in Great Ship Street, west of the Castle gardens.[81] Not residents of the Liberty per se, they were still close at hand, a proximity to the Deanery that cannot have afforded time for Bettesworth's turbulence to subside. As he had with Lord Blayney, Swift talked down his antagonist.[82]

Those resident in the Close did not take kindly to the news that Bettesworth had resolved to maim, or worse, "the Reverend the Dean of St. *Patrick*'s, our Neighbour, Benefactor, and Head of the Liberty of St. *Patrick*'s." Their purported response was stirring:

> We, the said Inhabitants of the said Liberty, and in the Neighbourhood thereof, from our great Love and Respect to the said Dean, to whom the whole Kingdom hath so many Obligations, as well as we of the Liberty, do unanimously declare, that we will endeavour to defend the Life and Limbs of the said Dean against the said Man, and all his Ruffians and Murderers, as far as the Law will allow, if he or any of them presume to come into the said Liberty with any wicked or malicious Intent, against the House, or Family, or Person, or Goods of the said Dean.[83]

---

80 Swift to the Duke of Dorset, [6-12] January 1733/4, *Correspondence*, ed. Woolley, III, 719; see also Luis R. Gámez, "Richard Bettesworth's Insult and 'The Yahoo's Overthrow,'" *Swift Studies*, 12 (1997), 80-84. The broader historiographical context, and comparisons with England, are discussed in Neal Garnham, "How Violent Was Eighteenth-Century Ireland?" *Irish Historical Studies*, 30 (1996-97), 377-92.

81 Landa notes that Worrall held "a portion of deanery property located in St. Kevin Street and Deanery Lane" by a lease of 1732 ("Swift's Deanery Income," p. 165), but the address in question undoubtedly lay outside the Liberty; see *Correspondence*, ed. Woolley, III, 721n4.

82 On this episode, see further Elias, "Swift's *Don Quixote*, Dunkin's *Virgil Travesty*, and Other New Intelligence," pp. 97-98.

83 "A Copy of the Paper with which several Persons of the Liberty of St. *Patrick*'s attended the Rev. Dr. J. *Swift*, Dean of St. *Patrick*'s *Dublin*," in *Prose Works*, V, 341-42.

Dated "January 8, 1733" (meaning 1734), this was signed by thirty-one men, a few of whom enjoyed distinctive surnames (Classon, Copstone, Curville, Pinckney), some of whom came from originally Welsh families (Jones, Lewis, Owens), but most of whom were of indigenous stock (Byrne, Carthy, Laughlin, Murphy, Reily). All of them were seized of the personal, local, and national importance of Swift's well-being. And he returned their consideration. "The Inhabitants of the Liberty, as well as those of the Neighbourhood," wrote their patron, "have lived with me in great Amity for near Twenty Years ... May God bless you and your Families in this World, and make you for ever happy in the next."[84]

Readers might still be forgiven for wondering about the texture of the prose in these various documents. Irvin Ehrenpreis doubts the independence of their content and expression, suspecting Swift's hand.[85] ("B - - - th, that booby, and S - - - l in grain," runs a companion piece to "On the Words – Brother Protestants," "Hath insulted us all by insulting the Dean."[86]) This is likely to have been the case. But that is no less material. Swift writes himself into the life of his own allod. The subtle distinction he draws, and reiterates, between residents of the Liberty and those who lived in adjacent "Neighbourhood[s]," in a context of popular unanimity, is analogous to the provocative local precedent he had contemplated setting over Wood's coinage, and which he hoped would be "followed in the whole City."[87] Contrasts of this colour sharpened his own self-approving view of the distinctiveness of Patrick's Close.

6. An Occasional Neighbour: Archbishop John Hoadly

What the second Archbishop of Dublin to serve alongside Swift thought about the alarms and excursions with Bettesworth is not readily apparent. William King had been succeeded in 1729 by John Hoadly (1678-1746), a former chaplain to Gilbert Burnet (1643-1715) and the younger brother of Benjamin Hoadly (1676-1761). These were not happy associations. The siblings were of much the same political and devotional mind.[88] Swift characterized Benjamin,

84 *Prose Works*, V, 343.

85 Ehrenpreis, *Dean Swift*, pp. 769-71.

86 Swift, "The Yahoo's Overthrow: or, The Kevan Bayl's New Ballad" (1734; published 1765), *Poems*, ed. Williams, III, 814, ll. 3-4.

87 Swift, "A Letter to the Lord Chancellor Middleton" (1724; published 1735), in *Prose Works*, X, 114.

88 William Gibson, "Brother of the More Famous Ben: The Theology of Archbishop John Hoadly," *Anglican and Episcopal History*, 75 (2006), 401-22.

the instigator of the Bangorian Controversy, as "a Champion for Resistance" (meaning his campaigns against the doctrines of hereditary right and passive obedience),[89] and he can hardly have been enthused by the prospect of John, a British interloper who had loyally supported the English interest in Ireland during his tenure as Bishop of Ferns and Leighlin.

For a third time, the Dean and his colleagues of the cloth began in dispute. An argument ensued at the second of Hoadly's enthronements, in St Patrick's in January 1730, when the Archbishop and his vicar general denied Swift the right he (mistakenly) claimed to administer the oaths. Invitations to dine at St Sepulchre's were declined for a period sufficient to mark his displeasure. Six months later, Gay may have provoked a thin smile from his friend when he invited him to stay at Amesbury Abbey, the Queensberrys' Wiltshire seat, and thus within Benjamin Hoadly's Salisbury diocese. "I thank you for offering me the neighbourhood of another Hoadly," Swift replied; "I have enough of one; he lives within 20 yards of me, our gardens joyn, but I never see him except upon business."[90]

The Dean's response may sound like continuing reserve, but the neighbours were only infrequently in the same place at the same time. Hoadly was seldom resident in St Sepulchre's. (His protracted absences may be the simplest explanation for the relative dearth of material documenting his vis-à-vis with Swift.) Shortly after his translation in 1729, he spent £2,500 on rebuilding Tallaght Castle, the dilapidated country seat of the Primates of Ireland which lay a few miles south-west of Dublin but which was nonetheless one of the constituent manors of the Archbishop's Liberty.[91] There he spent most of his time, "indefatigably promoting the improvement of agriculture by his skill, his purse, and his example."[92] A parliamentary lord spiritual, he also indefatigably promoted Whitehall's interest when important events drew him back to the Irish capital. In 1737, he attacked Swift for (again) opposing the import of halfpennies from England. "My Neighbor Prelate," the Dean recalled, "who politickly makes his Court to Sr R. W. by imitating that great Minister in every minute pulling up his Breeches ... harangued my Neighbors against me under the Name of *Some*

89 Swift, "The Publick Spirit of the Whigs" (1714), in *English Political Writings, 1711-1714*, eds Goldgar and Gadd, p. 254.

90 John Gay to Swift, [4 July 1730], *Correspondence*, ed. Woolley, III, 318; Swift to John Gay, 10 November 1730, III, 334.

91 See further Gabriel Stokes, "A Map of the House, Courts, Yards, Offices and Gardens, &c. at Tallagh" (1737), *A Catalogue of the Maps of the Estates of the Archbishops of Dublin, 1654-1850*, eds Raymond Refaussé and Mary Clark (Dublin: Four Courts Press, 2000), pp. 71-72.

92 Cited in Richard Mant, *History of the Church of Ireland*, 2 vols (London: Parker, 1840), II, 597.

wicked man about the new half-pence, but received no other answer than God bless the –."[93] The blank should read "Drapier," of course, and the passage evokes the larger – the truly national – response to the imposition of Wood's patent.

As with King, however, Swift gradually reached a modus vivendi with Hoadly. Some part of this rapprochement can be ascribed to his platonic affection for Sarah, the archdiocesan's only child, who appears from nowhere in his correspondence. "A murder now and then is all we have to trust to," he wrote to John Brandreth (d.1764), Dean of Armagh, complaining of having no news to "entertain ... a country correspondent":

> Our fruit is all destroyed with the long spring north-east winds; and I shall not have the tenth part of my last year's fruit. Miss Hoadly hath been nine days in the small-pox, which I never heard of till this minute; but they say, she is past danger. She would have been a terrible loss to the Archbishop.[94]

No earlier reference to her is to be found in his writing. The date of the letter, and the fact that he had been unaware of her condition, suggest that she was summering on her father's estate. (She married Bellingham Boyle [1690-1771] in the local church in 1740; her husband, Member of Parliament for Bandon in County Cork, was a member of the commission that examined Swift's mental capacity in 1742.) Similar associations can be heard in the letter in which he imagines her father "teach[ing] his neighbouring tenants and farmers a little English country management;" consonant with many of his teasingly disapproving letters to female friends, he then thanks her for the predial gifts she had sent from Tallaght – a quantity of butter and a slaughtered pig.[95]

7. "Not sent, by Mr Kings advice –"

Swift's concern for others in the prelate's household is more difficult to descry. The message he composed to Boleyn Whitney (1686-1758), the lawyer, alderman, and Hoadly's steward ("chief executive of the liberty, so to speak"),[96] is

93 Swift to Lord Orrery, [26-31 March 1737], *Correspondence*, ed. Woolley, IV, 410.

94 A letter of [30 June 1732], *Correspondence*, ed. Woolley, III, 495.

95 Swift to Miss Sarah Hoadly, 4 June 1734, *Correspondence*, ed. Woolley, III, 736-37.

96 Milne discusses the office of seneschal in *The Dublin Liberties, 1600-1850*, pp. 21-23, from which I cite here. Whitney served as MP for Philipstown, in King's County (now Daingean in County Offaly), between 1737 and 1758; the principal events of his life are recorded in Johnston-Liik, *History of the Irish Parliament, 1692-1800*, VI, 536.

particularly apropos. Wrought with fathomless contempt for its intended recipient, but neglected in biography and criticism, it may concern the "encroachments" of which he had written two years earlier. "I find that ever since you have been employd as Seneschall to my Ld Archbishop of Dublin," he begins (Whitney had held this position since 1731),

> you have been upon all occasions encroaching upon the Libertyes of the Dean and Chapter of St Patricks, in a most arbitrary and unpresedented manner. You know very well that our Libertyes were confirmed by an act of Parliament in the Reign of Edwd the 4th; which Act we have by us in the Book called Dignitas Decan:; and the Archbishop then alive was cast, although he did not act in a degree so arbitrarily and Magisteryally as You, who like a Lawyer call it a merit in any Court to extend your Jurisdiction. I resent this so highly, that knowing I am in the right, by having the Opinion for many years of severall able Lawyers, I will resist by force any of your people who dare to enter our Liberty, as having any Power here.
>
> I am Sr Your humble Ser^t^ Jonath: Swift

The author's postscript tries to pull rank. "If the Archbishop knew the foot we stand on, I believe he would not much approve of your proceedings."[97] This was not a letter between equals. That Whitney was both a lawyer, a profession for which Swift cultivated a lasting distaste (when they were not offering "Opinion[s]" in his favour), and, under a fancy job title, Hoadly's business agent, would only have exacerbated the dispute.[98] "Peter Walters –" is the contemptuously spare sum of one of the papers he thought of contributing to the *Intelligencer*, meaning the most infamously grasping steward of the day.[99]

But the kind of peculation in which Walters (*c*.1664-1746) indulged was not Whitney's métier. What angered Swift appears to have been the seneschal's attempts to enlarge the reach of his office. The Archbishop's bailiff evidently wished to enforce matters that fell under his purview in the Liberty of St Sepulchre's, but within the Liberty of St Patrick's. For that reason, he exceeded his authority, a secular arrogation of clerical privilege that was predictably noisome to the Dean. Swift invariably responded to slights to the dignity of holy orders with immitigable disdain. In his early dealings with the vicars

97 Swift to Boleyn Whitney, 15 April 1737, *Correspondence*, ed. Woolley, IV, 422-23.

98 On the expression of Swift's attitude to lawyers and the legal profession in *The Drapier's Letters*, a view with wider – but not absolute – application, see Joseph McMinn, "The Prosecution of Power: Swift's Defence of Ireland," *Reading Swift: Papers from The Fifth Münster Symposium*, ed. Real, pp. 365-73.

99 Jonathan Swift and Thomas Sheridan, *The Intelligencer*, ed. James Woolley (Oxford: Clarendon Press, 1992), p. 275.

choral, he had pronounced himself "very well instructed in [his] own Power." In his response to King's request for a proxy in May 1727, he was quick to challenge his neighbour to find a precedent for the demand "in any of your old records or of ours," a reference to the Liberties' parallel muniments, and thus their analogous jurisdictions. And in the message to Whitney, his invocation of Edward IV (1442-83) appeals to time out of mind. Conscious of his rights and responsibilities, alert to infractions and vigorous in prosecuting his response, Swift acted "not out of arrogance or a lust for power but out of respect, as he would have insisted, for order and decorum constitutionally and immemorially established."[100]

And yet the letter remained only in draft. Swift endorsed the copy, "Ap^{r}. 15 – 1737 Lett^{r} to A.Bs Senesc^{hll} not sent, by Mr Kings advice –."[101] This was a reference to James King (*c.*1699-1759), the curate of St Bride's (or St Bridget's), a resident of Kevin Street and "a very worthy usefull Clergy-man without any Reproach," his neighbour petitioned, "as well Principled in point of Loyalty and good notions, as your Grace can desire."[102] Why King urged Swift to think again, beyond an obvious reservation over the imperiousness of his patron's manner, resists explanation. Neither Ball nor Williams comments on this element of the message, David Woolley mentions the endorsement as evidence of King's "good notions" and Landa shrugs that the letter was "for some reason never sent."[103] Perhaps King was chary of the Dean's vow to "resist by force." What can be said is that the draft was written by a man of advancing years (Swift was sixty-nine at the time) but seemingly not sent on the counsel of a neighbour who was possibly thirty-five years his junior.[104] The message and its accompanying endorsement appear to be the only extant testimony of an opaquely juridical but very human episode, a principled but intemperate response to, and a friend's better judgement on, the compromises and inconveniences that attend the circumstance of being a neighbour of any kind.

---

100 Landa, *Swift and the Church of Ireland*, p. 71.

101 Swift to Boleyn Whitney, 15 April 1737, *Correspondence*, ed. Woolley, IV, 423.

102 W. G. Carroll, *Succession of Clergy in the Parishes of S. Bride, S. Michael le Pole, and S. Stephen, Dublin* (Dublin: J. Charles, 1884), pp. 21-22; Swift to John Hoadly, [1 June 1737], *Correspondence*, ed. Woolley, IV, 434.

103 *The Correspondence of Jonathan Swift, D.D.*, ed. F. Elrington Ball, 6 vols (London: G. Bell and Sons, 1910-14), VI, 9-10; *Correspondence*, ed. Williams, V, 32-33; *Correspondence*, ed. Woolley, IV, 435n2; Landa, *Swift and the Church of Ireland*, p. 69.

104 On Swift's regard for his neighbour, see his letters of [27 October 1735], *Correspondence*, ed. Woolley, IV, 207; and of [1739], IV, 600-1.

8. "The Laws of Charity, Neighbourhood, Alliance, and Hospitality"

Bettesworth's incursive threats, Whitney's encroachments, and Swift's promised response to the latter were all decidedly physical. Of still greater encroachments on his Liberty, however, he had little or nothing to say. The building of which he was the guardian did not stand apart from its environs. Thus houses crowded the north-eastern quarter of the precinct, backing into the walls of the Cathedral.[105] The parish church of St Nicholas Without, moreover, a part of which cure lay in the Archbishop's Liberty, was to be found within those walls, occupying much of the north transept, although the parochial house of worship was physically separated from the diocesan by a substantial partition, and the Dean and Chapter retained the right to collate ministers to the parish.[106] And St Patrick's was like many other Anglican cathedrals in accommodating its ecclesiastical court, and the court leet of the Liberty, within its fabric. A building was raised off the south aisle in the early 1720s. That the activities and success of those courts were dependent upon "a willingness by neighbours to mind each others' business" might be emphasized here.[107] The establishment of St Patrick's entertained the life of the district in which it stood.

This conjunction of the local and the spiritual epitomizes Swift's understanding of what it was to be a neighbour. Throughout his career, the neighbourly was often coterminous with the parochial, just as he seems to have regarded neighbourliness as a point in a spectrum of virtuous, generally Christian and more particularly Anglican, society.[108] Indeed, "the Laws of Charity, Neighbourhood,

105 Niall McCullough, *Dublin, an Urban History: The Plan of the City*, 3rd ed. (Dublin: Anne Street Press and Associated Editions, 2014), illustration 100 (p. 105). The presence of the spire indicates a date after 1749.

106 Milne, *The Dublin Liberties, 1600-1850*, p. 11; Canon John Crawford, "Some Extinct Churches of the Church of Ireland in the Liberties," *Dublin Historical Record*, 41 (1987-88), 46-54 (pp. 51-53). The disposition of the Cathedral is illustrated in Francis Grose, *The Antiquities of Ireland*, 2 vols (London: S. Hooper, 1791), I, Plate 21, a plan which is based on Kendrick's survey but which is much clearer in its identification of the constituent elements of the fabric.

107 Barnard, "St Patrick's Cathedral in the Age of Swift," pp. 208, 215; W. M. Jacob, "'In Love and Charity with Your Neighbours ...': Ecclesiastical Courts and Justices of the Peace in England in the Eighteenth Century," *Retribution, Repentance, and Reconciliation*, eds Kate Cooper and Jeremy Gregory, Studies in Church History, 40 (Woodbridge: The Boydell Press, 2004), 205-17 (p. 206).

108 See further James Woolley, "Friends and Enemies in *Verses on the Death of Dr. Swift*," *Studies in Eighteenth-Century Culture*, 8 (1979), 205-32; Joseph M. McMinn, "The Importance of Friendship in Swift's Writings," *Reading Swift: Papers from The Second Münster Symposium*, eds Richard H. Rodino and Hermann J. Real, with the assistance of Helgard Stöver-Leidig (Munich: Wilhelm Fink, 1993), pp. 71-80.

Alliance and Hospitality" required nothing less.[109] In like manner, his dealings with those amongst whom he lived were predicated on, or animated by, the position he held in the hierarchy of Church and State. Most of the neighbours we know by name (John Hoadly and Sarah Hoadly, James King, William King, Henry Land) were associated with the Cathedral in one form or another. Some were even tenants of the Dean. And when Swift was drawn into dispute with his neighbours in and around St Patrick's (not all his neighbours were resident in the Liberty), their disagreements generally concerned the exercise of his temporal powers as the head of a franchise long independent of the civic and ecclesiastical authorities, and the perpetuation of those prerogatives to future generations. Over their diminution or loss he would not let his successors – or the successors to the vicars choral – grieve.

So great were the privileges of his office, in fact, and the socio-economic consequences of those privileges, that Swift soon came to distinguish householders in the Liberty from the denizens of the capital's other districts. Even though Protestant weavers, impoverished widows, and pupils in charity were hardly unique to the enclave, they all became Swift's responsibility, in his mind, because they lodged in Patrick's Close. Not a cure of souls in the parochial sense, the manor and its residents nonetheless assumed a place in the Dean's affections. But we should not idealize. He did not always act out of disinterested virtue. Naming his orchard and paddock Naboth's Vineyard alluded to the truth that it was "a Garden [he] cheated one of [his] Neighbours out of," he told Laetitia Pilkington with less irony than becomes a national hero.[110] And he positively revelled in the position in which he found himself. Commanding Dublin's roads, having "Hackney Coaches, Carts & carriages" give way to him, allowed him to "make some advantage of the publick poverty," he explained in the letter in which he declared himself "Lord Mayor of 120 Houses": "These advantages contribute to my ease, & therefore I value them."[111] Only someone confident in his own sway could write in such terms. Swift may not have received the cathedral he felt was his due, but as a result of the particular circumstances of his Liberty, the Dean of St Patrick's was able to approach his neighbours with an authority beyond his standing in the Church.[112]

109 Swift, "The Sentiments of a Church-of-England Man, with Respect to Religion and Government" (1704-8; published 1711), in *Prose Works*, II, 24.

110 *Memoirs of Laetitia Pilkington*, ed. Elias, I, 34. The best account of the tract remains Edward Malins and The Knight of Glin, *Lost Demesnes: Irish Landscape Gardening, 1660-1845* (London: Barrie & Jenkins, 1976), pp. 33-35.

111 *Correspondence*, ed. Woolley, III, 663.

112 For their prompt help in facilitating the reproduction of Roger Kendrick's survey of the Liberty of St Patrick's, I am greatly obliged to Maria O'Shea of Marsh's Library and to Sarah Gearty of the Irish Historic Towns Atlas at the Royal Irish Academy.

RECEPTION AND ADAPTATION I

KIRSTEN JUHAS AND MASCHA HANSEN
Westfälische Wilhelms-Universität, Münster, and Universität Greifswald

Speaking with/of the Dead: Hester Thrale Piozzi and Swift

And now if I should *dye*! –
Why if I *should* dye! What does it signify?[1]

ABSTRACT. The work of the prolific writer, diarist, and *salonnière* Hester Lynch Piozzi (1741-1821), also known by her first husband's name as 'Mrs Thrale' and as Samuel Johnson's close friend and hostess, is no exception to the phenomenon described by Margaret Anne Doody that "much ... written by Englishwomen during the middle and later eighteenth century exhibits an awareness of Swift and a sense of his importance as a model." In addition to searching and securing traces of Swift in Thrale Piozzi's library and reading, this essay focuses on "Three Dialogues on the Death of Hester Lynch Thrale" (written in August 1779), a witty homage to the Dean's *Verses on the Death of Dr. Swift*. In the three true-to-life dialogues between the members of her Streatham circle, Thrale Piozzi skilfully amalgamates her admired predecessor's tone and content with the *Dialogues of the Dead* genre, much in fashion at the time, paradoxically creating an (authorial) presence in her own absence.

1

On 27 January 1777, the day she took to be her thirty-fifth birthday, Hester Lynch Thrale projected herself into the role of Stella, who had died on 28 January 1728, almost 49 years earlier. As Thrale Piozzi tells us in her *Anecdotes of the Late Samuel Johnson, LL.D.*, published in 1786, two years after the death of her famous friend, she likewise ascribed the role of Swift to Johnson by reminding her guest of Swift's habit of writing birthday poems for Stella:

> As I went into his room the morning of my birth-day ... and said to [Johnson], Nobody sends me verses now, because I am five-and-thirty years old; and Stella was fed with them till forty-six, I remember ... he burst out suddenly, for so he did without the least previous hesitation whatsoever, and without having entertained the smallest intention towards it half a minute before:

1 Hester Lynch Thrale, entry in *The Children's Book or rather Family Book* of 1 April 1778, reprinted in *The Thrales of Streatham Park*, ed. Mary Hyde (Cambridge, Massachusetts: Harvard University Press, 1977), p. 201 (italics reversed).

 | DOI:10.30965/9783846763971_023

Oft in danger, yet alive,
We are come to thirty-five;
Long may better years arrive,
Better years than thirty-five.
Could philosophers contrive
Life to stop at thirty-five,
Time his hours should never drive
O'er the bounds of thirty-five.
High to soar, and deep to dive,
Nature gives at thirty-five:
Ladies, stock and tend your hive,
Trifle not at thirty-five:
For howe'er we boast and strive,
Life declines from thirty-five:
He that ever hopes to thrive
Must begin by thirty-five;
And all who wisely wish to wive,
Must look on Thrale at thirty-five.[2]

Johnson's 'extempore verses' on Hester Thrale's thirty-fifth birthday and their repetition and variation of the number "thirty-five" recall the well-known first lines of Swift's first birthday poem, "On Stella's Birth-day. Written 1718-19": "Stella this Day is thirty four, / (We won't dispute a Year or more)."[3] The pun on Stella's age, who in fact turned thirty-eight, not thirty-four in 1719, sets the tone for the most light-hearted specimen of Swift's birthday poems to Stella, oscillating between raillery and praise.[4] That Hester Thrale was well aware of Esther Johnson's 'real' age at the time Swift wrote his poetic tribute and that she knew the addressee's exact life dates may be deduced from her remarking, correctly, to Johnson that "Stella was fed with [poems] until she was forty-six." Whereas Swift's birthday poems have been described as repeatedly and

2 *Anecdotes of the Late Samuel Johnson, LL.D., during the Last Twenty Years of his Life*, ed. Arthur Sherbo (London, New York, Toronto: Oxford University Press, 1974), p. 115. The same episode is also told in *Thraliana*. In *Thraliana*, however, the reference to Stella is missing, and the year is given as 1777 (*Thraliana*, ed. Katharine C. Balderston, 2nd ed., 2 vols [Oxford: Clarendon Press, 1951], I, 211-12; 319). The fact that Hester Lynch Salusbury was born on 16 January 1740/1 [O.S.] left her, when the calendar was changed in 1752, confused about her age (see also Volume VI of *The Yale Edition of the Works of Samuel Johnson*, Johnson's *Poems*, ed. E. L. McAdam, Jr, with George Milne [New Haven: Yale University Press, 1964], 292). It is legend that she took her seventy-ninth birthday to be her eightieth, which she celebrated accordingly with 600 guests and danced all night.

3 *Poems*, ed. Williams, II, 721, ll. 1-2.

4 See the similar 'mistake' in his second birthday poem, "Stella's Birth-day, Written AD. 1720-21": "Then Cloe, still go on to prate / Of thirty six, and thirty eight; / Pursue thy Trade of Scandall picking, / Thy hints that Stella is no Chickin" (*Poems*, ed. Williams, II, 735, ll. 39-42).

subtly transcending the conventions of congratulatory verse, Johnson's poem on Hester Thrale's thirty-fifth birthday rather closely follows the conventional threefold pattern of congratulating the recipient, celebrating the occasion, and offering good wishes for the future.[5] Presumably due to its rapid composition,[6] the birthday poem for Hester Thrale is much more formal and 'occasional' (in the very sense of the word) than any of Swift's, lacking its precursor's depth of intimate conversation and self-reflection. However, Johnson's first lines reveal at least a slight touch of the personal: "Oft in danger, yet alive / We are come to thirty-five" (ll. 1-2). As a regular guest of Hester and her husband Henry Thrale, a wealthy brewer, from 1766 to the latter's death in 1781, at both Streatham Park and the Thrale's city house next to the brewery in Southwark, Johnson enjoyed the status of an adopted family member and in this role, he was well acquainted with Hester's many and difficult pregnancies (thirteen between 1764 and 1779), the countless illnesses of the couple's children, numerous of them minutely recorded by their mother in the *Family Book* she kept from 1764 to 1778, and the oftentimes ensuing death of their young children (eight out of twelve did not survive to maturity).[7] In January 1777, the "danger" of Hester Thrale's health was real, not only because she was pregnant for the eleventh time (her daughter Cecilia was born only two weeks later on 8 February) and had but lately recovered from an illness,[8] but also, as she summed up herself in an entry in her *Family Book* of 7 January 1777, because she was physically and mentally exhausted from a series of losses and misfortunes and imagined herself dying in childbirth. At that time, she already envisaged the reactions of both her husband and Johnson to her own death:

> *I did pray earnestly for a Son ... but perhaps ... I may pay my own Life for it – Well no matter! I shall leave a Son of my own to inherit my paternal Estate & for the rest Mr Thrale may provide himself with Children & chuse a Wife where he will: it is not his Principle to lament much for the Dead, so my Loss will not break* his *Heart ... Poor Mr Johnson would have the greatest Loss of me, and he would be the most sensible of*

5 Charles Peake, "Swift's Birthday Verses to Stella," *Proceedings of The First Münster Symposium on Jonathan Swift*, eds Hermann J. Real and Heinz J. Vienken (Munich: Wilhelm Fink, 1985), pp. 175-86 (175, 186).

6 See James McLaverty, "Fixity and Instability in the Text of Johnson's Poems," *Samuel Johnson: The Arc of the Pendulum*, eds Freya Johnston and Linda Muggleton (Oxford: Oxford University Press, 2012), pp. 154-67 (156).

7 The mortality of Hester Thrale's children was high even for eighteenth-century standards and may have resulted from the rapid succession of pregnancies (James L. Clifford, *Hester Lynch Piozzi [Mrs. Thrale], With a New Introduction by Margaret Anne Doody*, 2nd ed. [Oxford: Clarendon Press, 1987], p. 144 and n2).

8 *Anecdotes of the Late Samuel Johnson*, ed. Sherbo, p. 115.

> *his Loss: he would willingly write my Epitaph I am sure if my Husband would treat me with a Monument.*[9]

The sense of continuing decay that is so characteristic of Swift's birthday poems,[10] most famously in his celebration of Stella's birthday, 1726/7, shortly before her death – "This Day then, let us not be told, / That you are sick, and I grown old"[11] – shines also through in Johnson's statement that "Life declines from thirty-five."[12] There is no "you ... and I" in Johnson's poem; Hester Thrale is addressed but indirectly through the third person singular and her last name: "And all who wisely wish to wive / Must look on Thrale at thirty-five." From a twenty-first century point of view, this last complimentary couplet not only leaves room for speculation – room that has, for example, been filled by James Boswell's malicious "Ode by Samuel Johnson to Mrs Thrale upon their Supposed Approaching Nuptials," celebrating Johnson's and the wealthy widow's upcoming marriage, only eight days after Henry Thrale's death[13] – it also shows a female writer and intellectual reduced to the conventional roles of wife and mother.

The speaker of Johnson's tribute to Hester's thirty-fifth birthday is virtually absent throughout the whole poem with one (possible) exception: the plural "We are come to thirty-five" may be interpreted as an example of *pluralis majestatis*. Johnson himself had reason to celebrate his being alive at his hostess's thirty-fifth birthday, after Hester and Henry Thrale had virtually 'saved' him in 1766 at a moment of crisis and continued to give him the domestic comfort and emotional stability he had been missing.[14] While Johnson does not refer to

9 *The Thrales of Streatham Park*, ed. Hyde, p. 175.

10 On Swift's awareness of Stella's continuing decay reflected in his poems to her, see John Irwin Fischer, "Faith, Hope, and Charity in Swift's Poems to Stella," *Contemporary Studies of Swift's Poetry*, eds John Irwin Fischer and Donald C. Mell, Jr (Newark: University of Delaware Press, London and Toronto: Associated University Presses, 1981), pp. 79-86 (80, 82 [courtesy]). See also Ronald Paulson, "Swift, Stella, and Permanence," *ELH*, 27 (1960), 298-314 (pp. 307-8).

11 *Poems*, ed. Williams, II, 763, ll. 3-4.

12 In a letter to Hester Thrale of 14 August 1780, Johnson later revealed that he took this thought from Galen: "If you try to plague me I shall tell you that according to Galen life begins to decline from *thirty five*" (quoted from Volume VI of *The Yale Edition of the Works of Samuel Johnson*, Johnson's *Poems*, eds McAdam and Milne, 293n14).

13 See *Thraliana*, ed. Balderston, II, 631n1.

14 *Anecdotes of the Late Samuel Johnson*, ed. Sherbo, p. 102. For further details, see Clifford, *Hester Lynch Piozzi (Mrs. Thrale)*, pp. 64-65; Martine Watson Brownley, "'Under the Dominion of *Some* Woman': The Friendship of Samuel Johnson and Hester Thrale," *Mothering the Mind*, eds Ruth Perry and Martine Watson Brownley (New York and London: Holmes and Meier, 1984), pp. 64-79; Elizabeth Hedrick, "The Duties of a Scholar:

their nurturing relationship, a central motif in the Swift-Stella poems ("You, to whose Care so oft I owe, That I'm alive to tell you so"[15]), in the *Anecdotes* and elsewhere, Hester makes no bones about the fact that Johnson was her "overgrown child"[16] and 'patient.'[17] In an entry of 1 May 1779 in *Thraliana*, Hester Thrale's unconventional diaries from 1776-1809,[18] Hester again compares herself to Stella:

> Pope & Swift, were *softened* by the Smiles of Patty Blount & Stella; & our stern Philosopher Johnson trusted me about the Years 1767 or 1768 – I know not which just now – with a Secret far dearer to him than his Life: such however is his nobleness, & such his partiality, that I sincerely believe he has never since that Day regretted his Confidence, or ever looked with less kind Affection on her who had him in her Power.[19]

Not wishing to join the speculations on the question what the "Secret far dearer to [Johnson] than his Life" he entrusted Hester Thrale with was, whether it is an allusion to his fear of going insane or whether Johnson suffered from "sexual fantasies involving restraint and bondage,"[20] we would rather like to draw

---

Samuel Johnson in Piozzi's *Anecdotes,*" *Mentoring in Eighteenth-Century British Literature and Culture*, ed. Anthony W. Lee (Farnham, Surrey: Ashgate, 2010), pp. 211-24 (211-12).

15 *Poems*, ed. Williams, II, 766, ll. 87-88; see also "To Stella, Visiting me in my Sickness" (II, 722-27).

16 Michael J. Franklin, "Piozzi, Hester Lynch (1741-1821)," ODNB, Oxford University Press, 2004, online edition (<http://www.oxforddnb.com/view/article22309>, accessed 27 March 2017).

17 "I shall for ever consider it as the greatest honour which could be conferred on any one, to have been the confidential friend of Dr. Johnson's health; and to have in some measure, with Mr. Thrale's assistance, saved from distress at least, if not from worse, a mind great beyond the comprehension of common mortals" (*Anecdotes of the Late Samuel Johnson*, ed. Sherbo, p. 156). She further claims, "To the assistance we gave him, the shelter our house afforded to his uneasy fancies, and to the pains we took to sooth or repress them, the world perhaps is indebted for the three political pamphlets, the new edition and correction of his Dictionary, and for the Poets Lives."

18 In the Introduction to her pioneering edition of *Thraliana*, Kathrine Balderston calls them "the first English ana" (I, xi). The six quarto blank volumes for putting down daily experiences, literary bon mots, etc. were given to Hester by her husband Henry Thrale in 1776.

19 *Thraliana*, ed. Balderston, I, 384-85 (emphasis added). This passage is quoted most frequently by scholars trying to investigate the "Mystery at the bottom" of Johnson's and Hester Thrale's relationship, as Swift would have put it (*A Tale of a Tub and Other Works*, ed. Marcus Walsh [Cambridge: Cambridge University Press, 2010], p. 123).

20 Francine Prose, *The Lives of the Muses: Nine Women and the Artists they Inspired* (Toronto, Ontario: HarperCollins, 2002), pp. 25-56 (36-37; see also 31-32); in addition, see Katherine C. Balderston, "Johnson's Vile Melancholy," *The Age of Johnson: Essays Presented to Chauncey Brewster Tinker*, ed. F. W. Hills (New Haven: Yale University Press, 1949),

attention to Mrs Thrale's phrase that Swift was "*softened*" by Stella's smiles. It is through the comparison with "Miss *Hester* Johnson," her "Namesake," as she calls Stella in one passage in *Thraliana*,[21] that she implies to have "softened" the rude and unruly temperament of Johnson herself more than once, not least by sitting up with him all night and making tea for him until four o'clock in the morning.[22] The thought that Stella had a favourable influence on Swift is not original,[23] but it is hardly a mere coincidence that a formulation similar to the one in *Thraliana* occurs in Johnson's "Life of Swift," according to which Esther Johnson's "conversation was to [Swift] the great *softener* of the ills of life."[24] Swift himself wrote in one of his poems to Stella, "on the Day of her Birth, but not on the Subject, when [he] was sick in bed": "when out my brutish passions break, / With gall in ev'ry word I speak, / She, with *soft* speech, my anguish chears."[25] Even if the thought that Stella softened his life seems to have originated with Swift, it is remarkable that both Hester Thrale and Johnson should have picked it up. Since they discussed proof sheets of the *Lives of the Poets* together with the family over breakfast[26] and since, chronologically, Hester Thrale was the first to note it down in *Thraliana*, the phrase may have been hers, not Johnson's. Moreover, it sheds as much light on their relationship as it does on Swift and Stella's, more especially so because it is supposed to have been Stella's "*conversation*" – notably Hester Thrale's strong point – that allegedly had the 'softening' effect.[27]

---

pp. 3-14 (10-14); and Ian McIntyre, *Hester: The Remarkable Life of Dr Johnson's 'Dear Mistress'* (London: Constable, 2008), pp. 54-55, 75-77.

21 *Thraliana*, ed. Balderston, I, 156 (italics in original). See also II, 625.

22 See *Anecdotes of the Late Samuel Johnson*, ed. Sherbo, p. 101; see also McIntyre, *Hester*, p. 123.

23 Compare, for example, Patrick Delany's *Observations upon Lord Orrery's Remarks on the Life and Writings of Dr. Jonathan Swift* (Dublin: for Robert Main, 1754), p. 99: "All these infelicities of temper, were remarkably augmented after the death of Mrs. JOHNSTON: whose cordial friendship, sweet temper, and lenient advice, poured balm and healing into his blood; and kept his spirits in some temperament" (reprinted in *The Lives of Jonathan Swift*, ed. Daniel Cook, 3 vols [London and New York: Routledge, 2011], I, 366).

24 Samuel Johnson, "Life of Swift," in *The Lives of the Poets*, ed. Roger Lonsdale, 4 vols (Oxford: Clarendon Press, 2006), III, 203 (emphasis added). Johnson goes even further in maintaining that she eventually "died under the tyranny of him" (III, 205).

25 *Poems*, ed. Williams, 754, ll. 11-13 [emphasis added].

26 Brownley, "'Under the Dominion of *Some* Woman': The Friendship of Samuel Johnson and Hester Thrale," p. 69. Johnson went to Brighton with the Thrales after finishing his "Life of Swift" on 18 October 1780 (*Lives of the Poets*, ed. Lonsdale, III, 426). On her reading a number of the *Lives* in manuscript, see *Thraliana*, ed. Balderston, I, 424, 448.

27 Felicity A. Nussbaum has lately argued that *The Letters to and from Samuel Johnson* also "followed in the tradition of the intimate exchanges between Jonathan Swift and Stella" ("Sociability and Life Writing: Hester Lynch Thrale Piozzi," *Women's Life Writing, 1700-1850:*

2

Jonathan Swift, whose personality and work have ever been prone to accusations of misogyny, is known to have encouraged a considerable number of his female acquaintances to write: Mary Davys, Laetitia Pilkington, Constantia Grierson, and Mary Barber. However, as Margaret Doody put it in her seminal essay on "Swift among the Women:"

> the case for Swift's influence on women writers cannot ... be made properly by considering only those women he himself knew ... Much of the poetry written by Englishwomen during the middle and later eighteenth century exhibits an awareness of Swift and a sense of his importance as a model.[28]

And Hester Thrale Piozzi was no exception, on the contrary. One of her recent biographers goes so far as to claim that "her chosen precursor was not Pope, nor even Johnson, but Swift, especially the Swift of *A Tale of a Tub* and the poems."[29] While this somewhat strong argument may be difficult to verify, it is possible to prove that Thrale Piozzi was well informed about Swift's life and that she owned, read, and admired many of his works. From early on, Hester Lynch Salusbury developed an avid taste for reading and books. At the age of four, she was given Ogilby's translation of Homer; before she was seven, she owned translations of Plutarch and Livy.[30]

There are three main sources of information about the impressive book collection she assembled during her lifetime: first, a sale catalogue recording the belongings of Streatham sold at auction in May 1816, including "*The Extensive and Well-Selected Library, containing near 3000 Volumes in the Various Departments of Literature.*"[31] By this time, maintaining Streatham Park had

Gender, Genre, and Authorship, eds Daniel Cook and Amy Cully [Houndmills, Basingstoke, and New York: Palgrave McMillan, 2012], pp. 55-70 [63]). Johnson even compared his own letters to "*Presto*'s" in one of his missives to Mrs Thrale on 18 May 1769 (*Letters to and from the Late Samuel Johnson, LL.D.*, ed. Hester Lynch Thrale, 2 vols [for A. Strahan and T. Cadell, 1788], I, 19). The British Library copy on ECCO has a note in Giuseppe Baretti's hand for this passage, which reads as follows: "Johnson disapproved of that Publication [i.e. *The Journal to Stella*] and would have highly disapproved of hers, if he had forseen it."

28 Margaret Anne Doody, "Swift among the Women," *The Yearbook of English Studies*, 18 (1988), 68-92 (p. 77).

29 William McCarthy, *Hester Thrale Piozzi: Portrait of a Literary Woman* (Chapel Hill and London: The University of North Carolina Press, 1985), p. 16.

30 McIntyre, *Hester*, p. 7.

31 An interleaved copy marked with prices and buyers' names was reprinted in *Sale Catalogues of Libraries of Eminent Persons: Poets and Men of Letters*, ed. Stephen Parks (London: Mansell, 1972), V, 391-480, as well as in *Sale Catalogues of the Libraries of Samuel*

become a serious strain on Hester Piozzi's finances, but the sale of the contents of the house freed her from serious financial worries for the rest of her life.[32] Many of the books sold at this auction had been bought by Johnson, who helped the Thrales gather a comprehensive collection.[33] Astonishingly, there is but one lot in which the name 'Swift' occurs. On the very first day of the sale, "seven odd vols. of Swift's Works" were purchased by a buyer named "Rogers" for ten shillings, along with Aaron Hill's works in four volumes.[34] The explanation why so little by Swift was sold at auction in 1816 probably was that Thrale Piozzi took her favourite books along with her as her personal library when she moved from Streatham Park to Brynbella, the new Welsh home she inhabited with her second husband, Gabriel Piozzi (1740-1809), since 1795.[35] Accordingly, the handwritten "Catalogue of the Books at Brynbella," kept by the John Rylands Library Manchester and consisting of ten densely written folio pages, is an important source of information.[36] In addition to the books she took along from Streatham, the handwritten catalogue begun in October 1806 lists the books she bought from 1784 onwards either in Bath or during her travels as well as additions up to the year 1813, all of them accurately arranged according to format. Among the octavos, she lists a two-volume edition of *Gulliver's Travels*, a two-volume "Broken Swift," *A Tale of a Tub*, and Orrery's *Life of Swift* (Figure 22.1); among the twelvemos, the *Poems* in eleven volumes, the second of which was missing, as well as a "broken" set of the *Miscellanies* in six (Figure 22.2).

The third source of information is another sale catalogue recording the books she had with her in Bath at her death in 1821, sold at auction two years

Johnson, Hester Lynch Thrale (Mrs. Piozzi), and James Boswell, ed. Donald D. Eddy (New Castle, Delaware: Oak Knoll Books, 1993), pp. 47-137. Another copy of the catalogue formerly belonging to the younger Charles Burney is now in the Osborn Collection at Yale.

32 The sum amounted to a total of £3,921.7s (Clifford, *Hester Lynch Piozzi [Mrs. Thrale]*, p. 441).

33 See *Sale Catalogues of Libraries of Eminent Persons*, ed. Parks, V, 388, and *Sale Catalogues of the Libraries of Samuel Johnson, Hester Lynch Thrale (Mrs. Piozzi), and James Boswell*, ed. Eddy, pp. 7-8.

34 *Sale Catalogues of Libraries of Eminent Persons*, ed. Parks, V, 402. From this scant information all that may be said is that this is likely to have been an incomplete set.

35 In 1814, Hester Piozzi made over Brynbella as a wedding gift to John Salusbury, her second husband's nephew whom she had adopted, establishing herself at Bath in somewhat reduced circumstances (Franklin, "Piozzi, Hester Lynch [1741-1821]," <http://www.oxforddnb.com/view/article22309>, accessed 27 March 2017).

36 The manuscript is in the possession of the John Rylands Library, Manchester, today (English MS 612).

later, among them, her collection of annotated Johnsoniana.[37] The outstanding feature of the books sold in 1823 is the high proportion of heavily annotated books – more than one hundred of the sets sold contained notes in her hand, some of them reproduced in the sale catalogue.[38] Thrale Piozzi, like Swift, was an inveterate scribbler of marginalia: "I have a Trick of writing in the Margins of my Books," she wrote into her *Thraliana* while reading Jeremy Collier's *Essays*, which were also in Swift's library, "it is not a good Trick, but one longs to say something & cannot stop to take out the *Thraliana*."[39] She did stop, however, to revise and copy her marginalia in Boswell's *Life of Johnson* from one edition to the next.[40] Her 1710 edition of the *Tale*, probably the very one from the "Catalogue of the Books at Brynbella," was sold in 1823 for 5 shillings and 6 pence, being adorned "with illustrative MS. Notes."[41] Her other Swiftiana include a two-volume edition of *Gulliver's Travels* (whose date of 1720 is an error, of course) as well as Orrery's *Life of Swift* (1752).[42]

Thrale Piozzi not only took an active interest in reading Swift's works, she also admired Swift's style, praising it as "beautiful" in the presence of Johnson.[43]

---

37 She bequeathed all her belongings to her adopted son John Salusbury, who sold many of them being perpetually in need of money. Reprints of the catalogue from the copy in the John Rylands Library, Manchester, are to be found in *Sale Catalogues of Libraries of Eminent Persons*, ed. Parks, V, 483-554, and *Sale Catalogues of the Libraries of Samuel Johnson, Hester Lynch Thrale (Mrs. Piozzi), and James Boswell*, ed. Eddy, pp. 139-212.

38 "Johnson imitates Fontenelle, not Bruyere in his comparison between Dryden and Pope," is one of the manuscript notes printed in the sale catalogue, in this case underneath lot 81, "Theophraste caracteres, par de Bruyere, 2 tom. Par. 1756" (p. 494). On the scholarly value of Thrale Piozzi's marginalia, see, in addition to *Sale Catalogues of Libraries of Eminent Persons*, ed. Parks, V, 387, Arthur Sherbo, "The Sale Catalogue of Mrs. Piozzi's Library: A Biographical Tool," *Notes and Queries*, 252 (2007), 497-504, and Marianna D'Ezio, *Hester Lynch Piozzi: A Taste for Eccentricity* (Newcastle upon Tyne: Cambridge Scholars Publishing, 2010), pp. 149-54.

39 *Thraliana*, ed. Balderston, II, 780.

40 See Lisa Berglund, "Hester Lynch Piozzi's Anecdotes versus the Editors," *The Age of Johnson*, 18 (2007), 273-90 (p. 278). Berglund treats Thrale Piozzi's marginalia as a distinct literary form. See also Morris R. Brownell, "Hester Lynch Piozzi's Marginalia," *Eighteenth-Century Life*, 3 (1977), 97-100; and the various references in H. J. Jackson, *Marginalia: Readers Writing in Books* (New Haven and London: Yale University Books, 2001).

41 We would like to thank William Hines and Timothy Cutts, both National Library of Wales, Aberystwyth, for making enquiries about Piozzi's annotated *Tale* edition.

42 *Sale Catalogues of Libraries of Eminent Persons*, ed. Parks, V, 504 (lot no 200); V, 501 (no lot 163); V, 538 (lot no 554). *Gulliver's Travels* was sold for nine shillings and Orrery's *Life of Swift* for four.

43 *Thraliana*, ed. Balderston, I, 172, see also *Anecdotes of the Late Samuel Johnson*, ed. Sherbo, p. 80. In *Anecdotes*, however, Hester Thrale claims that a "friend" praised Swift's style, whereas in *Thraliana* it is herself.

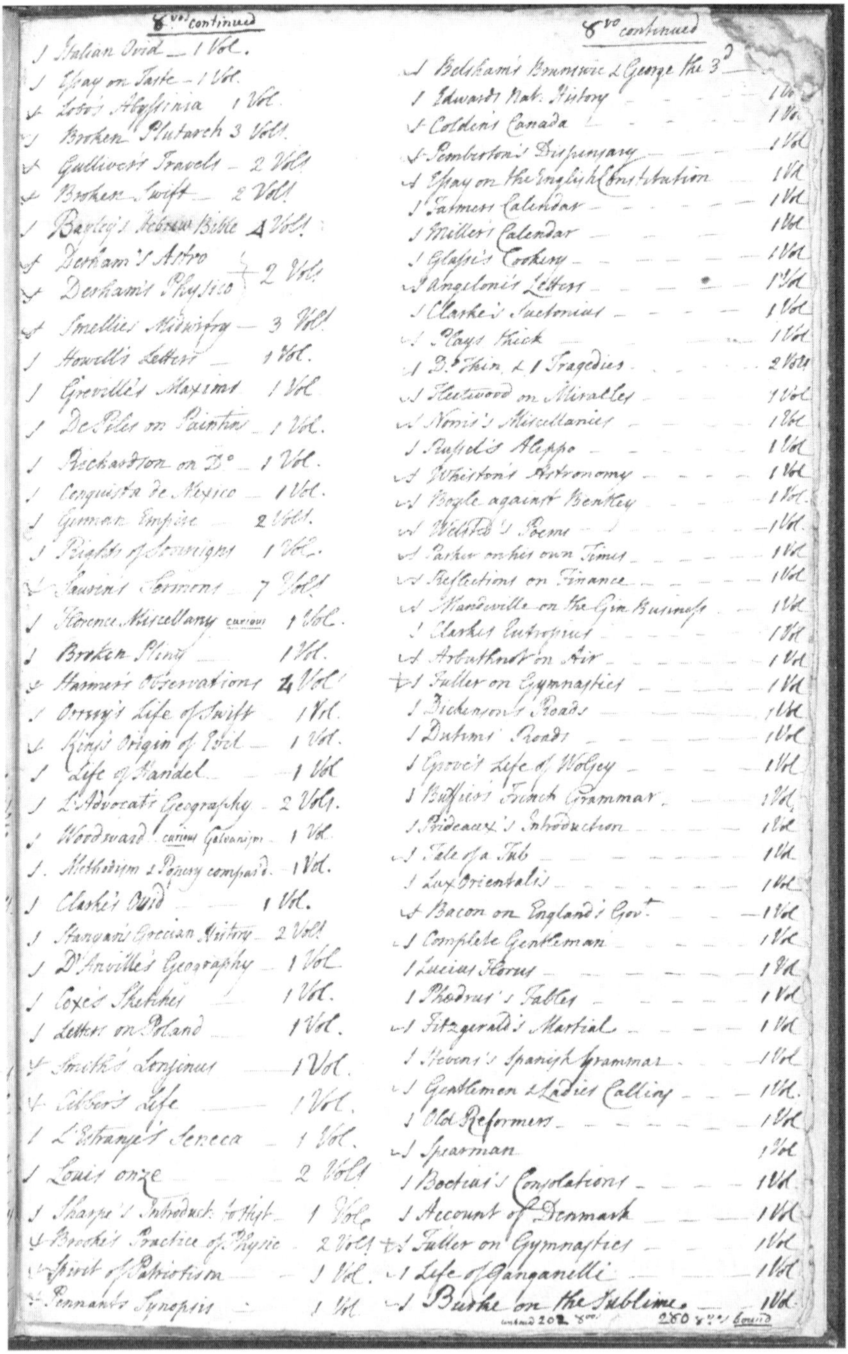

8vo continued
Italian Ovid — 1 Vol.
Essay on Taste — 1 Vol.
Lobo's Abyssinia 1 Vol.
Broken Plutarch 3 Vols.
Gulliver's Travels — 2 Vols
Broken Swift — 2 Vols
Bayley's Hebrew Bible 4 Vols
Derham's Astro / Derham's Physico — 2 Vols
Smellie's Midwifery — 3 Vols
Howell's Letters — 1 Vol.
Greville's Maxims 1 Vol
De Piles on Painting 1 Vol.
Richardson on Do 1 Vol.
Conquista de Mexico — 1 Vol.
German Empire 2 Vols.
Rights of Sovereigns 1 Vol.
Saurin's Sermons 7 Vols
Florence Miscellany curious 1 Vol.
Broken Pliny 1 Vol.
Harmer's Observations 4 Vol
Orrery's Life of Swift 1 Vol.
King's Origin of Evil 1 Vol.
Life of Handel 1 Vol
L'Advocat's Geography 2 Vols.
Woodward curious Galvanism 1 Vol
Methodism & Popery compared 1 Vol.
Clarke's Ovid 1 Vol.
Stanyan's Grecian History 2 Vols
D'Anville's Geography 1 Vol
Coxe's Sketches 1 Vol.
Letters on Poland 1 Vol.
Smith's Longinus 1 Vol.
Cibber's Life 1 Vol.
L'Estrange's Seneca 1 Vol.
Louis onze 2 Vols
Sharpe's Introduct. to Hist. 1 Vol.
Brooke's Practice of Physic 2 Vols
Spirit of Patriotism 1 Vol.
Pennant's Synopsis 1 Vol

8vo continued
Belsham's Brunswic & George the 3d
Edwards's Nat. History 1 Vol
Colden's Canada 1 Vol
Pemberton's Dispensary 1 Vol
Essay on the English Constitution 1 Vol
Farmer's Calendar 1 Vol
Miller's Calendar 1 Vol
Glasse's Cookery 1 Vol
Angeloni's Letters 1 Vol
Clarke's Suetonius 1 Vol
Plays thick 1 Vol
[illegible] & 1 Tragedies 2 Vols
Fleetwood on Miracles 1 Vol
Norris's Miscellanies 1 Vol
Russel's Aleppo 1 Vol
Whiston's Astronomy 1 Vol
Boyle against Bentley 1 Vol
Welsted's Poems 1 Vol
Parker on his own Times 1 Vol
Reflections on Finance 1 Vol
Mandeville on the Gin Business 1 Vol
Clarke's Eutropius 1 Vol
Arbuthnot on Air 1 Vol
Fuller on Gymnastics 1 Vol
Dickenson's Roads 1 Vol
Dutens' Roads 1 Vol
Grove's Life of Wolsey 1 Vol
Buffier's French Grammar 1 Vol
Prideaux's Introduction 1 Vol
Tale of a Tub 1 Vol
Lux Orientalis 1 Vol
Bacon on England's Govt 1 Vol
Complete Gentleman 1 Vol
Lucius Florus 1 Vol
Phaedrus's Fables 1 Vol
Fitzgerald's Martial 1 Vol
Stevens's Spanish Grammar 1 Vol
Gentlemen & Ladies Calling 1 Vol.
Old Reformers 1 Vol
Spearman 1 Vol
Boetius's Consolations 1 Vol
Account of Denmark 1 Vol
Fuller on Gymnastics 1 Vol
Life of Ganganelli 1 Vol
Burke on the Sublime 1 Vol
unbound 202 8vo — 280 8vo bound

FIGURES 22.1 AND 22.2 "Catalogue of Books at Brynbella, 18th October, 1806," with additions up to 1813, fols 3, 5 (The John Rylands Library, Manchester, GB 133 Eng MS 612).

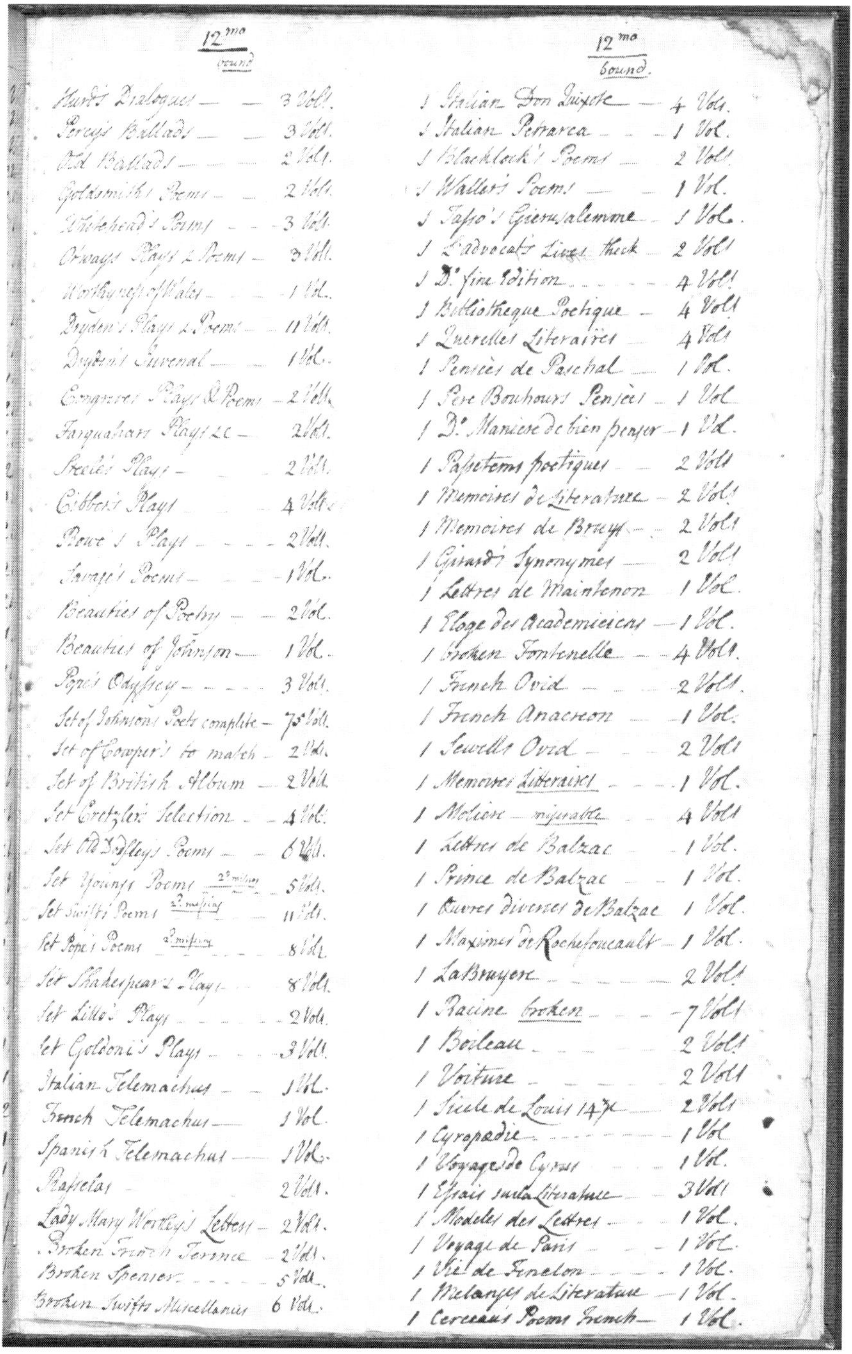

12mo
bound

Hurd's Dialogues — 3 Vols.
Percy's Ballads — 3 Vols.
Old Ballads — 2 Vols.
Goldsmith's Poems — 2 Vols.
Whitehead's Poems — 3 Vols.
Otways Plays & Poems — 3 Vols.
Worthyness of Wales — 1 Vol.
Dryden's Plays & Poems — 11 Vols.
Dryden's Juvenal — 1 Vol.
Congreve's Plays & Poems — 2 Vols.
Farquhars Plays &c — 2 Vols.
Steele's Plays — 2 Vols.
Cibbers Plays — 4 Vols.
Rowe's Plays — 2 Vols.
Savage's Poems — 1 Vol.
Beauties of Poetry — 2 Vol.
Beauties of Johnson — 1 Vol.
Pope's Odyssey — 3 Vols.
Set of Johnsons Poets complete — 75 Vols.
Set of Cowper's to match — 2 Vols.
Set of British Album — 2 Vols.
Set Cretzler's Selection — 4 Vols.
Set Old Dodsley's Poems — 6 Vols.
Set Youngs Poems 2d missing — 5 Vols.
Set Swift's Poems 2d missing — 11 Vols.
Set Pope's Poems 2d missing — 8 Vols.
Set Shakespears Plays — 8 Vols.
Set Lillo's Plays — 2 Vols.
Set Goldoni's Plays — 3 Vols.
Italian Telemachus — 1 Vol.
French Telemachus — 1 Vol.
Spanish Telemachus — 1 Vol.
Rasselas — 2 Vols.
Lady Mary Wortley's Letters — 2 Vols.
Broken French Terence — 2 Vols.
Broken Spenser — 5 Vols.
Broken Swifts Miscellanies 6 Vols.

12mo
bound.

1 Italian Don Quixote — 4 Vols.
1 Italian Petrarca — 1 Vol.
1 Blacklock's Poems — 2 Vols.
1 Waller's Poems — 1 Vol.
1 Tasso's Gierusalemme — 1 Vol.
1 L'Advocat's Lives thick — 2 Vols
1 Do. fine Edition — 4 Vols
1 Bibliotheque Poetique — 4 Vols
1 Querelles Literaires — 4 Vols
1 Pensées de Paschal — 1 Vol.
1 Pere Bouhours Pensées — 1 Vol
1 Do. Maniere de bien penser — 1 Vol.
1 Passetemps poetiques — 2 Vols
1 Memoires de Literature — 2 Vols
1 Memoires de Bruys — 2 Vols
1 Girard's Synonymes — 2 Vols
1 Lettres de Maintenon — 1 Vol.
1 Eloge des Academiciens — 1 Vol.
1 broken Fontenelle — 4 Vols.
1 French Ovid — 2 Vols.
1 French Anacreon — 1 Vol.
1 Sewell's Ovid — 2 Vols
1 Memoires Litteraires — 1 Vol.
1 Moliere miserable — 4 Vols
1 Lettres de Balzac — 1 Vol.
1 Prince de Balzac — 1 Vol.
1 Œuvres diverses de Balzac 1 Vol.
1 Maximes de Rochefoucault — 1 Vol.
1 La Bruyere — 2 Vols
1 Racine broken — 7 Vols
1 Boileau — 2 Vols
1 Voiture — 2 Vols
1 Siecle de Louis 14 — 2 Vols
1 Cyropedie — 1 Vol
1 Voyage de Cyrus — 1 Vol.
1 Essais sur la Literature — 3 Vols
1 Modeles des Lettres — 1 Vol.
1 Voyage de Paris — 1 Vol.
1 Vie de Fenelon — 1 Vol.
1 Melanges de Literature — 1 Vol.
1 Cereau's Poems French — 1 Vol.

Moreover, she recommended Swift as a writer to her eldest daughter Hester Maria, nick-named Queeney, who did not share her mother's enthusiasm about the Dean, and in an entry in *Thraliana* of December 1778, Mrs Thrale called "Dr Swift's Ballad on the South Sea" one of "the two *wittiest* things in our Language."[44] Further evidence of Thrale's partiality for Swift is provided by the numerous references to his works scattered through her own, to "The Beasts' Confession to the Priest," for example, and to *A Tale of a Tub* in "Pompey, or a Doggrel Epistle from Pompey in the Shades – to his Master" (1761), as well as to *A Meditation upon a Broomstick* and *The Conduct of the Allies* in *The British Synonymy: or, An Attempt to Regulate the Choice of Words in Familiar Conversation* (1794).[45] In addition to referring to Swift's works as a model, she tried to imitate (and emulate) him, most strikingly in "Three Dialogues on the Death of Hester Lynch Thrale."

3

The "Three Dialogues on the Death of Hester Lynch Thrale" were written in August 1779 and printed for the first time posthumously in 1932, "from the hitherto Unpublished Original Manuscript … in the Possession of the John Rylands Library."[46] The biographical and psychological reasons for imagining herself dead are similar to those entered into the *Family Book* shortly before Hester Thrale received Johnson's poem on her thirty-fifth birthday. She was still suffering from the loss of her mother, Hester Maria Salusbury, in 1773, from the loss of

44 "I was reading something of Swift one Day & commending him as a Writer – I cannot endure Swift replied my eldest Daughter; every thing of his seems to be *Froth* I think, and that Froth is *dirty*" (*Thraliana*, ed. Balderston, I, 524). For Hester Thrale's praise of Swift's poem on the South Sea Bubble, see *Thraliana*, ed. Balderston, I, 354.

45 For Swift's influence on "Pompey, or a Doggrel Epistle from Pompey in the Shades – to his Master" (1761), see McCarthy, *Hester Thrale Piozzi*, p. 16. Hester Lynch Piozzi, *British Synonymy: or, An Attempt at Regulating the Choice of Words in Familiar Conversation* (1794), 2 vols (Menston: Scolar Press, 1968), II, 202-3. For another reference to the *Tale*, see Hester Lynch Piozzi, *Observations and Reflections: Made in the Course of a Journey through France, Italy, and Germany*, ed. Herbert Barrows (Ann Arbor: The University of Michigan Press, 1967), p. 387.

46 "Three Dialogues on the Death of Hester Lynch Thrale: From the hitherto Unpublished Original Manuscript now in the Possession of the John Rylands Library," ed. M. Zamick, *John Rylands Library Bulletin*, 16 (1932), 77-114. All quotations are from this edition and will be given in parentheses within the text.

We would like to thank Dr Sophie Coulombeau and Dr Elizabeth Edwards for kindly sharing their photographs of the original manuscript with us.

seven children, among them, her beloved son Henry, who had died at the age of nine in 1776, leaving her husband without a male heir to inherit the brewery; additionally, there were financial problems concerning the brewery, a beautiful and witty rival in the attention of her husband as well as her husband's depression and first stroke in June 1779. But the immediate occasion for writing about her own death in literary form was probably the premature birth of a stillborn boy on 10 August, abruptly putting an end to her thirteenth pregnancy.[47] The question whether Hester Thrale really felt suicidal in the summer of 1779 remains controversial; in fact, she had several times mentioned her willingness to sacrifice her own life for the birth of a son.[48]

In the Preface of her morbidly comic dialogues on her own death as well as in her entry on their genesis in *Thraliana*, Thrale explicitly refers to Swift's *Verses on the Death of Dr. Swift* (published in 1739 but presumably composed in 1731) as her model: "One of Dean Swift's happiest Compositions is certainly the little poem on his own Death" (p. 97). This acknowledgment shows that she tried to imitate and compete with Swift's satirical stance, calling his long and multi-layered fictional obituary, which satirically juxtaposes multiple voices and views of the public, of both friends and enemies, his "happiest Composition" and a "little poem."[49] The majority of critics assume a tripartite structure of the Dean's anything but "happy" and "little" *Verses*: a proem (ll. 1-72), a second section (ll. 73-298), and, finally, the *Rose*-tavern eulogy (ll. 299-484). Particularly this last panegyrical section has produced numerous, often discordant, readings: it has been denounced as "unqualified" and "unworthy,"[50] considered to

47 This has also been pointed out lately by Felicity A. Nussbaum in "Hester Thrale: 'What Trace of the Wit?'" *Bluestockings Displayed: Portraiture, Performance, and Patronage, 1730-1830*, ed. Elizabeth Eger (Cambridge: Cambridge University Press, 2013), pp. 187-207 (191).

48 In her "New Introduction" to Clifford's groundbreaking monograph *Hester Lynch Piozzi (Mrs. Thrale)* (1987), Margaret Anne Doody speculates that "if Henry Thrale felt suicidal in 1772, perhaps Hester played with suicide in the dark recesses of the mind in the late summer of 1779" (p. xxix). See also *Thraliana*, ed. Balderston, I, 400 and n1, 401-2.

49 In a letter to John Gay of 1 December 1731, Swift himself ironically resorted to the adjective "pleasant": "I have been severall months writing near five hundred lines on a pleasant Subject, onely to tell what my friends and enemyes will say on me after I am dead" (*Correspondence*, ed. Woolley, III, 443). However, it is unlikely that Hester Thrale knew this letter.

50 John Middleton Murry, *Jonathan Swift: A Critical Biography* (London: Jonathan Cape, 1954), pp. 457 and 459.

be "serious" and truly (auto)biographical,[51] ironical and satirical,[52] and, most recently, to be basically "justified."[53]

Like the *Verses*, the "Three Dialogues" are built on a fundamental metaphysical paradox, that of an author writing about his or her own death. But while Swift opted for a long poem for his obituary, the *salonnière* Thrale resorted to the kind of satirical dialogue prefigured in the *Dialogues of the Dead* by the Greek-writing Syrian Lucian (*c.*115-180 AD). With the exception of a few stage directions, Thrale's text lacks a narrator or speaker, the kind of tart third-person commentator that is so characteristic of Swift's *Verses*: "The Queen, so Gracious, Mild, and Good, / Cries, "Is he gone? 'Tis time he shou'd. / He's dead you say; why let him rot; / I'm glad the Medals were forgot."[54] These lines, his scathing satire on the hypocrisy of the powerful exemplified by Queen Caroline, show Swift the satirist at his best. In the "Three Dialogues," by contrast, the satirical effect is achieved indirectly, either by a character discrediting him- or herself, or by characters coming verbally into conflict; due to the dramatic form, there is no third-person commentator to draw attention to any sore points. An example of the first group – a character discrediting himself – may be found at the beginning of the third dialogue, where Mr Seward, a hypochondriac, reads from the paper:

> Last Week died at Streatham the Wife of Henry Thrale Esqr. – who if he had any Feeling now, would himself be affected by the incessant recurrence of the paragraph ... I am not as much hurt at it myself as I thought I should have been, but then I had taken an Emetick the Night before I heard the News – and a Man is so different after the Bile is gone off his Stomach (p. 105).

This extract may also be taken as representative of the "Three Dialogues" in as much as it shows the shift away from the incident of Hester Thrale's death and gossip about her person to other topics of conversation, thus developing into a portraiture of the speakers rather than into a fuller portrait of Hester Thrale.

51 See James Woolley, "Autobiography in Swift's Verses on his Death," *Contemporary Studies of Swift's Poetry*, eds John Irwin Fisher and Donald C. Mell, Jr (Newark: University of Delaware Press; London and Toronto: Associated University Presses, 1981), pp. 112-22 (120).

52 See Barry Slepian, "The Ironic Intention of Swift's Verses on his own Death," *Essential Articles for the Study of Jonathan Swift's Poetry*, ed. David M. Vieth (Hamden, Connecticut: Archon Books, 1984), pp. 295-305 (301) (the article first appeared in *The Review of English Studies*, NS, 14 [1963], 249-56).

53 Eugene Hammond, *Jonathan Swift: Our Dean* (Newark: University of Delaware Press, 2016), p. 575.

54 *Poems*, ed. Williams, II, 553-72 (559, ll. 181-84). All quotations are from this edition and will be given in parentheses within the text.

Neither Johnson in the first dialogue nor Hester's husband nor their eldest daughter "Miss Hetty," generally called "Queeney," who are part of the second scene of the last dialogue, can be induced to say a single word about their confidante, wife, and mother; it is for the minor characters to mention her "Wit," her love of books, as well as her "prodigious strong Nerves … an admirable Quality for a Friend of Dr. Johnson's" (p. 101), a passage that has become the most frequently quoted one from the "Three Dialogues." But this is more or less all readers learn about the absent hostess whose satirical self-presentation appears less forceful, if also less hyperbolical and aggressive than Swift's (self-) portrait on the edge of hubris, voiced through his eulogist. Therefore, as the editor of the "Three Dialogues" noted, "a comparison with Swift holds only in those parts where some comment is introduced on Hester Thrale's own life and on the companions she thought fit for herself and her daughter" (p. 79).

Also, Hester Thrale hastens to emphasize in the Preface: "My Death would be a slight event indeed compared with his" (p. 97). For one, the 'topos of affected modesty' was a widespread means of (female) self-deprecation by women writers of the long eighteenth century.[55] For another, her argument that her death would not affect society at large, but only those "people [she] chiefly lived with" (p. 97) points to a central difference between Swift's *Verses* and Thrale's dialogues: unlike the Dean's savage satire on "VAIN human Kind" (l. 39) as represented by various strata of eighteenth-century society, Thrale stages true-to-life conversations satirizing the peculiarities and vanities of her acquaintances, no matter whether of her husband's partners in business or the members of her literary salon.[56] The author herself was very proud to have created authentic portraits of the "people she chiefly lived with," imitating their expressions and characteristic phrases:

> The Dialogues on my own Death … have some small merit too, from the perfect & finished Resemblance every Speaker's Speech & Phrase has to the person speaking – Mrs Montagu or Mr Norman, or Sir Philip Jennings Clerke – not a Creature says but what I am morally certain the people significant or insignificant would most certainly say, and that Time & in that Situation in which I put them.[57]

---

55 See Kirsten Juhas, *'I'le to My Self, and to My Muse Be True': Strategies of Self-Authorization in Eighteenth-Century Women Poetry* (Frankfurt on Main: Peter Lang, 2008), pp. 20-21.

56 Almost all of the characters that appear in the "The Three Dialogues" are also among the people rated by Hester Thrale at one point in *Thraliana* according to categories like "Religion," "Morality," "Scholarship," "General Knowledge," "Person & Voice," "Wit, Humour, and Good humour" (for the males), and "Worth of Heart," "Conversation Powers," "Person, Mien & Manner," "Good humour," "Useful Knowledge," and "Ornamental Knowledge" (for the females, including herself) (see *Thraliana*, ed. Balderston, I, 329-31).

57 *Thraliana*, ed. Balderston, I, 402.

4

While Hester Thrale claimed her dialogues to have been composed with the strictest attention to authenticity, a blithe disclaimer of all intentional satire, we nevertheless wish to argue, in this last part, that the result is both more original and more controversial: more original than a mere character sketch, since it merges Swift's *Verses* with the genre of the *Dialogues of the Dead*, and more controversial, since Thrale made her characters discuss not herself but topics that mattered to her, such as women's positions in society. It is therefore important to take a closer look at the topics discussed in the "Three Dialogues," to consider who raises these topics in the first place and how they are taken up or dropped again. In addition, we will briefly look at some of the genre conventions and traditions of *Dialogues of the Dead*, as these were exceedingly popular during the mid-eighteenth century but are less well-known today.[58]

The first dialogue takes place "a month after" Mrs Thrale's death at an assembly the Bluestocking hostess Elizabeth Vesey gives at her home in Bolton Street; its speakers are the writer and literary scholar Sir William Weller Pepys, the Bluestocking Elizabeth Montagu, Samuel Johnson, and Edmund Burke (p. 98). A month is the longest time Swift accords to one of his own mourners in *Verses* (to Pope, l. 207), and he, too, imagines a "Club assembled" at the *Rose*, "Where from Discourse of this and that, / [he grew] the Subject of their Chat" (ll. 300-2). Mrs Vesey, the hostess, does not appear 'in person' but is congratulated by Pepys on her superior assemblies. This compliment stings Mrs Montagu, who chimes in to take the limelight herself with a bright *bon mot*, a feat she will continually repeat throughout the piece. She is also the one to bring up the topic of Hester Thrale's death, almost literally so since she wishes to conjure her up in person (p. 98). In another corner of the room, Dr Johnson is then approached by the unfortunate Pepys who wishes to condole with him on the sad loss of Mrs Thrale (and of "Mrs Thrale's Dinners" [p. 99]). Yet Johnson brushes him off: "I do not like to talk of Mrs Thrale, sir." Pepys peevishly replies that Johnson was supposed to feel that loss to which Johnson replies: "Would you talk to your Friend (*sneeringly*) Keppel of the twenty-seventh of July?" (p. 100), his ferocity indicating that Mrs Thrale's death was of some momentum to him, after all.[59] On being attacked by Burke for his ill-temper, Johnson

58 Michael Prince notes that the genre was particularly popular in the decades from 1760-80 (*Philosophical Dialogue in the British Enlightenment: Theology, Aesthetics, and the Novel* [Cambridge: Cambridge University Press, 1996], p. 224).

59 Burke's reaction to Johnson's sneer may be significant even if it is unlikely that Thrale knew of Burke's letter to Admiral Augustus Keppel, congratulating him on his wise conduct at what is now known as the Battle of Ushant (27 July 1778), and offering "public

retorts that one cannot share pain with "a Creature" with whom one cannot even share pleasure (p. 100). The dialogue ends with Pepys "telling everybody what Mrs Montagu said last" and Johnson's leaving the room. The 'stage directions' – a narrative intrusion as well as a comment – claim that the conversation then changes to "a worthier subject" (p. 101).

The fact that this very first dialogue features Mrs Montagu invites comparison with Montagu's own *Dialogues of the Dead* (published among Lyttelton's *Dialogues*), witty but didactic both in intent and execution.[60] In 1779, Johnson had not yet written his life of Lyttelton, which would lead to his open quarrel with Montagu, and at the time of writing Mrs Thrale and Mrs Montagu seem to have genuinely liked and respected each other; indeed, all references to Mrs Montagu in the first part of *Thraliana* are supportive.[61] "Mrs Montagu's Bouquet is all out of the Hothouse – mine out of the Woods & Fields & many a Weed there is in it," Hester Thrale astutely commented on their different styles.[62] Clearly, Thrale does poke fun at Montagu's tendency to speak in 'bouquets from the hothouse' in her dialogue, yet Mrs Montagu is the one to mention Mrs Thrale in the first place and the one to subtly maintain that Mrs Thrale may have been more important to society than merely in her role as Johnson's hostess (the only praise that Pepys can think of).

The second dialogue is set at Beckenham Place, "after Suppers," present are the owner of the manor, the former timber merchant John Cator, his wife, another merchant called Mr Norman, and Guiseppe Baretti. In *Thraliana*, Hester Thrale calls John Cator "a purseproud Tradesman, coarse in his Expressions, & vulgar in Manners & Pronunciation; though very intelligent, and full both of Money and good sense."[63] Guiseppe Baretti (1719-89), the famously irascible linguist, taught Mrs Thrale's daughter Queeney Italian and stayed at Streatham

---

thanks" for the service done to the country (*The Correspondence of Edmund Burke, IV: July 1778-June 1782*, ed. John A. Woods [Cambridge and Chicago: Cambridge University Press and The University of Chicago Press, 1963], 13).

60 Elizabeth Montagu contributed three dialogues to George Lyttelton's *Dialogues of the Dead* (London: W. Sandby, 1760): XXVI: "CADMUS – HERCULES," XXVII: "MERCURY – And a modern fine LADY," and XXVIII: "PLUTARCH – CHARON – And a modern BOOKSELLER" (pp. 291-320). She wrote one more, "A Dialogue between Berenice and Cleopatra," which remained unpublished until after her death. Elizabeth Eger's edition of Montagu's works in the first volume of Gary Kelly's series prints all her *Dialogues of the Dead* (*Bluestocking Feminism: Writings of the Bluestocking Circle, 1738-1785, I: Elizabeth Montagu*, ed. Elizabeth Eger [London: Pickering and Chatto, 2004], 115-37).

61 Compare also Mrs Montagu's very high score (much higher than Thrale's own) in Mrs Thrale's classification of her acquaintances (*Thraliana*, ed. Balderston, I, 330).

62 Piozzi MS Rylands 629, 29a. Quoted from Clifford, *Hester Lynch Piozzi (Mrs. Thrale)*, p. 153.

63 *Thraliana*, ed. Balderston, I, 220.

for about three years until he broke with the Thrales in 1776.[64] In the dialogue, it is Baretti who jumps right into the topic by telling his host: "You have heard the News confirmed of the Death of Mrs Thrale" (p. 102). Unlike the lament in the first dialogue, Cator and Norman take this hint as a licence to wise-crack about Mrs Thrale's wit and "the monstrous Sight of Books" she has read. Cator cites Bacon as the source of a quotation actually taken from issue no 137 of Johnson's *Rambler*[65] while Norman self-importantly quotes "Senecar" (p. 103), "Magna Servitus est Magna Fortuna." The phrase was almost proverbial at the time; and Norman's claim to learning may safely be doubted: he is presented as a target similar to that of Swift's speaker in the *Verses*, who "laugh'd to hear an Idiot quote / A Verse from *Horace*, learn'd by Rote" (ll. 473-74).

In this second dialogue, Thrale's portrait of her characters is particularly spiteful, since she also picks up their habits of speech and 'vulgar' pronunciation – here played off against the perfect English of Baretti.[66] Cator's John-Bullish pride in his Englishness is likewise taken on: he talks of "our Countryman" Lord Bacon as a dig against Baretti the foreigner – who might have retorted that Mrs Thrale was Welsh, but does not. The dialogue then focuses on trade and the question of money: for Hester Thrale it remained a sore point that she had married into trade, and the Thrales had financial difficulties to contend with during those years.[67] All this is mentioned quite openly, but

64 Clifford, *Hester Lynch Piozzi (Mrs. Thrale)*, pp. 143-44, compare also p. 143n3. Mrs Thrale herself had named John Cator a trustee for her Welsh property in 1775, and the Cators and the Normans appear a few times in Frances Burney's journal letters written from Streatham: "The Party consisted of Mr Cator, who was formerly a Timber Merchant, but, having amassed a Fortune of 1.00:0000 [sic] pounds, he has left off Business. He is a good natured, busy sort of man. Mrs Cator, his Lady; – a sort of Mrs Nobody. Mr Norman, another Rich Business *leaver* off" (*The Early Journals and Letters of Fanny Burney, III: The Streatham Years, Part I, 1778-1779*, eds Lars Troide and Stewart Cooke [Montréal and Kingston: McGill-Queen's University Press, 1994], 124). In 1778, the Thrales and Baretti still seem to have occasionally met at the Cators' home. Susan Burney wrote to her sister on 1 August 1779 that Queeney had said she would visit "Cater" and see Baretti there: "She was to *meet Mr Baretti* that day wth M^{r} & M^{rs} T: at Mr *Cater's* I think -- & did not seem much delighted by the idea" (*The Journals and Letters of Susan Burney: Music and Society in Late Eighteenth-Century England*, ed. Philip Olleson [Farnham, Surrey: Ashgatre, 2012], p. 67).

65 "'Books, says Bacon, 'can never teach the use of books'" (*The Yale Edition of the Works of Samuel Johnson, IV: The Rambler*, eds W. J. Bate and Albrecht B. Strauss [New Haven and London: Yale University Press, 1969], 363). Seneca's phrase appears, for example, in David E. Macdonnel, *A Dictionary of Quotations in Most Frequent Use: Taken from the Greek, Latin, French, Spanish and Italian Languages, Translated into English*, 2nd rev. ed. (London, 1798), p. 106.

66 Cator's pronunciation was also made fun of at Streatham; see Joyce Hemlow, *The History of Fanny Burney* (Oxford: Clarendon Press, 1956), p. 126.

67 See, for instance, Clifford, *Hester Lynch Piozzi (Mrs. Thrale)*, pp. 167-68 and 201-2.

the main question discussed is whether a wife ought to have any influence at all on her husband, a point which calls forth Baretti's ire.[68] He jumps at Norman, who dares to contemplate that his son might marry a woman like Mrs Thrale: "If he is not the most ignorant the most impenetrable Blockhead that ever the Almighty has given Permission to infect the Earth with his Folly – he will not be governed by his Wife" (p. 104). Yet Cator sneeringly considers Baretti's outburst to be based on a foreign notion of marriage: "Do you say these things in Italy?" Indeed, in this dialogue Mrs Thrale is even less subtle about male exploitation of female services than in the first: Norman himself claims he has had two wives "& good Portions with each" but goes on to call women "a mere Drug" (p. 104). To Baretti, Mrs Thrale failed to fulfil her duty of wifely submissiveness, but by his very treatment of his companions, he has forfeited the right to be taken as an authority in these matters: Thrale cleverly portrays him as an intellectual superior but at the same time also as a bully who, being a foreigner, is not to be trusted when condemning English customs.[69] Mrs Cator, the only female present, remains fast asleep throughout and is only woken when Mr Cator suggests a toast, and revealingly calls his wife "General!"[70] Thrale's readers would have been aware of the widespread notions concerning women's influence on men's conversational politeness, so that even Mrs Cator's sleepiness should be considered a judgement on the male display of misogynist opinions.[71] It is tempting, too, to think of Swift's *Verses* again here (if slightly out of context) to illustrate how these men feel about being governed by their wives: "THEN hug themselves, and reason thus; / It is not yet so bad with us" (ll. 115-16).

The third dialogue begins with William Seward (1747-99), clearly depicted as one of the "rest," who, in Swift's words, "give a Shrug" when being faced with another's death (l. 211). Swift charged this "rest" with indifference and "stony Bowels" (l. 215), while Thrale's Seward, in turn, takes an emetic to move his own (p. 105). The real Seward was a rich young man much in favour at

68 Concerning Thrale's view of Baretti's irascible temper and general character, see *Thraliana*, ed. Balderston, I, 43.

69 When it came to wifely submission, Thrale considered her own conduct exemplary: "was I to die tomorrow I could swear I never oppos'd his Inclination three Times in the fifteen Years we have been married" (*Thraliana*, ed. Balderston, I, 369).

70 Baretti has the last word, declaring that while he wished a good husband to "[his] Hetty Thrale" (that is, Queeney), he supposes that Mr Thrale has had "Wife enough" in Hester Thrale.

71 Recording the life of her parents, Thrale argued that "for a Woman to contend with a Man She is shut up with at a Distance from Society, where the natural Roughness of the Sex is not restrained; & Gallantry can obtain no Reputation; is … dangerous" (*Thraliana*, ed. Balderston, I, 281).

Streatham at the time, though Hester Thrale, according to Burney, considered him "an Hypochondriac."[72] In the dialogue, he swallows yet another draught before Sir Richard Jebb enters. Jebb (1729-87) was the family physician of the Thrales and a favourite with Mrs Thrale, who enjoyed going to London to consult him, though he also occasionally joined the Streatham set.[73] On entering the scene in this Dialogue, Sir Richard immediately notices that Seward is "quacking" and by association of ideas wonders what Mrs Thrale must have done to ruin her own health.[74] Judging from the numbers of medical self-help books that were sold along with the rest of her library in 1816 – such as George Cheyne's *The English Malady: or, A Treatise of Nervous Diseases of All Kinds, as Spleen, Vapours, Lowness of Spirits, Hypochondriacal and Hysterical Distempers* (Dublin, 1733), or William Buchan's *Domestic Medicine: or, The Family Physician* (Edinburgh, 1769) – Mrs Thrale may well have been doctoring herself and her family.[75] Yet here it is probably the doctor who is being satirized since his intention seems to be to secure himself against any charge that he might have failed her as her physician – directly in line with Swift's suggestion that "THE Doctors tender of their Fame, / Wisely on me lay all the Blame: / 'We must confess his Case was nice; / But he would never take Advice'" (ll. 169-72). Worse still, Jebb's words seem to imply that Mrs Thrale might in fact have poisoned herself – a notion that piques Seward's curiosity: "What did She take? come tell, do" (p. 106). On Sir Richard's disclaiming that he ever thought of poison, Seward is even more intrigued: "Did she practise any clandestine cruelties upon her person? Any secret Mortifications?" (He goes so far as to mention a "Hair Cloth" [p. 107].) On Jebb's horrified response that he meant no such thing, Seward hurriedly claims that oddity and downright insanity were only to be expected, Thrale being both very pious and a wit. About to leave, Jebb recommends marriage to Seward to cure him – as Mrs Thrale actually heard him do

72 *The Early Journals and Letters of Fanny Burney, IV: The Streatham Years, Part II, 1780-1781*, ed. Betty Rizzo (Montréal and Kingston: McGill-Queen's University Press, 2003), 14. Hester Thrale considered Seward "beneficient though frigid" and remarked that "one loves him in spite both of one's self & him" (*Thraliana*, ed. Balderston, I, 221, see also 220n329).

73 See, for instance, *Thraliana*, ed. Balderston, I, 376. He had attended the Thrales' son, Henry, during his fatal illness in March 1776 (*Thraliana*, ed. Balderston, I, 319n1; Clifford, *Hester Lynch Piozzi* [*Mrs. Thrale*], pp. 136-37, 150).

74 *Thraliana* notes Seward's suggestion that Mr Cator should be "bled & Physicked well" to make him fit for company (I, 220).

75 In June 1779, an acquaintance of Mrs Thrale's, Peggy Pitches, died from Quackery: "I think She died of a Disorder common enough to young Women the Desire of Beauty; She had I fancy taken Quack Med'cines to prevent growing fat, or perhaps to repress Appetite, I have seen strange Stuff advertised in Ladies Memorandum books for such vile purposes" (*Thraliana*, ed. Balderston, I, 393).

in June 1779[76] – when another Streatham favourite, Sir Philip Jennings Clerke, enters and heartily agrees that there is no pleasure without women.[77] This is not quite what Jebb meant, though, since he clarifies: "Intellectual Pleasures go on most easily I believe without the Sexual Intercourse, but then a Man can't read always – " (p. 108). Seward chimes in with yet another witticism: "Women are like Bitters to be sure, they do give a Stimulus, but then Marriage is Chamomile Tea, a mere Emetick" (p. 108).

The scene then changes to a dinner-table conversation, hosted by Lady Lade, Hester Thrale's sister-in-law. Sir Philip Jennings Clerke is of the party, and so is Mr Seward. Besides, Mrs Thrale's husband Henry Thrale and their daughter Queeney attend, as does an unidentified Miss Dodson. She does not seem to have been part of either the Streatham or the Burney circles. Indeed, according to her treatment in the dialogue, she may have acted as a humble companion to Lady Lade, as she is sent on an errant which Sir Philip, for one, seems to think a servant's duty. Again, the topic of women's positions in society is subtly raised by the otherwise superfluous inclusion of her character. The talk now centres on just about anything but Mrs Thrale, though she is alluded to once as the friend several acquaintances have shed tears for. On hearing the Burneys mentioned, Mr Thrale grumbles that he does not want to see any of them, and Lady Lade rambles into a sneering speech disclaiming any new-fangled notion that wit in women could possibly be preferable to female beauty. She goes on to praise a singer whose ballads are, to her, "ten times more pleasing ... than all that fine Italian Stuff one can't understand" (p. 111). The conversation here stagnates since, rather like Dr Johnson in the first dialogue, Mr Thrale refuses to talk about anyone who might remind him of his wife. Clearly, the last dialogue again deals with the topic of gender relations, adding a third (and even a fourth) angle, the matter of sexual relations brought up by Jebb, while any notion of female solidarity is caricatured in the person of Lady Lade. Sir Philip eventually suggests that the party proceed to cards, a notion gladly assented to by all in yet another finely managed allusion to Swift's *Verses* ("'The Dean is dead, (*and what is Trumps?*)'" [l. 228]). Here, the "Three Dialogues" end.

While these dialogues are Thrale's "cleverest piece of creative writing," one reader contends, he considers them little more than "simple character sketches."[78] However, the very fact that Thrale raises issues as complicated as

---

76 See *The Early Journals and Letters of Fanny Burney, IV*, ed. Rizzo, 325.

77 Sir Philip Jennings Clerke (1722-88) was a Member of Parliament from 1768-1788. For his admiration of Mrs Thrale, and her reliance on his advice, see, for instance, *Thraliana*, ed. Balderston, I, 372-73.

78 Clifford, *Hester Lynch Piozzi* (*Mrs. Thrale*), p. 179.

women's role in society, even if she does so in a humorous mode, should make one admit the possibility of doubt. Shortly before, and also directly after writing these dialogues, Thrale herself bitterly lamented in *Thraliana* that she felt incapable of writing original compositions. She had thought about writing a comedy in May 1779, but added that she would have to take a French model as she had "not a Spark of Originality."[79] This may explain why she kept close to reality, and why she preferred the dialogue form to verses, despite being a prolific poet herself. Instead, Thrale's "Three Dialogues" are modelled on the *Dialogues of the Dead*, a literary genre that raises important moral, philosophical, and political issues in a light-hearted manner. Evidently, Thrale did not intend to adhere to established generic conventions; her dialogues are not spoken by the dead. And yet, she toyed with the genre, calling her work "Dialogues on [her] own Death."[80] Even so, the general purpose of *Dialogues of the Dead*, its didactic insistence on a palpable moral lesson to be gleaned, is at least partly maintained in Thrale's variation. To begin with, "there is no narrative; the dead [here: the living] are overheard."[81] According to Frederick Keener, this kind of dialogue does not emphasize its dramatic nature but uses a dramatic setting to focus on an exchange of ideas.[82] All of Thrale's dialogues foreground the speakers' opinions and (attempts at) wit, and at some point they all focus on the role of women and marriage, or on women's education and the impact of reading (the second one, for instance, raising the question whether "knowledge of the world" can be gained from books). Keener points out that "the dialogue of

79 *Thraliana*, ed. Balderston, I, 386-87; compare I, 402.

80 *Thraliana*, ed. Balderston, I, 402 and again I, 408.

81 Frederick M. Keener, *English Dialogues of the Dead: A Critical History, an Anthology, and a Check List* (New York: Columbia University Press, 1973), p. 4. According to Michael Prince, however, the genre suffered major upheavals throughout its popularity in the mid-eighteenth century; he argues that Johnson's *The Vanity of Human Wishes* and even *The History of Rasselas, Prince of Abyssinia* should be read as *Dialogues of the Dead* (*Philosophical Dialogue in the British Enlightenment*, p. 225). On the importance of the *Dialogue of the Dead* as a form useful to revive particular types of philosophical reasoning, see also Sibylle Baumbach, "*Speak, Dead, Speak*: Values, Virtues and Vices from Hades," *Literature and Values: Literature as a Medium for Representing, Disseminating, and Constructing Norms and Values*, eds Sibylle Baumbach, Herbert Grabes, and Ansgar Nünning (Trier: Wissenschaftlicher Verlag Trier, 2009), pp. 107-123; and, with more emphasis on George Lyttelton's and Elizabeth Montagu's contribution to the genre, the same author's "Totgesagte streiten länger: das Elysium als Austragungsort gelehrter Polemik in George Lytteltons *Dialogues of the Dead*," *Zeitsprünge: Forschungen zur Frühen Neuzeit*, 15 (2011), 404-24. In addition, Markman Ellis provides a significant discussion of the impact of Montagu's dialogues on her reputation ("'An Author in Form': Women Writers, Print Publication, and Elizabeth Montagu's 'Dialogues of the Dead,'" *ELH*, 79 [2012], 417-45).

82 See Keener, *English Dialogues of the Dead*, p. 15.

the dead is related to the dialogue proper and employs characters of known intellectual dispositions" who are typically "clustered" so as to prove a moral point.[83] Thrale, too, carefully places her characters to discuss, imply, and demonstrate various moral issues: Is it possible to share grief? Should a wife have influence over her husband? How should a humble companion be treated? A key feature of Lucian's dialogues, Keener continues, is the exchange between *alazons* – two or more self-deceiving, boastful men – rather than between *alazon* and *eiron*, as in comedy. The exchange between Johnson and Pepys is such an exchange, Pepys's vacuous chatter being self-deceiving and Johnson feeling superior to Pepys. In like manner, Baretti and his set may serve as a set of three vain boasters.[84]

As early as 1683, Fontenelle had introduced modern characters into the established form in his *Nouveaux dialogues des morts*, and Thrale knew his *Dialogues* well enough to quote from them freely.[85] She also owned a set of his collected works, besides those of Erasmus, Richard Hurd, and Lyttelton.[86] Thus, Thrale was familiar not only with most eighteenth-century versions of *Dialogues of the Dead* but also with philosophical dialogues in general. We cannot prove that Thrale knew Lucian's works, but it seems likely that she read one of the many translations produced throughout the century. She would have known Elizabeth Montagu's *Dialogues* as a matter of course, but her own are clearly different in style, closer to Lucian by far than to Lyttelton in their use of satire. Thrale may have wanted to prove that she could write better dialogues than Montagu because, unlike her friend, she was not afraid to insert 'weeds' (unlady-like expressions or unmentionable objects such as haircloths), or to acknowledge her debt to Swift as an inspiration.

More particularly, Thrale's "Three Dialogues" may have been inspired by William King, who had introduced female characters into the form in 1699, inventing a dialogue between a society hostess, Bellamira, and a learned lady, Calphurnia, called the "Affectation of the Learned Lady" (the very topic of Frances Burney's play *The Witlings*, which she completed while staying at Streatham in the first half of 1779). There are a few veiled references to King's dialogue in Thrale's version. In her second dialogue, Norman is horrified by the "monstrous" amount of books Thrale has read, while King's Bellamira

83 Keener, *English Dialogues of the Dead*, p. 9.

84 Keener, *English Dialogues of the Dead*, pp. 19-20.

85 *The Piozzi Letters*, eds Edward A. Bloom and Lillian D. Bloom, 6 vols (Newark: University of Delaware Press, and London: Associated University Presses, 1989-2002), V, 303n1.

86 In 1823, her set of the works of Fontenelle was sold with the auction catalogue quoting from her marginalia: *Sale Catalogues of Libraries of Eminent Persons*, ed. Parks, V, 496 (Fontenelle), 396 (Erasmus), 406 (Hurd), 420 (Lyttelton).

moralizes: "Reading may be allowable in our Sex, when we have little else to do, especially if the Subject be diverting, but your Toilette us'd always to be heap'd with such Books as frighted me to look into 'em."[87] King's characters then proceed to compare such works with the various dishes of a dinner, an idea that Hester puts into the mouth of William Pepys in the first dialogue: "Here is always at this house a mighty happy Selection – too many tho' I think Sir for the purposes of Conversation; any five of them would do better, a mere Galaxy of Wits this, too many good Dishes like poor Mrs. Thrale's Dinners" (p. 99).[88] Hester Thrale, too, was a learned lady by eighteenth-century standards, and she freely admitted that she did not enjoy the satiric butt of Burney's play. Her own dialogues may thus be meant to invite her readers to sample the difference between the stagnant witticisms of a Lady Lade, whose taste is in ballads and who prefers vacuous but beautiful girls to women of wit, and the conversational sallies she herself or Mrs Montagu were capable of.

The Thrales do not seem to have owend any of William King's works, a collected edition of which had been published in 1776, but King's life was included in Johnson's *Lives of the Poets* (1779-81), whose subjects were frequently discussed by the Streatham set, and is considered to have been composed throughout 1778/79, at the very time that Burney wrote *The Witlings* and Thrale the "Three Dialogues."[89] Apparently, Johnson did not like the genre of *Dialogues of the Dead*, considering it obsolete, and we do not know whether Thrale ever mentioned her own dialogues to her old friend. Yet we do know that they were read and enjoyed by Queeney Thrale and Frances Burney, according to *Thraliana*.[90]

Coming back to the question of authenticity raised by Thrale herself ("not a Creature says but what I am morally certain the people significant or insignificant would most certainly say"[91]), it is worth noting that the very fact that

87 King's dialogue is printed in Keener, *English Dialogues of the Dead*, pp. 189-91 (190). Calphurnia lists Jansen, Descartes, and Casaubon among the books on her table.

88 In *Thraliana*, Thrale records a parlour game in which people are compared to dishes at a dinner: Johnson is "a Haunch of Venison," Pepys a "Perigord Pye" and Mrs Montagu "Soup – à la *Reine*" (I, 347).

89 For Johnson, see *The Lives of the Poets*, ed. Lonsdale, II, 390; for discussions of the topics at Streatham, see, for instance, Keener, *English Dialogues of the Dead*, pp. 25-26, and *The Early Journals and Letters of Fanny Burney*, III, eds Troide and Cooke, 150-51.

90 Burney does not mention reading the dialogues in her *Journals*, but at that time she may have been preoccupied with the 'death' of her own first play: on 13 August 1779, she told her father: "down among the Dead Men sink the poor Witlings" (*The Early Journals and Letters of Fanny Burney*, III, eds Troide and Cooke, 345). As the editors point out, "down among the dead men" was the refrain of a familiar poem at the time but then, she may well have thought that *The Witlings*, never to be performed during her lifetime, had turned into a new variety of *Dialogues of the Dead*, too.

91 *Thraliana*, ed. Balderston, I, 402. Thrale did occasionally wonder whether she had in fact portrayed her characters accurately: "I repent that I have not made Pepys speak

several of her subjects are so significant and so familiar entices her readers into wondering whether her characters are portrayed authentically – or brazenly satirized. Without the voice of a narrator, the readers' imagination must supply some of the action, the tone of voices speaking, and the general atmosphere of each dialogue. Much depends on what is actually left out: the things not said, and even the people who do not appear. Thrale has eliminated herself from these dialogues, nominally at least, creating the (first) impression that she is not herself important. Unlike Swift in the *Verses*, her significance is barely discussed by her 'survivors,' her works are not mentioned, only her dinners are missed. Paradoxically, in most *Dialogues of the Dead* the dead speakers are very much alive when it comes to discussing what the living do. The "Three Dialogues," skilfully amalgamate Swift's *Verses* with the generic matrix of *Dialogues of the Dead*. At the same time, they provide us with a vivid glimpse of eighteenth-century sociability in practice as the conversations unfold. Thrale's last dialogue, however, seems to reverse that rule, showing the participants of Lady Lade's dinner to lack any such animation when deprived of Mrs Thrale's presence. Their stagnation highlights Thrale's own "extraordinary vitality," to borrow Marianna D'Ezio's words.[92] According to D'Ezio, "portraying her absence is much more effective for Mrs. Thrale than portraying a pale presence in her friends' thoughts and conversation." This is a particularly effective strategy since, for readers, Thrale remains at the centre of these dialogues, not least because they keep wondering when the characters will get round to mentioning her, and of course what they may then have to say about her. Thrale has managed to create an (authorial) presence in her own absence in salon-like conversations, with herself not in the role of hostess but in that of director or stage manager.[93] Like Swift, Thrale Piozzi now continues to live through her texts and in an increasing number of readings of her texts. Reading her, we take note of her originality as well as her impressive knowledge of contemporary literature. Certainly, Swift was one of the writers who inspired her most or, as one of Hester Thrale's biographers put it, "Swift's writings got into her blood early and stayed there."[94]

more tenderly of me in my Dialogues on my own death; he certainly does love me … This is no Skin deep Friendship – this is real Kindness & I shall for ever love him for it." Characteristically, however, she added: "Be his Friendship however what it will, his Vanity is still stronger; he would I believe speak & act just as he does in the Dialogue" (I, 408).

92 D'Ezio, *Hester Lynch Piozzi*, p. 30.

93 D'Ezio, *Hester Lynch Piozzi*, p. 161.

94 McCarthy, *Hester Thrale Piozzi*, p. 62.

Ian Higgins
The Australian National University, Canberra

Swift's Whig Pamphlet: Its Reception and Afterlife

Abstract. There is a rich body of scholarly work on the reception and afterlife of Swift's satiric fiction, poetry, and some of his Irish writings. Less attention has been paid to the reception and afterlife of some of his famous pamphlets written in the reigns of William III and Anne. This essay revisits Swift's first political pamphlet, *A Discourse of the Contests and Dissentions between the Nobles and the Commons in Athens and Rome* written at the end of William III's reign. It focuses on the tract's topical political eccentricity, contemporary Tory reception, republication in Swift's *Miscellanies in Prose and Verse* of 1711, continuities with some of Swift's other writings on parliaments, and its afterlife in the work of some anti-democratic writers.

1

A Discourse of the Contests and Dissentions between the Nobles and the Commons in Athens and Rome, with the Consequences they had upon both those States was published anonymously in 1701, under the imprint of John Nutt, a trade publisher used by the Tories.[1] The work appeared to be written in a Court Whig cause, defending William III's favourite, Hans Willem [William] Bentinck, Earl of Portland, and three Junto Whig Lords, John, Baron Somers, Charles Montagu,

1 Teerink and Scouten 478. For an annotated modern edition based on the 1701 text, see *A Discourse of the Contests and Dissentions between the Nobles and Commons in Athens and Rome, with the Consequences they had upon Both those States*, ed. Frank H. Ellis (Oxford: Clarendon Press, 1967; hereafter referred to as *Discourse*, ed. Ellis). For trenchant accounts of the *Discourse* and this edition of it, see Edward Rosenheim, Jr, "The Text and Context of Swift's *Contests and Dissentions*," *Modern Philology*, 66 (1968), 59-74, and J. A. Downie, "Swift's *Discourse*: Allegorical Satire or Parallel History?" *Swift Studies*, 2 (1987), 25-32. Nutt was in trouble for involvement with a Tory publication of 1701, printed by John Barber: Charles Davenant's *The True Picture of a Modern Whig* (see *Cobbett's Parliamentary History of England*, VI [London: T. C. Hansard, 1810], cols 21-22; see also Charles A. Rivington, *"TYRANT": The Story of John Barber, Jacobite Lord Mayor of London, and Printer and Friend to Dr Swift* [York: William Sessions, 1989], p. 9). One of the most popular of Tory works, Ned Ward's *The Secret History of the Calves-Head Club* (1703), came out under Nutt's imprint, and in 1713 the enlarged eighth edition was retitled *The Whigs Unmask'd: Being the Secret History of the Calf's-Head-Club* (London: J. Morphew, 1713). Nutt's business was taken on by John Morphew in 1706, under whose imprint Swift's *Miscellanies* of 1711 was published.

 | DOI:10.30965/9783846763971_024

Earl of Halifax, and Edward Russell, Earl of Orford, who had been impeached in April 1701 by a Tory House of Commons for their involvement in the secret partition treaty of 1698 and the second partition treaty of 1700. The tract is a polemical parallel history, and Swift's debut as a political pamphleteer.

The *Discourse* is patrician in tone, pitched above the Grub Street vulgar. Its Olympian survey of Athens and Rome requires readers to follow classical parallels and decode the innuendo applying the classical instances to topical persons and proceedings in 1701, though Swift ensures that readers do not miss the partisan point by devices such as emphatic italics and by supplying parenthetical modern political phrases and equivalents for classical persons and proceedings. Swift was chaplain to the Earl of Berkeley and in London from April to September 1701. The *Discourse* was conceived soon after his arrival in London from Dublin and was written over the spring and summer, while the Parliament was in session, and after its prorogation in June 1701, which is alluded to in Chapter V of the pamphlet. The work was published in October 1701 after Swift had returned to Ireland.[2] Upon publication, the work was noticed by Whigs and Tories. The erudite and ingenious audacity with which Swift finds and manipulates sources and forces parallels was announcing the arrival of a new propagandistic talent. The anonymous work was indeed attributed to the senior Whig leadership and the party's high-profile polemicists, John, Lord Somers, and to Bishop Gilbert Burnet, who told Swift he had "to disown it in a very public manner."[3] Swift allowed himself to be known in Whig circles as the author of the celebrated or notorious work when he returned to London.[4] It is paradoxical that he should reprint the Whig tract, in pride of place, as the opening work of the 1711 *Miscellanies in Prose and Verse*, when he was a Tory propagandist and proud of his current "greatness among the Tories."[5] The *Miscellanies* was his landmark mid-career retrospective, published by his bookseller Benjamin Tooke, Jr, a Tory publisher, printed by William Bowyer,

---

2 Jonathan Swift, *Memoirs, Relating to that Change which Happened in the Queen's Ministry in the Year 1710*, in *Prose Works*, VIII, 119; *The Account Books of Jonathan Swift*, eds Paul V. Thompson and Dorothy Jay Thompson (Newark: University of Delaware Press, and London: Scolar Press, 1984), pp. xiii-xv, 315; James Woolley, "Swift and Lord Berkeley, 1699-1701: Berkeley Castle Swiftiana," in *"The first wit of the age": Essays on Swift and his Contemporaries in Honour of Hermann J. Real*, eds Kirsten Juhas, Patrick Müller, and Mascha Hansen (Frankfurt on Main: Peter Lang, 2013), pp. 31-68 (46); *Discourse*, ed. Ellis, pp. 175-77; Ehrenpreis, *Dr Swift*, pp. 43, 46-47.

3 *Prose Works*, VIII, 119; *Discourse*, ed. Ellis, pp. 178-80.

4 *Prose Works*, VIII, 119.

5 *Journal to Stella: Letters to Esther Johnson and Rebecca Dingley, 1710-1713*, ed. Abigail Williams (Cambridge: Cambridge University Press, 2013), p. 44 (Letter 7, 20 October 1710).

and distributed by the Tory trade publisher John Morphew.[6] Swift was able to do so since there was presumably no practical difficulty in reprinting the *Discourse* in this collection: it must have belonged to Swift's bookseller Benjamin Tooke, Jr. The trade publisher John Morphew, in 1711, was the successor to Nutt, the trade publisher of the *Discourse* in 1701. As editor of Sir William Temple's *Miscellanea: The Third Part*, published in London by Benjamin Tooke in 1701, Swift had placed an anti-populist work, Temple's *An Essay on Popular Discontents* as the opening essay of the volume. He does the same for his own miscellaneous collection. There are commonplace parallels as well as differences between Temple's and Swift's works.[7] Yet the 1711 *Miscellanies* sought to establish Swift's Tory credentials, and so Swift must have felt that the *Discourse* did that.[8]

The work imputes parallels between the proceedings of the Tory-controlled House of Commons in 1701 and popular assemblies that ruined the liberties of Greece and Rome, destroying the ideal of a balanced mixed government of King, Lords, and Commons. As printed in the 1711 *Miscellanies*, the *Discourse* concludes with the political moral of his classical exempla:

---

6 All references to Swift's *Discourse* are to *A Discourse of the Contests and Dissentions between the Nobles and the Commons in Athens and Rome, with the Consequences they had upon both those States*, in [Jonathan Swift], *Miscellanies in Prose and Verse* (London: John Morphew, 1711), introd. C. P. Daw (Menston: Scolar Press, 1972), pp. 1-94, and will be cited hereafter as *Discourse* and *Miscellanies* within the text. This facsimile edition reproduces the British Library copy (shelf-mark 838.g.1) of the *Miscellanies*, which retains the cancelled leaves G6 and G7 (pp. 91-94), the cancelled paragraph about bribery, and, at A8, the substituted p. 91 for the 1711 edition. On Swift's printers, booksellers, and trade publishers, see Michael Treadwell, "Swift's Relations with the London Book Trade to 1714," *Author/Publisher Relations during the Eighteenth and Nineteenth Centuries*, eds Robin Myers and Michael Harris (Oxford: Oxford Polytechnic Press, 1983), pp. 1-36, and the same author's "London Trade Publishers, 1675-1750," *The Library*, 6th ser., 4 (1982), 99-134; Ian Gadd, "Leaving the Printer to his Liberty: Swift and the London Book Trade, 1701-1714," *Jonathan Swift and the Eighteenth-Century Book*, eds Paddy Bullard and James McLaverty (Cambridge: Cambridge University Press, 2013), pp. 51-64. On Bowyer as printer of the 1711 *Miscellanies*, see *The Bowyer Ledgers*, eds Keith Maslen and John Lancaster (London: The Bibliographical Society, and New York: The Bibliographical Society of America, 1991), no 60.

7 Swift, *A Tale of a Tub and Other Works*, ed. Marcus Walsh (Cambridge: Cambridge University Press, 2010), pp. 199-200, 533; F. P. Lock, *Swift's Tory Politics* (London: Duckworth, 1983), pp. 148, 161; Ashley Marshall, *Swift and History: Politics and the English Past* (Cambridge: Cambridge University Press, 2015), pp. 58-59.

8 I discuss the *Discourse* as part of the *Miscellanies* in a forthcoming essay "The Political Character of Jonathan Swift's *Miscellanies in Prose and Verse* (1711)," necessarily covering some of the same material as here. I wish to thank Dr Adrian Lashmore-Davies for his comments on my account of the *Discourse* in the 1711 *Miscellanies*.

> But whenever it comes to pass, that a popular Assembly, free from ... obstructions, and already possess'd of more Power, than an equal Balance will allow, shall continue to think they have not enough, but by cramping the Hand that holds the Balance, and by Impeachments or Dissentions with the Nobles, endeavour still for more; I cannot possibly see in the common course of things, how the same Causes can produce different Effects and Consequences among us, from what they did in *Greece* and *Rome*. (*Discourse*, p. 91)

In 1701, Swift was calling for the Commons to withdraw its impeachments of the Whig lords and more generally venting his indignation at the presumption of a Commons to encroach upon the King and Lords. The *Discourse* was anthologized in 1707, in a collection of Whig and Tory works, where it appears as a tract of the times, an artefact of the previous reign.[9] Reprinted in the *Miscellanies* of 1711, of course, the partisan work of 1701, divorced from its original polemical occasion, now just read as a work of anti-populist political-philosophical reflection and historical meditation on the traditional Tory theme of "*a Dominatio Plebis*, or Tyranny of the People" (*Discourse*, p. 50).[10] Placed at the beginning of the *Miscellanies*, the *Discourse* is implied to be a work consonant with the ideology of the current Tory government, for which Swift was propagandist.

But even as a Whig work in 1701, the *Discourse* was highly idiosyncratic. Its position on foreign policy and an international balance of power appears consonant with the Whig party line – the people recognize the threat from France, and the divisive conduct of the Commons in Parliament in impeaching Lords and constraining the King is threatening national security. Although the tract exhibits little of the Francophobia, strident warnings against popery, priestcraft, and Jacobitism, and adulation of William III characteristic of Whig productions, Swift's *Discourse* would seem to offer proleptic support for renewal of hostilities against Louis XIV and France, for what would be the War of the Spanish Succession, on the basis of balance-of-power alliances against France, and it offers measured praise of William III (see *Discourse*, pp. 76, 90-91).[11] But the dominant Whig line in the paper war of 1701 was populist, appealing to the people above their representatives in the Parliament, campaigning and petitioning against the Parliament, enunciating a democratic argument that

---

9 See *A Collection of State Tracts Publish'd during the Reign of King William III, Vol. III* (London: Printed in the Year 1707); Teerink and Scouten 478, p. 256; *Discourse*, ed. Ellis, pp. 185-86.

10 See also *Discourse*, pp. 9, 32.

11 Matthew Gertken, "Swift, Utrecht and Ireland," *Eighteenth-Century Ireland*, 30 (2015), 36-61 (pp. 44-46); and the same author's "Swift, Mottraye, and Charles XII of Sweden," *Swift Studies*, 32 (2017), 45-78 (p. 57).

the Parliament should be accountable to the people. The Tories in 1701 argued for the supremacy of Parliament and opposed the anarchy of appealing to the mob outside Parliament.[12] There is ambiguity or perhaps just incoherence in Swift's work. He may be read as saying that the legislature has an absolute unlimited Power, but also that it is not absolute, since the Power apparently remains in the body of the people who can resume it. But it is jarring in the context of 1701 that the main tenor of Swift's work is anti-populist. Swift is apprehensive of "the growing Power of the People" and he uses "*Tyranny*" of the "*People*" and "*Commons*" interchangeably (*Discourse*, pp. 44; 9, 32, 50). Swift's assertion in the opening of the tract of an "absolute unlimited Power" in the tripartite legislature of King, Lords, and Commons and the position that once original power is delegated it is irrevocable was the Tory position in the debate of 1701.[13] Such views reflect a post-Revolution Toryism reconstructed from Stuart absolutism, with supreme power now located in the sovereign legislature of the Crown-in-Parliament rather than in the Crown alone. The executive or administration was in the Crown (*Discourse*, pp. 1-5).[14] Swift distinguishes between the People and their elected representatives in Parliament. His appeal to the people is to "the Universal Bent and Current of a People" not to "the *bare Majority* of a few Representatives" (*Discourse*, p. 68). But "the Universal Bent and Current of the People" is something, apparently, that only the King and a patrician class or aristocratic elite can know. Swift's version of the Polybian mixed government is artfully monarchic and aristocratic. Polybius does not always say what Swift says that he does.[15] Polybius is used as a carapace for propagandistic purposes, and Polybius is useful for Swift in that in recommending a balanced mixed polity of the One, the Few, and the Many, he identifies as "the worst thing of all, mob rule."[16] The *Discourse*'s contention that "the Tyranny of the People" eventually ends in the tyranny "of a Single Person" is ancient

12 Mark Goldie, "Situating Swift's Politics in 1701," *Politics and Literature in the Age of Swift: English and Irish Perspectives*, ed. Claude Rawson (Cambridge: Cambridge University Press, 2010), pp. 31-51.

13 Goldie, "Situating Swift's Politics in 1701," pp. 39-41. For a reading of the tract as essentially Tory, see Lock, *Swift's Tory Politics*, pp. 146-61.

14 This view of the 'supreme power' as the legislative power lodged in the King and Parliament was of course the official Tory position defended at the Trial of Dr Henry Sacheverell in 1710; see Geoffrey Holmes, *The Trial of Doctor Sacheverell* (London: Eyre Methuen, 1973), VIII: "The Case for the Defence," especially pp. 182-84.

15 Downie, "Swift's *Discourse*: Allegorical Satire or Parallel History?," p. 28.

16 Polybius, *The Histories*, trans W. R. Paton, *et al.*, 6 vols (Cambridge, Massachusetts: Harvard University Press, and London, 2011 [1923]), III, 441 (Book VI, 57); in Swift's own copy of *Historiarum libri qui supersunt*, ed. Isaac Casaubon (Paris: H. Drouard, 1609), p. 499 (PASSMANN AND VIENKEN II, 1481-82). See also Marshall, *Swift and History*, p. 89.

(*Discourse*, p. 72).[17] But it is the great theme of the Tories of his day. The salient historical instance of the danger was the emergence of Cromwell out of the Puritan House of Commons – in Swift's later formulation, the "Tyranny of that Fanatick Anarchy."[18] The dangers of what is called in the *Discourse* a "*Tyranny of the People*" is Swift's usual default position in his political writing, though monarchical tyranny is a preoccupation, especially in late Swift, after the Hanoverian succession (*Discourse*, p. 32).

Swift could place the *Discourse* first in the *Miscellanies* because it had been shown to be ideologically a Tory work soon after its original publication. For Tory polemicists, Swift's *Discourse* had been a polemical gift, since its anti-populism and hostility to Protestant Dissent enabled them to convict the Whigs of inconsistency and hypocrisy. The Tory James Drake and Jacobite Charles Leslie criticized the *Discourse*. They both assumed that the work was by Bishop Gilbert Burnet, as is attested by their allusions to Burnet's political and theological tracts in their attacks on this new performance.[19] Swift wrote in his copy of Leslie's *New Association, Part II* that "Mr Lesley ... lays it to the Bp of Sarum Dr Burnet."[20] Drake detected absolutist tenets in Swift's account of the Crown's executive power in his version of the balanced mixed polity: "It is plain that the whole Power is in the *hand* that holds the Ballance." Drake finds that the "drift of all his Reasonings ... is to shew the Preferrableness of a Government by one or a few Persons, to a Government by many; that is, of an Absolute Monarchy, or an Aristocracy, to a Democracy, or a mixt Government, such as ours at present is."[21] Leslie also identified the anti-democratic character of the work. Indeed, the anti-populism of the tract reflects Leslie's own Bodinian and Filmerian political thought.[22] Exasperated by the inconsistency and incoherence of Whig populism, Leslie quotes the *Discourse*'s constitutional "Remedy" for the problem of popular encroachments from the Commons:

17 For example, see Plato, *Republic*, VIII, 544c-569c on "the transformation of a democracy into a tyranny" (*The Collected Dialogues of Plato*, eds Edith Hamilton and Huntington Cairns [Princeton: Princeton University Press, 1961], pp. 773-98 [798]; in Swift's own copy of *Platonis opera quæ extant omnia*, ed. J. Serranus, 3 vols [in 2] [{Paris}: Henricus Stephanus, 1578], p. 499 [PASSMANN AND VIENKEN II, 1438-40], II, 544-69).

18 *Prose Works*, XII, 264.

19 Goldie thinks Leslie thought it by Somers ("Situating Swift's Politics in 1701," p. 45). But Leslie's references to the author as a "Doctor" and to his career as a modern "*Vicar of Brey*" point to Burnet (*The New Association, Part II* [London: Printed and Sold by the Booksellers of London and Westminster, 1703], "Supplement," pp. 11, 13-14).

20 A. C. Elias, Jr, "Swift's Corrected Copy of *Contests and Dissensions*, with Other Pamphlets from his Library," *Philological Quarterly*, 75 (1996), 167-95 (p. 187).

21 [James Drake], *The Source of Our Present Fears Discover'd* (London: J. Nutt, 1703), pp. 52, 57.

22 See Lock, *Swift's Tory Politics*, pp. 157-61.

those "*to whom the rest of the Ballance is Entrusted, shou'd never give way so far to Popular Clamours*." Leslie welcomes the author's discovery of royalist absolutism, and jeers at the supposed author Gilbert Burnet: "Ah! *Doctor, Doctor*, Was this *Always* your *Doctrine*? Are you come to see it at last? And yet never *Mend*!"[23]

The anti-populism and hostility to the Commons in the *Discourse*'s politics has a provenance in Swift's High Church confession. Swift traces the origins of the contests and dissentions that have subverted the English mixed polity and led to Civil War and the military dictatorship of Cromwell to the rise of Puritanism. He writes:

> About the middle of Queen *Elizabeth*'s Reign, I take the Power between the Nobles and the Commons to have been in more equal Balance, than it was ever before or since. But then, or soon after, arose a Faction in *England*, which under the name of *Puritan*, began to grow Popular, by molding up their new Schemes of Religion with Republican Principles in Government; and gaining upon the *Prerogative*, as well as the *Nobles*, under several Denominations for the space of about sixty Years, did at last overthrow the Constitution, and according to the usual Course of such Revolutions, did introduce a Tyranny, first of the People, and then of a single Person. (*Discourse*, pp. 78-79)

Leslie commented: "This is a very Instructive Passage." Assuming that the work was by Burnet and alluding to Burnet's opposition to the Tory Occasional Conformity Bill of 1702 (which aimed at excluding Dissenters from public office), Leslie enquires: "What Reason the *Author* has since found out (except his being ever *In-consistent* with *Himself*) to Struggle so hard for letting the same *Faction* still have a *Share* in the *Ballance* of *Power*!"[24] Leslie found that despite its Whig provenance and appearances the essential grain of the work was unwhiggish. Swift's graphic anti-populist imagery (derived from Psalms 65:7) comparing the madness of the people to the raging of the sea would have been familiar to Leslie, since it was one of his favourite allusions, and one he had used in his first published Jacobite work, and uses in his answer to Swift's *Discourse* (*Discourse*, p. 80).[25]

---

23 [Leslie], *The New Association, Part II*. Added at the end of the pamphlet is a separately paginated "Supplement," dated "March 25. 1703;" the quotation is from the "Supplement," p. 11; see *Discourse*, p. 70. Extracts from Drake and Leslie are reprinted in *Discourse*, ed. Ellis, Appendices A-C, pp. 209-51.

24 [Leslie], *The New Association, Part II*, "Supplement," p. 12.

25 [Leslie], *An Answer to a Book, Intituled, The State of the Protestants in Ireland under the Late King James's Government* (London, 1692), p. 32; [Leslie], *The New Association, Part II*, "Supplement," p. 17.

Swift was 33 when the *Discourse* was published. He was certainly ambitious and possessed a sense of self-entitlement. He lacked perhaps experience and stature. But the personal chaplain to Lord Berkeley was not unreasonable in hoping for senior Church preferment. More than half of Anglican bishops appointed between 1689 and 1721 achieved the promotion by their thirty-ninth year.[26] Swift clearly thought the *Discourse* would advance his prospects with the Whigs. He reports that Lords Somers and Halifax, Bishop Burnet, and the Earl of Sunderland "were very liberal in promising me the greatest preferments I could hope for, if ever it came in their power."[27] Swift had not received preferment from Berkeley to the vacant deanery of Derry in 1700, and Swift's hostility to Ulster Dissenters and implacable support for the Church of Ireland's rights, if known to Berkeley, might have been a reason behind his being passed over for a more compliant safe Whig appointment.[28] The anti-Puritan 'Passage' in the *Discourse*, highlighted by Leslie, might indicate why the author of the *Discourse* did not receive senior clerical preferment from the Whigs when they did have power.

In the *Discourse*, addressing the problem of the influence "of *One* upon *Many*, which seems to be as great in a People *Represented*, as it was of old in the Commons *Collective*," Swift proposes a short way with the popular menace. He approves what Diodorus Siculus reports of Charondas the lawgiver who "provided a Statute, that whoever proposed any Alteration to be made, should step out, and do it with a Rope about his Neck." If the proposal was not generally approved, then "the Proposer" was "to be immediately *hang'd*." This would be an effectual way of "*taking off* (as the present Phrase is) those hot, unquiet Spirits, who disturb Assemblies, and obstruct Publick Affairs, by gratifying their Pride, their Malice, their Ambition, or their Avarice" (*Discourse*, pp. 86-87). The violence of Swift's pamphlet was remarked by Drake.[29] In its precise polemical moment of 1701, the unnamed targets were the Tory Commoners. But the menacing passage had other applications, which made it appropriate for the *Miscellanies* of 1711, where Whigs are Swift's satiric victims. The ringleaders of popular assemblies proposing to abolish old laws or establish new ones whom Swift wanted hanged were now Whigs soliciting for legislative repeal of the Test Act in favour of Dissenters, and Swift desired their impeachment. In 1708, Swift reports from London: "Here has the Irish Speaker [Alan Brodrick] been

26 *The Boulter Letters*, eds Kenneth Milne and Paddy McNally (Dublin: Four Courts Press, 2016), p. 23.

27 *Prose Works*, VIII, 119.

28 Woolley, "Swift and Lord Berkeley, 1699-1701: Berkeley Castle Swiftiana," p. 53.

29 *The Source of Our Present Fears Discover'd*, pp. 73-74, 77.

soliciting to get the Test Clause repealed by an Act here; for which I hope he will be impeached when [the Irish] Parliament meets again."[30] In *A Letter concerning the Sacramental Test*, Swift refers to the Speaker, Alan Brodrick, and to his brother Thomas Brodrick, "an honest *Bell-weather* of our House," who "had the Impudence some Years ago, in Parliament time, to shake my Lord Bishop of *Killaloo* by his Lawn Sleeve, and tell him in a threatning manner, *That he hoped to live to see the Day when there should not be one of his Order in the Kingdom*" (*Miscellanies*, p. 332). In the original edition, Swift adds a sentence proposing a short way with such parliamentary patriots as the Brodricks: "I can put him upon a much better way of serving his Countrey, which is to take some Course that himself and his *whole worthy Family* may be *Hang'd* tomorrow Morning."[31]

Concern over the manipulation of the populace and their representatives in the Commons prompts Swift in the *Discourse* to advance "a very unreasonable Paradox" that "the bribing of Elections, though a great and shameful Evil," is the necessary ill means the Crown has to counterbalance the pernicious influence of "popular Men" who for private ends obtain election by "servile Flatteries of the People" (*Discourse*, pp. 91-94). It was a startling acknowledgment of realpolitik in the 1701 Parliament. As a Country Whig member of the House of Commons, Sir Richard Cocks put it that "Bribery and corruption have been established and have taken firm root here." He noted how bribery used by the Old East India Company (the company supported by the Tories) was the occasion of the use of bribery by the New East India Company (supported by the Whigs) "to make a balance."[32] Cocks felt "that Athens, Rome and other popular governments owed the loss of their liberties and subversion of their constitutions to the largess and bounty ... bestowed by the candidates among the people."[33] But this fierce Country Whig opponent of corruption supported the impeached lords, and the peremptory political imperative of support for the King and his measures against the Tory Commoners.[34] In 1701, it was the Tories who were concerned that Williamite court influence through bribing at elections would corrupt parliamentary independence. Leslie read the *Discourse*'s justification for buying votes as totally undermining the whole Whig scheme of founding government upon election by the people. Swift's text was even capable of Jacobite application, since it exposed how William and his political managers courted support from Parliament. Leslie sardonically

30 Swift to Dean Stearne, 15 April 1708, *Correspondence*, ed. Woolley, I, 185.

31 *Prose Works*, II, 283.

32 *The Parliamentary Diary of Sir Richard Cocks, 1698-1702*, ed. D. W. Hayton (Oxford: Clarendon Press, 1996), pp. 66, 67.

33 Quoted in *The Parliamentary Diary of Sir Richard Cocks*, ed. Hayton, pp. xxviii.

34 *The Parliamentary Diary of Sir Richard Cocks*, ed. Hayton, pp. xlix, 105.

observed: "This is the *Bitterest* thing cou'd be said against the *Revolution*, as if it did not Proceed upon the General *Bent* and *Inclination* of the *People*; but only *Voted* by a Company of *Brib'd* Men; And cou'd stand no longer than the *People* were still *debarr'd* from the *Freedom* of their *Elections*."[35] Swift excised the compromising paragraph about bribing elections from the *Discourse* when it was reprinted in the *Miscellanies* of 1711. No doubt he felt that the recent election of a 'Church party' or Tory House of Commons showed that the people, for the moment, were not being swayed by enemies of the constitution in Church and State. Swift's deletion of the passage on bribery, however, was clearly a late decision (the cancelled passage is still in the British Library copy of the *Miscellanies*). He may have become aware that the practice was particularly deplored by Henry St John as a Whig court corruption.[36] It would have been embarrassingly impolitic for Swift, as the new author of the Tory *Examiner*, to be defending just such a corrupt practice. And as *Mr Examiner* Swift alludes to the *Discourse*, now included as the first essay in his *Miscellanies*, advancing a Tory revisionist understanding of the work's meaning. Swift's political warning about the evil of popular dissentions in 1701 had been heeded under Queen Anne and by the present Tory administration:

> Observing indeed some Time ago, that Seeds of Dissention had been plentifully scattered from a *certain Corner*; and fearing they began to rise and spread, I immediately writ a Paper on the Subject; which I treated with that Warmth, I thought it required: But the Prudence of those at the Helm soon prevented this growing Evil; and at present it seems likely to have no Consequences.[37]

But in 1701, Swift had accepted that the Crown's intervention was necessary to counter a corrupted Commons.

35 [Leslie], *The New Association, Part II*, "Supplement," p. 13.

36 On 10 November 1710, St John was wanting it observed "what a difference there is between the true strength of this nation and the fictitious one of the Whigs ... how much money must go to create a majority of the latter; on the other hand, take but off the opinion that the Crown is another way inclined, and the church interest rises with redoubled force, and by its natural genuine strength" (*Letters and Correspondence, Public and Private, of the Right Honourable Henry St. John, Lord Visc. Bolingbroke*, ed. Gilbert Parke, 4 vols [London: for G. G. and J. Robinson, 1798], I, 16-17). I am grateful to Dr Adrian Lashmore-Davies for this suggestion.

37 *The Examiner* (17 May 1711), in *Prose Works*, III, 153.

2

Aspects of Swift's *Discourse* were developed in his later work and had an afterlife in the writings of others. In the *Discourse*, Swift identifies indebtedness to creditors as an insidious cause of parliamentary corruption (*Discourse*, p. 42). His religious, economic, and political animus against usury became a theme of his later political writing, and informed his own later charities and lending practices. Hostility to usury is prominent in Tory polemic against the Williamite financial revolution and in their pacifist pamphlets throughout Anne's reign, as the work of James Drake and John Arbuthnot attests.[38] Swift uses the coinage "monied men" for the financiers, but it seems to be under-noticed in the scholarly commentary how explicit he is in attacking usury, and usurers called as such. But it was noticed by later writers such as William Cobbett, and by W. B. Yeats and Ezra Pound in the twentieth century, and indeed by Irish commentators on the global financial crisis of 2008 and subsequent Irish banking crisis and economic collapse, described as a 'Usury Crisis,' who invoke Swift. An editorial in *Church and State* of January 2011, for example, informs us:

> Jonathan Swift was a Tory Jacobite. He wrote a pamphlet which is credited with cutting short England's first Great War in the early 18th century. His opposition to the war was on the ground that it was being financed by National Debt, and that the increase in National Debt was bringing about a situation in which money would be the only value.[39]

In *Gulliver's Travels*, the King of Brobdingnag considers the "Management of our Treasury" and "such chargeable and extensive Wars" and asks Gulliver: "How a Kingdom could run out of its Estate like a private Person. He asked me, who were our Creditors? and, where we found Money to pay them?"[40] The answer, indeed, is found in *The Conduct of the Allies*: "The Answer is ready; We have been Fighting for the Ruin of the Publick Interest, and the Advancement of a Private. We have been fighting to raise the Wealth and Grandeur of a particular

---

38 [James Drake], *An Essay concerning the Necessity of Equal Taxes, and the Dangerous Consequences of the Encouragement Given to Usury among us of Late Years ... By the Author of the History of the Last Parliament* (London: Robert Gibson and Tho. Hodgson; sold by J. Nut, 1702); John Arbuthnot, *The History of John Bull*, eds Alan W. Bower and Robert A. Erickson (Oxford: Clarendon Press, 1976), on "*Usury*;" see especially pp. 15, 16, 36.

39 "The Usury Crisis," Editorial in *Church and State* (January 2011), Athol Books Magazine articles (<http://current-magazines.atholbooks.org/readers/full_article.php?article_id=77&title=The%20Usury%20Crisis>, accessed 23 January 2018).

40 *Gulliver's Travels*, ed. David Womersley (Cambridge: Cambridge University Press, 2012), pp. 185-86 (II, vi, 13).

Family; to enrich Usurers and Stock-jobbers; and to cultivate the pernicious Designs of a Faction, by destroying the Landed-Interest."[41] The "Continuance of the War" is imputed by Swift "to the Fears of the *Mony-changers*, lest their *Tables should be overthrown*" (invoking the great anti-usury text from the Gospel of St Matthew 21:12, where Jesus does precisely that to the moneychangers).[42] The pro-war Whig paper, the *Observator* of 29 November 1710, had taunted Swift's *Examiner* attacks on Marlborough pointing triumphantly to the success of Whig war aims in Marlborough's victories: "The *French* Standards and Colours that hang in *Westminster-Hall* as Trophies of his Conquests."[43] Swift is withering in the *Conduct*: "It will, no doubt, be a mighty Comfort to our Grandchildren, when they see a few Rags hang up in *Westminster-Hall*, which cost an hundred Millions, whereof they are paying the Arrears, and boasting, as Beggars do, that their Grandfathers were Rich and Great."[44] For Swift, it was the interest of usurers that had become the insidious priority in modern Britain since the Revolution. As the Whig *Observator* remarked in 1710: "I perceive twenty years past and the Revolution is a mighty Period with him ... 'tis from that time he deduces all our Calamities."[45] In Swift's ironic masterpiece of 1711 (written 1708), *An Argument against Abolishing Christianity*, the ultimate reason for why the legislature should not abolish England's nominal Christianity is the appeal to Mammon and the interest of the usurers. A parliamentary Act to abolish Christianity might lead to a fall in "the Bank, and *East-India* Stock" of "at least One *per Cent*," which is a great loss to endure just

41 *English Political Writings, 1711-1714: The Conduct of the Allies and Other Works*, eds Bertrand A. Goldgar and Ian Gadd (Cambridge: Cambridge University Press, 2008), p. 100. Compare similar passages: "It is the Folly of too many, to mistake the Eccho of a *London* Coffee-house for the Voice of the Kingdom. The City Coffee-houses have been for some Years filled with People, whose Fortunes depend upon the *Bank, East-India*, or some other Stock: Every new Fund to these, is like a new Mortgage to an Usurer, whose Compassion for a young Heir is exactly the same with that of a Stockjobber to the Landed Gentry" (p. 95). The new Tory ministry and its peace policy will be like a Steward to a "young extravagant Heir" who looks "into his Estate before things grew desperate, which made the Usurers forbear feeding him with Mony, as they used to do" (pp. 97-98).

42 *English Political Writings, 1711-1714: The Conduct of the Allies*, eds Goldgar and Gadd, p. 85.

43 *The Observator*, IX, no 92, 29 November-2 December 1710.

44 *English Political Writings, 1711-1714: The Conduct of the Allies*, eds Goldgar and Gadd, p. 97. Later Tory works echo this passage. Compare *A New Voyage to the Island of Fools* (London: John Morphew, 1713), p. 48: "great numbers of Colours and Standards ... lately taken from the Gauls in several memorable Battles ... *That never Trophies were purchas'd ... at the expence of so much Blood and Treasure*." See also Jeremy Black, "Foreign Policy and the Tory World in the Eighteenth Century," *Journal for Eighteenth-Century Studies*, 37 (2014), 285-97 (p. 286).

45 *The Observator*, IX, no 86, 8 November-11 November 1710.

for destroying Christianity (*Miscellanies*, p. 181). Swift in his Tory writings was clearly unprepared to support financing the war against France, or financing the maintenance of a standing army in Ireland against the Jacobite threat, if it meant benefiting usurers. A venomous instance of his loathing of usurers as corrupters of parliaments and nations is his gloating "Elegy on the Much Lamented Death of Mr Demar, the Famous Rich Usurer" (1720). According to this poem, the Irish nation was indebted to Demar: "Where'er he went he never saw his betters; / Lords, knights, and squires were all his humble debtors; / And under hand and seal, the Irish nation / Were forced to own to him their obligation."[46] Swift and usury is a subject in itself.

In the *Discourse*, Swift witnesses how the Commons is corrupted. Roman constitutional practice is idealized, where the People only meet occasionally and then only to vote and advise. As is well known, Swift supported annual parliaments, as did Old Whigs, Jacobites, and Irish patriots. Paradoxically, Swift's particular support for annual parliaments probably reflects the limited role he saw for them. Parliaments are there to advise and check the executive. Annual parliaments would prevent the corruption of standing parliaments, septennial parliaments, long parliaments. The distrust of elected parliaments in the *Discourse* reflects a continuity in Swift's political thinking. His contemporaneous but unfinished "History of England" (*c.*1700), covering the reigns of four kings – William II, Henry I, Stephen, and Henry II – displays this distrust. Swift wrote that he had been diverted from writing the "History," "chiefly by the indignation I conceived at the proceedings of a faction" that had led him to write the *Discourse of the Contests and Dissentions*.[47]

The account of the origins of the English Parliament in Swift's unpublished "History" accords with royalist and Tory historiography rather than with Whig parliamentarian accounts. The institution of parliament is said to have evolved over time and was not part of the pre-Conquest structure of the English polity. Popular assemblies were seldom called before Henry I's reign, and they were not superior to the Crown. Swift finds that from time immemorial "councils or assemblies were composed according to the pleasure of the prince who convened them, generally of nobles and bishops, sometimes were added some considerable commoners."[48] The "History" is usually read in relation to Temple's works and to historiography. The pamphlet wars of the early 1700s, however, show what was at stake in the history of these reigns, especially of King Stephen's. Swift's commentary on English history might be compared

46 *Poems*, ed. Rogers, pp. 214-15, ll. 15-18.

47 *Prose Works*, V, 11.

48 *Prose Works*, V, 35.

with Jacobite accounts of the dire consequences of deposing native hereditary kings in favour of foreigners. A notorious Jacobite pamphlet of 1703, *The Exorbitant Grants of William the III*, states:

> A Review of the *English* Chronicles will make it obvious to all People, that Foreigners and Usurpers have committed more Depredations here, than all the Hereditary Kings and Queens of *England*, &c. from the 1st of King *William* the First, to the last of *William* the 3d. and shew how our Ancestors labour'd against all such, as well in the Defence of their Liberties, as also to free the Nation from Insulting Strangers, as in the Case of *Stephen*, who having Usurp'd the Crown from the Empress *Mawde*, brought in the *Netherlanders*, and gave 'em large Territories in *England*, which so incens'd the Natives against *Stephen*, that as soon as he was dead, he was declar'd an Usurper, all his Grants revok'd, and the *Netherlanders* expell'd the Kingdom by King *Hen*. the Second.[49]

Swift's review of the chronicles accords attention to the controversial (in contemporary historiography and polemic) reign of Stephen, King of England from 1135-54. Stephen is clearly presented with William III in the lens. A nephew of the King, he is depicted as both a usurper and an elected king, intruded by a conspiracy, and "elected by those very persons who had so lately, and in so solemn a manner, more than once sworn fealty to another." He is a warmongering prince, who depredates the nation's treasure. Stephen is an historical parallel for William III with his "defective title," liberal distribution of lands to supporters, and employment of "*Flemings* in his wars" (William's Dutch guards). What brings satisfaction to subjects and quiet to the realm is the expulsion of foreigners.[50] The "History" laments the violation of oaths of allegiance and the disregard of hereditary right.[51] Swift considered publishing the "History" later in the Hanoverian era with a dedication to the Jacobite conspirator Karl, Count Gyllenborg, an appropriate dedicatee for a text containing such sentiments.[52]

49 *The Exorbitant Grants of William the III. Examin'd and Question'd: Shewing the Nature of Grants in Successive and Elective Monarchies ... and likewise Shewing that, where a Prince Hath No Hereditary Title, He Can Make No Hereditary Right* (London, 1703), p. 14. John Toland attributed the pamphlet to "*one* David Fitzgerald, *an* Irish *Papist*" ([John Toland], *High Church Display'd* [London, 1711], p. 204). For Whig answers, see *The Exorbitant Grants of William the III. Examin'd and Question'd ... with Reflections on Each Paragraph* (London: B. Bragg, 1703) and *Animadversions upon a Seditious Libel, Intituled, The Exorbitant Grants of William III. Examin'd and Question'd* (London: A. Baldwin, 1703).

50 *Prose Works*, V, 47-73 (pp. 48, 50, 72).

51 *Prose Works*, V, 63.

52 Ashley Marshall, however, finds the political content of the "History" "unlikely to have been seriously problematic" from the Government's view (*Swift and History*, p. 76, and pp. 71-73). The usual view in Swift studies is that the "History" "is written without any

The role of Parliament is also occluded in *A Project for the Advancement of Religion, and the Reformation of Manners: To the Countess of Berkeley,* first published in 1709, in *Gulliver's Travels,* and elsewhere. Swift's serious *Project* of authoritarian piety for the reform of the body politic is envisaged to be "in the Power of the Queen, without Interposition of the Legislature." Swift writes that what "[he] principally insist[s] on is a due Execution of the old" laws, "which lies wholly in the Crown, and in the Authority derived from thence" (*Miscellanies,* pp. 197, 225-26). The *Project* reflects the considerable power Swift is prepared to allow to the Crown, an absolutist bias critics noticed in the *Discourse.* In *Gulliver's Travels,* parliaments are hardly mentioned at all in the countries Gulliver visits. The primary focus is on the monarch and court.[53] In necromantic Glubbdubdrib in Book Three of the *Travels,* Swift offers another polemical classical parallel history in epitome. There is denunciation of modern parliaments. Gulliver "desired that the Senate of *Rome* might appear before me in one large Chamber, and a modern Representative, in Counterview, in another. The first seemed to be an Assembly of Heroes and Demy-Gods; the other a Knot of Pedlars, Pick-pockets, Highwaymen and Bullies." Swift attacks bribery and corruption. The modern English yeomanry "in selling their Votes, and managing at Elections have acquired every Vice and Corruption that can possibly be learned in a Court."[54]

One of Swift's last satires on affairs of state is an attack on a parliament, a poetic libel on the Irish House of Commons and the parliamentary attempt to remove tithes paid to the Church of Ireland.[55] *The Legion Club* of 1736 recalls the *Discourse* and the arguments against popular usurpation by the Many or the Commons. Swift reprises the terms of the 1701 controversy into this reprisal against an anticlerical Whig parliament. The poem reanimates the trope of 'legion' used in the controversy of 1701, especially Charles Leslie's deployment of it against Whig populism. Daniel Defoe's inflammatory *Memorial* of 1701, putting the views of the Kentish petitioners, had opposed the people to their Tory representatives in Parliament, threatening in conclusion: "Our Name is LEGION, and we are many."[56] The Whig self-characterization of the Many or the

evident political bias" (see Eugene Hammond, *Jonathan Swift: Irish Blow-In* [Newark: University of Delaware Press, 2016], p. 182).

53 See F. P. Lock, *The Politics of "Gulliver's Travels"* (Oxford: Clarendon Press, 1980), p. 37.

54 *Gulliver's Travels,* ed. Womersley, pp. 290-91, 304 (III, vii, 8, and III, viii, 12).

55 *The Legion Club* was published in a London miscellany in 1736 (*Poems,* ed. Rogers, pp. 550-56, and notes pp. 891-95; Stephen Karian, *Jonathan Swift in Print and Manuscript* [Cambridge: Cambridge University Press, 2010], pp. 133-65).

56 [Daniel Defoe], *Legion's Memorial* ([London, 1701]); *The Parliamentary Diary of Sir Richard Cocks,* ed. Hayton, pp. 126-27. The biblical phrase is from Mark 5:9.

people as 'Legion' was brilliantly accepted by Leslie, who applied the Gospel of St Luke: "And Jesus asked him, saying, What is thy name? And he said, Legion: because many devils were entered into him" (8:30). In *The New Association, Part II*, the pamphlet in which he had remarked on Swift's *Discourse*, Leslie attacks Whig populism and the Kentish petitioners. He writes: "The *Legion* which had so long *Possess'd* the Deluded *People*, with *Antimonarchical* and *Mob-Principles*" had "Produc'd a New *Crop* of *Devils*: Who are *Enter'd* into the *Herd* of *Swine*; We heard them lately *Grunt* from *Kent*."[57] In *The Legion Club*, and in his correspondence on the Irish Commons (where Swift refers to the *Legion Club* "putting 4l. a hogshead more duty on wine"),[58] the Dean happily reactivates Leslie's tropes against Whig populism in his animus against this Irish Whig parliament. Whether Swift was exorcizing his own demons in writing against Legion, since he had ostensibly been on the Whig side in 1701, he was now painting Whig populism and the House of Commons as a madhouse, a diabolical club for the demoniacally possessed.[59]

Swift's hostility to parliaments and anti-democratic animus in the *Discourse* was given a provocative Irish polemical charge in 1720. A passage from *A Discourse of the Contests and Dissentions* about the ruin resulting from a negligent people manipulated by a corrupted Commons was extracted by the Jacobite Tory printer Edward Waters and reprinted as *Hibernia's Passive Obedience*, published against the English Whig parliament's Declaratory Act of 1720.[60] The *Discourse*'s advocacy of a principle of aristocracy over the democratic principle sees its assimilation into Jacobite thought. The Chevalier Andrew Michael Ramsay's *Essay upon Civil Government ... with Observations on the Ancient Government of Rome and England*, which was published in French in 1721, the second French edition containing a dedication to the Pretender as King of Great Britain, translated into English and published in England in 1722 without the dedication, offers a Jacobite constitutional model of hereditary monarchy limited by law with an aristocratic senate. The work is explained by historians, reasonably enough, in relation to French absolutist political

57 [Leslie], *The New Association, Part II*, p. 36.

58 Swift and the Rev. Thomas Sheridan to Mrs. Whiteway, 28[-29] November 1735, *Correspondence*, ed. Woolley, IV, 240.

59 David Womersley, "'now deaf 1740': Entrapment, Foreboding, and Exorcism in Late Swift," *Politics and Literature in the Age of Swift: English and Irish Perspectives*, ed. Rawson, pp. 162-84 (176-82).

60 *Hibernia's Passive Obedience, Strain to Britannia* (Dublin: E. Waters, 1720). The extract is from the *Discourse*, p. 75.

philosophy.[61] But one of its possible English language sources, I suggest, is Swift's *Discourse*. Ramsay acknowledged his indebtedness to Swift's writings, and there was correspondence between them. Swift read Nathaniel Hooke's manuscript of the English translation of Ramsay's *Travels of Cyrus*, and his interest and attention to the manuscript and approbation of Ramsay's *Travels* was gratefully acknowledged by Ramsay in a letter to Swift of 1727.[62] In 1729, Ramsay tells Swift that "it is now many Years since I had the highest Esteem of your Genius and Writings."[63] Ramsay's later *Philosophical Principles of Natural and Revealed Religion* paraphrases *Gulliver's Travels* and the Swiftian passages are credited to "a modern humourist, well versed in the darkest side of human nature and of a very singular genius."[64] Ramsay's argument in the 1722 essay against popular government and the dangers of the Many upon the One and Few, his political model drawn from the exempla of Lycurgan Sparta and ancient Rome, and his hostility to parliaments and popular power with examples drawn from Athens and Rome, have similarities with Swift's *Discourse*.[65] Ramsay's history of the development of Parliament in England, like Swift's, gives the Commons a representative voice but not a deliberative one. The original constitutional order of monarch and aristocracy, Ramsay argues, had been altered by the increase of popular power. The consequences could eventually be seen in the emergence of Cromwell from the usurpation of the People upon the Crown and Lords, and Cromwell was a tyrant, more arbitrary and despotic than any monarch in Europe.

Swift's Whig *Discourse* has had an unwhiggish afterlife over the centuries. The *Discourse*, and Swift's other writings against parliaments and their corruption by usurers, are a presence in twentieth-century right-wing modernism, for example. A famous Irish case in point is W. B. Yeats's encounter with

---

61 See, for example, Doohwan Ahn, "From Greece to Babylon: The Political Thought of Andrew Michael Ramsay (1686-1743)," *History of European Ideas*, 37 (2011), 421-37; Andrew Mansfield, "The Wayward Political Apostle: Andrew Michael Ramsay," *International Journal of Humanities and Social Science*, 2, no 14 [special issue, July 2012], 79-88; and the same author's "Aristocratic Reform and the Extirpation of Parliament in Early Georgian Britain: Andrew Michael Ramsay and French Ideas of Monarchy," *History of European Ideas*, 40 (2014), 185-203; Scott Mandelbrote, "Ramsay, Andrew Michael," ODNB, accessed 22 March 2018.

62 BL, Add. MS 4805, fol. 162; *Correspondence*, ed. Woolley, III, 108.

63 BL, Add. MS 4805, fols 188, 189; *Correspondence*, ed. Woolley, III, 233.

64 D. G. Henderson, *Chevalier Ramsay* (London, *et al.*: Nelson, 1952), p. 137.

65 [Andrew Michael Ramsay], *An Essay upon Civil Government: Wherein Is Set forth, the Necessity, Origine, Rights, Boundaries, and Different Forms of Sovereignty. With Observations on the Ancient Government of Rome and England, according to the Principles of the Late Archbishop of Cambray. Translated from the French* (London: Randal Minshull, 1722).

Swift. This has been studied in detail, and his engagement with the *Discourse* may be briefly revisited here.[66] As his Rapallo notebooks and other sources attest, Yeats, from 1927 through the early 1930s, when he was in frequent contact with Ezra Pound, was reading Swift intensively. He described the *Discourse of the Contests and Dissentions* as Swift's "one philosophical work." He saw in it a rejection of the democratic principle for an aristocratic principle. According to Yeats, Swift proved "that Rome and Greece were destroyed by the war of the Many upon the Few." Swift "defines a tyranny as the predominance of the One, the Few, or the Many, but thinks that of the Many the immediate threat." The "tyranny of the Many produced that of Cromwell."[67] This Swiftian moral obsessed Yeats. In "An Horatian Ode upon Cromwell's Return from Ireland" of 1650, Andrew Marvell had described Cromwell as a "falcon" but still under the control, the servant, of the Parliament, the "Falc'ner."[68] It is interesting that in Yeats's famous "The Second Coming," an apocalyptic poem about the threat of bloody anarchy and the emergence of some bestial anti-Christ, we are told that the "falcon cannot hear the falconer."[69] In Yeats's "The Curse of Cromwell," a legacy of "Cromwell's house and Cromwell's murderous crew" is the extirpation of the aristocracy, and a new world where "money's rant is on."[70] Caesar figures in Swift's *Discourse* as a tyrant who uses his credit with the People to pull down the Nobles and subvert the Roman constitutional balance and liberty (*Discourse*, pp. 54, 57-59).[71] Yeats observes of Swift's *Discourse*:

66 There is a substantial corpus of work on Yeats's engagement with Swift, but see especially: Peter Faulkner, "Yeats and the Irish Eighteenth Century," *The Dolmen Press Yeats Centenary Papers, 1965*, ed. Liam Miller (Dublin: The Dolmen Press, 1968); Donald T. Torchiana, *W. B. Yeats and Georgian Ireland* (Evanston: Northwestern University Press, and London: Oxford University Press, 1966), especially pp. 120-67; Douglas N. Archibald, "*The Words upon the Window-Pane* and Yeats's Encounter with Jonathan Swift," *Yeats and the Theatre*, eds Robert O'Driscoll and Lorna Reynolds (New York: Maclean-Hunter Press, 1975), pp. 176-214; Robert Mahony, *Jonathan Swift: The Irish Identity* (New Haven and London: Yale University Press, 1995), especially pp. 144-47; R. F. Foster, *W. B. Yeats: A Life*, 2 vols (Oxford and New York: Oxford University Press, 1997-2003); Claude Rawson, "Savage Indignation Revisited: Swift, Yeats, and the 'Cry' of Liberty," in Claude Rawson, *Swift's Angers* (Cambridge: Cambridge University Press, 2014), pp. 239-67, 293-98. See also the remarks of Daniel Mulhall (then Irish Ambassador to Germany) in "Yeats, Swift, and Ireland's Contested Eighteenth Century," in *"The first wit of the age": Essays on Swift and his Contemporaries in Honour of Hermann J. Real*, eds Juhas, Müller, and Hansen, pp. 17-27.

67 W. B. Yeats, "Introduction to 'The Words upon the Window-Pane,'" in W. B. Yeats, *Explorations: Selected by Mrs W. B. Yeats* (London: Macmillan, 1962), pp. 351-52.

68 Andrew Marvell, *The Poems of Andrew Marvell*, ed. Nigel Smith (Harlow: Pearson Longman, 2007), pp. 267-79 (277-78, ll. 91, 96).

69 *The Collected Poems of W. B. Yeats*, 2nd ed. (London: Macmillan, 1950), p. 210.

70 *The Collected Poems of W. B. Yeats*, p. 350.

71 Marshall, *Swift and History*, p. 92.

"Whether the final tyranny is created by the Many – in his eyes all Caesars were tyrants – or imposed by foreign power, the result is the same. At the fall of liberty came 'a dark insipid period through all Greece' – had he Ireland in his mind also? – and the people became, in the words of Polybius, 'great reverencers of crowned heads.'"[72] Yeats understands from his reading of Swift that the Irish Ascendancy was naturally anti-Hanoverian. Swift is the inspiration for his censored poem "Crazy Jane on the King" with its refrain "May the Devil take King George."[73] Yeats finds in Swift hostility to popular and parliamentary democracy (which throws up tyrants like Cromwell), and hostility to foreign imposed tyranny. Swift is, for Yeats, the enemy of the tyranny of the Many and the tyranny of foreigners, as in Swift's sometimes monarcho-machic antipathy to Hanoverian crowned heads.

Yeats's recent modern biographer opines that Yeats at Rapallo in the later 1920s and early 1930s may have been "affected by the political atmosphere around him, and Pound's increasingly noisy admiration of Mussolini's authoritarian rule."[74] Yeats was certainly incorporating Swift's anti-democratic writing into his fascist vision at this time and into his vision of an independent Ireland under aristocratic leadership. He was struck by a particular Swiftian formulation in the *Discourse*, as indeed were Drake and Leslie back in 1703, writing in his Rapallo diary in 1930:

> Struck by this in Swift's *Discourse of the Contests and Dissentions between the Nobles and the Commons in Athens and Rome*. 'I think that the saying 'Vox populi vox Dei' ought to be understood of the universal bent and current of a people, not of the bare majority of a few representatives, which is often procured by little art, and great industry and application; wherein those who engage in the pursuits of malice and revenge, are much more sedulous than such as would prevent them' ... The whole essay leads up to Burke so clearly that one may claim that Anglo-Ireland re-created conservative thought as much in one as in the other. Indeed the *Discourse* with its law of history might be for us what Vico is to the Italians, had we a thinking nation.[75]

In the "Introduction to *The Words upon the Window-Pane*," his play about Swift, Yeats elides Swift's anti-democratic thinking in the *Discourse* and appropriation of Polybius into an approbation of Italian fascism, where the One is surrounded by an able Few guiding the Many.[76] Yeats, in Swift-infused poems

72 Yeats, *Explorations*, p. 353.
73 Foster, *W. B. Yeats*, II, 386-87.
74 Foster, *W. B. Yeats*, II, 397.
75 Yeats, *Explorations*, pp. 292-93.
76 Yeats, *Explorations*, p. 354; Foster, *W. B. Yeats*, II, 425.

such as "The Seven Sages," imagines an enlightened landed few, uncorrupted by money, guiding and reflecting the intuitive wisdom of the peasantry. Swift as Tory Examiner and as patriot Drapier is an exemplar, the guide of the people against the narrow interests of the financiers represented by the Whig faction. In 1939, Yeats recalled the *Discourse* again, and also a letter of Swift's to the Jacobite soldier Charles Wogan, when describing his imagined ideal Ireland as one where the masses would be shaped by the Few drawn from the Anglo-Irish Ascendancy and from the diasporic Jacobite gentry. Yeats writes:

> Although the Irish masses are vague and excitable because they have not yet been moulded and cast, we have as good blood as there is in Europe. Berkeley, Swift, Burke, Grattan, Parnell, Augusta Gregory, Synge, Kevin O'Higgins, are the true Irish people, and there is nothing too hard for such as these. If the Catholic names are few history will soon fill the gap. My imagination goes back to those Catholic exiled gentlemen of whom Swift said their bravery exceeded that of all nations.[77]

In Swift's one Whig political pamphlet, Yeats found an ally in his struggle against that capitalist middle-class materialist democracy which Yeats called "Whiggery."[78] Swift's literary-political legacy can be found on the Left and the Right in the nineteenth and twentieth centuries. He is a huge presence in H. G. Wells's scientific romances of the 1890s, for example. Features of Swift's writing have made him seem a literary precursor for the reactionary radicalism of the twentieth-century literary Right.[79] The *Discourse* contains some of these features: rhetorical violence, black humour, reactionary nostalgia for a world that has been lost but whose values should be cherished, hostility to a culture based on mammon and usury, contempt for parliaments, anti-democratic biases, and an animus against particular groups in society.

77 From "On the Boiler," "Ireland after the Revolution," in Yeats, *Explorations*, p. 442. See Swift to Charles Wogan, [July-] 2 August [1732], *Correspondence*, ed. Woolley, III, 514.

78 "The Seven Sages," *The Collected Poems of W. B. Yeats*, p. 272; Yeats, *Explorations*, p. 435.

79 On the literary Right, see Nicholas Hewitt, *Literature and the Right in Postwar France: The Story of the "Hussards"* (Oxford and Washington: Berg, 1996); Peter Wilkin, *The Strange Case of Tory Anarchism* (Faringdon: Libri Publishing, 2010).

Gregory Lynall
University of Liverpool

Swift among the Scientists, *ad infinitum*: Towards a History of Reading and Allusion

Abstract. This essay considers the afterlife of Swift's works amongst scientists and science writers, uncovering the contribution that reading Swift has made to the culture of science. In particular, it explores a tradition of Swiftian allusion, quotation, and critical engagement within scientific writing from the mid-eighteenth century to the present day, and shows how such remediations have supported the social acceptance (or rejection) of ideas, the construction of professional and intellectual identities, and the cultivation of a popular audience for the sciences. Swiftian allusion has also been deployed by those critical of science, who have found in Swift's caricatures provocative models for their own satiric figurations. Having remained part of the imaginative currency of scientific discourse for nearly three hundred years, references to Swift and his works can provide insights into the changing relationship between the sciences and humanities over this period.

Michael Faraday's Royal Institution Christmas lectures of 1848 (published as *The Chemical History of a Candle*, 1861) are a landmark in the popularization of the natural sciences. Faraday takes the unassuming theme of the burning of a candle to explain the fundamentals of chemistry and physics. Along the way, he makes reference to a handful of scientists, including John Tyndall, Humphry Davy, and Isaac Newton, but significantly only one 'literary' author. For Faraday, carbonic black smoke "brings to mind that old employment which Dean Swift recommended to servants for their amusement, namely, writing on the ceiling of a room with a candle" to "shew [their] Learning."[1] Faraday's allusion to *Directions for Servants* (1745) is itself a moment of "candle-writing," revealing his own literary sensibility whilst seeking to enliven his science with a passing reference to a text he presumably thought his audience would know. But how unique is Faraday as a scientist reader of Swift? What contribution has the reading of Swift made to the practice or writing of science? In particular, have Swiftian allusions and quotations helped scientists support their own or

1 Michael Faraday, *The Chemical History of a Candle: Sesquicentenary Edition*, ed. Frank A. J. L. James (Oxford: Oxford University Press, 2011), p. 23 (Lecture II); Swift, *Directions to Servants*, in *Prose Works*, XIII, 9-10.

 | DOI:10.30965/9783846763971_025

scrutinize others' work, aided them in the construction of scientific identities, and given them licence to adopt satiric or ironic modes?[2]

Much has been uncovered regarding Swift's understanding of, and relationship with, the forms of knowledge which would develop into and become known as the natural sciences. This work has included tracing Swift's reading of 'scientific' texts, his acquaintance and friendships with natural philosophers, mathematicians and others, and the social and political contexts which defined his response to natural knowledge.[3] Almost nothing has been said, however, regarding the afterlife of Swift's writing amongst scientists and science writers, unless we include Dr Arbuthnot, who found "the part of [*Gulliver's Travels* with] the projectors ... the least Brilliant."[4] Three hundred and fifty years since his birth (and Arbuthnot's, incidentally), it seems appropriate to assess Swift's legacy, including within the sciences: disciplines which have transformed and to some extent defined modernity. This essay, therefore, will explore the presence of Swift's works, from their publication until the present day, within the intellectual and cultural life of British science (with some references to further afield). I also include writers who were not themselves practitioners of science, but have called upon the writing of Swift when engaged in scientific debate or in popularizing scientific discoveries and theories.

Science and the scientist have long been considered "targets" of Swift's satires. Studying the responses of the supposed satiric "victims" of these works enables us to consider the agency of Swift's satire (whether or not the author himself intended it to vex or reform). Of course, science as we know it did not exist in Swift's time (knowledge was organized differently then), and the term "scientist" was coined in 1834 by William Whewell.[5] Indeed, given the evidence collected below, one might even (cautiously) argue that the ways in which science writers have remediated the works of Swift have played their own small part in the demarcation and professionalization of the practice and discourse of science, or have at least reflected and consolidated those social processes. As

2 The term "allusion" encompasses various kinds of intertextuality; see Gregory Machacek, "Allusion," *PMLA*, 122 (2007), 522-36. Where possible, Swift's influence upon prose style has been identified, although this kind of analysis is notoriously difficult.

3 See especially Marjorie Nicolson and Nora M. Mohler, "The Scientific Background of *Voyage to Laputa*" and "Swift's 'Flying Island' in the *Voyage to Laputa*," *Annals of Science*, 2 (1937), 299-334 and 405-30, and Gregory Lynall, *Swift and Science: The Satire, Politics, and Theology of Natural Knowledge, 1690-1730* (Houndmills, Basingstoke, Hampshire: Palgrave Macmillan, 2012).

4 Arbuthnot to Swift, 5 November 1726, *Correspondence*, ed. Woolley, III, 44. See Lynall, *Swift and Science*, pp. 116-17.

5 [William Whewell], "Review of Mary Somerville, *On The Connexion of the Physical Sciences*," *The Quarterly Review*, 51 (1834), 58-61 (p. 59).

we will see, distancing themselves from the Laputans, who characteristically dabble in "Matters where [they] have least Concern,"[6] has enabled the specialized scientist (particularly during the nineteenth century) to assert professionalism and rationality.

The continued popularity of *Gulliver's Travels* as a world 'classic' has ensured that Swift's satire has remained part of the imaginative currency of scientific discourse, contributing to a well-established and ongoing conversation about the status of the sciences and humanities. Reception history over several centuries is rarely pursued in literature and science studies, primarily because there are very few books and authors with the kind of wider cultural longevity viable for such research: *Frankenstein* is a notable exception.[7] Nevertheless, the history of allusion traced in this essay suggests that the sustained afterlife of literary texts within the history of science offers a unique perspective on the changing relationship between science and culture, and has the potential to change critical views of the original work.

Little evidence survives regarding what scientists thought and felt in the act of reading Swift, but their allusions leave a trace of how they interpreted and positioned themselves in relation to his satires. Perhaps more importantly, they provide an insight into the expectations of science audiences at a particular moment, and reflect the changing relationship between literary and scientific writing (if we can indeed make those distinctions). There is no 'common scientist reader' of Swift, nor an "interpretive community" in the Fishian sense[8] (especially because this essay considers a wide historical range), but there are some identifiable general trends in how science writers respond, and what these responses reveal about their attitudes to the source material. We can see, for instance, that Swift's writing is wielded variously as a repository of animus, a guarantor of writerly authority, and a source of tropic creativity. Unfortunately, little is known about which editions of Swift's works were read by the scientists and science writers included in this study, although in a small number of cases reading notebooks and library catalogues are extant

6 *Gulliver's Travels*, ed. David Womersley (Cambridge: Cambridge University Press, 2012), p. 236. Further references are to this edition and appear in parentheses within the text.

7 See especially Jon Turney, *Frankenstein's Footsteps: Science, Genetics, and Popular Culture* (New Haven, Connecticut, and London: Yale University Press, 1998). Since at least Gillian Beer's *Darwin's Plots: Evolutionary Narrative in Darwin, George Eliot and Nineteenth-Century Fiction* (Cambridge: Cambridge University Press, 1983), the field of literature and science has acknowledged the influence of literary upon scientific writing in its structures, metaphors, and modes.

8 See Stanley Fish, *Is there a Text in this Class? The Authority of Interpretive Communities* (Cambridge, Massachusetts: Harvard University Press, 1980).

(Charles Darwin's being a prime example).[9] Therefore, despite the emphasis on the material condition of the book within the history of reading, there is only a limited possibility of considering its effects here. We should also acknowledge that some scientists' interests in Swift neither related only to his representations of their profession, nor extended to a belief that his fictions could illustrate their scientific ideas. Instead, they have appreciated his writings in a variety of ways, not just as scientists. For instance, several of Benjamin Franklin's parodies and satires are clearly indebted to Swift, although they do not engage with natural philosophy *directly*: "Meditation on a Quart Mugg" (1733) joins "A Meditation upon a Broomstick" (1701) in parodying Robert Boyle's *Occasional Reflections* (1665); his astrological hoax *Poor Richard* (1743) is heavily indebted to the *Bickerstaff Papers* (1708), and *A Defense of the Rev. Mr. Hemphill's Observations* (1735) concludes with insect analogies reminiscent of the fable of the Spider and the Bee.[10] The physicist John Tyndall, like his father (the fervent Protestant John Tyndall, Sr), was fascinated by, but sought to refute the doctrine of transubstantiation, and this is probably one reason why a copy of the *Tale* was passed between them, with many "choice portions" marked by his father.[11] Another physicist, David Brewster, was (as a biographer of Sir Isaac Newton) only interested in Swift as an acquaintance of Catherine Barton, Newton's step-niece.[12] Charles Darwin's daughter, Henrietta Litchfield, reported that "every evening for many years" her parents would play backgammon, and when doing badly her father would often invoke the *Journal to Stella*

9 Darwin read the *Travels*, Hawkesworth's three-volume edition of the *Letters* (1766), "A Tale of a Tub" (generally thought to be Swift's, not Jonson's), Walter Scott's life of Swift (1814), and "Swift Stella's Journal" (Edinburgh, 1824). See Appendix IV: "Darwin's Reading Notebooks," *The Correspondence of Charles Darwin*, eds Frederick Burkhardt, *et al.*, 20 vols to date (Cambridge: Cambridge University Press, 1985-date), IV, 461, 462, 465, 476.

10 See "Meditation on a Quart Mugg," *Pennsylvania Gazette*, 19 July 1733, in *Benjamin Franklin: Writings*, ed. J. A. Leo Lemay (New York: The Library of America, 1987), pp. 216-17; *A Defense of the Rev. Mr. Hemphill's Observations* (Philadelphia: B. Franklin, 1735); [Richard Summers], *Poor Richard, 1743: An Almanack for the Year of Christ 1743* (Philadelphia: B. Franklin, 1743); and J. A. Leo Lemay, *The Life of Benjamin Franklin*, 3 vols (Philadelphia, Pennsylvania: University of Pennsylvania Press, 2006-9), I, 108, 264, 363; II, 72-74, 117, 131-32, 173-80, 211, 504, 523, 527, 538-39, 543-44, 560; III, 180, 352, 575.

11 John Tyndall to John Tyndall, Sr, 3 August 1841, *The Correspondence of John Tyndall*, eds James Elwick, Bernard Lightman, and Michael S. Reidy, 2 vols (London: Pickering and Chatto, 2014), I, 127 (and see I, 82-83, 84-85).

12 See Sir David Brewster, *Memoirs of the Life, Writings, and Discoveries of Sir Isaac Newton*, 2 vols (Edinburgh: Constable, *et al.*, 1855), II, 278, 492-95.

by exclaiming "bang your bones."[13] Darwin, however, would also draw upon Swift in his scientific writing, as we will see.

By 'science writing,' I do not mean a single genre. Swift appeared in various kinds of writing related to science: original essays and monographs, articles and books for a popular audience, reviews and opinion pieces in specialist science journals and more general publications, private correspondence, and public lectures. Transported into works of science, Swift's words, ideas, and complex rhetorical manoeuvrings are divorced from not only their original text, but also the generic and stylistic context in which that text operated. There is, for instance, a limit on how ironic one can be within a work of original (or even, popular) science. Whilst Swift's writings at times seem to be intentionally designed to undermine their own authority through multiple ironies, a writer of science is (to put it mildly) unlikely to bring into question the truth of their discourse, given the importance of representation to the cultural legitimation of scientific knowledge.[14] Swift's satiric and ironic subtlety might also be lost through misinterpretation or misplaced emphasis. One popular physics writer recently, for instance, argued that in the *Travels* "Swift goes into excruciating detail" and "really belabors the point" regarding numerical exactitude, with no mention that this is done to parody empirical and realistic modes of description, nor that it is Swift's narrator, not Swift himself, who narrates in this way.[15] Therefore, whilst Swiftian ideas might be adopted verbally, they are seldom manifested stylistically or structurally. Nevertheless, their deployment invariably reveals a deconstructive impulse which challenges the assumptions of their discourse, or registers an anxiety about the fragile authority of scientific knowledge (or its value to human life more generally).

In nineteenth-century Britain especially, there were strong connections between literary culture and organized science, and this was particularly apparent in the number of figures from the arts who engaged enthusiastically with scientific institutions.[16] The audiences for popular science and literature were evidently similar, and in the drive to popularize their new knowledge,

---

13 Henrietta Litchfield, ed., *Emma Darwin, A Century of Family Letters, 1792-1896*, 2 vols (London: John Murray, 1915), II, 221. For "bang your bones," see, for instance, *Journal to Stella. Letters to Esther Johnson and Rebecca Dingley, 1710-1713*, ed. Abigail Williams (Cambridge: Cambridge University Press, 2013), p. 91 (Letter 11 [14 December 1710]).

14 See especially Steven Shapin, "Pump and Circumstance: Robert Boyle's Literary Technology," *Social Studies of Science*, 14 (1984), 481-520.

15 Dave Goldberg, *The Universe in the Rearview Mirror: How Hidden Symmetries Shape Reality* (New York: Dutton, 2013), p. xix.

16 See Martin Willis, "Scientific Cultures and Institutions," *The Routledge Research Companion to Nineteenth-Century British Literature and Science*, eds John Holmes and Sharon Ruston (London: Routledge, 2017), pp. 30-40 (30).

scientists would draw upon literary sources as explanatory models or forms of critique. Shakespeare, Milton, Wordsworth, and Tennyson were probably the most popular literary authors, but Swift was also held in high esteem.[17] Alluding to such writers would both enliven their discourses with shared cultural reference points, and assert a literariness that belies the caricature of the narrow-minded scientist. As the passage from Faraday demonstrates, Swiftian allusions were not limited to the *Travels*. The nineteenth-century borrowings from Swift suggest in particular an audience au fait with lots of his writing and therefore not alienated by such literary references. They seem to draw upon a shared knowledge and understanding of Swift's works or, in the case of short, aphoristic passages from his more obscure writings, they assume that the name of Swift guarantees gnomic wisdom (an example of the Foucauldian "author function").[18] Indeed, nowadays, Swift is most likely to appear in a scientific paper in the form of an aphoristic quotation, often positioned as an epigraph, lending rhetorical weight to a paper from the offing.[19] Sometimes a science writer might put forward a "modest proposal," acknowledging the Swiftian origin of the phrase.[20] Swift's writing has also continued to contribute to scientific debate indirectly, through allusion within and/or broader influence upon later 'literary' works, including Thomas Carlyle's *Sartor Resartus* (1836), H. G. Wells's scientific romances of the 1890s, Derek Mahon's "St. Patrick's Day" (1999), Margaret Atwood's *Oryx and Crake* (2003), and (perhaps) Mary Shelley's *Frankenstein* (1818).[21]

---

17 A survey of the journal *Nature* between 1845 and 1900 finds the *name* of Shakespeare cited approximately 120 times, Milton 50, Tennyson 50, Wordsworth 25, and Swift 20 (although Swift's works and characters are likely to be cited without the author's name). *Nature*'s title page bore an epigraph from Wordsworth's sonnet "A Volant Tribe of Bards on Earth are Found" (1823) from the first issue (4 November 1869) until 1958; see Melinda Baldwin, *Making "Nature": The History of a Scientific Journal* (Chicago: University of Chicago Press, 2015), p. 33.

18 See Michel Foucault, "What Is an Author?" *Textual Strategies: Perspectives in Post-Structuralist Criticism*, ed. and introd. Josué V. Harari (Ithaca, New York: Cornell University Press, 1979), pp. 141-60 (148).

19 See, for instance, quotations from Swift in Frank M. van Bockxmeer, "ApoE and ACE Genes: Impact on Human Longevity," *Nature Genetics*, 6 (January 1994), 4-5 (p. 4), and Stephen Jay Gould, *The Structure of Evolutionary Theory* (Cambridge, Massachusetts: Harvard University Press, 2002), p. 53. On epigraphs, see Gerard Genette, *Paratexts: Thresholds of Interpretation*, trans. Jane E. Lewin (Cambridge: Cambridge University Press, 1997), pp. 156-60.

20 See DeWitt Stetten, "A Parable on Recombination," *Nature*, 266 (7 April 1977), 488.

21 See especially H. G. Wells, "Preface," in *The Scientific Romances* (London: Gollancz, 1935 [1933]), pp. vii-x (viii-ix). Shelley read *Gulliver's Travels* over several nights in November 1816, when she was working on her most famous novel, and curious parallels have been

One poetic passage from Swift has achieved a significant afterlife in particular. When reviewing a book on the idea of each particle perhaps holding a world in itself, the mathematician Augustus de Morgan (1806-71) adapted and extended the most famous lines of *On Poetry: A Rhapsody* (1733), becoming a kind of parasite himself:

> Great fleas have little fleas upon their backs to bite 'em,
> And little fleas have lesser fleas, and so *ad infinitum*.
> And the great fleas themselves, in turn, have greater fleas to go on;
> While these again have greater still, and greater still, and so on.[22]

In keeping with this trope of derivation generating derivatives itself, in his ground-breaking book on *Weather Prediction by Numerical Process* (1922), the meteorologist Lewis Fry Richardson (1881-1953) explained fractal wind patterns by remarking "big whirls have little whirls that feed on their velocity, and little whirls have lesser whirls and so on to viscosity – in the molecular sense."[23] Richardson does not cite de Morgan or Swift: he assumes that his readership are aware of the lines he imitates.[24] More recently, when Richard Dawkins quotes *On Poetry*, he tries to lambaste its (intentional) hypermetrics prosodically: "Swift's scansion ... is (surprisingly) so ungainly that we can understand why Augustus De Morgan came behind for another bite."[25]

---

suggested regarding the books' use of size, stasis, and ugliness. See 11, 13, 14, 15 November 1816, in *The Journals of Mary Shelley, 1814-1844*, eds Paula R. Feldman and Diana Scott-Kilvert, 2 vols (Oxford: Oxford University Press, 1987), I, 145-46, Philip Stevick, "*Frankenstein* and Comedy," *The Endurance of "Frankenstein": Essays on Mary Shelley's Novel*, eds George Levine and U. C. Knoepflmacher (Berkeley, Los Angeles, London: University of California Press, 1979), pp. 221-39 (225, 234-35), and Denise Gigante, "Facing the Ugly: The Case of *Frankenstein*," *ELH*, 67 (2000), 565-87 (pp. 573-74).

22 Augustus de Morgan, "Review of Nicholas Odgers, *The Mystery of Being; or Are Ultimate Atoms Inhabited Worlds?* (Redruth and London, 1863)," *A Budget of Paradoxes* (London: Longmans, Green, and Co., 1872), p. 377. For other allusions to Swift, see pp. 15, 79-80. See *On Poetry: A Rhapsody*, in *Poems*, ed. Rogers, p. 531, ll. 353-56.

23 Lewis Fry Richardson, *Weather Prediction by Numerical Process* (Cambridge: Cambridge University Press, 1922), p. 66.

24 *On Poetry: A Rhapsody* (often alongside Morgan's poem) continues to be quoted in scientific writing. See Ian Stewart, "Big Whorls Do Have Little Whorls," *Nature*, 338 (2 March 1989), 18-19 (p. 18); R. S. Siew, "Microbiology: Millennium Bug," *Nature*, 398 (1 April 1999), 376, and Brian G. Wybourne, "The Small and the Large in Physics," *Symmetry and Structural Properties of Condensed Matter*, eds T. Lulek, B. Lulek, and A. Wal (Singapore: World Scientific Publishing, 2003), pp. 3-8 (3, 8).

25 Richard Dawkins, *The Ancestor's Tale: A Pilgrimage to the Dawn of Life* (London: Weidenfeld and Nicolson, 2016 [2004]), p. 615.

Dawkins's pretensions at literary criticism aside, allusions to Swift in more recent scientific texts seem to signal not the embeddedness of the literary within scientific culture, but their dissimilarity. A relatively staid discussion of the MMR-autism controversy, for instance, quotes and footnotes *The Examiner* (that "*Falshood flies*, and *Truth* comes *limping* after"), which seems somewhat obtrusive stylistically, although its sentiment is not unwelcome within the debate itself (and is from a writer who was indeed concerned about the production of 'bad science').[26] Such quotations suggest a conscious need to communicate their science using discourses from outside the specialized discipline, including a shared literary heritage, which in its common frame of reference attempts to bridge the gap between elite scientist and general reader.

1. Outdoing Laputa

One of the first great communicators of Enlightenment natural philosophy was the Venetian polymath Francesco Algarotti (1712-64), whose *Newtonianism for the Ladies* (1737) did much to disseminate Newton's ideas and the culture of polite science across Europe. It was also the first popular science book to acknowledge the cultural penetration of *Gulliver's Travels*. This is perhaps not surprising: Algarotti was a big admirer of Swift, translating the *Tritical Essay* (under the title *Saggio tritico intorno alla facoltà della mente umana* [1745]) (although no copy of the volume is extant), and in his letters celebrating the Dean as "the English Lucian" and a man of "salty wit."[27]

Written as dialogues between the Marchioness of *E*--- and her male tutor, *Newtonianism for the Ladies* turns to the first two voyages of Gulliver when seeking to explain physical and perceptual relativism,[28] but also draws upon Laputa when considering cosmology. The Marchioness paraphrases Book III when she admits to being put into "terrible Apprehensions" through learning that "such a Quantity of Light should continually proceed from the Sun" and will perhaps run out. Her tutor almost predictably asks, "Have not you some Inclination ... to the learned Melancholy of the Inhabitants of *Dean Swift*'s

26 E. Fombonne and E. H. Cook, Jr, "MMR and Autistic Enterocolitis: Consistent Epidemiological Failure to Find an Association," *Molecular Psychiatry*, 8 (2003), 133-34; *The Examiner*, 14 (9 November 1710), in *Prose Works*, III, 11.

27 Flavio Gregori, "The Italian Reception of Swift," *The Reception of Jonathan Swift in Europe*, ed. Hermann J. Real (London: Thoemmes Continuum, 2005), pp. 17-56 (26).

28 Francesco Algarotti, *Sir Isaac Newton's Philosophy Explain'd for the Use of the Ladies*, trans. Elizabeth Carter, 2 vols (London: for E. Cave, 1739), I, 181, 66. Further quotations from this work are given in parentheses within the text.

flying Island?" and soon after repeats his comparison of her fears to "those of the *Laputian* school" (I, 39-40, 41, 42). Algarotti thereby introduces the Laputans as a paradigm against which natural philosophers should measure their potential for "astronomically induced panic."[29]

To reassure the Marchioness, the tutor brings forth a torrent of theories regarding the source of the Sun's energy:

> Atomists ... will find you a Method to recruit the Sun with that Facility which a Philosopher is Master of, who knows how to make all Nature subservient to his Schemes. They will make the Seeds of Light and Heat ... continually return back again into the Sun ... We will call certain Systems to our Assistance which will lend us Comets that from Time to Time shall fall into the Sun and afford him fresh Supplies: And if this be not sufficient, we will have Recourse to some Philosopher, who may find Means to make a Star fall into him ... Will you have any more? No, no, said she, the one half of these Things is sufficient to dissipate the Fears of a *Laputian* himself. (I, 41-42)

The tutor's uncritical faith in human "Systems" which will "make all Nature subservient" undermines an argument intended to set the Marchioness's mind at rest. The Swiftian allusion places an ironic frame around the passage, presumably intentional, given Algarotti's admiration for the Dean.

Later in the century, in the revolutionary atmosphere of the 1790s, Swift's satires were granted a place of more reactionary import. Conservative thinkers associated Enlightenment chemistry with radical politics and theology, and vice versa.[30] In so doing, they drew upon Swiftian tropes (themselves adaptations of Henry More's attacks on the hermeticist Thomas Vaughan)[31] which diagnosed the pursuit of pneumatical chemistry as a kind of enthusiasm. The "deep-seated affinity" Edmund Burke felt for Swift is well known,[32] and in his *Reflections upon the Revolution in France* (1790) he replicates the *Tale*'s pneumatical metaphors to characterize radical dissent as producing the "wild *gas*" of liberty. Burke also attributes the poor state of the French economy to its being "under the special direction of the learned academicians of Laputa

29 Lynall, *Swift and Science*, p. 90.

30 See especially Jan Golinski, *Science as Public Culture: Chemistry and Enlightenment in Britain, 1760-1820* (Cambridge: Cambridge University Press, 1992), p. 152.

31 See Phillip Harth, *Swift and Anglican Rationalism: The Religious Background of "A Tale of a Tub"* (Chicago and London: The University of Chicago Press, 1961), pp. 60-63, 66-67, 109-10.

32 See especially Carole Fabricant, "Colonial Sublimities and Sublimations: Swift, Burke, and Ireland," *ELH*, 72 (2005), 309-37 (p. 320).

and Balnibarbi."[33] As the decade progressed, advocates of enlightened science found themselves the subject of similar Swiftian attacks.

Between 1799 and 1802, at the Pneumatic Institution in Bristol, the physician Thomas Beddoes – together with a young chemist by the name of Humphry Davy – extolled the virtues of breathing nitrous oxide for human health, and inferred that the gas's effects (in providing a kind of spiritual transport) demonstrated a materialist basis for human emotions and perceptions. Reactionary thinkers, such as those who contributed to the *Anti-Jacobin Review*, were worried about the atheistical implications of this research, and drew upon the *Tale* and *Travels* in condemning Beddoes and Davy as "enthusiasts" fuelled by Enlightenment science.[34] The pertinence of these caricatures was not lost on the targets themselves, with Davy calling himself "a little of an enthusiast."[35]

Whilst these similitudes – which associated therapeutic pneumatics with social, political, and theological improprieties – were easy for the conservative satirists to deploy, the level of their Swiftian impersonation was significant, indicating a deep veneration for the *Tale*, and a recognition of its satirical potency. The anonymous *The Sceptic* (1800) caricatures Beddoes via the figure of the mountebank Dr Thistleton, "a dashing empiric of the new school, – called the Æolists, – or the quacks-pneumatic."[36] Like the "Polite Nation of *Laplanders*" in the *Tale* who "buy their *Winds* by wholesale" and "retail them,"[37] these new Æolists "brew quantities of *air*, or *gases*" and "retail [them] by the *bladder-full*" whilst publishing "wonderful accounts of wonderful cures, effected by

33 Edmund Burke, *Reflections on the Revolution in France* (London: J. Dodsley, 1790), pp. 8, 197. See Ronald Paulson, *Representations of Revolution, 1789-1820* (New Haven: Yale University Press, 1983), pp. 57-59. See also *A Letter from the Right Honourable Edmund Burke to a Noble Lord* (London: J. Owen, 1796), pp. 62, 65-66.

34 See Golinski, *Science as Public Culture*, p. 172, and Golinski, "The Literature of the New Sciences," *The Cambridge History of English Romantic Literature*, ed. James Chandler (Cambridge: Cambridge University Press, 2009), pp. 527-52 (542-43).

35 Royal Institution MSS, Humphry Davy papers, 20/b, 157, by courtesy of the Royal Institution of Great Britain. Davy was himself interested in the problem of "distinguishing genuine religious inspiration from superstition or enthusiasm." See Jan Golinski, *The Experimental Self: Humphry Davy and the Making of a Man of Science* (Chicago: The University of Chicago Press, 2016), p. 38.

36 Anon., *The Sceptic* (London: E. Peart, 1800), p. 62. Beddoes dedicated almost an entire essay to Swift's mental "disposition," whose "striking peculiarities" he attributed to obsessive masturbation. See Thomas Beddoes, *Hygëia: or, Essays Moral and Medical, on the Causes Affecting the Personal State of our Middling and Affluent Classes*, 3 vols (Bristol: R. Phillips, 1803), III, 187, 193-94, 195-96.

37 *A Tale of a Tub and Other Works*, ed. Marcus Walsh (Cambridge: Cambridge University Press, 2010), p. 104. Further quotations are from this edition, and references are given in parentheses within the text.

breathing so many bladders full of air a day."[38] Swift's satirical conflation of sectarian enthusiasm, radical Whiggery, mental illness, and pneumatical chemistry in Section VIII becomes particularly appropriate when applied nearly a century later to those who literally sell their gases for supposed therapeutic uses.[39] *The Sceptic*'s attack on Beddoes's suspected materialism, meanwhile, updates galvanically the parodic neuroanatomy of Section IX and the *Mechanical Operation*: "They [the Æolists] assure us that the brain is an electrical machine; the nerves conductors; and volition of course, is only *turning* the *handle* which sets the brain, at work, and the electrical fluid is put in motion."[40] There is a difference regarding the parodic immersion of these texts, however. *The Sceptic* maintains its clunky satirical critique throughout, as it relentlessly and brazenly pursues Davy and (especially) Beddoes; in contrast, the *Tale* and *Mechanical Operation* are subtler in their invective, and more indulgent in the discursive possibilities of materialist thought.[41]

A satirical partner-in-crime to *The Sceptic* was published anonymously in the socially conservative *Anti-Jacobin Review and Magazine* in May 1800, although its author was widely known to be the Cornish clergyman Richard Polwhele (1760-1838). "The Pneumatic Revellers: An Eclogue" depicts Beddoes as "Dr. B-," inviting his customers to participate in a kind of therapeutic communion:

> I call you, to take of the liquor of life;
> A fluid, to render as nimble and fresh,
> And purge from its drossy pollution, the flesh;
> To cherish each purified body, the blood in,
> The spirit of beef, and the essence of *pudding.[42]

This universal medicine is the product of a parodic transubstantiation, with Dr. B- assuming the role of Lord Peter. The poem's footnote reference "*Such was the brown loaf in Swift's Tale of a Tub" also imitates the fifth edition of the *Tale* paratextually. Similar to the "Assembly" of "*British Workmen*" who "move

38 *The Sceptic*, pp. 62-63.

39 See Gregory Lynall, "Swift's Pneumatics, Fanatics, and Satiric Mechanics," *Swift Studies*, 29 (2014), 6-23 (especially pp. 13-14).

40 *The Sceptic*, p. 64. See *A Tale of a Tub and Other Works*, ed. Walsh, pp. 105, 179.

41 On materialism in the *Tale*, see especially Roger D. Lund, "Strange Complicities: Atheism and Conspiracy in *A Tale of a Tub*," *Eighteenth-Century Life*, 13, no 3 (1989), 34-58, and Hermann J. Real, "A Taste of Composition Rare: The *Tale*'s Matter and Void," *Reading Swift: Papers from The Third Münster Symposium on Jonathan Swift*, eds Hermann J. Real and Helgard Stöver-Leidig (Munich: Wilhelm Fink, 1998), pp. 73-90.

42 [Richard Polwhele], "The Pneumatic Revellers: An Eclogue," *Anti-Jacobin Review and Magazine*, 6, no 23 (May 1800), 109-18 (p. 111). See also *A Tale of a Tub and Other Works*, ed. Walsh, p. 74.

their Bodies up and down" in the *Mechanical Operation* (pp. 175, 173, 176), Dr. B-'s customers are "Like grave Mandarins, their heads nodding together."[43] Much of the poem, however, works with broader tropes, as Dr. B- laments that the public "judge my fine medical airs but a bubble!" and see him "blown up wth vanity." Dr. B- eventually admits that his claims are mere flatulence: "The Gas, my good Sirs, [is] just emitted by me."[44] This Tubbean scatology is repeated in gross visuality in James Gillray's "Scientific Researches!" (1802), which questions the social decorum of public science by depicting an experimental participant at a Royal Institution lecture (possibly the politician and fellow of the Royal Society, Sir John Coxe Hippisley) both inhaling and farting, as lecturers (including Davy, and perhaps Thomas Garnett or Thomas Young) supply him with nitrous oxide.[45] Gillray might have been inspired by Swift directly, but it is likely that the satirical appropriateness of the Swiftian trope was confirmed to him by *The Sceptic* and "The Pneumatic Revellers."

Davy and Beddoes were also attacked by the Carlisle chemist and surgeon Robert Harrington, who had his own phlogiston theories and objected strongly not only to the French-led "chemical revolution," but also to the ideas of his scientific compatriots. In Harrington's view, Davy and Beddoes resembled not the Æolists of the *Tale*, but those "full of Volatile Spirits acquired in [the] Airy Region" of Laputa (*Gulliver's Travels*, ed. Womersley, p. 255). Davy and Beddoes's method of self-experimentation with nitrous oxide had undermined the authority of their claims, since the gas produces sensations "most ecstatic, (and I should say, *lunatic*; or, still more apropos, *Laputastic*)."[46] Indeed, Harrington refuses to drop the opportunity to construct satirical similitudes, persistently identifying "*Laputatic* extravagancies of modern nonsense," and in particular pointing out how the real natural philosophers' claims are wilder than those encountered in Swift's imagination: "If Swift had been now living, he would have seen his *Laputa* outdone," "Swift's imaginary island is at length eclipsed by bolder fictions," and so on.[47] Despite (or perhaps because of) the crudeness of these attacks, it has been suggested that they were very effective: in casting aspersions on the therapeutic effects of nitrous oxide, they scared off potential

43 "The Pneumatic Revellers: An Eclogue," p. 113.

44 "The Pneumatic Revellers: An Eclogue," pp. 116, 117.

45 James Gillray, "Scientific Researches! – New Discoveries in Pneumaticks! – or – an Experimental Lecture on the Powers of the Air" (London: by H. Humphry, 23 May 1802). The identities of the caricatures are suggested in June Z. Fullmer, "Letter," *Scientific American*, 203, no 2 (August 1960), 12-14.

46 Robert Harrington, *The Death-Warrant of the French Theory of Chemistry* (London: Longman, *et al.*, 1804), p. 96.

47 Harrington, *The Death-Warrant*, pp. 184, 286. See also pp. 27, 70, 102-3, 181, 183n, 262.

researchers, resulting in the gas's anaesthetic properties not being recognized until the 1840s.[48]

Whilst the terms "Laputastic" or "Laputatic" did not catch on in the hands of science writers, Laputa has been alluded to again and again in order to characterize particular scientific or technological endeavours as irrational, overreaching and delusionary utopian, pointless or over-abstracted: as the "vain pretensions of … the idly speculative tribes, who waste their precious time in visionary studies."[49] A typical example is a review of the third volume of Charles Lyell's *Principles of Geology* published in the *Gentleman's Magazine* in 1834. The anonymous reviewer celebrates the "great alteration and improvement which has taken place in the theory of Geology" through Lyell's work, and remarks that

> The older geologists were more fitted for the island of Laputa than for a Philosophical Society … With them it was assumed that enormous changes, and sudden and violent catastrophes, confounding and dislocating all the globe, were necessary to account for its present aspect … Now Mr Lyell's reasoning goes to the destruction of this ingenious but visionary fabric.[50]

The ideas of Georges Cuvier and others are displaced into a foreign, fantasy land associated with irrationality. Ironically, it is Lyell's gradualism which causes a kind of catastrophic collapse of the current theoretical system (like the "wandring *Bee*" sinking the "*Spider*'s Cittadel," another geological allegory).[51] References to Swift such as this one show us powerfully how literary allusions (including verbal, generic, and stylistic borrowings) are part of the social relations through which scientific ideas are accepted or debunked.

An abundance of other examples can be produced from the last two hundred and fifty years to illustrate the satiric power of the Laputan caricature within the discourse of science. Lord Monboddo, for instance, invoked Laputa as a cautionary example against the "very improper uses" of mathematics in the fields of medicine and ethics.[52] "Since the publication of Gulliver's

48 Golinski, "The Literature of the New Sciences," p. 543.

49 W. H. Dilworth, *The Life of Dr. Jonathan Swift* (London: for G. Wright, 1758), facsimile reprint in *Swiftiana XIII: Three Biographical Pamphlets, 1745-1758* (New York: Garland, 1975), p. 68.

50 Anon., "Review of Charles Lyell, *Principles of Geology*, Vol. III," *Gentleman's Magazine*, 155 (January 1834), 77-78 (p. 77).

51 See *A Tale of a Tub and Other Works*, ed. Walsh, p. 149, and Lynall, *Swift and Science*, especially pp. 54-56.

52 James Burnett, Lord Monboddo, *Antient Metaphysics: Volume Third* (London: T. Cadell, *et al.*, 1784), p. 319.

voyage to Laputa, nothing so ridiculous has ever been offered to the world," said Henry Peter, Lord Brougham (1778-1868), of William Herschel's ingenious (and correct) supposition that minimum sunspot activity recorded in the late seventeenth century was connected to the low production – and hence, high price – of grain during the same period.[53] In a letter to Peter Guthrie Tait, the physicist James Clerk Maxwell (1831-79) worked through the electrodynamics calculations of Bernard Riemann, voicing his suspicion of their reality (because they relied upon the concept of action at a distance) simply through a citation: "See Gulliver's Travels in Laputa."[54] For the naturalist Alfred Russel Wallace, state intervention in scientific development is "a process of forcing (in a kind of Laputa College)" in which "much power would have been wasted in the attempt to develop inventions and discoveries before the age was ripe for them."[55]

Allusions to the Third Voyage are not always so general, and some attempt to emulate Swift's verbal irony. Abstruse economic or statistical calculations have been compared to those of the "tailors of Laputa."[56] The physician William Marcet's (1828-1900) research on faecal matter had "realis[ed] experiments which Gulliver the veracious once saw" and "exhibits beautifully formed crystals of a new substance, to which he gives the name *excretine*."[57] For one mid-nineteenth-century essayist, panic regarding the "exhaustion" of coal made a passing resemblance to the Laputans "torment[ing] themselves with all

53 Henry Peter, Lord Brougham, "ART. XV: Observations on the Two Lately Discovered Celestial Bodies. By William Herschell," *The Edinburgh Review*, 1, no 2 (January 1803), 426-31 (p. 431).

54 Maxwell to Peter Guthrie Tait, 12 March 1868, in *The Scientific Letters and Papers of James Clerk Maxwell*, ed. P. M. Harman, 3 vols (Cambridge: Cambridge University Press, 1995), II, 355. See also Maxwell to Peter Guthrie Tait, 3 May 1871, in which he alludes to the *Memoirs of Scriblerus* (*Scientific Letters*, II, 636). When Maxwell eventually published his objection to Riemann's theories, there was no sign of the Laputan comparison, as he generously toned down his more sardonic side. See James Clerk Maxwell, *A Theory on Electricity and Magnetism*, 2 vols (Oxford: Clarendon Press, 1873), I, xi-xii.

55 Alfred Russel Wallace, *My Life: A Record of Events and Opinions*, 2 vols (London: Chapman and Hall, 1905), II, 58.

56 Anon., "Mortality Tables," *Nature*, 109, no 2734 (23 March 1922), 389-90 (p. 389), and see also Anon., "The Mathematical Theory of Political Economy" [review of Par Léon Walras, *Elements d'Economie Politique Pure* (1889)], *Nature*, 40 (5 September 1889), 434-36 (p. 435).

57 Anon., "The Month: Science and Arts," *Chambers's Journal of Popular Literature, Science, and Arts*, 173 (25 April 1857), 270-72 (p. 270). See William Marcet, "An Account of the Organic Chemical Constituents or Immediate Principles of the Excrements of Man and Animals in the Healthy State," *Philosophical Transactions*, 144 (1854), 265-83, and "On the Immediate Principles of Human Excrements in the Healthy State," *Philosophical Transactions*, 147 (1857), 403-13.

conceivable imaginary evils," especially because such warnings "would have been more successful if … less scientific … The imagination was hampered by the chemistry, and the question whether this and that were quite certain."[58]

Swiftian allusion also played its part in the discourse of Darwinian natural selection. Swift and Darwin each challenged anthropocentrism and traditional models of species-relations: from a certain perspective, the "theriophilic satire"[59] of the Yahoo had already tested out satirically some of the existential problems raised by Darwin's ideas. It has also been suggested that there are comically-anthropomorphic descriptions of animal species in Darwin which resemble Swift in style.[60] However, the *indirect* influence of Swift upon Darwin's writing is easier to prove. When John Herschel chose to voice his concern that the principle of natural selection was based on chance progress and excluded "intelligent direction," he invoked the simile of the Lagadan word-frame:

> We can no more accept the principle of arbitrary and casual variation and natural selection as a sufficient account, per se, of the past and present organic world, than we can receive the Laputan method of composing books (pushed *à outrance*) as a sufficient one of Shakespeare and the *Principia*.[61]

Herschel sent a copy of the book to Darwin, who was left "perplexed … beyond measure" by this point.[62] Although Herschel's criticism appeared merely in a footnote, it was brought out of the margins by William Thomson, Lord Kelvin, in his 1871 Presidential Address to the British Association. Near the conclusion of his lecture, Thomson laments that the "argument of design has been greatly too much lost sight of in recent zoological speculations," and remarks that Herschel's satirical comparison of natural selection to the Lagadan method of making books "seems to me a most valuable and instructive criticism."[63] A decade later, in a letter to the botanist Joseph Dalton Hooker (1817-1911), Darwin looked back on the original comments more calmly, acknowledging that

---

58 Anon., "The Coal Question," *Examiner*, 2903 (19 September 1863), 594.

59 See James E. Gill, "Beast over Man: Theriophilic Paradox in Gulliver's 'Voyage to the Country of the Houyhnhnms,'" *Studies in Philology*, 67 (1970), 532-49.

60 See Leslie Stephen, *Swift* (London: Macmillan, 1882), p. 200, and Gillian Beer, "Darwin's Reading and the Fictions of Development," *The Darwinian Heritage*, ed. David Kohn (Princeton, New Jersey: Princeton University Press, 1984), pp. 543-88 (563).

61 John F. W. Herschel, *Physical Geography of the Globe*, 5th ed. (Edinburgh: A. and C. Black, 1867 [1861]), p. 12n.

62 Darwin to John Frederick William Herschel, 23 May [1861], *The Correspondence of Charles Darwin*, eds Burkhardt, *et al.*, IX, 135.

63 William Thomson, Lord Kelvin, "Presidential Address to the British Association, Edinburgh, 1871," *Popular Lectures and Addresses*, 2nd ed., 3 vols (London: Macmillan, 1891-94), II, 132-205 (p. 204).

"Herschel's was a good sneer." Moreover, Darwin confessed that the Lagadan allusion inspired him to "put in the simile about Raphael's Madonna, when describing in the Descent of Man the manner of formations of the wondrous ball-and-socket ornaments" on the wings of the Argus pheasant (that to attribute this shading to natural selection "seems as incredible, as that one of Raphael's Madonnas should have been formed by the selection of chance daubs of paint made by a long succession of young artists").[64] As Darwin's rhetorical borrowing demonstrates, the influence of Swift upon scientific writing is present in a myriad of ways, not all of them verbal or at first-hand.

For some scientists and popularizers, appropriating Swift's writing introduces a critical self-reflexivity, at least half-seriously, in relation to how they perceive themselves and their peers in the production and application of scientific knowledge. For example, "Fancy never got astride Sir I. N[ewton]'s reason" claimed his assistant at the Mint, John Conduitt, echoing the *Tale* (although those aware of the great man's alchemical ambitions might see him differently).[65] More interestingly, Swift's caricatures have functioned as models of self-censure, helping to shape a scientist's understanding of what s/he seeks to avoid. So Charles Babbage (no doubt with the Lagadan word-frame in mind) self-deprecatingly recognized that his ambition to use a mechanical engine to calculate logarithm tables for navigational purposes "may perhaps be viewed as something more than Utopian, and that the philosophers of Laputa may be called up to dispute [his] claim to originality," although he "hope[d] the resemblance will be found to adhere to the nature of the subject rather than to the manner in which it has been treated."[66] Of course, by having the self-awareness to declare his potential to become a "mad scientist,"[67] Babbage demonstrates paradoxically that he could not become one, inoculating himself from potential attack through its pre-emption.

64 Darwin to J. D. Hooker, 6 August [1871], *The Correspondence of Charles Darwin*, eds Burkhardt, *et al.*, XIX, 528; Darwin, *The Descent of Man; and Selection in Relation to Sex*, 2 vols (London: John Murray, 1871), II, 141. See also Hooker to Darwin, 5 August 1871, *Correspondence*, eds Burkhardt, *et al.*, XIX, 525.

65 John Conduitt, "Notes on Newton's Character," in King's College Library, Cambridge, Keynes MS 130.7, f. 7^r^, in *The Newton Project*, <http://www.newtonproject.ox.ac.uk>, accessed 21 March 2018. See Lynall, *Swift and Science*, p. 146.

66 Charles Babbage, *A Letter to Sir Humphry Davy, Bart ... on the Application of Machinery to the Purpose of Calculating and Printing Mathematical Tables* (London: J. Booth, *et al.*, 1822), p. 11.

67 On the cultural image of the "mad scientist," see Roslynn D. Haynes, "Whatever Happened to the 'Mad, Bad' Scientist? Overturning the Stereotype," *Public Understanding of Science*, 25, no 1 (2016), 31-44.

Scientists' allusions to Swift have not only had a satirical or self-critical intent, but also positioned some of his scientific and technological ideas as kinds of futurology. A number of science writers have marvelled, for instance, at Swift's uncanny "prediction" of Mars' two moons and their orbits (in accordance with Kepler's third law), with a crater on Deimos named in his honour.[68] In his history of the art of printing (1797), Henry Lemoine even goes so far as to suggest that Swift's "ludicrous account" of the Lagadan word-machine did not only predict, but also might have inspired the invention of logographical printing (of type arranged in whole words, not single letters), although Swift "little imagined it might give rise, or at least be affording assistance to a science, in the communication of ideas, agreeable to that taciturnity his philosophers admire."[69] For others, time has proved Swift wrong. Calling attention to the vegetable and ultimately solar origin of coal, one essayist "question[s] whether the project of the Laputan sage to extract sunbeams from cucumbers was so very chimerical after all."[70] Meanwhile, another anonymous Victorian advocate of progress predicted that since science had come so far of late that "in the next hundred years ... The wonders of the Arabian Nights, the stories of Baron Munchausen, the flying island visited by Lemuel Gulliver, will be robbed of their attractions by sober facts which will outstrip ... the romantic imaginings of the wildest fiction."[71] Nevertheless, here, as elsewhere, Swift is recognized as an author whose speculative fictions inspire comparison with real scientific developments.

---

68 *Gulliver's Travels*, ed. Womersley, p. 245. See, for instance, Anon., "Science in Fiction" [review of H. G. Wells, *The War of the Worlds*], *Nature*, 57, no 1476 (10 February 1898), 339-40, and Roscoe Lamont, "The Moons of Mars," *Popular Astronomy*, 33 (1925), 496-99. On the prediction more generally, see especially S. H. Gould, "Gulliver and the Moons of Mars," *Journal of the History of Ideas*, 6 (1945), 91-101, and Hermann J. Real, "Gulliver and the Moons of Mars, Once More," *East-Central Intelligencer*, 15, no 2 (2001), 7-8. On the naming of the crater, see *Transactions of the International Astronomical Union*, Volume XVB, eds G. Contopoulos and A. Jappel (Dordrecht: D. Reidel, 1974), pp. 107, 221.

69 Henry Lemoine, *Typographical Antiquities: History, Origin, and Progress of the Art of Printing* (London: S. Fisher, 1797), p. 86.

70 Anon., "Article V. The Phasis of Force," *The National Review*, 8 (April 1857), 359-94 (p. 390). See also Anon., "The Place Where Light Dwelleth," *The British Quarterly Review*, 51 (1870), 409-41 (p. 420), and Anon., "Loan Collection of Scientific Apparatus: Section-Mechanics: Prime Movers," *Nature*, 14 (8 June 1876), 140-41 (p. 141). For Lord Ritchie-Calder, the scenario is not dissimilar to energy research in the 1970s; see "Sunshine out of Cucumbers, an Energy Perspective," *Environmental Science and Technology*, 13, no 9 (September 1979), 1068-75 (p. 1068).

71 Joseph Hatton, "Chiefly about the Future," *The Rose, the Shamrock, and the Thistle*, 1 (October 1862), 519-23 (p. 519).

2. Scale and Relativity

Science writers have not only been concerned with Laputa, however. It is of course commonplace to use "Lilliputian" and "Brobdingnagian" as adjectives of scale, but they had an extra currency within the discourse of science, since they also implied an exotic or otherworldly character.[72] The *Travels* emerged from within a culture of curiosity,[73] but they fed back and were assimilated into that culture, with new discoveries compared with Gulliver's encounters. Travel accounts, including those published in the *Philosophical Transactions*, might use the voyages of Gulliver to convey the unfamiliar scales they came across, including "such monstrous Precipices, and hideous Rocks, as bring all *Brobdingnag* before your Thoughts" (mediated by Pope's *Epistle to Burlington* [1731], in this case).[74] Furthermore, in the nineteenth century, "Lilliput was the imaginary space into which some of the most successful racial creations were projected."[75] Notably, the "Aztec Lilliputians" Maximo and Bartola, given this name because of their size and "exotic" origins, were exhibited in London in 1853.[76] Less controversially, writers of natural history would find ample occasion to draw upon the *Travels*. For example, in an article on "Insectivorous Plants," the botanist Asa Gray (1810-88) described the "Very curious, and even somewhat painful" sight of each bristle on the carnivorous drosera (or sundew) plant "by itself apparently feeble, but in their combination so effectual that the fly may be likened to the sleeping Gulliver made fast in the tiny but multitudinous toils of the Liliputians."[77] Meanwhile, Richard Proctor (1837-88) in his

72 Book Four has seldom attracted scientific interest. A rare exception is Lee Ehrman, who notes that the Houyhnhnms "practice not only sexual selection, but a type of birth control as well." See "Genetics and Sexual Selection," *Sexual Selection and the Descent of Man: The Darwinian Pivot*, ed. Bernard Grant Campbell (Chicago: Aldine, 1972), pp. 105-35 (106).

73 See Barbara M. Benedict, *Curiosity: A Cultural History of Early Modern Inquiry* (Chicago and London: The University of Chicago Press, 2001), p. 110.

74 Thomas Preston, "Two Letters from Mr. Thomas Preston to Mr. Joseph Ames, F. R. S. concerning the Island of Zetland," *Philosophical Transactions*, 43 (1744-45), 57-64 (pp. 58-59). See Alexander Pope, *Epistle to Burlington* (1731), in *The Twickenham Edition of the Works of Alexander Pope*, eds John Butt, *et al.*, 11 vols (London: Methuen, 1939-69), III, ii, 146, l. 104.

75 Jane Goodall, *Performance and Evolution in the Age of Darwin: Out of the Natural Order* (London: Routledge, 2002), p. 50.

76 See "The 'Aztec Lilliputians,'" *The Spectator*, 1308 (23 July 1853), 30.

77 Asa Gray, "Insectivorous Plants" (originally published in *The Nation*, 2 and 9 April 1874), in the same author's *Darwiniana: Essays and Reviews Pertaining to Darwinism* (New York: D. Appleton, 1888), p. 300. See also Asa Gray to Charles Darwin, 21 July 1863, *The Correspondence of Charles Darwin*, eds Burkhardt, *et al.*, XI, 547, and Fritz Müller's published letter to Darwin, "The Habits of Various Insects," *Nature*, 10 (11 June 1874), 102-3 (p. 103), in which the smallest species of honey-bee is nicknamed "Trigona lilliput."

book of popular astronomy explained that because gravity on the moons of Mars could be "equal to a six-hundredth only" of that on Earth, its inhabitants

> might be six hundred times as tall as terrestrial men, yet equally active ... The average height of a Brobdingnag was about 20 yards, or ten times the height of ordinary men. So that the inhabitants of a Martian moon ... would exceed a Brobdingnag sixty times in height, or six times more than a Brobdingnag exceeded Gulliver, or than Gulliver exceeded the King of Lilliput in height.[78]

One reviewer, however, dismissed such (convoluted) attempts to popularize as "whimsical puzzles," finding it "by no means clear to us that the interests of science or the edification of the reader are promoted by writing in such a vein as this."[79] This is not the only time the efficacy of Swiftian allusion within scientific works has been challenged, as we will soon see.

Given the structural importance of scale and perception to the *Travels*, combined with the attention the parodically empirical Gulliver pays to quantity and measurement, it is not a surprise that readers (from at least Henrietta Howard, the Countess of Suffolk, onwards) have been fascinated with its mathematics and physics of dimension.[80] Not only have science writers called upon the Lilliputians and Brobdingnagians as explanatory models, they have also analysed Swift's fictions of scale in themselves, as vehicles of popular science. Yet in subjecting the *Travels* to the demands of a strict, mathematical realism to which the work does not attain and, indeed, actively mocks, these writers become victims of Swift's satire.

Whilst Augustus de Morgan lavished praise on *On Poetry* through imitation, he was critical of the *Travels*, uncovering the mathematical questions which "Swift has masked with so much art." For example, in Gulliver's capture of the Blefuscuan fleet, Swift audaciously "supposes that a man, up to his neck in water, could drag by a rope a mass equal to 50-1728ths of a line-of-battle ship." Moreover, if Swift "means the force of gravity to be [the] same in Lilliput as

78 Richard A. Proctor, *The Poetry of Astronomy: A Series of Familiar Essays on the Heavenly Bodies, &c.* (London: Smith, Elder and Co, 1881), p. 321. See also William Henry Smyth, *A Cycle of Celestial Objects, for the Use of Naval, Military, and Private Astronomers*, 2 vols (London: John W. Parker, 1844), I, 92.

79 Anon., "Proctor's Poetry of Astronomy," *The Saturday Review*, 28 May 1881, 693-94 (p. 694).

80 See Henrietta Howard, Countess of Suffolk to Jonathan Swift, *c.*10 November 1726, *Correspondence*, ed. Woolley, III, 49-50; Anon., "Scientific Imagination," *The Speaker*, 15 (6 February 1897), 151-52; Anon., "Why Has Man Two Eyes?" *Saturday Review of Politics, Literature, Science, and Art*, 158, no 4127 (1 December 1934), 465, and James H. Newman, "Commentary on The Island of Laputa," *The World of Mathematics*, 4 vols (New York: Simon and Schuster, 1956), IV, 2210-13.

in England," then Lilliputian bodies "would not support their own weight."[81] He concedes, however, that Swift's "arithmetic is good. His diameter of 7837 yards does give his 10,000 acres; and his satellites of Mars are correctly placed," although he was "no doubt ... helped to the true answers" by someone such as Arbuthnot. As well as interrogating Swift's mathematical knowledge, de Morgan – defending his profession – also questions whether the "Laputan is a fair caricature."[82] A contemporary respondent accused de Morgan of being "slightly hypercritical" in his refusal to suspend disbelief, which only incited further censure.[83]

Not only was Swift apparently guilty of mathematical error. For Florence Moog, assistant professor of zoology at Washington University, St Louis, "Gulliver was a Bad Biologist," and yet his "book may serve as an unpremeditated textbook on biological absurdities and ... on the nicety with which all living organisms are tailored to the physical conditions of their existence."[84] Moog's essay, therefore, encapsulates the tension between the use of the literary work to explain scientific principles and a pedantic demonstration of its scientific flaws.[85] For a start, the Brobdingnagians could not exist: given that "the weight of a system increases as the cube of its linear dimensions ... a tremendous bulk could not be borne in a frame of human proportions."[86] Likewise, Lilliputians were "too small to be human," particularly because their brains would not be big enough to hold all of the cells needed. Their voices would be seven octaves higher, and inaudible to human hearing, and their faster metabolism would force them to eat 24 meals a day. Moog concludes, however, that "we must not be too hard on Gulliver ... His talents, like those of his friend and teacher, the unhappy Dean Swift of St Patrick's, were in the psychological realm."[87]

81 Augustus de Morgan, "Swift's *Gulliver's Travels*," *Notes and Queries*, 2nd ser., 6, no 137 (14 August 1858), 123-26 (p. 124).

82 de Morgan, "Swift's *Gulliver's Travels*," p. 125.

83 See Hilton Henbury, "*Gulliver's Travels*," *Notes and Queries*, 2nd ser., 6, no 141 (11 September 1858), 215-16 (p. 215), and Augustus de Morgan, "Swift's *Gulliver's Travels*," *Notes and Queries*, 2nd ser., 6, no 143 (25 September 1858), 251-53.

84 Florence Moog, "Gulliver was a Bad Biologist," *Scientific American*, 179 (1 November 1948), 52-55 (p. 52). See also David Robinson, "Biology's Big Idea" [review of John Whitfield, *In the Beat of a Heart* (2006)], *Nature*, 444 (15 November 2006), 272. Moog's criticism is deemed "excessive" in Colin Kiernan, "Swift and Science," *Historical Journal*, 14, no 4 (1971), 709-22 (p. 721).

85 See also J. B. S. Haldane's critique of the use of scale in *Pilgrim's Progress*: "On Being the Right Size" (1926), *Possible Worlds and Other Essays* (London: Chatto and Windus, 1927), pp. 18-26.

86 Moog, "Gulliver was a Bad Biologist," p. 52.

87 Moog, "Gulliver was a Bad Biologist," pp. 53, 55.

Using the *Travels* to explore scale was also the focus of the 1968 Royal Institution Christmas lectures. "Gulliver's Laws: The Physics of Large and Small," by MIT professor and popular science writer Philip Morrison, was an attempt to draw upon a story which the target audience of children would have encountered, perhaps capitalizing on the recent film adaptation, *The Three Worlds of Gulliver* (1960).[88] Whilst conceding, like Moog, that Swift had not written "a book of science ... His main interest was the nature of man,"[89] Morrison proceeded to take issue with some of the *Travels*' uses of scale in order to explore how the size of an object determines its properties. For instance, Morrison congratulated the Lilliputians because "they understood Euclid and they understood proportion and they understood scaling and respected geometry perfectly" in calculating Gulliver's relative volume (Lecture 2, p. 1).[90] Morrison goes on to show, however, that the calorific value needed by Gulliver is actually 12 cubed to the power of 0.73, therefore 230 Lilliputian rations (Lecture 3, p. 1). Gulliver's Lilliputian horse would have "no trouble at all [in] jumping over [Gulliver's] shoe," making it far from a "prodigious leap" (Lecture 3, p. 6). If Lilliputians' optics were in the same proportion to their bodies as humans' are, then their vision would have been very poor, since light has a fixed wavelength (Lecture 4, pp. 3-4). In their application of mathematics, physics and biology to the world of fantastical fiction, de Morgan, Moog, and Morrison therefore become like the Laputans, deploying their knowledge inappropriately, although none of them acknowledge that situational irony.

Whilst concentrating on Book One, and (to a lesser extent) on Book Two, in the fifth lecture Morrison did find time to include some aspects of Book Three, particularly the Lagadan word-frame. Here Morrison addressed the issue of Swift as a satirist of science, remarking that

> his purpose was to make fun of the Royal Society of his day, in which he succeeded very well. But ... in the end the scientist would prove the match for Dean Swift. We may well criticise science today and be concerned about its effect on our lives but not as Swift was concerned, because it was a waste of time ... That's not the problem of science and Swift was simply wrong in that point. (Lecture 5, p. 1)

88 *The Three Worlds of Gulliver*, dir. Jack Sher (Columbia Pictures, 1960).

89 Philip Morrison, "Broadcast Scripts Christmas Lectures 1968," Royal Institution MS AD/06/A/03/C/1968, Lecture 1, p. 2, by courtesy of the Royal Institution of Great Britain. Further quotations are from these manuscripts and will be given in parentheses within the text.

90 D'Arcy Wentworth Thompson is similarly complimentary in the revised edition of *On Growth and Form* (Cambridge: Cambridge University Press, 1945 [1942]), p. 22.

Morrison, who served for four years on the Manhattan Project, is silent on the military activities of the flying island (a veritable weapon of mass destruction), as one might expect in a lecture at Christmas, to an audience of children.[91]

The defamiliarization of scale in the *Travels* also developed an afterlife in the popularization of relativity theory. The chief protagonist in this endeavour was physicist Arthur Eddington (1882-1944), whose writings were often witty.[92] Eddington was the first to bring the theory of relativity to a popular audience and, acknowledging the strangeness of many of its concepts, he drew upon well-known stories. Most prominently, to explain space-contraction and time-retardation, Eddington made the case that both *Alice in Wonderland* and *Gulliver's Travels* were "elementary treatises on relativity":

> Both authors are describing the same phenomenon – a relative change of scale of observer and observed. Lewis Carroll took what is probably the ordinary scientific view, that the observer had changed ... Dean Swift took the truer view of the human mind when he made Gulliver attribute his own changes to the things around him.[93]

For "each party [to] think the other has contracted ... is a paradox beyond even the imagination of Dean Swift;" an idea "too absurd for fiction, and ... only to be found in the sober pages of science."[94] And yet, as relativity theory tells us, each observer thinks himself of greater size.[95]

Despite Eddington's best efforts, the science still seemed impenetrable for the lay reader, as one reviewer noted somewhat acerbically:

> In spite of its illustrations from "Gulliver's Travels," [and others] the volume cannot be recommended for holiday reading ... a conception so utterly opposed,

91 A brief biography of Morrison is given in Royal Institution MS AD/06/A/03/C/1968, Programme. In contrast to Morrison, Laputa showed Bertrand Russell "the possibility of scientific horrors." See "Books that Influenced me in Youth" (1957), in *The Collected Papers of Bertrand Russell, Volume 29: Détente or Destruction* (Abingdon: Routledge, 2005), p. 77.

92 See, for instance, Arthur Eddington, "The Internal Constitution of the Stars," *Nature*, 106, no 2653 (2 September 1920), 14-20 (p. 14).

93 Arthur Eddington, *Space Time and Gravitation: An Outline of the General Relativity Theory* (Cambridge: Cambridge University Press, 1921 [1920]), pp. 32-33. In using the *Travels* to explain relativity, Eddington perhaps draws upon the philosopher Herbert Wildon Carr; see "The Metaphysical Implications of the Principle of Relativity," *The Philosophical Review*, 24, no 1 (January 1915), 1-16 (pp. 3-5).

94 Eddington, *Space Time and Gravitation*, pp. 23-24.

95 See William Berkson, *Fields of Force: The Development of a World View from Faraday to Einstein* (Oxford: Routledge, 2014 [1974]), p. 305.

> not merely to ordinary habits of thought, but even to the geometry and physical science of our school-days ... cannot be visualised as a concrete whole.[96]

Unaware of, or at least unperturbed by, such criticism, Eddington's most famous lecture, his "Friday Evening Discourse in Physical Science" at the Royal Institution, on 22 January 1932, attempted to explain Einstein's theory to a popular audience again, and was subsequently published as *The Expanding Universe* (1933). To convey that length was relative, he alluded to the *Travels* once more, and again insisted on the importance of the observer: "Intrinsically Lilliput and Brobdingnag were just the same ... It needed an intruding Gulliver – an extraneous standard of length – to create a difference."[97]

The Swiftian allusion gives Eddington the licence to adopt a playful style in explaining that the real standard of length cannot be found at the International Bureau of Weights and Measures:

> The Gulliver of physics is generally supposed to be a certain bar of metal called the International Metre. But he is not much of a traveller; I do not think he has ever been away from Paris ... It is evident that the metre bar in Paris is not the real Gulliver. It is one of those practical devices which serve a useful purpose, but dim the clear light of theoretical understanding ... The radius of world-curvature is the real Gulliver.[98]

Channelling Swift in mode, Eddington revels in the apparent absurdity of his similes, bringing a kind of ludic consciousness to his explanations – a rarity in the scientific canon of Swiftian allusion.[99]

The allusion to *On Poetry: A Rhapsody* in the title of this essay perhaps suggested that we would discover Swift, like the writer in his extended simile, preyed upon by his scientist-readers. As we have seen, however, in most

96 Anon., "Getting outside Common-Sense" [review of Eddington, *Space Time and Gravitation*], *Saturday Review of Politics, Literature, Science, and Art*, 130, no 3384 (4 September 1920), 200-1 (p. 200). Following Eddington's allusions, Gulliver became part of the culture of relativity, with further references in newspapers and periodicals; see Katherine Ebury, *Modernism and Cosmology: Absurd Lights* (Basingstoke: Palgrave Macmillan, 2014), p. 179.

97 Eddington, *The Expanding Universe* (Cambridge: Cambridge University Press, 1933), p. 97. See also p. 102n.

98 Eddington, *Space Time and Gravitation*, pp. 96, 98-99.

99 In a similar vein more recently, for his regular column on recreational mathematics, Ian Stewart presents a supposedly found manuscript of a hitherto unknown chapter of the "Voyage to Laputa." It is an elaborate pastiche which explores Laputa's surface topology, with Gulliver emerging as an expert mathematician who corrects the calculations of the island's "Surveyor Royal." See Ian Stewart, "A Swift Trip over Rugged Terrain," *Scientific American*, 264, no 6 (June 1991), 89-91 (p. 89).

cases, science writers who allude to Swift do not do so in a hostile or critical way. This is perhaps because they do not recognize themselves in Swift's caricatures; as the "Preface" to *The Battel of the Books* (1704) asserts, "Satyr is a sort of *Glass*, wherein Beholders do generally discover every body's Face but their Own" (p. 142). Moreover, it is possible that those scientists who do feel offended by Swift's satires treat them in arguably the worst way: with silence.[100] Nevertheless, it seems significant that most science writers do not register themselves as targets of Swift, but instead interpret his satires as warnings against the 'errors' (of judgement, methodology, application, ethics) to which they or their rivals could potentially succumb.[101] His works, and allusions to them within scientific discourse, therefore have the ability to function as kinds of safety valve rather than explosive pressure. Indeed, we must look to 'literary' authors for the alternative view. Charles Dickens, for instance, is not alone in arguing that the Voyage to Laputa has a "comprehensive sneer, spreading over, not only speculative philosophy but practical science."[102]

The responses to Swift surveyed here therefore show us that, despite the specific cultural context in which he wrote and to some extent directed his satires, and the philosophical conservatism with which he is associated, there is much that his writings have offered and continue to offer the scientist reader and the science writer. Yet when re-deployed to serve these new interests, Swift's satiric and ironic subtlety is often lost. Seldom do the borrowings resonate with the same ludic intensity in their new contexts, although some writers (such as Algarotti and Eddington) come close, especially when trying to imitate Swift in mode and style.[103] As they police the boundaries of their disciplines (wary of what could be perceived to be banal, pedantic, or fanciful), or seek to disseminate new ideas to large audiences, science writers have used Swift to generate both dirt and poison *and* sweetness and light.

---

100 It seems somewhat strange, for instance, that the extensive writings of mathematician and amateur poet William Rowan Hamilton (1805-65), who spent his formative years living with his uncle James Hamilton, curate of Trim, make no reference to the most famous former local resident.

101 One exception is Sir George Thomson, whose presidential address to the British Association for the Advancement of Science defends the *a posteriori* scientific method whilst acknowledging it has been "made fun of" in Lagado. See George Thomson, "The Two Aspects of Science," *Nature*, 187, no 4740 (3 September 1960), 837-41 (p. 837).

102 Charles Dickens, "Cyrano de Bergerac," *Household Words*, 14, no 351 (13 December 1856), 524-28 (p. 524). See also Sir Walter Scott, ed., *The Works of Jonathan Swift, D.D.*, 2nd ed., 19 vols (Edinburgh: Archibald Constable, and London: Hearst and Robinson, 1824), XI, 10.

103 Although not in direct emulation, we might see the *Annals of Improbable Research* magazine and its associated annual *Ig Nobel* prizes as continuing a Swiftian tradition of satire on science. See Lynall, *Swift and Science*, p. 147.

RECEPTION AND ADAPTATION II

Peter Wagner
Universität Koblenz-Landau

The Little People in Art: A Note on a Lacuna in the Reception of *Gulliver's Travels* (Part 1)

Abstract. The Swift industry has paid little attention to the intricate ways in which the Dean's fiction and poetry are linked to visual art. Focusing on the initial scene in *Gulliver's Travels*, this article analyses some of the rhizomes connecting Swift's verbal representations with iconotexts and images of the Renaissance showing giants and pygmies. In doing so, the article is inspired by the work of Gilles Deleuze on the rhizome, that is, networks of representation that can be connected to any given artwork. The point here is not to show which paintings or graphic art Swift knew but to trace some of the rich fields of rhizomes with which his satire engages in multiple, ironic ways.

Swift critics have argued that the initial scene in *Gulliver's Travels* is mainly indebted to an ekphrasis in Philostratus' *Imagines* (of which Swift owned a copy published in 1608). Discussing visual art by Dosso Dossi and Cranach the Younger as well as engravings and emblem books showing Hercules (or Polyphemus) and the pygmies, this contribution shows how *Gulliver's Travels* draws on, and also plays with, images derived from Renaissance art.

Among the modern and postmodern novelists whose imagination was fired by *Gulliver's Travels* – from Flaubert to Conrad and Nabokov[1] – Jorge Luis Borges stands out as someone who engaged with Swift both in his fiction (as, for example, in "Brodie's Report")[2] and in his critical writing. Borges understood very well that Swift's ostensible account of travels to "Remote Nations of the World" was in essence a voyage through a library.[3] What Borges did not or could not see – he became totally blind at the age of 50 – is that this virtual library also contained visual material. While the Swift industry has paid extensive homage to the intertextual nature of the Dean's work, the visual underpinning of *Gulliver's Travels* deserves more critical attention.

* This piece would not have seen the light of day without the kind help of Erika Real, the incomparable, who facilitated my research in Münster in her own wonderful and friendly way – thank you for everything you did for me.

1 For details, see Jonathan Swift, *Gulliver's Travels*, ed. David Womersley (Cambridge: Cambridge University Press, 2012), p. civ, notes 240 and 241. Further quotations are from this edition and will be given in parentheses within the text.

2 Jorge Luis Borges, *Collected Fictions*, trans. Andrew Hurley (London: Penguin, 1999).

3 Jorge Luis Borges, *The Total Library: Non-Fiction, 1922-1986*, ed. Eliot Weinberger, trans. Esther Allen, Suzanne Jill Levine, and Eliot Weinberger (London: Penguin, 2007), pp. 214-16.

 | DOI:10.30965/9783846763971_026

In this contribution, I intend to provide an example of the far-reaching rhizomatous relations between Renaissance art and Swift's satire by focusing on just one scene at the opening of *Gulliver's Travels*. This is the incident when the shipwrecked hero upon waking up on an island finds himself fettered to the ground by little people eventually termed Lilliputians. Looking at this well-known episode, I let myself be guided by what Gilles Deleuze and Félix Guattari have termed rhizomatous reading. Given the intermedial nature of Swift's fiction, which engages with the snares of textual and visual representation – including mapping, cartography, and scientific recording – this approach strikes me as particularly suitable and rewarding, laying bare the visual artistic shoots and roots creating a network of sorts at the heart of thinking and writing about pygmies, midgets, and dwarfs, with an occasional look at their counterpart, the giants.

Although an established concept in theories of networks and hypertexts, the rhizome[4] is neither well known nor accepted or practised in literary theory.[5] Adapted from plant biology by Gilles Deleuze and Félix Guattari in 1976 to conceptualize non-linear relations in thinking (and reading/interpreting), the short treatise *Rhizome* was integrated into their major work *Mille Plateaux* in 1980, first translated into English in 1987 as *A Thousand Plateaus*. The two French critics are opposed to what they term the arboreal or tree-like concept, which operates with a major root and origins, proposing instead a schizo-analytic model with the rhizome as a figure for thinking multiplicity. They identify six key principles underpinning the rhizome[6]:

- connection: any point of the rhizome can be connected to anything other, there is no "correct" or "right" pathway
- heterogeneity: the rhizome connects not only signifier to signified, but entire semiotic chains to ideologies and specific historical circumstances

---

4 For detailed discussions of the rhizome as a critical concept in reading and interpreting representations, see Michael C. Frank, "Rhizom," *Metzler Lexikon Literatur- und Kulturtheorie*, 4th ed. Ansgar Nünning (Stuttgart: Metzler, 2008), pp. 626-27; Jörg Seidel, "Rhizom" (<http://seidel.jaiden.de/rhizom.php> [2014], accessed 16 October 2016), and Thomas Krämer, *Androgynie, Alterität und Alienität im britischen Glam, 1970-74* (Münster: LIT, 2014).

5 Thus, in Germany, the works of Klaus Theweleit initially faced a strong opposition in academic criticism, mainly because most of the critics failed to recognize the rhizomatous nature of Theweleit's fascinating approach (see especially *Männerphantasien*, 2 vols [München: Piper, 2000]; *Buch der Könige*, 3 vols [Frankfurt: Stroemfeld, 1988-94]; *Der Pocahontas Komplex*, 3 vols [Frankfurt: Stroemfeld, 1999-2013], and the English translation of *Männerphantasien*, *Male Fantasies*, published by Polity Press [London] in 1987).

6 The following six points are identified in the *Oxford Dictionary of Critical Theory*, ed. Ian Buchanan (Oxford: Oxford University Press, 2010), s.v. "rhizome."

- multiplicity: the rhizome is a complete entity and does not lack anything (such as a supplement)
- signifying rupture: the rhizome can be broken at any point, but it always restarts elsewhere (that is, ideas/concepts mutate)
- cartography: the rhizome is always mapped in a reading process, which thus contains performative elements
- decalcomania: the rhizome may contain pre-existing concepts/systems of thought plugged into its own heterogeneous process (like the notion of *mise-en-abyme*)

The critical reception of rhizomatous reading sketched by Deleuze and Guattari has largely ignored the fact that their model is not only marked by notions borrowed from psychoanalysis, biology, and cartography, but that it also includes a technical-mechanical dimension in that books as literary machines may be connected with great profit to machines of love, war, revolution, etc. As a critic or reader, it is important to know which "other machine can be connected to the literary machine."[7]

Art and art theory are two important rhizomes or machines that may be activated while reading the initial episode of "A Voyage to Lilliput." My aim, then, is not to identify Swift's sources but rather to uncover some of the Renaissance networks within which notions and concepts of pygmies (and giants) were (re)constructed.[8] In doing so, the focus will be on visual representations, although pictures never function without texts. In almost all cases, these texts attempt to limit or control the semantic richness of the images. This focus on pictures and iconotexts[9] circulating during the time Swift was educated and wrote his satires will help us better to understand his creation of the Lilliputians, of little people who are dangerous, wicked, evil, and potentially deadly. The visual discourse on little people in the Renaissance offers some answers to the question why Swift's giants in Brobdingnag are largely benevolent and wise, while the pygmies in Lilliput are the opposite. And the same applies

7 Gilles Deleuze and Félix Guattari, *Rhizom* (Berlin: Merve, 1977); the translation is mine.

8 I use the term (re)constructed because Renaissance writers, such as John Milton, Sir Thomas Browne, and Blaise de Vigenère (the French translator of Philostratus' *Imagines*), inherited specific notions concerning dwarfs and pygmies. Augustine's discussion of dwarfs in the context of monstrosity, for instance, still reverberates in Renaissance writings on the subject; see Karen L. Edwards, "Engaging with Pygmies: Thomas Browne and John Milton," *Sir Thomas Browne: The World Proposed*, eds Reid Barbour and Claire Preston (Oxford: Oxford University Press, 2008), pp. 100-17 (107).

9 For a detailed discussion of the term iconotext (representations containing both verbal and visual elements), with applications to eighteenth-century works, see Peter Wagner, *Reading Iconotexts: From Swift to the French Revolution* (London: Reaktion, 1995).

to Swift's satirical attempts in *Gulliver's Travels* if understood as a reaction to the belief in the reliability of vision and visual representation.

After wading ashore on the island of the Lilliputians, the shipwrecked Gulliver reports that he was extremely tired and fell asleep on the grass, not least because on leaving the ship he had drunk "about half a Pint of Brandy." Upon waking up after about nine hours, he found himself unable to stir:

> I happened to lie on my Back, I found my Arms and Legs were strongly fastened on each Side to the Ground; and my Hair, which was long and thick, tied down in the same Manner. I likewise felt several slender Ligatures across my Body, from my Armpits to my Thighs. (p. 34 [I, i, 5])

Gulliver soon realizes that he has been captured and fettered by "human Creatures not six Inches high" (p. 34 [I, i, 5]). He manages to free his left arm, yet the Lilliputians then threaten him with bows and arrows, shooting a "Flight into the Air, as we do Bombs in *Europe*; whereof many ... fell on my Body ... and some on my Face, which I immediately covered with my left Hand" (p. 35 [I, i, 5]).[10] Eventually, observing Gulliver quietening down, they "discharged no more Arrows" (p. 35 [I, i, 5]). Later in that scene (pp. 36-37 [I, i, 5]), Gulliver regales the watching Lilliputians, including the courtiers, with his "epic eating and drinking – not to mention sneezing, urinating, and defecating" that "recall Gargantua's similar feats in Rabelais's *Gargantua and Pantagruel*."[11] As Gulliver feels tempted during his Gargantuan feast "to seize Forty or Fifty of the first (Lilliputians) that came into my Reach, and dash them against the Ground" (p. 37 [I, i, 5]), any educated reader of the time would recognize the allusion to the giant Cyclops Polyphemus in the *Odyssey*, who killed six of Ulysses' crew members in the same manner.[12] Alternatively, Swift's annotators have identified as sources for the scene an episode in Philostratus' *Imagines* (Book 2) in which Hercules is attacked by pygmies, as well as the biblical narrative of

10 Gulliver's anxiety about his eyes is of course also an indirect allusion to the blinding of Polyphemus in the *Odyssey* (IX, 371-402). As we shall see, some Renaissance texts (and images) mingled the stories of Hercules and the pygmies, the blinding of Polyphemus, and of the biblical Samson who, when he had lost his strength, was blinded by the Philistines. Thus the French translation by Lefevre of the emblem showing Hercules and the pygmies in the Paris edition of Alciati's *Emblemata* (1536) describes pygmies trying to put out Hercules' eyes, so that he may lose his strength.

11 *Gulliver's Travels*, ed. Albert J. Rivero (New York and London: W. W. Norton, 2002), p. 19n2.

12 Drawing the reader's attention to the allusion, Womersley quotes the relevant passage from the *Odyssey* (IX, 287-90), adding that one finds a parallel allusion to Polyphemus in the Voyage to Brobdingnag, where Gulliver is compared to Polyphemus striding into the sea in pursuit of Ulysses' ship, an episode described in Virgil's *Aeneid* (III, 655-91) (see *Gulliver's Travels*, ed. Womersley, pp. 37n40 and 122n48).

Samson and Delilah, "Gulliver's long hair and strength [being] reminiscent of Samson's."[13] To these texts Milton's *Paradise Lost* (I, 50-75) has recently been added as there is "a general parallel with Satan returning to consciousness on the burning lake of Hell" (p. 34n31). Finally, there is no shortage of visual representations or sculptures of the cannibalistic giant, who is often shown as a one-eyed monster (Figure 25.1).[14]

If we add to these texts and motifs the impact of the Irish landscape on *Gulliver's Travels*,[15] as well as Swift's knowledge of contemporary travel

13 *Gulliver's Travels*, ed. Rivero, p. 17n7. The exact reference to the biblical passage in which Samson after having been betrayed by Delilah is shorn and blinded is Judges 16:4-21.

14 "Round-eyed" would be the correct translation of the Greek meaning of his name, Cyclops. In verbal and visual representations, Polyphemus is shown either with one eye in his forehead or with an additional third eye there. Swift plays with the Polyphemus episode in the *Odyssey* by way of several covert allusions: Gulliver's drinking of a half-pint of brandy before swimming ashore (p. 34 [I, i, 5]) recalls Ulysses' attempt to get Polyphemus drunk before blinding him; and Gulliver's concern that his eyes might be put out by arrows after capturing the Blefuscudan fleet (p. 74 [I, v, 1]) recalls the actual blinding of the Cyclops, as does the later punishment Gulliver is supposed to suffer by order of the King of Lilliput (p. 100 [I, vii, 14]). In a brief article on "Homeric Intertextuality" in *Gulliver's Travels*, Dieter Fuchs has explored the relationship between the Polyphemus episode in the *Odyssey* and Gulliver in Lilliput while stressing such aspects as vision and cannibalism (Dieter Fuchs, "Homeric Intertextuality: Odysseus and the Cyclops in *Gulliver's Travels*," *Swift Studies*, 28 [2013], 145-47). Like most editors of *Gulliver's Travels*, Fuchs assumes a direct textual relationship between Swift and its classical sources while disregarding the mediation of the text through visual representations. On paintings of Polyphemus, see E. W. Leach, "Polyphemus in a Landscape: Traditions of Pastoral Courtship," *The Pastoral Landscape*, ed. John Dixon Hunt (Washington, DC: National Gallery of Art, 1992), pp. 63-87.

The painting from which the detail of the blinding of Polyphemus is taken is held by Vassar College. It is part of two large rectangular panels forming a series of which the third panel, depicting the return of Ulysses, is lost. For additional pictures showing Polyphemus, see the various emblem books (reprinted in Arthur Henkel und Albrecht Schöne, *Emblemata: Handbuch zur Sinnbildkunst des XVI. und XVII. Jahrhunderts* [Stuttgart und Weimar: J. B. Metzler, 1996], cols 1692 and 1693) and the Pan-like giant Polyphemus in Blaise de Vigenère's French translation of Philostratus' *Eikones* (*Imagines*), *Les Images ou tableaux de platte peinture des deux Philostrates sophistes grecs* (Paris: La veuve Abel L'Angelier, 1615), p. 436.

15 In his brief article for the *Guardian*, Will Self argues: "For Swift, the long view of the Divis and Black Mountain massif from his parish to the South of Belfast, rather than filling him with awe at the sheer scale of nature, or calling forth the reverence accorded big things by the classical philosophers, reminded him instead of the prone form of a giant man, with the easternmost tumulus of Cave Hill forming its nose" ("Bigness and Littleness," *The Guardian*, Saturday, 28 August 2010, <https://www.theguardian.com/culture/2010/aug/28/will-self-bigness-and-littleness>, accessed 31 October 2018). Other critics refer to a visit by Swift in a country house where the view of people in the distance allegedly reminded him of dwarfs.

FIGURE 25.1 Unknown Italian artist (group of Lorenzo di Credi), *The Adventures of Ulysses: The Blinding of Polyphemus*.
Early 16th Century. Tempera on panel. 115.57 × 194.31 cm
DETAIL. VASSAR COLLEGE, USA

literature[16] and the "learned and scatological satire of Rabelais" (p. lxix), one can agree with this summary of intertextuality in the Dean's masterpiece:

> However, the travel literature of the later seventeenth and earlier eighteenth centuries provided Swift with only the wire-frame for *Gulliver's Travels*. He filled its spaces with material taken promiscuously from the description of ideal societies composed by Plato, by Plutarch and by Sir Thomas More ... from the scientific, poetic and ephemeral literature of the time; and from the tradition of the fantastic voyage which drew contributions from Lucian, from Cyrano de Bergerac and from Daniel Defoe. (p. lxix)

16 The standard study of this important discursive background for *Gulliver's Travels* is Dirk F. Passmann's detailed and meticulous monograph *"Full of Improbable Lies": "Gulliver's Travels" und die Reiseliteratur vor 1726* (Frankfurt am Main: Peter Lang, 1987). While Passmann traces the fictional, historical, philosophical, and scientific publications we need to consider vis-à-vis Swift's satire, he ignores visual discourse as an important genre per se. Passmann reproduces visual representations of dwarfs and giants (pp. 159 and 165), but their history in art remains in the dark. Passmann argues, for instance, that the picture of the Nile as a statue climbed by putti, from George Sandys's travel book (1673), reproduced on p. 165, might have inspired Swift for the initial scene in Lilliput. Yet the engraving in Sandys's *A Relation of a Journey* is borrowed from previous representations, such as Blaise de Vigenère's translation of Philostratus' *Imagines* (1615), in which we find a similar engraving of *Le Nil*, with extensive commentary (see *Les Images ou tableaux de platte peinture des deux Philostrates sophistes grecs*, pp. 31-34).

What is striking about annotations of *Gulliver's Travels*, generally, however, is that none of the editors mentions the possibility of any visual or theatrical influence. While one, for instance, notes that Swift owned a copy of Philostratus' *Imagines* (Paris, 1608), he never considers the illustrations in seventeenth-century editions of the book (see Figures 25.18-19), nor those spawned by these examples of classical Greek ekphrasis, which proved so influential for Renaissance art, literature, and music.[17] In addition, the same editor maintains that the initial scene in Lilliput is an "echo of Philostratus' description of Hercules tied down by pygmies" (p. 34n31), but fails to see that a close reading of the Latin source[18] unveils that the pygmies did not fetter Hercules at all. Nor did they, as in Swift's text, attempt to blind the hero (in the initial scene, with arrows, and later on as a punishment for his indecent urinating [pp. 35, 101 { I, i, 5; vii, 15}]). Since Philostratus' ekphrasis[19] of a painting he claims to have seen in or near Naples is an important rhizome, an English translation of it may be called for:

> While Heracles is asleep in Libya after conquering Antaeus, the Pygmies set upon him with the avowed intention of avenging Antaeus; for they claim to be brothers of Antaeus, high-spirited fellows, not athletes, indeed, nor his equals at wrestling, but earth-born and quite strong besides, and when they come up out of the earth the sand billows in waves. For the Pygmies dwell in the earth just like ants and store their provisions underground, and the food they eat is not the property of others but their own and raised by themselves. For they sow and reap and ride on a cart drawn by pigmy horses, and it is said that they use an axe

17 In his brief appendix on the frontispieces in the various editions of *Gulliver's Travels* (pp. 567-72), Womersley also refrains from a discussion of Swift's engagement with portraiture. Referring to Janine Barchas's monograph (*Graphic Design, Print Culture and the Eighteenth-Century Novel* [Cambridge: Cambridge University Press, 2003]), he fails to mention other discussions (such as the chapter on "Captain Gulliver and the Pictures," in Wagner, *Reading Iconotexts*, pp. 37-74).

The musical representation of Hercules and Polyphemus is yet another important rhizome I cannot discuss within the scope of this article. See, for instance, the treatment of Polyphemus in Georg Friedrich Händel and John Gay's *Acis and Galatea*, first performed in 1718.

18 Swift's text was an edition in Latin and Greek in which the educated reader could compare the two versions printed side by side (PASSMANN AND VIENKEN II, 1421-22). Most modern translations of Philostratus' *Eikones* seem to be based on the Latin text, with the exception of de Vigenère's French translation discussed below.

19 The matter becomes even more complicated when one considers the fact that there were several writers called Philostratus, probably related to each other. For a recent detailed study of Flavius Philostratus, the author of the first part of the *Eikones* (or *Imagines* in Latin), in which the Hercules episode appears, see Ewen Bowie and Jaś Elsner, eds, *Philostratus* (Cambridge: Cambridge University Press, 2009), especially Part I (life and work) and Part VII (on his *Imagines*).

> on stalks of grain, believing that these are trees. But ah, their boldness! Here they are advancing against Heracles and undertaking to kill him in his sleep; though they would not fear him even if he were awake. Meanwhile he sleeps on the soft sand, since weariness has crept over him in wrestling; and, filled with sleep, his mouth open, he draws full breaths deep in his chest, and Sleep himself stands over him in visible form, making much, I think, of his own part in the fall of Heracles. Antaeus also lies there, but whereas art paints Heracles as alive and warm, it represents Antaeus as dead and withered and abandons him to Earth.
>
> The army of the Pygmies envelops Heracles; while this one phalanx attacks his left hand, these other two companies march against his right hand as being stronger; bowmen and a host of slingers lay siege to his feet, amazed at the size of his shin; as for those who advance against his head, the Pygmy king has assumed the command at this point, which they think will offer the stoutest resistance, and they bring engines of war against it as if it were a citadel – fire for his hair, a mattock for his eyes, doors of a sort for his mouth, and these, I fancy, are gates to fasten on his nose, so that Heracles may not breathe when his head has been captured. All these things are being done, to be sure, around the sleeping Heracles; but lo! he stands erect and laughs at the danger, and sweeping together the hostile forces he puts them in his lion's skin, and I suppose he is carrying them to Eurystheus.[20]

The picture of the pygmies that comes across here differs to some extent from that of the Lilliputians: Philostratus' little people are compared to ants (in later accounts, lice and gnats), though in human shape; they are "high-spirited" and courageous, considering themselves to be relatives of the giant Antaeus, and as such not afraid of taking on Hercules even if he were wide awake. Irony does not seem to be in the foreground; if at all present in the text, it has to be construed indirectly by the reader.

The episode in Philostratus reached the Renaissance public in intermedial and interpreted forms, of which Swift's Latin source was just one. I will return to Philostratus in my attempt to show that the construction of Swift's Lilliputians owes a lot to the depiction of little people in the rendering of the Latin (or Greek) text in Renaissance painting and graphic art. While this art was without any doubt inspired by Philostratus' ekphrasis, it also enriched, extended, and thus changed the Greek and Latin versions of the text, especially the illustrated editions of *Eikones* or *Imagines*. In other words, Philostratus' Greek and Latin texts came down to the Renaissance public mostly in interpreted versions, and many of them were visual or iconotextual.

---

20 Philostratus, *Imagines*, trans. Arthur Fairbanks (London: William Heinemann, and Cambridge, Massachusetts: Harvard University Presss, 1960 [1931]), pp. 229-31 (II, 22).

In Swift's time, there was a plethora of discourse on the question whether or not pygmies and giants existed. In fact, this was almost an obsession of the age with roots all the way back to Greek and Roman authors.[21] This richly rhizomatic verbal (and iconotextual) discourse was re-enforced to some extent by a strong oral tradition and contemporary writings on little people.[22] Dwarfs also continued to be employed in royal and aristocratic households;[23] Lord

21 In addition to Passmann, *"Full of Improbable Lies"*, pp. 145-82, see also the medieval and early modern publications on the myth of a race of pygmies (listed in *Gulliver's Travels*, ed. Womersley, p. 29n1). In his French translation of Philostratus' *Imagines* (1615 and 1637), Blaise de Vigenère speculates at length about the origins and whereabouts of pygmies while quoting a long series of Greek and Roman writers who had dealt with the issue (*Les Images ou tableaux de platte peinture des deux Philostrates sophistes grecs* [Paris: Claude Sonnius, 1637], pp. 481-85).

22 These writings included academic treatises, such as Sir Thomas Browne's *Pseudodoxia Epidemica*, ed. Robin Robbins, 2 vols (Oxford: Clarendon Press, 1981), in which the author speculates on the existence of a nation of pygmies (I, 330-33, chapter xi). Browne concludes that the evidence available to him (including travel reports) did not persuade him of the existence of such people (as nations). On the rhizomatous background of Browne's discussion of pygmies, see Edwards, "Engaging with Pygmies: Thomas Browne and John Milton," pp. 100-17.

Equally important were works for the general public, such as the anonymous *Elegy on the Much Lamented Death of Matthew Buckinger, the Famous Little-Man (without Arms and Legs) who Departed this Life at Cork, Sept. 28. 1722* (FOXON E67). On this popular background, with respect to giants, see Daniel Woolf, "Of Danes and Giants: Popular Beliefs about the Past in Early Modern England," *Dalhousie Review*, 71 (1991), 166-209. Woolf's discussion of popular beliefs about giants in early modern England can also be applied to dwarfs or pygmies. Focusing on the belief that giants lived in the past, he argues in particular that "from the late 16th to the 18th centuries, beliefs about the past increasingly worked their way from oral into written or printed form," especially in ballads and chapbooks, "as the writers, readers and hearers of stories, anecdotes, ballads and legends conversed" (pp. 180-81). See also Jennifer B. Westwood and Jacqueline Simpson, *The Law of the Land: A Guide to England's Legends* (London: Penguin, 2005) on the role of giants in local legend. According to these authors, giants had two main roles in this form of discourse: "as creatures of landscape features which appear to be artificial yet are beyond the strength of ordinary men, and as the butt of jokes about their foolishness" (p. 628). See also Jacqueline Simpson and Steve Roud, *A Dictionary of English Folklore* (Oxford: Oxford University Press, 2000), s.v. "Giants." The discourse about pygmies was of course also fired by the presence of dwarfs as jesters or fools in aristocratic houses, in popular shows, and in portraiture. Hogarth includes a giant in his print *Southwark Fair* (1734), and Swift saw "dwarfs" in a London show (Leo Damrosch, *Jonathan Swift: His Life and his World* [New Haven and London: Yale University Press, 2013], p. 119).

23 As Edwards explains, the early modern period made a distinction between pygmies and dwarfs. "Uncertainty about where they belong on the map," she writes, "seems to encode uncertainty about where they belong in relation to the human" ("Engaging with Pygmies: Thomas Browne and John Milton," p. 107). Dwarfs were considered an anomaly, a variety

Minimus (also known as Jeffrey Hudson, 1619-81), who was painted by Anthony van Dyck in 1633 (Figure 25.2) and featured in a court masque written by Ben Jonson and staged by Inigo Jones, is just one of the better known examples.[24] Clearly, there was a concomitant and equally important visual and theatrical discourse to which literary critics have paid far too little attention.

The reluctance of literary scholars to consider Renaissance art or iconotexts (such as illustrated classical texts) in the discussion of Swift's satire may be due to the assumption that the Dean cared little about visual art.[25] Yet Swift's attitudes towards the arts disclose a Janus-faced personality. On the one hand, there is the author who, in his role as satirist, never failed to express his suspicion vis-à-vis painting in particular. A student of Plato, or so the argument goes, he equated visual art with deceitful rhetoric, arguing invariably that art created falsity and illusion, especially dangerous aspects when men's view of women was at stake. He also attacked the alleged reliability and verisimilitude in portraiture often put in the service of mendacious travel literature.[26] On the other hand, Swift the private person, who was perhaps not so much in love

---

of monstrosity, while the existence of pygmies as a people was discussed as a possibility (though Sir Thomas Browne and Blaise de Vigenère express scepticism about this idea).

24 Hudson was presented to King Charles I by the Earl of Buckingham. He became Queen Henrietta Maria's confidant and counsellor and appears in the portrait of the Queen by van Dyck. The website for this painting in the National Gallery of Art, Washington, DC, describes him thus: "The queen's love of entertainment is symbolized by the presence of 14-year-old Sir Jeffrey Hudson and Pug the monkey, both royal favorites. Hudson, a perfectly proportioned dwarf whose services had been offered to the queen as a young boy, possessed a ready wit, and became one of the Queen's trusted advisors, even joining her in exile in France in the early years of the English Civil Wars (1642-1651)" (<https://www.nga.gov/collection/art-object-page.41651.html>, accessed 31 October 2018). Hudson also featured in various roles in court masques staged by Inigo Jones (especially the last two masques). Apparently, there is a life-size statue of Lord Minimus in the public bar of the Boat Inn in Portumna, Galway. On Hudson (also known as Lord Minimus), see Nick Page, *Lord Minimus: The Extraordinary Life of Britain's Smallest Man* (London: HarperCollins, 2001).

25 Thus *The Cambridge Companion to Jonathan Swift*, ed. Christopher Fox (Cambridge: Cambridge University Press, 2003), features an exhaustive essay by Brean Hammond on "Swift's Reading" (pp. 73-86) but nothing on the Dean's knowledge or use of art, the silent assumption being that it was unimportant for Swift's work.

26 See my discussion of the strategic satirical functions of the portrait frontispieces in *Gulliver's Travels* in *Reading Iconotexts*, pp. 37-74; Barchas, *Graphic Design, Print Culture and the Eighteenth-Century Novel*, pp. 28-34, draws on this chapter, extending it to the different portraits in the Dublin editions of 1735. For a discussion of Swift's satirical employment of Rococo art, see my "Of Painted and Graven Images: On the Function of Pictures in Swift's Writings," *Reading Swift: Papers from The Third Münster Symposium on Jonathan Swift*, eds Hermann J. Real and Helgard Stöver-Leidig (Munich: Wilhelm Fink, 1998), pp. 269-92.

FIGURE 25.2
Anthony van Dyck, *Henrietta Maria with Sir Jeffrey Hudson* (1633).
Oil on canvas. 219.1 × 134.8 cm
NATIONAL GALLERY OF ART. WASHINGTON, DC

with pictures as he was with texts, still owned paintings and went to picture auctions.[27] From Ehrenpreis down to the most recent biographer, one notices the consistent, seemingly ineradicable belief of critics that the Dean had "little interest" in the arts.[28] The fact that Swift's library contained an edition, in Latin and Greek, of Philostratus' *Imagines* does not mean that the story of "Hercules inter Pygmaeos" described in it was the only one he knew. Nor does it mean that the Gulliver episode is related exclusively to verbal sources. While we do

27 Joseph McMinn notes that Swift records at least seven visits to picture auctions in London with Benjamin Pratt, Provost of Trinity College. He also saw pictures in the possession of the Duke of Ormonde, who "had amassed Ireland's greatest collection of paintings at Kilkenny Castle, largely as a result of his travels through France during Charles II's exile" (*Jonathan Swift and the Arts* [Newark: University of Delaware Press, 2010], p. 134).

28 While Damrosch criticizes Ehrenpreis for his (Freudian) projections and misreadings of Swift (*Jonathan Swift*, pp. 5-6), he later silently adopts and supports Ehrenpreis's allegedly mistaken views, for example, Swift's attitudes towards the arts. This is most surprising since Damrosch claims to have read McMinn's monograph (*Jonathan Swift and the Arts*, p. 502n19). If he had really read it, he should have corrected or at least qualified his statement that the Dean had "little interest ... in the arts" (*Jonathan Swift*, p. 185).

not know which paintings and prints inspired Swift, we can at least map the discursive visual space in which representations of the episode circulated.[29]

Since rhizomes have neither beginning nor end, we may as well start in fifteenth-century Italy, tracing the rhizomatous connections from an Italian Renaissance painting backwards and forwards in temporal and geographical space. In 1535, Dosso Dossi (*c.*1486-1542; also called Giovanni di Lutero) painted Hercules and the pygmies[30] (Figure 25.3), giving the Hercules figure the facial features of his patron, Ercole II d'Este (1508-59) (Figure 25.4).

Educated contemporaries would remember the story depicted here. Just before accomplishing his tenth labour, the stealing of Geryon's cattle, Hercules arrived in Libya, where he fought and killed the tyrannical, evil giant Antaeus. Falling asleep, Hercules was attacked by pygmies, but they were unable to harm him. The painter adapts the story (in Philostratus, it is set in the Libyan sands) to an Italian-Arcadian landscape and to the situation at the court of Ferrara, with a benevolent ruler substituting for his classical namesake and obviously bemused at the attempts of dwarfs to harm him. The painting alludes to some of the details in Philostratus' *Imagines* (for example, Hercules' lion's skin) while leaving out Antaeus as well as the personification of Sleep. At the same time, Dossi renders the little people as contemporary (Italian) soldiers or courtiers, perhaps also as lansquenets. These Italian pygmies, according to the general impression, seem to overestimate themselves or their force. The Italian Hercules is not afraid of them, an implicit message of Ercole II to his enemies. Another most interesting rhizome in this painting is the play with sexual identity and virility, such as the pose of Hercules' body so reminiscent of Renaissance female nudes as we find them, for example, in Dürer's *Das Meerwunder* (*c.*1498)

29 We should consider the fact that many libraries contained illustrated editions in addition to pure textual versions of important classical texts. Thus the library of Alexander Seton, first Earl of Dunfermline, whose decorations at Pinkie House, Musselburgh, are discussed below, held a copy of Philostratus' *Imagines* in Latin and Greek as well as Blaise de Vigenère's beautifully illustrated *Les Images ou tableaux de platte peinture* (1615), which served as a direct source for some of the wall paintings decorating the Earl's picture gallery, built in imitation of the gallery Philostratus claimed to have visited near Naples (Michael Bath, "Philostratus Comes to Scotland: A New Source for the Pictures at Pinkey," *Journal of the Northern Renaissance*, 5 [2013], 1-25 [p. 6]).

30 My brief discussion of the painting is indebted to *Cranach: mit einem Bestandskatalog der Gemälde in den Staatlichen Kunstsammlungen Dresden*, eds Harald Marx und Ingrid Mössinger (Köln: Wienand, 2005), p. 415.

FIGURE 25.3 Dosso Dossi (Giovanni di Lutero), *Hercules and the Pygmies* (1535). Oil on canvas. 114 × 146.5 cm
LANDESMUSEUM JOANNEUM. ALTE GALERIE. GRAZ, AUSTRIA

FIGURE 25.4
Dosso Dossi, *Portrait of Ercole II d'Este, Duke of Ferrara* (1508-59), the eldest son of Lucrezia Borgia.

FIGURE 25.5 Albrecht Dürer, *Das Meerwunder* (c.1498). Copper engraving. 24.8 × 18.9 cm

(Figure 25.5) or in the sleeping or reclining Venuses of Giorgione, Titian, Bardone, and Palma Vecchio (Figures 25.6-7).[31]

These, in turn, have strong rhizomatous connections with a woodcut illustration in one of the most influential iconotexts of the Renaissance, Francesco Colonna's *Hypnerotomachia Poliphili* (Venice, 1499), which appeared in an incomplete English translation in 1592 (*The Strife of Love in a Dream*).[32] The interest among humanists and artists in mythical Greek and Roman characters and stories was no doubt also fanned by the presence of Andrea Alciati in Ferrara between 1542 and 1546. First circulating in manuscript among his friends, his collection of *Emblemata* proved one of the most powerful iconotextual sources for artists and writers after its first publication in Augsburg in 1531.[33]

In 1551, sixteen years after the Dossi painting, Lucas Cranach the Younger painted two scenes with Hercules and the pygmies at the behest of his patron, Elector Moritz of Saxony. Like Ercole II, Moritz faced strong enemies around him and kept up close political relations with the court at Ferrara: "During his trip to Ferrara in early 1549, Elector Moritz may have seen the paintings representing … Hercules fighting the Pygmies, done by Dosso and Battista Dossi for

31 In addition to the Venuses by Giorgione and Titan reproduced here, see, for instance, Palma Vecchio's *Resting Venus* (*c.*1520, Staatliche Kunstsammlungen Dresden), and Paris Bardone's *Sleeping Venus with Cupid* (*c.*1540, Galleria Franchetti, Venice). D. M. Field's chapter on "The Renaissance Nude" in his *The Nude in Art* (London: Hamlyn, 1981) is still rather useful, because it outlines the male and female ideals in relation to classical sources.

Another rhizome to be traced is the visual representation of Polyphemus; what goes for Cranach's Hercules is, to some extent, also applicable to Dossi. See my brief discussion of Polyphemus in the context of Cranach's two pictures below.

32 See the full-page illustration of a nymph eyed by a lustful and aroused satyr (Francesco Colonna, *Hypnerotomachia Poliphili* [Venice: Aldus Manutius, 1499], trans. Joscelyn Godwin as *The Strife of Love in a Dream* [London: Thames and Hudson, 1999], p. 73). Attributed to Francesco Colonna (1431-1527), a Dominican monk, the *Hypnerotomachia Poliphili* is one of the most beautiful if mysterious books of the Italian Renaissance, first printed by Aldus Manutius. An allegorical romance written in a unique Latinized Italian, it is studded with allusions to archaeology, mythology, magic, and folklore. With impressive woodcuts from the school of Andrea Mantegna, the love story of Poliphilus and Polia (reported in a dreamlike manner) was especially influential for visual art, from Dürer to Bernini. Interestingly, the representation of the nymph observed by a lustful satyr is the ekphrasis of a marble monument the hero sees in his short dream. The first complete English translation of the book appeared in 1999. Colonna's book was also important for Alciati's *Emblems* (especially its use of hieroglyphs). We thus find endless meanderings or rhizomatous networks stretching from Dossi to early Renaissance art and iconotexts.

33 Andrea Alciati, *Emblematum liber* (Augsburg: Heinrich Steyner, 1531).

FIGURE 25.6 Giorgione, *Sleeping Venus* (1508-10).
Oil on canvas. 108.5 × 175 cm
STAATLICHE KUNSTSAMMLUNGEN DRESDEN. GEMÄLDEGALERIE ALTE MEISTER

FIGURE 25.7 Titian, *Venus of Urbino* (before 1538).
Oil on canvas. 119 × 165 cm
GALLERIA DEGLI UFFIZI. FLORENCE, ITALY

FIGURE 25.8 Lucas Cranach d. J., *Der schlafende Herkules und die Pygmäen* (1551). Oil on wood. 189 × 259 cm
STAATLICHE KUNSTSAMMLUNGEN DRESDEN. GEMÄLDEGALERIE ALTE MEISTER

Duke Ercole II d'Este."[34] Dossi placed his scene in an Italian landscape and a political context, and Cranach's paintings of 1551 (Figures 25.8-9) operate in a similar way.

The painter anchors the episode in a contemporary German location, transposing the myth to a Saxon setting in the mid-sixteenth century and depicting the pygmies as dwarf-like, heavily armed figures in contemporary clothing. With their long beards and costumes, the dwarfs take up a large space of the picture, giving Cranach ample opportunity to represent them as individuals, no doubt also inspired by oral history. Since the location is Saxony (the *Sächsische Schweiz*, near Dresden), the Greek hero is transformed into a "Hercules Germanicus;"[35] he is shown asleep under an oak tree while the wicked dwarfs

---

34 Barbara Marx, "Wandering Objects, Migrating Artists: The Appropriation of Italian Renaissance Art by German Courts," *Forging European Identities, 1400-1700*, ed. Herman Roodenburg (Cambridge: Cambridge University Press, 2007), pp. 178-226 (203).

35 Jürgen Müller, "Moritz von Sachsen als 'Hercules Germanicus': zur Deutung der Herkulestafeln Lukas Cranach des Jüngeren," *"Man könnt vom Paradies nicht angenehmer*

FIGURE 25.9 Lucas Cranach d. J., *Der erwachte Herkules vertreibt die Pygmäen* (1551). Oil on wood. 188 × 261 cm
STAATLICHE KUNSTSAMMLUNGEN DRESDEN. GEMÄLDEGALERIE ALTE MEISTER

attack him with a variety of arms. Larger than Dossi's pygmies, they carry all sorts of dangerous weapons; two dwarfs are about to saw off Hercules' right foot. In *Der erwachte Herkules vertreibt die Pygmäen*, Cranach presents a scene within a scene on the left, as – in the manner mentioned by Philostratus – Hercules carries off some of the midgets in his lion's skin, thus demonstrating that in the contemporary imagination the size of pygmies varied between the length of a fist (the meaning of the word in Old Greek) and a lower arm. In 1646, Sir Thomas Browne, in his chapter "Of Pigmies" in *Pseudodoxia epidemica*, defined the pygmies as "a dwarfish race of people, or lowest diminution of mankinde, comprehended in one cubit, or as some will have it, in two foot, or three spans."[36] Like Dossi's painting, Cranach's two scenes carry a political

träumen": Festschrift für Prof. Dr. Harald Marx (Berlin: Deutscher Kunstverlag, 2009), pp. 50-57.

36 Browne doubted the existence of a people of pygmies, arguing that "there is, or ever was such a race or Nation … our strictest enquiry receaves no satisfaction" (*Pseudodoxia Epidemica*, ed. Robbins, I, 330). The *Online Etymology Dictionary* has this entry on the noun pygmy:

FIGURE 25.10
Lucas Cranach d. J., *Kurfürst Moritz von Sachsen* (1578).
Oil on canvas. 121.5 × 93 cm
STAATLICHE KUNSTSAMMLUNGEN DRESDEN. RÜSTKAMMER

message that is strengthened by Hercules' straight look at the viewer in the second painting. If the Greek demi-god stands for Moritz of Saxony (entangled in the religious wars of his time; see Figure 25.10, Cranach's posthumous portrait of 1578), then the message is clear: "Enemies beware, for if necessary I will defeat you, crushing you as I am doing with these dwarfs."[37]

Late 14c, *Pigmei*, 'member of the fabulous race of dwarfs,' described by Homer and Herodotus and said to inhabit Egypt or Ethiopia and India, from Latin *Pygmaei* (singular *Pygmaeus*), from Greek *Pygmaioi*, plural of *Pygmaios* 'a Pygme,' noun use of adjective meaning 'dwarfish,' literally 'of the length of a *pygme*, a *pygme* tall,' from *pgyme* 'cubit,' literally 'fist,' the measure of length from the elbow to the knuckle; related to *pyx* 'with clenched fist' and to Latin *pugnus* 'fist' (see pugnacious).

Figurative use for 'person of small importance' is from 1590s. Believed in 17c. to refer to chimpanzees or orang-utans, and occasionally the word was used in this sense. The ancient word was applied by Europeans to the equatorial African race 1863, but the tribes were known to the ancients and likely were the original inspiration for the legend. As an adjective from 1590s.

37 Barbara Marx notes that in the *Awakened Hercules* Cranach "presents the portrait features of Elector Moritz as a red-bearded 'wild man' fighting his dwarflike enemies" ("Wandering Objects, Migrating Artists: The Appropriation of Italian Renaissance Art by German Courts," p. 203).

There is also a structural and thematic relationship between Cranach's sleeping Hercules and visual representations of Polyphemus in art (see Figure 25.1) and in emblem books. The Polyphemus, for instance, who appears in Joannes Sambuccus' *Emblemata*, might pass for a picture of Hercules.[38] Yet the context in which Polyphemus is situated is *Principum Negligentia* (Negligence of Princes) – the title of the emblem. The context of the Polyphemus story would make sense, too, the implicit warning being that Moritz is not as stupid as the Cyclops and that he will be neither blinded nor vanquished.[39]

While both Dossi and Cranach politicized the Hercules figure to praise their patrons and to ridicule their enemies as presumptuous pygmies, one wonders whether Swift's idea of a giant fettered by dwarfs has visual antecedents. One example (Figure 25.11) was painted in the wake of Cranach's Hercules scenes; it is undated and was initially given the title "ein Pigmei Streit;" in the Cranach catalogue of 2005, it is listed under the title *Der gefesselte Herkules ringt mit den Pygmäen*.[40]

What is remarkable about this picture, apart from the fact that it shows another bemused Hercules who does not seem to mind his fetters, is the unusually large space taken up by the pygmies. Reminiscent of the crowds of little people in the Dossi and Cranach paintings, with individualized faces and arms, banners and musical instruments,[41] their representation seems to be inspired more by northern European tales of dwarfs than by Philostratus. It appears that in paintings pygmies were often associated with madness or shown in scenes demonstrating human follies. A good example is Frans Verbeeck's undated painting entitled *The Mocking of Human Follies* (Figure 25.12), which was also produced around the time Cranach painted his scenes.[42]

38 *Emblemata et aliquot nummi antiqui operis* (Antwerp: Christopher Plantin, 1566).

39 This is also true for Dossi's picture of Ercole II as Hercules discussed above. A simpler explanation for the resemblance between images of Hercules and Polyphemus would be the adoption of Hercules images by artists in search of pictures for Polyphemus. It is also interesting that in some commentaries on the emblem the translators of the Latin texts seem to mingle the stories of Hercules and the pygmies, Polyphemus and Odysseus, and the biblical Samson. See, for instance, the French text published by Christian Wechel in Paris in 1536, where the translator Lefevre has the pygmies attack Hercules' eyes "pour ce qu'il ne sembloit fort homme [that he may not appear to be a strong man]."

40 In *Cranach 2005*, eds Marx and Mössinger, a date around 1600 is suggested, but the inventory in Berlin dates it at 1551, the year when Cranach painted his two scenes (p. 422).

41 This scene as well as the pygmy figures in the Dossi painting remind me immediately of the "cortège" during the "Morgestraich" held each year during carnival in Basle, Switzerland, with people in bizarre masks and bands of musicians playing Renaissance (military) tunes mainly with drums and pipes.

42 Verbeeck lived and worked in Mechelen, Belgium (*c*.1510-70), in a group of Verbeeck painters between the time of Bosch and Brueghel.

FIGURE 25.11 Unknown artist. *Der gefesselte Herkules ringt mit den Pygmäen* (*c*.1600). Oil on wood
STAATLICHE MUSEEN ZU BERLIN. GEMÄLDEGALERIE (DEPOT FREMDBESITZ). REPRODUCED FROM MARX AND MÖSSINGER, *CRANACH* (2005), P. 422

Here is a short ekphrasis of this intriguing picture sold at auction in Vienna in October 2014 under the title *Der Narrenhandel* at the humble price of more than three million Euros:[43]

> This crowded scene ... seems to be incomprehensible at first sight ... In an open landscape covered with green meadows, small figurines are being traded beneath a tall tree. Some of them, wearing caps and bells, are recognisable as fools. On the right-hand side of the composition is an inn, while the coast and ships appear on the left. The whole scenery is interspersed with merchants and buyers, all of whom are busy dealing with the tiny fools: fools en miniature (fantastic diminutions reminiscent of Jonathan Swift's *Gulliver's Travels*) are being offered for sale and purchased as if they were articles of trade. The absurdity of these

43 A detailed discussion of the painting in Dutch can be found in Jan op de Beeck, "De Familie Verbeeck: een raar schildersgeslacht uit Mechelen," *De zotte schilders: moraalridders van het penseel rond Bosch, Brueghel en Brouwer*, eds Eric de Bruyn and Jan op de Beeck (Gent: Snoek Ducaju & Zoon, 2003), pp. 88-93.

FIGURE 25.12 Frans Verbeeck (*c.*1510-70), *The Mocking of Human Follies* (*Der Narrenhandel*). Oil on canvas. N. d. 135 × 188cm
PRIVATE COLLECTION

transactions can only be interpreted as an allegory that appears to illustrate that human folly will always be circulating and is therefore inextinguishable. The painting is thus an allegorical satire on man's follies.

In the foreground, several merchants are depicted sitting at a table and cradling some of the tiny fools, while a traveling vendor and his wife offer small fools for sale from a sack and baskets. The vendor is depicted harnassed like a horse, and on his forehead sits one of the little fools with a hammer – an allusion to the well-known 'stone operation.' This surgical removal of a stone through the forehead was a subject that originated in the art of Hieronymus Bosch and was widespread in the 16th and 17th centuries in the form of numerous representations and variations. The motif's message is quite simple: it is impossible to cure stupidity through surgery.

In the left background appears another vendor, who sits under a tree, as well as a covered set of scales that is obviously used for weighing the fools, who are delivered by waggons and even by boat. In the right middle foreground appears a man at a table selling fools, while another vendor ... is based next to the inn.

Inspirations and instructions for the numerous allusive and enigmatic details contained in the present composition can be found in the satirical rhymes of the Guild of Rhetoricians, the so-called 'rederijkers' (comparable to today's carnival speakers), which made fun of vices and follies ... The clergy and Catholicism are ridiculed ... the amorous couple at the right margin ... a friar and a nun ... indulge in the folly of love. Left to the principal scene, a couple of pilgrims kneeling

> down in adoration in front of a couple of aged fools is just as peculiar. The female fool nurses a baby fool, feeding him some kind of mash.[44]
>
> Numerous further allusions to satirical texts ... can be found in the catalogue (by Op de Beeck). Just one more example is the cage in the right background suspended above a group of dancers: it contains a fool hatching a large egg from which emerges a small fool. The motif refers to the proverb 'men mag geen zot eieren laten uitbroeden', which means that one should not allow fools to hatch eggs as they will only produce more fools.[45]

The stylistic uniqueness and iconographic wealth and autonomy of the painting puts this example of Verbeeck family art on an equal footing with that of Bosch and Brueghel. The painting parades figure types from Flemish folklore "that have been brought to the brink of scurrility and caricature."[46]

As far as the representation of pgymies or little people is concerned, the painting widens the scope of what we have seen so far. For the small figures represented here are not only fools but also representations of hobgoblins, imps, and evil dwarfs as they peopled the oral folklore tradition of Northern Europe during the Renaissance.[47] These notions of pygmies seem to conflate in other paintings by Verbeeck, such as his *Burlesque Feast* of 1550 (Figure 25.13), in which perspective is dramatized in a way strongly reminiscent of Swift's handling it in *Gulliver's Travels*.[48]

Art historical research has unearthed additional rhizomatous shoots that would connect Cranach's rendering of the myth with the Bible – Samson's fight with the Philistines, for instance,[49] and with previous or contemporary paint-

44 Perhaps this scene, just like the one on the right, belongs to the anti-Catholic satire of the painting, as the Catholic practice of adoring saints during pilgrimages is ridiculed.

45 Alexander Wied, *The Mocking of Human Follies: Auction Catalogue at the Vienna Dorotheum*, p. 2 (<www.dorotheum.com/en/auction-detail/auction-10841>, accessed 8 October 2014).

46 Wied, *The Mocking of Human Follies*, p. 2.

47 The English language offers a great variety of words for little beings – from spirits to small humans – predominantly associated with negative ideas; to the imp and the hobgoblin one might add goblin, kobold, gnome, pixy, elf, and comparable creatures from the Celtic tradition, such as the Irish leprechaun.

48 By the laws of perspective, the figures in the centre foreground and to the left in this painting should appear larger than those seated at the table. But in the burlesque spirit of the entire mocking of a wedding, they are rendered as misshapen dwarfs. Or they are pygmies mocked in the cruel spirit of a time when physical handicaps were still considered funny. On this particular satirical handling of perspective in connection with the representation of giants and Lilliputians in *Gulliver's Travels* and baroque art, see Thomas R. Cleary, "Big People and Little People: Size, Distance and Value in *Gulliver's Travels* and Baroque *trompe-l'oeil*," *Studies on Voltaire and the Eighteenth Century*, 305 (1992), 1493-95.

49 *Cranach 2005*, eds Marx and Mössinger, p. 415; see also the sketch by Dürer mentioned there.

FIGURE 25.13 Frans Verbeeck, *Burlesque Feast* (c.1550). Oil on oak. 98.5 × 147 cm
MUSEO DE BELLAS ARTES DE BILBAO

ers, such as Holbein.[50] However, some of the rhizomes established by emblem books proved even more influential with their representations of giants and pygmies alike. The most important emblem book in this context was Andrea Alciati's (or Alciato's) *Emblematum liber*: "Both Dossi and Cranach," art historians have pointed out, "used Alciati's emblem for the motto *in eos qui supra vires quicquam audent*."[51] Cranach's conception of the sleeping Hercules, too, is indebted to an emblem in the 1548 French edition of this book (Figure 25.14).[52]

Alciati lived in Ferrara between 1542 and 1546, and while there adopted the episode of Hercules and the pygmies in his collection, which probably first appeared in print in 1531.[53] From their first appearance in Latin, Alciati's emblems were enormously influential, extending their impact over the whole of Europe. As an historian has noted, "Andrea Alciati's book of emblems is the most re-

50 See Müller, "Moritz von Sachsen als 'Hercules Germanicus': zur Deutung der Herkulestafeln Lukas Cranach des Jüngeren," pp. 50-57.

51 Marx, "Wandering Objects, Migrating Artists: The Appropriation of Italian Renaissance Art by German Courts," p. 203.

52 Werner Schade, "Maler am Hofe Moritz' von Sachsen," *Zeitschrift des deutschen Vereins für Kunstwissenschaft*, 22 (1968), 29-44 (p. 33).

53 *Cranach 2005*, eds Marx and Mössinger, pp. 419-22.

56 STVLTITIA.

In eos qui ſupra vires quic-
quam audent.

Dum dormit: dulci recreat dum corpora ſomno
Sub picea, & clauam cæteráque arma tenet,
Alciden pygmæa manus proſternere letho
Poſſe putat: uires non bene docta ſuas.
Excitus ipſe, uelut pulices, ſic proterit hoſtem,
Et ſæui implicitum pelle leonis agit.

FIGURE 25.14 Woodcut from Andrea Alciati, *Emblemata* (Lyon, 1548 and 1550).

printed emblem book in history. It appeared in over two hundred editions in the sixteenth and seventeenth centuries" – in addition to Latin, also in French, German, Italian, and Spanish,[54] with many of the emblems also published in English in Geffrey Whitney's *Choice of Emblems* of 1586.

What is important about Alciati's book of emblems is that, in addition to its international history of production and publication (by Italian, German, and French artists and writers), it established ways of thinking about little people that seemed to have survived several centuries. Alciati's emblems first circulated without any illustrations among his friends in Italy and France. A legal scholar who also stayed in Bourges from 1529 to 1534, his major work was on Roman law; he "saw his emblems as essentially recreative and entertaining: a relief and respite from his graver labours as a lawyer and academic."[55] We do not know how his emblems came into the hands of the Augsburg printer Heinrich Steyner. In any case, Steyner commissioned illustrations (woodcuts by Hans Schäufelein after the Augsburg painter Jörg Breu) for most of Alciati's mottoes and emblems, thus inadvertently establishing the modern tripartite form of the emblem with his first illustrated Augsburg edition of 1531.

Since Alciati did not approve of the Augsburg edition of 1531, he entrusted a Paris printer, Christian Wechel, with corrected and augmented editions that appeared with new cuts between 1534 and 1542, including French and German translations. After the mid-1540s, Alciati collaborated with various printers, the editions by Guillaume Rouillé (and his partner Macé Bonhomme), who published thirty-five editions between 1548 and 1616, being among the most important. These printers also rearranged the previous rather erratic and arbitrary sequence into one structured by theme or topic: "Alciato's *Emblemata* were turned into a handy work of reference, a succour and support for an author's flagging rhetorical invention."[56] One might add that the book, as Cranach's paintings demonstrate, was equally important for painters, not to mention theologians and rhetoricians.[57]

The tripartite structure of the emblem consists of a motto or *inscriptio*(*n*), a picture (*pictura*) and a short text or epigram in verse, the *subscriptio*(n). This iconographic tradition was maintained for more than one hundred years. Looking at the relevant emblem of the 1531 edition (Figure 25.15), one notices

---

54 For more extensive discussions of the genesis and printing history of the *Emblematum liber*, see John Manning's introduction to the reprint of the Lyon edition of 1550 ([Aldershot: Scolar Press, 1996], pp. ix-xxi [xi]), and the introduction in Henkel and Schöne, *Emblemata*, pp. ix-xxv, which also explains the general set-up of emblem books and the way they were composed and read.

55 *Emblematum liber*, introd. Manning, p. x.

56 *Emblematum liber*, introd. Manning, p. xiii.

57 Henkel and Schöne, *Emblemata*, p. xviii.

FIGURE 25.15 Woodcut from Andrea Alciati, *Emblematum liber* (Augsburg, 1531).

that in the *pictura* the Hercules episode is told in two scenes contained in one, the action moving from right to left.

More importantly, however, the scene is framed, both textually and ideologically, for emblems were supposed to represent and explicate.[58] While there were different pictorial representations of the encounter between the Greek hero and the pygmies in the various subsequent editions of the book, the emblem remains in essence an iconotext made up of words and an image in which the verbal parts force the picture into a generally moral direction. The various national varieties of the emblem books as they developed in the sixteenth century strengthened this moralistic trend. Thus even in the very first (German) edition, the motto above the picture reads: "In eos qui supra vires quicquam audent [Against those who venture what is beyond their powers]," rendered in German as "Wider dise die wieder jr vermügen dörffen etwas anfahen." The epigram below the picture provides a Latin text briefly explaining the stupidity of the pygmies in attacking someone too strong for them. This 'moral' is close to the Latin version offered in Philostratus' *Icones* (or *Imagines*), it is true, but Alciati lifted most of these epigrams from the *Anthologica Graeca*, translating its short poems into Latin and adapting them for his purposes.[59] The various national editions subsequently also contained translations of the Latin. Here is the Augsburg edition of 1531:

58 Henkel and Schöne, *Emblemata*, pp. xii-xiii; xvii.

59 Henkel and Schöne, *Emblemata*, p. xi.

Dum dormit, dulci recreat dum corpora somno,
Sub picea et clavam caeteraque arma tenet,
Alcyden pygmea manus prosternere laetho,
Posse putat, vires non bene docta suas.
Exitus ipse velut pulices, sic proterit hostem,
Et saevi implicitum pelle leonis agit.

Dieweil da schlafft und ruht so süß
Under einr Thannen Hercules
Und helt bey sich sein Kolben groß
Mit anderen Waffen ubermaß
Meinen die kleinen Zwergen schon
Sie woollen jin wol meistern thon
Wölln alsbald jn reiben auff
Bdenkt nit jr sterck der kleine hauff
Dann er auffgwegt sie zerknitst doch
Als werens nur gar kleine Flöch
Verwirrts und wickelts also eyn
Mit der großen Löwen Haut seyn.[60]

Moreover, the editions that adopted Rouillé's thematic order after the 1550s group the episode with Hercules and the pygmies under two further categories. The encounter is listed under the general title "vitia [vices]" and the subtitle "stultitia [stupidity or foolishness]." This emblematic interpretation of the mythical scene is remarkable since the Latin of Philostratus does not really interpret the conduct of the pygmies as foolish. On the contrary, in the *Imagines*, the pygmies are described as fearless, strong, and "high-spirited fellows" claiming "to be brothers of Antaeus," who "would not fear [Hercules] even if he were awake" (II, 22).

In the course of history, the pictorial part of emblems gradually became more important until the illustrations assumed a general priority in the ensemble.[61] But textual changes also occurred when national languages replaced the Latin, the lingua franca of the Renaissance. Thus, in the first major English collection of emblems, Geffrey Whitney's *A Choice of Emblemes* (1586), the pictorial part was borrowed from previous Continental editions, accompanied by an English translation of the Latin subscription in which lice become "gnattes" (Figure 25.16).

More importantly, this translation is followed by a poetic explication warning readers not to undertake anything "above [their] power." An interesting socio-political dimension is added as "the pore" are admonished not to "strife

60 Henkel and Schöne, *Emblemata*, p. 1653.
61 Henkel and Schöne, *Emblemata*, p. xv.

16

Quod potes, tenta.

WHILE, HERCVLES, with mightie clubbe in hande
In Lyons ſkinne did ſleepe, and take his eaſe:
About him ſtraighte approch'de the Pigmeis bande,
And for to kill this conquerour aſſaies,
But fooliſhe dwarffes? theire force was all to ſmalle,
For when he wak'de, like gnattes hee cruſh'd them all.

Hi homunciones extremas Ægypti partes inhabitant agricolationi dediti, Subinde cum gruibus bellum gerunt. Plinius lib. 7. cap. 2. & Aul. Gellius lib. 9. cap. 4.

This warneth vs, that nothinge paſte our ſtrengthe
Wee ſhoulde attempte: nor anie worke pretende,
Aboue our power: leſt that with ſhame at lengthe
Wee weakelinges prooue, and fainte before the ende.
The pore, that ſtriue with mightie, this doth blame:
And ſottes, that ſeeke the learned to defame.

Propertius.

Turpe eſt quod nequeas capiti ſubmittere pondus,
Et preſſum inflexo mox dare terga genu.

Ludus

FIGURE 25.16 Woodcut from Geffrey Whitney, *A Choice of Emblemes* (Leiden, 1586). REPRODUCED FROM THE FACSIMILE REPRINT ED. HENRY GREEN. LONDON: LOVELL, 1866. P. 16.

with mightie," and "sottes" (foolish people) to abstain from defaming the learned.[62] Curiously, however, this emblem appears with a motto, "Quod potes, tenta [Try as much as you can; or strive to your utmost]," which contradicts the explication of the *subscriptio*.

However, Alciati's epigrammatic text seems to have been as influential as Philostratus' ekphrasis of a picture he allegedly saw in or near Naples. For quite a few engravings of the sixteenth and seventeenth centuries illustrating the episode also contain Alciati's Latin text, thus obstructing or even preventing the potential disseminating power of the picture. Unlike paintings, which were mostly reserved for the upper classes, copper engravings saw a much wider circulation among the public since they were affordable for members of the middle class, too. These constitute an important discursive field which was shot through with verbal and visual rhizomes stretching from Philostratus to the early Renaissance. A case in point is a print by Cornelis Cort (1533-78) after a lost painting by Frans Floris. Entitled *Hercules Besieged by Pygmies* (Figure 25.17), it is dated 1562 (the second state being dated 1563). It should be clear by now that the source for the sleeping Hercules besieged by pygmies is not necessarily the *Icones* or *Imagines* by Philostratus.

Neither was the subject unusual nor can the picture be explained by one source only. While there are clear echoes of Philostratus (for example, the inclusion of the dead Antaeus and the representation of Sleep, Somnus, hovering above Hercules), here is a summary of the various representations of the scene in different media:

> The combination of illustration with moralistic epigram derives from the emblem Hercules besieged by Pygmies by Alciati. His moral is directed to the Pygmies, 'who venture on something beyond their powers.' It could be more specifically related to the poor who rise against the powerful, or to fools who try to defame the reputation of the learned. In the 1534 woodcut ... in which Hercules figures twice, he appears to let the Pygmies have their way. The momentarily good-natured aspect was imitated by Dosso and Battista Dosso in a painting made ... during the reign of Ercole II of Ferrara. Alciati taught in Ferrara from 1542 to 1546 and it will have been these Pygmies that inspired him to have depicted them as lansquenets in the new edition of his Emblemata published in Lyon in 1548 ... Sleep here reveals himself by his bat wings and the strange snake growing out of one of them ... He is the Devil in disguise. Hercules lies in the seductive pose of Ariadne, or rather of Endymion visited by Sleep ... The tree under which Hercules lies has bare branches, while the part above his head looks like the head of an adder, symbols of his sinister situation. Antaeus lies with his arm on a root near a hollow tree from which a new shoot is sprouting,

62 A similar turn in the explication of the meaning of the scene can be found in Artus Thomas's poetic lines as a *subscriptio* to the picture of Hercules in de Vigenère's translation into French of Philostratus' *Imagines* (1614); see the discussion below.

FIGURE 25.17 Cornelis Cort, *Hercules Besieged by Pygmies.* Engraving. 1562/63. 32.8 × 46.9 cm

> for Hercules has not conquered evil for ever ... [The] Pygmies are naked, but they are not all youthful ... Nor are they rash and unthinking. Admittedly one group swarming out of caves at bottom right and centre are foolishly trying to roll away the club with their bare hands and one is about to throw a stone, but the king leading out his orderly army appears to come from a well-run country, while gesticulating Pygmy philosophers have wisely decided that it is better not to fight the hero at all.[63]

This visual example of the myth of Hercules and the pygmies demonstrates the iconotextual nature of such Renaissance representations, with their rhizomes reaching back to Alciati and Philostratus.

At this point, I suggest taking a closer look at the dissemination of Philostratus' ekphrastic description of a mythological scene, particularly at the way it was received in the Renaissance and the early modern period. Swift scholars tell us that "Swift owned a copy of *Imagines* (Paris, 1608)" and that he "annotated the volume with the praise that it was 'neither disagreeable nor useless' ('nec illepida nec inutilia')," adding that "he had been greatly pleased by it ('quae autem mihi maxime arriserunt')."[64] Swift commented in Latin

63 J. P. Guépin, "Hercules belegerd door de Pygmeeën, schilderijen van Jan van Sorel en Frans Floris naar een Icon van Philostratus," *Oud Holland: Quarterly for Dutch Art History*, 102, no 2 (1988), 155-72.

64 *Gulliver's Travels*, ed. Womersley, p. 34n31; see also PASSMANN AND VIENKEN II, 1421-23.

because he usually annotated the authors he was reading in their own tongue; his edition of *Imagines* contained Philostratus' text in Greek and Latin, side by side, making it easy for educated readers to compare the two versions.[65]

But in the seventeenth century, this edition of Philostratus was neither the most popular nor the most influential one. In fact, it was the first French illustrated edition of *Images* of 1614, and its numerous subsequent editions, to which Philostratus' text owed its enormous influence.[66] It is important to bear in mind that there were two authors called Philostratus, and that their texts were often published together with descriptions of statues by Callistratus. Swift's personal copy of 1608, for instance, contained *Philostrati Lemni Opera ... Philostrati Iunioris Imagines et Callistrati Ecphrases*. The *Eikones* or *Imagines* as we know them today are the work of two Greek philosophers from the third century, one called Flavius Philostratus the Elder (from Lemnos, *c.*190-230 AD), and the other Philostratus the Younger, probably his grandson.[67] In descriptions of 64 paintings (written by the Elder) and 17 additional pictures (described by the Younger), the two philosophers produced ekphrases of works of art they claimed to have seen in a gallery near or in Naples. These paintings allegedly showed mythological figures described by Greek and Roman poets. While it is unknown whether these works of art really existed, it is the generic nature of the *Imagines* that is most important: ekphrasis, the description of images (or statues),[68] is really a pretext for the two authors who wanted to demonstrate their skills as rhetoricians. While doing so, they speculated on the relationship between the visual arts and reality, elaborating along the way a complex theory of imitation (*mimesis*) and observations on the truth of

65 The episode with Hercules and the Pygmies appears on pp. 816-17.

66 H. Bardon, "Sur les 'Images ou Tableaux de Platte Peinture' de Blaise de Vigenère," *Revue belge de philologie et d'histoire*, 55, no 1 (1977), 106-21.

67 On the authors and their texts, see Raichel A. Le Goff's thesis, "Philostratus Illustrated: The Reception of 'The Imagines' in Renaissance Art and Culure," doctoral dissertation, University of Newcastle, Australia, 2012, and the excellent summary of the textual history, including the French illustrated versions, by Jean Balsamo, "Le Livre du mois: Philostrate," pp. 1-4 (<www.bib.ens.fr/mars-2013-Philostr.615.0.html>, accessed 31 October 2018). Le Goff, in particular, describes how the *Imagines* were rediscovered, translated, read, and interpreted by humanists, artists, and their patrons, from the time of the first printed edition in 1503 to the beginning of the seventeenth century. I disagree with her argument, though, that its popularity diminished in the early seventeenth century. This may have been true of editions without illustrations, but as the history of the de Vigenère edition shows, there was an actual revival of the Philostratus texts after 1614, with rhizomatous shoots and roots stretching into art, decoration, book illustration, and music.

68 On ekphrasis as such, and the variety of notional ekphrases, see Wagner, *Reading Iconotexts*, pp. 81, 126.

fables and their capacity to offer an access to higher levels of reality.[69] These dimensions situate the *Imagines* at the crossroads of the theory of art and philosophy, literature, and mere intellectual speculation; no wonder then that it became a key text for humanists and artists when it was rediscovered in the Renaissance, and no wonder that Swift found it delightful, too.[70] Originally circulating in manuscript, the Greek text of the *Eikones*, together with the *Ekphraseis* of Callistratus, were first published in Florence in 1496.[71] The two Philostrati and Callistratus eventually had a "mutual Latin *editio princeps* in 1503, entitled *Icones Philostrati*; *Descriptiones Callistrati*, published in Venice by Aldus Manutius in 1503.[72] A French translation, ordered by King Henri III and executed by Blaise de Vigenère, was published in 1578, and in 1597 a second edition appeared with the second series of ekphrases and Callistratus' descriptions of statues; this was reprinted in 1602. The editor, Abel l'Angelier, of Paris, then decided to market a revised version of *Imagines*, based on de Vigenère's French translation, revised and corrected by Fédéric Morel and augmented by engravings, which in turn were accompanied by epigrams of Artus Thomas d'Embry. L'Angelier took his colleague Mathieu Guillemot aboard for this venture, but they both died before the publication of the illustrated volume, which was finally taken on by their widows in 1614.[73] The frontispiece of this newly illustrated *Imagines* hints at the geographical origin of the ekphrases by the two Philostrati (Figure 25.18).

Although rather expensive because of its richly adorned engravings, *Les Images ou tableaux de platte peinture des deux Philostrates sophists grecs et les statues de Callistrate mis en françois par Blaise de Vigenere* was reprinted in 1615, with further editions in 1629 and 1630, and a revised one in 1637. Two aspects rendered this edition remarkable and unique. On the one hand, it was Blaise de Vigenère's French translation[74] of the *Imagines* (used in the 1614 edi-

69 Balsamo, "Le Livre du mois: Philostrate," p. 2.

70 On the influence of *Imagines* as an exemplar for later ekphrastic treatments, see Graeme Miles, "Genres of Painting and Genres of Text in the *Imagines* of Philostratus," *Approaches to Genre in the Ancient World*, eds Michelle Borag and Graeme Miles (Newcastle upon Tyne: Cambridge Scholars, 2013), pp. 123-41, and *Musée de mots: l'héritage de Philostrate dans la littérature occidentale*, eds Sylvie Ballestra-Puech, *et al.* (Geneva: Droz, 2010).

71 John F. Moffit, *Caravaggio in Context: Learned Naturalism and Renaissance Humanism* (Jefferson, North Carolina: McFarland, 2004), pp. 219-20n53.

72 Moffit, *Caravaggio in Context*, pp. 219-20n53. Moffit also underlines the "great popularity among Renaissance painters of Philostratus' descriptions of ancient paintings" (p. 220n54).

73 Balsamo, "Le Livre du mois: Philostrate," p. 2.

74 Blaise de Vigenère (1523-96) was a "French diplomat and author of over twenty books, of which his *Traicté des Chiffres* on cryptography has attracted modern interest since it is

FIGURE 25.18 Frontispiece of *Les Images ou Tableaux de platte peinture* … trans. Blaise de Vigenère (Paris, 1614/15). Engraving

tion and later ones), allegedly based on the Greek original,[75] together with annotations and commentaries (by Fédéric Morel and de Vigenère himself); on the other, it was the illustrations, which constituted a novelty and a "major attraction" for a wider audience.[76] Interestingly, the first engravings were done by Thomas de Leu and Léonard Gaultier after drawings by the painter Antoine Caron (d.1599); they were then continued by Jaspar Isaac and his crew, with a final result that has been termed "franco-flamand," with a shot of "maniérisme praguois,"[77] in other words, a truly European venture.

Each description in the de Vigenère edition starts with an elaborate engraving (Figure 25.19), taking up an entire page, in each case with an epigram by Artus Thomas, followed in some cases by Morel's Avertissement and by de Vigenère's Argument in italics. De Vigenère's translation of the Philostratus text then appears in regular type, and finally, commentaries and often rather elaborate annotations.[78] The illustrations thus added an important dimension

---

thought to have invented the first intelligence cipher of its type not to be easily broken" (Bath, "Philostratus Comes to Scotland: A New Source for the Pictures at Pinkey," p. 4). He died in 1596 and did not live to see the beautiful, illustrated result of his labours as translator.

75 As far as I could ascertain, there are hardly any analyses of the differences between the Greek and Latin versions of *Eikones / Imagines*. This is all the more surprising since our modern understanding of the text seems to be largely based on the Latin translation. Comparisons of brief passages do show differences. Since I suspected that in II, 22 (Hercules among the Pygmies) there might be a reference to the fettering of Hercules in the Greek version, I asked Hermann J. Real for help with this passage in Greek and Latin. His important finding was that the Latin version contains the verb "circumvallarunt," that is, they surrounded him, whereas the Greek rendering is more complicated and ambivalent, with meanings such as surround, beleaguer, hold – and thus perhaps also fetter.

Largely unnoticed by modern critics, Blaise de Vigenère's translation leaned heavily on a Latin translation from 1515 by Stefano Negri, published in Milan in 1521 and reprinted in Basle in 1532. Vigenère's knowledge of Greek was apparently not very good and Fédéric Morel, the best Greek scholar of his time and translator to the king, discovered this plagiarism of sorts. This did not, however, keep Morel (presumably the "docte personage de ce temps en la langue Grecque" mentioned in the title, who corrected and annotated the edition of 1614) from also using Negri's translation when he published a full translation of the texts by the two Philostratus in 1608. For details, see Bardon, "Sur les 'Images ou Tableaux de Platte Peinture' de Blaise de Vigenère," pp. 113-14.

76 Balsamo, "Le Livre du mois: Philostrate," p. 3.

77 Balsamo, "Le Livre du mois: Philostrate," p. 3.

78 Bardon notes that Morel's actual corrections of de Vigenère's translation from Latin (in relation to the Greek original he claims to have used) are few and far between ("Sur les 'Images ou Tableaux de Platte Peinture' de Blaise de Vigenère," p. 114).

480 HERCVLES PARMY

C'eſt vn mal-heur extreme
De s'ignorer ſoy-meſme,
Vn Geant triomphant
Eſt braué d'vn enfant.
Le plus chetif eſclaue
S'eſtime le plus braue,

Lors que ſon iugement
A cet aueuglement :
Car ſi-toſt qu'on ouure la porte
A quelque bonne opinion,
La vanité ſe rend ſi forte
Qu'elle perd de preſomption.

HERCVLES

FIGURE 25.19 "Hercules parmy les Pygmées." Engraving from *Les Images ou Tableaux de platte peinture* … trans. Blaise de Vigenère (Paris, 1614/15).

to the dissemination of the *Imagines*; what had originally been a book for educated readers also became a book for artists.[79]

Two examples may demonstrate the rhizomatous shoots of the French translation of the *Imagines* in various media and in surprising foreign locations. Around 1615, when Alexander Seton, first Earl of Dunfermline, decorated his neo-Stoic gallery (imitating the one the Philostrati claimed to have seen) in his newly erected Pinkie House, Musselburgh, the ceiling was painted with 30 emblems. These were done after the iconotexts in two emblem books, and one was modelled after an "engraved illustration to Blaise de Vigenère's French translation of the *Imagines* of Philostratus." We can thus trace and map the rhizomatous links between Blaise de Vigenère's iconotext and the "deliberate attempt by the Scottish Chancellor to recreate in early-modern Scotland a building which would reconstitute the arts of antiquity."[80] The French edition of the *Imagines* of 1614 may also have inspired Ben Jonson for his masque *Pleasure Reconciled to Virtue*, performed at Court on Twelfth Night, 6 January 1618, in which four pygmies[81] attempt to kill the sleeping Hercules:

> The masque dramatizes the expulsion by Hercules of gross sensuality from the world ... In the 'second Antimasque' Hercules is roused from his sleep at the foot of Mount Atlas by a chorus of pygmies whom he sweeps from the land; they enter the stage with the words '*Antaeus* dead? And Hercules yet live? (Jonson 1925-52 7: ll. 87-89, 135). The pygmies vaingloriously resolve to attack him, and attempt to steal his club, an action which we find pictured in the illustration to de Vigenère's 'Hercules Furieux' showing Hercules destroying a host of pigmies who have attacked him.[82]

---

79 On the iconotextual nature of the text of the *Imagines*, see Miles, "Genres of Painting and Genres of Text in the *Imagines* of Philostratus," pp. 123-41. For discussions of the two Philostrati texts as examples of ekphrasis, see Stephen M. Beall, "Word-Painting in the 'Imagines' of the Elder Philostratus," *Hermes*, 121 (1993), 350-63; Mario Baumann, *Bilder schreiben: virtuose Ekphrasis in Philostrats "Eikones"* (Berlin: Walter de Gruyter, 2011), and Cordula Bachmann, *Wenn man die Welt als Gemälde betrachtet: Studien zu den Eikones Philostrats des Älteren* (Heidelberg: Verlag Antike, 2015).

80 Michael Bath notes: "Of the 30 emblems painted on the gallery ceiling eight are copied from the *Emblemata Horatiana* (Antwerp, 1607) of Otto van Veen ('Vaenius'), and three copy examples from the *Emblemata* (Frankfurt, 1596) of Denis Lebey de Batilly" ("Philostratus Comes to Scotland: A New Source for the Pictures at Pinkey," pp. 2, 3).

81 These were played by boys dressed as frogs (see David Lindley's explanatory footnote in *Court Masques: Jacobean and Caroline Entertainments, 1605-1640* [Oxford: Oxford University Press, 1995], p. 250). Frogs conveyed the ideas of excrement and earth, as Edwards explains ("Engaging with Pygmies: Thomas Browne and John Milton," p. 110), one dominant notion of the pygmies being of sensuous, earthbound creatures lacking human morality or ethics.

82 Bath, "Philostratus Comes to Scotland: A New Source for the Pictures at Pinkey," p. 13. It has to be added here, however, that Bath's commentary refers to the wrong illustration,

Bardon has argued that the engravings are the "commentaire linéaire du texte,"[83] closely following the Greek version. Indeed, one recognizes some of the details of the story, with the walls and towers of Troy in the background, the dead Antaeus in the middle distance, and a reclining, sleeping Hercules on his lion's skin in the centre. In the tradition of Renaissance painting showing classical heroes, the athletic body of Hercules is naked (as in Cornelis Cort's engraving from 1562), echoing as it does the triumphant mythical males in painting and sculpture by Leonardo, Michelangelo, Raphael, and Titian.[84] Baccio Bandinelli's gigantic Hercules in the Piazza della Signorina, Florence, of 1530 (*Ercole e Caco*), originally to be sculpted by Michelangelo, is just one of many examples (Figure 25.20). The Hercules in de Vigenère's *Les Images*, then, is not the one described by Philostratus but rather the visual embodiment of the male ideal of beauty as imagined by Renaissance artists.

Philostratus' *Eikones* is also recalled in the representation of the pygmies in the engraving illustrating the Hercules episode (Figure 25.19). While two are trying to set fire to the hero's hair, a 'phalanx' of warriors attempt to carry away his club, and others appear from caves below the ground. Unlike the nude pygmies in Cort's print, those in the French engraving are wearing military clothes or uniforms (as the Renaissance imagined Greek or Roman soldiers). The danger emanating from the pygmies in this picture seems, however, less than that in Cranach's paintings – apart from the two figures attempting to set fire to Hercules' hair, they are busy trying to steal the hero's club. Perhaps as a tribute to Philostratus' comparison of the pygmies with ants, they are also rendered smaller in size than Cranach's dwarfs and closer in size and spirit to the seemingly harmless little people in the Dossi painting of 1535.

As a French Renaissance rendering of the myth told by Philostratus, the picture is both intertextual and intermedial. Its format closely resembles sixteenth-century emblem books. Instead of the motto above the *pictura*, a title

---

the "Hercules Furieux" from the 1614 edition illustrating the hero's killing of his own children. "Hercules parmy les Pygmées" appears before this incident.

The entire scene in Jonson's court masque presupposes a certain knowledge among the audience of the story of Hercules and the pygmies, no doubt as interpreted in Renaissance art and such iconotexts as *Les Images* by de Vigenère. The text mentions, for instance, the pygmies' belief that Antaeus is their brother, and when Hercules wakes up, they "run into holes." See the reprint of the masque in *Court Masques*, ed. Lindley, p. 120.

83 Bardon, "Sur les 'Images ou Tableaux de Platte Peinture' de Blaise de Vigenère," p. 115.

84 Vigenère seems to have believed that in their ekphrases the two Philostrati described real works of art by classical painters such as Apelles, Zeuxis, and others, whose details we can still study in those Renaissance painters and sculptors who drew on the texts of the two Greek sophists; for example, Leonardo, Michelangelo, Mantegna, and Raphael (Bardon, "Sur les 'Images ou Tableaux de Platte Peinture' de Blaise de Vigenère," p. 116).

FIGURE 25.20
Baccio Bandinelli, *Ercole e Caco* (*Hercules and Cacus*) (1530).
PIAZZA DELLA SIGNORINA. FLORENCE, ITALY

spreads over two pages, while the verses below show the same moralizing and explanatory function as the emblematic epigram, the traditional *subscriptio*. Severely reducing the semantic richness of the image, Artus Thomas's clumsy couplets read:

> C'est un mal-heur extreme
> De s'ignorer soy-mesme,
> Un Geant triumphant
> Est brave d'un enfant.
> Le plus chetif esclave
> S'estime le plus brave,
> Lors que son iugement
> A cet aveuglement:
> Car si tost qu'on ouvre la porte
> A quelque bonne opinion,
> La vanité se rend si forte
> Que'elle pert de presumption.

Rather than comment on the picture, however, these moralizing verses repeat the interpretation of the myth as offered in previous emblem books: not to overestimate oneself and one's talents. The iambic trimeter couplets extend this warning to inferior social classes while suggesting that such thinking leads to vanity and presumption. It is interesting that in de Vigenère's annotations the motto from Alciati's emblem book (which is also part of Cort's engraving) should actually be quoted verbatim in Latin (p. 485), underlining the ostensible moral message of the picture and the mythical story as a whole.[85] In brief, the engraving is a highly intermedial iconotext, a *mise-en-scène* of the classical mythological story with rhizomatous links to Italian painting and sculpture, emblem books and the verbal re-creation of a painting by a classical artist in the text of Philostratus' *Imagines*.[86]

Several ideas emerge from this discussion of the rhizomatous connections between iconotextual representations of pygmies in the Renaissance on the one hand, and Philostratus' text on the other. For one, the size and nature of the pygmies become a matter of interpretation, as the visual re-creations of

85 The French commentary on the Hercules episode represented in the picture is entirely by Blaise de Vigenère. In the Argument (*Les Images ou tableaux de platte peinture des deux Philostrates sophistes grecs* [1615], pp. 481-82), he first laments the fact that man, like Hercules, is never carefree but has to be prepared for new troubles at any time. Describing the pygmies attacking the hero as "une petite racaille d'arriere-parens (sic) du deffunt" (relatives of the deceased Antaeus) coming out of the earth like ants while ignoring their force, Vigenère introduces another text as the moral of the tale: the oracle of Delphi – "Know thyself." He also suggests to compare this episode with the previous one, in which Hercules kills Antaeus, who embodies violent, tyrannical, and cruel giants. Vigenère claims that the pygmies are known for their "voluptez ... delices et concupiscens" and that humans should not give in to such sensual drives.

In his summary of the story, Vigenère does not really refer to the engraving on p. 480, arguing that the pygmy families are related to Antaeus as "enfans de la terre," a point underlined again in the marginalia. In the subsequent "Annotations" (pp. 483-84), he comments on verbal and visual representations of pygmies by poets, historians, and "naturalistes." Mentioning "nains" (dwarfs) he saw during a meal in Rome at the home of Cardinal de Vitelli (34 misshapen dwarfs), he finally casts doubt on the existence of pygmies as a people or nation (as some other Renaissance writers like Sir Thomas Browne). This does not, however, keep him from speculating about their potential homeland (India, Egypt, Ethiopia, and Greece). The commentary then drifts off into discussions of the alleged animal nature of pygmies, myths about them (for example, that their women bear children from the age of 5 to 8) and about "hommes sauvages." He also quotes the full Latin *subscriptio* from the Alciati emblem showing Hercules and the pygmies, finishing with an interesting story lifted from Suidas: Hercules had two evil brothers, Passalus and Alcmon, who conspired to kill him and whom he caught and fettered, hanging them on his club like rabbits. This reminds one of Cranach's rendering of the rather large pygmies carried away in his lion's skin by the furious hero.

86 Bardon claims that the engraving follows the Greek text very closely ("la gravure est le commentaire linéaire du texte" ["Sur les 'Images ou Tableaux de Platte Peinture' de Blaise de Vigenère," p. 115]), presupposing differences between the Latin and Greek versions of Philostratus' ekphrasis. Unlike other critics (like Michael Bath) who consider the engravings in de Vigenère's translation rather influential, Bardon thinks that Ovid was more important for Renaissance artists than Philostratus (pp. 119-20).

Lilliputians are embedded not only in new artistic environments but also in socio-political contexts. For another, while in Philostratus' *Imagines* they are part of a rhetorical strategy that has little truck with their moral nature and, in fact, does not really criticize them, the visual discourse on pygmies in the Renaissance instrumentalizes them in new ways. This occurs in the context of the moral and political ideologies of humanism, and particularly in the visual satire it created. More often than not, Philostratus' courageous and hardy pygmies become ludicrous or mad dwarfs, sometimes even potentially lethal and evil little people who are not afraid of killing a sleeping, innocent giant. It would be wrong to assume that one particular version or 'reading' of the pygmies dominated. In terms of the Deleuzian 'machines' activated when reading a text, the nature of the pygmies depends precisely on the rhizomes in which they are set with each new artistic creation.

Finally, Swift's own re-creation of little people should be seen at the crossroads of this rhizomatous network. To be sure, he read and annotated the Latin version in his bilingual edition of Philostratus' *Imagines* of 1608; but Swift's pygmies are very unlike those we find in this classical source. They are closer to the little people created by the verbal and visual discourse of the Renaissance, iconotextual products that haunted the minds of writers and artists, who altered and adapted the text of the Greek philosopher to suit their own purposes. The outstanding quality of Swift's satire may be seen in the fact that it draws not on one single source but on entire rhizomatous fields – oral, musical, verbal, and visual. Thus, the brief episode at the beginning of the "Voyage to Lilliput" is an invitation to the reader to consider the historical representations of Lilliputians in literature and the arts.[87] Swift, too, employs the pygmies for his own satirical and political purposes closely connected with an Enlightenment critique of seeing and of perspective in representation. The literary quality of his venture becomes more obvious when considered within the rich fields of rhizomes with which his satire plays in intertextual and intermedial ways. The pleasure created by the pygmies in *Gulliver's Travels* derives to a large extent from the fact that they are *mises-en-abymes* of representations seen or read before. It is not least in the satirical manner in which Swift re-organizes and re-evaluates and thus questions the mental images of Renaissance little people that makes one recognize the quality of his writing. More often than not, the Dean's texts urge the reader to re-consider preconceived ideas, and the way this is done in the Voyage to Lilliput may safely be called masterly.

87 By extension, this also applies to giants (Gulliver as giant in Book One, and as Lilliputian in Book Two). Hercules and Polyphemus in their various representations in word and image come into play here.

Howard D. Weinbrot
The University of Wisconsin, Madison

"Toujours il faut adoucir": Jonathan Swift, the Abbé Yart, Albin Hennet, and "le bon goût qui règne en France"

Abstract. In October of 1749, the *Journal de Trévoux* reviewed both the final volume of Pierre-Antoine de la Place's *Le Théâtre Anglois* (1745/6-49) and the first volume of the Abbé Antoine Yart's *Idée de la poësie Angloise* (1749-53). La Place provided the first French translations of Shakespeare. Yart provided translations and the first moderately full French overview of English poetry. Each sympathetic translator was thirty-eight years old. Each represented a young generation of mid-century French men of letters. Each well-reviewed set of volumes was an epochal event in Anglo-French literary relations. Each has been largely ignored. I hope to rectify that oversight regarding the Abbé Yart, his colleagues, and his contexts. I will discuss the French view of Jonathan Swift that Yart inherited, how and why he at the least softened his translations of Swift's poems, and how he hoped thereby to change Swift's reputation in eighteenth-century France. I then will suggest the degree to which those *adoucissements* and post-Orrery publication influenced further appreciation and transmission of Swift's poetry and reputation, most particularly in Albin-Joseph-Ulpien Hennet's *La Poétique Anglaise* (1806).[1]

1. The Most Savage of All Nations

Enlightened Gaul was not divided in its opinion of Jonathan Swift the political commentator. He was brilliant, famous, illustrious, original, and witty. Some of

1 These important, concurrent, publishing events were functions of growing anglomania. For one eighteenth-century discussion of such interest, together with English disdain for the French, see Louis Charles Fougeret de Montbron, *Préservatif contre l'Anglomanie* (Minorque, 1757). Josephine Grieder adds a modern overview: *Anglomania in France, 1740-1789: Fact, Fiction, and Political Discourse* (Geneva and Paris: Librairie Droz, 1985). See also Michael Maurer, *Aufklärung und Anglophilie in Deutschland* (Göttingen und Zürich: Vandenhoeck und Ruprecht, 1987), pp. 20-32, and *passim*. Abbé Antoine Yart, *Idée de la poësie Angloise: ou, traduction des meilleurs poetes Anglois, qui n'ont point encore paru dans notre langue, avec un jugement sur leurs ouvrages, & une comparaison de leurs poësies avec celles des auteurs anciens & modernes, & un grand nombre d'anecdotes & de notes critiques*, 7 vols (Paris: Briasson, 1749-56). For Albin-Joseph-Ulpien Hennet, see *La Poétique Anglaise*, 3 vols (Paris: de Valade and Barrois, 1806). References to these editions will be cited parenthetically in the text. I am indebted to Hermann J. Real and his colleagues at the Ehrenpreis Centre for several German and French sources cited within this essay.

 | DOI:10.30965/9783846763971_027

that justified praise was based on his fame across the Channel, and some was based on translators' enlargement of his anger at Britain's long and generally successful War of the Spanish Succession against France. Swift's *Conduct of the Allies* (1711) begins with mock admiration for "the Industry of a sort of Men, wholly out of Favour with the Prince and People." In the French *Conduit des alliez* (1712), Swift is astonished by certain men "tout à fait ennemis du Prince & du Peuple."[2] His *Publick Spirit of the Whigs* (1714) alludes to Whigs as "the Heads and Principal Members of a struggling Faction." The French *L'Esprit des Whigs* (1714) transmogrifies "struggling" into "violente."[3] Hostility to British conduct of that war and to Britain generally extended beyond the Seven Years War (1754-63). Swift's *History of the Four Last Years of the Queen* appeared posthumously in 1758. It was translated in 1765 as *Histoire du règne de la reine Anne d'Angleterre*. The English editor writes that Swift was not content with repeating Marlborough's known faults, "but insinuated a new crime by seeming to attempt to acquit him of aspiring to the throne." The French version is even more unsettling: in attempting to clear him from the crime, "il s'en acquitte d'une maniere à l'en faire soupçonner."[4] English "seeming" becomes French suspect-

---

2 Jonathan Swift, Preface to *The Conduct of the Allies, and of the Late Ministry, in Beginning and Carrying on the Present War* (London: John Morphew, 1711), in *English Political Writings, 1711-1714*, eds Bertrand A. Goldgar and Ian Gadd (Cambridge: Cambridge University Press, 2008), pp. 47, 243; italics inverted. All subsequent quotations are from this edition. *La Conduite des alliez, et du dernier ministere, en commençant & en continuent la guerre*, 2nd ed. (Liege: Guillaume-Henry Streel, 1712), unsigned but cited as sig. a2r with the title page called a1r; in italics. The translator of another edition complained that he found his predecessor's text "Fausse en plusieurs Endroits, jusqu'à alterer le Sens." His version of Swift's words above cite "certains Hommes ... qui, quoique tout à fait disgraciez du Prince & du Peuple" nonetheless dare to oppose the peace (*La Conduite des alliez, et du ministere precedent, en commençant la presente guerre*, 7th ed. [Luxembourg: André Chevalier, 1712], pp. i, viij, in italics).

3 Jonathan Swift, *The Publick Spirit of the Whigs, Set forth in the Generous Encouragement of the Author of the Crisis*, in *English Political Writings, 1711-1714*, eds Goldgar and Gadd, pp. 47, 243. *L'Esprit des Whigs, manifesté par le genéreux encouragement qu'ils donnnent à l'auteur de la crise* (London [=Amsterdam]: Jean Morphew, 1714), p. [1] (Teerink and Scouten 601). Swift was most useful for contemporary political events, as in "*les affaires du tems presents*," in *Recueil de quelques pieces nouvelles concernant les affaires du tems present, qui ont paruës en Angleterre & en Hollande* ([Paris], 1712). The collection includes translations of *The Conduct of the Allies* and *Some Remarks on the Barrier Treaty*. See the French Bibliothèque Nationale Catalogue Général and Teerink and Scouten 552. For other French translations of political tracts, see Teerink and Scouten 545-52, 563-64. *The History of the Four Last Years of the Queen*, in *Prose Works*, VII, 175, italics and roman type reversed, Appendix A, Preface by Charles Lucas, who adds at the end of the sentence quoted above, "But this is done in a manner peculiar to this author."

4 *The History of the Four Last Years of the Queen*, in *Prose Works*, VII, 175, italics and roman type reversed, Appendix A, Preface by Charles Lucas, who adds at the end of the sentence

ing. From Swift's earliest to at least this posthumous political appearance in France, translators have him say what he should say for French purposes. Such political alteration anticipates and reflects literary alterations that adapt, that is often change, Swift for French taste. Translators do this because they must if a version of Jonathan Swift is safely to cross la Manche.

Fuller acceptance of Swift's voice was made more difficult by linguistic divergence. The French regularly complained that bloody and violent Britons were flattered by authors keen on pleasing "the people" rather than the proper more elevated guardians of polite civilization. French discomfort and often disgust with English drama and culture embodied that sensibility. This is clear in Robert-Martin Lesuire's *Les Sauvages de l'Europe: satyr contre les anglois* (1760), translated as *The Savages of Europe* (1764). It is hostile to cruel, drunken, Francophobic, homicidal, irreligious, lawless, pathological, suicidal, violent, vulgar England, which lacks redeeming traits. Chapter 5 exemplifies such horrors when a naive young French couple and their wise Chinese escort visit an English theatre. The grim experience shows them staged "murders, ghosts, death-heads, scaffolds, wheels and gibbets, accompanied by a due number of executioners." Kin Foe concludes that "the whole world look[s] on the English as a bloody, savage race." He prays "that these barbarous islanders may, for ever, remain inclosed within their own bounds, nor pollute with their dangerous commerce, that amiable humanity which every other part of Europe may justly boast of." England is "the most savage of all nations." France is "the most civilized of people."[5]

---

quoted above, "But this is done in a manner peculiar to this author." Swift, *Histoire du règne de la reine Anne d'Angleterre*, trans. [Marc-Antoine Eidous] (Amsterdam: Marc-Michel Rey and Arkstée & Merkus, 1765), p. xviii: "Non content de rappeller au Lecteur les fauts dont le Duc de Marlborough fut convaincu publiquement, il l'accuse d'avoir aspiré à la Couronne: & lors même qu'il entreprend de le justifier de ce crime, il s'en acquitte d'une maniere à l'en fair soupçonner, & qui n'est propre qu'à lui" (Teerink and Scouten 814) (p. xviii). Eidous uses "justifier" in the sense of "Montrer, prouver, déclarer qu'un qui était accusé est innocent" (*Dictionnaire de l'Académie Françoise*, 2 vols [Avignon: Pierre Beaume, 1777], I, s.v.). I use this edition of the *Dictionnaire* because it is closer to the date of Eidous' translation. The *Journal de Trévoux* was lukewarm regarding Swift's work. He violates his remark that he writes only facts, with neither panegyric nor satire. In fact, he regularly praises Queen Anne and her ministers and is bitterly hostile to those whose "crime" is merely not to applaud all the Court's operations. The *Journal* admires but appears ambiguous regarding Swift's style: "il peint avec une force qui lui est propre" (65, no 2 [July 1765], 356-58).

5 Robert-Martin Lesuire, *Les Sauvages de l'Europe: satyre contre les Anglois* (Berlin, 1760), trans. James Pettit Andrews as *The Savages of Europe: From the French* (London: Dryden Leach for T. Davies, 1764), pp. 40 (murders), 55 (whole world), 67 (barbarous), 138 (savage, civilized). There was a second edition in Berlin in 1762, and a softened adaptation as *Amants François à Londres: ou, Les Délices de l'Angleterre* in 1780. *L'Année littéraire* provides long extracts and

Swift's major products in that commerce sometimes provided instruction and delight, but when altered to fit French needs. Changes were necessary because the English language was as boldly violent as the people who wrote and spoke it. French commonplaces repeat that the English language is extravagant, excessive, undisciplined, and, as Voltaire said, too much like Hebrew, too metaphoric.[6] Almost by definition the English other than Addison and Pope lack *goût*. That term connotes more than the word "taste." Slowly acquired cultural progress is cognate with French *goût*, as it develops "peu-à-peu l'esprit des bons artistes."[7] In a world of *goût*, Swift as the enemy of extended war is replaced by Swift as an admired but feared emblem of British incoherence, so different from the French image of itself as an imperial civilizing nation. Benign Bourbon *ad exemplum regis* denotes national improvement by means of a monarch whose achievements improve the nation, and glorify

---

comments. It thinks Lesuire excessive by far, but is appalled at its insufficiently condemnatory description of Mr Blickman, who murders his wife and children and then commits suicide (2 [1760], 240-55, with 253-55 the evaluative pages). Lesuire's catalogue of English brutal, bloody scenes on stage was commonplace. See [Pierre-Joseph Fiquet du Bocage], *Lettre sur le théâtre Anglois*, 2 vols ([Paris], 1752), who objects to "le fer, le poison, l'assassinat, les tortures, les gibets, les enterremans, les sorciers, les Demons même" (I, 14-15).

6 Voltaire, *Letters concerning the English Nation* (London: C. Davis and A. Lyon, 1733), pp. 177-78; for English as "too much inflated, too unnatural, too closely copied from the *Hebrew* writers who abound so much with the *Asiatic* Fustian," Voltaire had already included a theory of causation. English liberty of conscience makes the English "more conversant in the Scripture, and hath rendered the Language of the Prophets so familiar to them, that their Poetry savours very much of that *Eastern* out-of-the-way Sublimity." See his *Essay upon the Civil Wars of France ... And also upon the Epick Poetry of the European Nations from Homer down to Milton*, 4th ed. (London: N. Prevost, 1731), p. 84. The "Asian" and "Eastern" sublime is an inflated, unnatural, out-of-the-way, false sublimity inferior to a European, largely French, restrained and elegant style. For further discussion of English and its relationship to Hebrew in the seventeenth and eighteenth centuries, see Howard D. Weinbrot, *Britannia's Issue: The Rise of British Literature from Dryden to Ossian* (Cambridge: Cambridge University Press, 1993), pp. 408-45.

7 Voltaire, entry on "Goüt," in *Encyclopédie ou Dictionnaire raisonné des sciences, des artes, et des métiers* (Berne, 1764), XVI, 337. *Goüt* involves intelligent choice, restraint, adherence to rules like the three unities, and consequent distinctions between *bon* and *mauvais goüt*. Alexander Gerard mined several essays from the *Encyclopédie* for his own *An Essay on Taste ... The Second Edition: To which are added, Three Dissertations on the Same Subject* (Edinburgh: A. Millar, *et al.*, 1764), by Gerard's French guides, Voltaire, d'Alembert, and Montesquieu. Voltaire stresses cultural acquisition; d'Alembert discusses an already internal sense that needs nurturing; and Montesquieu describes taste as the quality of discovering what gives us the degree of pleasure from each object we see or experience. All agree that the "vulgar," that is those who have not been properly educated, are at the least less likely to have or to acquire taste. Gerard himself also stresses that taste must exercise judgement, discernment, and careful analysis, as in Aristotle, Bouhours, and Bossu. See especially pp. 88-92 for his stress on literary analysis that must hone internal response.

the ruler – Louis XIV and his great arts, arms, political, and religious regime. France's Reason and cultivation transcend its British neighbours, because France is more civilized than its British neighbours. The *Journal de Trévoux* knew this to be true: one reads the Ancients and not the English to form *goût*, which they indeed receive from France: "c'est de nous qu'ils peuvent en recevoir." We recall that French commentators were especially keen on this theory of tasteful art regarding drama. Corneille and Racine surpass the Ancients by being more ancient, or more regular, than the Ancients. French tragedy venerates the three unities, preserves the unbridgeable gap between comedy and tragedy, and rejects overt sexual passion, blood, and death on stage. In contrast, the Abbé Desfontaines said, Shakespeare sacrificed propriety, probability, and good sense for typically English drama. It is "toujours noir, cruel & sanguinaire" and thus banished from other, civilized, nations' stages.[8] French cultural historians attributed much of this supremacy to Louis XIV's polished monarchy. Boileau's seminal *Art poëtique* (1674), the epistle dedicatory and preface to the *Dictionnaire* of the Académie Française (1694), and Voltaire's *Siècle de Louis XIV* (1751) are among the many examples of this theory of causation. As Voltaire said in his retrospective Introduction, France was primitive under Louis XIII, but Louis XIV created the stage of civilization that "approaches the nearest to perfection." Reason and true philosophy were only discovered then, and "from the last years of cardinal Richlieu to the death of Lewis XIV" France produced a revolution in "government ... arts, minds, and manners; which ought to be an eternal epocha of the true glory of our country." Jean-Arnold Trochereau extended the argument on regnal change as cultural progress, but applied it to backward England. The English overpraise their authors and underpraise the superior French. Poetry in mid-seventeenth-century England was primitive, "lorsque sous Louis XIII. & le commencement du Regne de Louis XIV." Immortal French authors rivalled the best of Greece and Rome when English literature was "au berceau," in its cradle.[9]

---

8 *Journal de Trévoux* (*Mémoires pour l'histoire des sciences & des beaux arts*) reviewing volume three (1753) of the Abbé Yart's *Idée de la poësie Angloise: ou, Traduction des meilleurs poëtes Anglois* (Paris: chez Briasson, 1753), (September 1753), p. 1950. Abbé Pierre-François Guyot Desfontaines, "Le Théâtre Anglois," in *Jugemens sur quelques ouvrages nouveaux*, 9 vols (Avignon: Pierre Girou, 1744-46), IX, 16. Desfontaines comments, harshly, upon the first two volumes (1745) of Pierre-Antoine de la Place's *Théâtre Anglois* and its non-Voltairean introduction of Shakespeare to French readers.

9 Voltaire, *The Age of Lewis XIV: Translated from the French of M. de Voltaire*, trans. [Anonymous], 2 vols (London: R. Dodsley, 1752), I, 3-4. France "carried taste" and learning in varied ways to England, Germany, Russia, Italy, "and Europe, in general, owes its politeness to the court of Lewis XIV" (p. 4). Jean-Arnold Trochereau de la Berlière, *Choix de differens morceaux de poësie traduits de l'Anglois* (Paris: Pissot and Pissost Fils, 1749),

Swift himself often seemed to work within dark and low areas that typified much licentious English art; hence frequent likening of him to rude Rabelais, another comic master with a libertine's, if not libidinous, imagination. The analogy was not a compliment. Antoine de Courtin's *Rules of Civility: or, The Maxims of Genteel Behaviour* makes plain that "we must not be immodest in our Raillery, touching upon things that ought to be conceal'd," as with the "Famous Pattern of merry Ribaldry," Rabelais. Fontenelle's *Histoire des oracles* (1686) notes that Rabelais was learned, agreeable, witty, and mixed crass comedy with learning. Alas, he did not live in a century that obliged him to be more forthright and polite. John Oldmixon excoriates Swift's concept of an English-language academy like that of the Académie Française. He cites La Bruyère on Rabelais as abominable, beastly, enigmatic, incomprehensible, inexplicable, and fit only to divert the rabble. For Jacques Auguste de Thou, Rabelais reflected the debauchery, intemperance, and the indiscriminate laughter "of a *Democritus* ... in a scurrilous Stile." Voltaire later adds that only a blockhead would try to comment upon "smart Sayings and Repartees." That is why "the Works of the ingenious Dean *Swift*, who has been call'd the *English Rabelais*, will never be well-understood in *France*."[10] Rabelais surely was some readers' secret or forbidden pleasure, but he lacked the *politesse* that reflected civilization's triumph over barbarism.

p. xli. Trochereau had earlier criticized English authors for lacking the order, precision, and "arrangement Méthodique" that spread advantageous light over a work (p. xix).

10 Antoine de Courtin, *The Rules of Civility: or, The Maxims of Genteel Behaviour, as they are Practis'd and Observ'd by Persons of Quality, upon Several Occasions. Newly Done out of the Twelfth Edition in French* (London: R. Scott, *et al.*, 1703), p. 198; Bernard le Bovier de Fontenelle, *Histoire des oracles ... nouvelle edition augmentée* (London: Paul & Isaac Vaillant, 1721), p. 219: "Il est certain que Rabelais avoit beaucoup d'esprit & de lecture, & un art très-particulier de debiter des choses savantes comme des pures fadaises, & de dire de pures fadaises le plus souvent sans ennuyer. C'est dommage qu'il n'ai vêcu dans un Siècle qui l'eut obligé à plus d'honnêteté, & de politesse;" John Oldmixon, *Reflections on Dr. Swift's Letter to the Earl of Oxford, about the English Tongue* (London: A. Baldwin, 1712), pp. 28-29; Jacques Auguste de Thou, *Monsieur de Thou's History of his Own Time ... Translated from the Geneva Edition of 1620*, trans. Bernard Williams, 2 vols (London: E. Say, W. Meadows, *et al.*, 1729-30), II, cxxvii; Voltaire, *Letters concerning the English Nation*, p. 213. Voltaire praises Swift for being superior to Rabelais in taste and delicacy. He offers unusual praise for Swift's poetry as well, but follows with greater praise, and long extracts, of Pope's elegant, more correct, poetry (pp. 215-20). In contrast, see Abbé Antoine Yart, *Idée de la poësie Angloise*, VII, 195-96: "il est absurde de comparer Swift avec Rabelais." Yart's remarks are consistent with his view of Swift as a great man, artist, *philosophe*, religious and political thinker, if not always consistent with French cultural values. Nathalie Zimpfer has discussed Swift and Rabelais in "Swift and Religion: From Myth to Reality," *Swift Studies*, 24 (2009), 46-69.

French literati overwhelmingly thought Jonathan Swift embodied that perhaps great but certainly dangerous pre-Louis XIV dark bad taste. The famous Dean's works recalled an age of licence, lack of control, and Democritus' crude merciless laughter rather than Horace's subtle insinuation. Swift lived in the right century but the wrong country. His frame of mind was less fit for France than for England; it was harmful to himself and perhaps to the reader. Swift's career is a warning. He should be admired, but cautioned against, censored, refined, and made fit for the drawing room rather than for Bedlam or the jakes that un-retouched Swift suggests.

2. "Outrez & libres à l'excès": Swift's Major Texts in France, 1721-27

René Macé attempted the reorientation that Swift's major prose works required. His translation of *A Tale of a Tub* as *Les Trois Justaucorps* (1721) changes London to Paris, eliminates all of Swift's digressions, the appended but cognate *Battle of the Books*, the *Mechanical Operation of the Spirit*, and the Bookseller's Advertisement. He turns the complex 332-page 1704 *Tale* into a seventy-nine page reasonably direct narrative of the three coats. Swift concludes with Peter and Jack conspiring to trap and humiliate Martin, who escapes on the run. Thereafter, the Modern narrator praises "*Invention*" as the master of its servants "*Method* and *Reason*." Macé concludes with an attack upon some fifteen Huguenots all of whom he baptizes with the name Jean. These and others were "rendus célébres pour quelque folie." Unlike Swift behind his own *Tale*'s narrator, the Huguenot Jeans are subject to the author's control and punishment. Macé also hopes to make Swift seem European. He cites Boccaccio's "The Three Rings" (*Les Trois Anneaux*) from the third day of the *Decameron* (*c*.1353) as Swift's source and reprints the tale in verse stanzas at the end of his book. Thus viewed, Swift is only the tale teller in a work that is "*proprement le Conte d'un Conte Anglois*" by someone versed in Continental heritage. Macé has adapted Swift for readers "*de se faire lire avec plaisir*."[11] What little attention

11 *A Tale of a Tub and Other Works*, ed. Marcus Walsh (Cambridge: Cambridge University Press, 2010), p. 136. René Macé, *Les Trois Justaucorps, conte bleu, tiré de l'Anglois du Révérend Mr. Jonathan Swif* (sic) (Dublin [The Hague?], 1721), p. 78 (rendu), sigs *2r (*proprement*), *2v (*de se faire*). Macé acknowledges the *Tale*'s singular greatness and his inability to make it seem so in a foreign language (sig. *2v). Macé had been visiting in Dublin, heard a great deal about the Dean, and translated *A Tale of a Tub* at least in part to profit from Swift's Dublin omnipresence perhaps transferable to France and environs. The *Journal des sçavans* was among those many who thought that the *Trois Justaucorps* offered neither instruction nor delight. The translator was correct to hide his name: "il ne sçauroit faire

the book drew denied that possible pleasure, but did produce much indignation regarding its attacks upon religion. This became a familiar complaint.

The Dutch Protestant Justus van Effen also translated that famously clever but puzzling visitor's *A Tale of a Tub*. The Preface to *Le Conte du tonneau* (1721) both attracts and warns. It is difficult to find any work in any language so full of fire and imagination, but nor is there anything so bizarre – by definition, "Fantastique, extravagant, capricieux ... Il signifie aussi fig. Extraordinaire & hors de l'usage commun." Swift interrupts his principal narrative with digressions that are more numerous than the tale itself. Van Effen acknowledges that this is part of Swift's point in his attack upon the Moderns and praise of the Ancients. He nonetheless is "peut-étre Partisan outré,"[12] one of the terms, like *hardie, license*, and *déreglée*, that Francophones used for British texts and subjects.

Van Effen knows that bizarre Swift makes demands French readers cannot meet. The *Tale*'s digressions are so specific to his context, and so full of ingenious and idiosyncratic banter that it is "impossible" even for a wise and learned reader to acquire the solid knowledge to understand these ironies. Some of this difficulty is a function of Swift's character. The *Tale* suffers from his ribald turns and apparent mockery of sacred writ that revolt more sensitive imaginations and offend less perceptive readers (I, sig. *7v). Much of "la difficulté terrible" of the translation also is a function of the British national temper. "Les Anglois sont outrez, & libres à l'excès, dans leur tour d'Esprit, comme dans leur conduite, & dans leurs manieres." Their "bisarrerie d' imagination"

---

honneur à son Auteur." The work's flat and crude raillery regarding religion could not please any sect, much less the regularly mocked Catholics. The tale from Boccaccio "est une Piece impie" (*Journal des sçavans* [May 1721], pp. 299-300).

12 Justus van Effen, *Le Conte du tonneau contenant tout ce que les arts, & le sciences ont de plus sublimes*, 2 vols (in one) (The Hague: Henri Scheurleer, 1721), I, sig.*2v: It is difficult "de trouver dans aucune langue un Ouvrage si plein de feu, & d'imagination. Il est vrai en même tems qu'il ne se peut rien de plus bisarre; la narration est interrompuë continuellement par des digressions, qui occupent plus de place que le sujet principal;" it may be "outré" but it also insinuates itself "dans l'Esprit du Lecteur par un badinage élegant, & par un raillerie délicate" (I, sig. *3r). Further quotations from this edition will be cited parenthetically in the text. For "bizarre," see the *Dictionnaire de l'Académie Françoise* (Paris: Jean Baptiste Coignard, 1694), henceforth cited as *Dictionnaire*. Judgement that Swift's talent was both great and greatly unsettling was familiar in England as well. As one among many examples, see ["Sir" John Hill], *Some Observations on the Writers of the Present Age, and their Manner of Treating Each Other* (London: M. Sheepy, *et al.*, 1752), p. 24: Orrery demonstrates "the real Character of *Swift*; and while we admire, his Wit must tremble at the Lengths it often carried him." See below for further discussion of Orrery's influence upon both British and French views of Swift.

leads them to elaborate metaphors so different from the Ancient simplicity they claim to revere (I, sig. *9r).

Van Effen is sufficiently intimidated by Swift's imagination to lower the *Tale*'s temperature and reduce its real and perceived offenses against civility. Readers will not find anything in this translation with "le moindre air de libertinage" (I, sig. *6v). "J'ai adoucir ces endroits" when confronted with certain verbal "tours gaillards," ribald expressions (I, sig. *7v). Never mind those lacunae in the text to make it look like an old manuscript: "je l'ignore absolument, & le public peut l'ignorer avec moi sans y perdre beaucoup" (I, sig. *8r). Unlike Macé, and much to the *Journal des sçavans*' annoyance, van Effen preserves Swift's basic devices of Modern digression and disruption, Ancients on dubious defence, and Martin's Church of England fleeing from Peter and Jack (I, 290-91).[13] Van Effen softens Swift's "imagination libertine" (I, sig. *3r) on behalf of "la pudeur du Public François" (I, *sig. 7v); he nonetheless does not annihilate the rough mentality he feared. He includes both the *Battle of the Books* and the *Mechanical Operation of the Spirit*, but his comments on each again portray Swift as both dangerous and uniquely brilliant. The *Mechanical Operation of the Spirit* is "un Chef-d'œuvre de profanation" (II, sig. *1v), but the *Battle of the Books* is "un des plus heureuses Allegories, qui soient jamais sorties de l'Esprit humain" (II, sig. *3r).

None of this, partial, praise of excellence could compensate for the *Conte du tonneau*'s apparent attack upon Christian religion of any confession. For the Huguenot Prosper Marchand (1678-1756) that "criminel" text proposes "rien moins que de tourner cruellement en ridicule les trois principales Sects de Christianisme Occidental." Swift's 1710 "Apology" defends the Church of England and insists that the *Tale* says nothing "*contrary to Religion or Morality*," which Marchand thinks absurd: "Rien ne seroit plus étonnant." He would have found an ally in the Marquis de Saint-Simon. In August of 1755, Saint-Simon asked Horace Walpole

> to look over a translation he had made of the *Tale of a Tub* – the proposal was soon followed by a folio, and a letter of three sides to press [him] seriously to revise it ... In the description of the tailor as an idol, and his goose as the symbol, he says in a note, the *goose* means the dove, and is a concealed satire on the Holy Ghost.[14]

13 See the *Journal des sçavans* for May, 1721, pp. 310-15. This version is even more defective than Macé's *Les Trois Justaucorps* because its narrative progress is regularly interrupted by digressions: "qui ne sont pas moins fades & moins grossieres que le Conte même" (p. 310).

14 Prosper Marchand, *Dictionnaire historique: ou, Memoires critiques et littéraires, concernant la vie et les ouvrages de divers personnages distingués*, ed. Jean Nicolas Sebastien Allamand, 2 vols (The Hague: Pierre de Hondt, 1758-59), I, 326-27, with further, stern,

Few were surprised when on 17 May 1734 the *Tale* was placed on the papal Index, and thereby brought the satire more republication.[15] Swift the political ally of France had become Swift the religious and cultural enemy of France. This perception improved but marginally. Whether in England or France, *A Tale of a Tub* was at once stunning, difficult, and often alienating. Thereafter, *Gulliver's*

---

comments on the translations by Mace and van Effen. The *Dictionnaire* appeared posthumously in 1758, but collected many of his earlier observations. See also Marchand's article on Imposters ("Imposteribus") as well as *Horace Walpole's Correspondence with John Chute, Richard Bentley*, eds W. S. Lewis, *et al.* (New Haven: Yale University Press, 1973), XXXV, 241, and Saint-Simon's letter of 19 July 1755 to Walpole, in *Horace Walpole's Miscellaneous Correspondence*, eds W. S. Lewis and John Riely (1980), XL, 82-83. So far as I know, Saint-Simon's manuscript has not surfaced. What little we know about it testifies to the ongoing French sense of Swift as profane. Voltaire did not use the word "profane," but he placed Swift among the English writers who ridiculed Christianity, as in *A Tale of a Tub*. See, among other places, Voltaires's "Lettres a S. A. M[sr] le Prince De ***," in *Oeuvres complètes de Voltaire*, ed. Louis Moland, 54 vols (Paris: Garnier Freres, 1877-85), XXVI, 490-91. The titled recipient was Karl Wilhelm Ferdinand, Duke of Braunschweig-Luneburg.

15 Sybil Goulding notes the papal condemnation for the *Conte* on 17 May 1734; see *Swift en France* (Paris: Edouard Champion, 1924), p. 38 and n1. It is a pleasure to acknowledge my debt to Goulding in particular and to the generations of Franco-English comparatists who made enduring contributions to our understanding of the relationships between two great cultures, whether in peace or war. See also Astrid Krake, Hermann J. Real, and Marie-Luise Spieckermann, "The Dean's Voyages into Germany," *The Reception of Jonathan Swift in Europe*, ed. Hermann J. Real (London and New York: Bloomsbury, 2013 [2005]), pp. 96-97 on Van Effen's translation and p. 96 on the Papal *Index Librorum Prohibitorum* (Rome, 1721); Jonathan Swift, *A Tale of a Tub and Other Works*, ed. Walsh, p. 6. Meanwhile, new evidence has surfaced which makes us see the proceedings of the Congregazione dell'Indice in a clearer light. The investigation regarding van Effen's translation of the *Tale* was set in motion by the Congregation around 1727/28. The Congregatio generalis reached a decision on 11 January 1734. The relator was Gianfrancesco Baldini CRS (*Systematisches Repertorium zur Buchzensur, 1701-1813: Indexkongregation*, eds Hubert Wolf, *et al.* [Paderborn, München, Wien: Ferdinand Schöningh, 2009], p. 1014). The recommendation to put the book on the Index was forwarded to the Pope, who alone was authorized to do so (Gustavo Costa, "La Congregazione dell'Indice e Jonathan Swift [Documenti sulla ricezione Italiana di *Tale of a Tub*]," *Paratesto: rivista internazionale*, 1 [2004], 145-65; Hermann J. Real, "*A Tale of a Tub* on the Roman Index: Further Evidence," *The Eighteenth-Century Intelligencer*, 32, no 1 [2018], 25-28). See also the Huguenot emigré Armand Boisbeleau de la Chapelle's Préface du Traducteur, in *Le Babillard: ou, Le nouvelliste philosophe. Traduit de l'Anglois*, 2 vols (Amsterdam: François Changuion, 1724), I, 5. Boisbeleau de la Chapelle regards Swift as well known in England. He is the author of "petites Pièces ... presque toutes d'un tour assez singulier pour venir d'un Hommes d'Eglise. Il se pique fort de penser & d'écrire en Cavalier & en Homme du belair." Swift's *Tale* in England was of course regularly criticized as irreligious, as in one of many examples, *A Letter from a Clergyman to his Friend, with an Account of the Travels of Captain Lemuel Gulliver* (London: A. Moore, 1726), p. 19. The *Tale* is profane, impious, and "Jests at Almighty God." The author clearly is a Whig who detests Swift's Tory politics hostile to Walpole and his administration.

Travels (1726, 1735) produced numerous critics, but its demonstrable genius, broad circulation, and British popularity also made it attractive in France. For all its amusing initial two books, however, its best-known French translator responded about the same way as Macé and van Effen did to *A Tale of a Tub: Gulliver* was offensive, needed to learn proper manners, and both what to say and what not to say in France.

Abbé Pierre-François Guyot Desfontaines's version of *Gulliver's Travels* (1727) praised Swift as brilliant, energetic, exciting, imaginative, original – and vulgar. *Gulliver*'s bêtises include *basse, bizarre, ennuïeuse, fade, foible, grosse, impénétrable, impertinent, indécente, insipide, mauvais, pitoïable, puerile*, and *triviale.*[16] Desfontaines hopes to have banished all such blemishes from his translation (I, xxxiii), for a literal version of so imaginative but crude an effort must embarrass its translator and offend "le bon goût qui règne en France" (I, xvi). Desfontaines thus has "retranché tout ce qui m'a paru grossier & incontėnent" (p. xxxvii), or a great deal of what made *Gulliver* attractive as a shocking but acute questioner of conventional wisdom. Desfontaines thus claims to have improved upon his original (I, xxxiii), perhaps by excluding images of the woman's body and sexual impulses.

Gulliver in Brobdingnag witnesses a nurse breastfeeding an infant and desentimentalizes this endearing natural act. The woman's breast is monstrous, nauseous, pimpled, freckled, spotted, six feet high and sixteen feet in circumference. Gulliver reflects upon the imagined beauty of his own countrywomen, but he is keen to show what reality is like when one has "a near sight" of whatever one idealizes. Swift uses almost a page for his detailed description (*Prose Works*, XI, 91-92 [II, i, 11]). Desfontaines uses a sentence, says that nothing so

16 Abbé Pierre-François Guyot Desfontaines, *Voyages de Gulliver*, 2 vols (Paris: Gabriel Martin, 1727), I, xv-xvi for all these terms. Subsequent quotations are given parenthetically in the text. Hostile English response to *Gulliver* included terms like abominable, ridiculous, ludicrous, out of life, and worn out. See Jonathan Smedley, *Gulliveriana: or, A Fourth Volume of Miscellanies. Being a Sequel of the Three Volumes Published by Pope and Swift* (London: J. Roberts, 1728), p. xix, among other places. Smedley shares another tactic, or term, with French detractors and reluctant allies – Swift as bizarre (pp. viii, xix).

The first French translation was the unsigned three-volume set from The Hague, *Voyages du Capitaine Lemuel Gulliver en divers pays eloignez*, 3 vols (in one) (The Hague: P. Gosse and J. K. Neaulme, 1727-28), with the third volume containing pseudonymous material like the *Voyage des Severambes* and several "Observations" on the earlier voyages. I have found no reason to question received wisdom from Sybil Goulding forward (pp. 57-58): the book was slightly known and broadly ignored once Desfontaines's version appeared. See also Melanie Maria Just, "The Reception of *Gulliver's Travels* in Britain and Ireland, France, and Germany," *Les Voyages du Gulliver*, eds François Boulaire and Daniel Carey (Caen: Presses Universitaires de Caen, 2002; 2012 Open Edition), pp. 81-100, specifically, paragraphs 31-44 in the Open Edition.

much disgusted Gulliver as those breasts, and that "je ne sçai à quoi je puis les comparer" (I, 146). Brobdingnagian teenaged girls get their turn as well. A sixteen-year-old maid of honour uses naked Gulliver as a sex-toy, dances him upon her nipple and performs dildo-like tricks about which Gulliver prefers not to speak (*Prose Works*, XI, 118-19 [II, v, 6]). Desfontaines turns this scene into a vanity of human wishes regarding the folly of adoring beautiful women, whose bodies smell badly. As for the rest, *politesse* knows that certain subjects may not be discussed, "Je ne dis rien touchant d'autres endroits énormes de leurs corps" (I, 180).

Desfontaines's Gulliver is also amusingly Francophile. The Brobingnagian King is astounded that Britain has a standing army in peace and fights wars abroad. A nation need only defend its borders and secure its trade (*Prose Works*, XI, 131 [II, vi, 14]). Desfontaines agrees, but adds what sounds like mockery: "Devés-vous songer à faire des conquêtes?" (I, 206). The Abbé enhances this approach with a far less subtle intervention: he makes Swift acknowledge Sun-King splendour at English expense. Gulliver tells his Houyhnhnm master about the War of the Spanish Succession begun by William of Orange and continued by Queen Anne (*Prose Works*, XI, 245 [IV, v, 2]). Desfontaines transforms Swift's "*Revolution* under the Prince of *Orange*" to the "invasion du Prince d'*Orange*" (II, 178). This "Prince ambitieux" began a war against the "Roi de France, le Monarque le plus puissant de l'Europe, dont la gloire étoit répanduë dans tout l'Univers, et qui possédoit toutes les vertus Royales" (II, 178). Desfontaines's Gulliver is Louis XIV's apologist, and Britain is an idiosyncratic opponent of universally acknowledged French royal virtue.[17] Desfontaines indeed adjusts *Gulliver* "au goût de la France." Swift's works are "très estimé en Angleterre," but to be "très estimé en France" must also be "très adouci" (I, xl-xli).[18]

---

17 The British Swift is of course generally hostile to Louis XIV, most especially in *A Tale of a Tub*. For some such remarks, see *Ode to the King: On his Irish Expedition, and the Success of his Arms in General* (1691), in *Poems*, ed. Williams, I, 10, Stanza VII, ll. 119-46; *A Discourse of the Contests and Dissentions between the Nobles and the Commons in Athens and Rome* (1701), ed. Frank H. Ellis (Oxford: Clarendon Press, 1967), pp. 90-91; Section IX, "Digression concerning Madness," in *A Tale of a Tub and Other Works*, ed. Walsh, p. 107. The list is selective.

18 Whether by arrogance, ambition, naivety, native blindness, or all of the above, Desfontaines sent Swift a copy of the second edition of the *Voyages*, unaware that Swift had already seen the first edition and its cascade of insults. Swift's delayed response replaced putative French polish with Swiftian irony and annoyance. He read Desfontaines's Preface and, Swift mocks, was pleased that he did not see special excellence in his author: "vous au contraire avez bien le justice de dire au commencement que votre auteur est plein de polissonades de sottisses, des puerilitez &c." The translator wrongly cites Swift's book as responses to specifically English concerns. All vices are the same in all countries,

Desfontaines was a learned ninny, but he was in the mainstream of troubled commentary upon Swift's alien imagination. His great travel narrative was annoying, boring, mediocre, and in need of French lessons that Desfontaines supplied. Both *A Tale of a Tub* and *Gulliver's Travels* offended reigning French good taste. The Abbé Augustin-Simon Irailh affirmed that judgement. In 1761, he noted that translations of this difficult author needed improvement: he is an "écrivain plein d'esprit & original; mais à qui l'on reproche, en Angleterre même, d'être un *à low author*, un auteur qui tombe souvent dans le bas."[19] Eighteenth-century French readers thought Jonathan Swift famous, original, and brilliantly imaginative. He was also low, gross, indecent, revolting, impious, and someone about whom his audience needed to be warned, and whose best-known works needed cleansing. Could these views change if readers were introduced to Swift the poet rather than to Swift the prose satirist? The Abbé Antoine Yart tried.

---

certainly including France thus subject to Swift's correction. Swift was also annoyed with Desfontaines's adherence to conventional assumptions regarding the English language and nation.

From the second edition forward, Desfontaines shortened the paragraph with those several insults. He uses one sentence but still gets the grumpy job done: he has found "des endroits foibles & négligés, même très mauvais, des allégories impénêrables, des allusions insipides, des détails puériles, des réflexions triviales, des pensées basses," and so on with the like endearing sentiments. See Desfontaines's "Préface du traducteur, mise à la tête de l'edition de 1728," in *Voyages de Gulliver: Nouvelle Edition*, 2 vols (Paris: H. L. Guerin and F. Delatour, 1762), I, xii-xiii. See also *Correspondence*, ed. Woolley, III, 111. Swift wrote an earlier draft of his letter and then made corrections for this one in August of 1727, perhaps with Bolingbroke's improvements (See David Woolley, "Swift's Letter to Desfontaines, 1727: The Autograph First Draft," *Swift Studies*, 2 [1987], 107-13). Desfontaines wrote to Swift on 23 June 1727, OS (*Correspondence*, ed. Woolley, III, 97-98). He knew that he was treading on thin ice, but was pleased with the rapid sale of his *Voyages* and pretended to look forward to seeing Swift in Paris, where he would treat him royally. Desfontaines made his nominal adjustments in foolish hopes of mollifying Swift and of receiving an audience should he indeed visit France. Swift was not amused and not travelling.

19 Abbé Augustin-Simon Irailh, *Querelles littéraires: ou, Mémoires pour servera l'histoire des révolutions à la république des lettres, de puis Homere jusqu' à nos jours*, 4 vols (Paris: Durand, 1761), II, 125-26. This is part of a longer section on varied conflicts among different translators (pp. 125-44). Desfontaines himself moved from translation to his own version of a proper Gallic *Gulliver*, the invented *Le Nouveau Gulliver: ou voyage de Jean Gulliver, fils du capitaine Gulliver*, 2 vols (Paris: La veuve Clouzier and François le Breton, 1730 [1729]). Paul Gabriel Boucé discusses "Gulliver's Frenchified Travels to Blefuscu: The First Two Translations," *Reading Swift: Papers from The Fourth Münster Symposium on Jonathan Swift*, eds Hermann J. Real and Helgard Stöver-Leidig (Munich: Wilhelm Fink, 2003), pp. 379-86.

3. Abbé Antoine Yart's *Traduction des meilleurs poëtes Anglois*

Voltaire's *Letters concerning the English Nation* (1733) include one of his more sensible observations regarding British literature: "The poetical Numbers of Dean *Swift* are of a singular and almost inimitable Taste; true Humour, whether in Prose or Verse, seems to be his peculiar Talent" (p. 215). Like most French readers, Jean-Arnold Trochereau paid this observation no mind. His *Choix de differens morceaux de poësie traduits de l'Anglois* (1749) omits Swift's poetry. Abbé Antoine Yart knew that in 1749 Swift's fame in France was limited to his prose works; but as Trocherau put it, "le goût pour les Ouvrages Anglois est devenu presque universel."[20] Yart hoped to meet that demand and to fill the French poetical vacuum. He thus featured Swift in his eight-volume *Idée de la poësie Angloise* (1749-56). Yart sought to expand French respect for English poetry in order to create new or correct old opinions of, say, Jonathan Swift. Reviewers recognized his method and reasonable success. The *Journal de Trévoux* promptly reviewed the first volume, printed its full historical, narrative, title and told readers that each English author's newly translated poems were prefaced by a biographical notice and a critical *discours*. Yart includes several historical or analytic critiques and comparison of the Ancients, the Moderns, the English, and the French. The *Journal de Trévoux* admires this contribution to French letters: "Tout ceci est bien entendu, & nous felicitons notre Littérature d'avoir acquis un Ecrivain aussi attentif & aussi judicieux que M. L'Abbé Yart" (October 1749, 2194-95).

That attentive and judicious author knew that Swift came trailing clouds of idiosyncrasy and almost by definition needed retrenchment and *adoucissement*. The *Journal des sçavans*' review of Yart's first volume demonstrates the difficulty of bringing the outré English poet Swift into mainstream French letters. Jacques Calot drew pictures of men hanged, as monsters, deformed dwarfs, and bizarre *commedia dell'arte* performers. Such crude subjects typified his life span (1592-1635) during the dark centuries that Louis XIV banished while creating "an eternal epocha" of French true glory. Swift is agreeable, playful, singular, and elegantly translated. Whether these compensate for grotesque disorder is another matter. The *Journal des sçavans* quotes much of Yart's own evaluation:

---

20 Jean-Arnold Trochereau de la Berlière, "Discours préliminaire," *Choix de differens morceaux de poësie traduits de l'Angloise*, p. iv. Voltaire also noted that Swift enjoyed more polite company than Rabelais and in "the Justness, the Choice, the good Taste, in all of which Particulars our giggling rural Vicar *Rabelais* is wanting" (*Letters concerning the English Nation*, p. 215). Yart and Hennet, among many other French commentators, clearly thought Voltaire wrong.

> Notre élégant Traducteur se flate avec raison, que l'enjouement des pensées du Docteur Swift, & la singularité de ses images, dont le caractère est déjà fort connu par les traductions du Conte du Tonneau & de Gulliver feront passer sur le désordre grotesque des tableaux de cet agréable Autour. (April 1750, p. 393; Yart, I, 214)

Disorder and singularity to the contrary, Swift now appeared in France as a poet and not only as a great but disturbing prose satirist and political partisan. Yart begins the difficult job of assimilating Swift into varied poetic traditions nurtured by major poets from an alien nation across the Channel. To do so, Yart both admits, and where possible compensates for, Swift's "désordre grotesque." As the *Journal des sçavans* put it with Yart's help, "Il faut, dit il, avoir la même indulgence pour le calot de la Poësie Angloise, que nous en avons pour les portraits ridicules de notre Calot, en faveur de la gayeté originale qu' l'un & l'autre ont répandu dans leurs ouvrages" (December 1749, p. 822; Yart I, 215).

Abbé Yart of course hoped to encourage this indulgence. His *Idée de la poësie Angloise*'s evaluative subtitle places Swift's poetry in the best company: *Traduction des meilleurs poëtes Anglois, qui n'ont point encore paru dans notre langue.* Yart alerts readers to excellence, novelty, cultural transfer, and critical estimates across space and time. He offers judgements *sur leurs Ouvrages, & une comparaison de leurs Poësies avec celles des Auteurs anciens & modernes.* Yart works as if he is editing an established poet who requires proper critical machinery: bibliography, critical discourse, explanatory footnotes, and analyses of structure, national taste, language, and characterization. This novice commentator-translator is neither a French Academy Immortal nor among the *philosophe* Movers and Shakers in Paris or Ferney. He nonetheless was a member of Rouen's academy founded by Louis XV on 17 January 1744. He was little known but intellectually respectable. His important project thus received royal approval and was printed by Antoine-Claude Briasson (1700-75), who in 1751 became one of the *Encyclopédie*'s printers.

Yart moved carefully and was applauded by many of France's, and therefore Europe's, major literati for handsomely serving French letters and even, modestly, changing French opinion of the brutal British. Some general praise noted the benign importation of hitherto ignored English poets. In July of 1754, for example, the *Mercure de France* reviewed volumes five and six of "Cet ouvrage estimable," which has merited the public's unanimous warm welcome. The *Mercure* exhorts Yart to continue "de nous enricher des trésors littéraires d'une nation aussi spirituelle & aussi féconde en bons ouvrages que la nation Angloise" (67, p. 106). Other approbation specified authors, as did the *Journal des sçavans.* It was both admiring and suspicious of Jonathan Swift, who melded originality, agreeable playfulness, and grotesque disorder. This shared respect and suspicion was probably transferred to Swift's poetry and perhaps especially so in Yart's later volumes. His conception of the task, however, is consistent if not uniform, throughout the *Idée de la poësie Angloise.*

Yart is likely to have used the term *idée* in the *Dictionnaire de l'Académie François*'s first sense: "La notion, & l'image que l'esprit se forme de quelque chose." So joint a platonic and practical view helps to define the English character as portrayed in English poetry. Yart announces that goal in the first volume's Preface, which also states why France should want this new *idée*. Poetry, he says in a familiar concept, reached its perfection under Louis XIV, when the Ancients inspired French dramatists who banished bad taste. Modern poets continue to imitate those masters, produce a multitude of similar copies, and thus add little to the stores of excellence. Even those who open apparently new paths soon follow roads already taken (I, i-ii).

France can reanimate the nation's taste for poetry by determining how distinguished authors of polished nations read antiquity's great authors to find "dans les ouvrages des étrangers de nouvelles manières d'imiter les Anciens" (I, ii). Yart offers a paradigm change. We recall the eighteenth-century French view of England and its literature: with some exceptions, these were violent uncivilized people with a violent undisciplined language. Yart acknowledges that highly figurative English is outré, but its best traits fill a void in French art and character. "Le génie de l'invention est rare parmi nous," who are better at embellishing than discovering beauties (I, iii). Other nations have improved themselves by borrowing from French authors; they now can borrow from the English and render "un service important à la France." French poetry has improved imprecise, bold, and confused English poetry with Gallic order, decency, precision, clarity, and polish (I, iv). Now is the time to dig in the deep English mines, separate the gold from the soil that covers it, enrich and cultivate our own soil with those foreign plants, and provide France with new sources of beauty (I, v). English poetry will improve French art's energy and originality and reduce copying of the Ancients' copiers. France now has a source "de mille beautés nouvelles pour des Ecrivains judicieux & habiles" (I, vi).

Le Conte du tonneau puzzled and alienated many readers. The *Voyages de Gulliver* generally pleased them, but they were told that Swift's original violated French taste and that Desfontaines improved and cleansed those journeys. Yart hopes to improve on those responses. His strategy in the *Idée* is to explain to, or ingratiate Swift with, his French audience. His tactics are to grant and then reorient that uncertain reception: Swift is an English poet who offends French taste, but he is imaginative in ways that his French colleagues are not. Yart must make that case for Swift without making a case against France.

Yart includes Swift's verse in five of his eight volumes. The broad selection includes several genres and shows Swift's ability to use complex poetic kinds. Yart also shrewdly ignores fierce poems, like *A Character, Panegyric, and Description of the Legion Club* (1736), and moving ones, like the final poem to Stella. The first would rekindle the question of Swift's low mind. The second would rekindle what we will see is the painful matter of Swift's offensive conduct towards his unacknowledged but beloved wife. Yart eliminates most controversy in favour of the witty, convivial, safely parodic, and social Swift also respectful, if arch, to his betters like Lord Oxford.[21]

Yart begins his campaign to assimilate Swift the poet in the important first volume of the *Idée de la poësie Angloise*. It includes "Parody on an Epigram of Martial," *Description of a City Shower, Description of the Morning, Epistle to Lord Oxford, Imitation of the Sixth Satire of the Second Book of Horace*, and most importantly, *Baucis and Philemon*. Swift's poems are variously *originaux* and *ingénieuse*; they have *singularité* and are *singuliéres*; some of the burlesques are "fort plaisans" (I, 193). The poems and their genres in volume one, however, are reasonably congenial both with French practice and with one of Yart's main intentions – to show how the English deal with the Ancients and other poetic traditions in ways from which sympathetic French can learn. We see this in Swift's adaptation of classical texts and forms for modern purposes. He is an English original talent but still connected to the Ancients and to his modern French colleagues, like Scarron in burlesque and even the sacred Boileau in adapting Horace.

The Abbé knows that Swift's *Baucis and Philemon* from Ovid's *Metamorphoses* (VIII, 618-724) has collegial French competitors. One is by that paragon of French easy narrative and intelligent commentary on life, Jean de La Fontaine (Book XII, Fable 25).[22] Yart observes that if La Fontaine does not always render Ovid's sentiments and images, he at least replaces them with others equally pleasant, as perhaps in the transfer of the metamorphosed trees to a beautiful valley near the Duc de Vendôme's Château d'Ant. In an adaptation of Longinus on the Sublime (13, 3-4), we hear that La Fontaine is "un grand Poëte, qui lutte, pour ainsi dire, contre un autre grand Poëte" (I, 193). Pierre-Charles Roy's "Ballet de la Paix" (1738) adds a new version of Baucis and Philemon that trades

21 Here are Swift's poems in the rest of *Idée de la poësie Angloise*: Volume IV: *Epistle to Dr. Delany*; Volume V: *Elegy on the Death of Partridge, Elegy on the Death of Old Bennet* (wrongly attributed); Volume VI: *Verses to Biddy Floyd, Two Epigrams*; Volume VII: *Cadenus and Vanessa*.

22 In Swift's edition in *Suite des fables choisies*, Book VII, Fable 15 [1694], pp. 39-45 (PASSMANN AND VIENKEN II, 1026-27).

the elderly husband and wife rewarded by the visiting gods for "deux jeunes Amans, dont la fidélité est éprouvée & couronnée par les Dieux" (I, 193). Yart's Swift functions within poets' familiar practice of borrowing from one author to comment on their own individual and cultural needs. By implication, La Fontaine, Roy, and others authorize Swift's comparable practice of variation and expansion of the source-text, if not of every aspect of that practice.

Yart grants readers' preconceptions regarding Swift, but suggests that those preconceptions need not deny the instruction and delight that Swift's poetry offers. Yart thus already had reminded readers of what they probably knew: in *Baucis and Philemon* as elsewhere, Swift's images can be too gross for poetry (I, 197n), others are "quelquesfois ridicules & peu agréables," and yet others indeed seem to reflect what the *Journal des sçavans* agreed was grotesque disorder (I, 214). We are not surprised that Swift has banished most of what can move the heart and elevate the soul: "tout est burlesque & ridicule dans son Poëme" (I, 193). Swift includes pleasant details as well as nasty if original traits, which Yart will not present to the reader, but mentions in subtextual remarks (I, 194). Hence, "j'ai retranché quelques traits, qui m'ont paru trop satyriques ou contraires au respect dû à la Religion" (I, 211; italics reversed). Yart retrenches when singularity becomes offensive peculiarity, but he has already established the wisdom of adapting the ancient to the modern poet's needs. Swift goes too far, but he fits Yart's conception for why English poetry is useful for French readers and men of letters: he teaches a way of imitating the Ancients that is both new and familiar, as in *Baucis and Philemon.*

The poem, however, was among works that some English commentators regarded as hostile to religion. According to the author of *Saint Patrick's Purgatory* (1716), Swift's diary confirms that he wrote *A Tale of a Tub* "to the utter Confusion of all Religion, Morals, and Manners, and to the Establishment of *Wit* and *Drollery* in their place." He also ridiculed "the Church in *Baucis* and *Philemon.*"[23] Yart recognized what he thought such ridicule and soon responded as he had promised. In Swift's poem, Ovid's Jupiter and Mercury who seek hospitality become "Two Brother Hermits, Saints by Trade" (l. 7). The humble cottage later becomes a handsome church rather than an elegant marble-columned pagan temple, with Baucis and Philemon as two trees growing from one trunk. Swift gives his virtuous couple a short respite as beautiful yew trees in front of the church transformed from their modest home,

23 [J. S.], *Saint Patrick's Purgatory: or, Dr. S—t's Expostulation with his Distressed Friends in the Tower and Elsewhere* (London: R. Burleigh, 1716), pp. 3-4. The diary is reprinted in *Gulliveriana: or, A Fourth Volume of Miscellanies*, see pp. 132-33 for these remarks. I quote *Baucis and Philemon* as in *Poems*, ed. Williams, I, 111-17.

Till once, a Parson of our Town,
To mend his Barn, cut *Baucis* down;
At which, 'tis hard to be believ'd,
How much the other Tree was griev'd,
Grew Scrubby, dy'd a-top, was stunted:
So, the next Parson stub'd and burnt it. (ll. 173-78)

Ovid's couple is permanently exalted and shares desired death together as the gods' reward for domestic virtue. Swift's couple is temporarily exalted before each transformed member is murdered for timber by unthinking Anglican clergymen. Ovid concludes his tale with affirmation of the divine and the secular: those who worship the gods are as gods; those who have worshipped the gods should be worshipped. Swift concludes with the inadequacy of those most responsible for worship and for the worshippers. Baucis as an emblem of the unity of God and Man in service and in love becomes secular lumber for a clergyman's secular barn and is removed from any place of worship. Philemon as an emblem of spousal devotion suffers as a decaying and then a destroyed tree: "the next Parson stub'd and burnt it" (l. 178). Samuel Johnson used Swift's line to illustrate the meaning of the verb "to stub": "To force up; to extirpate."[24]

Abbé Yart is largely faithful to Swift's final paragraph but uses his note to comment in a firm editorial voice. He is surprised that Swift the paragon of imagination has not sustained his allegory and terminated the couple's lives "par des adieux plus tendres," as Ovid and the French authors did. He could have had the superstitious people revere the two trees. Instead, we are offended that they are slaughtered and burned "comme des Arbres vulgaires," which of course is Swift's point (I, 209n). Here as elsewhere, Yart fears that Swift has fallen into crude observation unfit for poetry: "Notre goût, sur ce point, est fort différent de celui des Anglois" (I, 197n). Swift nonetheless often includes "des

24 Samuel Johnson, *A Dictionary of the English Language*, 2 vols (London: by W. Strahan for J. and P. Knapton, *et al.*, 1755), s.v. I speculate that Swift may also be adapting or imitating the conclusion to La Fontaine's fable, a copy of which he would have seen in several editions of the *Fables choisies*, 1705 and 1708 for example, as well as the 1693 version which he owned (PASSMANN AND VIENKEN II, 1025-27). La Fontaine's loyal couple find their new home and valley transported intact to the Duc de Vendôme's Château d'Ant, near Dreux. Swift's contrasting loyal couple is destroyed *in situ*. For Swift's knowledge of the *Fables*, see, in addition to PASSMANN AND VIENKEN's admirable catalogue, Brean Hammond, "Swift's Reading," *The Cambridge Companion to Jonathan Swift*, ed. Christopher Fox (Cambridge: Cambridge University Press, 2003), pp. 73-86 (80). Jonathan Smedley also saw the similarity to La Fontaine, but in a darker way. *Baucis and Philemon* is a good poem, "but whoever reads *Fountaine's* Fables, will discover that the *Captain* is but an *Imitator*, and a *Plagiary*" (*Gulliveriana*, p. xxx).

détails fort plaisans" and "plaisante & ingénieuse" and "originaux" (I, 193, 198n), but also much that is malign (I, 193, 198n). Some of Swift's images are gross (I, 197n); others are "ridicules & peu agréables." He banishes what moves the heart and elevates the soul and is wholly burlesque (I, 193). Yart mates such reservations with Swift's original way of adapting the ancient for modern purposes. Swift is crudely un-French, but *Baucis and Philemon* teaches French poets how to imitate the Ancients and be both new and familiar. Justus van Effen thought *A Tale of a Tub* bizarre. Desfontaines thought *Gulliver's Travels* indecent and bizarre as well as entertaining in his superior French version. Yart only thinks Swift often unworthy of himself, too English and outré, but with rich imagination buttressed by pleasant and ingenious humour that requires a reader's adjustment and then brings pleasure.

Desfontaines's *révoltant* Swift clearly has not become Yart's *salutaire* Swift; he is flawed but is less bizarre than the uniqueness of *Le Conte du tonneau* or *Gulliver* imply. Instead, Swift the poet is part of long traditions among "*des Auteurs anciens & modernes*" and thereby part of ongoing critical discussion. Comparison and contrast with other masters suggest that Swift himself ranks among masters. As Yart later says, "Tous les Poëtes que je traduis sont dignes d'être connus" (III [1753], xxvii). He made this possible with several of Swift's good but modest poems in volumes four (1753), five (1754), and six (1754). Volume seven (1756) became Yart's most important contribution regarding Swift's legacy as poet and as man in eighteenth-century France. By 1756, alas, affirming that legacy had become more difficult than ever. Without such an affirmation, Swift might only have had a brilliant future behind him.

4. *Cadenus and Vanessa*: "Le barbare" Swift

Two major factors make volume seven in Yart's *Idée* urgent as an attempt to cleanse Swift's reputation. That volume includes the great and controversial *Cadenus and Vanessa*. It also appears after François Lacombe translated Lord Orerry's harsh *Remarks on the Life and Writings* of Swift as *Lettres historiques et philologiques du Comte d'Orreri* (1753). Unlike its English parent, the *Lettres historiques* evoked neither a version of Patrick Delany's *Observations upon Lord Orrery's Remarks* (London: W. Reeve and A. Linde, 1754) nor Deane Swift's less helpful *Essay upon the Life, Writings, and Character of Dr. Jonathan Swift* (London: Charles Bathurst, 1755).[25] Few French readers saw these partial

25 Deane Swift's hysterical attacks upon Patrick Delany tainted his defence of Jonathan. See Delany's aggrieved response in *A Letter to Dean[e] Swift, Esq; on his Essay upon the Life,*

counter-weights to Orrery’s often grim version of Swift. One cannot overstate the damage his *Remarks* did to Swift’s reputation on either side of the Channel.

Sybil Goulding long ago called Orrery-Lacombe scarcely more than defamation. That would be an unpleasant but not defining issue if French readers took it as such. Instead, they generally assumed that Orrery’s book was the ugly truth regarding an ugly man. Lacombe is likely to have believed that as well when he translated those *Remarks* on Swift, with which Orrery hoped to form his son’s heart and soul. He spares nothing because he is less concerned with working for his friend’s glory “que d’instruire & de précautionner un jeune homme contre l’abus qu’on peut faire des talens.”[26]

Pierre Clément’s discussion in *Cinq années littéraires* (1756) reflects this view of the *Remarks* even before Lacombe’s translation. The angry Clément writes from London on 21 January 1752: “Ah le vilain homme … ce fameux *Doyen!*” Orrery has played an evaluator’s and not a friend’s role in writing Swift’s life “avec tant de candeur.”[27] Orrery the “ami impartial” gives Swift all the justice he merits – not much (p. 222). Clément lists Swift’s varied social and moral sins, including pride, rudeness, misanthropy, and cruelty: “voilà son caractère.” He is “ce tigre, de race obscure & probablement fils postiche lui-même” (p. 220), that is, false, counterfeit, or bluntly perhaps a bastard.[28] Everything he seems

---

Writings, and Character of Dr. J. Swift. By the Author of the Observations on Lord Orrery’s Remarks (London: W. Reeve and A. Linde, 1755). Delany engages Deane Swift regarding Jonathan’s alleged marriage to Stella (pp. 23-24). Deane Swift of course was hardly alone in denigrating Orrery’s *Remarks* and defending Jonathan. See, for example, Charles Jones, *An Epistle from the Hon. R[ichard] E[dgcumbe] to his Dear Nanny: To which is added, A Satire on L–d O–ry’s Remarks on the Life and Writings of Dean S–ft* (London: R. Lyon, 1752), p. 8. Resentment should have ended after Swift’s death, “But his Last Act bespoke their Favour, / He left an Hospital for Fools.”

26 Goulding, *Swift en France*, p. 131; John Boyle, fifth Earl of Cork and Orrery, *Lettres historiques et philologiques du Comte d’Orreri sur la vie et les ouvrages de Swift* (London and Paris: Lambert, 1753), sig. [A4r]; the translator was François Lacombe. John Stubbs is among those who second Goulding’s view. He laments that Orrery was “the most shocking contemporary denouncer” of Swift and was a prime mover of his “demonization;” see John Stubbs, *Jonathan Swift: The Reluctant Rebel* (New York and London: W. W. Norton, 2016), pp. 626-27, and more broadly pp. 626-33. My own view is that hostility to *A Tale of a Tub*, Whig hostility to Swift’s politics and political pamphlets, and Book Four of *Gulliver’s Travels* allowed Orrery to provide a “friend’s” evidence for what Swift’s enemies already wanted to believe was true.

27 Pierre Clément, *Les Cinq années littéraires: ou, Lettres de M. Clément sur les ouvrages de littérature qui ont paru dans les années 1748, 1749, 1750, 1751 & 1752* (Berlin, 1756), II, 219. Subsequent references to the edition and volume are cited parenthetically in the text.

28 For “postiche,” see *Dictionnaire*, II, 292: “Fait & ajousté après coup … On appelle des fausses Dents & des faux cheveux, *Des dents postiches, des cheveux postiches.* On appelle *Postiche*, ce qui est ajousté & ne convient point.”

to have done for the good is suspect. Nor can one defend his works (p. 221), Clément's estimate of which was probably coloured by the estimate of Swift's "vilain" nature. Most of these works are "sans goût," weighed down by "des détails puériles, désintéressans, choquans, indécens, & même odieux." Clément acknowledges that Swift's literary achievements nonetheless are good enough almost to require pardon for their author: "mais *Stella, Stella*" (p. 222). Swift's conduct towards that unfortunate woman is one of the chief reasons that Swift provoked "l'aversion cordiale" which nearly drummed him out of French, and sometimes British, civilized life. He seduced and married the virtuous, talented, beautiful Stella, raised by Temple but thought his steward's daughter and for Swift therefore unworthy of being publicly recognized as his wife (p. 220). Clément quotes Orrery's remark that Swift regarded women merely as busts and not as complete human creatures. Clément replies: "Ah! C'est qu'il étoit buste lui-même, & buste du marbre le plus dur & le plus froid" (p. 221).

"*Stella, Stella*" was but half the reason Swift seemed to many of Orrery's readers a cold, heartless tiger feeding on vulnerable women. Vanessa was a would-be wife and a consequent corpse. The *Journal étranger* savages Swift's "inhumanité" regarding Stella; and his "odieux & ... inhumain" conduct regarding Vanessa.[29] Such continued assaults transcended Orrery's catalogue of Swift's personal failures.[30] The *Journal des sçavans* reviewed Lacombe's translation, repeated many of its complaints regarding Swift's conduct, and related them

29 As a parallel to the *Journal des sçavans*, the *Monthly Review* blames Swift's "barbarity to *Stella*'s person" and after "Good God!" laments his mingled crime, pride, avarice, and "deliberate ensnarements." The full review is in the *Monthly Review*, 11 (1754), 56-77. Delany's *Observations* on Orrery tactfully corrected some of Orrery's remarks, but also agreed with many others. Such post-Orrery remarks were familiar. See Robert Shiels, *The Lives of the Poets of Great-Britain and Ireland, to the Time of Dean Swift*, 5 vols (London: R. Griffiths, 1753), V, 81, 95-97, and *A New and General Biographical Dictionary*, 11 vols (London: T. Osborne, *et al.*, 1761), XI, 56-60. Of course, Swift's relationships with Stella and Vanessa appear in major biographies, like those of Hawkesworth (1768) and Johnson (1781), among others. Across the Channel, see the *Journal étranger*'s review of Delany's *Observations* (January 1754), pp. 64-90; pp. 80 (inhumanity), 83 (odieux and inhumain) quoted. The *Journal* extends the review to February, pp. 83-100, which also labels Swift's writing as libertine, licentious, obscene, and thus perhaps irreligious enough for him to be excluded from a bishopric (p. 89).

30 Readers nonetheless were sceptical regarding some of Orrery's other claims regarding Swift, whose works they often denigrated. The *Journal de Trévoux* rejects his Lordship's view that Swift, who reflects "de raison & de bizarrerie," is the author who most closely approached Horace. The proper analogy is with a remnant of seventeenth-century crudity and the author who apologized to his patron, the Duke d'Arpajon, for dedicating his early, capricious, foolish, works to him. *Trévoux* limits Swift to the class of Cyrano de Bergerac, who certainly is not, as Orrery believes, either a great mind or a transcendent genius (November 1753), 2652-53.

directly to a familiar victim. That vain, proud, ambitious, intractable, capricious, inconstant man was unworthy of so excellent a woman as Stella. The *Journal des sçavans* uses a term that often described Swift's works now to describe his mind: his refusal to share a home with Stella signals "la bizarrerie de son caractère" by a man unworthy "d'une femme de ce mérite." The *Journal de Trévoux* also cites Swift's bizarre mind, and adds that in some respects he is the Socrates and in others "le Rabelais de l'Angleterre," that is, an outmoded writer unacceptable within enlightened polite worlds. The *Mercure de France* is pleasingly astonished by the variety of Swift's talents and the breadth of his knowledge. It also more frankly states its response to Lacombe's Orrery: "On y verra cet homme célèbre décomposé en quelque manière." The *Journal des sçavans* adds that Orrery is especially troubled by *Cadenus and Vanessa*, but "nous ne connoissons point de traduction en François."[31] Yart cautiously fills that void.

Swift's fractured celebrity was nasty in its own right but potentially catastrophic regarding views of his relationships with both Vanessa and Stella. Abbé Yart had the usual job of relating, placing, and evaluating Swift's poems within ongoing genres; he now also had to defend or perhaps explain the Anglican Dean of St Patrick's misconduct in life and art. It seemed that he ensnared Vanessa who loved him, sought to marry him, and had been corrupted by him as her teacher. Orrery-Lacombe made such a defence difficult and for some impossible.

Their Swift is a malign tutor. As in Orrery's English to which Lacombe tends to be but modestly unfaithful, his "rules were certainly of a most extraordinary kind. He taught her, that vice, as soon as it defied shame, was immediately changed into virtue. That vulgar forms were not binding upon *certain choice*

31 *Journal des sçavans* (October 1753), 671-72 (bizarrerie, mérite); *Journal de Trévoux*, 53 (November 1753), 2652 (Socrates); *Mercure de France*, 65 (October 1753), 128 (Lacombe); *Journal des sçavans* (October 1753), 674 (connoissons). For other germane harsh comments on Swift's writings that many regarded as "bizarre" as his personal conduct, see "Swift," in *Nouveau dictionnaire historique-portatif: ou, Histoire abrégée de tous les hommes qui se sont fait un nom par des talens, des vertus, des forfaits, des erreurs, &c.*, ed. Louis Mayeul Chaudon, 4 vols (Amsterdam: Marc Michel Rey, 1774), IV, 308-9. *Cadenus and Vanessa*, as in Swift's other poems, has imagination and good verses, but all are "trop d'écarts & trop peu de corrections." That poem indeed is "l'histoire de ses amours" or rather, he says, Swift's indifference to Vanessa who futilely burned for him. *Gulliver's Travels* is original of its kind, and offers both a well-sustained narrative and "des contes puèriles, des allégories plaisantes, & de froides allusions, des ironies fines & des plaisanteries grossieres, une morale sensée & des polissoneries révoltantes" (IV, 308-9). It is insipid, low, repetitive, and boring. These remarks, borrowed from Desfontaines, also characterize the van Effen translation of the *Tale of a Tub* as the *Conte du tonneau*.

spirits, to whom either the writings, or the persons of men of wit were acceptable" (p. 111). This suited what Vanessa thought her own "exalted turn of mind;" if the theory was "so charming, the practice must be much more delightful." So close a connection of body and soul convinced her that "each should succeed the other in all pleasurable enjoyments." The soul was happy; now the body should be as well. She courts Swift, to which he feigns ignorance and speaks of friendship, reason, "gratitude, respect and esteem." Orrery sees little of Swift's respect for decorum or religious values. "He almost preached upon virtue, and he muttered some indistinct phrases concerning chastity" (p. 112), or as Lacombe put it, "il lui débita quelques maximes hardies sur la chasteté." Orrery calls Cadenus's conduct "unaccountable;" Lacombe more darkly calls it "bisarre" (p. 113). The French term for Swift's literary transgressions again becomes the term for his character's transgressions, and then for his social transgressions, "bizarre" conduct that is "Fantastique, extravagant, capricieux," and beyond normal behaviour (*Dictionnaire*, s.v.).

Swift's "defects in nature" join with his "distant manner" and "indifference" to his wife Stella after their marriage, what Lacombe again heightens as "plus extraordinaire." More extraordinary yet, Swift's poem included a paragraph of sexual innuendo designed as much to protect his own reputation as to wound Vanessa's. Lacombe slightly abbreviates and heightens Orrery's anger: "Je blâmerai tout ma vie le Doyen d'avoir si librement, & avec des couleurs si frappantes, ce qu'il aurait dû se cacher à lui-même" (p. 114). Lacombe's bizarre Swift is a bad tutor, a bad husband, a bad preacher, and a bad chooser of a potential mistress. French readers conditioned to seek *politesse* in their literature would have been alarmed. Swift's grotesque literary tableaux have become grotesque moral tableaux.

Swift adds bad or savage manners to his already bad conduct towards Vanessa. He harshly rejects her request that he marry her, throws a brutal letter of rejection upon the table and treats her with "insolence and disdain." She receives reproach instead of love, tyranny instead of affection, and is morally, spiritually, psychologically, and physically destroyed. Lacombe's frightened Vanessa sees Swift in "colère;" it was nearly impossible "de le regarder sans frayeur." Orrery refers to "the inward contents of his letter" (p. 116). Lacombe labels its contents "fatale" and the cause of her death (p. 117). Orrery likens Vanessa to Dido abandoned by Aeneas, quotes Virgil's Latin (*Aeneid*, IV, 450-51), and alludes to her impending death. Lacombe explains the allusion rather than hides its meaning in a learned language. Vanessa is "Semblable à Didon qui ne pouvant plus supporter la rigueur de son sort" and, in a partial paraphrase of Orrery's quotation, calls death "à son secours, lasse de jouir de la-céleste clarté" (pp. 117-18). Lacombe offers victimized Vanessa a reward that the Anglican Dean of St Patrick's seemed to have done his best to deny – Vanessa's heavenly respite. As the allusion to the *Aeneid* suggests, and as we shall see, whatever the poem's controversial paragraph's nuance, for both Orrery and Lacombe Cadenus may have seduced, but certainly attracted and abandoned a princess who welcomed him, loved him, and who was fatally rejected by him.

Both author and translator state that Vanessa survived just a few days after having received Swift's letter. Each version of this event is painful. Orrery's Vanessa "perished ... under all the agonies of despair." Lacombe's Vanessa "périt misérablement" (each, p. 118). Elie Catherine Fréron knew the appropriate words for Swift's "imperfection naturelle" and both Stella's and Vanessa's consequent death-by-deprivation. Vanessa was "la seconde femme que le barbare *Swift* fit mourir d'amour & de langueur."[32]

Yart had placed Swift among the best of the English poets not yet translated into French. He recognized that Swift's imaginative excesses stretched French ability to enjoy or even to understand his works. His genius is worth the effort, but his conduct in romantic concerns was deadly. Both Stella the wife and Vanessa the apparent mistress died of intentionally unrequited love for a gravely flawed eminent churchman. Yart needs to neutralize those images or else abandon Swift to the world of "le bas" and "le barbare." The first step in this hopeful process is to place *Cadenus and Vanessa* within its international contexts in the fluid genre of the *conte*.

32 Elie Catherine Fréron, *Lettres sur quelques écrits de ce tems*, 13 vols (London and Paris: Duchesne, 1751-54), X, 296. Fréron extensively reviews Lacombe's translation of Orrery, comments broadly upon Swift, shares some of Orrery's reservations, and offers a familiar French observation: in Swift one finds "partout ... un génie surprenant & bizarre," and that "sa satyre un peu trop libre va quelquefois jusqu'à la basse plaisanterie" (X, 294, 297). Fréron reviews the fourth volume of Yart's *Idée de la poësie Angloise* in the same number. He expresses the general French approbation of Yart's softening of English excess and elimination of "des images ou des expressions basses & ridicules," but adds a caution. These changes make reading English works "beaucoup moins desagréable," but also stop one from forming "une idée juste de la Poèsie Angloise." Yart's notes properly alert his readers to those changes (X, 323), but not, I add, in the compromising portion of *Cadenus and Vanessa*, for which see below. See also Fréron's review of Yart's first three volumes, in *Lettres*, 9 (1752), 240-58, and on Swift, pp. 244-46. Fréron admires Yart's "histoire abrégée des plus grands Poëtes Anglois" (IX, 253).

5. Apologie des Moeurs et des Ecrits de M. Swift

Yart establishes the *conte*'s proper limits. In so doing, he uses a term that characterizes his approach to the English in *Idée de la poësie Angloise*. They are "nos voisins" and not the uncivilized brutes across the Channel. Neighbours are part of a shared culture in which art investigates and portrays "la connoisance la plus délicate de l'esprit & du cœur humain" (VII, 1-2). As the Académie's *Dictionnaire* put the commonplace, a "voisin" is one who is near and remains near ("Qui est proche ... qui demeure auprés"). The verb "voisener" is to visit one's neighbour familiarly ("visiter familierement ses voisins"). Johnson later enlarged upon what is implicit in such visits. A neighbour is "one who lives in familiarity with another; a word of civility." Being neighbourly is to be "kind; civil" (*Dictionary*, s.v.). Yart surely has such thoughts in mind as he briefly outlines the genre's several traits, its history, and its progress from the Orient to Continental Europe and to France's neighbour England. The *conte*'s narrative concerns acts by humans not gods; it is of modest length without superfluous details or excessive brevity; as a lesser form of the epic, it avoids sublime actions like "la perte du Paradis" or "la ruine de Troie" (VII, 6). One might say that the *conte* hopes to depict kind, civil, neighbourly relations among its actors.

National character conditions national poetry. The English regularly transgress the *conte*'s clear and known rules. Yart wonders whether this is the spirit of contradiction or of misguided creativity ("fécondité mal entendue" [VII, 12]). The French are best at the *conte* because their light and rapid spirit carries them from the tale's beginning to its end without wandering among "des images & des pensées" (VII, 14). A long generic history allows several kinds of excellence: images dominate the Greek *contes*, thoughts the Latin, "les réflexions dans les Anglois, & les faits dans les nôtres" (VII, 15). Yart has skilfully granted specifically English traits while still including English practice within the *conte*'s generic framework that accommodates Greek, French, and English modes of proceeding.

The *conte*'s young audience requires protection. A tale must be morally decent and not disturb an innocent reader, "ménager la pudeur."[33] Yart has a

---

33 Yart is consistent with Samuel Johnson's contemporaneous discussion of the novel in the *Rambler*, no 4 (1750): "These books are written chiefly to the young, the ignorant, and the idle, to whom they serve as lectures of conduct, and introductions into life." Consequently, "the highest degree of reverence should be paid to youth, and ... nothing indecent should be suffered to approach their eyes or ears." Caution is required "to secure them from unjust prejudices, perverse opinions, and incongruous combinations of images" (see *The Rambler*, in *The Yale Edition of the Works of Samuel Johnson*, III, eds W. J. Bate and Albrecht B. Strauss [New Haven: Yale University Press, 1969], 21).

tactical problem: how can *Cadenus and Vanessa* be seen to protect modesty? He answers that question, in part, by analysing La Fontaine's practice in the *conte*, who lived among licentious libertines, was inadequately educated in morality, and was too self-centred. In words that recall literary and cultural crudity prior to Louis XIV, he lived in a century "où le langage n'étoit pas plus reglé que les moeurs." He thus wrote *contes* "extrèmement dangereux" (VII, 19). Gross expressions show little genius in the author and little respect for his reader; proper and delicate expressions regarding love are necessary for the yet uneducated and unsophisticated "jeune cœur" (VII, 22). French readers nonetheless revere La Fontaine. It seems reasonable to make the same decision regarding Swift. That analogy, however, is not nearly enough to exonerate a famous man labelled a fatal brute regarding women. Yart responds to that problem in a familiar French way. This first French translation of *Cadenus and Vanessa* must protect or at least not endanger its young and especially its female readers. The second part of Yart's attempt to cleanse Swift's reputation is to practise the suppression that he had already warned against regarding English poetry: "S'ils parlent trop librement, je supprime ou je réfute ce qui est trop libre" (III, xxvii). At least as important, Yart adds his "Apologie des Mœurs et des Ecrits de M. Swift. *Tirée de ses lettres & de quelques autres Mémoires*."

One claim against Swift was that his dubious works expressed his dubious conduct. Yart over-compensates by portraying a nearly saint-like Jonathan Swift and by directly and indirectly challenging Orrery. Swift's ancestry denotes loyalty to the Crown. His family left England for Ireland because they refused to be subject to Cromwell, the "usurpateur" (VII, 175). Swift immortalized St George Ashe, his tutor at Trinity College, Dublin, and Sir William Temple at Moor Park. Swift then served the Anglican Church, and Queen Anne's ministers and Court. He writes the *Examiner* papers that help to remove the aggressive Marlborough from office, but upon the accession of George I he returns to Dublin. He becomes a zealous patriotic churchman, friend, and "grand philosophe," who regularly protests "l'esclavage où le gouvernement Anglois réduisoit l'Irlande" (VII, 179). He urges his Irish compatriots to buy local goods and resist debased English coinage. He troubles "les tyrans de l'Irlande" (VII, 180), is never discouraged, helps the poor, lends money without interest, and founds a hospital for the mentally ill. He is the father and the benefactor of the Irish people, who in turn love him. "Il régnoit sur les Irlandois, le Roi d'Angleterre ne régnoit que sur l'Irlande" (VII, 181): "son zele pour sa patrie remplissoient son coeur" (VII, 172n).

Yart tactfully and tactically begins discussion of Swift's works with Abbé Desfontaines's version of *Gulliver's Travels*, regarding which he quotes Gay as writing to Swift on 17 November 1726, "tout le monde lut avec transport"

(VII, 181). Its satire indeed is severe, but its misanthropy "n'étoit ni chagrine ni méchante" (VII, 184). Swift so confirms in his letter of 29 September 1725, in which he tells Pope that "his chief end ... is to vex (Yart: "tourmenter" [VII, 185]) the world rather than divert it." Swift laughs at Mankind rather than hates it. In fact, he was a valued colleague and beloved friend who always was helpful, faithful, and loved in return. As a devout Anglican, he mocked only fanaticism, superstition, and atheism. Those who reproach him for *A Tale of a Tub* really reproach him for being a Protestant, but perhaps he did not even write that work, which he never acknowledged.

The "Apologie" confronts Orrery's claim that Swift was vain, ambitious, caustic, avaricious, and impious. The evidence Yart had already cited, he says, refutes such libels, and especially the "odieux" claim that Swift was impious, "reproche aussi injuste que les autres" (VII, 189). One of those others is that Swift was a recluse. Yart quoted long letters from or to Gay and Pope, which are among the many "jolis morceaux" and "lettres charmantes" to friends (VII, 191). He thereby shows Swift in a social world among distinguished *littérateurs*. Such a man can easily embrace the world of benevolent Irish power enjoyed at Lady Acheson's country estate. In personal, literary, and character-matters, Swift is superior to "la plupart des Auteurs" (VII, 193). His political papers were "profonds & ingénieux;" his style was exemplary; his "raissonnemens les plus solides;" his instruction propelled by laughter. Jonathan Swift is "l'Auteur le plus original que l'Angleterre ait jamais eu" (VII, 194). As Voltaire said, he is not like Rabelais or Scarron or Cervantes or Cyrano. Swift is unique, fine, delicate, and certainly not "de bas" in his language (VII, 194-95). Yart again likens Swift to a received master of proper French style, whose morality he questions. Swift is "aussi original dans son genre, que la Fontaine l'est dans le sien" (VII, 196). Yart ends his "Apologie" with an important footnote. He finished this *discours* on *contes* and his defence of Swift at the end of 1753. The *Journal étranger* for January and February of 1755 alerted him to Patrick Delany's defence of Swift and polite rebuttal, where possible, of Orrery's severe judgements. This gives Yart both "le plus grand plaisir" and an Anglophone argument on authority that supports his own conclusion: Swift's few "petits défauts" are insignificant when set against "la foule de ses vertus." Delany is not as uniformly positive as Yart hopes, but he suggests that Swift's rich life and art provide the "lumière vive & immense" that Yart also sees (VII, 198-99n). He now must translate *Cadenus and Vanessa*, a darkly brilliant example of that art, on whose compromising paragraph Orrery and Delany agreed, and which Yart is obliged to consider in his own selective way.

6. *Cadenus and Vanessa*: "On ne peut soupçonner aucun crime dans leur commerce"

Yart attends to readers' needs. He enlarges their generic expectations, includes a prefatory discourse, and uses explanatory footnotes to prompt further interpretation. These illumine the poet's meaning, point out special virtues, and in some cases tell why the translator omitted certain lines. He cites special excellence: "Peut-on voir une plus charmante allégorie?" he asks (VII, 146n a). At another place, he adds "Que cette idée est noble & juste!" (VII, 158n a). He places Swift within known traditions, as with his likeness to the generally approved if not generally virtuous La Fontaine (VII, 148n b). When Swift offers especially original or even outré English phrasing, Yart says with apparent admiration: "Voilà du style de Docteur" (VII, 150n). Even if a comic image seems excessive, it is "ni moins ingénieuse ni moins morale" for all that (VII, 159n a). Yes, Vanessa was distraught that Cadenus had only esteem for her merit rather than attraction for her charms, but he was innocent of her death. She herself "abrégea sa vie par l'usage immodéré des liqueurs" (VII, 172n).

Yart also alerts readers that he adapts Swift to the more polite French world, for which, he hopes, Swift can be made to fit. Young women are moral, decent, beautiful, and worthy of being the *beau sexe*; they are not pedants and do not bother with legal cant or learned allusions. Yart thus drops most references to classical figures other than ones like Pallas and Venus, who cannot be detached from the plot. Swift's poem is particularized and eclectic in its allusions to classical and to English places and names. One energetic eight-line section includes Fleta, Brackton, Coke, Ovid, Virgil, Dido, Tibullus, Cowley, and Waller (ll. 107-15). Yart's version excludes all of these (VII, 144). Swift's colloquial "Old Queen *Bess*" (l. 397) yields to Yart's dignified "la Reine Elisabeth" (VII, 156).

The French world requires a *conte* to protect the young reader. Yart thus reshapes Swift's different kind of poem. This *Cadenus and Vanessa* avoids the slightest possible apparent deviation from *politesse* and *pudeur*. Yart banishes Swift's references to female parts and physical or possible sexual position. For example, the men's celestial lawyer in Venus' court denigrates modern women's superficial emotional and sensual lives. They should be losers in the battle of the sexes. The ancient practice of intense shared mutual affection between a man and a woman in love is gone. Women now have "gross Desire; / Their Passions move in lower Spheres" (ll. 37-38). Women's amusements are fashionable "Toys" – fans, flounces and the like – that fill their heads and rob their time "Between their Toylets and their Beds" (ll. 47-50). Yart translates neither women's "lower Spheres" nor "their Beds." One suggests carnal desire; the other is where desire becomes practice. Each suggests inadequate concern for protecting a naive reader.

These unacceptable words were spoken by an attorney who is the men's misguided advocate, and whose insults Swift should not have permitted. Yart's note to this passage complains that the lawyer strangely abuses the right of his clients to insult women, who require respect. There are certain reproaches one should not make against them, and which they will never forget. Yart states the method that he also exercises later in the poem: "J'ai extrêmement adouci ce plaidoyer" (VII, 142n a). He softens the lawyer's charges and retrenches the ugly legal terms of art.[34]

Swift's *conte* needs much *adoucissement* in part of course because of its setting. He draws Vanessa as baptized in a classical, celestial, domain. He replaces Holy Water with nectar and amarinthian flowers that give the infant moral cleanliness, modesty, and such "Decency of Mind" that she never blushes (l. 164). In contrast, spuriously virtuous women "blush because they understand" sexual innuendo (l. 171). Yart's respect for women again permits him to censor the apparent insult. He concludes his paragraph's version with praise of future blushless Vanessa as part of a virtuous gender that shares "cette décence si aimable dans le beau sexe" (VII, 146). Yart knows that the word "virgin" evokes a woman's innocent body, whose attractive parts should not be mentioned. Swift's "young Virgins" (l. 311) thus become a singular "jeune personne" (VII, 152). We read that Pallas would be jealous "to see a Mortal Virgin deck'd" with graces hitherto unknown to human "Female Breasts" (ll. 271, 273). Yart's Vanessa has the graces of "une simple mortelle" who apparently absorbs those talents in some place other than her heart beneath the unmentioned breast (VII, 150). "Deep transfix'd her Bosom" (l. 519) becomes "pénétra le cœur de Vanessa," and "pierc'd her Breast" (l. 521) is "augmenterent la blessure" (VII, 161).

Moreover, a proper lady does not want a poet publicly to discuss her finances. Yart eliminates a section (ll. 211-27) in which Pallas insures that Vanessa has good economic sense and an estate of some five thousand pounds. Stating the ample sum troubles Yart, whose note tells us: "J'omets quelques détails, qui ne plairoient point, sur l'économie & les revenus de Vanessa" (VII, 148n a). Yart's *conte* also omits lines (772-89) in which Swift proclaims the sort of complex, mingled, form of love he hopes for, but in which he cannot engage. Nor,

---

34 See Yart, VII, 142n.a: "L'Avocat des hommes abuse ici étrangement du droit que ses confreres prétendent avoir de dire des injures à leurs parties; quelque sujet qu'on eût de se plaindre des femmes, on doit les respecter; il est des reproches qu'on ne doit point leur faire, & qu'elles ne pardonnent jamais. J'ai extrémement adouci ce plaidoyer: j'en ai aussi retranché une foule de terms de Palais qui déparent ce Poëme."

we shall see, can Yart offer readers a section (ll. 790-818) in which idealized Vanessa behaves more like a man than a proper woman who should not make "the Government ... her own" (l. 801).

Yart's limiting, polishing, and excluding are necessary and demonstrable when he reaches the poem's interpretative and often thought scandalous crux. We can anticipate and understand his practice by means of the nearly concluding pages of the "Apologie de M. Swift." Yart there tells us that Swift's style is not "bourgeois & burlesque." It is extremely natural, pure, and as elegant as that of Pope and Bolingbroke. Swift's ideas are "plaisantes & comiques," but in his own unique way, and not in Scarron's or Rabelais's manner – unpolished, and bereft of modern *politesse*. Swift's ideas in fact are fine if comic, and delicate if joking. The artisan's names he introduces were not low in his own language. When well placed, they make a charming contrast to the elevated grave characters with whom they contrast (VII, 195).

Yart extends this praise to Swift's political, philosophical, and other writings that educate all ages and all nations, and certainly apply to the poetry that Yart has long been translating. He then offers a summary panegyric of Swift's verse, the "agréable" shorter poems, *Baucis and Philemon*, and then *Cadenus and Vanessa*. Yart puffs its elegant style, fine thoughts, natural characterization, moral instruction disguised beneath pleasantries, original fiction, "le tout ensemble neuf & comique" (VII, 196).

There are necessary omissions. Yart hopes to have answered familiar French condemnation of Swift's style, and argues on a selection of acceptable poems rather than on several others less tactful, more violent, crude, or variously romantic. He excludes these because some violate French taste and some violate conventions, at their best, regarding a cleric's distance from an apparently seductive woman. Such poems would soil Yart's case for Swift's "agréable" poetry. These reasons also explain much of the bowdlerized *Cadenus and Vanessa*. Yart normally informs readers that he has expunged certain lines but does not do so regarding the hinted seduction paragraph. He cannot alert readers to the offence that he must hide and that would remove *Cadenus and Vanessa* from even the margins of the protective *conte*.

Yart clearly admired Swift the poet and the man. He may also have known, or known about, the harsh responses to what many in Britain thought a rude if not hostile compromise of Vanessa that gave his enemies abundant ammunition and, for some, enhanced Swift's reputation as a philanderer. Jonathan Smedley thought *Cadenus and Vanessa* the best of Swift's poems in the third volume of the *Miscellanies*, but he should have "buried it in Silence": its subject "can never afford him any thing but Matter of Shame and Sorrow." Leonard Welsted drew an image of "unbutton'd" Swift languishing in Vanessa's arms and indifferent to virtue, the Church, the State, or Ireland. For one nominal playwright, Vanessa was a good name to use for a court-woman with a previous lover and now impregnated by Prince Adonis. Deane Swift defended the real Vanessa who, he said, "was extreamly angry with the DOCTOR on Account of" the dubious lines. He also quotes a couplet from her verse elegy: "Nor can, alas! The grave secure / Her virtues uncorrupt and pure!" Swift's friend Patrick Delany was comparably troubled by "these ill-judged lines." They do "not necessarily infer" sexual union, but they "seem to have designedly drawn it into a doubt. O that they were annihilated, or rather, that neither they, nor their cause (idle vanity) had ever existed in a breast, which should have abhorred *all appearance of evil*."[35] French response to the paragraph and awareness of Swift's "idle vanity" could have hardly been any milder. Whether or not Orrery defamed Swift, for many British and French readers, Swift certainly defamed Vanessa. If Yart wished to preserve Swift either as a poet worth knowing or as a proper advocate of the moral tale, he had no choice but to censor it and eliminate its most troubling paragraph. Here is the poem's context for that section (ll. 818-27).

Shepherds and nymphs take their case against one another to Venus' law court. The women say that love and marriage are debased and the men are to blame. The men say that love and marriage are debased and the women are to blame. Venus postpones a decision for sixteen years, but then sees beautiful, virtuous, infant Vanessa, tricks Pallas into thinking that Vanessa is a boy and gifts him / her with the best male virtues of learning, wit, modesty, and

---

35 Smedley, *Gulliveriana*, pp. xxix-xxx, and see p. 3; Leonard Welsted, *One Epistle to Mr. A. Pope, Occasion'd by Two Epistles Lately Published* (London: J. Roberts, 1730), p. 20; *The Humours of the Court: or, Modern Gallantry. A New Ballad Opera* (London: W. James, 1732), p. [viii]. Deane Swift defends Vanessa and Swift's innocent relationship with her: *An Essay upon the Life, Writings, and Character, of Dr. Jonathan Swift* (London: Charles Bathurst, 1755), pp. 253 (angry), 265 (alas!); Delany, *Observations upon Lord Orrery's Remarks*, p. 115. For a discussion of Swift as putative philandering libertine, see Howard D. Weinbrot, "'Tis Well an Old Age is Out': Johnson, Swift, and his Generation," first published in *Reading Swift: Papers from The Sixth Münster Symposium on Jonathan Swift*, eds Kirsten Juhas, Hermann J. Real, and Sandra Simon (Munich: Wilhelm Fink, 2013), pp. 595-620, and reprinted in *Samuel Johnson: New Contexts for a New Century* (San Marino, California: Huntington Library Press, 2014), pp. 47-68. Some later readers acknowledged that the poem was ambiguous but did not confirm sexual union. See [Quentin Craufurd], *Essai historique sur le Docteur Swift, et sur son influence dans le gouvernement de la Grande Bretagne* (Paris, 1808), pp. 266-67. British Craufurd (1743-1819) made his fortune in India and retired to Paris, where he lived as a wealthy gentleman and mingled in the royal court. He and his mistress Anna Eleanor Sullivan facilitated, and were part of, the royal family's unsuccessful flight to Varennes and hoped-for escape from revolutionary France. Craufurd wrote about French literature and generally admired Swift.

restraint, to no avail. Women insult her and men ignore her, until Cupid provides Cadenus as tutor and pierces her heart with love for him. Swift soon changes Vanessa's role to recipient rather than seeker of love. Her gift of male values includes her control of personal "Government" (l. 801) and "The Science she designs to teach" (l. 811). She courts the reluctant, but pleased and tempted Cadenus, who knows that she has made "a kind Advance" (l. 817).

Swift adds the troubling paragraph that places Vanessa in a lose-lose situation. Either she has immorally seduced Cadenus, or she has been rejected but remains culpable for the desire and attempt. Cadenus himself has violated the terms of shifted roles, to which he agreed when he "fairly abdicates his Throne" (l. 800) and enables Vanessa's "vows to take him at his Word" (l. 803) in those changed roles. Cadenus nonetheless here seems a fallible but stolid cleric who admits to temptation, but will "descend" no farther. He makes clear that his pupil is the aggressor. Such a view is likely to have been in Orrery / Lacombe's mind when they say: "Je blâmerai tout ma vie le Doyen" for that distressing paragraph:

> But what Success *Vanessa* met,
> Is to the World a Secret yet:
> Whether the Nymph, to please her Swain,
> Talks in a high Romantick Strain;
> Or whether he at last descends
> To like with less Seraphick Ends;
> Or, to compound the Business, whether
> They temper Love and Books together;
> Must never to Mankind be told,
> Nor shall the conscious Muse unfold. (ll. 818-27)

Swift then returns to the poem's initial setting. Venus again arrives at the court, has learned from Vanessa's experience, hears closing arguments, and decides the case against the men (l. 853). She blames them for not courting virtuous Vanessa, leaves the rest of love matters to Cupid, and flies back to classical heaven, but not before including a hint that exonerates Cadenus in "the Business" of Vanessa's courtship. Venus complains that though the young woman was "A Model for her Sex design'd" she "never cou'd one Lover find" (ll. 866-67). Venus' departure leaves the mortals "all below at Six and Sev'n" (l. 888). Cupid now in charge of love has already shown poor judgement. Swift leaves his poem's world "in confusion, commonly said of a room where the furniture, &c. is scattered about, or of a business left unsettled."[36] Venus as

36 See Francis Grose, *A Classical Dictionary of the Vulgar Tongue* (London: S. Hooper, 1785), s.v. "Six." For some of such repeated uses earlier in the century, see Thomas Brown, *The*

goddess of love abdicates her responsibility properly to order romantic affairs on earth. Cadenus as tutor in charge of Vanessa's education abandons his responsibility properly to order her mind and not court her heart or another part of her anatomy. Swift as poet abdicates his responsibility to the reader properly to give order and moral values to his poem and portrays himself as the man subject to the woman's "descent" upon him. Swift's poem and its reversal of roles ends in a confused, unsettled, and isolated quotidian world. Venus has gone; Vanessa has gone; Swift as Cadenus is present, but at sixes and sevens, and justifying himself.

Abbé Yart's typical omissions end his translation, which becomes a work very different from Swift's. Yart precedes the ambiguous paragraph with tactical exclusions, as with Swift's Cadenus who had never before loved (ll. 768-72). Love leads to sexual desire, which should be purged from a *conte* in which a young and still innocent woman is a model for comparable readers. Yart thus tellingly omits the section in which Cadenus and Vanessa reverse roles. The male becomes subject and pupil. The female becomes governor and tutor, who hopes to instruct him in the ways of love. The Abbé who turned "breast" into "cœur" cannot translate lines that show a bold young woman who offers Cadenus the sexual "Science she designs to teach" (l. 811). Yart prepares French readers for a message very different from Swift's. Omitting the role-reversal prepares for omission of what happened during the consequent possible tempering of "Love and Books together" (l. 825). Yart's Cadenus remains in control. Vanessa remains only a mild temptation. The threat of seduction, sexual licence, and a cleric's fall into love or lust disappears.[37]

Third Volume of the Works of Mr. Thomas Brown, 3 vols (London: B. Bragg, 1708), p. 170; John Bunyan, *The Barren Fig-Tree: or, The Doom and Downfal of the Fruitless Professor*, 6th ed. (London: Jonathan Robinson, 1709); *A Collection of Poems, &c. for and against Dr. Sacheverell: The Third Part* (London, 1710), pp. 11, 16; John Arbuthnot, *John Bull Still in his Senses: Being the Third Part of Law is a Bottomless Pit* (London: John Morphew, 1712), p. 6.

37 Yart does not announce his copy text. It is possible but unlikely that he would have worked from a version lacking the compromising paragraph. I have examined twenty-six editions of *Cadenus and Vanessa* either as a free-standing poem or as part of larger miscellanies, and have seen the following without the relevant paragraph: the first edition by N. Blandford and sold by J. Peele (London, 1726), *Cadenus and Vanessa: or, The Judgment of Venus ... Written by Dr. Sw-ft, upon Himself and Mrs. Vanh----y, his Favourite Lady*, 2nd ed. (London: J. Roberts, 1726), and *Cadenus and Vanessa: A Poem. From the Original Copy* (Dublin, 2726 [sic]: no printer cited). For a fuller discussion of the different versions, see Herman Teerink, "Swift's *Cadenus and Vanessa*" and "Swift's *Cadenus and Vanessa* again," *Harvard Library Bulletin* 2, no 2 (1948), 254-57, and 3, no 3 (1949), 435-36, respectively. TEERINK AND SCOUTEN list the several editions as well (pp. 324-27), and so does FOXON S814-S829. One suspects pressure of varied sorts regarding whether to include or exclude the ten lines. Roberts's first edition includes the lines; the second edition excludes them;

The conclusion to Yart's *conte* only approximates Swift's. Venus as judge decides in favour of the women. She quits the bench, leaves the world of love to Cupid to manage, harnesses her doves to her chariot and flies upwards. The world below apparently remains secure and orderly as in Yart's last sentence: Venus "quitta la terre, & monta dans les Cieux" (VII, 171). Yart's final omission is Swift's line in which Venus "left all below at Six and Sev'n." Yart's text avoids moral confusion because it neither permits nor admits ambiguity or worse in the relationship between Cadenus and Vanessa. He insists on Swift's innocence: "On ne peut soupçonner aucun crime dans leur commerce" (VII, 172). *Adoucissement* and the educational, protective, *conte* supersede Swift's piercing ironies and complex characterization of actors in what seemed to many not a world left in proper order, but a pending and then real tragedy.

The Abbé Yart bravely introduced and discussed poetry by a transcendent apocalyptic satirist. Swift offered French readers and poets images and original approaches to ancient poems for which some in his culture were grateful; but it was generally not willing to follow him beyond the edge of benevolent illusion. Voltaire said that to appreciate Swift's poetry one needed to visit England.[38] In *Idée de la poësie Angloise*, Yart preferred to visit through books, but to stay in la belle France.

---

the third edition includes them. In sum, though, almost all editions of *Cadenus and Vanessa* and the *Miscellanies* include the compromising lines. See three germane essays: Peter J. Schakel, "What Success It Met: The Reception of *Cadenus and Vanessa*," *Reading Swift: Papers from The Third Münster Symposium on Jonathan Swift*, eds Hermann J. Real and Helgard Stöver-Leidig (Munich: Wilhelm Fink, 1998), pp. 215-24; John Irwin Fischer, "'Love and Books': Some Early Texts of *Cadenus and Vanessa*, and a Few Words about Love," *Reading Swift: Papers from The Fourth Münster Symposium on Jonathan Swift*, eds Real and Stöver-Leidig, pp. 285-310; Daniel Cook, "*Cadenus and Vanessa*: The Self-Conscious Muse," *Reading Swift: Papers from The Sixth Münster Symposium on Jonathan Swift*, eds Kirsten Juhas, Hermann J. Real, and Sandra Simon (Munich: Wilhelm Fink, 2013), pp. 400 16.

Of course, there are other copies that I have not seen, but even if Yart worked from a text without the paragraph, he would have been made aware of it by means of Lacombe's Orrery, which he clearly knew and which clearly troubled him. The omission is consistent with his broader practice of *adoucissement* that eliminated unacceptable words, phrases, and paragraphs. He may also have known several of the other harsh responses to Swift and all the more felt it necessary to preserve his readers from such responses in *Cadenus and Vanessa*.

38 Voltaire, *Letters concerning the English Nation*, p. 215.

7. "Plus hardi, moins gallant": Did *Adoucissement* Integrate Swift into French Culture?

Abbé Yart worked bravely to convince his readers that Swift was not a dangerous author. Omission and frequent genteel softening helped Yart to give that impression. His efforts nonetheless failed. We know that after Orrery / Lacombe there was broad dismay with Swift's conduct towards Stella as his unacknowledged wife, and towards Vanessa as his apparent paramour. This included condemnation of Swift's disrespect in the censored, compromising, paragraph to which Orrery / Lacombe alerted readers.

These issues were part of larger concerns with Swift's generally hostile attitudes towards women. For all the Abbé Yart's creative efforts, *Cadenus and Vanessa* was hardly a protective *conte*. Readers after his *Idée de la poësie Angloise* continued to condemn Swift's inability to respond properly to women who loved him, to whom he was attracted, and whom he variously spurned. The *Dictionnaire historique-portatif* was indebted to Orrery and acknowledged the "bisarrerie" of a husband who would only see his wife "en présence de Témoins." Thereafter, Louis Mayeul Chaudon insisted that Swift's treatment of Stella was "aussi cruel que bizarre." His rejection of Vanessa threw her into "une mélancolie dont elle mourut."[39]

Such familiar denigration had predictable consequences for Swift's reputation in early nineteenth-century France. Albin-Joseph-Ulpien Hennet's *La Poétique Anglaise* of 1806 is a bilingual anthology and series of biographies and critical commentaries. He was influenced by Johnson's *Lives of the Poets* (1779-81), admired English poetry, and was attracted, pleased, and cautious regarding its freedom, energy, originality, and "hardi" styles and language. He also reflects much by then conventional French wisdom concerning Jonathan Swift, who, thanks in significant part both to Yart and to Johnson, French readers accepted within "la poétique Anglaise."

Hennet recognizes Swift's special brilliance as "le plus original des poëtes" (II, 257) and as a stunning if controversial artist: "il étonne souvent et n'ennuie jamais" (II, 284). In a virtual leitmotif, however, he is also "le plus bizarre des hommes" (II, 257), "toujours bizarre" regarding Stella (II, 275), for whom he is a "bizarre époux" (II, 281) and whose devastating death justly punishes him for

39 "Swift," in *Dictionnaire historique-portatif, contenant l'histoire des patriarches, des princes, Hebreux, des empereurs, des rois*, ed. Abbé Jean-Baptiste l'Advocat, 2 vols (Paris: Didot, 1761 [1755]), II, 556 (Stella), 557 (Orrery); "Swift" in Chaudon, *Nouveau dictionnaire historique-portatif*, II, 308. In each case, Swift's clear attraction and clear indifference to a woman who loved him was a major cause of their deaths.

"une bizarrerie" that was his tyranny over her. He exhibits "toute la bizarrerie de son caractère" (II, 276) in personal relations and has a "bizarre amour" with Vanessa (II, 278).

In a related commonplace, within a five-year period, "deux femmes charmantes" died for love of Swift (II, 282). Hennet makes a telling allusion regarding that sad attraction. Swift, he says, was a dark-toned man who never lightened his expression; he washed himself with oriental scrupulosity, had a gloomy aspect, never smiled, always was original and sometimes mad. He was a poet, philosopher, politician, theologian, great walker, and "très économe," or stingy. Such a man might know love, but not inspire it. That, Hennet continues, is precisely the opposite of what happened: two women as spiritual but more beautiful than Sappho competed in vain for the conquest of an ecclesiastic "sous sa robe noire, ne ressemblait en rien à Phaon" (II, 262).

Hennet alludes to Ovid's broadly known *Heroides*, Epistle 15, which Pope translated for Tonson's *Ovid* in 1712 and reprinted in his own *Works* in 1717. Phaon, the aged and ugly boatman, ferries Aphrodite, disguised as an aged woman, from Lesbos to Asia Minor. He does not demand a fee, in return for which Aphrodite gives him a magic ointment that makes him young, handsome, and irresistible to women. Sappho falls desperately in love with him; he rejects her charms; and in despair she throws herself from the rocks of Leucas into the sea and drowns.[40] The story of Sappho and Phaon is a story of the woman's death through misplaced love, and was so portrayed in several eighteenth-century Ovidian and other works.[41] Hennet makes the paradox plain when he says that Stella and Vanessa were more beautiful than Sappho, but that Swift was no Phaon: these lovely women died for an unlovely man.

40 *Ovid's Epistles, Translated by Several Hands. The Eighth Edition. With a New Translation of Three Epistles* (London: Jacob Tonson, 1712), pp. 7-20; *The Works of Mr. Alexander Pope* (London: W. Bowyer and Bernard Lintott, 1717), pp. [273]-86. The story was widely known and, among many other places, summarized and commented upon in the revised Pierre Bayle, *A General Dictionary, Historical and Critical: In which a New and Accurate Translation of that of the Celebrated Mr. Bayle is Included*, 10 vols (London: G. Strahan, *et al.*, 1739), "Sappho," IX, 68-73. In some versions of the tale, he sleeps with her; in others, she seeks to do so and is rejected. In Pope's version, they consummate their relationship, after which Phaon grew tired of her (p. 276).

41 For some of these, see Bezaleel Morrice, *The Muse's Treat: or, A Collation of Wit and Love* (London: Henry Morris, 1702), pp. 60-65; *The Third Volume of the Works of Mr. William Congreve* (London: Jacob Tonson, 1710), p. 1059; William Harrison, *The Passion of Sappho, and Feast of Alexander Set to Musick* (London: Jacob Tonson, 1711), pp. 1-6; *Miscellaneous Poems and Translations by Several Hands* (London: Bernard Lintott, 1712), pp. 230-43; *Poetical Miscellanies, Consisting of Original Poems and Translations: By the Best Hands* (London: Jacob Tonson, 1714), p. 250; *Poems of Love and Gallantry: Written in the Marshalsea and Newgate, by Several of the Prisoners Taken at Preston* (London: J. Grantham, 1716), p. 18.

Hennet remains puzzled and outraged at the disparity of charm and beauty between the women and Swift. "Je ne sais comment qualifier [un attachement] avec miss Stella Johnson" (II, 262). He again makes the allusion overt regarding Vanessa the "Héloïse nouvelle" (II, 272): she composes a loving rebus for the insensible Dean, while within she shines in "l'âme et l'esprit de Sapho" (II, 274). I suspect that Hennet comments upon these deadly relationships when he ends his selections from Swift's poetry with Swift on himself shortly before his death. He is alone, deaf, without power or authority, and "Nay, what's incredible, alack! / I hardly hear a Woman's Clack" (III, 184).[42]

Swift's poetry often exemplifies that difficult relationship with women, clacking or otherwise. Hennet complains about "les traits caustiques qu'il lance sans cesse contre les femmes" (II, 284), for which he must "sollicite l'indulgence des dames." He adapts the Abbé Yart's method for the longest of the five poems he translates, *Strephon and Chloc* as "Rosette et Mondor": "J'ai ... adoucir les traits d'un pinceau beaucoup hardi" (III, ix-x).[43] Hennet's version and its no-longer-bold brush strokes retrench about 100 lines of the facing poem, makes it Parisian and reasonably polite if arch, and either eliminates crudities, or changes its often caustic into circumspect lines. It even includes an admonition to Jonathan Swift himself.

For example, Strephon has courted, won, and wed the glorious, the divine, the impeccable, the perfect Chloe / Rosette. He now lies abed anxiously lusting for his goddess and fretting about his own rough manhood unworthy of a nymph "so high" and "unsusceptible of stain." He cleanses his "hands, his neck, his mouth, his feet" and "other parts that shall be nameless" in order not to offend the ladies (III, 172, 174). Swift nonetheless hints at what Strephon does to prepare one part of his male anatomy to act because his love is "hot": "Why, let it go, if I must tell it – / He'll sweat, and then the Nymph may smell it" (*Poems*, ed. Williams, II, 586, ll. 83-84). The rest of the paragraph particularizes

42 Hennet's translation shifts the meaning wholly from Swift's isolation to the husband's relief: "Le croirez-vous, pauvres maris? / Femme qui jette les hautes cris / Ne m'étourdit plus les oreilles" (III, 185). Swift says nothing about poor husbands; "clack" becomes high cries. For the poem, see "Written by the Reverend Dr. Swift. On his Own Deafness," together with Swift's Latin version and answering lines perhaps by Thomas Sheridan (*Poems*, ed. Williams, II, 672-74).

43 The poems are "Verses Wrote in a Lady's Ivory Table-Book" ("Sur les tablettes d'ivoir d'une dame"), "Stella's Birth-Day" ("A Stella le jour de naissance"), "On Mrs Biddy Floyd: or, The Receipt to Form a Beauty" ("Virginie H ... Recette pour faire un beauté"), "Strephon and Chloe" ("Rosette et Mondor"), and "Swift on Himself Sometime before his Death" ("Swift sur lui-même quelque tems avant sa mort"). I quote *Strephon* from Hennet's English text, the better to set it against the facing French version. See also *Poems*, ed. Williams, II, 584-93.

Strephon's image: his coarse beard, hairy chest, and laced nightcap contrast with the fantasized delicate, fragrant, perfection of Chloe as goddess (III, 174). Hennet limits all this to one line: "Mondor, hélas! N'est qu'un homme" with a large blank space beneath it to signal the facing omissions necessary for French readers (III, 175).

Thereafter, Chloe enters the bed with a tea-full bladder, reaches for the chamber pot beneath her, and emits an audible, ample, and smelly stream of urine. She is all too human: "ye Gods! what sound is this? / Can Chloe, heavenly Chloe----?" Strephon asks rhetorically (III, 180). Not to be outdone in urinary waterfalls, Strephon reaches for his own chamber pot "And, as he fill'd the reeking vase, / Let fly a rouser in her face." The fancied attending cupids and consequent passion fly away (III, 180, 182). Hennet ignores the noisy and noisome stream but is mischievous enough to suggest what Rosette is doing and to have Mondor proclaim: "Quoi, ma Rosette fait pipi!" which he will more discreetly do as well (III, 181, 183). Thus far and no farther, and certainly not to a gentleman on his wedding night farting in his wife's face. Hennet breaks translator's protocol and berates Swift for including such matters. The French poet will not say to French women what Swift alone says to English women:

> J'épargne aux lectrices françaises
> Les suites de cet accident;
> Swift seul, plus hardi, moins galant,
> Peut conter, aux dames anglaises,
> Comme quoi Mondor assuré
> Que Rosette était une femme,
> D'être homme aussi se but bon gré
> Et fit ce qu'avait fait madame. (III, 183)

Such admonition of the author one translates may not be unique. It certainly is unusual and certainly expresses Hennet's and other French readers' response to Swift. He is original, never bores, but also is "Swift seul, plus hardi, moins galant" than Hennet's audience preferred.

8. Further Reasons for Restraint

Whether in prose satire or in poetry, Swift as Swift could not make a major impact on eighteenth-century French culture; it admired his skill but rejected his message, the way it was communicated, and those he apparently harmed in the process. After all, his "bizarre" conduct towards Stella and Vanessa remained both puzzling and disturbing on either side of the Channel. Some of that concern ameliorated as time passed and Swift's relationship with Vanessa could be thought "la matière d'un roman."[44] Nonetheless, Swift at his brilliant best is hardly a romance novelist. He often grimly tells us what is wrong, rather than celebrates what is right. His genius includes an ability to look over the edge, to examine received wisdom and dismantle its pieties. He stresses the fragility of civilized life, the need to buttress it with the fences that religion or monarchy might supply, and the probability that the fences will collapse if they have not already done so. He regularly expresses anger at the collapse and those who caused it. Swift's few satiric norms regularly are in danger. He writes his own "Verses" on his death (1731, 1739) because only he can understand his fears and achievements and, the darkest Walpole opposition excepted, because too few others would join him in characterizing Britain's "dire destructive Scene" (*Poems*, ed. Williams, II, 568, l. 392) that defeats unguarded virtue.[45]

Many in France agreed that virtue needed protection, including from Swift's own perceived attacks. We recall that Prosper Marchand thought *A Tale of a Tub* criminal. The Abbé Le Blanc agreed regarding *A Modest Proposal* (1729), which he read during his London residence in 1737-38 and discussed in his *Letters on the English and French Nations* (1747). Le Blanc knew that it satirized English oppression of the Irish, yet within lines omitted from the Dublin edition, he asks "Who can relish" that ridiculous and disgusting work. Its "wretched detail" is insipid, offensive, and "makes it drop out of the reader's hands."[46] Le Blanc may have read *A Modest Proposal* in English or in its especially hostile French translation. In either case, it made clear that though Swift was indeed

44 [Craufurd], *Essai historique sur le Docteur Swift*, regarding Vanessa and *Cadenus and Vanessa*: "Leurs amours présentent un épisode intéressant, qui fourniroit à lui seul la matière d'un roman" (p. xix). Craufurd includes a long chapter concerning Vanessa together with much about Stella (pp. 236-68). He also argues that "le véritable caractère de Swift est encore plus méconnu en France" (p. vii), but many thought that they indeed understood his character and thought it too "bizarre" for comfort. Craufurd's British ancestry and of course comfort with his native language make it far easier for him to accept and promote the excellence of Swift's character and style.

45 For such matters, see Howard D. Weinbrot, "Jonathan Swift: Defeat, Isolation, and the Price of Failed Norms," *Swift Studies*, 32 (2017), 79-100.

46 Abbé Jean-Bernard le Blanc, *Letters on the English and French Nations*, 2 vols (London: J. Brindley, *et al.*, 1747), I, 217n*. He praises Swift's *Proposal for Correcting the English Tongue* (II, 77 [Letter XII]) and then wrongly adds that "we have given a kind reception to all the works of Dr. SWIFT, that have been translated" (II, 302 [Letter XXXIX]). Le Blanc's remarks regarding *A Modest Proposal* offended William Scott and George Faulkner, le Blanc's publishers in Dublin. They repeat only the first sentence: "He is one of the English authors, who has best succeeded in pleasantry" (Le Blanc, *Letters on the English and French Nations* [Dublin: William Scott and George Faulkner, 1747], I, 156 n*).

famous, many French readers thought him unclerical, troubling, libertine, bizarre, verbally licentious, and dangerous.[47]

The Abbé Antoine Yart nobly introduced and discussed Swift's poetry, which he softened and censored for French readers; he also offered Swift as a model for French poets, but only as a shadow of his true poetic and satiric nature. Yart could not present the Dean as a great apocalyptic satirist second only to the Hebrew prophets. Albin-Joseph-Ulpien Hennet added a new set of Swift's poems, which again cleansed the longest and scolded its author for lack of *politesse*. Swift offered French readers and poets images and original approaches to ancient poems and modern circumstances, for which Hennet's culture was grateful; but it was generally not willing to follow him to the collapse of benevolent illusion. Voltaire said that Swift would never be well understood in France. He might also have said that Swift was well understood in France, and therefore needed to be changed into something that he was not.

47 So far as I can tell, there was only one translation of *A Modest Proposal* into French (TEERINK AND SCOUTEN 680). It appeared in Rotterdam in a larger anti-Catholic volume: "Projet facile, equitable et modeste, pour rendre utile à nôtre Nation un très grand nombre de pauvres Enfans, qui lui sont maintentenant fort à charge. Traduit de l'Anglois," *Recueil de pièces curieuses sur les matiéres les plus intéressantes. Par Albert Radicati, Comte de Passeran* ([Rotterdam, 1736], pp. 369-84 [369]). Radicati does not identify Swift as the author, but The Hague Royal Library copy includes a manuscript note "(van Swift)." The Latin tag beneath the title is *Castigat ridendo mores*, "castigate manners by laughing." Not all English or Irish editions of *A Modest Proposal* included Swift's name, but by the mid-1730s his authorship was well known, and the *Recueil* was published in Rotterdam by Thomas Johnson and his son. An English bookseller would surely know Swift's authorship. This translation concludes the book and follows a long attack upon transubstantiation as modern cannibalism (see Frank Lestringant, *Une sainte horreur ou le voyage en Eucharistie, XVIe-XVIIIe siècle* [Paris: Presses Universitaires de France, 1996]). It is grimly possible that Radicati saw the "Project facile" as a proper way to rid Ireland of the Papists he so abhorred.

As a sign of changing times, see Paul Max Simon, who writes in *Swift: Étude psychologique et littéraire*: the "étrange composition" *A Modest Proposal* reflects "ce flegme sérieux et spirituel que nous avons appelé humour ... Le ton de cet écrit est si juste, si sérieux, si naturel, que je ne sais quel économiste le prit à la lettre, et ne craignit pas de l'invoquer comme un exemple de la misère qui désolait l'Irlande" ([Paris: J.-B. Baillière, 1893], pp. 30-31).

Contributors

DAVID ALVAREZ is Associate Professor of English at DePauw University, Greencastle, Indiana. He has published on Joseph Addison, Mary Astell, Alexander Pope, the third Earl of Shaftesbury, and John Locke. He is currently co-editing a collection of essays titled *Imagining Religious Toleration, 1600-1800.*

SABINE BALTES-ELLERMANN is a senior civil servant at the German Federal Office of Languages. Her academic interests are Irish studies and eighteenth-century literature. Publications include a monograph on *The Controversy about Wood's Halfpence* (*1722-25*) *and the Tradition of Irish Constitutional Nationalism* (2003), an edited collection of eighteenth-century pamphlets entitled *Jonathan Swift's Allies: The Wood's Halfpence Controversy in Ireland, 1724/5* (2nd ed. 2017), as well as numerous articles on Swift and his contemporaries, eighteenth-century drama, and popular culture.

JANIKA BISCHOF works as research associate for the *Online.Swift* project. She was a member of the collaborative research centre *Symbolische Kommunikation und gesellschaftliche Wertesysteme* at the Westfälische Wilhelms-Universität, Münster, and completed her doctoral dissertation on book gifts in medieval England in 2011. From 2012 until 2016, she worked as research assistant for the edition project *Acta et Documenta Synodi Nationalis Dordrechtanae* at the Johannes a Lasco Bibliothek in Emden. The focus of her work for *Online.Swift* is the technical implementation.

ANDREW CARPENTER is Professor Emeritus of English at University College, Dublin, and a member of the Royal Irish Academy. He has published many books and articles on seventeenth- and eighteenth-century Irish poetry in English, as well as several on Swift. He is best known for two anthologies, *Verse in English from Tudor and Stuart Ireland* (2003) and *Verse in English from Eighteenth-Century Ireland* (1997). His most recent publications are *The Irish Poet and the Natural World: An Anthology of Verse in English from the Tudors to the Romantics* (co-edited with Lucy Collins, 2014) and an edition of *The Poems of Olivia Elder* (2017).

NORBERT COL is Professor of English at the Université de Bretagne-Sud, Lorient, where he teaches British history and literature. Specializing in the History of Ideas, more specifically on Edmund Burke and Jonathan Swift, he has authored a bilingual edition of Edmund Burke's *An Appeal from the New to*

 | DOI:10.30965/9783846763971_028

the Old Whigs (1996), and, in addition to numerous articles, two monographs: *Burke, le contrat social et les révolutions* (2001) and *À la recherche du conservatisme britannique: historiographie, britannicité, modernité* (*XVII*^{e}-*XX*^{e} *siècles*) (2007). He has also edited *Écritures de soi* (2007) and co-edited, with Allan Ingram, *Utopie, individu et société: la sociabilité en question* (2015).

DANIEL COOK is a Senior Lecturer in English and Associate Director of the Centre for Scottish Culture at the University of Dundee, with research and teaching interests in Scottish and Irish literature of the long eighteenth century. He is the author of *Thomas Chatterton and Neglected Genius, 1760-1830* and editor of *The Lives of Jonathan Swift*, *The Afterlives of Eighteenth-Century Fiction* (with Nicholas Seager), and *Women's Life Writing, 1700-1850* (with Amy Culley).

J. A. DOWNIE is Professor of English Emeritus at Goldsmiths' College, University of London. His books include a biography of Swift, *Jonathan Swift, Political Writer* (1984; re-issued 2014). He is the editor of *The Oxford Handbook of the Eighteenth-Century Novel* (2016) and is currently editing *The Oxford Handbook of Daniel Defoe* (with Nicholas Seager).

CHRISTOPHER J. FAUSKE is Professor of Communications at Salem State University, Salem, Massachusetts, and the author of books on Jonathan Swift, and Archbishop William King, as well as John Frederick MacNeice and Louis MacNeice. He has edited and co-edited works on Maria Edgeworth and on late seventeenth- and early eighteenth-century economic policy, pamphlets, and politics.

REBECCA FERGUSON graduated from the Universities of Southampton (BA) and London (PhD). From 1979 to 2013, she was a lecturer at the University of Wales, Lampeter, today University of Wales Trinity Saint David, where she is now an Honorary Research Fellow. In 1988-89, she spent a year as a Fulbright Exchange Lecturer at the University of Massachusetts, Dartmouth, USA, and has given various conference papers and British Council-funded guest lectures in Britain, Europe, and America. She has published widely on Alexander Pope, Toni Morrison, and Jonathan Swift, and is the author of *Th'Unbalanced Mind: Pope and the Rule of Passion* (1986) and *Reading Black Identities: Transition and Exchange in the Novels of Toni Morrison* (2007), for which she received a Recognition Award from the Toni Morrison Society in 2008. Her articles have appeared in various book collections and in journals including *Critical Survey*, *MELUS* and, most recently, *Swift Studies*.

RUDOLF FREIBURG is Professor of English Literature at the Friedrich-Alexander-Universität, Erlangen-Nürnberg. He is co-editor of several books, including *Swift: The Enigmatic Dean* (1998), *"But Vindicate the Ways of God to Man": Literature and* Theodicy (2004), *Kultbücher* (2004), *Literatur und Holocaust* (2009), *Träume* (2015), *Unendlichkeit* (2016), and *D@tenflut* (2016). He has also written numerous essays ranging on authors from the eighteenth to the twenty-first century.

EUGENE HAMMOND is Professor of English and Writing at the State University of New York at Stony Brook. He is the author of *Jonathan Swift: Irish Blow-In* and *Jonathan Swift: Our Dean* (2016), of the textbook *Thoughtful Writing* (third edition, 2009), and of, among others, articles on "Irony and Criticism of Rhetoric in Erasmus' *Praise of Folly* and Swift's *Tale of a Tub*" (1983), and on "Justice in Thomas More's *Utopia* and in Swift's *Gulliver's Travels*" (1982), published in distinguished journals in the field.

MASCHA HANSEN is Lecturer in English Literature at the University of Greifswald. She has published on Frances Burney, Queen Charlotte, and the Bluestockings, and has recently co-edited a collection entitled *"The first wit of the age": Essays on Swift and his Contemporaries* (2013). She is currently working on a project addressing eighteenth-century women's attitudes to, and visions of, the future.

MOYRA HASLETT is Professor of Eighteenth-Century and Romantic Literature at Queen's University Belfast. Her publications include a chapter on contemporary responses to *Gulliver's Travels* (in her monograph on *Pope to Burney, Scriblerians to Bluestockings*), an essay on "Swift and Conversational Culture" (in *Eighteenth-Century Ireland*), and an essay on "The Poet as Clubman" (in the *Oxford Handbook of British Poetry, 1660-1800*). An essay on the tradition of writing birthday poems addressed to Swift is forthcoming in *Swift Studies*. She has recently served as Principal Investigator for the Irish Song Project and has been invited to many public talks on the topic of the Wood's Halfpence affair as part of that project.

DAVID HAYTON is Visiting Professor in the School of English and History at Ulster University and a Member of the Royal Irish Academy. He was previously Professor of Early Modern Irish and British History at Queen's University Belfast, where he is Professor Emeritus. His publications have been concentrated on Irish and British history, c.1680-1750 and include two major collections of essays, *Ruling Ireland, 1685-1742* (2004), and *The Anglo-Irish Experience, 1680-1730*

(2012), as well as several scholarly editions, most notably *Letters of Marmaduke Coghill, 1722-1738* (2004) and *Irish Political Writings after 1725: A Modest Proposal and Other Works* in *The Cambridge Edition of the Works of Jonathan Swift* (2018). In 2017, he was awarded a Leverhulme Emeritus Fellowship to work on a book on parliamentary elections in Ireland, 1692-1768.

IAN HIGGINS is a Reader in English at the Australian National University in Canberra, Australia, where he lectures on literature from the seventeenth to the twentieth centuries. In addition to a monograph on *Swift* (2004), he has published many essays on Swift and his era, and (with Claude Rawson) has edited *Gulliver's Travels* for Oxford University Press (2005) and *The Essential Writings of Jonathan Swift* for Norton (2010). He is a foundation general editor of *The Cambridge Edition of the Works of Jonathan Swift*, currently in progress.

ALLAN INGRAM is Professor Emeritus of English at the University of Northumbria at Newcastle. He has published books on James Boswell, on Swift and Pope (1986), and on eighteenth-century insanity and its representation, as well as edited collections of primary material on the relations between insanity and medicine in the period. He has also edited *Gulliver's Travels* for Broadview Press (2012). Between 2006 and 2009, he was Director of a Leverhulme Trust project, *Before Depression, 1660-1800*, as part of which he was co-general editor of a four-volume collection, *Depression and Melancholy, 1660-1800* (2012) and co-author of *Melancholy Experience in the Long Eighteenth Century* (2011). He was Co-Director of a second Leverhulme Trust project, *Fashionable Diseases: Medicine, Literature and Culture, 1660-1830* and co-edited a volume of essays, *Disease and Death in Eighteenth-Century Literature and Culture: Fashioning the Unfashionable* (2016) He also co-edited a memorial volume for Bill Overton, *Voice and Context in Eighteenth-Century Verse: Order in Variety* (2015), and is co-editor of the English Association journal, *English*. He is currently working on relations between Swift, Pope, and the medical profession.

KIRSTEN JUHAS works as research associate for the *Online.Swift* project, for which she has edited, co-edited, and annotated a number of texts, among them, *An Answer to a Scurrilous Pamphlet* and *A Meditation upon a Broomstick*. In addition to various essays on topics related to Jonathan Swift, she is author of a study on eighteenth-century women poets (2008) and co-author of a teacher's manual on Don DeLillo's *Falling Man* (2011, 2013). She has co-edited the volumes *Reading Swift: Papers from The Sixth Münster Symposium on Jonathan Swift* and *"The first wit of the age": Essays on Swift and his Contemporaries* (both published in 2013). In 2009, she became an assistant editor of *Swift Studies* and since 2015 has been co-editor of this annual.

STEPHEN KARIAN is an Associate Professor of English at the University of Missouri. His publications include a monograph on *Jonathan Swift in Print and Manuscript* (2010) and numerous articles in *The Age of Johnson*; *The Huntington Library Quarterly*; *Irish Historical Studies*; *SEL Studies in English Literature, 1500-1900*; *Studies in Bibliography*; *Swift Studies*, and elsewhere. With James Woolley, he is co-editing Swift's complete poems in four volumes for *The Cambridge Edition of the Works of Jonathan Swift.*

FLORIAN KLAEGER is Professor of English at the University of Bayreuth. He holds a PhD in English literature from the University of Düsseldorf and has published on early modern literature, diasporic fiction, and the contemporary novel, most notably in *Reading into the Stars: Cosmopoetics in the Contemporary Novel* (2018). His research interests are linked by the question after the formal resources of literature for the creation of social cohesion. He has recently co-edited a collection of essays on *Literarische Form: Literary Form* (Heidelberg: Winter, 2018).

GREGORY LYNALL is Reader in English at the University of Liverpool. His publications include *Swift and Science: The Satire, Politics, and Theology of Natural Knowledge, 1690-1730* (2012). In 2013, he was awarded the Richard H. Rodino Prize from the Ehrenpreis Centre for Swift Studies for his essay on "Swift's 'Poetical Chymistry'" (*Review of English Studies*, 2012). He is currently writing a cultural history of solar energy and a biography of Dr John Arbuthnot.

ASHLEY MARSHALL is Professor of English at the University of Nevada, Reno. She is the author of *The Practice of Satire in England, 1658-1770* (2013) and *Swift and History: Politics and the English Past* (2015), as well as numerous articles in *Eighteenth-Century Life*, *Huntington Library Quarterly*, *Modern Philology*, *The Review of English Studies*, *Swift Studies*, and other journals. She has recently completed a monograph on the beginnings of political journalism in London, 1695-1720.

JAMES E. MAY, has for over two decades surveyed rare book and manuscript sales for *The Scriblerian* and edited *The Eighteenth-Century Intelligencer* newsletter. He has written on bibliographical and textual problems in early editions of Oliver Goldsmith, George Lyttelton, Tobias Smollett, Jonathan Swift, and Edward Young. He is presently writing a descriptive bibliography of Edward Young (to 1775) and identifying the ornament stocks of early eighteenth-century Dublin and London printers.

PATRICK MÜLLER is a civil servant and teacher of English for the German Federal Office of Languages. Alongside the work he did for the Shaftesbury Project at Friedrich-Alexander-Universität, Erlangen-Nürnberg, he has written numerous articles on Shaftesbury and other eighteenth-century authors as well as on contemporary British and American fiction. He is co-editor of *"The first wit of the age": Essays on Swift and his Contemporaries* (2013).

DIRK F. PASSMANN is author of *"Full of Improbable Lies": "Gulliver's Travels" und die Reiseliteratur vor 1726* (1987) as well as numerous essays on Swiftian matters. His publications include a four-volume handbook on *Swift's Library and Reading*, co-authored with Heinz J. Vienken (2003), and, most recently, the Index to David Woolley's edition of *The Correspondence of Jonathan Swift* (1999-2007), co-compiled with Hermann J. Real (2014). He works as a publisher in Münster.

JONATHAN PRITCHARD has held teaching positions in the United States and Germany. He has published articles on the literature and literary history of the long eighteenth century in, amongst others, *The Huntington Library Quarterly, The Review of English Studies, Studies in Philology, Swift Studies*, and *The Transactions of the Cambridge Bibliographical Society.*

MELINDA ALLIKER RABB is Professor of English at Brown University. She is the author of *Satire and Secrecy in English Literature from 1650 to 1750* and of *Miniature and the English Imagination: Literature, Cognition, and Small-Scale Culture, 1650-1765*. She has also published widely in scholarly journals on topics pertaining to the long eighteenth century. Her essays include studies of Swift, Pope, Fielding, and Richardson, among others, as well as women writers, satire, and the canon.

HERMANN JOSEF REAL is Professor Emeritus of English and Director of the Ehrenpreis Centre for Swift Studies at the Westfälische Wilhelms-Universität, Münster. He is editor of Swift's *The Battle of the Books* (1978) and co-editor of *Swift and his Contexts* (1989). He has convened seven Münster symposia on Jonathan Swift since 1984, and edited and co-edited their transactions (1985-2019). He has also co-authored a monograph on *Gulliver's Travels* (1984), co-translated and annotated the *Travels* into German (1987; 4th ed., 2011), and annotated a new translation of *A Tale of a Tub* in German (1994). He has been Editor of the annual *Swift Studies* since its inception (1986). Among his book publications are three anthologies of edited essays: *Securing Swift: Selected*

Essays (2001), *The Reception and Reputation of Jonathan Swift in Germany: Essays and Investigations* (2002), and *The Reception of Jonathan Swift in Europe* (2005), reissued in a revised version in paperback (2012). In 2014, his Index to David Woolley's edition of *The Correspondence of Jonathan Swift* (1999-2007), compiled with Dirk F. Passmann, was published. For the past years, Hermann Josef Real has been working as co-editor on a new critical online edition of the Prose Works of Jonathan Swift (*Online.Swift*), with introductions and variorum commentaries.

HANS-PETER WAGNER is Professor Emeritus of English and American Literature at the Landau campus of Universität Koblenz-Landau. He has taught at German, British, French, American, and African universities and was Distinguished Visiting Professor at Dartmouth College. The editor of several English Enlightenment novels in the Penguin Classics series and of LAPASEC (Landau-Paris Studies on the Eighteenth Century), he has published widely on colonial American culture, postmodern American literature, Enlightenment literature, and the graphic art of William Hogarth as well as on text-image relations. Recent publications include a two-volume *Survey of American Literature: 1900-2000* (2017); *A Survey of British Literature, Part I: Renaissance to Romanticism*, also in two volumes (2016); *An Introduction to British and Irish Fiction: Renaissance to Romanticism* (2014); *William Hogarth: das graphische Werk* (2013), and the second revised edition of *A History of British, Irish, and American Literature* (2010). He lives in Saarbrücken and, with great ardour, in Lannion, Brittany.

MARCUS WALSH is Professor Emeritus of English Literature at the University of Liverpool. He edited *A Tale of a Tub and Other Works* for *The Cambridge Edition of The Works of Jonathan Swift* (2010). He has written on Swift, Smart, Johnson, Sterne, and Malone; on the theory, practice, and history of literary editing; and on biblical interpretation and scholarship in the seventeenth and eighteenth centuries. He is currently a General Editor and a volume editor for the Oxford University Press edition of *The Writings of Alexander Pope.*

HOWARD WEINBROT is Ricardo Quintana Professor of English Emeritus, and William Freeman Vilas Research Professor in the College of Letters and Science Emeritus at the University of Wisconsin, Madison. He is currently a reader at the Huntington Library, San Marino, California. His research concerns the religion and sermons of Jonathan Swift and of Samuel Johnson, after which he will return to the influence of Samuel Johnson's edition of Shakespeare in France.

James Woolley is Frank Lee and Edna M. Smith Professor of English Emeritus at Lafayette College. His papers on Swift and his contemporaries include "Swift's Most Popular Poems," in *Reading Swift: Papers from The Sixth Münster Symposium on Jonathan Swift*; "Swift and Lord Berkeley, 1699-1701," in *"The first wit of the age"*; "The Circulation of Verse in Jonathan Swift's Dublin," *Eighteenth-Century Ireland*, 32; and, with Daniel Cook, "Charles Ford's Library," *Swift Studies*, 32. He is co-editor of the Swift Poems Project and its digital archive and with Stephen Karian is editing Swift's poems for Cambridge University Press.

Index